A History of Western Society

FOURTH EDITION

Volume II *From Absolutism to the Present*

John P. McKay
UNIVERSITY OF ILLINOIS AT URBANA–CHAMPAIGN

Bennett D. Hill
GEORGETOWN UNIVERSITY

John Buckler
UNIVERSITY OF ILLINOIS AT URBANA–CHAMPAIGN

HOUGHTON MIFFLIN COMPANY   BOSTON
DALLAS   GENEVA, ILLINOIS
PALO ALTO   PRINCETON, NEW JERSEY

About the Authors

John P. McKay Born in St. Louis, Missouri, John P. McKay received his B.A. from Wesleyan University (1961), his M.A. from the Fletcher School of Law and Diplomacy (1962), and his Ph.D. from the University of California, Berkeley (1968). He began teaching history at the University of Illinois in 1966 and became a professor there in 1976. John won the Herbert Baxter Adams Prize for his book *Pioneers for Profit: Foreign Entrepreneurship and Russian Industrialization, 1885–1913* (1970). He has also written *Tramways and Trolleys: The Rise of Urban Mass Transport in Europe* (1976) and has translated Jules Michelet's *The People* (1973). His research has been supported by fellowships from the Ford Foundation, the Guggenheim Foundation, the National Endowment for the Humanities, and IREX. His articles and reviews have appeared in numerous journals, including *The American Historical Review, Business History Review, The Journal of Economic History,* and *Slavic Review.* He edits *Industrial Development and the Social Fabric: An International Series of Historical Monographs.*

Bennett D. Hill A native of Philadelphia, Bennett D. Hill earned an A.B. at Princeton (1956) and advanced degrees from Harvard (A.M., 1958) and Princeton (Ph.D., 1963). He taught history at the University of Illinois at Urbana, where he was department chairman from 1978 to 1981. He has published *English Cistercian Monasteries and Their Patrons in the Twelfth Century (1968)* and *Church and State in the Middle Ages* (1970); and articles in *Analecta Cisterciensia, The New Catholic Encyclopaedia, The American Benedictine Review,* and *The Dictionary of the Middle Ages.* His reviews have appeared in *The American Historical Review, Speculum, The Historian, The Catholic Historical Review,* and *Library Journal.* He has been a fellow of the American Council of Learned Societies and has served on committees for the National Endowment for the Humanities. Now a Benedictine monk of St. Anselm's Abbey, Washington, D.C., he is also a Visiting Professor at Georgetown University.

John Buckler Born in Louisville, Kentucky, John Buckler received his B.A. from the University of Louisville in 1967. Harvard University awarded him the Ph.D. in 1973. From 1984 to 1986 he was the Alexander von Humboldt Fellow at Institut für Alte Geschichte, University of Munich. He is currently a professor at the University of Illinois. In 1980 Harvard University Press published his *The Theban Hegemony, 371–362 B.C..* He has also published *Philip II and the Sacred War* (Leiden 1989), and co-edited *BOIOTIKA: Vorträge vom 5. International Böotien-Kolloquium* (Munich 1989). His articles have appeared in journals both here and abroad, like the *American Journal of Ancient History, Classical Philology, Rheinisches Museum für Philologie, Classical Quarterly, Wiener Studien,* and *Symbolae Osloenses.*

Contents in Brief

Contents

16

ABSOLUTISM AND CONSTITUTIONALISM IN WESTERN EUROPE (CA 1589–1715)

17

ABSOLUTISM IN EASTERN EUROPE TO 1740

18

TOWARD A NEW WORLD-VIEW

Civil War in the United States in Chapter 25 to facilitate more continuous transatlantic comparisons, a revised discussion of intellectual trends in Chapter 28 that emphasizes the connection between these movements and subsequent political developments, and a unified account of the Second World War in Chapter 29. We have also taken special care to explain terms and concepts as soon as they are introduced.

Third, the addition of more problems of historical interpretation in the third edition was well received, and we have continued in that direction in this edition. We believe that the problematic element helps the reader develop the critical-thinking skills that are among the most precious benefits of studying history. New examples of this more open-ended, more interpretive approach include the debate over Alexander the Great and his achievements (Chapter 4), the controversy regarding the causes of Rome's decline (Chapter 6), the significance of abandoned children in the Middle Ages (Chapter 10), the social costs of English enclosure (Chapter 19), and the impact of industrialization on women and the standard of living (Chapter 22).

Finally, the illustrative component of our work has been completely revised. There are many new illustrations, including nearly two hundred color reproductions that let both great art and important events come alive. As in earlier editions, all illustrations have been carefully selected to complement the text, and all carry captions that enhance their value. Artwork remains an integral part of our book, for the past can speak in pictures as well as in words.

The use of full color throughout this edition also serves to clarify the maps and graphs and to enrich the textual material. Again for improved clarity, maps from the third edition have been completely redesigned to provide easily read and distinguished labels and prominent boundaries and typographical relief. We have also added new maps that illustrate social as well as political developments, including maps on Cistercian expansion and economic activity, seventeenth-century Dutch commerce, Europe at 1715, the ethnic and political boundaries of the Soviet republics, and the reform movements of 1989 in eastern Europe.

In addition to the many maps that support text discussion, we offer a new, full-color map essay at the beginning of each volume. Our purpose is twofold. First, by reproducing and describing such cartographic landmarks as the Babylonian world map, the medieval Ebstorf map, maps of the Americas, Africa, and the British Empire based on Ptolemy and Mercator, and contemporary global projections and satellite images, we hope to demonstrate for students the evolution of Western cartography and to guide them toward an understanding of the varied functions and uses of maps. Second, the map essay is intended to reveal the changing European world-view and its expansion from antiquity to the present. In this sense, the map essay may serve as an introduction to the course as well as to cartography.

Distinctive Features

Distinctive features from earlier editions remain in the fourth. To help guide the reader toward historical understanding we have posed specific historical questions at the beginning of each chapter. These questions are then answered in the course of the chapter, each of which concludes with a concise summary of the chapter's findings. The timelines added in the third edition have proved useful, and still more are found in this edition, including double-page timelines that allow students to compare simultaneous political, economic, religious, and cultural developments.

We have also tried to suggest how historians actually work and think. We have quoted extensively from a wide variety of primary sources and have demonstrated in our use of these quotations how historians sift and weigh evidence. We want the reader to think critically and to realize that history is neither a list of cut-and-dried facts nor a senseless jumble of conflicting opinions. It is our further hope that the primary quotations, so carefully fitted into their historical context, will give the reader a sense that even in the earliest and most remote periods of human experience, history has been shaped by individual men and women, some of them great aristocrats, others ordinary folk.

Each chapter concludes with carefully selected suggestions for further reading. These suggestions are briefly described to help readers know where to turn to continue thinking and learning about the Western world. The chapter bibliographies have been revised and expanded to keep them current with the vast and complex new work being done in many fields.

Western civilization courses differ widely in chronological structure from one campus to another. To accommodate the various divisions of historical time into intervals that fit a two-quarter, three-quarter, or two-semester period, *A History of Western Society* is being published in four versions, three of which embrace the complete work:

One-volume hardcover edition, A HISTORY OF WESTERN SOCIETY; two-volume paperback, A HISTORY OF WESTERN SOCIETY *Volume I: From Antiquity to the Enlightenment* (Chapters 1–17), *Volume II: From Absolutism to the Present* (Chapters 16–32); three-volume paperback, A HISTORY OF WESTERN SOCIETY *Volume A: From Antiquity to 1500* (Chapters 1–13), *Volume B: From the Renaissance to 1815* (Chapters 12–21), *Volume C: From the Revolutionary Era to the Present* (Chapters 21–32). For courses on Europe since the Renaissance, we are offering A HISTORY OF WESTERN SOCIETY *Since 1400* (Chapters 13–32) for the first time in the fourth edition.

Note that overlapping chapters in both the two- and the three-volume sets permit still wider flexibility in matching the appropriate volume with the opening and closing dates of a course term.

Ancillaries

Learning and teaching ancillaries, including a *Study Guide, MicroStudy Plus* (a computerized version of the *Study Guide*) *Instructor's Resource Manual, Test Items, MicroTest* (a computerized version of the *Test Items*), and *Map Transparencies,* also contribute to the usefulness of the text. The excellent *Study Guide* has been thoroughly revised by Professor James Schmiechen of Central Michigan University. Professor Schmiechen has been a tower of strength ever since he critiqued our initial prospectus, and he has continued to give us many valuable suggestions and his warmly appreciated support. His *Study Guide* contains chapter summaries, chapter outlines, review questions, extensive multiple-choice exercises, self-check lists of important concepts and events, and a variety of study aids and suggestions. New to the fourth edition are study-review exercises on the interpretation of visual sources and major political ideas as well as suggested issues for discussion and essay and chronology reviews. Another major addition is the section, Understanding the Past Through Primary Sources. Seven primary source documents widely used by

historians are included, each preceded by a description of the author and source and followed by questions for analysis. The *Study Guide* also retains the very successful sections on studying effectively. These sections take the student by ostensive example through reading and studying activities like underlining, summarizing, identifying main points, classifying information according to sequence, and making historical comparisons. To enable both students and instructors to use the *Study Guide* with the greatest possible flexibility, the guide is available in two volumes, with considerable overlapping of chapters. Instructors and students who use only Volumes A and B of the text have all the pertinent study materials in a single volume, *Study Guide, Volume 1* (Chapters 1–21); likewise, those who use only Volumes B and C of the text also have all the necessary materials in one volume, *Study Guide, Volume 2* (Chapters 12–32). The multiple-choice sections of the *Study Guide* are also available as *Micro-Study Plus,* a computerized, tutorial version that tells students not only which response is correct but also why each of the other choices is wrong and provides the page numbers of the text where each question is discussed. These "rejoinders" to the multiple-choice questions also appear in printed form at the end of the *Study Guide. MicroStudy Plus* is available for both IBM and Macintosh computers.

The *Instructor's Resource Manual,* prepared by Professor John Marshall Carter of Oglethorpe University, contains learning objectives, chapter synopses, suggestions for lectures and discussion, paper and class activity topics, and lists of audio-visual resources. The accompanying *Test Items,* by Professor Charles Crouch of St. John's University in Collegeville, Minnesota offer identification, multiple-choice, and essay questions for a total of approximately 2000 test items. These test items are available to adopters in both IBM and Macintosh versions, both of which include editing capabilities. In addition, a set of full-color *Map Transparencies* of all the maps in the text is available on adoption.

JOHN P. MCKAY

BENNETT D. HILL

JOHN BUCKLER

Though the medieval religious framework had broken down, people still thought largely in religious terms. Europeans explained what they did politically and economically in terms of religious doctrine. Religious ideology served as a justification for many goals: the opposition of the French nobility to the crown, the Dutch struggle for political and economic independence from Spain. In Germany religious pluralism and the intervention of the French and the Swedes led to the long and devastating Thirty Years' War (1618–1648). After 1648 the divisions between Protestants and Catholics in Germany tended to become permanent. In France the bitter civil wars between the Catholic monarchy and Protestant nobility contributed to the growth of religious skepticism. The religious pluralism and skepticism that mark modern society are largely the legacy of this age of religious struggle.

Expanding Horizons: Mapmaking in the West

Today cartography, the art of making maps, is as widespread as typography, the process of printing. Maps are so much a part of daily life that people take them for granted. But people are not born with maps in their heads, as they are with fingers on their hands. The very concept of a map is a human invention of vast intellectual and practical importance. Like writing itself, cartography depends on people's use of visual and symbolic means to portray reality. Earth is not a flat table, devoid of physical features. Instead it is marked by mountains, valleys, rivers, oceans, and distances among them all. The knowledge of these features and the accurate portrayal of them allow people to understand their relationship to the planet on which they live. That is the basic reason for a map or an atlas.

The intellectual motivations of cartographers are easily overlooked, but they contribute something singular to the understanding of people. Human beings have a natural curiosity about their world and a joy in discovering new parts of it or learning more about regions not so well known. The Roman statesman and orator Cicero once asked, "*Ubinam gentium sumus?*" ("Where in the world are we?") Although he used this question as a figure of speech, many people were quite serious about finding an accurate answer to it. This curiosity and desire have led people to examine not only the earth but its relation to the cosmos of which it is a part. Early cartographers learned to use the stars as fixed points for the measurement of place and distance. Even today American nuclear submarines depend on celestial

MAP 1 Babylonian world map, ca 600 B.C. *(Source: Courtesy of the Trustees of the British Museum)*

navigation, transmitted by satellite, to determine their course and position. Once people looked to the stars, they began to wonder about the shape, nature, and content of the universe itself. Mapping of the earth was no longer enough; people now charted the cosmos. The Hubble Space Satellite, launched in May 1990, is a sign that the quest continues today.

For ordinary purposes cartography fills a host of practical needs. Maps were first used as a way to describe people's immediate environment—to illustrate the shape of villages and the boundaries of fields. As knowledge of the earth grew, maps became indispensable for travel, both on land and sea. People needed to know where their destination lay, how to reach it, and what to expect along the way. Mariners used the geographical knowledge provided by maps to sail from one port to another.

Other uses of early maps were economic. As people came into contact with one another, they saw new opportunities for barter and trade. It was no longer enough to know how to travel to different locations. Merchants needed to understand the geography of their markets and to know what foreign lands produced and what trading partners wanted in return for their goods. In short, economic contact itself increased knowledge of the face of the land, which could be preserved on maps by symbols to indicate the natural resources and products of various lands.

A third important function of early maps was military. Rulers and generals needed exact knowledge of distances and terrain through which their armies could move and fight. Their needs spurred interest in *topography,* the detailed description and representation of the natural and artificial features of a landscape. The military need for detail led to greater accuracy of maps and better definition of the physical environment.

The demands of empire were not only military but also administrative. The only effective way to govern an area is to know where each part of it is located and what its importance is. Rulers need precise maps to enforce their authority, dispatch commands, collect taxes, and maintain order. Thus the value to historians of some maps lies in their illustration of people's knowledge of the world in relation to the needs of government and the exercise of authority over broad distances.

These are only a few of the uses of cartography, but what of the maps themselves? How do people depict visually and accurately large sections of land or the entire face of the globe? The ways are numerous and some more exact than others. The earliest maps are only pictures of towns showing spatial relationships within a very limited context.

A more accurate way of making a map was derived from land surveys. Beginning about 1500 B.C., surveyors trained in geometry and trigonometry began to study the land in question and to divide its physical features into a series of measured angles and elevations. Cartographers then placed this information onto a grid, so that they could represent visually, according to a consistent and logical system, relations among areas. Although the method sounds simple, it presented early cartographers with a daunting problem, one that still exists today. Mapmakers must represent on a two-dimensional surface the face of a three-dimensional globe. To complicate matters even further, the earth is not a perfect sphere. How cartographers have grappled with these problems can best be seen from the maps illustrated here.

Since maps are basically visual, it is best to trace their evolution in their own context. People of other cultures also mapped their lands, but the Western tradition of cartography enjoyed its own singular path of development. The earliest known map of the Western world is the Babylonian world map, which dates to about 600 B.C. (Map 1). Babylon, with its neighbors around it, lies at the center of the world. Surrounding the land is the ocean, depicted as a circle. Quite interesting are the triangles beyond the ocean, which indicate that the Babylonians knew of peoples beyond the ocean. Here for the first time is evidence of a people who attempted to put themselves geographically into the context of their larger world.

The greatest geographer of the Greco-Roman period was unquestionably Claudius Ptolemaeus, better known as Ptolemy, who lived in Alexandria in the second century A.D. He advanced far beyond the schematic Babylonian world map to produce a scientific atlas based on data. He knew from previous scholars that the world was spherical, so he devised a way of using conic lines of *longitude,* angular distances east and west, and of *latitude,* angular distances north and south, to plot the positions and distances of the earth's features. Despite its distortions, Ptolemy's *Geographia* became the standard Western work on geography until the Age of Discovery (ca 1450–1650) in the early modern period.

The best illustration of his brilliant vision actually dates much later than its first representation to a manuscript produced in the German city of Ulm in 1482 (Map 2). Ptolemy put cartography on a scientific basis.

Some of the practical fruits of Ptolemy's labor can be seen in the series of maps known as the Peutinger Table, which probably dates to ca A.D. 500. The Table is a good example of how cartography served the Roman Empire. The section illustrated here is typical of the entire series: it indicates roads, rivers, mountains, cities, and towns in Greece (Map 3). In that respect it is an ancient road map, for its purpose was not to define the known world, as Ptolemy had done, but to inform the emperor and his bureaucracy how they could most easily administer and communicate with the provinces. Although alien to modern notions of the shape of Europe, the Peutinger Table is a remarkably accurate atlas of routes and distances and thus displays vividly and beautifully one of the most practical functions of cartography.

Europeans in the Middle Ages, like their predecessors, drew maps of the world, but now religion became an ingredient of cartography. Ptolemy's concepts of geography remained in force, but maps also served another and different purpose for society. The Ebstorf Map, drawn during the thirteenth century, shows the world surrounded by the ocean, a conception dating to antiquity (Map 4). Yet the

MAP 2 Map from Ptolemy's *Geographica (Source: Michael Holford)*

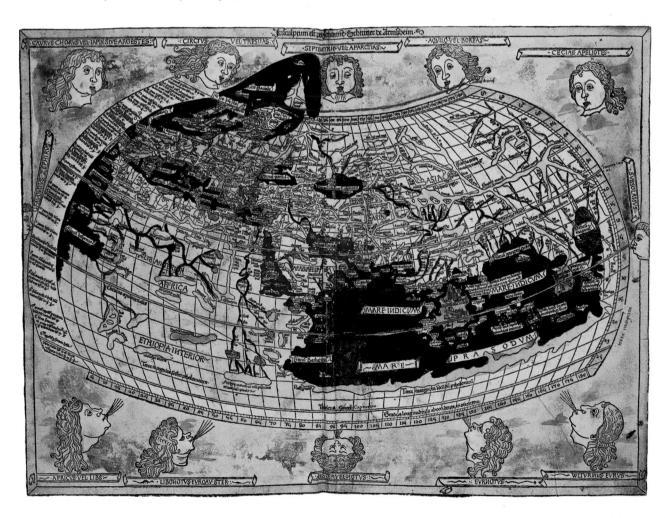

MAP 6 Catalan Atlas of 1375 *(Source: Bibliothèque Nationale, Paris/Photo Hubert Josse)*

tion to survey the land and to navigate the seas. Cartographers chose several major points to serve as hubs of a series of lines extended to other major points. The face of the globe was thereby cut up into a pattern of triangles, rectangles, and occasionally squares. Although this system proved complicated and unwieldy, triangulation did improve the utility of maps for explorers. An excellent example of a triangulated map comes from the Catalan Atlas of 1375 (Map 6). To make the atlas even more functional, the cartographer has indicated orientation, so that users may locate their position according to a compass.

Only with the Age of Discovery did European explorers and cartographers make significant advances over Ptolemy's view of the world. Sailors and navigators who voyaged to find new lands or to become better acquainted with familiar places dealt in an aspect of reality that is essential to map-making: they had to be able to calculate where they were. They knew that the world was curved, and they used the stars as fixed points to guide them. It is thus ironic that one of the most important advances in geographical knowledge came by mistake. In 1492 Christopher Columbus discovered the New World by sailing westward from Europe, looking for a sea passage to India. Although Columbus himself did not immediately recognize the full significance of his achievement, his discovery revolutionized geographical thinking. There was more to the world than Ptolemy had known, and the basic features of the earth had to be explored, relationships rethought, and a new way of looking at the globe found.

Perhaps nothing better indicates the fluid state of geography and cartography at the time than the map of Juan de la Cosa of Columbus's second voyage to the Americas (Map 7). A navigator and an explorer, de la Cosa charted the newly found coast of Central America using the points of the compass to orient the fall of the land and triangulation to project his findings inland. Although he

MAP 7 Juan de la Cosa's map of Columbus's discoveries, 1493 (*Source: Museo Naval de Madrid*)

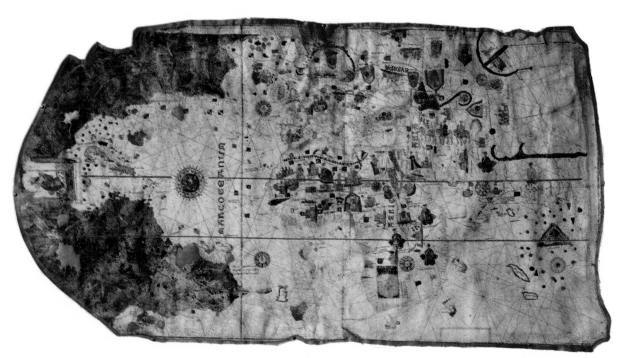

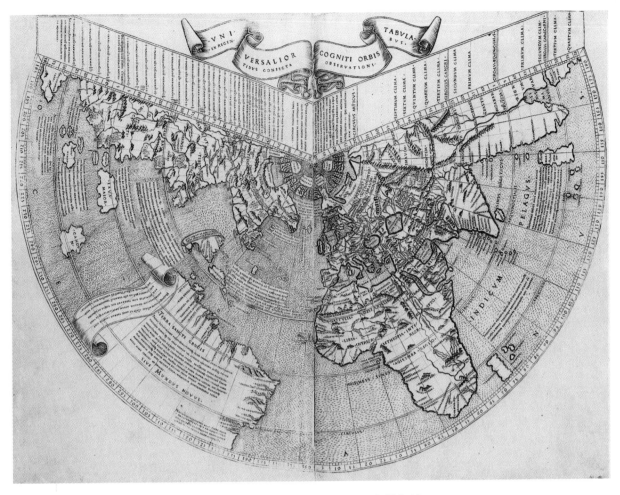

MAP 8 World map of Johannes Ruysch, 1507 and 1508 *(Source: British Library, Department of Maps)*

could depict the coastline accurately because of direct observation, de la Cosa could reveal little about the land beyond.

The discoveries of the European explorers opened a new era, both in how people thought of the world and in how to depict the new findings. The first person to apply effectively Ptolemaic geography to the discoveries of his age was perhaps Johannes Ruysch, who included material on the the New World in his editions of Ptolemy, printed in Rome in 1507 and 1508 (Map 8). Yet the real breakthrough came with Geradus Mercator (1512–1594). Mercator improved Ptolemy's system of latitude and longitude by substituting straight lines for Ptolemy's curved lines. He used this grid to incorporate the discoveries in a completely new atlas. Admittedly Mercator's method distorts the actual physical relations of the land masses over broad spaces. (A weakness of Mercator's system is that areas in the polar regions appear larger than lands near the equator. For instance, Greenland on Mercator's grid is larger than South America.) More important, however, his concept has proved that every portion of the world may be seen as possessing four right angles to orient users of his maps to every other portion of it. Mercator's grid, in one form or another, has endured as a cartographic staple to this day.

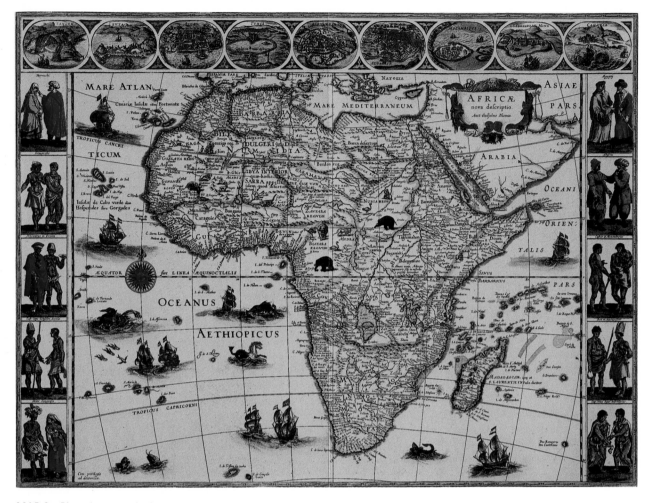

MAP 9 Blaeu's map of Africa, early seventeenth century *(Source: Courtesy, R. V. Tooley)*

The cumulative effects of the advance of knowledge in geography and cartography can best be seen in the three maps that demonstrate an increasingly precise familiarity with Africa. The map of Blaeu, dating to the early seventeenth century, combines the concepts of scale maps and picture maps (Map 9). Obviously explorers had an accurate idea only of the shape of the continent. The inland was *terra incognita,* unknown territory where fabulous beasts and peoples dwelt. The amazing progress of human knowledge of the land and how to map it can immediately be seen by comparing Blaeu's map of Africa with that of d'Anville, which was published in 1747 (Map 10). D'Anville made excellent use of Mercator's system to produce a profile of Africa that could find its place in any modern atlas. Yet d'Anville was intellectually honest enough to leave the interior of Africa largely blank. True d'Anville's map is not so visually delightful as Blaeu's, but in terms of cartography it is far more important. It showed its users what was yet to be discovered and how to proceed with finding it.

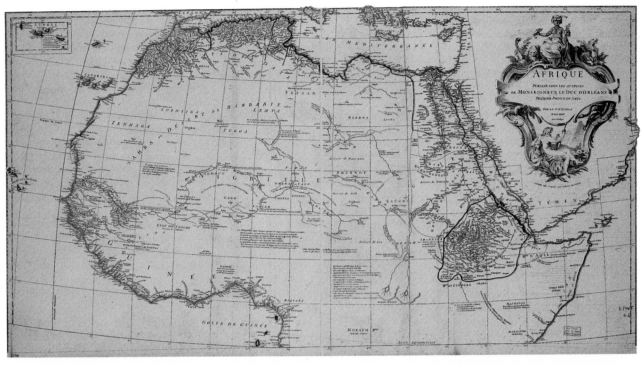

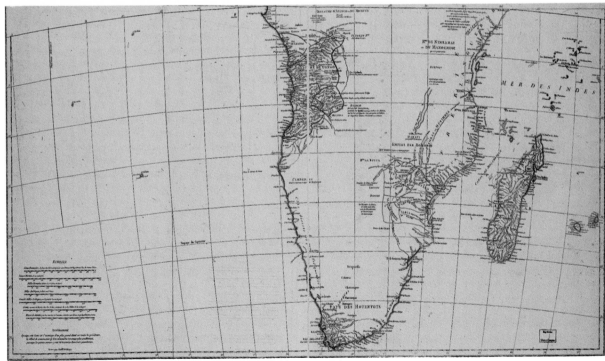

MAP 10 D'Anville's map of Africa, 1747 *(Source: Library of Congress)*

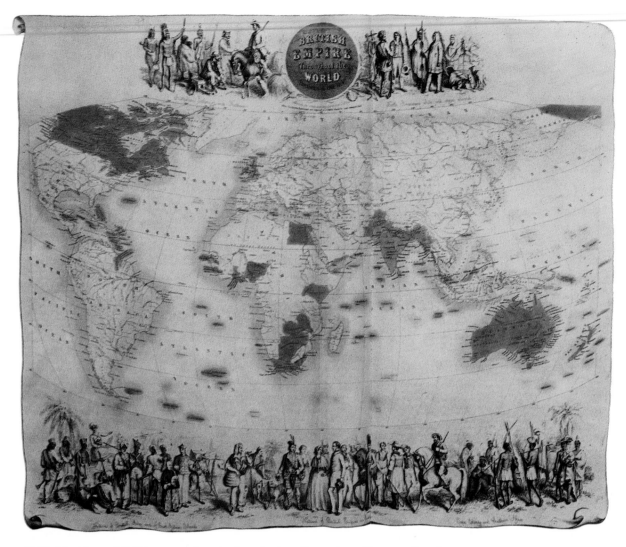

MAP 11 Map of British possessions in the nineteenth century *(Source: Courtesy, David Nash)*

Modern research has put maps to new tasks. After the basic shape and distances of the earth's features were reasonably known, it became possible to plot information on maps that illustrated the findings of scholars and scientists. Thus maps assumed an additional importance because they could record novel aspects of human life and history. The map of the British Empire illustrates when and where the British extended their control of portions of the earth (Map 11). The use of color to indicate the extent of British rule is another application of symbols to convey information. The same is true of the nineteenth-century thematic map of the spread of disease throughout the world (Map 12). Such maps give cartography a new dimension. They show not only where people are on earth but also what they have done in time. In short, they are historical maps that have as much to do with people as with places.

Mapmakers today continue to grapple with the age-old problem of how accurately to portray landmasses, their shapes, and their spatial relationships on an earth that is not a perfect sphere. The problem has been that no matter what projection is used, some geographical areas will be distorted.

In struggling with this problem, cartographers

have used circles, ovals, and rectangles to portray maps on a flat surface. The orthographic projection (the circular maps at the four corners of Maps 13, 14, and 15) uses circles and is one of the oldest. Because it shows only one hemisphere at a time, distortion is minimized, especially at the center of the map where attention is focused. It is a realistic view of the globe, but it is not possible to display more than one hemisphere at a time. As you look at the other projections, it will be useful to compare them to the orthographic projection to see where they are distorted.

The greatest distortion occurs in world maps because of their greater geographical area. Not only are the sizes of regions distorted, but so are their shapes. Different projections are able to minimize some of these distortions. Both the Sinusoidal (Map 13) and the Mollweide (Map 14) map projections provide fairly accurate area representation; that is, the relative size of the continents is correct.

MAP 12 Map illustrating the spread of disease during the nineteenth century *(Source: British Library, Department of Maps)*

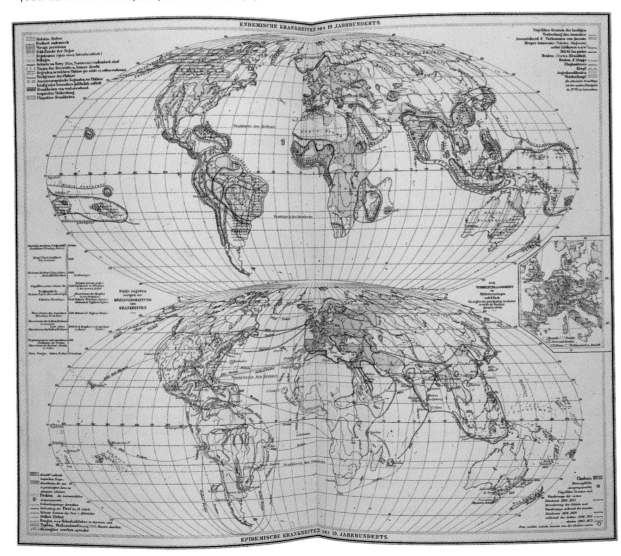

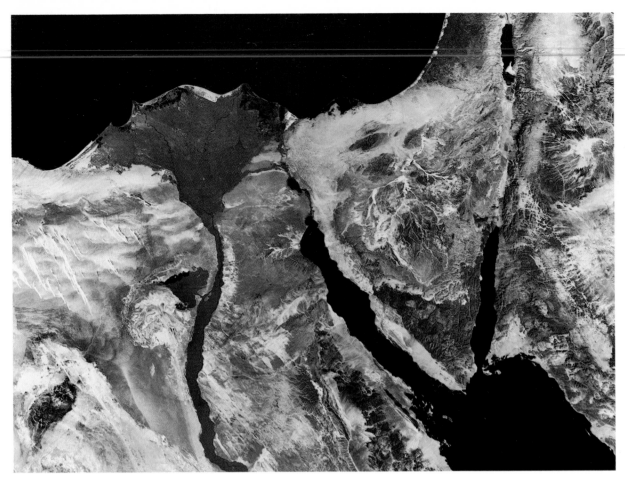

MAP 16 Landsat image of the Nile Delta *(Source: Earth Satellite Corporation)*

ellite image of the Nile Delta (Map 16) gives an excellent idea of how much more there is to learn about the planet that we often take for granted, our home, the earth.

JOHN BUCKLER

SUGGESTED READING

Bagrow, Leo. *History of Cartography.* 2nd ed. Chicago: Precedent Publishing, Inc., 1985. Brown, Lloyd A. *The Story of Maps.* New York: Dover Publications, 1979. Dilke, O. A. W. *Greek and Roman Maps.* Ithaca: Cornell University Press, 1985. Harley, J. B., and D. Woodward, eds. *The History of Cartography,* Vol. 1: Cartography in Prehistoric, Ancient and Medieval Europe and the Mediterranean. Chicago and London: University of Chicago Press, 1967. Harvey, Paul D. A. *The History of Topographical Maps.* London: Thames & Hudson, 1980. Hodgkiss, Alan G. *Understanding Maps: A Systematic History of Their Use and Development.* Folkestone: Dawson, 1981. Skelton, Raleigh A. *Decorative Printed Maps of the Fifteenth to Eighteenth Centuries.* London: Staples Press, 1952. Reprinted by Spring Books, 1970. Skelton, Raleigh A. *Explorers' Maps: Chapters in the Cartographic Record of Geographical Discovery.* London: Routledge and Kegan Paul, 1958. Reprinted by Spring Books, 1970. Thrower, Norman J. W. *Maps & Man: An Examination of Cartography in Relation to Culture and Civilization.* Englewood Cliffs, N.J.: Prentice-Hall, 1978. Tooley, R. V., Cand Bricker, and G. R. Crone. *A History of Cartography: 2500 Years of Maps and Mapmakers.* London: Thames & Hudson, 1969.

16

Absolutism and Constitutionalism in Western Europe (ca 1589–1715)

The seventeenth century was a period of revolutionary transformation. The century witnessed agricultural and manufacturing crises that had profound political consequences. A colder and wetter climate through most of the period meant a shorter farming season. Grain yields declined. In an age when cereals constituted the bulk of the diet for most people everywhere, smaller harvests led to food shortages and starvation. Food shortages in turn meant population decline or stagnation. Industry also suffered. While the evidence does not permit broad generalizations, it appears that the output of woolen textiles, one of the most important manufactures, declined sharply in the first half of the century. The economic crisis was not universal: it struck various sections of Europe at different times and to different degrees. In the middle decades of the century, Spain, France, Germany, and England all experienced great economic difficulties; but these years saw the golden age of the Netherlands.

Meanwhile, governments increased their spending, primarily for state armies; in the seventeenth century, armies grew larger than they had been since the time of the Roman Empire. To pay for these armies, governments taxed. The greatly increased burden of taxation, falling on a population already existing at a subsistence level, triggered revolts. All across Europe peasant revolts were extremely common, and everywhere "New taxes or the increase of old ones played a part in provoking almost every revolt" during the period.[1]

Governments struggled to free themselves from the restrictions of custom, powerful social groups, or competing institutions. Spanish and French monarchs gained control of the major institution in their domains, the Roman Catholic church. Rulers of England and some of the German principalities, who could not completely regulate the church, set up national churches. In the German Empire, the Treaty of Westphalia placed territorial sovereignty in the princes' hands. The kings of France, England, and Spain claimed the basic loyalty of their subjects. Monarchs made laws, to which everyone within their borders was subject. These powers added up to something close to sovereignty.

A state may be termed *sovereign* when it possesses a monopoly over the instruments of justice and the use of force within clearly defined boundaries. In a sovereign state no system of courts, such as ecclesiastical tribunals, competes with state courts in the dispensation of justice; and private armies, such as those of feudal lords, present no threat to royal authority because the state's army is stronger. Royal law touches all persons within the country. Sovereignty had been evolving during the late sixteenth century. Seventeenth-century governments now needed to address the problem of *which* authority within the state would possess sovereignty—the Crown or privileged groups.

In the period between roughly 1589 and 1715, two basic patterns of government emerged in Europe: absolute monarchy and the constitutional state. Almost all subsequent governments have been modeled on one of these patterns.

- How did these forms of government differ from the feudal and dynastic monarchies of earlier centuries?

- In what sense were they "modern"?

- What social and economic factors limited absolute monarchs?

- Which Western countries most clearly illustrate the new patterns of political organization?

This chapter will explore these questions.

ABSOLUTISM

In the *absolutist* state, sovereignty is embodied in the person of the ruler. Absolute kings claim to rule by divine right, meaning they are responsible to God alone. (Medieval kings governed "by the grace of God," but invariably they acknowledged that they had to respect and obey the law.) Absolute monarchs in the seventeenth and eighteenth centuries had to respect the fundamental laws of the land, though they claimed to rule by divine right.

Absolute rulers tried to control competing jurisdictions, institutions, or interest groups in their territories. They regulated religious sects. They abolished the liberties long held by certain areas, groups, or provinces. Absolute kings also secured the cooperation of the one class that historically had posed the greatest threat to monarchy, the nobility. Medieval governments, restrained by the church, the feudal nobility, and their own financial limitations, had been able to exert none of these controls.

In some respects, the key to the power and success of absolute monarchs lay in how they solved their financial problems. Medieval kings frequently had found temporary financial support through bargains with the nobility: the nobility agreed to an ad hoc grant in return for freedom from future taxation. In contrast, the absolutist solution was the creation of new state bureaucracies, which directed the economic life of the country in the interests of the king, either forcing taxes ever higher or devising alternative methods of raising revenue.

Bureaucracies were composed of career officials, appointed by and solely accountable to the king. The backgrounds of these civil servants varied. Absolute monarchs sometimes drew on the middle class, as in France, or utilized members of the nobility, as in Spain and eastern Europe. Where there was no middle class or an insignificant one, as in Austria, Prussia, Spain, and Russia, the government of the absolutist state consisted of an interlocking elite of monarchy, aristocracy, and bureaucracy.

Royal agents in medieval and Renaissance kingdoms had used their public offices and positions to benefit themselves and their families. In England, for example, Crown servants from Thomas Becket to Thomas Wolsey had treated their high offices as their private property and reaped considerable profit from them. The most striking difference between seventeenth-century bureaucracies and their predecessors was that seventeenth-century civil servants served the state as represented by the king. Bureaucrats recognized that the offices they held were public, or state, positions. The state paid them salaries to handle revenues that belonged to the Crown, and they were not supposed to use their positions for private gain. Bureaucrats gradually came to distinguish between public duties and private property.

Absolute monarchs also maintained permanent standing armies. Medieval armies had been raised by feudal lords for particular wars or campaigns, after which the troops were disbanded. In the seventeenth century, monarchs alone recruited and maintained armies—in peacetime as well as during war. Kings deployed their troops both inside and outside the country in the interests of the monarchy. Armies became basic features of absolutist, and modern, states. Absolute rulers also invented new methods of compulsion. They concerned themselves with the private lives of potentially troublesome subjects, often through the use of secret police.

Rule of absolute monarchs was not all-embracing, because they lacked the financial and military resources and the technology to make it so. Thus the absolutist state was not the same as a totalitarian state. *Totalitarianism* is a twentieth-century phenomenon; it seeks to direct all facets of a state's culture—art, education, religion, the economy, and politics—in the interests of the state. By definition totalitarian rule is *total* regulation. By twentieth-century standards, the ambitions of absolute monarchs were quite limited: each sought the exaltation of himself or herself as the embodiment of the state. Whether or not Louis XIV of France actually said, "L'état, c'est moi!" ("I am the state!"), the remark expresses his belief that he personified the French nation. Yet the absolutist state did foreshadow recent totalitarian regimes in two fundamental respects: in the glorification of the state over all other aspects of the culture, and in the use of war and an expansionist foreign policy to divert attention from domestic ills.

All of this is best illustrated by the experience of France, aptly known as the model of absolute monarchy.

The Foundations of French Absolutism: Sully and Richelieu

The ingenious Huguenot-turned-Catholic Henry IV (see pages 471–472) ended the French religious wars with the Edict of Nantes (1598). The first of the Bourbon dynasty, and probably the first French ruler since Louis IX in the thirteenth century genuinely to care about the French people, Henry IV and his great minister Maximilian de Béthune, duke of Sully (1560–1641), laid the foundations of later French absolutism. Henry denied influence on the royal council to the nobility, which had harassed the countryside for half a century. Maintaining that "if we are without compassion for the people, they must succumb and we all perish with them," Henry also lowered the severe taxes on the overburdened peasantry.

Sully proved himself a financial genius. He reduced the crushing royal debt accumulated during the era of religious conflict and began to build up the treasury. He levied an annual tax, the *paulette*, on people who had purchased judicial and financial offices and had consequently been exempt from taxation. The paulette provided a specific amount of revenue each year, and Sully assigned specific expenses against that revenue. One of the first French officials to appreciate the significance of overseas trade, Sully subsidized the Company for Trade with the Indies. He started a countrywide highway system and even dreamed of an international organization for the maintenance of peace.

In twelve short years, Henry IV and Sully restored public order in France and laid the foundations for economic prosperity. By the standards of the time, Henry IV's government was progressive and promising. His murder in 1610 by a crazed fanatic led to a severe crisis.

After the death of Henry IV, the queen-regent Marie de' Medici led the government for the child-king Louis XIII (r. 1610–1643), but in fact feudal nobles and princes of the blood dominated the political scene. In 1624 Marie de' Medici secured the appointment of Armand Jean du Plessis—Cardinal Richelieu (1585–1642)—to the council of ministers. It was a remarkable appointment. The next year Richelieu became president of the council, and after 1628 he was first minister of the French crown. Richelieu used his strong influence over King Louis XIII to exalt the French monarchy as the embodiment of the French state. One of the greatest servants of the French state, Richelieu set in place the cornerstone of French absolutism, and his work served as the basis for France's cultural domination of Europe in the later seventeenth century.

Richelieu's policy was the total subordination of all groups and institutions to the French monarchy. The French nobility, with its selfish and independent interests, had long constituted the foremost threat to the centralizing goals of the Crown and to a strong national state. Therefore, Richelieu tried to break the power of the nobility. He leveled castles, long the symbol of feudal independence. He crushed aristocratic conspiracies with quick executions. For example, when the duke of Montmorency, the first peer of France and the godson of Henry IV, became involved in a revolt in 1632, he was summarily put to death.

The constructive genius of Cardinal Richelieu is best reflected in the administrative system he established. He extended the use of the royal commissioners called intendants. France was divided into thirty-two *généralités* ("districts"), in each of which a royal intendant had extensive responsibility for justice, police, and finances. The intendants were authorized "to decide, order and execute all that they see good to do." Usually members of the upper middle class or minor nobility, the intendants were appointed directly by the monarch, to whom they were solely responsible. They could not be natives of the districts where they held authority; thus they had no vested interest in their localities. The intendants recruited men for the army, supervised the collection of taxes, presided over the administration of local law, checked up on the local nobility, and regulated economic activities—commerce, trade, the guilds, marketplaces—in their districts. They were to use their power for two related purposes: to enforce royal orders in the généralités of their jurisdiction and to weaken the power and influence of the regional nobility. The system of government by intendants derived from Philip Augustus's baillis and seneschals, and ultimately from Charlemagne's missi dominici. As the intendants' power grew during Richelieu's administration, so did the power of the centralized state.

The cardinal perceived that Protestantism often served as a cloak for the political intrigues of ambitious lords. When the Huguenots revolted in 1625, under the duke of Rohan, Richelieu personally supervised the siege of their walled city, La Rochelle, and forced it to surrender. Thereafter, fortified cities were abolished. Huguenots were allowed to practice their faith, but they no longer possessed armed strongholds or the means to be an independent party in the state. Another aristocratic prop was knocked down.

French foreign policy under Richelieu was aimed at the destruction of the fence of Habsburg territories that surrounded France. Consequently, Richelieu supported the Habsburgs' enemies. In 1631 he signed a treaty with the Lutheran king Gustavus Adolphus, promising French support against the Catholic Habsburgs in what has been called the Swedish phase of the Thirty Years' War (see page 478). French influence became an important factor in the political future of the German Empire. Richelieu acquired for France extensive rights in Alsace in the east and Arras in the north.

Richelieu's efforts at centralization extended even to literature. In 1635 he gave official recognition to a group of philologists who were interested in grammar and rhetoric. Thus was born the French Academy. With Richelieu's encouragement, the Academy began the preparation of a dictionary to standardize the French language; it was completed in 1694. The French Academy survives as a prestigious society and its membership now includes people outside the field of literature.

All of these new policies, especially war, cost money. In his *Political Testament* Richelieu wrote, "I have always said that finances are the sinews of the state." He fully realized that revenues determine a government's ability to inaugurate and enforce policies and programs. A state secures its revenues through taxation. But the political and economic structure of France greatly limited the government's ability to tax. Seventeenth-century France remained "a collection of local economies and local societies dominated by local elites." The rights of some assemblies in some provinces, such as Brittany, to vote their own taxes; the hereditary exemption from taxation of many wealthy members of the nobility and the middle class; and the royal pension system drastically limited the government's power to tax.

Richelieu—and later Louis XIV—temporarily solved their financial problems by securing the cooperation of local elites. The central government shared the proceeds of tax revenue with local powers. It never gained all the income it needed. Because the French monarchy could not tax at will, it never completely controlled the financial system. In practice, therefore, French absolutism was strictly limited.[2]

In building the French state, Richelieu believed he had to resort to drastic measures against persons and groups within France and to conduct a tough anti-Habsburg foreign policy. He knew also that his approach sometimes seemed to contradict traditional Christian teaching. As a priest and bishop, how did he justify his policies? He developed his own *raison d'état* ("reason of state"): "What is done for the state is done for God, who is the basis and foundation of it." Richelieu had no doubt that "the French state was a Christian state . . . governed by a Christian monarch with the valuable aid of an enlightened Cardinal Minister." "Where the interests of the state are concerned," the cardinal himself wrote, God absolves actions which, if privately committed, would be a crime."[3]

Richelieu persuaded Louis XIII to appoint his protégé Jules Mazarin (1602–1661) as his successor. An Italian diplomat of great charm, Mazarin had served on the council of state under Richelieu, acquiring considerable political experience. He became a cardinal in 1641 and a French citizen in 1643. When Louis XIII followed Richelieu to the grave in 1643 and a regency headed by Queen Anne of Austria governed for the child-king Louis XIV, Mazarin became the dominant power in the

Philippe de Champaigne: Cardinal Richelieu This portrait, with its penetrating eyes, expression of haughty and imperturable cynicism, and dramatic sweep of red robes, suggests the authority, grandeur, and power that Richelieu wished to convey as first minister of France. *(Source: Reproduced by courtesy of the Trustees, The National Gallery, London)*

government. He continued the centralizing policies of Richelieu, but his attempts to increase royal revenues led to the civil wars known as the "Fronde."

The word *fronde* means "slingshot" or "catapult," and a *frondeur* was originally a street urchin who threw mud at the passing carriages of the rich.

The term came to be used for anyone who opposed the policies of the government. The policies of Richelieu and Mazarin had vastly increased the political power of the monarchy. By 1660 the state bureaucracy included about sixty thousand officeholders who represented a great expansion of the royal presence, a broad means of extracting the wealth of the working people. Naturally, these officeholders and state bureaucrats were the bitter tar-

Coysevox: Louis XIV (1687–1689) The French court envisioned a new classical age with the Sun King as emperor and his court a new Rome. This statue depicts Louis in a classical pose, clothed (except for the wig) as for a Roman military triumph. *(Source: Caisse Nationale des Monuments Historiques et des Sites, Paris)*

gets of the exploited peasants and artisans. On the other hand, these officials, who considered their positions the path to economic and social advancement, felt they were manipulated by the Crown and their interests ignored.[4] When in 1648 Mazarin proposed new methods of raising state income, bitter civil war ensued between the monarchy on the one side and the frondeurs (the nobility and middle class) on the other. Riots and public turmoil wracked Paris and the nation. Violence continued intermittently for the next twelve years.

The conflicts of the Fronde had three significant results for the future. It became apparent that the government would have to compromise with the bureaucrats and social elites who controlled local institutions and constituted the state bureaucracy. These groups were already largely exempt from taxation, and Louis XIV confirmed their privileged social status. Second, the French economy was badly disrupted and would take years to rebuild. Finally, the Fronde had a traumatic effect on the young Louis XIV. The king and his mother were frequently threatened and sometimes treated as prisoners by aristocratic factions. On one occasion a mob broke into the royal bedchamber to make sure the king was actually there; it succeeded in giving him a bad fright. Louis never forgot such humiliations. The period of the Fronde formed the cornerstone of his political education and of his conviction that the sole alternative to anarchy was absolute monarchy. The personal rule of Louis XIV represented the culmination of the process of centralization, but it also witnessed the institutionalization of procedures that would ultimately undermine the absolute monarchy.

The Absolute Monarchy of Louis XIV

According to the court theologian Bossuet, the clergy at the coronation of Louis XIV in Reims Cathedral asked God to cause the splendors of the French court to fill all who beheld it with awe. God subsequently granted that prayer. In the reign of Louis XIV (1643–1715), the longest in European history, the French monarchy reached the peak of absolutist development. In the magnificence of his court, in his absolute power, in the brilliance of the culture over which he presided and which permeated all of Europe, and in his remarkably long life, the "Sun King" dominated his age. No wonder scholars have characterized the second half of the seventeenth century as the "Grand Century," the "Age of Magnificence," and, echoing the eighteenth-century philosopher Voltaire, the "Age of Louis XIV."

Who was this phenomenon, of whom it was said that when Louis sneezed, all Europe caught cold? Born in 1638, king at the age of five, he entered into personal, or independent, rule in 1661. One of the first tales recorded about him gained wide circulation during his lifetime. Taken as a small child to his father's deathbed, he identified himself as *Louis Quatorze* ("Louis the fourteenth"). Since neither Louis nor his father referred to himself with numerals, the story is probably untrue. But it reveals the incredible sense of self that contemporaries, both French and foreign, believed that Louis possessed throughout his life.

In old age, Louis claimed that he had grown up learning very little, but recent historians think he was being modest. True, he knew little Latin and only the rudiments of arithmetic and thus by Renaissance standards was not well educated. On the other hand, he learned to speak Italian and Spanish fluently; he spoke and wrote elegant French; he knew some French history and more European geography than the ambassadors accredited to his court. He imbibed the devout Catholicism of his mother, Anne of Austria, and throughout his long life scrupulously performed his religious duties. Religion, Anne, and Mazarin all taught Louis that God had established kings as his rulers on earth. The royal coronation consecrated him to God's service, and he was certain—to use Shakespeare's phrase—that there was a divinity that doth hedge a king. Though kings were a race apart, they could not do as they pleased: they must obey God's laws and rule for the good of the people.

Louis's education was more practical than formal. Under Mazarin's instruction, he studied state papers as they arrived, and he attended council meetings and sessions at which French ambassadors were dispatched abroad and foreign ambassadors received. He learned by direct experience and gained professional training in the work of government. Above all, the misery he suffered during the Fronde gave Louis an eternal distrust of the nobility and a profound sense of his own isolation. Accordingly, silence, caution, and secrecy became political tools for the achievement of his goals. His characteristic answer to requests of all kinds became the enigmatic "Je verrai" ("I shall see").

Louis grew up with an absolute sense of his royal dignity. Contemporaries considered him tall and distinguished in appearance but inclined to heaviness because of the gargantuan meals in which he indulged. A highly sensual man easily aroused by an attractive female face and figure, Louis nonetheless ruled without the political influence of either his wife, Queen Maria Theresa, whom he married as the result of a diplomatic agreement with Spain, or his mistresses. One contemporary described him this way: "He has an elevated, distinguished, proud, intrepid, agreeable air . . . a face that is at the same time sweet and majestic. . . . His manner is cold; he speaks little except to people with whom he is familiar . . . [and then] he speaks well and effectively, and says what is apropos. . . . [H]e has natural goodness, is charitable, liberal, and properly acts out the role of king."[5] Louis XIV was a consummate actor, and his "terrifying majesty" awed all who saw him. He worked extremely hard and succeeded in being "every moment and every inch a king." Because he so relished the role of monarch, historians have had difficulty distinguishing the man from the monarch.

Historians have often said that Louis XIV introduced significant governmental innovations, the greatest of which was "the complete domestication of the nobility." By this phrase scholars meant that he exercised complete control over the powerful social class that historically had opposed the centralizing goals of the French monarchy. Recent research has demonstrated that notions of "domestication" represent a gross exaggeration. What Louis XIV actually achieved was the cooperation or collaboration of the nobility. Throughout France the nobility agreed to participate in projects that both exalted the monarchy and reinforced the aristocrats' ancient prestige. Thus the relationship between the Crown and the nobility constituted collaboration, rather than absolute control.

In the province of Languedoc, for example, Louis and his agents persuaded the notables to support the construction of the Canal des Deux Mers, a waterway linking the Mediterranean Sea and the Atlantic Ocean. Royal encouragement for the manufacture of luxury draperies in Languedocian towns likewise tied provincial business people to national goals, although French cloths subsequently proved unable to compete with cheaper Dutch ones. Above all, in the campaign for the repression of the Huguenots, the interests of the monarchy and nobility coincided. Aristocrats repeatedly petitioned Louis XIV to close Protestant churches and schools and to expel Huguenot ministers. In 1685 the king ultimately agreed. In each instance, through mutual collaboration, the nobility and the king achieved goals that neither could have won without the other. For his part, Louis won increased military taxation from the Estates of Languedoc. In return, Louis graciously granted the nobility and dignitaries privileged social status and increased access to his person, which meant access to the enormous patronage the king had to dispense. French government rested on the social and political structure of seventeenth-century France, a structure in which the nobility historically exercised great influence. In this respect, therefore, French absolutism was not so much modern as the last phase of a historical feudal society.[6]

Louis XIV installed his royal court at Versailles, a small town 10 miles from Paris. He required all the great nobility of France, at the peril of social, political, and sometimes economic disaster, to come live at Versailles for at least part of the year. Today Versailles stands as the best surviving museum of a vanished society on earth. In the seventeenth century, it became a model of rational order, the center of France and thus the center of Western civilization, the perfect symbol of the king's power.

Louis XIII began Versailles as a hunting lodge, a retreat from a queen he did not like. His son's architects, Le Nôtre and Le Vau, turned what the duke of Saint-Simon called "the most dismal and thankless of sights" into a veritable paradise. Wings were added to the original building to make the palace U-shaped. Everywhere at Versailles the viewer had a sense of grandeur, vastness, and elegance. Enormous state rooms became display galleries for inlaid tables, Italian marble statuary, Gobelin tapestries woven at the state factory in Paris, silver ewers, and beautiful (if uncomfortable) furniture. If genius means attention to detail, Louis XIV and his designers had it: the decor was perfected down to the last doorknob and keyhole. In the gigantic Hall of Mirrors, later to reflect so much of German as well as French history, hundreds of candles illuminated the domed ceiling, where allegorical paintings celebrated the king's victories.

The art and architecture of Versailles served as fundamental tools of state policy under Louis XIV. Architecture was another device the king used to overawe his subjects and foreign visitors. Versailles was seen as a reflection of French genius. Thus the Russian tsar Peter the Great imitated Versailles in the construction of his palace, Peterhof, as did the Prussian emperor Frederick the Great in his palace at Potsdam outside Berlin.

As in architecture, so too in language. Beginning in the reign of Louis XIV, French became the language of polite society and the vehicle of diplomatic exchange. French also gradually replaced Latin as the language of international scholarship and learning. The wish of other kings to ape the courtly style of Louis XIV and the imitation of French intellectuals and artists spread the language all over Europe. The royal courts of Sweden, Russia, Poland, and Germany all spoke French. In the eighteenth century, the great Russian aristocrats were more fluent in French than in Russian. In England the first Hanoverian king, George I, spoke fluent French and only halting English. France inspired a cosmopolitan European culture in the late seventeenth century, and that culture was inspired by the king. That is why the French today revere Louis XIV as one of their greatest national heroes: because of the culture that he inspired and symbolized.

Against this background of magnificent splendor, as Saint-Simon describes him, Louis XIV

. . . reduced everyone to subjection, and brought to his court those very persons he cared least about. Whoever was old enough to serve did not dare demur. It was still another device to ruin the nobles by accustoming them to equality and forcing them to mingle with everyone indiscriminately. . . .

Upon rising, at bedtime, during meals, in his apartments, in the gardens of Versailles, everywhere the courtiers had a right to follow, he would glance right and left to see who was there; he saw and noted everyone; he missed no one, even those who were hoping they would not be seen. . . .

Louis XIV took great pains to inform himself on what was happening everywhere, in public places, private homes, and even on the international scene. . . . Spies and informers of all kinds were numberless. . . .

But the King's most vicious method of securing information was opening letters.[7]

Though this passage was written by one of Louis's severest critics, all agree that the king used court ceremonial to undermine the power of the great nobility. By excluding the highest nobles from his councils, he weakened their ancient right to advise the king and to participate in government; they became mere instruments of royal policy. Operas, fetes, balls, gossip, and trivia occupied the nobles' time and attention. Through painstaking attention to detail and precisely calculated showmanship, Louis XIV reduced the major threat to his power. He separated power from status and grandeur: he secured the nobles' cooperation, and the nobility enjoyed the status and grandeur in which they lived.

Louis dominated the court, and in his scheme of things, the court was more significant than the government. In government Louis utilized several councils of state, which he personally attended, and the intendants, who acted for the councils throughout France. A stream of questions and instructions flowed between local districts and Versailles, and under Louis XIV a uniform and centralized administration was imposed on the country. In 1685 France was the strongest and most highly centralized state in Europe.

Councilors of state came from the recently ennobled or the upper middle class. Royal service provided a means of social mobility. These professional bureaucrats served the state in the person of the king, but they did not share power with him. Louis stated that he chose bourgeois officials because he wanted "people to know by the rank of the men who served him that he had no intention of sharing power with them."[8] If great ones were the king's advisers, they would seem to share the royal authority; professional administrators from the middle class would not.

Throughout his long reign and despite increasing financial problems, he never called a meeting of the Estates General. The nobility, therefore, had no means of united expression or action. Nor did Louis have a first minister; he kept himself free from worry about the inordinate power of a Richelieu. Louis's use of spying and terror—a secret police force, a system of informers, and the practice of opening private letters—foreshadowed some of the devices of the modern state. French government remained highly structured, bureaucratic, centered at Versailles, and responsible to Louis XIV.

Financial and Economic Management Under Louis XIV: Colbert

Finance was the grave weakness of Louis XIV's absolutism. An expanding professional bureaucracy, the court of Versailles, and extensive military reforms (discussed later in this chapter) cost a great amount of money. The French method of collecting taxes consistently failed to produce enough revenue. Tax farmers, agents who purchased from the Crown the right to collect taxes in a particular district, pocketed the difference between what they raked in and what they handed over to the state. Consequently, the tax farmers profited, while the government got far less than the people paid. In addition, by an old agreement between the Crown and the nobility, the king could freely tax the common people, provided he did not tax the nobles. The nobility thereby relinquished a role in government: since they did not pay taxes, they could not legitimately claim a say in how taxes were spent. Louis, however, lost enormous potential revenue. The middle classes, moreover, secured many tax exemptions. With the rich and prosperous classes exempt, the tax burden fell heavily on those least able to pay, the poor peasants.

Hall of Mirrors, Versailles The grandeur and elegance of the Sun King's reign are reflected in the Hall of Mirrors, where the king's victories were celebrated in paintings on the domed ceiling. Hundreds of candles lit up the dome. (Source: Michael Holford)

The Spider and the Fly   In reference to the insect symbolism (upper left), the caption on the lower left side of this illustration states, "The noble is the spider, the peasant the fly." The other caption (upper right) notes, "The more people have, the more they want. The poor man brings everything—wheat, fruit, money, vegetables. The greedy lord sitting there ready to take everything will not even give him the favor of a glance." This satirical print summarizes peasant grievances. *(Source: New York Public Library)*

The king named Jean-Baptiste Colbert (1619–1683), the son of a wealthy merchant-financier of Reims, as controller-general of finances. Colbert came to manage the entire royal administration and proved himself a financial genius. Colbert's central principle was that the wealth and the economy of France should serve the state. He did not invent the system called "mercantilism," but he rigorously applied it to France.

Mercantilism is a collection of governmental policies for the regulation of economic activities, especially commercial activities, by and for the state. In seventeenth- and eighteenth-century economic theory, a nation's international power was thought to be based on its wealth, specifically its gold supply. To accumulate gold, a country should always

sell more goods abroad than it bought. Colbert believed that a successful economic policy meant more than a favorable balance of trade, however. He insisted that the French sell abroad and buy *nothing* back. France should be self-sufficient, able to produce within its borders everything the subjects of the French king needed. Consequently, the outflow of gold would be halted, debtor states would pay in bullion, and, with the wealth of the nation increased, its power and prestige would be enhanced.

Colbert attempted to accomplish self-sufficiency through state support for both old industries and newly created ones. He subsidized the established cloth industries at Abbeville, Saint-Quentin, and Carcassonne. He granted special royal privileges to the rug and tapestry industries at Paris, Gobelin, and Beauvais. New factories at Saint-Antoine in Paris manufactured mirrors to replace Venetian imports. Looms at Chantilly and Alençon competed with English lacemaking, and foundries at Saint-Étienne made steel and firearms that reduced Swedish imports. To ensure a high-quality finished product, Colbert set up a system of state inspection and regulation. To ensure order within every industry, he compelled all craftsmen to organize into guilds, and within every guild he gave the masters absolute power over their workers. Colbert encouraged skilled foreign craftsmen and manufacturers to immigrate to France, and he gave them special privileges. To improve communications, he built roads and canals, the most famous linking the Mediterranean and the Bay of Biscay. To protect French goods, he abolished many domestic tariffs and enacted high foreign tariffs, which prevented foreign products from competing with French ones.

Colbert's most important work was the creation of a powerful merchant marine to transport French goods. He gave bonuses to French shipowners and shipbuilders and established a method of maritime conscription, arsenals, and academies for the training of sailors. In 1661 France possessed 18 unseaworthy vessels; by 1681 it had 276 frigates, galleys, and ships of the line. Colbert tried to organize and regulate the entire French economy for the glory of the French state as embodied in the king.

Colbert hoped to make Canada—rich in untapped minerals and some of the best agricultural land in the world—part of a vast French empire. He gathered four thousand peasants from western

France and shipped them to Canada, where they peopled the province of Quebec. (In 1608, one year after the English arrived at Jamestown, Virginia, Sully had established the city of Quebec, which became the capital of French Canada.) Subsequently, the Jesuit Marquette and the merchant Joliet sailed down the Mississippi River and took possession of the land on both sides, as far south as present-day Arkansas. In 1684 the French explorer La Salle continued down the Mississippi to its mouth and claimed vast territories and the rich delta for Louis XIV. The area was called, naturally, "Louisiana."

How successful were Colbert's policies? His achievement in the development of manufacturing was prodigious. The textile industry, especially in woolens, expanded enormously, and "France . . . had become in 1683 the leading nation of the world in industrial productivity."[9] The commercial classes prospered, and between 1660 and 1700 their position steadily improved. The national economy, however, rested on agriculture. Although French peasants did not become serfs, as did the peasants of eastern Europe, they were mercilessly taxed. After 1685 other hardships afflicted them: poor harvests, continuing deflation of the currency, and fluctuation in the price of grain. Many peasants emigrated. With the decline in population and thus in the number of taxable people (the poorest), the state's resources fell. A totally inadequate tax base and heavy expenditure for war in the later years of the reign made Colbert's goals unattainable.

The Revocation of the Edict of Nantes

We now see with the proper gratitude what we owe to God . . . for the best and largest part of our subjects of the so-called reformed religion have embraced Catholicism, and now that, to the extent that the execution of the Edict of Nantes remains useless, we have judged that we can do nothing better to wipe out the memory of the troubles, of the confusion, of the evils that the progress of this false religion has caused our kingdom . . . than to revoke entirely the said Edict.[10]

Thus, in 1685, Louis XIV revoked the Edict of Nantes, by which his grandfather Henry IV had granted liberty of conscience to French Huguenots. The new law ordered the destruction of

churches, the closing of schools, the Catholic baptism of Huguenots, and the exile of Huguenot pastors who refused to renounce their faith. Why? There had been so many mass conversions during previous years (many of them forced) that Madame de Maintenon, Louis's second wife, could say that "nearly all the Huguenots were converted." Some Huguenots had emigrated. Richelieu had already deprived French Calvinists of political rights. Why, then, did Louis, by revoking the edict, persecute some of his most loyal and industrially skilled subjects, force others to flee abroad, and provoke the outrage of Protestant Europe?

Recent scholarship has convincingly shown that Louis XIV was basically tolerant. He insisted on religious unity not for religious but for political reasons. His goal was "one king, one law, one faith." He hated division within the realm and insisted that religious unity was essential to his royal dignity and to the security of the state. The seventeenth century, moreover, was not a tolerant one. While France in the early years of Louis's reign permitted religious liberty, it was not a popular policy. In fact, as mentioned earlier, aristocrats had petitioned Louis to crack down on Protestants. But the revocation was solely the king's decision, and it won him enormous praise. "If the flood of congratulation means anything, it . . . was probably the one act of his reign that, at the time, was popular with the majority of his subjects."[11]

While contemporaries applauded Louis XIV, scholars in the eighteenth century and later damned him for the adverse impact that revocation had on the economy and foreign affairs. Tens of thousands of Huguenot craftsmen, soldiers, and business people emigrated, depriving France of their skills and tax revenues and carrying their bitterness to Holland, England, and Prussia. Modern scholarship has greatly modified this picture. While Huguenot settlers in northern Europe aggravated Protestant hatred for Louis, the revocation of the Edict of Nantes had only minor and scattered effects on French economic development.[12]

French Classicism

Scholars characterize the art and literature of the age of Louis XIV as "French classicism." By this they mean that the artists and writers of the late seventeenth century deliberately imitated the subject matter and style of classical antiquity; that their work resembled that of Renaissance Italy; and that French art possessed the classical qualities of discipline, balance, and restraint. Classicism was the official style of Louis's court. In painting, however, French classicism had already reached its peak before 1661, the beginning of the king's personal government.

Nicholas Poussin (1594–1665) is generally considered the finest example of French classicist painting. Poussin spent all but eighteen months of his creative life in Rome because he found the atmosphere in Paris uncongenial. Deeply attached to classical antiquity, he believed that the highest aim of painting was to represent noble actions in a logical and orderly, but not realistic, way. His masterpiece, *The Rape of the Sabine Women,* exhibits these qualities. Its subject is an incident in Roman history; the figures of people and horses are ideal representations, and the emotions expressed are studied, not spontaneous. Even the buildings are exact architectural models of ancient Roman structures.

Poussin, whose paintings still had individualistic features, did his work before 1661. After Louis's accession to power, the principles of absolutism molded the ideals of French classicism. Individualism was not allowed, and artists' efforts were directed to the glorification of the state as personified

Poussin: The Rape of the Sabine Women (ca 1636) Considered the greatest French painter of the seventeenth century, Poussin in this dramatic work shows his complete devotion to the ideals of classicism. The heroic figures are superb physical specimens, but hardly life-like. *(Source: The Metropolitan Museum of Art, New York, Harris Brisbane Dick Fund, 1946 (46.160)).*

by the king. Precise rules governed all aspects of culture, with the goal of formal and restrained perfection.

Contemporaries said that Louis XIV never ceased playing the role of grand monarch on the stage of his court. If the king never fully relaxed from the pressures and intrigues of government, he did enjoy music and theater and used them as a backdrop for court ceremonial. Louis favored Jean-Baptiste Lully (1632–1687), whose orchestral works combine lively animation with the restrained austerity typical of French classicism. Lully also composed court ballets, and his operatic productions achieved a powerful influence throughout Europe. Louis supported François Couperin (1668–1733), whose harpsichord and organ works possess the regal grandeur the king loved, and Marc-Antoine Charpentier (1634–1704), whose solemn religious music entertained him at meals. Charpentier received a pension for the *Te Deums,* hymns of thanksgiving, he composed to celebrate French military victories.

Louis XIV loved the stage, and in the plays of Molière and Racine his court witnessed the finest achievements in the history of the French theater. When Jean-Baptiste Poquelin (1622–1673), the son of a prosperous tapestry maker, refused to join his father's business and entered the theater, he took the stage name "Molière." As playwright, stage manager, director, and actor, Molière produced comedies that exposed the hypocrisies and follies of society through brilliant caricature. *Tartuffe* satirized the religious hypocrite, *Le Bourgeois Gentilhomme* attacked the social parvenu, and *Les Femmes Savantes (The Learned Women)* mocked the fashionable pseudo-intellectuals of the day. In structure Molière's plays followed classical models, but they were based on careful social observation. Molière made the bourgeoisie the butt of his ridicule; he stopped short of criticizing the nobility, thus reflecting the policy of his royal patron.

While Molière dissected social mores, his contemporary Jean Racine (1639–1699) analyzed the power of love. Racine based his tragic dramas on Greek and Roman legends, and his persistent theme is the conflict of good and evil. Several plays —*Andromaque, Bérénice, Iphigénie,* and *Phèdre*— bear the names of women and deal with the power of passion in women. Louis preferred *Mithridate* and *Britannicus* because of the "grandeur" of their themes. For simplicity of language, symmetrical structure, and calm restraint, the plays of Racine represent the finest examples of French classicism. His tragedies and Molière's comedies are still produced today.

Louis XIV's Wars

Just as the architecture and court life at Versailles served to reflect the king's glory, and as the economy of the state under Colbert was managed to advance the king's prestige, so did Louis XIV use war to exalt himself above the other rulers and nations of Europe. He visualized himself as a great military hero. "The character of a conqueror," he remarked, "is regarded as the noblest and highest of titles." Military glory was his aim. In 1666 Louis appointed François le Tellier (later marquis of Louvois) as secretary of war. Louvois created a professional army, which was modern in the sense that the French state, rather than private nobles, employed the soldiers. The king himself took personal command of the army and directly supervised all aspects and details of military affairs.

A commissariat was established to feed the troops, in place of their ancient practice of living off the countryside. An ambulance corps was designed to look after the wounded. Uniforms and weapons were standardized. Finally, a rational system of recruitment, training, discipline, and promotion was imposed. With this new military machine, for the first time in Europe's history one national state, France, was able to dominate the politics of Europe.

Louis continued on a broader scale the expansionist policy begun by Cardinal Richelieu. In 1667, using a dynastic excuse, he invaded Flanders, part of the Spanish Netherlands, and Franche-Comté in the east. In consequence he acquired twelve towns, including the important commercial centers of Lille and Tournai (Map 16.1). Five years later, Louis personally led an army of over a hundred thousand men into Holland, and the Dutch ultimately saved themselves only by opening the dikes and flooding the countryside. This war, which lasted six years and eventually involved the Holy Roman Empire and Spain, was concluded by the Treaty of Nijmegen (1678). Louis gained additional Flemish towns and all of Franche-Comté.

Encouraged by his successes, by the weakness of the German Empire, and by divisions among the

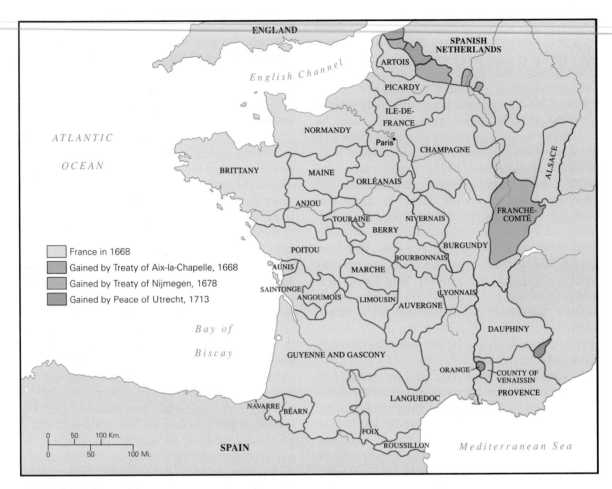

MAP 16.1 The Acquisitions of Louis XIV, 1668–1713 The desire for glory and the weakness of his German neighbors encouraged Louis' expansionist policy. But he paid a high price for his acquisitions.

other European powers, Louis continued his aggression. In 1681 he seized the city of Strasbourg and three years later sent his armies into the province of Lorraine. At that moment the king seemed invincible. In fact, Louis had reached the limit of his expansion at Nijmegen. The wars of the 1680s and 1690s brought him no additional territories. In 1689 the Dutch prince William of Orange, a bitter foe of Louis XIV, became king of England. William joined the League of Augsburg—which included the Habsburg emperor, the kings of Spain and Sweden, and the electors of Bavaria, Saxony, and the Palatinate—adding British resources and men to the alliance. Neither the French nor the league won any decisive victories. France lacked the means to win; it was financially exhausted.

Louis was attempting to support an army of 200,000 men, in several different theaters of war, against the great nations of Europe, the powerful Bank of Amsterdam, and (after 1694) the Bank of England. This task far exceeded French resources. Le Peletier, Colbert's successor as minister of finance, resorted to devaluation of the currency and to the old device of creating and selling offices, tax exemptions, and titles of nobility. These measures failed to produce adequate revenue. So the weight of taxation fell on the already overburdened peasants. They expressed their frustrations in widespread revolts that hit all parts of France in the last decades of the century.

A series of bad harvests between 1688 and 1694 brought catastrophe. Cold, wet summers reduced the harvests by an estimated one-third to two-thirds. The price of wheat skyrocketed. The result was widespread starvation, and in many provinces the death rate rose to several times the normal figure. Parish registers reveal that France buried at least a tenth of its population in those years. Rising grain prices, new taxes for war on top of old ones, a slump in manufacturing and thus in exports, and the constant nuisance of pillaging troops—all these meant great suffering for the French people. France wanted peace at any price. Louis XIV granted a respite for five years, while he prepared for the conflict later known as the War of the Spanish Succession.

This struggle (1701–1713), provoked by the territorial disputes of the past century, also involved the dynastic question of the succession to the Spanish throne. It was an open secret in Europe that the king of Spain, Charles II (r. 1665–1700), was mentally defective and sexually impotent. In 1698 the European powers, including France, agreed by treaty to partition, or divide, the vast Spanish possessions between the king of France and the Holy Roman Emperor, who were Charles II's brothers-in-law. When Charles died in 1700, however, his will left the Spanish crown and the worldwide Spanish Empire to Philip of Anjou, Louis XIV's grandson. While the will specifically rejected union of the French and Spanish crowns, Louis was obviously the power in France, not his seventeen-year-old grandson. Louis reneged on the treaty and accepted the will.

The Dutch and the English would not accept French acquisition of the Spanish Netherlands and of the rich trade with the Spanish colonies. The union of the Spanish and French crowns, moreover, would have totally upset the European balance of power. The Versailles declaration that "the Pyrenees no longer exist" provoked the long-anticipated crisis.

In 1701 the English, Dutch, Austrians, and Prussians formed the Grand Alliance against Louis XIV. They claimed that they were fighting to prevent France from becoming too strong in Europe, but during the previous half-century, overseas maritime rivalry among France, Holland, and England had created serious international tension. The secondary motive of the allied powers was to check France's expanding commercial power in North America, Asia, and Africa. In the ensuing series of conflicts, two great soldiers dominated the alliance

against France: Eugene, prince of Savoy, representing the Holy Roman Empire, and the Englishman John Churchill, subsequently duke of Marlborough. Eugene and Churchill inflicted a severe defeat on Louis in 1704 at Blenheim in Bavaria. Marlborough followed with another victory at Ramillies near Namur in Brabant.

The war was finally concluded at Utrecht in 1713, where the principle of partition was applied. Louis's grandson Philip remained the first Bourbon king of Spain on the understanding that the French and Spanish crowns would never be united. France surrendered Newfoundland, Nova Scotia, and the Hudson Bay territory to England, which also acquired Gibraltar, Minorca, and control of the African slave trade from Spain. The Dutch gained little because Austria received the former Spanish Netherlands (Map 16.2)

The Peace of Utrecht had important international consequences. It represented the balance-of-power principle in operation, setting limits on the extent to which any one power, in this case France, could expand. The treaty completed the decline of Spain as a great power. It vastly expanded the British Empire. Finally, Utrecht gave European powers experience in international cooperation, thus preparing them for the alliances against France at the end of the century.

The Peace of Utrecht marked the end of French expansionist policy. In Louis's thirty-five-year quest for military glory, his main territorial acquisition was Strasbourg. Even revisionist historians, who portray the aging monarch as responsible in negotiation and moderate in his demands, acknowledge "that the widespread misery in France during the period was in part due to royal policies, especially the incessant wars."[13] To raise revenue for the wars, forty thousand additional offices had been sold, thus increasing the number of families exempt from future taxation. In 1714 France hovered on the brink of financial bankruptcy. Louis had exhausted the country without much compensation. It is no wonder that when he died on September I, 1715, Saint-Simon wrote, "Those . . . wearied by the heavy and oppressive rule of the King and his ministers, felt a delighted freedom. . . . Paris . . . found relief in the hope of liberation. . . . The provinces . . . quivered with delight . . . [and] the people, ruined, abused, despairing, now thanked God for a deliverance which answered their most ardent desires."[14]

Spanish aristocrats, attempting to maintain an extravagant lifestyle they could no longer afford, increased the rents on their estates. High rents and heavy taxes in turn drove the peasants from the land. Agricultural production suffered, and the peasants departed for the large cities, where they swelled the ranks of unemployed beggars.

Their most Catholic majesties, the kings of Spain, had no solutions to these dire problems. If one can discern personality from pictures, the portraits of Philip III (r. 1598–1622), Philip IV (r. 1622–1665), and Charles II hanging in the Prado, the Spanish national museum in Madrid, reflect the increasing weakness of the dynasty. Their faces—the small, beady eyes, the long noses, the jutting Habsburg jaws, the pathetically stupid expressions—tell a story of excessive inbreeding and decaying monarchy. The Spanish kings all lacked force of character. Philip III, a pallid, melancholy, and deeply pious man "whose only virtue appeared to reside in a total absence of vice," handed the government over to the lazy duke of Lerma, who used it to advance his personal and familial wealth. Philip IV left the management of his several kingdoms to Count Olivares.

Olivares was an able administrator. He did not lack energy and ideas; he devised new sources of revenue. But he clung to the grandiose belief that the solution to Spain's difficulties rested in a return to the imperial tradition. Unfortunately, the imperial tradition demanded the revival of war with the Dutch, at the expiration of a twelve-year truce in 1622, and a long war with France over Mantua (1628–1659). Spain thus became embroiled in the Thirty Years' War. These conflicts, on top of an empty treasury, brought disaster.

In 1640 Spain faced serious revolts in Catalonia and Portugal; in 1643 the French inflicted a crushing defeat on a Spanish army in Belgium. By the Treaty of the Pyrenees of 1659, which ended the French-Spanish wars, Spain was compelled to surrender extensive territories to France. This treaty marked the end of Spain as a great power.

Seventeenth-century Spain was the victim of its past. It could not forget the grandeur of the sixteenth century and look to the future. The bureaucratic councils of state continued to function as symbols of the absolute Spanish monarchy. But because those councils were staffed by aristocrats, it was the aristocracy that held the real power. Spanish absolutism had been built largely on slave-pro-

duced gold and silver. When the supply of bullion decreased, the power and standing of the Spanish state declined.

The most cherished Spanish ideals were military glory and strong Roman Catholic faith. In the seventeenth century, Spain lacked the finances and the manpower to fight the expensive wars in which it foolishly got involved. Spain also ignored the new mercantile ideas and scientific methods, because they came from heretical nations, Holland and England. The incredible wealth of South America destroyed what remained of the Spanish middle class and created contempt for business and manual labor.

The decadence of the Habsburg dynasty and the lack of effective royal councilors also contributed to Spanish failure. Spanish leaders seemed to lack the will to reform. Pessimism and fatalism permeated national life. In the reign of Philip IV, a royal council was appointed to plan the construction of a canal linking the Tagus and Manzanares rivers in Spain. After interminable debate, the committee decided that "if God had intended the rivers to be navigable, He would have made them so."

In the brilliant novel *Don Quixote*, the Spanish writer Miguel de Cervantes (1547–1616) produced one of the great masterpieces of world literature. *Don Quixote*—on which the modern play *Man of La Mancha* is based—delineates the whole fabric of sixteenth-century Spanish society. The main character, Don Quixote, lives in a world of dreams, traveling about the countryside seeking military glory. From the title of the book, the English language has borrowed the word *quixotic*. Meaning "idealistic but impractical," the term characterizes seventeenth-century Spain. As a leading scholar has written, "The Spaniard convinced himself that reality was what he felt, believed, imagined. He filled the world with heroic reverberations. Don Quixote was born and grew."[16]

CONSTITUTIONALISM

The seventeenth century, which witnessed the development of absolute monarchy, also saw the appearance of the constitutional state. While France and later Prussia, Russia, and Austria (see Chapter 17) solved the question of sovereignty with the absolutist state, England and Holland evolved to-

Diego Velázquez: The Spinners (1599–1600) Spain's master of realism captures women workers in a tapestry workshop and three ladies inspecting a tapestry in the background. Or so people long believed. Modern critics see a mythological weaving competition between the low-born Arachne on the right and the goddess of arts and crafts on the left. (The gutsy Arachne lost and was turned into a spider.) Art historians also have their debates and conflicting interpretations. *(Source: Museo del Prado, Madrid)*

ward the constitutional state. What is constitutionalism? Is it identical to democracy?

Constitutionalism is the limitation of government by law. Constitutionalism also implies a balance between the authority and power of the government on the one hand and the rights and liberties of the subjects on the other. The balance is often very delicate.

A nation's constitution may be written or unwritten. It may be embodied in one basic document, occasionally revised by amendment or judi-

cial decision, like the Constitution of the United States. Or a constitution may be partly written and partly unwritten and include parliamentary statutes, judicial decisions, and a body of traditional procedures and practices, like the English and Canadian constitutions. Whether written or unwritten, a constitution gets its binding force from the government's acknowledgment that it must respect that constitution—that is, that the state must govern according to the laws. Likewise, in a constitutional state, the people look on the law and the constitution as the protectors of their rights, liberties, and property.

Modern constitutional governments may take either a republican or a monarchial form. In a constitutional republic, the sovereign power resides in the electorate and is exercised by the electorate's representatives. In a constitutional monarchy, a king or queen serves as the head of state and possesses some residual political authority, but again the ultimate or sovereign power rests in the electorate.

A constitutional government is not, however, quite the same as a democratic government. In a complete democracy, *all* the people have the right to participate either directly, or indirectly through their elected representatives, in the government of the state. Democratic government, therefore, is intimately tied up with the *franchise* (the vote). Most men could not vote until the late nineteenth century. Even then, women—probably the majority in Western societies—lacked the franchise; they gained the right to vote only in the twentieth century. Consequently, although constitutionalism developed in the seventeenth century, full democracy was achieved only in very recent times.

The Decline of Royal Absolutism in England (1603–1649)

In 1588 Queen Elizabeth I of England exercised very great personal power; by 1689 the English monarchy was severely circumscribed. Change in England was anything but orderly. Seventeenth-century England displayed little political stability. It executed one king, experienced a bloody civil war, experimented with military dictatorship, then restored the son of the murdered king, and finally, after a bloodless revolution, established constitutional monarchy. Political stability came only in the 1690s. How do we account for the fact that, after such a violent and tumultuous century, England laid the foundations for constitutional monarchy? What combination of political, socioeconomic, and religious factors brought on a civil war in 1642 to 1649 and then the constitutional settlement of 1688 to 1689?

The extraordinary success of Elizabeth I had rested on her political shrewdness and flexibility, her careful management of finances, her wise selection of ministers, her clever manipulation of Parliament, and her sense of royal dignity and devotion to hard work. The aging queen had always refused to discuss the succession. After her Scottish cousin James Stuart succeeded her as James I (r. 1603–1625), Elizabeth's strengths seemed even greater than they actually had been.

King James was well educated, learned, and, with thirty-five years' experience as king of Scotland, politically shrewd. But he was not as interested in displaying the majesty and mystique of monarchy as Elizabeth had been. He also lacked the common touch. Urged to wave at the crowds who waited to greet their new ruler, James complained that he was tired and threatened to drop his breeches "so they can cheer at my arse." The new king failed to live up to the role expected of him in England. Moreover, James's Scottish accent, in a society already hostile to the Scots and where proper spoken English was becoming a matter of concern, proved another disadvantage.[17]

James was devoted to the theory of the divine right of kings. He expressed his ideas about divine right in his essay "The Trew Law of Free Monarchy." According to James I, a monarch has a divine (or God-given) right to his authority and is responsible only to God. Rebellion is the worst of political crimes. If a king orders something evil, the subject should respond with passive disobedience but should be prepared to accept any penalty for noncompliance.

Unfortunately, he lectured the House of Commons: "There are no privileges and immunities which can stand against a divinely appointed King." This notion, implying total royal jurisdiction over the liberties, persons, and properties of English men and women, formed the basis of the Stuart concept of absolutism. Such a view ran directly counter to the long-standing English idea that a person's property could not be taken away without due process of law. James's expression of such views before the English House of Commons constituted a grave political mistake.

The House of Commons guarded the state's pocketbook, and James and later Stuart kings badly needed to open that pocketbook. Elizabeth had bequeathed to James a sizable royal debt. Through prudent management the debt could have been gradually reduced, but James I looked on all revenues as a happy windfall to be squandered on a lavish court and favorite courtiers. In reality, the extravagance displayed in James's court, as well as the public flaunting of his male lovers, weakened respect for the monarchy.

Elizabeth had also left to her Stuart successors a House of Commons that appreciated its own financial strength and intended to use that strength to acquire a greater say in the government of the state. The knights and burgesses who sat at Westminster in the late sixteenth and early seventeenth centuries wanted to discuss royal expenditures, religious reform, and foreign affairs. In short, the Commons wanted what amounted to sovereignty.

Profound social changes had occurred since the sixteenth century. The English House of Commons during the reigns of James I and his son Charles I (r. 1625–1649) was very different from the assembly Henry VIII had manipulated into passing his Reformation legislation. A social revolution had brought about the change. The dissolution of the monasteries and the sale of monastic land had enriched many people. Agricultural techniques like the draining of wasteland and the application of fertilizers improved the land and its yield. In the seventeenth century old manorial common land was enclosed and turned into sheep runs; breeding was carefully supervised, and the size of the flocks increased. In these activities, as well as in renting and leasing parcels of land, precise accounts were kept.

Many people invested in commercial ventures at home, such as the expanding cloth industry, and through partnerships and joint stock companies engaged in foreign enterprises. Many also made prudent marriages. All these developments led to a great deal of social mobility. Both in commerce and in argiculture, the English in the late sixteenth and early seventeenth centuries were capitalists, investing their profits to make more money. Though the international inflation of the period hit everywhere, in England commercial and agricultural income rose faster than prices. Wealthy country gentry, rich city merchants, and financiers invested abroad.

The typical pattern was for the commercially successful to set themselves up as country gentry, thus creating an elite group that possessed a far greater proportion of land and of the national wealth in 1640 than had been the case in 1540. Small wonder that in 1640 someone could declare in the House of Commons, probably accurately, "We could buy the House of Lords three times over." Increased wealth had also produced a better-educated and more articulate House of Commons. Many members had acquired at least a smattering of legal knowledge, and they used that knowledge to search for medieval precedents from which to argue against the king. The class that dominated the Commons wanted political power corresponding to its economic strength.

In England, unlike France, there was no social stigma attached to paying taxes. Members of the House of Commons were willing to tax themselves provided they had some say in the expenditure of those taxes and in the formulation of state policies. The Stuart kings, however, considered such ambitions intolerable presumption and a threat to their divine-right prerogative. Consequently, at every Parliament between 1603 and 1640, bitter squabbles erupted between the Crown and the wealthy, articulate, and legal-minded Commons. Charles I's attempt to govern without Parliament (1629–1640), and to finance his government by arbitrary nonparliamentary levies, brought the country to a crisis.

An issue graver than royal extravagance and Parliament's desire to make law also disturbed the English and embittered relations between the king and the House of Commons. That problem was religion. In the early seventeenth century, increasing numbers of English people felt dissatisfied with the Church of England established by Henry VIII and reformed by Elizabeth. Many Puritans (see page 444) believed that Reformation had not gone far enough. They wanted to "purify" the Anglican church of Roman Catholic elements—elaborate vestments and ceremonial, the position of the altar in the church, even the giving and wearing of wedding rings.

It is very difficult to establish what proportion of the English population was Puritan. According to the present scholarly consensus, the dominant religious groups in the early seventeenth century were Calvinist; their more zealous members were Puritans. It also seems clear that many English men and women were attracted by the socioeconomic implications of John Calvin's theology. Calvinism emphasized hard work, sobriety, thrift, competition, and postponement of pleasure, and it tended to link sin and poverty with weakness and moral corruption. These attitudes fit in precisely with the economic approaches and practices of many (successful) business people and farmers. These values have frequently been called the "Protestant ethic," "middle-class ethic," or "capitalist ethic." While it is hazardous to identify capitalism and progress with Protestantism—there were many successful Catholic capitalists—the "Protestant virtues" represented the prevailing values of members of the House of Commons.

James I and Charles I both gave the impression of being highly sympathetic to Roman Catholicism. Charles supported the policies of William Laud (1573–1645), archbishop of Canterbury, who tried to impose elaborate ritual and rich ceremonial on all churches. Laud insisted on complete uniformity of church services and enforced that uniformity through an ecclesiastical court called the "Court of High Commission." People believed the country was being led back to Roman Catholicism. In 1637 Laud attempted to impose two new elements on the church organization in Scotland: a new prayer book, modeled on the Anglican *Book of Common Prayer,* and bishoprics, which the Presbyterian Scots firmly rejected. The Scots therefore revolted. In order to finance an army to put down the Scots, King Charles was compelled to summon Parliament in November 1640.

For eleven years Charles I had ruled without Parliament, financing his government through extraordinary stopgap levies, considered illegal by most English people. For example, the king revived a medieval law requiring coastal districts to help pay the cost of ships for defense, but levied the tax, called "ship money," on inland as well as coastal countries. When the issue was tested in the courts, the judges, having been suborned, decided in the king's favor.

Most members of Parliament believed that such taxation without consent amounted to arbitrary and absolute despotism. Consequently, they were not willing to trust the king with an army. Accordingly, this Parliament, commonly called the "Long Parliament" because it sat from 1640 to 1660, proceeded to enact legislation that limited the power of the monarch and made arbitrary government impossible.

In 1641 the Commons passed the Triennial Act, which compelled the king to summon Parliament every three years. The Commons impeached Archbishop Laud and abolished the House of Lords and the Court of High Commission. It went further and threatened to abolish the institution of episcopacy. King Charles, fearful of a Scottish invasion—the original reason for summoning Parliament—

accepted these measures. Understanding and peace were not achieved, however, partly because radical members of the Commons pushed increasingly revolutionary propositions, partly because Charles maneuvered to rescind those he had already approved. An uprising in Ireland precipitated civil war.

Ever since Henry II had conquered Ireland in 1171, English governors had mercilessly ruled the land, and English landlords had ruthlessly exploited the Irish people. The English Reformation had made a bad situation worse: because the Irish remained Catholic, religious differences became united with economic and political oppression. Without an army, Charles I could neither come to terms with the Scots nor put down the Irish rebellion, and the Long Parliament remained unwilling to place an army under a king it did not trust. Charles thus instigated military action against parliamentary forces. He recruited an army drawn from the nobility and their cavalry staff, the rural gentry, and mercenaries. The parliamentary army was composed of the militia of the city of London, country squires with business connections, and men with a firm belief in the spiritual duty of serving.

The English civil war (1642–1649) tested whether sovereignty in England was to reside in the king or in Parliament. The civil war did not resolve that problem, although it ended in 1649 with the execution of King Charles on the charge of high treason—a severe blow to the theory of divine-right monarchy. The period between 1649 and 1660, called the "Interregnum" because it separated two monarchial periods, witnessed England's solitary experience of military dictatorship.

Puritanical Absolutism in England: Cromwell and the Protectorate

The problem of sovereignty was vigorously debated in the middle years of the seventeenth century. In *Leviathan,* the English philosopher and political theorist Thomas Hobbes (1588–1679) maintained that sovereignty is ultimately derived from the people, who transfer it to the monarchy by implicit contract. The power of the ruler is absolute, but kings do not hold their power by divine right. This view pleased no one in the seventeenth century.

When Charles I was beheaded on January 30, 1649, the kingship was abolished. A *commonwealth*, or republican form of government, was proclaimed. Theoretically, legislative power rested in the surviving members of Parliament and executive power in a council of state. In fact, the army that had defeated the royal forces controlled the government, and Oliver Cromwell controlled the army. Though called the "Protectorate," the rule of Cromwell (1653–1658) constituted military dictatorship.

Oliver Cromwell (1599–1658) came from the country gentry, the class that dominated the House of Commons in the early seventeenth century. He himself had sat in the Long Parliament. Cromwell rose in the parliamentary army and achieved nationwide fame by infusing the army with his Puritan convictions and molding it into the highly effective military machine, called the "New Model Army," that defeated the royalist forces.

Parliament had written a constitution, the Instrument of Government (1653), that invested executive power in a lord protector (Cromwell) and a council of state. The instrument provided for triennial parliaments and gave Parliament the sole power to raise taxes. But after repeated disputes, Cromwell tore the document up. He continued the standing army and proclaimed quasi-martial law. He divided England into twelve military districts, each governed by a major general. The major generals acted through the justices of the peace, though they sometimes overrode them. On the issue of religion, Cromwell favored broad toleration, and the Instrument of Government gave all Christians, except Roman Catholics, the right to practice their faith. Toleration meant state protection of many different Protestant sects, however, and most English people had no enthusiasm for such a notion; the idea was far ahead of its time. As for Irish Catholicism, Cromwell identified it with sedition. In 1649 he crushed rebellion in Ireland with merciless savagery, leaving a legacy of Irish hatred for England that has not yet subsided. The state rigorously censored the press, forbade sports, and kept the theaters closed in England.

Cromwell's regulation of the nation's economy had features typical of seventeenth-century absolutism. The lord protector's policies were mercantilist, similar to those Colbert established in France. Cromwell enforced a navigation act requiring that English goods be transported on English ships.

The navigation act was a great boost to the development of an English merchant marine and brought about a short but successful war with the commercially threatened Dutch. Cromwell also welcomed the immigration of Jews, because of their skills, and they began to return to England after four centuries of absence.

Absolute government collapsed when Cromwell died in 1658. Fed up with military rule, the English

Periodical Sheet on the Civil War Single sheets or broadsides spread the positions of the opposing sides to the nonliterate public. *Mercurius Rusticus,* intended for country people, conveyed the royalist argument. *(Source: The British Library)*

Cromwell Dismisses the Rump Parliament   In 1648 the army disposed of its enemies in Parliament; those who remained were known as the Rump Parliament. After the execution of Charles I and the establishment of the Commonwealth, legislative power in England theoretically rested in Parliament. But in 1653, concluding that he could not work with this body, Cromwell turned out the Rump. In this satirical Dutch print, Cromwell ordered members to go home. The sign on the wall reads, "This house is to let." *(Source: The British Library/Pat Hodgson Library)*

longed for a return to civilian government, restoration of the common law, and social stability. Moreover, the strain of creating a community of puritanical saints proved too psychologically exhausting. Government by military dictatorship was an unfortunate experiment that the English never forgot or repeated. By 1660 they were ready to restore the monarchy.

The Restoration of the English Monarchy

The Restoration of 1660 re-established the monarchy in the person of Charles II (r. 1660–1685), eldest son of Charles I. At the same time both houses of Parliament were restored, together with the established Anglican church, the courts of law, and the system of local government through justices of the peace. The Restoration failed to resolve two serious problems. What was to be the attitude of the state toward Puritans, Catholics, and dissenters from the established church? And what was to be the constitutional position of the king—that is, what was to be the relationship between the king and Parliament?

About the first of these issues, Charles II, a relaxed, easygoing, and sensual man, was basically indifferent. He was not interested in doctrinal issues. The new members of Parliament were, and they proceeded to enact a body of laws that sought to compel religious uniformity. Those who refused to receive the sacrament of the Church of England could not vote, hold public office, preach, teach, attend the universities, or even assemble for meetings, according to the Test Act of 1673. These restrictions could not be enforced. When the Quaker William Penn held a meeting of his Friends and was arrested, the jury refused to convict him.

In politics, Charles II was determined "not to set out in his travels again," which meant that he intended to get along with Parliament. Charles II's solution to the problem of the relationship between the king and the House of Commons had profound importance for later constitutional development. Generally good rapport existed between the king and the strongly royalist Parliament that had restored him. This rapport was due largely to the king's appointment of a council of five men who served both as his major advisers and as members of Parliament, thus acting as liaison agents between the executive and the legislature. This body —known as the "Cabal" from the names of its five members (Clifford, Arlington, Buckingham, Ashley-Cooper, and Lauderdale)—was an ancestor of the later cabinet system (see page 524). It gradually came to be accepted that the Cabal was answerable in Parliament for the decisions of the king. This development gave rise to the concept of ministerial responsibility: royal ministers must answer to the Commons.

Harmony between the Crown and Parliament rested on the understanding that Charles would summon frequent parliaments and that Parliament would vote him sufficient revenues. However, although Parliament believed Charles had a virtual divine right to govern, it did not grant him an adequate income. Accordingly, in 1670 Charles entered into a secret agreement with Louis XIV. The French king would give Charles £200,000 annually, and in return Charles would relax the laws against Catholics, gradually re-Catholicize England, support French policy against the Dutch, and convert to Catholicism himself.

When the details of this secret treaty leaked out, a great wave of anti-Catholic fear swept England. This fear was compounded by a crucial fact: although Charles had produced several bastards, he had no legitimate children. It therefore appeared that his brother and heir, James, duke of York, who had publicly acknowledged his Catholicism, would inaugurate a Catholic dynasty. The combination of hatred for the French absolutism embodied in Louis XIV, hostility to Roman Catholicism, and fear of a permanent Catholic dynasty produced virtual hysteria. The Commons passed an exclusion bill denying the succession to a Roman Catholic, but Charles quickly dissolved Parliament and the bill never became law.

James II (r. 1685–1688) did succeed his brother. Almost at once the worst English anti-Catholic fears, already aroused by Louis XIV's revocation of the Edict of Nantes, were realized. In direct violation of the Test Act, James appointed Roman Catholics to positions in the army, the universities, and local government. When these actions were tested in the courts, the judges, whom James had appointed, decided for the king. The king was suspending the law at will and appeared to be reviving the absolutism of his father and grandfather. He went further. Attempting to broaden his base of support with Protestant dissenters and nonconformists, James issued a declaration of indulgence granting religious freedom to all.

Two events gave the signals for revolution. First, seven bishops of the Church of England petitioned the king that they not be forced to read the declaration of indulgence because of their belief that it was an illegal act. They were imprisoned in the Tower of London but subsequently acquitted amid great public enthusiasm. Second, in June 1688 James's second wife produced a male heir. A Catholic dynasty seemed assured. The fear of a Roman Catholic monarchy, supported by France and ruling outside the law, prompted a group of eminent persons to offer the English throne to James's Protestant daughter, Mary, and her Dutch husband, Prince William of Orange. In December 1688 James II, his queen, and their infant son fled to France and became pensioners of Louis XIV. Early in 1689, William and Mary were crowned king and queen of England.

The Triumph of England's Parliament: Constitutional Monarchy and Cabinet Government

The English call the events of 1688 to 1689 the "Glorious Revolution." The revolution was indeed glorious in the sense that it replaced one king with another with a minimum of bloodshed. It also represented the destruction, once and for all, of the idea of divine-right monarchy. William and Mary accepted the English throne from Parliament and in so doing explicitly recognized the supremacy of Parliament. The revolution of 1688 established the principle that sovereignty, the ultimate power in the state, was divided between king and Parliament and that the king ruled with the consent of the governed.

The men who brought about the revolution quickly framed their intentions in the Bill of Rights, the cornerstone of the modern British constitution. The basic principles of the Bill of Rights were formulated in direct response to Stuart absolutism. Law was to be made in Parliament; once made, it could not be suspended by the Crown. Parliament had to be called at least every three years. Both elections to and debate in Parliament were to be free, in the sense that the Crown was not to interfere in them (this aspect of the bill was widely disregarded in the eighteenth century). Judges would hold their offices "during good behavior," a provision that assured the independence of the judiciary. No longer could the Crown get the judicial decisions it wanted by threats of removal. There was to be no standing army in peacetime—a limitation designed to prevent the repetition of either Stuart or Cromwellian military government. The Bill of Rights granted "that the subjects which are Protestants may have arms for their defense suitable to their conditions and as allowed by law,"[18] meaning that Catholics could not possess firearms because the Protestant majority feared them. Additional legislation granted freedom of worship to Protestant dissenters and nonconformists and required that the English monarch always be Protestant.

The Glorious Revolution found its best defense in the political philosopher John Locke's *Second Treatise of Civil Government* (1690). Locke (1632–1704) maintained that people set up civil governments in order to protect life, liberty, and property. A government that oversteps its proper function—protecting the natural rights of life, liberty, and property—becomes a tyranny. (By "natural" rights, Locke meant rights basic to all men because all have the ability to reason.) Under a tyrannical government, the people have the natural right to rebellion. Rebellion can be avoided if the government carefully respects the rights of citizens and if the people zealously defend their liberty. Recognizing the close relationship between economic and political freedom, Locke linked economic liberty and private property with political freedom. Locke

served as the great spokesman for the liberal English revolution of 1688 to 1689 and for representative government. His idea, inherited from ancient Greece and Rome (see Chapter 4), that there are natural or universal rights, equally valid for all peoples and societies, played a powerful role in eighteenth-century Enlightenment thought. His ideas on liberty and tyranny were especially popular in colonial America.

The events of 1688 to 1689 did not constitute a *democratic* revolution. The revolution placed sovereignty in Parliament, and Parliament represented the upper classes. The great majority of English people acquired no say in their government. The English revolution established a constitutional monarchy; it also inaugurated an age of aristocratic government, which lasted at least until 1832 and in many ways until 1914.

In the course of the eighteenth century, the cabinet system of government evolved. The term *cabinet* derives from the small private room in which English rulers consulted their chief ministers. In a cabinet system, the leading ministers, who must have seats in and the support of a majority of the House of Commons, formulate common policy and conduct the business of the country. During the administration of one royal minister, Sir Robert Walpole, who led the cabinet from 1721 to 1742, the idea developed that the cabinet was responsible to the House of Commons. The Hanoverian king George I (r. 1714–1727) normally presided at cabinet meetings throughout his reign, but his son and heir George II (r. 1727–1760) discontinued the practice. The influence of the Crown in decision making accordingly declined. Walpole enjoyed the favor of the monarchy and of the House of Commons and came to be called the king's first, or "prime," minister. In the English cabinet system, both legislative and executive power are held by the leading ministers, who form the government.

The Dutch Republic in the Seventeenth Century

In the late sixteenth century, the seven northern provinces of the Netherlands, of which Holland and Zeeland were the most prosperous, had succeeded in throwing off Spanish domination. This success was based on their geographical lines of defense, the wealth of their cities, the military strategy of William the Silent, the preoccupation of Philip II of Spain with so many additional concerns, and the northern provinces' vigorous Calvinism. In 1581 the seven provinces of the Union of Utrecht had formed the United Provinces (see page 474). Philip II continued to try to crush the Dutch, but in 1609 his son Philip III agreed to a truce that implicitly recognized the independence of the United Provinces. At the time neither side expected the peace to be permanent. The Peace of Westphalia in 1648, however, confirmed the Dutch republic's independence.

The seventeenth century witnessed an unparalleled flowering of Dutch scientific, artistic, and literary achievement. In this period, often called the "golden age of the Netherlands," Dutch ideas and

Vermeer: A Woman Weighing Gold (ca 1657) Vermeer painted pictures of middle-class women involved in ordinary activities in the quiet interiors of their homes. Unrivaled among Dutch masters for his superb control of light, in this painting Vermeer illuminates the pregnant woman weighing gold on her scales, as Christ in the painting on the wall weighs the saved and the damned. *(Source: National Gallery of Art, Washington; Widener Collection)*

attitudes played a profound role in shaping a new and modern world-view. At the same time, the Republic of the United Provinces of the Netherlands represents another model of the development of the modern constitutional state.

Within each province an oligarchy of wealthy merchants called "regents" handled domestic affairs in the local Estates. The provincial Estates held virtually all the power. A federal assembly, or States General, handled matters of foreign affairs, such as war. But the States General did not possess sovereign authority, since all issues had to be referred back to the local Estates for approval. The States General appointed a representative, the *stadholder,* in each province. As the highest executive there, the stadholder carried out ceremonial functions and was responsible for defense and good order. The sons of William the Silent, Maurice and William Louis, held the office of stadholder in all seven provinces. As members of the House of Orange, they were closely identified with Dutch patriotism. The regents in each province jealously guarded local independence and resisted efforts at centralization. Nevertheless, Holland, which had the largest navy and the most wealth, dominated the republic and the States General. Significantly, the Estates assembled at Holland's capital, The Hague.

The government of the United Provinces fits none of the standard categories of seventeenth-century political organization. The Dutch were not monarchial, but fiercely republican. The government was controlled by wealthy merchants and financiers. Though rich, their values were not aristocratic but strongly middle class, emphasizing thrift, hard work, and simplicity in living. The Dutch republic was not a strong federation but a confederation—that is, a weak union of strong provinces. The provinces were a temptation to powerful neighbors, yet the Dutch resisted the long Spanish effort at reconquest and withstood both French and English attacks in the second half of the century. Louis XIV's hatred of the Dutch was proverbial. They represented all that he despised—middle-class values, religious toleration, and political independence.

The political success of the Dutch rested on the phenomenal commercial prosperity of the Netherlands. The moral and ethical bases of that commercial wealth were thrift, frugality, and religious toleration. John Calvin had written, "From where do the merchant's profits come except from his own diligence and industry." This attitude undoubtedly encouraged a sturdy people who had waged a centuries-old struggle against the sea.

Alone of all European peoples in the seventeenth century, the Dutch practiced religious toleration. Peoples of all faiths were welcome within their borders. Although there is scattered evidence of anti-Semitism, Jews enjoyed a level of acceptance and absorption in Dutch business and general culture unique in early modern Europe. It is a testimony to the urbanity of Dutch society that in a century when patriotism was closely identified with religious uniformity, the Calvinist province of Holland allowed its highest official, Jan van Oldenbarneveldt, to continue to practice his Roman Catholic faith. As long as business people conducted their religion in private, the government did not interfere with them.

Toleration also paid off: it attracted a great deal of foreign capital and investment. Deposits at the Bank of Amsterdam were guaranteed by the city council, and in the middle years of the century the bank became Europe's best source of cheap credit and commercial intelligence and the main clearinghouse for bills of exchange. People of all races and creeds traded in Amsterdam, at whose docks on the Amstel River five thousand ships were berthed. Joost van den Vondel, the poet of Dutch imperialism, exulted:

God, God, the Lord of Amstel cried, hold every
*   conscience free;*
And Liberty ride, on Holland's tide, with billowing sails
*   to sea,*
And run our Amstel out and in; let freedom gird the
*   bold,*
And merchant in his counting house stand elbow deep in
*   gold.*[19]

The fishing industry was the cornerstone of the Dutch economy. For half the year, from June to December, fishing fleets combed the dangerous English coast and the North Sea, raking in tiny herring. Profits from herring stimulated shipbuilding, and even before 1600 the Dutch were offering the lowest shipping rates in Europe. The merchant marine was the largest in Europe. In 1650 contemporaries estimated that the Dutch had sixteen thousand merchant ships, half the European total. All the wood for these ships had to be imported: the Dutch bought whole forests from Norway. They also bought entire vineyards from French growers before the grapes were harvested. They controlled the Baltic grain trade, buying entire wheat and rye crops in Poland, east Prussia, and Swedish Pomerania. Because they dealt in bulk, nobody could undersell the Dutch. Foreign merchants coming to Amsterdam could buy anything from precision lenses for the newly invented microscope to muskets for an army of five thousand. Although Dutch cities became famous for their exports—diamonds and linens from Haarlem, pottery from Delft—Dutch wealth depended less on exports than on transport.

In 1602 a group of the regents of Holland formed the Dutch East India Company, a joint stock company. The investors each received a percentage of the profits proportional to the amount of money they had put in. Within half a century, the Dutch East India Company had cut heavily into Portuguese trading in East Asia. The Dutch seized the Cape of Good Hope, Ceylon, and Malacca and established trading posts in each place. In the 1630s the Dutch East India Company was paying its investors about a 35 percent annual return on their investments. The Dutch West India

Job Berckheyde: The Amsterdam Stock Exchange Small shareholders (through brokers) as well as rich capitalists could buy and sell and, by various combinations, speculate without having any money at all in the Amsterdam stock market. Shares in the Dutch East India Company were major objects of speculation. The volume, fluidity, and publicity of the Exchange were its new and distinctly modern features. *(Source: Museum Boymans-van Beuningen, Rotterdam)*

Company, founded in 1621, traded extensively with Latin America and Africa (Map 16.3).

Trade and commerce brought the Dutch prodigious wealth. In the seventeenth century, the Dutch enjoyed the highest standard of living in Europe, perhaps in the world. Amsterdam and Rotterdam built massive granaries where the surplus of one year could be stored against possible shortages the next. Thus, excepting the 1650s when bad harvests reduced supplies, food prices fluctuated very little. By the standards of Cologne, Paris, or London, salaries were high for all workers—except women. All classes of society, including unskilled laborers, ate well. The low price of bread meant that, compared to other places in Europe, a higher percentage of the worker's income could be spent on fish, cheese, butter, vegetables, even meat. A

scholar recently described the Netherlands as "an island of plenty in a sea of want." Consequently, the Netherlands experienced very few of the food riots that characterized the rest of Europe.[20]

Although the initial purpose of the Dutch East and West India Companies was commercial—the import of spices and silks to Europe—the Dutch found themselves involved in the imperialist exploitation of parts of East Asia and Latin America, with great success. In 1652 the Dutch founded Cape Town on the southern tip of Africa as a fueling station for ships planning to cross the Pacific. But war with France and England in the 1670s hurt the United Provinces. The long War of the Spanish Succession, in which the Dutch supported England against France, was a costly drain on Dutch manpower and financial resources. The peace signed in

MAP 16.3 Seventeenth-century Dutch Commerce Dutch wealth rested on commerce, and commerce depended on the huge Dutch merchant marine, manned by perhaps 48,000 sailors. The fleet carried goods from all parts of the globe to the port of Amsterdam.

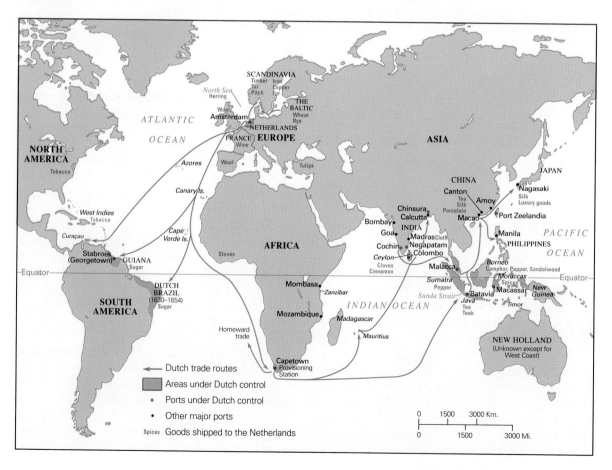

Pieter Claesz: Still Life   The term "still life" became popular after 1650 as a reference to paintings of inanimate objects—flowers, fruit, all kinds of food, tableware, musical instruments—and the term was usually applied to Dutch paintings. As this scene suggests, the enormously successful Dutch commercial society took great pleasure in sensuous materialism. Yet the tortoise, a symbol of long life, and the watch, a reminder of the passage of time, imply that all is vanity. *(Source: Louvre/Cliché des Musées Nationaux, Paris)*

1715 to end the war marked the beginning of Dutch economic decline.

SUMMARY

According to Thomas Hobbes, the central drive in every human is "a perpetual and restless desire of Power, after Power, that ceaseth only in Death." The seventeenth century solved the problem of sovereign power in two fundamental ways: absolutism and constitutionalism. The France of Louis XIV witnessed the emergence of the fully absolutist state. The king commanded all the powers of the state: judicial, military, political, and, to a great extent, ecclesiastical. France developed a centralized bureaucracy, a professional army, a state-directed economy, all of which Louis personally supervised. For the first time in history, all the institutions and powers of the national state were effectively controlled by a single person. The king saw himself as the representative of God on earth, and it has been said that "to the seventeenth century imagination God was a sort of image of Louis XIV."[21]

As Louis XIV personifies absolutism, so Stuart England exemplifies the evolution of the first modern constitutional state. The conflicts between Parliament and the first two Stuart rulers, James I and Charles I, tested where sovereign power would rest in the state. The resulting civil war did not solve the problem. The Instrument of Government, the document produced in 1653 by the victorious parliamentary army, provided for a balance of governmental authority and recognition of popular rights; as such, the Instrument has been called the first modern constitution. Unfortunately, it lacked public support. James II's absolutist tendencies brought on the Glorious Revolution of 1688 to 1689, and the people who made that revolution settled three basic issues. Sovereign power was divided between king and Parliament, with Parliament enjoying the greater share. Government was to be based on the rule of law. And the liberties of English people were made explicit in written form, in the Bill of Rights. The framers of the English constitution left to later generations the task of making constitutional government work.

The models of governmental power established by seventeenth-century England and France strongly influenced other states then and ever since. As the American novelist William Faulkner wrote, "The past isn't dead; it's not even past."

NOTES

1. G. Parker and L. M. Smith, "Introduction," and N. Steensgaard, "The Seventeenth Century Crisis," in *The General Crisis of the Seventeenth Century,* ed. G. Parker and L. M. Smith (London: Routledge & Kegan Paul, 1985), pp. 1–53, esp. p. 12.
2. J. B. Collins, *Fiscal Limits of Absolutism: Direct Taxation in Early Seventeenth Century France* (Berkeley: University of California Press, 1988), pp. 1, 3–4, 215–222.
3. Cited in J. H. Elliot, *Richelieu and Olivares* (Cambridge: Cambridge University Press, 1984), p. 135; and in W. F. Church, *Richelieu and Reason of State* (Princeton, N.J.: Princeton University Press, 1972), p. 507.
4. D. Parker, *The Making of French Absolutism* (New York: St. Martin's Press, 1983), pp. 146–148.
5. Quoted in J. Wolf, *Louis XIV* (New York: W. W. Norton, 1968), p. 115.
6. See W. Beik, *Absolutism and Society in Seventeenth Century France: State Power and Provincial Aristocracy in Languedoc* (Cambridge: Cambridge University Press, 1985), pp. 279–302.
7. S. de Gramont, ed., *The Age of Magnificence: Memoirs of the Court of Louis XIV by the Duc de Saint Simon* (New York: Capricorn Books, 1964), pp. 141–145.
8. Quoted in Wolf, p. 146.
9. Quoted in A. Trout, *Jean-Baptiste Colbert* (Boston: Twayne, 1978), p. 128.
10. Quoted in Wolf, p. 394.
11. Ibid.
12. See W. C. Scoville, *The Persecution of the Huguenots and French Economic Development: 1680–1720* (Berkeley: University of California Press, 1960).
13. W. F. Church, *Louis XIV in Historical Thought: From Voltaire to the Annales School* (New York: W. W. Norton, 1976), p. 92.
14. Gramont, p. 183.
15. J. H. Elliott, *Imperial Spain, 1469–1716* (New York: Mentor Books, 1963), pp. 306–308.
16. B. Bennassar, *The Spanish Character: Attitudes and Mentalities from the Sixteenth to the Nineteenth Century* trans. B. Keen (Berkeley: University of California Press, 1979), p. 125.
17. For a revisionist interpretation, see J. Wormald, "James VI and I: Two Kings or One?" *History* 62 (June 1983): 187–209.
18. C. Stephenson and G. F. Marcham, *Sources of English Constitutional History* (New York: Harper & Row, 1937), p. 601.
19. Quoted in D. Maland, *Europe in the Seventeenth Century* (New York: Macmillan, 1967), pp. 198–199.
20. S. Schama, *The Embarrassment of Riches: An Interpretation of Dutch Culture in the Golden Age* (New York: Alfred A. Knopf, 1987), pp. 165–170.
21. Quoted in C. J. Friedrich and C. Blitzer, *The Age of Power* (Ithaca, N.Y.: Cornell University Press, 1957), p. 112.

SUGGESTED READING

Students who wish to explore the problems presented in this chapter in greater depth will easily find a rich and exciting literature, with many titles available in paperback editions. The following surveys all provide good background material. G. Parker, *Europe in Crisis, 1598–1618* (1980), provides a sound introduction to the social, economic, and religious tensions of the period. R. S. Dunn, *The Age of Religious Wars, 1559–1715,* 2d ed. (1979), examines the period from the perspective of the confessional strife between Protestants and Catholics, but there is also stimulating material on absolutism and constitutionalism. T. Aston, ed., *Crisis in Europe, 1560–1660* (1967), contains essays by leading historians. P. Anderson, *Lineages of the Absolutist State* (1974), is a Marxist interpretation of absolutism in western and eastern Europe. M. Beloff, *The Age of Absolutism* (1967), concentrates on the social forces that underlay administrative change. H. Rosenberg, "Absolute Monarchy and Its Legacy," in N. F. Cantor and S. Werthman, eds., *Early Modern Europe, 1450–1650* (1967), is a seminal study. The classic treatment of constitutionalism remains that of C. H. McIlwain, *Constitutionalism: Ancient and Modern* (1940), written by a great scholar during the rise of German fascism. S. B. Crimes, *English Constitutional History* (1967), is an excellent survey with useful chapters on the sixteenth and seventeenth centuries.

Louis XIV and his age have predictably attracted the attention of many scholars. J. Wolf's *Louis XIV,* cited in the Notes, remains the best available biography. Two works of W. H. Lewis, *The Splendid Century* (1957) and *The Sunset of the Splendid Century* (1963), make delightful light reading, especially for the beginning student. The advanced student will want to consult the excellent historiographical analysis by W. F. Church mentioned in the Notes, *Louis XIV in Historical Thought.* Perhaps the best works of the Annales school on the period are P.

Goubert, *Louis XIV and Twenty Million Frenchmen* (1972), and his heavily detailed *The Ancien Régime: French Society, 1600–1750,* 2 vols. (1969–1973), which contains invaluable material on the lives and work of ordinary people. For the French economy and financial conditions, the old study of C. W. Cole, *Colbert and a Century of French Mercantilism,* 2 vols. (1939), is still valuable but should be supplemented by R. Bonney, *The King's Debts: Finance and Politics in France, 1589–1661* (1981), and by the works of Trout and Scoville listed in the Notes. Scoville's book is a significant contribution to revisionist history. For Louis XIV's foreign policy and wars, see R. Hatton, "Louis XIV: Recent Gains in Historical Knowledge," *Journal of Modern History* 45 (1973), and her edited work *Louis XIV and Europe* (1976), an important collection of essays. Hatton's *Europe in the Age of Louis XIV* (1979) is a splendidly illustrated survey of many aspects of seventeenth-century European culture. O. Ranum, *Paris in the Age of Absolutism* (1968), describes the geographical, political, economic, and architectural significance of the cultural capital of Europe, while V. L. Tapie, *The Age of Grandeur: Baroque Art and Architecture* (1960), also emphasizes the relationship between art and politics with excellent illustrations.

For Spain and Portugal, in addition to the works in the Notes, see M. Defourneaux, *Daily Life in Spain in the Golden Age* (1976), highly useful for an understanding of ordinary people and of Spanish society; and C. R. Phillips, *Ciudad Real, 1500–1750: Growth, Crisis, and Readjustment in the Spanish Economy* (1979), a significant case study.

The following works all offer solid material on English political and social issues of the seventeenth century: M. Ashley, *England in the Seventeenth Century,* rev. ed. (1980), and *The House of Stuart: Its Rise and Fall* (1980); C. Hill, *A Century of Revolution* (1961); J. P. Kenyon, *Stuart England* (1978); and K. Wrightson, *English Society, 1580–1680* (1982). Perhaps the most comprehensive treatments of Parliament are C. Russell's *Crisis of Parliaments, 1509–1660* (1971) and *Parliaments and English Politics, 1621–1629* (1979). On the background of the English civil war, L. Stone, *The Crisis of the Aristocracy* (1965) and *The Causes of the English Revolution* (1972), are standard works, while both B. Manning, *The English People and the English Revolution* (1976), and D. Underdown, *Revel, Riot, and Rebellion* (1985), discuss the extent of popular involvement; Underdown's is the more sophisticated treatment. For English intellectual currents, see J. O. Appleby, *Economic Thought and Ideology in Seventeenth Century England* (1978); and C. Hill, *Intellectual Origins of the English Revolution* (1966) and *Society and Puritanism in Pre-revolutionary England* (1964).

For the several shades of Protestant sentiment in the early seventeenth century, see P. Collinson, *The Religion of Protestants* (1982). C. M. Hibbard, *Charles I and the Po-*

pish Plot (1983), treats Roman Catholic influence; like Collinson's work, it is an excellent, fundamental reference for religious issues, though the older work of W. Haller, *The Rise of Puritanism* (1957), is still valuable. For women, see R. Thompson, *Women in Stuart England and America* (1974), and A. Fraser, *The Weaker Vessel* (1985). For Cromwell and the Interregnum, C. Firth, *Oliver Cromwell and the Rule of the Puritans in England* (1956); C. Hill, *God's Englishman* (1972); and A. Fraser, *Cromwell, the Lord Protector* (1973), are all valuable. J. Morrill, *The Revolt of the Provinces,* 2d ed. (1980), is the best study of religious neutralism, while C. Hill, *The World Turned Upside Down* (1972), discusses radical thought during the period.

For the Restoration and the Glorious Revolution, see R. Hutton, *Charles II: King of England, Scotland and Ireland* (1989), and A. Fraser, *Royal Charles: Charles II and the Restoration* (1979), two highly readable biographies; R. Ollard, *The Image of the King: Charles I and Charles II* (1980), which examines the nature of monarchy; J. Miller, *James II: A Study in Kingship* (1977); J. Childs, *The Army, James II, and the Glorious Revolution* (1980); J. R. Jones, *The Revolution of 1688 in England* (1972); and L. G. Schwoerer, *The Declaration of Rights, 1689* (1981), a fine assessment of that fundamental document. The ideas of John Locke are analyzed by J. P. Kenyon, *Revolution Principles: The Politics of Party, 1689–1720* (1977). R. Hutton, *The Restoration, 1658–1667* (1985), is a thorough if somewhat difficult narrative.

On Holland, K. H. D. Haley, *The Dutch Republic in the Seventeenth Century* (1972), is a splendidly illustrated appreciation of Dutch commercial and artistic achievements, while J. L. Price, *Culture and Society in the Dutch Republic During the Seventeenth Century* (1974), is a sound scholarly work. R. Boxer, *The Dutch Seaborne Empire* (1980), and the appropriate chapters of D. Maland's *Europe in the Seventeenth Century,* cited in the Notes, are useful for Dutch overseas expansion and the reasons for Dutch prosperity. The following works focus on the economic and cultural life of the leading Dutch city: V. Barbour, *Capitalism in Amsterdam in the Seventeenth Century* (1950), and D. Regin, *Traders, Artists, Burghers: A Cultural History of Amsterdam in the Seventeenth Century* (1977). J. M. Montias, *Artists and Artisans in Delft: A Socioeconomic Study of the Seventeenth Century* (1982), examines another major city. The leading statesmen of the period may be studied in these biographies: H. H. Rowen, *John de Witt, Grand Pensionary of Holland, 1625–1672* (1978); S. B. Baxter, *William the III and the Defense of European Liberty, 1650–1702* (1966); and J. den Tex, *Oldenbarnevelt,* 2 vols. (1973).

Many facets of the lives of ordinary French, Spanish, English, and Dutch people are discussed by P. Burke, *Popular Culture in Early Modern Europe* (1978), an important and provocative study.

17

Absolutism in Eastern Europe to 1740

A Prussian Giant Grenadier Frederick William I wanted tall, handsome soldiers. He dressed them in tight bright uniforms to distinguish them from the peasant population from which most soldiers came. He also ordered several portraits of his favorites from his court painter, J. C. Merk. Grenadiers wore the distinctive mitre cap instead of an ordinary hat so that they could hurl their heavy hand grenades unimpeded by a broad brim. *(Source: Copyright reserved to Her Majesty Queen Elizabeth II)*

was still a novelty. Moreover, the Great Elector's successor, Elector Frederick III, "the Ostentatious" (r. 1688–1713), was weak of body and mind.

Like so many of the small princes of Germany and Italy at the time, Frederick III imitated Louis XIV in every possible way. He built his own very expensive version of Versailles. He surrounded himself with cultivated artists and musicians and basked in the praise of toadies and sycophants. His only real political accomplishment was to gain the title of king from the Holy Roman emperor, a Habsburg, in return for military aid in the War of the Spanish Succession, and in 1701 he was crowned King Frederick I.

This tendency toward luxury-loving, happy, and harmless petty tyranny was completely reversed by Frederick William I, "the Soldiers' King" (r. 1713–1740). A crude, dangerous psychoneurotic, Frederick William I was nevertheless the most talented reformer ever produced by the Hohenzollern family. It was he who truly established Prussian absolutism and gave it its unique character. It was he who created the the best army in Europe, for its size, and who infused military values into a whole society. In the words of a leading historian of Prussia:

For a whole generation, the Hohenzollern subjects were victimized by a royal bully, imbued with an obsessive bent for military organization and military scales of value. This left a deep mark upon the institutions of Prussiandom and upon the molding of the "Prussian spirit."[3]

Frederick William's attachment to the army and military life was intensely emotional. He had, for example, a bizarre, almost pathological love for tall soldiers, whom he credited with superior strength and endurance. Austere and always faithful to his wife, he confided to the French ambassador: "The most beautiful girl or woman in the world would be a matter of indifference to me, but tall soldiers —they are my weakness." Like some fanatical modern-day basketball coach in search of a championship team, he sent his agents throughout both Prussia and all of Europe, tricking, buying, and kidnaping top recruits. Neighboring princes sent him their giants as gifts to win his gratitude. Prussian mothers told their sons: "Stop growing or the recruiting agents will get you."[4]

Profoundly military in temperament, Frederick William always wore an army uniform, and he lived the highly disciplined life of the professional soldier. He began his work by five or six in the morning; at ten he almost always went to the parade ground to drill or inspect his troops. A man of violent temper, Frederick William personally punished the most minor infractions on the spot: a missing button off a soldier's coat quickly provoked a savage beating with his heavy walking stick.

Frederick William's love of the army was also based on a hardheaded conception of the struggle for power and a dog-eat-dog view of international politics. Even before ascending the throne, he bitterly criticized his father's ministers: "They say that they will obtain land and power for the king with the pen; but I say it can be done only with the sword." Years later he summed up his life's philosophy in his instructions to his son: "A formidable army and a war chest large enough to make this army mobile in times of need can create great respect for you in the world, so that you can speak a word like the other powers."[5] This unshakable belief that the welfare of king and state depended on the army above all else reinforced Frederick William's passion for playing soldier.

The cult of military power provided the rationale for a great expansion of royal absolutism. As the ruthless king himself put it: "I must be served with life and limb, with house and wealth, with honour and conscience, everything must be committed except eternal salvation—that belongs to God, but all else is mine."[6] To make good these extraordinary demands, Frederick William created a strong centralized bureaucracy. More commoners probably rose to top positions in the civil government than at any other time in Prussia's history. The last traces of the parliamentary Estates and local self-government vanished.

The king's grab for power brought him into considerable conflict with the noble landowners, the Junkers. In his early years, he even threatened to destroy them; yet, in the end, the Prussian nobility was not destroyed but enlisted—into the army. Responding to a combination of threats and opportunities, the Junkers became the officer caste. By 1739 all but 5 of 245 officers with the rank of major or above were aristocrats, and most of them were native Prussians. A new compromise had been worked out, whereby the proud nobility imperiously commanded the peasantry in the army as well as on its estates.

Coarse and crude, penny-pinching and hardworking, Frederick William achieved results.

Above all, he built a first-rate army on the basis of third-rate resources. The standing army increased from 38,000 to 83,000 during his reign. Prussia, twelfth in Europe in population, had the fourth largest army by 1740. Only the much more populous states of France, Russia, and Austria had larger forces, and even France's army was only twice as large as Prussia's. Moreover, soldier for soldier, the Prussian army became the best in Europe, astonishing foreign observers with its precision, skill, and discipline. For the next two hundred years, Prussia and then Prussianized Germany would almost always win the crucial military battles.

Frederick William and his ministers also built an exceptionally honest and conscientious bureaucracy, which not only administered the country but tried with some success to develop it economically. Finally, like the miser he was, living very frugally off the income of his own landholdings, the king loved his "blue boys" so much that he hated to "spend" them. This most militaristic of kings was, paradoxically, almost always at peace.

Nevertheless, the Prussian people paid a heavy and lasting price for the obsessions of the royal drillmaster. Civil society became rigid and highly disciplined. Prussia became the "Sparta of the North"; unquestioning obedience was the highest virtue. As a Prussian minister later summed up, "To keep quiet is the first civic duty."[7] Thus the policies of Frederick William I combined with harsh peasant bondage and Junker tyranny to lay the foundations for probably the most militaristic country of modern times.

THE DEVELOPMENT OF RUSSIA

One of the favorite parlor games of nineteenth-century Russian (and non-Russian) intellectuals was debating whether Russia was a Western and European or a non-Western Asiatic society. This question was particularly fascinating because it was unanswerable. To this day Russia differs fundamentally from the West in some basic ways, though Russian history has paralleled that of the West in other ways. A good case can be made for either position: thus the hypnotic attraction of Russian history.

The differences between Russia and the West were particularly striking before 1700, when

St. Basil's Cathedral in Moscow, with its sloping roofs and colorful onion-shaped domes, is a striking example of powerful Byzantine influences on Russian culture. According to tradition, an enchanted Ivan the Terrible blinded the cathedral's architects to ensure that they would never duplicate their fantastic achievement, which still dazzles the beholder in today's Red Square. *(Source: George Holton/Photo Researchers)*

competing princes left to turn to, the boyars had to yield.

The rise of the new service nobility accelerated under Ivan IV (r. 1533–1584), the famous Ivan the Terrible. Having ascended the throne at age three, Ivan suffered insults and neglect at the hands of the haughty boyars after his mother mysteriously died, possibly poisoned, when he was just eight. At age sixteen he suddenly pushed aside his hated boyar advisers. In an awe-inspiring ceremony, complete with gold coins pouring down on his head, he majestically crowned himself and officially took the august title of tsar for the first time.

Selecting the beautiful and kind Anastasia of the popular Romanov family for his wife and queen, the young tsar soon declared war on the remnants

of Mongol power. He defeated the faltering khanates of Kazan and Astrakhan between 1552 and 1556, adding vast new territories to Russia. In the course of these wars, Ivan virtually abolished the old distinction between hereditary boyar private property and land granted temporarily for service. All nobles, old and new, had to serve the tsar in order to hold any land.

The process of transforming the entire nobility into a service nobility was completed in the second part of Ivan the Terrible's reign. In 1557 Ivan turned westward, and for the next twenty-five years Muscovy waged an exhausting, unsuccessful war primarily with the large Polish-Lithuanian state, which controlled not only Poland but much of the Ukraine in the sixteenth century. Quarreling with the boyars over the war and blaming them for the sudden death of his beloved Anastasia in 1560, the increasingly cruel and demented Ivan turned to strike down all who stood in his way.

Above all, he struck down the ancient Muscovite boyars with a reign of terror. Leading boyars, their relatives, and even their peasants and servants were executed en masse by a special corps of unquestioning servants. Dressed in black and riding black horses, they were forerunners of the modern dictator's secret police. Large estates were confiscated, broken up, and reapportioned to the lower service nobility. The great boyar families were severely reduced. The newer, poorer, more nearly equal service nobility, still less than half a percent of the total population, was totally dependent on the autocrat.

Ivan also took giant strides toward making all commoners servants of the tsar. His endless wars and demonic purges left much of central Russia depopulated. It grew increasingly difficult for the lower service nobility to squeeze a living for themselves out of the peasants left on their landholdings. As the service nobles demanded more from the remaining peasants, more and more peasants fled toward the wild, recently conquered territories to the east and south. There they formed free groups and outlaw armies known as "Cossacks." The Cossacks maintained a precarious independence beyond the reach of the oppressive landholders and the tsar's hated officials. The solution to this problem was to complete the tying of the peasants to the land, making them serfs perpetually bound to serve the noble landholders, who were bound in turn to serve the tsar.

In the time of Ivan the Terrible, urban traders and artisans were also bound to their towns and jobs, so that the tsar could tax them more heavily. Ivan assumed that the tsar owned Russia's trade and industry, just as he owned all the land. In the course of the sixteenth and seventeenth centuries, the tsars therefore took over the mines and industries and monopolized the country's important commercial activities. The urban classes had no security in their work or property, and even the wealthiest merchants were basically dependent agents of the tsar. If a new commercial activity became profitable, it was often taken over by the tsar and made a royal monopoly. This royal monopolization was in sharp contrast to developments in western Europe, where the capitalist middle classes were gaining strength and security in their private property. The tsar's service obligations checked the growth of the Russian middle classes, just as they led to decline of the boyars, rise of the lower nobility, and the final enserfment of the peasants.

Ivan the Terrible's system of autocracy and compulsory service struck foreign observers forcibly. Sigismund Herberstein, a German traveler to Russia, wrote in 1571: "All the people consider themselves to be *kholops*, that is slaves of their Prince." At the same time, Jean Bodin, the French thinker who did so much to develop the modern concept of sovereignty, concluded that Russia's political system was fundamentally different from those of all other European monarchies and comparable only to that of the Turkish empire. In both Turkey and Russia, as in other parts of Asia and Africa, "the prince is become lord of the goods and persons of his subjects . . . governing them as a master of a family does his slaves."[12] The Mongol inheritance weighed heavily on Russia.

Ivan the Terrible Ivan IV, the first to take the title Tsar of Russia, executed many Muscovite boyars and their peasants and servants. His ownership of all the land, trade, and industry restricted economic development. *(Source: National Museum, Copenhagen, Denmark)*

and able-bodied men were desperately needed on the farm in the busy summer months. Thus beautiful St. Petersburg was built on the shoveling, carting, and paving of a mass of conscripted serfs.

Peter also drafted more privileged groups to his city, but on a permanent basis. Nobles were summarily ordered to build costly stone houses and palaces in St. Petersburg and to live in them most of the year. The more serfs a noble possessed, the bigger his dwelling had to be. Merchants and artisans were also commanded to settle and build in St. Petersburg. These nobles and merchants were then required to pay for the city's avenues, parks, canals, embankments, pilings, and bridges, all of which were very costly in terms of both money and lives because they were built on a swamp. The building of St. Petersburg was, in truth, an enormous direct tax levied on the wealthy, who in turn forced the peasantry to do most of the work. The only immediate beneficiaries were the foreign architects and urban planners. No wonder so many Russians hated Peter's new city.

Yet the tsar had his way. By the time of his death in 1725, there were at least six thousand houses and numerous impressive government buildings in St. Petersburg. Under the remarkable women who ruled Russia throughout most of the eighteenth century, St. Petersburg blossomed fully as a majestic and well-organized city, at least in its wealthy showpiece sections. Peter's youngest daughter, the quick-witted, sensual beauty, Elizabeth (r. 1741–1762), named as her chief architect Bartolomeo Rastrelli, who had come to Russia from Italy as a boy of fifteen in 1715. Combining Italian and Russian traditions into a unique, wildly colorful St. Petersburg style, Rastrelli built many palaces for the nobility and all the larger government buildings erected during Elizabeth's reign. He also rebuilt the Winter Palace as an enormous, aqua-colored royal residence, now the Hermitage Museum. There Elizabeth established a flashy, luxury-loving, and slightly crude court, which Catherine the Great in turn made truly imperial. All the while St. Petersburg grew rapidly, and its almost 300,000 inhabitants in 1782 made it one of the world's largest cities. Peter and his successors had created out of nothing a magnificent and harmonious royal city, which unmistakably proclaimed the power of Russia's rulers and the creative potential of the absolutist state.

SUMMARY

From about 1400 to 1650, social and economic developments in eastern Europe increasingly diverged from those in western Europe. In the east, peasants and townspeople lost precious freedoms, while the nobility increased its power and prestige. It was within this framework of resurgent serfdom and entrenched nobility that Austrian and Prussian monarchs fashioned absolutist states in the seventeenth and early eighteenth centuries. These monarchs won absolutist control over standing armies, permanent taxes, and legislative bodies. But they did not question the underlying social and economic relationships. Indeed, they enhanced the privileges of the nobility, which furnished the leading servitors for enlarged armies and growing state bureaucracies.

In Russia, the social and economic trends were similar, but the timing of political absolutism was different. Mongol conquest and rule was a crucial experience, and a harsh, indigenous tsarist autocracy was firmly in place by the reign of Ivan the Terrible in the sixteenth century. More than a century later, Peter the Great succeeded in tightening up Russia's traditional absolutism and modernizing it by reforming the army, the bureaucracy, and the defense industry. In Russia and throughout eastern Europe, war and the needs of the state in time of war weighed heavily in the triumph of absolutism.

Triumphant absolutism interacted spectacularly with the arts. Baroque art, which had grown out of the Catholic Reformation's desire to move the faithful and exalt the true faith, admirably suited the secular aspirations of eastern European rulers. They built grandiose baroque palaces, monumental public squares, and even whole cities to glorify their power and majesty. Thus baroque art attained magnificent heights in eastern Europe, symbolizing the ideal and harmonizing with the reality of imperious royal absolutism.

NOTES

1. Quoted in F. L. Carsten, *The Origins of Prussia* (Oxford: Clarendon Press, 1954), p. 152.
2. Ibid., p. 175.

3. H. Rosenberg, *Bureaucracy, Aristocracy, and Autocracy: The Prussian Experience, 1660–1815* (Boston: Beacon Press, 1966), p. 38.

4. Quoted in R. Ergang, *The Potsdam Fuhrer: Frederick William I, Father of Prussian Militarism* (New York: Octagon Books, 1972), pp. 85, 87.

5. Ibid., pp. 6–7, 43.

6. Quoted in R. A. Dorwart, *The Administrative Reforms of Frederick William I of Prussia* (Cambridge, Mass.: Harvard University Press, 1953), p. 226.

7. Quoted in Rosenberg, p. 40.

8. Quoted in R. Pipes, *Russia Under the Old Regime* (New York: Charles Scribner's Sons, 1974), p. 48.

9. Quoted in N. V. Riasanovsky, *A History of Russia* (New York: Oxford University Press, 1963), p. 79.

10. Quoted in I. Grey, *Ivan III and the Unification of Russia* (New York: Collier Books, 1967), p. 39.

11. Quoted in Grey, p. 42.

12. Both quoted in Pipes, pp. 65, 85.

13. Quoted in Ergang, p. 13.

14. Quoted in J. Summerson, in *The Eighteenth Century: Europe in the Age of Enlightenment,* ed. A. Cobban (New York: McGraw-Hill, 1969), p. 80.

15. Quoted in L. Mumford, *The Culture of Cities* (New York: Harcourt Brace Jovanovich, 1938), p. 97.

SUGGESTED READING

All of the books cited in the Notes are highly recommended. Carsten's *The Origin of Prussia* is the best study on early Prussian history, and Rosenberg's *Bureaucracy, Aristocracy, and Autocracy* is a masterful analysis of the social context of Prussian absolutism. In addition to Ergang's *The Potsdam Fuhrer,* an exciting and critical biography of ramrod Frederick William I, there is G. Ritter, *Frederick the Great* (1968), a more sympathetic study of the talented son by one of Germany's leading conservative historians. G. Craig, *The Politics of the Prussian Army, 1640–1945* (1964), expertly traces the great influence of the military on the Prussian state over three hundred years. R. J. Evans, *The Making of the Habsburg Empire, 1550–1770* (1979), and R. A. Kann, *A History of the Habsburg Empire, 1526–1918* (1974), analyze the development of absolutism in Austria, as does A. Wandruszka, *The House of Habsburg* (1964). J. Stoye, *The Siege of Vienna* (1964), is a fascinating account of the last great Ottoman offensive, which is also treated in the interesting study by P. Coles, *The Ottoman Impact on Europe, 1350–1699* (1968). The Austro-Ottoman conflict is also a theme of L. S. Stavrianos, *The Balkans Since 1453* (1958), and D. McKay's fine biography, *Prince Eugene of Savoy* (1978). A good general account is provided in D. McKay and H. Scott, *The Rise of the Great Powers, 1648–1815* (1983), and R. Vierhaus, *Germany in the Age of Absolutism* (1988), offers a good survey of the different German states.

On eastern European peasants and serfdom, D. Chirot, ed., *The Origins of Backwardness in Eastern Europe: Economics and Politics from the Middle Ages Until the Twentieth Century* (1989), is a wide-ranging introduction, which may be compared with J. Blum, "The Rise of Serfdom in Eastern Europe," *American Historical Review* 62 (July 1957): 807–836. E. Levin, *Sex and Society in the World of the Orthodox Slavs, 900–1700* (1989), carries family history to eastern Europe, while R. Mousnier, *Peasant Uprisings in Seventeenth-Century France, Russia, and China* (1970), is a fine comparative study. J. Blum, *Lord and Peasant in Russia from the Ninth to the Nineteenth Century* (1961), provides a good look at conditions in rural Russia, and P. Avrich, *Russian Rebels, 1600–1800* (1972), treats some of the violent peasant upheavals those conditions produced. R. Hellie, *Enserfment and Military Change in Muscovy* (1971), is outstanding, as is A. Yanov's provocative *Origins of Autocracy: Ivan the Terrible in Russian History* (1981). In addition to the fine surveys by Pipes and Riasanovsky cited in the Notes, J. Billington, *The Icon and the Axe* (1970), is a stimulating history of early Russian intellectual and cultural developments, such as the great split in the church. M. Raeff, *Origins of the Russian Intelligentsia* (1966), skillfully probes the mind of the Russian nobility in the eighteenth century. B. H. Sumner, *Peter the Great and the Emergence of Russia* (1962), is a fine brief introduction, which may be compared with the brilliant biography by Russia's greatest prerevolutionary historian, V. Klyuchevsky, *Peter the Great* (English trans., 1958), and with N. Riasanovsky, *The Image of Peter the Great in Russian History and Thought* (1985). G. Vernadsky and R. Fisher, eds., *A Source Book of Russian History from Early Times to 1917,* 3 vols. (1972), is an invaluable, highly recommended collection of documents and contemporary writings.

Three good books on art and architecture are E. Hempel, *Baroque Art and Architecture in Central Europe* (1965); G. Hamilton, *The Art and Architecture of Russia* (1954); and N. Pevsner, *An Outline of European Architecture,* 6th ed. (1960).

18

Toward a New World-view

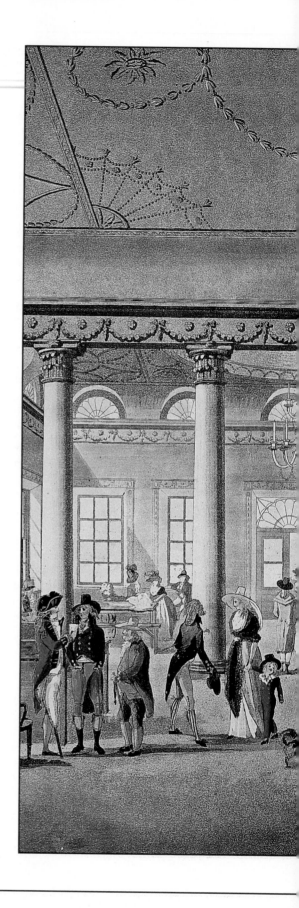

René Descartes dismissed the scientific theories of Aristotle and his medieval disciples as outdated dogma. A brilliant philosopher and mathematician, he formulated rules for abstract, deductive reasoning and the search for comprehensive scientific laws. *(Source: Royal Museum of Fine Arts, Copenhagen)*

mathematics. As a twenty-three-year-old soldier serving in the Thirty Years' War, he experienced on a single night in 1619 a life-changing intellectual vision. Descartes saw that there was a perfect correspondence between geometry and algebra and that geometrical, spatial figures could be expressed as algebraic equations and vice versa. A great step forward in the history of mathematics, Descartes' discovery of analytic geometry provided scientists with an important new tool. Descartes also made contributions to the science of optics, but his greatest achievement was to develop his initial vision into a whole philosophy of knowledge and science.

Like Bacon, Descartes scorned traditional science and had great faith in the powers of the human mind. Yet Descartes was much more sys-tematic and mathematical than Bacon. He decided it was necessary to doubt everything that could reasonably be doubted and then, as in geometry, to use deductive reasoning from self-evident principles to ascertain scientific laws. Descartes' reasoning ultimately reduced all substances to "matter" and "mind"—that is, to the physical and the spiritual. His view of the world as consisting of two fundamental entities is known as *Cartesian dualism*. Descartes was a profoundly original and extremely influential thinker.

It is important to realize that the modern scientific method, which began to crystallize in the late seventeenth century, has combined Bacon's inductive experimentalism and Descartes' deductive, mathematical rationalism. Neither of these extreme approaches was sufficient by itself. Bacon's inability to appreciate the importance of mathematics and his obsession with practical results clearly showed the limitations of antitheoretical empiricism. Like-wise, some of Descartes' positions—he believed, for example, that it was possible to deduce the whole science of medicine from first principles—aptly demonstrated the inadequacy of rigid, dogmatic rationalism. Significantly, Bacon faulted Galileo for his use of abstract formulas, while Descartes criticized the great Italian for being too experimental and insufficiently theoretical. Thus the modern scientific method has typically combined Bacon and Descartes. It has joined precise observations and experimentalism with the search for general laws that may be expressed in rigorously logical, mathematical language.

Finally, there is the question of science and religion. Just as some historians have argued that Protestantism led to the rise of capitalism, others have concluded that Protestantism was a fundamental factor in the rise of modern science. Protestantism, particularly in its Calvinist varieties, supposedly made scientific inquiry a question of individual conscience and not of religious doctrine. The Catholic church, on the other hand, supposedly suppressed scientific theories that conflicted with its teachings and thus discouraged scientific progress.

The truth of the matter is more complicated. *All* religious authorities—Catholic, Protestant, and Jewish—opposed the Copernican system to a greater or lesser extent until about 1630, by which time the scientific revolution was definitely in progress. The Catholic church was initially less hostile than Protestant and Jewish religious leaders.

This early Catholic toleration and the scientific interests of Renaissance Italy help account for the undeniable fact that Italian scientists played a crucial role in scientific progress right up to the trial of Galileo in 1633. Thereafter, the Counter-Reformation church became more hostile to science, a change that helps account for the decline of science in Italy (but not in Catholic France) after 1640. At the same time, some Protestant countries became quite "pro-science," especially if the country lacked a strong religious authority capable of imposing religious orthodoxy on scientific questions.

This was the case with England after 1630. English religious conflicts became so intense that it was impossible for the authorities to impose religious unity on anything, including science. It is significant that the forerunners of the Royal Society agreed to discuss only "neutral" scientific questions, so as not to come to blows over closely related religious and political disputes. The work of Bacon's many followers during Cromwell's commonwealth helped solidify the neutrality and independence of science. Bacon advocated the experimental approach precisely because it was open-minded and independent of any preconceived religious or philosophical ideas. Neutral and useful, science became an accepted part of life and developed rapidly in England after about 1640.

Some Consequences of the Scientific Revolution

The rise of modern science had many consequences, some of which are still unfolding. First, it went hand in hand with the rise of a new and expanding social group—the scientific community. Members of this community were linked together by learned societies, common interests, and shared values. Expansion of knowledge was the primary goal of this community, and scientists' material and psychological rewards depended on their success in this endeavor. Thus science became quite competitive, and even more scientific advance was inevitable.

Second, the scientific revolution introduced not only new knowledge about nature but also a new and revolutionary way of obtaining such knowledge—the modern scientific method. In addition to being both theoretical and experimental, this method was highly critical, and it differed profoundly from the old way of getting knowledge about nature. It refused to base its conclusions on tradition and established sources, on ancient authorities and sacred texts.

The scientific revolution had few consequences for economic life and the living standards of the masses until the late eighteenth century at the very earliest. True, improvements in the techniques of navigation facilitated overseas trade and helped enrich leading merchants. But science had relatively few practical economic applications, and the hopes of the early Baconians were frustrated. The close link between theoretical, or pure, science and applied technology, which we take for granted today, simply did not exist before the nineteenth century. Thus the scientific revolution of the seventeenth century was first and foremost an intellectual revolution. It is not surprising that for more than a hundred years its greatest impact was on how people thought and believed.

THE ENLIGHTENMENT

The scientific revolution was the single most important factor in the creation of the new world-view of the eighteenth-century Enlightenment. This world-view, which has played a large role in shaping the modern mind, was based on a rich mix of ideas, sometimes conflicting, for intellectuals delight in playing with ideas just as athletes delight in playing games. Despite this diversity, three central concepts stand out.

The most important and original idea of the Enlightenment was that the methods of natural science could and should be used to examine and understand all aspects of life. This was what intellectuals meant by *reason*, a favorite word of Enlightenment thinkers. Nothing was to be accepted on faith. Everything was to be submitted to the rational, critical, scientific way of thinking. This approach brought the Enlightenment into a head-on conflict with the established churches, which rested their beliefs on the special authority of the Bible and Christian theology. A second important Enlightenment concept was that the scientific method was capable of discovering the laws of human society as well as those of nature. Thus was social science born. Its birth led to the third key idea, that of progress. Armed with the proper method of discovering the laws of human existence, Enlightenment thinkers believed it was at least possible to create better societies and better people. Their belief was strengthened by some genuine improvements in economic and social life during the eighteenth century (see Chapters 19 and 20).

The Enlightenment was therefore profoundly secular. It revived and expanded the Renaissance concentration on worldly explanations. In the course of the eighteenth century, the Enlightenment had a profound impact on the thought and culture of the urban middle and upper classes. It did not have much appeal for the poor and the peasants.

The Emergence of the Enlightenment

The Enlightenment did not reach its maturity until about 1750. Yet it was the generation that came of age between the publication of Newton's masterpiece in 1687 and the death of Louis XIV in 1715 that tied the crucial knot between the scientific revolution and a new outlook on life.

Talented writers of that generation popularized hard-to-understand scientific achievements for the educated elite. The most famous and influential popularizer was a versatile French man of letters, Bernard de Fontenelle (1657–1757). Fontenelle practically invented the technique of making highly complicated scientific findings understandable to a broad nonscientific audience. He set out to make science witty and entertaining, as easy to read as a novel. This was a tall order, but Fontenelle largely succeeded.

His most famous work, *Conversations on the Plurality of Worlds* of 1686, begins with two elegant figures walking in the gathering shadows of a large park. One is a woman, a sophisticated aristocrat, and the other is her friend, perhaps even her lover. They gaze at the stars, and their talk turns to a passionate discussion of . . . astronomy! He confides that "each star may well be a different world." She is intrigued by his novel idea: "Teach me about these stars of yours." And he does, gently but persistently stressing how error is giving way to truth. At one point he explains:

There came on the scene . . . one Copernicus, who made short work of all those various circles, all those solid skies, which the ancients had pictured to themselves. The former he abolished; the latter he broke in pieces. Fired with the noble zeal of a true astronomer, he took the earth and spun it very far away from the center of the universe, where it had been installed, and in that center he put the sun, which had a far better title to the honor.[9]

Rather than tremble in despair in the face of these revelations, Fontenelle's lady rejoices in the advance of knowledge. Fontenelle thus went beyond entertainment to instruction, suggesting that the human mind was capable of making great progress.

This idea of progress was essentially a new idea of the later seventeenth century. Medieval and Reformation thinkers had been concerned primarily with sin and salvation. The humanists of the Renaissance had emphasized worldly matters, but they had been backward-looking. They had believed it might be possible to equal the magnificent accomplishments of the ancients, but they did not ask for more. Fontenelle and like-minded writers had come to believe that, at least in science and mathematics, their era had gone far *beyond* antiquity. Progress, at least intellectual progress, was clearly possible. During the eighteenth century, this idea would sink deeply into the consciousness of the European elite.

Fontenelle and other literary figures of his generation were also instrumental in bringing science into conflict with religion. Contrary to what is often assumed, many seventeenth-century scientists, both Catholic and Protestant, believed that their work exalted God. They did not draw antireligious implications from their scientific findings. The greatest scientist of them all, Isaac Newton, was a devout if unorthodox Christian who saw all of his studies as directed toward explaining God's message. Newton devoted far more of his time to angels and biblical prophecies than to universal gravitation, and he was convinced that all of his inquiries were equally scientific.

Fontenelle, on the other hand, was skeptical about absolute truth and cynical about the claims of organized religion. Since such unorthodox views could not be stated openly in Louis XIV's France, Fontenelle made his point through subtle editorializing about science. His depiction of the cautious Copernicus as a self-conscious revolutionary was typical. In his *Eulogies of Scientists,* Fontenelle exploited with endless variations the basic theme of rational, progressive scientists versus prejudiced, reactionary priests. Time and time again, Fontenelle's fledgling scientists attended church and studied theology; then, at some crucial moment, each was converted from the obscurity of religion to the clarity of science.

The progressive and antireligious implications that writers like Fontenelle drew from the scientific revolution reflected a very real crisis in European thought at the end of the seventeenth century. This crisis had its roots in several intellectual uncertainties and dissatisfactions, of which the demolition of Aristotelian-medieval science was only one.

A second uncertainty involved the whole question of religious truth. The destructive wars of religion had been fought, in part, because religious freedom was an intolerable idea in the early seventeenth century. Both Catholics and Protestants had believed that religious truth was absolute and therefore worth fighting and dying for. It was also generally believed that a strong state required unity in religious faith. Yet the disastrous results of the many attempts to impose such religious unity, such as Louis XIV's expulsion of the French Huguenots in 1685, led some people to ask if ideological conformity in religious matters was really necessary. Others skeptically asked if religious truth could ever be known with absolute certainty and concluded that it could not.

The most famous of these skeptics was Pierre Bayle (1647–1706), a French Huguenot who took refuge in Holland. A teacher by profession and a crusading journalist by inclination, Bayle critically examined the religious beliefs and persecutions of the past in his *Historical and Critical Dictionary*, published in 1697. Demonstrating that human beliefs had been extremely varied and very often mistaken, Bayle concluded that nothing can ever be known beyond all doubt. In religion as in philosophy, humanity's best hope was open-minded toleration. Bayle's skeptical views were very influential. Many eighteenth-century writers mined his inexhaustible vein of critical skepticism for ammunition in their attacks on superstition and theology. Bayle's four-volume *Dictionary* was found in more private libraries of eighteenth-century France than any other book.

The rapidly growing travel literature on non-European lands and cultures was a third cause of uncertainty. In the wake of the great discoveries, Europeans were learning that the peoples of China, India, Africa, and the Americas all had their own very different beliefs and customs. Europeans

shaved their faces and let their hair grow. The Turks shaved their heads and let their beards grow. In Europe a man bowed before a woman to show respect. In Siam a man turned his back on a woman when he met her, because it was disrespectful to look directly at her. Countless similar examples discussed in the travel accounts helped change the perspective of educated Europeans. They began to look at truth and morality in relative rather than absolute terms. Anything was possible, and who could say what was right or wrong? As one Frenchman wrote: "There is nothing that opinion, prejudice, custom, hope, and a sense of honor cannot do." Another wrote disapprovingly of religious skeptics who were corrupted "by extensive travel

Popularizing Science The frontispiece illustration of Fontenelle's *Conversations on the Plurality of Worlds* invites the reader to share the pleasures of astronomy with an elegant lady and an entertaining teacher. *(Source: University of Illinois, Champaign)*

and lose whatever shreds of religion that remained with them. Every day they see a new religion, new customs, new rites."[10]

A fourth cause and manifestation of European intellectual turmoil was John Locke's epoch-making *Essay Concerning Human Understanding.* Published in 1690—the same year Locke published his famous *Second Treatise of Civil Government* (see page 524)—Locke's essay brilliantly set forth a new theory about how human beings learn and form their ideas. In doing so, he rejected the prevailing view of Descartes, who had held that all people are born with certain basic ideas and ways of thinking. Locke insisted that all ideas are derived from experience. The human mind is like a blank tablet (*tabula rasa*) at birth, a tablet on which environment writes the individual's understanding and beliefs. Human development is therefore determined by education and social institutions, for good or for evil. Locke's *Essay Concerning Human Understanding* passed through many editions and translations. It was, along with Newton's *Principia,* one of the dominant intellectual inspirations of the Enlightenment.

The Philosophes and Their Ideas

By the death of Louis XIV in 1715, many of the ideas that would soon coalesce into the new world-view had been assembled. Yet Christian Europe was still strongly attached to its traditional beliefs, as witnessed by the powerful revival of religious orthodoxy in the first half of the eighteenth century. By the outbreak of the American Revolution in 1775, however, a large portion of western Europe's educated elite had embraced many of the new ideas. This acceptance was the work of one of history's most influential groups of intellectuals, the *philosophes.* It was the philosophes who proudly and effectively proclaimed that they, at long last, were bringing the light of knowledge to their ignorant fellow creatures in a great Age of Enlightenment.

Philosophe is the French word for "philosopher," and it was in France that the Enlightenment reached its highest development. The French philosophes were indeed philosophers. They asked fundamental philosophical questions about the meaning of life, about God, human nature, good and evil, and cause and effect. But, in the tradition of Bayle and Fontenelle, they were not content with abstract arguments or ivory-tower speculations among a tiny minority of scholars and professors. They wanted to influence and convince a broad audience.

The philosophes were intensely committed to reforming society and humanity, yet they were not free to write as they wished, since it was illegal in France to criticize openly either church or state. Their most radical works had to circulate in France in manuscript form, very much as critical works are passed from hand to hand in unpublished form in dictatorships today. Knowing that direct attacks would probably be banned or burned, the philosophes wrote novels and plays, histories and philosophies, dictionaries and encyclopedias, all filled with satire and double meanings to spread the message.

One of the greatest philosophes, the baron de Montesquieu (1689–1755), brilliantly pioneered this approach in *The Persian Letters,* an extremely influential social satire published in 1721. Montesquieu's work consisted of amusing letters supposedly written by Persian travelers, who see European customs in unique ways and thereby cleverly criticize existing practices and beliefs.

Having gained fame using wit as a weapon against cruelty and superstition, Montesquieu settled down on his family estate to study history and politics. His interest was partly personal for, like many members of the high French nobility, he was dismayed that royal absolutism had triumphed in France under Louis XIV. But Montesquieu was also inspired by the example of the physical sciences, and he set out to apply the critical method to the problem of government in *The Spirit of Laws* (1748). The result was a complex comparative study of republics, monarchies, and despotisms—a great pioneering inquiry in the emerging social sciences.

Showing that forms of government were related to history, geography, and customs, Montesquieu focused on the conditions that would promote liberty and prevent tyranny. He argued that despotism could be avoided if political power were divided and shared by a diversity of classes and orders holding unequal rights and privileges. A strong, independent upper class was especially important, according to Montesquieu, because in order to prevent the abuse of power, "it is necessary that by the arrangement of things, power checks power." Admiring greatly the English balance of power among the king, the houses of Parliament, and the independent courts, Montesquieu believed that in France the thirteen high courts—the *parlements*—were front-line defenders of liberty against royal despotism. Apprehensive about the uneducated poor, Montesquieu was clearly no democrat, but his theory of separation of powers had a great impact on France's wealthy, well-educated elite. The constitutions of the young United States in 1789 and of France in 1791 were based in large part on this theory.

The most famous and in many ways most representative philosophe was François Marie Arouet, who was known by the pen name of Voltaire (1694–1778). In his long career, this son of a comfortable middle-class family wrote over seventy witty volumes, hobnobbed with kings and queens, and died a millionaire because of shrewd business speculations. His early career, however, was turbulent. In 1717 Voltaire was imprisoned for eleven months in the Bastille in Paris for insulting the regent of France. In 1726 a barb from his sharp tongue led a great French nobleman to have him beaten and arrested. This experience made a deep impression on Voltaire. All his life he struggled against legal injustice and class inequalities before the law.

Released from prison after promising to leave the country, Voltaire lived in England for three years. Sharing Montesquieu's enthusiasm for English institutions, Voltaire then wrote various works praising England and popularizing English scientific progress. Newton, he wrote, was history's greatest man, for he had used his genius for the benefit of humanity. "It is," wrote Voltaire, "the man who sways our minds by the prevalence of reason and the native force of truth, not they who reduce mankind to a state of slavery by force and downright violence . . . that claims our reverence and admiration."[11] In the true style of the Enlightenment, Voltaire mixed the glorification of science and reason with an appeal for better people and institutions.

Yet, like almost all of the philosophes, Voltaire was a reformer and not a revolutionary in social and political matters. Returning to France, he was eventually appointed royal historian in 1743, and his *Age of Louis XIV* portrayed Louis as the dignified leader of his age. Voltaire also began a long correspondence with Frederick the Great, and he accepted Frederick's invitation to come brighten up the Prussian court in Berlin. The two men later quarreled, but Voltaire always admired Frederick as a free thinker and an enlightened monarch.

Unlike Montesquieu, Voltaire pessimistically concluded that the best one could hope for in the way of government was a good monarch, since human beings "are very rarely worthy to govern themselves." Nor did he believe in social equality in human affairs. The idea of making servants equal to their masters was "absurd and impossible." The only realizable equality, Voltaire thought, was that "by which the citizen only depends on the laws which protect the freedom of the feeble against the ambitions of the strong."[12]

Voltaire's philosophical and religious positions were much more radical. In the tradition of Bayle, his voluminous writings challenged—often indirectly—the Catholic church and Christian theology at almost every point. Though he was considered by many devout Christians to be a shallow blasphemer, Voltaire's religious views were influential and quite typical of the mature Enlightenment. The essay on religion from his widely read *Philosophical Dictionary* sums up many of his criticisms and beliefs:

I meditated last night; I was absorbed in the contemplation of nature; I admired the immensity, the course, the harmony of these infinite globes which the vulgar do not know how to admire.

I admired still more the intelligence which directs these vast forces. I said to myself: "One must be blind not to be dazzled by this spectacle; one must be stupid not to recognize its author; one must be mad not to worship the Supreme Being."

I was deep in these ideas when one of those genii who fill the intermundane spaces came down to me . . . and transported me into a desert all covered with piles of bones. . . . He began with the first pile. "These," he said, "are the twenty-three thousand Jews who danced before a calf, with the twenty-four thousand who were killed while lying with Midianitish women. The number of those massacred for such errors and offences amounts to nearly three hundred thousand.

"In the other piles are the bones of the Christians slaughtered by each other because of metaphysical disputes. . . ."

"What!" I cried, "brothers have treated their brothers like this, and I have the misfortune to be of this brotherhood! . . . Why assemble here all these abominable monuments to barbarism and fanaticism?"

Voltaire leans forward at left to exchange ideas with Frederick the Great across the table, as Prussian officials look on. As this painting suggests, Voltaire's radicalism was mainly intellectual and philosophical, not social or political. *(Source: Bildarchiv Preussischer Kulturbesitz)*

"To instruct you. . . . Follow me now." . . .

I saw a man with a gentle, simple face, who seemed to me to be about thirty-five years old. From afar he looked with compassion upon those piles of whitened bones, through which I had been led to reach the sage's dwelling place. I was astonished to find his feet swollen and bleeding, his hands likewise, his side pierced, and his ribs laid bare by the cut of the lash. "Good God!" I said to him, "is it possible for a just man, a sage, to be in this state? . . . Was it . . . by priests and judges that you were so cruelly assassinated?"

With great courtesy he answered, "Yes."

"And who were these monsters?"

"They were hypocrites."

"Ah! that says everything; I understand by that one word that they would have condemned you to the cruelest punishment. Had you then proved to them, as Socrates

did, that the Moon was not a goddess, and that Mercury was not a god?"

"No, it was not a question of planets. My countrymen did not even know what a planet was; they were all arrant ignoramuses. Their superstitions were quite different from those of the Greeks."

"Then you wanted to teach them a new religion?"

"Not at all; I told them simply: 'Love God with all your heart and your neighbor as yourself, for that is the whole of mankind's duty.' Judge yourself if this precept is not as old as the universe; judge yourself if I brought them a new religion." . . .

"Did you not say once that you were come not to bring peace, but a sword?"

"It was a scribe's error; I told them that I brought peace and not a sword. I never wrote anything; what I said can have been changed without evil intention."

"You did not then contribute in any way by your teaching, either badly reported or badly interpreted, to those frightful piles of bones which I saw on my way to consult with you?"

"I have only looked with horror upon those who have made themselves guilty of all these murders."

. . . [Finally] I asked him to tell me in what true religion consisted.

"Have I not already told you? Love God and your neighbor as yourself." . . .

"Well, if that is so, I take you for my only master."[13]

This passage requires careful study, for it suggests several Enlightenment themes of religion and philosophy. As the opening paragraphs show, Voltaire clearly believed in a God. But the God of Voltaire and most philosophes was a distant, deistic God, a great Clockmaker who built an orderly universe and then stepped aside and let it run. The passage also reflects the philosophes' hatred of all forms of religious intolerance. They believed that people had to be wary of dogmatic certainty and religious disputes, which often led to fanaticism and savage, inhuman action. Simple piety and human kindness—the love of God and the golden rule— were religion enough, even Christianity enough, as Voltaire's interpretation of Christ suggests.

The ultimate strength of the philosophes lay in their numbers, dedication, and organization. The philosophes felt keenly that they were engaged in a common undertaking that transcended individuals. Their greatest and most representative intellectual achievement was, quite fittingly, a group effort— the seventeen-volume *Encyclopedia: The Rational Dictionary of the Sciences, the Arts, and the Crafts*, edited by Denis Diderot (1713–1784) and Jean le Rond d'Alembert (1717–1783). Diderot and d'Alembert made a curious pair. Diderot began his career as a hack writer, first attracting attention with a skeptical tract on religion that was quickly

Canal with Locks The articles on science and the industrial arts in the *Encyclopedia* carried lavish explanatory illustrations. This typical engraving from the section on water and its uses shows advances in canal building and reflects the encyclopedists' faith in technical progress. *(Source: University of Illinois, Champaign)*

burned by the judges of Paris. D'Alembert was one of Europe's leading scientists and mathematicians, the orphaned and illegitimate son of celebrated aristocrats. Moving in different circles and with different interests, the two men set out to find coauthors who would examine the rapidly expanding whole of human knowledge. Even more fundamentally, they set out to teach people how to think critically and objectively about all matters. As Diderot said, he wanted the *Encyclopedia* to "change the general way of thinking."[14]

The editors of the *Encyclopedia* had to conquer innumerable obstacles. After the appearance in 1751 of the first volume, which dealt with such controversial subjects as atheism, the soul, and blind people—all words beginning with *a* in French—the government temporarily banned publication. The pope later placed the work on the Index and pronounced excommunication on all who read or bought it. The timid publisher mutilated some of the articles in the last ten volumes without the editors' consent in an attempt to appease the authorities. Yet Diderot's unwavering belief in the importance of his mission held the encyclopedists together for fifteen years, and the enormous work was completed in 1765. Hundreds of thousands of articles by leading scientists and famous writers, skilled workers and progressive priests, treated every aspect of life and knowledge.

Not every article was daring or original, but the overall effect was little short of revolutionary. Science and the industrial arts were exalted, religion and immortality questioned. Intolerance, legal injustice, and out-of-date social institutions were openly criticized. More generally, the writers of the *Encyclopedia* showed that human beings could use the process of reasoning to expand human knowledge. Encyclopedists were convinced that greater knowledge would result in greater human happiness, for knowledge was useful and made possible economic, social, and political progress. The *Encyclopedia* was widely read and extremely influential in France and throughout western Europe as well. It summed up the new world-view of the Enlightenment.

The Later Enlightenment

After about 1770, the harmonious unity of the philosophes and their thought began to break down. As the new world-view became increasingly accepted by the educated public, some thinkers sought originality by exaggerating certain ideas of the Enlightenment to the exclusion of others. These latter-day philosophes often built rigid, dogmatic systems.

In his *System of Nature* (1770) and other works, the wealthy, aristocratic Baron Paul d'Holbach (1723–1789) argued that human beings were machines completely determined by outside forces. Free will, God, and immortality of the soul were foolish myths. D'Holbach's aggressive atheism and determinism, which were coupled with deep hostility toward Christianity and all other religions, dealt the unity of the Enlightenment movement a severe blow. *Deists* such as Voltaire, who believed in God but not in established churches, were repelled by the inflexible atheism they found in the *System of Nature*. They saw in it the same dogmatic intolerance they had been fighting all their lives.

D'Holbach published his philosophically radical works anonymously to avoid possible prosecution, and in his lifetime he was best known to the public as the generous patron and witty host of writers and intellectuals. At his twice-weekly dinner parties, an inner circle of regulars who knew the baron's secret exchanged ideas with aspiring philosophes and distinguished visitors. One of the most important was the Scottish philosopher David Hume (1711–1776), whose carefully argued skepticism had a powerful long-term influence.

Building on John Locke's teachings on learning, Hume argued that the human mind is really nothing but a bundle of impressions. These impressions originate only in sense experiences and our habits of joining these experiences together. Since our ideas ultimately reflect only our sense experiences, our reason cannot tell us anything about questions like the origin of the universe or the existence of God, questions that cannot be verified by sense experience (in the form of controlled experiments or mathematics). Paradoxically, Hume's rationalistic inquiry ended up undermining the Enlightenment's faith in the very power of reason itself.

Another French aristocrat, Marie-Jean Caritat, the marquis de Condorcet (1743–1794), transformed the Enlightenment belief in gradual, hard-won progress into fanciful utopianism. In his *Progress of the Human Mind*, written in 1793 during the French Revolution, Condorcet tracked the nine stages of human progress that had already occurred and predicted that the tenth would bring perfection. Ironically, Condorcet wrote this work while fleeing for his life. Caught and condemned by revolutionary extremists, he preferred death by his own hand to the blade of the guillotine.

Other thinkers and writers after about 1770 began to attack the Enlightenment's faith in reason, progress, and moderation. The most famous of these was the Swiss Jean-Jacques Rousseau (1712–1778), a brilliant but difficult thinker, an appealing but neurotic individual. Born into a poor family of watchmakers in Geneva, Rousseau went to Paris and was greatly influenced by Diderot and Voltaire. Always extraordinarily sensitive and suspicious, Rousseau came to believe his philosophe friends were plotting against him. In the mid-1750s he broke with them personally and intellectually, living thereafter as a lonely outsider with his uneducated common-law wife and going in his own highly original direction.

Like other Enlightenment thinkers, Rousseau was passionately committed to individual freedom. Unlike them, however, he attacked rationalism and civilization as destroying rather than liberating the individual. Warm, spontaneous feeling had to complement and correct the cold intellect. Moreover, the individual's basic goodness had to be protected from the cruel refinements of civilization. These ideas greatly influenced the early romantic movement (see Chapter 23), which rebelled against the culture of the Enlightenment in the late eighteenth century.

Applying his heartfelt ideas to children, Rousseau had a powerful impact on the development of modern education. In his famous pedagogical novel *Émile* (1762), he argued that education must shield the naturally unspoiled child from the corrupting influences of civilization and too many books. According to Rousseau, children must develop naturally and spontaneously, although the sexes were by nature intended for different occupations. At the proper time, Émile might tackle difficult academic subjects and enter a demanding profession. But Sophie, his future wife, needed to learn only how to manage the home and to be a good mother and an obedient wife. This idea—that girls and boys should be educated to operate in "separate spheres"—was to gain wide acceptance in Europe among the middle classes in the nineteenth century.

Rousseau also made an important contribution to political theory in *The Social Contract* (1762). His fundamental ideas were the general will and popular sovereignty. According to Rousseau, the general will is sacred and absolute, reflecting the common interests of the people, who have displaced the monarch as the holder of the sovereign power. The general will is not necessarily the will of the majority, however, although minorities have to subordinate themselves to it without question. Little noticed before the French Revolution, Rousseau's concept of the general will appealed greatly to democrats and nationalists after 1789. The concept has also been used since 1789 by many dictators, who have claimed that they, rather than some momentary majority of the voters, represent the general will and thus the true interests of democracy and the sovereign masses.

The Social Setting of the Enlightenment

The philosophes were splendid talkers as well as effective writers. Indeed, sparkling conversation in private homes spread Enlightenment ideas to Europe's upper middle class and aristocracy. Paris set the example, and other French cities and European capitals followed. In Paris a number of talented and often rich women presided over regular social gatherings of the great and near-great in their elegant drawing rooms, or *salons*. There they encouraged a d'Alembert and a Fontenelle to exchange witty, uncensored observations on literature, science, and philosophy with great aristocrats, wealthy middle-class financiers, high-ranking officials, and noteworthy foreigners. Thus talented hostesses brought the various French elites together and mediated the spread of Enlightenment thought.

Elite women also exercised an unprecedented feminine influence on artistic taste. Soft pastels, ornate interiors, sentimental portraits, and starry-eyed lovers protected by hovering Cupids were all hallmarks of the style they favored. And it has been argued that feminine influence in the drawing room went hand in hand with the emergence of polite society and the general attempt to civilize a rough military nobility. Similarly, some philosophes championed greater rights and expanded education for women, claiming that the position and treatment of women were the best indicators of a society's level of civilization and decency.[15] To be sure, for these male philosophes, greater rights for women did not mean equal rights, except perhaps in a very abstract, theoretical way. Elite women remained legally subordinate to men in economic and political affairs.

One of the most famous salons was that of Madame Geoffrin, the unofficial godmother of the *Encyclopedia*. Having lost her parents at an early age, the future Madame Geoffrin was married at fifteen by her well-meaning grandmother to a rich and boring businessman of forty-eight. It was the classic marriage of convenience—the poor young girl and the rich old man—and neither side ever pretended that love was a consideration. After dutifully raising her children, Madame Geoffrin sought to break out of her gilded cage as she entered middle age. The very proper businessman's wife became friendly with a neighbor, the marquise de Tencin, an aristocratic beauty who had settled down to run a salon that counted Fontenelle and the philosopher Montesquieu among its regular guests.

When the marquise died in 1749, Madame Geoffrin tactfully transferred these luminaries to her spacious mansion for regular dinners. At first Madame Geoffrin's husband loudly protested the arrival of this horde of "parasites." But his wife's will was much stronger than his, and he soon opened his purse and even appeared at the twice-weekly dinners. "Who was that old man at the end of the table who never said anything?" an innocent newcomer asked one evening. "That," replied Madame Geoffrin without the slightest emotion, "was my husband. He's dead."[16]

When Monsieur Geoffrin's death became official, Madame Geoffrin put the large fortune and spacious mansion she inherited to good use. She welcomed the encyclopedists, and her generous financial aid helped to save their enterprise from collapse, especially after the first eight volumes were burned by the authorities in 1759. She also corresponded with the king of Sweden and Catherine the Great of Russia. Madame Geoffrin was, however, her own woman. She remained a practicing

Madame Geoffrin's Salon   In this stylized group portrait a famous actor reads to a gathering of leading philosophes and aristocrats in 1755. Third from the right presiding over her gathering is Madame Geoffrin, next to the sleepy ninety-eight-year-old Bernard de Fontenelle. *(Source: Giraudon/Art Resource)*

Christian and would not tolerate attacks on the church in her house. The plain and long-neglected Madame Geoffrin managed to become the most renowned hostess of the eighteenth century.

There were many other hostesses, but Madame Geoffrin's greatest rival, Madame du Deffand, was one of the most interesting. While Madame Geoffrin was middle-class, pious, and chaste, Madame du Deffand was a skeptic from the nobility who lived fast and easy, at least in her early years. Another difference was that women—mostly highly intelligent, worldly members of the nobility—were fully the equal of men in Madame du Deffand's intellectual salon. Forever pursuing fulfillment in love and life, Madame du Deffand was an accomplished and liberated woman. An exceptionally fine letter writer, she carried on a vast correspondence and counted Voltaire as her most enduring friend.

The salons seem to have functioned as informal schools, where established hostesses bonded with younger women and passed their skills to them. Madame du Deffand's closest female friend was Julie de Lespinasse, a beautiful, talented young woman whom she befriended and made her protégée. The never-acknowledged illegitimate daughter of noble parents, Julie de Lespinasse had a hard youth, but she flowered in Madame du Deffand's drawing room—so much so that she was eventually dismissed by her jealous patroness.

Once again Julie de Lespinasse triumphed. Her friends gave her money so that she could form her own salon. Her highly informal gatherings—she was not rich enough to supply more than tea and cake—attracted the keenest minds in France and Europe. As one philosophe wrote:

She could unite the different types, even the most antagonistic, sustaining the conversation by a well-aimed phrase, animating and guiding it at will. . . . Politics, religion, philosophy, news: nothing was excluded. Her circle met daily from five to nine. There one found men of all ranks in the State, the Church, and the Court, soldiers and foreigners, and the leading writers of the day.[17]

Thus in France the ideas of the Enlightenment thrived in a social setting that graciously united members of the intellectual, economic, and social elites. Never before and never again would social and intellectual life be so closely and so pleasantly joined. In such an atmosphere, the philosophes, the French nobility, and the upper middle class intermingled and increasingly influenced one another. Critical thinking became fashionable and flourished alongside hopes for human progress through greater knowledge.

THE DEVELOPMENT OF ABSOLUTISM

How did the Enlightenment influence political developments? To this important question there is no easy answer. On the one hand, the philosophes were primarily interested in converting people to critical scientific thinking and were not particularly concerned with politics. On the other hand, such thinking naturally led to political criticism and interest in political reform. Educated people, who belonged mainly to the nobility and middle class, came to regard political change as both possible and desirable. A further problem is that Enlightenment thinkers had different views on politics. Some, led by the nobleman Montesquieu, argued for curbs on monarchial power in order to promote liberty, and some French judges applied such theories in practical questions.

Until the American Revolution, however, most Enlightenment thinkers believed that political change could best come from above—from the ruler—rather than from below, especially in central and eastern Europe. There were several reasons for this essentially moderate belief. First, royal absolutism was a fact of life, and the kings and queens of Europe's leading states clearly had no intention of giving up their great powers. Therefore, the philosophes realistically concluded that a benevolent absolutism offered the best opportunities for improving society. Critical thinking was turning the art of good government into an exact science. It was necessary only to educate and "enlighten" the monarch, who could then make good laws and promote human happiness. Second, philosophes turned toward rulers because rulers seemed to be listening, treating them with respect, and seeking their advice. Finally, although the philosophes did not dwell on this fact, they distrusted the masses. Known simply as "the people" in the eighteenth century, the peasant masses and the urban poor were, according to the philosophes, still enchained by religious superstitions and violent passions. No doubt the people were maturing, but they were still children in need of firm parental guidance.

Encouraged and instructed by the philosophes, several absolutist rulers of the later eighteenth century tried to govern in an "enlightened" manner. Yet, because European monarchs had long been locked in an intense international competition, a more enlightened state often meant in practice a more effective state, a state capable of expanding its territory and defeating its enemies. Moreover, reforms from above had to be grafted onto previous historical developments and existing social structures. Little wonder, then, that the actual programs and accomplishments of these rulers varied greatly. Let us therefore examine the evolution of monarchial absolutism at close range before trying to form any overall judgment regarding the meaning of what historians have often called the "enlightened absolutism" of the later eighteenth century.

✳ The "Greats": Frederick of Prussia and Catherine of Russia

Just as the French culture and absolutism of Louis XIV provided models for European rulers in the late seventeenth century, the Enlightenment teachings of the French philosophes inspired European monarchs in the second half of the eighteenth century. French was the international language of the educated classes, and the education of future kings and queens across Europe lay in the hands of French tutors espousing Enlightenment ideas. France's cultural leadership was reinforced by the fact that it was still the wealthiest and most populous country in Europe. Thus absolutist monarchs in several west German and Italian states, as well as in Spain and Portugal, proclaimed themselves more enlightened. By far the most influential of the new-style monarchs were Frederick II of Prussia and Catherine II of Russia, both styled "the Great."

Frederick the Great   Frederick II (r. 1740–1786), commonly known as Frederick the Great, built masterfully on the work of his father, Frederick William I (see pages 543–545). This was somewhat surprising for, like many children with tyrannical parents, he rebelled against his family's wishes in his early years. Rejecting the crude life of the barracks, Frederick embraced culture and literature, even writing poetry and fine prose in French, a language his father detested. He threw off his father's dour Calvinism and dabbled with atheism. After

trying unsuccessfully to run away at age eighteen in 1730, he was virtually imprisoned and even compelled to watch his companion in flight beheaded at his father's command. Yet, like many other rebellious youths, Frederick eventually reached a reconciliation with his father, and by the time he came to the throne ten years later, Frederick was determined to use the splendid army that his father had left him.

When, therefore, the emperor of Austria, Charles VI, also died in 1740 and his young and beautiful daughter, Maria Theresa, became ruler of the Habsburg dominions, Frederick suddenly and without warning invaded her rich, all-German province of Silesia. This action defied solemn Prussian promises to respect the Pragmatic Sanction, which guaranteed Maria Theresa's succession—but no matter. For Frederick, it was the opportunity of a lifetime to expand the size and power of Prussia. Although Maria Theresa succeeded in dramatically rallying the normally quarrelsome Hungarian nobility, her multinational army was no match for Prussian precision. In 1742, as other greedy powers were falling on her lands in the general European War of the Austrian Succession (1740–1748), she was forced to cede all of Silesia to Prussia (see Map 17.2). In one stroke, Prussia doubled its population to six million people. Now Prussia unquestionably towered above all the other German states and stood as a European Great Power.

Though successful in 1742, Frederick had to spend much of his reign fighting against great odds to save Prussia from total destruction. Maria Theresa was determined to regain Silesia, and when the ongoing competition between Britain and France for colonial empire brought renewed conflict in 1756, her able chief minister fashioned an aggressive alliance with France and Russia. During the Seven Years' War (1756–1763), the aim of the alliance was to conquer Prussia and divide up its territory, just as Frederick II and other monarchs had so recently sought to partition the Austrian Empire. Frederick led his army brilliantly, striking repeatedly at vastly superior forces invading from all sides. At times he believed all was lost, but he fought on with stoic courage. In the end, he was miraculously saved: Peter III came to the Russian throne in 1762 and called off the attack against Frederick, whom he greatly admired.

In the early years of his reign, Frederick II had kept his enthusiasm for Enlightenment culture strictly separated from a brutal concept of international politics. He wrote:

Of all States, from the smallest to the biggest, one can safely say that the fundamental rule of government is the principle of extending their territories. . . . The passions of rulers have no other curb but the limits of their power. Those are the fixed laws of European politics to which every politician submits.[18]

But the terrible struggle of the Seven Years' War tempered Frederick and brought him to consider how more humane policies for his subjects might also strengthen the state.

Thus Frederick went beyond a superficial commitment to Enlightenment culture for himself and his circle. He tolerantly allowed his subjects to believe as they wished in religious and philosophical matters. He promoted the advancement of knowledge, improving his country's schools and universities. Moreover, Frederick tried to improve the lives of his subjects more directly. As he wrote his friend Voltaire, "I must enlighten my people, cultivate their manners and morals, and make them as happy as human beings can be, or as happy as the means at my disposal permit." The legal system and the bureaucracy were Frederick's primary tools. Prussia's laws were simplified, torture of prisoners was abolished, and judges decided cases quickly and impartially. Prussian officials became famous for their hard work and honesty. After the Seven Years' War ended in 1763, Frederick's government also energetically promoted the reconstruction of agriculture and industry in his war-torn country. In all this Frederick set a good example. He worked hard and lived modestly, claiming that he was "only the first servant of the state." Thus Frederick justified monarchy in terms of practical results and said nothing of the divine right of kings.

Frederick's dedication to high-minded principles went only so far, however. He never tried to change Prussia's existing social structure. True, he condemned serfdom in the abstract, but he accepted it in practice and did not even free the serfs on his own estates. He accepted and extended the privileges of the nobility, which he saw as his primary ally in the defense and extension of his realm. It became practically impossible for a middle-class person to gain a top position in the government. The Junker nobility remained the backbone of the army and the entire Prussian state.

Catherine the Great   Catherine the Great of Russia (r. 1762–1796) was one of the most remarkable rulers who ever lived, and the philosophes adored her. Catherine was a German princess from Anhalt-Zerbst, a totally insignificant principality sandwiched between Prussia and Saxony. Her father commanded a regiment of the Prussian army, but her mother was related to the Romanovs of Russia, and that proved to be her chance.

Peter the Great had abolished the hereditary succession of tsars so that he could name his successor and thus preserve his policies. This move opened a period of palace intrigue and a rapid turnover of rulers until Peter's youngest daughter Elizabeth came to the Russian throne in 1741. A crude, shrewd woman noted for her hard drinking and hard loving—one of her official lovers was an illiterate shepherd boy—Elizabeth named her nephew Peter heir to the throne and chose Catherine to be his wife in 1744. It was a mismatch from the beginning. The fifteen-year-old Catherine was intelligent and attractive; her husband was stupid and ugly, his face badly scarred by smallpox. Ignored by her childish husband, Catherine carefully studied Russian, endlessly read writers like Bayle and Voltaire, and made friends at court. Soon she knew what she wanted. "I did not care about Peter," she wrote in her *Memoirs*, "but I did care about the crown."[19]

As the old empress Elizabeth approached death, Catherine plotted against her unpopular husband. A dynamic, sensuous woman, Catherine used her sexuality to good political advantage. She selected as her new lover a tall, dashing young officer named Gregory Orlov, who with his four officer brothers commanded considerable support among the soldiers stationed in St. Petersburg. When Peter came to the throne in 1762, his decision to withdraw Russian troops from the coalition against Prussia alienated the army. Nor did Peter III's attempt to gain support from the Russian nobility by freeing it from compulsory state service succeed. At the end of six months, Catherine and the military conspirators deposed Peter III in a palace revolution. Then the Orlov brothers murdered him. The German princess became empress of Russia.

Catherine had drunk deeply at the Enlightenment well. Never questioning the common assumption that absolute monarchy was the best form of government, she set out to rule in an enlightened manner. One of her most enduring goals was to bring the sophisticated culture of western

Catherine as Equestrian Catherine took advantage of her intelligence and good looks to maneuver her husband Peter III off the throne and get herself crowned as Russia's new monarch. Strongly influenced by the Enlightenment, she cultivated the French philosophes and instituted moderate domestic reforms only to reverse them in the aftermath of Pugachev's rebellion. *(Source: Sovfoto)*

Europe to backward Russia. To do so, she imported Western architects, sculptors, musicians, and intellectuals. She bought masterpieces of Western art in wholesale lots and patronized the philosophes. An enthusiastic letter writer, she corresponded extensively with Voltaire and praised him as the "champion of the human race." When the French government banned the *Encyclopedia,* she offered to publish it in St. Petersburg. She discussed reform with Diderot in St. Petersburg; and when Diderot needed money, she purchased his library for a small fortune but allowed him to keep it during his lifetime. With these and countless similar actions, Catherine skillfully won a good press for herself and for her country in the West. Moreover, this intellectual ruler, who wrote plays and loved good talk, set the tone for the entire Russian nobility. Peter the Great westernized Russian armies, but it was Catherine who westernized the thinking of the Russian nobility.

Catherine's second goal was domestic reform, and she began her reign with sincere and ambitious projects. Better laws were a major concern. In 1767 she drew up enlightened instructions for the special legislative commission she appointed to prepare a new law code. No new unified code was ever produced, but Catherine did restrict the practice of torture and allowed limited religious toleration. She also tried to improve education and strengthen local government. The philosophes applauded these measures and hoped more would follow.

Such was not the case. In 1773 a simple Cossack soldier named Emelian Pugachev sparked a gigantic uprising of serfs, very much as Stenka Razin had done a century earlier (see page 552). Proclaiming himself the true tsar, Pugachev issued "decrees" abolishing serfdom, taxes, and army service. Thousands joined his cause, slaughtering landlords and officials over a vast area of southwestern Russia. Pugachev's untrained hordes eventually proved no match for Catherine's noble-led regular army. Betrayed by his own company, Pugachev was captured and savagely executed.

Pugachev's rebellion was a decisive turning point in Catherine's domestic policy. On coming to the throne she had condemned serfdom in theory, but she was smart enough to realize that any changes would have to be very gradual or else she would quickly follow her departed husband. Pugachev's rebellion put an end to any illusions she might have had about reforming serfdom. The peasants were clearly dangerous, and her empire rested on the support of the nobility. After 1775 Catherine gave the nobles absolute control of their serfs. She extended serfdom into new areas, such as the Ukraine. In 1785 she formalized the nobility's privileged position, freeing them forever from taxes and state service. She also confiscated the lands of the Russian Orthodox church and gave them to favorite officials. Under Catherine, the Russian nobility attained its most exalted position, and serfdom entered its most oppressive phase.

Catherine's third goal was territorial expansion, and in this respect she was extremely successful. Her armies subjugated the last descendants of the Mongols, the Crimean Tartars, and began the conquest of the Caucasus.

Her greatest coup by far was the partitioning of Poland. Poland showed the dangers of failing to build a strong absolutist state. For decades all important decisions had required the unanimous agreement of all the Polish nobles, which meant that nothing could ever be done. When between 1768 and 1772 Catherine's armies scored unprecedented victories against the Turks and thereby threatened to disturb the balance of power between Russia and Austria in eastern Europe, Frederick of Prussia obligingly came forward with a deal. He proposed that Turkey be let off easily, and that Prussia, Austria, and Russia each compensate itself by taking a gigantic slice of Polish territory. Catherine jumped at the chance. The first partition of Poland took place in 1772. Two more partitions, in 1793 and 1795, gave all three powers more Polish territory, and the kingdom of Poland simply vanished from the map (Map 18.1).

Expansion helped Catherine keep the nobility happy, for it provided her with vast new lands to give to her faithful servants. Expansion also helped Catherine reward her lovers, of whom twenty-one have been definitely identified. On all these royal favorites she lavished large estates with many serfs,

as if to make sure there were no hard feelings when her interest cooled. Until the end this remarkable woman—who always believed that, in spite of her domestic setbacks, she was slowly civilizing Russia—kept her zest for life. Fascinated by a new twenty-two-year-old flame when she was a roly-poly grandmother in her sixties, she happily reported her good fortune to a favorite former lover: "I have come back to life like a frozen fly; I am gay and well."[20]

Absolutism in France and Austria

The Enlightenment's influence on political developments in France and Austria was complex. In France, the monarchy maintained its absolutist claims, and some philosophes like Voltaire believed that the king was still the best source of needed reform. At the same time, discontented nobles and learned judges drew on thinkers such as Montesquieu for liberal arguments, and they sought with some success to limit the king's power. In Austria, two talented rulers did manage to introduce major reforms, although traditional power politics were more important than Enlightenment teachings.

Louis XV of France   In building French absolutism, Louis XIV had successfully drawn on the middle class to curb the political power of the nobility. As long as the Grand Monarch lived, the nobility could only grumble and, like the duke of Saint-Simon in his *Memoirs,* scornfully lament the rise of "the vile bourgeoisie." But when Louis XIV finally died in 1715, to be succeeded by his five-year-old great-grandson, Louis XV (r. 1715–1774), the Sun King's elaborate system of absolutist rule was challenged in a general reaction. Favored by the duke of Orléans, who governed as regent until 1723, the nobility made a strong comeback.

Most important, the duke restored to the high court of Paris—the Parlement—the right to "register" and thereby approve the king's decrees. This was a fateful step. The judges of the Parlement of Paris had originally come from the middle class, and their high position reflected the way that Louis XIV (and earlier French monarchs) had chosen to use that class to build the royal bureaucracy so necessary for an absolutist state. By the eighteenth century, however, these middle-class judges had risen to become hereditary nobles. Moreover, although Louis XIV had curbed the political power of the nobility, he had never challenged its enormous social prestige. Thus high position in the government continued to bestow the noble status that middle-class officials wanted, either immediately or after three generations of continuous service. The judges of Paris, like many high-ranking officials, actually owned their government jobs and freely passed them on as private property from father to son. By supporting the claim of this well-entrenched and increasingly aristocratic group to register the king's laws, the duke of Orléans sanctioned a counter-weight to absolute power.

These implications became clear when the heavy expenses of the War of the Austrian Succession plunged France into financial crisis. In 1748 Louis XV appointed a finance minister who decreed a 5 percent income tax on every individual, regardless of social status. Exemption from most taxation had long been a hallowed privilege of the nobility, and other important groups—the clergy, the large towns, and some wealthy bourgeoisie—had also gained special tax advantages over time. The result

was a vigorous protest from many sides, and the Parlement of Paris refused to ratify the tax law. The monarchy retreated; the new tax was dropped.

Following the disastrously expensive Seven Years' War, the conflict re-emerged. The government tried to maintain emergency taxes after the war ended. The Parlement of Paris protested and even challenged the basis of royal authority, claiming that the king's power must necessarily be limited to protect liberty. Once again the government caved in and withdrew the wartime taxes in 1764. Emboldened by its striking victory and widespread support from France's educated elite, the judicial opposition in Paris and the provinces pressed its demands. In a barrage of pamphlets and legal briefs, it asserted that the king could not levy taxes without the consent of the Parlement of Paris acting as the representative of the entire nation.

Indolent and sensual by nature, more interested in his many mistresses than in affairs of state, Louis XV finally roused himself for a determined defense of his absolutist inheritance. "The magistrates," he

MAP 18.1 The Partition of Poland and Russia's Expansion, 1772–1795   Though all three of the great eastern absolutist states profited from the division of large but weak Poland, Catherine's Russia gained the most.

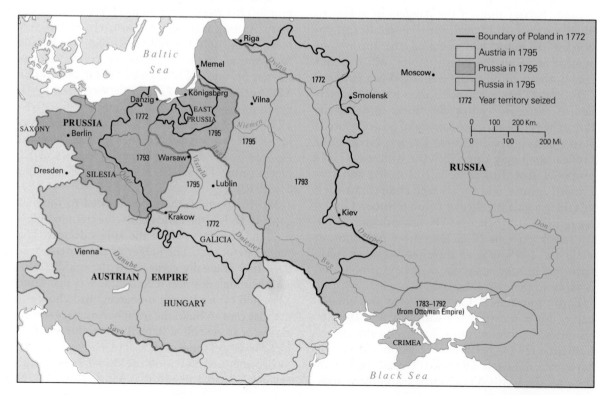

angrily told the Parlement of Paris in a famous face-to-face confrontation, "are my officers. . . . In my person only does the sovereign power rest."[21] In 1768 Louis appointed a tough career official named René de Maupeou as chancellor and ordered him to crush the judicial opposition.

Maupeou abolished the Parlement of Paris and exiled its members to isolated backwaters in the provinces. He created a new and docile parlement of royal officials, and he began once again to tax the privileged groups. A few philosophes like Voltaire applauded these measures: the sovereign was using his power to introduce badly needed reforms that had been blocked by a self-serving aristocratic elite. Most philosophes and educated public opinion as a whole sided with the old parlements, however, and there was widespread dissatisfaction with royal despotism. Yet the monarchy's power was still great enough for Maupeou simply to ride over the opposition, and Louis XV would probably have prevailed—if he had lived to a very ripe old age.

But Louis XV died in 1774. The new king, Louis XVI (r. 1774–1792), was a shy twenty-year-old with good intentions. Taking the throne, he is reported to have said: "What I should like most is to be loved."[22] The eager-to-please monarch decided to yield in the face of such strong criticism from so much of France's elite. He dismissed Maupeou and repudiated the strong-willed minister's work. The old Parlement of Paris was reinstated, as enlightened public opinion cheered and people hoped for moves toward representative government. Such moves were not forthcoming. Instead, a weakened but unrepentant monarchy faced a judicial opposition that claimed to speak for the entire French nation. Increasingly locked in stalemate, the country was drifting toward renewed financial crisis and political upheaval.

The Austrian Habsburgs   Joseph II (r. 1780–1790) was a fascinating individual. For an earlier generation of historians he was the "revolutionary emperor," a tragic hero whose lofty reforms were undone by the landowning nobility he dared to challenge. More recent scholarship has revised this romantic interpretation and stressed how Joseph II continued the state-building work of his mother, the empress Maria Theresa, a remarkable but old-fashioned absolutist.

Maria Theresa's long reign (1740–1780) began with her neighbors, led by Frederick II of Prussia, invading her lands and trying to dismember them (see page 584). Emerging from the long War of the Austrian Succession in 1748 with only the serious loss of Silesia, Maria Theresa and her closest ministers were determined to introduce reforms that would make the state stronger and more efficient. Three aspects were most important in these reforms. First, Maria Theresa introduced measures to bring relations between church and state under government control. Like some medieval rulers, the most devout and very Catholic Maria Theresa aimed at limiting the papacy's political influence in her realm. Second, a whole series of administrative reforms strengthened the central bureaucracy, smoothed out some provincial differences, and revamped the tax system, taxing even the lands of nobles without special exemptions. Finally, the government sought to improve the lot of the agricultural population, cautiously reducing the power of lords over both their hereditary serfs and their partially free peasant tenants.

Coregent with his mother from 1765 onward and a strong supporter of change, Joseph II moved forward rapidly when he came to the throne in 1780. He controlled the established Catholic church even more closely, in an attempt to ensure that it produced better citizens. He granted religious toleration and civic rights to Protestants and Jews—a radical innovation that impressed his contemporaries. In even more spectacular peasant reforms, Joseph abolished serfdom in 1781, and in 1789 he decreed that all peasant labor obligations be converted into cash payments. This ill-conceived measure was violently rejected not only by the nobility but by the peasants it was intended to help, since their primitive barter economy was woefully lacking in money. When a disillusioned Joseph died prematurely at forty-nine, the entire Habsburg empire was in turmoil. His brother Leopold (r. 1790–1792) was forced to cancel Joseph's radical edicts in order to re-establish order. Peasants lost most of their recent gains, and once again they were required to do forced labor for their lords, as in the 1770s under Maria Theresa.

An Overall Evaluation

Having examined the evolution of monarchial absolutism in four leading states, we can begin to look for meaningful generalizations and to evaluate the overall influence of Enlightenment thought on politics. That thought, it will be remembered,

Maria Theresa and her husband pose with eleven of their sixteen children at Schön-brunn palace. Joseph, the heir to the throne, stands at the center of the star pattern. Wealthy women often had very large families, in part because they seldom nursed their babies as poor women usually did. *(Source: Kunsthistorisches Museum, Vienna)*

was clustered in two distinct schools: the liberal critique of unregulated monarchy promoted by Montesquieu and the defenders of royal absolutism led by Voltaire.

It is clear that France diverged from its eastern neighbors in its political development in the eighteenth century. Although neither the French monarchy nor the eastern rulers abandoned the absolutist claims and institutions they had inherited, the monarch's capacity to govern in a truly absolutist manner declined substantially in France, and this was not the case in eastern Europe. The immediate cause of this divergence was the political resurgence of the French nobility after 1715 and the growth of judicial opposition, led by the Parlement

of Paris. More fundamentally, however, the judicial and aristocratic opposition in France achieved its still rather modest successes because it received major support from educated public opinion, which increasingly made the liberal critique of unregulated royal authority its own. In France, then, the proponents of absolute monarchy were increasingly on the defensive, as was the French monarchy itself.

The situation in eastern Europe was different. The liberal critique of absolute monarchy remained an intellectual curiosity, and proponents of reform from above held sway. Moreover, despite their differences, the leading eastern European monarchs of the later eighteenth century all claimed that they were acting on the principles of the Enlightenment. The philosophes generally agreed with this assessment and cheered them on. Beginning in the mid-nineteenth century, historians developed the idea of a common "enlightened despotism" or "enlightened absolutism," and they canonized Frederick, Catherine, and Joseph as its most outstanding examples. More recent research has raised doubts about this old interpretation and has led to a fundamental re-evaluation.

First, there is general agreement that these absolutists, especially Catherine and Frederick, did encourage and spread the cultural values of the Enlightenment. Perhaps this was their greatest achievement. Skeptical in religion and intensely secular in basic orientation, they unabashedly accepted the here and now and sought their happiness in the enjoyment of it. At the same time, they were proud of their intellectual accomplishments and good taste, and they supported knowledge, education, and the arts. No wonder the philosophes felt the monarchs were kindred spirits.

Historians also agree that the absolutists believed in change from above and tried to enact needed reforms. Yet the results of these efforts brought only very modest improvements, and the life of the peasantry remained very hard in the eighteenth century. Thus some historians have concluded that these monarchs were not really sincere in their reform efforts. Others disagree, arguing that powerful nobilities blocked the absolutists' genuine commitment to reform. (The old interpretation of Joseph II as the tragic "revolutionary emperor" forms part of this argument.)

The emerging answer to this confusion is that the later eastern absolutists were indeed committed to reform, but that humanitarian objectives were of quite secondary importance. Above all, the absolutists wanted reforms that would strengthen the state and allow them to compete militarily with their neighbors. Modern scholarship has stressed, therefore, how Catherine, Frederick, and Joseph were in many ways simply continuing the state building of their predecessors, reorganizing their armies and expanding their bureaucracies to raise more taxes and troops. The reason for this continuation was simple. The international political struggle was brutal, and the stakes were high. First Austria under Maria Theresa, and then Prussia under Frederick the Great, had to engage in bitter fighting to escape dismemberment, while decentralized Poland was coldly divided and eventually liquidated.

Yet, in their drive for more state power, the later absolutists were also innovators, and the idea of an era of enlightened absolutism retains a certain validity. Sharing the Enlightenment faith in critical thinking and believing that knowledge meant power, these absolutists really were more enlightened because they put their state-building reforms in a new, broader perspective. Above all, they considered how more humane laws and practices could help their populations become more productive and satisfied, and thus able to contribute more substantially to the welfare of the state. It was from this perspective that they introduced many of their most progressive reforms, tolerating religious minorities, simplifying legal codes, and promoting practical education.

The primacy of state as opposed to individual interests—a concept foreign to North Americans long accustomed to easy dominion over a vast continent—also helps to explain some puzzling variations in social policies. For example, Catherine the Great took measures that worsened the peasants' condition because she looked increasingly to the nobility as her natural ally and sought to strengthen it. Frederick the Great basically favored the status quo, limiting only the counterproductive excesses of his trusted nobility against its peasants. On the other hand, Joseph II believed that greater freedom for peasants was the means to strengthen his realm, and he acted accordingly. Each enlightened absolutist sought greater state power, but each believed a different policy would attain it.

In conclusion, the eastern European absolutists of the later eighteenth century combined old-fashioned state building with the culture and critical thinking of the Enlightenment. In doing so, they succeeded in expanding the role of the state in the life of society. Unlike the successors of Louis XIV, they perfected bureaucratic machines that were to prove surprisingly adaptive and capable of enduring into the twentieth century.

SUMMARY

This chapter has focused on the complex development of a new world-view in Western civilization. This new view of the world was essentially critical and secular, drawing its inspiration from the scientific revolution and crystallizing in the Enlightenment.

The decisive breakthroughs in astronomy and physics in the seventeenth century, which demolished the imposing medieval synthesis of Aristotelian philosophy and Christian theology, had only limited practical consequences despite the expectations of scientific enthusiasts like Bacon. Yet the impact of new scientific knowledge on intellectual life became great. Interpreting scientific findings and Newtonian laws in an antitraditional, antireligious manner, the French philosophes of the Enlightenment extolled the superiority of rational, critical thinking. This new method, they believed, promised not just increased knowledge but even the discovery of the fundamental laws of human society. Although they reached different conclusions when they turned to social and political realities, the philosophes nevertheless succeeded in spreading their radically new world-view. That was a momentous accomplishment.

NOTES

1. H. Butterfield, *The Origins of Modern Science* (New York: Macmillan, 1951), p. viii.
2. Quoted in A. G. R. Smith, *Science and Society in the Sixteenth and Seventeenth Centuries* (New York: Harcourt Brace Jovanovich, 1972), p. 97.
3. Quoted in Butterfield, p. 47.
4. Quoted in Smith, p. 100.
5. Ibid., pp. 115–116.
6. Ibid., p. 120.
7. A. R. Hall, *From Galileo to Newton, 1630–1720* (New York: Harper & Row, 1963), p. 290.
8. Quoted in R. K. Merton, *Science, Technology and Society in Seventeenth-century England*, rev. ed. (New York: Harper & Row, 1970), p. 164.
9. Quoted in P. Hazard, *The European Mind, 1680–1715* (Cleveland: Meridian Books, 1963), pp. 304–305.
10. Ibid., pp. 11–12.
11. Quoted in L. M. Marsak, ed., *The Enlightenment* (New York: John Wiley & Sons, 1972), p. 56.
12. Quoted in G. L. Mosse et al., eds., *Europe in Review* (Chicago: Rand McNally, 1964), p. 156.
13. F. M. Arouet de Voltaire, *Oeuvres completes,* vol. 8 (Paris: Firmin-Didot, 1875), pp. 188–190.
14. Quoted in P. Gay, "The Unity of the Enlightenment," *History* 3 (1960): 25.
15. See E. Fox-Genovese, "Women in the Enlightenment," in *Becoming Visible: Women in European History,* 2d ed., ed. R. Bridenthal, C. Koonz, and S.
Stuard (Boston: Houghton Mifflin, 1987), esp. pp. 252–259 and 263–265.
16. Quoted in G. P. Gooch, *Catherine the Great and Other Studies* (Hamden, Conn.: Archon Books, 1966), p. 112.
17. Ibid., p. 149.
18. Quoted in L. Krieger, *Kings and Philosophers, 1689–1789* (New York: W. W. Norton, 1970), p. 257.
19. Ibid., p. 15.
20. Ibid., p. 53.
21. Quoted in R. R. Palmer, *The Age of Democratic Revolution,* vol. 1 (Princeton, N.J.: Princeton University Press, 1959), pp. 95–96.
22. Quoted in G. Wright, *France in Modern Times* (Chicago: Rand McNally, 1960), p. 42.

SUGGESTED READING

The first three authors cited in the Notes—H. Butterfield, A. G. R. Smith, and A. R. Hall—have written excellent general interpretations of the scientific revolution. These may be compared with an outstanding recent work by M. Jacob, *The Cultural Meaning of the Scientific Revolution* (1988), which has a useful bibliography. The older study of England by R. Merton, mentioned in the Notes, also analyzes ties between science and the larger community. A. Debus, *Man and Nature in the Renaissance* (1978), is good on the Copernican revolution, while M. Boas, *The Scientific Renaissance, 1450–1630* (1966), is especially insightful about the influence of magic on science and about Galileo's trial. T. Kuhn, *The Structure of Scientific Revolutions* (1962), is a challenging, much-discussed attempt to understand major breakthroughs in scientific thought over time. E. Andrade, *Sir Isaac Newton* (1958), is a good short biography, which may be compared with F. Manuel, *The Religion of Isaac Newton* (1974).

The work of P. Hazard listed in the Notes is a classic study of the formative years of Enlightenment thought, and his *European Thought in the Eighteenth Century* (1954) is also recommended. A famous, controversial interpretation of the Enlightenment is that of C. Becker, *The Heavenly City of the Eighteenth Century Philosophes* (1932), which maintains that the world-view of medieval Christianity continued to influence the philosophes greatly. Becker's ideas are discussed interestingly in R. O. Rockwood, ed., *Carl Becker's Heavenly City Revisited* (1958). P. Gay has written several major studies on the Enlightenment: *Voltaire's Politics* (1959) and *The Party of Humanity* (1971) are two of the best. I. Wade, *The Structure and Form of the French Enlightenment* (1977), is a major synthesis. F. Baumer's *Religion and the Rise of Skepticism*

(1969), H. Payne's *The Philosophes and the People* (1976), and H. Chisick, *The Limits of Reform in the Enlightenment: Attitudes Toward the Education of the Lower Classes in Eighteenth-Century France* (1981), are interesting studies of important aspects of Enlightenment thought. On women, see the stimulating study by E. Fox-Genovese cited in the Notes, as well as S. Spencer, ed., *French Women and the Age of Enlightenment* (1984), and K. Rogers's *Feminism in Eighteenth-Century England* (1982). Above all, one should read some of the philosophes and let them speak for themselves. Two good anthologies are C. Brinton, ed., *The Portable Age of Reason* (1956), and F. Manuel, ed., *The Enlightenment* (1951). Voltaire's most famous and very amusing novel *Candide* is highly recommended, as are S. Gendzier, ed., *Denis Diderot: The Encyclopedia: Selections* (1967), and A. Wilson's biography, *Diderot* (1972).

In addition to the works mentioned in the Suggested Reading for Chapters 16 and 17, the monarchies of Europe are carefully analyzed in C. Tilly, ed., *The Formation of National States in Western Europe* (1975), and in J. Gagliardo, *Enlightened Despotism* (1967), both of which have useful bibliographies. M. Anderson, *Historians and Eighteenth-Century Europe* (1979), is a valuable introduction to modern scholarship. Other recommended studies on the struggle for power and reform in different countries are: F. Ford, *Robe and Sword* (1953), which discusses the resurgence of the French nobility after the death of Louis XIV; R. Herr, *The Eighteenth-Century Revolution in Spain* (1958), on the impact of Enlightenment thought in Spain; and P. Bernard, *Joseph II* (1968). There are several fine works on Russia. J. Alexander, *Catherine the Great: Life and Legend* (1989), is the best biography of the famous ruler. I. de Madariaga's masterful *Russia in the Age of Catherine the Great* (1981) and D. Ransel's solid *Politics of Catherinean Russia* (1975) are recommended. The ambitious reader should also look at A. N. Radishchev, *A Journey from St. Petersburg to Moscow* (English trans., 1958), a famous 1790 attack on Russian serfdom and an appeal to Catherine the Great to free the serfs, for which Radishchev was exiled to Siberia.

The culture of the time may be approached through A. Cobban, ed., *The Eighteenth Century* (1969), a richly illustrated work with excellent essays, and C. B. Behrens, *The Ancien Régime* (1967). C. Rosen, *The Classical Style: Haydn, Mozart, Beethoven* (1972), brilliantly synthesizes music and society, as did Mozart himself in his great opera *The Marriage of Figaro*, where the count is the buffoon and his servant the hero.

19

The Expansion of Europe in the Eighteenth Century

variety of jobs. It was a constant scramble for a meager living. And this was in a rich agricultural region in a country where peasants were comparatively well off. The privileges of Europe's ruling elites weighed heavily on the people of the land.

Agricultural Revolution

One possible way for European peasants to improve their difficult position was to take land from those who owned but did not labor. Yet the social and political conditions that enabled the ruling elites to squeeze the peasants were ancient and deep-rooted, and powerful forces stood ready to crush any protest. Only with the coming of the French Revolution were European peasants, mainly in France, able to improve their position by means of radical mass action.

Technological progress offered another possibility. The great need was for new farming methods that would enable Europeans to produce more and eat more. The uncultivated fields were the heart of the matter. If peasants (and their noble landlords) could replace the idle fallow with crops, they could increase the land under cultivation by 50 percent. So remarkable were the possibilities and the results that historians have often spoken of the progressive

Enclosing the Fields This remarkable aerial photograph captures key aspects of the agricultural revolution. Though the long ridges and furrows of the old open-field system still stretch across the whole picture, hedge rows now cut through the long strips to divide the land into several enclosed fields. *(Source: Cambridge University Collection)*

elimination of the fallow, which occurred slowly throughout Europe from the mid-seventeenth century on, as an agricultural revolution.

This agricultural revolution, which took longer than historians used to believe, was a great milestone in human development. The famous French scholar Marc Bloch, who gave his life in the resistance to the Nazis in World War Two, summed it up well: "The history of the conquest of the fallow by new crops, a fresh triumph of man over the earth that is just as moving as the great land clearing of the Middle Ages, [is] one of the noblest stories that can be told."[1]

Because grain crops exhaust the soil and make fallowing necessary, the secret to eliminating the fallow lies in alternating grain with certain nitrogen-storing crops. Such crops not only rejuvenate the soil even better than fallowing, but give more produce as well. The most important of these land-reviving crops are peas and beans, root crops such as turnips and potatoes, and clovers and grasses. In the eighteenth century, peas and beans were old standbys; turnips, potatoes, and clover were newcomers to the fields. As time went on, the number of crops that were systematically rotated grew, and farmers developed increasingly sophisticated patterns of rotation to suit different kinds of soils. For example, farmers in French Flanders near Lille in the late eighteenth century used a ten-year rotation, alternating a number of grain, root, and hay crops in a given field on a ten-year schedule. Continuous experimentation led to more scientific farming.

Improvements in farming had multiple effects. The new crops made ideal feed for animals. Because peasants and larger farmers had more fodder —hay and root crops—for the winter months, they could build up their small herds of cattle and sheep. More animals meant more meat and better diets for the people. More animals also meant more manure for fertilizer, and therefore more grain for bread and porridge. The vicious cycle in which few animals meant inadequate manure, which meant little grain and less fodder, which led to fewer animals, and so on, could be broken. The cycle became positive: more animals meant more manure, which meant more grain and more fodder, which meant more animals, which meant better diets.

Advocates of the new rotations, who included an emerging group of experimental scientists, some government officials, and a few big landowners, believed that new methods were scarcely possible

Surveyors Measuring   Enclosing open farmland met with much resistance, especially from poorer peasants and some nobility. It was more successful in England as illustrated in this scene from a nineteenth-century map of Bedfordshire. *(Source: Courtesy, Bedfordshire County Council)*

within the traditional framework of open fields and common rights. A farmer who wanted to experiment with new methods would have to get all the landholders in a village to agree to the plan, and advocates of improvement maintained that this would be difficult if not impossible, given peasant caution and the force of tradition. Therefore, they argued that innovating agriculturalists needed to enclose and consolidate their scattered holdings into compact, fenced-in fields, in order to farm more effectively. In doing so, the innovators also needed to enclose their individual shares of the natural pasture, the common. According to this view, a revolution in village life and organization was the necessary price of technical progress.

That price seemed too high to many rural people. Above all, the village poor believed that they were being asked to pay an unfair and disproportionate share of the bill. With land distributed very unequally all across Europe by 1700, large groups of village poor held small, inadequate holdings, or very little land at all. Common rights were precious to these poor peasants. The rights to glean and to graze a cow on the common, to gather firewood in the lord's forest and pick berries in the marsh, were vital because they helped poor peasants retain a modicum of independence and status and avoid falling into the growing group of landless, "proletarian" wage workers. Thus, when the small landholders and the village poor could effectively oppose the enclosure of the open fields and the common pasture, they did so. Moreover, in many countries they usually found allies among the larger, predominately noble landowners, who were also wary of enclosure because it required large investments and posed risks for them as well. Only powerful social and political pressures could overcome the combined opposition.

The old system of unenclosed open fields and the new system of continuous rotation coexisted in Europe for a very long time. In large parts of central Russia, for example, the old system did not disappear until after the Bolshevik Revolution in 1917. It could also be found in much of France and Germany in the early years of the nineteenth century, because peasants there had successfully opposed efforts to introduce the new techniques in the late eighteenth century. Indeed, until the end of the eighteenth century, the promise of the new system was extensively realized only in the Low Countries and in England.

The Leadership of the Low Countries and England

The new methods of the agricultural revolution originated in the Low Countries. The vibrant, dynamic middle-class society of seventeenth-century republican Holland was the most advanced in Europe in many areas of human endeavor. In shipbuilding and navigation, in commerce and banking, in drainage and agriculture, the people of the Low Countries, especially the Dutch, provided models the jealous English and French sought to copy or to cripple.

By the middle of the seventeenth century, intensive farming was well established throughout much of the Low Countries. Enclosed fields, continuous rotation, heavy manuring, and a wide variety of crops—all these innovations were present. Agriculture was highly specialized and commercialized. The same skills that grew turnips produced flax to be spun into linen for clothes and tulip bulbs to lighten the heart with their beauty. The fat cattle of Holland, so beloved by Dutch painters, gave the most milk in Europe. Dutch cheeses were already world-renowned.

The reasons for early Dutch leadership in farming were basically twofold. In the first place, since the end of the Middle Ages the Low Countries had been one of the most densely populated areas in Europe. Thus, in order to feed themselves and provide employment, the Dutch were forced at an early date to seek maximum yields from their land and to increase the cultivated area through the steady draining of marshes and swamps. Even so, they had to import wheat from Poland and eastern Germany.

The pressure of population was connected with the second cause, the growth of towns and cities in the Low Countries. Stimulated by commerce and overseas trade, Amsterdam grew from 30,000 inhabitants to 200,000 in its golden seventeenth century. The growth of urban population provided Dutch peasants with good markets for all they could produce and allowed each region to specialize in what it did best. Thus the Dutch could develop their potential, and the Low Countries became "the Mecca of foreign agricultural experts who came . . . to see Flemish agriculture with their own eyes, to write about it and to propagate its methods in their home lands."[2]

The English were the best students. Indeed, they were such good students it is often forgotten that they had teachers at all. Drainage and water control was one subject in which they received instruction. Large parts of seventeenth-century Holland had once been sea and sea marsh, and the efforts of centuries had made the Dutch the world's leaders in the skills of drainage. In the first half of the seventeenth century, Dutch experts made a great contribution to draining the extensive marshes, or fens, of wet and rainy England.

The most famous of these Dutch engineers, Cornelius Vermuyden, directed one large drainage project in Yorkshire and another in Cambridgeshire. The project in Yorkshire was supported by Charles I and financed by a group of Dutch capitalists, who were to receive one-third of all land reclaimed in return for their investment. Despite local opposition, Vermuyden drained the land by means of a large canal—his so-called Dutch river—and settlers cultivated the new fields in the Dutch fashion. In the Cambridge fens, Vermuyden and his Dutch workers eventually reclaimed 40,000 acres, which were then farmed intensively in the Dutch manner. Although all these efforts were disrupted in the turbulent 1640s by the English civil war, Ver-

Dutch Villagers turned perishable milk into valuable cheeses that could be conveniently shipped to many markets. In this workshop scene a girl carries buckets of milk to women who are pressing curds together to form a solid. The finished cheeses—big red rounds of Gouda—stand on shelves to the right. *(Source: Courtesy, Dutch Dairy Bureau)*

muyden and his countrymen largely succeeded. Swampy wilderness was converted into thousands of acres of some of the best land in England. On such new land, where traditions and common rights were not firmly established yet, farmers introduced new crops and new rotations fairly easily.

Dutch experience was also important to Viscount Charles Townsend (1674–1738), one of the pioneers of English agricultural improvement. This lord from the upper reaches of the English aristocracy learned about turnips and clover while serving as English ambassador to Holland. In the 1710s, he was using these crops in the sandy soil of his large estates in Norfolk in eastern England, already one of the most innovative agricultural areas in the country. When Lord Charles retired from politics in 1730 and returned to Norfolk, it was said that he spoke of turnips, turnips, and nothing but turnips.

This led some wit to nickname his lordship "Turnip" Townsend. But Townsend had the last laugh. Draining extensively, manuring heavily, and sowing crops in regular rotation without fallowing, the farmers who leased Townsend's lands produced larger crops. They and he earned higher incomes. Those who had scoffed reconsidered. By 1740 agricultural improvement in various forms had become something of a craze among the English aristocracy.

Jethro Tull (1674–1741), part crank and part genius, was another important English innovator. A true son of the early Enlightenment, Tull constantly tested accepted ideas about farming in an effort to develop better methods through empirical research. He was especially enthusiastic about using horses for plowing, in preference to slower-moving oxen. He also advocated sowing seed with drilling equipment, rather than scattering it by

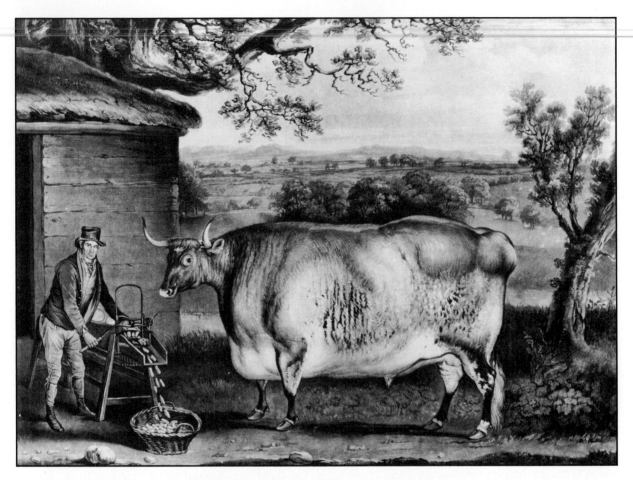

Selective Breeding meant bigger livestock and more meat on English tables. This gigantic champion, one of the new improved shorthorn breed, was known as the Newbus Ox. Such great fat beasts were pictured in the press and praised by poets. *(Source: Institute of Agricultural History and Museum of English Rural Life, University of Reading)*

hand. Drilling distributed seed evenly and at the proper depth. There were also improvements in livestock, inspired in part by the earlier successes of English country gentlemen in breeding ever-faster horses for the races and fox hunts that were their passions. Selective breeding of ordinary livestock was a marked improvement over the old pattern, which has been graphically described as little more than "the haphazard union of nobody's son with everybody's daughter."

By the mid-eighteenth century, English agriculture was in the process of a radical transformation. The eventual result was that by 1870 English farmers produced 300 percent more food than they had produced in 1700, although the number of people working the land had increased by only 14 percent. This great surge of agricultural production provided food for England's rapidly growing urban population. It was a tremendous achievement.

The Cost of Enclosure

What was the cost of technical progress in England, and to what extent did its payment result in social injustice? Scholars agree that the impetus for enclosing the fields came mainly from the powerful ruling class, the English aristocracy. Owning large estates, the aristocracy benefited directly from higher yields that could support higher rents, and it was able and ready to make expensive investments in the new technology. Beyond these certainties, there are important differences of interpretation among historians.

Many historians stress the initiative and enterprise of the big English landowners, which they contrast with the inertia and conservatism of continental landowners, big and small. They also assert that the open fields were enclosed fairly, with both large and small owners receiving their fair share after the strips were surveyed and consolidated.

Other historians argue that fairness was more apparent than real. The large landowners controlled Parliament, which made the laws. They had Parliament pass hundreds of "enclosure acts," each of which authorized the fencing of open fields in a given village and the division of the common in proportion to one's property in the open fields. The heavy legal and surveying costs of enclosure were also divided among the landowners. This meant that many peasants who had small holdings had to sell out to pay their share of the expenses. Similarly, the landless cottagers lost their age-old access to the common pasture without any compensation whatsoever. This dealt landless families a serious blow, because it deprived women of the means to raise animals for market and earn vital income. In the spirited words of one critical historian, "Enclosure (when all the sophistications are allowed for) was a plain enough case of class robbery, played according to the fair rules of property and law laid down by a Parliament of property-owners and lawyers."[3]

In assessing these conflicting interpretations, one needs to put eighteenth-century developments in a longer historical perspective. In the first place, as much as half of English farmland was already enclosed by 1750. A great wave of enclosure of English open fields into sheep pastures had already occurred in the sixteenth and early seventeenth centuries, a wave that had already dispossessed many English peasants in order to produce wool for the growing textile industry. In the later seventeenth and early eighteenth centuries, many open fields were enclosed fairly harmoniously by mutual agreement among all classes of landowners in English villages. Thus parliamentary enclosure, the great bulk of which occurred after 1760 and particularly during the Napoleonic wars early in the nineteenth century, only completed a process that was in full swing. Nor did an army of landless cottagers and farm laborers appear only in the last years of the eighteenth century. Much earlier, and certainly by 1700 because of the early enclosures for sheep runs, there were perhaps two landless agricultural workers in England for every independent farmer. In 1830, after the enclosures were complete, the proportion of landless laborers on the land was not substantially greater.

Indeed, by 1700 a highly distinctive pattern of landownership and production existed in England. At one extreme were a few large landowners, at the other a large mass of landless cottagers, who labored mainly for wages and who could graze only a pig or a cow on the village common. In between stood two other groups: small, independent peasants farmers who owned their own land, and substantial tenant farmers who rented land from the big landowners, hired wage laborers, and sold their output on a cash market. Yet the small, independent English peasant farmers had been declining in number since the sixteenth-century enclosures (and even before), and they continued to do so in the eighteenth century. They could not compete with the rising group of profit-minded, market-oriented tenant farmers.

These tenant farmers, many of whom had formerly been independent owners, were the key to mastering the new methods of farming. Well financed by the large landowners, the tenant farmers fenced fields, built drains, and improved the soil with fertilizers. Such improvements actually increased employment opportunities for wage workers in some areas. So did new methods of farming, for land was farmed more intensively without the fallow, and new crops like turnips required more care and effort. Thus enclosure did not force people off the land and into the towns by eliminating jobs, as has sometimes been claimed.

At the same time, by eliminating common rights and greatly reducing the access of poor men and women to the land, the eighteenth-century enclosure movement marked the completion of two major historical developments in England—the rise of market-oriented estate agriculture and the emergence of a landless rural proletariat. By 1815 a tiny minority of wealthy English (and Scottish) landowners held most of the land and pursued profits aggressively, leasing their holdings through agents at competitive prices to middle-sized farmers. These farmers produced mainly for cash markets and relied on landless laborers for their workforce. These landless laborers may have lived as well in 1800 as in 1700 in strictly economic terms. But they had lost that bit of independence and self-respect that common rights had provided. They had become completely dependent on cash wages earned in agriculture or in rural industry for their survival. In no other European country had this "proletarianization"—this transformation of large numbers of small peasant farmers into landless rural wage earners—gone so far as it had in England by the late eighteenth century. And, as in the earlier English enclosure movement, the village poor found the cost of economic change and technical progress heavy and unjust.

THE BEGINNING OF THE POPULATION EXPLOSION

Another factor that affected the existing order of life and forced economic changes in the eighteenth century was the remarkable growth of European population, the beginning of the "population explosion." This population explosion continued in Europe until the twentieth century, by which time it was affecting non-Western areas of the globe. What caused the growth of population, and what did the challenge of more mouths to feed and more hands to employ do to the European economy?

FIGURE 19.1 The Growth of Population in England, 1000–1800 England is a good example of both the uneven increase of European population before 1700 and the third great surge of growth, which began in the eighteenth century. *(Source: E. A. Wrigley,* Population and History. *New York: McGraw-Hill, 1969)*

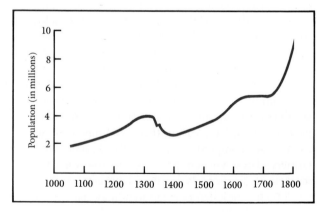

Limitations on Population Growth

Many commonly held ideas about population in the past are wrong. One such mistaken idea is that people always married young and had large families. A related error is the belief that past societies were so ignorant that they could do nothing to control their numbers and that population was always growing too fast. On the contrary, until 1700 the total population of Europe grew slowly much of the time, and it followed an irregular cyclical pattern (Figure 19.1).

The cyclical pattern of European population growth had a great influence on many aspects of social and economic life over time, although striking local and regional differences often make generalization difficult. As we have seen, the terrible ravages of the Black Death caused a sharp drop in population and prices after 1350 and also created a labor shortage throughout Europe (see page 534). Lords in eastern Europe responded to this labor shortage by reversing the trend toward personal freedom and gradually reinstituting serfdom. This landlord reaction failed in western Europe, however, where serf obligations had declined or even disappeared by 1500. Moreover, the era of labor shortages and low food prices after the Black Death resulted in an increased standard of living for peasants and artisans. Indeed, some economic historians calculate that, for those common people in western Europe who managed to steer clear of warfare and of power struggles within the ruling class, the later Middle Ages was an era of exceptional well-being.

But peasant and artisan well-being was eroded in the course of the sixteenth century. The second great surge of population growth indicated by Figure 19.1 outstripped the growth of agricultural production after about 1500. There was less food per person, and food prices rose more rapidly than wages, a development intensified by the inflow of precious metals from the Americas and a general if uneven European price revolution. The result was a substantial decline in living standards for the great majority of people throughout Europe. This decline aggravated especially the plight of both the urban and the rural poor. By 1600 the pressure of population on resources was severe in much of Europe, and widespread poverty was an undeniable reality.

For this reason, population growth slowed and stopped in seventeenth-century Europe. Births and deaths, fertility and mortality, were in a crude but effective balance. The birthrate—annual births as a proportion of the population—was fairly high, but far lower than it would have been if all women between ages fifteen and forty-five had been having as many children as biologically possible. The death rate in normal years was also high, though somewhat lower than the birthrate. As a result, the population grew modestly in normal years at a rate of perhaps 0.5 to 1 percent, or enough to double the population in 70 to 140 years. This is, of course, a generalization encompassing many different patterns. In areas like Russia and colonial New England, where there was a great deal of frontier to be settled, the annual rate of increase might well have exceeded 1 percent. In a country like France, where the land had long been densely settled, the rate of increase might have been less than 0.5 percent.

Although population growth of even 1 percent per year is fairly modest by the standards of many African and Latin American countries today—some of which are growing at about 3 percent annually—it will produce a very large increase over a long period. An annual increase of even 1 percent will result in sixteen times as many people in three hundred years. Such gigantic increases simply did not occur in agrarian Europe before the eighteenth century. In certain abnormal years and tragic periods—the Black Death was only the most extreme and extensive example—many more people died than were born. Total population fell sharply, even catastrophically. A number of years of modest growth would then be necessary to make up for those who had died in an abnormal year. Such savage increases in deaths occurred periodically in the seventeenth century on a local and regional scale, and these demographic crises combined with birthrates far below the biological potential to check the growth of population until after 1700.

The grim reapers of demographic crisis were famine, epidemic disease, and war. Famine, the inevitable result of poor farming methods and periodic crop failures, was particularly murderous because it was accompanied by disease. With a brutal one-two punch, famine stunned and weakened a population, and disease finished it off. Disease could also ravage independently, even in years of adequate harvests. Bubonic plague returned again and again in Europe for more than three hundred years after its ravages in the fourteenth century. Epidemics of dysentery and smallpox also operated independently of famine.

War was another scourge. The indirect effects were more harmful than the organized killing. War spread disease. Soldiers and camp followers passed venereal disease through the countryside to scar and kill. Armies requisitioned scarce food supplies for their own use and disrupted the agricultural cycle. The Thirty Years' War (see pages 477–481) witnessed all possible combinations of distress. In the German states, the number of inhabitants declined by more than *two-thirds* in some large areas and by at least one-third almost everywhere else. The Thirty Years' War reduced the total German population by no less than 40 percent. But numbers inadequately convey the dimensions of such human tragedy. One needs the vision of the artist. The great sixteenth-century artist Albrecht Dürer captured the horror of demographic crisis in his chilling woodcut *The Four Horsemen of the Apocalypse* (see page 382). Death, accompanied by his trusty companions War, Famine, and Conflict, takes his merciless ride of destruction. The narrow victory of life over death that prevails in normal times is being undone.

The New Pattern of the Eighteenth Century

In the eighteenth century, the population of Europe began to grow markedly. This increase in numbers occurred in all areas of Europe—western and eastern, northern and southern, dynamic and stagnant. Growth was especially dramatic after about 1750, as Figure 19.2 shows.

Although it is certain that Europe's population grew greatly, it is less clear why. Painstaking and innovative research in population history has shown that, because population grew everywhere, it is best to look first for general factors, rather than focus on those limited to individual countries or to certain levels of social and economic development. What, then, caused fewer people to die or, possibly, more babies to be born? In some kinds of families in some areas, women may have had more babies than before (see page 631). Yet the basic cause was a decline in mortality—fewer deaths.

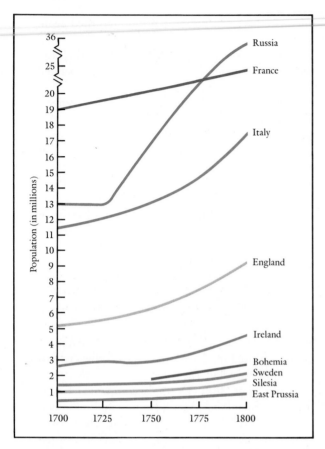

FIGURE 19.2 The Increase of Population in Europe in the Eighteenth Century France's large population continued to support French political and intellectual leadership. Russia emerged as Europe's most populous state because natural increase was complemented by growth from territorial expansion.

The bubonic plague mysteriously disappeared. Following the Black Death in the fourteenth century, plagues had remained a part of the European experience, striking again and again with savage force, particularly in towns. As a German writer of the early sixteenth century noted, "It is remarkable and astonishing that the plague should never wholly cease, but it should appear every year here and there, making its way from one place to another. Having subsided at one time, it returns within a few years by a circuitous route."[4]

As late as 1720, a ship from Syria and the Levant, where plague was ever-present, brought the monstrous disease to Marseilles. In a few weeks, forty thousand of the city's ninety thousand inhabitants died. The epidemic swept southern France, killing

one-third, one-half, even three-fourths of those in the larger towns. Once again an awful fear swept across Europe. But the epidemic passed, and that was the last time plague fell on western and central Europe. The final disappearance of plague was due in part to stricter measures of quarantine in Mediterranean ports and along the Austrian border with Turkey. Human carriers of plague were carefully isolated. Chance and plain good luck were more important, however.

It is now understood that bubonic plague is, above all, a disease of rats. More precisely, it is the black rat that spreads major epidemics, for the black rat's flea is the principal carrier of the plague bacillus. After 1600, for reasons unknown, a new rat of Asiatic origin—the brown, or wander, rat—began to drive out and eventually eliminate its black competitor. In the words of a noted authority, "This revolution in the animal kingdom must have gone far to break the lethal link between rat and man."[5] Although the brown rat also contracts the plague, another kind of flea is its main parasite. That flea carries the plague poorly and, for good measure, has little taste for human blood.

Advances in medical knowledge did not contribute much to reducing the death rate in the eighteenth century. The most important advance in preventive medicine in this period was inoculation against smallpox. This great improvement was long confined mainly to England and probably did little to reduce deaths throughout Europe until the latter part of the century. However, improvements in the water supply and sewerage promoted somewhat better public health and helped reduce such diseases as typhoid and typhus in some urban areas of western Europe. It has also been argued recently that eighteenth-century improvements in water supply and in the drainage of swamps and marshes reduced Europe's large and dangerous insect population. Filthy flies and mosquitoes played a major role in spreading serious epidemics and also in transmitting common diseases, especially those striking children and young adults. Thus early public health measures were probably more important than historians have previously believed, and they helped the decline in mortality that began with the disappearance of plague to continue into the early nineteenth century.

Human beings also became more successful in their efforts to safeguard the supply of food and protect against famine. The eighteenth century was a time of considerable canal and road building in western Europe. These advances in transportation, which were among the more positive aspects of strong absolutist states, lessened the impact of local crop failure and famine. Emergency supplies could be brought in. The age-old spectacle of localized starvation became less frequent. Wars became more gentlemanly and less destructive than in the seventeenth century and spread fewer epidemics. New foods, particularly the potato, were introduced. Potatoes served as an important alternative source of vitamins A and C for the poor, especially when the grain crops were skimpy or failed. In short, population grew in the eighteenth century primarily because years of abnormal death rates were less catastrophic. Famines, epidemics, and wars continued to occur, but their severity moderated.

The growth of population in the eighteenth century cannot be interpreted as a sign of human progress, however. As we have seen, serious population pressure on resources existed by 1600 and continued throughout the seventeenth century. Thus renewed population growth in the eighteenth century maintained or even increased the imbalance between the number of people and the economic opportunities available to them. There was only so much land available, and tradition slowed the adoption of better farming methods. Therefore, agriculture could not provide enough work for the rapidly growing labor force, and poor people in the countryside had to look for new ways to make a living.

THE GROWTH OF COTTAGE INDUSTRY

The growth of population increased the number of rural workers with little or no land, and this in turn contributed to the development of industry in rural areas. The poor in the countryside needed increasingly to supplement their earnings from agriculture with other types of work, and capitalists from the city were eager to employ them, often at lower wages than urban workers usually commanded. Manufacturing with hand tools in peasant cottages and worksheds grew markedly in the eighteenth century. Rural industry became a crucial feature of the European economy.

To be sure, peasant communities had always made some clothing, processed some food, and

constructed some housing for their own use. But in the High Middle Ages, peasants did not produce manufactured goods on a large scale for sale in a market. Industry in the Middle Ages was dominated and organized by urban craft guilds and urban merchants, who jealously regulated handicraft production and sought to maintain it as an urban monopoly. By the eighteenth century, however, the pressures of rural poverty and the need to employ landless proletarians were overwhelming the efforts of urban artisans to maintain their traditional control over industrial production. A new system was expanding lustily.

Doctor in Protective Clothing   Most doctors believed, incorrectly, that poisonous smells carried the plague. This doctor has placed strong-smelling salts in his "beak" to protect himself against deadly plague vapors. *(Source: Germanisches Nationalmuseum, Nuremberg)*

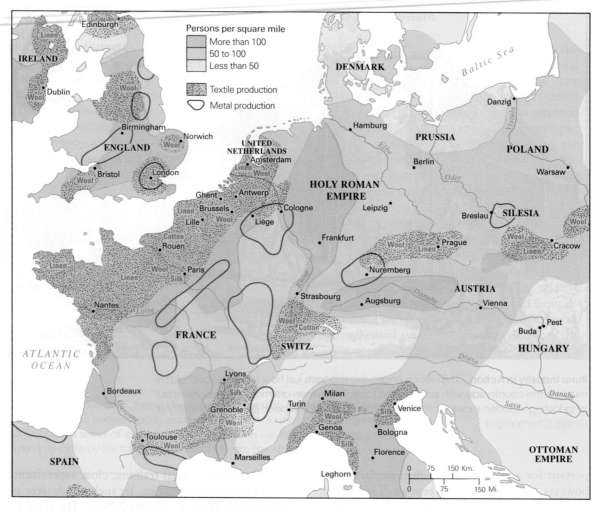

MAP 19.1 Industry and Population in Eighteenth-Century Europe The growth of cottage manufacturing in rural areas helped country people to increase their income and contributed to increases in the population. This putting-out system began in England, and most of the work was in the textile industry.

poor in the countryside was to encourage the growth of cottage manufacturing. Thus in France, as in Germany and other areas, the later part of the eighteenth century witnessed a remarkable expansion of rural industry in certain densely populated regions (Map 19.1). The pattern established in England was spreading to the Continent.

The Textile Industry

Throughout most of history, until at least the nineteenth century, the industry that has employed the most people has been textiles. The making of linen, woolen, and eventually cotton cloth was the typical activity of cottage workers engaged in the putting-out system. A look inside the cottage of the English rural textile worker illustrates a way of life as well as an economic system.

The rural worker lived in a small cottage, with tiny windows and little space. Indeed, the worker's cottage was often a single room that served as workshop, kitchen, and bedroom. There were only a few pieces of furniture, of which the weaver's loom was by far the largest and most important. That loom had changed somewhat in the early eighteenth century, when John Kay's invention of the flying shuttle enabled the weaver to throw the shuttle back and forth between the threads with one hand. Aside from that improvement, however, the loom was as it had been for much of history. In the cottage there were also spinning wheels, tubs for dyeing cloth and washing raw wool, and carding pieces to comb and prepare the raw material.

These different pieces of equipment were necessary because cottage industry was first and foremost a family enterprise. All the members of the family helped in the work, so that "every person from seven to eighty (who retained their sight and who could move their hands) could earn their bread," as one eighteenth-century English observer put it.[6] While the women and children prepared the raw material and spun the thread, the man of the house wove the cloth. There was work for everyone, even the youngest. After the dirt was beaten out of the raw cotton, it had to be thoroughly cleaned with strong soap in a tub, where tiny feet took the place of the agitator in a washing machine. George Crompton, the son of Samuel Crompton, who in 1784 invented the mule for cotton spinning, recalled that "soon after I was able to walk I was employed in the cotton manufacture. . . . My mother tucked up my petticoats about my waist, and put me into the tub to tread upon the cotton at the bottom."[7] Slightly older children and aged relatives carded and combed the cotton or wool, so

The Weaver's Repose   This painting by Decker Cornelis Gerritz (1594–1637) captures the pleasure of release from long hours of toil in cottage industry. The loom realistically dominates the cramped living space and the family's modest possessions. *(Source: Musées Royaux des Beaux-Arts, Brussels. Copyright A.C.I.)*

that the woman and the older daughter she had taught could spin it into thread. Each member had a task. The very young and very old worked in the family unit as a matter of course.

There was always a serious imbalance in this family enterprise: the work of four or five spinners was needed to keep one weaver steadily employed. Therefore, the wife and the husband had constantly to try to find more thread and more spinners. Widows and unmarried women—those "spinsters" who spun for their living—were recruited by the wife. Or perhaps the weaver's son went off on horseback to seek thread. The need for more thread might even lead the weaver and his wife to become small capitalist employers. At the end of the week, when they received the raw wool or cotton from the merchant-manufacturer, they would put out some of this raw material to other cottages. The following week they would return to pick up the thread and pay for the spinning—spinning that would help keep the weaver busy for a week until the merchant came for the finished cloth.

Relations between workers and employers were often marked by sharp conflict. An English popular song written about 1700, called "The Clothier's Delight, or the Rich Men's Joy and the Poor Men's Sorrow," has the merchant boasting of his countless tricks used to "beat down wages":

We heapeth up riches and treasure great store
Which we get by griping and grinding the poor.
  And this is a way for to fill up our purse
  Although we do get it with many a curse.[8]

There were constant disputes over weights of materials and the quality of the cloth. Merchants accused workers of stealing raw materials, and weavers complained that merchants delivered underweight bales. Suspicions abounded.

There was another problem, at least from the merchant-capitalist's point of view. Rural labor was cheap, scattered, and poorly organized. For these reasons it was hard to control. Cottage workers tended to work in spurts. After they got paid on Saturday afternoon, the men in particular tended to drink and relax for two or three days. Indeed, Monday was called "holy Monday" because inactivity was so religiously observed. By the end of the week the weaver was probably working feverishly to make his quota. But if he did not succeed, there was little the merchant could do. When times were

good and the merchant could easily sell everything produced, the weaver and his family did fairly well and were particularly inclined to loaf, to the dismay of the capitalist. Thus the putting-out system in the textile industry had definite shortcomings from the employer's point of view. There was an imbalance between spinning and weaving. Labor relations were often poor, and the merchant was unable to control the quality of the cloth or the schedule of the workers. Ambitious merchant-capitalists therefore intensified their search for ways to produce more efficiently and to squeeze still more work out of "undisciplined" cottage workers.

BUILDING THE ATLANTIC ECONOMY

In addition to agricultural improvement, population pressure, and expanding cottage industry, the expansion of Europe in the eighteenth century was characterized by the growth of world trade. Spain and Portugal revitalized their empires and began drawing more wealth from renewed development. Yet, once again, the countries of northwestern Europe—the Netherlands, France, and above all Great Britain—benefited most. Great Britain (formed in 1707 by the union of England and Scotland in a single kingdom) gradually became the leading maritime power. In the eighteenth century, British ships and merchants succeeded in dominating long-distance trade, particularly the fast-growing intercontinental trade across the Atlantic Ocean. The British played the critical role in building a fairly unified Atlantic economy, which offered remarkable opportunities for them and their colonists.

Mercantilism and Colonial Wars

Britain's commercial leadership in the eighteenth century had its origins in the mercantilism of the seventeenth century (see page 508). European mercantilism was a system of economic regulations aimed at increasing the power of the state. As practiced by a leading advocate like Colbert under Louis XIV, mercantilism aimed particularly at creating a favorable balance of foreign trade in order to increase a country's stock of gold. A country's gold holdings served as an all-important treas-

The East India Dock, London   This painting by Samuel Scott captures the spirit and excitement of British maritime expansion. Great sailing ships line the quay, bringing profit and romance from far-off India. London grew in population from 350,000 in 1650 to 900,000 in 1800, when it was twice as big as Paris, its nearest rival. *(Source: Courtesy of Board of Trustees of the Victoria & Albert Museum)*

ure chest, to be opened periodically to pay for war in a violent age.

Early English mercantilists shared these views. What distinguished English mercantilism was the unusual idea that governmental economic regulations could and should serve the private interest of individuals and groups as well as the public needs of the state. As Josiah Child, a very wealthy brewer and director of the East India Company, put it, in the ideal economy "Profit and Power ought jointly to be considered."[9] In France and other continental countries, by contrast, seventeenth-century mercantilists generally put the needs of the state far above those of business people and workers. And

COLONIAL COMPETITION AND WAR, 1651–1763

1651–1663	British Navigation Acts create the mercantile system, which is not seriously modified until 1786
1652–1674	Three Anglo-Dutch wars damage Dutch shipping and commerce
1664	New Amsterdam is seized and renamed New York
1701–1714	War of the Spanish Succession
1713	Peace of Utrecht: Britain wins parts of Canada from France and control of the western African slave trade from Spain
1740–1748	War of the Austrian Succession, resulting in no change in territorial holdings in North America
1756–1763	Seven Years' War (known in North America as the French and Indian War), a decisive victory for Britain
1763	Treaty of Paris: Britain receives all French territory on the North American mainland and achieves dominance in India

they seldom saw a possible union of public and private interests for a common good.

The result of the English desire to increase both military power and private wealth was the mercantile system of the Navigation Acts. Oliver Cromwell established the first of these laws in 1651, and the restored monarchy of Charles II extended them further in 1660 and 1663; these Navigation Acts of the seventeenth century were not seriously modified until 1786. The acts required that most goods imported from Europe into England and Scotland be carried on British-owned ships with British crews or on ships of the country producing the article. Moreover, these laws gave British merchants and shipowners a virtual monopoly on trade with the colonies. The colonists were required to ship their products—sugar, tobacco, and cotton—on British (or American) ships and to buy almost all of their European goods from Britain. It was believed that these economic regulations would provide British merchants and workers with profits and employment, and colonial plantation owners and farmers with a guaranteed market for their products. And the the emerging British empire would develop a shipping industry with a large number of tough, experienced deep-water seamen, who could be drafted when necessary into the Royal Navy to protect the island nation and its colonial possessions.

The Navigation Acts were a form of economic warfare. Their initial target was the Dutch, who were far ahead of the English in shipping and foreign trade in the mid-seventeenth century. The Navigation Acts, in conjunction with three Anglo-Dutch wars between 1652 and 1674, did seriously damage Dutch shipping and commerce. The thriving Dutch colony of New Amsterdam was seized in 1664 and renamed "New York." By the later seventeenth century, when the Dutch and the English became allies to stop the expansion of France's Louis XIV, the Netherlands was falling behind England in shipping, trade, and colonies.

As the Netherlands followed Spain into relative decline, France stood clearly as England's most serious rival in the competition for overseas empire. Rich in natural resources and endowed with a population three or four times that of England, continental Europe's leading military power was already building a powerful fleet and a worldwide system of rigidly monopolized colonial trade. And France, aware that Great Britain coveted large parts of Spain's American empire, was determined to revitalize its Spanish ally. Thus, from 1701 to 1763, Britain and France were locked in a series of wars to decide, in part, which nation would become the leading maritime power and claim a lion's share of the profits of Europe's overseas expansion (Map 19.2).

MAP 19.2 The Economy of the Atlantic Basin in 1701
The growth of trade encouraged both economic development and military conflict in the Atlantic Basin.

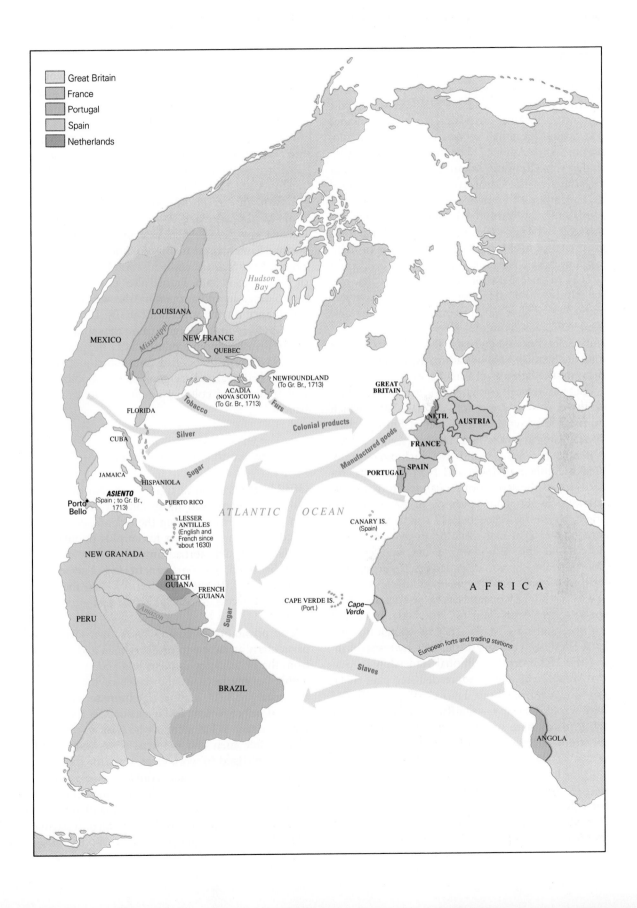

Great Britain
France
Portugal
Spain
Netherlands

Hudson Bay

LOUISIANA

MEXICO

NEW FRANCE

QUEBEC

NEWFOUNDLAND
(To Gr. Br., 1713)

ACADIA
(NOVA SCOTIA)
(To Gr. Br., 1713)

Tobacco

FLORIDA

Furs

GREAT
BRITAIN

Silver

CUBA

Colonial products

NETH.

AUSTRIA

Sugar

Manufactured goods

JAMAICA

HISPANIOLA

FRANCE

ASIENTO
(Spain ; to Gr. Br.,
1713)

PUERTO RICO

PORTUGAL

SPAIN

Porto
Bello

LESSER
ANTILLES
(English and
French since
about 1630)

ATLANTIC OCEAN

CANARY IS.
(Spain)

NEW GRANADA

AFRICA

DUTCH
GUIANA

FRENCH
GUIANA

CAPE VERDE IS.
(Port.)

*Cape
Verde*

PERU

Amazon

Sugar

European forts and trading stations

BRAZIL

Slaves

ANGOLA

The first round was the War of the Spanish Succession (see page 513), which started when Louis XIV declared his willingness to accept the Spanish crown willed to his grandson. Besides upsetting the continental balance of power, a union of France and Spain threatened to destroy the British colonies in North America. The thin ribbon of British settlements along the Atlantic seaboard from Massachusetts to the Carolinas would be surrounded by a great arc of Franco-Spanish power stretching south and west from French Canada to Florida and the Gulf of Mexico (see Map 19.2). Defeated by a great coalition of states after twelve years of fighting, Louis XIV was forced in the Peace of Utrecht (1713) to cede Newfoundland, Nova Scotia, and the Hudson Bay territory to Britain. Spain was compelled to give Britain control of the lucrative West African slave trade—the so-called *asiento*—and to let Britain send one ship of merchandise into the Spanish colonies annually, through Porto Bello on the Isthmus of Panama.

France was still a mighty competitor. The War of the Austrian Succession (1740–1748), which started when Frederick the Great of Prussia seized Silesia from Austria's Maria Theresa (see page 584), gradually became a world war, including Anglo-French conflicts in India and North America. Indeed, it was the seizure of French territory in Canada by New England colonists in 1745 that led France to sue for peace in 1748 and to accept a return to the territorial situation existing in North America at the beginning of the war. France's Bourbon ally, Spain, defended itself surprisingly well, and Spain's empire remained intact.

This inconclusive stand-off helped set the stage for the Seven Years' War (1756–1763). In central Europe, Austria's Maria Theresa sought to win back Silesia and crush Prussia, thereby re-establishing the Habsburgs' traditional leadership in German affairs. She almost succeeded (see page 584), skillfully winning both France—the Habsburgs' long-standing enemy—and Russia to her cause. Yet the Prussian state survived, saved by its army and the sudden decision of Russia to withdraw from the war in 1762.

Outside of Europe, the Seven Years' War was the decisive round in the Franco-British competition for colonial empire (Map 19.3). Led by William Pitt, whose grandfather had made a fortune as a trader in India, the British concentrated on using superior sea power to destroy the French fleet and choke off French commerce around the world. Capturing Quebec in 1759 and winning a great naval victory at Quiberon Bay, the British also strangled France's valuable sugar trade with its Caribbean islands and smashed French forts in India. After Spain entered the war on France's side in 1761, the surging British temporarily occupied Havana in Cuba and Manila in the Philippines. With the Treaty of Paris (1763), France lost all its possessions on the mainland of North America. French Canada as well as French territory east of the Mississippi River passed to Britain, and France ceded Louisiana to Spain as compensation for Spain's loss of Florida to Britain. France also gave up most of its holdings in India, opening the way to British dominance on the subcontinent. By 1763 British naval power, built in large part on the rapid growth of the British shipping industry after the passage of the Navigation Acts, had triumphed decisively. Britain had realized its goal of monopolizing a vast trading and colonial empire for its exclusive benefit.

Land and Wealth in North America

Of all Britain's colonies, those on the North American mainland proved most valuable in the long run. The settlements along the Atlantic coast provided an important outlet for surplus population, so that migration abroad limited poverty in England, Scotland, and northern Ireland. The settlers also benefited. In the mainland colonies, they had privileged access to virtually free and unlimited land.

The possibility of having one's own farm was particularly attractive to ordinary men and women from the British Isles. Land in England was already highly concentrated in the hands of the nobility and gentry in 1700 and became more so with agricultural improvement and enclosures in the eighteenth century. White settlers who came to the colonies as free men and women, or as indentured servants pledged to work seven years for their passage, or as prisoners and convicts, could obtain their own farms on easy terms as soon as they had their personal freedom. Life in the mainland colonies was hard, but the settlers succeeded in paying little or no rent to grasping landlords, and taxes

MAP 19.3 European Claims in North America Before and After the Seven Year's War (1756–1763)   France lost its vast claims in North America, though the British government then prohibited colonists from settling west of a line drawn in 1763. The British wanted to avoid costly wars with Indians living in the newly conquered territory.

were very low. Unlike the great majority of European peasants, who had to accept high rents and taxes as part of the order of things, American farmers could keep most of what they managed to produce.

The availability of land made labor expensive in the colonies. This basic fact, rather than any repressive aspects of the Navigation Acts, limited the growth of industry in the colonies. The advantage for colonists was in farming, and farm they did.

Cheap land and scarce labor were also critical factors in the growth of slavery in the southern colonies. By 1700 British indentured servants were carefully avoiding the Virginia lowlands, where black slavery was spreading, and by 1730 the large

plantations there had gone over completely to black slaves. Slave labor permitted an astonishing tenfold increase in tobacco production between 1700 and 1774 and created a wealthy aristocratic planter class in Maryland and Virginia.

In the course of the eighteenth century, the farmers of New England and the middle colonies began to produce more food than they needed. They exported ever more foodstuffs, primarily to the West Indies. There the owners of the sugar plantations came to depend on the mainland colonies for grain and dried fish to feed their slaves. The plantation owners, whether they grew tobacco in Virginia and Maryland or sugar in the West Indies, had the exclusive privilege of supplying the British

Tobacco was a key commodity in the Atlantic trade. This engraving from 1775 shows a merchant and his slaves preparing a cargo for sail. *(Source: The British Library)*

Isles with their products. Englishmen could not buy cheaper sugar from Brazil, nor were they allowed to grow tobacco in the home islands. Thus the colonists, too, had their place in the protective mercantile system of the Navigation Acts. The American shipping industry grew rapidly in the eighteenth century, for example, because colonial shippers enjoyed the same advantages as their fellow citizens in Britain.

The abundance of almost-free land resulted in a rapid increase in the colonial population in the eighteenth century. In a mere three-quarters of a century after 1700, the white population of the mainland colonies multiplied a staggering ten times, as immigrants arrived and colonial couples raised large families. In 1774, 2.2 million whites and 330,000 blacks inhabited what would soon become the independent United States.

Rapid population growth did not reduce the settlers to poverty. On the contrary, agricultural development resulted in fairly high standards of living, in eighteenth-century terms, for mainland colonists. There was also an unusual degree of economic equality by European standards. Few people were extremely rich, and few were extremely poor. Remarkably, on the eve of the American Revolution, white men or women in the mainland British colonies probably had the highest average income and standard of living in the world.[10] Thus

it is clear just how much the colonists benefited from hard work and the mercantile system created by the Navigation Acts.

The Growth of Foreign Trade

England also profited greatly from the mercantile system. Above all, the rapidly growing and increasingly wealthy agricultural populations of the mainland colonies provided an expanding market for English manufactured goods. This situation was extremely fortunate, for England in the eighteenth century was gradually losing, or only slowly expanding, its sales to many of its traditional European markets. However, rising demand for manufactured goods in North America, as well as in the West Indies, Africa, and Latin America, allowed English cottage industry to continue to grow and diversify. Merchant-capitalists and manufacturers found new and exciting opportunities for profit and wealth.

Since the late Middle Ages, England had relied very heavily on the sale of woolen cloth in foreign markets. Indeed, as late as 1700, woolen cloth was the only important manufactured good exported from England, and fully 90 percent of it was sold to Europeans. In the course of the eighteenth century, the states of continental Europe were trying to develop their own cottage textile industries in an effort to deal with rural poverty and overpopulation. Like England earlier, these states adopted protectionist, mercantilist policies. They tried by means of tariffs and other measures to exclude competing goods from abroad, whether English woolens or the cheap but beautiful cotton calicos the English East India Company brought from India and sold in Europe.

France had already closed its markets to the English in the seventeenth century. In the eighteenth century, German states purchased much less woolen cloth from England and encouraged cottage production of coarse, cheap linens, which became a feared competitor in all of central and southern Europe. By 1773 England was selling only about two-thirds as much woolen cloth to northern and western Europe as it had in 1700. The decline of many markets on the Continent meant that the English economy badly needed new markets and new products in order to develop and prosper.

Protected colonial markets came to the rescue, more than offsetting stagnating trade with Europe. The markets of the Atlantic economy led the way, as may be seen in Figure 19.3. English exports of manufactured goods to continental Europe increased very modestly, from roughly £2.9 million in 1700 to only £3.3 million in 1773. Meanwhile, sales of manufactured products to the Atlantic economy—primarily the mainland colonies of North America and the West Indian sugar islands, with an important assist from West Africa and Latin America—soared from £500,000 to £4.0 million. Sales to other "colonies"—Ireland and India—also rose substantially in the eighteenth century.

English exports became much more balanced and diversified. To America and Africa went large quantities of metal items—axes to frontier settlers, firearms, chains for slaveowners. There were also clocks and coaches, buttons and saddles, china and furniture, musical instruments and scientific equipment, and a host of other things. By 1750 half the nails made in England were going to the colonies. Foreign trade became the bread and butter of some industries.

Thus the mercantile system formed in the seventeenth century to attack the Dutch and to win power and profit for England continued to shape

trade in the eighteenth century. The English concentrated in their hands much of the demand for manufactured goods from the growing Atlantic economy. The pressure of demand from three continents on the cottage industry of one medium-sized country heightened the efforts of English merchant-capitalists to find new and improved ways to produce more goods. By the 1770s England stood on the threshold of epoch-making industrial changes which will be described later in Chapter 22.

Revival in Colonial Latin America

When the last Spanish Habsburg, the feeble-minded Charles II, died in 1700 (see page 513), Spain's vast empire lay ready for dismemberment. Yet, in one of those striking reversals with which history is replete, Spain revived. The empire held together and even prospered, while a European-oriented landowning aristocracy enhanced its position in colonial society.

FIGURE 19.3 Exports of English Manufactured Goods, 1700–1774 While trade between England and Europe stagnated after 1700, English exports to Africa and the Americas boomed and greatly stimulated English economic development. *(Source: R. Davis, English Foreign Trade, 1700–1774, Economic History Review, 2d series, 15 (1962); 302–303)*

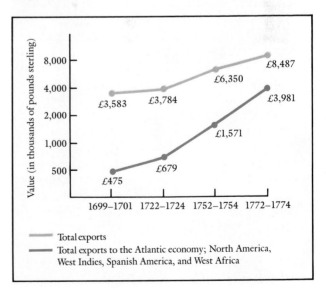

Total exports

Total exports to the Atlantic economy; North America, West Indies, Spanish America, and West Africa

Spain recovered in part because of better leadership. Louis XIV's grandson, who took the throne as Philip V (r. 1700–1746), brought new men and fresh ideas with him from France and rallied the Spanish people to his Bourbon dynasty in the long War of the Spanish Succession. When peace was restored, a series of reforming ministers reasserted royal authority, overhauling state finances and strengthening defense.

Revitalization in Madrid had positive results in the colonies. The colonies succeeded in defending themselves from numerous British attacks and even increased in size. Spain received Louisiana from France in 1763, and missionaries and ranchers extended Spanish influence all the way to northern California.

Political success was matched by economic improvement. After declining markedly in the seventeenth century, silver mining recovered in Mexico and Peru. Output quadrupled between 1700 and 1800, when Spanish America accounted for half of world silver production. Silver mining also encouraged food production for large mining camps and gave the *Creoles*—people of Spanish blood born in America—the means to purchase more and more European luxuries and manufactured goods. A class of wealthy merchants arose to handle this flourishing trade, which often relied on smuggled goods from Great Britain. As in British North America, industry remained weak, although workshops employing forced Indian labor were occupied with fashioning Mexican and Peruvian wool into coarse fabrics for purchase by the Latin American masses. Spain's colonies were an important element of the Atlantic economy.

Economic development strengthened the Creole elite, which came to rival the top government officials dispatched from Spain. Creole estate owners controlled much of the land, the main source of wealth. Small independent farmers were rare. The estate owners strove to become a genuine European aristocracy, and they believed that work in the fields was the proper occupation of an impoverished peasantry. The defenseless Indians suited their needs. As the Indian population recovered in numbers, slavery and periodic forced labor gave way to widespread debt peonage from 1600 on. Under this system, a planter or rancher would keep the estate's Christianized, increasingly Hispanicized Indians in perpetual debt bondage by periodically advancing food, shelter, and a little money. In this way, debt peonage was a form of agricultural serfdom.

There were also Creoles of modest means, especially in the cities. The large middle group in Spanish colonies consisted of racially mixed *mestizos,* the offspring of Spanish men and Indian women. The most talented mestizos realistically aspired to join the Creoles, for enough wealth and power could make one white. This ambition siphoned off the most energetic mestizos and lessened the buildup of any lower-class discontent. Thus, by the end of the colonial era, roughly 20 percent of the population was classified as white and about 30 percent as

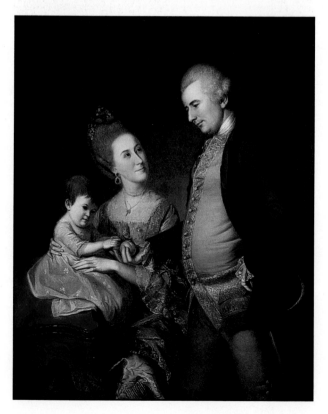

Charles Willson Peale: General John Cadwalader, His First Wife Elizabeth Lloyd, and Their Daughter Anne With their rich imported satins and elegant household furnishings, represented by the elaborately carved table on the left, this colonial American family proclaims its prosperity, refinement, and high social standing. American demand for foreign goods was voracious. *(Source: Philadelphia Museum of Art; The Cadwalader Collection)*

Porto Bello   Located on the isthmus of Panama, little Porto Bello was a major port in Spanish America. When ships arrived for 40-day trade fairs, it bustled with the energy of merchants, slaves, and soldiers. *(Source: The Pierpont Morgan Library)*

mestizo. Pure-blooded Indians accounted for most of the remainder, for only on the sugar plantations of Cuba and Puerto Rico did black slavery ever take firm root in Spanish America.

The situation was quite the opposite in Portuguese Brazil. As in the West Indies, enormous numbers of blacks were brought in chains to work the sugar plantations. About half the population of Brazil was of African origin in the early nineteenth century. Even more than in the Spanish territories, the people of Brazil intermingled sexually and culturally. In contrast to North America, where racial lines were hard and fast, at least in theory, colonial Brazil made a virtue of miscegenation, and the population grew to include every color in the racial rainbow.

SUMMARY

While some European intellectual elites were developing a new view of the world in the eighteenth century, Europe as a whole was experiencing a gradual but far-reaching expansion. As agriculture showed signs of modest improvement across the Continent, first the Low Countries and then England launched changes that gradually revolutionized agriculture. Plague disappeared, and the populations of all countries grew significantly, encouraging the growth of wage labor, cottage industry, and merchant capitalism.

Europeans also continued their overseas expansion, fighting for empire and profit and, in particular, consolidating their hold on the Americas. A revived Spain and its Latin American colonies participated fully in this expansion. As in agriculture and cottage industry, however, England and its empire proved most successful. The English concentrated much of the growing Atlantic trade in their hands, a development that challenged and enriched English industry and intensified the search for new methods of production. Thus, by the 1770s, England was approaching an economic breakthrough fully as significant as the great political upheaval destined to develop shortly in neighboring France.

NOTES

1. M. Bloch, *Les caractères originaux de l'histoire rurale française,* vol. 1 (Paris: Librarie Armand Colin, 1960), pp. 244–245.
2. B. H. Slicher van Bath, *The Agrarian History of Western Europe, A.D. 500–1850* (New York: St. Martin's Press, 1963), p. 240.
3. E. P. Thompson, *The Making of the English Working Class* (New York: Vintage Books, 1966), p. 218.
4. Quoted in E. E. Rich and C. H. Wilson, eds., *The Cambridge Economic History of Europe,* vol. 4 (Cambridge: Cambridge University Press, 1967), p. 74.
5. Ibid., p. 85.
6. Quoted in I. Pinchbeck, *Women Workers and the Industrial Revolution, 1750–1850* (New York: F. S. Crofts, 1930), p. 113.
7. Quoted in S. Chapman, *The Lancashire Cotton Industry* (Manchester, Eng.: Manchester University Press, 1903), p. 13.
8. Quoted in P. Mantoux, *The Industrial Revolution in the Eighteenth Century* (New York: Harper & Row, 1961), p. 75.
9. Quoted in C. Wilson, *England's Apprenticeship, 1603–1763* (London: Longmans, Green, 1965), p. 169.
10. G. Taylor, "America's Growth Before 1840," *Journal of Economic History* 24 (December 1970): pp. 427–444.

SUGGESTED READING

The works by B. H. Slicher van Bath and M. Bloch listed in the Notes are wide-ranging general introductions to the gradual transformation of European agriculture. Bloch's classic has been translated as *French Rural History*

(1966). J. Blum, *The End of the Old Order in Rural Europe* (1978), is an impressive comparative study. J. de Vries, *The Dutch Rural Economy in the Golden Age, 1500–1700* (1974), skillfully examines the causes of early Dutch leadership in farming, while A. Kussmaul, *A General View of the Rural Economy of England, 1538–1840* (1989), charts the path of agricultural progress in England. Two recommended and complementary studies on landowning nobilities are R. Forster, *The Nobility of Toulouse in the Eighteenth Century* (1960), and G. E. Mingay, *English Landed Society in the Eighteenth Century* (1963). A. Goodwin, ed., *The European Nobility in the Eighteenth Century* (1967), is an exciting group of essays on aristocrats in different countries. R. and E. Forster, eds., *European Society in the Eighteenth Century* (1969), assembles a rich collection of contemporary writing on a variety of economic and social topics. E. Le Roy Ladurie, *The Peasants of Languedoc* (1976), a brilliant and challenging study of rural life in southern France for several centuries, complements J. Goody et al., eds., *Family and Inheritance: Rural Society in Western Europe, 1200–1800* (1976). Life in small-town France comes alive in P. Higonnet, *Pont-de-Montvert: Social Structure and Politics in a French Village, 1700–1914* (1971), while O. Hufton deals vividly and sympathetically with rural migration, work, women, and much more in *The Poor in Eighteenth-Century France* (1974).

An ambitious reexamination with extensive bibliographical references by M. Gutman, *Toward the Modern Economy: Early Modern Industry in Europe, 1500–1800* (1988), highlights the creativity of rural industry, as do J. Goodman and K. Honeyman in *Gainful Pursuits: The Making of Industrial Europe, 1600–1914* (1988). The classic study by P. Mantoux, cited in the Notes, and D. Landes, *The Unbound Prometheus* (1969), lay more stress on the growing limitations of cottage production. G. Gullickson, *Spinners and Weavers of Auffay: Rural Industry and the Sexual Division of Labor in a French Village, 1750–1850* (1986), and M. Sonenscher, *The Hatters of Eighteenth-Century France* (1987), are valuable studies.

Two excellent multivolume series, *The Cambridge Economic History of Europe,* mentioned in the Notes, and C. Cipolla, ed., *The Fontana Economic History of Europe,* cover the sweep of economic developments from the Middle Ages to the present and have extensive bibliographies. So does R. Cameron, *A Concise Economic History of the World* (1989), which deals mainly with Europe. F. Braudel, *Civilization and Capitalism, Fifteenth–Eighteenth Century* (1981–1984), is a monumental and highly recommended three-volume synthesis. In the area of trade and colonial competition, V. Barbour, *Capitalism in Amsterdam* (1963), and C. R. Boxer, *The Dutch Seaborne Empire* (1970), are very interesting on Holland. J. Brewer, *The Sinews of Power: War, Money, and the English State, 1688–1783* (1989), looks at English victories, while G. Parker,

The Military Revolution: Military Technology in the Rise of the West (1988), a masterful, beautifully illustrated work, explores the roots of European power and conquest. W. Dorn, *The Competition for Empire, 1740–1763* (1963), D. K. Fieldhouse, *The Colonial Empires* (1971), and R. Davies, *The Rise of Atlantic Economies* (1973), are all valuable works on the struggle for empire. R. Pares, *Yankees and Creoles* (1956), is a short, lively work on trade between the mainland colonies and the West Indies, and M. Rediker, *Between the Devil and the Deep Blue Sea: Merchant Seamen, Pirates, and the Anglo-American Maritime World, 1700–1750* (1987), captures the spirit of ships and sailors. E. Williams, *Capitalism and Slavery* (1966), provocatively argues that slavery provided the wealth necessary for England's industrial development. Another exciting work is J. Nef, *War and Human Progress* (1968), which examines the impact of war on economic and industrial development in European history between about 1500 and 1800.

Three very fine books on the growth of population are M. Flinn's concise *The European Demographic System, 1500–1800* (1981); E. A. Wrigley's demanding *Population and History* (1969); and T. McKeown's scholarly *The Modern Rise of Population* (1977). J. Komlos, *Nutrition and Economic Development in the Eighteenth-Century Habsburg Monarchy* (1989), and W. McNeill, *Plagues and Peoples* (1976), are both noteworthy. For England, C. Wilson's volume mentioned in the Notes is highly recommended, as is P. Langford, *A Polite and Commercial People: England, 1727–1783* (1989). Further works on England can be found in the Suggested Reading for Chapter 22. The greatest novel of eighteenth-century English society is Henry Fielding's unforgettable *Tom Jones,* although Jane Austen's novels about country society, *Emma* and *Pride and Prejudice,* are not far behind.

20

The Life of the People

The discussion of agriculture and industry in the last chapter showed the ordinary man and woman at work, straining to make ends meet and earn a living. Yet work is only part of human experience. What about the rest?

- What changes occurred in marriage and the family by the end of the eighteenth century?
- What was life like for children?
- What did people eat, and how did diet and medical care affect people's health?
- What were the patterns of popular religion in the era of the Enlightenment?

These questions help us better understand how the peasant masses and urban poor really lived in western Europe before the age of revolution at the end of the eighteenth century. They are the focus of this chapter.

MARRIAGE AND THE FAMILY

The basic unit of social organization is the family. It is within the structure of the family that human beings love, mate, and reproduce themselves. It is primarily the family that teaches the child, imparting values and customs that condition an individual's behavior for a lifetime. The family is also an institution woven into the web of history. It evolves and changes, assuming different forms in different times and places.

Extended and Nuclear Families

In many traditional Asian and African societies, the typical family has often been an extended family. A newly married couple, instead of establishing their own home, will go to live with either the bride's or the groom's family. The couple raise their children while living under the same roof with their own brothers and sisters, who may also be married. The family is a big, three- or four-generation clan, headed by a patriarch or perhaps a matriarch, and encompassing everyone from the youngest infant to the oldest grandparent.

Extended families, it is often said, provide security for adults and children in traditional agrarian peasant economies. Everyone has a place within the extended family, from cradle to grave. Sociologists frequently assume that the extended family gives way to the conjugal, or nuclear, family with the advent of industrialization and urbanization. In a society characterized by nuclear families, couples establish their own households and their own family identities when they marry. They live with the children they raise, apart from their parents. Something like this is indeed happening in much of Asia and Africa today. And since Europe was once agrarian and preindustrial, it has often been believed that the extended family must also have prevailed in Europe before being destroyed by the Industrial Revolution.

In recent years innovative historians have developed new ways to test such old ideas. Above all, historians have analyzed the entries in previously neglected parish registers, in which local priests and pastors recorded the births, deaths, and marriages of the people in their church parishes. As a result, knowledge about the details of family life for the mass of people before the nineteenth century has greatly increased. Many simplistic old beliefs have been disproved by one of the most exciting advances in historical scholarship in the last generation. Yet it is important to realize that only a tiny percentage of all European villages have been studied, while perplexing local and regional variations have also been discovered. Thus many questions remain, and there is still much research to be done.

Despite these qualifications, it seems clear that the extended, three-generation family was a great rarity in western and central Europe by 1700. Indeed, the extended family may never have been common in Europe, although it is hard to know about the Middle Ages because fewer records survive. When young European couples married, they normally established their own households and lived apart from their parents. When a three-generation household came into existence, it was usually a parent who moved in with a married child, rather than a newly married couple moving in with either set of parents. The married couple, and the children that were sure to follow, were on their own from the beginning.

Perhaps because European couples set up separate households when they married, people did not marry young in the seventeenth and early eighteenth centuries. Indeed, the average person, who was neither rich nor aristocratic, married surprisingly late, many years after reaching adulthood and many more after beginning to work. In one well-studied, apparently typical English village, both men and women married for the first time at an average age of twenty-seven or older in the seventeenth and eighteenth centuries. A similar pattern existed in early-eighteenth-century France. Moreover, a substantial portion of men and women never married at all.

Between two-fifths and three-fifths of European women capable of bearing children—that is, women between fifteen and forty-four—were unmarried at any given time. The contrast with traditional non-Western societies is once again striking. In those societies, the pattern has very often been almost universal and very early marriage. The union of a teenage bride and teenage groom has been the general rule.

The custom of late marriage combined with a nuclear-family household was a distinctive characteristic of European society. The consequences have been tremendous, though still only partially explored. It seems likely that the agressive dynamism and creativity that have characterized European society were due in large part to the pattern of marriage and family. This pattern fostered and required self-reliance and independence. In preindustrial western Europe in the sixteenth through eighteenth centuries, marriage normally joined a mature man and a mature woman—two adults who had already experienced a great deal of life and could transmit self-reliance and real skills to the next generation.

Why was marriage delayed? The main reason was that couples normally could not marry until they could support themselves economically. The land was still the main source of income. The peasant son often needed to wait until his father's death to inherit the family farm and marry his sweetheart. Similarly, the peasant daughter and her family needed to accumulate a small dowry to help her fiancé buy land or build a house.

There were also laws and regulations to temper impetuous love and physical attraction. In some areas, couples needed the legal permission or tacit approval of the local lord or landowner in order to marry. In Austria and Germany, there were legal restrictions on marriage, and well into the nineteenth century poor couples had particular difficulty securing the approval of local officials. These officials believed that freedom to marry for the lower classes would mean more landless paupers, more abandoned children, and more money for welfare. Thus prudence, custom, and law combined to postpone the march to the altar. This pattern helped society maintain some kind of balance between the number of people and the available economic resources.

Work away from Home

Many young people worked within their families until they could start their own households. Boys plowed and wove; girls spun and tended the cows. Many others left home temporarily to work elsewhere. In the towns, a lad might be apprenticed to a craftsman for seven or fourteen years to learn a trade. During that time he would not be permitted to marry. In most trades he earned little and worked hard, but if he were lucky he might eventually be admitted to a guild and establish his economic independence. More often, the young man would drift from one tough job to another: hired hand for a small farmer, wage laborer on a new road, carrier of water in a nearby town. He was always subject to economic fluctuations, and unemployment was a constant threat.

Girls also temporarily left their families to work, at an early age and in large numbers. The range of opportunities open to them was more limited, however. Service in another family's household was by far the most common job. Even middle-class families often sent their daughters into service and hired others as servants in return. Thus a few years away from home as a servant were often a normal part of growing up. If all went well, the girl (or boy) would work hard and save some money for parents and marriage. At the least, there would be one less mouth to feed at home.

The legions of young servant girls worked hard but had little real independence. Sometimes the employer paid the girl's wages directly to her parents. Constantly under the eye of her mistress, the servant girl found her tasks were many—cleaning, shopping, cooking, caring for the baby. Often the work was endless, for there were no laws to limit

Chardin: The Kitchen Maid Lost in thought as she pauses in her work, perhaps this young servant is thinking about her village and loved ones there. Chardin was one of eighteenth-century France's greatest painters, and his scenes from everyday life provide valuable evidence for the historian. *(Source: National Gallery of Art, Washington, D.C. Samuel H. Kress Collection)*

exploitation. Few girls were so brutalized that they snapped under the strain of such treatment like Varka—the Russian servant girl in Chekhov's chilling story "Sleepy"—who, driven beyond exhaustion, finally quieted her mistress's screaming child by strangling it in its cradle. But court records are full of complaints by servant girls of physical mistreatment by their mistresses. There were many others like the fifteen-year-old English girl in the early eighteenth century who told the judge that her mistress had not only called her "very opprobrious names, as Bitch, Whore and the like," but also "beat her without provocation and beyond measure."[1]

There was also the pressure of seducers and sexual attack. In theory, domestic service offered protection and security for a young girl leaving home. The girl had food, lodging, and a new family. She did not drift in a strange and often dangerous environment. But, in practice, she was often the easy prey of a lecherous master, or his sons, or his friends. Indeed, "the evidence suggests that in all European countries, from Britain to Russia, the upper classes felt perfectly free to exploit sexually girls who were at their mercy."[2] If the girl became pregnant, she was quickly fired and thrown out in disgrace to make her own way. Prostitution and petty thievery were often the harsh consequences of unwanted pregnancy. "What are we?" exclaimed a bitter Parisian prostitute. "Most of us are unfortunate women, without origins, without education, servants and maids for the most part."[3]

Premarital Sex and Birth-control Practices

Did the plight of some ex-servant girls mean that late marriage in preindustrial Europe went hand in hand with premarital sex and many illegitimate children? For most of western and central Europe, until at least 1750, the answer seems to be no. English parish registers, in which the clergy recorded the births and deaths of the population, seldom list more than one bastard out of every twenty children baptized. Some French parishes in the seventeenth century had extraordinarily low rates of illegitimacy, with less than 1 percent of the babies born out of wedlock. Illegitimate babies were apparently a rarity, at least as far as the official church records are concerned.

At the same time, premarital sex was clearly commonplace. In one well-studied English village, one-third of all first children were conceived before the couple was married, and many were born within three months of the marriage ceremony. In the mid-eighteenth century, one-fifth of the French women in the village of Auffay, in Normandy, were pregnant when they got married, although only 2 percent of all babies in the village were born to unwed mothers. No doubt many of these French and English couples were already betrothed, or at least "going steady," before they entered into an intimate relationship, and pregnancy simply set the marriage date once and for all. But the very low rates of illegitimate birth also reflect the powerful social controls of the traditional village, particularly the open-field village with its pattern of cooperation and common action. Irate parents and village elders, indignant priests and authoritative landlords, all combined to pressure any young people who wavered about marriage in the face of unexpected pregnancy. These controls meant that premarital sex was not entered into lightly. In the countryside it was generally limited to those contemplating marriage.

Once a woman was married, she generally had several children. This does not mean that birth control within marriage was unknown in western and central Europe before the nineteenth century. But it was primitive and quite undependable. The most common method was *coitus interruptus*—withdrawal by the male before ejaculation. The French, who were apparently early leaders in contraception, were using this method extensively to limit family size by the end of the eighteenth century. Withdrawal as a method of birth control was in keeping with the European pattern of nuclear family, in which the father bore the direct responsibility of supporting his children. Withdrawal—a male technique—was one way to meet that responsibility.

Mechanical and other means of contraception were not unknown in the eighteenth century, but they appear to have been used mainly by certain sectors of the urban population. The "fast set" of London used the "sheath" regularly, although primarily to protect against venereal disease, not pregnancy. Prostitutes used various contraceptive techniques to prevent pregnancy, and such information was probably available to anyone who really sought it. The second part of an indictment for adultery against a late-sixteenth-century English vicar charged that the wayward minister was "also an instructor of young folks [in] how to commit the sin of adultery or fornication and not to beget or bring forth children."[4]

New Patterns of Marriage and Illegitimacy

In the second half of the eighteenth century, the pattern of late marriage and few illegitimate children began to break down. It is hard to say why. Certainly, changes in the economy had a gradual but profound impact. The growth of cottage industry created new opportunities for earning a living, opportunities not tied to the land. Cottage industry tended to develop in areas where the land was poor in quality and divided into small, inadequate holdings. As cottage industry took hold in such areas, young people attained greater independence and did not have to wait to inherit a farm in order to get married. A scrap of ground for a garden and a cottage for the loom and spinning wheel could be quite enough for a modest living. A contemporary observer of an area of rapidly growing cottage industry in Switzerland at the end of the eighteenth century described these changes: "The increased and sure income offered by the combination of cottage manufacture with farming hastened and multiplied marriages and encouraged the division of landholdings, while enhancing their value; it also promoted the expansion and embellishment of houses and villages."[5] The pattern of cottage industry stimulating a lower age of marriage and thus more rapid population growth was also widely observed in England.

Cottage workers married not only earlier but for different reasons. Nothing could be so businesslike, so calculating, as a peasant marriage that was often dictated by the needs of the couple's families. After 1750, however, courtship became more extensive and freer as cottage industry grew. It was easier to yield to the attraction of the opposite sex and fall in love. Members of the older generation were often shocked by the lack of responsibility they saw in the early marriages of the poor, the union of "people with only two spinning wheels and not even a bed." But the laws and regulations they imposed, especially in Germany, were often disregarded. Unions based on love rather than on economic considerations were increasingly the pattern for cottage workers. Factory workers, numbers of whom first began to appear in England after about 1780, followed the path blazed by cottage workers.

Changes in the timing and motivation of marriage went hand in hand with a rapid increase in illegitimate births between about 1750 and 1850. Some historians even speak of an "illegitimacy explosion." In Frankfurt, Germany, for example, only about 2 percent of all births were illegitimate in the early 1700s. This figure rose to 5 percent in about 1760, to about 10 percent in 1800, and peaked at about 25 percent around 1850. In Bordeaux, France, illegitimate births rose steadily until by 1840 one out of every three babies was born out of wedlock. Small towns and villages less frequently experienced such startlingly high illegitimacy rates, but increases from a range of 1 to 3 percent initially to 10 to 20 percent between 1750 and 1850 were commonplace. A profound sexual and cultural transformation was taking place. Fewer girls were abstaining from premarital intercourse, and, more important, fewer boys were marrying the girls they got pregnant.

It is hard to know exactly why this change occurred and what it meant. The old idea of a safe, late, economically secure marriage did not reflect economic and social realities. The growing freedom of thought in the turbulent years beginning with the French Revolution in 1789 influenced sexual and marital behavior in both towns and villages. And illegitimate births, particularly in Germany, were also the result of open rebellion against class laws limiting the right of the poor to marry. Unable to show a solid financial position and thereby obtain a marriage license, couples asserted their independence and lived together anyway. Children were the natural and desired result of "true love" and greater freedom. Eventually, when the stuffy, old-fashioned propertied classes gave in and repealed their laws against "imprudent marriage," poor couples once again went to the altar, often accompanied by their children, and the number of illegitimate children declined.

More fundamentally, the need of a growing population to seek work outside farming and the village made young people more mobile. Mobility in turn encouraged new sexual and marital relationships, which were less subject to parental pressure and village tradition. As in the case of young servant girls who became pregnant and were then forced to fend for themselves, some of these relationships promoted loose living or prostitution. This resulted in more illegitimate births and strengthened an urban subculture of habitual illegitimacy.

Early Sexual Emancipation?

It has been suggested that the increase in illegitimate births represented a stage in the emancipation of women. According to this view, new economic opportunities outside the home, in the city and later in the factory, revolutionized women's attitudes about themselves. Young working women became individualistic and rebelled against old restrictions like late marriage. They sought fulfillment in the pleasure of sexuality. Since there was little birth control, freer sex for single women meant more illegitimate babies.

No doubt single working women in towns and cities were of necessity more independent and self-reliant. Yet, until at least the late nineteenth century, it seems unlikely that such young women were motivated primarily by visions of emancipation and sexual liberation. Most women were servants or textile workers. These jobs paid poorly, and the possibility of a truly independent, "liberated" life was correspondingly limited. Most women in the city probably looked to marriage and family life as an escape from hard, poorly paid work

and as the foundation of a satisfying life. Moreover, illegitimacy increased in rural areas as well as in urban ones, so an interpretation based on changed attitudes in towns and cities does not account for the entire phenomenon.

Promises of marriage from men of the working girl's own class led naturally enough to sex, which was widely viewed as part of serious courtship. In one medium-sized French city in 1787 to 1788, the great majority of unwed mothers stated that sexual intimacy had followed promises of marriage. Their sisters in rural Normandy reported again and again that they had been "seduced in anticipation of marriage."[6] Many soldiers, day laborers, and male servants were no doubt sincere in their proposals. But their lives were insecure, and many hesitated to

Peasants Begging In seventeenth-century France, many heavily taxed peasants found it very difficult to afford enough to eat. Although charity was becoming more fashionable, many peasant families were reduced to begging. *(Source: The Metropolitan Museum of Art)*

take on the heavy economic burdens of wife and child. Nor were their backbones any longer stiffened by the traditional pressures of the village.

Thus it became increasingly difficult for a woman to convert pregnancy into marriage, and in a growing number of cases the intended marriage did not take place. The romantic yet practical dreams and aspirations of many young working women and men in towns and villages were frustrated by low wages, inequality, and changing economic and social conditions. Old patterns of marriage and family were breaking down among the common people. Only in the late nineteenth century would more stable patterns reappear.

INFANTS AND CHILDREN

In the traditional framework of agrarian Europe, women married late but then began bearing children rapidly. If a woman married before she was thirty, and if both she and her husband lived to forty-five, the chances were roughly one in two that she would give birth to six or more children. The newborn child entered a dangerous world. Infant mortality was high. One in five was sure to die, and one in three was quite likely to, in the poorer areas. Newborn children were very likely to catch infectious diseases of the stomach and chest, which were not understood. Thus little could be done for an ailing child, even in rich families. Childhood itself was dangerous because of adult indifference, neglect, and even brutality. Parents in early modern Europe could count themselves fortunate if half their children lived to adulthood.

Child Care and Nursing

Women of the lower classes generally breast-fed their infants, and for much longer periods than is customary today. Breast-feeding decreases the likelihood of pregnancy for the average woman by delaying the resumption of ovulation. Although women may have been only vaguely aware of the link between nursing and not getting pregnant, they were spacing their children—from two to three years apart—and limiting their fertility by nursing their babies. If a newborn baby died, nursing stopped and a new life could be created. Nursing also saved lives: the breast-fed infant was more likely to survive on its mother's milk than on any artificial foods. In many areas of Russia, where common practice was to give a new child a sweetened (and germ-laden) rag to suck on for its subsistence, half the babies did not survive the first year.

In contrast to the laboring poor, the women of the aristocracy and upper middle class seldom nursed their own children. The upper-class woman felt that breast-feeding was crude, common, and well beneath her dignity. Instead, she hired a wet nurse to suckle her child. The urban mother of more modest means—the wife of a shopkeeper or artisan—also commonly used a wet nurse, sending her baby to some poor woman in the country as soon as possible.

Wet-nursing was a very widespread and flourishing business in the eighteenth century, a dismal business within the framework of the putting-out system. The traffic was in babies rather than in wool and cloth, and two or three years often passed before the wet-nurse worker finished her task. The great French historian Jules Michelet described with compassion the plight of the wet nurse, who was still going to the homes of the rich in early-nineteenth-century France:

People do not know how much these poor women are exploited and abused, first by the vehicles which transport them (often barely out of their confinement), and afterward by the employment offices which place them. Taken as nurses on the spot, they must send their own child away, and consequently it often dies. They have no contact with the family that hires them, and they may be dismissed at the first caprice of the mother or doctor. If the change of air and place should dry up their milk, they are discharged without any compensation. If they stay here [in the city] they pick up the habits of the easy life, and they suffer enormously when they are forced to return to their life of [rural] poverty. A good number become servants in order to stay in the town. They never rejoin their husbands, and the family is broken.[7]

Other observers noted the flaws of wet-nursing. It was a common belief that a nurse passed her bad traits to the baby with her milk. When a child turned out poorly, it was assumed that "the nurse changed it." Many observers charged that nurses were often negligent and greedy. They claimed that there were large numbers of "killing nurses" with whom no child ever survived. The nurse let the child die quickly, so that she could take another child and another fee. No matter how the adults fared in the wet-nurse business, the child was a certain loser.

Foundlings and Infanticide

In the ancient world and in Asian societies, it was not uncommon to allow or force newborn babies, particularly girl babies, to die when there were too many mouths to feed. To its great and eternal credit, the early medieval church, strongly influenced by Jewish law, denounced infanticide as a pagan practice and insisted that every human life was sacred. The willful destruction of newborn children became a crime punishable by death. And yet, as the reference to "killing nurses" suggests, direct and indirect methods of eliminating unwanted babies did not disappear. There were, for example, many cases of "overlaying"—parents rolling over and suffocating the child placed between them in their bed. Such parents claimed they were drunk and had acted unintentionally. In Austria in 1784, suspicious authorities made it illegal for parents to take children under five into bed with them. Severe poverty on the one hand and increasing illegitimacy on the other conspired to force the very poor to thin their own ranks.

The young girl—very likely a servant—who could not provide for her child had few choices. If she would not stoop to abortion or the services of a killing nurse, she could bundle up her baby and leave it on the doorstep of a church. In the late seventeenth century, Saint Vincent de Paul was so distressed by the number of babies brought to the steps of Notre Dame in Paris that he established a home for foundlings. Others followed his example. In England the government acted on a petition calling for a foundling hospital "to prevent the frequent murders of poor, miserable infants at birth" and "to suppress the inhuman custom of exposing newborn children to perish in the streets."

In much of Europe in the eighteenth century, foundling homes became a favorite charity of the rich and powerful. Great sums were spent on them. The foundling home in St. Petersburg, perhaps the most elaborate and lavish of its kind, occupied the

Abandoned Children   At this Italian foundlings' home a frightened, secretive mother could discreetly deposit her baby. (Source: The Bettmann Archive)

former palaces of two members of the high nobility. In the early nineteenth century it had 25,000 children in its care and was receiving 5,000 new babies a year. At their best, the foundling homes of the eighteenth century were a good example of Christian charity and social concern in an age of great poverty and inequality.

Yet the foundling home was no panacea. By the 1770s one-third of all babies born in Paris were immediately abandoned to the foundling home by their mothers. Fully a third of all those foundlings were abandoned by married couples, a powerful commentary on the standard of living among the

A Chance for Children This seventeenth-century lottery ticket offered French citizens an opportunity to support a Paris foundling home. Most homes had to rely on private charity to survive. *(Source: Jean-Loup Charmet)*

working poor, for whom an additional mouth to feed often meant tragedy. In London competition for space in the foundling home soon became so great that it led "to the disgraceful scene of women scrambling and fighting to get to the door, that they might be of the fortunate few to reap the benefit of the Asylum."[8]

Furthermore, great numbers of babies entered, but few left. Even in the best of these homes, half the babies normally died within a year. In the worst, fully 90 percent did not survive. They succumbed to long journeys over rough roads, the intentional and unintentional neglect of their wet nurses, and the customary childhood illnesses. So great was the carnage that some contemporaries called the foundling hospitals "legalized infanticide."

Certainly some parents and officials looked on the hospitals as a dump for unwanted babies. In the early 1760s, when the London Foundling Hospital was obliged to accept all babies offered, it was deluged with babies from the countryside. Many parish officers placed with the foundling home the abandoned children in their care, just as others apprenticed five-year-old children to work in factories. Both practices reduced the cost of welfare at the local level. Throughout the eighteenth century, millions of children of the poor continued to exit after the briefest of appearances on the earthly stage. True, they died after being properly baptized, an important consideration in still-Christian Europe. Yet those who dream of an idyllic past would do well to ponder the foundling's fate.

Attitudes Toward Children

What were the more typical circumstances of children's lives? Did the treatment of foundlings reflect the attitudes of normal parents? Although some scholars argue otherwise, it seems that the young child was often of little concern to its parents and to society in the eighteenth century. This indifference toward children was found in all classes; rich children were by no means exempt. The practice of using wet nurses, who were casually selected and often negligent, is one example of how even the rich and the prosperous put the child out of sight and out of mind. One French moralist, writing in 1756 about how to improve humanity, observed that "one blushes to think of loving one's children." It has been said that the English gentleman of the period "had more interest in the diseases of his horses than of his children."[9]

Parents believed that the world of the child was an uninteresting one. When parents did stop to notice their offspring, they often treated them as dolls or playthings—little puppies to fondle and cuddle in a moment of relaxation. The psychological distance between parent and child remained vast.

Feelings toward children were conditioned by the terrible frequency of death among children of all classes. Doctors and clergymen urged parents not to become too emotionally involved with their children, who were so unlikely to survive. Mothers, especially, did not always heed such warnings, but the risk of emotional devastation was real. The great eighteenth-century English historian Edward Gibbon (1737–1794) wrote that "the death of a new born child before that of its parents may seem unnatural but it is a strictly probable event, since of any given number the greater part are extinguished before the ninth year, before they possess the faculties of the mind and the body." Gibbon's father named all his boys Edward, hoping that at least one of them would survive to carry his name. His prudence was not misplaced. Edward the future historian and eldest survived. Five brothers and sisters who followed him all died in infancy.

Doctors were seldom interested in the care of children. One contemporary observer quoted a famous doctor as saying that "he never wished to be called to a young child because he was really at a loss to know what to offer for it." There were "physicians of note who make no scruple to assert that there is nothing to be done for children when they are ill." Children were caught in a vicious circle: they were neglected because they were very likely to die, and they were likely to die because they were neglected.

Indifference toward children often shaded off into brutality. When parents and other adults did turn toward children, it was normally to discipline and control them. The novelist Daniel Defoe (1660?–1731), always delighted when he saw very young children working hard in cottage industry, coined the axiom "Spare the rod and spoil the child." He meant it. So did Susannah Wesley, mother of John Wesley (1703–1791), the founder of Methodism. According to her, the first task of a parent toward her children was "to conquer the will, and bring them to an obedient temper." She reported that her babies were "taught to fear the rod, and to cry softly; by which means they escaped the abundance of correction they might otherwise have had, and that most odious noise of the crying of children was rarely heard in the house."[10]

It was hardly surprising that, when English parish officials dumped their paupers into the first factories late in the eighteenth century, the children were beaten and brutalized (see Chapter 22). That was part of the child-rearing pattern—widespread indifference on the one hand and strict physical discipline on the other—that prevailed through most of the eighteenth century.

From the middle of the century, this pattern came under increasing attack. Critics like Jean-Jacques Rousseau called for greater love, tenderness, and understanding toward children. In addition to supporting foundling homes to discourage infanticide and urging wealthy women to nurse their own babies, these new voices ridiculed the practice of swaddling. Wrapping youngsters in tight-fitting clothes and blankets was generally believed to form babies properly by "straightening them out." By the end of the eighteenth century, small children were often dressed in simpler, more comfortable clothing, allowing much greater freedom of movement. More parents expressed a delight in the love and intimacy of the child and found real pleasure in raising their offspring. These changes were part of the general growth of humanitarianism and optimism about human potential that characterized the eighteenth-century Enlightenment.

Schools and Education

The role of formal education outside the home, in those special institutions called schools, was growing more important. The aristocracy and the rich had led the way in the sixteenth century with special colleges, often run by the Jesuits. But "little schools," charged with elementary education of the children of the masses, did not appear until the seventeenth century. Unlike medieval schools, which mingled all age groups, the little schools specialized in boys and girls from seven to twelve, who were instructed in basic literacy and religion.

Although large numbers of common people got no education at all in the eighteenth century, the beginnings of popular education were recognizable. For example, France made a start in 1682

The Five Senses   Published in 1774, J. B. Basedow's *Elementary Reader* helped spread new attitudes toward child development and education. Drawing heavily on the theories of Locke and Rousseau, the German educator advocated nature study and contact with everyday life. In this illustration for Basedow's reader, gentle teachers allow uncorrupted children to learn about the five senses through direct experience. *(Source: Caroline Buckler)*

with the establishment of Christian schools, which taught the catechism and prayers as well as reading and writing. The Church of England and the dissenting congregations established "charity schools" to instruct the children of the poor. As early as 1717, Prussia made attendance at elementary schools compulsory. Inspired by the old Protestant idea that every believer should be able to read and study the Bible in the quest for personal salvation, and by the new idea of a population capable of effectively serving the state, Prussia led the way in the development of universal education. Religious mo-

tives were also extremely important elsewhere. From the middle of the seventeenth century, Presbyterian Scotland was convinced that the path to salvation lay in careful study of the Scriptures, and this belief led to an effective network of parish schools for rich and poor alike. The Enlightenment commitment to greater knowledge through critical thinking reinforced interest in education in the eighteenth century.

The result of these efforts was a remarkable growth of basic literacy between 1600 and 1800, especially after 1700. Whereas in 1600 only one male in six was barely literate in France and Scotland, and one in four in England, by 1800 almost 90 percent of the Scottish male population was literate. At the same time, two out of three males were literate in France; and in advanced areas such as Normandy, literacy approached 90 percent (Map 20.1). More than half of English males were literate by 1800. In all three countries the bulk of the jump occurred in the eighteenth century. Women were also increasingly literate, although they probably lagged behind men somewhat in most countries. Some elementary education was becoming a reality for European peoples, and schools were of growing significance in everyday life.

THE EUROPEAN'S FOOD

Plague and starvation, which recurred often in the seventeenth century, gradually disappeared in the eighteenth century. This phenomenon probably accounts in large part for the rapid growth in the total number of Europeans and for their longer lives. The increase in the average life span, allowing for regional variations, was substantial. In 1700 the average European could expect at birth to live only twenty-five years. A century later, a newborn European could expect to live fully ten years longer, to age thirty-five. The doubling of the adult life span meant that there was more time to produce and create, and more reason for parents to stress learning and preparation for adulthood.

People also lived longer because ordinary years were progressively less deadly. People ate better and somewhat more wisely. Doctors and hospitals probably saved a few more lives than they had in the past. How and why did health and life expectancy improve, and how much did they improve? And what were the differences between rich and poor? To answer these questions, it is necessary first to follow the eighteenth-century family to the table and then to see what contribution doctors made.

Diets and Nutrition

Although the accomplishments of doctors and hospitals are constantly in the limelight today, the greater, if less spectacular, part of medicine is preventive medicine. The great breakthrough of the second half of the nineteenth century was the development of public health techniques—proper sanitation and mass vaccinations—to prevent outbreaks of communicable diseases. Even before the nineteenth century, when medical knowledge was slight and doctors were of limited value, prevention was the key to longer life. Warm, dry housing, good clothing, and plentiful food make for healthier populations, much more capable of battling disease. Clothing and housing for the masses probably improved only modestly in the eighteenth century, but the new agricultural methods and increased agricultural output had a beneficial effect. The average European ate more and better food and was healthier as a result in 1800 than in 1700. This pattern is apparent if we look at the fare of the laboring poor.

At the beginning of the eighteenth century, ordinary men and women depended on grain as fully as they had in the past. Bread was quite literally the staff of life. Peasants in the Beauvais region of France ate two pounds of bread a day, washing it down with water, green wine, beer, or a little skimmed milk. Their dark bread was made from a

MAP 20.1 Literacy in France on the Eve of the French Revolution Literacy rates varied widely between and within states in eighteenth-century Europe. Northern France was clearly ahead of southern France.

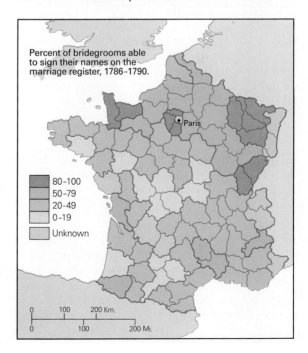

Percent of bridegrooms able to sign their names on the marriage register, 1786–1790.

Paris

80–100
50–79
20–49
0–19
Unknown

0   100   200 Km.

0   100   200 Mi.

mixture of rough-ground wheat and rye—the standard flour of the poor. The poor also ate grains in soup and gruel. In rocky northern Scotland, for example, people depended on oatmeal, which they often ate half-cooked so it would swell in their stomachs and make them feel full. No wonder, then, that the supply of grain and the price of bread were critical questions for most people.

The poor, rural and urban, also ate a fair quantity of vegetables. Indeed, vegetables were considered "poor people's food." Peas and beans were probably the most common; grown as field crops in much of Europe since the Middle Ages, they were eaten fresh in late spring and summer. Dried, they became the basic ingredients in the soups and stews of the long winter months. In most regions, other vegetables appeared in season on the tables of the poor, primarily cabbages, carrots, and wild greens. Fruit was uncommon and limited to the summer months.

The European poor loved meat and eggs, but even in England—the wealthiest country in Europe in 1700—they seldom ate their fill. Indeed, the poor ate less meat in 1700 than in 1500, because their general standard of living had declined as the population surged in the sixteenth century (see page 606). Now meat was just too expensive. When the poor did eat meat—on a religious holiday or at a wedding or other special occasion—it was most likely lamb or mutton. Sheep could survive on rocky soils and did not compete directly with humans for the slender resources of grain.

Le Nain: Peasant Family   A little wine and a great deal of dark bread: the traditional food of the poor French peasantry accentuates the poetic dignity of this masterpiece, painted about 1640 by Louis Le Nain. *(Source: Louvre/Cliché des Musées Nationaux, Paris)*

Milk was rarely drunk. It was widely believed that milk caused sore eyes, headaches, and a variety of ills, except among the very young and very old. Milk was used primarily to make cheese and butter, which the poor liked but could afford only occasionally. Medical and popular opinion considered whey, the watery liquid left after milk was churned, "an excellent temperate drink."

The diet of the rich—aristocrats, officials, and the comfortable bourgeoisie—was traditionally quite different from that of the poor. The men and women of the upper classes were rapacious carnivores, and a person's standard of living and economic well-being were often judged by the amount of meat eaten. A truly elegant dinner among the great and powerful consisted of one rich meat after another: a chicken pie, a leg of lamb, a grilled steak, for example. Three separate meat courses might be followed by three fish courses, laced with piquant sauces and complemented with sweets, cheeses, and nuts of all kinds. Fruits and vegetables were not often found on the tables of the rich. The longstanding dominance of meat and fish in the diet of the upper classes continued throughout the eighteenth century. There was extravagant living, and undoubtedly great overeating and gluttony, not only among the aristocracy but also among the prosperous professional classes.

There was also an enormous amount of overdrinking among the rich. The English squire, for example, who loved to ride with his hounds, loved drink with a similar passion. He became famous as the "four-bottle man." With his dinner he drank red wine from France or white wine from the Rhineland, and with his dessert he took sweet but strong port or Madeira from Portugal. Sometimes he ended the evening under the table in a drunken stupor, but very often he did not. The wine and the meat were consumed together in long hours of sustained excess, permitting the gentleman and his guests to drink enormous quantities.

The diet of small traders, master craftsmen, minor bureaucrats—the people of the towns and cities—was probably less monotonous than that of the peasantry. The markets, stocked by market gardens in the outskirts, provided a substantial variety of meats, vegetables, and fruits, although bread and beans still formed the bulk of the poor family's diet.

There were also regional dietary differences in 1700. Generally speaking, northern, Atlantic Europe ate better than southern, Mediterranean Europe. The poor of England probably ate best of all. Contemporaries on both sides of the Channel often contrasted the Englishman's consumption of meat with the French peasant's greater dependence on bread and vegetables. The Dutch were also considerably better fed than the average European, in large part because of their advanced agriculture and diversified gardens.

The Impact of Diet on Health

How were the poor and the rich served by their quite different diets? Good nutrition depends on a balanced supply of food as well as on an adequate number of calories. Modern research has shown that the chief determinant of nutritional balance is the relationship between carbohydrates (sugar and starch) and proteins. A diet consisting primarily of carbohydrates is seriously incomplete.

At first glance, the diet of the laboring poor, relying as it did on carbohydrates, seems very unsatisfactory. Even when a peasant got his daily two or three pounds of bread, his supply of protein and essential vitamins would appear too low. A closer look reveals a somewhat brighter picture. Most bread was "brown" or "black," made from wheat or rye. The flour of the eighteenth century was a whole-meal flour, produced by stone grinding. It contained most of the bran—the ground-up husk—and the all-important wheat germ. The bran and germ contain higher proportions of some minerals, vitamins, and good-quality proteins than does the rest of the grain. Only when they are removed does bread become a foodstuff providing relatively more starch and less of the essential nutrients.

In addition, the field peas and beans eaten by poor people since Carolingian days contained protein that complemented the proteins in whole-meal bread. The proteins in whey, cheese, and eggs, which the poor ate at least occasionally, also supplemented the bread and vegetables. Indeed, a leading authority concludes that if a pint of milk and some cheese and whey were eaten each day, the balance of the poor people's diet "was excellent, far better indeed than in many of our modern diets."[11]

The basic bread-and-vegetables diet of the poor *in normal times* was adequate. It protected effectively against most of the disorders associated with a deficiency of the vitamin B complex, for example.

other practical work. The number of monks plunged from 65,000 to 27,000. The state also expropriated the dissolved monasteries and used their great wealth for charitable purposes and higher salaries for ordinary priests.

Catholic Piety

Catholic territorial churches also sought to purify religious practice somewhat. As might be expected, Joseph II went the furthest. Above all, he and his agents sought to root out what they considered to be idolatry and superstition. Yet pious peasants saw only an incomprehensible attack on the true faith and drew back in anger. Joseph's sledgehammer approach and the resulting reaction dramatized an underlying tension between Christian reform and popular piety after the Reformation.

Protestant reformers had taken very seriously the commandment that "Thou shalt not make any graven image" (Exodus 20:4), and their radical reforms had reordered church interiors. Relics and crucifixes had been permanently removed from crypt and altar, while stained-glass windows had been smashed and walls and murals covered with whitewash. Processions and pilgrimages, saints and shrines—all such nonessentials had been rigorously suppressed in the attempt to recapture the vital core of the Christian religion. Such revolutionary changes had often troubled ordinary churchgoers, but by the late seventeenth century,

Planting Crosses After their small wooden crosses were blessed at church as part of the Rogation Days' ceremonies in early May, French peasants traditionally placed them in their fields and pastures to protect the seed and help the crops grow. This illustration shows the custom being performed in the French Alps in the mid-nineteenth century, when it was still widely practiced. *(Source: Library of Congress)*

"Clipping the Church"   The ancient English ceremony of dancing around the church once each year on the night before Lent undoubtedly had pre-Christian origins, for its purpose was to create a magical protective chain against evil spirits and the devil. The Protestant reformers did their best to stamp them out, but such "pagan practices" sometimes lingered on. *(Source: Somerset Archaeological and Natural History Society)*

these reforms had been thoroughly routinized by official Protestant churches.

The situation was quite different in Catholic Europe around 1700. First of all, the visual contrast was striking; baroque art (see Chapter 15) had lavished rich and emotionally exhilarating figures and images on Catholic churches, just as Protestants had removed theirs. From almost every indication, people in Catholic Europe remained intensely religious. More than 95 percent of the population probably attended church for Easter Communion, the climax of the Catholic church year.

The tremendous popular strength of religion in Catholic countries reflected the fact that religious practice went far beyond Sunday churchgoing and was an important part of community life. Thus, although Catholics reluctantly confessed their sins to the priest, they enthusiastically joined together in public processions to celebrate the passage of the liturgical year. In addition to the great processional days—such as Palm Sunday, the joyful re-enactment of Jesus' triumphal entry into Jerusalem, or Rogations, with its chanted supplications and penances three days before the bodily ascent of Jesus into heaven on Ascension Day—each parish had its own local processions. Led by its priest, a congregation might march around the village, or across the countryside to a local shrine or chapel. There were endless variations. In the southern French Alps, the people looked forward especially to "high-mountain" processions in late spring. Parishes came together from miles around on some high mountain. There the assembled priests asked God to bless the people with healthy flocks and pure waters, and then all joined together in an enormous picnic. Before each procession, the priest explained its religious significance to kindle group piety. But processions were also folklore and tradition, an escape from work and a form of recreation. A holiday atmosphere sometimes reigned on longer processions, with drinking and dancing and couples disappearing into the woods.

Devout Catholics held many religious beliefs that were marginal to the Christian faith, often of obscure or even pagan origin. On the feast of Saint Anthony, priests were expected to bless salt and bread for farm animals to protect them from disease. One saint's relics could help cure a child of fear, and there were healing springs for many ailments. The ordinary person combined a strong Christian faith with a wealth of time-honored superstitions.

Parish priests and Catholic hierarchies were frequently troubled by the limitations of their parishioners' Christian understanding. One parish priest in France, who kept an invaluable daily diary, lamented that his parishioners were "more superstitious than devout . . . and sometimes appear as baptized idolators."[14]

Many parish priests in France, often acting on instructions from their bishops, made an effort to purify popular religious culture. For example, one priest tried to abolish pilgrimages to a local sacred spring of Our Lady, reputed to revive dead babies long enough for a proper baptism. French priests denounced particularly the "various remnants of paganism" found in popular bonfire ceremonies during Lent, in which young men, "yelling and screaming like madmen," tried to jump over the bonfires in order to help the crops grow and protect themselves from illness. One priest saw rational Christians turning back into pagan animals —"the triumph of Hell and the shame of Christianity."[15]

Yet, whereas Protestant reformers had already used the power of the territorial state to crush such practices, Catholic church leaders generally proceeded cautiously in the eighteenth century. They knew that old beliefs—such as the belief common throughout Europe that the priest's energetic ringing of church bells and his recitation of ritual prayers would protect the village from hail and thunderstorms—were an integral part of the people's religion. Thus Catholic priests and hierarchies generally preferred a compromise between theological purity and the people's piety, realizing perhaps that the line between divine truth and mere superstition is not easily drawn.

Protestant Revival

By the late seventeenth century, official Protestant churches had completed their vast reforms and had generally settled into a smug complacency. In the Reformation heartland, one concerned German minister wrote that the Lutheran church "had become paralyzed in forms of dead doctrinal conformity" and badly needed a return to its original inspiration.[16] This voice was one of many that would prepare and then guide a powerful Protestant revival, a revival largely successful because it answered the intense but increasingly unsatisfied needs of common people.

The Protestant revival began in Germany. It was known as "Pietism," and three aspects helped explain its powerful appeal. First, Pietism called for warm emotional religion that everyone could experience. Enthusiasm—in prayer, in worship, in preaching, in life itself—was the key concept. "Just as a drunkard becomes full of wine, so must the congregation become filled with spirit," declared one exuberant writer. Another said simply, "The heart must burn."[17]

Second, Pietism reasserted the earlier radical stress on the "priesthood of all believers," thereby reducing the large gulf between the official clergy and the Lutheran laity. Bible reading and study were enthusiastically extended to all classes, and this provided a powerful spur for popular education as well as individual religious development. Finally, Pietists believed in the practical power of Christian rebirth in everyday affairs. Reborn Christians were expected to lead good, moral lives and come from all walks of life.

Pietism had a major impact on John Wesley (1703–1791), who served as the catalyst for popular religious revival in England. Wesley came from a long line of ministers, and when he went to Oxford University to prepare for the clergy, he mapped a fanatically earnest "scheme of religion." Like some students during final-exam period, he organized every waking moment. After becoming a teaching fellow at Oxford, he organized a Holy Club for similarly minded students, who were soon known contemptuously as "Methodists" because they were so methodical in their devotion. Yet, like the young Luther, Wesley remained intensely troubled about his own salvation, even after his ordination as an Anglican priest in 1728.

Wesley's anxieties related to grave problems of the faith in England. The Church of England was shamelessly used by the government to provide favorites with high-paying jobs and sinecures. Building of churches practically stopped while the population grew, and in many parishes there was a grave shortage of pews. Services and sermons had settled into an uninspiring routine. That the properly purified religion had been separated from local customs and social life was symbolized by church doors that were customarily locked on weekdays. Moreover, the skepticism of the Enlightenment was making inroads among the educated classes, and deism was becoming popular. Some bishops and church leaders acted as if they believed that doctrines like the Virgin Birth or the Ascension were little more than particularly elegant superstitions.

Living in an atmosphere of religious decline and uncertainty, Wesley became profoundly troubled by his lack of faith in his own salvation. Yet spiritual counseling from a sympathetic Pietist minister from Germany prepared Wesley for a mystical, emotional "conversion" in 1738. He described this critical turning point in his *Journal*:

*In the evening I went to a [Christian] society in Aldersgate Street where one was reading Luther's preface to the Epis-*tle to the Romans. *About a quarter before nine, while he was describing the change which God works in the heart through faith in Christ, I felt my heart strangely warmed. I felt I did trust in Christ, Christ alone for salvation; and an assurance was given me that he had taken away* my sins, even, mine, *and saved* me *from the law of sin and death.*[18]

Wesley's emotional experience resolved his intellectual doubts. Moreover, he was convinced that any person, no matter how poor or simple, might have a similar heartfelt conversion and gain the same blessed assurance.

Wesley took the good news to the people. Since existing churches were often overcrowded and the

John Wesley preached that all who truly believe in Christ may gain eternal salvation. Shown here preaching from his father's tomb, Wesley waited until the 1780s to organize the Methodists into a separate denomination. *(Source: E. T. Archive)*

Pluralism reflected corruption in the Church of England. With the help of powerful friends, the "pluralist" parson satirized in this eighteenth-century cartoon has received appointments to four different parishes. Employing poor assistants to do the preaching, he collects a handsome unearned income. *(Source: Bettmann/Hulton)*

church-state establishment was hostile, Wesley preached in open fields. People came in large numbers. Of critical importance was Wesley's rejection of Calvinist predestination—the doctrine of salvation granted only to a select few (see Chapter 14). Expanding on earlier Dutch theologians' views, he preached that *all* men and women who earnestly sought salvation might be saved. It was a message of hope and joy, of free will and universal salvation.

Traveling some 225,000 miles by horseback and preaching more than 40,000 sermons in fifty years, Wesley's ministry won converts, formed Methodist cells, and eventually resulted in a new denomination. Evangelicals in the Church of England and the old dissenting groups also followed Wesley's

example, giving impetus to an even broader awakening among the lower classes. That result showed that in England, as throughout Europe despite different churches and different practices, religion remained a vital force in the lives of the people.

SUMMARY

In recent years, imaginative research has greatly increased the specialist's understanding of ordinary life and social patterns in the past. The human experience, as recounted by historians, has become richer and more meaningful, and many mistaken ideas have fallen. This has been particularly true of eighteenth-century, agrarian Europe. The intimacies of family life, the contours of women's history and of childhood, and vital problems of medicine and religion are emerging from obscurity. Nor is this all. A deeper, truer understanding of the life of common people can shed light on the great economic and political developments of long-standing concern, to be seen in the next chapter.

NOTES

1. Quoted in J. M. Beattie, "The Criminality of Women in Eighteenth-century England," *Journal of Social History* 8 (Summer 1975): 86.
2. W. L. Langer, "Infanticide: A Historical Survey," *History of Childhood Quarterly* 1 (Winter 1974): 357.
3. Quoted in R. Cobb, *The Police and the People: French Popular Protest, 1789–1820* (Oxford: Clarendon Press, 1970), p. 238.
4. Quoted in E. A. Wrigley, *Population and History* (New York: McGraw-Hill, 1969), p. 127.
5. Quoted in D. S. Landes, ed., *The Rise of Capitalism* (New York: Macmillan, 1966), pp. 56–57.
6. G. Gullickson, *Spinners and Weavers of Auffay: Rural Industry and the Sexual Division of Labor in a French Village, 1750–1850* (Cambridge: Cambridge University Press, 1986), p. 186. Also see L. A. Tilly, J. W. Scott, and M. Cohen, "Women's Work and European Fertility Patterns," *Journal of Interdisciplinary History* 6 (Winter 1976): 447–476.
7. J. Michelet, *The People,* trans. with an introduction by J. P. McKay (Urbana: University of Illinois Press, 1973; original publication, 1846), pp. 38–39.
8. J. Brownlow, *The History and Design of the Foundling Hospital* (London, 1868), p. 7.
9. Quoted in B. W. Lorence, "Parents and Children in Eighteenth-century Europe," *History of Childhood Quarterly* 2 (Summer 1974): 1–2.
10. Ibid., pp. 13, 16.
11. J. C. Drummond and A. Wilbraham, *The Englishman's Food: A History of Five Centuries of English Diet* 2d ed. (London: Jonathan Cape, 1958), p. 75.
12. Quoted in L. S. King, *The Medical World of the Eighteenth Century* (Chicago: University of Chicago Press, 1958), p. 320.
13. Quoted in R. Sand, *The Advance to Social Medicine* (London: Staples Press, 1952), pp. 86–87.
14. Quoted in I. Woloch, *Eighteenth-century Europe: Tradition and Progress, 1715–1789* (New York: W. W. Norton, 1982), p. 292.
15. Quoted in T. Tackett, *Priest and Parish in Eighteenth-century France* (Princeton, N.J.: Princeton University Press, 1977), p. 214.
16. Quoted in K. Pinson, *Pietism as a Factor in the Rise of German Nationalism* (New York: Columbia University Press, 1934), p. 13.
17. Ibid., pp. 43–44.
18. Quoted in S. Andrews, *Methodism and Society* (London: Longmans, Green, 1970), p. 327.

SUGGESTED READING

Though long ignored in many general histories of the Western world, social topics of the kind considered in this chapter have come into their own in recent years. The articles cited in the Notes are typical of the exciting work being done, and the reader is strongly advised to take time to look through recent volumes of some leading journals: *Journal of Social History, Past and Present,* and *Journal of Interdisciplinary History.* In addition, the number of book-length studies has expanded rapidly and continues to do so. Several of these studies are mentioned in the Notes, and the books by Wrigley, Drummond and Wilbraham, and Tackett are especially useful.

Among general introductions to the history of the family, women, and children, J. Casey, *The History of the Family* (1989), is recommended. P. Laslett, *The World We Have Lost* (1965), is an exciting, pioneering investigation of England before the Industrial Revolution, though some of his conclusions have been weakened by further research. L. Stone, *The Family, Sex and Marriage in England, 1500–1800* (1977), is a provocative general interpretation, and L. Tilly and J. Scott, *Women, Work and Family* (1978), is excellent. Two valuable works on women, both with good bibliographies, are M. Boxer and J. Quataert, eds., *Connecting Spheres: Women in the Western World, 1500 to the Present* (1987), and R. Bridenthal, C. Koonz, and S. Stuard, eds., *Becoming Visible: Women in European History,* 2d ed. (1987). P. Aries, *Centuries of Childhood: A Social History of Family Life* (1962), is another stimulating study. E. Shorter, *The Making of the Modern Family* (1975), is a lively controversial interpretation, which should be compared with the excellent study by M. Segalen, *Love and Power in the Peasant Family: Rural France in the Nineteenth Century* (1983). T. Rabb and R. I. Rothberg, eds., *The Family in History* (1973), is a good collection of articles dealing with both Europe and the United States. A. MacFarlane, *The Family Life of Ralph Josselin* (1970), is a brilliant re-creation of the intimate family circle of a seventeenth-century English clergyman who kept a detailed diary; MacFarlane's *Origins of English Individualism: The Family, Property and Social Transi-*

tion (1978) is a major work. I. Pinchbeck and M. Hewitt, *Children in English Society* (1973), is a good introduction. Various aspects of sexual relationships are treated imaginatively by M. Foucault, *The History of Sexuality* (1981), and R. Wheaton and T. Hareven, eds., *Family and Sexuality in French History* (1980).

J. Burnett, *A History of the Cost of Living* (1969), has a great deal of interesting information about what people spent their money on in the past. J. Knyveton, *Diary of a Surgeon in the Year 1751–1752* (1937), gives a contemporary's unforgettable picture of both eighteenth-century medicine and social customs, as do D. and R. Porter, *Patient's Progress: Doctors and Doctoring in Eighteenth-Century England* (1989), and M. Romsey, *Professional and Popular Medicine in France, 1770–1830: The Social World of Medical Practice* (1988). Good introductions to the evolution of medical practices are B. Ingles, *History of Medicine* (1965); O. Bettmann, *A Pictorial History of Medicine* (1956); and H. Haggard's old but interesting *Devils, Drugs, and Doctors* (1929). W. Boyd, *History of Western Education* (1966), is a standard survey, while R. Houston, *Literacy in Early Modern Europe: Culture and Education, 1500–1800* (1988), is brief and engaging. M. D. George, *London Life in the Eighteenth Century* (1965), is a delightfully written book, while D. Roche, *The People of Paris* (1987), presents an unforgettable portrait of the Paris poor in the eighteenth century. G. Rude, *The Crowd in History, 1730–1848* (1964), is an innovative effort to see politics and popular protest from below. An important series edited by R. Forster and O. Ranuum considers neglected social questions such as diet, abandoned children, and deviants, as does P. Burke's excellent study, *Popular Culture in Early Modern Europe* (1978). J. Gillis, *For Better, for Worse: Marriage in Britain Since 1500* (1985), admirably covers the subject.

Good works on religious life include J. Delumeau, *Catholicism Between Luther and Voltaire: A New View of the Counter-Reformation* (1977); B. Semmel, *The Methodist Revolution* (1973); and J. Bettey, *Church and Community: The Parish Church in English Life* (1979).

21

The Revolution in Politics, 1775–1815

The last years of the eighteenth century were a time of great upheaval. A series of revolutions and revolutionary wars challenged the old order of kings and aristocrats. The ideas of freedom and equality, ideas that have not stopped shaping the world since that era, flourished and spread. The revolution began in North America in 1775. Then in 1789 France, the most influential country in Europe, became the leading revolutionary nation. It established first a constitutional monarchy, then a radical republic, and finally a new empire under Napoleon. The armies of France also joined forces with patriots and radicals abroad in an effort to establish new governments based on new principles throughout much of Europe. The world of modern domestic and international politics was born.

- What caused this era of revolution?
- What were the ideas and objectives of the men and women who rose up violently to undo the established system?
- What were the gains and losses for privileged groups and for ordinary people in a generation of war and upheaval?

These are the questions underlying this chapter's examination of the French and American revolutions.

LIBERTY AND EQUALITY

Two ideas fueled the revolutionary period in both America and Europe: liberty and equality. What did eighteenth-century politicians and other people mean by liberty and equality, and why were those ideas so radical and revolutionary in their day?

The call for liberty was first of all a call for individual human rights. Even the most enlightened monarchs customarily claimed that it was their duty to regulate what people wrote and believed. Liberals of the revolutionary era protested such controls from on high. They demanded freedom to worship according to the dictates of their consciences instead of according to the politics of their prince. They demanded the end of censorship and the right to express their beliefs freely in print and at public meetings. They demanded freedom from

arbitrary laws and from judges who simply obeyed orders from the government.

These demands for basic personal freedoms, which were incorporated into the American Bill of Rights and other liberal constitutions, were very far-reaching. Indeed, eighteenth-century revolutionaries demanded more freedom than most governments today believe it is desirable to grant. The Declaration of the Rights of Man, issued at the beginning of the French Revolution, proclaimed, "Liberty consists in being able to do anything that does not harm another person." A citizen's rights had, therefore, "no limits except those which assure to the other members of society the enjoyment of these same rights." Liberals called for the freedom of the individual to develop and to create to the fullest possible extent. In the context of the aristocratic and monarchial forms of government that then dominated Europe, this was a truly radical idea.

The call for liberty was also a call for a new kind of government. The revolutionary liberals believed that the people were sovereign—that is, that the people alone had the authority to make laws limiting the individual's freedom of action. In practice, this system of government meant choosing legislators who represented the people and who were accountable to them. Moreover, liberals of the revolutionary era believed that every people— that is, every ethnic group—had this right of self-determination and, thus, the right to form a free nation.

By equality, eighteenth-century liberals meant that all citizens were to have identical rights and civil liberties. Above all, the nobility had no right to special privileges based on the accident of birth.

Liberals did not define equality as meaning that everyone should be equal economically. Quite the contrary. As Thomas Jefferson wrote in an early draft of the American Declaration of Independence, before changing "property" to the more noble-sounding "happiness," everyone was equal in "the pursuit of property." Jefferson and other liberals certainly did not expect equal success in that pursuit. Great differences in wealth and income between rich and poor were perfectly acceptable to liberals. The essential point was that everyone should legally have an equal chance. French liberals and revolutionaries said they wanted "careers opened to talent." They wanted employment in government, in business, and in the professions to be based on ability, not on family background or legal status.

Equality of opportunity was a very revolutionary idea in eighteenth-century Europe. Legal inequality between classes and groups was the rule, not the exception. Society was still legally divided into groups with special privileges, such as the nobility and the clergy, and groups with special burdens, like the peasantry. In many countries, various middle-class groups—professionals, business people, townspeople, and craftsmen—enjoyed privileges that allowed them to monopolize all sorts of economic activity. It was this kind of economic inequality, an inequality based on artificial legal distinctions, against which liberals protested.

The Roots of Liberalism

The ideas of liberty and equality—the central ideas of classical liberalism—have deep roots in Western history. The ancient Greeks and the Judeo-Christian tradition had affirmed for hundreds of years the sanctity and value of the individual human being. The Judeo-Christian tradition, reinforced by the Reformation, had long stressed personal responsibility on the part of both common folk and exalted rulers, thereby promoting the self-discipline without which liberty becomes anarchy. The hounded and persecuted Protestant radicals of the later sixteenth century had died for the revolutionary idea that individuals were entitled to their own religious beliefs.

Although the liberal creed had roots deep in the Western tradition, classical liberalism first crystallized at the end of the seventeenth century and during the Enlightenment of the eighteenth century. Liberal ideas reflected the Enlightenment's stress on human dignity and human happiness on earth. Liberals shared the Enlightenment's general faith in science, rationality, and progress: the adoption of liberal principles meant better government and a better society for all. Almost all the writers of the Enlightenment were passionately committed to greater personal liberty. They preached religious toleration, freedom of press and speech, and fair and equal treatment before the law.

Certain English and French thinkers were mainly responsible for joining the Enlightenment's concern for personal freedom and legal equality to a theoretical justification of liberal self-government.

The two most important were John Locke and the baron de Montesquieu, considered earlier. Locke (see page 524) maintained that England's long political tradition rested on "the rights of Englishmen" and on representative government through Parliament. Locke admired especially the great Whig nobles who had made the bloodless revolution of 1688 to 1689, and he argued that if a government oversteps its proper function of protecting the natural rights of life, liberty, and private property, it becomes a tyranny. Montesquieu (see page 576) was also inspired by English constitutional history. He, too, believed that powerful "intermediary groups"—such as the judicial nobility of which he was a proud member—offered the best defense of liberty against despotism.

The Marquis de Lafayette was the most famous great noble to embrace the liberal revolution. Shown here directing a battle in the American Revolution, he returned to champion liberty and equality in France. For admirers he was the "hero of two worlds." *(Source: Jean-Loup Charmet)*

The Attraction of Liberalism

The belief that representative institutions could defend their liberty and interests appealed powerfully to ambitious and educated bourgeois. Yet it is important to realize that liberal ideas about individual rights and political freedom also appealed to much of the aristocracy, at least in western Europe and as formulated by Montesquieu. Representative government did not mean democracy, which liberal thinkers tended to equate with mob rule. Rather, they envisioned voting for representatives as being restricted to those who owned property, those with "a stake in society." England had shown the way. After 1688 it had combined a parliamentary system and considerable individual liberty with a restricted franchise and unquestionable aristocratic pre-eminence. In the course of the eighteenth century, many leading French nobles, led by a judicial nobility inspired by Montesquieu, were increasingly eager to follow the English example.

Eighteenth-century liberalism, then, appealed not only to the middle class, but also to some aristocrats. It found broad support among the educated elite and the substantial classes in western Europe. What it lacked from the beginning was strong mass support. For comfortable liberals, the really important questions were theoretical and political. They had no need to worry about their stomachs and the price of bread. For the much more numerous laboring poor, the great questions were immediate and economic. Getting enough to eat was the crucial challenge. These differences in outlook and well-being were to lead to many misunderstandings and disappointments for both groups in the revolutionary era.

THE AMERICAN REVOLUTION, 1775–1789

The era of liberal revolution began in the New World. The thirteen mainland colonies of British North America revolted against their home country and then succeeded in establishing a new unified government.

Americans have long debated the meaning of their revolution. Some have even questioned whether or not it was a real revolution, as opposed to a war for independence. According to some scholars, the Revolution was conservative and defensive in that its demands were for the traditional liberties of English citizens; Americans were united against the British, but otherwise they were a satisfied people, not torn by internal conflict. Other scholars have argued that, on the contrary, the American Revolution was quite radical. It split families between patriots and Loyalists and divided the country. It achieved goals that were fully as advanced as those obtained by the French in their great revolution a few years later.

How does one reconcile these positions? Both contain large elements of truth. The American revolutionaries did believe they were demanding only the traditional rights of English men and women. But those traditional rights were liberal rights, and in the American context they had very strong democratic and popular overtones. Thus the American Revolution was fought in the name of established ideals that were still quite radical in the context of the times. And in founding a government firmly based on liberal principles, the Americans set an example that had a forceful impact on Europe and speeded up political development there.

The Origins of the Revolution

The American Revolution had its immediate origins in a squabble over increased taxes. The British government had fought and decisively won the Seven Years' War (see page 618) on the strength of its professional army and navy. The American colonists had furnished little real aid. The high cost of the war to the British, however, had led to a doubling of the British national debt. Anticipating further expense defending its recently conquered western lands from Indian uprisings like that of Pontiac, the British government in London set about reorganizing the empire with a series of bold, largely unprecedented measures. Breaking with tradition, the British decided to maintain a large army in North America after peace was restored in 1763. Moreover, they sought to exercise strict control over their newly conquered western lands and to tax the colonies directly. In 1765 the government pushed through Parliament the Stamp Act, which levied taxes on a long list of commercial and legal documents, diplomas, pamphlets, newspapers, almanacs, dice, and playing cards. A stamp glued to each article indicated the tax had been paid.

The effort to increase taxes as part of tightening up the empire seemed perfectly reasonable to the British. Heavier stamp taxes had been collected in

The Boston Tea Party   This contemporary illustration shows men disguised as Indians dumping East India Company tea into Boston's harbor. The enthusiastic crowd cheering from the wharf indicates widespread popular support. *(Source: Library of Congress)*

Great Britain for two generations, and Americans were being asked only to pay a share of their own defense costs. Moreover, Americans had been paying only very low local taxes. The Stamp Act would have doubled taxes to about 2 shillings per person per year. No other people in the European or colonial world (except the Poles) paid so little. The British, meanwhile, paid the highest taxes in the Western world in about 1765—26 shillings per person. It is not surprising that taxes per person in the newly independent American nation were much higher in 1785 than in 1765, when the British no longer subsidized American defense. The colonists protested the Stamp Act vigorously and violently, however, and after rioting and boycotts against British goods, Parliament reluctantly repealed the new tax.

As the fury of the Stamp Act controversy revealed, much more was involved than taxes. The key question was political. To what extent could the home government refashion the empire and reassert its power while limiting the authority of colonial legislatures and their elected representatives? Accordingly, who should represent the colonies,

and who had the right to make laws for Americans? While a troubled majority of Americans searched hard for a compromise, some radicals began to proclaim that "taxation without representation is tyranny." The British government replied that Americans were represented in Parliament, albeit indirectly (like most English people themselves), and that the absolute supremacy of Parliament throughout the empire could not be questioned. Many Americans felt otherwise. As John Adams put it, "A Parliament of Great Britain can have no more rights to tax the colonies than a Parliament of Paris." Thus imperial reorganization and parliamentary supremacy came to appear as grave threats to Americans' existing liberties and time-honored institutions.

Americans had long exercised a great deal of independence and gone their own way. In British North America, unlike England and Europe, no powerful established church existed, and personal freedom in questions of religion was taken for granted. The colonial assemblies made the important laws, which were seldom overturned by the home government. The right to vote was much more widespread than in England. In many parts of colonial Massachusetts, for example, as many as 95 percent of the adult males could vote.

Moreover, greater political equality was matched by greater social and economic equality. Neither a hereditary nobility nor a hereditary serf population existed, although the slavery of the Americas consigned blacks to a legally oppressed caste. Independent farmers were the largest group in the country and set much of its tone. In short, the colonial experience had slowly formed a people who felt themselves separate and distinct from the home country. The controversies over taxation intensified those feelings of distinctiveness and separation and brought them to the fore.

In 1773 the dispute over taxes and representation flared up again. The British government had permitted the financially hard-pressed East India Company to ship its tea from China directly to its agents in the colonies, rather than through London middlemen who sold to independent merchants in the colonies. Thus the company secured a vital monopoly on the tea trade, and colonial merchants were suddenly excluded from a highly profitable business. The colonists were quick to protest.

In Boston, men disguised as Indians had a rowdy "tea party" and threw the company's tea into the harbor. This led to extreme measures. The so-called Coercive Acts closed the port of Boston, curtailed local elections and town meetings, and greatly expanded the royal governor's power. County conventions in Massachusetts protested vehemently and urged that the acts be "rejected as the attempts of a wicked administration to enslave America." Other colonial assemblies joined in the denunciations. In September 1774, the First Continental Congress met in Philadelphia, where the more radical members argued successfully against conces-

The Signing of the Declaration, July 4, 1776 John Trumbull's famous painting shows the dignity and determination of America's revolutionary leaders. An extraordinarily talented group, they succeeded in rallying popular support without losing power to more radical forces in the process. *(Source: Yale University Art Gallery)*

sions to the Crown. Compromise was also rejected by the British Parliament, and in April 1775 fighting began at Lexington and Concord.

Independence

The fighting spread, and the colonists moved slowly but inevitably toward open rebellion and a declaration of independence. The uncompromising attitude of the British government and its use of German mercenaries went a long way toward dissolving long-standing loyalties to the home country and rivalries among the separate colonies. *Common Sense* (1775), a brilliant attack by the recently arrived English radical Thomas Paine (1737–1809), also mobilized public opinion in favor of independence. A runaway best seller with sales of 120,000 copies in a few months, Paine's tract ridiculed the idea of a small island ruling a great continent. In his call for freedom and republican government, Paine expressed Americans' growing sense of separateness and moral superiority.

On July 4, 1776, the Second Continental Congress adopted the Declaration of Independence. Written by Thomas Jefferson, the Declaration of Independence boldly listed the tyrannical acts committed by George III (r. 1760–1820) and confidently proclaimed the natural rights of humankind and the sovereignty of the American states. Sometimes called the world's greatest political editorial, the Declaration of Independence in effect universalized the traditional rights of English people and made them the rights of all humanity. It stated that "all men are created equal . . . they are endowed by their Creator with certain unalienable rights . . . among these are life, liberty, and the pursuit of happiness." No other American political document has ever caused such excitement, both at home and abroad.

Many American families remained loyal to Britain; many others divided bitterly. After the Declaration of Independence, the conflict often took the form of a civil war pitting patriot against Loyalist. The Loyalists tended to be wealthy and politically moderate. Many patriots, too, were wealthy—individuals such as John Hancock and George Washington—but willingly allied themselves with farmers and artisans in a broad coalition. This coalition harassed the Loyalists and confiscated their property to help pay for the American war effort. The broad social base of the revolutionaries tended

to make the liberal revolution democratic. State governments extended the right to vote to many more people in the course of the war and re-established themselves as republics.

On the international scene, the French sympathized with the rebels from the beginning. They wanted revenge for the humiliating defeats of the Seven Years' War. Officially neutral until 1778, they supplied the great bulk of guns and gunpowder used by the American revolutionaries, very much as neutral great powers supply weapons for "wars of national liberation" in our day. By 1777 French volunteers were arriving in Virginia, and a dashing young nobleman, the marquis de Lafayette (1757–1834), quickly became one of Washington's most trusted generals. In 1778 the French government offered a formal alliance to the American ambassador in Paris, Benjamin Franklin, and in 1779 and 1780 the Spanish and Dutch declared war on Britain. Catherine the Great of Russia helped organize a League of Armed Neutrality in order to protect neutral shipping rights, which Britain refused to recognize.

Thus by 1780 Great Britain was engaged in an imperial war against most of Europe as well as the thirteen colonies. In these circumstances, and in the face of severe reverses in India, the West Indies, and at Yorktown in Virginia, a new British government decided to cut its losses. American negotiators in Paris were receptive. They feared that France wanted a treaty that would bottle up the new United States east of the Alleghenies and give British holdings west of the Alleghenies to France's ally, Spain. Thus the American negotiators ditched the French and accepted the extraordinarily favorable terms Britain offered.

By the Treaty of Paris of 1783, Britain recognized the independence of the thirteen colonies and ceded all its territory between the Appalachians and the Mississippi River to the Americans. Out of the bitter rivalries of the Old World, the Americans snatched dominion over half a continent.

Framing the Constitution

The liberal program of the American Revolution was consolidated by the federal Constitution, the Bill of Rights, and the creation of a national republic. Assembling in Philadelphia in the summer of 1787, the delegates to the Constitutional Convention were determined to end the period of economic depression, social uncertainty, and very weak central government that had followed independence. The delegates decided, therefore, to grant the federal, or central, government important powers: regulation of domestic and foreign trade, the right to levy taxes, and the means to enforce its laws.

Strong rule was placed squarely in the context of representative self-government. Senators and congressmen would be the lawmaking delegates of the voters, and the president of the republic would be an elected official. The central government was to operate in Montesquieu's framework of checks and balances. The executive, legislative, and judicial branches would systematically balance each other. The power of the federal government would in turn be checked by the powers of the individual states.

When the results of the secret deliberations of the Constitutional Convention were presented to the states for ratification, a great public debate began. The opponents of the proposed constitution—the Anti-Federalists—charged that the framers of the new document had taken too much power from the individual states and made the federal government too strong. Moreover, many Anti-Federalists feared for the personal liberties and individual freedoms for which they had just fought. In order to overcome these objections, the Federalists solemnly promised to spell out these basic freedoms as soon as the new constitution was adopted. The result was the first ten amendments to the Constitution, which the first Congress passed shortly after it met in New York in March 1789. These amendments formed an effective bill of rights to safeguard the individual. Most of them—trial by jury, due process of law, right to assemble, freedom from unreasonable search—had their origins in English law and the English Bill of Rights of 1689. Others—the freedoms of speech, the press, and religion—reflected natural-law theory and the American experience.

The American Constitution and the Bill of Rights exemplified the great strengths and the limits of what came to be called "classical liberalism." Liberty meant individual freedoms and political safeguards. Liberty also meant representative government but did not necessarily mean democracy with its principle of one person, one vote.

Equality—slaves excepted—meant equality before the law, not equality of political participation or economic well-being. Indeed, economic inequal-

ity was resolutely defended by the elite who framed the Constitution. The right to own property was guaranteed by the Fifth Amendment, and if the government took private property, the owner was to receive "just compensation." The radicalism of liberal revolution in America was primarily legal and political, not economic or social.

The Revolution's Impact on Europe

Hundreds of books, pamphlets, and articles analyzed and romanticized the American upheaval. Thoughtful Europeans noted, first of all, its enormous long-term implications for international politics. A secret report by the Venetian ambassador to Paris in 1783 stated what many felt: "If only the union of the Provinces is preserved, it is reasonable to expect that, with the favorable effects of time, and of European arts and sciences, it will become the most formidable power in the world."[1] More generally, American independence fired the imaginations of those few aristocrats who were uneasy with their privileges and of those commoners who yearned for greater equality. Many Europeans believed that the world was advancing now and that America was leading the way. As one French writer put it in 1789: "This vast continent which the seas surround will soon change Europe and the universe."

Europeans who dreamed of a new era were fascinated by the political lessons of the American Revolution. The Americans had begun with a revolutionary defense against tyrannical oppression, and they had been victorious. They had then shown how rational beings could assemble together to exercise sovereignty and write a permanent constitution—a new social contract. All this gave greater reality to the concepts of individual liberty and representative government. It reinforced one of the primary ideas of the Enlightenment, the idea that a better world was possible.

THE FRENCH REVOLUTION, 1789–1791

No country felt the consequences of the American Revolution more directly than France. Hundreds of French officers served in America and were inspired by the experience. The most famous of these, the young and impressionable marquis de Lafayette, left home as a great aristocrat determined only to fight France's traditional foe, England. He returned with a love of liberty and firm republican convictions. French intellectuals and publicists engaged in passionate analysis of the federal Constitution, as well as the constitutions of the various states of the new United States. The American Revolution undeniably hastened upheaval in France.

Yet the French Revolution did not mirror the American example. It was more violent and more complex, more influential and more controversial, more loved and more hated. For Europeans and most of the rest of the world, it was the great revolution of the eighteenth century, *the* revolution that opened the modern era in politics.

The Breakdown of the Old Order

Like the American Revolution, the French Revolution had its immediate origins in the financial difficulties of the government. As we noted in Chapter 18, the efforts of Louis XV's ministers to raise taxes had been thwarted by the Parlement of Paris, strengthened in its opposition by widespread popular support (see pages 588–589). When renewed efforts to reform the tax system met a similar fate in 1776, the government was forced to finance all of its enormous expenditures during the American war with borrowed money. The national debt and the annual budget deficit soared. By the 1780s fully half of France's annual budget went for ever-increasing interest payments on the ever-increasing debt. Another quarter went to maintain the military, while 6 percent was absorbed by the costly and extravagant king and his court at Versailles. Less than one-fifth of the entire national budget was available for the productive functions of the state, such as transportation and general administration. It was an impossible financial situation.

One way out would have been for the government to declare partial bankruptcy, forcing its creditors to accept greatly reduced payments on the debt. The powerful Spanish monarchy had regularly repudiated large portions of its debt in earlier times, and France had done likewise, after an attempt to establish a French national bank ended in financial disaster in 1720. Yet by the 1780s the French debt was held by an army of aristocratic and bourgeois creditors, and the French monarchy, though absolute in theory, had become far too weak for such a drastic and unpopular action.

France and America   Made in France about 1784, this figurine commemorates the vital support that France gave to the colonists in the American Revolution. Arrayed in Roman armor, a majestic Louis XVI hands documents entitled ''American independence'' and ''freedom of the seas'' to Benjamin Franklin. Franklin was lionized as a sage and a liberator while American ambassador to France. *(Source: The Providence Athenaeum, Providence, Rhode Island)*

Nor could the king and his ministers, unlike modern governments, print money and create inflation to cover their deficits. Unlike England and Holland, which had far larger national debts relative to their populations, France had no central bank, no paper currency, and no means of creating credit. French money was good gold coin. Therefore, when a depressed economy and a lack of public confidence made it increasingly difficult for the government to obtain new gold loans in 1786, it had no alternative but to try to increase taxes. And since France's tax system was unfair and out of date, increased revenues were possible only through fundamental reforms. Such reforms, which would affect all groups in France's complex and fragmented society, opened a Pandora's box of social and political demands.

demands with a surprise maneuver on the night of August 4, 1789. The duke of Aiguillon, one of France's greatest noble landowners, declared that

in several provinces the whole people forms a kind of league for the destruction of the manor houses, the ravaging of the lands, and especially for the seizure of the archives where the title deeds to feudal properties are kept. It seeks to throw off at last a yoke that has for many centuries weighted it down.[3]

He urged equality in taxation and the elimination of feudal dues. In the end, all the old exactions were abolished, generally without compensation: serfdom where it still existed, exclusive hunting rights for nobles, fees for justice, village monopolies, the right to make peasants work on the roads,

and a host of other dues. Though a clarifying law passed a week later was less generous, the peasants ignored the "fine print." They never paid feudal dues again. Thus the French peasantry, which already owned about 30 percent of all the land, quickly achieved a great and unprecedented victory. Henceforth, the French peasants would seek mainly to consolidate their triumph. As the Great Fear subsided, they became a force for order and stability.

A Limited Monarchy

The National Assembly moved forward. On August 27, 1789, it issued the Declaration of the Rights of Man. This great liberal document had a

Storming the Bastille   This representation by an untrained contemporary artist shows civilians and members of the Paris militia—the "conquerors of the Bastille"—on the attack. This successful action had enormous practical and symbolic significance, and July 14 has long been France's most important national holiday. *(Source: Musée Carnavalet/Photo Hubert Josse)*

"To Versailles" This print is one of many commemorating the women's march on Versailles. Notice on the left that the fashionable lady from the well-to-do is a most reluctant revolutionary. *(Source: Photo Flammarion)*

very American flavor, and Lafayette even discussed his draft in detail with the American ambassador in Paris, Thomas Jefferson, the author of the American Declaration of Independence. According to the French declaration, "men are born and remain free and equal in rights." Mankind's natural rights are "liberty, property, security, and resistance to oppression." Also, "every man is presumed innocent until he is proven guilty." As for law, "it is an expression of the general will; all citizens have the right to concur personally or through their representatives in its formation. . . . Free expression of thoughts and opinions is one of the most precious rights of mankind: every citizen may therefore speak, write, and publish freely." In short, this clarion call of the liberal revolutionary ideal guaranteed equality before the law, representative government for a sovereign people, and individual freedom. This revolutionary credo, only two pages long, was propagandized throughout France and Europe and around the world.

Moving beyond general principles to draft a constitution proved difficult. The questions of how much power the king should retain and whether he could permanently veto legislation led to another deadlock. Once again the decisive answer came from the poor, in this instance the poor women of Paris.

To understand what happened, one must remember that the work and wages of women and children were essential in the family economy of the laboring poor. In Paris great numbers of women worked, particularly within the putting-out system in the garment industry—making lace, fancy dresses, embroidery, ribbons, bonnets, corsets, and so on. Many of these goods were beautiful luxury items, destined for an aristocratic and international clientele.[4] Immediately after the fall of the Bastille, many of France's great court nobles began to leave Versailles for foreign lands, so that a plummeting demand for luxuries intensified the general economic crisis. International markets also declined, and the church was no longer able to give its traditional grants of food and money to the poor. Unemployment and hunger increased further, and the result was another popular explosion.

On October 5 some seven thousand desperate women marched the 12 miles from Paris to Versailles to demand action. A middle-class deputy looking out from the Assembly saw "multitudes

French armies occupied Madrid, but the foes of Napoleon fled to the hills and waged uncompromising guerrilla warfare. Spain was a clear warning. Resistance to French imperialism was growing.

Yet Napoleon pushed on, determined to hold his complex and far-flung empire together. In 1810, when the Grand Empire was at its height, Britain still remained at war with France, helping the guerrillas in Spain and Portugal. The continental system, organized to exclude British goods from the Continent and force that "nation of shopkeepers" to its knees, was a failure. Instead, it was France that suffered from Britain's counter-blockade, which created hard times for French artisans and the middle class. Perhaps looking for a scapegoat, Napoleon turned on Alexander I of Russia, who had been fully supporting Napoleon's war of prohibitions against British goods.

Napoleon's invasion of Russia began in June 1812 with a force that eventually numbered 600,000, probably the largest force yet assembled in a single army. Only one-third of this force was French, however; nationals of all the satellites and allies were drafted into the operation. Originally planning to winter in the Russian city of Smolensk if Alexander did not sue for peace, Napoleon reached Smolensk and recklessly pressed on. The great battle of Borodino that followed was a draw, and the Russians retreated in good order. Alexander ordered the evacuation of Moscow, which then burned, and refused to negotiate. Finally, after five weeks in the burned-out city, Napoleon or-

Goya: The Third of May, 1808   This great painting screams in outrage at the horrors of war, which Goya witnessed in Spain. Spanish rebels, focused around the Christ-like figure at the center, are gunned down by anonymous French soldiers, grim forerunners of modern death squads and their atrocities. *(Source: Museo del Prado, Madrid)*

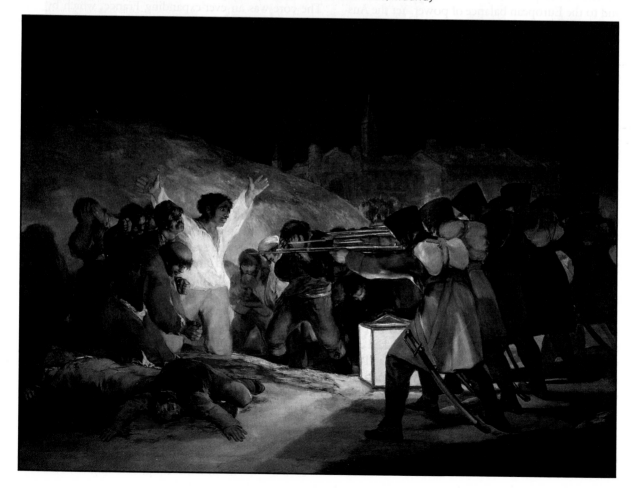

THE NAPOLEONIC ERA

November 1799	Napoleon overthrows the Directory
December 1799	French voters overwhelmingly approve Napoleon's new constitution
1800	Napoleon founds the Bank of France
1801	France defeats Austria and acquires Italian and German territories in the Treaty of Lunéville
	Napoleon signs a concordat with the pope
1802	Treaty of Amiens with Britain
December 1804	Napoleon crowns himself emperor
October 1805	Battle of Trafalgar: Britain defeats the French and Spanish fleets
December 1805	Battle of Austerlitz: Napoleon defeats Austria and Prussia
1807	Treaties of Tilsit: Napoleon redraws the map of Europe
1810	Height of the Grand Empire
June 1812	Napoleon invades Russia with 600,000 men
Winter 1812	Disastrous retreat from Russia
March 1814	Russia, Prussia, Austria, and Britain form the Quadruple Alliance to defeat France
April 1814	Napoleon abdicates and is exiled to Elba
February–June 1815	Napoleon escapes from Elba and rules France until suffering defeat at Battle of Waterloo

dered a retreat. That retreat was one of the great military disasters in history. The Russian army and the Russian winter cut Napoleon's army to pieces. Only 30,000 men returned to their homelands.

Leaving his troops to their fate, Napoleon raced to Paris to raise yet another army. Possibly he might still have saved his throne if he had been willing to accept a France reduced to its historical size—the proposal offered by Austria's foreign minister Metternich. But Napoleon refused. Austria and Prussia deserted Napoleon and joined Russia and Great Britain in the Fourth Coalition. All across Europe, patriots called for a "war of liberation" against Napoleon's oppression, and the well-disciplined regular armies of Napoleon's enemies closed in for the kill. This time the coalition held together, cemented by the Treaty of Chaumont, which created a Quadruple Alliance to last for twenty years. Less than a month later, on April 4, 1814, a defeated, abandoned Napoleon abdicated his throne. After this unconditional abdication, the victorious allies granted Napoleon the island of Elba off the coast of Italy as his own tiny state. Napoleon was even allowed to keep his imperial title, and France was required to pay him a large yearly income of 2 million francs.

The allies also agreed to the restoration of the Bourbon dynasty, in part because demonstrations led by a few dedicated French monarchists indicated some support among the French people for that course of action. The new monarch, Louis XVIII (r. 1814–1824), tried to consolidate that support by issuing the Constitutional Charter, which accepted many of France's revolutionary changes and guaranteed civil liberties. Indeed, the Charter gave France a constitutional monarchy roughly similar to that established in 1791, although far fewer people had the right to vote for representatives to the resurrected Chamber of Deputies. Moreover, after Louis XVIII stated firmly that his government would not pay any war reparations, France was treated leniently by the allies, who agreed to meet in Vienna to work out a general peace settlement.

Yet Louis XVIII—old, ugly, and crippled by gout—totally lacked the glory and magic of Napoleon. Hearing of political unrest in France and diplomatic tensions in Vienna, Napoleon staged a daring escape from Elba in February 1815. Landing in France, he issued appeals for support and marched on Paris with a small band of followers. French officers and soldiers who had fought so long for their

22

The Revolution in Energy and Industry

done in the open air with animals and hand tools. Many landless farm laborers and poor peasants, long accustomed to leaving their villages for temporary employment, went to build railroads. By the time the work was finished, life back home in the village often seemed dull and unappealing, and many men drifted to towns in search of work—with the railroad companies, in construction, in factories. By the time they sent for their wives and sweethearts to join them, they had become urban workers.

The railroad changed the outlook and values of the entire society. The last and culminating invention of the Industrial Revolution, the railroad dramatically revealed the power and increased the speed of the new age. Racing down a track at 16 miles per hour or, by 1850, at a phenomenal 50 miles per hour was a new and awesome experience.

As a noted French economist put it after a ride on the Liverpool and Manchester in 1833, "There are certain impressions that one cannot put into words!"

Some great painters, notably J. M. W. Turner (1775–1851) and Claude Monet (1840–1926), succeeded in expressing this sense of power and awe. So did the massive new train stations, the cathedrals of the industrial age. Leading railway engineers like Isambard Kingdom Brunel and Thomas Brassey, whose tunnels pierced mountains and whose bridges spanned valleys, became public idols —the astronauts of their day. Everyday speech absorbed the images of railroading. After you got up a "full head of steam," you "highballed" along. And if you didn't "go off the track," you might "toot your own whistle." The railroad fired the imagination.

The Liverpool and Manchester Railway This hand-colored engraving celebrates the opening of the world's first major railroad on September 15, 1830. Railroad construction reshaped the built environment and proclaimed the coming of a new age. *(Source: Mr. and Mrs. M. G. Powell)*

The Third-Class Carriage   The French artist Honoré Daumier was fascinated by the railroad and its human significance. This great painting focuses on the peasant grandmother, absorbed in memories. The nursing mother represents love and creativity; the sleeping boy, innocence. *(Source: The Metropolitan Museum of Art. Bequest of Mrs. H. O. Havemeyer, 1929. The H. O. Havemeyer Collection (29. 100. 129))*

Industry and Population

In 1851 London was the site of a famous industrial fair. This Great Exposition was held in the newly built Crystal Palace, an architectural masterpiece made entirely of glass and iron, both of which were now cheap and abundant. For the millions who visited, one fact stood out. The little island of Britain —England, Wales, and Scotland—was the "workshop of the world." It alone produced two-thirds of the world's coal and more than half of its iron and cotton cloth. More generally, it has been carefully estimated that, in 1860, Britain produced a truly remarkable 20 percent of the entire world's output of industrial goods, whereas it had produced only about 2 percent of the world total

in 1750.[2] Experiencing revolutionary industrial change, Britain became the first industrial nation (Map 22.2).

As the British economy significantly increased its production of manufactured goods, the gross national product (GNP) rose roughly fourfold at constant prices between 1780 and 1851. In other words, the British people increased their wealth and their national income dramatically. At the same time, the population of Great Britain boomed, growing from about 9 million in 1780 to almost 21 million in 1851. Thus growing numbers consumed much of the increase in total production. According to one recent study, average consumption per person increased by only 75 percent between 1780 and 1851, as the growth in the total

"Be United and Industrious" This handsome membership certificate of the "new model" Amalgamated Society of Engineers exalts the nobility of skilled labor and the labor movement. Union members are shown rejecting the call of Mars, the God of War, and accepting well-deserved honors from the Goddess of Peace. Other figures represent the strength of union solidarity, famous English inventors, and the trades of the members. *(Source: E. T. Archive)*

British workers also engaged in direct political activity in defense of their own interests. After the collapse of Owen's national trade union, a great deal of the energy of working people went into the Chartist movement, whose goal was political democracy. The key Chartist demand—that all men be given the right to vote—became the great hope of millions of aroused people. Workers were also active in campaigns to limit the workday in the factories to ten hours and to permit duty-free importation of wheat into Great Britain to secure cheap bread. Thus working people played an active role in shaping the new industrial system. Clearly, they were neither helpless victims nor passive beneficiaries.

The Sexual Division of Labor

The era of the Industrial Revolution witnessed major changes in the sexual division of labor. In preindustrial Europe most people generally worked in family units. By tradition, certain jobs were defined by sex—women and girls for milking and spinning, men and boys for plowing and weaving. But many tasks might go to either sex, because particular circumstances dictated a family's response in its battle for economic survival. This pattern of family employment carried over into early factories and subcontracting, but it collapsed as child labor was restricted and new attitudes emerged. A different sexual division of labor gradually arose to take its place. The man emerged as the family's primary wage earner, while the woman found only limited job opportunities. Generally denied good jobs at good wages in the growing urban economy, women were expected to concentrate on unpaid housework, child care, and craft work at home.

This new pattern of "separate spheres" had several aspects. First, all studies agree that married women were much less likely to work full-time for wages outside the house after the first child arrived, although they often earned small amounts doing putting-out handicrafts at home and taking in boarders. Second, when married women did work for wages outside the house, they usually came from the poorest, most desperate families, where the husbands were poorly paid, sick, unemployed, or missing. Third, these poor married (or widowed) women were joined by legions of young unmarried women, who worked full-time but only in certain jobs. Fourth, all women were generally con-

workers. After 1815 he experimented with cooperative and socialist communities, including one at New Harmony, Indiana. Then, in 1834, Owen organized one of the largest and most visionary of the early national unions, the Grand National Consolidated Trades Union. When this and other grandiose schemes collapsed, the British labor movement moved once again after 1851 in the direction of craft unions. The most famous of these "new model unions" was the Amalgamated Society of Engineers. These unions won real benefits for members by fairly conservative means and thus became an accepted part of the industrial scene.

fined to low-paying, dead-end jobs. Virtually no occupation open to women paid a living wage—a wage sufficient for a person to live independently. Men predominated in the better-paying, more promising employments. Evolving gradually as family labor declined, but largely in place in the urban sector of the British economy by 1850, the new sexual division of labor constituted a major development in the history of women and of the family.

If the reorganization of paid work along gender lines is widely recognized, there is as yet no agreement on its causes. One school of scholars sees little connection with industrialization and finds the answer in the deeply ingrained sexist attitudes of a "patriarchal tradition," which predated the economic transformation. These scholars stress the role of male-dominated craft unions in denying women access to good jobs and in reducing them to unpaid maids dependent on their husbands. Other scholars, believing that the gender roles of women and men can vary enormously with time and culture, look more to a combination of economic and biological factors in order to explain why the mass of women were either unwilling or unable to halt the emergence of a sex-segregated division of labor.

Three ideas stand out in this more recent interpretation. First, the new and unfamiliar discipline of the clock and the machine was especially hard on married women. Above all, relentless factory discipline conflicted with child care in a way that labor on the farm or in the cottage had not. A woman operating ear-splitting spinning machinery could mind a child of seven or eight working beside her (until such work was outlawed), but she could no longer pace herself through pregnancy, even though overwork during pregnancy heightened the already high risks of childbirth. Nor could a woman breast-feed her baby on the job, although breast-feeding saved lives. Thus a working-class woman had strong incentives to concentrate on child care within her home, if her family could afford it.

Second, running a household in conditions of primitive urban poverty was an extremely demanding job in its own right. There were no supermarkets or discount department stores, no running water or public transportation. Everything had to be done on foot. As in the poor sections of many inner cities today, shopping and feeding the family constituted a never-ending challenge. The woman marched from one tiny shop to another, dragging her tired children (for who was to watch them?) and struggling valiantly with heavy sacks, tricky shopkeepers, and walk-up apartments. Yet another brutal job outside the house—a "second shift"—had limited appeal for the average married woman. Thus women might well accept the emerging division of labor as the best available strategy for family survival in the industrializing society.[10]

Third, why were the women who did work for wages outside the home segregated and confined to certain "women's jobs"? No doubt the desire of males to monopolize the best opportunities and hold women down provides part of the answer. Yet, as Jane Humphries has argued, sex-segregated employment also formed a collective response to the new industrial system. Previously, at least in theory, young people worked under a watchful parental eye. The growth of factories and mines brought unheard-of opportunities for girls and boys to mix on the job, free of familial supervision. Continuing to mix after work, they were "more likely to form liaisons, initiate courtships, and respond to advances."[11] Such intimacy also led to more unplanned pregnancies and fueled the illegitimacy explosion that had begun in the late eighteenth century and that gathered force until at least 1850 (see pages 631–632). Thus segregation of jobs by gender was partly an effort by older people to help control the sexuality of working-class youth.

Investigations into the British coal industry before 1842 provide a graphic example of this concern. The middle-class men leading the inquiry often failed to appreciate the physical effort of the girls and women who dragged with belt and chain the unwheeled carts of coal along narrow underground passages. But they professed horror at the sight of girls and women working without shirts, which was a common practice because of the heat, and they quickly assumed the prevalence of licentious sex with the male miners, who also wore very little clothing. In fact, most girls and married women worked for related males in a family unit that provided considerable protection and restraint. Yet many witnesses from the working class believed that "blackguardism and debauchery" were common and that "They are best out of the pits, the lasses." Some miners stressed particularly the sexual danger of letting girls work past puberty. As one explained,

"I consider it a scandal for girls to work in the pits. Till they are 12 or 14 they may work very well but after that

it's an abomination. . . . The work of the pit does not hurt them, it is the effect on their morals that I complain of, and after 14 they should not be allowed to go. . . . [A]fter that age it is dreadful for them."[12]

The Mines Act of 1842 prohibited underground work for all women, as well as for boys under ten.

Some women who had to support themselves protested against being excluded from coal mining, which paid higher wages than most other jobs open to women. But provided they were part of families that could manage economically, the girls and the women who had worked underground were generally pleased with the law. In explaining her satisfaction in 1844, one mother of four provided a real insight into why many women accepted the emerging sexual division of labor:

While working in the pit I was worth to my [miner] husband seven shillings a week, out of which we had to pay 2½ shillings to a woman for looking after the younger children. I used to take them to her house at 4 o'clock in the morning, out of their own beds, to put them into hers. Then there was one shilling a week for washing; besides, there was mending to pay for, and other things. The house was not guided. The other children broke things; they did not go to school when they were sent; they would be playing about, and get ill-used by other children, and their clothes torn. Then when I came home in the evening, everything was to do after the day's labor, and I was so tired I had no heart for it; no fire lit, nothing cooked, no water fetched, the house dirty, and nothing comfortable for my husband. It is all far better now, and I wouldn't go down again.[13]

Industrial Revolution in England greatly increased output in certain radically altered industries, stimulated the large handicraft and commercial sectors, and speeded up overall economic growth. Rugged Scotland industrialized at least as fast as England, and Great Britain became the first industrial nation. By 1850 the level of British per capita industrial production surpassed continental levels by a growing margin, and Britain savored a near monopoly in world markets for mass-produced goods. Thus continental countries inevitably took rather different paths to the urban industrial society. They relied more on handicraft production in both towns and villages, and only in the 1840s did railroad construction begin to create a strong demand for iron, coal, and railway equipment that speeded up the process of industrialization.

The rise of modern industry had a profound impact on people and their lives. In the early stages Britain again led the way, experiencing in a striking manner the long-term social changes accompanying the economic transformation. Factory discipline and Britain's stern capitalist economy weighed heavily on working people, who, however, actively fashioned their destinies, refusing to be passive victims. Improvements in the standard of living came slowly, although they were substantial by 1850. The era of industrialization fostered new attitudes toward child labor, encouraged protective factory legislation, and called forth an assertive labor movement. It also promoted a more rigid division of roles and responsibilities within the family that was detrimental to women, another gradual but profound change of revolutionary proportions.

SUMMARY

Western society's industrial breakthrough grew out of a long process of economic and social change, in which the rise of capitalism, overseas expansion, and the growth of rural industry stood out as critical preparatory developments. Eventually taking the lead in all of these developments, and also profiting from stable government, abundant natural resources, and a flexible labor force, England experienced between roughly the 1780s and the 1850s an epoch-making transformation, one that is still aptly termed the Industrial Revolution.

Building on technical breakthroughs, power-driven equipment, and large-scale enterprise, the

NOTES

1. N. F. R. Crafts, *British Economic Growth During the Industrial Revolution* (Oxford: Oxford University Press, 1985), p. 32. These estimates are for Great Britain as a whole.
2. P. Bairoch, "International Industrialization Levels from 1750 to 1980," *Journal of European Economic History* 11 (Spring 1982): 269–333.
3. Crafts, pp. 45, 95–102.
4. M. Lévy-Leboyer, *Les banques européennes et l'industrialisation dans la première moitié du XIXe siècle* (Paris: Presses Universitaires de France, 1964), p. 29.
5. J. Michelet, *The People,* trans. with an introduction by J. P. McKay (Urbana: University of Illinois Press, 1973; original publication, 1846), p. 64.

6. F. Engels, *The Condition of the Working Class in England,* trans. and ed. W. O. Henderson and W. H. Chaloner (Stanford, Calif.: Stanford University Press, 1968), p. xxiii.

7. Quoted in W. A. Hayek, ed., *Capitalism and the Historians* (Chicago: University of Chicago Press, 1954), p. 126.

8. Crafts, p. 95.

9. Quoted in E. R. Pike, *"Hard Times": Human Documents of the Industrial Revolution* (New York: Praeger, 1966), p. 109.

10. See, especially, J. Brenner and M. Rama, "Rethinking Women's Oppression," *New Left Review* 144 (March–April 1984): 33–71, and sources cited there.

11. J. Humphries, " '. . . The Most Free from Objection . . .' The Sexual Division of Labor and Women's Work in Nineteenth-Century England," *Journal of Economic History* 47 (December 1987): 948.

12. Ibid., p. 941; Pike, p. 266.

13. Quoted in Pike, p. 208.

SUGGESTED READING

There is a vast and exciting literature on the Industrial Revolution. R. Cameron, *A Concise Economic History of the World* (1989), provides an introduction to the issues and has a carefully annotated bibliography. J. Goodman and K. Honeyman, *Gainful Pursuits: The Making of Industrial Europe, 1600–1914* (1988); D. S. Landes, *The Unbound Prometheus: Technological Change and Industrial Development in Western Europe from 1750 to the Present* (1969); and S. Pollard, *Peaceful Conquest: The Industrialization of Europe* (1981), are excellent general treatments of European industrial growth. These studies also suggest the range of issues and interpretations. M. Berg, *The Age of Manufactures: Industry, Innovation and Work in Britain, 1700–1820* (1985); P. Mathias, *The First Industrial Nation: An Economic History of Britain, 1700–1914* (1969); P. Mantoux, *The Industrial Revolution in the Eighteenth Century* (1961), admirably discuss the various aspects of the English breakthrough and offer good bibliographies, as does the work by Crafts mentioned in the Notes. W. Rostow, *The Stages of Economic Growth: A Non-Communist Manifesto* (1960), is a popular, provocative study.

H. Kirsch, *From Domestic Manufacturing to Industrial Revolution: The Case of the Rhineland Textile Districts* (1989), and M. Neufeld, *The Skilled Metalworkers of Nuremberg: Craft and Class in the Industrial Revolution* (1985), examine the persistence and gradual transformation of handicraft techniques. R. Cameron brilliantly traces the spread of railroads and industry across Europe in *France and the Economic Development of Europe, 1800–1914*

(1961). The works of A. S. Milward and S. B. Saul, *The Economic Development of Continental Europe, 1780–1870* (1973) and *The Development of the Economies of Continental Europe, 1850–1914* (1977), may be compared with J. Clapham's old-fashioned classic, *Economic Development of France and Germany* (1963). C. Kindleberger, *Economic Growth in France and Britain, 1851–1950* (1964), is a stimulating study, especially for those with some background in economics. Other important works in recent years on industrial developments are C. Tilly and E. Shorter, *Strikes in France, 1830–1848* (1974); D. Ringrose, *Transportation and Economic Stagnation in Spain, 1750–1850* (1970); L. Schofer, *The Formation of a Modern Labor Force* (1975), which focuses on the Silesian part of Germany; and W. Blackwell, *The Industrialization of Russia,* 2d ed. (1982). L. Moch, *Paths to the City: Regional Migration in Nineteenth-century France* (1983), and W. Schivelbusch, *Disenchanted Night: The Industrialization of Light in the Nineteenth Century* (1983), imaginatively analyze quite different aspects of industrialization's many consequences.

The debate between "optimists" and "pessimists" about the consequences of industrialization in England goes on. P. Taylor, ed., *The Industrial Revolution: Triumph or Disaster?* (1970), is a useful introduction to different viewpoints, while Hayek's collection of essays, cited in the Notes, stresses positive aspects. It is also fascinating to compare Friedrich Engels's classic condemnation, *The Condition of the Working Class in England,* with Andrew Ure's optimistic defense, *The Philosophy of Manufactures,* first published in 1835 and reprinted recently. E. P. Thompson continues and enriches the Engels tradition in *The Making of the English Working Class* (1963), an exciting book rich in detail and early working-class lore. E. R. Pike's documentary collection, *"Hard Times,"* cited in the Notes, provides fascinating insights into the lives of working people. An unorthodox but moving account of a doomed group is D. Bythell, *The Handloom Weavers* (1969). F. Klingender, *Art and the Industrial Revolution,* rev. ed. (1968), is justly famous, and M. Ignatieff, *A Just Measure of Pain* (1980), is an engrossing study of prisons during English industrialization. D. S. Landes, *Revolution in Time: Clocks and the Making of the Modern World* (1983), is a brilliant integration of industrial and cultural history.

Among general studies, G. S. R. Kitson Clark, *The Making of Victorian England* (1967), is particularly imaginative. A. Briggs, *Victorian People* (1955), provides an engrossing series of brief biographies. H. Ausubel discusses a major reformer in *John Bright* (1966), and B. Harrison skillfully illuminates the problem of heavy drinking in *Drink and the Victorians* (1971). The most famous contemporary novel dealing with the new industrial society is Charles Dickens's *Hard Times,* an entertaining but exaggerated story. *Mary Barton* and *North and South* by Elizabeth Gaskell are more realistic portrayals, and both are highly recommended.

23

Ideologies and Upheavals, 1815–1850

The momentous economic and political transformation of modern times began in the late eighteenth century with the Industrial Revolution in England and then the French Revolution. Until about 1815, these economic and political revolutions were separate, involving different countries and activities and proceeding at very different paces. The Industrial Revolution created the factory system and new groups of capitalists and industrial workers in northern England, but almost continuous warfare with France checked its spread to continental Europe. Meanwhile, England's ruling aristocracy suppressed all forms of political radicalism at home and joined with crowned heads abroad to oppose and eventually defeat revolutionary and Napoleonic France. The economic and political revolutions worked at cross-purposes and even neutralized each other.

After peace returned in 1815, the situation changed. Economic and political changes tended to fuse, reinforcing each other and bringing about what the historian Eric Hobsbawm has incisively called the "dual revolution." For instance, the growth of the industrial middle class encouraged the drive for representative government, while the demands of the French sans-culottes in 1793 and 1794 inspired many socialist thinkers. Gathering strength and threatening almost every aspect of the existing political and social framework, the dual revolution rushed on to alter completely first Europe and then the world. Much of world history in the last two centuries can be seen as the progressive unfolding of the dual revolution.

Yet three qualifications must be kept firmly in mind. In Europe in the nineteenth century, as in Asia and Africa in more recent times, the dual revolution was not some inexorable mechanical monster grinding peoples and cultures into a homogenized mass. The economic and political transformation it wrought was built on complicated histories, strong traditions, and highly diverse cultures. Radical change was eventually a constant, but the particular results varied enormously.

Nor should the strength of the old forces be underestimated. In central and eastern Europe especially, the traditional elites—the monarchs, noble landowners, and bureaucrats—long proved capable of defending their privileges and even of redirecting the dual revolution to serve their interests.

Finally, the dual revolution posed a tremendous intellectual challenge. The meanings of the economic, political, and social changes that were occurring, as well as the ways they could be shaped by human action, were anything but clear. These questions fascinated observers and stimulated new ideas and ideologies.

- What ideas did thinkers develop to describe and shape the transformation going on before their eyes?

- How did the artists and writers of the Romantic movement also reflect and influence changes in this era?

- How did the political revolution, derailed in France and resisted by European monarchs, eventually break out again after 1815?

- Why did the revolutionary surge triumph briefly in 1848, then fail almost completely?

These are the questions this chapter will explore.

THE PEACE SETTLEMENT

The eventual triumph of revolutionary economic and political forces was by no means certain in 1814. Quite the contrary. The conservative, aristocratic monarchies with their preindustrial armies and economies (Great Britain excepted) appeared firmly in control once again. France had been decisively defeated by the off-again, on-again alliance of Russia, Prussia, Austria, and Great Britain. That alliance had been strengthened and reaffirmed in March 1814, when the allies pledged not only to defeat France but to hold it in line for twenty years thereafter. The Quadruple Alliance had then forced Napoleon to abdicate in April 1814 and restored the Bourbon dynasty to the French throne (see page 687). But there were many other international questions outstanding, and the allies agreed to meet in Vienna to fashion a general peace settlement. Interrupted by Napoleon's desperate gamble during the Hundred Days, the allies concluded their negotiations at the Congress of Vienna after Napoleon's defeat at Waterloo.

Most people felt profound longing for peace. The great challenge for political leaders in 1814 was to construct a peace settlement that would last and not sow the seeds of another war. Their efforts were largely successful and contributed to a century

The Great Powers negotiated the main questions of the peace settlement in intimate sessions at the Congress of Vienna. This painting shows the Duke of Wellington, standing at the far left; seated at far left is the Prussian Prince of Hardinberg. Wellington had just led the allied forces to victory against Napoleon at Waterloo. *(Source: Windsor Castle, Royal Library© 1990. Her Majesty Queen Elizabeth II)*

unmarred by destructive, generalized war (Map 23.1).

The Congress of Vienna

The allied powers were concerned first and foremost with the defeated enemy, France. Agreeing to the restoration of the Bourbon dynasty, the allies signed the first Peace of Paris with Louis XVIII on May 30, 1814.

The allies were quite lenient toward France. France was given the boundaries it possessed in 1792, which were larger than those of 1789. France lost only the territories it had conquered in Italy, Germany, and the Low Countries, in addition to a few colonial possessions. Although there was some

sentiment for levying a fine on France to pay for the war, the allies did not press the matter when Louis XVIII stated firmly that his government would not pay any reparations. France was even allowed to keep the art treasures Napoleon's agents had looted from the museums of Europe. Thus the victorious powers did not punish harshly, and they did not foment a spirit of injustice and revenge in the defeated country.

When the four allies met together at the Congress of Vienna, assisted in a minor way by a host of delegates from the smaller European states, they also agreed to raise a number of formidable barriers against renewed French aggression. The Low Countries—Belgium and Holland—were united under an enlarged Dutch monarchy capable of opposing France more effectively. Moreover, Prussia

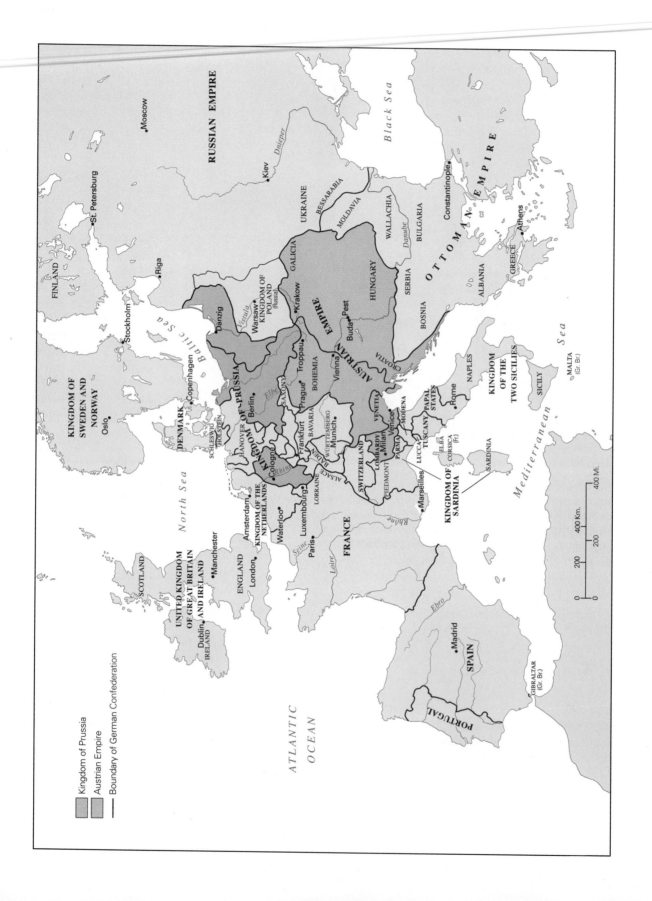

Kingdom of Prussia
Austrian Empire
Boundary of German Confederation

ATLANTIC OCEAN

SCOTLAND

UNITED KINGDOM OF GREAT BRITAIN AND IRELAND

ENGLAND
•Manchester
London•
Dublin•
IRELAND

North Sea

KINGDOM OF SWEDEN AND NORWAY
Oslo•
Stockholm•

FINLAND

St. Petersburg•

•Moscow

RUSSIAN EMPIRE

Riga•

Baltic Sea

Copenhagen•
DENMARK
SCHLESWIG
HOLSTEIN

Amsterdam•
KINGDOM OF THE NETHERLANDS
Waterloo•
Luxembourg•
Cologne•
Rhine
HANOVER
KINGDOM OF PRUSSIA
Berlin•
Elbe
SAXONY
Frankfurt•
BADEN
BAVARIA
WÜRTTEMBERG
Munich•

Danzig•
Vistula
Warsaw•
KINGDOM OF POLAND (Russia)

Kiev•
Dnieper

UKRAINE

GALICIA
Krakow•

BESSARABIA

MOLDAVIA

Black Sea

Constantinople•

OTTOMAN EMPIRE

AUSTRIAN EMPIRE
Troppau•
BOHEMIA
Prague•
Vienna•
Buda•Pest
HUNGARY
CROATIA

WALLACHIA
Danube
BULGARIA
SERBIA
BOSNIA

ALBANIA
GREECE
Athens•

FRANCE
Paris•
Seine
Loire
Rhône

SWITZERLAND
ALSACE
LORRAINE
PIEDMONT
LOMBARDY
Milan•
KINGDOM OF SARDINIA
Marseilles•
VENETIA
Venice•
PARMA
MODENA
LUCCA
TUSCANY
PAPAL STATES
Rome•
ELBA
CORSICA (Fr.)
SARDINIA

NAPLES
KINGDOM OF THE TWO SICILIES
SICILY

MALTA (Gr. Br.)

Mediterranean Sea

SPAIN
Madrid•
PORTUGAL
GIBRALTAR (Gr. Br.)

0   200   400 Mi.
0   200   400 Km.

received considerably more territory on France's eastern border, so as to stand as the "sentinel on the Rhine" against France. In these ways the Quadruple Alliance combined leniency toward France with strong defensive measures. They held out a carrot with one hand and picked up a bigger stick with the other.

In their moderation toward France the allies were motivated by self-interest and traditional ideas about the balance of power. To Metternich and Castlereagh, the foreign ministers of Austria and Great Britain, as well as their French counterpart Talleyrand, the balance of power meant an international equilibrium of political and military forces, which would preserve the freedom and independence of each of the Great Powers. Such a balance would discourage aggression by any combination of states or, worse, the domination of Europe by any single state. As they saw it, the task of the powers was thus twofold. They had to make sure that France would not dominate Europe again, and they also had to arrange international relations so that none of the victors would be tempted to strive for domination in its turn. Such a balance involved many considerations and all of Europe.

The balance of power was the mechanism used by the Great Powers—Austria, Britain, Prussia, Russia, and France—to settle their own dangerous disputes at the Congress of Vienna. There was general agreement among the victors that each of them should receive compensation in the form of territory for their successful struggle against the French. Great Britain had already won colonies and strategic outposts during the long wars, and these it retained. Metternich's Austria gave up territories in Belgium and southern Germany but expanded greatly elsewhere, taking the rich provinces of Venetia and Lombardy in northern Italy as well as its former Polish possessions and new lands on the eastern coast of the Adriatic (see Map 23.1). There was also agreement that Prussia and Russia should be compensated. But where, and to what extent? That was the ticklish question that almost led to renewed war in January 1815.

The vaguely progressive, impetuous Alexander I of Russia had already taken Finland and Bessarabia

on his northern and southern borders. Yet he burned with ambition to restore the ancient kingdom of Poland, on which he expected to bestow the benefits of his rule. The Prussians were willing to go along and give up their Polish territories, provided they could swallow up the large and wealthy kingdom of Saxony, their German neighbor to the south.

These demands were too much for Castlereagh and Metternich, who feared an unbalancing of forces in central Europe. In an astonishing about-face, they turned for diplomatic support to the wily Talleyrand and the defeated France he represented. On January 3, 1815, Great Britain, Austria, and France signed a secret alliance directed against Russia and Prussia. As Castlereagh concluded somberly, it appeared that the "peace we have so dearly purchased will be of short duration."[1]

The outcome, however, was compromise rather than war. When rumors of the alliance were intentionally leaked, the threat of war caused the rulers of Russia and Prussia to moderate their demands. They accepted Metternich's proposal: Russia established a small Polish kingdom, and Prussia received two-fifths rather than all of Saxony (see Map 23.1). This compromise was very much within the framework of balance-of-power ideology and eighteenth-century diplomacy: Great Powers became greater, but not too much greater. In addition, France had been able to intervene and tip the scales in favor of the side seeking to prevent undue expansion of Russia and Prussia. In so doing, France regained its Great Power status and was no longer isolated, as Talleyrand gleefully reported to Louis XVIII.

Unfortunately for France, as the final touches were being put on the peace settlement at Vienna, Napoleon suddenly reappeared on the scene. Escaping from his "comic kingdom" on the island of Elba in February 1815 and rallying his supporters for one last campaign during the Hundred Days, Napoleon was defeated at Waterloo and exiled to St. Helena. Yet the resulting peace—the second Peace of Paris—was still relatively moderate toward France. Fat old Louis XVIII was restored to his throne for a second time. France lost some territory, had to pay an indemnity of 700 million francs, and had to support a large army of occupation for five years.

The rest of the settlement already concluded at the Congress of Vienna was left intact. The members of the Quadruple Alliance did, however, agree

MAP 23.1 Europe in 1815 Europe's leaders re-established a balance of political power after the defeat of Napoleon.

to meet periodically to discuss their common interests and to consider appropriate measures for the maintenance of peace in Europe. This agreement marked the beginning of the European "congress system," which lasted long into the nineteenth century and settled international crises through diplomatic conferences.

Intervention and Repression

There was also a domestic political side to the re-establishment of peace. Within their own countries, the leaders of the victorious states were much less flexible. In 1815, under Metternich's leadership, Austria, Prussia, and Russia embarked on a crusade against the ideas and politics of the dual revolution. The crusade lasted until 1848.

The first step was the Holy Alliance, formed by Austria, Prussia, and Russia in September 1815. First proposed by Russia's Alexander I, the alliance proclaimed the intention of the three eastern monarchs to rule exclusively on the basis of Christian principles and to work together to maintain peace and justice on all occasions. Castlereagh refused to sign, characterizing the vague statement of principle as "a piece of sublime mysticism and nonsense." Yet it soon became a symbol of the repression of liberal and revolutionary movements all over Europe.

In 1820 revolutionaries succeeded in forcing the monarchs of Spain and the southern Italian kingdom of the Two Sicilies to grant liberal constitutions against their wills. Metternich was horrified: revolution was rising once again. Calling a conference at Troppau in Austria, under the provisions of the Quadruple Alliance, he and Alexander I proclaimed the principle of active intervention to maintain all autocratic regimes whenever they were threatened. Austrian forces then marched into Naples and restored Ferdinand I to the throne of the Two Sicilies. The French armies of Louis XVIII likewise restored the Spanish regime—after the Congress of Troppau had rejected Alexander's offer to send his Cossacks across Europe to teach the Spanish an unforgettable lesson.

Great Britain remained aloof, arguing that intervention in the domestic politics of foreign states was not an object of British diplomacy. In particular, Great Britain opposed any attempts by the restored Spanish monarchy to reconquer its former Latin American possessions, which had gained their independence during and after the Napoleonic wars. Encouraged by the British position, the young United States proclaimed its celebrated Monroe Doctrine in 1823. This bold document declared that European powers were to keep their hands off the New World and in no way attempt to re-establish their political system there. In the United States, constitutional liberalism, an ongoing challenge to the conservatism of continental Europe, retained its cutting edge.

In the years following the crushing of liberal revolution in southern Italy in 1821 and in Spain in 1823, Metternich continued to battle against liberal political change. Sometimes he could do little, as in the case of the new Latin American republics. Nor could he undo the dynastic changes of 1830 and 1831 in France and Belgium. Nonetheless, until 1848 Metternich's system proved quite effective in central Europe, where his power was the greatest.

Metternich's policies dominated not only Austria and the Italian peninsula but the entire German Confederation, which the peace settlement of Vienna had called into being. The confederation was composed of thirty-eight independent German states, including Prussia and Austria. (Neither Prussia's eastern territories nor the Hungarian half of the Austrian Empire was included in the confederation.) These states met in complicated assemblies dominated by Austria, with Prussia a willing junior partner in the planning and execution of repressive measures.

It was through the German Confederation that Metternich had the infamous Carlsbad Decrees issued in 1819. The decrees required the thirty-eight German member states to root out subversive ideas in their universities and newspapers. The decrees also established a permanent committee with spies and informers to investigate and punish any liberal or radical organizations. Metternich's ruthless imposition of repressive internal policies on the governments of central Europe contrasted with the intelligent moderation he had displayed in the general peace settlement of 1815.

Metternich and Conservatism

Metternich's determined defense of the status quo made him a villain in the eyes of most progressive, optimistic historians of the nineteenth century. Yet rather than denounce the man, it is more useful to try to understand him and the general conservatism he represented.

Born into the middle ranks of the landed nobility of the Rhineland, Prince Klemens von Metternich (1773–1859) was an internationally oriented aristocrat. In 1795 his splendid marriage to Eleonora von Kaunitz, granddaughter of a famous Austrian statesman and heiress to vast estates, opened the door to the highest court circles and a brilliant diplomatic career. Austrian ambassador to Napoleon's court in 1806 and Austrian foreign minister from 1809 to 1848, the cosmopolitan Metternich always remained loyal to his class and jealously defended its rights and privileges to the day he died. Like most other conservatives of his time, he did so with a clear conscience. The nobility was one of Europe's most ancient institutions, and conservatives regarded tradition as the basic source of human institutions. In their view, the proper state and society remained that of pre-1789 Europe, which rested on a judicious blend of monarchy, bureaucracy, and aristocracy.

Metternich's commitment to conservatism was coupled with a passionate hatred of liberalism. He firmly believed that liberalism, as embodied in revolutionary America and France, had been responsible for a generation of war with untold bloodshed and suffering. Liberal demands for representative government and civil liberties had unfortunately captured the imaginations of some middle-class lawyers, business people, and intellectuals. Metternich thought that these groups had been and still were engaged in a vast conspiracy to impose their beliefs on society and destroy the existing order. Like many other conservatives then and since, Metternich blamed liberal revolutionaries for stirring up the lower classes, whom he believed to be indifferent or hostile to liberal ideas, desiring nothing more than peace and quiet.

The threat of liberalism appeared doubly dangerous to Metternich because it generally went with national aspirations. Liberals, especially liberals in central Europe, believed that each people, each national group, had a right to establish its own independent government and seek to fulfill its own destiny. The idea of national self-determination was repellent to Metternich. It not only threatened the existence of the aristocracy, it also threatened to destroy the Austrian Empire and revolutionize central Europe.

The vast Austrian Empire of the Habsburgs was a great dynastic state. Formed over centuries by war, marriage, and luck, it was made up of many peoples speaking many languages (Map 23.2). The Germans, long the dominant element, had supported and profited by the long-term territorial expansion of Austria; yet they accounted for only a quarter of the population. The Magyars (Hungarians), a substantially smaller group, dominated the kingdom of Hungary—which was part of the Austrian Empire—though they did not account for a majority of the population even there.

The Czechs, the third major group, were concentrated in Bohemia and Moravia. There were also large numbers of Italians, Poles, and Ukrainians, as well as smaller groups of Slovenes, Croats, Serbs, Ruthenians, and Rumanians. The various Slavic peoples, together with the Italians and the Rumanians, represented a widely scattered and completely divided majority in an empire dominated by

Metternich   This portrait by Sir Thomas Lawrence reveals much of Metternich the man. Handsome, refined, and intelligent, Metternich was a great aristocrat passionately devoted to the defense of his class and its interests. *(Source: Copyright reserved to Her Majesty Queen Elizabeth II)*

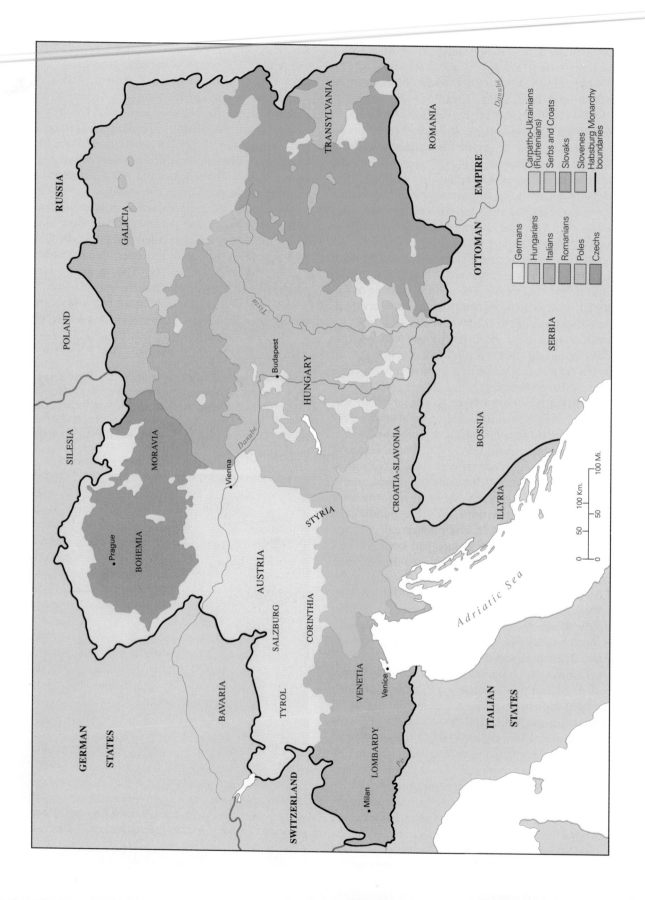

Germans and Hungarians. Different ethnic groups often lived in the same provinces and even the same villages. Thus the different parts and provinces of the empire differed in languages, customs, and institutions. They were held together primarily by their ties to the Habsburg emperor.

The multinational state Metternich served was both strong and weak. It was strong because of its large population and vast territories; it was weak because of its many and potentially dissatisfied nationalities. In these circumstances, Metternich virtually had to oppose liberalism and nationalism, for Austria was simply unable to accommodate those ideologies of the dual revolution. Other conservatives supported Austria because they could imagine no better fate for the jumble of small nationalities wedged precariously between masses of Germans and hordes of Russians in east central Europe. Castlereagh even went so far as to say that Austria was the "great hinge upon which the fate of Europe must ultimately depend." Metternich's repressive conservatism may not hold appeal for many people today, but it had understandable roots in the dilemma of a multinational state in an age of rising nationalism.

RADICAL IDEAS AND EARLY SOCIALISM

The years following the peace settlement of 1815 were years of profound intellectual activity. Intellectuals and social observers were seeking to understand the revolutionary changes that had occurred and were still taking place. These efforts led to ideas that still motivate the world.

Almost all of these basic ideas were radical. In one way or another they opposed the old, deeply felt conservatism that Metternich exemplified so well. The revived conservatism, with its stress on tradition, a hereditary monarchy, a strong and privileged landowning aristocracy, and an official church, was rejected by radicals. Instead, radicals developed and refined alternative visions—alterna-

MAP 23.2 Peoples of the Habsburg Monarchy, 1815 The old dynastic state was a patchwork of nationalities. Note the widely scattered pockets of Germans and Hungarians.

tive ideologies—and tried to convince society to act on them. With time, they were very successful.

Liberalism

The principal ideas of liberalism—liberty and equality—were by no means defeated in 1815. First realized successfully in the American Revolution and then achieved in part in the French Revolution, this political and social philosophy continued to pose a radical challenge to revived conservatism. Liberalism demanded representative government as opposed to autocratic monarchy, equality before the law as opposed to legally separate classes. The idea of liberty also continued to mean specific individual freedoms: freedom of the press, freedom of speech, freedom of assembly, and freedom from arbitrary arrest. In Europe, only France with Louis XVIII's Constitutional Charter and Great Britain with its Parliament and historic rights of English men and women had realized much of the liberal program in 1815. Even in those countries, liberalism had not fully succeeded; and elsewhere, liberal demands were still a call for revolutionary change.

Although liberalism still had its cutting edge, it was not as sharp a tool as it had been. This was true because liberalism in the early nineteenth century resolutely opposed government intervention in social and economic affairs, even if the need for action seemed great to social critics and reformers. This form of liberalism is often called "classical" liberalism in the United States, in order to distinguish it sharply from modern American liberalism, which usually favors more government programs to meet social needs and to regulate the economy. Classical liberalism's decline in radicalism was especially evident in its economic principles, which called for unrestricted private enterprise and no government interference in the economy. This philosophy was popularly known as the doctrine of *laissez faire.*

The idea of a free economy had first been persuasively formulated by a Scottish professor of philosophy, Adam Smith (1723–1790). Smith, whose *Inquiry into the Nature and Causes of the Wealth of Nations* (1776) founded modern economics, was highly critical of eighteenth-century mercantilism. Mercantilism, he said, meant stifling government regulations as well as unjust privileges for private monopolies and government favorites. Far preferable was free competition, which would give all citizens a fair and equal opportunity to do what they did best. Smith argued effectively that freely competitive private enterprise would result in greater income for everyone, not just the rich.

Unlike some of his contemporaries, Smith applauded the modest rise in real wages of British workers in the eighteenth century and went so far as to say, "No society can surely be flourishing and happy, of which the far greater part of the members are poor and miserable." Smith also believed that greater competition meant higher wages for workers, since manufacturers and "masters are always and everywhere in a sort of tacit, but constant and uniform, combination, not to raise the wages of laborers above their actual rate." In short, Adam Smith was a spokesman for general economic development, not narrow business interests.

In the early nineteenth century, the British economy was progressively liberalized, as old restrictions on trade and industry were relaxed or eliminated. This liberalization promoted continued economic growth in the Industrial Revolution. At the same time, however, economic liberalism and laissez-faire economic thought were tending to become a doctrine serving business interests. Businessmen used the doctrine to defend their right to do exactly as they wished in their factories. Labor unions were outlawed because they supposedly restricted free competition and the individual's "right to work."

The teachings of Thomas Malthus (1766–1834) and David Ricardo (1772–1823) helped especially to make economic liberalism an ideology of business interests in many people's minds. As we have seen (page 702), Malthus argued that population would always tend to grow faster than the supply of food. This led Ricardo to formulate his "iron law of wages," which said that, because of the pressure of population growth, wages would be just high enough to keep the workers from starving. Malthus and Ricardo thought of themselves as objective social scientists. Yet their teachings were often used by industrial and middle-class interests in England, the Continent, and the United States to justify opposing any kind of government action to protect or improve the lot of workers: if workers were poor, it was their own fault, the result of their breeding like rabbits.

In the early nineteenth century, liberal political ideals also became more closely associated with narrow class interests. Early-nineteenth-century liberals favored representative government, but they generally wanted property qualifications attached to the right to vote. In practice, this meant limiting the vote to well-to-do aristocratic landowners, substantial businessmen, and successful members of the professions. Workers and peasants as well as the lower middle class of shopkeepers, clerks, and artisans did not own the necessary property and thus could not vote.

As liberalism became increasingly middle-class after 1815, some intellectuals and foes of conservatism felt that it did not go nearly far enough. Inspired by memories of the French Revolution and the contemporary example of exuberant Jacksonian democracy in the young American republic, they called for universal voting rights, at least for males. Giving all men the vote, they felt, would allow the masses to join in government and would lead to democracy.

Many people who believed in democracy also believed in the republican form of government. They detested the power of the monarchy, the privileges of the aristocracy, and the great wealth of the upper middle class. These democrats and republicans were more radical than the liberals. Taking for granted much of the liberal program, they sought to go beyond it. Democrats and republicans were also more willing than most liberals to endorse violent upheaval to achieve goals. All of this meant that liberals and radical, democratic republicans could join forces against conservatives only up to a point.

Nationalism

Nationalism was a second radical idea in the years after 1815, an idea destined to have an enormous influence in the modern world. In a summation of this complex ideology, three points stand out. First, nationalism has normally evolved from a real or imagined *cultural* unity, manifesting itself especially in a common language, history, and territory. Second, nationalists have usually sought to turn this cultural unity into *political* reality, so that the territory of each people coincides with its state boundaries. It was this goal that made nationalism so potentially explosive in central and eastern Europe after 1815, when there were either too few states (Austria, Russia, and the Ottoman Empire) or too many (the Italian peninsula and the German Confederation) and when different peoples overlapped and intermingled. Third, modern nationalism had its immediate origins in the French Revolution and the Napoleonic wars. Nationalism was effectively harnessed by the French republic during the Reign of Terror to help repel foreign foes, and all across Europe patriots tried to kindle nationalist flames in the war against Napoleon. Thus by 1815 there were already hints of nationalism's remarkable ability to spread and develop.

Between 1815 and 1850, most people who believed in nationalism also believed in either liberalism or radical, democratic republicanism. In more recent times, however, many governments have been very nationalistic without favoring liberty and democracy. Why, then, was love of liberty almost synonymous with love of nation in the early nineteenth century?

A common faith in the creativity and nobility of the people was perhaps the single most important reason for linking these two concepts. Liberals and especially democrats saw the people as the ultimate source of all government. The people (or some of them) elected their officials and governed themselves within a framework of personal liberty. Yet such self-government would be possible only if the people were united by common traditions and common loyalties. In practice, common loyalties rested above all on a common language. Thus liberals and nationalists agreed that a shared language forged the basic unity of a people, a unity that transcended local or provincial interests and even class differences.

Early nationalists usually believed that every nation, like every citizen, had the right to exist in freedom and to develop its character and spirit. They were confident that the independence and freedom of other nations, as in the case of other citizens within a nation, would not lessen the freedom of their own country. Rather, the symphony of nations would promote the harmony and ultimate unity of all peoples. As the French historian Jules Michelet put it in *The People* in 1846, each citizen "learns to recognize his country . . . as a note in the grand concert; through it he himself participates and loves the world." Similarly, the Italian patriot

Giuseppe Mazzini believed that "in laboring according to the true principles of our country we are laboring for Humanity." Thus the liberty of the individual and the love of a free nation overlapped greatly in the early nineteenth century.

Nationalism also had a negative side to it. Even as they talked of serving the cause of humanity, early nationalists stressed the differences among peoples. The German pastor and philosopher Johann Herder (1744–1803) had argued that every people has its own particular spirit and genius, which it expresses through its culture and language. Yet Herder (and others after him) could not define the uniqueness of the French, German, and Slavic peoples without comparing and contrasting one people with another. Thus, even early nationalism developed a strong sense of "we" and "they."

"They" were often the enemy. The leader of the Czech cultural revival, the passionate democrat and nationalist historian Francis Palacký, is a good example of this tendency. In his histories he lauded the achievements of the Czech people, which he characterized as a long struggle against brutal German domination. To this "we–they" outlook, it was all too easy for nationalists to add two other highly volatile ingredients: a sense of national mission and a sense of national superiority. As Mazzini characteristically wrote, "Peoples never stop before they have achieved the ultimate aim of their existence, before having fulfilled their mission." Even Michelet, so alive to the aspirations of other peoples, could not help speaking in 1846 of the "superiority of France"; the principles espoused in the French Revolution had made France the "salvation of mankind."

German and Spanish nationalists had a very different opinion of France. To them the French often seemed as oppressive as the Germans seemed to the Czechs, as hateful as the Russians seemed to the Poles. The despised enemy's mission might seem as oppressive as the American national mission seemed to the Mexicans after the U.S. annexation of Texas. In 1845 the American journalist and strident nationalist John Louis O'Sullivan wrote that taking land from an "imbecile and distracted Mexico" was a laudable step in the "fulfillment of our manifest destiny to overspread the continent allotted by Providence for the free development of our yearly multiplying millions."[2]

Early nationalism was thus ambiguous. Its main thrust was liberal and democratic. But below the surface lurked ideas of national superiority and national mission, which could lead to aggressive crusades and counter-crusades, as had happened in the French Revolution and in the "wars of liberation" against Napoleon.

French Utopian Socialism

To understand the rise of socialism, one must begin with France. Despite the fact that France lagged far behind Great Britain in developing modern industry, almost all the early socialists were French. Although they differed on many specific points, these French thinkers were acutely aware that the political revolution in France and the rise of modern industry in England had begun a transformation of society. Yet they were disturbed by what they saw. Liberal practices in politics and economics appeared to be fomenting selfish individualism and splitting the community into isolated fragments. There was, they believed, an urgent need for a further reorganization of society to establish cooperation and a new sense of community. Starting from this shared outlook, individual French thinkers went in many different directions. They searched the past, analyzed existing conditions, and fashioned luxurious utopias. Yet certain ideas tied their critiques and visions together.

Early French socialists believed in economic planning. Inspired by the emergency measures of 1793 and 1794 in France, they argued that the government should rationally organize the economy and not depend on destructive competition to do the job. Early socialists also shared an intense desire to help the poor and to protect them from the rich. With passionate moral fervor, they preached that the rich and the poor should be more nearly equal economically. Finally, socialists believed that most private property should be abolished and replaced by state or community ownership. Planning, greater economic equality, and state ownership of property: these were the key ideas of early French socialism and of all socialism since.

One of the most influential early socialist thinkers was a nobleman, Count Henri de Saint-Simon (1760–1825). A curious combination of radical thinker and successful land speculator, Saint-Simon optimistically proclaimed the tremendous possibilities of industrial development: "The age of gold is before us!" The key to progress was proper social organization. Such an arrangement of society required the "parasites"—the court, the aristocracy, lawyers, churchmen—to give way, once and for all, to the "doers"—the leading scientists, engineers, and industrialists. The doers would carefully plan the economy and guide it forward by undertaking vast public works projects and establishing investment banks. Saint-Simon also stressed in highly moralistic terms that every social institution ought to have as its main goal improved conditions for the poor. Saint-Simon's stress on industry and science inspired middle-class industrialists and bankers, like the Pereire brothers, founders of the Crédit Mobilier (see page 708).

After 1830 the socialist critique of capitalism became sharper. Charles Fourier (1772–1837), a lonely, saintly man with a tenuous hold on reality, described a socialist utopia in lavish mathematical detail. Hating the urban wage system, Fourier envisaged self-sufficient communities of 1,620 people living communally on 5,000 acres devoted to a combination of agriculture and industry. Although Fourier waited in vain each day at noon in his apartment for a wealthy philanthropist to endow his visionary schemes, he was very influential. Several utopian communities were founded along the lines he prescribed, mainly in the United States.

Fourier was also an early proponent of the total emancipation of women. Extremely critical of middle-class family life, Fourier believed that most marriages were only another kind of prostitution. According to Fourier, young single women were shamelessly "sold" to their future husbands for dowries and other financial considerations. Therefore, Fourier called for the abolition of marriage, free unions based only on love, and complete sexual freedom. Many middle-class men and women found these ideas, which were shared and even practiced by some followers of Saint Simon, shocking and immoral. The socialist program for the liberation of women as well as workers appeared to them as doubly dangerous and revolutionary.

Louis Blanc (1811–1882), a sharp-eyed, intelligent journalist, was much more practical. In his *Organization of Work* (1839), he urged workers to agitate for universal voting rights and to take control of the state peacefully. Blanc believed that the full power of the state should be directed at setting up government-backed workshops and factories to

Fourier's Utopia   The vision of a harmonious planned community freed from capitalism and selfish individualism radiates from this 1847 illustration of Fourier's principles. *(Source: Mary Evans Picture Library/Photo Researchers)*

guarantee full employment. The right to work had to become as sacred as any other right. Finally, there was Pierre Joseph Proudhon (1809–1865), a self-educated printer, who wrote a pamphlet in 1840 entitled *What Is Property?* His answer was that it was nothing but theft. Property was profit that was stolen from the worker, who was the source of all wealth. Unlike most socialists, Proudhon feared the power of the state and was often considered an anarchist.

Thus a variety of French thinkers blazed the way with utopian socialism in the 1830s and 1840s. Their ideas were very influential, particularly in Paris, where poverty-stricken workers with a revolutionary tradition were attentive students. Yet the economic arguments of the French utopians were weak, and their specific programs usually seemed too fanciful to be taken seriously. To Karl Marx was left the task of establishing firm foundations for modern socialism.

The Birth of Marxian Socialism

In 1848 the thirty-year-old Karl Marx (1818–1883) and the twenty-eight-year-old Friedrich Engels (1820–1895) published the *Communist Manifesto,* the bible of socialism. The son of a Jewish lawyer who had converted to Christianity, the atheistic young Marx had studied philosophy at the University of Berlin before turning to journalism and economics. He read widely in French socialist thought and was influenced by it. He shared Fourier's view of middle-class marriage as legalized prostitution, and he too looked forward to the emancipation of women and the abolition of the family. But by the time he was twenty-five, he was developing his own socialist ideas.

Early French socialists often appealed to the middle class and the state to help the poor. Marx ridiculed such appeals as naive. He argued that the interests of the middle class and those of the

The Marx Family In 1849 the exiled Marx settled in London. There he wrote *Capital,* the weighty exposition of his socialist theories, and worked to organize the working class. With his coauthor and financial supporter Friedrich Engels (right), Marx is shown here with his daughters, ironically a picture of middle-class respectability. *(Source: Culver Pictures)*

industrial working class are inevitably opposed to each other. Indeed, according to the *Manifesto,* the "history of all previously existing society is the history of class struggles." In Marx's view, one class had always exploited the other, and with the advent of modern industry, society was split more clearly than ever before: between the middle class—the bourgeoisie—and the modern working class—the proletariat. Moreover, the bourgeoisie had reduced everything to a matter of money and "naked self-interest." "In a word, for exploitation, veiled by religious and political illusions, the bourgeoisie had substituted naked, shameless, direct brutal exploitation."

Just as the bourgeoisie had triumphed over the feudal aristocracy, Marx predicted, the proletariat was destined to conquer the bourgeoisie in a violent revolution. While a tiny minority owned the means of production and grew richer, the ever-poorer proletariat was constantly growing in size and in class consciousness. In this process, the proletariat was aided, according to Marx, by a portion of the bourgeoisie who had gone over to the proletariat and who (like Marx and Engels) "had raised themselves to the level of comprehending theoretically the historical moment." And the critical moment was very near. "Let the ruling classes tremble at a Communist revolution. The proletarians have nothing to lose but their chains. They have a world to win. WORKING MEN OF ALL COUNTRIES, UNITE!" So ends the *Communist Manifesto.*

In brief outline, Marx's ideas may seem to differ only slightly from the wild and improbable ideas of the utopians of his day. Yet whatever one may think of the validity of Marx's analysis, he must be taken seriously. He united sociology, economics, and all human history in a vast and imposing edifice. He synthesized in his socialism not only French utopian schemes but English classical economics and German philosophy—the major intellectual currents of his day. Moreover, after the young Marx fled to England as a penniless political refugee following the revolutions of 1848, he continued to show a rare flair for combining complex theorization with both lively popular writing and practical organizational ability. This combination of theoretical and practical skills contributed greatly to the subsequent diffusion of Marx's socialist synthesis after 1860, as will be shown in Chapter 25 (see page 817).

Marx's debt to England was great. He was the last of the classical economists. Following David Ricardo, who had taught that labor was the source of all value, Marx went on to argue that profits were really wages stolen from the workers. Moreover, Marx incorporated Engels's charges of terrible oppression of the new class of factory workers in England; thus his doctrines seemed to be based on hard facts.

Marx's theory of historical evolution was built on the philosophy of the German Georg Hegel (1770–1831). Hegel believed that history is "ideas in motion": each age is characterized by a dominant set of ideas, which produces opposing ideas and eventually a new synthesis. The idea of being had been dominant initially, for example, and it had produced its antithesis, the idea of nonbeing. This idea in turn had resulted in the synthesis of becoming. Thus history has pattern and purpose.

Marx retained Hegel's view of history as a dialectic process of change but made economic relationships between classes the driving force. This dialectic explained the decline of agrarian feudalism and the rise of industrial capitalism. And Marx stressed again and again that the "bourgeoisie, historically, has played a most revolutionary part. . . . During its rule of scarcely one hundred years the bourgeoisie has created more massive and more colossal productive forces than have all preceding generations together." Here was a convincing explanation for people trying to make sense of the dual revolution. Marx's next idea, that it was now the bourgeoisie's turn to give way to the socialism of revolutionary workers, appeared to many the irrefutable capstone of a brilliant interpretation of humanity's long development. Thus Marx pulled together powerful ideas and insights to create one of the great secular religions out of the intellectual ferment of the early nineteenth century.

THE ROMANTIC MOVEMENT

Radical concepts of politics and society were accompanied by comparable changes in literature and other arts during the dual revolution. The early nineteenth century marked the acme of the romantic movement, which profoundly influenced the arts and enriched European culture immeasurably.

The romantic movement was in part a revolt against classicism and the Enlightenment. Classicism was essentially a set of artistic rules and standards that went hand in glove with the Enlightenment's belief in rationality, order, and restraint. The classicists believed that the ancient Greeks and Romans had discovered eternally valid aesthetic rules and that playwrights and painters should continue to follow them. Classicists could enforce these rules in the eighteenth century because they dominated the courts and academies for which artists worked.

Forerunners of the romantic movement appeared from about 1750 on. Of these, Rousseau (see page 581)—the passionate advocate of feeling, freedom, and natural goodness—was the most influential. Romanticism then crystallized fully in the 1790s, primarily in England and Germany. The French Revolution kindled the belief that radical reconstruction was also possible in cultural and artistic life (even though many early English and German romantics became disillusioned with events in France and turned from liberalism to conservatism in politics). Romanticism gained strength until the 1840s.

Romanticism

Romanticism was characterized by a belief in emotional exuberance, unrestrained imagination, and spontaneity in both art and personal life. In Germany early romantics of the 1770s and 1780s called themselves the "Storm and Stress" (*Sturm und Drang*) group, and many romantic artists of the early nineteenth century lived lives of tremendous emotional intensity. Suicide, duels to the death, madness, and strange illnesses were not uncommon among leading romantics. Romantic artists typically led bohemian lives, wearing their hair long and uncombed in preference to powdered wigs and living in cold garrets rather than frequenting stiff drawing rooms. They rejected materialism and sought to escape to lofty spiritual heights through their art. Great individualists, the romantics believed the full development of one's unique human potential to be the supreme purpose in life. The romantics were driven by a sense of an unlimited universe and by a yearning for the unattained, the unknown, the unknowable.

Nowhere was the break with classicism more apparent than in romanticism's general conception of nature. Classicism was not particularly interested in nature. In the words of the eighteenth-century English author Samuel Johnson, "A blade of grass is always a blade of grass; men and women are my subjects of inquiry." Nature was portrayed by classicists as beautiful and chaste, like an eighteenth-century formal garden. The romantics, on the other hand, were enchanted by nature. Sometimes they found it awesome and tempestuous, as in Théodore Géricault's painting *The Raft of the Medusa,* which shows the survivors of a shipwreck adrift in a turbulent sea. Others saw nature as a source of spiritual inspiration. As the great English landscape artist John Constable declared, "Nature is Spirit visible."

Most romantics saw the growth of modern industry as an ugly, brutal attack on their beloved nature and on the human personality. They sought escape—in the unspoiled Lake District of northern England, in exotic North Africa, in an idealized Middle Ages. Yet some romantics found a vast, awesome, terribly moving power in the new industrial landscape. In ironworks and cotton mills they saw the flames of hell and the evil genius of Satan himself. One of John Martin's last and greatest paintings, *The Great Day of His Wrath* (1850), vividly depicts the Last Judgment foretold in Revelation 6, when the "sun became black as sackcloth of hair, and the moon became as blood; and the stars of heaven fell unto the earth." Martin's romantic masterpiece was inspired directly by a journey through the "Black country" of the industrial Midlands in the dead of night. According to Martin's son:

The glow of the furnaces, the red blaze of light, together with the liquid fire, seemed to him truly sublime and awful. He could not imagine anything more terrible even in the regions of everlasting punishment. All he had done or attempted in ideal painting fell far short, very far short, of the fearful sublimity.[3]

Fascinated by color and diversity, the romantic imagination turned toward the study and writing of history with a passion. For romantics, history was not a minor branch of philosophy from which philosophers picked suitable examples to illustrate their teachings. History was beautiful, exciting, and important in its own right. It was the art of change over time—the key to a universe that was now perceived to be organic and dynamic. It was no longer perceived to be mechanical and static as it had to

Constable: The Hay Wain Constable's love of a spiritualized and poetic nature radiates from this masterpiece of romantic art. Exhibited in Paris in 1824, *The Hay Wain* created a sensation and made a profound impression on the young Delacroix. *(Source: Courtesy of the Trustees, The National Gallery, London)*

the philosophes of the eighteenth-century Enlightenment.

Historical studies supported the development of national aspirations and encouraged entire peoples to seek in the past their special destinies. This trend was especially strong in Germany and eastern Europe. As the famous English historian Lord Acton put it, the growth of historical thinking associated with the romantic movement was a most fateful step in the story of European thought.

Literature

Britain was the first country where romanticism flowered fully in poetry and prose, and the British romantic writers were among the most prominent in Europe. Wordsworth, Coleridge, and Scott were all active by 1800, to be followed shortly by Byron, Shelley, and Keats. All were poets: romanticism found its distinctive voice in poetry, as the Enlightenment had in prose.

A towering leader of English romanticism, William Wordsworth (1770–1850) traveled in France after his graduation from Cambridge. There he fell passionately in love with a French woman, who bore him a daughter. He was deeply influenced by the philosophy of Rousseau and the spirit of the early French Revolution. Back in England, prevented by war and the Terror from returning to France, Wordsworth settled in the countryside with his sister Dorothy and Samuel Taylor Coleridge (1772–1834).

In 1798 the two poets published their *Lyrical Ballads,* one of the most influential literary works in the history of the English language. In defiance of classical rules, Wordsworth and Coleridge abandoned flowery poetic conventions for the language of ordinary speech, simultaneously endowing simple subjects with the loftiest majesty. This twofold rejection of classical practice was at first ignored and then harshly criticized, but by 1830 Wordsworth had triumphed.

One of the best examples of Wordsworth's romantic credo and genius is "Daffodils":

I wandered lonely as a cloud
That floats on high o'er vales and hills,
When all at once I saw a crowd,
A host, of golden daffodils;
Beside the lake, beneath the trees,
Fluttering and dancing in the breeze.

Continuous as the stars that shine
And twinkle on the Milky Way,
They stretched in never-ending line
Along the margin of a bay:
Ten thousand saw I at a glance,
Tossing their heads in sprightly dance.

The waves beside them danced, but they
Out-did the sparkling waves in glee:
A poet could not but be gay,
In such a jocund company:
I gazed—and gazed—but little thought
What wealth the show to me had brought:

For oft, when on my couch I lie
In vacant or in pensive mood,
They flash upon that inward eye
Which is the bliss of solitude;
And then my heart with pleasure fills,
And dances with the daffodils.

Here indeed are simplicity and love of nature in commonplace forms. Here, too, is Wordsworth's romantic conviction that nature has the power to elevate and instruct, especially when interpreted by a high-minded poetic genius. Wordsworth's conception of poetry as the "spontaneous overflow of powerful feeling recollected in tranquility" is well illustrated by the last stanza.

Born in Edinburgh, Walter Scott (1771–1832) personified the romantic movement's fascination with history. Raised on his grandfather's farm, Scott fell under the spell of the old ballads and tales of the Scottish border. He was also deeply influenced by German romanticism, particularly by the immortal poet and dramatist Johann Wolfgang von Goethe (1749–1832). Scott translated Goethe's famous *Gotz von Berlichingen,* a play about a sixteenth-century knight who revolted against centralized authority and championed individual freedom—at least in Goethe's romantic drama. A natural storyteller, Scott then composed long narrative poems and a series of historical novels. Scott excelled in faithfully recreating the spirit of bygone ages and great historical events, especially those of Scotland.

At first, the strength of classicism in France inhibited the growth of romanticism there. Then, between 1820 and 1850, the romantic impulse broke through in the poetry and prose of Lamartine, Alfred de Vigny, Victor Hugo, Alexander Dumas, and George Sand. Of these, Victor Hugo (1802–1885) was the greatest in both poetry and prose.

Son of a Napoleonic general, Hugo achieved an amazing range of rhythm, language, and image in his lyric poetry. His powerful novels exemplified the romantic fascination with fantastic characters, strange settings, and human emotions. The hero of Hugo's famous *Hunchback of Notre Dame* (1831) is the great cathedral's deformed bellringer, a "human gargoyle" overlooking the teeming life of fifteenth-century Paris. A great admirer of Shakespeare, whom classical critics had derided as undisciplined and excessive, Hugo also championed romanticism in drama. His play *Hernani* (1830) consciously broke all the old rules, as Hugo renounced his early conservatism and equated freedom in literature with liberty in politics and society. Hugo's political evolution was thus exactly the opposite of Wordsworth's, in whom youthful radicalism gave way to middle-aged caution. As the contrast between the two artists suggests, romanticism was a cultural movement compatible with many political beliefs.

Amandine Aurore Lucie Dupin (1804–1876), a strong-willed and gifted woman generally known by her pen name, George Sand, defied the narrow conventions of her time in an unending search for self-fulfillment. After eight years of unhappy marriage in the provinces, she abandoned her dullard of a husband and took her two children to Paris to pursue a career as a writer. There Sand soon achieved fame and wealth, eventually writing over eighty novels on a variety of romantic and social themes. All were shot through with a typically romantic love of nature and moral idealism. George Sand's striking individualism went far beyond her flamboyant preference for men's clothing and cigars and her notorious affairs with the poet Alfred de Musset and the composer Frédéric Chopin, among others. Her semi-autobiographical novel *Lélia* was shockingly modern, delving deeply into her tortuous quest for sexual and personal freedom.

In central and eastern Europe, literary romanticism and early nationalism often reinforced each other. Seeking a unique greatness in every people, well-educated romantics plumbed their own histories and cultures. Like modern anthropologists, they turned their attention to peasant life and transcribed the folk songs, tales, and proverbs that the cosmopolitan Enlightenment had disdained. The brothers Jacob and Wilhelm Grimm were particularly successful at rescuing German fairy tales from oblivion. In the Slavic lands, romantics played a decisive role in converting spoken peasant languages into modern written languages. The greatest of all Russian poets, Alexander Pushkin (1799–1837), rejecting eighteenth-century attempts to force Russian poetry into a classical strait jacket, used his lyric genius to mold the modern literary language.

Art and Music

The greatest and most moving romantic painter in France was Eugène Delacroix (1798–1863), probably the illegitimate son of the French foreign minister Talleyrand. Delacroix was a master of dramatic, colorful scenes that stir the emotions. He was fascinated with remote and exotic subjects, whether lion hunts in Morocco or the languishing, sensuous women of a sultan's harem. Yet he was also a passionate spokesman for freedom. His masterpiece, *Liberty Leading the People,* celebrated the nobility of popular revolution in general and revolution in France in particular.

In England the most notable romantic painters were J. M. W. Turner (1775–1851) and John Constable (1776–1837). Both were fascinated by nature, but their interpretations of it contrasted sharply, aptly symbolizing the tremendous emotional range of the romantic movement. Turner depicted nature's power and terror; wild storms and sinking ships were favorite subjects. Constable painted gentle Wordsworthian landscapes in which human beings were at one with their environment, the comforting countryside of unspoiled rural England.

It was in music that romanticism realized most fully and permanently its goals of free expression and emotional intensity. Whereas the composers of the eighteenth century had remained true to well-defined structures, like the classical symphony, the great romantics used a great range of forms to create a thousand musical landscapes and evoke a host of powerful emotions. Romantic composers also transformed the small classical orchestra, tripling its size by adding wind instruments, percussion, and more brass and strings. The crashing chords evoking the surge of the masses in Chopin's "Revolutionary" etude, the bottomless despair of the funeral march in Beethoven's Third Symphony, the solemn majesty of a great religious event in Schumann's Rhenish Symphony—such were the modern orchestra's musical paintings that plumbed the depths of human feeling.

This range and intensity gave music and musicians much greater prestige than in the past. Music no longer simply complemented a church service or helped a nobleman digest his dinner. Music became a sublime end in itself. It became for many the greatest of the arts, precisely because it achieved the most ecstatic effect and most perfectly realized the endless yearning of the soul. It was worthy of great concert halls and the most dedicated sacrifice. The unbelievable one-in-a-million performer—the great virtuoso who could transport the listener to ecstasy and hysteria—became a cultural hero. The composer Franz Liszt (1811–1886) vowed to do for the piano what Paganini had done for the violin, and he was lionized as the greatest pianist of his age. People swooned for Liszt as they scream for rock stars today.

Though romanticism dominated music until late in the nineteenth century, no composer ever surpassed its first great master, Ludwig van Beethoven (1770–1827). Extending and breaking open classical forms, Beethoven used contrasting themes and tones to produce dramatic conflict and inspiring resolutions. As the contemporary German novelist Ernst Hoffmann (1776–1822) wrote, "Beethoven's music sets in motion the lever of fear, of awe,

Heroes of Romanticism   Observed by a portrait of Byron and bust of Beethoven, Liszt plays for friends. From left to right sit Alexander Dumas, George Sand (characteristically wearing men's garb), and Marie d'Agoult, Liszt's mistress. Standing are Victor Hugo, Paganini, and Rossini. *(Source: Bildarchiv Preussischer Kulturbesitz)*

of horror, of suffering, and awakens just that infinite longing which is the essence of Romanticism." Beethoven's range was tremendous; his output included symphonies, chamber music, sonatas for violin and piano, masses, an opera, and a great many songs.

At the peak of his fame, in constant demand as a composer and recognized as the leading concert pianist of his day, Beethoven began to lose his hearing. He considered suicide but eventually overcame despair: "I will take fate by the throat; it will not bend me completely to its will."[4] Beethoven continued to pour out immortal music. Among other achievements, he fully exploited for the first time the richness and beauty of the piano. Beethoven never heard much of his later work, including the unforgettable choral finale to the Ninth Symphony, for his last years were silent, spent in total deafness.

REFORMS AND REVOLUTIONS

While the romantic movement was developing, liberal, national, and socialist forces battered against the conservatism of 1815. In some countries, change occurred gradually and peacefully. Elsewhere, pressure built up like steam in a pressure cooker without a safety valve and eventually caused an explosion in 1848. Three important countries —Greece, Great Britain, and France—experienced variations on this basic theme.

National Liberation in Greece

National, liberal revolution, frustrated in Italy and Spain by conservative statesmen, succeeded first after 1815 in Greece. Since the fifteenth century, the Greeks had been living under the domination of the Ottoman Turks. In spite of centuries of foreign rule, the Greeks had survived as a people, united by their language and the Greek Orthodox religion. It was perfectly natural that the general growth of national aspirations and a desire for independence would inspire some Greeks in the early nineteenth century. This rising national movement led to the formation of secret societies and then to revolt in 1821, led by Alexander Ypsilanti, a Greek patriot and a general in the Russian army.

The Great Powers, particularly Metternich, were opposed to all revolution, even revolution against the Islamic Turks. They refused to back Ypsilanti and supported the Ottoman Empire. Yet for many Europeans the Greek cause became a holy one. Educated Americans and Europeans were in love with the culture of classical Greece; Russians were stirred by the piety of their Orthodox brethren. Writers and artists, moved by the romantic impulse, responded enthusiastically to the Greek struggle. The flamboyant, radical poet Lord Byron went to Greece and died there in the struggle "that Greece might still be free." Turkish atrocities toward the rebels fanned the fires of European outrage and Greek determination. One of Delacroix's romantic masterpieces memorialized the massacre at Chios, where the Turks slaughtered nearly 100,000 Greeks.

The Greeks, though often quarreling among themselves, battled on against the Turks and hoped for the eventual support of European governments. In 1827 Great Britain, France, and Russia responded to popular demands at home and directed Turkey to accept an armistice. When the Turks refused, the navies of these three powers trapped the Turkish fleet at Navarino and destroyed it. Russia then declared another of its periodic wars of expansion against the Turks. This led to the establishment of a Russian protectorate over much of present-day Rumania, which had also been under Turkish rule. Great Britain, France, and Russia finally declared Greece independent in 1830 and installed a German prince as king of the new country in 1832. In the end the Greeks had won: a small nation had gained its independence in a heroic war against a foreign empire.

Liberal Reform in Great Britain

Eighteenth-century British society had been both flexible and remarkably stable. It was dominated by the landowning aristocracy, but that class was neither closed nor rigidly defined. Successful business and professional people could buy land and become gentlefolk, while the common people had more than the usual opportunities of the preindustrial world. Basic civil rights for all were balanced by a tradition of deference to one's social superiors. Parliament was manipulated by the king and was thoroughly undemocratic. Only about 6 percent of

Delacroix: Massacre at Chios   The Greek struggle for freedom and independence won the enthusiastic support of liberals, nationalists, and romantics. The Ottoman Turks were seen as cruel oppressors holding back the course of history, as in this powerful masterpiece by Delacroix. *(Source: Louvre/Cliché des Musées Nationaux, Paris)*

the population could vote for representatives to Parliament, and by the 1780s there was growing interest in some kind of political reform.

But the French Revolution threw the aristocracy into a panic for a generation, making it extremely hostile to any attempts to change the status quo. The Tory party, completely controlled by the landed aristocracy, was particularly fearful of radical movements at home and abroad. Castlereagh

initially worked closely with Metternich to restrain France and restore a conservative balance in central Europe. This same intense conservatism motivated the Tory government at home. After 1815 the aristocracy defended its ruling position by repressing every kind of popular protest.

The first step in this direction began with revision of the Corn Laws in 1815. Corn Laws to regulate the foreign grain trade had long existed, but

escaped famine. Thereafter, free trade became almost sacred doctrine in Great Britain.

The following year, the Tories passed a bill designed to help the working classes, but in a different way. This was the Ten Hours Act of 1847, which limited the workday for women and young people in factories to ten hours. Tory aristocrats continued to champion legislation regulating factory conditions. They were competing vigorously with the middle class for the support of the working class. This healthy competition between a still-vigorous aristocracy and a strong middle class was a crucial factor in Great Britain's peaceful evolution. The working classes could make temporary alliances with either competitor to better their own conditions.

The people of Ireland did not benefit from this political competition. Long ruled as a conquered people, the great mass of the population (outside the northern counties of Ulster, which were partly Presbyterian) were Irish Catholic peasants, who rented their land from a tiny minority of Church of England Protestants, many of whom lived in England (see Chapter 20). Ruthlessly exploited and growing rapidly in numbers, Irish peasants had come to depend on the potato crop, the size of which varied substantially from year to year. Potato failures cannot be detected in time to plant other crops, nor can potatoes be stored for more than a year. Moreover, Ireland's precarious potato economy was a subsistence economy, which therefore lacked a well-developed network of roads and trade capable of distributing other foods in time of disaster. When the crop failed in 1845, the Irish were very vulnerable.

In 1846, 1848, and 1851, the potato crop failed again in Ireland and throughout much of Europe. The general result was high food prices, widespread

Evictions of Irish Peasants who could not pay their rent continued for decades after the famine. Surrounded by a few meager possessions, this family has been turned out of its cottage in the 1880s. The door is nailed shut to prevent their return. *(Source: Lawrence Collection, National Library of Ireland, Dublin)*

Delacroix: Liberty Leading the People   This great romantic painting glorifies the July Revolution in Paris in 1830. Raising high the revolutionary tricolor, Liberty unites the worker, bourgeois, and street child in a righteous crusade against privilege and oppression. *(Source: Louvre/Cliché des Musées Nationaux, Paris)*

suffering, and, frequently, social upheaval. In Ireland, the result was unmitigated disaster—the Great Famine. Blight attacked the young plants, and the tubers rotted. Widespread starvation and mass fever epidemics followed. Total losses of population were staggering. Fully 1 million emigrants fled the famine between 1845 and 1851, going primarily to the United States and Great Britain, and at least 1.5 million people died or went unborn because of the disaster. The British government's efforts at famine relief were too little and too late. At the same time, the government energetically supported the heartless demands of landowners with armed force. Tenants who could not pay their rents

were evicted and their homes broken up or burned. Famine or no, Ireland remained a coquered province, a poor agricultural land that had gained little from the liberal reforms and the industrial developments that were transforming Great Britain.

The Revolution of 1830 in France

Louis XVIII's Constitutional Charter of 1814—theoretically a gift from the king but actually a response to political pressures—was basically a liberal constitution (see page 687). The economic gains of the middle class and the prosperous peasantry were fully protected; great intellectual and artistic freedom was permitted; and a real parliament with upper and lower houses was created. Immediately after Napoleon's abortive Hundred Days, the moderate, worldly-wise king refused to bow to the wishes of diehard aristocrats like his brother Charles, who wished to sweep away all the revolutionary changes and return to a bygone age of royal absolutism and aristocratic pretension. Instead, Louis appointed as his ministers moderate royalists, who sought and obtained the support of a majority of the representatives elected to the lower Chamber of Deputies between 1816 and Louis's death in 1824.

Louis XVIII's charter was anything but democratic. Only about 100,000 of the wealthiest people out of a total population of 30 million had the right to vote for the deputies who, with the king and his ministers, made the laws of the nation. Nonetheless, the "notable people" who did vote came from very different backgrounds. There were wealthy businessmen, war profiteers, successful professionals, ex-revolutionaries, large landowners from the middle class, Bourbons, and Bonapartists.

The old aristocracy with its pre-1789 mentality was a minority within the voting population. It was this situation that Louis's successor, Charles X (r. 1824–1830), could not abide. Crowned in a lavish, utterly medieval, five-hour ceremony in the cathedral of Reims in 1824, Charles was a true reactionary. He wanted to re-establish the old order in France. Increasingly blocked by the opposition of the deputies, Charles finally repudiated the Constitutional Charter in an attempted coup in July 1830. He issued decrees stripping much of the wealthy middle class of its voting rights, and he censored the press. The reaction was an immediate insurrection. In "three glorious days" the government collapsed. Paris boiled with revolutionary excitement, and Charles fled. Then the upper middle class, which had fomented the revolt, skillfully seated Charles's cousin, Louis Philippe, duke of Orléans, on the vacant throne.

Louis Philippe (r. 1830–1848) accepted the Constitutional Charter of 1814, adopted the red, white, and blue flag of the French Revolution, and admitted that he was merely the "king of the French people." In spite of such symbolic actions, the situation in France remained fundamentally unchanged. Casimir Périer, a wealthy banker and Louis Philippe's new chief minister, bluntly told a deputy who complained when the vote was extended only from 100,000 to 170,000 citizens, "The trouble with this country is that there are too many people like you who imagine that there has been a revolution in France."[5] The wealthy "notable" elite actually tightened its control as the old aristocracy retreated to the provinces to sulk harmlessly. For the upper middle class there had been a change in dynasty, in order to protect the status quo and the narrowly liberal institutions of 1815. Republicans, democrats, social reformers, and the poor of Paris were bitterly disappointed. They had made a revolution, but it seemed for naught.

THE REVOLUTIONS OF 1848

In 1848 revolutionary political and social ideologies combined with economic crisis and the romantic impulse to produce a vast upheaval. Only the most advanced and the most backward major countries—reforming Great Britain and immobile Russia—escaped untouched. Governments toppled; monarchs and ministers bowed or fled. National independence, liberal-democratic constitutions, and social reform: the lofty aspirations of a generation seemed at hand. Yet, in the end, the revolutions failed. Why was this so?

A Democratic Republic in France

The late 1840s in Europe were hard economically and tense politically. The potato famine in Ireland in 1845 and in 1846 had echoes on the Continent. Bad harvests jacked up food prices and caused misery and unemployment in the cities. "Prerevolutionary" outbreaks occurred all across Europe: an abortive Polish revolution in the northern part of Austria in 1846, a civil war between radicals and conservatives in Switzerland in 1847, and an armed uprising in Naples, Italy, in January 1848. Revolution was almost universally expected, but it took revolution in Paris—once again—to turn expectations into realities.

From its beginning in 1830, Louis Philippe's "bourgeois monarchy" was characterized by stubborn inaction. There was a glaring lack of social legislation, and politics was dominated by corruption and selfish special interests. The king's chief minister in the 1840s, François Guizot, was complacency personified. Guizot was especially satisfied with the electoral system. Only the rich could vote for deputies, and many of the deputies were docile government bureaucrats. It was the government's stubborn refusal to consider electoral reform that touched off popular revolt in Paris. Barricades went up on the night of February 22, 1848, and by February 24 Louis Philippe had abdicated in favor of his grandson. But the common people in arms would tolerate no more monarchy. This refusal led to the proclamation of a provisional republic, headed by a ten-man executive committee and certified by cries of approval from the revolutionary crowd.

In the flush of victory, there was much about which Parisian revolutionaries could agree. A generation of historians and journalists had praised the First French Republic, and their work had borne fruit: the revolutionaries were firmly committed to a republic as opposed to any form of constitutional monarchy, and they immediately set about drafting a constitution for France's Second Republic. Moreover, they wanted a truly popular and democratic republic, so that the healthy, life-giving forces of the common people—the peasants and the workers —could reform society with wise legislation. In practice, building such a republic meant giving the right to vote to every adult male, and this was quickly done. Revolutionary compassion and sympathy for freedom were expressed in the freeing of all slaves in French colonies, abolition of the death penalty, and the establishment of a ten-hour workday for Paris.

Yet there were profound differences within the revolutionary coalition in Paris. On the one hand, there were the moderate, liberal republicans of the middle class. They viewed universal manhood suffrage as the ultimate concession to be made to popular forces and strongly opposed any further radical social measures. On the other hand were the radical republicans. Influenced by the critique of capitalism and unbridled individualism elaborated by a generation of utopian socialists, and appalled by the poverty and misery of the urban poor, the radical republicans were committed to socialism. To be sure, socialism came in many utopian shapes and sizes for the Parisian working poor and their leaders, but that did not make their commitment to it any less real. Finally, wedged in between these groups were individuals like the poet Lamartine and the democrat Ledru-Rollin, who were neither doctrinaire socialists nor stand-pat liberals and who sought to escape an impending tragedy.

Daumier: The Legislative Belly Protected by freedom of the press after 1830, French radicals bitterly attacked the do-nothing government of Louis Philippe. Here Daumier savagely ridicules the corruption of the Chamber of Deputies. *(Source: ©1990 The Art Institute of Chicago. All Rights Reserved.)*

blood-spattered corpses of workers who had fallen in an uprising on March 18, the nearly hysterical king finally caved in. On March 21 he promised to grant Prussia a liberal constitution and to merge it into a new national German state that was to be created. He appointed two wealthy businessmen from the Rhineland—perfect representatives of moderate liberalism—to form a new government.

The situation might have stabilized at this point if the workers had not wanted much more and the Prussian aristocracy much less. On March 26 the workers issued a series of radical and vaguely socialist demands that troubled their middle-class allies: universal voting rights, a ministry of labor, a minimum wage, and a ten-hour day. At the same time, a wild-tempered Prussian landowner and aristocrat,

Revolutionary Justice in Vienna   As part of the conservative resurgence, in October 1848 the Austrian minister of war ordered up reinforcements for an army marching on Hungary. In a last defiant gesture the outraged revolutionaries in Vienna seized the minister and lynched him from a lamppost for treason. The army then reconquered the city in a week of bitter fighting. *(Source: Mary Evans Picture Library/Photo Researchers)*

Otto von Bismarck, joined the conservative clique gathered around the king to urge counter-revolution. While these tensions in Prussia were growing, an elected assembly met in Berlin to write a constitution for the Prussian state.

To add to the complexity of the situation, a self-appointed committee of liberals from various German states successfully called for the formation of a national constituent assembly to begin writing a federal constitution for a unified German state. That body met for the first time on May 18 in Saint Paul's Church in Frankfurt. The Frankfurt National Assembly was a most curious revolutionary body. It was really a serious middle-class body whose 820 members included some 200 lawyers; 100 professors; many doctors, judges, and officials; and 140 businessmen for good measure.

Convened to write a constitution, the learned body was soon absorbed in a battle with Denmark over the provinces of Schleswig and Holstein. Jurisdiction over them was a hopelessly complicated issue from a legal point of view. Britain's foreign minister Lord Palmerston once said that only three people had ever understood the Schleswig-Holstein question, and of those one had died, another had gone mad, and he himself had forgotten the answer. The provinces were inhabited primarily by Germans but were ruled by the king of Denmark, although Holstein was a member of the German Confederation. When Frederick VII, the new nationalistic king of Denmark, tried to integrate both provinces into the rest of his state, the Germans there revolted.

Hypnotized by this conflict, the National Assembly at Frankfurt debated ponderously and finally called on the Prussian army to oppose Denmark in the name of the German nation. Prussia responded and began war with Denmark. As the Schleswig-Holstein issue demonstrated, the national ideal was a crucial factor motivating the German middle classes in 1848.

Almost obsessed with the fate of Germans under Danish rule, many members of the National Assembly also wanted to bring the German-speaking provinces of Austria into the new German state. Yet resurgent Austria resolutely opposed any division of its territory. Once this Austrian action made a "big German state" impossible, the National Assembly completed its drafting of a liberal constitution. Finally, in March 1849, the Assembly elected King Frederick William of Prussia emperor of the new German national state (minus Austria and Schleswig-Holstein).

By early 1849, however, reaction had been successful almost everywhere. Frederick William reasserted his royal authority, disbanded the Prussian Constituent Assembly, and granted his subjects a limited, essentially conservative, constitution. Reasserting that he ruled by divine right, Frederick William contemptuously refused to accept the "crown from the gutter." The reluctant revolutionaries in Frankfurt had waited too long and acted too timidly.

When Frederick William, who really wanted to be emperor but only on his own authoritarian terms, tried to get the small monarchs of Germany to elect him emperor, Austria balked. Supported by Russia, Austria forced Prussia to renounce all its schemes of unification in late 1850. The German Confederation was re-established. After two turbulent years, the political map of the German states remained unchanged. Attempts to unite the Germans—first in a liberal national state and then in a conservative Prussian empire—had failed completely.

SUMMARY

In 1814 the victorious allied powers sought to restore peace and stability in Europe. Dealing moderately with France and wisely settling their own differences, the allies laid the foundations for beneficial international cooperation throughout much of the nineteenth century. Led by Metternich, the conservative powers also sought to prevent the spread of subversive ideas and radical changes in domestic politics. Yet European thought has seldom been more powerfully creative than after 1815, and ideologies of liberalism, nationalism, and socialism all developed to challenge the existing order. The Romantic movement, breaking decisively with the dictates of classicism, reinforced the spirit of change and revolutionary anticipation.

All of these forces culminated in the liberal and nationalistic revolutions of 1848. Political, economic, and social pressures that had been building since 1815 exploded dramatically, but the upheavals of 1848 were abortive and very few revolutionary goals were realized. The moderate, nationalistic middle classes were unable to consolidate their initial victories in France or elsewhere in Europe. Instead, they drew back when artisans, factory workers, and radical socialists rose up to present their own much more revolutionary demands. This retreat facilitated the efforts of dedicated aristocrats in central Europe and made possible the crushing of Parisian workers by a coalition of solid bourgeoisie and landowning peasantry in France. A host of fears, a sea of blood, and a torrent of disillusion had drowned the lofty ideals and utopian visions of a generation. The age of romantic revolution was over.

NOTES

1. Quoted in A. J. May, *The Age of Metternich, 1814–1848* rev. ed. (New York: Holt, Rinehart & Winston, 1963), p. 11.
2. Quoted in H. Kohn, *Nationalism* (New York: Van Nostrand, 1955), pp. 141–142.
3. Quoted in F. D. Klingender, *Art and the Industrial Revolution* (St. Albans, Eng.: Paladin, 1972), p. 117.
4. Quoted in F. B. Artz, *From the Renaissance to Romanticism: Trends in Style in Art, Literature, and Music, 1300–1830* (Chicago: University of Chicago Press, 1962), pp. 276, 278.
5. Quoted in G. Wright, *France in Modern Times* (Chicago: Rand McNally, 1960), p. 145.
6. A. de Tocqueville, *Recollections* (New York: Columbia University Press, 1949), p. 94.
7. M. Agulhon, *1848* (Paris: Éditions du Seuil, 1973), pp. 68–69.
8. Quoted in W. L. Langer, *Political and Social Upheaval, 1832–1852* (New York: Harper & Row, 1969), p. 361.

SUGGESTED READING

All of the works cited in the Notes are highly recommended. May's is a good brief survey, while Kohn has written perceptively on nationalism in many books. Wright's *France in Modern Times* is a lively introduction to French history with stimulating biographical discussions; Langer's is a balanced synthesis with an excellent bibliography. Among general studies, C. Moraze, *The Triumph of the Middle Classes* (1968), a wide-ranging procapitalist interpretation, may be compared with E. J. Hobsbawm's flexible Marxism in *The Age of Revolution,* *1789–1848* (1962). For English history, A. Briggs's socially oriented *The Making of Modern England, 1784–1867* (1967) and D. Thomson's *England in the Nineteenth Century, 1815–1914* (1951) are excellent. Restoration France is sympathetically portrayed by G. de Bertier de Sauvigny in *The Bourbon Restoration* (1967), while R. Price, *A Social History of Nineteenth-Century France* (1987), is a fine synthesis incorporating recent research. T. Hamerow studies the social implications of the dual revolution in Germany in *Restoration, Revolution, Reaction 1815–1871* (1966), which may be compared with H. Treitschke's bombastic, pro-Prussian *History of Germany in the Nineteenth Century* (1915–1919), a classic of nationalistic history, and L. Snyder, *Roots of German Nationalism* (1978). H. James, *A German Identity, 1770–1990* (1989), and J. Sheehan, *Germany, 1770–1866* (1989), are stimulating general histories that skillfully incorporate recent research. E. Kedourie, *Nationalism* (1960), is a stimulating critique of the new faith. H. Kissinger, *A World Restored* (1957), offers not only a provocative interpretation of the Congress of Vienna but also insights into the mind of Richard Nixon's famous secretary of state. Compare that volume with H. Nicolson's entertaining *The Congress of Vienna* (1946). On 1848, L. B. Namier's highly critical *1848: The Revolution of the Intellectuals* (1964) and P. Robertson's *Revolutions of 1848: A Social History* (1960) are outstanding. I. Deak, *The Lawful Revolution: Louis Kossuth and the Hungarians, 1848–49* (1979), is a noteworthy study of an interesting figure.

On early socialism and Marxism, there are A. Lindemann's stimulating survey, *A History of European Socialism* (1983), and W. Sewell, Jr.'s *Work and Revolution in France: The Language of Labor from the Old Regime to 1848* (1980), as well as G. Lichtheim's high-powered *Marxism* (1961) and his *Short History of Socialism* (1970). Fourier is treated sympathetically in J. Beecher, *Charles Fourier* (1986). J. Schumpeter, *Capitalism, Socialism and Democracy* (1947), is magnificent but difficult, a real mind-stretcher. Also highly recommended is B. Taylor, *Eve and the New Jerusalem: Socialism and Feminism in the Nineteenth Century* (1983), which explores fascinating English attempts to emancipate workers and women at the same time. On liberalism, there are R. Heilbroner's entertaining *The Worldly Philosophers* (1967) and G. de Ruggiero's classic *History of European Liberalism* (1959). J. Barzun, *Classic, Ro-*

mantic and Modern (1961), skillfully discusses the emergence of romanticism. R. Stromberg, *An Intellectual History of Modern Europe,* 3d ed. (1981), and F. Baumer, *Modern European Thought: Continuity and Change in Ideas, 1600–1950* (1970), are valuable surveys. The important place of religion in nineteenth-century thought is considered from different perspectives in H. McLeod, *Religion and the People of Western Europe* (1981), and O. Chadwick, *The Secularization of the European Mind in the Nineteenth Century* (1976). Two good church histories with useful bibliographies are J. Altholz, *The Churches in the Nineteenth Century* (1967), and A. Vidler, *The Church in an Age of Revolution: 1789 to the Present Day* (1961).

The thoughtful reader is strongly advised to delve into the incredibly rich writing of contemporaries. J. Bowditch and C. Ramsland, eds., *Voices of the Industrial Revolution* (1961), is an excellent starting point, with well-chosen selections from leading economic thinkers and early socialists. H. Hugo, ed., *The Romantic Reader,* is another fine anthology. Mary Shelley's *Frankenstein,* a great romantic novel, draws an almost lovable picture of the famous monster and is highly recommended. Jules Michelet's compassionate masterpiece *The People,* a famous historian's anguished examination of French social divisions on the eve of 1848, draws one into the heart of the period and is highly recommended. Alexis de Tocqueville covers some of the same ground less romantically in his *Recollections,* which may be compared with Karl Marx's white-hot "instant history," *Class Struggles in France, 1848–1850* (1850). Great novels that accurately portray aspects of the times are Victor Hugo, *Les Misérables,* an exciting story of crime and passion among France's poor; Honoré de Balzac, *La Cousine Bette* and *Le Père Goriot;* and Thomas Mann, *Buddenbrooks,* a wonderful historical novel that traces the rise and fall of a prosperous German family over three generations during the nineteenth century.

24

Life in Urban Society

The era of intellectual and political upheaval that culminated in the revolutions of 1848 was also an era of rapid urbanization. After 1848, Western political development veered off in a novel and uncharted direction, but the growth of towns and cities rushed forward with undiminished force. Thus Western society was urban and industrial in 1900, as surely as it had been rural and agrarian in 1800. The urbanization of society was both a result of the Industrial Revolution and a reflection of its enormous long-term impact.

- What was life like in the cities, and how did it change?
- What did the emergence of urban industrial society mean for rich and poor and those in between?
- How did families cope with the challenges and respond to the opportunities of the developing urban civilization?
- Finally, what changes in science and thought inspired and gave expression to this new civilization?

These are the questions this chapter will investigate.

TAMING THE CITY

The growth of industry posed enormous challenges for all elements of Western society, from young factory workers confronting relentless discipline to aristocratic elites maneuvering to retain political power. As we saw in Chapter 22, the early consequences of economic transformation were mixed and far-reaching, and by no means wholly negative. By 1850 at the latest, working conditions were improving and real wages were definitely rising for the mass of the population, and they continued to do so until 1914. Thus, given the poverty and uncertainty of preindustrial life, some historians maintain that the history of industrialization in the nineteenth century is probably better written in terms of increasing opportunities than of greater hardships.

Critics of this relatively optimistic view of industrialization claim that it neglects the quality of life in urban areas. They stress that the new industrial towns and cities were awful places, where people, especially poor people, suffered from bad housing, lack of sanitation, and a sense of hopelessness. They ask if these drawbacks did not more than cancel out higher wages and greater opportunity. An examination of urban development provides some answers to this complex question.

Industry and the Growth of Cities

Since the Middle Ages, European cities had been centers of government, culture, and large-scale commerce. They had also been congested, dirty, and unhealthy. People were packed together almost as tightly as possible within the city limits. The typical city was a "walking city": for all but the wealthiest classes, walking was the only available form of transportation.

Infectious disease spread with deadly speed in cities, and people were always more likely to die in the city than in the countryside. In the larger towns, more people died each year than were born, on the average, and urban populations were able to maintain their numbers only because newcomers were continuously arriving from rural areas. Little could be done to improve these conditions. Given the pervasive poverty, absence of urban transportation, and lack of medical knowledge, the deadly and overcrowded conditions could only be accepted fatalistically. They were the urban equivalents of bad weather and poor crops, the price of urban excitement and opportunity.

Clearly, deplorable urban conditions did not originate with the Industrial Revolution. What the Industrial Revolution did was to reveal those conditions more nakedly than ever before. The steam engine freed industrialists from dependence on the energy of fast-flowing streams and rivers, so that by 1800 there was every incentive to build new factories in urban areas. Cities had better shipping facilities than the countryside and thus better supplies of coal and raw materials. There were also many hands wanting work in the cities, for cities drew people like a magnet. And it was a great advantage for a manufacturer to have other factories nearby to supply the business's needs and buy its products. Therefore, as industry grew, there was also a rapid expansion of already overcrowded and unhealthy cities.

The challenge of the urban environment was felt first and most acutely in Great Britain. The number

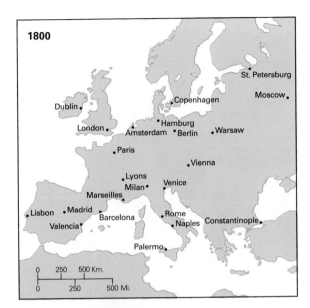

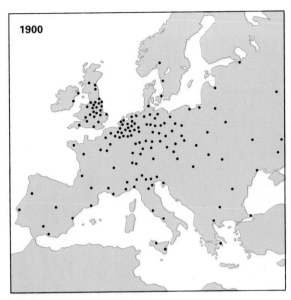

MAP 24.1 European Cities of 100,000 or More, 1800 and 1900   There were more large cities in Great Britain in 1900 than in all Europe in 1800.

of people living in cities of 20,000 or more in England and Wales jumped from 1.5 million in 1801 to 6.3 million in 1851 and reached 15.6 million by 1891. Such cities accounted for 17 percent of the total English population in 1801, 35 percent as early as 1851, and fully 54 percent in 1891. Other countries duplicated the English pattern as they industrialized. An American observer was hardly exaggerating when he wrote in 1899 that "the most remarkable social phenomenon of the present century is the concentration of population in cities" (Map 24.1).[1]

In the 1820s and 1830s, people in Britain and France began to worry about the condition of their cities. In those years, the populations of a number of British cities were increasing by 40 to 70 percent each decade. With urban areas expanding at such previously undreamed-of rates, people's fatalistic acceptance of overcrowded, unsanitary urban living conditions began to give way to active concern. Something had to be done.

On one point everyone could agree: except on the outskirts, each town and city was using every scrap of land to the fullest extent. Parks and open areas were almost nonexistent. A British parliamentary committee reported in 1833 that "with a rapidly increasing population, lodged for the most part in narrow courts and confined streets, the means of occasional exercise and recreation in fresh air are every day lessened, as inclosures [of vacant areas] take place and buildings spread themselves on every side."[2] Buildings were erected on the smallest possible lots, in order to pack the maximum number of people into a given space. Narrow houses were built wall to wall, in long rows. These row houses had neither front nor back yards, and only a narrow alley in back separated one row from the next. Or buildings were built around tiny courtyards completely enclosed on all four sides. Many people lived in cellars and attics. These tiny rooms were often overcrowded. "Six, eight, and even ten occupying one room is anything but uncommon," wrote a doctor from Aberdeen in Scotland for a government investigation in 1842.

These highly concentrated urban populations lived in extremely unsanitary and unhealthy conditions. Open drains and sewers flowed alongside or down the middle of unpaved streets. Because of poor construction and an absence of running water, the sewers often filled with garbage and excrement. Toilet facilities were primitive in the extreme. In parts of Manchester, as many as two hundred people shared a single outhouse. Such privies filled up rapidly, and since they were infrequently emptied, sewage often overflowed and seeped into cellar dwellings.

The extent to which filth lay underfoot and the smell of excrement filled the air is hard to believe;

A COURT FOR KING CHOLERA.

Filth and Disease This 1852 drawing from *Punch* tells volumes about the unhealthy living conditions of the urban poor. In the foreground children play with a dead rat and a woman scavenges a dungheap. Cheap rooming houses provide shelter for the frightfully overcrowded population. *(Source: The British Library)*

yet it was abundantly documented between 1830 and 1850. One London construction engineer found, for example, that the cellars of two large houses on a major road were "full of night-soil [human excrement], to the depth of three feet, which had been permitted for years to accumulate from the overflow of the cesspools." Moreover, some courtyards in poorer neighborhoods became dunghills, collecting excrement that was sometimes sold as fertilizer. By the 1840s there was among the better-off classes a growing, shocking "realization that, to put it as mildly as possible, millions of English men, women, and children were living in shit."[3]

Who or what was responsible for these awful conditions? The crucial factors were the tremendous pressure of more people and the *total* absence of public transportation. People simply had to jam themselves together if they were to be able to walk to shops and factories. Another factor was that government in Great Britain, both local and national, was slow to provide sanitary facilities and establish adequate building codes. This slow pace was probably attributable more to a need to explore and identify what precisely should be done than to rigid middle-class opposition to government action. Certainly Great Britain had no monopoly on overcrowded and unhealthy urban conditions; many continental cities were every bit as bad.

Most responsible of all was the sad legacy of rural housing conditions in preindustrial society, combined with appalling ignorance. As the author of a recent study concludes, there "were rural slums of a horror not surpassed by the rookeries of London. . . . The evidence shows that the decent cottage was the exception, the hovel the rule."[4]

Thus housing was far down on the newcomer's list of priorities, and it is not surprising that many people carried the filth of the mud floor and the dung of the barnyard with them to the city.

Indeed, ordinary people generally took dirt and filth for granted, and some even prized it. One English miner told an investigator, "I do not think it usual for the lasses [in the coal mines] to wash their bodies; my sisters never wash themselves." As for the men, "their legs and bodies are as black as your hat." When poor people were admitted to English workhouses, they often resisted the required bath. One man protested that it was "equal to robbing him of a great coat which he had had for some years."[5]

The Public Health Movement

Although cleanliness was not next to godliness in most people's eyes, it was becoming so for some reformers. The most famous of these was Edwin Chadwick, one of the commissioners charged with the administration of relief to paupers under the revised Poor Law of 1834. Chadwick was a good *Benthamite*—that is, a follower of the radical philosopher Jeremy Bentham (1748–1832). Bentham had taught that public problems ought to be dealt with on a rational, scientific basis and according to the "greatest good for the greatest number." Applying these principles, Chadwick soon saw that much more than economics was involved in the problems of poverty and the welfare budget. Indeed, he soon became convinced that disease and death actually caused poverty, simply because a sick worker was an unemployed worker and orphaned children were poor children. Most important, Chadwick believed that disease could be prevented by quite literally cleaning up the urban environment. That was his "sanitary idea."

Building on a growing number of medical and sociological studies, Chadwick collected detailed reports from local Poor Law officials on the "sanitary conditions of the laboring population." After three years of investigation, these reports and Chadwick's hard-hitting commentary were published in 1842 to wide publicity. This mass of evidence proved that disease was related to filthy environmental conditions, which were in turn caused largely by lack of drainage, sewers, and garbage collection. Putrefying, smelly excrement was no longer simply disgusting. For reformers like Chadwick, it was a threat to the entire community. It polluted the atmosphere and caused disease.

The key to the energetic action Chadwick proposed was an adequate supply of clean piped water. Such water was essential for personal hygiene, public bathhouses, street cleaning, firefighting, and industry. Chadwick correctly believed that the stinking excrement of communal outhouses could be dependably carried off by water through sewers at less than one-twentieth the cost of removing it by hand. The cheap iron pipes and tile drains of the industrial age would provide running water and sewerage for all sections of town, not just the wealthy ones. In 1848, with the cause strengthened by the cholera epidemic of 1846, Chadwick's report became the basis of Great Britain's first public health law, which created a national health board and gave

Sewer Scavenger Growing cities had many rubbish collectors, who sifted through garbage for things to sell and "recycle." Some worked in the sewers, like this London scavenger. Sewer scavengers occasionally found valuable items, but their occupation was unhealthy and extremely dangerous. *(Source: Museum of London)*

cities broad authority to build modern sanitary systems.

The public health movement won dedicated supporters in the United States, France, and Germany from the 1840s on. As in Great Britain, governments accepted at least limited responsibility for the health of all citizens. Moreover, they adopted increasingly concrete programs of action, programs that broke decisively with the age-old fatalism of urban populations in the face of shockingly high mortality. Thus, despite many people's skepticism about sanitation, European cities were making real progress toward adequate water supplies and sewage systems by the 1860s and 1870s. And city dwellers were beginning to reap the reward of better health.

The Bacterial Revolution

Effective control of communicable disease required a great leap forward in medical knowledge and biological theory as well as clean water supply and good sewers. Reformers like Chadwick were seriously handicapped by the prevailing *miasmatic theory* of disease—the belief that people contract disease when they breathe the bad odors of decay and putrefying excrement; in short, the theory that smells cause disease. The miasmatic theory was a reasonable deduction from empirical observations: cleaning up filth did produce laudable results. Yet the theory was very incomplete.

Keen observation by doctors and public health officials in the 1840s and 1850s pinpointed the role of bad drinking water in the transmission of disease and suggested that contagion was *spread through* filth and not caused by it. Moreover, some particularly horrid stenches, such as that of the sewage-glutted Thames River at London in 1858, did not lead to widely feared epidemics, and this fact also weakened the miasmatic idea.

The breakthrough was the development of the *germ theory* of disease by Louis Pasteur (1822–1895), a French chemist who began studying fermentation in 1854. For ages people had used fermentation to make bread and wine, beer and cheese, but without really understanding what was going on. And from time to time, beer and wine would mysteriously spoil for no apparent reason. Responding to the calls of big brewers for help, Pasteur used his microscope to develop a simple test brewers could use to monitor the fermentation process and avoid spoilage. Continuing his investigations, Pasteur found that fermentation depended on the growth of living organisms, and that the activity of these organisms could be suppressed by heating the beverage—by *pasteurizing* it. The breathtaking implication was that specific diseases were caused by specific living organisms—germs—and that those organisms could be controlled in people as well as in beer, wine, and milk.

By 1870 the work of Pasteur and others had demonstrated the general connection between germs and disease. When, in the middle of the 1870s, the German country doctor Robert Koch and his coworkers developed pure cultures of harmful bacteria and described their life cycles, the dam broke. Over the next twenty years, researchers—mainly Germans—identified the organisms responsible for disease after disease, often identifying several in a single year. These discoveries led to the development of a number of effective vaccines and the emergence of modern immunology.

Acceptance of the germ theory brought about dramatic improvements in the deadly environment of hospitals and surgery. The English surgeon Joseph Lister (1827–1912) had noticed that patients with simple fractures were much less likely to die than those with compound fractures, in which the skin was broken and internal tissues were exposed to the air. In 1865, when Pasteur showed that the air was full of bacteria, Lister immediately grasped the connection between aerial bacteria and the problem of wound infection. He reasoned that a chemical disinfectant applied to a wound dressing would "destroy the life of the floating particles." Lister's "antiseptic principle" worked wonders. In the 1880s, German surgeons developed the more sophisticated practice of sterilizing not only the wound but everything—hands, instruments, clothing—that entered the operating room.

The achievements of the bacterial revolution coupled with the ever-more-sophisticated public health movement saved millions of lives, particularly after about 1890. Mortality rates began to decline dramatically in European countries (Figure 24.1), as the awful death sentences of the past—diphtheria, typhoid and typhus, cholera, yellow fever—became vanishing diseases. City dwellers benefited especially from these developments. By 1910 the death rates for people of all ages in urban areas were generally no greater than in rural areas, and sometimes they were less. Particularly striking was the decline in infant mortality in the cities after 1890. By 1910, in many countries, an urban mother was less likely than a rural mother to see her child die before its first birthday. A great silent revolution had occurred: the terrible ferocity of death from disease-carrying bacteria in the cities had almost been tamed.

Urban Planning and Public Transportation

Public health was only part of the urban challenge. Overcrowding, bad housing, and lack of transportation could not be solved by sewers and better medicine; yet in these areas, too, important transformations significantly improved the quality of urban life after midcentury.

More effective urban planning was one of the keys to improvement. Urban planning was in decline by the early nineteenth century, but after 1850 its practice was revived and extended. France took the lead during the rule of Napoleon III (1848–1870), who sought to stand above class conflict and promote the welfare of all his subjects through government action. He believed that rebuilding much of Paris would provide employment, improve living conditions, and testify to the power and glory of his empire. In the baron Georges Haussmann, an aggressive, impatient Alsatian whom he placed in charge of Paris, Napoleon III found an authoritarian planner capable of bulldozing both buildings and opposition. In twenty years Paris was quite literally transformed (Map 24.2).

The Paris of 1850 was a labyrinth of narrow, dark streets, the results of desperate overcrowding. In a central city not twice the size of New York's Central Park lived more than one-third of the city's one million inhabitants. Terrible slum conditions and extremely high death rates were facts of life. There were few open spaces and only two public parks for the entire metropolis. Public transportation played a very small role in this enormous walking city.

Haussmann and his fellow planners proceeded on many interrelated fronts. With a bold energy that often shocked their contemporaries, they razed old buildings in order to cut broad, straight, tree-lined boulevards through the center of the city as well as in new quarters on the outskirts. These boulevards, designed in part to prevent the easy construction and defense of barricades by revolutionary crowds, permitted traffic to flow freely. Their

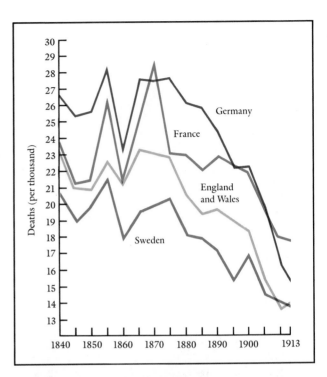

FIGURE 24.1 The Decline of Death Rates in England and Wales, Germany, France, and Sweden, 1840–1913 A rising standard of living, improvements in public health, and better medical knowledge all contributed to the dramatic decline of death rates in the nineteenth century.

creation also demolished some of the worst slums. New streets stimulated the construction of better housing, especially for the middle classes. Small neighborhood parks and open spaces were created throughout the city, and two very large parks suitable for all kinds of holiday activities were developed on either side of the city. The city also improved its sewers, and a system of aqueducts more than doubled the city's supply of good fresh water.

Haussmann and Napoleon III tried to make Paris a more beautiful city, and to a large extent they succeeded. The broad, straight boulevards, such as those radiating out like the spokes of a wheel from the Arch of Triumph and those centering on the new Opera House, afforded impressive vistas. If for most people Paris remains one of the world's most beautiful and enchanting cities, it is in part because of the transformations of Napoleon III's Second Empire.

Rebuilding Paris provided a new model for urban planning and stimulated modern urbanism

Apartment Living in Paris This drawing shows how different social classes lived close together in European cities about 1850. Passing the middle-class family on the first (American second) floor, the economic condition of the tenants declined until one reached abject poverty in the garret. *(Source: Bibliothéque Nationale, Paris)*

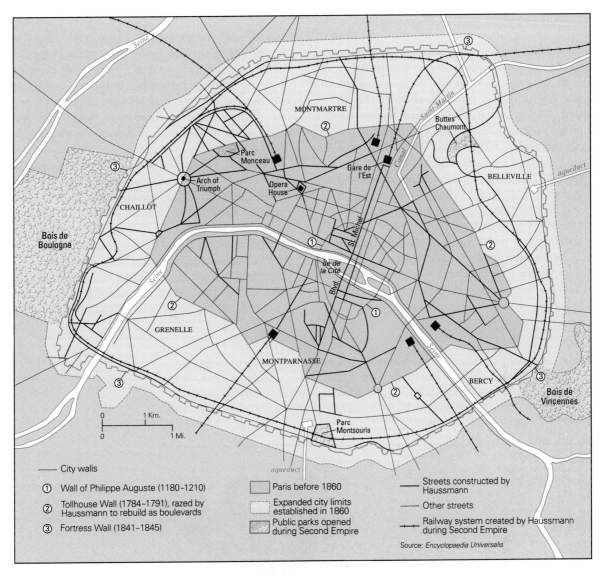

MAP 24.2 The Modernization of Paris, ca 1850–1870   Broad boulevards, large parks, and grandiose train stations transformed Paris. The cutting of the new north-south axis —known as the Boulevard Saint-Michel—was one of Haussmann's most controversial projects. It razed much of Paris's medieval core and filled the Île de la Cité with massive government buildings.

throughout Europe, particularly after 1870. In city after city, public authorities mounted a coordinated attack on many of the interrelated problems of the urban environment. As in Paris, improvements in public health through better water supply and waste disposal often went hand in hand with new boulevard construction. Cities like Vienna and Cologne followed the Parisian example of tearing down old walled fortifications and replacing them with broad, circular boulevards on which office buildings, town halls, theaters, opera houses, and museums were erected. These ring roads and the new boulevards that radiated out from them toward the outskirts eased movement and encouraged urban expansion (see Map 24.2). *Zoning expropriation laws,* which allowed a majority of the owners of land in a given quarter of the city to impose major street or sanitation improvements on a reluctant minority, were an important mechanism of the new urbanism.

The development of mass public transportation was also of great importance in the improvement of urban living conditions. Such transportation came late, but in a powerful rush. In the 1870s, many European cities authorized private companies to operate horse-drawn streetcars, which had been developed in the United States, to carry riders along the growing number of major thoroughfares. Then, in the 1890s, occurred the real revolution: European countries adopted another American transit innovation, the electric streetcar.

Electric streetcars were cheaper, faster, more dependable, and more comfortable than their horse-drawn counterparts. Service improved dramatically. Millions of Europeans—workers, shoppers, schoolchildren—hopped on board during the workweek. And on weekends and holidays, street-cars carried millions on happy outings to parks and countryside, racetracks and music halls. In 1886 the horse-drawn streetcars of Austria-Hungary, France, Germany, and Great Britain were carrying about 900 million riders. By 1910 electric streetcar systems in the four countries were carrying 6.7 billion riders.[6] Each man, woman, and child was using public transportation four times as often in 1910 as in 1886.

Good mass transit helped greatly in the struggle for decent housing. The new boulevards and horse-drawn streetcars had facilitated a middle-class move to better housing in the 1860s and 1870s; similarly, after 1890, electric streetcars gave people of modest means access to new, improved housing. The still-crowded city was able to expand and become less congested. In England in 1901, only 9 percent of the urban population was "over-crowded" in terms of the official definition of

Mass Public Transportation   Before the 1890s, urban Europeans relied on horse-drawn streetcars for transportation. Electric trolleys—faster, cheaper, bigger, and cleaner than their horse-drawn counterparts—improved service dramatically. This photograph of Berlin dates from 1901 when electric street cars were rapidly replacing horse-drawn buses. *(Source: Ullstein Bilderdienst)*

more than two persons per room. On the Continent, many city governments in the early twentieth century were building electric streetcar systems that provided transportation to new public and private housing developments in outlying areas of the city for the working classes. Poor, overcrowded housing, long one of the blackest blots on the urban landscape, was in retreat—another example of the gradual taming of the urban environment.

RICH AND POOR AND IN BETWEEN

General improvements in health and in the urban environment had beneficial consequences for all kinds of people. Yet differences in living conditions between social classes remained gigantic.

Social Structure

How much had the almost-completed journey to an urban, industrialized world changed the social framework of rich and poor? The first great change was a substantial and undeniable increase in the standard of living for the average person. The real wages of British workers, for example, which had already risen by 1850, almost doubled between 1850 and 1906. Similar unmistakable increases occurred in continental countries as industrial development quickened after 1850. Ordinary people took a major step forward in the centuries-old battle against poverty, reinforcing efforts to improve many aspects of human existence.

There is another side to the income coin, however, and it must be stressed as well. Greater economic rewards for the average person did *not* eliminate poverty, nor did they make the wealth and income of the rich and the poor significantly more equal. In almost every advanced country around 1900, the richest 5 percent of all households in the population received one-third of all national income. The richest one-fifth of households received anywhere from 50 to 60 percent of all national income, while the entire bottom four-fifths received only 40 to 50 percent. Moreover, the bottom 30 percent of households received 10 percent or less of all income. These enormous differences are illustrated in Figure 24.2.

The middle classes, smaller than they are today, accounted for less than 20 percent of the popula-

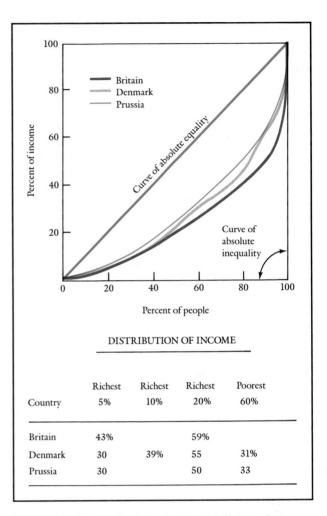

FIGURE 24.2 The Distribution of Income in Britain, Denmark, and Prussia in 1913 The so-called Lorenz curve is useful for showing the degree of economic inequality in a given society. The closer the actual distribution of income lies to the (theoretical) curve of absolute equality, where each 20 percent of the population receives 20 percent of all income, the more incomes are nearly equal. European society was very far from any such equality before World War One. Notice that incomes in Prussia were somewhat more equal than those in Britain. *(Source: S. Kuznets,* Modern Economic Growth, *Yale University Press, New Haven, 1966, pp. 208–209)*

tion; thus the statistics show that the upper and middle classes alone received more than one-half of all income. The poorest four-fifths—the working classes, including peasants and agricultural laborers—received less altogether than the two richest classes. And since many wives and teenagers in poor families worked for wages, these figures actually understate the enduring gap between rich and poor. Moreover, income taxes on the wealthy were light or nonexistent. Thus the gap between rich and poor remained enormous at the beginning of the twentieth century. It was probably almost as great as it had been in the age of agriculture and aristocracy, before the Industrial Revolution.

The great gap between rich and poor endured, in part, because industrial and urban development made society more diverse and less unified. By no means did society split into two sharply defined opposing classes, as Marx had predicted. Instead, economic specialization enabled society to produce more effectively and in the process created more new social groups than it destroyed. There developed an almost unlimited range of jobs, skills, and earnings; one group or subclass shaded off into another in a complex, confusing hierarchy. Thus the tiny elite of the very rich and the sizable mass of the dreadfully poor were separated from each other by many subclasses, each filled with individuals struggling to rise or at least to hold their own in the social order. In this atmosphere of competition and hierarchy, neither the middle classes nor the working classes acted as a unified force. The age-old pattern of great economic inequality remained firmly intact.

The Middle Classes

By the beginning of the twentieth century, the diversity and range within the urban middle class were striking. Indeed, it is more meaningful to think of a confederation of middle classes, loosely united by occupations requiring mental rather than physical skill. At the top stood the upper middle class, composed mainly of the most successful business families from banking, industry, and large-scale commerce. These families were the prime beneficiaries of modern industry and scientific progress. As people in the upper middle class gained in income and progressively lost all traces of radicalism after the trauma of 1848, they were almost irresistibly drawn toward the aristocratic lifestyle.

As the aristocracy had long divided the year between palatial country estates and lavish townhouses during "the season," so the upper middle class purchased country places or built beach houses for weekend and summer use. (Little wonder that a favorite scenario in late-nineteenth-century middle-class novels was a mother and children summering gloriously in the country home, with only sporadic weekend intrusions by a distant, shadowy father.) The number of servants was an important indicator of wealth and standing for the middle class, as it had always been for the aristocracy. Private coaches and carriages, ever an expensive item in the city, were also signs of rising social status. More generally, the rich businessman and certainly his son devoted less time to business and more to "culture" and easy living than was the case in less wealthy or well-established commercial families.

The topmost reaches of the upper middle class tended to shade off into the old aristocracy to form a new upper class. This was the 5 percent of the population that, as we have seen, received roughly one-third of the national income in European countries before 1914. Much of the aristocracy welcomed this development. Having experienced a sharp decline in its relative income in the course of industrialization, the landed aristocracy had met big business coming up the staircase and was often delighted to trade titles, country homes, and snobbish elegance for good hard cash. Some of the best bargains were made through marriages to American heiresses. Correspondingly, wealthy aristocrats tended increasingly to exploit their agricultural and mineral resources as if they were business people. Bismarck was not the only proud nobleman to make a fortune distilling brandy on his estates.

Below the wealthy upper middle class were much larger, much less wealthy, and increasingly diversified middle-class groups. Here one found the moderately successful industrialists and merchants, as well as professionals in law and medicine. This was the middle middle class, solid and quite comfortable but lacking great wealth. Below them were independent shopkeepers, small traders, and tiny manufacturers—the lower middle class. Both of these traditional elements of the middle class expanded modestly in size with economic development.

Meanwhile, the traditional middle class was gaining two particularly important additions. The expansion of industry and technology created a growing demand for experts with specialized knowledge. The most valuable of the specialties became solid middle-class professions. Engineering, for example, emerged from the world of skilled labor as a full-fledged profession of great importance, considerable prestige, and many branches.

Architects, chemists, accountants, and surveyors—to name only a few—first achieved professional standing in this period. They established criteria for advanced training and certification and banded together in organizations to promote and defend their interests.

Management of large public and private institutions also emerged as a kind of profession, as governments provided more services and as very large corporations like railroads came into being. Government officials and many private executives were not capitalists in the sense that they owned business enterprises. But public and private managers did have specialized knowledge and the capacity to earn a good living. And they shared most of the values of the business-owning entrepreneurs and the older professionals.

Industrialization also expanded and diversified the lower middle class. The number of independent, property-owning shopkeepers and small business people grew and so did the number of white-collar employees—a mixed group of traveling salesmen, bookkeepers, store managers, and clerks who staffed the offices and branch stores of large corporations. White-collar employees were propertyless and often earned no more than the better-paid skilled or semiskilled workers did. Yet white-collar workers were fiercely committed to the middle class and to the ideal of moving up in society. In the Balkans, for example, clerks let their fingernails grow very long to distinguish themselves from people who worked with their hands. The tie, the suit, and soft clean hands were no-less-subtle marks of class distinction than wages.

Relatively well educated but without complex technical skills, many white-collar groups aimed at achieving professional standing and the accompanying middle-class status. Elementary school teachers largely succeeded in this effort. From being miserably paid part-time workers in the early nineteenth century, teachers rode the wave of mass education to respectable middle-class status and income. Nurses also rose from the lower ranks of unskilled labor to precarious middle-class standing. Dentistry was taken out of the hands of the working-class barbers and placed in the hands of highly trained (and middle-class) professionals.

In spite of their growing occupational diversity and conflicting interests, the middle classes were loosely united by a certain style of life. Food was the largest item in the household budget, for middle-class people liked to eat very well. In France and Italy, the middle classes' love of good eating meant that, even in large cities, activity ground almost to a halt between half past twelve and half past two on weekdays, as husbands and schoolchildren returned home for the midday meal. Around eight in the evening, the serious business of eating was taken up once again.

The English were equally attached to substantial meals, which they ate three times a day if income allowed. The typical English breakfast of bacon and eggs, toast and marmalade, and stewed fruits—not to mention sardines, kidneys, or fresh fish—always astonished French and German travelers, though large-breakfast enthusiasts like the Dutch and Scandinavians were less awed. The European middle classes consumed meat in abundance, and a well-off family might spend 10 percent of its substantial earnings on meat alone. In the 1890s, even a very prosperous English family—with an income of, say, $10,000 a year while the average working-class family earned perhaps $400 a year—spent fully a quarter of its income on food and drink.

Spending on food was also great because the dinner party was this class's favored social occasion. A wealthy family might give a lavish party for eight to twelve almost every week, while more modest households would settle for once a month. Throughout middle-class Europe, such dinners were served in the "French manner" (which the French had borrowed from the Russian aristocracy): eight or nine separate courses, from appetizers at the beginning to coffee and liqueurs at the end. In summer, a picnic was in order. But what a picnic! For a party of ten, one English cookbook suggested 5 pounds of cold salmon, a quarter of lamb, 8 pounds of pickled brisket, a beef tongue, a chicken pie, salads, cakes, and 6 pounds of strawberries. An ordinary family meal normally consisted of only four courses—soup, fish, meat, and dessert.

The middle-class wife could cope with this endless procession of meals, courses, and dishes because she had both servants and money at her disposal. The middle classes were solid members of what some contemporary observers called the "servant-keeping classes." Indeed, the employment of at least one enormously helpful full-time maid to cook and clean was the best single sign that a family had crossed the vague line separating the working classes from the middle classes. The greater its income, the greater the number of servants a family employed. The all-purpose servant gave way to a

"A Corner of the Table"   With photographic precision this 1904 oil painting by the French academic artist Paul-Émile Chabas (1867–1937) skillfully idealizes the elegance and intimacy of a sumptuous dinner party. *(Source: Bibliothèque des Arts Decoratifs/ Jean-Loup Charmet)*

cook and a maid, then to a cook, a maid, and a boy, and so on. A prosperous English family, far up the line with $10,000 a year, in 1900 spent fully one-fourth of its income on a hierarchy of ten servants: a manservant, a cook, a kitchen maid, two house-maids, a serving maid, a governess, a gardener, a coachman, and a stable boy. Domestic servants were the second largest item in the budget of the middle classes. Food and servants together ab-sorbed about one-half of income at all levels of the middle classes.

Well fed and well served, the middle classes were also well housed by 1900. Many quite prosperous families rented rather than owned their homes. Apartment living, complete with tiny rooms for servants under the eaves of the top floor, was com-monplace (outside Great Britain), and wealthy in-vestors and speculative builders found good prof-

its in middle-class housing. By 1900 the middle classes were also quite clothes-conscious. The fac-tory, the sewing machine, and the department store had all helped to reduce the cost and expand the va-riety of clothing. Middle-class women were particu-larly attentive to the fickle dictates of fashion.

Education was another growing expense, as mid-dle-class parents tried to provide their children with ever-more-crucial advanced education. The key-stones of culture and leisure were books, music, and travel. The long realistic novel, the heroics of Wagner and Verdi, the diligent striving of the duti-ful daughter on a piano, and the packaged tour to a foreign country were all sources of middle-class pleasure.

Finally, the middle classes were loosely united by a shared code of expected behavior and morality. This code was strict and demanding. It laid great stress on hard work, self-discipline, and personal achievement. Men and women who fell into crime or poverty were generally assumed to be responsible for their own circumstances. Traditional Christian morality was reaffirmed by this code and preached tirelessly by middle-class people who took pride in their own good conduct and regular church attendance. Drinking and gambling were denounced as vices; sexual purity and fidelity were celebrated as virtues. In short, the middle-class person was supposed to know right from wrong and was expected to act accordingly.

The Working Classes

About four out of five people belonged to the working classes at the turn of the century. Many members of the working classes—that is, people whose livelihoods depended on physical labor and who did not employ domestic servants—were still small landowning peasants and hired farm hands. This was especially true in eastern Europe. In western and central Europe, however, the typical worker had left the land. In Great Britain, less than 8 percent of the people worked in agriculture, while in rapidly industrializing Germany only one person in four was employed in agriculture and forestry. Even in less industrialized France, less than half the people depended on the land in 1900.

The urban working classes were even less unified and homogeneous than the middle classes. In the first place, economic development and increased specialization expanded the traditional range of working-class skills, earnings, and experiences. Meanwhile, the old sharp distinction between highly skilled artisans and unskilled manual workers was gradually breaking down. To be sure, highly skilled printers and masons, as well as unskilled dock workers and common laborers, continued to exist. But between these extremes there were ever-more semiskilled groups, many of which were composed of factory workers and machine tenders (Figure 24.3).

In the second place, skilled, semiskilled, and unskilled workers had widely divergent lifestyles and cultural values, and their differences contributed to a keen sense of social status and hierarchy within the working classes. The result was great variety and limited class unity.

Highly skilled workers, who comprised about 15 percent of the working classes, were a real "labor aristocracy." By 1900 they were earning about £2 a week in Great Britain, or roughly $10 a week and $500 per year. This was only about two-thirds the income of the bottom ranks of the servant-keeping classes. But it was fully twice as much as the earnings of unskilled workers, who averaged about $5 per week, and substantially more than the earnings of semiskilled workers, who averaged perhaps $7 per week. Other European countries had a similar range of earnings.

The most "aristocratic" of the highly skilled workers were construction bosses and factory foremen, men who had risen from the ranks and were fiercely proud of their achievement. The labor aristocracy also included members of the traditional highly skilled handicraft trades that had not been mechanized or placed in factories. These included makers of scientific and musical instruments, cabinetmakers, potters, jewelers, bookbinders, engravers, and printers. This group as a whole was under constant long-term pressure. Irregularly but inexorably, factory methods were being extended to more crafts, and many skilled artisans were being replaced by lower-paid semiskilled factory workers. Traditional woodcarvers and watchmakers virtually disappeared, for example, as the making of furniture and timepieces was put into the factory.

At the same time, a contrary movement was occurring. The labor aristocracy was consistently being enlarged by the growing need for highly skilled workers, such as shipbuilders, machine-tool makers, railway locomotive engineers, fine cotton textile spinners, and some metalworkers. Thus the labor elite was in a state of flux as individuals and whole crafts moved in and out of it.

FIGURE 24.3 The Urban Social Hierarchy

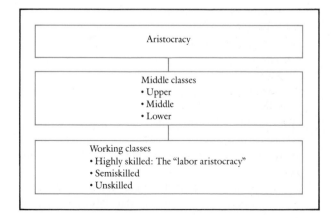

To maintain its precarious standing, the upper working class adopted distinctive values and strait-laced, almost puritanical, behavior. Like the middle classes, the labor aristocracy was strongly committed to the family and to economic improvement. Families in the upper working class saved money regularly, worried about their children's education, and valued good housing. Despite these similarities, which superficial observers were quick to exaggerate, skilled workers viewed themselves not as aspirants to the middle class but as the pacesetters and natural leaders of all the working classes. Well aware of the degradation not so far below them, they practiced self-discipline and stern morality.

The upper working class in general frowned on heavy drinking and sexual permissiveness. The organized temperance movement was strong in the countries of northern Europe, such as Great Britain, where a generation advocated tea as the "cup that cheers but does not inebriate." As one German labor aristocrat somberly warned, "the path to the brothel leads through the tavern" and from there quite possibly to drastic decline or total ruin for person and family.[7]

Men and women of the labor aristocracy were quick to find fault with those below them who failed to meet their standards. In 1868 William Lovett, an English labor aristocrat if ever there was one, denounced "this ignorant recklessness and improvidence that produce the swarms of half--starved, neglected, and ignorant children we see in all directions; who mostly grow up to become the burdens and often the pests of society, which the industrious and frugal have to support."[8] Finally, many members of the labor aristocracy had definite political and philosophical beliefs, whether Christian or socialist or both. Such beliefs further strengthened the firm moral code of the upper working class.

Below the labor aristocracy stood semiskilled and unskilled urban workers. The enormous complexity of this sector of the world of labor is not easily summarized. Workers in the established crafts—carpenters, bricklayers, pipefitters—stood near the top of the semiskilled hierarchy, often flirting with (or having backslid from) the labor elite. A large number of the semiskilled were factory workers, who earned highly variable but relatively good wages and whose relative importance in the labor force was increasing.

Below the semiskilled workers was a larger group of unskilled, who included day laborers such as longshoremen, wagon-driving teamsters, teen-agers, and every kind of "helper." Many of these people had real skills and performed valuable services, but they were unorganized and divided, united only by the common fate of meager earnings. The same lack of unity characterized street vendors and market people—self-employed workers who competed savagely with each other and with the established shopkeepers of the lower middle class.

One of the largest components of the unskilled group was domestic servants, whose numbers grew steadily in the nineteenth century. In advanced Great Britain, for example, one out of every seven employed persons was a domestic servant in 1911. The great majority were women; indeed, one out of every three girls in Britain between the ages of fifteen and twenty was a domestic servant. Throughout Europe and America, a great many female domestics in the cities were recent migrants from rural areas. As in earlier times, domestic service was still hard work at low pay with limited personal independence. For the full-time general maid in a lower-middle-class family, there was an unending routine of babysitting, shopping, cooking, and cleaning. In the great households, the girl was at the bottom of a rigid hierarchy; status-conscious butlers and housekeepers were determined to stand almost as far above her as the wealthy master and mistress.

Nonetheless, domestic service had real attractions for "rough country girls" with strong hands and few specialized skills. Marriage prospects were better, or at least more varied, in the city. And though wages were low, they were higher and more regular than in hard agricultural work. Finally, as one London observer noted, young girls and other migrants were drawn to the city by "the contagion of numbers, the sense of something going on, the theaters and the music halls, the brightly lighted streets and busy crowds—all, in short, that makes the difference between the Mile End fair on a Saturday night, and a dark and muddy country lane, with no glimmer of gas and with nothing to do."[9]

Many young domestics from the countryside made a successful transition to working-class wife and mother. Yet, with an unskilled or unemployed husband and a growing family, such a woman often had to join the broad ranks of working women in the "sweated industries." These industries resembled the old putting-out and cottage industries of the eighteenth and early nineteenth cen-

Sweated Industry About 1900   This moving photograph shows an English family making cheap toys at home for low wages. Women and children were the backbone of sweated industry, and this husband may be filling in while unemployed. *(Source: University of Reading, Institute of Agricultural History and Museum of English Rural Life)*

turies. The women normally worked at home, though sometimes together in some loft or garret, for tiny merchant-manufacturers. Paid by the piece and not by the hour, these women (and their young daughters), for whom organization was impossible, earned pitiful wages and lacked any job security.

Some women did hand-decorating of every conceivable kind of object; the majority, however, made clothing, especially after the advent of the sewing machine. Foot-powered sewing machines allowed the poorest wife or widow in the foulest dwelling to rival and eventually supplant the most highly skilled male tailor. By 1900 only a few such tailors lingered on in high-priced "tailor-made" shops. An army of poor women accounted for the bulk of the inexpensive "ready-made" clothes displayed on department store racks and in tiny shops. All of these considerations graphically illustrate the rise and fall of groups and individuals within the working classes.

The urban working classes sought fun and recreation, and they found it. Across the face of Europe, drinking was unquestionably the favorite leisure-time activity of working people. For many middle-class moralists, as well as moralizing historians since, love of drink has been a curse of the modern age—a sign of social dislocation and popular suffering. Certainly, drinking was deadly serious business. One English slum dweller recalled that "drunkenness was by far the commonest cause of dispute and misery in working class homes. On account of it one saw many a decent family drift down through poverty into total want."[10]

Generally, however, heavy "problem" drinking declined by the late nineteenth century, as it became less and less socially acceptable. This decline reflected in part the moral leadership of the upper working class. At the same time, drinking became more public and social, especially as on-the-job drinking, an ancient custom of field laborers and urban artisans, declined. Cafés and pubs became increasingly bright, friendly places. Working-class political activities, both moderate and radical, were also concentrated in taverns and pubs. Moreover, social drinking by married couples and sweethearts became an accepted and widespread practice for the

Renoir: Le Moulin de la Galette à Montmartre   In this 1876 masterpiece the impressionist painter Auguste Renoir (1841–1919) has transformed a popular outdoor dance hall of the Parisian masses into an enchanted fairyland. Renoir was a joyous artist, and his work optimistically affirmed the beauty and value of modern life. *(Source: Musée d'Orsay/Cliché des Musées Nationaux, Paris)*

first time. This greater participation by women undoubtedly helped to civilize the world of drink and hard liquor.

The two other leisure-time passions of the working classes were sports and music halls. By the late nineteenth century there had been a great decline in "cruel sports," such as bullbaiting and cockfighting, throughout Europe. Their place was filled by modern spectator sports, of which racing and soccer were the most popular. There was a great deal of gambling on sports events, and for many a working person the desire to decipher the racing forms was a powerful incentive toward literacy. Music halls and vaudeville theaters, the working-class counterparts of middle-class opera and classical theater, were enormously popular throughout Europe. In the words of one English printer, "It is to the music halls that the vast body of working people look for recreation and entertainment."[11] In 1900 there were more than fifty in London alone. Music hall audiences were thoroughly mixed, which may account for the fact that drunkenness, sexual intercourse and pregnancy before marriage, marital difficulties, and problems with mothers-in-law were favorite themes of broad jokes and bittersweet songs.

In more serious moments, religion and the Christian churches continued to provide working people with solace and meaning. The eighteenth-century vitality of popular religion in Catholic countries and the Protestant rejuvenation exemplified by German Pietism and English Methodism (see pages 652–654) carried over into the nineteenth century. Indeed, many historians see the early early nineteenth century as an age of religious revival. Yet historians also recognize that, by the last two or three decades of the nineteenth century, a considerable decline in both church attendance and church donations was occurring in most European countries. And it seems clear that this decline was greater for the urban working classes than for their rural counterparts or for the middle classes.

What did the decline in working-class church attendance really mean? Some have argued that it accurately reflected a general decline in faith and religious belief. Others disagree, noting correctly that most working-class families still baptized their children and considered themselves Christians. Although more research is necessary, it appears that the urban working classes in Europe did become more secular and less religious in the late nineteenth and early twentieth centuries. They rarely repudiated the Christian religion, but it tended to play a diminishing role in their daily lives.

Part of the reason was that the construction of churches failed to keep up with the rapid growth of urban population, especially in new working-class neighborhoods. Thus the vibrant, materialistic urban environment undermined popular religious impulses, which were poorly served in the cities. Equally important, however, was the fact that throughout the nineteenth century both Catholic and Protestant churches were normally seen as they saw themselves—as conservative institutions defending social order and custom. Therefore, as the European working classes became more politically conscious, they tended to see the established (or quasi-established) "territorial church" as defending what they wished to change and allied with their political opponents. Especially the men of the urban working classes developed vaguely anti-church attitudes, even though they remained neutral or positive toward religion. They tended to regard regular church attendance as "not our kind of thing"—not part of urban working-class culture.

The pattern was different in the United States. There, most churches also preached social conservatism in the nineteenth century. But because church and state had always been separated and because there was always a host of competing denominations and even different religions, working people identified churches much less with the political and social status quo. Instead, individual churches in the United States were often closely identified with an ethnic group rather than with a social class; and churches thrived, in part, as a means of asserting ethnic identity.

THE FAMILY

Urban life wrought many fundamental changes in the family. Although much is still unknown, it seems clear that by the late nineteenth century the family had stabilized considerably after the disruption of the late eighteenth and early nineteenth centuries. The home became more important for both men and women. The role of women and attitudes toward children underwent substantial change, and adolescence emerged as a distinct stage of life. These are but a few of the transformations that affected all social classes in varying degrees.

Premarital Sex and Marriage

By 1850 the preindustrial pattern of lengthy courtship and mercenary marriage was pretty well dead among the working classes. In its place, the ideal of romantic love had triumphed. As one French observer in a small seaport remarked about 1850, "The young men are constantly letting partners with handsome dowries go begging. When they marry, it's ordinarily for inclination and not for advantage."[12]

Couples were ever more likely to come from different, even distant, towns and to be more nearly the same age, further indicating that romantic sentiment was replacing tradition and financial considerations. The calculating practice whereby wealthy old craftsmen took pretty young brides, who as comfortable middle-aged widows later married poor apprentices, was increasingly heard of only in old tales and folk songs.

Economic considerations in marriage long remained much more important to the middle classes than to the working classes. In France, dowries and elaborate legal marriage contracts were standard practice among the middle classes, and marriage was for many families life's most crucial financial transaction. A popular author advised young Frenchmen that "marriage is in general a means of increasing one's credit and one's fortune and of insuring one's success in the world."[13] This preoccupation with money led many middle-class men, in France and elsewhere, to marry late, after they were established economically, and to choose women considerably younger and less sexually experienced than themselves. These differences between husband and wife became a source of tension in many middle-class marriages.

A young woman of the middle class found her romantic life carefully supervised by her well-meaning mother, who schemed for a proper marriage and guarded her daughter's virginity like the family's credit. After marriage, middle-class morality sternly demanded fidelity.

Middle-class boys were watched, too, but not as vigilantly. By the time they reached late adolescence, they had usually attained considerable sexual experience with maids or prostitutes. With marriage a distant, uncertain possibility, it was all too easy for the young man of the middle classes to turn to the urban underworld of whoredom and sexual exploitation to satisfy his desires.

In the early nineteenth century, sexual experimentation before marriage had also triumphed, as had illegitimacy. There was an "illegitimacy explosion" between 1750 and 1850 (see page 632). By the 1840s, as many as one birth in three was occurring outside of wedlock in many large cities. Although poverty and economic uncertainty undoubtedly prevented many lovers from marrying, there were also many among the poor and propertyless who saw little wrong with having illegitimate offspring. One young Bavarian woman answered happily when asked why she kept having illegitimate children: "It's O.K. to make babies. . . . The king has o.k.'d it!"[14] Thus the pattern of romantic ideals, premarital sexual activity, and widespread illegitimacy was firmly established by midcentury among the urban working classes.

It is hard to know how European couples managed sex, pregnancy, and marriage after 1850, because such questions were considered improper both in polite conversation and in public opinion polls. Yet there are many telltale clues. In the second half of the century the rising rate of illegitimacy was reversed: more babies were born to married mothers. Some observers have argued that this shift reflected the growth of puritanism and a lessening of sexual permissiveness among the unmarried. This explanation, however, is unconvincing.

The percentage of brides who were pregnant continued to be high and showed little or no tendency to decline. In many parts of urban Europe around 1900, as many as one woman in three was going to the altar an expectant mother. Moreover, unmarried people almost certainly used the cheap condoms and diaphragms the industrial age had made available to prevent pregnancy, at least in predominately Protestant countries.

Unmarried young people were probably engaging in just as much sexual activity as their parents and grandparents who had created the illegitimacy explosion of 1750 to 1850. But toward the end of the nineteenth century, pregnancy usually meant marriage and the establishment of a two-parent household. This important development reflected the growing respectability of the working classes, as well as their gradual economic improvement. Skipping out was less acceptable, and marriage was less of an economic disaster. Thus the urban working-class couple became more stable, and their stability strengthened the family as an institution.

Prostitution

In Paris alone, 155,000 women were registered as prostitutes between 1871 and 1903, and 750,000 others were suspected of prostitution in the same years. Men of all classes visited prostitutes, but the middle and upper classes supplied much of the motivating cash. Thus, though many middle-class men abided by the publicly professed code of stern puritanical morality, others indulged their appetites for prostitutes and sexual promiscuity.

My Secret Life, the anonymous eleven-volume autobiography of an English sexual adventurer from the servant-keeping classes, provides a remarkable picture of such a man. Beginning at an early age with a maid, the author becomes progressively obsessed with sex and devotes his life to living his sexual fantasies. In almost every one of his innumerable encounters all across Europe, this man of wealth simply buys his pleasure. Usually meetings are arranged in a businesslike manner: regular and part-time prostitutes quote their prices; working-class girls are corrupted by hot meals and baths.

At one point, he offers a young girl a sixpence for a kiss and gets it. Learning that the pretty, unskilled working girl earns nine pence a day, he offers her the equivalent of a week's salary for a few moments of fondling. When she finally agrees, he savagely exults that "*her* want was my opportunity."[15] Later he offers more money for more gratification, and when she refuses, he tries unsuccessfully to rape her in a hackney cab. On another occasion he takes a farm worker by force: "Her tears ran down. If I had not committed a rape, it looked uncommonly like one." He then forces his victim to take money to prevent a threatened lawsuit, while the foreman advises the girl to keep quiet and realize that "you be in luck if he likes you."

Obviously atypical in its excesses, the encyclopedic thoroughness of *My Secret Life* does reveal the dark side of sex and class in urban society. Thinking of their wives largely in terms of money and social position, the men of the comfortable classes often purchased sex and even affection from poor girls both before and after marriage. Moreover, the great continuing differences between rich and poor made for every kind of debauchery and sexual exploitation, including the brisk trade in poor virgins that the author of *My Secret Life* particularly relished. Brutal sexist behavior was part of life—a part the sternly moral women (and men) of the upper working class detested and tried to shield their daughters from. For many poor young women, prostitution, like domestic service, was a stage of life. Having passed through it for two or three years in their early twenties, they went on in their mid-twenties to marry (or live with) men of their own class and establish homes and families.

Kinship Ties

Within working-class homes, ties to relatives after marriage—kinship ties—were in general much stronger than superficial social observers have recognized. Most newlyweds tried to live near their parents, though not in the same house. Indeed, for many married couples in the cities, ties to mothers and fathers, uncles and aunts, became more important, and ties to nonrelated acquaintances became weaker.

Toulouse-Lautrec: à La Mie   Nobleman by birth and cripple by accident, Henri de Toulouse-Lautrec (1864–1901) was irresistibly drawn to the night life of Paris and its sexual underworld. This portrait of an aging prostitute and her reptilian companion is a powerful study in degradation. *(Source: Courtesy, Museum of Fine Arts, Boston)*

social position and that of their children. Children were no longer an economic asset. By having fewer youngsters, parents could give those they had valuable advantages, from music lessons and summer vacations to long, expensive university educations and suitable dowries. A young German skilled worker with only one child spoke for many in his class when he said, "We want to get ahead, and our daughter should have things better than my wife and sisters did."[22] Thus the growing tendency of couples in the late nineteenth century to use a variety of contraceptive methods—rhythm, withdrawal, and mechanical devices—certainly reflected increased concern for children.

Indeed, many parents were probably *too* concerned about their children, unwittingly subjecting

them to an emotional pressure cooker of almost unbearable intensity. The result was that many children and especially adolescents came to feel trapped and in desperate need of greater independence.

Biological and medical theories led parents to believe in the possibility that their own emotional characteristics were passed on to their offspring and that they were thus directly responsible for any abnormality in a child. The moment the child was conceived was thought to be of enormous importance. "Never run the risk of conception when you are sick or over-tired or unhappy," wrote one influential American woman. "For the bodily condition of the child, its vigor and magnetic qualities, are much affected by conditions ruling this great moment."[23] So might the youthful "sexual excess" of the father curse future generations. Although this was true in the case of syphilis, which could be transmitted to unborn children, the rigid determinism of such views left little scope for the child's individual development.

Another area of excessive parental concern was the sexual behavior of the child. Masturbation was viewed with horror, for it represented an act of independence and even defiance. Diet, clothing, games, and sleeping were carefully regulated. Girls were discouraged from riding horses and bicycling because rhythmic friction simulated masturbation. Boys were dressed in trousers with shallow and widely separated pockets. Between 1850 and 1880, there were surgical operations for children who persisted in masturbating. Thereafter until about 1905, various restraining apparatuses were more often used.

These and less blatant attempts to repress the child's sexuality were a source of unhealthy tension, often made worse by the rigid division of sexual roles within the family. It was widely believed that mother and child love each other easily, but that relations between father and child are necessarily difficult and often tragic. The father was a stranger; his world of business was far removed from the maternal world of spontaneous affection. Moreover, the father was demanding, often expecting the child to succeed where he himself had failed and making his love conditional on achievement. Little wonder that the imaginative literature of the late nineteenth century came to deal with the emotional and destructive elements of father-son relationships. In the Russian Feodor Dostoevsky's great novel *The Brothers Karamazov* (1880–1881),

The Drawing Room The middle-class ideal of raising cultured, educated, and properly protected young women is captured in this illustration. A serious mother lovingly teachers her youngest child while the older daughters practice their genteel skills. A drawing room was a kind of nineteenth-century family room, mercifully spared the tyranny of television. (Source: Bettmann/Hulton)

for example, four sons work knowingly or unknowingly to destroy their father. Later, at the murder trial, one of the brothers claims to speak for all mankind and screams out: "Who doesn't wish his father dead?"

Sigmund Freud (1856–1939), the Viennese founder of psychoanalysis, formulated the most striking analysis of the explosive dynamics of the family, particularly the middle-class family in the late nineteenth century. A physician by training, Freud began his career treating mentally ill patients. He noted that the hysteria of his patients appeared to originate in bitter early childhood experiences, wherein the child had been obliged to repress strong feelings. When these painful experiences were recalled and reproduced under hypnosis or through the patient's free association of ideas, the patient could be brought to understand his or her unhappiness and eventually to deal with it.

One of Freud's most influential ideas concerned the Oedipal tensions resulting from the son's instinctive competition with the father for the mother's love and affection. More generally, Freud postulated that much of human behavior is motivated by unconscious emotional needs, whose nature and origins are kept from conscious awareness by various mental devices he called "defense mechanisms." Freud concluded that much unconscious psychological energy is sexual energy, which is repressed and precariously controlled by rational thinking and moral rules. If Freud exaggerated the sexual and familial roots of adult behavior, that exaggeration was itself a reflection of the tremendous emotional intensity of family life in the late nineteenth century.

The working classes probably had more avenues of escape from such tensions than did the middle classes. Unlike their middle-class counterparts, who remained economically dependent on their families until a long education was finished or a proper marriage secured, working-class boys and girls went to work when they reached adolescence. Earning wages on their own, they could bargain with their parents for greater independence within the household by the time they were sixteen or seventeen. If they were unsuccessful, they could and did leave home, to live cheaply as paying lodgers in other working-class homes. Thus the young person from the working classes broke away from the family more easily when emotional ties became oppressive. In the twentieth century, middle-class youth would follow this lead.

SCIENCE AND THOUGHT

Major changes in Western thought accompanied the emergence of urban society. Two aspects of these complex intellectual developments stand out as especially significant. Scientific knowledge expanded rapidly and came to influence the Western world-view even more profoundly than it had since the Scientific Revolution and the early Enlightenment. And, between about the 1840s and the 1890s, European literature underwent a shift from soaring romanticism to tough-minded realism.

The Triumph of Science

As the pace of scientific advance quickened and as theoretical advances resulted in great practical benefits, science exercised growing influence on human thought. The intellectual achievements of the Scientific Revolution had resulted in few such benefits, and theoretical knowledge had also played a relatively small role in the Industrial Revolution in England. But breakthroughs in industrial technology enormously stimulated basic scientific inquiry, as researchers sought to explain theoretically how such things as steam engines and blast furnaces actually worked. The result was an explosive growth of fundamental scientific discoveries from the 1830s onward. And in contrast to earlier periods, these theoretical discoveries were increasingly transformed into material improvements for the general population.

A perfect example of the translation of better scientific knowledge into practical human benefits was the work of Pasteur and his followers in biology and the medical sciences. Another was the development of the branch of physics known as *thermodynamics*. Building on Newton's laws of mechanics and on studies of steam engines, thermodynamics investigated the relationship between heat and mechanical energy. By midcentury, physicists had formulated the fundamental laws of thermodynamics, which were then applied to mechanical engineering, chemical processes, and many other fields. The *law of conservation of energy* held that different forms of energy—such as heat, electricity, and magnetism—could be converted but neither created nor destroyed. Nineteenth-century thermodynamics demonstrated that the physical world is governed by firm, unchanging laws.

ever-greater specialization and progress by the brutal economic struggle that efficiently determined the "survival of the fittest." The poor were the ill-fated weak, the prosperous the chosen strong. Understandably, Spencer and other Social Darwinists were especially popular with the upper middle class.

Realism in Literature

In 1868 Émile Zola (1840–1902), the giant of the realist movement in literature, defended his violently criticized first novel against charges of pornography and corruption of morals. Such accusations were meaningless, Zola claimed: he was only a purely objective scientist using "the modern method, the universal instrument of inquiry of which this age makes such ardent use to open up the future."

I chose characters completely dominated by their nerves and their blood, deprived of free-will, pushed to each action of their lives by the fatality of their flesh. . . . I have simply done on living bodies the work of analysis which surgeons perform on corpses.[25]

Zola's literary manifesto articulated the key themes of realism, which had emerged in the 1840s and continued to dominate Western culture and style until the 1890s. Realist writers believed that literature should depict life exactly as it was. Forsaking poetry for prose and the personal, emotional viewpoint of the romantics for strict, scientific objectivity, the realists simply observed and recorded —content to let the facts speak for themselves.

The major realist writers focused their extraordinary powers of observation on contemporary everyday life. Emphatically rejecting the romantic search for the exotic and the sublime, they energetically pursued the typical and the commonplace. Beginning with a dissection of the middle classes, from which most of them sprang, many realists eventually focused on the working classes, especially the urban working classes, who had been neglected in imaginative literature before this time. They put a microscope to many unexplored and taboo subjects—sex, strikes, violence, alcoholism —and hastened to report that slums and factories teemed with savage behavior. Many shocked middle-class critics denounced realism as ugly sensationalism, wrapped provocatively in pseudoscientific declarations and crude language.

The realists' claims of objectivity did not prevent the elaboration of a definite world-view. Unlike the romantics, who had gloried in individual freedom and an unlimited universe, realists such as Zola were strict determinists. Human beings, like atoms, were components of the physical world, and all human actions were caused by unalterable natural laws. Heredity and environment determined human behavior; good and evil were merely social conventions.

The realist movement began in France, where romanticism had never been completely dominant, and three of its greatest practitioners—Balzac, Flaubert, and Zola—were French. Honoré de Balzac (1799–1850) spent thirty years writing a vastly ambitious panorama of postrevolutionary French life. Known collectively as *The Human Comedy,* this series of nearly one hundred books vividly portrays more than two thousand characters from virtually all sectors of French society. Balzac pictures urban society as grasping, amoral, and brutal, characterized by a Darwinian struggle for wealth and power. In *Le Père Goriot* (1835), the hero, a poor student from the provinces, eventually surrenders his idealistic integrity to feverish ambition and society's all-pervasive greed.

Madame Bovary (1857), the masterpiece of Gustave Flaubert (1821–1880), is far narrower in scope than Balzac's work but unparalleled in its depth and accuracy of psychological insight. Unsuccessfully prosecuted as an outrage against public morality and religion, Flaubert's carefully crafted novel tells the ordinary, even banal, story of a frustrated middle-class housewife who has an adulterous love affair and is betrayed by her lover. Without moralizing, Flaubert portrays the provincial middle class as petty, smug, and hypocritical.

Zola was most famous for his seamy, animalistic view of working-class life. But he also wrote gripping, carefully researched stories featuring the stock exchange, the big department store, and the army, as well as urban slums and bloody coal strikes. Like many later realists, Zola sympathized with socialism, a sympathy evident in his overpowering *Germinal* (1885).

Realism quickly spread beyond France. In England, Mary Ann Evans (1819–1880), who wrote under the pen name George Eliot, brilliantly achieved a more deeply felt, less sensational kind of realism. "It is the habit of my imagination," George Eliot wrote, "to strive after as full a vision of the medium in which a character moves as one of the character itself." Her great novel *Middle-march: A Study of Provincial Life* examines masterfully the ways in which people are shaped by their social medium as well as their own inner strivings, conflicts, and moral choices. Thomas Hardy (1840–1928) was more in the Zola tradition. His novels, such as *Tess of the D'Urbervilles* and *Return of the Native,* depicted men and women frustrated and crushed by fate and bad luck.

The greatest Russian realist, Count Leo Tolstoy (1828–1910), combined realism in description and character development with an atypical moralizing, which came to dominate his later work. Tolstoy's greatest work was *War and Peace,* a monumental novel set against the historical background of Napoleon's invasion of Russia in 1812. Tolstoy probes deeply into the lives of a multitude of unforgettable characters, such as the ill-fated Prince Andrei; the shy, fumbling Pierre; and the enchanting, level-headed Natasha. Tolstoy goes to great pains to develop his fatalistic theory of history, which regards free will as an illusion and the achievements of even the greatest leaders as only the channeling of historical necessity. Yet Tolstoy's central message is one that most of the people discussed in this chapter would readily accept: human love, trust, and everyday family ties are life's enduring values.

Thoroughgoing realism (or "naturalism," as it was often called) arrived late in the United States, most arrestingly in the work of Theodore Dreiser (1871–1945). Dreiser's first novel, *Sister Carrie* (1900), the story of an ordinary farm girl who does well going wrong in Chicago, so outraged conventional morality that the publisher withdrew the book. The United States subsequently became a bastion of literary realism in the twentieth century after the movement had faded away in Europe.

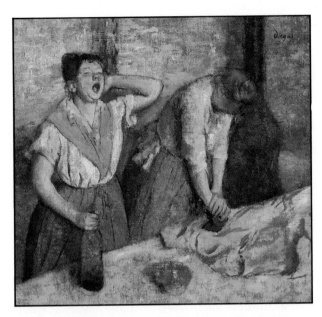

Degas: Women Ironing   Realism replaced romanticism as the dominant trend in the visual arts for a long generation after 1850. This French work by Edgar Degas (1834–1917) accurately captures the hard work and fatigue of unskilled labor. *(Source: Musée d'Orsay/Cliché des Musées Nationaux, Paris)*

SUMMARY

The Industrial Revolution had a decisive influence on the urban environment. The populations of towns and cities grew rapidly because it was economically advantageous to locate factories and offices in urban areas. This rapid growth worsened long-standing overcrowding and unhealthy living conditions and posed a frightening challenge for society. Eventually government leaders, city planners, reformers, scientists, and ordinary citizens responded. They took effective action in public

health and provided themselves with other badly needed urban services. Gradually they tamed the ferocious savagery of the traditional city.

As urban civilization came to prevail, there were major changes in family life. Especially among the lower classes, family life became more stable, more loving, and less mercenary. These improvements had a price, though. Sex roles for men and women became sharply defined and rigidly separate. Women especially tended to be locked into a subordinate and stereotypical role. Nonetheless, on balance, the quality of family life improved for all family members. Better, more stable family relations reinforced the benefits for the masses of higher real wages, increased social security, political participation, and education.

While the quality of urban and family life improved, the class structure became more complex and diversified than before. Urban society featured many distinct social groups, which existed in a state of constant flux and competition. The gap between rich and poor remained enormous and really quite traditional in mature urban society, although there were countless gradations between the extremes. Large numbers of poor women in particular continued to labor as workers in sweated industries, as domestic servants, and as prostitutes in order to satisfy the demands of their masters in the servant-keeping classes. Urban society in the late nineteenth century represented a great step forward for humanity, but it remained very unequal.

Inequality was a favorite theme of realist novelists like Balzac and Zola. More generally, literary realism reflected Western society's growing faith in science, progress, and evolutionary thinking. The emergence of urban, industrial civilization accelerated the secularization of the Western world-view.

NOTES

1. A. Weber, *The Growth of Cities in the Nineteenth Century* (New York: Columbia University Press, 1899), p. 1.
2. Quoted in W. Ashworth, *The Genesis of Modern British Town Planning* (London: Routledge & Kegan Paul, 1954), p. 17.
3. S. Marcus, "Reading the Illegible," in *The Victorian City: Images and Realities,* ed. H. J. Dyos and Michael Wolff, vol. 1 (London: Routledge & Kegan Paul, 1973), p. 266.
4. E. Gauldie, *Cruel Habitations: A History of Working-Class Housing, 1780–1918* (London: George Allen & Unwin, 1974), p. 21.
5. Quoted in E. Chadwick, *Report on the Sanitary Condition of the Labouring Population of Great Britain,* ed. M. W. Flinn (Edinburgh: University of Edinburgh Press, 1965; original publication, 1842), pp. 315–316.
6. J. P. McKay, *Tramways and Trolleys: The Rise of Urban Mass Transport in Europe* (Princeton, N.J.: Princeton University Press, 1976), p. 81.
7. Quoted in R. P. Neuman, "The Sexual Question and Social Democracy in Imperial Germany," *Journal of Social History* 7 (Winter 1974): 276.
8. Quoted in B. Harrison, "Underneath the Victorians," *Victorian Studies* 10 (March 1967): 260.
9. Quoted in J. A. Banks, "The Contagion of Numbers," in Dyos and Wolff, vol. 1, p. 112.
10. Quoted in R. Roberts, *The Classic Slum: Salford Life in the First Quarter of the Century* (Manchester, Eng.: University of Manchester Press, 1971), p. 95.
11. Quoted in B. Harrison, "Pubs," in Dyos and Wolff, vol. 1, p. 175.
12. Quoted in E. Shorter, *The Making of the Modern Family* (New York: Basic Books, 1975), p. 150.
13. Quoted in T. Zeldin, *France, 1848–1945* (Oxford, Eng.: Clarendon Press, 1973), vol. 1, p. 288.
14. Quoted in J. M. Phayer, "Lower-Class Morality: The Case of Bavaria," *Journal of Social History* 8 (Fall 1974): 89.
15. Quoted in S. Marcus, *The Other Victorians: A Study of Sexuality and Pornography in Mid-Nineteenth-Century England* (New York: Basic Books, 1966), p. 142.
16. Quoted in G. S. Jones, "Working-Class Culture and Working-Class Politics in London, 1870–1900: Notes on the Remaking of a Working Class," *Journal of Social History* 7 (Summer 1974): 486.
17. Quoted in Zeldin, vol. 1, p. 346.
18. Quoted in Shorter, pp. 230–231.
19. Roberts, p. 35.
20. Quoted in Zeldin, vol. 1, p. 295.
21. Ibid., vol. 1, p. 328.
22. Quoted in Neuman, p. 281.
23. Quoted by S. Kern, "Explosive Intimacy: Psychodynamics of the Victorian Family," *History of Childhood Quarterly* 1 (Winter 1974): 439.
24. A. Comte, *The Positive Philosophy of Auguste Comte,* trans. H. Martineau, vol. 1 (London: J. Chapman, 1853), pp. 1–2.
25. Quoted in G. J. Becker, ed., *Documents of Modern Literary Realism* (Princeton, N.J.: Princeton University Press, 1963), p. 159.

SUGGESTED READING

All of the books and articles cited in the Notes are highly recommended; each in its own way is an important contribution to social history and the study of life in the urban society. Note that the *Journal of Social History,* which has a strong European orientation, is excellent both for its articles and for its reviews of new books. The book mentioned by T. Zeldin, *France, 1848–1945,* 2 vols. (1973, 1977), is a pioneering social history that opens many doors, as is the ambitious synthesis by T. Hamerow, *The Birth of a New Europe: State and Society in the Nineteenth Century* (1983).

On the European city, D. Harvey, *Consciousness and the Urban Experience* (1985), is provocative, and D. Pickney, *Napoleon III and the Rebuilding of Paris* (1972), is fascinating, as are G. Masur, *Imperial Berlin* (1970), and M. Hamm, ed., *The City in Russian History* (1976). So also are N. Evenson's beautifully illustrated *Paris: A Century of Change, 1878–1978* (1979); and D. Grew's authoritative *Town in the Ruhr: A Social History of Bochum, 1860–1914* (1979). J. Siegel, *Bohemian Paris: Culture, Politics, and the Boundaries of Bourgeois Life, 1830–1930* (1986), and J. Merriman, ed., *French Cities in the Nineteenth Century: Class, Power, and Urbanization* (1982), are important works on France. D. Olsen's scholarly *Growth of Victorian*

London (1978) complements H. Mayhew's wonderful contemporary study, *London Labour and the Labouring Poor* (1861), reprinted recently. M. Crichton's realistic historical novel on organized crime, *The Great Train Robbery* (1976), is excellent. J. J. Tobias, *Urban Crime in Victorian England* (1972), is a lively, scholarly approach to declining criminal activity in the nineteenth century, with a wealth of detail. J. P. Goubert, *The Conquest of Water: The Advent of Health in the Industrial Age* (1989), and G. Rosen, *History of Public Health* (1958), are excellent introductions to sanitary and medical developments. For society as a whole, J. Burnett, *History of the Cost of Living* (1969), cleverly shows how different classes spent their money, and B. Tuchman, *The Proud Tower* (1966), draws an unforgettable portrait of people and classes before 1914. J. Laver's handsomely illustrated *Manners and Morals in the Age of Optimism, 1848–1914* (1966) investigates the urban underworld and relations between the sexes. Sexual attitudes are also examined by E. Trudgill, *Madonnas and Magdalenas: The Origin and Development of Victorian Sexual Attitudes* (1976), and J. Phayer, *Sexual Liberation and Religion in Nineteenth Century Europe* (1977). G. Alter, *Family and Female Life Course: The Women of Verviers, Belgium, 1849–1880* (1988), and A. McLaren, *Sexuality and Social Order: Birth Control in Nineteenth-Century France* (1982), explore attitudes toward family planning.

Women are coming into their own in historical studies. In addition to the general works by Shorter, Wrigley, Stone, and Tilly and Scott cited in Chapter 20, there are a growing number of eye-opening specialized investigations. These include L. Davidoff, *The Best Circles* (1973), and P. Jalland, *Women, Marriage and Politics, 1860–1914* (1986), on upper-class society types; O. Banks, *Feminism and Family Planning in Victorian England* (1964); and P. Branca, *Women in Europe Since 1750* (1978). M. J. Peterson, *Love and Work in the Lives of Victorian Gentlewomen* (1989), and L. Holcombe, *Victorian Ladies at Work* (1973), examine middle-class women at work. M. Vicinus, ed., *Suffer and Be Still* (1972) and *A Widening Sphere* (1981), are far-ranging collections of essays on women's history, as is R. Bridenthal, C. Koonz, and S. Stuard, eds., *Becoming Visible: Women in European History,* 2d ed.

(1987). Feminism is treated perceptively in R. Evans, *The Feminists: Women's Emancipation in Europe, America, and Australia* (1979); K. Blair, *The Clubwoman as Feminist: True Womanhood Redefined, 1868–1914* (1980); and C. Moses, *French Feminism in the Nineteenth Century* (1984). J. Gillis, *Youth and History* (1974), is a good introduction. D. Ransel, ed., *The Family in Imperial Russia* (1978), is an important work on the subject, as is J. Donzelot, *The Policing of Families* (1979), which stresses the loss of family control of all aspects of life to government agencies.

Among studies of special groups, J. Scott, *The Glass-Workers of Carmaux* (1974), is outstanding on skilled French craftsmen, and D. Lockwood, *The Blackcoated Worker* (1958), carefully examines class consciousness in the English lower middle class. J. R. Wegs, *Growing Up Working Class: Continuity and Change Among Viennese Youth, 1890–1938* (1989), is recommended. Two fine studies on universities and their professors are S. Rothblatt, *Revolution of the Dons: Cambridge and Society in Victorian England* (1968), and F. Ringer, *The Decline of the German Mandarins* (1969). Servants and their employers receive excellent treatment in T. McBride, *The Domestic Revolution: The Modernization of Household Service in England and France, 1820–1920* (1976), and B. Smith, *Ladies of the Leisure Class: The Bourgeoises of Northern France in the Nineteenth Century* (1981), which may be compared with the innovative study by M. Miller, *The Bon Marché: Bourgeois Culture and the Department Store, 1869–1920* (1981).

On Darwin, M. Ruse, *The Darwinian Revolution* (1979), is a good starting point, as are P. Bowler, *Evolution: The History of an Idea*, rev. ed. (1989), and G. Himmelfarb, *Darwin and the Darwinian Revolution* (1968). O. Chadwick, *The Secularization of the European Mind in the Nineteenth Century* (1976), analyzes the impact of science (and other factors) on religious belief. The masterpieces of the great realist social novelists remain one of the best and most memorable introductions to nineteenth-century culture and thought. In addition to the novels discussed in this chapter, and those cited in the Suggested Reading for Chapters 22 and 23, I. Turgenev's *Fathers and Sons* and Zola's *The Dram-Shop (L'Assommoir)* are especially recommended.

25

The Age of Nationalism,
1850–1914

The revolutions of 1848 closed one era and opened another. Urban industrial society began to take strong hold on the Continent and in the young United States, as it already had in Great Britain. Internationally, the repressive peace and diplomatic stability of Metternich's time were replaced by a period of war and rapid change. In thought and culture, exuberant romanticism gave way to hard-headed realism. In the Atlantic economy, the hard years of the 1840s were followed by good times and prosperity throughout most of the 1850s and 1860s. Perhaps most important of all, Western society progressively found, for better or worse, a new and effective organizing principle, capable of coping with the many-sided challenge of the dual revolution and the emerging urban civilization. That principle was nationalism—dedication to and identification with the nation-state.

The triumph of nationalism is a development of enormous historical significance. It was by no means completely predictable. After all, nationalism had been a powerful force since at least 1789. Yet it had repeatedly failed to realize its goals, most spectacularly so in 1848.

- Why, then, did nationalism become in one way or another an almost universal faith in Europe and in the United States between 1850 and 1914?

- More specifically, how did nationalism evolve so that it appealed not only to predominately middle-class liberals but to the broad masses of society as well?

These are the weighty questions this chapter will seek to answer.

NAPOLEON III IN FRANCE

Early nationalism was at least liberal and idealistic and often democratic and radical as well. The ideas of nationhood and popular sovereignty posed an awesome revolutionary threat to conservatives like Metternich. Yet, from the vantage point of the twentieth century, it is clear that nationalism wears many masks: it may be democratic and radical, as it was for Mazzini and Michelet; but it can also flourish in dictatorial states, which may be conservative,

fascist, or communist. Napoleon I's France had already combined national devotion with authoritarian rule. Significantly, it was Napoleon's nephew, Louis Napoleon, who revived and extended this merger. It was he who showed how governments could reconcile popular and conservative forces in an authoritarian nationalism. In doing so, he provided a model for political leaders elsewhere.

The Second Republic and Louis Napoleon

The overwhelming victory of Louis Napoleon Bonaparte in the French presidential election of December 1848 has long puzzled historians. The nephew of Napoleon I, Louis Napoleon had lived most of his life outside of France and played no part in French politics before 1848. Why did universal manhood suffrage give such an unproven nobody 5.5 million votes, while the runner-up, General Cavaignac of June Days fame (see page 746), polled only 1.5 million and the other three candidates (including the poet Lamartine) received insignificant support?

The usual explanation is that, though Louis Napoleon had only his great name in common with his uncle, that was enough. According to some historians, the Napoleonic legend—a monument to the power of romanticism between 1820 and 1848—had transformed a dictator into a demigod in the minds of the unsophisticated French masses. Another explanation, popularized by Karl Marx, has stressed the fears of middle-class and peasant property owners in the face of the socialist challenge of urban workers. These classes wanted protection. They wanted a tough cop with a big stick on the beat. They found him in Louis Napoleon, who had indeed served briefly as a special constable in London at the height of the Chartist agitation.

These explanations are not wrong, but there was more to Louis Napoleon's popularity than stupidity and fear. In late 1848 Louis Napoleon had a positive "program" for France, which was to guide him throughout most of his long reign. This program had been elaborated earlier in two pamphlets, *Napoleonic Ideas* and *The Elimination of Poverty,* which Louis Napoleon had written while imprisoned for a farcical attempt to overthrow Louis Philippe's government. The pamphlets had been widely circulated prior to the presidential election.

Louis Napoleon believed that the government should represent the people and that it should also try hard to help them economically. How was this to be done? Parliaments and political parties were not the answer, according to Louis Napoleon. Politicians represented special-interest groups, particularly middle-class ones. When they ran a parliamentary government, they stirred up class hatred because they were not interested in helping the poor. This had occurred under Louis Philippe, and it was occurring again under the Second Republic. The answer was a strong, even authoritarian, national leader, like the first Napoleon, who would serve all the people, rich and poor. This leader would be linked to the people by direct democracy and universal male suffrage. Sovereignty would flow from the entire population to the leader and would not be diluted or corrupted by politicians and legislative bodies.

These political ideas went hand in hand with Louis Napoleon's vision of national unity and social progress. Rather than doing nothing or providing only temporary relief for the awful poverty of the poor, the state and its leader had a sacred duty to provide jobs and stimulate the economy. All classes would benefit by such action.

Louis Napoleon's political and social ideas were at least vaguely understood by large numbers of French peasants and workers in December 1848. To many common people he appeared to be both a strong man *and* a forward-looking champion of their interests, and that is why they voted for him.

Elected to a four-year term, President Louis Napoleon had to share power with a conservative National Assembly. With some misgivings he signed a bill to increase greatly the role of the Catholic church in primary and secondary education. In France, as elsewhere in Europe after 1848, the anxious well-to-do saw religion as a bulwark against radicalism. As one leader of the church in France put it, "There is only one recipe for making those who own nothing believe in property-rights: that is to make them believe in God, who dictated the Ten Commandments and who promises eternal punishment to those who steal."[1] Very reluctantly, Louis Napoleon also signed another conservative law depriving many poor people of the right to vote. He took these conservative measures for two main reasons: he wanted the Assembly to vote funds to pay his personal debts, and he wanted it to change the constitution so he could run for a second term.

The Assembly did neither. Thus in 1851 Louis Napoleon began to organize a conspiracy with key army officers. On December 2, 1851, he illegally dismissed the Assembly and seized power in a *coup d'état*. There was some armed resistance in Paris and other cities, but the actions of the Assembly had left the Second Republic with few defenders. Restoring universal male suffrage, Louis Napoleon called on the French people, as his uncle had done, to legalize his actions. They did: 92 percent voted to make him a strong president for ten years. A year later, 97 percent agreed in a national plebiscite to make him hereditary emperor. For the third time, and by the greatest margin yet, the authoritarian Louis Napoleon was overwhelmingly elected to lead the French nation.

Napoleon III's Second Empire

Louis Napoleon—now Emperor Napoleon III—experienced both success and failure between 1852 and 1870. His greatest success was with the economy, particularly in the 1850s. His government encouraged the new investment banks and massive railroad construction that were at the heart of the Industrial Revolution on the Continent. General economic expansion was also fostered by the government's ambitious program of public works, which included the rebuilding of Paris to improve the urban environment. The profits of business people soared with prosperity, and the working classes did not fare poorly either. Their wages more than kept up with inflation, and jobs were much easier to find.

Louis Napoleon always hoped that economic progress would reduce social and political tensions. This hope was at least partially realized. Until the mid-1860s, there was little active opposition and even considerable support for his government from France's most dissatisfied group, the urban workers. Napoleon III's regulation of pawnshops and his support of credit unions and better housing for the working class were evidence of positive concern in the 1850s. In the 1860s he granted workers the right to form unions and the right to strike—important economic rights denied by earlier governments.

At first, political power remained in the hands of the emperor. He alone chose his ministers, and they had great freedom of action. At the same time, Napoleon III restricted but did not abolish the Assembly. Members were elected by universal male suffrage every six years, and Louis Napoleon and his government took the parliamentary elections

Rebuilding Paris Expensive and time consuming, boulevard construction in Paris brought massive demolition, considerable slum clearance, and protests of ruin to the old city. In addition to expecting economic benefits, Napoleon III rightly believed that broad boulevards would be harder for revolutionaries to barricade than narrow twisting streets. *(Source: The Mansell Collection)*

very seriously. They tried to entice notable people, even those who had opposed the regime, to stand as government candidates in order to expand the base of support. Moreover, the government used its officials and appointed mayors to spread the word that the election of the government's candidates—and the defeat of the opposition—was the key to roads, schools, tax rebates, and a thousand other local concerns.

In 1857 and again in 1863, Louis Napoleon's system worked brilliantly and produced overwhelming electoral victories. Yet in the course of the 1860s Napoleon III's electoral system gradually disintegrated, for several reasons. France's problems in Italy and the rising power of Prussia led to increasing criticism at home from his Catholic and nationalist supporters. With increasing effectiveness, the middle-class liberals who had

always detested his dictatorship continued to denounce his rule as a disgrace to France's republican tradition.

Napoleon was always sensitive to the public mood. Public opinion, he once said, always wins the last victory. Thus in the 1860s he progressively liberalized his empire. He gave the Assembly greater powers and the opposition candidates greater freedom, which they used to good advantage. In 1869 the opposition, consisting of republicans, monarchists, and liberals, polled almost 45 percent of the vote.

The following year, a sick and weary Louis Napoleon once again granted France a new constitution, which combined a basically parliamentary regime with a hereditary emperor as chief of state. In a final great plebiscite on the eve of a disastrous war with Prussia, 7.5 million Frenchmen voted in favor of the new constitution, and only 1.5 million opposed it. Napoleon III's attempt to reconcile a strong national state with universal manhood suffrage was still evolving, in a democratic direction.

NATION BUILDING IN ITALY AND GERMANY

Louis Napoleon's triumph in 1848 and his authoritarian rule in the 1850s provided the old ruling classes of Europe with a new model in politics. To what extent was it possible that the expanding urban middle classes and even the growing working classes might, like people in rural areas, rally to a strong and essentially conservative national state? This was one of the great political questions in the 1850s and 1860s. In central Europe, a resounding and definitive answer came with the national unification of Italy and Germany.

Italy to 1850

Italy had never been a united nation prior to 1860. Part of Rome's great empire in ancient times, the Italian peninsula was divided in the Middle Ages into competing city-states, which led the commercial and cultural revival of the West with amazing creativity. A battleground for great powers after 1494, Italy had been reorganized in 1815 at the Congress of Vienna. The rich northern provinces of Lombardy and Venetia were taken by Metternich's Austria. Sardinia and Piedmont were under the rule of an Italian monarch, and Tuscany with its famous capital of Florence shared north central Italy with several smaller states. Central Italy and Rome were ruled by the papacy, which had always considered an independent political existence necessary to fulfill its spiritual mission. Naples and Sicily were ruled, as they had been for almost a hundred years, by a branch of the Bourbons. Metternich was not wrong in dismissing Italy as "a geographical expression" (Map 25.1).

Between 1815 and 1848, the goal of a unified Italian nation captured the imaginations of increasing numbers of Italians. There were three basic approaches. The first was the radical program of the idealistic patriot Mazzini, who preached a centralized democratic republic based on universal suffrage and the will of the people. The second was that of Gioberti, a Catholic priest, who called for a federation of existing states under the presidency of a progressive pope. Finally, there were those who looked for leadership toward the autocratic kingdom of Sardinia-Piedmont, much as many Germans looked toward Prussia.

The third alternative was strengthened by the failures of 1848, when Austria smashed and discredited Mazzini's republicanism. Almost by accident, Sardinia's monarch Victor Emmanuel retained the liberal constitution granted under duress in March 1848. This constitution provided for a fair degree of civil liberties and real parliamentary government, complete with elections and parliamentary control of taxes. To the Italian middle classes, Sardinia appeared to be a liberal, progressive state, ideally suited to achieve the goal of national unification. By contrast, Mazzini's brand of democratic republicanism seemed quixotic and too radical. As for the papacy, the initial cautious support by Pius IX (1846–1878) for unification had given way to fear and hostility after he was temporarily driven from Rome during the upheavals of 1848. For a long generation, the papacy would stand resolutely opposed not only to national unification but to most modern trends. In 1864, in the *Syllabus of Errors,* Pius IX strongly denounced rationalism, socialism, separation of church and state, and religious liberty, denying that "the Roman pontiff can and ought to reconcile and align himself with progress, liberalism, and modern civilization."

Cavour and Garibaldi

Sardinia had the good fortune of being led by a brilliant statesman, Count Camillo Benso di Cavour, the dominant figure in the Sardinian government from 1850 until his death in 1861. Cavour's development was an early sign of the coming tacit alliance between the aristocracy and the solid middle class throughout much of Europe. Beginning as a successful manager of his father's large landed estates in Piedmont, Cavour was also an economic liberal. He turned toward industry and made a substantial fortune in sugar mills, steamships, banks, and railroads. Economically secure, he then entered the world of politics and became chief minister in the liberalized Sardinian monarchy. Cavour's national goals were limited and realistic. Until 1859 he sought unity only for the states of northern and perhaps central Italy in a greatly expanded

MAP 25.1 The Unification of Italy, 1859–1870 The leadership of Sardinia-Piedmont and nationalist fervor were decisive factors in the unification of Italy.

kingdom of Sardinia. It was not one of his goals to incorporate the Papal States or the kingdom of the Two Sicilies, with their very different cultures and governments, into an Italy of all the Italians. Cavour was a moderate nationalist.

In the 1850s Cavour worked to consolidate Sardinia as a liberal state capable of leading northern Italy. His program of highways and railroads, of civil liberties and opposition to clerical privilege, increased support for Sardinia throughout northern Italy. Yet Cavour realized that Sardinia could not drive Austria out of Lombardy and Venetia and unify northern Italy under Victor Emmanuel without the help of a powerful ally. He sought that ally in the person of Napoleon III, who sincerely believed in the general principle of nationality, as well as modest expansion for France.

In a complicated series of diplomatic maneuvers, Cavour worked for a secret diplomatic alliance with Napoleon III against Austria. Finally, in July 1858, he succeeded and goaded Austria into attacking Sardinia. Napoleon III came to Sardinia's defense. Then, after the victory of the combined Franco-Sardinian forces, Napoleon III did a complete about-face. Nauseated by the gore of war and criticized by French Catholics for supporting the pope's declared enemy, Napoleon III abandoned Cavour. He made a compromise peace with the Austrians at Villafranca in July 1859. Sardinia would receive only Lombardy, the area around Milan. The rest of the map of Italy would remain essentially unchanged. Cavour resigned in a rage.

Yet Cavour's plans were salvaged by popular revolts and Italian nationalism. While the war against Austria had raged in the north, dedicated nationalists in central Italy had risen and driven out their rulers. Nationalist fervor seized the urban masses. Large crowds demonstrated, chanting, "Italy and Victor Emmanuel!" and singing passionately, "Foreigners, get out of Italy!" Buoyed up by this enthusiasm, the leaders of the nationalist movement in central Italy ignored the compromise peace of Villafranca and called for fusion with Sardinia. This was not at all what France and the other Great Powers wanted, but the nationalists held firm and eventually had their way. Cavour returned to power in early 1860, and the people of central Italy voted overwhelmingly to join a greatly enlarged kingdom of Sardinia. Cavour had achieved his original goal of a north Italian state (see Map 25.1).

For superpatriots like Giuseppe Garibaldi (1807–1882), the job of unification was still only half done. The son of a poor sailor, Garibaldi personified the romantic, revolutionary nationalism of

Garibaldi and His Red Shirts   Four days after landing in western Sicily, Garibaldi's forces won the Battle of Calatafimi, pictured here with the flamboyant patriot exhorting his troops at the center. Within two weeks Garibaldi took Palermo and established a provisional government in Sicily. *(Source: Museo del Risorgimento, Milan. Photo: Giancarlo Costa)*

Mazzini and 1848. As a lad of seventeen, he had traveled to Rome and been converted to the "New Italy, the Italy of all the Italians." As he later wrote in his *Autobiography,* "The Rome that I beheld with the eyes of youthful imagination was the Rome of the future—the dominant thought of my whole life." Sentenced to death in 1834 for his part in an uprising in Genoa, Garibaldi escaped to South America. For twelve years he led a guerrilla band in Uruguay's struggle for independence. "Shipwrecked, ambushed, shot through the neck," he found in a tough young woman, Anna da Silva, a mate and companion in arms. Their first children nearly starved in the jungle while Garibaldi, clad in his long red shirt, fashioned a legend not unlike that of the Cuban Ché Guevara in recent times. He returned to Italy to fight in 1848 and led a corps of volunteers against Austria in 1859. By the spring of 1860, Garibaldi had emerged as a powerful independent force in Italian politics.

Partly to use him and partly to get rid of him, Cavour secretly supported Garibaldi's bold plan to "liberate" Sicily. Landing in Sicily in May 1860, Garibaldi's guerrilla band of a thousand "Red Shirts" captured the imagination of the Sicilian peasantry. Outwitting the twenty-thousand-man royal army, the guerrilla leader took Palermo. Then he and his men crossed to the mainland, marched triumphantly toward Naples, and prepared to attack Rome and the pope. But the wily Cavour quickly sent Sardinian forces to occupy most of the Papal States (but not Rome) and to intercept Garibaldi.

Cavour realized that an attack on Rome would bring about war with France, and he also feared Garibaldi's popular appeal. Therefore, he immediately organized a plebiscite in the conquered territories. Despite the urging of some of his more radical supporters, the patriotic Garibaldi did not oppose Cavour, and the people of the south voted to join Sardinia. When Garibaldi and Victor Emmanuel rode through Naples to cheering crowds, they symbolically sealed the union of north and south, of monarch and people.

Cavour had succeeded. He had controlled Garibaldi and had turned popular nationalism in a conservative direction. The new kingdom of Italy, which did not include Venice until 1866 or Rome until 1870, was neither radical nor democratic. Italy was a parliamentary monarchy under Victor Emmanuel, but in accordance with the Sardinian constitution only a small minority of Italians had the right to vote. There was a definite division between the propertied classes and the common people. There was also a great social and cultural gap between the progressive, industrializing north and the stagnant, agrarian south. This gap would increase, since peasant industries in the south would not be able to survive. Italy was united politically. Other divisions remained.

Germany Before Bismarck

In the aftermath of 1848, while Louis Napoleon consolidated his rule and Cavour schemed, the German states were locked in a political stalemate. With Russian diplomatic support, Austria had blocked the halfhearted attempt of Frederick William IV of Prussia (r. 1840–1861) to unify Germany "from above." This action contributed to a growing tension between Austria and Prussia, as each power sought to block the other within the reorganized German Confederation (see pages 724–751). Stalemate also prevailed in the domestic politics of the individual states, as Austria, Prussia, and the smaller German kingdoms entered a period of reaction and immobility.

At the same time, powerful economic forces were undermining the political status quo. As we have seen, modern industry grew rapidly in Europe throughout the 1850s. Nowhere was this growth more rapid than within the German customs union (*Zollverein*). Developing gradually under Prussian leadership after 1818 and founded officially in 1834 to stimulate trade and increase the revenues of member states, the customs union had not included Austria. After 1848 it became a crucial factor in the Austro-Prussian rivalry.

Tariff duties were substantially reduced so that Austria's highly protected industry could not bear to join. In retaliation, Austria tried to destroy the Zollverein by inducing the south German states to leave it, but without success. Indeed, by the end of 1853 all the German states except Austria had joined the customs union. A new Germany excluding Austria was becoming an economic reality, and the middle class and business groups were finding solid economic reasons to bolster their idealistic support of national unification. Thus economic developments helped Prussia greatly in its struggle against Austria's supremacy in German affairs.

The national uprising in Italy in 1859 made a profound impression in the German states. In Prussia, great political change and war—perhaps with Austria, perhaps with France—seemed quite possible. Along with his top military advisers, the tough-minded William I of Prussia (r. 1861–1888), who had replaced the unstable Frederick William IV as regent in 1858 and become king himself in 1861, was convinced of the need for major army reforms. William I wanted to double the size of the highly disciplined regular army. He also wanted to reduce the importance of the reserve militia, a semipopular force created during the Napoleonic wars. Of course, reform of the army meant a bigger defense budget and higher taxes.

Prussia had emerged from 1848 with a parliament of sorts, and by 1859 the Prussian parliament was in the hands of the liberal middle class. The middle class, like the landed aristocracy, was overrepresented by the Prussian electoral system, and it wanted society to be less, not more, militaristic. Above all, middle-class representatives wanted to establish once and for all that the parliament, not the king, had the ultimate political power. They also wanted to ensure that the army was responsible to the people and not a "state within a state." These demands were popular. The parliament rejected the military budget in 1862, and the liberals triumphed so completely in new elections that the conservatives "could ride to the parliament building in a single coach." King William considered abdicating in favor of his more liberal son. In the end, he called on Count Otto von Bismarck to head a new ministry and defy the parliament. It was a momentous choice.

Otto von Bismarck A fierce political fighter with a commanding personality and a brilliant mind, Bismarck was devoted to Prussia and its king and aristocracy. Uniforms were worn by civilian officials as well as by soldiers in Prussia. *(Source: Brown Brothers)*

Bismarck Takes Command

The most important figure in German history between Luther and Hitler, Otto von Bismarck (1815–1898) has been the object of enormous interest and debate. A great hero to some, a great villain to others, Bismarck was above all a master of politics. Born into the Prussian landowning aristocracy, the young Bismarck was a wild and tempestuous student, given to duels and drinking. Proud of his Junker heritage—"my fathers have been born and have lived and died in the same rooms for centuries"—and always devoted to his Prussian sovereign, Bismarck had a strong personality and an unbounded desire for power.

Bismarck entered the civil service, which was the only socially acceptable career except the army for a Prussian aristocrat. But he soon found bureaucratic life unbearable and fled to his ancestral estate. "My pride," he admitted, "bids me command rather than obey."[2] Yet in his drive for power, power for himself and for Prussia, Bismarck was extraordinarily flexible and pragmatic. "One must always have two irons in the fire," he once said. He kept his options open, pursuing one policy and then another as he moved with skill and cunning toward his goal.

Bismarck first honed his political skills as a diplomat. Acquiring a reputation as an ultraconservative in the Prussian assembly in 1848, he fought against Austria as the Prussian ambassador to the German Confederation from 1851 to 1859. Transferred next to St. Petersburg and then to Paris, Bismarck worked toward a basic goal that was well known by 1862—to build up Prussia's strength and consolidate Prussia's precarious Great Power status.

To achieve this goal, Bismarck was convinced that Prussia had to control completely the northern, predominately Protestant part of the German Confederation. He saw three possible paths open before him. He might work with Austria to divide up the smaller German states lying between them. Or he might combine with foreign powers—France and Italy, or even Russia—against Austria. Or he might ally with the forces of German nationalism to defeat and expel Austria from German affairs. Each possibility was explored in many complicated diplomatic maneuvers, but in the end the last path was the one Bismarck took.

That Bismarck would join with the forces of German nationalism to increase Prussia's power seemed unlikely when he took office as chief minister in 1862. Bismarck's appointment made a strong but unfavorable impression. His speeches were a sensation and a scandal. Declaring that the government would rule without parliamentary consent, Bismarck lashed out at the middle-class opposition: "The great questions of the day will not be decided by speeches and resolutions—that was the blunder of 1848 and 1849—but by blood and iron." In 1863 he told the Prussian parliament, "If a compromise cannot be arrived at and a conflict arises, then the conflict becomes a question of power. Whoever has the power then acts according to his opinion." Denounced for this view that "might makes right," Bismarck had the bureaucracy go right on collecting taxes, even though the parliament refused to approve the budget. Bismarck reorganized the army. And for four years, from 1862 to 1866, the voters of Prussia continued to express their opposition by sending large liberal majorities to the parliament.

The Austro-Prussian War of 1866

Opposition at home spurred the search for success abroad. The ever-knotty question of Schleswig-Holstein provided a welcome opportunity. When the Danish king tried again, as in 1848, to bring the provinces into a centralized Danish state against the will of the German Confederation, Prussia joined Austria in a short and successful war against Denmark in 1864. Then Bismarck maneuvered Austria into a tricky position. Prussia and

Austria agreed to joint administration of the conquered provinces, thereby giving Bismarck a weapon he could use either to force Austria into peacefully accepting Prussian domination in northern Germany or to start a war against Austria.

Bismarck knew that a war with Austria would have to be a localized war. He had to be certain that Prussian expansion did not provoke a mighty armed coalition, such as the coalition that had almost crushed Frederick the Great in the eighteenth century. Russia, the great bear to the east, was no problem. Bismarck had already gained Alexander II's gratitude by supporting Russia's repression of a Polish uprising in 1863. Napoleon III—the "sphinx without a riddle," according to Bismarck—was another matter. But Bismarck charmed him into neutrality with vague promises of more territory along the Rhine. Thus, when Austria proved unwilling to give up its historic role in German affairs, Bismarck was in a position to engage in a war of his own making.

The Austro-Prussian War of 1866 lasted only seven weeks. Utilizing railroads to mass troops and the new breechloading needle gun for maximum firepower, the reorganized Prussian army overran northern Germany and defeated Austria decisively at the Battle of Sadowa in Bohemia. Anticipating Prussia's future needs, Bismarck offered Austria realistic, even generous, peace terms. Austria paid no reparations and lost no territory to Prussia, although Venice was ceded to Italy. But the German Confederation was dissolved, and Austria agreed to withdraw from German affairs. The states north of the Main River were grouped in a new North German Confederation led by an expanded Prussia. The mainly Catholic states of the south were permitted to remain independent, while forming military alliances with Prussia. Bismarck's fundamental goal of Prussian expansion was being realized (Map 25.2).

The Taming of the Parliament

Bismarck had long been convinced that the old order he so ardently defended should make peace —on its own terms—with the liberal middle class and the nationalist movement. Inspired somewhat by Louis Napoleon, he realized that nationalism was not necessarily hostile to conservative, authoritarian government. Moreover, Bismarck believed that, because of the events of 1848, the German

MAP 25.2 The Unification of Germany, 1866–1871 This map deserves careful study. Note how Prussian expansion, Austrian expulsion from the old German Confederation, and the creation of a new German Empire went hand in hand. Austria lost no territory but Prussia's neighbors in the north suffered grievously or simply disappeared.

Legend:

Prussia before 1866

Conquered by Prussia in Austro-Prussian War, 1866

Austrian territories excluded from German Confederation, 1867

Joined with Prussia to form German Confederation, 1867

South German states joining with Prussia to form German Empire, 1871

Won by Prussia in Franco-Prussian War, 1871

✕ Major battles

—— German Confederation boundary, 1815–1866

—— Bismarck's German Empire, 1871

middle class could be led to prefer the reality of national unity to a long, uncertain battle for truly liberal institutions. During the constitutional struggle over army reform and parliamentary authority, he had delayed but not abandoned this goal. Thus, during the attack on Austria in 1866, he increasingly identified Prussia's fate with the "national development of Germany."

In the aftermath of victory, Bismarck fashioned a federal constitution for the new North German Confederation. Each state retained its own local government, but the king of Prussia was to be president of the confederation and the chancellor—

"His First Thought"   This 1896 cartoon provides a brilliant commentary on German middle-class attitudes. Suddenly crippled, the man's first thought is "Disaster! Now I can no longer be an army reserve officer." Being a part-time junior officer, below the dominant aristocratic career officers, became a great middle-class status symbol. *(Source: Caroline Buckler)*

Bismarck—was to be responsible only to the president. The federal government—William I and Bismarck—controlled the army and foreign affairs. There was also a legislature, consisting of two houses that shared equally in the making of laws. Delegates to the upper house were appointed by the different states, but members of the lower house were elected by universal, equal manhood suffrage. With this radical innovation, Bismarck opened the door to popular participation and went over the head of the middle class directly to the people. All the while, however, ultimate power rested as securely as ever in the hands of Prussia and its king and army.

Events within Prussia itself were even more significant than those at the federal level. In the flush of victory, the ultraconservatives expected Bismarck to suspend the Prussian constitution or perhaps abolish the Prussian parliament altogether. Yet he did nothing of the sort. Instead, he held out an olive branch to the parliamentary opposition. Marshaling all his diplomatic skill, Bismarck asked the parliament to pass a special indemnity bill to approve after the fact all of the government's spending between 1862 and 1866. Most of the liberals snatched at the chance to cooperate. For four long years, they had opposed and criticized Bismarck's "illegal" measures. And what had happened? Bismarck, the king, and the army had persevered, and in the end these conservative forces had succeeded beyond the wildest dreams of the liberal middle class. In 1866 German unity was in sight, and the people were going to be allowed to participate actively in the new state. Many liberals repented their "sins" and were overjoyed that Bismarck would forgive them.

None repented more ardently or more typically than Hermann Baumgarten, a mild-mannered, thoroughly decent history professor and member of the liberal opposition. In his essay "A Self Criticism of German Liberalism," he confessed in 1866:

We thought by agitation we could transform Germany. But . . . almost all the elements of our political system have been shown erroneous by the facts themselves. . . . Yet we have experienced a miracle almost without parallel. The victory of our principles would have brought us misery, whereas the defeat of our principles has brought boundless salvation.[3]

The constitutional struggle was over. The German middle class was bowing respectfully before Bismarck and the monarchial authority and aristocratic superiority he represented. The middle class did not stand upright again in the years before 1914.

The Franco-Prussian War of 1870–1871

The rest of the story of German unification is anticlimactic. In 1867 Bismarck brought the four south German states into the customs union and established a customs parliament. But the south Germans were reluctant to go further because of their different religious and political traditions. Bismarck realized that a patriotic war with France would drive the south German states into his arms. The French obligingly played their part. The apparent issue—whether a distant relative of Prussia's William I (and France's Napoleon III) might become king of Spain—was only a diplomatic pretext. By 1870 the French leaders of the Second Empire, alarmed by their powerful new neighbor on the Rhine, had decided on a war to teach Prussia a lesson.

As soon as war against France began in 1870, Bismarck had the wholehearted support of the south German states. With other governments standing still—Bismarck's generosity to Austria in 1866 was paying big dividends—German forces under Prussian leadership decisively defeated Louis Napoleon's armies at Sedan on September 1, 1870. Three days later, French patriots in Paris proclaimed yet another French republic and vowed to continue fighting. But after five months, in January 1871, a starving Paris surrendered, and France went on to accept Bismarck's harsh peace terms. By this time, the south German states had agreed to join a new German Empire. The victorious William I was proclaimed emperor of Germany in the Hall of Mirrors in the palace of Versailles. Europe had a nineteenth-century German "sun king." As in the 1866 constitution, the king of Prussia and his ministers had ultimate power in the new empire, and the lower house of the legislature was elected popularly by universal male suffrage.

The Franco-Prussian War of 1870 to 1871, which Europeans generally saw as a test of nations in a pitiless Darwinian struggle for existence, released an enormous surge of patriotic feeling in Germany. Bismarck's genius, the invincible Prussian army, the solidarity of king and people in a unified nation—these and similar themes were trumpeted endlessly during and after the war. The weakest of the Great Powers in 1862—after Austria, Britain, France, and Russia—Prussia fortified by the other Germans states had become the most powerful state in Europe in less than a decade. Most Germans were enormously proud, enormously relieved. And they were somewhat drunk with success, blissfully imagining themselves the fittest and best of the European species. Semi-authoritarian nationalism had triumphed. Only a few critics remained dedicated to the liberal ideal of truly responsible parliamentary government.

NATION BUILDING IN THE UNITED STATES

Closely linked to general European developments in the nineteenth century, the United States experienced the full drama of midcentury nation building and felt the power of nationalism to refashion politics and remake states. Yet in the United States competing national aspirations served first to divide rather than unite. Only after a bitter civil war was nationalism successfully harnessed to the building of a transcontinental giant.

Slavery and Territorial Expansion

Formed in the process of revolt against Great Britain, the young "United" States was divided by slavery from its birth. Then, as the new federal Constitution was being written, the Northwest Ordinance of 1787 effectively extended the seaboard patterns of free and slave labor into the vast area west of the Appalachian Mountains and east of the Mississippi, with the Ohio River serving as the fatal dividing line. The purchase of the entire Louisiana Territory from France in 1803 opened another enormous area for settlement, as the native American Indians continued to be pushed to the fringes or decimated. Thus the stage was set for growing regional tensions as American economic development carried the free and the slaveholding states in very different directions.

In the North, white settlers broke the soil north of the Ohio and extended the pattern of family farm agriculture. Ingenious Yankees began building English-model factories, drawing first on New England farm girls housed in company dormitories and then on families of Irish immigrants. By 1850

Slavery and Cotton   The intense activity and the systematic exploitation of slave labor on large cotton plantations come alive in this contemporary painting. Slaves of both sexes and of all ages pick the cotton and transport it to smoke-belching worksheds, shown in the background, for later processing in cotton gins. (Source: Courtesy Jay P. Altmayer)

an industrializing, urbanizing North was also building an efficient system of canals and railroads and attracting most of the rising tide of European immigrants.

In the South, by contrast, industry and cities did not develop, and newcomers avoided the region. And while fully three-quarters of all Southern white families were small farmers and owned no slaves in 1850, plantation owners holding twenty or more slaves and producing a market crop dominated the economy and the society, as they had since colonial times. Turning increasingly from tobacco, sugar cane, and rice, the rich, profit-minded slaveowners used gangs of black slaves to claim a vast new kingdom, a kingdom where cotton was the king. Expanding into fertile virgin lands and relying after 1793 on Eli Whitney's newly invented cotton engine (or "gin," for short), which separated the sticky green seeds from the fluffy fiber and did the work of fifty workers, the cotton kingdom eventually stretched across most of the Deep South, from the Carolinas westward to Arkansas and eastern

Texas. By 1850, it produced 5 million bales a year (as opposed to only 4,000 bales in 1791) and profitably satisfied an apparently insatiable demand from cotton mills in Great Britain, other European countries, and New England.

The rise of the slave-based cotton empire had momentous consequences for the republic. First, it revitalized slave-based agriculture and created great wealth, and not just for rich Southern slaveholders. Cotton accounted for two-thirds of the value of all American exports by the 1850s, and many economic historians believe it provided the critical "leading sector" that ignited rapid economic growth in the United States. Second, the large profits flowing from cotton production led influential Southerners to defend slavery and even argue that it benefited slaves as well as masters (and, indirectly, poor whites). In defending their "peculiar institution," Southern whites developed a strong cultural identity and saw themselves as a close-knit "we" distinct from a Northern "they." Third, prodded by bitter battles over the protective tariff and by passionate antislavery crusaders, Northern whites also came to see their free-labor system as being no less economically and morally superior. Thus regional antagonisms intensified.

These antagonisms came to a climax after 1848, when a recently defeated Mexico ceded to the United States half a million square miles of territory stretching from west Texas to the Pacific Ocean. Whether and to what extent Congress should permit slavery in this conquered area became the all-absorbing and highly divisive political issue. Attitudes hardened on both sides, and outbreaks of violence multiplied, involving even the U.S. Congress. In one famous incident in 1856, a hotheaded representative from South Carolina used his heavy cane to beat an abolitionist senator from Massachusetts almost to death as he sat at his desk on the Senate floor. By 1860 many Northerners warned ominously of a "Slave Power" plot to destroy freedom everywhere, and Southerners denounced the power of "lord King Numbers" to strangle and ruin the South (Map 25.3). In

MAP 25.3 Slavery in the United States, 1860 This map illustrates the nation on the eve of the Civil War. Although many issues contributed to the developing opposition between North and South, slavery was the fundamental, enduring force that underlay all others. Lincoln's prediction, "I believe this government cannot endure permanently half slave and half free," tragically proved correct.

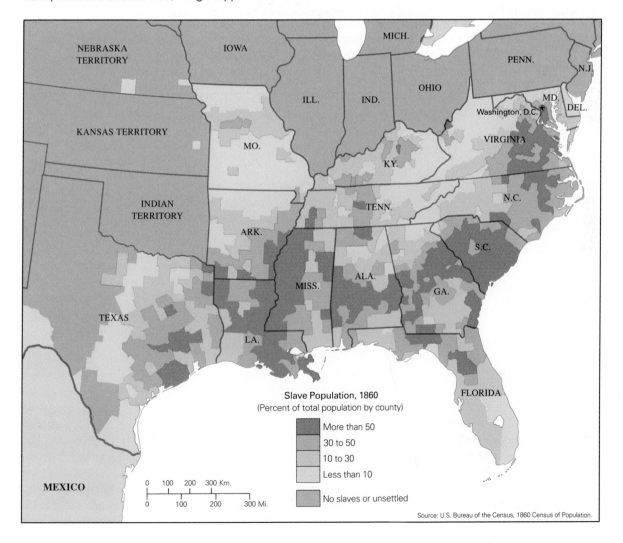

Slave Population, 1860
(Percent of total population by county)

More than 50
30 to 50
10 to 30
Less than 10

No slaves or unsettled

0   100   200   300 Km.
0   100   200   300 Mi.

Source: U.S. Bureau of the Census, 1860 Census of Population.

Abraham Lincoln's famous words, the United States was a "house divided" by contradictory economic systems and conflicting values.

Civil War and Reunification

Lincoln's election as president in 1860 gave Southern "fire-eaters" the chance they had been waiting for. Having agitated for years for the end of the Union, they now trumpeted the fact that Lincoln had not even campaigned in the South as an insult and called for secession and Southern independence. Southern moderates countered that secession would lead to war and then to emancipation, possibly through bloody slave revolts. Alexander H. Stephens, future vice-president of the Southern Confederacy, declared prophetically, "I consider slavery much more secure in the Union than out of it."[4] But radicals in South Carolina quickly voted to leave the Union, and the rest of the Deep South followed suit. Confederate troops then fired on an indefensible federal fort in the heart of South Carolina's Charleston harbor, in a successful effort to provoke Northern retaliation and thus cause the cautious but proud Upper South—Virginia, Ten-

The Battle of Gettysburg, July 1–3, 1863 marked the high point of the Confederate advance and was the greatest battle of the war. This painting commemorates the climax on the third day, when Confederate General Robert E. Lee commanded Pickett's division to charge the Union center. Coming toward the viewer in the face of terrible fire, the brave Southerners have reached the first Union line. But General Hancock, shown with arm extended in the left foreground, is ordering the Northern counterattack that will decimate Prickett's troops and force the Confederates back into Virginia. *(Source: Photograph by Al Freni© 1985 Time-Life Books, Inc. Courtesy, The Seventh Regiment Fund, Inc.)*

nessee, and North Carolina—to join the gamble for an independent Southern nation.

The long Civil War (1861–1865) was the bloodiest conflict in all of American history, but in the end the South was decisively defeated and the Union was preserved. To historians explaining this outcome, it is clear that the vastly superior population, industry, and transportation of the North placed the South at a great, probably fatal disadvantage. Yet less obvious factors tied to morale and national purpose were also extremely important. The enormous gap between the slaveowning elite and the poor whites made it impossible for the South to build effectively on the patriotism of 1861. As the war ground on, many ordinary whites felt that the burden of war was falling mainly on their shoulders, because big planters resisted taxation and used loopholes to avoid the draft. Desertions from Southern armies mounted rapidly from the summer of 1863, as soldiers became disillusioned and responded to moving calls for help at home. "Before God, Edward, unless you come home we must die," wrote one of many desperate wives with sick and hungry children.[5]

Slavery itself weakened the South's war effort. Although blacks were used on the home front in countless ways, owners generally tried to keep their valuable property on their plantations, in order to prevent runaways and possible slave rebellion. Nor would planters accept the idea of a black Southern soldier or of freedom for blacks as a last-ditch means of fully mobilizing the South.

In the North, by contrast, most people prospered during the war years. Enthusiasm remained high, and certain dominant characteristics of American life and national culture took shape. Powerful business corporations emerged, steadfastly supported by the Republican party during and after the war. The vision of an ethnically diverse but still unified nation gained strength, for on the battlefield immigrants and native-born were all "damn Yankees" in Southern eyes. The Homestead Act of 1862, which gave western land to those who would settle it, and the Emancipation Proclamation of 1863, which freed the slaves in rebellious states, reinforced tremendously the concept of free labor taking its chances in a market economy. Finally, the success of Lincoln and the North in holding the Union together seemed to confirm that the "manifest destiny" of the United States was indeed to straddle a continent as a great (and presumably virtuous)

world power. Thus a new American nationalism grew out of the war to prevent the realization of Southern nationhood.

Northern victory also led to a "national" policy of sorts toward American blacks, although the path was complicated and often contradictory. With Northern armies occupying large parts of the Southern states until 1877, Congress guaranteed the legal freedom of blacks during the Reconstruction era and thwarted devious efforts of former masters to virtually re-enslave the freed black population. But Northern efforts to "reconstruct" the South did not include land reform. Freed blacks were generally forced to continue laboring for whites, but now as tenants under unfavorable sharecropping conditions. Blacks also faced very pervasive discrimination. Thus, as a result of war and reunification, the life of blacks in the Southern states moved much closer to that of the small number of blacks in the North, who had long been free but unequal citizens.

THE MODERNIZATION OF RUSSIA

In Russia, unlike Italy and Germany, there was no need to build a single state out of a jumble of principalities. The Russian Empire was already an enormous multinational state, a state that contained all the ethnic Russians and many other nationalities as well. As in the United States at midcentury, the long-term challenge facing the government was to hold the existing state together, either by means of political compromise or by military force. Thus Russia's rulers saw nationalism as a subversive ideology in the early nineteenth century, and they tried with some success to limit its development among their non-Russian subjects.

Yet old autocratic Russia found itself in serious trouble after 1853. It became clear to Russia's leaders that the country had to embrace the process of *modernization*. A vague and often overworked term, modernization is a great umbrella under which some writers place most of the major developments of the last two hundred or even five hundred years. Yet defined narrowly—as changes that enable a country to compete effectively with the leading countries at a given time—modernization can be a useful concept. It fits Russia after the Crimean War particularly well.

The "Great Reforms"

In the 1850s Russia was a poor agrarian society. Industry was little developed, and almost 90 percent of the population lived on the land. Agricultural techniques were backward: the ancient open-field system reigned supreme. Serfdom was still the basic social institution. Bound to the lord on a hereditary basis, the peasant serf was little more than a slave. Individual serfs and serf families were regularly sold, with and without land, in the early nineteenth century. Serfs were obliged to furnish labor services or money payments as the lord saw fit. Moreover, the lord could choose freely among the serfs for army recruits, who had to serve for twenty-five years, and he could punish a serf with deportation to Siberia whenever he wished. Sexual exploitation of female serfs by their lords was common.

Serfdom had become the great moral and political issue for the government by the 1840s, but it might still have lasted many more years had it not been for the Crimean War of 1853 to 1856. The war began as a dispute with France over who should protect certain Christian shrines in the Ottoman Empire. Because the fighting was concentrated in the Crimean peninsula on the Black Sea, Russia's transportation network of rivers and wagons failed to supply the distant Russian armies adequately. France and Great Britain, aided by Sardinia and the Ottoman Empire, inflicted a humiliating defeat on Russia.

The military defeat marked a turning point in Russian history. The Russian state had been built on the military, and Russia had not lost a major war for a century and a half. This defeat demonstrated that Russia had fallen behind the rapidly industrializing nations of western Europe in many areas. At the very least, Russia needed railroads, better armaments, and reorganization of the army if it was to maintain its international position. Moreover, the disastrous war had caused hardship and raised the specter of massive peasant rebellion. Reform of serfdom was imperative. And, as the new tsar, Alexander II (r. 1855–1881), told the serf owners, it would be better if reform came from above. Military disaster thus forced Alexander II and his ministers along the path of rapid social change and general modernization.

The first and greatest of the reforms was the freeing of the serfs in 1861. Human bondage was abolished forever, and the emancipated peasants received, on the average, about half of the land. Yet they had to pay fairly high prices for their land, and because the land was owned collectively, each peasant village was jointly responsible for the payments of all the families in the village. The government hoped that collective responsibility would strengthen the peasant village as a social unit and prevent the development of a class of landless peasants. In practice, collective ownership and responsibility made it very difficult for individual peasants to improve agricultural methods or leave their villages. Thus the effects of the reform were limited, for it did not encourage peasants to change their old habits and attitudes.

Most of the later reforms were also halfway measures. In 1864 the government established a new institution of local government, the *zemstvo*. Members of this local assembly were elected by a three-class system of towns, peasant villages, and noble landowners. A zemstvo executive council dealt with local problems. The establishment of the zemstvos marked a significant step toward popular participation, and Russian liberals hoped it would lead to a national parliament. They were soon disappointed. The local zemstvo remained subordinate to the traditional bureaucracy and the local nobility, who were heavily favored by the property-based voting system. More successful was reform of the legal system, which established independent courts and equality before the law. Education was also liberalized somewhat, and censorship was relaxed but not removed.

The Industrialization of Russia

Until the twentieth century, Russia's greatest strides toward modernization were economic rather than political. Industry and transport, both so vital to the military, were transformed in two industrial surges. The first of these came after 1860. The government encouraged and subsidized private railway companies, and construction boomed. In 1860 the empire had only about 1,250 miles of railroads; by 1880 it had about 15,500 miles. The railroads enabled agricultural Russia to export grain and thus earn money for further industrialization. Domestic manufacturing was stimulated, and by the end of the 1870s Russia had a well-developed railway-equipment industry. Industrial suburbs grew up around Moscow and St. Petersburg, and a class of modern factory workers began to take shape.

Novgorod Merchants Drinking Tea This late nineteenth-century photograph suggests how Russian businessmen were slow to abandon traditional dress and attitudes. Stern authoritarians and staunchly devoted to church and tsar, they were often suspicious of foreigners as well as the lawyers and journalists who claimed to speak for the nation's middle class. *(Source: Bettmann/Hulton)*

Industrial development strengthened Russia's military forces and gave rise to territorial expansion to the south and east. Imperial expansion greatly excited many ardent Russian nationalists and superpatriots, who became some of the government's most enthusiastic supporters. Industrial development also contributed mightily to the spread of Marxian thought and the transformation of the Russian revolutionary movement after 1890.

In 1881 Alexander II was assassinated by a small group of terrorists. The era of reform came to an abrupt end, for the new tsar, Alexander III (r. 1881–1894), was a determined reactionary. Russia, and indeed all of Europe, experienced hard times economically in the 1880s. Political modernization remained frozen until 1905, but economic modernization sped forward in the massive industrial surge of the 1890s. As it had after the Crimean

War, nationalism played a decisive role. The key leader was Sergei Witte, the tough, competent minister of finance from 1892 to 1903. Early in his career, Witte found in the writings of Friedrich List (see page 707) an analysis and a program for action. List had stressed the peril for Germany of remaining behind England in the 1830s and 1840s. Witte saw the same threat of industrial backwardness threatening Russia's power and greatness.

Witte moved forward on several fronts. A railroad manager by training, he believed that railroads were "a very powerful weapon . . . for the direction of the economic development of the country."[6] Therefore, the government built railroads rapidly, doubling the network to 35,000 miles by the end of the century. The gigantic trans-Siberian line connecting Moscow with Vladivostok on the Pacific Ocean 5,000 miles away was Witte's

Building the Trans-Siberian Railroad Constructed largely in the 1890s as part of Witte's industrialization drive, the world's longest railroad facilitated Russian penetration of northern China and Korea. That penetration then led to war with Japan. *(Source: Bettmann/Hulton)*

pride, and it was largely completed during his term of office. Following List's advice, Witte established high protective tariffs to build Russian industry, and he put the country on the gold standard of the "civilized world" in order to strengthen Russian finances.

Witte's greatest innovation, however, was to use the West to catch up with the West. He aggressively encouraged foreigners to use their abundant capital and advanced technology to build great factories in backward Russia. As he told the tsar, "The inflow of foreign capital is . . . the only way by which our industry will be able to supply our country quickly with abundant and cheap products."[7] This policy was brilliantly successful, especially in southern Russia. There, in the eastern Ukraine, foreign capitalists and their engineers built an enormous and very modern steel and coal industry almost from scratch in little more than a decade. By 1900 only the United States, Germany, and Great Britain were producing more steel than Russia. The Russian petroleum industry had even pulled up alongside that of the United States and was producing and refining half the world's output of oil.

Witte knew how to keep foreigners in line. Once a leading foreign businessman came to him and an-

grily demanded that the Russian government fulfill a contract it had signed and pay certain debts immediately. Witte asked to see the contract. He read it and then carefully tore it to pieces and threw it in the wastepaper basket without a word of explanation. It was just such a fiercely independent Russia that was catching up with the advanced nations of the West.

The Revolution of 1905

Catching up partly meant vigorous territorial expansion, for this was the age of Western imperialism. By 1903 Russia had established a sphere of influence in Chinese Manchuria and was casting greedy eyes on northern Korea. When the protests of equally imperialistic Japan were ignored, the Japanese launched a surprise attack in February 1904. To the world's amazement, Russia suffered repeated losses and was forced in August 1905 to accept a humiliating defeat.

As is often the case, military disaster abroad brought political upheaval at home. The business and professional classes had long wanted to match economic with political modernization. Their minimal goal was to turn the last of Europe's absolutist monarchies into a liberal, representative regime. Factory workers, strategically concentrated in the large cities, had all the grievances of early industrialization and were organized in a radical labor movement. Peasants had gained little from the era of reforms and were suffering from poverty and overpopulation. Finally, nationalist sentiment was emerging among the empire's minorities. The politically and culturally dominant ethnic Russians were only about 45 percent of the population, and by 1900 some intellectuals among the subject nationalities were calling for self-rule and autonomy. Separatist nationalism was strongest among the Poles and Ukrainians. With the army pinned down in Manchuria, all these currents of discontent converged in the revolution of 1905.

The beginning of the revolution pointed up the incompetence of the government. On a Sunday in January 1905, a massive crowd of workers and their families converged peacefully on the Winter Palace in St. Petersburg to present a petition to the tsar. The workers were led by a trade-unionist priest named Father Gapon, who had been secretly supported by the police as a preferable alternative to more radical unions. Carrying icons and respectfully singing "God Save the Tsar," the workers did not know Nicholas II had fled the city. Suddenly troops opened fire, killing and wounding hundreds. The "Bloody Sunday" massacre turned ordinary workers against the tsar and produced a wave of general indignation.

Outlawed political parties came out into the open, and by the summer of 1905 strikes, peasant uprisings, revolts among minority nationalities, and troop mutinies were sweeping the country. The revolutionary surge culminated in October 1905 in a great paralyzing general strike, which forced the government to capitulate. The tsar issued the October Manifesto, which granted full civil rights and promised a popularly elected Duma (parliament) with real legislative power. The manifesto split the opposition. It satisfied most moderate and liberal demands, but the Social Democrats rejected it and led a bloody workers' uprising in Moscow in December 1905. Frightened middle-class moderates helped the government repress the uprising and survive as a constitutional monarchy.

On the eve of the opening of the first Duma in May 1906, the government issued the new constitution, the Fundamental Laws. The tsar retained great powers. The Duma, elected indirectly by universal male suffrage, and a largely appointive upper house could debate and pass laws, but the tsar had an absolute veto. As in Bismarck's Germany, the emperor appointed his ministers, who did not need to command a majority in the Duma.

The disappointed, predominately middle-class liberals, the largest group in the newly elected Duma, saw the Fundamental Laws as a great step backward. Efforts to cooperate with the tsar's ministers soon broke down. The government then dismissed the Duma, only to find that a more hostile and radical opposition was elected in 1907. After three months of deadlock, the second Duma was also dismissed. Thereupon the tsar and his reactionary advisers unilaterally rewrote the electoral law so as to increase greatly the weight of the propertied classes at the expense of workers, peasants, and national minorities.

The new law had the intended effect. With landowners assured half the seats in the Duma, the government finally secured a loyal majority in 1907 and again in 1912. Thus armed, the tough, energetic chief minister, Peter Stolypin, pushed through important agrarian reforms designed to break down collective village ownership of land and to encourage the more enterprising peasants—the so-called wager on the strong. On the eve of the First World War, Russia was partially modernized, a conservative constitutional monarchy with a peasant-based but industrializing economy.

THE RESPONSIVE NATIONAL STATE, 1871–1914

For central and western Europe, the unification of Italy and Germany by "blood and iron" marked the end of a dramatic period of nation building. After 1871 the heartland of Europe was organized in strong national states. Only on the borders of Europe—in Ireland and Russia, in Austria-Hungary and the Balkans—did subject peoples still strive for political unity and independence. Despite national differences, European domestic politics after 1871 had a common framework, the firmly established national state. The common themes within that framework were the emergence of mass politics and growing mass loyalty toward the national state.

For good reason, ordinary people—the masses of an industrializing, urbanizing society—felt increasing loyalty to their governments. More and more people could vote. By 1914 universal manhood suffrage was the rule rather than the exception. This development had as much psychological as political significance. Ordinary men were no longer denied the right to vote because they lacked wealth or education. They counted; they could influence the government to some extent. They were becoming "part of the system."

Women also began to demand the right to vote. The women's suffrage movement achieved its first success in the western United States, and by 1913 women could vote in twelve states. Europe, too, moved slowly in this direction. In 1914 Norway gave the vote to most women. Elsewhere, women like the English Emmeline Pankhurst were very militant in their demands. They heckled politicians and held public demonstrations. These efforts generally failed before 1914, but they prepared the way for the triumph of the women's suffrage movement immediately after World War One.

As the right to vote spread, politicians and parties in national parliaments represented the people more responsively. Most countries soon had many political parties. The multiparty system meant that parliamentary majorities were built on shifting coalitions, which were unstable but did give parties leverage. Parties could obtain benefits for their supporters. Governments increasingly passed laws to alleviate general problems and to help specific groups. Governments seemed to care, and they seemed more worthy of support.

The German Empire

Politics in Germany after 1871 reflected many of these developments. The new German Empire was a federal union of Prussia and twenty-four smaller states. Much of the everyday business of government was conducted by the separate states, but there was a strong national government with a chancellor—until 1890, Bismarck—and a popularly elected parliament, called the *Reichstag.* Although Bismarck refused to be bound by a parliamentary majority, he tried nonetheless to maintain such a majority. This situation gave the political parties opportunities. Until 1878 Bismarck relied mainly on the National Liberals, who had rallied to him after 1866. They supported legislation useful for further economic and legal unification of the country.

Less wisely, they backed Bismarck's attack on the Catholic church, the so-called *Kulturkampf,* or "struggle for civilization." Like Bismarck, the middle-class National Liberals were particularly alarmed by Pius IX's declaration of papal infallibility in 1870. That dogma seemed to ask German Catholics to put loyalty to their church above loyalty to their nation. Only in Protestant Prussia did the Kulturkampf have even limited success. Catholics throughout the country generally voted for the Catholic Center party, which blocked passage of national laws hostile to the church. Finally, in 1878, Bismarck abandoned his attack. Indeed, he and the Catholic Center party entered into an uneasy but mutually advantageous alliance. The reasons were largely economic.

After a worldwide financial bust in 1873, European agriculture was in an increasingly difficult position. Wheat prices plummeted as cheap grain poured in from the United States, Canada, and Russia. New lands were opening up in North America and Russia, and the combination of railroads and technical improvements in shipping cut freight rates for grain drastically. European peasants with their smaller, less efficient farms could not compete in cereal production, especially in western and southern Germany. The peasantry there was largely Catholic, and the Catholic Center party was thus converted to the cause of higher tariffs to protect the economic interests of its supporters.

The same competitive pressures caused the Protestant Junkers, who owned large estates in eastern Germany, to embrace the cause of higher tariffs. They were joined by some of the iron and steel magnates of the Prussian Rhineland and Westphalia, who had previously favored free trade. With three such influential groups lobbying energetically, Bismarck was happy to go along with a new protective tariff in 1879. In doing so, he won new supporters in the parliament—the Center party of the Catholics and the Conservative party of the Prussian landowners—and he held on to most of the National Liberals.

Bismarck had been looking for a way to increase taxes and raise more money for the government. The solution was higher tariffs. Many other governments acted similarly. The 1880s and 1890s saw a widespread return to protectionism. France, in particular, established very high tariffs to protect agriculture and industry, peasants and manufacturers. Thus the German government and other

Bismarck and William II   Shown here visiting Bismarck's country estate in 1888, shortly after he became emperor of Germany (and king of Prussia), the young and impetuous William II soon quarrelled with his chief minister. Determined to rule, not merely to reign, his dismissal of Bismarck in 1890 was a fatal decision. *(Source: Bildarchiv Preussicher Kulturbesitz)*

governments responded to a major economic problem and simultaneously won greater loyalty.

At the same time, Bismarck tried to stop the growth of German socialism because he genuinely feared its revolutionary language and allegiance to a movement transcending the nation-state. In 1878, after two attempts on the life of William I by radicals (though not socialists), Bismarck succeeded in ramming through the Reichstag a law repressing socialists. Socialist meetings and publications were strictly controlled. The Social Democratic party was outlawed and driven underground. However, German socialists displayed a discipline and organization worthy of the Prussian army itself. Bismarck had to try another tack.

Thus Bismarck's state pioneered with social measures designed to win the support of working-class people. In 1883 he pushed through the parliament the first of several modern social security laws to help wage earners. The laws of 1883 and 1884 established national sickness and accident insur-

ance; the law of 1889 established old-age pensions and retirement benefits. Henceforth sick, injured, and retired workers could look forward to regular weekly benefits from the state. This national social security system, paid for through compulsory contributions by wage earners and employers as well as grants from the state, was the first of its kind anywhere. It was to be fifty years before similar measures would be taken in the United States. Bismarck's social security system did not wean workers from socialism, but it did protect them from some of the uncertainties of the complex urban industrial world. This enormously significant development was a product of political competition and governmental efforts to win popular support.

Increasingly, the great issues in German domestic politics were socialism and the Marxian Social Democratic party. In 1890 the new emperor, the young, idealistic, and unstable William II (r. 1888–1918), opposed Bismarck's attempt to renew the law outlawing the Social Democratic party. Eager to rule in his own right, as well as to earn the support of the workers, William II forced Bismarck to resign. After the "dropping of the pilot," German foreign policy changed profoundly and mostly for the worse, but the government did pass new laws to aid workers and to legalize socialist political activity.

Yet William II was no more successful than Bismarck in getting workers to renounce socialism. Indeed, socialist ideas spread rapidly, and more and more Social Democrats were elected to the parliament in the 1890s. After opposing a colonial war in German Southwest Africa in 1906 and thus suffering important losses in the general elections of 1907, the German Social Democratic party broadened its base in the years before World War One. In the elections of 1912, the party scored a great victory, becoming the largest single party in the Reichstag. The "revolutionary" socialists were, however, becoming less and less revolutionary in Germany. In the years before World War One, the strength of socialist opposition to greater military spending and imperialist expansion declined greatly. German socialists marched under the national banner.

Republican France

In 1871 France seemed hopelessly divided once again. The patriotic republicans who proclaimed the Third Republic in Paris after the military disaster at Sedan refused to admit defeat. They defended Paris with great heroism for weeks, living off rats and zoo animals, until they were quite literally starved into submission by German armies in January 1871. When national elections then sent a large majority of conservatives and monarchists to the National Assembly, the traumatized Parisians exploded and proclaimed the Paris Commune in March 1871. Vaguely radical, the leaders of the Commune wanted to govern Paris without interference by the conservative French countryside. The National Assembly, led by the aging politician Adolphe Thiers, would hear none of it. The Assembly ordered the French army into Paris and brutally crushed the Commune. Twenty thousand people died in the fighting. As in June 1848, it was Paris against the provinces, French against French.

Out of this tragedy France slowly formed a new national unity, achieving considerable stability before 1914. How is one to account for this? Luck

played a part. Until 1875 the monarchists in the "republican" National Assembly had a majority but could not agree who should be king. The compromise Bourbon candidate refused to rule except under the white flag of his ancestors—a completely unacceptable condition. In the meantime, Thiers's slaying of the radical Commune and his other firm measures showed the fearful provinces and the middle class that the Third Republic might be moderate and socially conservative. France therefore retained the republic, though reluctantly. As President Thiers cautiously said, it was "the government which divides us least."

Another stabilizing factor was the skill and determination of the moderate republican leaders in the early years. The most famous of these was Léon Gambetta, the son of an Italian grocer, a warm, easygoing, unsuccessful lawyer turned professional politician. A master of emerging mass politics, Gambetta combined eloquence with the personal touch as he preached a republic of truly equal opportunity. Gambetta was also instrumental in establishing absolute parliamentary supremacy between 1877 and 1879, when the deputies challenged Marshall MacMahon and forced the somewhat autocratic president to resign. By 1879 the great majority of members of both the upper and the lower houses of the parliament were republicans. Although these republicans were split among many parliamentary groups and later among several parties—a situation that led to constant coalition politics and the rapid turnover of ministers—the Third Republic had firm foundations after almost a decade.

The moderate republicans sought to preserve their creation by winning the hearts and minds of the next generation. Trade unions were fully legalized, and France acquired a colonial empire. More important, under the leadership of Jules Ferry, the moderate republicans of small towns and villages passed a series of laws between 1879 and 1886 establishing free compulsory elementary education for both girls and boys. At the same time, they greatly expanded the state system of public tax-supported schools. Thus France shared fully in the general expansion of public education, which served as a critical nation-building tool throughout the Western world in the late nineteenth century.

In France most elementary and much secondary education had traditionally been in the parochial schools of the Catholic church, which had long been hostile to republics and to much of secular life. Free compulsory elementary education in France became secular republican education. The pledge of allegiance and the national anthem replaced the catechism and the "Ave Maria." Militant young elementary teachers carried the ideology of patriotic republicanism into every corner of France. In their classes, they sought to win the loyalty of the young citizens to the republic, so that France would never again vote en masse for dictators like the two Napoleons.

Although these reforms disturbed French Catholics, many of them rallied to the republic in the 1890s. The limited acceptance of the modern world by the more liberal Pope Leo XIII (1878–1903) eased tensions between church and state. Unfortunately, the Dreyfus affair changed all that.

Alfred Dreyfus, a Jewish captain in the French army, was falsely accused and convicted of treason. His family never doubted his innocence and fought unceasingly to reopen the case, enlisting the sup-

port of prominent republicans and intellectuals such as the novelist Émile Zola. In 1898 and 1899, the case split France apart. On one side was the army, which had manufactured evidence against Dreyfus, joined by anti-Semites and most of the Catholic establishment. On the other side stood the civil libertarians and most of the more radical republicans.

This battle, which eventually led to Dreyfus's being declared innocent, revived republican feeling against the church. Between 1901 and 1905, the government severed all ties between the state and the Catholic church, after centuries of close relations. The salaries of priests and bishops were no longer paid by the government, and all churches were given to local committees of lay Catholics. Catholic schools were put completely on their own financially, and in a short time they lost a third of their students. The state school system's power of indoctrination was greatly strengthened. In France,

Captain Alfred Dreyfus   Leaving an 1899 reconsideration of his original court martial, Dreyfus receives an insulting "guard of dishonor" from soldiers whose backs are turned. Top army leaders were determined to brand Dreyfus as a traitor. *(Source: Bibliothèque Nationale, Paris)*

only the growing socialist movement, with its very different and thoroughly secular ideology, stood in opposition to patriotic, republican nationalism.

Great Britain and Ireland

Britain in the late nineteenth century has often been seen as a shining example of peaceful and successful political evolution. Germany was stuck with a manipulated parliament that gave an irresponsible emperor too much power; France had a quarrelsome parliament that gave its presidents too little power. Great Britain, in contrast, seemed to enjoy an effective two-party parliament that skillfully guided the country from classical liberalism to full-fledged democracy with hardly a misstep.

This view of Great Britain is not so much wrong as incomplete. After the right to vote was granted to males of the solid middle class in 1832, opinion leaders and politicians wrestled with the uncertainties of a further extension of the franchise. In his famous essay *On Liberty,* published in 1859, the philosopher John Stuart Mill (1806–1873), the leading heir to the Benthamite tradition (see page 759), probed the problem of how to protect the rights of individuals and minorities in the emerging age of mass electoral participation. Mill pleaded eloquently for the practical and moral value inherent in safeguarding individual differences and unpopular opinions. In 1867 Benjamin Disraeli and the Conservatives extended the vote to all middle-class males and the best-paid workers. The son of a Jewish stockbroker, himself a novelist and urban dandy, the ever-fascinating Disraeli (1804–1881) was willing to risk this "leap in the dark" in order to gain new supporters. The Conservative party, he believed, needed to broaden its traditional base of aristocratic and landed support if it was to survive. After 1867 English political parties and electoral campaigns became more modern, and the "lower orders" appeared to vote as responsibly as their "betters." Hence the Third Reform Bill of 1884 gave the vote to almost every adult male.

While the House of Commons was drifting toward democracy, the House of Lords was content to slumber nobly. Between 1901 and 1910, however, that bastion of aristocratic conservatism tried to reassert itself. Acting as supreme court of the land, it ruled against labor unions in two important decisions. And after the Liberal party came to power in 1906, the Lords vetoed several measures passed by the Commons, including the so-called People's Budget. The Lords finally capitulated, as they had done in 1832, when the king threatened to create enough new peers to pass the bill.

Aristocratic conservatism yielded to popular democracy, once and for all. The result was that extensive social welfare measures, slow to come to Great Britain, were passed in a spectacular rush between 1906 and 1914. During those years, the Liberal party, inspired by the fiery Welshman David Lloyd George (1863–1945), substantially raised taxes on the rich as part of the People's Budget. This income helped the government pay for national health insurance, unemployment benefits, old-age pensions, and a host of other social measures. The state was integrating the urban masses socially as well as politically.

This record of accomplishment was only part of the story, though. On the eve of World War One, the ever-emotional, ever-unanswered question of Ireland brought Great Britain to the brink of civil war. In the 1840s, Ireland had been decimated by famine, which fueled an Irish revolutionary movement. Thereafter, the English slowly granted concessions, such as the abolition of the privileges of the Anglican church and rights for Irish peasants. The Liberal prime minister William Gladstone (1809–1898), who had proclaimed twenty years earlier that "my mission is to pacify Ireland," introduced bills to give Ireland self-government in 1886 and in 1893. They failed to pass. After two decades of relative quiet, Irish nationalists in the British Parliament saw their chance. They supported the Liberals in their battle for the People's Budget and received a home-rule bill for Ireland in return.

Thus Ireland, the emerald isle, achieved self-government—but not quite, for Ireland is composed of two peoples. As much as the Irish Catholic majority in the southern counties wanted home rule, precisely that much did the Irish Protestants of the northern counties of Ulster come to oppose it. Motivated by the accumulated fears and hostilities of generations, the Protestants of Ulster refused to submerge themselves in a Catholic Ireland, just as Irish Catholics had refused to submit to a Protestant Britain.

The Ulsterites vowed to resist home rule in northern Ireland. By December 1913 they had raised 100,000 armed volunteers, and they were supported by much of English public opinion.

Thus in 1914 the Liberals in the House of Lords introduced a compromise home-rule law that did not apply to the northern counties. This bill, which openly betrayed promises made to Irish nationalists, was rejected and in September the original home-rule plan was passed but simultaneously suspended for the duration of the hostilities. The momentous Irish question had been overtaken by earth-shattering world war in August 1914.

Irish developments illustrated once again the power of national feeling and national movements in the nineteenth century. Moreover, they were proof that governments could not elicit greater loyalty unless they could capture and control that elemental current of national feeling. Though Great Britain had much going for it—power, Parliament, prosperity—none of these availed in the face of the conflicting nationalisms espoused by Catholics and Protestants in northern Ireland. Similarly, progressive Sweden was powerless to stop the growth of the Norwegian national movement, which culminated in Norway's breaking away from Sweden and becoming a fully independent nation in 1905. In this light, one can also see how hopeless was the case of the Ottoman Empire in Europe in the later nineteenth century. It was only a matter of time before the Serbs, Bulgarians, and Romanians would break away, and they did.

The Austro-Hungarian Empire

The dilemma of conflicting nationalisms in Ireland also helps one appreciate how desperate the situation in the Austro-Hungarian Empire had become by the early twentieth century. In 1849 Magyar nationalism had driven Hungarian patriots to declare an independent Hungarian republic, which was savagely crushed by Russian and Austrian armies (see pages 746–749). Throughout the 1850s, Hungary was ruled as a conquered territory, and Emperor Francis Joseph and his bureaucracy tried hard to centralize the state and Germanize the language and culture of the different nationalities.

Then, in the wake of defeat by Prussia in 1866, a weakened Austria was forced to strike a compromise and establish the so-called dual monarchy. The empire was divided in two, and the nationalistic Magyars gained virtual independence for Hungary. Henceforth each half of the empire agreed to deal with its own "barbarians"—its own minorities

"No Home Rule"   Posters like this one helped to foment pro-British, anti-Catholic sentiment in the northern Irish counties of Ulster before the First World War. The rifle raised defiantly and the accompanying rhyme are a thinly veiled threat of armed rebellion and civil war. *(Source: Courtesy, Ulster Museum, Belfast)*

—as it saw fit. The two states were joined only by a shared monarch and common ministries for finance, defense, and foreign affairs. After 1867 the disintegrating force of competing nationalisms continued unabated, for both Austria and Hungary had several "Irelands" within their borders.

In Austria, ethnic Germans were only one-third of the population, and by the late 1890s many Germans saw their traditional dominance threatened by Czechs, Poles, and other Slavs. A particularly emotional and divisive issue in the Austrian parliament was the language used in government and elementary education at the local level. From 1900 to 1914, the parliament was so divided that ministries generally could not obtain a majority and ruled instead by decree. Efforts by both conservatives and socialists to defuse national antagonisms by stressing economic issues cutting across ethnic lines—endeavors that led to the introduction of universal male suffrage in 1907—proved largely unsuccessful.

One aspect of such national antagonisms was anti-Semitism, which was particularly virulent in Austria. The Jewish populations of Austrian cities grew very rapidly after Jews obtained full legal equality in 1867, and by 1900 Jews constituted 10 percent of the population of Vienna. Many Jewish business people were quite successful in banking and retail trade, while Jewish artists, intellectuals, and scientists, like the world-famous Sigmund Freud, played a major role in making Vienna a leading center of European culture and modern thought. When extremists charged the Jews with controlling the economy and corrupting German culture with alien ideas and ultramodern art, anxious Germans of all classes tended to listen. The popular mayor of Vienna from 1897 to 1910, Dr. Karl Lueger, combined anti-Semitic rhetoric with calls for "Christian socialism" and municipal ownership of basic services. Lueger appealed especially to the German lower middle class—and to an unsuccessful young artist named Adolf Hitler.

In Hungary, the Magyar nobility in 1867 restored the constitution of 1848 and used it to dominate both the Magyar peasantry and the minority populations until 1914. Only the wealthiest one-fourth of adult males had the right to vote, making

The Language Ordinances of 1897, which were intended to satisfy the Czechs by establishing equality between German and the local language in non-German districts of Austria, produced a powerful backlash among Germans. This wood engraving shows troops dispersing German protesters of the new law before the parliament building. (Source: Österveichische Nationalbibliothek)

the parliament the creature of the Magyar elite. Laws promoting use of the Magyar (Hungarian) language in schools and government were rammed through and bitterly resented, especially by the Croatians and Rumanians. While Magyar extremists campaigned loudly for total separation from Austria, the radical leaders of the subject nationalities dreamed in turn of independence from Hungary. Unlike most major countries, which harnessed nationalism to strengthen the state after 1871, the Austro-Hungarian Empire was progressively weakened and destroyed by it.

MARXISM AND THE SOCIALIST MOVEMENT

Nationalism served, for better or worse, as a new unifying principle. But what about socialism? Did the rapid growth of socialist parties, which were generally Marxian parties, dedicated to an international proletarian revolution, mean that national states had failed to gain the support of workers? Certainly, many prosperous and conservative citizens were greatly troubled by the socialist movement. And many historians have portrayed the years before 1914 as a time of increasing conflict between revolutionary socialism on the one hand and a nationalist alliance between conservative aristocracy and the prosperous middle class on the other. This question requires close examination.

The Socialist International

The growth of socialist parties after 1871 was phenomenal. Neither Bismarck's antisocialist laws nor his extensive social security system checked the growth of the German Social Democratic party, which espoused the Marxian ideology. By 1912 it had attracted millions of followers and was the largest party in the parliament. Socialist parties also grew in other countries, though nowhere else with quite such success. In 1883 Russian exiles in Switzerland founded a Russian Social Democratic party, which grew rapidly in the 1890s and thereafter, despite internal disputes. In France, various socialist parties re-emerged in the 1880s after the carnage of the Commune. Most of them were finally unified in a single, increasingly powerful Marxian party, called the French Section of the Workers International, in 1905. Belgium and Austria-Hungary also had strong socialist parties of the Marxian persuasion.

As the name of the French party suggests, Marxian socialist parties were eventually linked together in an international organization. As early as 1848, Marx had laid out his intellectual system in the *Communist Manifesto* (see pages 731–733). He had declared that "the working men have no country," and he had urged proletarians of all nations to unite against their governments. Joining the flood of radicals and republicans who fled continental Europe for England and America after the revolutions of 1848, Marx settled in London. Poor and depressed, he lived on his meager earnings as a journalist and on the gifts of his friend Engels. Marx never stopped thinking of revolution. Digging deeply into economics and history, he concluded that revolution follows economic crisis and tried to prove it in *Critique of Political Economy* (1859) and his greatest theoretical work, *Capital* (1867).

The bookish Marx also excelled as a practical organizer. In 1864 he played an important role in founding the First International of socialists—the International Working Men's Association. In the following years, he battled successfully to control the organization and used its annual meetings as a means of spreading his realistic, "scientific" doctrines of inevitable socialist revolution. Then Marx enthusiastically embraced the passionate, vaguely radical patriotism of the Paris Commune and its terrible conflict with the French National Assembly as a giant step toward socialist revolution. This impetuous action frightened many of his early supporters, especially the more moderate British labor leaders. The First International collapsed.

Yet international proletarian solidarity remained an important objective for Marxists. In 1889, as the individual parties in different countries grew stronger, socialist leaders came together to form the Second International, which lasted until 1914. Although the International was only a federation of various national socialist parties, it had great psychological impact. Every three years, delegates from the different parties met to interpret Marxian doctrines and plan coordinated action. May 1— May Day—was declared an annual international one-day strike, a day of marches and demonstrations. A permanent executive for the International was established. Many feared and many others rejoiced in the growing power of socialism and the Second International.

Socialist Clubs helped spread Marxian doctrines among the working classes. There workers (and intellectuals) from different backgrounds debated the fine points and developed a sense of solidarity. *(Source: Bildarchiv Preussischer Kulturbesitz)*

Unions and Revisionism

Was socialism really radical and revolutionary in these years? On the whole, it was not. Indeed, as socialist parties grew and attracted large numbers of members, they looked more and more toward gradual change and steady improvement for the working class, less and less toward revolution. The mainstream of European socialism became militantly moderate; that is, socialists increasingly combined radical rhetoric with sober action.

Workers themselves were progressively less inclined to follow radical programs. There were several reasons for this. As workers gained the right to vote and to participate politically in the nation-state, their attention focused more on elections than on revolutions. And as workers won real, tangible benefits, this furthered the process. Workers were not immune to patriotic education and indoc-

trination during military service, however ardently socialist intellectuals might wish the contrary. Nor were workers a unified social group.

Perhaps most important of all, workers' standard of living rose substantially after 1850 as the promise of the Industrial Revolution was at least partially realized. In Great Britain, for example, workers could buy almost twice as much with their wages in 1906 as in 1850, and most of the increase came after 1870. Workers experienced similar increases in most continental countries after 1850, though much less strikingly in late-developing Russia. Improvement in the standard of living was much more than merely a matter of higher wages. The quality of life improved dramatically in urban areas. For all these reasons, workers tended more and more to become militantly moderate: they demanded gains, but they were less likely to take to the barricades in pursuit of them.

The growth of labor unions reinforced this trend toward moderation. In the early stages of industrialization, modern unions were generally prohibited by law. A famous law of the French Revolution had declared all guilds and unions illegal in the name of "liberty" in 1791. In Great Britain, attempts by workers to unite were considered criminal conspiracies after 1799. Other countries had similar laws, and these obviously hampered union development. In France, for example, about two hundred workers were imprisoned each year between 1825 and 1847 for taking part in illegal combinations. Unions were considered subversive bodies, only to be hounded and crushed.

From this sad position workers struggled to escape. Great Britain led the way in 1824 and 1825, when unions won the right to exist but (generally) not the right to strike. After the collapse of Robert Owen's attempt to form one big union in the 1830s (see page 713), new and more practical kinds of unions appeared. Limited primarily to highly skilled workers such as machinists and carpenters, the "new model unions" avoided both radical politics and costly strikes. Instead, their sober, respectable leaders concentrated on winning better wages and hours for their members through collective bargaining and compromise. This approach helped pave the way to full acceptance in Britain in the 1870s, when unions won the right to strike without being held legally liable for the financial damage inflicted on employers. After 1890 unions for unskilled workers developed, and between 1901 and 1906 the legal position of British unions was further strengthened.

Germany was the most industrialized, socialized, and unionized continental country by 1914. German unions were not granted important rights until 1869, and until the antisocialist law was repealed in 1890, they were frequently harassed by the government as socialist fronts. Nor were socialist leaders particularly interested in union activity, believing as they did in the iron law of low wages and the need for political revolution. The result was that, as late as 1895, there were only about 270,000 union members in a male industrial workforce of nearly 8 million. Then, with German industrialization still storming ahead and almost all legal harassment eliminated, union membership skyrocketed to roughly 3 million in 1912.

This great expansion both reflected and influenced the changing character of German unions. Increasingly, unions in Germany focused on bread-and-butter issues—wages, hours, working conditions—rather than on instilling pure socialist doctrine. Genuine collective bargaining, long opposed by socialist intellectuals as a "sellout," was officially recognized as desirable by the German Trade Union Congress in 1899. When employers proved unwilling to bargain, a series of strikes forced them to change their minds.

Between 1906 and 1913, successful collective bargaining was gaining a prominent place in German industrial relations. In 1913 alone, over 10,000 collective bargaining agreements affecting 1.25 million workers were signed. Further gradual improvement, not revolution, was becoming the primary objective of the German trade-union movement.

The German trade unions and their leaders were —in fact, if not in name—thoroughgoing revisionists. *Revisionism*—that most awful of sins in the eyes of militant Marxists in the twentieth century—was an effort by various socialists to update Marxian doctrines to reflect the realities of the time. Thus the socialist Edward Bernstein argued in 1899 in his *Evolutionary Socialism* that Marx's predictions of ever-greater poverty for workers and ever-greater concentration of wealth in ever-fewer hands had been proved false. Therefore, Bernstein suggested, socialists should reform their doctrines and tactics. They should combine with other progressive forces to win gradual evolutionary gains for workers through legislation, unions, and further economic development. These views were formally denounced as heresy by the German Social Democratic party and later by the entire Second International. Nevertheless, the revisionist, gradualist approach continued to gain the tacit acceptance of many German socialists, particularly in the trade unions.

Moderation found followers elsewhere. In France, the great humanist and socialist leader Jean Jaurès formally repudiated revisionist doctrines in order to establish a unified socialist party, but he remained at heart a gradualist. Questions of revolutionary versus gradualist policies split Russian Marxists.

Socialist parties before 1914 had clear-cut national characteristics. Russians and socialists in the Austro-Hungarian Empire tended to be the most radical. The German party talked revolution and practiced reformism, greatly influenced by its enormous trade-union movement. The French party talked revolution and tried to practice it, unrestrained by a trade-union movement that was both very weak and very radical. In England, the socialist but non-Marxian Labour party, reflecting the well-established union movement, was formally committed to gradual reform. In Spain and Italy, Marxian socialism was very weak. There anarchism, seeking to smash the state rather than the bourgeoisie, dominated radical thought and action.

In short, socialist policies and doctrines varied from country to country. Socialism itself was to a large extent "nationalized" behind the imposing façade of international unity. This helps explain why, when war came in 1914, socialist leaders almost without exception supported their governments.

SUMMARY

From the mid-nineteenth century on, Western society became nationalistic as well as urban and industrial. Nation-states and strong-minded national leaders gradually enlisted widespread support and gave men and women a sense of belonging. Even socialism became increasingly national in orientation, gathering strength as a champion of working-class interests in domestic politics. Yet, while nationalism served to unite peoples, it also drove them apart. Though most obvious in the United States before the Civil War and in Austria-Hungary and Ireland, this was in a real sense true for all of Western civilization. The universal national faith, which reduced social tensions within states, promoted a bitter, almost Darwinian competition between states and thus ominously threatened the progress and unity it had helped to build.

NOTES

1. Quoted in G. Wright, *France in Modern Times* (Chicago: Rand McNally, 1960), p. 179.
2. Quoted in O. Pflanze, *Bismarck and the Development of Germany: The Period of Unification, 1815–1871* (Princeton, N.J.: Princeton University Press, 1963), p. 60.
3. Quoted in H. Kohn, *The Mind of Germany: The Education of a Nation* (New York: Charles Scribner's Sons & Macmillan, 1960), pp. 156–161.
4. Quoted in R. Sewell, *A House Divided: Sectionalism and Civil War, 1848–1865* (Baltimore: Johns Hopkins University Press, 1988), p. 79.
5. Ibid., p. 124.
6. Quoted in T. von Laue, *Sergei Witte and the Industrialization of Russia* (New York: Columbia University Press, 1963), p. 78.
7. Quoted in J. P. McKay, *Pioneers for Profit: Foreign Entrepreneurship and Russian Industrialization, 1885–1913* (Chicago: University of Chicago Press, 1970), p. 11.

SUGGESTED READING

In addition to the general works mentioned in the Suggested Reading for Chapter 23, which treat the entire nineteenth century, G. Craig, *Germany, 1866–1945* (1980), and B. Moore, *Social Origins of Dictatorship and Democracy* (1966), are outstanding. R. Anderson, *France, 1870–1914* (1977), provides a good introduction and has a useful bibliography.

Among specialized works of high quality, D. Harvey, *Napoleon III and His Comic Empire* (1988), and R. Williams, *Gaslight and Shadows* (1957), brings the world of Napoleon III vibrantly alive, while Karl Marx's *The Eighteenth Brumaire of Louis Napoleon* is a famous denunciation of the *coup d'état*. E. Weber, *France, Fin de Siècle* (1986) and the engaging collective biography by R. Shattuck, *The Banquet Years* (1968), capture the spirit of Paris at the end of the century. E. Weber, *Peasants into Frenchmen* (1976), stresses the role of education and modern communications in the transformation of rural France after 1870. E. Thomas, *The Women Incendiaries* (1966), examines radical women in the Paris Commune. G. Chapman, *The Dreyfus Case: A Reassessment* (1955), and D. Johnson, *France and the Dreyfus Affair* (1967), are careful examinations of the famous case. In *Jean Barois*, Nobel Prize winner R. M. Du Gard accurately recreates in novel form the Dreyfus affair, and Émile Zola's novel *The Debacle* treats the Franco-Prussian War realistically.

D. M. Smith has written widely on Italy, and his *Garibaldi* (1956) and *Italy: A Modern History*, rev. ed. (1969) are recommended. P. Schroeder, *Austria, Great Britain and the Crimean War* (1972), is an outstanding and highly original diplomatic study. In addition to the important studies on Bismarck and Germany by Pflanze and Kohn cited in the Notes, see E. Eyck, *Bismarck and the German Empire* (1964). F. Stern, *Gold and Iron* (1977), is a fascinating examination of relations between Bismarck and his financial adviser, the Jewish banker Bleichröder. L. Cecil, *Wilhelm II: Prince and Emperor, 1859–1900* (1989), probes the character and politics of Germany's ruler. G.

Iggers, *The German Conception of History* (1968); K. D. Barkin, *The Controversy over German Industrialization, 1890–1902* (1970); and E. Spencer, *Management and Labor in Imperial Germany: Ruhr Industrialists as Employers* (1984), are valuable in-depth investigations. H. Glasser, ed., *The German Mind in the Nineteenth Century* (1981), is an outstanding anthology, as are R. E. Joeres and M. Maynes, eds., *German Women in the Eighteenth and Nineteenth Centuries* (1986), and P. Mendes-Flohr, ed., *The Jew in the Modern World: A Documentary History* (1980). C. Schorske, *Fin de Siècle Vienna: Politics and Culture* (1980), and P. Gay, *Freud, Jews, and Other Germans* (1978), are brilliant on aspects of modern culture. A. Sked, *The Decline and Fall of the Habsburg Empire, 1815–1918* (1989), and R. Kann, *The Multinational Empire*, 2 vols. (1950, 1964), probe the intricacies of the nationality problem in Austria-Hungary, while S. Stavrianos has written extensively on southeastern Europe, including *The Balkans, 1815–1914* (1963). In addition to the excellent introduction to the United States in the era of regional conflict by Sewell, which is cited in the Notes and which has an annotated bibliography, Southern nationalism has been interpreted from different perspectives by P. Escott, *After Secession: Jefferson Davis and the Failure of Confederate Nationalism* (1974), and D. Faust, *The Creation of Confederate Nationalism* (1988). E. Foner, *A Short History of Reconstruction* (1989), is highly recommended.

In addition to the studies on Russian industrial development by von Laue and McKay cited in the Notes, P. Gatrell, *The Tsarist Economy, 1850–1917* (1986), and A. Rieber, *Merchants and Entrepreneurs in Imperial Russia* (1982), are recommended. Among fine studies on Russian development, H. Rogger, *Russia in the Age of Modernization and Revolution, 1881–1917* (1983), which has an excellent bibliography; T. Emmons, *The Russian Landed Gentry and the Peasant Emancipation of 1861* (1968); and H. Troyat, *Daily Life in Russia Under the Last Tsar* (1962), are especially recommended. T. Friedgut, *Iuzovka and Revolution: Life and Work in Russia's Donbass, 1869–1924* (1989); R. Zelnik, *Labor and Society in Tsarist Russia, 1855–1870* (1971); and R. Johnson, *Peasant and Proletarian: The Working Class of Moscow at the End of the Nineteenth Century* (1979), skillfully treat different aspects of working-class life and politics. W. E. Mosse, *Alexander II and the Modernization of Russia* (1958), provides a good discussion of midcentury reforms, while C. Black, ed., *The Transformation of Russian Society* (1960), offers a collection of essays on Russian modernization. I. Turgenev's great novel *Fathers and Sons* probes the age-old conflict of generations as well as nineteenth-century Russian revolutionary thought.

G. Dangerfield, *The Strange Death of Liberal England* (1961), brilliantly examines social tensions in Ireland as well as Englishwomen's struggle for the vote before 1914. W. Arnstein convincingly shows how the Victorian aristocracy survived and even flourished in nineteenth-century Britain in F. Jaher, ed., *The Rich, the Well-Born, and the Powerful* (1973), an interesting collection of essays on social elites in history. The theme of aristocratic strength and survival is expanded in A. Mayer's provocative *Persistence of the Old Regime: Europe to the Great War* (1981).

On late-nineteenth-century socialism, C. Schorske, *German Social Democracy, 1905–1917* (1955), is a modern classic. V. Lidtke, *The Outlawed Party* (1966), and J. Quataert, *Reluctant Feminists in German Social Democracy, 1885–1917* (1979), are also recommended for the study of the German socialists. H. Goldberg, *The Life of Jean Jaurès* (1962), is a sympathetic account of the great French socialist leader. P. Stearns, who has written several books on European labor history, considers radical labor leaders in *Revolutionary Syndicalism and French Labor* (1971). D. Geary, ed., *Labour and Socialist Movements in Europe Before 1914* (1989), contains excellent studies on developments in different countries and has up-to-date bibliographies.

26

The West and the World

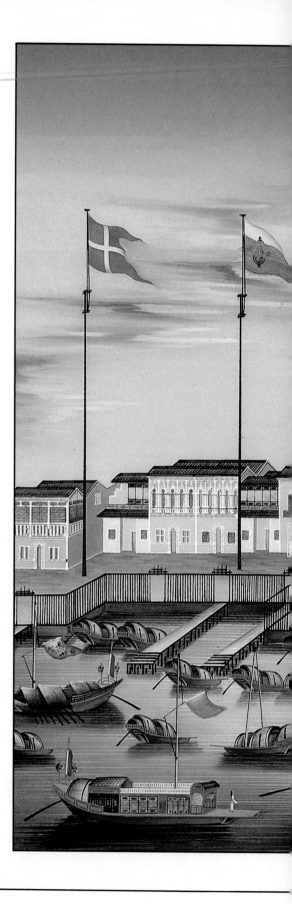

While industrialization and nationalism were transforming urban life and Western society, Western society itself was reshaping the world. At the peak of its power and pride, the West entered the third and most dynamic phase of the aggressive expansion that began with the Crusades and continued with the great discoveries and the rise of seaborne colonial empires. An ever-growing stream of products, people, and ideas flowed out of Europe in the nineteenth century. Hardly any corner of the globe was left untouched. The most spectacular manifestations of Western expansion came in the late nineteenth century, when the leading European nations established or enlarged their far-flung political empires. The political annexation of territory in the 1880s—the "new imperialism," as it is often called by historians—was the capstone of a profound underlying economic and technological process.

- How and why did this many-sided, epoch-making expansion occur in the nineteenth century?
- What were some of its consequences for the West and the rest of the world?

These are the questions this chapter will examine.

INDUSTRIALIZATION AND THE WORLD ECONOMY

The Industrial Revolution created, first in Great Britain and then in continental Europe and North America, a growing and tremendously dynamic economic system. In the course of the nineteenth century, that system was extended across the face of the earth. Some of this extension into non-Western areas was peaceful and beneficial for all concerned, for the West had many products and techniques the rest of the world desired. If peaceful methods failed, however, Europeans did not stand on ceremony. They used their superior military power to force non-Western nations to open their doors to Western economic interests. In general, Westerners fashioned the global economic system so that the largest share of the ever increasing gains from trade, technology, and migration flowed to the West and its propertied classes.

The Industrial Revolution in Europe marked a momentous turning point in human history. Indeed, it is only by placing Europe's economic breakthrough in a global perspective that one can truly appreciate its revolutionary implications and consequences.

From such a global perspective, the ultimate significance of the Industrial Revolution was that it allowed those regions of the world that industrialized in the nineteenth century to increase their wealth and power enormously in comparison to those that did not. As a result, a gap between the industrializing regions—mainly Europe and North America—and the nonindustrializing ones—mainly Africa, Asia, and Latin America—opened up and grew steadily throughout the nineteenth century. Moreover, this pattern of uneven global development became institutionalized, or built into the structure of the world economy. Thus we evolved a "lopsided world," a world of rich lands and poor.

Historians have long been aware of this gap, but it is only recently that historical economists have begun to chart its long-term evolution with some precision. Their findings are extremely revealing, although one must understand that they contain a margin of error and other limitations as well. The findings of one such study are summarized in Figure 26.1. This figure compares the long-term evolution of average income per person in today's "developed" (or industrialized) regions—defined as western and eastern Europe, North America, and Japan—with that found in the "Third World"—a term that is now widely used by international organizations and by scholars to group Africa, Asia, and Latin America into a single unit. To get these individual income figures, researchers estimate a country's gross national product (GNP) at different points in time, convert those estimates to some common currency, and divide by the total population.

Figure 26.1 highlights three main points. First, in 1750 the average standard of living was no higher in Europe as a whole than in the rest of the world. In 1750 Europe was still a poor agricultural society. Moreover, the average per-person income in the wealthiest European country (Great Britain) was less than twice that in the poorest non-Western land. By 1970, however, the average person in the wealthiest countries had an income fully twenty-five times as great as that received by the average person in the poorest countries of Africa and Asia.

Second, it was industrialization that opened the gaps in average wealth and well-being among countries and regions. One sees that Great Britain had jumped well above the European average by 1830, when the first industrial nation was well in advance of its continental competitors. One also sees how Great Britain's lead gradually narrowed, as other European countries and the United States successfully industrialized in the course of the nineteenth century.

Finally, income per person stagnated in the Third World before 1913, in striking contrast to the industrializing regions. Only after 1945, in the era of political independence and decolonization, did Third World countries finally make some real economic progress, beginning in their turn the critical process of industrialization.

The rise of these enormous income disparities, which are poignant indicators of equal disparities in food and clothing, health and education, life expectancy and general material well-being, has generated a great deal of debate. One school of interpretation stresses that the West used science, technology, capitalist organization, and even its critical world-view to create its wealth and greater physical well-being. Another school argues that the West used its political and economic power to steal much of its riches, continuing in the nineteenth (and twentieth) century the rapacious colonialism born of the era of expansion.

These issues are complex, and there are few simple answers. As noted in Chapter 22, the wealth-creating potential of technological improvement and more intensive capitalist organization was indeed great. At the same time, those breakthroughs rested, in part, on Great Britain's having already used political force to dominate the world economy in the nineteenth century. Wealth—unprecedented wealth—was indeed created, but the lion's share of that new wealth flowed to the West and its propertied classes.

Trade and Foreign Investment

Commerce between nations has always been a powerful stimulus to economic development. Never was this more true than in the nineteenth century,

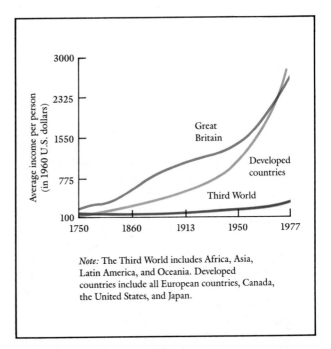

FIGURE 26.1 The Growth of Average Income per Person in the Third World, Developed Countries, and Great Britain, 1750–1970, in 1960 U.S. dollars and prices. *(Source: P. Bairoch and M. Lévy-Leboyer, eds., Disparities in Economic Development Since the Industrial Revolution. New York: St. Martin's Press, 1981, pp. 7–8, 10)*

when world trade grew prodigiously. World trade grew modestly until about 1840, and then it took off. After a slowdown in the last years of the century, another surge lasted until World War One. In 1913 the value of world trade was roughly $38 billion, or about *twenty-five* times what it had been in 1800. (This amount actually understates the growth, since average prices of both manufactured goods and raw materials were lower in 1913 than in 1800.) In a general way, the enormous increase in international commerce summed up the growth of an interlocking world economy, centered in and directed by Europe.

Great Britain played a key role in using trade to tie the world together economically. In 1815 Britain already had a colonial empire, for India, Canada, Australia, and other scattered areas remained British possessions after American independence. The technological breakthroughs of the Industrial Revolution allowed Britain to manufacture cotton textiles, iron, and other goods more cheaply and to far outstrip domestic demand for such products.

Thus British manufacturers sought export markets, first in Europe and then around the world.

Take the case of cotton textiles. By 1820 Britain was exporting half of its production. Europe bought half of these cotton textile exports, while India bought only 6 percent. Then, as European nations and the United States exercised sovereignty to erect protective tariff barriers and promote domestic industry, British cotton textile manufacturers aggressively sought and found other foreign markets in non-Western areas. By 1850 India bought 25 percent and Europe only 16 percent of a much larger total. As a British colony, India could not raise tariffs to protect its ancient cotton textile industry, and thousands of Indian weavers lost their livelihoods.

After the repeal of the Corn Laws in 1846 (see page 741), Britain also became the world's single best market. The decisive argument in the battle against tariffs on imported grain had been, "We must give, if we mean honestly to receive, and buy as well as sell." Until 1914 Britain thus remained the world's emporium, where not only agricultural products and raw materials but also manufactured goods entered freely. Free access to the enormous market of Britain stimulated the development of mines and plantations in many non-Western areas.

The growth of trade was facilitated by the conquest of distance. The earliest railroad construction occurred in Europe (including Russia) and in America north of the Rio Grande; other parts of the globe saw the building of rail lines after 1860. By 1920 more than one-quarter of the world's railroads were in Latin America, Asia, Africa, and Australia. Wherever railroads were built, they drastically reduced transportation costs, opened new economic opportunities, and called forth new skills and attitudes. Moreover, in the areas of massive European settlement—North America and Australia—they were built in advance of the population and provided a means of settling the land.

The power of steam revolutionized transportation by sea as well as by land. In 1807 inhabitants of the Hudson Valley in New York saw the "Devil on the way to Albany in a saw-mill," as Robert Fulton's steamship *Clermont* traveled 150 miles upstream in thirty-two hours. Steam power, long used to drive paddle-wheelers on rivers, particularly in Russia and North America, finally began to supplant sails on the oceans of the world in the late 1860s. Lighter, stronger, cheaper steel replaced iron, which had replaced wood. Screw propellers superseded paddle wheels, while mighty compound steam engines cut fuel consumption by half. Passenger and freight rates tumbled, and the intercontinental shipment of low-priced raw materials became feasible. In addition to the large passenger liners and freighters of the great shipping companies, there were innumerable independent tramp steamers searching endlessly for cargo around the world.

An account of an actual voyage by a typical tramp freighter will highlight nineteenth-century developments in global trade. The ship left England in 1910, carrying rails and general freight to western Australia. From there, it carried lumber to Melbourne in southeastern Australia, where it took on harvester combines for Argentina. In Buenos Aires it loaded wheat for Calcutta, and in Calcutta it took on jute for New York. From New York it carried a variety of industrial products to Australia before returning to England with lead, wool, and wheat after a voyage of approximately 72,000 miles to six continents in seventeen months.

The revolution in land and sea transportation helped European pioneers to open up vast new territories and to produce agricultural products and raw materials there for sale in Europe. Moreover, the development of refrigerated railway cars and, from the 1880s, refrigerator ships enabled first Argentina and then the United States, Australia, and New Zealand to ship mountains of chilled or frozen beef and mutton to European (mainly British) consumers. From Asia, Africa, and Latin America came not only the traditional tropical products—spices, tea, sugar, coffee—but new raw materials for industry, such as jute, rubber, cotton, and coconut oil.

Intercontinental trade was enormously facilitated by the Suez and Panama canals. Of great importance, too, was large and continuous investment in modern port facilities, which made loading and unloading cheaper, faster, and more dependable. Finally, transoceanic telegraph cables inaugurated rapid communications among the financial centers of the world. While a British tramp freighter steamed from Calcutta to New York, a broker in London was arranging by telegram for it to carry an American cargo to Australia. World commodity prices were also instantaneously conveyed by the same network of communications.

The growth of trade and the conquest of distance encouraged the expanding European economy to make massive foreign investments. Begin-

The Suez Canal   Completed in 1869, the hundred-mile canal cut in half the length of the journey between Europe and Asia. This picture from a popular weekly newspaper shows a line of ships passing through the canal on the opening day. *(Source: Girandon/Art Resource)*

ning about 1840, European capitalists started to invest large sums in foreign lands. They did not stop until the outbreak of World War One in 1914. By that year, Europeans had invested more than $40 billion abroad. Great Britain, France, and Germany were the principal investing countries, although by 1913 the United States was emerging as a substantial foreign investor. The sums involved were enormous (Map 26.1). In the decade before 1914, Great Britain was investing 7 percent of its annual national income abroad, or slightly more than it was investing in its entire domestic economy. The great gap between rich and poor within Europe meant that the wealthy and moderately well-to-do could and did send great sums abroad in search of interest and dividends.

Most of the capital exported did not go to European colonies or protectorates in Asia and Africa. About three-quarters of total European investment went to other European countries, the United States and Canada, Australia and New Zealand, and Latin America. Europe found its most profitable opportunities for investment in construction of the railroads, ports, and utilities that were necessary to settle and develop the almost-vacant lands in such places as Australia and the Americas. By lending money for a railroad in Argentina or in Canada's prairie provinces, for example, Europeans not only

collected interest but also enabled white settlers to buy European rails and locomotives, developed sources of cheap wheat, and opened still more territory for European settlement. Much of this investment—such as in American railroads, fully a third of whose capital in 1890 was European, or in Russian railroads, which drew heavily on loans from France—was peaceful and mutually beneficial. The victims were native American Indians and Australian aborigines, who were decimated by the diseases, liquor, and weapons of an aggressively expanding Western society.

The Opening of China and Japan

Europe's relatively peaceful development of robust offshoots in sparsely populated North America, Australia, and much of Latin America absorbed huge quantities of goods, investments, and migrants. From a Western point of view, that was the most important aspect of Europe's global thrust. Yet Europe's economic and cultural penetration of old, densely populated civilizations was also profoundly significant, especially for the non-European peoples affected by it. With such civilizations Europeans also increased their trade and profit. Moreover, as had been the case ever since Vasco da

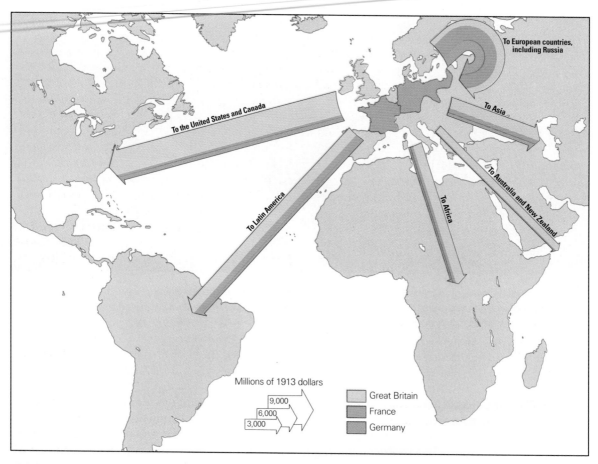

MAP 26.1 European Investment to 1914   Foreign investment grew rapidly after 1850, and Britain, France, and Germany were the major investing nations. As shown above, most European investment was not directed to the area seized by the "new imperialism."

Gama and Christopher Columbus, the expanding Western society was prepared to use force to attain its desires, if necessary. This was what happened in China and Japan, two crucial examples of the general pattern of intrusion into non-Western lands.

Traditional Chinese civilization was self-sufficient. For centuries China had sent more to Europe in the way of goods and inventions than it received, and this was still the case in the eighteenth century. Europeans and the English in particular had developed a taste for Chinese tea, but they had to pay for it with hard silver since China was supremely uninterested in European wares. Trade with Europe was carefully regulated by the Chinese imperial government—the Manchu Dynasty—which was more interested in isolating and controlling the strange "sea barbarians" than in pursuing commercial exchange. The imperial government refused to estab-

lish diplomatic relations with the "inferior" European states, and it required all foreign merchants to live in the southern city of Canton and to buy and sell only from the local merchant monopoly. Practices considered harmful to Chinese interests, such as the sale of opium and the export of silver from China, were strictly forbidden.

For years the little community of foreign merchants in Canton had to accept the Chinese system. By the 1820s, however, the dominant group, the British, were flexing their muscles. Moreover, in the smoking of opium—that "destructive and ensnaring vice" denounced by Chinese decrees—they had found something the Chinese really wanted. Grown legally in British-occupied India, opium was smuggled into China by means of fast ships and bribed officials. The more this rich trade developed, the greedier British merchants became and the more they resented the patriotic attempts of the Chinese government to stem the tide of drug addiction. By 1836 the aggressive goal of the British merchants in Canton was an independent British colony in China and "safe and unrestricted liberty" in trade. They pressured the British government to take decisive action and enlisted the support of British manufacturers with visions of vast Chinese markets to be opened.

At the same time, the Manchu government decided that the opium trade had to be stamped out. It was ruining the people and stripping the empire of its silver, which was going to British merchants to pay for the opium. The government began to prosecute Chinese drug dealers vigorously and in 1839 sent special envoy Lin Tse-hsü to Canton. Lin Tse-hsü ordered the foreign merchants to obey China's laws, "for our great unified Manchu Empire regards itself as responsible for the habits and morals of its subjects and cannot rest content to see any of them become victims of a deadly poison."[1] The British merchants refused and were expelled, whereupon war soon broke out.

Using troops from India and in control of the seas, the British occupied several coastal cities and forced China to surrender. In the Treaty of Nanking in 1842, the imperial government was forced to cede the island of Hong Kong to Britain forever, pay an indemnity of $100 million, and open up four large cities to foreign trade with low tariffs.

Thereafter the opium trade flourished, and Hong Kong developed rapidly as an Anglo-Chinese enclave. China continued to nurture illusions of superiority and isolation, however, and refused to accept foreign diplomats in Peking, the imperial capital. Finally, there was a second round of foreign attack between 1856 and 1860, culminating in the occupation of Peking by seventeen thousand British and French troops and the intentional burning of the emperor's summer palace. Another round of harsh treaties gave European merchants and missionaries greater privileges and protection. Thus did Europeans use military aggression to blow a hole in the wall of Chinese seclusion and open the country to foreign trade and foreign ideas. Blasting away at Chinese sovereignty as well, they forced the Chinese to accept trade and investment on unfavorable terms for the foreseeable future.

China's neighbor, Japan, had its own highly distinctive civilization and even less use for Westerners. European traders and missionaries first arrived in Japan in the sixteenth century. By 1640 Japan had reacted quite negatively to their presence. The government decided to seal off the country from all European influences, in order to preserve traditional Japanese culture and society. Officials ruthlessly persecuted Japanese Christians and expelled all but a few Dutch merchants, who were virtually imprisoned in a single port and rigidly controlled. When American and British whaling ships began to appear off Japanese coasts almost two hundred years later, the policy of exclusion was still in effect. An order of 1825 commanded Japanese officials to "drive away foreign vessels without second thought."[2]

Japan's unbending isolation seemed hostile and barbaric to the West, particularly to the United States. It complicated the practical problems of shipwrecked American sailors and the provisioning of whaling ships and China traders sailing in the eastern Pacific. It also thwarted the hope of trade and profit. Moreover, Americans shared the self-confidence and dynamism of expanding Western society. They had taken California from Mexico in 1848, and Americans felt destined to play a great role in the Pacific. It seemed, therefore, the United States' duty to force the Japanese to share their ports and behave like a "civilized" nation.

After several unsuccessful American attempts to establish commercial relations with Japan, Commodore Matthew Perry steamed into Edo (now Tokyo) Bay in 1853 and demanded diplomatic negotiations with the emperor. Japan entered a grave crisis. Some Japanese warriors urged resistance, but senior officials realized how defenseless their cities were against naval bombardment. Shocked and humiliated, they reluctantly signed a treaty with the United States that opened two ports and permitted trade. Over the next five years, more treaties spelled out the rights and privileges of the Western nations and their merchants in Japan. Japan was "opened." What the British had done in China with war, the Americans had done in Japan with the threat of war.

Western Penetration of Egypt

Egypt's experience illustrates not only the explosive power of the expanding European economy and society but also their seductive appeal in non-Western lands. Of great importance in African and Middle Eastern history, the ancient land of the pharaohs had since 525 B.C. been ruled by a succession of foreigners, most recently by the Ottoman Turks. In 1798 French armies under young General Napoleon Bonaparte invaded the Egyptian part of the Ottoman Empire and occupied the territory for three years. Into the power vacuum left by the French withdrawal stepped an extraordinary Albanian-born Turkish general, Muhammad Ali (1769–1849).

First appointed governor of Egypt by the Turkish sultan, Muhammad Ali soon disposed of his political rivals and set out to build his own state on the strength of a large, powerful army organized along European lines. He drafted for the first time the illiterate, despised peasant masses of Egypt, and he hired French and Italian army officers to train these raw recruits and their Turkish officers. The government was also reformed, new lands were cultivated, and communications were improved. By the time of his death in 1849, Muhammad Ali had established a strong and virtually independent Egyptian state, to be ruled by his family on a hereditary basis within the Turkish empire.

Muhammad Ali's policies of modernization attracted large numbers of Europeans to the banks of the Nile. As one Arab sheik of the Ottoman Empire remarked in the 1830s, "Englishmen are like ants; if one finds a bit of meat, hundreds follow."[3] The port city of Alexandria had more than fifty thousand Europeans by 1864, most of them Italians, Greeks, French, and English. Europeans served not only as army officers but also as engineers, doctors, high government officials, and police officers. Others found their "meat" in trade, finance, and shipping.

To pay for a modern army as well as for European services and manufactured goods, Muhammad Ali encouraged the development of commercial agriculture geared to the European market. This development had profound implications. Egyptian peasants had been poor but largely self-sufficient, growing food for their own consumption on state-owned lands allotted to them by tradition. Faced with the possibility of export agriculture, high-ranking officials and members of Muhammad Ali's family began carving large private landholdings out of the state domain. The new landlords made the peasants their tenants and forced them to grow cash crops for European markets. Borrowing money from European lenders at high rates and still making good profits, Egyptian landowners "modernized" agriculture, but to the detriment of peasant well-being.

East Meets West   This painting gives a Japanese view of the first audience of the American Consul and his staff with the shogun, Japan's hereditary military governor, in 1859. The Americans appear strange and ill at ease. *(Source: Laurie Platt Winfrey, Inc.)*

British in Egypt   In this photograph Scottish soldiers pose with the ancient and mysterious Great Sphinx like school children on an outing. *(Source: Bettmann/Hulton)*

These trends continued under Muhammad Ali's grandson Ismail, who in 1863 began his sixteen-year rule as Egypt's *khedive,* or prince. Educated at France's leading military academy, Ismail was a westernizing autocrat. He dreamed of using European technology and capital to modernize Egypt quickly and build a vast empire in northeast Africa. The large irrigation networks he promoted caused cotton production and exports to Europe to boom. Ismail also borrowed large sums to install modern communications, and with his support the Suez Canal was completed by a French company in 1869. The Arabic of the masses rather than the Turkish of the conquerors became the official language, and young Egyptians educated in Europe helped spread new skills and new ideas in the bureaucracy. Cairo acquired modern boulevards, Western hotels, and an opera house. As Ismail proudly declared, "My country is no longer in Africa, we now form part of Europe."[4]

Yet Ismail was too impatient and too reckless. His projects were enormously expensive, and the sale of his stock in the Suez Canal to the British

government did not relieve the situation. By 1876 Egypt owed foreign bondholders a colossal $450 million and could not pay the interest on its debt. Rather than let Egypt go bankrupt and repudiate its loans, as had some Latin American countries and U.S. state governments in the early nineteenth century, the governments of France and Great Britain intervened politically to protect the European bankers who held the Egyptian bonds. They forced Ismail to appoint French and British commissioners to oversee Egyptian finances, in order that the Egyptian debt would be paid in full. This was a momentous decision. It implied direct European political control and was a sharp break with the previous pattern of trade and investment. Throughout most of the nineteenth century, Europeans had used naked military might and political force primarily to make sure that non-Western lands would accept European trade and investment. Now Europeans were going to determine the state budget and effectively rule Egypt.

Foreign financial control evoked a violent nationalistic reaction among Egyptian religious

Ellis Island in New York's harbor was the main entry point into the United States after 1892. For millions of immigrants the first frightening experience in the new land was being inspected and processed through its crowded "pens." (Source: Culver Pictures)

cimated Arabi's forces and, as a result, occupied all of Egypt.

The British said their occupation was temporary, but British armies remained in Egypt until 1956. They maintained the façade of the khedive's government as an autonomous province of the Ottoman Empire, but the khedive was a mere puppet. The able British consul general Evelyn Baring, later Lord Cromer, ruled the country after 1883. Once a vocal opponent of involvement in Egypt, Baring was a paternalistic reformer who had come to believe that "without European interference and initiative reform is impossible here." Baring's rule did result in tax reforms and better conditions for peasants, while foreign bondholders tranquilly clipped their coupons and Egyptian nationalists nursed their injured pride.

In Egypt, Baring and the British reluctantly but spectacularly provided a new model for European expansion in densely populated lands. Such expansion was based on military force, political domination, and a self-justifying ideology of beneficial reform. This model was to predominate until 1914. Thus did Europe's Industrial Revolution lead to tremendous political as well as economic expansion throughout the world.

THE GREAT MIGRATION

A poignant human drama was interwoven with economic expansion: literally millions of people picked up stakes and left their ancestral lands in the course of history's greatest migration. To millions of ordinary people, for whom the opening of China and the interest on the Egyptian debt had not the slightest significance, this great movement was the central experience in the saga of Western expansion. It was, in part, because of this great migration that the West's impact on the world in the nineteenth century was so powerful and many-sided.

The Pressure of Population

In the early eighteenth century, the growth of European population entered its third and decisive stage, which continued unabated until the twentieth century (see Chapter 19). Birthrates eventually declined in the nineteenth century, but so did death rates, mainly because of the rising standard

leaders, young intellectuals, and army officers. In 1879, under the leadership of Colonel Ahmed Arabi, they formed the Egyptian Nationalist party. Continuing diplomatic pressure, which forced Ismail to abdicate in favor of his weak son Tewfiq (r. 1879–1892), resulted in bloody anti-European riots in Alexandria in 1882. A number of Europeans were killed, and Tewfiq and his court had to flee to British ships for safety. When the British fleet bombarded Alexandria, more riots swept the country, and Colonel Arabi declared that "an irreconcilable war existed between the Egyptians and the English." But a British expeditionary force de-of living and secondarily because of the medical revolution. Thus the population of Europe (including Asiatic Russia) more than doubled, from approximately 188 million in 1800 to roughly 432 million in 1900.

These figures actually understate Europe's population explosion, for between 1815 and 1932 more than 60 million people left Europe. These migrants went primarily to the "areas of European settlement"—North and South America, Australia, New Zealand, and Siberia—where they contributed to a rapid growth in numbers. The population of North America (the United States and Canada) alone grew from 6 million to 81 million between 1800 and 1900 because of continuous immigration and the high fertility rates of North American women. Since population grew more slowly in Africa and Asia than in Europe, as Figure 26.2 shows, Europeans and people of European origin jumped from about 22 percent of the world's total to about 38 percent on the eve of World War One.

The growing number of Europeans provided further impetus for Western expansion. It was a driving force behind emigration. As in the eighteenth century, the rapid increase in numbers put pressure on the land and led to land hunger and relative overpopulation in area after area. In most countries, migration increased twenty years after a rapid growth in population, as many children of the baby boom grew up, saw little available land and few opportunities, and migrated. This pattern was especially prevalent when rapid population increase predated extensive industrial development, which offered the best long-term hope of creating jobs within the country and reducing poverty. Thus millions of country folk went abroad, as well as to nearby cities, in search of work and economic opportunity. The case of the Irish, who left in large numbers for Britain during the Industrial Revolution and for the United States after the potato famine, was extreme but not unique.

Before looking at the people who migrated, let us consider three facts. First, the number of men and women who left Europe increased rapidly before World War One. As Figure 26.3 shows, more than 11 million left in the first decade of the twentieth century, over five times the number departing in the 1850s. The outflow of migrants was clearly an enduring characteristic of European society for the entire period.

Second, different countries had very different patterns of movement. As Figure 26.3 also shows,

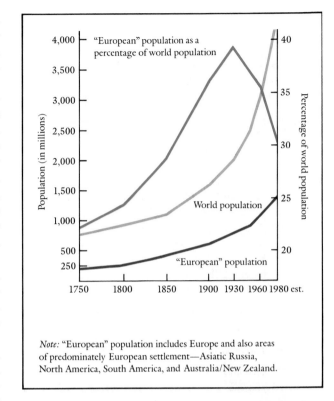

FIGURE 26.2 The Increase of European and World Populations 1750–1980 *(Sources: W. Woodruff,* Impact of Western Man: A Study of Europe's Role in the World Economy. *St. Martin's Press, New York, 1967. p. 103; United Nations.* Statistical Yearbook, *1982, 1985, pp. 2–3.)*

people left Britain and Ireland (which are not distinguished in the British figures) in large numbers from the 1840s on. This emigration reflected not only rural poverty but also the movement of skilled, industrial technicians and the preferences shown to British migrants in the British Empire. Ultimately, about one-third of all European migrants between 1840 and 1920 came from the British Isles. German migration was quite different. It grew irregularly after about 1830, reaching a first peak in the early 1850s and another in the early 1880s. Thereafter it declined rapidly, for Germany's rapid industrialization was providing adequate jobs at home. This pattern contrasted sharply with that of Italy. More and more Italians left the country right up to 1914, reflecting severe problems in Italian villages and relatively slow industrial growth. In sum, migration patterns mirrored social and economic conditions in the various European countries and provinces.

The Jewish Market on New York's lower East Side was a bustling center of economic and social life in 1900. Jewish immigrants could usually find work with Jewish employers, and New York's Jewish population soared from 73 thousand in 1880 to 1.1 million in 1910. *(Source: The Granger Collection)*

Many landless young European men and women were spurred to leave by a spirit of revolt and independence. In Sweden and in Norway, in Jewish Russia and in Italy, these young people felt frustrated by the small privileged classes, who often controlled both church and government and resisted demands for change and greater opportunity. Many a young Norwegian seconded the passionate cry of Norway's national poet, Bjørnson: "Forth will I! Forth! I will be crushed and consumed if I stay."[5]

Many young Jews wholeheartedly agreed with a spokesman of Kiev's Jewish community in 1882, who declared, "Our human dignity is being trampled upon, our wives and daughters are being dishonored, we are looted and pillaged: either we get decent human rights or else let us go wherever our eyes may lead us."[6] Thus, for many, migration was

a radical way to "get out from under." Migration slowed down when the people won basic political and social reforms, such as the right to vote and social security.

Asian Migrants

Not all migration was from Europe. A substantial number of Chinese, Japanese, Indians, and Filipinos—to name only four key groups—responded to rural hardship with temporary or permanent migration. At least 3 million Asians (as opposed to more than 60 million Europeans) moved abroad before 1920. Most went as indentured laborers to work under incredibly difficult conditions on the plantations or in the gold fields of Latin America, southern Asia, Africa, California, Hawaii, and Australia. White estate owners very often used Asians to replace or supplement blacks after the suppression of the slave trade.

In the 1840s, for example, there was a strong demand for field hands in Cuba, and the Spanish government actively recruited Chinese laborers. They came under eight-year contracts, were paid about twenty-five cents a day, and were fed potatoes and salted beef. Between 1853 and 1873, when such migration was stopped, more than 130,000 Chinese laborers went to Cuba. The majority spent their lives as virtual slaves. The great landlords of Peru also brought in more than 100,000 workers from China in the nineteenth century, and there were similar movements of Asians elsewhere.

Such migration from Asia would undoubtedly have grown to much greater proportions if planters and mine owners in search of cheap labor had had their way. But they did not. Asians fled the plantations and gold fields as soon as possible, seeking greater opportunities in trade and towns. There they came into conflict with other brown-skinned peoples—as in Malaya and East Africa—and with white settlers in areas of European settlement.

These settlers demanded a halt to Asian migration. One Australian brutally summed up the typical view: "The Chinaman knows nothing about Caucasian civilization. . . . It would be less objectionable to drive a flock of sheep to the poll than to allow Chinamen to vote. The sheep at all events would be harmless."[7] By the 1880s Americans and Australians were building "great white walls"—discriminatory laws designed to keep Asians out. Thus a final, crucial factor in the migrations before 1914 was the general policy of "whites only" in the open lands of possible permanent settlement. This, too, was part of Western dominance in the increasingly lopsided world. Largely successful in monopolizing the best overseas opportunities, Europeans and people of European ancestry reaped the main benefits from the great migration. By 1913 people in Australia, Canada, and the United States all had higher average incomes than people in Great Britain, still Europe's wealthiest nation.

The Chinese Exclusion Act   This vicious cartoon from a San Francisco newspaper celebrates American anti-migration laws. Americans and Europeans generally shared the same attitudes regarding the non-Western world. *(Source: Caroline Buckler)*

WESTERN IMPERIALISM

The expansion of Western society reached its apex between about 1880 and 1914. In those years, the leading European nations not only continued to send massive streams of migrants, money, and manufactured goods around the world, but also rushed to create or enlarge vast *political* empires abroad. This political empire building contrasted sharply with the economic penetration of non-Western territories between 1816 and 1880, which had left a China or a Japan "opened" but politically independent. By contrast, the empires of the late nineteenth century recalled the old European colonial empires of the seventeenth and eighteenth centuries and led contemporaries to speak of the new imperialism.

Characterized by a frantic rush to plant the flag over as many people and as much territory as possible, the new imperialism had momentous consequences. It resulted in new tensions among competing European states, and it led to wars and rumors of war with non-European powers. The new imperialism was aimed primarily at Africa and Asia. It put millions of black, brown, and tan peoples directly under the rule of whites. How and why did whites come to rule these peoples?

The Scramble for Africa

The most spectacular manifestation of the new imperialism was the seizure of Africa, which broke sharply with previous patterns and fascinated contemporary Europeans and Americans.

As late as 1880, European nations controlled only 10 percent of the African continent, and their possessions were hardly increasing. The French had begun conquering Algeria in 1830, and within fifty years substantial numbers of French, Italian, and Spanish colonists had settled among the overwhelming Arab majority.

At the other end of the continent, in South Africa, the British had taken possession of the Dutch settlements at Cape Town during the wars with Napoleon I. This takeover had led disgruntled Dutch cattle ranchers and farmers in 1835 to make their so-called Great Trek into the interior, where they fought the Zulu and Xhosa peoples for land. After 1853, while British colonies like Canada and

Australia were beginning to evolve toward self-government, the Boers, or Afrikaners (as the descendants of the Dutch in the Cape Colony were beginning to call themselves), proclaimed their political independence and defended it against British armies. By 1880 Afrikaner and British settlers, who detested each other, had wrested control of much of South Africa from the Zulu, Xhosa, and other African peoples.

European trading posts and forts dating back to the Age of Discovery and the slave trade dotted the coast of West Africa. The Portuguese proudly but ineffectively held their old possessions in Angola and Mozambique. Elsewhere, over the great mass of the continent, Europeans did not rule.

Between 1880 and 1900, the situation changed drastically. Britain, France, Germany, and Italy scrambled for African possessions as if their national livelihood depended on it. By 1900 nearly the whole continent had been carved up and placed under European rule: only Ethiopia in northeast Africa and Liberia on the West African coast remained independent. Even the Dutch settler republics of southern Africa were conquered by the British in the bloody Boer War (1899–1902). In the years before 1914, the European powers tightened their control and established colonial governments to rule their gigantic empires (Map 26.2).

In the complexity of the European seizure of Africa, certain events and individuals stand out. Of enormous importance was the British occupation of Egypt, which established the new model of formal political control. There was also the role of Leopold II of Belgium (r. 1865–1909), an energetic, strong-willed monarch with a lust for distant territory. "The sea bathes our coast, the world lies before us," he had exclaimed in 1861. "Steam and electricity have annihilated distance, and all the non-appropriated lands on the surface of the globe can become the field of our operations and of our success."[8] By 1876 Leopold was focusing on central Africa. Subsequently he formed a financial syndicate under his personal control to send H. M. Stanley, a sensation-seeking journalist and part-time explorer, to the Congo basin. Stanley was able

MAP 26.2 The Partition of Africa European nations carved up Africa after 1880 and built vast political empires.

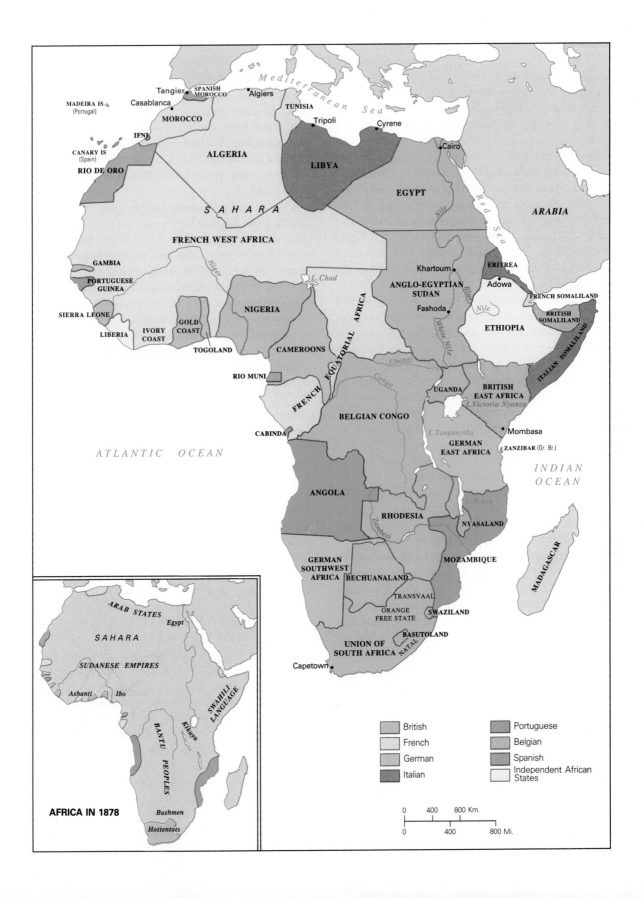

Mediterranean Sea

Tangier
SPANISH MOROCCO
Casablanca
Algiers
MADEIRA IS. (Portugal)
TUNISIA
Tripoli
Cyrene
MOROCCO
Cairo
IFNI
CANARY IS (Spain)
ALGERIA
LIBYA
RIO DE ORO
EGYPT
S A H A R A
ARABIA
FRENCH WEST AFRICA
Red Sea
Nile
GAMBIA
L. Chad
Khartoum
ERITREA
PORTUGUESE GUINEA
ANGLO-EGYPTIAN SUDAN
Adowa
FRENCH SOMALILAND
SIERRA LEONE
NIGERIA
Blue Nile
Fashoda
BRITISH SOMALILAND
LIBERIA
IVORY COAST
GOLD COAST
ETHIOPIA
White Nile
ITALIAN SOMALILAND
TOGOLAND
CAMEROONS
FRENCH EQUATORIAL AFRICA
Ubangi
RIO MUNI
Congo
UGANDA
BRITISH EAST AFRICA
CABINDA
BELGIAN CONGO
L.Victoria Nyanza
ATLANTIC OCEAN
L.Tanganyika
Mombasa
GERMAN EAST AFRICA
ZANZIBAR (Gr. Br.)
INDIAN OCEAN
ANGOLA
L.Nyasa
RHODESIA
NYASALAND
Zambesi
MOZAMBIQUE
MADAGASCAR
GERMAN SOUTHWEST AFRICA
BECHUANALAND
TRANSVAAL
ORANGE FREE STATE
SWAZILAND
BASUTOLAND
UNION OF SOUTH AFRICA
NATAL
Capetown

ARAB STATES
Egypt
SAHARA
SUDANESE EMPIRES
Ashanti
Ibo
SWAHILI LANGUAGE
BANTU PEOPLES
Kikuyu
Bushmen
Hottentots

AFRICA IN 1878

	British		Portuguese
	French		Belgian
	German		Spanish
	Italian		Independent African States

0   400   800 Km.

0   400   800 Mi.

to establish trading stations, sign "treaties" with African chiefs, and plant Leopold's flag. Leopold's actions alarmed the French, who quickly sent out an expedition under Pierre de Brazza. In 1880 de Brazza signed a treaty of protection with the chief of the large Teke tribe and began to establish a French protectorate on the north bank of the Congo River.

Leopold's buccaneering intrusion into the Congo area raised the question of the political fate of black Africa—Africa south of the Sahara. By 1882, when the British successfully invaded and occupied Egypt, the richest and most developed land in Africa, Europe had caught "African fever." There was a gold-rush mentality, and the race for territory was on.

To lay down some basic rules for this new and dangerous game of imperialist competition, Jules Ferry of France and Bismarck of Germany arranged an international conference on Africa in Berlin in 1884 and 1885. The conference established the principle that European claims to African territory had to rest on "effective occupation" in order to be recognized by other states. This principle was very important. It meant that Europeans would push relentlessly into interior regions from all sides and that no single European power would be able to claim the entire continent. The conference recognized Leopold's personal rule over a neutral Congo Free State and declared all of the Congo basin a free-trade zone. The conference also agreed to work to stop slavery and the slave trade in Africa.

The Berlin conference coincided with Germany's sudden emergence as an imperial power. Prior to about 1880, Bismarck, like many other European leaders at the time, had seen little value in colonies. Colonies reminded him, he said, of a poor but proud nobleman who wore a fur coat when he could not afford a shirt underneath. Then, in 1884 and 1885, as political agitation for expansion increased, Bismarck did an abrupt about-face, and Germany established protectorates over a number of small African kingdoms and tribes in Togo, Cameroon, southwest Africa, and later in East Africa.

In acquiring colonies, Bismarck cooperated against the British with France's Jules Ferry, who was as ardent for empire as he was for education. With Bismarck's tacit approval, the French pressed vigorously southward from Algeria, eastward from their old forts on the Senegal coast, and northward from de Brazza's newly formed protectorate on the Congo River. The object of these three thrusts was Lake Chad, a malaria-infested swamp on the edge of the Sahara Desert.

Meanwhile, the British began enlarging their West African enclaves and impatiently pushing northward from the Cape Colony and westward from Zanzibar. Their thrust southward from Egypt was blocked in the Sudan by fiercely independent Muslims, who massacred a British force at Khartoum in 1885.

A decade later, another British force under General Horatio H. Kitchener moved cautiously and more successfully up the Nile River, building a railroad to supply arms and reinforcements as it went. Finally, in 1898, these British troops met their foe at Omdurman, where Muslim tribesmen charged time and time again only to be cut down by the recently invented machine gun. For one smug participant, the young British officer Winston Churchill, it was "like a pantomime scene" in a play. "These extraordinary foreign figures . . . march up one by one from the darkness of Barbarism to the footlights of civilization . . . and their conquerors, taking their possessions, forget even their names. Nor will history record such trash." For another, more somber English observer, "It was not a battle but an execution. The bodies were not in heaps . . . but they spread evenly over acres and acres."[9] In the end, eleven thousand fanatical Muslim tribesmen lay dead, while only twenty-eight Britons had been killed.

Continuing up the Nile after the Battle of Omdurman, Kitchener's armies found that a small French force had already occupied the village of Fashoda. Locked in imperial competition with Britain ever since the British occupation of Egypt, France had tried to beat the British to one of Africa's last unclaimed areas—the upper reaches of the Nile. The result was a serious diplomatic crisis, and even the threat of war. Eventually, wracked by the Dreyfus affair (see page 813) and unwilling to fight, France backed down and withdrew its forces.

The British conquest of the Sudan exemplifies the general process of empire building in Africa. The fate of the Muslim force at Omdurman was eventually inflicted on all native peoples who resisted European rule: they were blown away by vastly superior military force. But however much the European powers squabbled for territory and privilege around the world, they always had the sense to stop short of actually fighting each other

Omdurman, 1898 European machine guns cut down the charging Muslim tribesmen again and again. "It was not a battle but an execution," said one witness. Thus the Sudan was conquered and one million square miles added to the British empire. *(Source: E. T. Archive)*

for it. Imperial ambitions were not worth a great European war.

Imperialism in Asia

Although the sudden division of Africa was more spectacular, Europeans also extended their political control in Asia. In 1815 the Dutch ruled little more than the island of Java in the East Indies. Thereafter they gradually brought almost all of the 3,000-mile archipelago under their political authority, though—in good imperialist fashion— they had to share some of the spoils with Britain and Germany. In the critical decade of the 1880s, the French under the leadership of Jules Ferry took Indochina. India, Japan, and China also experienced a profound imperialist impact (Map 26.3).

Two other great imperialist powers, Russia and the United States, also acquired rich territories in Asia. Russia, whose history since the later Middle Ages had been marked by almost continuous expansion, moved steadily forward on two fronts throughout the nineteenth century. Russians conquered Muslim areas to the south in the Caucasus and in central Asia and also proceeded to nibble greedily on China's outlying provinces in the Far East, especially in the 1890s.

The United States' great conquest was the Philippines, taken from Spain in 1898 after the Spanish-American War. When it quickly became clear that the United States had no intention of granting independence, Philippine patriots rose in revolt and were suppressed only after long, bitter fighting. (Not until 1934 was a timetable for independence established.) Some Americans protested the taking

repeatedly conquered by Muslim and Mongol invaders. It was as if Europe, with its many states and varieties of Christianity, had been conquered and united in a single great empire.

In spite of these achievements, the decisive reaction to European rule was the rise of nationalism among the Indian elite. No matter how anglicized and necessary a member of the educated classes became, he or she could never become the white ruler's equal. The top jobs, the best clubs, the modern hotels, and even certain railroad compartments were sealed off to brown-skinned men and women. The peasant masses might accept such inequality as the latest version of age-old oppression, but the well-educated, English-speaking elite eventually could not. For the elite, racial discrimination meant not only injured pride but bitter injustice. It flagrantly contradicted those cherished Western concepts of human rights and equality. Moreover, it was based on dictatorship, no matter how benign.

By 1885, when educated Indians came together to found the predominately Hindu Indian National Congress, demands were increasing for the equality and self-government Britain enjoyed and had already granted white-settler colonies, such as Canada and Australia. By 1907, emboldened in part by Japan's success (see the next section), the radicals in the Indian National Congress were calling for complete independence. Even the moderates were demanding home rule for India through an elected parliament. Although there were sharp divisions between Hindus and Muslims, Indians were finding an answer to the foreign challenge. The common heritage of British rule and Western ideals, along with the reform and revitalization of the Hindu religion, had created a genuine movement for national independence.

The Example of Japan

When Commodore Perry arrived in Japan in 1853 with his crude but effective gunboat diplomacy, Japan was a complex feudal society. At the top stood a figurehead emperor; but for more than two hundred years, real power had been in the hands of a hereditary military governor, the *shogun.* With the help of a warrior-nobility known as *samurai,* the shogun governed a country of hard-working, productive peasants and city dwellers. Often poor and restless, the intensely proud samurai were deeply humiliated by the sudden American intrusion and the unequal treaties with Western countries.

When foreign diplomats and merchants began to settle in Yokohama, radical samurai reacted with a wave of antiforeign terrorism and antigovernment assassinations between 1858 and 1863. The imperialist response was swift and unambiguous. An allied fleet of American, British, Dutch, and French warships demolished key forts, further weakening the power and prestige of the shogun's government. Then, in 1867, a coalition led by patriotic samurai seized control of the government with hardly any bloodshed and restored the political power of the emperor. This was the Meiji Restoration, a great turning point in Japanese development.

The immediate, all-important goal of the new government was to meet the foreign threat. The battle cry of the Meiji reformers was "enrich the state and strengthen the armed forces." Yet how was this to be done? In an about-face that was one of history's most remarkable chapters, the young but well-trained, idealistic but flexible, leaders of Meiji Japan dropped their antiforeign attacks. Convinced that Western civilization was indeed superior in its military and industrial aspects, they initiated from above a series of measures to reform Japan along modern lines. They were convinced that "Japan must be reborn with America its mother and France its father."[17] In the broadest sense, the Meiji leaders tried to harness the power inherent in Europe's dual revolution, in order to protect their country and catch up with the West.

In 1871 the new leaders abolished the old feudal structure of aristocratic, decentralized government and formed a strong unified state. Following the example of the French Revolution, they dismantled the four-class legal system and declared social equality. They decreed freedom of movement in a country where traveling abroad had been a most serious crime. They created a free, competitive, government-stimulated economy. Japan began to build railroads and modern factories. Thus the new generation adopted many principles of a free, liberal society; and, as in Europe, such freedom resulted in a tremendously creative release of human energy.

Yet the overriding concern of Japan's political leadership was always a powerful state, and to achieve this, more than liberalism was borrowed from the West. A powerful modern navy was created, and the army was completely reorganized along French and German lines, with three-year military service for all males and a professional officer corps. This army of draftees effectively put down disturbances in the countryside, and in 1877 it was used to crush a major rebellion by feudal elements protesting the loss of their privileges. Japan also borrowed rapidly and adapted skillfully the West's science and modern technology, particularly in industry, medicine, and education. Many Japanese were encouraged to study abroad, and the government paid large salaries to attract foreign experts. These experts were always carefully controlled, though, and replaced by trained Japanese as soon as possible.

By 1890, when the new state was firmly established, the wholesale borrowing of the early restora-

tion had given way to more selective emphasis on those things foreign that were in keeping with Japanese tradition. Following the model of the German Empire, Japan established an authoritarian constitution and rejected democracy. The power of the emperor and his ministers was vast, that of the legislature limited.

Japan successfully copied the imperialism of Western society. Expansion not only proved that Japan was strong; it also cemented the nation together in a great mission. Having "opened" Korea with the gunboat diplomacy of imperialism in 1876, Japan decisively defeated China in a war over Korea in 1894 to 1895 and took Formosa. In the next years, Japan competed aggressively with the leading European powers for influence and terri-

Japanese Industrialization   The famous Tomioka silk reeling factory pioneered with mass-production techniques and women factory workers in the 1870s. The combination shown here of European technology with native dress symbolizes Japan's successful integration of Western practices into the traditional culture of its society. *(Source: Laurie Platt Winfrey, Inc.)*

tory in China, particularly Manchuria. There Japanese and Russian imperialism met and collided. In 1904 Japan attacked Russia without warning, and after a bloody war, Japan emerged with a valuable foothold in China, Russia's former protectorate over Port Arthur (see Map 26.3). By 1910, when it annexed Korea, Japan was a major imperial power, continuously expanding its influence in China in spite of sharp protests from its distant Pacific neighbor, the United States.

Japan became the first non-Western country to use an ancient love of country to transform itself and thereby meet the many-sided challenge of Western expansion. Moreover, Japan demonstrated convincingly that a modern Asian nation could defeat and humble a great Western power. Many

Chinese nationalists were fascinated by Japan's achievement. A group of patriots in French-ruled southern Vietnam sent Vietnamese students to Japan to learn the island empire's secret of success. Japan provided patriots in Asia and Africa with an inspiring example of national recovery and liberation.

Toward Revolution in China

In 1860 the two-hundred-year-old Manchu Dynasty in China appeared on the verge of collapse. Efforts to repel the foreigner had failed, and rebellion and chaos wracked the country. Yet the government drew on its traditional strengths and made

The Empress Dowager Tzu Hsi drew on conservative forces, like the court eunuchs surrounding her here, to maintain her power. Three years after her death in 1908, a revolution broke out and forced the last Chinese emperor, a boy of six, to abdicate. *(Source: Courtesy of the Freer Gallery of Art, Smithsonian Institution, Washington, D.C.)*

a surprising comeback that lasted more than thirty years.

Two factors were crucial in this reversal. First, the traditional ruling groups temporarily produced new and effective leadership. Loyal scholar-statesmen and generals quelled disturbances like the great Tai Ping rebellion. A truly remarkable woman, the empress dowager Tzu Hsi, governed in the name of her young son and combined shrewd insight with vigorous action to revitalize the bureaucracy.

Second, destructive foreign aggression lessened, for the Europeans had obtained their primary goal of commercial and diplomatic relations. Indeed, some Europeans contributed to the dynasty's recovery. A talented Irishman effectively reorganized China's customs office and increased the government tax receipts, while a sympathetic American diplomat represented China in foreign lands and helped strengthen the central government. Such efforts dovetailed with the dynasty's efforts to adopt some aspects of Western government and technology while maintaining traditional Chinese values and beliefs.

The parallel movement toward domestic reform and limited cooperation with the West collapsed under the blows of Japanese imperialism. The Sino-Japanese war of 1894 to 1895 and the subsequent harsh peace treaty revealed China's helplessness in the face of aggression, triggering a rush for foreign concessions and protectorates in China. At the high point of this rush in 1898, it appeared that the European powers might actually divide China among themselves, as they had recently divided Africa. Probably only the jealousy each nation felt toward its imperial competitors saved China from partition, although the United States' Open Door policy, which opposed formal annexation of Chinese territory, may have helped tip the balance. In any event, the tempo and impact of foreign penetration greatly accelerated after 1894.

So, too, did the intensity and radicalism of the Chinese reaction. Like the leaders of the Meiji Restoration, some modernizers saw salvation in Western institutions. In 1898 the government launched a desperate "hundred days of reform" in an attempt to meet the foreign challenge. More radical reformers like the revolutionary Sun Yat-sen (1866–1925), who came from the peasantry and was educated in Hawaii by Christian missionaries, sought to overthrow the dynasty altogether and establish a republic.

On the other side, some traditionalists turned back toward ancient practices, political conservatism, and fanatical hatred of the "foreign devils." "Protect the country, destroy the foreigner" was their simple motto. Such conservative, antiforeign patriots had often clashed with foreign missionaries, whom they charged with undermining reverence for ancestors and thereby threatening the Chinese family and the entire society. In the agony of defeat and unwanted reforms, secret societies like the Boxers rebelled. In northeastern China, more than two hundred foreign missionaries and several thousand Chinese Christians were killed. Once again, the imperialist response was swift and harsh. Peking was occupied and plundered by foreign armies. A heavy indemnity was imposed.

The years after the Boxer Rebellion (1900–1903) were ever more troubled. Anarchy and foreign influence spread, as the power and prestige of the Manchu Dynasty declined still further. Antiforeign, antigovernment revolutionary groups agitated and plotted. Finally, in 1912, a spontaneous uprising toppled the Manchu Dynasty. After thousands of years of emperors and empires, a loose coalition of revolutionaries proclaimed a Western-style republic and called for an elected parliament. The transformation of China under the impact of expanding Western society entered a new phase, and the end was not in sight.

SUMMARY

In the nineteenth century the industrializing West entered the third and most dynamic phase of its centuries-old expansion into non-Western lands. In so doing, Western nations profitably subordinated those lands to their economic interests, sent forth millions of emigrants, and established political influence in Asia and vast political empires in Africa. The reasons for this culminating surge were many, but the economic thrust of robust industrial capitalism, an ever-growing lead in technology, and the competitive pressures of European nationalism were particularly important.

Western expansion had far-reaching consequences. For the first time in human history, the world became in many ways a single unit. Moreover, European expansion diffused the ideas and techniques of a highly developed civilization. Yet the West relied on force to conquer and rule, and

it treated non-Western peoples as racial inferiors. Thus non-Western elites, often armed with Western doctrines, gradually responded to the Western challenge. They launched a national, anti-imperialist struggle for dignity, genuine independence, and modernization. This struggle would emerge as a central drama of world history after the great European civil war of 1914 to 1918, which reduced the West's technological advantage and shattered its self-confidence and complacent moral superiority.

NOTES

1. Quoted in A. Waley, *The Opium War Through Chinese Eyes* (New York: Macmillan, 1958), p. 29.
2. Quoted in J. W. Hall, *Japan, from Prehistory to Modern Times* (New York: Delacorte Press, 1970), p. 250.
3. Quoted in R. Hallett, *Africa to 1875* (Ann Arbor: University of Michigan Press, 1970), p. 109.
4. Quoted in Earl of Cromer, *Modern Egypt* (London, 1911), p. 48.
5. Quoted in T. Blegen, *Norwegian Migration to America,* vol. 2 (Northfield, Minn.: Norwegian-American Historical Association, 1940), p. 468.
6. Quoted in I. Howe, *World of Our Fathers* (New York: Harcourt Brace Jovanovich, 1976), p. 25.
7. Quoted in C. A. Price, *The Great White Walls Are Built: Restrictive Immigration to North America and Australia, 1836–1888* (Canberra: Australian National University Press, 1974), p. 175.
8. Quoted in W. L. Langer, *European Alliances and Alignments, 1871–1890* (New York: Vintage Books, 1931), p. 290.
9. Quoted in J. Ellis, *The Social History of the Machine Gun* (New York: Pantheon Books, 1975), pp. 86, 101.
10. Quoted in G. H. Nadel and P. Curtis, eds., *Imperialism and Colonialism* (New York: Macmillan, 1964), p. 94.
11. Quoted in W. L. Langer, *The Diplomacy of Imperialism,* 2d ed. (New York: Alfred A. Knopf, 1951), pp. 86, 88.
12. Rudyard Kipling, *The Five Nations* (London, 1903), quoted by the permission of Mrs. George Bambridge, Methuen & Company, and Doubleday & Company, Inc.
13. E. H. Berman, "African Responses to Christian Mission Education," *African Studies Review* 17 (1974): 530.
14. Quoted in Langer, *Diplomacy of Imperialism,* p. 88.
15. Quoted in Ellis, pp. 99–100.
16. Quoted in K. M. Panikkar, *Asia and Western Dominance: A Survey of the Vasco da Gama Epoch of Asian History* (London: George Allen & Unwin, 1959), p. 116.
17. Quoted in Hall, p. 289.

SUGGESTED READING

General surveys of European expansion in a broad perspective include R. Betts, *Europe Overseas* (1968); A. Thornton, *Imperialism in the Twentieth Century* (1977); T. Smith, *The Patterns of Imperialism* (1981); and W. Woodruff, *Impact of Western Man* (1967), which has an extensive bibliography. D. K. Fieldhouse has also written two fine surveys, *Economics and Empire, 1830–1914* (1970) and *Colonialism, 1870–1945* (1981). G. Barraclough, *An Introduction to Contemporary History* (1964), argues powerfully that Western imperialism and the non-Western reaction to it have been crucial in world history since about 1890. J. A. Hobson's classic *Imperialism* (1902) is readily available, and the Marxist-Leninist case is effectively presented in V. G. Kieran, *Marxism and Imperialism* (1975). Two excellent anthologies on the problem of European expansion are the volume by Nadel and Curtis cited in the Notes and H. Wright, ed., *The "New Imperialism,"* rev. ed. (1975).

Britain's leading position in European imperialism is examined in a lively way by B. Porter, *The Lion's Share* (1976); J. Morris, *Pax Britannica* (1968); and D. Judd, *The Victorian Empire* (1970), a stunning pictorial history. B. Semmel has written widely on the intellectual foundations of English expansion, as in *The Rise of Free Trade Imperialism* (1970). J. Gallegher and R. Robinson, *Africa and the Victorians: The Climax of Imperialism* (1961), is an influential reassessment. H. Brunschwig, *French Colonialism, 1871–1914* (1966), and W. Baumgart, *Imperialism: The Idea and Reality of British and French Colonial Expansion* (1982), are well-balanced studies. A. Moorehead, *The White Nile* (1971), tells the fascinating story of the European exploration of the mysterious upper Nile. Volumes 5 and 6 of K. Latourette, *History of the Expansion of Christianity,* 7 vols. (1937–1945), examine the powerful impulse for missionary work in non-European areas. D. Headrick stresses Western technological superiority in *Tools of Empire* (1981).

Howe and Blegen, cited in the Notes, provide dramatic accounts of Jewish and Norwegian migration to the United States. Most other migrant groups have also found their historians: M. Walker, *Germany and the Emigration, 1816–1885* (1964), and W. Adams, *Ireland and Irish Emigration to the New World* (reissued 1967), are outstanding. Langer's volumes consider the diplomatic aspects of imperialism in exhaustive detail. Ellis's well-illustrated study of the machine gun is fascinating, as is Price on the restriction of Asian migration to Australia. All these works are cited in the Notes.

E. Wolf, *Europe and the People Without History* (1982), considers the impact of imperialism on non-Western peoples with skill and compassion. Two unusual and provocative studies on personal relations between European rulers and non-European subjects are D. Mannoni, *Prospero and Caliban: The Psychology of Colonialization* (1964), and F. Fanon, *Wretched of the Earth* (1965), a bitter attack on white racism by a black psychologist active in the Algerian revolution. Novels also bring the psychological and human dimensions of imperialism alive. H. Rider Haggard, *King Solomon's Mines,* portrays the powerful appeal of adventure in exotic lands, while Rudyard Kipling, the greatest writer of European expansion, is at his stirring best in *Kim* and *Soldiers Three.* Joseph Conrad unforgettably probes European motives in *Heart of Darkness,* while André Gide, *The Immoralist,* closely examines European moral corruption in North Africa.

Hall, cited in the Notes, is an excellent introduction to the history of Japan. Waley, also cited in the Notes, has written extensively and well on China. I. Hsü, *The Rise of Modern China,* 2d ed. (1975), and K. Latourette, *The Chinese: Their History and Culture,* rev. ed. (1964), are fine histories with many suggestions for further reading. E. Reischauer's topical survey, *Japan: The Story of a Nation* (1981), is recommended, as are T. Huber, *The Revolutionary Origins of Modern Japan* (1981), and Y. Fukuzawa, *Autobiography* (1966), the personal account of a leading intellectual who witnessed the emergence of modern Japan.

G. Perry, *The Middle East: Fourteen Islamic Centuries* (1983), concisely surveys nineteenth-century developments and provides up-to-date bibliographies. B. Lewis, *The Middle East and the West* (1963), is a penetrating analysis of the impact of Western ideas on Middle Eastern thought. Hallett, cited in the Notes, and R. July, *A History of the African People* (1970), contain excellent introductions to Africa in the age of imperialism. J. D. Fage, *A History of Africa* (1978), is also recommended. A classic study of Western expansion from an Indian viewpoint is Panikkar's volume mentioned in the Notes. S. Wolpert, *A New History of India,* 2d ed. (1982), incorporates recent scholarship in a wide-ranging study that is highly recommended.

27

The Great Break:
War and Revolution

In the summer of 1914 the nations of Europe went willingly to war. They believed they had no other choice. Moreover, both peoples and governments confidently expected a short war leading to a decisive victory. Such a war, they believed, would "clear the air," and European society would be able to go on as before.

These expectations were almost totally mistaken. The First World War was long, indecisive, and tremendously destructive. To the shell-shocked generation of survivors, it was known simply as the Great War: the war of unprecedented scope and intensity. From today's perspective it is clear that the First World War marked a great break in the course of Western historical development since the French and Industrial revolutions. A noted British political scientist has gone so far as to say that even in victorious and relatively fortunate Great Britain, the First World War was *the* great turning point in government and society, "as in everything else in modern British history. . . . There's a much greater difference between the Britain of 1914 and, say, 1920, than between the Britain of 1920 and today."[1]

This is a strong statement, but it contains a great amount of truth, for all of Europe as well as for Britain. It suggests three questions this chapter will try to answer.

- What caused the Great War?
- How and why did war and revolution have such enormous and destructive consequences?
- And how did the years of trauma and bloodshed form elements of today's world, many of which people now accept and even cherish?

THE FIRST WORLD WAR

The First World War was so long and destructive because it involved all the Great Powers and because it quickly degenerated into a senseless military stalemate. Like evenly matched boxers in a championship bout, the two sides tried to wear each other down. There was no referee to call a draw, only the blind hammering of a life-or-death struggle.

The Franco-Prussian War and the foundation of the German Empire opened a new era in international relations. France was decisively defeated in 1871 and forced to pay a large war indemnity and give up Alsace-Lorraine. In ten short years, from 1862 to 1871, Bismarck had made Prussia-Germany—traditionally the weakest of the Great Powers—the most powerful nation in Europe (see pages 797–801). Had Bismarck been a Napoleon I or a Hitler, for whom no gain was ever sufficient, continued expansion would no doubt sooner or later have raised a powerful coalition against the new German Empire. Yet he was not. As Bismarck never tired of repeating after 1871, Germany was a "satisfied" power. Within Europe, Germany had no territorial ambitions and only wanted peace.

But how was peace to be preserved? The most serious threat to peace came from the east, from Austria-Hungary and from Russia. Those two enormous multinational empires had many conflicting interests, particularly in the Balkans, where the Ottoman Empire—the "sick man of Europe"—was ebbing fast. There was a real threat that Germany might be dragged into a great war between the two rival empires. Bismarck's solution was a system of alliances (Figure 27.1) to restrain both Russia and Austria-Hungary, to prevent conflict between them, and to isolate a hostile France.

A first step was the creation in 1873 of the conservative Three Emperors' League, which linked the monarchs of Austria-Hungary, Germany, and Russia in an alliance against radical movements. In 1877 and 1878, when Russia's victories over the Ottoman Empire threatened the balance of Austrian and Russian interests in the Balkans and the balance of British and Russian interests in the Middle East, Bismarck played the role of sincere peacemaker. At the Congress of Berlin in 1878, he saw that Austria obtained the right to "occupy and administer" the Ottoman provinces of Bosnia and Herzegovina to counterbalance Russian gains, while independent Balkan states were also carved from the disintegrating Ottoman Empire.

Bismarck's balancing efforts at the Congress of Berlin infuriated Russian nationalists, and this led Bismarck to conclude a defensive military alliance with Austria against Russia in 1879. Motivated by tensions with France, Italy joined Germany and

The Congress of Berlin, 1878   With the Austrian representative on his right and with other participants looking on, Bismarck the mediator symbolically seals the hard-won agreement by shaking hands with the chief Russian negotiator. The Great Powers often relied on such special conferences to settle their international disputes. *(Source: The Bettmann Archive)*

Austria in 1882, thereby forming what became known as the Triple Alliance.

Bismarck continued to work for peace in eastern Europe, seeking to neutralize tensions between Austria-Hungary and Russia. In 1881 he capitalized on their mutual fears and cajoled them both into a secret alliance with Germany. This Alliance of the Three Emperors lasted until 1887. It established the principle of cooperation among all three powers in any further division of the Ottoman Empire, while each state pledged friendly neutrality in case one of the three found itself at war with a fourth power (except the Ottoman Empire).

Bismarck also maintained good relations with Britain and Italy, while cooperating with France in Africa but keeping France isolated in Europe. In 1887 Russia declined to renew the Alliance of the Three Emperors because of new tensions in the Balkans. Bismarck craftily substituted a Russian-German Reinsurance Treaty, by which both states promised neutrality if the other were attacked.

Bismarck's accomplishments in foreign policy after 1871 were great. For almost a generation, he maintained German leadership in international affairs, and he worked successfully for peace by managing conflicts and by restraining Austria-Hungary and Russia with defensive alliances.

The Rival Blocs

In 1890 the young, impetuous emperor William II dismissed Bismarck, in part because of the chancellor's friendly policy toward Russia since the 1870s. William then adamantly refused to renew the Russian-German Reinsurance Treaty, in spite of Russian willingness to do so. This fateful departure in foreign affairs prompted long-isolated republican

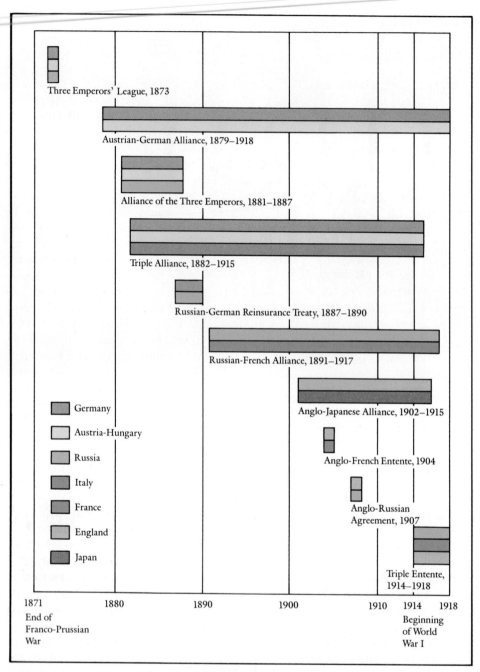

FIGURE 27.1 The Alliance System After 1871   Bismarck's subtle diplomacy maintained reasonably good relations among the eastern monarchies—Germany, Russia, and Austria-Hungary—and kept France isolated. The situation changed dramatically in 1891, when the Russian-French Alliance divided the Great Powers into two fairly equal military blocs.

France to court absolutist Russia, offering loans, arms, and friendship. In both countries there were enthusiastic public demonstrations, and in St. Petersburg harbor the autocratic Alexander III stood bareheaded on a French battleship while a band played the *Marseillaise,* the hymn of the Revolution. A preliminary agreement between the two countries was reached in 1891, and in early 1894 France and Russia became military allies. This alliance (see Figure 27.1) was to remain in effect as long as the Triple Alliance of Austria, Germany, and Italy: continental Europe was dangerously divided into two rival blocs.

The policy of Great Britain became increasingly crucial. Long content with "splendid isolation" and no permanent alliances, Britain after 1891 was the only uncommitted Great Power. Could Britain afford to remain isolated, or would it feel compelled to take sides? Alliance with France or Russia certainly seemed highly unlikely. With its vast and rapidly expanding empire, Britain was often in serious conflict with these countries around the world in the heyday of imperialism.

Britain also squabbled with Germany, for Emperor William II was a master of tactless public statements, and Britain found Germany's pursuit of greater world power after about 1897 vaguely disquieting. Nevertheless, many Germans and some Britons believed that their leaders would eventually formalize the "natural alliance" they felt already united the advanced, racially related Germanic and Anglo-Saxon peoples. Alas, such an understanding never materialized. Instead, the generally good relations that had prevailed between Prussia and Great Britain ever since the mid-eighteenth century, and certainly under Bismarck, gave way to a bitter Anglo-German rivalry.

There were several reasons for this tragic development. The hard-fought Boer War (1899–1902) between the British and the tiny Dutch republics of South Africa had a major impact on British policy. British political leaders saw that Britain was overextended around the world. The Boer War also brought into the open widespread anti-British feeling, as editorial writers in many nations denounced the latest manifestation of British imperialism. There was even talk of Germany, Austria, France, and Russia forming a grand alliance against the bloated but insatiable British Empire. Therefore, British leaders prudently set about shoring up their exposed position with alliance and agreements.

Britain improved its often-strained relations with the United States and in 1902 concluded a formal alliance with Japan (see Figure 27.1). Britain then responded favorably to the advances of France's skillful foreign minister, Théophile Delcassé, who wanted better relations with Britain and was willing to accept British rule in Egypt in return for British support of French plans to dominate Morocco. The resulting Anglo-French Entente of 1904 settled all outstanding colonial disputes between Britain and France.

Frustrated by Britain's turn toward France in 1904, Germany decided to test the strength of the entente and drive Britain and France apart. First Germany threatened and bullied France into dismissing Delcassé. However, rather than accept the typical territorial payoff of imperial competition—a slice of French jungle in Africa or a port in Morocco—in return for French primacy in Morocco, the Germans foolishly rattled their swords in 1905. They insisted on an international conference on the whole Moroccan question without presenting precise or reasonable demands. Germany's crude bullying forced France and Britain closer together, and Germany left the Algeciras Conference of 1906 empty-handed and isolated (except for Austria-Hungary).

The result of the Moroccan crisis and the Algeciras Conference was something of a diplomatic revolution. Britain, France, Russia, and even the United States began to see Germany as a potential threat, a would-be intimidator that might seek to dominate all Europe. At the same time, German leaders began to see sinister plots to "encircle" Germany and block its development as a world power. In 1907 Russia, battered by the disastrous war with Japan and the revolution of 1905, agreed to settle its quarrels with Great Britain in Persia and central Asia with a special Anglo-Russian Agreement (see Figure 27.1). As a result of that agreement, Germany's blustering paranoia increased and so did Britain's thinly disguised hostility.

Germany's decision to add a large, enormously expensive fleet of big-gun battleships to its already expanding navy also heightened tensions after 1907. German nationalists, led by the all-too-persuasive Admiral Tirpitz, saw a large navy as the legitimate mark of a great world power. But British leaders like Lloyd George saw it as a detestable military challenge, which forced them to spend the "People's Budget" on battleships rather than social welfare. As Germany's rapid industrial growth allowed it to overcome Britain's early lead, economic rivalry also contributed to distrust and hostility between the two nations. Unscrupulous journalists and special-interest groups in both countries portrayed healthy competition in foreign trade and investment as a form of economic warfare.

Many educated shapers of public opinion and ordinary people in Britain and Germany were increasingly locked in a fateful "love-hate" relationship between the two countries. Proud nationalists in both countries simultaneously admired and feared the power and accomplishments of their nearly equal rival. In 1909 the mass-circulation London *Daily Mail* hysterically informed its readers in a series of reports that "Germany is deliberately preparing to destroy the British Empire."[2] By then, Britain was psychologically, if not officially, in the Franco-Russian camp. The leading nations of Europe were divided into two hostile blocs, both ill prepared to deal with upheaval on Europe's southeastern frontier.

The Outbreak of War

In the early years of this century, war in the Balkans was as inevitable as anything can be in human history. The reason was simple: nationalism was destroying the Ottoman Empire and threatening to break up the Austro-Hungarian Empire. The only questions were what kinds of wars would occur and where they would lead.

Greece had long before led the struggle for national liberation, winning its independence in 1832. In 1875 widespread nationalist rebellion in the Ottoman Empire had resulted in Turkish repression, Russian intervention, and Great Power tensions. Bismarck had helped resolve this crisis at the 1878 Congress of Berlin, which worked out the

German Warships Under Full Steam   As these impressive ships engaged in battle exercises in 1907 suggest, Germany did succeed in building a large modern navy. But Britain was equally determined to maintain its naval superiority, and the spiraling arms race helped poison relations between the two countries. *(Source: Bibliothéque des Arts Décoratifs/Jean-Loup Charmet)*

MAP 27.1 The Balkans After the Congress of Berlin, 1878 The Ottoman Empire suffered large territorial losses but remained a power in the Balkans.

MAP 27.2 The Balkans in 1914 Ethnic boundaries did not follow political boundaries, and Serbian national aspirations threatened Austria-Hungary.

partial division of Turkish possessions in Europe. Austria-Hungary obtained the right to "occupy and administer" Bosnia and Herzegovina. Serbia and Rumania won independence, and a part of Bulgaria won local autonomy. The Ottoman Empire retained important Balkan holdings, for Austria-Hungary and Russia each feared the other's domination of totally independent states in the area (Map 27.1).

After 1878 the siren call of imperialism lured European energies, particularly Russian energies, away from the Balkans. This diversion helped preserve the fragile balance of interests in southeastern Europe. By 1903, however, Balkan nationalism was on the rise once again. Serbia led the way, becoming openly hostile toward both Austria-Hungary and the Ottoman Empire. The Serbs, a Slavic

people, looked to Slavic Russia for support of their national aspirations. To block Serbian expansion and to take advantage of Russia's weakness after the revolution of 1905, Austria in 1908 formally annexed Bosnia and Herzegovina with their predominately Serbian populations. The kingdom of Serbia erupted in rage but could do nothing without Russian support.

Then in 1912, in the First Balkan War, Serbia turned southward. With Greece and Bulgaria it took Macedonia from the Ottoman Empire and then quarreled with its ally Bulgaria over the spoils of victory—a dispute that led in 1913 to the Second Balkan War. Austria intervened in 1913 and forced Serbia to give up Albania. After centuries, nationalism had finally destroyed the Ottoman Empire in Europe (Map 27.2). This sudden but long-awaited event elated the Balkan nationalists and dismayed the leaders of multinational Austria-Hungary. The former hoped and the latter feared that Austria might be next to be broken apart.

Within this tense context, Archduke Francis Ferdinand, heir to the Austrian and Hungarian thrones, and his wife Sophie were assassinated by Bosnian revolutionaries on June 28, 1914, during a state visit to the Bosnian capital of Sarajevo. The assassins were closely connected to the ultranationalist Serbian society The Black Hand. This revolutionary group was secretly supported by members of the Serbian government and was dedicated to uniting all Serbians in a single state. Although the leaders of Austria-Hungary did not and could not know all the details of Serbia's involvement in the assassination plot, they concluded after some hesitation that Serbia had to be severely punished once and for all. After a month of maneuvering, Austria-Hungary presented Serbia with an unconditional ultimatum, on July 23.

The Serbian government had just forty-eight hours in which to agree to cease all subversion in Austria and all anti-Austrian propaganda in Serbia. Moreover, a thorough investigation of all aspects of the assassination at Sarajevo was to be undertaken in Serbia by a joint commission of Serbian and Austrian officials. These demands amounted to control of the Serbian state. When Serbia replied moderately but evasively, Austria began to mobilize and then declared war on Serbia on July 28. Thus a desperate multinational Austria-Hungary deliberately chose war in a last-ditch attempt to stem the rising tide of hostile nationalism. The "Third Balkan War" had begun.

Of prime importance in Austria-Hungary's fateful decision was Germany's unconditional support. Emperor William II and his chancellor Theobald von Bethmann-Hollweg gave Austria-Hungary a "blank check" and urged aggressive measures in early July, even though they realized that war between Austria and Russia was the most probable result. They knew Russian pan-Slavs saw Russia not only as the protector, but also as the eventual liberator, of southern Slavs. As one pan-Slav had said much earlier, "Austria can hold her part of the Slavonian mass as long as Turkey holds hers and vice versa."[3] At the very least a resurgent Russia could not stand by, as in the Bosnian crisis, and simply watch the Serbs be crushed. Yet Bethmann-Hollweg apparently hoped that while Russia (and therefore France) would go to war, Great Britain would remain neutral, unwilling to fight for "Russian aggression" in the distant Balkans. After all, Britain had reached only "friendly understandings" with France and Russia on colonial questions and had no alliance with either power.

In fact, the diplomatic situation was already out of control. Military plans and timetables began to dictate policy. Russia, a vast country, would require much longer to mobilize its armies than Germany and Austria-Hungary. On July 28, as Austrian armies bombarded Belgrade, Tsar Nicholas II ordered a partial mobilization against Austria-Hungary. Almost immediately he found that this was impossible. All the complicated mobilization plans of the Russian general staff had assumed a war with both Austria and Germany: Russia could not mobilize against one without mobilizing against the other. On July 29, therefore, Russia ordered full mobilization and in effect declared general war. For, as the French general Boisdeffre had said to the agreeing Russian tsar when the Franco-Russian military convention was being negotiated in 1892, "mobilization is a declaration of war."[4]

The same tragic subordination of political considerations to military strategy descended on Germany. The German general staff had also thought only in terms of a two-front war. Their plan for war—the Schlieffen plan, the work of Count Alfred von Schlieffen, chief of the German general staff from 1891 to 1906 and a professional military man—called for knocking out France first with a lightning attack through neutral Belgium before turning on Russia.

Thus, on August 2, 1914, General Helmuth von Moltke, "acting under a dictate of self-preservation," demanded that Belgium permit German armies to pass through its territory. Belgium, whose neutrality had been solemnly guaranteed in 1839 by all the great states including Prussia, refused. Germany attacked. Thus Germany's terrible, politically disastrous response to a war in the Balkans was an all-out invasion of France by way of the plains of neutral Belgium on August 3. In the face of this act of aggression, Great Britain joined France and declared war on Germany the following day. The First World War had begun.

Reflections on the Origins of the War

Although few events in history have aroused such interest and controversy as the coming of the First

World War, the question of immediate causes and responsibilities can be answered with considerable certainty. Austria-Hungary deliberately started the "Third Balkan War." A war for the right to survive was Austria-Hungary's desperate, although understandable, response to the aggressive, yet understandable, revolutionary drive of Serbian nationalists to unify their people in a single state. In spite of Russian intervention in the quarrel, it is clear from the beginning of the crisis that Germany not only pushed and goaded Austria-Hungary but was also responsible for turning a little war into the Great War by means of its sledgehammer attack on Belgium and France.

After Bismarck's resignation in 1890, German leaders lost control of the international system. They felt increasingly that Germany's status as a world power was declining while that of Britain, France, Russia, and the United States was growing. Indeed, the powers of what officially became in August 1914 the Triple Entente—Great Britain, France, and Russia—were checking Germany's vague but real aspirations, as well as working to strangle Austria-Hungary, Germany's only real ally. Germany's aggression in 1914 reflected the failure of all European leaders, not just those in Germany, to incorporate Bismarck's mighty empire permanently and peacefully into the international system.

There were other underlying causes. The new overseas expansion—imperialism—did not play a direct role, since the European powers always settled their colonial conflicts peacefully. Yet the easy imperialist victories did contribute to a general European overconfidence and reinforced national rivalries. In this respect imperialism was thought to be influential.

The triumph of nationalism was a crucial underlying precondition of the Great War. Nationalism was at the heart of the Balkan wars, in the form of Serbian aspirations and the grandiose pan-German versus pan-Slavic racism of some fanatics. Nationalism drove the spiraling arms race. More generally, as shown in Chapter 25, the aristocracy and middle classes arrived at nationalistic compromises, while ordinary people looked toward increasingly responsive states for psychological and material well-being.

Broad popular commitment to "my country right or wrong" weakened groups that thought in terms of international communities and consequences. Thus the big international bankers, who

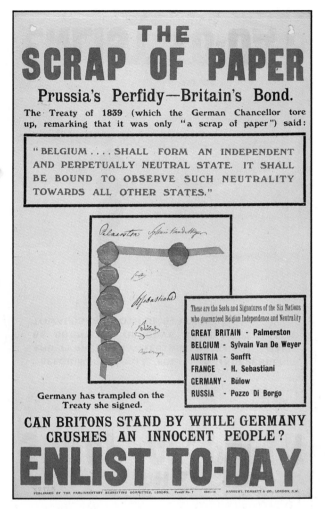

This British Poster shows the signature page of the 1839 treaty guaranteeing the neutrality of Belgium. When German armies invaded Belgium in 1914, Chancellor Bethmann-Hollweg cynically dismissed the treaty as a "scrap of paper"—a perfect line for anti-German propaganda. *(Source: By courtesy of the Trustees of the Imperial War Museum)*

were frightened by the prospect of war in July 1914, and the extreme-left socialists, who believed that the enemy was at home and not abroad, were equally out of step with national feeling.

Finally, the wealthy governing classes underestimated the risk of war in 1914. They had forgotten that great wars and great social revolutions very often go together in history. Metternich's alliance of conservative forces in support of international peace and the domestic status quo had become only a distant memory.

Preparing the Attack   The great offenses of the First World War required the mobilization of men and material on an unprecedented scale. This photo shows American troops moving up. *(Source: U.S. Army Signal Corps)*

The First Battle of the Marne

When the Germans invaded Belgium in August 1914, they and everyone else believed that the war would be short, for urban society rested on the food and raw materials of the world economy: "The boys will be home by Christmas." The Belgian army heroically defended its homeland, however, and fell back in good order to join a rapidly landed British army corps near the Franco-Belgian border. This action complicated the original Schlieffen plan of concentrating German armies on the right wing and boldly capturing Paris in a vast encircling movement. Moreover, the German left wing in Lorraine failed to retreat, thwarting the plan to suck French armies into Germany and then annihilate them. Instead, by the end of August, dead-tired German soldiers were advancing along an enormous front in the scorching summer heat. The neatly designed prewar plan to surround Paris from the north and west had been thrown into confusion.

French armies totaling 1 million, reinforced by more than 100,000 British troops, had retreated in orderly fashion before Germany's 1.5 million men in the field. Under the leadership of the steel-nerved General Joseph Joffre, the French attacked a gap in the German line at the Battle of the Marne on September 6. For three days, France threw everything into the attack. At one point, the French government desperately requisitioned all the taxis of Paris to rush reserves to the troops at the front. Finally, the Germans fell back. Paris and France had been miraculously saved.

Stalemate and Slaughter

The attempts of French and British armies to turn the German retreat into a rout were unsuccessful, and so were moves by both sides to outflank each other in northern France. As a result, both sides began to dig trenches to protect themselves from machine gun fire. By November 1914 an unbroken line of trenches extended from the Belgian ports through northern France past the fortress of Verdun and on to the Swiss frontier.

In the face of this unexpected stalemate, slaughter on the western front began in earnest. The defenders on both sides dug in behind rows of trenches, mines, and barbed wire. For days and even weeks, ceaseless shelling by heavy artillery supposedly "softened up" the enemy in a given area (and also signaled the coming attack). Then young draftees and their junior officers went "over the top" of the trenches in frontal attacks on the enemy's line.

The cost in lives was staggering, the gains in territory minuscule. The massive French and British offensives during 1915 never gained more than three miles of blood-soaked earth from the enemy. In the Battle of the Somme in the summer of 1916, the British and French gained an insignificant 125 square miles at the cost of 600,000 dead or wounded, while the Germans lost half a million men. That same year, the unsuccessful German campaign against Verdun cost 700,000 lives on both sides. The British poet Siegfried Sassoon (1886–1967) wrote of the Somme offensive: "I am staring at a sunlit picture of Hell."

Terrible 1917 saw General Robert Nivelle's French army almost destroyed in a grand spring attack at Champagne, while at Passchendaele in the fall, the British traded 400,000 casualties for 50

The Fruits of War   The extent of carnage, the emotional damage, and the physical destruction were equally unprecedented. Once great cathedrals standing in ruin symbolized the disaster. *(Source: UPI/Bettmann Newsphotos)*

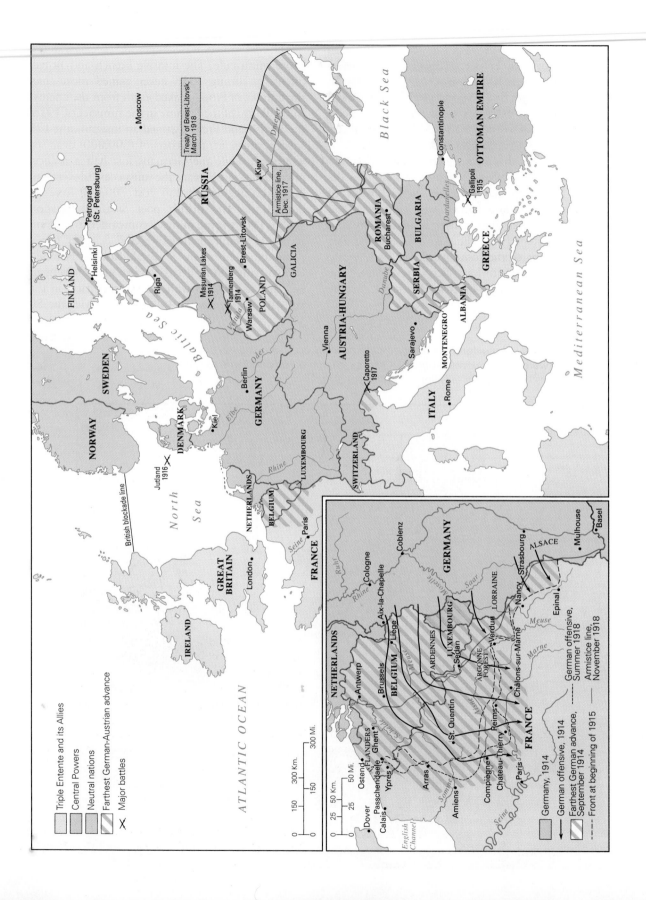

Main Map

Triple Entente and its Allies
Central Powers
Neutral nations
Farthest German-Austrian advance
✕ Major battles

ATLANTIC OCEAN

IRELAND

GREAT BRITAIN
London

North Sea

British blockade line

NORWAY

SWEDEN

DENMARK
Kiel

Jutland 1916 ✕✕

Baltic Sea

FINLAND
Helsinki

Riga

Petrograd (St. Petersburg)

RUSSIA

Moscow

Treaty of Brest-Litovsk, March 1918

Kiev

Armistice line, Dec. 1917

Masurian Lakes 1914 ✕
Tannenberg 1914 ✕

Warsaw
Vistula
POLAND

Brest-Litovsk

Dnieper

GALICIA

Black Sea

OTTOMAN EMPIRE
Constantinople

Gallipoli 1915 ✕

Dardanelles

GREECE

ALBANIA
MONTENEGRO

BULGARIA

ROMANIA
Bucharest

SERBIA
Sarajevo

Danube

AUSTRIA-HUNGARY
Vienna

Caporetto 1917 ✕

ITALY
Rome

Mediterranean Sea

NETHERLANDS
BELGIUM
LUXEMBOURG

GERMANY
Berlin
Elbe
Oder
Rhine

SWITZERLAND

FRANCE
Paris
Seine

0   150   300 Km.
0   150   300 Mi.

Inset Map

Germany, 1914
German offensive, 1914 →
Farthest German advance, September 1914
Front at beginning of 1915
German offensive, Summer 1918
Armistice line, November 1918

0   25   50 Km.
0   25   50 Mi.

English Channel

Dover
Calais
Ostend
Passchendaele
Ypres
FLANDERS

NETHERLANDS
Antwerp
Ghent
Brussels
BELGIUM

Aix-la-Chapelle
Liège

Cologne
Coblenz

GERMANY

Rhine
Ruhr
Moselle
Saar

Arras
Amiens
Somme
St. Quentin

ARDENNES
Sedan
LUXEMBOURG
Verdun
ARGONNE FOREST
Meuse

LORRAINE
Nancy
Strasbourg
ALSACE
Mulhouse
Basel

Compiègne
Château-Thierry
Reims
Châlons-sur-Marne
Marne
Epinal

Paris
Seine

FRANCE

square miles of Belgian Flanders. The hero of Erich Remarque's great novel *All Quiet on the Western Front* (1929) describes one such attack:

We see men living with their skulls blown open; we see soldiers run with their two feet cut off. . . . Still the little piece of convulsed earth in which we lie is held. We have yielded no more than a few hundred yards of it as a prize to the enemy. But on every yard there lies a dead man.

Such was war on the western front.

The war of the trenches shattered an entire generation of young men. Millions who could have provided political creativity and leadership after the war were forever missing. Moreover, those who lived through the holocaust were maimed, shell-shocked, embittered, and profoundly disillusioned. The young soldiers went to war believing in the world of their leaders and elders, the pre-1914 world of order, progress, and patriotism. Then, in Remarque's words, the "first bombardment showed us our mistake, and under it the world as they had taught it to us broke in pieces." For many, the sacrifice and comradeship of the battlefield became life's crucial experience, an experience that "soft" civilians could never understand. A chasm opened up between veterans and civilians, making the difficult postwar reconstruction all the more difficult.

The Widening War

On the eastern front, slaughter did not degenerate into suicidal trench warfare. With the outbreak of the war, the "Russian steamroller" immediately moved into eastern Germany. Very badly damaged by the Germans under Generals Paul von Hindenburg and Erich Ludendorff at the battles of Tannenberg and the Masurian Lakes in August and September 1914, Russia never threatened Germany again. On the Austrian front, enormous armies seesawed back and forth, suffering enormous losses. Austro-Hungarian armies were repulsed twice by little Serbia in bitter fighting. But with the help of German forces, they reversed the Russian advances

MAP 27.3 The First World War in Europe The trench war on the western front was concentrated in Belgium and northern France, while the war in the east encompassed an enormous territory.

of 1914 and forced the Russians to retreat deep into their own territory in the eastern campaign of 1915. A staggering 2.5 million Russians were killed, wounded, or taken prisoner that year.

These changing tides of victory and defeat brought neutral countries into the war (Map 27.3). Italy, a member of the Triple Alliance since 1882, had declared its neutrality in 1914 on the grounds that Austria had launched a war of aggression. Then, in May 1915, Italy joined the Triple Entente of Great Britain, France, and Russia in return for promises of Austrian territory. Bulgaria allied with Austria and Germany, now known as the Central Powers, in September 1915 in order to settle old scores with Serbia.

The entry of Italy and Bulgaria in 1915 was part of a general widening of the war. The Balkans, with the exception of Greece, came to be occupied by the Central Powers, and British forces were badly defeated in 1915 trying to take the Dardanelles from Turkey, Germany's ally. More successful was the entente's attempt to incite Arab nationalists against their Turkish overlords. An enigmatic British colonel, soon known to millions as Lawrence of Arabia, aroused the Arab princes to revolt in early 1917. In 1918 British armies from Egypt smashed the Ottoman Empire once and for all. In their Middle East campaign, the British drew on forces from Australia, New Zealand, and India. Contrary to German hopes, the colonial subjects of the British (and French) did not revolt but loyally supported their foreign masters. The European war extended around the globe as Great Britain, France, and Japan seized Germany's colonies.

A crucial development in the expanding conflict came in April 1917, when the United States declared war on Germany. American intervention grew out of the war at sea, sympathy for the Triple Entente, and the increasing desperation of total war. At the beginning of the war, Britain and France had established a total naval blockade to strangle the Central Powers and prevent deliveries of food and raw materials from overseas. No neutral ship was permitted to sail to Germany with any cargo. The blockade annoyed Americans, but effective propaganda over German atrocities in occupied Belgium, as well as lush profits from selling war supplies to Britain and France, blunted American indignation.

Moreover, in early 1915 Germany launched a counter-blockade using the murderously effective submarine, a new weapon that violated traditional niceties of fair warning under international law. In May 1915, after sinking about ninety ships in the British war zone, a German submarine sank the British passenger liner *Lusitania,* which was also carrying arms and munitions. More than a thousand lives, among them 139 Americans, were lost. President Woodrow Wilson protested vigorously. Germany was forced to relax its submarine warfare for almost two years; the alternative was almost certain war with the United States.

Early in 1917, the German military command—confident that improved submarines could starve their island enemy, Britain, into submission before the United States could come to its rescue—resumed unrestricted submarine warfare. Like the invasion of Belgium, this was a reckless gamble. British shipping losses reached staggering proportions, though by late 1917 naval strategists came up with the inevitable effective response: the convoy system for safe transatlantic shipping. In the meantime, the embattled President Wilson had told a sympathetic Congress and people that the "German submarine warfare against commerce is a warfare against mankind." Thus the last uncommitted great nation, as fresh and enthusiastic as Europe had been in 1914, entered the world war in April 1917, almost three years after it began. Eventually the United States was to tip the balance in favor of the Triple Entente and its allies.

THE HOME FRONT

Before looking at the last year of the Great War, let us turn our attention to the people on the home front. The people behind the lines were tremendously involved in the titanic struggle. War's impact on them was no less massive than on the men crouched in the trenches.

Mobilizing for Total War

In August 1914 most people had greeted the outbreak of hostilities enthusiastically. In every country, the masses believed that their nation was in the right and defending itself from aggression. With the exception of a few extreme left-wingers, even socialists supported the war. Tough standby plans to imprison socialist leaders and break general

strikes protesting the war proved quite unnecessary in 1914. In Germany, for example, the trade unions voted not to strike, and socialists in the parliament voted money for war credits in order to counter the threat of Russian despotism. A German socialist volunteered for the front, explaining to fellow members of the Reichstag that "to shed one's blood for the fatherland is not difficult: it is enveloped in romantic heroism."[5] Everywhere the support of the masses and working class contributed to national unity and an energetic war effort.

By mid-October generals and politicians began to realize that more than patriotism would be needed to win the war, whose end was not in sight. Each country experienced a relentless, desperate demand for men and weapons. In France, for example, the generals found themselves needing 100,000 heavy artillery shells a day, as opposed to the 12,000 they had anticipated using. This enormous quantity had to come from a French steel industry that had lost three-fourths of its iron resources in the first days of the war, when Germany seized the mines of French Lorraine. Each belligerent quickly faced countless shortages, for prewar Europe had depended on foreign trade and a great international division of labor. In each country economic life and organization had to change and change fast to keep the war machine from sputtering to a stop. And change they did.

In each country a government of national unity began to plan and control economic and social life in order to wage "total war." Free-market capitalism was abandoned, at least "for the duration." Instead, government planning boards established priorities and decided what was to be produced and consumed. Rationing, price and wage controls, and even restrictions on workers' freedom of movement were imposed by government. Only through such regimentation could a country make the greatest possible military effort. Thus, though there were national variations, the great nations all moved toward planned economies commanded by the established political leadership.

This revolutionary development would burn deeply into the twentieth-century consciousness. The planned economy of total war released the tremendous energies first harnessed by the French under Robespierre during the French Revolution. Total war, however, was based on tremendously productive industrial economies not confined to a single nation. The result was an effective—and therefore destructive—war effort on all sides.

Waging Total War   A British war plant strains to meet the insatiable demand for trench-smashing heavy artillery shells. Quite typically, many of these defense workers are women. *(Source: By courtesy of the Trustees of the Imperial War Museum)*

Moreover, the economy of total war blurred the old distinction between soldiers on the battlefield and civilians at home. As President Wilson told Americans shortly after the United States entered the war, there were no armies in the struggle in the traditional sense. Rather, "there are entire nations armed. Thus the men [and women] who remain to till the soil and man the factories are not less a part of the army than the men beneath the battle flags."[6] The war was a war of whole peoples and entire populations, and the loser would be the society that cracked first.

Finally, however awful the war was, the ability of governments to manage and control highly complicated economies strengthened the cause of socialism. With the First World War, socialism became for the first time a realistic economic blueprint rather than a utopian program.

Germany illustrates the general trend. It also went furthest in developing a planned economy to wage total war. As soon as war began, Walter Rathenau, the talented, foresighted Jewish industrialist in charge of Germany's largest electrical com-

pany, convinced the government to set up a War Raw Materials Board to ration and distribute raw materials. Under Rathenau's direction, every useful material from foreign oil to barnyard manure was inventoried and rationed. Moreover, the board launched successful attempts to produce substitutes, such as synthetic rubber and synthetic nitrates. Without the spectacular double achievement of discovering a way to "fix" nitrogen present in the air and then producing synthetic nitrates in enormous quantity, the blockaded German war machine would have stalled in a matter of months.

Food was also rationed in accordance with physical need. Men and women doing hard manual work were given extra rations. During the last two years of the war, only children and expectant mothers received milk rations. Sometimes mistakes were made that would have been funny if they had not been tragic. In early 1915 German authorities calculated that greedy pigs were eating food that hungry people needed, and they ordered a "hog massacre" only to find that there were too few pigs left to eat an abundant potato crop. Germany also failed to tax the war profits of private firms heavily enough. This contributed to massive deficit financing, inflation, the growth of a black market, and the eventual re-emergence of class conflict.

Following the terrible battles of Verdun and the Somme in 1916, the military leaders Hindenburg and Ludendorff became the real rulers of Germany, and they decreed the ultimate mobilization for total war. Germany, said Hindenburg, could win only "if all the treasures of our soil that agriculture and industry can produce are used exclusively for the conduct of War. . . . All other considerations must come second."[7] This goal, they believed, required that every German man, woman, and child be drafted into the service of the war. Thus, in December 1916, the military leaders rammed through the parliament the Auxiliary Service Law, which required all males between seventeen and sixty to work only at jobs considered critical to the war effort.

Although women and children were not specifically mentioned, this forced-labor law was also aimed at them. Many women already worked in war factories, mines, and steel mills, where they labored like men at the heaviest and most dangerous jobs. With the passage of the Auxiliary Service Law, many more women followed. Children were organized by their teachers into garbage brigades to collect every scrap of useful materials: grease strained from dishwater, coffee grounds, waste paper, tin cans, metal door knockers, bottles, rags, hair, bones, and so forth, as well as acorns, chestnuts, pine cones, and rotting leaves. Potatoes gave way to turnips, and people averaged little more than a thousand calories a day. Thus in Germany total war led to the establishment of history's first "totalitarian" society, and war production increased while some people literally starved to death.

Great Britain mobilized for total war less rapidly and less completely than Germany, for it could import materials from its empire and from the United States. By 1915, however, a serious shortage of shells led to the establishment of a Ministry of Munitions under David Lloyd George. The ministry organized private industry to produce for the war, controlled profits, allocated labor, fixed wage rates, and settled labor disputes. By December 1916, when Lloyd George became prime minister, the British economy was largely planned and regulated. More than two hundred factories and 90 percent of all imports were bought and allocated directly by the state. Subsequently, even food was strictly rationed, while war production continued to soar. Great Britain had followed successfully in Germany's footsteps.

The Social Impact

The social impact of total war was no less profound than the economic, though again there were important national variations. The millions of men at the front and the insatiable needs of the military created a tremendous demand for workers. Jobs were available for everyone. This situation had seldom if ever been seen before 1914, when unemployment and poverty had been facts of urban life. The exceptional demand for labor brought about momentous changes.

One such change was greater power and prestige for labor unions. Having proved their loyalty in August 1914, labor unions became an indispensable partner of government and private industry in the planned war economy. Unions cooperated with war governments on work rules, wages, and production schedules in return for real participation in important decisions. This entry of labor leaders and unions into policy-making councils paralleled the entry of socialist leaders into the war governments.

The role of women changed dramatically. In every country, large numbers of women left home work and domestic service to work in industry, transportation, and offices. By 1917 women formed fully 43 percent of the labor force in Russia. The number of women driving buses and streetcars increased tenfold in Great Britain. Moreover, women became highly visible—not only as munitions workers but as bank tellers, mail carriers, even policewomen.

At first, the male-dominated unions were hostile to women moving into new occupations, believing that their presence would lower wages and change work rules. But government pressure and the principle of equal pay for equal work (at least until the end of the war) overcame these objections. Women also served as nurses and doctors at the front. In general, the war greatly expanded the range of women's activities and changed attitudes toward women. As a direct result of their many-sided war effort, Britain, Germany, and Austria granted women the right to vote immediately after the war. Women also showed a growing spirit of independence during the war, as they started to bob their hair, shorten their skirts, and smoke in public.

War also promoted greater social equality, blurring class distinctions and lessening the gap between rich and poor. This blurring was most apparent in Great Britain, where wartime hardship was never extreme. In fact, the bottom third of the population generally lived *better* than ever before, for the poorest gained most from the severe shortage of labor. The English writer Robert Roberts recalled how his parents' tiny grocery store in the slums of Manchester thrived as never before during the war, when people who had scrimped to buy bread and soup bones were able to afford fancy cakes and thick steaks. In 1924 a British government study revealed that the distribution of income had indeed shifted in favor of the poorest; only half as many families lived in severe poverty as in 1911, even though total production of goods had not increased. In continental countries greater equality was reflected in full employment, rationing according to physical needs, and a sharing of hardships. There, too, society became more uniform and more egalitarian, in spite of some war profiteering.

Finally, death itself had no respect for traditional social distinctions. It savagely decimated the young aristocratic officers who led the charge, and it fell heavily on the mass of drafted peasants and unskilled workers who followed. Yet death often spared the aristocrats of labor, the skilled workers and foremen. Their lives were too valuable to squander at the front, for they were needed to train

Wartime Propaganda was skillful and effective. The poster on the left spurred men to volunteer for military service before the draft was introduced in Britain in 1916. The poster on the right appeals to patriotism and the love of family as it urges the French to buy another batch of war bonds. *(Source: By courtesy of the Trustees of the Imperial War Museum)*

the newly recruited women and older unskilled men laboring valiantly in war plants at home.

Growing Political Tensions

During the first two years of war, most soldiers and civilians supported their governments. Even in Austria-Hungary—the most vulnerable of the belligerents, with its competing nationalities—loyalty to the state and monarchy remained astonishingly strong through 1916. Belief in a just cause, patriotic nationalism, the planned economy, and a sharing of burdens united peoples behind their various national leaders. Furthermore, each government did its best to control public opinion to bolster morale. Newspapers, letters, and public addresses were rigorously censored. Good news was overstated; bad news was repressed or distorted.

Each government used both crude and subtle propaganda to maintain popular support. German propaganda hysterically pictured black soldiers from France's African empire raping German women, while German atrocities in Belgium and elsewhere were ceaselessly recounted and exaggerated by the French and British. Patriotic posters and slogans, slanted news and biased editorials inflamed national hatreds and helped sustain superhuman efforts.

By the spring of 1916, however, people were beginning to crack under the strain of total war. In April 1916 Irish nationalists in Dublin tried to take advantage of this situation and rose up against British rule in their great Easter Rebellion. A week of bitter fighting passed before the rebels were crushed and their leaders executed. Strikes and protest marches over inadequate food began to flare up on every home front. Soldiers' morale began to decline. Italian troops mutinied. Numerous French units refused to fight after General Nivelle's disastrous offensive of May 1917. Only tough military justice and a tacit agreement with his troops that there would be no more grand offensives enabled the new general in chief, Henri Philippe Pétain, to restore order. A rising tide of war-weariness and defeatism also swept France's civilian population before Georges Clemenceau emerged as a ruthless and effective wartime leader in November 1917. Clemenceau established a virtual dictatorship, pouncing on strikers and jailing without trial jour-

Irish Nationalists   Organized in 1913 to press for Home Rule in Ireland, the unofficial Irish Citizen Army was committed to complete independence from Great Britain. Shown here beneath a defiant pro-republican banner, it fought with other militant groups in the Easter Rebellion. (Source: Lawrence Collection. National Library of Ireland, Dublin)

nalists and politicians who dared to suggest a compromise peace with Germany.

The strains were worse for the Central Powers. In October 1916 the chief minister of Austria was assassinated by a young socialist crying, "Down with Absolutism! We want peace!"[8] The following month, when the feeble old Emperor Francis Joseph died sixty-eight years after his mother Sophia had pushed him onto the throne in 1848 (see page 749), a symbol of unity disappeared. In spite of absolute censorship, political dissatisfaction and conflicts among nationalities grew. In April 1917 Austria's chief minister summed up the situation in the gloomiest possible terms. The country and army were exhausted. Another winter of war would bring revolution and disintegration. "If the monarchs of the Central Powers cannot make peace in the coming months," he wrote, "it will be made for them by their peoples."[9] Both Czech and Yugoslav leaders demanded autonomous democratic states for their peoples. The British blockade kept tightening; people were starving.

The strain of total war and the Auxiliary Service Law was also evident in Germany. In the winter of 1916 to 1917, Germany's military position appeared increasingly desperate. Stalemates and losses in the west were matched by temporary Russian advances in the east: hence the military's insistence on the all-or-nothing gamble of unrestricted submarine warfare when the Triple Entente refused in December 1916 to consider peace on terms that were favorable to the Central Powers.

Also, the national political unity of the first two years of war was collapsing as the social conflict of prewar Germany re-emerged. A growing minority of socialists in the parliament began to vote against war credits, calling for a compromise "peace without annexations or reparations." In July 1917 a coalition of socialists and Catholics passed a resolution in the parliament to that effect. Such a peace was unthinkable for conservatives and military leaders. So also was the surge in revolutionary agitation and strikes by war-weary workers that occurred in early 1917. When the bread ration was further reduced in April, more than 200,000 workers struck and demonstrated for a week in Berlin, returning to work only under the threat of prison and military discipline. Thus militaristic Germany, like its ally Austria-Hungary (and its enemy France), was beginning to crack in 1917. Yet it was Russia that collapsed first and saved the Central Powers, for a time.

THE RUSSIAN REVOLUTION

The Russian Revolution of 1917 was one of modern history's most momentous events. Directly related to the growing tensions of World War One, it had a significance far beyond the wartime agonies of a single European nation. The Russian Revolution opened a new era. For some, it was Marx's socialist vision come true; for others, it was the triumph of dictatorship. To all, it presented a radically new prototype of state and society.

The Fall of Imperial Russia

Like its allies and its enemies, Russia embraced war with patriotic enthusiasm in 1914. At the Winter Palace, while throngs of people knelt and sang "God Save the Tsar," Tsar Nicholas II (r. 1894–1917) repeated the oath Alexander I had sworn in 1812 and vowed never to make peace as long as the enemy stood on Russian soil. Russia's lower house, the Duma, voted war credits. Conservatives anticipated expansion in the Balkans, while liberals and most socialists believed alliance with Britain and France would bring democratic reforms. For a moment, Russia was united.

Soon, however, the strains of war began to take their toll. The unprecedented artillery barrages used up Russia's supplies of shells and ammunition, and better-equipped German armies inflicted terrible losses. For a time in 1915, substantial numbers of Russian soldiers were sent to the front without rifles; they were told to find their arms among the dead. There were two million Russian casualties in 1915 alone. Morale declined among soldiers and civilians. Nonetheless, Russia's battered peasant army did not collapse but continued to fight courageously until early 1917.

Under the shock of defeat, Russia moved toward full mobilization on the home front. The Duma and organs of local government took the lead, setting up special committees to coordinate defense, industry, transportation, and agriculture. These efforts improved the military situation, and Russian factories produced more than twice as many shells in 1916 as in 1915. Yet there were many failures, and Russia mobilized less effectively for total war than the other warring nations.

The great problem was leadership. Under the constitution resulting from the revolution of 1905 (see pages 808–809), the tsar had retained complete control over the bureaucracy and the army. Legislation proposed by the Duma, which was weighted in favor of the wealthy and conservative classes, was subject to the tsar's veto. Moreover, Nicholas II fervently wished to maintain the sacred inheritance of supreme royal power, which with the Orthodox church was for him the key to Russia's greatness. A kindly, slightly stupid man, of whom a friend said he "would have been an ideal country gentleman, devoting his life to wife and children, his farms and his sport," Nicholas failed to form a close partnership with his citizens in order to fight the war more effectively. He relied instead on the old bureaucratic apparatus, distrusting the moderate Duma, rejecting popular involvement, and resisting calls to share power.

As a result the Duma, the educated middle classes, and the masses became increasingly critical of the tsar's leadership. Following Nicholas's belated dismissal of the incompetent minister of war, demands for more democratic and responsive government exploded in the Duma in the summer of 1915. "From the beginning of the war," declared one young liberal, "public opinion has understood the character and magnitude of the struggle; it has understood that short of organizing the whole country for war, victory is impossible. But the Government has rejected every offer of help with disdain."[10] In September, parties ranging from conservative to moderate socialist formed the Progressive Bloc, which called for a completely new government responsible to the Duma instead of the tsar. In answer, Nicholas temporarily adjourned the Duma and announced that he was traveling to the front in order to lead and rally Russia's armies.

His departure was a fatal turning point. With the tsar in the field with the troops, control of the government was taken over by the hysterical empress, Tsarina Alexandra, and a debauched adventurer, the monk Rasputin. A minor German princess and granddaughter of England's Queen Victoria, Nicholas's wife was a devoted mother with a sick child, a strong-willed woman with a hatred of parliaments. Having constantly urged her husband to rule absolutely, Alexandra tried to do so herself in his absence. She seated and unseated the top ministers. Her most trusted adviser was "our Friend Grigori," an uneducated Siberian preacher who was appropriately nicknamed Rasputin—the "Degenerate."

Rasputin began his career with a sect noted for mixing sexual orgies with religious ecstasies, and his influence rested on mysterious healing powers. Alexis, Alexandra's fifth child and heir to the throne, suffered from a rare disease, hemophilia. The tiniest cut meant uncontrollable bleeding, terrible pain, and possible death. Medical science could do nothing. Only Rasputin could miraculously stop the bleeding, perhaps through hypnosis. The empress's faith in Rasputin was limitless. "Believe more in our Friend," she wrote her husband in 1916. "He lives for you and Russia." In this atmosphere of unreality, the government slid steadily toward revolution.

In a desperate attempt to right the situation and end unfounded rumors that Rasputin was the empress's lover, three members of the high aristocracy murdered Rasputin in December 1916. The empress went into semipermanent shock, her mind haunted by the dead man's prophecy: "If I die or you desert me, in six months you will lose your son and your throne."[11] Food shortages in the cities worsened, morale declined. On March 8, women calling for bread in Petrograd (formerly St. Petersburg) started riots, which spontaneously spread to the factories and throughout the city. From the front the tsar ordered the troops to restore order, but discipline broke down and the soldiers joined the revolutionary crowd. The Duma responded by declaring a provisional government on March 12, 1917. Three days later, Nicholas abdicated.

The Provisional Government

The March revolution was the result of an unplanned uprising of hungry, angry people in the capital, but it was joyfully accepted throughout the country. The patriotic upper and middle classes rejoiced at the prospect of a more determined and effective war effort, while workers happily anticipated better wages and more food. All classes and political parties called for liberty and democracy. They were not disappointed. As Lenin said, Russia became the freest country in the world. After generations of arbitrary authoritarianism, the provisional government quickly established equality before the law; freedom of religion, speech, and assembly; the right of unions to organize and strike; and the rest of the classic liberal program.

Yet both the liberal and moderate socialist leaders of the provisional government rejected social revolution. The reorganized government formed in May 1917, which included the fiery agrarian socialist Alexander Kerensky, refused to confiscate large landholdings and give them to peasants, fearing that such drastic action in the countryside would only complete the disintegration of Russia's peasant army. For the patriotic Kerensky, as for other moderate socialists, the continuation of war was still the all-important national duty. There would be plenty of time for land reform later, and thus all the government's efforts were directed toward a last offensive in July. Human suffering and war-weariness grew, sapping the limited strength of the provisional government.

From its first day, the provisional government had to share power with a formidable rival—the Petrograd Soviet (or council) of Workers' and Soldiers' Deputies. Modeled on the revolutionary soviets of 1905, the Petrograd Soviet was a huge, fluctuating mass meeting of two to three thousand workers, soldiers, and socialist intellectuals. Seeing itself as a true grassroots revolutionary democracy, this counter- or half-government suspiciously watched the provisional government and issued its own radical orders, further weakening the provisional government. Most famous of these was Army Order No. 1, issued to all Russian military forces as the provisional government was forming.

Order No. 1 stripped officers of their authority and placed power in the hands of elected committees of common soldiers. Designed primarily to protect the revolution from some counter-revolutionary Bonaparte on horseback, Army Order No. 1 instead led to a total collapse of army discipline. Many an officer was hanged for his sins. Meanwhile, following the foolhardy summer offensive, masses of peasant soldiers began "voting with their feet," to use Lenin's graphic phrase. That is, they began returning to their villages to help their families get a share of the land, land that peasants were simply seizing as they settled old scores in a great agrarian upheaval. All across the country, liberty was turning into anarchy in the summer of 1917. It was an unparalleled opportunity for the most radical and most talented of Russia's many socialist leaders, Vladimir Ilyich Lenin (1870–1924).

Lenin and the Bolshevik Revolution

From his youth, Lenin's whole life was dedicated to the cause of revolution. Born into the middle class, Lenin became an implacable enemy of imperial Russia when his older brother was executed for plotting to kill the tsar in 1887. As a law student he began searching for a revolutionary faith. He found it in Marxian socialism, which began to win converts among radical intellectuals as industrialization surged forward in Russia in the 1890s. Exiled to Siberia for three years because of socialist agitation, Lenin studied Marxian doctrines with religious intensity. After his release, the young priest of socialism joined fellow believers in western Europe. There he lived for seventeen years and developed his own revolutionary interpretations of the body of Marxian thought.

Three interrelated ideas were central for Lenin. First, turning to the early fire-breathing Marx of 1848 and the *Communist Manifesto* for inspiration, Lenin stressed that capitalism could be destroyed only by violent revolution. He tirelessly denounced all revisionist theories of a peaceful evolution to socialism as betraying Marx's message of unending class conflict. Lenin's second, more original, idea was that, under certain conditions, a socialist revolution was possible even in a relatively backward country like Russia. Though capitalism was not fully developed there and the industrial working class was small, the peasants were poor and thus potential revolutionaries.

Lenin believed that at a given moment revolution was determined more by human leadership than by vast historical laws. Thus Lenin's third basic idea: the necessity of a highly disciplined workers' party, strictly controlled by a dedicated elite of intellectuals and full-time revolutionaries like Lenin himself. Unlike ordinary workers and trade-union officials, this elite would never be seduced by short-term gains. It would not stop until revolution brought it to power.

Lenin's theories and methods did not go unchallenged by other Russian Marxists. At the meetings of the Russian Social Democratic Labor party in London in 1903, matters came to a head. Lenin demanded a small, disciplined, elitist party, while his opponents wanted a more democratic party with mass membership. The Russian party of Marxian socialism promptly split into two rival factions. Lenin's camp was called *Bolsheviks,* or "majority group"; his opponents were *Mensheviks,* or "minority group." Lenin's majority did not last, but Lenin did not care. He kept the fine-sounding name Bolshevik and developed the party he wanted: tough, disciplined, revolutionary.

Mass Demonstrations in Petrograd   in June 1917 showed a surge of working-class support for the Bolsheviks. In this photo a few banners of the Mensheviks and other moderate socialists are drowned in a sea of Bolshevik slogans. *(Source: Sovfoto)*

Unlike most other socialists, Lenin did not rally
round the national flag in 1914. Observing events
from neutral Switzerland, he saw the war as a product of imperialistic rivalries and as a marvelous opportunity for class war and socialist upheaval. The
March revolution was, Lenin felt, a step in that direction. Since propaganda and internal subversion
were accepted weapons of total war, the German
government graciously provided the impatient
Lenin, his wife, and about twenty trusted colleagues with safe passage across Germany and back
into Russia in April 1917. The Germans hoped
that Lenin would undermine the sagging war effort
of the world's freest society. They were not disappointed.

Arriving triumphantly at Petrograd's Finland
Station on April 3, Lenin attacked at once. To the

great astonishment of the local Bolsheviks, he rejected all cooperation with the "bourgeois" provisional government of the liberals and moderate socialists. His slogans were radical in the extreme:
"All power to the soviets." "All land to the peasants." "Stop the war now." Never a slave to Marxian determinism, the brilliant but not unduly intellectual Lenin was a superb tactician. The moment
was now.

Yet Lenin almost overplayed his hand. An attempt by the Bolsheviks to seize power in July collapsed, and Lenin fled and went into hiding. He
was charged with being a German agent, and indeed he and the Bolsheviks were getting money
from Germany.[12] But no matter. Intrigue between
Kerensky, who became prime minister in July, and
his commander in chief General Lavr Kornilov, a

popular war hero "with the heart of a lion and the brains of a sheep," resulted in Kornilov's leading a feeble attack against the provisional government in September. In the face of this rightist "counter-revolutionary" threat, the Bolsheviks were rearmed and redeemed. Kornilov's forces disintegrated, but Kerensky lost all credit with the army, the only force that might have saved him and democratic government in Russia.

Trotsky and the Seizure of Power

Throughout the summer, the Bolsheviks had appealed very effectively to the workers and soldiers of Petrograd, markedly increasing their popular support. Party membership had soared from 50,000 to 240,000, and in October the Bolsheviks gained a fragile majority in the Petrograd Soviet. Moreover, Lenin had found a strong right arm—Leon Trotsky, the second most important person in the Russian Revolution.

A spellbinding revolutionary orator and independent radical Marxist, Trotsky (1879–1940) supported Lenin wholeheartedly in 1917. It was he who brilliantly executed the Bolshevik seizure of power. Painting a vivid but untruthful picture of German and counter-revolutionary plots, Trotsky first convinced the Petrograd Soviet to form a special Military-Revolutionary Committee in October and make him its leader. Military power in the capital passed into Bolshevik hands. Trotsky's second master stroke was to insist that the Bolsheviks reduce opposition to their coup by taking power in the name, not of the Bolsheviks, but of the more popular and democratic soviets, which were meeting in Petrograd from all over Russia in early November. On the night of November 6, militants from Trotsky's committee joined with trusty Bolshevik soldiers to seize government buildings and pounce on members of the provisional government. Then on to the congress of soviets! There a Bolshevik majority—roughly 390 of 650 turbulent delegates—declared that all power had passed to the soviets and named Lenin head of the new government.

The Bolsheviks came to power for three key reasons. First, by late 1917 democracy had given way to anarchy: power was there for those who would take it. Second, in Lenin and Trotsky the Bolsheviks had an utterly determined and truly superior leadership, which both the tsarist government and the provisional government lacked. Third, in 1917 the Bolsheviks succeeded in appealing to many soldiers and urban workers, people who were exhausted by war and eager for socialism. With time, many workers would become bitterly disappointed, but for the moment they had good reason to believe they had won what they wanted.

Dictatorship and Civil War

History is full of short-lived coups and unsuccessful revolutions. The truly monumental accomplishment of Lenin, Trotsky, and the rest of the Bolsheviks was not taking power but keeping it. In the next four years, the Bolsheviks went on to conquer the chaos they had helped to create, and they began to build their kind of dictatorial socialist society. The conspirators became conquerors. How was this done?

Lenin had the genius to profit from developments over which he and the Bolsheviks had no control. Since summer, a peasant revolution had been sweeping across Russia, as the tillers of the soil invaded and divided among themselves the great and not-so-great estates of the landlords and the church. Peasant seizure of the land—a Russian 1789—was not very Marxian, but it was quite unstoppable in 1917. Thus Lenin's first law, which supposedly gave land to the peasants, actually merely approved what peasants were already doing. Urban workers' great demand in November was direct control of individual factories by local workers' committees. This, too, Lenin ratified with a decree in November.

Unlike many of his colleagues, Lenin acknowledged that Russia had lost the war with Germany, that the Russian army had ceased to exist, and that the only realistic goal was peace at any price. The price was very high. Germany demanded in December 1917 that the Soviet government give up all its western territories. These areas were inhabited by Poles, Finns, Lithuanians, and other non-Russians—all those peoples who had been conquered by the tsars over three centuries and put into the "prisonhouse of nationalities," as Lenin had earlier called the Russian Empire.

At first, Lenin's fellow Bolsheviks would not accept such great territorial losses. But when German armies resumed their unopposed march into Russia

THE RUSSIAN REVOLUTION

1914	Russia enthusiastically enters the First World War
1915	Two million Russian casualties
	Progressive Bloc calls for a new government responsible to the Duma rather than to the tsar
	Tsar Nicholas adjourns the Duma and departs for the front; control of the government falls to Alexandra and Rasputin
December 1916	Murder of Rasputin
March 8, 1917	Bread riots in Petrograd (St. Petersburg)
March 12, 1917	Duma declares a provisional government
March 15, 1917	Tsar Nicholas abdicates without protest
April 3, 1917	Lenin returns from exile and denounces the provisional government
May 1917	Reorganized provisional government, including Kerensky, continues the war Petrograd Soviet issues Army Order no. 1, granting military power to committees of common soldiers
Summer 1917	Agrarian upheavals: peasants seize estates, peasant soldiers desert the army to participate
October 1917	Bolsheviks gain a majority in the Petrograd Soviet
November 6, 1917	Bolsheviks seize power; Lenin heads the new "provisional workers' and peasants' government"
November 1917	Lenin ratifies peasant seizure of land and worker control of factories; all banks nationalized
January 1918	Lenin permanently disbands the Constituent Assembly
February 1918	Lenin convinces the Bolshevik Central Committee to accept a humiliating peace with Germany in order to pursue the revolution
March 1918	Treaty of Brest-Litovsk: Russia loses one-third of its population
	Trotsky as war commissar begins to rebuild the Russian army
	Government moves from Petrograd to Moscow
1918–1920	Great Civil War
Summer 1918	Eighteen competing regional governments; White armies oppose the Bolshevik revolution
1919	White armies on the offensive but divided politically; they receive little benefit from Allied intervention
1920	Lenin and Red armies victorious, retaking Belorussia and the Ukraine

in February 1918, Lenin had his way in a very close vote in the Central Committee of the party. "Not even his greatest enemy can deny that at this moment Lenin towered like a giant over his Bolshevik colleagues."[13] A third of old Russia's population was sliced away by the German meat ax in the Treaty of Brest-Litovsk in March 1918. With peace, Lenin had escaped the certain disaster of continued war and could uncompromisingly pursue his goal of absolute political power for the Bolsheviks—now renamed Communists—within Russia.

In November 1917 the Bolsheviks had cleverly proclaimed their regime only a "provisional workers' and peasants' government," promising that a freely elected Constituent Assembly would draw up a new constitution. But free elections produced a stunning setback for the Bolsheviks, who won less than one-fourth of the elected delegates. The Socialist Revolutionaries—the peasants' party —had a clear majority. The Constituent Assembly met for only one day, on January 18, 1918. It was then permanently disbanded by Bolshevik soldiers acting under Lenin's orders. Thus, even before the peace with Germany, Lenin was forming a one-party government.

The destruction of the democratically elected Constituent Assembly helped feed the flames of civil war. People who had risen up for self-rule in November saw that once again they were getting dictatorship from the capital. For the next three years, "Long live the [democratic] soviets; down with the Bolsheviks" was to be a popular slogan. The officers of the old army took the lead in organizing the so-called White opposition to the Bolsheviks in southern Russia and the Ukraine, in Siberia, and to the west of Petrograd. The Whites came from many social groups and were united only by their hatred of the Bolsheviks—the Reds.

By the summer of 1918, fully eighteen self-proclaimed regional governments—several of which represented minority nationalities—competed with Lenin's Bolsheviks in Moscow. By the end of the year, White armies were on the attack. In October 1919 it appeared they might triumph, as they closed in on Lenin's government from three sides. Yet they did not. By the spring of 1920, the White armies had been almost completely defeated, and the Bolshevik Red Army had retaken Belorussia and the Ukraine. The following year, the Communists also reconquered the independent nationalist governments of the Caucasus. The civil war was over; Lenin had won.

Lenin and the Bolsheviks won for several reasons. Strategically, they controlled the center, while the Whites were always on the fringes and disunited. Moreover, the poorly defined political program of the Whites was vaguely conservative, and it did not unite all the foes of the Bolsheviks under a progressive, democratic banner. For example, the most gifted of the White generals, the nationalistic General Anton Denikin, refused to call for a democratic republic and a federation of nationalities, although he knew that doing so would help his cause. Most important, the Communists quickly developed a better army, an army for which the divided Whites were no match.

Once again, Trotsky's leadership was decisive. The Bolsheviks had preached democracy in the army and elected officers in 1917. But beginning in March 1918, Trotsky as war commissar re-established the draft and the most drastic discipline for the newly formed Red Army. Soldiers deserting or

Vladimir Lenin Dramatically displaying both his burning determination and his skill as a revolutionary orator, Lenin addresses the victorious May Day celebration of 1918 in Moscow's Red Square. (Source: Culver Pictures)

disobeying an order were summarily shot. Moreover, Trotsky made effective use of former tsarist army officers, who were actively recruited and given unprecedented powers of discipline over their troops. In short, Trotsky formed a disciplined and effective fighting force.

The Bolsheviks also mobilized the home front. Establishing "war communism"—the application of the total war concept to a civil conflict—they seized grain from peasants, introduced rationing, nationalized all banks and industry, and required everyone to work. Although these measures contributed to a breakdown of normal economic activity, they also served to maintain labor discipline and to keep the Red Army supplied.

"Revolutionary terror" also contributed to the Communist victory. The old tsarist secret police was re-established as the Cheka, which hunted down and executed thousands of real or supposed foes, such as the tsar and his family and other "class enemies." At one point, shortly after the government moved from Petrograd to Moscow in March 1918, a circus clown in Moscow was making fun of the Bolsheviks to an appreciative audience. Chekists in the crowd quickly pulled out their guns and shot several laughing people. Moreover, people were shot or threatened with being shot for minor nonpolitical failures. The terror caused by the secret police became a tool of the government. The Cheka sowed fear, and fear silenced opposition.

Finally, foreign military intervention in the civil war ended up helping the Communists. After Lenin made peace with Germany, the Allies (the Americans, British, and Japanese) sent troops to Archangel and Vladivostok to prevent war materiel they had sent the provisional government from being captured by the Germans. After the Soviet government nationalized all foreign-owned factories without compensation and refused to pay all of Russia's foreign debts, Western governments and particularly France began to support White armies. Yet these efforts were small and halfhearted. In 1919 Western peoples were sick of war, and few Western politicians believed in a military crusade against the Bolsheviks. Thus Allied intervention in the civil war did not aid the Whites effectively, though it did permit the Communists to appeal to the patriotic nationalism of ethnic Russians, in particular the former tsarist army officers. Allied intervention was both too little and too much.

Together, the Russian Revolution and the Bolshevik triumph were one of the reasons why the First World War was such a great turning point in modern history. A radically new government, based on socialism and one-party dictatorship, came to power in a great European state, maintained power, and eagerly encouraged worldwide revolution. Although halfheartedly constitutional monarchy in Russia was undoubtedly headed for some kind of political crisis before 1914, it is hard to imagine the triumph of the most radical proponents of change and reform except in a situation of total collapse. That was precisely what happened to Russia in the First World War.

THE PEACE SETTLEMENT

Victory over revolutionary Russia boosted sagging German morale, and in the spring of 1918 the Germans launched their last major attack against France. Yet this offensive failed like those before it. With breathtaking rapidity, the United States, Great Britain, and France decisively defeated Germany militarily. The guns of world war finally fell silent. Then, as civil war spread in Russia and as chaos engulfed much of eastern Europe, the victorious Western Allies came together in Paris to establish a lasting peace.

Expectations were high; optimism was almost unlimited. The Allies labored intensively and soon worked out terms for peace with Germany and for the creation of the peace-keeping League of Nations. Nevertheless, the hopes of peoples and politicians were soon disappointed, for the peace settlement of 1919 turned out to be a failure. Rather than creating conditions for peace, it sowed the seeds of another war. Surely this was the ultimate tragedy of the Great War, a war that directly and indirectly cost $332 billion and left 10 million dead and another 20 million wounded. How did it happen? Why was the peace settlement unsuccessful?

The End of the War

In early 1917 the strain of total war was showing everywhere. After the Russian Revolution in March, there were major strikes in Germany. In July a coalition of moderates passed a "peace resolution" in the German parliament, calling for peace without territorial annexations. To counter this moderation born of war-weariness, the German military established a virtual dictatorship. The military also aggressively exploited the collapse of Russian armies after the Bolshevik Revolution. Advancing almost unopposed on the eastern front in early 1918, the German high command won great concessions from Lenin in the Treaty of Brest-Litovsk in March 1918, as we have seen.

With victory in the east quieting German moderates, General Ludendorff and company fell on France once more in the great spring offensive of 1918. For a time, German armies pushed forward, coming within 35 miles of Paris. But Ludendorff's exhausted, overextended forces never broke through. They were decisively stopped in July at the second Battle of the Marne, where 140,000 fresh American soldiers saw action. Adding 2 million men in arms to the war effort by August, the late but massive American intervention decisively tipped the scales in favor of Allied victory.

By September, British, French, and American armies were advancing steadily on all fronts, and a panicky General Ludendorff realized that Germany had lost the war. Yet he insolently insisted that moderate politicians shoulder the shame of defeat, and on October 4 the emperor formed a new, more liberal German government to sue for peace. As negotiations over an armistice dragged on, an angry and frustrated German people finally rose up. On November 3, sailors in Kiel mutinied, and throughout northern Germany soldiers and workers began to establish revolutionary councils on the Russian soviet model. The same day, Austria-Hungary surrendered to the Allies and began breaking apart. Revolution broke out in Germany, and masses of workers demonstrated for peace in Berlin. With army discipline collapsing, the emperor abdicated and fled to Holland. Socialist leaders in Berlin proclaimed a German republic on November 9 and simultaneously agreed to tough Allied terms of surrender. The armistice went into effect on November 11, 1918. The war was over.

Revolution in Germany

Military defeat brought political revolution to Germany and Austria-Hungary, as it had to Russia. In Austria-Hungary, the revolution was primarily nationalistic and republican in character. Having started the war to preserve an antinationalist dynastic state, the Habsburg empire had perished in the attempt. In its place, independent Austrian, Hungarian, and Czechoslovak republics were proclaimed, while a greatly expanded Serbian monarchy united the south Slavs and took the name of Yugoslavia. The prospect of firmly establishing the new national states overrode class considerations for most people in east central Europe.

The German Revolution of November 1918 resembled the Russian Revolution of March 1917. In both cases, a genuine popular uprising toppled an authoritarian monarchy and established a liberal provisional republic. In both countries, liberals and moderate socialists took control of the central government, while workers' and soldiers' councils formed a counter-government. In Germany, however, the moderate socialists won and the Lenin-like radical revolutionaries in the councils lost. In communist terms, the liberal, republican revolution in Germany in 1918 was only half a revolution: a bourgeois political revolution without a communist second installment. It was Russia without Lenin's Bolshevik triumph.

There were several reasons for the German outcome. The great majority of Marxian socialist leaders in the Social Democratic party were, as before the war, really pink and not red. They wanted to establish real political democracy and civil liberties, and they favored the gradual elimination of capitalism. They were also German nationalists, appalled by the prospect of civil war and revolutionary terror. Moreover, there was much less popular

Rosa Luxemburg A brilliant writer and a leader in the German Social Democratic party, Luxemburg scorned moderate socialism and stressed the revolutionary character of Marxism. Murdered by army officers in 1919, she was cannonized by the faithful as a communist saint. *(Source: Courtesy, Centralne Archiwum KCPZPR, Warsaw, Poland)*

support among workers and soldiers for the extreme radicals than in Russia. Nor did the German peasantry, which already had most of the land, at least in western Germany, provide the elemental force that has driven all great modern revolutions, from the French to the Chinese.

Of crucial importance also was the fact that the moderate German Social Democrats, unlike Kerensky and company, accepted defeat and ended the war the day they took power. This act ended the decline in morale among soldiers and prevented the regular army with its conservative officer corps from disintegrating. When radicals, headed by Karl Liebknecht and Rosa Luxemburg and their supporters in the councils, tried to seize control of the government in Berlin in January, the moderate socialists called on the army to crush the uprising. Liebknecht and Luxemburg were arrested and then brutally murdered by army leaders, an act that caused the radicals in the Social Democratic party to break away in anger and form a pro-Lenin German Communist party shortly thereafter. Finally, even if the moderate socialists had followed Liebknecht and Luxemburg on the Leninist path, it is very unlikely they would have succeeded. Civil war in Germany would certainly have followed, and the Allies, who were already occupying western Germany according to the terms of the armistice, would have marched on to Berlin and ruled Germany directly. Historians have often been unduly hard on Germany's moderate socialists.

The Treaty of Versailles

The peace conference opened in Paris in January 1919 with seventy delegates representing twenty-seven victorious nations. There were great expectations. A young British diplomat later wrote that the victors "were convinced that they would never commit the blunders and iniquities of the Congress of Vienna [of 1815]." Then the "misguided, reactionary, pathetic aristocrats" had cynically shuffled populations; now "we believed in nationalism, we believed in the self-determination of peoples." Indeed, "we were journeying to Paris . . . to found a new order in Europe. We were preparing not Peace only, but Eternal Peace."[14] The general optimism and idealism had been greatly strengthened by President Wilson's January 1918 peace proposal, the Fourteen Points, which stressed national self-determination and the rights of small countries.

The real powers at the conference were the United States, Great Britain, and France, for Germany was not allowed to participate, and Russia was locked in civil war and did not attend. Italy was considered part of the Big Four, but its role was quite limited. Almost immediately the three great allies began to quarrel. President Wilson, who was wildly cheered by European crowds as the spokesman for a new idealistic and democratic international cooperation, was almost obsessed with creating a League of Nations. Wilson insisted that this question come first, for he passionately believed that only a permanent international organization could protect member states from aggression and avert future wars. Wilson had his way, although Lloyd George of Great Britain and especially Clemenceau of France were unenthusiastic. They were primarily concerned with punishing Germany.

Playing on British nationalism, Lloyd George had already won a smashing electoral victory in December on the popular platform of making Germany pay for the war. "We shall," he promised, "squeeze the orange until the pips squeak." Personally inclined to make a somewhat moderate peace with Germany, Lloyd George was to a considerable extent a captive of demands for a total victory worthy of the sacrifices of total war against a totally depraved enemy. As Kipling summed up the general British feeling at the end of the war, the Germans were "a people with the heart of beasts."[15]

France's Georges Clemenceau, "the Tiger" who had broken wartime defeatism and led his country to victory, wholeheartedly agreed. Like most French people, Clemenceau wanted old-fashioned revenge. He also wanted lasting security for France. This, he believed, required the creation of a buffer state between France and Germany, the permanent demilitarization of Germany, and vast German reparations. He feared that sooner or later Germany with its sixty million people would attack France with its forty million, unless the Germans were permanently weakened. Moreover, France had no English Channel (or Atlantic Ocean) as a reassuring barrier against German aggression. Wilson, supported by Lloyd George, would hear none of it. Clemenceau's demands seemed vindictive, violating morality and the principle of national self-determination. By April the conference was deadlocked on the German question, and Wilson packed his bags to go home.

Clemenceau's obsession with security reflected his anxiety about France's long-term weakness. In

The Treaty of Versailles was signed in the magnificent Hall of Mirrors, part of the vast palace that Louis XIV had built to celebrate his glory. The Allies did not allow Germany to participate in the negotiation of the treaty. *(Source: National Archives, Washington)*

the end, convinced that France should not break with its allies because France could not afford to face Germany alone in the future, he agreed to a compromise. He gave up the French demand for a Rhineland buffer state in return for a formal defensive alliance with the United States and Great Britain. Under the terms of this alliance, both Wilson and Lloyd George promised that their countries would come to France's aid in the event of a German attack. Thus Clemenceau appeared to win his goal of French security, as Wilson had won his of a permanent international organization. The Allies moved quickly to finish the settlement, believing that any adjustments would later be possible within the dual framework of a strong Western alliance and the League of Nations (Map 27.4).

The Treaty of Versailles between the Allies and Germany was the key to the settlement, and the terms were not unreasonable as a first step toward re-establishing international order. (Had Germany won, it seems certain that France and Belgium would have been treated with greater severity, as Russia had been at Brest-Litovsk.) Germany's colonies were given to France, Britain, and Japan as League of Nations mandates. Germany's territorial losses within Europe were minor, thanks to Wilson. Alsace-Lorraine was returned to France. Parts of Germany inhabited primarily by Poles were ceded to the new Polish state, in keeping with the principle of national self-determination. Predominately German Danzig was also placed within the Polish tariff lines, but as a self-governing city under League of Nations protection. Germany had to limit its army to 100,000 men and agree to build no military fortifications in the Rhineland.

More harshly, the Allies declared that Germany (with Austria) was responsible for the war and had therefore to pay reparations equal to all civilian damages caused by the war. This unfortunate and much-criticized clause expressed inescapable popular demands for German blood, but the actual figure was not set, and there was the clear possibility that reparations might be set at a reasonable level in the future, when tempers had cooled.

When presented with the treaty, the German government protested vigorously. But there was no

MAP 27.4 Shattered Empires and Territorial Changes After World War One The Great War brought tremendous changes in eastern Europe. New nations were established, and a dangerous power vacuum was created between Germany and Soviet Russia.

alternative, especially considering that Germany was still starving because the Allies had not yet lifted their naval blockade. On June 28, 1919, German representatives of the ruling moderate Social Democrats and the Catholic party signed the treaty in the Sun King's Hall of Mirrors at Versailles, where Bismarck's empire had been joyously proclaimed almost fifty years before.

Separate peace treaties were concluded with the other defeated powers—Austria, Hungary, Bulgaria, and Turkey. For the most part, these treaties merely ratified the existing situation in east central Europe following the breakup of the Austro-Hungarian Empire. Like Austria, Hungary was a particularly big loser, as its "captive" nationalities (and some interspersed Hungarians) were ceded to Rumania, Czechoslovakia, Poland, and Yugoslavia. Italy got some Austrian territory. The Turkish empire was broken up. France received Lebanon and Syria, while Britain took Iraq and Palestine, which was to include a Jewish national homeland first promised by Britain in 1917. Officially League of Nations mandates, these acquisitions of the Western powers were one of the more imperialistic elements of the peace settlement. Another was mandating Germany's holdings in China to Japan. The age of Western imperialism lived on. National self-determination remained a reality only for Europeans and their offspring.

American Rejection of the Versailles Treaty

The rapidly concluded peace settlement of early 1919 was not perfect, but within the context of war-shattered Europe it was an acceptable beginning. The principle of national self-determination, which had played such a large role in starting the war, was accepted and served as an organizing framework. Germany had been punished but not dismembered. A new world organization complemented a traditional defensive alliance of satisfied powers. The serious remaining problems could be worked out in the future. Moreover, Allied leaders had seen speed as essential for another reason: they detested Lenin and feared that his Bolshevik Revolution might spread. They realized that their best answer to Lenin's unending calls for worldwide upheaval was peace and tranquility for war-weary peoples.

There were, however, two great interrelated obstacles to such peace: Germany and the United States. Plagued by communist uprisings, reactionary plots, and popular disillusionment with losing the war at the last minute, Germany's moderate socialists and their liberal and Catholic supporters faced an enormous challenge. Like French republicans after 1871, they needed time (and luck) if they were to establish firmly a peaceful and democratic republic. Progress in this direction required understanding yet firm treatment of Germany by the victorious Western Allies, and particularly by the United States.

However, the United States Senate and, to a lesser extent, the American people rejected Wilson's handiwork. Republican senators led by Henry Cabot Lodge refused to ratify the Treaty of Versailles without changes in the articles creating the League of Nations. The key issue was the League's power—more apparent than real—to require member states to take collective action against aggression.

Lodge and others believed that this requirement gave away Congress's constitutional right to declare war. No doubt Wilson would have been wise to accept some reservations. But, in failing health, Wilson with narrow-minded self-righteousness rejected all attempts at compromise. He instructed loyal Democratic senators to vote against any reservations whatsoever to the Treaty of Versailles. In doing so, Wilson assured that the treaty was never ratified by the United States in any form and that the United States never joined the League of Nations. Moreover, the Senate refused to ratify Wilson's defensive alliance with France and Great Britain. America turned its back on Europe.

Perhaps understandable in the light of American traditions and the volatility of mass politics, the Wilson-Lodge fiasco and the new-found gospel of isolationism nevertheless represented a tragic and cowardly renunciation of America's responsibility. Using America's action as an excuse, Great Britain, too, refused to ratify its defensive alliance with France. Bitterly betrayed by its allies, France stood alone. Very shortly, France was to take actions against Germany that would feed the fires of German resentment and seriously undermine democratic forces in the new republic. The great hopes of early 1919 were turning to ashes by the end of the year. The Western alliance had collapsed, and a grandiose plan for permanent peace had given way to a fragile truce. For this and for what came later, the United States must share a large part of the guilt.

SUMMARY

Why did World War One have such revolutionary consequences? Why was it such a great break with the past? World War One was, first of all, a war of committed peoples. In France, Britain, and Germany in particular, governments drew on genuine popular support. This support reflected not only the diplomatic origins of the war but also the way western European society had been effectively unified under the nationalist banner in the later nineteenth century. The relentlessness of total war helps explain why so many died, why so many were crippled physically and psychologically, and why Western civilization would in so many ways never be the same again. More concretely, the war swept away monarchs and multinational empires. National self-determination apparently triumphed, not only in Austria-Hungary but in many of Russia's western borderlands as well. Except in Ireland and parts of Soviet Russia, the revolutionary dream of national unity, born of the French Revolution, had finally come true.

Two other revolutions were products of the war. In Russia, the Bolsheviks established a radical regime, smashed existing capitalist institutions, and stayed in power with a new kind of authoritarian rule. Whether the new Russian regime was truly Marxian or socialist was questionable, but it indisputably posed a powerful, ongoing revolutionary challenge in Europe and Europe's colonial empires.

More subtle, but quite universal in its impact, was an administrative revolution. This revolution, born of the need to mobilize entire societies and economies for total war, greatly increased the power of government. And after the guns grew still, government planning and wholesale involvement in economic and social life did not disappear in Europe. Liberal market capitalism and a well-integrated world economy were among the many casualties of the administrative revolution, and greater social equality was everywhere one of its results. Thus, even in European countries where a communist takeover never came close to occurring, society still experienced a great revolution.

Finally, the "war to end war" did not bring peace but only a fragile truce: in the West the Allies failed to maintain their wartime solidarity. Germany remained unrepentant and would soon have more grievances to nurse. Moreover, the victory of national self-determination in eastern Europe created a power vacuum between a still-powerful Germany and a potentially mighty communist Russia. A vast area lay open to military aggression from two sides.

NOTES

1. M. Beloff, quoted in *U.S. News and World Report,* March 8, 1976, p. 53.
2. Quoted in J. Remak, *The Origins of World War I* (New York: Holt, Rinehart & Winston, 1967), p. 84.
3. Quoted in W. E. Mosse, *Alexander II and the Modernization of Russia* (New York: Collier Books, 1962), pp. 125–126.
4. Quoted in Remak, p. 123.
5. Quoted in J. E. Rodes, *The Quest for Unity: Modern Germany 1848–1970* (New York: Holt, Rinehart & Winston, 1971), p. 178.
6. Quoted in F. P. Chambers, *The War Behind the War, 1914–1918* (London: Faber & Faber, 1939), p. 444.
7. Ibid., p. 168.
8. Quoted in R. O. Paxton, *Europe in the Twentieth Century* (New York: Harcourt Brace Jovanovich, 1975), p. 109.
9. Quoted in Chambers, p. 378.
10. Ibid., p. 110.
11. Ibid., pp. 302, 304.
12. A. B. Ulam, *The Bolsheviks* (New York: Collier Books, 1968), p. 349.
13. Ibid., p. 405.
14. H. Nicolson, *Peacemaking 1919* (New York: Grosset & Dunlap Universal Library, 1965), pp. 8, 31–32.
15. Ibid., p. 24.

SUGGESTED READING

O. Hale, *The Great Illusion,* 1900–1914 (1971), is a thorough account of the prewar era. Both Remak's volume cited in the Notes and L. Lafore, *The Long Fuse* (1971), are highly recommended studies of the causes of the First World War. A. J. P. Taylor, *The Struggle for Mastery in Europe, 1848–1919* (1954), is an outstanding survey of diplomatic developments with an exhaustive bibliography. V. Steiner, *Britain and the Origins of the First World War* (1978), and G. Kennan, *The Decline of Bismarck's European Order: Franco-Russian Relations, 1875–1890* (1979), are also major contributions. K. Jarausch's *The Enigmatic Chancellor* (1973) is an important recent study on Bethmann-Hollweg and German policy in 1914. C. Falls, *The Great War* (1961), is the best brief introduction to military aspects of the war. B. Tuchman, *The Guns of*

August (1962), is a marvelous account of the dramatic first month of the war and the beginning of military stalemate. G. Ritter provides an able study in *The Schlieffen Plan* (1958). J. Winter, *The Experience of World War I* (1988), is a strikingly illustrated history of the war, and A. Horne, *The Price of Glory: Verdun 1916* (1979), is a moving account of the famous siege. J. Ellis, *Eye-Deep in Hell* (1976), is a vivid account of trench warfare. Vera Brittain's *Testament of Youth,* the moving autobiography of a nurse in wartime, shows lives buffeted by new ideas and personal tragedies.

F. L. Carsten, *War Against War* (1982), considers radical movements in Britain and Germany. The best single volume on the home fronts is still the one by Chambers mentioned in the Notes. Chambers drew heavily on the many fine books on the social and economic impact of the war in different countries published by the Carnegie Endowment for International Peace under the general editorship of J. T. Shotwell. A. Marwick, *The Deluge* (1970), is a lively account of war and society in Britain, while G. Feldman, *Army, Industry, and Labor in Germany, 1914–1918* (1966), shows the impact of total war and military dictatorship on Germany. Three excellent collections of essays, R. Wall and J. Winter, eds., *The Upheaval of War: Family, Work, and Welfare in Europe, 1914–1918* (1988), J. Roth, ed., *World War I* (1967), and R. Albrecht-Carrié, ed., *The Meaning of the First World War* (1965), probe the enormous consequences of the war for people and society. The debate over Germany's guilt and aggression, which has been reopened in recent years, may be best approached through G. Feldman, ed., *German Imperialism, 1914–1918* (1972), and A. Hillgruber, *Germany and the Two World Wars* (1981). M. Fainsod, *International Socialism and the World War* (1935), ably discusses the splits between radical and moderate socialists during the conflict. In addition to Erich Maria Remarque's great novel *All Quiet on the Western Front,* Henri Barbusse, *Under Fire* (1917), and Jules Romains, *Verdun* (1939), are highly recommended for their fictional yet realistic re-creations of the war. P. Fussell, *The Great War*

and Modern Memory (1975), probes all the powerful literature inspired by the war.

R. Suny and A. Adams, eds., *The Russian Revolution and Bolshevik Victory,* 3d ed. (1990), presents a wide range of old and new interpretations. A. Ulam's work cited in the Notes, which focuses on Lenin, is a masterful introduction to the Russian Revolution, while S. Fitzpatrick, *The Russian Revolution* (1982), provides a provocative reconsideration. B. Wolfe, *Three Who Made a Revolution* (1955), a collective biography of Lenin, Trotsky, and Stalin, and R. Conquest, *V. I. Lenin* (1972), are recommended. Leon Trotsky himself wrote the colorful and exciting *History of the Russian Revolution* (1932), which may be compared with the classic eyewitness account of the young, pro-Bolshevik American John Reed, *Ten Days That Shook the World* (1919). R. Daniels, *Red October* (1969), provides a clear account of the Bolshevik seizure of power, and R. Pipes, *The Formation of the Soviet Union* (1968), is recommended for its excellent treatment of the nationality problem during the revolution. D. Koenker, W. Rosenberg, and R. Suny, eds., *Party, State and Society in the Russian Civil War* (1989), probes the social foundations of Bolshevik victory. A. Wildman, *The End of the Russian Imperial Army* (1980), is a fine account of the soldiers' revolt, and G. Leggett, *The Cheka: Lenin's Secret Police* (1981), shows revolutionary terror in action. Boris Pasternak's justly celebrated *Doctor Zhivago* is a great historical novel of the revolutionary era. R. Massie, *Nicholas and Alexandra* (1971), is a moving popular biography of Russia's last royal family and the terrible health problem of the heir to the throne. H. Nicolson's study listed in the Notes captures the spirit of the Versailles settlement. T. Bailey, *Woodrow Wilson and the Lost Peace* (1963), and W. Widenor, *Henry Cabot Lodge and the Search for an American Foreign Policy* (1981), are also highly recommended. A. Mayer provocatively stresses the influence of domestic social tensions and widespread fear of further communist revolt in *The Politics and Diplomacy of Peacemaking* (1969).

28

The Age of Anxiety

Isaac So

When Allied diplomats met in Paris in early 1919 with their optimistic plans for building a lasting peace, most people looked forward to happier times. They hoped that life would return to normal after the terrible trauma of total war. They hoped that once again life would make sense in the familiar prewar terms of peace, prosperity, and progress. These hopes were in vain. The Great Break—the First World War and the Russian Revolution—had mangled too many things beyond repair. Life would no longer fit neatly into the old molds.

Instead, great numbers of men and women felt themselves increasingly adrift in a strange, uncertain, and uncontrollable world. They saw themselves living in an age of anxiety, an age of continuous crisis, which lasted until at least the early 1950s. In almost every area of human experience, people went searching for ways to put meaning back into life.

- What did the doubts and searching mean for Western thought, art, and culture?

- How did political leaders try to re-establish real peace and prosperity between 1919 and 1939?

- And why did those leaders fail?

These are questions this chapter will explore.

UNCERTAINTY IN MODERN THOUGHT

A complex revolution in thought and ideas was under way before the First World War, but only small, unusual groups were aware of it. After the war, new and upsetting ideas began to spread through the entire population. Western society began to question and even abandon many cherished values and beliefs that had guided it since the eighteenth-century Enlightenment and the nineteenth-century triumph of industrial development, scientific advances, and evolutionary thought.

Before 1914 most people still believed in progress, reason, and the rights of the individual. Progress was a daily reality, apparent in the rising standard of living, the taming of the city, and the steady increase in popular education. Such developments also encouraged the comforting belief in the logical universe of Newtonian physics, as well as faith in the ability of a rational human mind to understand that universe through intellectual investigation. And just as there were laws of science, so were there laws of society that rational human beings could discover and then wisely act on. Finally, the rights of the individual were not just taken for granted, they were actually increasing. Well-established rights were gradually spreading to women and workers, and new "social rights" like old-age pensions were emerging. In short, before World War One, most Europeans had a moderately optimistic view of the world, and with good reason.

From the 1880s on, however, a small band of serious thinkers and creative writers began to attack these well-worn optimistic ideas. These critics rejected the general faith in progress and the power of the rational human mind. Such views were greatly strengthened by the experience of history's most destructive war, which suggested to many that human beings were a pack of violent, irrational animals quite capable of tearing the individual and his or her rights to shreds. There was growing pessimism and a general crisis of the mind, and a growing chorus of thinkers, creative writers, and scientists echoed and enlarged on the themes first expressed by the small group of critics between 1880 and 1914. People did not know what to think. This disorientation was particularly acute in the 1930s, when the rapid rise of harsh dictatorships and the Great Depression transformed old certainties into bitter illusions.

No one expressed this state of uncertainty better than the French poet and critic Paul Valéry (1871–1945) in the early 1920s. Speaking of the "crisis of the mind," Valéry noted that Europe was looking at its future with dark foreboding:

The storm has died away, and still we are restless, uneasy, as if the storm were about to break. Almost all the affairs of men remain in a terrible uncertainty. We think of what has disappeared, and we are almost destroyed by what has been destroyed; we do not know what will be born, and we fear the future, not without reason. . . . Doubt and disorder are in us and with us. There is no thinking man, however shrewd or learned he may be, who can hope to dominate this anxiety, to escape from this impression of darkness.[1]

In the midst of economic, political, and social disruptions Valéry saw the "cruelly injured mind," besieged by doubts and suffering from anxieties. This was the general intellectual crisis of the twentieth century, which touched almost every field of

"The War, as I Saw It"   This was the title of a series of grotesque drawings that appeared in 1920 in *Simplicissimus,* Germany's leading satirical magazine. Nothing shows better the terrible impact of World War One than this profoundly disturbing example of expressionist art. *(Source: Caroline Buckler)*

thought. The implications of new ideas and discoveries in philosophy, physics, psychology, and literature played a central role in this crisis, disturbing "thinking people" everywhere.

Modern Philosophy

Among those thinkers in the late nineteenth century who challenged the belief in progress and the general faith in the rational human mind, the German philosopher Friedrich Nietzsche (1844–1900) was particularly influential. Nietzsche believed that Western civilization had lost its creativity and decayed into mediocrity. Christianity's "slave morality" had glorified weakness and humility. Furthermore, human beings in the West had overstressed rational thinking at the expense of passion and emotion. Nietzsche viewed the pillars of conventional morality—reason, democracy, progress, respectability—as outworn social and psychological constructs whose influence was suffocating any

creativity. The only hope of revival was for a few superior individuals to free themselves from the hum-
drum thinking of the masses and embrace life passionately. Such individuals would become true
heroes, supermen capable of leading the dumb
herd of inferior men and women. Nietzsche also
condemned both political democracy and greater
social equality.

The growing dissatisfaction with established
ideas before 1914 was apparent in other important
thinkers. In the 1890s, the French philosophy professor Henri Bergson (1859–1941) convinced
many young people through his writing that immediate experience and intuition are as important as
rational and scientific thinking for understanding
reality. Indeed, according to Bergson, a religious
experience or a mystical poem is often more accessible to human comprehension than a scientific law
or a mathematical equation.

Another thinker who agreed about the limits of
rational thinking was the French socialist Georges
Sorel (1847–1922). Sorel frankly characterized
Marxian socialism as an inspiring but unprovable
religion rather than a rational scientific truth. Socialism would come to power, he believed, through
a great, violent strike of all working people, which
would miraculously shatter capitalist society. Sorel
rejected democracy and believed that the masses of
the new socialist society would have to be tightly
controlled by a small revolutionary elite.

The First World War accelerated the revolt
against established certainties in philosophy, but
that revolt went in two very different directions. In
English-speaking countries, the main development
was the acceptance of logical empiricism (or logical
positivism) in university circles. In continental
countries, where esoteric and remote logical empiricism has never won many converts, the primary
development in philosophy was existentialism.

Logical empiricism was truly revolutionary. It
quite simply rejected most of the concerns of traditional philosophy, from the existence of God to the
meaning of happiness, as nonsense and hot air.
This outlook began primarily with the Austrian
philosopher Ludwig Wittgenstein (1889–1951),
who later emigrated to England, where he trained
numerous disciples.

Wittgenstein argued in his pugnacious *Tractatus
Logico-Philosophicus (Essay on Logical Philosophy)* in
1922 that philosophy is only the logical clarification of thoughts, and therefore it becomes the
study of language, which expresses thoughts. The
great philosophical issues of the ages—God, freedom, morality, and so on—are quite literally senseless, a great waste of time, for statements about
them can neither be tested by scientific experiments
nor demonstrated by the logic of mathematics.
Statements about such matters reflect only the personal preferences of a given individual. As Wittgenstein put it in the famous last sentence of his work,
"Of what one cannot speak, of that one must keep
silent." Logical empiricism, which has remained
dominant in England and the United States to this
day, drastically reduced the scope of philosophical
inquiry. Anxious people could find few if any answers in this direction.

Highly diverse and even contradictory, *existential*
thinkers were loosely united in a courageous search
for moral values in a world of terror and uncertainty. Theirs were true voices of the age of anxiety.

Most existential thinkers in the twentieth century have been atheists. Like Nietzsche, who had already proclaimed that "God is dead," they did not
believe a supreme being had established humanity's
fundamental nature and given life its meaning. In
the words of the famous French existentialist Jean-
Paul Sartre (1905–1980), human beings simply
exist: "They turn up, appear on the scene." Only
after they "turn up" do they seek to define themselves. Honest human beings are terribly alone, for
there is no God to help them. They are hounded by
despair and the meaninglessness of life. The crisis
of the existential thinker epitomized the modern
intellectual crisis—the shattering of traditional beliefs in God, reason, and progress.

Existentialists did recognize that human beings,
unless they kill themselves, must act. Indeed, in the
words of Sartre, "man is condemned to be free."
There is, therefore, the possibility—indeed, the necessity—of giving meaning to life through actions,
of defining oneself through choices. To do so, individuals must become "engaged" and choose their
own actions courageously, consistently, and in full
awareness of their inescapable responsibility for
their own behavior. In the end, existentialists argued, human beings can overcome the absurdity
that existentialists saw in life.

Modern existentialism developed first in Germany in the 1920s, when the philosophers Martin
Heidegger and Karl Jaspers found a sympathetic
audience among disillusioned postwar university
students. But it was in France during the years immediately after World War Two that existentialism
came of age. The terrible conditions of the war

reinforced the existential view of life and the existential approach to it. On the one hand, the armies of the German dictator Hitler had conquered most of Europe and unleashed a hideous reign of barbarism. On the other, men and women had more than ever to define themselves by their actions. Specifically, each individual had to choose whether to join the Resistance against Hitler or to accept and even abet tyranny. The writings of Sartre, who along with Albert Camus (1913–1960) was the leading French existentialist, became enormously influential. Himself active in the Resistance, Sartre and his colleagues offered a powerful answer to profound moral issues and the contemporary crisis.

The Revival of Christianity

Christianity and religion in general had been on the defensive in intellectual circles since the Enlightenment, especially during the late nineteenth century. But the loss of faith in human reason and in continual progress now led to a renewed interest in the Christian view of the world in the twentieth century. A number of thinkers and theologians began to revitalize the fundamentals of Christianity, especially after World War One. They had a powerful impact on society. Sometimes described as Christian existentialists because they shared the loneliness and despair of atheistic existentialists, they revived the tradition of Saint Augustine. They stressed human beings' sinful nature, the need for faith, and the mystery of God's forgiveness.

This development was a break with the late nineteenth century. In the years before 1914, some theologians, especially Protestant theologians, had felt the need to interpret Christian doctrine and the Bible so that they did not seem to contradict science, evolution, and common sense. Christ was therefore seen primarily as the greatest moral teacher, and the "supernatural" aspects of his divinity were strenuously played down. An important if extreme example of this tendency was the young Albert Schweitzer's *Quest of the Historical Jesus* (1906). A theologian and later a famous medical missionary and musician of note, Schweitzer (1875–1965) argued that Christ while on earth was a completely natural man whose teachings had been only temporary rules to prepare himself and his disciples for the end of the world, which they were erroneously expecting. In short, some modern theologians were embarrassed by the miraculous, unscientific aspects of Christianity and turned away from them.

The revival of fundamental Christian belief after World War One was fed by rediscovery of the work of the nineteenth-century Danish religious philosopher Søren Kierkegaard (1813–1855), whose ideas became extremely influential. Kierkegaard had rejected formalistic religion and denounced the worldliness of the Danish Lutheran church. He had eventually resolved his personal anguish over his imperfect nature by making a total religious commitment to a remote and majestic God.

Similar ideas were brilliantly developed by the Swiss Protestant theologian Karl Barth (1886–1968), whose many influential writings after 1920 sought to re-create the religious intensity of the Reformation. For Barth, the basic fact about human beings is that they are imperfect, sinful creatures, whose reason and will are hopelessly flawed. Religious truth is therefore made known to human beings only through God's grace. People have to accept God's word and the supernatural revelation of Jesus Christ with awe, trust, and obedience. Lowly mortals should not expect to "reason out" God and his ways.

Among Catholics, the leading existential Christian thinker was Gabriel Marcel (1887–1973). Born into a cultivated French family, where his atheistic father was "gratefully aware of all that . . . art owed to Catholicism but regarded Catholic thought itself as obsolete and tainted with absurd superstitions,"[2] Marcel found in the Catholic church an answer to what he called the postwar "broken world." Catholicism and religious belief provided the hope, humanity, honesty, and piety for which he hungered. Flexible and gentle, Marcel and his countryman Jacques Maritain (1882–1973) denounced anti-Semitism and supported closer ties with non-Catholics.

After 1914 religion became much more relevant and meaningful to thinking people than it was before the war. In addition to Marcel and Maritain, many other illustrious individuals turned to religion between about 1920 and 1950. The poets T. S. Eliot and W. H. Auden, the novelists Evelyn Waugh and Aldous Huxley, the historian Arnold Toynbee, the Oxford professor C. S. Lewis, the psychoanalyst Karl Stern, and the physicist Max Planck were all either converted to religion or attracted to it for the first time. Religion, often of a despairing, existential variety, was one meaningful answer to terror and anxiety. In the words of another famous

Roman Catholic convert, English novelist Graham Greene, "One began to believe in heaven because one believed in hell."[3]

The New Physics

Ever since the Scientific Revolution of the seventeenth century, scientific advances and their implications have greatly influenced the beliefs of thinking people. By the late nineteenth century, science was one of the main pillars supporting Western society's optimistic and rationalistic view of the world. The Darwinian concept of evolution had been accepted and assimilated in most intellectual circles. Progressive minds believed that science, unlike religion and philosophical speculation, was based on hard facts and controlled experiments. Science seemed to have achieved an unerring and almost completed picture of reality. Unchanging natural laws seemed to determine physical processes and permit useful solutions to more and more problems. All this was comforting, especially to people who were no longer committed to traditional religious beliefs. And all this was challenged by the new physics.

An important first step toward the new physics was the discovery at the end of the century that atoms were not like hard, permanent little billiard balls. They were actually composed of many far-smaller, fast-moving particles, such as electrons and protons. The Polish-born physicist Marie Curie (1867–1934) and her French husband discovered that radium constantly emits subatomic particles and thus does not have a constant atomic weight. Building on this and other work in radiation, the German physicist Max Planck (1858–1947) showed in 1900 that subatomic energy is emitted in uneven little spurts, which Planck called "quanta," and not in a steady stream as previously believed. Planck's discovery called into question the old sharp distinction between matter and energy; the implication was that matter and energy might be different forms of the same thing. The old view of atoms as the stable, basic building blocks of nature, with a different kind of unbreakable atom for each of the ninety-two chemical elements, was badly shaken.

In 1905 the German-born Jewish genius Albert Einstein (1879–1955) went further than the Curies and Planck in challenging Newtonian physics. His famous theory of special relativity postulated that time and space are not absolute, but relative to the viewpoint of the observer. To clarify Einstein's idea, consider a person riding on a train. From the viewpoint of an observer outside the train, the passenger's net speed is exactly the same whether the passenger is walking or sitting. From the passenger's viewpoint, walking to the restaurant car is different from sitting in a seat. The closed framework of Newtonian physics was quite limited compared to that of Einsteinian physics,

Lord Rutherford   The great physicist Ernest Rutherford split the atom in 1919 with a small device he could hold in his hands. Here he is seen with a colleague in Cambridge University's renowned Cavendish Laboratory in 1932, when scientific laboratories engaged in pure research were still relatively small. *(Source: Cavendish Laboratory, Cambridge University/C. E. Wynn-Williams)*

which unified an apparently infinite universe with the incredibly small, fast-moving subatomic world. Moreover, Einstein's theory stated clearly that matter and energy are interchangeable and that all matter contains enormous levels of potential energy.

The 1920s opened the "heroic age of physics," in the apt words of one of its leading pioneers, Ernest Rutherford (1871–1937). Breakthrough followed breakthrough. In 1919 Rutherford showed that the atom could be split. By 1944 seven subatomic particles had been identified, of which the most important was the neutron. The neutron's capacity to pass through other atoms allowed for even more intense experimental bombardment of matter, leading to chain reactions of unbelievable force. This was the road to the atomic bomb.

Although few nonscientists understood the revolution in physics, the implications of the new theories and discoveries, as presented by newspapers and popular writers, were disturbing to millions of men and women in the 1920s and 1930s. The new universe was strange and troubling. It lacked any absolute objective reality. Everything was "relative," that is, dependent on the observer's frame of reference. Moreover, the universe was uncertain and undetermined, without stable building blocks. In 1927 the German physicist Werner Heisenberg (1901–1976) formulated the "principle of uncertainty." Heisenberg's principle postulates that, because it is impossible to know the position and speed of an individual electron, it is therefore impossible to predict its behavior. Instead of Newton's dependable, rational laws, there seemed to be only tendencies and probabilities in an extraordinarily complex and uncertain universe.

Moreover, a universe described by abstract mathematical symbols seemed to have little to do with human experience and human problems. When, for example, Max Planck was asked what science could contribute to resolving conflicts of values, his response was simple: "Science is not qualified to speak to this question." Physics, the queen of the sciences, no longer provided people easy, optimistic answers—nor, for that matter, did it provide any answers at all.

Freudian Psychology

With physics presenting an uncertain universe so unrelated to ordinary human experience, questions regarding the power and potential of the human mind assumed special significance. The findings and speculations of the leading psychologist, Sigmund Freud (see page 781), were particularly disturbing.

Before Freud, poets and mystics had probed the unconscious and irrational aspects of human behavior. But most professional, "scientific" psychologists assumed that a single, unified conscious mind processed sense experiences in a rational and logical way. Human behavior in turn was the result of rational calculation—of "thinking"—by the conscious mind. Basing his insights on the analysis of dreams and of hysteria, Freud developed a very different view of the human psyche beginning in the late 1880s.

According to Freud, human behavior is basically irrational. The key to understanding the mind is the primitive, irrational unconscious, which he called the *id*. The unconscious is driven by sexual, aggressive, and pleasure-seeking desires and is locked in a constant battle with the other parts of the mind: the rationalizing conscious (the *ego*), which mediates what a person *can* do, and ingrained moral values (the *superego*), which tell what a person *should* do. Human behavior is a product of fragile compromise between instinctual drives and the controls of rational thinking and moral values. Since the instinctual drives are extremely powerful, the ever-present danger for individuals and whole societies is that unacknowledged drives will overwhelm the control mechanisms in a violent, distorted way. Yet Freud also agreed with Nietzsche that the mechanisms of rational thinking and traditional moral values can be too strong. They can repress sexual desires too effectively, crippling individuals and entire peoples with guilt and neurotic fears.

Freudian psychology and clinical psychiatry had become an international movement by 1910, but only after 1918 did they receive popular attention, especially in the Protestant countries of northern Europe and in the United States. Many opponents and even some enthusiasts interpreted Freud as saying that the first requirement for mental health is an uninhibited sex life. Thus, after the First World War, the popular interpretation of Freud reflected and encouraged growing sexual experimentation, particularly among middle-class women. For more serious students, the psychology of Freud and his followers drastically undermined the old, easy optimism about the rational and progressive nature of the human mind.

Munch: The Dance of Life Like his contemporary Sigmund Freud, the expressionist painter Edvard Munch studied the turmoil and fragility of human thought and action. Solitary figures struggling with fear and uncertainty dominate his work. Here the girl in white represents innocence, the tense woman in black stands for mourning and rejection and the woman in red evokes the joy of passing pleasure. *(Source: © Nasjonalgalleriet, Oslo. Photo: Jacques Lathion)*

Twentieth-century Literature

Literature articulated the general intellectual climate of pessimism, relativism, and alienation. Novelists developed new techniques to express new realities. The great nineteenth-century novelists had typically written as all-knowing narrators, describing realistic characters and their relationship to an understandable if sometimes harsh society. In the twentieth century, most major writers adopted the limited, often confused viewpoint of a single individual. Like Freud, these novelists focused their attention on the complexity and irrationality of the human mind, where feelings, memories, and desires are forever scrambled. The great French novelist Marcel Proust (1871–1922), in his semi-autobiographical *Remembrance of Things Past*

(1913–1927), recalled bittersweet memories of childhood and youthful love and tried to discover their innermost meaning. To do so, Proust lived like a hermit in a soundproof Paris apartment for ten years, withdrawing from the present to dwell on the past.

Serious novelists also used the "stream-of-consciousness" technique to explore the psyche. In *Jacob's Room* (1922), Virginia Woolf (1882–1941) turned the novel into a series of internal monologues, in which ideas and emotions from different periods of time bubble up as randomly as from a patient on a psychoanalyst's couch. William Faulkner (1897–1962), perhaps America's greatest twentieth-century novelist, used the same technique in *The Sound and the Fury*, much of whose intense drama is confusedly seen through the eyes of an idiot. The most famous stream-of-consciousness novel—and surely the most disturbing novel of its generation—is *Ulysses,* which the Irish novelist James Joyce (1882–1941) published in 1922. Into *Ulysses'* account of an ordinary day in the life of an ordinary man, Joyce weaves an extended ironic parallel between his hero's aimless wanderings through the streets and pubs of Dublin and the adventures of Homer's hero *Ulysses* on his way home from Troy. Abandoning conventional grammar and blending foreign words, puns, bits of knowledge, and scraps of memory together in bewildering confusion, the language of Ulysses is intended to mirror modern life itself: a gigantic riddle waiting to be unraveled.

As creative writers turned their attention from society to the individual and from realism to psychological relativity, they rejected the idea of progress. Some even described "anti-utopias," nightmare visions of things to come. In 1918 an obscure German high school teacher named Oswald Spengler (1880–1936) published *The Decline of the West,* which quickly became an international sensation. According to Spengler, every culture experiences a life cycle of growth and decline. Western civilization, in Spengler's opinion, was in its old age, and death was approaching in the form of conquest by the yellow race. T. S. Eliot (1888–1965), in his famous poem *The Waste Land* (1922), depicted a world of growing desolation, although after his conversion to Anglo-Catholicism in 1927, Eliot came to hope cautiously for humanity's salvation. No such hope appeared in the work of Franz Kafka (1883–1924), whose novels *The Trial* and *The Castle,* as well as several of his greatest short stories, portray helpless individuals crushed by inexplicably hostile forces. The German-Jewish Kafka died young, at forty-one, and so did not see the world of his nightmares materialize in the Nazi state.

The Englishman George Orwell (1903–1950), however, had seen both that reality and its Stalinist counterpart by 1949 when he wrote perhaps the ultimate in anti-utopian literature: *1984.* Orwell set the action in the future, in 1984. Big Brother—the dictator—and his totalitarian state use a new kind of language, sophisticated technology, and psychological terror to strip a weak individual of his last shred of human dignity. The supremely self-confident chief of the Thought Police tells the tortured, broken, and framed Winston Smith: "If you want a picture of the future, imagine a boot stamping on a human face—forever."[4] A phenomenal best seller, *1984* spoke to millions of people in the closing years of the age of anxiety.

MODERN ART AND MUSIC

Throughout the twentieth century, there has been considerable unity in the arts. The "modernism" of the immediate prewar years and the 1920s is still strikingly modern. Manifestations of modernism in art, architecture, and music have of course been highly varied, just as in physics, psychology, and philosophy; yet there are resemblances, for artists, scientists, and original thinkers partake of the same

Virginia Woolf Her novels captured sensations like impressionist paintings, and her home attracted a circle of artists and writers known as the Bloomsbury Group. Many of Woolf's essays dealt with women's issues and urged greater opportunity for women's creativity. *(Source: © Gisèle Freund/Photo Researchers)*

culture. Creative artists rejected old forms and old values. Modernism in art and music meant constant experimentation and a search for new kinds of expression. And though many people find the modern visions of the arts strange, disturbing, and even ugly, the twentieth century, so dismal in many respects, will probably stand as one of Western civilization's great artistic eras.

Architecture and Design

Modernism in the arts was loosely unified by a revolution in architecture. The architectural revolution not only gave the other arts striking new settings, it intended nothing less than to transform the physical framework of the urban society according to a new principle: *functionalism*. Buildings, like

Frank Lloyd Wright: The "Falling Water" House Often considered Wright's masterpiece, Falling Water combines modern architectural concepts with close attention to a spectacular site. Anchored to a high rock ledge by means of reinforced concrete, the house soars out over a cascading waterfall at Bear Run in western Pennsylvania. Built in 1937 for a Pittsburgh businessman, Falling Water is now open to the public and attracts 70,000 visitors each year. *(Source: Western Pennsylvania Conservancy/Art Resource)*

industrial products, should be useful and "functional": that is, they should serve, as well as possible, the purpose for which they were made. Thus architects and designers had to work with engineers, town planners, and even sanitation experts. Moreover, they had to throw away useless ornamentation and find beauty and aesthetic pleasure in the clean lines of practical constructions and efficient machinery. The Viennese pioneer Adolf Loos (1870–1933) quite typically equated ornamentation with crime, and the Franco-Swiss genius Le Corbusier (1887–1965) insisted that "a house is a machine for living in."[5]

The United States, with its rapid urban growth and lack of rigid building traditions, pioneered in the new architecture. In the 1890s the Chicago school of architects, led by Louis H. Sullivan (1856–1924), used cheap steel, reinforced concrete, and electric elevators to build skyscrapers and office buildings lacking almost any exterior ornamentation. In the first decade of the twentieth century, Sullivan's student Frank Lloyd Wright (1869–1959) built a series of radically new and truly modern houses featuring low lines, open interiors, and mass-produced building materials. Europeans were inspired by these and other American examples of functional construction as the massive, unadorned grain elevators of the Midwest.

Around 1905, when the first really modern buildings were going up in Europe, architectural leadership shifted to the German-speaking countries and remained there until Hitler took power in 1933. In 1911 the twenty-eight-year-old Walter Gropius (1883–1969) broke sharply with the past in his design of the Fagus shoe factory at Alfeld, Germany. A clean, light, elegant building of glass and iron, Gropius's new factory represented a jump right into the middle of the century.

After the First World War, the new German republic gave Gropius the authority to merge the schools of fine and applied arts at Weimar into a single, interdisciplinary school, the Bauhaus. In spite of intense criticism from conservative politicians and university professors, the Bauhaus brought together many leading modern architects, artists, designers, and theatrical innovators, who worked as an effective, inspired team. Throwing out traditional teaching methods, they combined the study of fine art, such as painting and sculpture, with the study of applied art in the crafts of printing, weaving, and furniture making. Through-

out the 1920s, the Bauhaus, with its stress on functionalism and good design for everyday life, attracted enthusiastic students from all over the world. It had a great and continuing impact.

Along with Gropius, the architect and town planner Le Corbusier had a revolutionary influence on the development of modern architecture. Often drawing his inspiration from industrial forms, such as ocean liners, automobiles, and airplanes, Le Corbusier designed houses with flat roofs, open interior spaces, and clear, clean lines. His famous Savoy Villa at Poissy rested on concrete pillars and seemed to float on air. A true visionary, Le Corbusier sketched plans for a city of the future, with tall buildings surrounded by playgrounds and parks.

Another leader in the modern or "international" style was Ludwig Mies van der Rohe (1886–1969), who followed Gropius as director of the Bauhaus in 1930 and emigrated to the United States in 1937. His classic Lake Shore Apartments in Chicago, built between 1948 and 1951, symbolize the triumph of steel-frame and glass-wall modern architecture, which had grown out of Sullivan's skyscrapers and German functionalism in the great building boom after the Second World War.

Modern Painting

Modern painting grew out of a revolt against French impressionism. The *impressionism* of such French painters as Claude Monet (1840–1926), Pierre Auguste Renoir (1841–1919), and Camille Pissarro (1830–1903) was, in part, a kind of "superrealism." Leaving exact copying of objects to photography, these artists sought to capture the momentary overall feeling, or impression, of light falling on a real-life scene before their eyes. By 1890, when impressionism was finally established, a few artists known as *postimpressionists,* or *expressionists,* were already striking out in new directions. After 1905 art took on the abstract, nonrepresentational character that it generally retains today.

Though individualistic in their styles, postimpressionists were united in their desire to know and depict worlds other than the visible world of fact. Like the early nineteenth-century romantics, they wanted to portray unseen, inner worlds of emotion and imagination. Like modern novelists, they wanted to express a complicated psychological view of reality as well as an overwhelming emotional intensity. In *The Starry Night* (1889), for example, the great Dutch expressionist Vincent van Gogh (1853–1890) painted the vision of his mind's eye. Flaming cypress trees, exploding stars, and a cometlike Milky Way swirl together in one great cosmic rhythm. Paul Gauguin (1848–1903), the French stockbroker-turned-painter, pioneered in expressionist techniques, though he used them to infuse his work with tranquility and mysticism. In 1891 he fled to the South Pacific in search of unspoiled beauty and a primitive way of life. Gauguin believed that the form and design of a picture was important in itself and that the painter need not try to represent objects on canvas as the eye actually saw them.

Fascination with form, as opposed to light, was characteristic of postimpressionism and expressionism. Paul Cézanne (1839–1906), who had a profound influence on twentieth-century painting, was particularly committed to form and ordered design. He told a young painter, "You must see in nature the cylinder, the sphere, and the cone."[6] As Cézanne's later work became increasingly abstract and nonrepresentational, it also moved away from the traditional three-dimensional perspective toward the two-dimensional plane, which has characterized so much of modern art. The expressionism of a group of painters led by Henri Matisse (1869–1954) was so extreme that an exhibition of their work in Paris in 1905 prompted shocked critics to call them *les fauves*—"the wild beasts." Matisse and his followers were primarily concerned, not with real objects, but with the arrangement of color, line, and form as an end in itself.

In 1907 a young Spaniard in Paris, Pablo Picasso (1881–1973), founded another movement—cubism. Cubism concentrated on a complex geometry of zigzagging lines and sharp-angled, overlapping planes. About three years later came the ultimate stage in the development of abstract, nonrepresentational art. Artists such as the Russian-born Wassily Kandinsky (1866–1944) turned away from nature completely. "The observer," said Kandinsky, "must learn to look at [my] pictures . . . as form and color combinations . . . as a representation of mood and not as a representation of *objects*."[7] On the eve of the First World War, extreme expressionism and abstract painting were developing rapidly not only in Paris but also in Russia and Germany. Modern art had become international.

In the 1920s and 1930s, the artistic movements of the prewar years were extended and consolidated. The most notable new developments were *dadaism* and *surrealism.* Dadaism attacked all accepted standards of art and behavior, delighting in outrageous conduct. Its name, from the French word *dada,* meaning "hobbyhorse," is deliberately nonsensical. A famous example of dadaism was a reproduction of Leonardo da Vinci's Mona Lisa in which the famous woman with the mysterious smile sports a mustache and is ridiculed with an obscene inscription. After 1924 many dadaists were attracted to surrealism, which became very influential in art in the late 1920s and 1930s. Surrealism was inspired to a great extent by Freudian psychology. Surrealists painted a fantastic world of wild dreams and complex symbols, where watches melted and giant metronomes beat time in precisely drawn but impossible alien landscapes.

Refusing to depict ordinary visual reality, surrealist painters made powerful statements about the age of anxiety. Picasso's 26-foot-long mural *Guernica* (1937) masterfully unites several powerful strands in twentieth-century art. Inspired by the Spanish Civil War, the painting commemorates the bombing of the ancient Spanish town of Guernica by fascist planes, an attack that took the lives of a thousand people—one out of every eight inhabitants—in a single night of terror. Combining the free distortion of expressionism, the overlapping planes of cubism, and the surrealist fascination with grotesque subject matter, *Guernica* is what Picasso meant it to be: an unforgettable attack on "brutality and darkness."

Modern Music

Developments in modern music were strikingly parallel to those in painting. Composers, too, were attracted by the emotional intensity of expressionism. The ballet *The Rite of Spring* by Igor Stravinsky (1882–1971) practically caused a riot when it was first performed in Paris in 1913 by Sergei Diaghilev's famous Russian dance company. The combination of pulsating, barbaric rhythms from the orchestra pit and an earthy representation of lovemaking by the dancers on the stage seemed a shocking, almost pornographic enactment of a primitive fertility rite.

Picasso: Guernica In this rich, complex work a shrieking woman falls from a burning house on the far right. On the left a woman holds a dead child, while toward the center are fragments of a warrior and a screaming horse pierced by a spear. Picasso has used only the mournful colors of black, white, and gray. *(Source: Pablo Picasso, Guernica (1937, May–early June). Oil on canvas.© SPADEM, Paris/VAGA, New York, 1982)*

After the experience of the First World War, when irrationality and violence seemed to pervade the human experience, expressionism in opera and ballet flourished. One of the most famous and powerful examples is the opera *Wozzeck* by Alban Berg (1885–1935), first performed in Berlin in 1925. Blending a half-sung, half-spoken kind of dialogue with harsh, atonal music, *Wozzeck* is a gruesome tale of a soldier driven by Kafka-like inner terrors and vague suspicions of unfaithfulness to murder his mistress.

Some composers turned their backs on long-established musical conventions. As abstract painters arranged lines and color but did not draw identifiable objects, so modern composers arranged sounds without creating recognizable harmonies. Led by the Viennese composer Arnold Schönberg (1874–1951), they abandoned traditional harmony and tonality. The musical notes in a given piece were no longer united and organized by a key; instead they were independent and unrelated. Schönberg's twelve-tone music of the 1920s arranged all twelve notes of the scale in an abstract, mathematical pattern, or "tone row." This pattern sounded like no pattern at all to the ordinary listener and could be detected only by a highly trained eye studying the musical score. Accustomed to the harmonies of classical and romantic music, audiences generally resisted modern atonal music. Only after the Second World War did it begin to win acceptance.

MOVIES AND RADIO

Until after World War Two at the earliest, these revolutionary changes in art and music appealed mainly to a minority of "highbrows" and not to the general public. That public was primarily and enthusiastically wrapped up in movies and radio. The long-declining traditional arts and amusements of people in villages and small towns almost vanished, replaced by standardized, commercial entertainment.

Moving pictures were first shown as a popular novelty in naughty peepshows—"What the Butler Saw"—and penny arcades in the 1890s, especially in Paris. The first movie houses date from an experiment in Los Angeles in 1902. They quickly attracted large audiences and led to the production of short, silent action films like the eight-minute

The Great Dictator In 1940 the great actor and director, Charlie Chaplin, abandoned the little tramp to satirize the great dictator, Adolph Hitler. Chaplin had strong political views and made a number of films with political themes as the escapist fare of the Great Depression gave way to the reality of the Second World War. *(Source: The Museum of Modern Art/Still Film Archives)*

Great Train Robbery of 1903. American directors and business people then set up "movie factories," at first in the New York area and after 1910 in Los Angeles. These factories churned out two short films each week. On the eve of the First World War, full-length feature films like the Italian *Quo Vadis* and the American *Birth of a Nation,* coupled with improvements in the quality of pictures, suggested the screen's vast possibilities.

During the First World War the United States became the dominant force in the rapidly expanding silent-film industry. In the 1920s, Mack Sennett (1884–1960) and his zany Keystone Cops specialized in short, slapstick comedies noted for frantic automobile chases, custard-pie battles, and gorgeous bathing beauties. Screen stars such as Mary Pickford and Lillian Gish, Douglas Fairbanks and

Rudolph Valentino became household names, with their own "fan clubs." Yet Charlie Chaplin (1889–1978), a funny little Englishman working in Hollywood, was unquestionably the king of the "silver screen" in the 1920s. In his enormously popular role as a lonely tramp, complete with baggy trousers, battered derby, and an awkward, shuffling walk, Chaplin symbolized the "gay spirit of laughter in a cruel, crazy world."[8] Chaplin also demonstrated that, in the hands of a genius, the new medium could combine mass entertainment and artistic accomplishment.

The early 1920s were also the great age of German films. Protected and developed during the war, the large German studios excelled in bizarre expressionist dramas, beginning with *The Cabinet of Dr. Caligari* in 1919. Unfortunately, their period of creativity was short-lived. By 1926 American money was drawing the leading German talents to Hollywood and consolidating America's international domination. Film making was big business, and European theater owners were forced to book whole blocks of American films to get the few pictures they really wanted. This system put European producers at a great disadvantage until "talkies" permitted a revival of national film industries in the 1930s, particularly in France.

Whether foreign or domestic, motion pictures became the main entertainment of the masses until after the Second World War. In Great Britain one in every four adults went to the movies twice a week in the late 1930s, and two in five went at least once a week. Continental countries had similar figures. The greatest appeal of motion pictures was that they offered ordinary people a temporary escape from the hard realities of everyday life. For an hour or two the moviegoer could flee the world of international tensions, uncertainty, unemployment, and personal frustrations. The appeal of escapist entertainment was especially strong during the Great Depression. Millions flocked to musical comedies featuring glittering stars such as Ginger Rogers and Fred Astaire and to the fanciful cartoons of Mickey Mouse and his friends.

Radio became possible with the transatlantic "wireless" communication of Guglielmo Marconi (1874–1937) in 1901 and the development of the vacuum tube in 1904, which permitted the transmission of speech and music. But only in 1920 were the first major public broadcasts of special events made in Great Britain and the United States. Lord Northcliffe, who had pioneered in journalism with the inexpensive, mass-circulation *Daily Mail,* sponsored a broadcast of "only one artist . . . the world's very best, the soprano Nellie Melba."[9] Singing from London in English, Italian, and French, Melba was heard simultaneously all over Europe on June 16, 1920. This historic event captured the public's imagination. The meteoric career of radio was launched.

Every major country quickly established national broadcasting networks. In the United States, such networks were privately owned and financed by advertising. In Great Britain, Parliament set up an independent, high-minded public corporation, the British Broadcasting Corporation (BBC), which was supported by licensing fees. Elsewhere in Europe, the typical pattern was direct control by the government.

Whatever the institutional framework, radio became popular and influential. By the late 1930s, more than three out of every four households in both democratic Great Britain and dictatorial Germany had at least one cheap, mass-produced radio. In other European countries, radio ownership was not quite so widespread, but the new medium was no less important.

Radio in unscrupulous hands was particularly well suited for political propaganda. Dictators like Mussolini and Hitler controlled the airwaves and could reach enormous national audiences with their frequent, dramatic speeches. In democratic countries, politicians such as President Franklin Roosevelt and Prime Minister Stanley Baldwin effectively used informal "fireside chats" to bolster their support.

Motion pictures also became powerful tools of indoctrination, especially in countries with dictatorial regimes. Lenin himself encouraged the development of Soviet film making, believing that the new medium was essential to the social and ideological transformation of the country. Beginning in the mid-1920s, a series of epic films, the most famous of which were directed by Sergei Eisenstein (1898–1948), brilliantly dramatized the communist view of Russian history.

In Germany, Hitler turned to a young and immensely talented woman film maker, Leni Riefenstahl (b. 1902), for a masterpiece of documentary propaganda, *The Triumph of the Will,* based on the Nazi party rally at Nuremberg in 1934. Riefenstahl combined stunning aerial photography, joyful crowds welcoming Hitler, and mass processions of young Nazi fanatics. Her film was a brilliant and all-too-powerful documentary of Germany's "Nazi rebirth." The new media of mass culture were potentially dangerous instruments of political manipulation.

THE SEARCH FOR PEACE AND POLITICAL STABILITY

As established patterns of thought and culture were challenged and mangled by the ferocious impact of World War One, so also was the political fabric stretched and torn by the consequences of the great conflict. The Versailles settlement had established a shaky truce, not a solid peace. Thus politicians and national leaders faced a gigantic task as they struggled to create a stable international order within the general context of intellectual crisis and revolutionary artistic experimentation.

The pursuit of real and lasting peace proved difficult for many reasons. Germany hated the Treaty of Versailles. France was fearful and isolated. Britain was undependable, and the United States had turned its back on European problems. Eastern Europe was in ferment, and no one could predict the future of communist Russia. Moreover, the international economic situation was poor and greatly complicated by war debts and disrupted patterns of trade. Yet for a time, from 1925 to late 1929, it appeared that peace and stability were within reach. When the subsequent collapse of the 1930s mocked these hopes, the disillusionment of liberals in the democracies was intensified.

Germany and the Western Powers

Germany was the key to lasting peace. Only under the pressure of the Allies' naval blockade and threat to extend their military occupation from the Rhineland to the rest of the country had Germany's new republican government signed the Treaty of Versailles in June 1919. To Germans of all political parties, the treaty represented a harsh, dictated peace, to be revised or repudiated as soon as possible. The treaty had neither broken nor reduced Germany, which was potentially still the strongest country in Europe. Thus the treaty had fallen between two stools: too harsh for a peace of reconciliation, too soft for a peace of conquest.

Moreover, with ominous implications for the future, France and Great Britain did not see eye to eye on Germany. By the end of 1919, France wanted to stress the harsh elements in the Treaty of Versailles. Most of the war in the west had been fought on French soil, and much of rich, industrialized northern France had been devastated. The expected costs of reconstruction were staggering; like Great Britain, France had also borrowed large sums from the United States during the war, which had to be repaid. Thus French politicians believed that massive reparations from Germany were a vital economic necessity. Moreover, if the Germans had to suffer to make the payments, the French would not be overly concerned. Having compromised with President Wilson only to be betrayed by America's failure to ratify the treaty, many French leaders saw strict implementation of all provisions of the Treaty of Versailles as France's last best hope. Large reparation payments could hold Germany down indefinitely, and France would realize its goal of security.

The British soon felt differently. Prewar Germany had been Great Britain's second-best market in the entire world, and after the war a healthy, prosperous Germany appeared to be essential to the British economy. Indeed, many English people agreed with the analysis of the young English economist John Maynard Keynes (1883–1946), who eloquently denounced the Treaty of Versailles in his famous *Economic Consequences of the Peace* (1919). According to Keynes's interpretation, astronomical reparations and harsh economic measures would indeed reduce Germany to the position of an impoverished second-rate power, but such impoverishment would increase economic hardship in all countries. Only a complete revision of the foolish treaty could save Germany—and Europe. Keynes's attack exploded like a bombshell and became very influential. It stirred deep guilt feelings about Germany in the English-speaking world, feelings that often paralyzed English and American leaders in their relations with Germany and its leaders between the First and Second World Wars.

The British were also suspicious of France's army —momentarily the largest in Europe—and France's foreign policy. Ever since 1890, France had looked to Russia as a powerful ally against Germany. But with Russia hostile and socialist, and with Britain and the United States unwilling to make any firm commitments, France turned to the newly formed states of eastern Europe for diplomatic support. In 1921 France signed a mutual defense pact with Poland and associated itself closely with the so-called Little Entente, an alliance that joined Czechoslovakia, Rumania, and Yugoslavia against defeated and bitter Hungary. The British and the French were also on cool terms because of conflicts relating to their League of Nations mandates in the Middle East.

While French and British leaders drifted in different directions, the Allied reparations commission completed its work. In April 1921 it announced that Germany had to pay the enormous sum of 132 billion gold marks ($33 billion) in annual installments of 2.5 billion gold marks. Facing possible occupation of more of its territory, the young German republic, which had been founded in Weimar but moved back to Berlin, made its first payment in 1921. Then in 1922, wracked by rapid inflation and political assassinations, and motivated by hostility and arrogance as well, the Weimar Republic announced its inability to pay more. It proposed a moratorium on reparations for three years, with the clear implication that thereafter reparations would either be drastically reduced or eliminated entirely.

The British were willing to accept this offer, but the French were not. Led by their tough-minded, legalistic prime minister, Raymond Poincaré, they decided they either had to call Germany's bluff or see the entire peace settlement dissolve to France's great disadvantage. So, despite strong British protests, France and its ally Belgium decided to pursue a firm policy. In early January 1923, French and Belgian armies began to occupy the Ruhr district, the heartland of industrial Germany, creating the most serious international crisis of the 1920s.

The Occupation of the Ruhr

The strategy of Poincaré and his French supporters was simple. Since Germany would not pay reparations in hard currency or gold, France and Belgium would collect reparations in kind—coal, steel, and machinery. If forcible collection proved impossible, France would use occupation to paralyze Germany and force it to accept the Treaty of Versailles.

Strengthened by a wave of patriotism, the German government ordered the people of the Ruhr to stop working and start resisting—passively—the French occupation. The coal mines and steel mills of the Ruhr grew silent, leaving 10 percent of Germany's total population in need of relief. The

French answer to passive resistance was to seal off, not only the Ruhr, but the entire Rhineland from the rest of Germany, letting in only enough food to prevent starvation. The French also revived plans for a separate state in the Rhineland.

By the summer of 1923, France and Germany were engaged in a great test of wills. As the German government had anticipated, French armies could not collect reparations from striking workers at gunpoint. But French occupation was indeed paralyzing Germany and its economy, for the Ruhr district normally produced 80 percent of Germany's steel and coal. Moreover, the occupation of the Ruhr turned rapid German inflation into runaway inflation. Faced with the need to support the striking Ruhr workers and their employers, the German government began to print money to pay its bills. Prices soared. People went to the store with a big bag of paper money; they returned home with a handful of groceries. German money rapidly lost all value, and so did anything else with a stated fixed value.

Runaway inflation brought about a social revolution. The accumulated savings of many retired and middle-class people were wiped out. The old middle-class virtues of thrift, caution, and self-reliance were cruelly mocked by catastrophic inflation. People told themselves that nothing had real value anymore, not even money. The German middle and lower middle classes, feeling cheated, burned with resentment. Many hated and blamed the Western governments, their own government, big business, the Jews, the workers, the communists for their misfortune. They were psychologically prepared to follow radical leaders in a crisis.

In August 1923, as the mark fell and political unrest grew throughout Germany, Gustav Stresemann assumed leadership of the government. Stresemann adopted a compromising attitude. He called off passive resistance in the Ruhr and in October agreed in principle to pay reparations, but asked for a reexamination of Germany's ability to pay. Poincaré accepted. His hard line was becoming increasingly unpopular with French citizens, and it was hated in Britain and the United States. Moreover, occupation was dreadfully expensive, and France's own currency was beginning to lose value on foreign exchange markets.

More generally, in both Germany and France, power was finally passing to the moderates, who realized that continued confrontation was a destructive, no-win situation. Thus, after five long years of

"Hands Off the Ruhr" The French occupation of the Ruhr to collect reparations payments raised a storm of patriotic protest, including this anti-French poster of 1923. *(Source: Internationaal Instituut voor Sociale Geschiedenis)*

hostility and tension culminating in a kind of undeclared war in the Ruhr in 1923, Germany and France decided to give compromise and cooperation a try. The British, and even the Americans, were willing to help. The first step was a reasonable compromise on the reparations question.

Hope in Foreign Affairs, 1924–1929

The reparations commission appointed an international committee of financial experts headed by an American banker, Charles G. Dawes, to reexamine reparations from a broad perspective. The committee made a series of recommendations known as the Dawes Plan (1924), and the plan was accepted by France, Germany, and Britain. German reparations were reduced and placed on a sliding scale, like an income tax, whereby yearly payments depended on the level of German economic prosperity. The Dawes Plan also recommended large loans to Germany, loans that could come only from the United States. These loans were to help Stresemann's government put its new currency on a firm basis and promote German recovery. In short, Germany would get private loans from the United States and pay reparations to France and Britain, thus enabling those countries to repay the large sums they owed the United States.

This circular flow of international payments was complicated and risky. For a time, though, it worked. The German republic experienced a spectacular economic recovery. By 1929 Germany's wealth and income were 50 percent greater than in 1913. With prosperity and large, continuous inflows of American capital, Germany easily paid about $1.3 billion in reparations in 1927 and 1928, enabling France and Britain to pay the United States. In 1929 the Young Plan, named after an American businessman, further reduced German reparations and formalized the link between German reparations and French-British debts to the United States. In this way the Americans, who did not have armies but who did have money, belatedly played a part in the general economic settlement, which though far from ideal facilitated the worldwide recovery of the late 1920s.

The economic settlement was matched by a political settlement. In 1925 the leaders of Europe signed a number of agreements at Locarno, Switzerland. Stresemann, who guided Germany's foreign policy until his death in 1929, had suggested a treaty with France's conciliatory Aristide Briand,

The Fruits of Germany's Inflation   In the end, currency had value only as waste paper. Here bank notes are being purchased by the bail for paper mills, along with old rags (Lumpen) and bones (Knochen). (Source: Archiv für Kunst u. Geschichte)

who had returned to office in 1924 after French voters rejected the bellicose Poincaré. By this treaty Germany and France solemnly pledged to accept their common border, and both Britain and Italy agreed to fight either country if it invaded the other. Stresemann also agreed to settle boundary disputes with Poland and Czechoslovakia by peaceful means, and France promised those countries military aid if they were attacked by Germany. For their efforts Stresemann and Briand shared the Nobel Peace Prize in 1926. The effect of the treaties of Locarno was far-reaching. For years, a "spirit of Locarno" gave Europeans a sense of growing security and stability in international affairs.

Hopes were strengthened by other developments. In 1926 Germany joined the League of Nations, where Stresemann continued his "peace offensive." In 1928 fifteen countries signed the Kellogg-Briand Pact, which "condemned and renounced war as an instrument of national policy." The signing states agreed to settle international disputes peacefully. Often seen as idealistic nonsense because it made no provisions for action in case war actually occurred, the pact was nevertheless a hopeful step. It grew out of a suggestion by Briand that France and the United States renounce the possibility of war between their two countries. Briand was gently and subtly trying to draw the United States back into involvement with Europe. When Secretary of State Frank B. Kellogg proposed a multinational pact, Briand appeared close to success. Thus the cautious optimism of the late 1920s also rested on the hope that the United States would accept its responsibilities as a great world power and consequently contribute to European stability.

Hope in Democratic Government

Domestic politics also offered reason to hope. During the occupation of the Ruhr and the great inflation, republican government in Germany had appeared on the verge of collapse. In 1923 Communists momentarily entered provincial governments, and in November an obscure nobody named Adolf Hitler leaped on a table in a beer hall in Munich and proclaimed a "national socialist revolution." But Hitler's plot was poorly organized and easily crushed, and Hitler was sentenced to prison, where he outlined his theories and program

in his book *Mein Kampf (My Struggle).* Throughout the 1920s, Hitler's National Socialist party attracted support only from a few fanatical anti-Semites, ultranationalists, and disgruntled ex-servicemen. In 1928 his party had an insignificant twelve seats in the national parliament. Indeed, after 1923 democracy seemed to take root in Weimar Germany. A new currency was established, and the economy boomed.

The moderate businessmen who tended to dominate the various German coalition governments were convinced that economic prosperity demanded good relations with the Western powers, and they supported parliamentary government at home. Stresemann himself was a man of this class, and he was the key figure in every government until his death in 1929. Elections were held regularly, and republican democracy appeared to have growing support among a majority of the Germans.

There were, however, sharp political divisions in the country. Many unrepentant nationalists and monarchists populated the right and the army. Germany's Communists were noisy and active on the left. The Communists, directed from Moscow, reserved their greatest hatred and sharpest barbs for their cousins the Social Democrats, whom they endlessly accused of betraying the revolution. The working classes were divided politically, but most supported the nonrevolutionary but socialist Social Democrats.

The situation in France had numerous similarities to that in Germany. Communists and Socialists battled for the support of the workers. After 1924 the democratically elected government rested mainly in the hands of coalitions of moderates, and business interests were well represented. France's great accomplishment was rapid rebuilding of its war-torn northern region. The expense of this undertaking led, however, to a large deficit and substantial inflation. By early 1926 the franc had fallen to 10 percent of its prewar value, causing a severe crisis. Poincaré was recalled to office, while Briand remained minister for foreign affairs. The Poincaré government proceeded to slash spending and raise taxes, restoring confidence in the economy. The franc was "saved," stabilized at about one-fifth of its prewar value. Good times prevailed until 1930.

Despite its political shortcomings, France attracted artists and writers from all over the world in the 1920s. Much of the intellectual and artistic ferment of the times flourished in Paris. As the writer

An American in Paris   The young Josephine Baker suddenly became a star when she brought an exotic African eroticism to French music halls in 1925. American blacks and Africans had a powerful impact on entertainment in Europe in the 1920s and 1930s. *(Source: Bettmann/Hulton)*

Gertrude Stein (1874–1946), a leader of the large colony of American expatriates living in Paris, later recalled, "Paris was where the twentieth century was."[10] More generally, France appealed to foreigners and the French as a harmonious combination of small businesses and family farms, of bold innovation and solid traditions.

Britain, too, faced challenges after 1920. The wartime trend toward greater social equality continued, however, helping to maintain social harmony. The great problem was unemployment. Many of Britain's best markets had been lost dur-

ing the war. In June 1921 almost 2.2 million people—23 percent of the labor force—were out of work, and throughout the 1920s unemployment hovered around 12 percent. Yet the state provided unemployment benefits of equal size to all those without jobs and supplemented those payments with subsidized housing, medical aid, and increased old-age pensions. These and other measures kept living standards from seriously declining, defused class tensions, and pointed the way toward the welfare state Britain established after World War Two.

Relative social harmony was accompanied by the rise of the Labour party as a determined champion of the working classes and of greater social equality. Committed to the kind of moderate, "revisionist" socialism that had emerged before World War One (see page 908), the Labour party replaced the Liberal party as the main opposition to the Conservatives. The new prominence of the Labour party reflected the decline of old liberal ideals of competitive capitalism, limited government control, and individual responsibility. In 1924 and 1929, the Labour party under Ramsay MacDonald governed the country with the support of the smaller Liberal party. Yet Labour moved toward socialism gradually and democratically, so that the middle classes were not overly frightened as the working classes won new benefits.

The Conservatives under Stanley Baldwin showed the same compromising spirit on social issues. The last line of Baldwin's greatest speech in March 1925 summarized his international and domestic programs: "Give us peace in our time, O Lord." Thus, in spite of such conflicts as the 1926 strike by hard-pressed coal miners, which ended in an unsuccessful general strike, social unrest in Britain was limited in the 1920s and in the 1930s as well. In 1922 Britain granted southern, Catholic Ireland full autonomy after a bitter guerrilla war, thus removing another source of prewar friction. In summary, developments in both international relations and in the domestic politics of the leading democracies gave cause for cautious optimism in the late 1920s.

THE GREAT DEPRESSION, 1929–1939

Like the Great War, the Great Depression must be spelled with capital letters. Economic depression was nothing new. Depressions occurred throughout the nineteenth century with predictable regularity, as they recur in the form of recessions and slumps to this day. What was new about this depression was its severity and duration. It struck with ever-greater intensity from 1929 to 1933, and recovery was uneven and slow. Only with the Second World War did the depression disappear in much of the world.

The social and political consequences of prolonged economic collapse were enormous. The depression shattered the fragile optimism of political leaders in the late 1920s. Mass unemployment made insecurity a reality for millions of ordinary people, who had paid little attention to the intellectual crisis or to new directions in art and ideas (Map 28.1). In desperation, people looked for leaders who would "do something." They were willing to support radical attempts to deal with the crisis by both democratic leaders and dictators.

The Economic Crisis

There is no agreement among historians and economists about why the Great Depression was so deep and lasted so long. Thus it is best to trace the course of the great collapse before trying to identify what caused it.

Though economic activity was already declining moderately in many countries by early 1929, the crash of the stock market in the United States in October of that year really started the Great Depression. The American stock market boom, which had seen stock prices double between early 1928 and September 1929, was built on borrowed money. Many wealthy investors, speculators, and people of modest means had bought stocks by paying only a small fraction of the total purchase price and borrowing the remainder from their stockbrokers. Such buying "on margin" was extremely dangerous. When prices started falling, the hard-pressed margin buyers either had to put up more money, which was often impossible, or sell their shares to pay off their brokers. Thus thousands of people started selling all at once. The result was a financial panic. Countless investors and speculators were wiped out in a matter of days or weeks.

The general economic consequences were swift and severe. Stripped of their wealth and confidence, battered investors and their fellow citizens started buying fewer goods. Production began to slow down, and unemployment began to rise. Soon the entire American economy was caught in a vicious, spiraling decline.

The financial panic in the United States triggered a worldwide financial crisis, and that crisis resulted in a drastic decline in production in country after country. Throughout the 1920s American bankers and investors had lent large amounts of capital not only to Germany but to many other countries. Many of these loans were short-term, and once

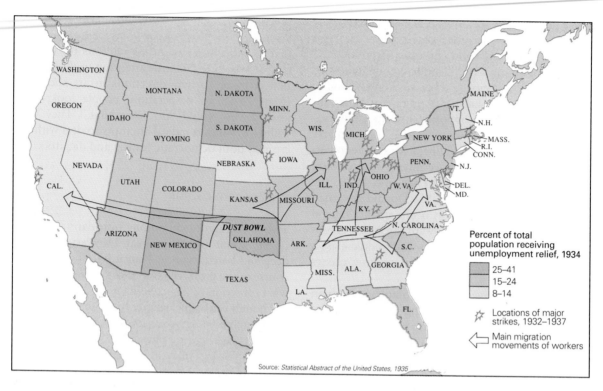

Percent of total
population receiving
unemployment relief, 1934

- 25–41
- 15–24
- 8–14

☆ Locations of major
strikes, 1932–1937

⇐ Main migration
movements of workers

Source: *Statistical Abstract of the United States, 1935*

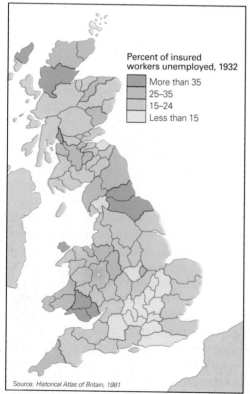

Percent of insured
workers unemployed, 1932

- More than 35
- 25–35
- 15–24
- Less than 15

Source: *Historical Atlas of Britain, 1981*

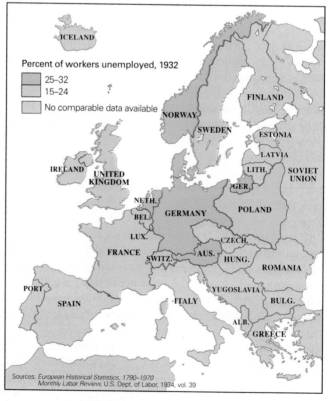

Percent of workers unemployed, 1932

- 25–32
- 15–24
- No comparable data available

Sources: *European Historical Statistics, 1790–1970*
Monthly Labor Review, U.S. Dept. of Labor, 1934, vol. 39

MAP 28.1 The Great Depression in the United States, Britain, and Europe National
and regional differences were substantial. Germany, industrial northern Britain, and
the American Middle West were particularly hard-hit.

panic broke, New York bankers began recalling them. Gold reserves thus began to flow out of European countries, particularly Germany and Austria, toward the United States. It became very hard for European business people to borrow money, and the panicky public began to withdraw its savings from the banks. These banking problems eventually led to the crash of the largest bank in Austria in 1931 and then to general financial chaos. The recall of private loans by American bankers also accelerated the collapse in world prices, as business people around the world dumped industrial goods and agricultural commodities in a frantic attempt to get cash to pay what they owed.

The financial crisis led to a general crisis of production: between 1929 and 1933, world output of goods fell by an estimated 38 percent. As this happened, each country turned inward and tried to go it alone. In 1931, for example, Britain went off the gold standard, refusing to convert bank notes into gold, and reduced the value of its money. Britain's goal was to make its goods cheaper and therefore more salable in the world market. But because more than twenty nations, including the United States in 1934, also went off the gold standard, no country gained a real advantage. Similarly, country after country followed the example of the United States when it raised protective tariffs to their highest levels ever in 1930 and tried to seal off shrinking national markets for American producers only. Within this context of fragmented and destructive economic nationalism, recovery finally began in 1933.

Although opinions differ, two factors probably best explain the relentless slide to the bottom from 1929 to early 1933. First, the international economy lacked a leadership able to maintain stability when the crisis came. Specifically, as a noted American economic historian concludes, the seriously weakened British, the traditional leaders of the world economy, "couldn't and the United States wouldn't" stabilize the international economic system in 1929.[11] The United States, which had momentarily played a positive role after the occupation of the Ruhr, cut back its international lending and erected high tariffs.

The second factor was poor national economic policy in almost every country. Governments generally cut their budgets and reduced spending when they should have run large deficits in an attempt to stimulate their economies. Since World War Two, such a "counter-cyclical policy," advocated by John

Maynard Keynes, has become a well-established weapon against depression. But in the 1930s Keynes's prescription was generally regarded with horror by orthodox economists.

Mass Unemployment

The need for large-scale government spending was tied to mass unemployment. As the financial crisis led to cuts in production, workers lost their jobs and had little money to buy goods. This led to still more cuts in production and still more unemployment, until millions were out of work. In Britain, unemployment had averaged 12 percent in the 1920s; between 1930 and 1935, it averaged more

Middle-Class Unemployment   An English office worker's unusual sandwich board poignantly summarizes the bitter despair of the unemployed in the 1930s. (*Source: Bettmann/Hulton*)

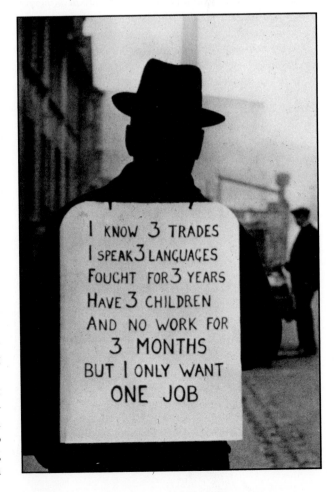

than 18 percent. Far worse was the case of the United States, where unemployment had averaged only 5 percent in the 1920s. In 1932 unemployment soared to about *one-third* of the entire labor force: fourteen million people were out of work (see Map 28.1). Only by pumping new money into the economy could the government increase demand and break the vicious cycle of decline.

Along with its economic effects, mass unemployment posed a great social problem that mere numbers cannot adequately express. Millions of people lost their spirit and dignity in an apparently hopeless search for work. Homes and ways of life were disrupted in millions of personal tragedies. Young people postponed marriages they could not afford, and birthrates fell sharply. There was an increase in suicide and mental illness. Poverty or the threat of poverty became a grinding reality. In 1932 the workers of Manchester, England, appealed to their city officials—a typical appeal echoed throughout the Western world:

We tell you that thousands of people . . . are in desperate straits. We tell you that men, women, and children are going hungry. . . . We tell you that great numbers are being rendered distraught through the stress and worry of trying to exist without work. . . .

If you do not do this—if you do not provide useful work for the unemployed—what, we ask, is your alternative? Do not imagine that this colossal tragedy of unemployment is going on endlessly without some fateful catastrophe. Hungry men are angry men.[12]

Mass unemployment was a terrible time bomb preparing to explode.

The New Deal in the United States

Of all the major industrial countries, only Germany was harder hit by the Great Depression, or reacted more radically to it, than the United States. Depression was so traumatic in the United States because the 1920s had been a period of complacent prosperity. The Great Depression and the response to it marked a major turning point in American history.

President Herbert Hoover and his administration initially reacted to the stock market crash and economic decline with dogged optimism and limited action. In May 1930 Hoover told a group of business and farm leaders, "I am convinced that we

have now passed the worst and with continued unity of effort we shall rapidly recover." When, however, the full force of the financial crisis struck Europe in the summer of 1931 and boomeranged back to the United States, people's worst fears became reality. Banks failed; unemployment soared. In 1932 industrial production fell to about 50 percent of its level in 1929. In these tragic circumstances Franklin Delano Roosevelt, an inspiring wheelchair aristocrat previously crippled by polio, won a landslide electoral victory with grand but vague promises of a "New Deal for the forgotten man."

Roosevelt's basic goal was to reform capitalism in order to preserve it. In his words, "A frank examination of the profit system in the spring of 1933 showed it to be in collapse; but substantially everybody in the United States, in public office and out of public office, from the very rich to the very poor, was as determined as was my Administration to save it."[13] Roosevelt rejected socialism and government ownership of industry in 1933. To right the situation, he chose forceful government intervention in the economy.

In this choice, Roosevelt and his advisers were greatly influenced by American experience in World War One. During the wartime emergency, the American economy had been thoroughly planned and regulated. Roosevelt and his "brain trust" of advisers adopted similar policies to restore prosperity and reduce social inequality. Roosevelt was flexible, pragmatic, and willing to experiment. Government intervention and experimentation were combined in some of the New Deal's most significant measures.

The most ambitious attempt to control and plan the economy was the National Recovery Administration (NRA), established by Congress right after Roosevelt took office. The key idea behind the NRA was to reduce competition and fix prices and wages for everyone's benefit. This goal required government, business, and labor to hammer out detailed regulations for each industry. Along with this kind of national planning in the private sector of the economy, the government believed it could sponsor enough public works projects to assure recovery. Because the NRA broke with the cherished American tradition of free competition and aroused conflicts among business people, consumers, and bureaucrats, it did not work well. By the time the NRA was declared unconstitutional in

President Roosevelt used his famous "fireside chats" to explain his changing policies and to reassure the American people that the New Deal initiatives were working. This photo captures Roosevelt's forceful personality and contagious confidence, which he conveyed over the air waves. *(Source: Brown Brothers)*

1935, Roosevelt and the New Deal were already moving away from government efforts to plan and control the entire economy.

Instead, Roosevelt and his advisers attacked the key problem of mass unemployment directly. The federal government accepted the responsibility of employing directly as many people as financially possible, something Hoover had consistently rejected. Thus, when it became clear in late 1933 that the initial program of public works was too small, new agencies were created to undertake a vast range of projects.

The most famous of these was the Works Progress Administration (WPA), set up in 1935. At its peak in late 1938, this government agency employed more than three million individuals. One-fifth of the entire labor force worked for the WPA at some point in the 1930s. To this day, thousands of public buildings, bridges, and highways built by the WPA stand as monuments to energetic govern-

ment efforts to provide people with meaningful work. The WPA was enormously popular in a nation long schooled in self-reliance and the work ethic. The hope of a job with the government helped check the threat of social revolution in the United States.

Other social measures aimed in the same direction. Following the path blazed by Germany's Bismarck in the 1880s, the U.S. government in 1935 established a national social security system, with old-age pensions and unemployment benefits, to protect many workers against some of life's uncertainties. The National Labor Relations Act of 1935 gave union organizers the green light by declaring collective bargaining to be the policy of the United States. Following some bitter strikes, such as the sit-down strike at General Motors in early 1937, union membership more than doubled, from four million in 1935 to nine million in 1940. In general, between 1935 and 1938 government rulings and social reforms chipped away at the privileges of the wealthy and tried to help ordinary people.

Yet, despite its undeniable accomplishments in social reform, the New Deal was only partly successful as a response to the Great Depression. At the height of the recovery, in May 1937, seven million workers were still unemployed. The economic situation then worsened seriously in the recession of 1937 and 1938. Production fell sharply, and although unemployment never again reached the fifteen million mark of 1933, it hit eleven million in 1938 and was still a staggering ten million when war broke out in Europe in September 1939.

The New Deal never did pull the United States out of the depression. This failure frustrated Americans then, and it is still puzzling today. Perhaps, as some have claimed, Roosevelt should have used his enormous popularity and prestige in 1933 to nationalize the banks, the railroads, and some heavy industry, so that national economic planning could have been successful. On the other hand, Roosevelt's sharp attack on big business and the wealthy after 1935 had popular appeal but also damaged business confidence and made the great capitalists uncooperative. Given the low level of profit and the underutilization of many factories, however, it is questionable whether business would have behaved much differently even if the New Deal had catered to it.

Finally, it is often argued that the New Deal did not put enough money into the economy through deficit financing. Like his predecessors in the White House, Roosevelt was attached to the ideal of the balanced budget. His largest deficit was only $4.4 billion in 1936. Compare this figure with deficits of $21.5 billion in 1942 and $57.4 billion in 1943, when the nation was prosperously engaged in total war and unemployment had vanished. By 1945 many economists concluded that the New Deal's deficit-financed public works had been too small a step in the right direction. These Keynesian views were to be very influential in economic policy in Europe and America after the Second World War.

The Scandinavian Response to Depression

Of all the Western democracies, the Scandinavian countries under Socialist leadership responded most successfully to the challenge of the Great Depression. Having grown steadily in number in the late nineteenth century, the Socialists became the largest political party in Sweden and then in Norway after the First World War. In the 1920s they passed important social reform legislation for both peasants and workers, gained practical administrative experience, and developed a unique kind of socialism. Flexible and nonrevolutionary, Scandinavian socialism grew out of a strong tradition of cooperative community action. Even before 1900, Scandinavian agricultural cooperatives had shown how individual peasant families could join together for everyone's benefit. Labor leaders and capitalists were also inclined to work together.

When the economic crisis struck in 1929, Socialist governments in Scandinavia built on this pattern of cooperative social action. Sweden in particular pioneered in the use of large-scale deficits to finance public works and thereby maintain production and employment. Scandinavian governments also increased social welfare benefits, from old-age pensions and unemployment insurance to subsidized housing and maternity allowances. All this spending required a large bureaucracy and high taxes, first on the rich and then on practically everyone. Yet both private and cooperative enterprise thrived, as did democracy. Some observers saw Scandinavia's welfare socialism as an appealing "middle way" between sick capitalism and cruel communism or fascism.

Recovery and Reform in Britain and France

In Britain, MacDonald's Labour government and then, after 1931, the Conservative-dominated coalition government followed orthodox economic theory. The budget was balanced, but unemployed workers received barely enough welfare to live. Despite government lethargy, the economy recovered considerably after 1932. By 1937 total production was about 20 percent higher than in 1929. In fact, for Britain the years after 1932 were actually somewhat better than the 1920s had been, quite the opposite of the situation in the United States and France.

This good, but by no means brilliant, performance reflected the gradual reorientation of the British economy. After going off the gold standard in 1931 and establishing protective tariffs in 1932, Britain concentrated increasingly on the national rather than the international market. The old export industries of the Industrial Revolution, such as textiles and coal, continued to decline, but the new industries like automobiles and electrical appliances grew in response to British home demand. Moreover, low interest rates encouraged a housing boom. By the end of the decade there were highly visible differences between the old, depressed industrial areas of the north and the new, growing areas of the south. These developments encouraged Britain to look inward and avoid unpleasant foreign questions.

Because France was relatively less industrialized and more isolated from the world economy, the Great Depression came late. But once the depression hit France, it stayed and stayed. Decline was steady until 1935, and the short-lived recovery never brought production or employment back up to predepression levels. Economic stagnation both reflected and heightened an ongoing political crisis. There was no stability in government. As before 1914, the French parliament was made up of many political parties, which could never cooperate for very long. In 1933, for example, five coalition cabinets formed and fell in rapid succession.

The French lost the underlying unity that had made governmental instability bearable before 1914. Fascist-type organizations agitated against parliamentary democracy and looked to Mussolini's Italy and Hitler's Germany for inspiration. In February 1934, French fascists and semifascists rioted and threatened to overturn the republic. At the same time, the Communist party and many workers opposed to the existing system were looking to Stalin's Russia for guidance. The vital center of moderate republicanism was sapped from both sides.

Frightened by the growing strength of the fascists at home and abroad, the Communists, the Socialists, and the Radicals formed an alliance—the Popular Front—for the national elections of May 1936. Their clear victory reflected the trend toward polarization. The number of Communists in the parliament jumped dramatically from 10 to 72, while the Socialists, led by Léon Blum, became the strongest party in France with 146 seats. The really quite moderate Radicals slipped badly, and the conservatives lost ground to the semifascists.

In the next few months, Blum's Popular Front government made the first and only real attempt to deal with the social and economic problems of the 1930s in France. Inspired by Roosevelt's New Deal, the Popular Front encouraged the union movement and launched a far-reaching program of social reform, complete with paid vacations and a forty-hour workweek. Popular with workers and the lower middle class, these measures were quickly sabotaged by rapid inflation and cries of revolution from fascists and frightened conservatives. Wealthy people sneaked their money out of the country, labor unrest grew, and France entered a severe financial crisis. Blum was forced to announce a "breathing spell" in social reform.

The fires of political dissension were also fanned by civil war in Spain. The Communists demanded that France support the Spanish republicans, while many French conservatives would gladly have joined Hitler and Mussolini in aiding the attack of Spanish fascists. Extremism grew, and France itself was within sight of civil war. Blum was forced to resign in June 1937, and the Popular Front quickly collapsed. An anxious and divided France drifted aimlessly once again, preoccupied by Hitler and German rearmament.

SUMMARY

After the First World War, Western society entered a complex and difficult era—truly an age of anxiety. Intellectual life underwent a crisis marked by pessimism, uncertainty, and fascination with irrational forces. Ceaseless experimentation and rejection of old forms characterized art and music, while motion pictures and radio provided a new, standardized entertainment for the masses. Intellectual and artistic developments that had been confined to small avant-garde groups before 1914 gained wider currency along with the insecure state of mind they expressed.

Politics and economics were similarly disrupted. In the 1920s political leaders groped to create an enduring peace and rebuild the prewar prosperity, and for a brief period late in the decade they even seemed to have succeeded. Then the Great Depression shattered the fragile stability. Uncertainty returned with redoubled force in the 1930s. The international economy collapsed, and unemployment struck millions. The democracies turned inward as they sought to cope with massive domestic problems and widespread disillusionment. Generally speaking, they were not very successful. The old liberal ideals of individual rights and responsibilities, elected government, and economic freedom seemed ineffective and outmoded to many, even when they managed to survive. And in many countries they were abandoned completely.

NOTES

1. P. Valéry, *Variety,* trans. M. Cowley (New York: Harcourt, Brace, 1927), pp. 27–28.
2. G. Marcel, as quoted in S. Hughes, *The Obstructed Path: French Social Thought in the Years of Desperation, 1930–1960* (New York: Harper & Row, 1967), p. 82.
3. G. Greene, *Another Mexico* (New York: Viking Press, 1939), p. 3.
4. G. Orwell, *1984* (New York: New American Library, 1950), p. 220.
5. C. E. Jeanneret-Gris (Le Corbusier), *Towards a New Architecture* (London: J. Rodker, 1931), p. 15.
6. Quoted in A. H. Barr, Jr., *What Is Modern Painting?,* 9th ed. (New York: Museum of Modern Art, 1966), p. 27.
7. Ibid., p. 25.
8. R. Graves and A. Hodge, *The Long Week End: A Social History of Great Britain, 1918–1939* (New York: Macmillan, 1941), p. 131.
9. Quoted in A. Briggs, *The Birth of Broadcasting,* vol. 1 (London: Oxford University Press, 1961), p. 47.
10. Quoted in R. J. Sontag, *A Broken World, 1919–1939* (New York: Harper & Row, 1971), p. 129.
11. C. P. Kindleberger, *The World in Depression, 1929–1939* (Berkeley: University of California Press, 1973), p. 292.
12. Quoted in S. B. Clough et al., eds., *Economic History of Europe: Twentieth Century* (New York: Harper & Row, 1968), pp. 243–245.
13. Quoted in D. Dillard, *Economic Development of the North Atlantic Community* (Englewood Cliffs, N.J.: Prentice-Hall, 1967), p. 591.

SUGGESTED READING

Among general works, E. Wiskemann's, *Europe of the Dictators, 1919–1945* (1966) and Sontag's study cited in the Notes are particularly recommended. The latter has an excellent bibliography. A. Bullock, ed., *The Twentieth Century* (1971), is a lavish visual feast combined with penetrating essays on major developments since 1900. Two excellent accounts of contemporary history—one with a liberal and the other with a conservative point of view—are R. Paxton, *Europe in the Twentieth Century* (1975), and P. Johnson, *Modern Times: The World from the Twenties to the Eighties* (1983). Crucial changes in thought before and after World War One are discussed in three rewarding intellectual histories: G. Masur, *Prophets of Yesterday* (1961); H. S. Hughes, *Consciousness and Society* (1956); and M. Biddiss, *Age of the Masses: Ideas and Society Since 1870* (1977). R. Stromberg, *European Intellectual History Since 1789,* 4th ed. (1986), and F. Baumer, *Modern European Thought: Continuity and Change in Ideas, 1600–1950* (1970), are recommended general surveys.

J. Rewald's, *The History of Impressionism,* rev. ed. (1961) and *Post-Impressionism* (1956) are excellent, as is the work by Barr cited in the Notes. P. Collaer, *A History of Modern Music* (1961), and H. R. Hitchcock, *Architecture: Nineteenth and Twentieth Centuries* (1958), are good introductions, while T. Wolfe, *From Bauhaus to My House* (1981), is a lively critique of modern architecture. L. Barnett, *The Universe and Dr. Einstein* (1952), is a fascinating study of the new physics. A. Storr, *Freud* (1989), and P. Rieff, *Freud* (1956), consider the man and how his theories have stood the test of time. M. White, ed., *The Age of Analysis* (1955), opens up basic questions of twentieth-century psychology and philosophy. H. Liebersohn, *Fate and Utopia in German Sociology* (1988), analyzes developments in German social science, and P. Gay, *Weimar Culture* (1970), is a brilliant exploration of the many-sided artistic renaissance in Germany in the 1920s. M. Marrus, ed., *Emergence of Leisure* (1974), is a pioneering inquiry into an important aspect of mass culture. H. Daniels-Rops, *A Fight for God,* 2 vols. (1966), is a sympathetic history of the Catholic church between 1870 and 1939.

G. Ambrosius and W. Hibbard, *A Social and Economic History of Twentieth-Century Europe* (1989), provides a good survey, while C. Maier, *Recasting Bourgeois Europe* (1975), is an ambitious comparative study of social classes and conflicts in France, Germany, and Italy after World War One. P. Fritzsche, *Rehearsals for Fascism: Populism and Political Mobilization in Weimar Germany* (1990); R. Wohl, *The Generation of 1914* (1979); R. Kuisel, *Capital and State in Modern France: Renovation and Economic Management* (1982); and W. McDougall, *France's Rhineland Diplomacy, 1914–1924* (1978), are four more important studies on aspects of the postwar challenge. M. Childs, *Sweden: The Middle Way* (1961), applauds Sweden's efforts at social reform. W. Neuman, *The Balance of Power in the Interwar Years, 1919–1939* (1968), perceptively examines international politics after the Locarno treaties of 1925. In addition to the contemporary works discussed in the text, the crisis of the interwar period comes alive in R. Crossman, ed., *The God That Failed* (1950), in which famous Western writers tell why they were attracted to and later repelled by communism; J. Ortega y Gasset's renowned *The Revolt of the Masses* (1932); and

F. A. Hayek's *The Road to Serfdom* (1944), a famous warning of the dangers to democratic freedoms.

In addition to Kindleberger's excellent study of the Great Depression cited in the Notes, there is J. Galbraith's very lively and understandable account of the stock market collapse, *The Great Crash* (1955). J. Garraty, *Unemployment in History* (1978), is noteworthy, though novels best portray the human tragedy of economic decline. W. Holtby, *South Riding* (1936), and W. Greenwood, *Love on the Dole* (1933), are moving stories of the Great Depression in England; H. Fallada, *Little Man, What Now?* (1932), is the classic counterpart for Germany. Also highly recommended as commentaries on English life between the wars are R. Graves, *Goodbye to All That,* rev. ed. (1957), and G. Orwell, *The Road to Wigan Pier* (1972). Among French novelists, A. Gide painstakingly examines the French middle class and its values in *The Counterfeiters,* while A. Camus, the greatest of the existential novelists, is at his unforgettable best in *The Stranger* and *The Plague.*

29

Dictatorships and the Second World War

power and eliminated his enemies in the mid-1920s. Then in 1928, as undisputed leader of the ruling Communist party, he launched the first five-year plan—the "revolution from above," as he so aptly termed it.

The five-year plans were extremely ambitious. Often incorrectly considered a mere set of economic measures to speed up Soviet Russia's industrial development, the five-year plans actually marked the beginning of a renewed attempt to mobilize and transform Soviet society along socialist lines. The goal was to create a new way of life and to generate new attitudes and new loyalties. The means Stalin and the small Communist party elite chose were constant propaganda, enormous sacrifice, and unlimited violence and state control. Thus the Soviet Union in the 1930s became a dynamic, modern totalitarian state.

From Lenin to Stalin

By spring 1921 Lenin and the Bolsheviks had won the civil war, but they ruled a shattered and devastated land. Many farms were in ruins, and food supplies were exhausted. In southern Russia, drought combined with the ravages of war to produce the worst famine in generations. By 1920, according to the government, from 50 to 90 percent of the population in seventeen provinces was starving. Industrial production also broke down completely. In 1921, for example, output of steel and

Lenin and Stalin in 1922.   Lenin re-established limited economic freedom throughout Russia in 1921, but he ran the country and the Communist party in an increasingly authoritarian way. Stalin carried the process much further and eventually built a regime based on harsh dictatorship. *(Source: Sovfoto)*

cotton textiles was only about 4 percent of what it had been in 1913. The revolutionary Trotsky later wrote that the "collapse of the productive forces surpassed anything of the kind history had ever seen. The country, and the government with it, were at the very edge of the abyss."[2] The Bolsheviks had destroyed the economy as well as their foes.

In the face of economic disintegration and rioting by peasants and workers, as well as an open rebellion by previously pro-Bolshevik sailors at Kronstadt—a rebellion that had to be quelled with machine guns, the tough but ever-flexible Lenin changed course. In March 1921 he announced the New Economic Policy (NEP), which re-established limited economic freedom in an attempt to rebuild agriculture and industry. During the civil war, the Communists had simply seized grain without payment. Lenin in 1921 substituted a grain tax on the country's peasant producers, who were permitted to sell their surpluses in free markets. Peasants were also encouraged to buy as many goods as they could afford from private traders and small handicraft manufacturers, groups that were now allowed to reappear. Heavy industry, railroads, and banks, however, remained wholly nationalized. Thus NEP saw only a limited restoration of capitalism.

Lenin's New Economic Policy was shrewd and successful, from two points of view. Politically, it was a necessary but temporary compromise with Russia's overwhelming peasant majority. Flushed with victory after their revolutionary gains of 1917, the peasants would have fought to hold onto their land. With fond hopes of immediate worldwide revolution fading by 1921, Lenin realized that his government was not strong enough to take it from them. As he had accepted Germany's harsh terms at Brest-Litovsk in 1918, Lenin made a deal with the only force capable of overturning his government.

Economically, NEP brought rapid recovery. In 1926 industrial output had surpassed the level of 1913, and Russian peasants were producing almost as much grain as before the war. Counting shorter hours and increased social benefits, workers were living somewhat better than they had in the past.

As the economy recovered and the government partially relaxed its censorship and repression, an intense struggle for power began in the inner circles of the Communist party, for Lenin had left no chosen successor when he died in 1924. The principal contenders were the stolid Stalin and the flamboyant Trotsky.

The son of a shoemaker, Joseph Dzhugashvili—later known as Stalin—studied for the priesthood but was expelled from his theological seminary, probably for rude rebelliousness. By 1903 he had joined the Bolsheviks. In the years before the First World War, he engaged in many revolutionary activities in the Transcaucasian area of southern Russia, including a daring bank robbery to get money for the Bolsheviks. This raid gained Lenin's attention and approval. Ethnically a Georgian and not a Russian, Stalin in his early writings focused on the oppression of minority peoples in the Russian Empire. Stalin was a good organizer but a poor speaker and writer, with no experience outside of Russia.

Leon Trotsky, a great and inspiring leader who had planned the 1917 takeover (see page 878) and then created the victorious Red Army, appeared to have all the advantages. Yet it was Stalin who succeeded Lenin. Stalin won because he was more effective at gaining the all-important support of the party, the only genuine source of power in the one-party state. Rising to general secretary of the party's Central Committee just before Lenin's first stroke in 1922, Stalin used his office to win friends and allies with jobs and promises. Stalin also won recognition as commissar of nationalities, a key position in which he governed many of Russia's minorities.

The "practical" Stalin also won because he appeared better able than the brilliant Trotsky to relate Marxist teaching to Russian realities in the 1920s. First, as commissar of nationalities, he built on Lenin's idea of granting minority groups a certain degree of freedom in culture and language while maintaining rigorous political control through carefully selected local Communists. Stalin could loudly claim, therefore, to have found a way to solve the ancient problem of ethnic demands for independence in the multinational state. And of course he did.

Second, Stalin developed a theory of "socialism in one country," which was more appealing to the majority of Communists than Trotsky's doctrine of "permanent revolution." Stalin argued that Russia had the ability to build socialism on its own. Trotsky maintained that socialism in Russia could succeed only if revolution occurred quickly throughout Europe. To many Communists, Trotsky's views seemed to sell Russia short and to promise risky conflicts with capitalist countries by recklessly encouraging revolutionary movements around the world. Stalin's willingness to break with NEP and push socialism at home appealed to young militants. In short, Stalin's theory of socialism in one country provided many in the party with a glimmer of hope in the midst of the capitalist-appearing NEP, which they had come to detest.

With cunning skill Stalin gradually achieved absolute power between 1922 and 1927. First, he allied with Trotsky's personal enemies to crush Trotsky, who was expelled from the Soviet Union in 1929 and eventually was murdered in Mexico in 1940, undoubtedly on Stalin's order. Stalin then aligned with the moderates, who wanted to go slow at home, to suppress Trotsky's radical followers. Finally, having defeated all the radicals, he turned against his allies, the moderates, and destroyed them as well. Stalin's final triumph came at the Party Congress of December 1927, which condemned all "deviation from the general party line" formulated by Stalin. The dictator was then ready to launch his "revolution from above"—the real Russian revolution for millions of ordinary citizens.

The Five-Year Plans

The Party Congress of 1927, which ratified Stalin's seizure of power, marked the end of the New Economic Policy and the beginning of the era of socialist five-year plans. The first five-year plan had staggering economic objectives. In just five years, total industrial output was to increase by 250 percent. Heavy industry, the preferred sector, was to grow even faster; steel production, for example, was to jump almost 300 percent. Agricultural production was slated to increase by 150 percent, and one-fifth of Russia's peasants were scheduled to give up their private plots and join socialist collective farms. In spite of warnings from moderate Communists that these goals were unrealistic, Stalin raised them higher as the plan got under way. By 1930 a whirlwind of economic and social change was sweeping the country.

Stalin unleashed his "second revolution" for a variety of interrelated reasons. There were, first of all, ideological considerations. Like Lenin, Stalin and his militant supporters were deeply committed to socialism as they understood it. Since the country had recovered economically and their rule was secure, they burned to stamp out NEP's private

traders, independent artisans, and few well-to-do peasants. Purely economic motivations were also important. Although the economy had recovered, it seemed to have stalled in 1927 and 1928. A new socialist offensive seemed necessary if industry and agriculture were to grow rapidly.

Political considerations were most important. Internationally, there was the old problem, remaining from prerevolutionary times, of catching up with the advanced and presumably hostile capitalist nations of the West. Stalin said in 1931, when he pressed for ever-greater speed and sacrifice: "We are fifty or a hundred years behind the advanced countries. We must make good this distance in ten years. Either we do it, or we shall go under."[3]

Domestically, there was what Communist writers of the 1920s called the "cursed problem"— the problem of the Russian peasants. For centuries, Russian peasants had wanted to own the land, and finally they had it. Sooner or later, the Communists reasoned, the peasants would become conservative little capitalists and pose a threat to the regime. Therefore, Stalin decided on a preventive war against the peasantry, in order to bring it under the absolute control of the state.

That war was *collectivization*—the forcible consolidation of individual peasant farms into large, state-controlled enterprises. Beginning in 1929, peasants all over the Soviet Union were ordered to give up their land and animals and to become members of collective farms, although they continued to live in their own homes. As for the *kulaks,* the better-off peasants, Stalin instructed party workers to "liquidate them as a class." Stripped of their land and livestock, the kulaks were generally not even permitted to join the collective farms. Many starved or were deported to forced-labor camps for "re-education."

Since almost all peasants were in fact poor, the term *kulak* soon meant any peasant who opposed the new system. Whole villages were often attacked. One conscience-stricken colonel in the secret police confessed to a foreign journalist: "I am an old Bolshevik. I worked in the underground against the Tsar and then I fought in the Civil War. Did I do all that in order that I should now surround villages with machineguns and order my men to fire indiscriminately into crowds of peasants? Oh, no, no!"[4]

Forced collectivization of the peasants led to economic and human disaster. Large numbers of peas-

Plastov: Collective Farm Threshing   This example of socialist realism portrays the results of collectivization in positive terms, but the propaganda message does not seem heavy-handed. These peasants have become employees of a large collective farm and are threshing its wheat crop. Socialist realism was expected to depict—and to glorify— the achievements of the New Soviet society. *(Source: A. M. Gork: Museum of Art, Kiev)*

ants slaughtered their animals and burned their crops in sullen, hopeless protest. Between 1929 and 1933, the number of horses, cattle, sheep, and goats in the Soviet Union fell by at least half. Nor were the state-controlled collective farms more productive. The output of grain barely increased between 1928 and 1938, when it was almost identical to that of 1913. Communist economists had expected collectivized agriculture to pay for new factories. Instead, the state had to invest heavily in agriculture, building thousands of tractors to replace slaughtered draft horses. Collectivized agriculture was unable to make any substantial financial contribution to Soviet industrial development in the first five-year plan. The human dimension of the tragedy was shocking. Collectivization created man-made famine in 1932 and 1933, and many perished. Indeed, Stalin confided to Churchill at Yalta in 1945 that ten million people had died in the course of collectivization.

Yet collectivization was a political victory of sorts. By the end of 1932, fully 60 percent of Rus-

sian peasant families had been herded onto collective farms; by 1938, 93 percent. Regimented and indoctrinated as employees of an all-powerful state, the peasants were no longer even a potential political threat to Stalin and the Communist party. Moreover, the state was assured of grain for bread for urban workers, who were much more important politically than the peasants. Collective farmers had to meet their grain quotas first and worry about feeding themselves second. Many collectivized peasants drew much of their own food from tiny, grudgingly tolerated garden plots that they worked in their off hours. No wonder some peasants joked, with that grim humor peculiar to the totalitarian society, that the initials then used by the Communist party actually stood for "The Second Serfdom, That of the Bolsheviks."

The industrial side of the five-year plans was more successful—indeed, quite spectacular. The output of industry doubled in the first five-year plan and doubled again in the second. Soviet industry produced about four times as much in 1937

Adult Education.   Illiteracy, especially among women, was a serious problem after the Russian Revolution. This early photo shows how adults successfully learned to read and write throughout the Soviet Union. *(Source: Sovfoto)*

"In Soviet Russia there is no capital except education. If a person does not want to become a collective farmer or just a cleaning woman, the only means you have to get something is through education."[6]

Women in Soviet Russia

Women's lives were radically altered by Stalinist society. Marxists had traditionally believed that both capitalism and the middle-class husband exploited women. The Russian Revolution of 1917 immediately proclaimed complete equality of rights for women. In the 1920s divorce and abortion were made very easy, and women were urged to work outside the home and liberate themselves sexually. A prominent and influential Bolshevik feminist,

Alexandra Kollontai, went so far as to declare that the sexual act had no more significance than "drinking a glass of water." This observation drew a sharp rebuke from the rather prudish Lenin, who said that "no sane man would lie down to drink from a puddle in the gutter or even drink from a dirty glass."[7] After Stalin came to power, sexual and familial liberation was played down, and the most lasting changes for women involved work and education.

The changes were truly revolutionary. Young women were constantly told that they must be fully equal to men, that they could and should do anything men could do. Russian peasant women had long experienced the equality of backbreaking physical labor in the countryside, and they continued to enjoy that equality on collective farms. With the advent of the five-year plans, millions of women also began to toil in factories and in heavy construction, building dams, roads, and steel mills in summer heat and winter frost. Yet most of the opportunities open to men through education were also opened to women. Determined women pursued their studies and entered the ranks of the better-paid specialists in industry and science. Medicine practically became a woman's profession. By 1950, 75 percent of all doctors in Soviet Russia were women.

Thus Stalinist society gave women great opportunities but demanded great sacrifices as well. The vast majority of women simply *had* to work outside the home. Wages were so low that it was almost impossible for a family or couple to live only on the husband's earnings. Moreover, the full-time working woman had a heavy burden of household tasks in her off hours, for most Soviet men in the 1930s still considered the home and the children the woman's responsibility. Finally, rapid change and economic hardship led to many broken families, creating further physical, emotional, and mental strains for women. In any event, the often-neglected human resource of women was ruthlessly mobilized in Stalinist society. This, too, was an aspect of the Soviet totalitarian state.

MUSSOLINI'S ITALY

Before turning to Hitler's Germany, it is necessary to look briefly at Mussolini's role in Italy. Like all the other emerging dictators, Mussolini hated liberalism, and he destroyed it in Italy. But that was not all. Mussolini and his supporters were the first to call themselves "fascists"—revolutionaries determined to create a certain kind of totalitarian state. As Mussolini's famous slogan of 1926 put it, "Everything in the state, nothing outside the state, nothing against the state." But Mussolini in power, unlike Stalin and Hitler, did not in fact create a real totalitarian state. His dictatorship was rather an instructive hybrid, a halfway house between conservative authoritarianism and modern totalitarianism.

The Seizure of Power

Before the First World War, Italy was a liberal state moving gradually toward democracy. But there were serious problems. Much of the Italian population was still poor, and class differences were extreme. Many peasants were more attached to their villages and local interests than to the national state. Moreover, the papacy and many devout Catholics, as well as the socialists, were strongly opposed to the heirs of Cavour and Garibaldi, middle-class lawyers and politicians who ran the country largely for their own benefit. Relations between church and state were often tense.

The war worsened the political situation. Having fought on the side of the Allies almost exclusively for purposes of territorial expansion, Italian nationalists were bitterly disappointed with Italy's modest gains at Versailles. Workers and peasants also felt cheated: to win their support during the war, the government had promised social and land reform, which it did not deliver after the war.

Encouraged by the Russian Revolution of 1917, radical workers and peasants began occupying factories and seizing land in 1920. These actions scared and radicalized the property-owning classes. The Italian middle classes were already in an ugly mood, having suffered from inflation during the war. Moreover, after the war, the pope lifted his ban on participation by Catholics in Italian politics, and a strong Catholic party quickly emerged. Thus by 1922 almost all the major groups in Italian society were opposed—though for different reasons—to the liberal parliamentary government.

Into these crosscurrents of unrest and frustration stepped the blustering, bullying Benito Mussolini (1883–1945). Son of a village schoolteacher and a poor blacksmith, Mussolini began his political career as a Socialist leader and radical newspaper editor before World War One. In 1914, powerfully influenced by antiliberal cults of violent action, the young Mussolini urged that Italy join the Allies, a stand for which he was expelled from the Italian Socialist party by its antiwar majority. Later Mussolini fought at the front and was wounded in 1917. Returning home, he began organizing bitter war veterans like himself into a band of Fascists—from the Italian word for "a union of forces."

At first, Mussolini's program was a radical combination of nationalist and socialist demands, including territorial expansion, benefits for workers, and land reform for peasants. As such, it competed with the better-organized Socialist party and failed to get off the ground. When Mussolini saw that his violent verbal assaults on the rival Socialists won him growing support from the frightened middle classes, he shifted gears in 1920. In thought and action, Mussolini was a striking example of the turbulence of the age of anxiety.

Mussolini and his growing private army of Black Shirts began to grow violent. Typically, a band of Fascist toughs would roar off in trucks at night and swoop down on a few isolated Socialist organizers, beating them up and force-feeding them almost deadly doses of castor oil. Few people were killed, but Socialist newspapers, union halls, and local Socialist party headquarters were destroyed. Mussolini's toughs pushed Communists and Socialists out of the city governments of northern Italy.

Mussolini, a skillful politician, refused to become a puppet of frightened conservatives and capitalists. He allowed his followers to convince themselves that they were not just opposing the "reds," but making a real revolution of their own. Many believed that they were not only destroying parliamentary government, but forming a strong, dynamic movement that would help the little people against the established interests.

With the government breaking down in 1922, largely because of the chaos created by his direct-action bands, Mussolini stepped forward as the savior of order and property. Striking a conservative note in his speeches and gaining the sympathetic neutrality of army leaders, Mussolini demanded the resignation of the existing government and his own appointment by the king. In October 1922, to force matters, a large group of Fascists marched on Rome to threaten the king and force him to call on Mussolini. The threat worked. Victor Emmanuel III (r. 1900–1946), who had no love for the old liberal politicians, asked Mussolini to form a new cabinet. Thus, after widespread violence and a threat of armed uprising, Mussolini seized power "legally." He was immediately granted dictatorial authority for one year by the king and the parliament.

The Regime in Action

Mussolini became dictator on the strength of Italians' rejection of parliamentary government, coupled with fears of Russian-style revolution. Yet what he intended to do with his power was by no means clear until 1924. Some of his dedicated supporters pressed for a "second revolution." Mussolini's ministers, however, included old conservatives, moderates, and even two reform-minded Socialists.

A new electoral law was passed giving two-thirds of the representatives in the parliament to the party that won the most votes, a change that allowed the Fascists and their allies to win an overwhelming majority in 1924. Shortly thereafter, five of Mussolini's Fascist thugs kidnaped and murdered Giacomo Matteotti, the leader of the Socialists in the parliament. In the face of this outrage, the opposition demanded that Mussolini's armed squads be dissolved and all violence be banned.

Although he may or may not have ordered Matteotti's murder, Mussolini stood at the crossroads of a severe political crisis. After some hesitation, he charged forward. Declaring his desire to "make the nation Fascist," he imposed a series of repressive measures. Freedom of the press was abolished, elections were fixed, and the government ruled by decree. Mussolini arrested his political opponents, disbanded all independent labor unions, and put dedicated Fascists in control of Italy's schools. Moreover, he created a Fascist youth movement, Fascist labor unions, and many other Fascist organizations. By the end of 1926, Italy was a one-party dictatorship under Mussolini's unquestioned leadership.

Yet Mussolini did not complete the establishment of a modern totalitarian state. His Fascist party never became all-powerful. It never destroyed the old power structure, as the Communists did in Soviet Russia, or succeeded in dominating it, as the Nazis did in Germany. Membership in the Fascist party was more a sign of an Italian's respectability than a commitment to radical change. Interested primarily in personal power, Mussolini was content to compromise with the old conservative classes that controlled the army, the economy, and the state. He never tried to purge these classes or even move very vigorously against them. He controlled and propagandized labor, but left big business to regulate itself, profitably and securely. There was no land reform.

Mussolini also came to draw on the support of the Catholic church. In the Lateran Agreement of 1929, he recognized the Vatican as a tiny independent state, and he agreed to give the church heavy financial support. The pope expressed his satisfaction and urged Italians to support Mussolini's government.

Nothing better illustrates Mussolini's unwillingness to harness everyone and everything for dynamic action than his treatment of women. He abolished divorce and told women to stay at home

Mussolini loved to swagger and bully. Here in his office he instinctively strikes his favorite theatrical pose, even as he discusses with its painter a less aggressive portrait of himself. *(Source: Courtesy, Gabriele Stocchi, Rome)*

and produce children. To promote that goal, he decreed a special tax on bachelors in 1934. In 1938 women were limited by law to a maximum of 10 percent of the better-paying jobs in industry and government. Italian women, as women, appear not to have changed their attitudes or behavior in any important way under Fascist rule.

It is also noteworthy that Mussolini's government did not persecute Jews until late in the Second World War, when Italy was under Nazi control. Nor did Mussolini establish a truly ruthless police state. Only twenty-three political prisoners were condemned to death between 1926 and 1944. In spite of much pompous posing by the chauvinist leader and in spite of mass meetings, salutes, and a certain copying of Hitler's aggression in foreign policy after 1933, Mussolini's Italy, though undemocratic, was never really totalitarian.

HITLER'S GERMANY

The most frightening totalitarian state was Nazi Germany. A product of Hitler's evil genius as well as of Germany's social and political situation and the general attack on liberalism and rationality in the age of anxiety, Nazi Germany emerged rapidly after Hitler came to power in 1933. The Nazis quickly smashed or took over most independent organizations, mobilized the economy, and began brutally persecuting the Jewish population. From the start, all major decisions were in the hands of the aggressive dictator Adolf Hitler.

The Roots of Nazism

Nazism grew out of many complex developments, of which the most influential were extreme nationalism and racism. These two ideas captured the mind of the young Hitler, and it was he who dominated Nazism for as long as it lasted.

Born the fourth child of a successful Austrian customs official and an indulgent mother, Adolf Hitler (1889–1945) spent his childhood happily in small towns in Austria. A good student in grade school, Hitler did poorly on reaching high school and dropped out at age fourteen after the death of his father. After four years of unfocused loafing, Hitler finally left for Vienna to become an artist. Denied admission to the Imperial Academy of Fine Arts because he lacked talent, the dejected Hitler stayed on in Vienna. There he lived a comfortable, lazy life on his generous orphan's pension and found most of the perverted beliefs that guided his life.

In Vienna Hitler soaked up extreme German nationalism, which was particularly strong there. Austro-German nationalists, as if to compensate for their declining position in the Austro-Hungarian Empire, believed Germans to be a superior people and the natural rulers of central Europe. They often advocated union with Germany and violent expulsion of "inferior" peoples as the means of maintaining German domination of the Austro-Hungarian Empire.

Hitler was deeply impressed by Vienna's mayor, Karl Lueger, whom he called the "mightiest mayor of all times." Lueger claimed to be a "Christian socialist." With the help of the Catholic trade unions, he had succeeded in winning the support of the little people of Vienna for an attack on capitalism and liberalism, which he held responsible for un-Christian behavior and excessive individualism. A master of mass politics in the urban world, Lueger showed Hitler the enormous potential of anticapitalist and antiliberal propaganda.

From Lueger and others, Hitler eagerly absorbed virulent anti-Semitism, racism, and hatred of Slavs. He was particularly inspired by the racist ravings of an ex-monk named Lanz von Liebenfels. Preaching the crudest, most exaggerated distortions of the Darwinian theory of survival, Liebenfels stressed the superiority of Germanic races, the inevitability of racial conflict, and the inferiority of the Jews. Liebenfels even anticipated the breeding and extermination policies of the Nazi state. He claimed that the master race had to multiply its numbers by means of polygamy and breeding stations, while it systematically sterilized and liquidated inferior races. Anti-Semitism and racism became Hitler's most passionate convictions, his explanation for everything. He believed inferior races—the Slavs and the Jews in particular—were responsible for Austria's woes. The Jews, he claimed, directed an international conspiracy of finance capitalism and Marxian socialism against German culture, German unity, and the German race. Hitler's belief was totally irrational, but he never doubted it.

Although he moved to Munich in 1913 to avoid being drafted in the Austrian army, the lonely Hitler greeted the outbreak of the First World War as a salvation. He later wrote in his autobiography, *Mein Kampf,* that, "overcome by passionate enthusiasm, I fell to my knees and thanked heaven out of an overflowing heart." The struggle and discipline of war gave life meaning, and Hitler served bravely as a dispatch carrier on the western front.

When Germany was suddenly defeated in 1918, Hitler's world was shattered. Not only was he a fanatical nationalist, but war was his reason for living. Convinced that Jews and Marxists had "stabbed Germany in the back," he vowed to fight on. And in the bitterness and uncertainty of postwar Germany, his wild speeches began to attract attention.

In late 1919 Hitler joined a tiny extremist group in Munich called the German Workers' party. In addition to denouncing Jews, Marxists, and democrats, the German Workers' party promised unity under a uniquely German "national socialism," which would abolish the injustices of capitalism and create a mighty "people's community." By 1921 Hitler had gained absolute control of this small but growing party. Moreover, Hitler was already a master of mass propaganda and political showmanship. Party members sported badges and uniforms, gave victory salutes, and marched like robots through the streets of Munich. But Hitler's most effective tool was the mass rally, a kind of political revival meeting. Songs, slogans, and demonstrations built up the tension until Hitler finally arrived. He then often worked his audience into a frenzy with wild, demagogic attacks on the Versailles treaty, the Jews, the war profiteers, and Germany's Weimar Republic.

Party membership multiplied tenfold after early 1922. In late 1923, when the Weimar Republic seemed on the verge of collapse, Hitler decided on an armed uprising in Munich. Inspired by Mussolini's recent easy victory, Hitler had found an ally in General Ludendorff of First World War fame. After Hitler had overthrown the Bavarian government, Ludendorff was supposed to march on Berlin with Hitler's support. The plot was poorly organized, however, and it was crushed by the police, backed up by the army, in less than a day. Hitler was arrested, tried, and sentenced to five years in prison. He had failed for the moment. But Nazism had been born, and it did not die.

Hitler's Road to Power

At his trial, Hitler violently denounced the Weimar Republic and skillfully presented his own program. In doing so he gained enormous publicity and attention. Moreover, he learned from his unsuccessful revolt. Hitler concluded that he had to undermine rather than overthrow the government, that he had to use its tolerant democratic framework to intimidate the opposition and come to power through electoral competition. He forced his more violent supporters to accept his new strategy. Finally, Hitler used his brief prison term—he was released in less than a year—to dictate *Mein Kampf.* There he expounded on his basic themes: "race," with the stress on anti-Semitism; "living space," with a sweeping vision of war and conquered territory; and the leader-dictator (Führer) with unlimited, arbitrary power. Hitler's followers had their bible.

In the years of prosperity and relative stability between 1924 and 1929, Hitler concentrated on building his National Socialist German Workers' party, or Nazi party. By 1928 the party had a hundred thousand highly disciplined members under Hitler's absolute control. To appeal to the middle classes, Hitler de-emphasized the anticapitalist elements of national socialism and vowed to fight Bolshevism.

Hitler in Opposition Hitler returns the salut of his Brown Shirts in this photograph from the third party day rally in Nuremberg in 1927. The Brown Shirts formed a private army within the Nazi movement, and their uniforms, marches, saluts, and vandalism helped keep Hitler in the public eye in the 1920s. *(Source: Courtesy, Bison Books, London)*

"Hitler, Our Last Hope"   So reads the very effective Nazi campaign poster, which is attracting attention with its gaunt and haggard faces. By 1932 almost half of all Germans, like these in Berlin, had come to agree. *(Source: Bildarchiv Preussischer Kulturbesitz. Photo: Herbert Hoffman, 1932)*

The Nazis were still a small splinter group in 1928, when they received only 2.6 percent of the vote in the general elections and twelve Nazis won seats in the parliament. There the Nazi deputies pursued the legal strategy of using democracy to destroy democracy. As Hitler's talented future minister of propaganda Joseph Goebbels (1897–1945) explained in 1928 in the party newspaper, "We become Reichstag deputies in order to paralyze the spirit of Weimar with its own aid. . . . We come as enemies! As the wolf breaks into the sheepfold, so we come."[8]

In 1929 the Great Depression began striking down economic prosperity, one of the barriers that had kept the wolf at bay. Unemployment jumped from 1.3 million in 1929 to 5 million in 1930; that year Germany had almost as many unemployed as all the other countries of Europe combined. Industrial production fell by one-half between 1929 and 1932. By the end of 1932, an incredible 43 percent of the labor force was unemployed, and it was estimated that only one in every three union members was working full-time. No factor contributed more to Hitler's success than the economic crisis. Never very interested in economics before, Hitler began promising German voters economic as well as political and military salvation.

Hitler focused his promises on the middle and lower middle class—small business people, office workers, artisans, and peasants. Already disillusioned by the great inflation of 1923, these people were seized by panic as bankruptcies increased, unemployment soared, and the dreaded Communists made dramatic election gains. The middle and lower middle classes deserted the conservative and moderate parties for the Nazis in great numbers.

The Nazis also appealed strongly to German youth. Indeed, in some ways the Nazi movement was a mass movement of young Germans. Hitler himself was only forty in 1929, and he and most of his top aides were much younger than other leading German politicians. "National Socialism is the organized will of the youth," proclaimed the official Nazi slogan, and the battle cry of Gregor Strasser, a leading Nazi organizer, was "Make way, you old ones."[9] In 1931 almost 40 percent of Nazi party members were under thirty, compared with 20 percent of Social Democrats. Two-thirds of Nazi members were under forty. National recovery, exciting and rapid change, and personal advancement: these were the appeals of Nazism to millions of German youths.

In the election of 1930, the Nazis won 6.5 million votes and 107 seats, which made them second in strength only to the Social Democrats, the moderate socialists. The economic situation continued to deteriorate, and Hitler kept promising he would bring recovery. In 1932 the Nazi vote leaped to 14.5 million, and the Nazis became the largest party in the Reichstag.

Another reason Hitler came to power was the breakdown of democratic government as early as May 1930. Unable to gain support of a majority in the Reichstag, Chancellor (chief minister) Heinrich Brüning convinced the president, the aging war hero General Hindenburg, to authorize rule by decree. The Weimar Republic's constitution permitted such rule in emergency situations, but the rather authoritarian, self-righteous Brüning intended to use it indefinitely. Moreover, Brüning was determined to overcome the economic crisis by cutting back government spending and ruthlessly forcing down prices and wages. Brüning's ultraorthodox policies not only intensified the economic collapse in Germany, they also convinced the lower middle classes that the country's republican leaders were stupid and corrupt. These classes were pleased rather than dismayed by Hitler's attacks on the republican system. After President Hindenburg forced Brüning to resign in May 1932, the new government headed by Franz von Papen continued to rule by decree.

The continuation of the struggle between the Social Democrats and Communists, right up until the moment Hitler took power, was another aspect of the breakdown of democratic government. The

The Mobilization of Young People was a prime objective of the Nazi leadership. Here boys in a Nazi youth group, some of whom are only children, are disciplined and conditioned to devote themselves to the regime. *(Source: Bettmann/Hulton)*

Hitler ruled a vast European empire stretching from the outskirts of Moscow to the English Channel. Hitler and the top Nazi leadership began building their "New Order," and they continued their efforts until their final collapse in 1945. In doing so, they showed what Nazi victory would have meant.

Hitler's New Order was based firmly on the guiding principle of Nazi totalitarianism: racial imperialism. Within this New Order, the Nordic peoples—the Dutch, the Norwegians, and the Danes—received preferential treatment, for they were racially related to the Germans. The French, an "inferior" Latin people, occupied the middle position. They were heavily taxed to support the Nazi war effort, but were tolerated as a race. Once Nazi reverses began to mount in late 1942, however, all the occupied territories of western and northern Europe were exploited with increasing intensity. Material shortages and both mental and physical suffering afflicted millions of people.

Slavs in the conquered territories to the east were treated with harsh hatred as "subhumans." At the height of his success in 1941 to 1942, Hitler painted for his intimate circle the fantastic details of a vast eastern colonial empire, where the Poles, Ukrainians, and Russians would be enslaved and forced to die out, while Germanic peasants resettled their abandoned lands. Himmler and the elite corps of S.S. volunteers struggled loyally, sometimes against the German army, to implement part of this general program even before victory was secured. In parts of Poland, the S.S. arrested and evacuated Polish peasants to create a German

Prelude to Murder: This photo captures the terrible inhumanity of Nazi racism. Frightened and bewildered families from the soon-to-be destroyed Warsaw ghetto are being forced out of their homes by German soldiers for deportation to concentration camps. There they face murder in the gas chambers. *(Source: Collection VIOLLET)*

"mass settlement space." Polish workers and Russian prisoners of war were transported to Germany, where they did most of the heavy labor and were systematically worked to death. The conditions of Russian slave labor in Germany were so harsh that four out of five Russian prisoners did not survive the war.

Finally, Jews were condemned to extermination, along with Gypsies, Jehovah's Witnesses, and captured Communists. By 1939 German Jews had lost all their civil rights, and after the fall of Warsaw the Nazis began deporting them to Poland. There they and Jews from all over Europe were concentrated in ghettos, compelled to wear the Jewish star, and turned into slave laborers. But by 1941 Himmler's S.S. was carrying out the "final solution of the Jewish question"—the murder of every single Jew. All over Hitler's empire, Jews were arrested, packed like cattle onto freight trains, and dispatched to extermination camps.

There the victims were taken by force or deception to "shower rooms," which were actually gas chambers. These gas chambers, first perfected in the quiet, efficient execution of seventy thousand mentally ill Germans between 1938 and 1941, permitted rapid, hideous, and thoroughly bureaucratized mass murder. For fifteen to twenty minutes came the terrible screams and gasping sobs of men, women, and children choking to death on poison gas. Then, only silence. Special camp workers quickly tore the victims' gold teeth from their jaws and cut off their hair for use as chair stuffing. The bodies were then cremated, or sometimes boiled for oil to make soap, while the bones were crushed to produce fertilizers. At Auschwitz, the most infamous of the Nazi death factories, as many as twelve thousand human beings were slaughtered each day. On the turbulent Russian front, the S.S. death squads forced the Jewish population to dig giant pits, which became mass graves as the victims were lined up on the edge and cut down by machine guns. The extermination of European Jews was the ultimate monstrosity of Nazi racism and racial imperialism. By 1945 six million Jews had been murdered.

The Grand Alliance

While the Nazis built their savage empire, the Allies faced the hard fact that chance, rather than choice, brought them together. Stalin had been cooperating fully with Hitler between August 1939 and June 1941, and only the Japanese attack on Pearl Harbor in December 1941 and Hitler's immediate declaration of war had overwhelmed powerful isolationism in the United States. The Allies' first task was to try to overcome their mutual suspicions and build an unshakable alliance on the quicksand of accident. By means of three interrelated policies they succeeded.

First, President Roosevelt accepted Churchill's contention that the United States should concentrate first on defeating Hitler. Only after victory in Europe would the United States turn toward the Pacific for an all-out attack on Japan, the lesser threat. Therefore, the United States promised and sent large amounts of military aid to Britain and Russia, and American and British forces in each combat zone were tightly integrated under a single commander. America's policy of "Europe first" helped solidify the anti-Hitler coalition.

Second, within the European framework, the Americans and the British put immediate military needs first. They consistently postponed tough political questions relating to the eventual peace settlement and thereby avoided conflicts that might have split the alliance until after the war.

Third, to further encourage mutual trust, the Allies adopted the principle of the "unconditional surrender" of Germany and Japan. The policy of unconditional surrender cemented the Grand Alliance because it denied Hitler any hope of dividing his foes. It probably also discouraged Germans and Japanese who might have tried to overthrow their dictators in order to make a compromise peace. Of great importance for the postwar shape of Europe, it meant that Russian and Anglo-American armies would almost certainly come together to divide all of Germany, and most of the Continent, among themselves.

The military resources of the Grand Alliance were awesome. The strengths of the United States were its mighty industry, its large population, and its national unity. Even before Pearl Harbor, President Roosevelt had called America the "arsenal of democracy" and given military aid to Britain and Russia. Now the United States geared up rapidly for all-out war production and drew heavily on a generally cooperative Latin America for resources. It not only equipped its own armies but eventually gave its allies about $50 billion of arms and equip-

"For the Motherland's Sake, Go Forward, Heroes" Joining the historic Russian warrior and the young Soviet soldier in the common cause, this poster portrays the defense of the nation as a sacred mission and illustrates the way Soviet leaders successfully appealed to Russian nationalism during the war. *(Sorce: Library of Congress)*

ment. Britain received by far the most, but about one-fifth of the total went to Russia in the form of badly needed trucks, planes, and munitions.

Too strong to lose and too weak to win when it stood alone, Britain, too, continued to make a great contribution. The British economy was totally and effectively mobilized, and the sharing of burdens through rationing and heavy taxes on war profits maintained social harmony. Moreover, as

1942 wore on, Britain could increasingly draw on the enormous physical and human resources of its empire and the United States. By early 1943 the Americans and the British combined small aircraft carriers with radar-guided bombers to rid the Atlantic of German submarines. Britain, the impregnable floating fortress, became a gigantic front-line staging area for the decisive blow to the heart of Germany.

As for Soviet Russia, so great was its strength that it might well have defeated Germany without Western help. In the face of the German advance, whole factories and populations were successfully evacuated to eastern Russia and Siberia. There, war production was reorganized and expanded, and the Red Army was increasingly well supplied. The Red Army was also well led, for a new generation of talented military leaders quickly arose to replace those so recently purged. Most important of all, Stalin drew on the massive support and heroic determination of the Soviet people. Broad-based Russian nationalism, as opposed to narrow communist ideology, became the powerful unifying force in what was appropriately called the "Great Patriotic War of the Fatherland."

Finally, the United States, Britain, and Soviet Russia were not alone. They had the resources of much of the world at their command. And, to a greater or lesser extent, they were aided by a growing resistance movement against the Nazis throughout Europe, even in Germany. Thus, although Ukrainian peasants often welcomed the Germans as liberators, the barbaric occupation policies of the Nazis quickly drove them to join and support behind-the-lines guerrilla forces. More generally, after Russia was invaded in June 1941, Communists throughout Europe took the lead in the underground Resistance, joined by a growing number of patriots and Christians. Anti-Nazi leaders from occupied countries established governments-in-exile in London, like that of the "Free French" under the intensely proud General Charles De Gaulle. These governments gathered valuable

MAP 29.2 World War Two in Europe The map shows the extent of Hitler's empire at its height, before the battle of Stalingrad in late 1942, and the subsequent advances of the Allies until Germany surrendered on May 7, 1945.

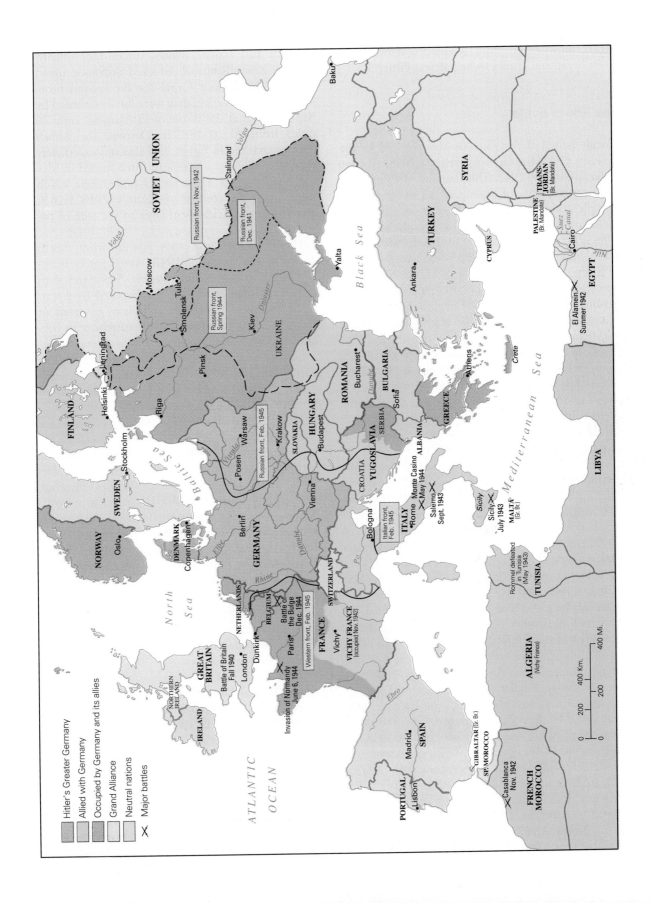

Hitler's Greater Germany
Allied with Germany
Occupied by Germany and its allies
Grand Alliance
Neutral nations
X **Major battles**

ATLANTIC
OCEAN

North
Sea

IRELAND

NORTHERN
IRELAND

GREAT
BRITAIN

London•

•Dunkirk
Battle of Britain
Fall 1940

Invasion of Normandy
June 6, 1944

Paris•

FRANCE
Vichy•

VICHY FRANCE
(occupied Nov. 1942)

Western front, Feb. 1945

NETHERLANDS

BELGIUM
X Battle of
the Bulge
Dec. 1944

SWITZERLAND

PORTUGAL
Lisbon•

SPAIN
Madrid•

GIBRALTAR (Gr. Br.)

SP. MOROCCO

X Casablanca
Nov. 1942

FRENCH
MOROCCO

ALGERIA
(Vichy France)

0   200   400 Km.
0   200   400 Mi.

NORWAY
Oslo•

SWEDEN

Stockholm•

DENMARK
Copenhagen•

Elbe

Rhine

GERMANY
Berlin•

Vienna•

Danube

Po

Baltic Sea

FINLAND

Helsinki•

Leningrad•

Riga•

Vistula

Posen•
Warsaw•
Russian front, Feb. 1945

Krakow•

SLOVAKIA

HUNGARY
Budapest•

CROATIA

YUGOSLAVIA
SERBIA

ALBANIA

ITALY
Rome• •Monte Casino
May 1944

Bologna•
Italian front,
Feb. 1945

Salerno× X
Sept. 1943

Sicily× July 1943

Sicily

MALTA
(Gr. Br.)

Mediterranean Sea

Rommel defeated
in Tunisia
(May 1943)

TUNISIA

LIBYA

MOSCOW•

Smolensk•
Tula•

Pinsk•

UKRAINE

Kiev•

Dnieper

Russian front,
Spring 1944

SOVIET UNION

Volga

Volga

Don

× Stalingrad

Russian front, Nov. 1942

Russian front,
Dec. 1941

ROMANIA
Bucharest•

Danube

BULGARIA
Sofia•

GREECE
Athens•

Crete

Black Sea

Yalta•

Ankara•

TURKEY

Baku•

SYRIA

CYPRUS

TRANS-
JORDAN
(Br. Mandate)

PALESTINE
(Br. Mandate)
Suez
Canal
Cairo•
Nile

EGYPT

El Alamein ×
Summer 1942

Ebro

secret information from Resistance fighters and even organized armies to help defeat Hitler.

The Tide of Battle

Barely halted at the gates of Moscow and Leningrad in 1941, the Germans renewed their Russian offensive in July 1942. This time they drove toward the southern city of Stalingrad, in an attempt to cripple communications and seize the crucial oil fields of Baku. Reaching Stalingrad, the Germans slowly occupied most of the ruined city in a month of incredibly savage house-to-house fighting.

Then, in November 1942, Soviet armies counterattacked. They rolled over Romanian and Italian troops to the north and south of Stalingrad, quickly closing the trap and surrounding the entire German Sixth Army of 300,000 men. The surrounded Germans were systematically destroyed, until by the end of January 1943 only 123,000 soldiers were left to surrender. Hitler, who had refused to allow a retreat, had suffered a catastrophic defeat. In the summer of 1943, the larger, better-equipped Soviet armies took the offensive and began moving forward (Map 29.2).

In late 1942 the tide also turned in the Pacific and in North Africa. By late spring 1942, Japan had established a great empire in East Asia (Map 29.3). Unlike the Nazis, the Japanese made clever appeals to local nationalists, who hated European imperial domination and preferred Japan's so-called Greater Asian Co-prosperity Sphere.

Then, in the Battle of the Coral Sea in May 1942, Allied naval and air power stopped the Japanese advance and also relieved Australia from the threat of invasion. This victory was followed by the Battle of Midway Island, in which American pilots sank all four of the attacking Japanese aircraft carriers and established American naval superiority in the Pacific. In August 1942, American marines attacked Guadalcanal in the Solomon Islands. Badly hampered by the policy of "Europe first"—only 15 percent of Allied resources were going to fight the war in the Pacific in early 1943—the Americans, under General Douglas MacArthur and Admiral Chester Nimitz, and the Australians nevertheless began "island hopping" toward Japan. Japanese forces were on the defensive.

In North Africa, the war had been seesawing back and forth since 1940. In May 1942, combined German and Italian armies, under the brilliant General Erwin Rommel, attacked British-occupied Egypt and the Suez Canal for the second time. After a rapid advance, they were finally defeated by British forces at the Battle of El Alamein, only 70 miles from Alexandria. In October the British counterattacked in Egypt, and almost immediately thereafter an Anglo-American force landed in Morocco and Algeria. These French possessions, which were under the control of Pétain's Vichy French government, quickly went over to the side of the Allies.

Having driven the Axis powers from North Africa by the spring of 1943, Allied forces maintained the initiative by invading Sicily and then mainland Italy. Mussolini was deposed by a war-weary people, and the new Italian government publicly accepted unconditional surrender in September 1943. Italy, it seemed, was liberated. Yet Mussolini was rescued by German commandos in a daring raid and put at the head of a puppet government. German armies seized Rome and all of northern Italy. Fighting continued in Italy.

Indeed, bitter fighting continued in Europe for almost two years. Germany, less fully mobilized for war than Britain in 1941, applied itself to total war in 1942 and enlisted millions of prisoners of war and slave laborers from all across occupied Europe in that effort. Between early 1942 and July 1944, German war production actually tripled. Although British and American bombing raids killed many German civilians, they were surprisingly ineffective from a military point of view. Also, German resistance against Hitler failed. After an unsuccessful attempt on Hitler's life in July 1944, thousands of Germans were brutally liquidated by S.S. fanatics. Terrorized at home and frightened by the prospect of unconditional surrender, the Germans fought on with suicidal stoicism.

On June 6, 1944, American and British forces under General Dwight Eisenhower landed on the beaches of Normandy in history's greatest naval invasion. Having tricked the Germans into believing that the attack would come near the Belgian border, the Allies secured a foothold on the coast of Normandy. In a hundred dramatic days, more than two million men and almost a half-million vehicles pushed inland and broke through German lines. Rejecting proposals to strike straight at Berlin in a massive attack, Eisenhower moved forward cautiously on a broad front. Not until March 1945

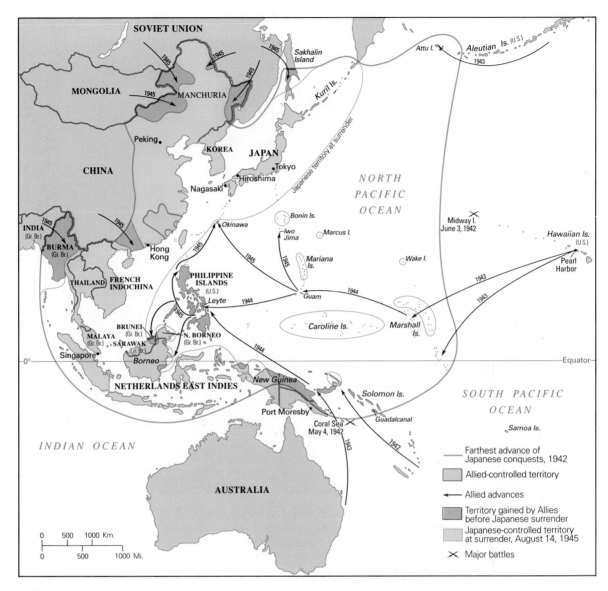

MAP 29.3 World War Two in the Pacific   Japanese forces also overran an enormous territory in 1942, which the Allies slowly recaptured in a long bitter struggle. As this map shows, Japan still held a large Asian empire in August 1945, when the unprecedented devastation of atomic warfare suddenly forced it to surrender.

did American troops cross the Rhine and enter Germany.

The Russians, who had been advancing steadily since July 1943, reached the outskirts of Warsaw by August 1944. For the next six months they moved southward into Romania, Hungary, and Yugoslavia. In January 1945, Red armies again moved westward through Poland, and on April 26 they met American forces on the Elbe River. The Allies

had closed their vise on Nazi Germany and overrun Europe. As Soviet forces fought their way into Berlin, Hitler committed suicide in his bunker, and on May 7 the remaining German commanders capitulated.

Three months later, the United States dropped atomic bombs on Hiroshima and Nagasaki in Japan. Mass bombing of cities and civilians, one of the terrible new practices of World War Two, had

The Normandy Invasion   The first American and British troops hit the beaches at 6:30 A.M. on June 6, 1944. The enemy poured down murderous fire on these Americans at Omaha Beach, but a naval bombardment eventually silenced the German guns. Thousands of Allied planes provided air cover and bombed German troops trying to move up from the interior. *(Source: National Archives, Washington)*

ended in the final nightmare—unprecedented human destruction in a single blinding flash. The Japanese surrendered. The Second World War, which had claimed the lives of more than fifty million soldiers and civilians, was over.

SUMMARY

The Second World War marked the climax of the tremendous practical and spiritual maladies of the age of anxiety, which led in many lands to the rise of dictatorships. Many of these dictatorships were variations on conservative authoritarianism, but there was also a fateful innovation—the modern totalitarian regime, most fully developed in Communist Russia and Nazi Germany. The totalitarian regimes utterly rejected the liberalism of the nineteenth century. Inspired by the lessons of total war and Lenin's one-party rule, they tried to subordinate everything to the state. Although some areas of life escaped them, state control increased to a staggering, unprecedented degree. The totalitarian regimes trampled on basic human rights with unrestrained brutality and police terror. Moreover, these regimes were armed with the weapons of modern technology, rendering opposition almost impossible.

Both Communist Russia and Nazi Germany tried to gain the *willing* support of their populations. Monopolizing the means of expression and communication, they claimed to represent the masses and to be building new, more equal societies. Many people believed them. Both regimes also won enthusiastic supporters by offering tough, ruthless people from modest backgrounds enormous rewards for loyal and effective service. Thus these totalitarian dictatorships rested on considerable genuine popular support, as well as on police terror. This combination gave them their awesome power and dynamism. That dynamism was, how-

ever, channeled in quite different directions. Stalin and the Communist party aimed at building their kind of socialism and the new socialist personality at home. Hitler and the Nazi elite aimed at unlimited territorial and racial aggression on behalf of a master race; domestic recovery was only a means to that end.

Unlimited Nazi aggression made war inevitable, first with the western European democracies, then with Germany's totalitarian neighbor, and finally with the United States. Plunging Europe into the ultimate nightmare, unlimited aggression unwittingly forged a mighty coalition that smashed the racist Nazi empire and its leader. In the words of the ancient Greeks, he whom the gods would destroy, they first make mad.

The City of Nagasaki A second atomic bomb struck Nagasaki on August 9, 1945, three days after the first giant fireball incinerated Hiroshima. Approximately 75,000 Japanese were killed or injured at Nagasaki. In this grim photo, taken about a month after the attack, a Japanese survivor pushes his bicycle along a path cleared through the ruins. (Source: UPI/Bettmann Newsphotos)

30

The Recovery of Europe and the Americas

The total defeat of the Nazis and their allies laid the basis for one of Western civilization's most remarkable recoveries. A battered western Europe dug itself out from under the rubble and experienced a great renaissance in the postwar era, which lasted into the late 1960s.

The western hemisphere, with its strong European heritage, also made exemplary progress. Soviet Russia eventually became more humane and less totalitarian. Yet there was also a tragic setback. The Grand Alliance against Hitler gave way to an apparently endless cold war, in which conflict between East and West threatened world peace and troubled domestic politics.

- What were the causes of the cold war, which was the most disappointing development of the postwar era?

- How and why, in spite of the tragic division of the Continent into two hostile camps, did Europe recover so successfully from the ravages of war and Nazism?

- To what extent did communist eastern Europe and the Americas experience a similar recovery?

- How and why did European empires collapse and Asian and African peoples gain political independence?

These are the questions this chapter will seek to answer.

THE COLD WAR, 1942–1953

In 1945 triumphant American and Russian soldiers came together and embraced on the banks of the Elbe River in the heart of vanquished Germany. At home, in the United States and in the Soviet Union, their loved ones erupted in joyous celebration. Yet victory was flawed. The Allies could not cooperate politically when it came to peacemaking. Motivated by different goals and hounded by misunderstandings, the United States and Soviet Russia soon found themselves at loggerheads. By the end of 1947, Europe was rigidly divided. It was West versus East in the cold war.

The most powerful allies in the wartime coalition —Soviet Russia and the United States—began to quarrel almost as soon as the unifying threat of Nazi Germany disappeared. The hostility between the Eastern and Western superpowers was a tragic disappointment for millions of people, but it was not really so surprising. It grew sadly but logically out of military developments, wartime agreements, and long-standing political and ideological differences.

In the early phases of the war, the Americans and the British made military victory their highest priority. They consistently avoided discussion of Stalin's war aims and the shape of the eventual peace settlement. This policy was evident in December 1941 and again in May 1942, when Stalin asked the United States and Britain to agree to Russia's moving its western border of 1938 farther west at the expense of Poland, in effect ratifying the gains Stalin had made from his deal with Hitler in 1939.

Stalin's request ran counter to the moralistic Anglo-American Atlantic Charter of August 1941. In good Wilsonian fashion, the Atlantic Charter had called for peace without territorial expansion or secret agreements, and for free elections and self-determination for all liberated nations. In this spirit, the British and Americans declined to promise Polish territory to Russia; Stalin received only a military alliance and no postwar commitments. Yet the United States and Britain did not try to take advantage of Russia's precarious position in 1942; in fact, they soothed Stalin by promising an invasion of continental Europe as soon as possible. They feared that hard bargaining would anger Stalin and encourage him to consider making a separate peace with Hitler. So they focused on the policy of unconditional surrender to solidify the alliance.

By late 1943, as Allied armies scored major victories, specific issues related to the shape of the postwar world could no longer be postponed. The conference Stalin, Roosevelt, and Churchill held in the Iranian capital of Teheran in November 1943 thus proved of crucial importance in determining subsequent events. There, the Big Three jovially reaffirmed their determination to crush Germany and searched for the appropriate military strategy. Churchill, fearful of the military dangers of a direct attack and anxious to protect Britain's political in-

The Big Three In 1945 a triumphant Winston Churchill, an ailing Franklin Roosevelt, and a determined Joseph Stalin met at Yalta in southern Russia to plan for peace. Cooperation soon gave way to bitter hostility. *(Source: F.D.R. Library)*

terests in the eastern Mediterranean, argued that American and British forces should follow up their North African and Italian campaigns with an indirect attack on Germany through the Balkans. Roosevelt, however, agreed with Stalin that an American-British frontal assault through France would be better. This agreement was part of Roosevelt's general effort to meet Stalin's wartime demands whenever possible. Roosevelt reportedly told his friend William Bullitt, formerly American ambassador to the Soviet Union, before the Teheran Conference, "I have just a hunch that Stalin doesn't want anything but security for his country, and I think that if I give him everything I possibly can and ask nothing from him in return, *noblesse oblige,* he won't try to annex anything and will work for a world of democracy and peace."[1]

At Teheran, the Normandy invasion was set for the spring of 1944. Although military considerations probably largely dictated this decision, it had momentous political implications: it meant that the Russian and the American-British armies would come together in defeated Germany along a north-south line and that only Russian troops would liberate eastern Europe. Thus the basic shape of postwar Europe was emerging even as the fighting continued. Real differences over questions like Poland were carefully ignored.

When the Big Three met again at Yalta on the Black Sea in southern Russia in February 1945, rapidly advancing Soviet armies were within a hundred miles of Berlin. The Red Army had occupied not only Poland but also Bulgaria, Romania, Hungary, part of Yugoslavia, and much of Czechoslovakia. The temporarily stalled American-British forces had yet to cross the Rhine into Germany. Moreover, the United States was far from defeating Japan. Indeed, it was believed that the invasion and occupation of Japan would cost a million American casualties—an estimate that led to the subsequent decision to drop atomic bombs in order to save American lives. In short, Russia's position was strong and America's weak.

There was little the increasingly sick and apprehensive Roosevelt could do but double his bet on Stalin's peaceful intentions. It was agreed at Yalta that Germany would be divided into zones of occupation and would pay heavy reparations to the Soviet Union in the form of agricultural and industrial goods, though many details remained unsettled. At American insistence, Stalin agreed to declare war on Japan after Germany was defeated. He also agreed to join the proposed United Nations, which the Americans believed would help preserve peace after the war; it was founded in April 1945 in San Francisco.

For Poland and eastern Europe—"that Pandora's Box of infinite troubles," according to American Secretary of State Cordell Hull—the Big Three struggled to reach an ambiguous compromise at Yalta: eastern European governments were to be freely elected but pro-Russian. As Churchill put it at the time, "The Poles will have their future in their own hands, with the single limitation that they must honestly follow in harmony with their allies, a policy friendly to Russia."[2]

The Yalta compromise over eastern Europe broke down almost immediately. Even before the Yalta Conference, Bulgaria and Poland were in the hands of Communists, who arrived home in the baggage of the Red Army. Minor concessions to noncommunist groups thereafter did not change this situation. Elsewhere in eastern Europe, pro-Russian "coalition" governments of several parties were formed, but the key ministerial posts were reserved for Moscow-trained Communists.

At the postwar Potsdam Conference of July 1945, the long-ignored differences over eastern Europe finally surged to the fore. The compromising Roosevelt had died and been succeeded by the more determined President Harry Truman, who demanded immediate free elections throughout eastern Europe. Stalin refused pointblank. "A freely elected government in any of these East European countries would be anti-Soviet," he admitted simply, "and that we cannot allow."[3]

Here, then, is the key to the much-debated origins of the cold war. American ideals, pumped up by the crusade against Hitler, and American politics, heavily influenced by millions of voters from eastern Europe, demanded free elections in Soviet-occupied eastern Europe. On the other hand, Stalin, who had lived through two enormously destructive German invasions, wanted absolute military security from Germany and its potential Eastern allies, once and for all. Suspicious by nature, he believed that only communist states could truly be devoted allies, and he feared that free elections would result in independent and quite possibly hostile governments on his western border. Moreover, by the middle of 1945 there was no way short of war that the United States and its Western allies could really influence developments in eastern Europe, and war was out of the question. Stalin was bound to have his way.

West versus East

The American response to Stalin's exaggerated conception of security was to "get tough." In May 1945 Truman abruptly cut off all aid to Russia. In October he declared that the United States would never recognize any government established by force against the free will of its people. In March 1946 former British prime minister Churchill ominously informed an American audience that an "iron curtain" had fallen across the Continent, dividing Germany and all of Europe into two antagonistic camps. Soon emotional, moralistic denunciations of Stalin and communist Russia re-emerged as part of American political life. Yet the United States also responded to the popular desire to "bring the boys home" and demobilized with incredible speed. When the war against Japan ended in September 1945, there were 12 million Americans in the armed forces; by 1947 there were only 1.5 million, as opposed to 6 million for Soviet Russia. Some historians have argued that American leaders believed that the atomic bomb gave the

United States all the power it needed; but "getting tough" really meant "talking tough."

Stalin's agents quickly reheated the "ideological struggle against capitalist imperialism." Moreover, the large, well-organized Communist parties of France and Italy obediently started to uncover American plots to take over Europe and aggressively challenged their own governments with violent criticisms and large strikes. The Soviet Union also put pressure on Iran and Turkey, and while Greek Communists battled Greek royalists, another bitter civil war raged in China. By the spring of 1947, it appeared to many Americans that Stalin wanted much more than just puppet regimes in Soviet-occupied eastern Europe. He seemed determined to export communism by subversion throughout Europe and around the world.

The American response to this challenge was the Truman Doctrine, which was aimed at "containing" communism in areas already occupied by the Red Army. Truman told Congress in March 1947: "I believe it must be the policy of the United States to support free people who are resisting attempted subjugation by armed minorities or by outside pressure." To begin, Truman asked Congress for military aid to Greece and Turkey. Then, in June, Secretary of State George C. Marshall offered Europe economic aid—the "Marshall Plan"—to help it rebuild.

Stalin refused Marshall Plan assistance for all of eastern Europe. He purged the last remaining noncommunist elements from the coalition governments of eastern Europe and established Soviet-style, one-party communist dictatorships. The

The Berlin Air Lift Standing in the rubble of their bombed-out city, a German crowd in the American sector awaits the arrival of a U.S. transport plane flying in over the Soviet blockade in 1948. The crisis over Berlin was a dramatic indication of growing tensions among the Allies, which resulted in the division of Europe into two hostile camps. *(Source: Walter Sanders, LIFE MAGAZINE © Time Inc.)*

seizure of power in Czechoslovakia in February 1948 was particularly brutal and antidemocratic, and it greatly strengthened Western fears of limitless communist expansion, beginning with Germany. Thus, when Stalin blocked all traffic through the Soviet zone of Germany to the former capital of Berlin, which had also been divided into sectors at the end of the war by the occupying powers, the Western Allies responded firmly but not provocatively. Hundreds of planes began flying over the Russian roadblocks around the clock, supplying provisions to the people of West Berlin and thwarting Soviet efforts to swallow them up. After 324 days the Russians backed down: containment seemed to work. In 1949, therefore, the United States formed an anti-Soviet military alliance of Western governments, the North Atlantic Treaty Organization (NATO); in response, Stalin tightened his hold on his satellites, later united in the Warsaw Pact. Europe was divided into two hostile blocs.

In late 1949 the Communists triumphed in China, frightening and infuriating many Americans, who saw an all-powerful worldwide communist conspiracy extending even into the upper reaches of the American government. When the Russian-backed communist forces of northern Korea invaded southern Korea in 1950, President Truman's response was swift. American-led United Nations armies intervened. The cold war had spread around the world and become very hot.

It seems clear that the rapid descent from victorious Grand Alliance to bitter cold war was intimately connected with the tragic fate of eastern Europe. After 1932, when the eastern European power vacuum invited Nazi racist imperialism, the appeasing Western democracies mistakenly did nothing. They did, however, have one telling insight: how, they asked themselves, could they unite with Stalin to stop Hitler without giving Stalin great gains on his western borders? After Hitler's invasion of Soviet Russia, the Western powers preferred to ignore this question and hope for the best. But when Stalin later began to claim the spoils of victory, a helpless but moralistic United States refused to cooperate and professed outrage. One cannot help but feel that Western opposition immediately after the war came too late and quite possibly encouraged even more aggressive measures by the always-suspicious Stalin. And it helped explode the quarrel over eastern Europe into a global confrontation, which became institutionalized and lasted until the late 1980s despite intermittent periods of relaxation.

THE WESTERN EUROPEAN RENAISSANCE

As the cold war divided Europe into two blocs, the future appeared bleak on both sides of the iron curtain. Economic conditions were the worst in generations, and millions of people lived on the verge of starvation. Politically, Europe was weak and divided, a battleground for cold war ambitions. Moreover, long-cherished European empires were crumbling in the face of Asian and African nationalism. Yet Europe recovered, and the Western nations led the way. In less than a generation, western Europe achieved unprecedented economic prosperity and regained much of its traditional prominence in world affairs. It was an amazing rebirth— a true renaissance.

The Postwar Challenge

After the war, economic conditions in western Europe were terrible. Simply finding enough to eat was a real problem. Runaway inflation and black markets testified to severe shortages and hardship. The bread ration in Paris in 1946 was little more than it had been in 1942 under the Nazi occupation. Rationing of bread had to be introduced in Britain in 1946 for the first time. Both France and Italy produced only about half as much in 1946 as before the war. Many people believed that Europe was quite simply finished. The prominent British historian Arnold Toynbee felt that, at best, western Europeans might seek to civilize the crude but all-powerful Americans, somewhat as the ancient Greeks had civilized their Roman conquerors.

Suffering was most intense in defeated Germany. The major territorial change of the war had moved Soviet Russia's border far to the west. Poland was in turn compensated for this loss to Russia with land taken from Germany (Map 30.1). To solidify these boundary changes, thirteen million people were driven from their homes in eastern Germany (and other countries in eastern Europe) and forced to resettle in a greatly reduced Germany. The Russians were also seizing factories and equipment as reparations, even tearing up railroad tracks and sending the rails to the Soviet Union. The com-

MAP 30.1 Europe After World War Two Both the Soviet Union and Poland took land from Germany, which the Allies partitioned into occupation zones. Those zones subsequently formed the basis of the East and the West German states, as the Iron Curtain fell to divide both Germany and Europe.

mand "Come here, woman," from a Russian soldier was the sound of terror, the prelude to many a rape.

In 1945 and 1946, conditions were not much better in the Western zones. There was the same soul-numbing devastation. Walking through Munich, a survivor wrote that

You could often see for miles, and then you went through canyons, as in the mountains, the rubble towering up on both sides. . . . I wandered like a sleepwalker through this wasteland. . . . There was no city. There was only the ghost, the feeling, the sensation of a devastated, stunned wasteland. The creatures in this wasteland resembled ghosts. . . . Their faces were without expression, their eyes sunken and listless. . . . A huge solitude and despair seized me.[4]

The Western Allies also treated the German population with great severity at first. By February 1946 the average daily diet of a German in the Ruhr had been reduced to two slices of bread, a pat of margarine, a spoonful of porridge, and two small potatoes. Countless Germans sold many of their possessions to American soldiers to buy food. Cigarettes replaced worthless money as currency. The winter of 1946 to 1947 was one of the coldest in memory, and there were widespread signs of actual starvation. By the spring of 1947, refugee-clogged, hungry, prostrate Germany was on the verge of total collapse and threatening to drag down the rest of Europe.

Yet western Europe was not finished. The Nazi occupation and the war had discredited old ideas and old leaders. All over Europe, many people were willing to change and experiment in hopes of building a new and better Europe out of the rubble. New groups and new leaders were coming to the fore to guide these aspirations. Progressive Catholics and revitalized Catholic political parties —the Christian Democrats—were particularly influential.

In Italy the Christian Democrats emerged as the leading party in the first postwar elections in 1946, and in early 1948 they won an absolute majority in the parliament in a landslide victory. Their very able leader was Alcide De Gasperi, a courageous antifascist and former Vatican librarian, firmly committed to political democracy, economic reconstruction, and moderate social reform. In France, too, the Catholic party provided some of the best

postwar leaders, like Robert Schuman. This was particularly true after January 1946, when General De Gaulle, the inspiring wartime leader of the Free French, resigned after having re-established the free and democratic Fourth Republic. As Germany was partitioned by the cold war, a radically purified Federal Republic of Germany found new and able leadership among its Catholics. In 1949 Konrad Adenauer, the former mayor of Cologne and a long-time anti-Nazi, began his long, highly successful democratic rule; the Christian Democrats became West Germany's majority party for a generation. In providing effective leadership for their respective countries, the Christian Democrats were inspired and united by a common Christian and European heritage. They steadfastly rejected totalitarianism and narrow nationalism and placed their faith in democracy and cooperation.

The Socialists and the Communists, active in the Resistance against Hitler, also emerged from the war with increased power and prestige, especially in France and Italy. They, too, provided fresh leadership and pushed for social change and economic reform with considerable success. In the immediate postwar years, welfare measures such as family allowances, health insurance, and increased public housing were enacted throughout much of Europe. In Italy social benefits from the state came to equal a large part of the average worker's wages. In France large banks, insurance companies, public utilities, coal mines, and the Renault auto company were nationalized by the government. Britain followed the same trend. The voters threw out Churchill and the Conservatives in 1945, and the socialist Labour party under Clement Attlee moved toward establishment of the "welfare state." Many industries were nationalized, and the government provided each citizen with free medical service and taxed the middle and upper classes heavily. Thus, all across Europe, social reform complemented political transformation, creating solid foundations for a great European renaissance.

The United States also supplied strong and creative leadership. Frightened by fears of Soviet expansion, the United States provided western Europe with both massive economic aid and ongoing military protection. Economic aid was channeled through the Marshall Plan, which required that the participating countries coordinate their efforts for maximum effectiveness. This requirement led to the establishment of the Organization of European

Economic Cooperation (OEEC). Between early 1948 and late 1952, the United States furnished foreign countries roughly $22.5 billion, of which seven-eighths was in the form of outright gifts rather than loans. Military security was provided through NATO, established as a regional alliance for self-defense and featuring American troops stationed permanently in Europe as well as the protection of the American nuclear umbrella. Thus the United States assumed its international responsibilities after the Second World War, exercising the leadership it had shunned in the tragic years after 1919.

Economic "Miracles"

As Marshall Plan aid poured in, the battered economies of western Europe began to turn the corner in 1948. Impoverished West Germany led the way with a spectacular advance after the Allies permitted Adenauer's government to reform the currency and stimulate private enterprise. Other countries were not far behind. The outbreak of the Korean War in 1950 further stimulated economic activity, and Europe entered a period of rapid, sustained economic progress that lasted into the late 1960s. By 1963 western Europe was producing more than two-and-one-half times as much as it had before the war. Never before had the European economy grown so fast. For politicians and economists, for workers and business leaders, it was a time of astonishing, loudly proclaimed economic "miracles."

There were many reasons for western Europe's brilliant economic performance. American aid helped the process get off to a fast start. Europe received equipment to repair damaged plants and even whole new specialized factories when necessary. Thus critical shortages were quickly overcome. Moreover, since European nations coordinated the distribution of American aid, many barriers to European trade and cooperation were quickly dropped. Aid from the United States helped, therefore, to promote both a resurgence of economic liberalism with its healthy competition and an international division of labor.

As in most of the world, economic growth became a basic objective of all western European governments, for leaders and voters were determined to avoid a return to the dangerous and demoralizing stagnation of the 1930s. Governments gener-

ally accepted Keynesian economics (see Chapter 28) and sought to stimulate their economies, and some also adopted a number of imaginative strategies. Those in Germany and France were particularly successful and influential.

Under Minister of Economy Ludwig Erhard, a roly-poly, cigar-smoking ex-professor, postwar West Germany broke decisively with the totally regulated, strait-jacketed Nazi economy. Erhard bet on the free-market economy, while maintaining the extensive social welfare network inherited from the Hitler era. He and his teachers believed, not only that capitalism was more efficient, but also that political and social freedom could thrive only if there were real economic freedom. Erhard's first step was to reform the currency and abolish rationing and price controls in 1948. He boldly declared, "The only ration coupon is the Mark."[5] At first, profits jumped sharply, prompting business people to employ more people and produce more. By the late 1950s, Germany had a prospering economy and full employment, a strong currency and stable prices. Germany's success aroused renewed respect for free-market capitalism and encouraged freer trade among other European nations.

In France the major innovation was a new kind of planning. Under the guidance of Jean Monnet, an economic pragmatist and apostle of European unity, a planning commission set ambitious but flexible goals for the French economy. It used Marshall aid money and the nationalized banks to funnel money into key industries, several of which were state owned. At the same time, the planning commission and the French bureaucracy encouraged private enterprise to "think big." The often-cautious French business community responded, investing heavily in new equipment and modern factories. Thus France combined flexible planning and a "mixed" state and private economy to achieve the most rapid economic development in its long history. Throughout the 1950s and 1960s, there was hardly any unemployment in France. The average person's standard of living improved dramatically. France, too, was an economic "miracle."

Other factors also contributed to western Europe's economic boom. In most countries after the war, there were large numbers of men and women ready to work hard for low wages and the hope of a better future. Germany had millions of impoverished refugees, while France and Italy still had millions of poor peasants. Expanding industries in

Postwar Reconstruction   The Hamburg apartments on the left were bombed-out shells in 1945, along with 300,000 other housing units in the city. Yet by 1951 these same apartments were replaced, or ingeniously rebuilt (right). In half of the shells, crushed rubble mixed with concrete was poured to provide missing walls and to achieve a quick and economical rehabilitation. *(Source: National Archives, Washington)*

those countries thus had a great asset to draw on. More fully urbanized Britain had no such rural labor pool; this lack, along with a welfare socialism that stressed "fair shares" rather than rapid growth, helps account for its fairly poor postwar economic performance.

In 1945 impoverished Europe was still rich in the sense that it had the human skills of an advanced industrial society. Skilled workers, engineers, managers, and professionals knew what could and should be done, and they did it.

Many consumer products had been invented or perfected since the late 1920s, but few Europeans had been able to buy them during the depression and war. In 1945 the electric refrigerator, the washing machine, and the automobile were rare luxuries. There was, therefore, a great potential demand, which the economic system moved to satisfy.

Finally, ever since 1919 the nations of Europe had suffered from high tariffs and small national markets, which made for small and therefore inefficient factories. In the postwar era, European countries junked many of these economic barriers and gradually created a large unified market—the Common Market. This action, which stimulated the economy, was part of the postwar search for a new European unity.

Toward European Unity

Western Europe's political recovery was spectacular. Republics were re-established in France, West Germany, and Italy. Constitutional monarchs were restored in Belgium, Holland, and Norway. These democratic governments took root once again and thrived. To be sure, only West Germany established a two-party system on the British-American model; states like France and Italy returned to multiparty politics and shifting parliamentary coalitions. Yet the middle-of-the-road parties—primarily the Christian Democrats and the Socialists—dominated and provided continuing leadership. National self-determination was accompanied by civil liberties and great individual freedom. All of this was itself an extraordinary achievement.

Even more remarkable was the still-unfinished, still-continuing movement toward a united Europe. The Christian Democrats with their shared Catholic heritage were particularly committed to "building Europe," and other groups shared their dedication. Many Europeans believed that narrow, exaggerated nationalism had been a fundamental cause of both world wars, and that only through unity could European conflict be avoided in the future. Many western Europeans also realized how very weak their countries were in comparison with the United States and the Soviet Union, the two superpowers that had divided Europe from outside and made it into a cold war battleground. Thus the cold war encouraged some visionaries to seek a new "European nation," a superpower capable of controlling western Europe's destiny and reasserting its influence in world affairs.

The close cooperation among European states required by the Marshall Plan led to the creation of both the OEEC and the Council of Europe in 1948. European federalists hoped that the Council of Europe would quickly evolve into a true European parliament with sovereign rights, but this did not happen. Britain, with its empire and its "special relationship" with the United States, consistently opposed giving any real political power—any sovereignty—to the council. Many old-fashioned continental nationalists and Communists felt similarly. The Council of Europe became little more than a multinational debating society.

Frustrated in the direct political approach, European federalists turned toward economics. As one of them explained, "Politics and economics are closely related. Let us try, then, for progress in economic matters. Let us suppress those obstacles of an economic nature which divide and compartmentalize the nations of Europe."[6] In this they were quite successful.

Two far-seeing French statesmen, the planner Jean Monnet and Foreign Minister Robert Schuman, courageously took the lead in 1950. The Schuman Plan called for a special international organization to control and integrate all European steel and coal production. West Germany, Italy, Belgium, the Netherlands, and Luxembourg accepted the French idea in 1952; the British would have none of it. The immediate economic goal—a single competitive market without national tariffs or quotas—was rapidly realized. By 1958 coal and steel moved as freely among the six nations of the European Coal and Steel Community as among the states of the United States. The more far-reaching political goal was to bind the six member nations so closely together economically that war among them would become unthinkable and virtually impossible. This brilliant strategy did much to reduce tragic old rivalries, particularly that of France and Germany.

The Coal and Steel Community was so successful that it encouraged further technical and economic cooperation among "the Six." In 1957 the same six nations formed Euratom to pursue joint research in atomic energy; they also signed the Treaty of Rome, which created the European Economic Community, generally known as the Common Market (Map 30.2). The first goal of the treaty was gradual reduction of all tariffs among the Six to create a large free trade area. Other goals included the free movement of capital and labor and common economic policies and institutions.

An epoch-making stride toward unity, the Common Market was a tremendous success. Tariffs were rapidly reduced, and the European economy was stimulated. Companies and regions specialized in what they did best. Western Europe was being united in a single market almost as large as that of the United States. Many medium-sized American companies rushed to Europe, for a single modern factory in, say, Belgium or southern Italy had a vast potential market of 170 million customers.

The development of the Common Market fired imaginations and encouraged hopes of rapid progress toward political as well as economic union. In the 1960s, however, these hopes were frustrated by a resurgence of more traditional nationalism. Once again, France took the lead. Mired in a bitter colonial war in Algeria, the country turned in 1958 to General De Gaulle, who established the Fifth French Republic and ruled as its president until 1969. A towering giant both literally and figuratively, De Gaulle was the last of the bigger-than-life wartime leaders. A complex man who aroused a strong and sometimes negative response, especially in the United States, De Gaulle was at heart a romantic nationalist dedicated to reasserting France's greatness and glory. Once he had resolved the Algerian conflict, he labored to re-create a powerful, truly independent France, which would lead and even dictate to the other Common Market states.

De Gaulle personified the political resurgence of the leading nations of western Europe, as well as declining fears of the Soviet Union in the 1960s. Viewing the United States as the main threat to genuine French (and European) independence, he withdrew all French military forces from the "American-controlled" NATO command, which had to move from Paris to Brussels. De Gaulle tried to create financial difficulties for the United States by demanding gold for the American dollars France had accumulated. France also developed its own nuclear weapons. Within the Common Market, De Gaulle in 1963 and again in 1967 vetoed the application of the pro-American British, who were having second thoughts and wanted to join.

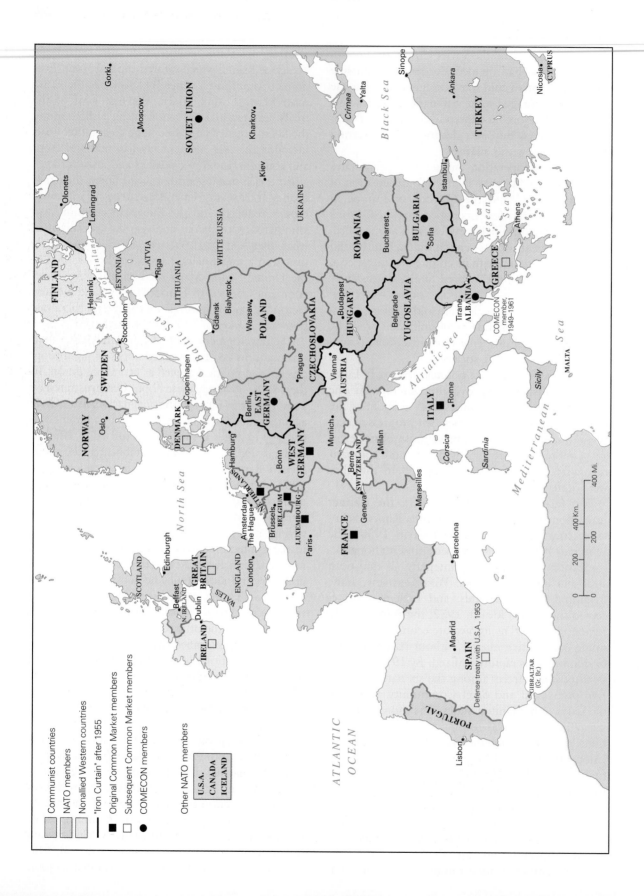

Communist countries

NATO members

Nonallied Western countries

"Iron Curtain" after 1955

■ Original Common Market members

□ Subsequent Common Market members

● COMECON members

Other NATO members

U.S.A.
CANADA
ICELAND

FINLAND

Olonets•

•Leningrad

Helsinki•

Gorki•

•Moscow

SOVIET UNION

Kharkov•

•Kiev

ESTONIA

LATVIA

LITHUANIA

WHITE RUSSIA

UKRAINE

Crimea

•Yalta

Sinope•

Black Sea

Ankara•

TURKEY

Nicosia•
CYPRUS

NORWAY

Oslo•

SWEDEN

Stockholm•

Gulf of Finland

Riga•

Bialystok•

Gdansk•

POLAND

Warsaw•

•Istanbul

ROMANIA

Bucharest•

BULGARIA

•Sofia

Aegean Sea

Athens•

GREECE

Baltic Sea

Copenhagen•

DENMARK

Berlin•
EAST
GERMANY

Prague•

CZECHOSLOVAKIA

Budapest•

HUNGARY

Belgrade•

YUGOSLAVIA

Tirane•
ALBANIA

COMECON
member,
1949–1961

North Sea

Hamburg•

Bonn•

WEST
GERMANY

Munich•

Vienna•

AUSTRIA

Berne•
SWITZERLAND

Adriatic Sea

ITALY

•Rome

Mediterranean Sea

Sicily

MALTA

Corsica

Sardinia

Edinburgh•

SCOTLAND

Belfast•
N. IRELAND

Dublin•

IRELAND

ENGLAND

London•

GREAT
BRITAIN

WALES

NETHERLANDS

Amsterdam•
The Hague•

Brussels•
BELGIUM

LUXEMBOURG

Paris•

FRANCE

Geneva•

Milan•

Marseilles•

Barcelona•

ATLANTIC
OCEAN

PORTUGAL

Lisbon•

SPAIN

Madrid•

Defense treaty with U.S.A., 1953

GIBRALTAR
(Gr. Br.)

0   200   400 Km.

0   200   400 Mi.

More generally, he refused to permit the scheduled advent of majority rule within the Common Market, and he forced his partners to accept many of his views. Thus, throughout the 1960s the Common Market thrived economically, but it did not transcend deep-seated nationalism; it remained a union of sovereign states.

Decolonization

The postwar era saw the total collapse of colonial empires. Between 1947 and 1962, almost every colonial territory gained independence. Europe's long expansion, which had reached a high point in the late nineteenth century, was completely reversed (Map 30.3). The spectacular collapse of Western political empires fully reflected old Europe's eclipsed power after 1945. Yet the new nations of Asia and Africa have been so deeply influenced by Western ideas and achievements that the "westernization" of the world has continued to rush forward.

Modern nationalism, with its demands for political self-determination and racial equality, spread from intellectuals to the masses in virtually every colonial territory after the First World War. Economic suffering created bitter popular resentment, and thousands of colonial subjects had been unwillingly drafted into French and British armies. Nationalist leaders stepped up their demands. By 1919 one high-ranking British official mournfully wrote: "A wave of unrest is sweeping over the Empire, as over the rest of the world. Almost every day brings some disturbance or other at our Imperial outposts."[7] The Russian Revolution also encouraged the growth of nationalism, and Soviet Russia verbally and militarily supported nationalist independence movements.

Furthermore, European empires had been based on an enormous power differential between the rulers and the ruled, a difference that had declined

French President De Gaulle and his wife bid farewell to President and Mrs. Kennedy at the presidential palace in Paris in 1961. A proud statesman who never forgot the snubs received from his American and British allies during the war, De Gaulle challenged American leadership in Western Europe. *(Source: Wide World Photos)*

almost to the vanishing point by 1945. Not only was western Europe poor and battered immediately after the war, but Japan had demonstrated that whites were not invincible. With its political power and moral authority in tatters, Europe's only choice was either to submit gracefully or to enter into risky wars of reconquest.

Most Europeans regarded their empires very differently after 1945 than before 1914, or even before 1939. Empire had rested on self-confidence and a sense of righteousness; Europeans had believed their superiority to be not only technical and military but spiritual and moral as well. The horrors of the Second World War and the near-destruction of Western civilization destroyed such complacent arrogance and gave opponents of imperialism the upper hand in Europe. After 1945 most Europeans were willing to let go of their colonies more or less voluntarily and to concentrate on rebuilding at home.

MAP 30.2 European Alliance Systems After the Cold War divided Europe into two hostile military alliances, six Western European countries formed the Common Market in 1957. The Common Market grew later to include most of Western Europe, while the Communist states organized their own economic association—COMECON.

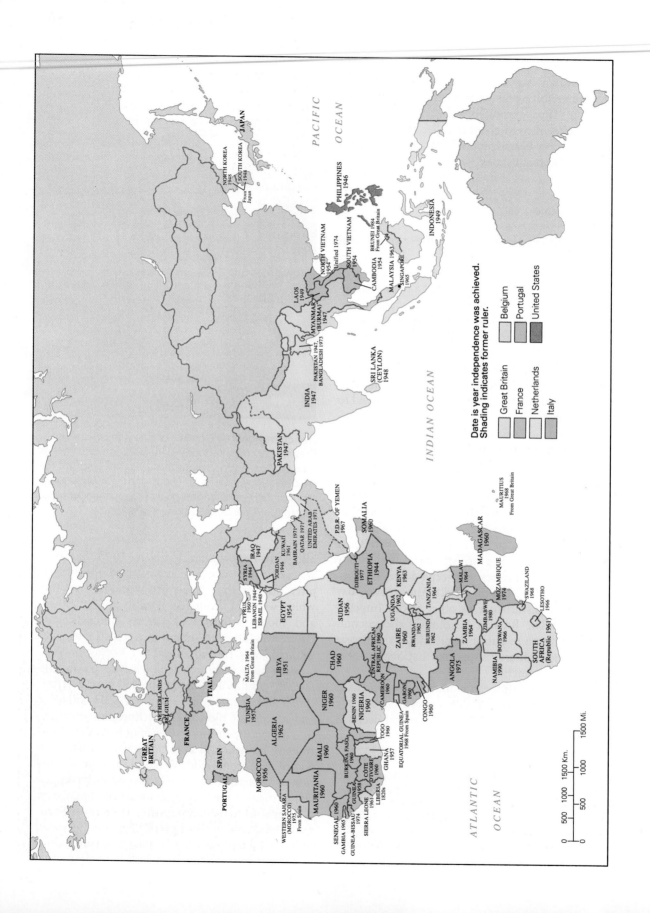

Date is year independence was achieved.
Shading indicates former ruler.

Great Britain
France
Netherlands
Italy
Belgium
Portugal
United States

India played a key role in decolonization and the end of empire. India was Britain's oldest, largest, and most lucrative nonwhite possession, and Britain had by far the largest colonial empire. Nationalist opposition to British rule coalesced after the First World War under the leadership of the British-educated lawyer Mahatma Gandhi (1869–1948), who preached nonviolent "noncooperation" with the British. Indian intellectuals effectively argued the old liberal case for equality and self-determination. In response, Britain's rulers gradually introduced political reforms and limited self-government. When the war ended, independence followed very rapidly. The new Labour government was determined to leave India; radicals and socialists had always opposed imperialism, and the heavy cost of governing India had become an intolerable financial burden. The obstacle posed by conflict between India's Hindu and Muslim populations was resolved in 1947 by creating two states, predominantly Hindu India and Muslim Pakistan.

If Indian nationalism drew on Western parliamentary liberalism, Chinese nationalism developed and triumphed in the framework of Marxist-Leninist totalitarianism. In the turbulent early 1920s, a broad alliance of nationalist forces within the Russian-supported *Kuomintang*—the National People's party—was dedicated to unifying China and abolishing European concessions. But in 1927 Chiang Kai-shek (1887–1975), the successor to Sun Yat-sen (see page 851) and the leader of the Kuomintang, broke with his more radical Communist allies, headed by Mao Tse-tung.

In 1931 Mao Tse-tung (1893–1976) led his followers on an incredible 5,000-mile march to remote northern China and dug in. Even war against the Japanese army of occupation could not force Mao and Chiang to cooperate. By late 1945 the long-standing quarrel erupted in civil war. Stalin gave Mao some aid, and the Americans gave Chiang much more. Winning the support of the peasantry by promising to expropriate the big landowners, the tougher, better-organized Communists

forced the Nationalists to withdraw to the island of Taiwan (formerly known as Formosa) in 1949.

Mao and the Communists united China's 550 million inhabitants in a strong centralized state, expelled foreigners, and began building a new society along Soviet lines, with mass arrests, forced-labor camps, and ceaseless propaganda. The peasantry was collectivized, and the inevitable five-year plans concentrated quite successfully on the expansion of heavy industry.

Most Asian countries followed the pattern of either India or China. Britain quickly gave Sri Lanka (Ceylon) and Burma independence in 1948; the Philippines became independent of the United States in 1946. The Dutch attempt to reconquer the Netherlands East Indies was unsuccessful, and in 1949 Indonesia emerged independent.

The French similarly sought to re-establish colonial rule in Indochina, but despite American aid they were defeated in 1954 by forces under the communist and nationalist guerrilla leader Ho Chi Minh (1890–1969), who was supported by Russia and China. At the subsequent international peace conference in Geneva, French Indochina gained

Chinese Red Guards   line up before a giant picture of Mao Tse-tung in about 1967. They are waving the "Little Red Book," which contains a collection of Mao's slogans and teachings. *(Source: Wide World Photos)*

MAP 30.3 The New States in Africa and Asia   Divided primarily along religious lines into two states, British India led the way to political independence in 1947. Most African territories achieved statehood by the mid-1960s, as European empires passed away, unlamented.

independence. Vietnam was divided into two hostile zones, one communist and one anticommunist, pending unification on the basis of internationally supervised free elections. But the elections were never held, and civil war soon broke out between the North and the South.

In Africa, Arab nationalism was an important factor in the ending of empire. Sharing a common language and culture, Arab nationalists were also loosely united by their opposition to the colonial powers and to the migration of Jewish refugees to Palestine. The British, whose occupation policies in Palestine were condemned by Arabs and Jews, by Russians and Americans, announced their withdrawal from Palestine in 1948. The United Nations voted for the creation of two states, one Arab and one Jewish. The Arab countries immediately attacked the new Jewish nation and suffered a humiliating defeat. In the course of the fighting, thousands of Arab refugees fled from the territory that became the Jewish state of Israel.

Many of these Arab refugees refused to accept defeat. They vowed to fight on, for generations if necessary, until the state of Israel was destroyed or until they established their own independent Palestinian state. The Palestinian refugees also sought the support of existing Arab states, claiming that Israel was the great enemy of Arab interests and Arab nationalism. The Arab-Israeli conflict was destined to outlive the postwar era, enduring to this day.

The Arab defeat in 1948 triggered a nationalist revolution in Egypt in 1952, where a young army officer named Gamal Abdel Nasser (1918–1970) drove out the pro-Western king. In 1956 Nasser abruptly nationalized the Suez Canal, the last symbol and substance of Western power in the Middle East. Infuriated, the British and French, along with the Israelis, invaded Egypt. This was, however, to be the dying gasp of imperial power: the moralistic, anti-imperialist Americans joined with the Russians to force the British, French, and Israelis to withdraw.

The failure of the Western powers to unseat Nasser in 1956 in turn encouraged Arab nationalists in Algeria. Algeria's large French population considered Algeria an integral part of France. It was this feeling that made the ensuing war so bitter and so atypical of decolonization. In the end, General De Gaulle, who had returned to power as part of a movement to keep Algeria French, accepted the principle of Algerian self-determination. In 1962,

after more than a century of French rule, Algeria became independent and the European population quickly fled.

In most of Africa south of the Sahara, decolonization proceeded much more smoothly. Beginning in 1957, Britain's colonies won independence with little or no bloodshed. In 1958 the clever De Gaulle offered the leaders of French black Africa the choice of a total break with France or immediate independence within a kind of French commonwealth. Heavily dependent on France for economic aid and technology, all but one of the new states chose association with France. Throughout the 1960s France (and its western European partners) successfully used economic and cultural ties with former colonies, such as special trading privileges with the Common Market and heavy investment in French-based education, to maintain a powerful European presence in black Africa. Radicals charged France (and Europe generally) with "neocolonialism," designed to perpetuate European economic domination indefinitely. In any event, enduring aid and influence in black Africa was an important manifestation of western Europe's political recovery and even of its possible emergence as a genuine superpower.

SOVIET EASTERN EUROPE

While western Europe surged ahead economically, regaining political independence as American influence gradually waned, eastern Europe followed a different path. Soviet Russia first tightened its grip on the "liberated" nations of eastern Europe under Stalin and then refused to let go. Economic recovery in eastern Europe proceeded, therefore, along Soviet lines, and political and social developments were largely determined by changes in the Soviet Union. Thus one must look primarily at Soviet Russia to understand the achievements and failures of eastern European peoples after the Second World War.

Stalin's Last Years

The unwillingness of the United States to accept what Stalin did to territories occupied by the triumphant Red Army was at least partly responsible for the outbreak and institutionalization of the cold war. Yet Americans were not the only ones who felt disappointed and even betrayed by Stalin's actions.

The Great Patriotic War of the Fatherland—World War Two as seen from the Soviet perspective—had fostered Russian nationalism and a relaxation of totalitarian terror. It also produced a rare but real unity between Soviet rulers and most Russian people. When an American correspondent asked a distinguished sixty-year-old Jewish scientist, who had decided to leave Russia for Israel in 1972, what had been the best period in Russian history, he received a startling answer: the Second World War. The scientist explained: "At that time we all felt closer to our government than at any other time in our lives. It was not *their* country then, but *our* country. . . . It was not *their* war, but *our* war."[8] Having made such a heroic war effort, the vast majority of the Soviet people hoped in 1945 that a grateful party and government would grant greater freedom and democracy. Such hopes were soon crushed.

Even before the war ended, Stalin was moving his country back toward rigid dictatorship. As early as 1944, the leading members of the Communist party were being given a new motivating slogan: "The war on Fascism ends, the war on capitalism begins."[9] By early 1946, Stalin was publicly singing the old tune that war was inevitable as long as capitalism existed. Stalin's invention of a new foreign foe was mainly an excuse for re-establishing totalitarian measures, for the totalitarian state cannot live without enemies. Unfortunately, as dissident Russian historians have argued, Stalin's language at home and his actions in eastern Europe were so crudely extreme that he managed to turn an imaginary threat into a real one, as the cold war took hold.

One of Stalin's first postwar goals was to repress the millions of Soviet citizens who were outside Soviet borders when the war ended. Many had been captured by the Nazis; others were ordinary civilians who had been living abroad. Many were opposed to Stalin; some had fought for the Germans. Determined to hush up the fact that large numbers of Soviet citizens hated his regime so much that they had willingly supported the Germans and refused to go home, Stalin demanded that all these "traitors" be returned to him. At Yalta, Roosevelt and Churchill agreed, and they kept their word. American and British military commanders refused to recognize the right of political asylum under any circumstances.

Roughly two million people were delivered to Stalin against their will. Most were immediately arrested and sent to forced-labor camps, where about 50 percent perished. The revival of many forced-labor camps, which had accounted for roughly one-sixth of all new construction in Soviet Russia before the war, was further stimulated by large-scale purges, particularly in 1945 and 1946, of many people who had never left the Soviet Union.

Culture and art were also purged. Rigid anti-Western ideological conformity was reimposed in violent campaigns led by Stalin's trusted henchman, Andrei Zhdanov. Zhdanov denounced many artists, including the composers Sergei Prokofiev and Dimitri Shostakovich and the outstanding film director Sergei Eisenstein. The great poet Anna Akhmatova was condemned as "a harlot and nun who mixes harlotry and prayer" and, like many others, was driven out of the writers' union, thus practically ensuring that her work would not be published. In 1949 Stalin launched a savage verbal attack on Soviet Jews, who were accused of being pro-Western and antisocialist.

In the political realm, Stalin reasserted the Communist party's complete control of the government and his absolute mastery of the party. Five-year plans were reintroduced to cope with the enormous task of economic reconstruction. Once again, heavy and military industry were given top priority, and consumer goods, housing, and still-collectivized agriculture were neglected. Everyday life was very hard: in 1952 the wages of ordinary people still bought 25 to 40 percent *less* than in 1928. In short, it was the 1930s all over again in Soviet Russia, although police terror was less intense than during that era's purges.

Stalin's prime postwar innovation was to export the Stalinist system to the countries of eastern Europe. The Communist parties of eastern Europe had established one-party states by 1948, thanks to the help of the Red Army and the Russian secret police. Rigid ideological indoctrination, attacks on religion, and a lack of civil liberties were soon facts of life. Industry was nationalized, and the middle class was stripped of its possessions. Economic life was then faithfully recast in the Stalinist mold. Forced industrialization, with five-year plans and a stress on heavy industry, lurched forward without regard for human costs. For the sake of ideological uniformity, agriculture had to be collectivized; this process went much faster in Bulgaria and Czechoslovakia than in Hungary and Poland. Finally, the

Frenz: Pink Snow   This light-hearted, fanciful rendition of traditional Russian themes hardly seems a threat to the Stalinist state. Yet it failed to conform to the official style of socialist realism and thus was suppressed with a host of other works during Zhdanov's brutal cultural purge. *(Source: Sovfoto)*

satellite countries were forced to trade heavily with Soviet Russia on very unfavorable terms, as traditional economic ties with western Europe were forcibly severed.

Only Josip Tito (1892–1980), the popular Resistance leader and Communist chief of Yugoslavia, was able to resist Russian economic exploitation successfully. Tito openly broke with Stalin in 1948, and since there was no Russian army in Yugoslavia, he got away with it. Tito's successful proclamation of Communist independence led the infuriated and humiliated Stalin to purge the Communist parties of eastern Europe. Hundreds of thousands who had joined the party after the war were expelled. Popular Communist leaders who, like Tito, had led the Resistance against Germany, were made to star in reruns of the great show trials of the 1930s, com-

plete with charges of treason, unbelievable confessions, and merciless executions. Thus did history repeat itself as Stalin sought to create absolutely obedient instruments of domination in eastern Europe.

Reform and De-Stalinization

In 1953 the aging Stalin finally died, and a new era slowly began in Soviet eastern Europe. Even as they struggled for power, Stalin's heirs realized that change and reform were necessary. There was, first of all, widespread fear and hatred of Stalin's political terrorism, which had struck both high and low with its endless purges and unjust arrests. Even Stalin's secret-police chief, Lavrenti Beria, publicly advocated a relaxation of controls in an unsuccessful attempt to seize power. Beria was arrested and shot, after which the power of the secret police was curbed and many of its infamous forced-labor camps were gradually closed. Change was also necessary for economic reasons. Agriculture was in bad shape, and shortages of consumer goods were discouraging hard work and initiative. Finally, Stalin's aggressive foreign policy had led directly to an ongoing American commitment to western Europe and a strong Western alliance. Soviet Russia was isolated and contained.

On the question of just how much change should be permitted, the Communist leadership was badly split. The conservatives, led by Stalin's long-time foreign minister, the stone-faced Vyacheslav Molotov, wanted to make as few changes as possible. The reformers, led by Nikita Khrushchev, argued for major innovations. Khrushchev (1894–1971), who had joined the party as an uneducated coal miner in 1918 at twenty-four and had risen steadily to a high-level position in the 1930s, was emerging as the new ruler by 1955.

To strengthen his position and that of his fellow reformers within the party, Khrushchev launched an all-out attack on Stalin and his crimes at a closed session of the Twentieth Party Congress in 1956. In gory detail he described to the startled Communist delegates how Stalin had tortured and murdered thousands of loyal Communists, how he had trusted Hitler completely and bungled the country's defense, and how he had "supported the glorification of his own person with all conceivable methods." For hours Soviet Russia's top leader delivered an attack whose content would previously have been dismissed as "anticommunist hysteria" in many circles throughout the Western world.

Khrushchev's "secret speech," read to Communist party meetings throughout the country, strengthened the reform movement. The liberalization—or "de-Stalinization," as it was called in the West—of Soviet Russia was genuine. The Communist party jealously maintained its monopoly on political power, but Khrushchev shook it up and brought in new blood. The economy was made more responsive to the needs and even some of the desires of the people, as some resources were shifted from heavy industry and the military toward consumer goods and agriculture. Stalinist controls over workers were relaxed, and independent courts rather than the secret police judged and punished nonpolitical crimes.

Russia's very low standard of living finally began to improve and continued to rise throughout the 1960s. By 1970 Russians were able to buy twice as much food, three times as much clothing, and twelve times as many appliances as in 1950. (Even so, the standard of living in Soviet Russia was only about half that of the wealthier western European countries in 1970 and well below that of eastern European countries as well.)

De-Stalinization created great ferment among writers and intellectuals, who hungered for cultural freedom. The poet Boris Pasternak (1890–1960), who survived the Stalinist years by turning his talents to translating Shakespeare, finished his great novel *Doctor Zhivago* in 1956. Published in the West but not in Russia, *Doctor Zhivago* is both a literary masterpiece and a powerful challenge to communism. It tells the story of a prerevolutionary intellectual who rejects the violence and brutality of the revolution of 1917 and the Stalinist years. Even as he is destroyed, he triumphs because of his humanity and Christian spirit. Pasternak was forced by Khrushchev himself to refuse the Nobel Prize in 1958—but he was not shot. Other talented writers followed Pasternak's lead, and courageous editors let the sparks fly.

The writer Alexander Solzhenitsyn (b. 1918) created a sensation when his *One Day in the Life of Ivan Denisovich* was published in Russia in 1962. Solzhenitsyn's novel portrays in grim detail life in a Stalinist concentration camp—a life to which Solzhenitsyn himself had been unjustly condemned—and is a damning indictment of the Stalinist past.

Khrushchev also de-Stalinized Soviet foreign policy. "Peaceful coexistence" with capitalism was possible, he argued, and great wars were not inevitable. Khrushchev made positive concessions: he met with U.S. President Dwight Eisenhower at the first summit meeting since Potsdam, and he agreed in 1955 to real independence for a neutral Austria after ten long years of Allied occupation. Thus there was considerable relaxation of cold war tensions between 1955 and 1957. At the same time, Khrushchev began wooing the new nations of Asia and Africa—even if they were not communist—with promises and aid. He also proclaimed that there could be different paths to socialism, thus calling a halt to the little cold war with Tito's Yugoslavia.

De-Stalinization stimulated rebelliousness in the eastern European satellites. Having suffered in silence under Stalin, Communist reformers and the masses were quickly emboldened to seek much greater liberty and national independence. Poland took the lead in March 1956: riots there resulted in the release of more than nine thousand political prisoners, including the previously purged Wladyslaw Gomulka. Taking charge of the government, Gomulka skillfully managed to win greater autonomy for Poland while calming anti-Russian feeling.

Hungary experienced a real and very tragic revolution. Led by students and workers—the classic urban revolutionaries—the people of Budapest installed a liberal Communist reformer as their new chief in October 1956. Soviet troops were forced to leave the country. One-party rule was abolished, and the new government promised free elections, freedom of expression, and massive social changes. Worst of all from the Russian point of view, the new government declared Hungarian neutrality and renounced Hungary's military alliance with Moscow. As in 1849, the Russian answer was to invade Hungary with a large army and to crush, once again, a national, democratic revolution.

Fighting was bitter until the end, for the Hungarians hoped that the United States would fulfill its earlier propaganda promises and come to their aid. When this did not occur because of American unwillingness to risk a general war, the people of eastern Europe realized that their only hope was to strive for small domestic gains while following Russia obediently in foreign affairs. This cautious approach produced some results. In Poland, for example, the peasants were not collectivized, and Catholics were allowed to practice their faith. Thus eastern Europe profited, however modestly, from Khrushchev's policy of de-Stalinization and could hope for still greater freedom in the future.

The Fall of Khrushchev

In October 1962 a remarkable poem entitled "Stalin's Heirs," by the popular young poet Yevgeny Yevtushenko (b. 1933), appeared in *Pravda,* the official newspaper of the Communist party and the most important one in Soviet Russia. Yevtushenko wrote:

Some of his heirs are in retirement pruning their
   rosebushes,
   and secretly thinking that their time will come again.
Others even attack Stalin from the rostrum but at
   home, at night-time, think back to bygone days.[10]

Like Solzhenitsyn's novel about Stalin's concentration camps, published a month later, this very political poem was authorized by Communist party boss Khrushchev himself. It was part of his last, desperate offensive against the many well-entrenched conservative Stalinists in the party and government, who were indeed "secretly thinking that their time will come again." And it did.

Within two years Khrushchev had fallen in a bloodless palace revolution. Under Leonid Brezhnev (1906–1982), Soviet Russia began a period of limited "re-Stalinization." The basic reason for this development was that Khrushchev's Communist colleagues saw de-Stalinization as a dangerous, two-sided threat. How could Khrushchev denounce the dead dictator without eventually denouncing and perhaps even arresting his still-powerful henchmen? In a heated secret debate in 1957, when the conservatives had tried without success to depose the menacing reformer, Khrushchev had pointed at two of Stalin's most devoted followers, Molotov and Kaganovich, and exclaimed: "Your hands are stained with the blood of our party leaders and of innumerable innocent Bolsheviks!" "So are yours!" Molotov and Kaganovich shouted back at him. "Yes, so are mine," Khrushchev replied. "I admit this. But during the purges I was merely carrying out your order. . . . I was not responsible. You were."[11] Moreover, the widening campaign of de-Stalinization posed a clear threat to the dictatorial authority of the party. It was producing growing, perhaps uncontrollable, criticism of the whole communist system. The party had to tighten up while there was still time. It was clear that Khrushchev had to go.

Another reason for conservative opposition was Khrushchev's foreign policy. Although he scored some diplomatic victories, notably with Egypt and India, Khrushchev's policy toward the West was highly erratic and ultimately unsuccessful. In 1958 he ordered the Western Allies to evacuate West Berlin within six months, which led only to a reaffirmation of Allied unity and to Khrushchev's backing down. Then in 1961, as relations with Communist China deteriorated dramatically, Khrushchev ordered the East Germans to build a wall between East and West Berlin, thereby sealing off West Berlin in clear violation of existing access agreements among the Great Powers. The recently elected U.S. president, John F. Kennedy, acquiesced. Emboldened and seeing a chance to change the balance of military power decisively,

Khrushchev ordered missiles with nuclear warheads installed in Fidel Castro's communist Cuba. President Kennedy countered with a naval blockade of Cuba, and after a tense diplomatic crisis, Khrushchev was forced to remove the Russian missiles in return for American pledges not to disturb Castro's regime. Khrushchev looked like a bumbling buffoon; his influence, already slipping, declined rapidly after the Cuban fiasco, and in October 1964 he was forced to resign by the Communist party's Central Committee.

After Brezhnev and his supporters took over in 1964, they started talking cautiously of Stalin's "good points" and ignoring his crimes. Their praise of the whole Stalinist era, with its rapid industrialization and wartime victories, informed Soviet citizens that no fundamental break with the past had occurred at home. Russian leaders also launched a massive arms buildup, determined never to suffer Khrushchev's humiliation in the face of American nuclear superiority. And they began building the large navy and air force necessary for intervention in faraway places, like Cuba, around the globe. Yet Brezhnev and company proceeded cautiously in the mid-1960s. They avoided direct confrontation with the United States and seemed more solidly committed to peaceful coexistence than the deposed Khrushchev—to the great relief of people in the West.

THE WESTERN HEMISPHERE

One way to think of what historians used to call the New World is as a vigorous offshoot of Western civilization, an offshoot that has gradually developed its own characteristics while retaining European roots. From this perspective, one can see many illuminating parallels and divergences in the histories of Europe and the Americas. So it was after the Second World War. The western hemisphere experienced a many-faceted postwar recovery, somewhat similar to that of Europe, though it began earlier, especially in Latin America.

Postwar Prosperity in the United States

The Second World War cured the depression in the United States and brought about the greatest boom in American history. Unemployment practically vanished, as millions of new workers, half of them women, found jobs. Personal income doubled, and the well-being of Americans increased dramatically. Yet the experience of the 1930s weighed heavily on people's minds, feeding fears that peace would bring renewed depression.

In fact, conversion to a peacetime economy went smoothly, marred only by a spurt of inflation accompanying the removal of government controls. Moreover, the U.S. economy continued to advance fairly steadily for a long generation. Though cold war fears marked American relations with the rest of the world, economic prosperity kept the public generally satisfied at home.

This helps explain why postwar domestic politics consisted largely of modest adjustments to the status quo until the 1960s. After a flurry of unpopular postwar strikes, a conservative Republican Congress chopped away at the power of labor unions by means of the Taft-Hartley Act of 1947. But Truman's upset victory in 1948 demonstrated that Americans had no interest in undoing Roosevelt's social and economic reforms. The Congress proceeded to increase social security benefits, subsidize middle- and lower-class housing, and raise the minimum wage. These and other liberal measures consolidated the New Deal. But true innovations, whether in health or civil rights, were rejected, and in 1952 the Republican party and the voters turned to General Eisenhower, a national hero and self-described moderate.

The federal government's only major new undertaking during the "Eisenhower years" was the interstate highway system, a suitable symbol of the basic satisfaction of the vast majority. Some Americans feared that the United States was becoming a "blocked society," obsessed with stability and incapable of wholesome change. This feeling contributed in 1960 to the election of the young, attractive John F. Kennedy, who promised to "get the country moving again." President Kennedy captured the popular imagination with his flair and rhetoric, revitalized the old Roosevelt coalition, and modestly expanded existing liberal legislation before he was struck down by an assassin's bullet in 1963.

The Civil Rights Revolution

Belatedly and reluctantly, complacent postwar America experienced a genuine social revolution:

after a long and sometimes bloody struggle, blacks (and their white supporters) threw off a deeply entrenched system of segregation, discrimination, and repression. This movement for civil rights advanced on several fronts. Eloquent lawyers from the National Association for the Advancement of Colored People (NAACP) challenged school segregation in the courts and in 1954 won a landmark decision in the Supreme Court that "separate educational facilities are inherently unequal."

While state and local governments in the South were refusing to comply, blacks were effectively challenging institutionalized inequality with bus boycotts, sit-ins, and demonstrations. As Martin Luther King told the white power structure, "We will not hate you, but we will not obey your evil laws."[12]

Blacks also used their growing political power in key northern states to gain the support of the liberal wing of the Democratic party. All these efforts culminated after the liberal landslide that elected Lyndon Johnson in 1964. The Civil Rights Act of 1964 categorically prohibited discrimination in public services and on the job. In the follow-up Voting Rights Act of 1965, the federal government firmly guaranteed all blacks the right to vote. By the 1970s, substantial numbers of blacks had been elected to public and private office throughout the southern states, showing proof positive that dramatic changes had occurred in American race relations.

Black voters and political leaders enthusiastically supported the accompanying surge of new liberal social legislation in the mid-1960s. President Johnson, reviving the New Deal approach of his early congressional years, solemnly declared "unconditional war on poverty." Congress and the administration created a host of antipoverty projects, such as the domestic peace corps, free preschools for slum children, and community-action programs. Although these programs were directed to all poor Americans—the majority of whom are white— they were also intended to extend greater equality for blacks to the realm of economics. More generally, the United States promoted in the mid-1960s the kind of fundamental social reform that western Europe had embraced immediately after World War Two. The United States became much more of a welfare state, as government spending for social benefits rose dramatically and approached European levels.

Economic Nationalism in Latin America

Although the countries of Latin America share a European heritage, specifically a Spanish-Portuguese heritage, their striking differences make it difficult to generalize meaningfully about modern Latin American history. Yet a growing economic nationalism seems unmistakable. As the early nineteenth century saw Spanish and Portuguese colonies win wars of political independence, recent history has been an ongoing quest for genuine economic independence through local control and industrialization, which has sometimes brought Latin American countries into sharp conflict with Europe and the United States.

To understand the rise of economic nationalism, one must remember that Latin American countries developed as producers of foodstuffs and raw materials, which were exported to Europe and the United States in return for manufactured goods and capital investment. This exchange was mutually beneficial, especially in the later nineteenth century, and the countries that participated most actively, like Argentina and southern Brazil, became the wealthiest and most advanced. There was, however, a heavy price to pay. Latin America became very dependent on foreign markets, products, and investments. Industry did not develop, and large landowners profited most, further enhancing their social and political power.

The old international division of labor, disrupted by the First World War but re-established in the 1920s, was finally destroyed by the Great Depression—a historical turning point as critical for Latin America as for the United States. Prices and exports of Latin American commodities collapsed as Europe and the United States drastically reduced their purchases and raised tariffs to protect domestic producers. With foreign sales plummeting, Latin American countries could not buy industrial goods abroad. Latin America suffered the full force of the global economic crisis.

The result in the larger, more important Latin American countries was a profound shift in the direction of economic nationalism after 1930. The more popularly based governments worked to reduce foreign influence and gain control of their own economies and natural resources. They energetically promoted national industry by means of high tariffs, government grants, and even state enterprise. They favored the lower middle and urban

The March on Washington   in August 1963 marked a dramatic climax in the civil rights struggle. More than 200,000 people gathered at the Lincoln Memorial to hear the young Martin Luther King deliver his greatest address, his "I have a dream" speech. *(Source: Francis Miller, LIFE MAGAZINE © Time Warner Inc.)*

working classes with social benefits and higher wages in order to increase their purchasing power and gain their support. These efforts at recovery were fairly successful. By the late 1940s, the factories of Argentina, Brazil, and Chile could generally satisfy domestic consumer demand for the products of light industry. In the 1950s, some countries began moving into heavy industry. Economic nationalism and the rise of industry are particularly striking in the two largest and most influential countries, Mexico and Brazil, which together account for half the population of Latin America.

Mexico   Overthrowing the elitist, upper-class rule of the tyrant Porfirio Díaz, the spasmodic, often-chaotic Mexican Revolution of 1910 culminated in 1917 in a new constitution. This radical nationalistic document called for universal suffrage, massive land reform, benefits for labor, and strict control of foreign capital. Actual progress was quite modest until 1934, when a charismatic young Indian from a poor family, Lázaro Cárdenas, became president and dramatically revived the languishing revolution. Under Cárdenas, many large estates were divided up among small farmers or returned undivided to Indian communities.

Meanwhile, because foreign capitalists were being discouraged, Mexican business people built many small factories and managed to thrive. The government also championed the cause of industrial workers. In 1938, when Mexican workers became locked in a bitter dispute with British and American oil companies, Cárdenas nationalized the petroleum industry—to the astonishment of a world unaccustomed to such actions. Finally, the 1930s saw the flowering of a distinctive Mexican culture, which proudly embraced its Indian past and gloried in the modern national revolution.

Diego Rivera (1886–1957) was one of the great and committed painters of the Mexican Revolution. Rivera believed that art should reflect the "new order of things" and inspire the common people—the workers and the peasants. One of Rivera's many wall paintings, this vibrant central mural in the National Palace in Mexico City, depicts a brutal Spanish conquest and a liberating revolution. *(Source: Robert Frerck/Odyssey Productions)*

In 1940 the official, semi-authoritarian party that has governed Mexico continuously since the revolution selected the first of a series of more moderate presidents. Steadfast in their radical, occasionally anti-American rhetoric, these presidents used the full power of the state to promote industrialization through a judicious mixture of public, private, and even foreign enterprise. The Mexican economy grew rapidly, at about 6 percent per year from the early 1940s to the late 1960s, with the upper and middle classes reaping the lion's share of the benefits.

Brazil   After the fall of the monarchy in 1889, politics had largely been dominated by the coffee barons and by regional rivalries. These rivalries and deteriorating economic conditions allowed a military revolt led by Getulio Vargas, governor of one of Brazil's larger states, to seize control of the federal government in 1930. Vargas, who proved to be a consummate politician, fragmented the opposition and established a mild dictatorship that lasted until 1945. Vargas's rule was generally popular, combining as it did effective economic nationalism and moderate social reform.

Somewhat like President Franklin Roosevelt in the United States, Vargas decisively tipped the balance of political power away from the Brazilian states to the ever-expanding federal government, which became a truly national government for the first time. Vargas and his allies also set out to industrialize Brazil and gain economic independence. While the national coffee board used mountains of surplus coffee beans to fire railroad locomotives, the government supported Brazilian manufacturers with high tariffs, generous loans, and labor peace. This probusiness policy did not prevent new social legislation: workers received shorter hours, pensions, health and accident insurance, paid vacations, and other benefits. Finally, Vargas shrewdly upheld the nationalist cause in his relations with the giant to the north. Early in the Second World War, for example, he traded acceptance of U.S. military bases in Brazil for American construction of Brazil's first huge steel-making complex. By 1945, when the authoritarian Vargas fell in a bloodless military coup that called for greater political liberty, Brazil was modernizing rapidly.

Modernization continued for the next fifteen years. The economy boomed. Presidential politics were re-established, while the military kept a watchful eye for extremism among the civilian politicians. Economic nationalism was especially vigorous under the flamboyant President Kubitschek (1956–1960), a doctor of German-Czech descent. The government borrowed heavily from international bankers to promote industry and built the extravagant new capital of Brasília in the midst of a wilderness. When Brazil's creditors demanded more conservative policies to stem inflation, Kubitschek delighted the nationalists with his firm and successful refusal. His slogan was "Fifty Years' Progress in Five," and he seemed to mean it.

The Brazilian and Mexican formula of national economic development, varying degrees of electoral competition, and social reform was shared by some other Latin American countries, notably Argentina and Chile. By the late 1950s, optimism was widespread, if cautious. Economic and social progress seemed to promise less violent, more democratic politics. These expectations were profoundly shaken by the Cuban Revolution.

The Cuban Revolution

Although many aspects of the Cuban Revolution are obscured by controversy, certain background conditions are clear. First, after achieving independence in 1898, Cuba was for many years virtually an American protectorate. The Cuban constitution gave the United States the legal right to intervene in Cuban affairs, a right that was frequently exercised until Roosevelt renounced it in 1934. Second, and partly because the American army had often been the real power, Cuba's political institutions were weak and its politicians were extraordinarily corrupt. Under the strongman Fulgencio Batista, an opportunistic ex-sergeant who controlled the government almost continually from 1933 to 1958, graft and outright looting were a way of life. Third, Cuba was one of Latin America's most prosperous and advanced countries by the 1950s, but its sugar-and-tourist economy was dependent on the United States. Finally, the enormous differences between rich and poor in Cuba were typical of Latin America. But Cuba also had a strong Communist party, which was highly unusual.

Fidel Castro, a magnetic leader with the gift of oratory and a flair for propaganda, managed to unify anti-Batista elements in a revolutionary front. When Castro's guerrilla forces triumphed in late 1958, the new government's goals were unclear.

Castro had promised a "real" revolution but had always laughed at charges that he was a communist. As the regime consolidated its power in 1959 and 1960, it became increasingly clear that "real" meant "communist" in Castro's mind. Wealthy Cubans, who owned three-quarters of the sugar industry and many profitable businesses, fled to Miami. Soon the middle class began to follow.

Meanwhile, relations with the Eisenhower administration—which had indirectly supported Castro by refusing to sell arms to Batista after March 1958—deteriorated rapidly. Thus, in April 1961, newly elected President Kennedy went ahead with a pre-existing CIA plan to use Cuban exiles to topple Castro. But the Kennedy administration lost its nerve and abandoned the exiles as soon as they were put ashore at the Bay of Pigs. This doomed the invasion, and the exiles were quickly captured, to be ransomed later for $60 million.

The Bay of Pigs invasion—a triumph for Castro and a humiliating, roundly criticized fiasco for the United States—had significant consequences. It freed Castro to build his version of a communist society, and he did. Political life in Cuba featured "anti-imperialism," an alliance with the Soviet bloc, the dictatorship of the party, and a vigorously promoted Castro cult. Revolutionary enthusiasm was genuine among party activists, much of Cuba's youth, and some of the masses some of the time. Prisons and emigration silenced opposition. The economy was characterized by all-pervasive state ownership, collective farms, and Soviet trade and aid. Early efforts to industrialize ran aground, and sugar production at pre-Castro levels continued to dominate the economy. Socially, the regime pursued equality and the creation of a new socialist personality. In short, revolutionary totalitarianism came to the Americas.

The failure of the United States' halfhearted effort to derail Castro probably encouraged Khrushchev to start putting nuclear missiles in Cuba, leading directly to the most serious East-West crisis since the Korean War. And, although the Russians backed down (see page 979), Castro's survival heightened both hopes and fears that the Cuban Revolution could spread throughout Latin America. As leftists were emboldened to try guerrilla warfare, conservatives became more rigid and suspicious of calls for change. In the United States, fear of communism aroused heightened cold war–style interest in Latin America. Using the Organization of American States to isolate Cuba, the United States in 1961 pledged $10 billion in aid over ten years to a new hemispheric "Alliance for Progress." The alliance was intended to promote long-term economic development and social reform, which American liberals hoped would immunize Latin America from the Cuban disease.

U.S. aid did contribute modestly to continued Latin America economic development in the 1960s, although population growth canceled out two-thirds of the increase on a per capita basis. Democratic social reforms—the other half of the Alliance for Progress formula—proceeded slowly, however. Instead, the period following the Cuban Revolution saw the rise of extremism and a revival of conservative authoritarianism in Latin America. These developments marked the turbulent beginnings of a new era in the late 1960s.

SUMMARY

The recovery of Europe and the Americas after World War Two is one of the most striking chapters in the long, uneven course of Western civilization. Although the dangerous tensions of the cold war frustrated fond hopes for a truly peaceful international order, the transition from imperialism to decolonization proceeded rapidly, surprisingly smoothly, and without serious damage to western Europe. Instead, as eastern Europe fell under harsh one-party Communist rule, genuine political democracy gained unprecedented strength in the West, and economic progress quickened the pace of ongoing social and cultural transformation. Thus the tremendous promise inherent in Western society's fateful embrace of the "dual revolution," which had begun in France and England in the late eighteenth century and which had been momentarily halted by the agonies of the Great Depression and the horrors of Nazi totalitarianism, was largely if perhaps only temporarily realized in the shining achievements of the postwar era.

NOTES

1. W. Bullitt, "How We Won the War and Lost the Peace," *Life*, August 30, 1948, p. 94.
2. Quoted in N. Graebner, *Cold War Diplomacy, 1945–1960* (Princeton, N.J.: Van Nostrand, 1962), p. 17.
3. Ibid.

4. Quoted in F. Prinz, ed., *Trümmerzeit in München* (Munich: Münchner Stadtmuseum, 1984), p. 273; trans. J. Buckler.

5. Quoted in J. Hennessy, *Economic "Miracles"* (London: André Deutsch, 1964), p. 5.

6. P. Van Zeeland, in *European Integration*, ed. C. G. Haines (Baltimore: Johns Hopkins Press, 1957), Preface, p. xi.

7. Lord Milner, quoted in R. von Albertini, "The Impact of Two World Wars on the Decline of Colonialism," *Journal of Contemporary History* 4 (January 1969): 17.

8. Quoted in H. Smith, *The Russians* (New York: Quadrangle Books/New York Times, 1976), p. 303.

9. Quoted in D. Treadgold, *Twentieth Century Russia*, 5th ed. (Boston: Houghton Mifflin, 1981), p. 442.

10. Quoted in M. Tatu, *Power in the Kremlin: From Khrushchev to Kosygin* (New York: Viking Press, 1968), p. 248.

11. Quoted in I. Deutscher, "The U.S.S.R. Under Khrushchev," in *Soviet Society*, ed. A. Inkeles and K. Geiger (Boston: Houghton Mifflin, 1961), p. 41.

12. Quoted in S. E. Morison et al., *A Concise History of the American Republic* (New York: Oxford University Press, 1977), p. 697.

SUGGESTED READING

An excellent way to approach wartime diplomacy is through the accounts of the statesmen involved. Great leaders and matchless stylists, Winston Churchill and Charles De Gaulle have both written histories of the war in the form of memoirs. Other interesting memoirs are those of Harry Truman (1958); Dwight Eisenhower, *Crusade in Europe* (1948); and Dean Acheson, *Present at the Creation* (1969), a beautifully written defense of American foreign policy in the early cold war. W. A. Williams, *The Tragedy of American Diplomacy* (1962), and W. La Feber, *America, Russia, and the Cold War* (1967), claim, on the contrary, that the United States was primarily responsible for the conflict with the Soviet Union. Two other important studies focusing on American policy are J. Gaddis, *The United States and the Origins of the Cold War* (1972), and D. Yergin, *Shattered Peace: The Origins of the Cold War and the National Security Council* (1977). A. Fontaine, a French journalist, provides a balanced general approach in his *History of the Cold War*, 2 vols. (1968). V. Mastny's thorough investigation of Stalin's war aims, *Russia's Road to the Cold War* (1979), is highly recommended.

R. Mayne, *The Recovery of Europe, 1945–1973*, rev. ed. (1973), and N. Luxenburg, *Europe Since World War II*, rev. ed. (1979), are recommended general surveys, as are two important works: W. Laqueur, *Europe Since Hitler*, rev. ed. (1982), and P. Johnson, *Modern Times: The World from the Twenties to the Eighties* (1983). T. White, *Fire in the Ashes* (1953), is a vivid view of European resurgence and Marshall Plan aid by an outstanding journalist. I. and D. Unger, *Postwar America: The United States Since 1945* (1989), and W. Leuchtenberg, *In the Shadow of FDR: From Harry Truman to Ronald Reagan*, rev. ed. (1989), ably discuss developments in the United States. Postwar economic and technological developments are analyzed in G. Ambrosius and W. Hibbard, *A Social and Economic History of Twentieth-Century Europe* (1989). A. Shonfield, *Modern Capitalism* (1965), provides an engaging, optimistic assessment of the growing importance of government investment and planning in European economic life. F. R. Willis, *France, Germany, and the New Europe, 1945–1967* (1968), is useful for postwar European diplomacy. Three outstanding works on France are J. Ardagh, *The New French Revolution* (1969), which puts the momentous social changes since 1945 in human terms; G. Wright, *Rural Revolution in France: The Peasantry in the Twentieth Century* (1964); and D. L. Hanley et al., eds., *France: Politics and Society Since 1945* (1979). R. Dahrendorf, *Society and Democracy in Germany* (1971), and H. S. Hughes, *The United States and Italy* (1968), are excellent introductions to modern German and Italian history. A. Marwick, *British Society Since 1945* (1982), and A. H. Halsey, *Change in British Society*, 2d ed. (1981), are good on postwar developments.

H. Seton-Watson, *The East European Revolution* (1965), is a good history of the communization of eastern Europe, and S. Fischer-Galati, ed., *Eastern Europe in the Sixties* (1963), discusses major developments. P. Zinner's, *National Communism and Popular Revolt in Eastern Europe* (1956) and *Revolution in Hungary* (1962) are excellent on the tragic events of 1956. Z. Brzezinski, *The Soviet Bloc: Unity and Conflict* (1967), is a major inquiry. W. Connor, *Socialism, Politics and Equality: Hierarchy and Change in Eastern Europe and the USSR* (1979), and J. Hough and M. Fainsod, *How the Soviet Union Is Governed* (1978), are important general studies. A. Amalrik, *Will the Soviet Union Survive Until 1984?* (1970), is a fascinating interpretation of Soviet society and politics in the 1960s by a Russian who paid for his criticism with prison and exile. A. Lee, *Russian Journal* (1981), and H. Smith's, *The Russians*, cited in the Notes, are excellent journalistic yet comprehensive reports by perceptive American observers.

R. von Albertini, *Decolonialization* (1971), is a good history of the decline and fall of European empires. The tremendous economic problems of the newly independent countries of Asia and Africa are discussed sympathetically by B. Ward, *Rich Nations and Poor Nations* (1962), and R. Heilbroner, *The Great Ascent* (1953). Two excellent general studies on Latin America are J. E. Fagg, *Latin America: A General History*, 3d ed. (1977), and R. J. Shafer, *A History of Latin America* (1978). Both contain detailed suggestions for further reading.

31

Life in the Postwar Era

While Europe staged its astonishing political and economic recovery from the Nazi nightmare, the patterns of everyday life and the structure of Western society were changing no less rapidly and remarkably. Epoch-making inventions and new technologies—the atomic bomb, television, computers, jet planes, and contraceptive pills, to name only a few—profoundly affected human existence. Important groups in society formulated new attitudes and demands, which were reflected in such diverse phenomena as the ever-expanding role of government, the revolt of youth in the late 1960s, and the women's movement. Rapid social change was clearly a fact of life in the Western world.

It was by no means easy to make sense out of all these changes while they were happening. Many "revolutions" and "crises" proved to be merely passing fads, sensationally ballyhooed by the media one day and forgotten the next. Some genuinely critical developments, such as those involving the family, were complex and contradictory, making it hard to understand what was really happening, much less explain why. Yet, by the 1980s, the great changes in social structure and everyday life that took place after the Second World War were coming into sharper focus. Above all, the historian was gaining vital perspective, for it became increasingly clear that the years from about 1968 to 1974 marked the end of the postwar period, as shall be seen in Chapter 32. Thus the startling postwar renaissance emerged in its turn as a separate era in the long evolution of the West, an era with its own distinctive social characteristics but still linked to what came before and after.

- How, then, did Western society and everyday life change in the postwar era, and why?
- What did these changes mean to people?

These are the questions this chapter will seek to answer.

SCIENCE AND TECHNOLOGY

Ever since the Scientific Revolution of the seventeenth century and the Industrial Revolution at the end of the eighteenth century, scientific and technical developments have powerfully influenced attitudes, society, and everyday life. Never was this influence stronger than after about 1940. Fantastic pipe dreams of science fiction a brief century ago became realities. Submarines passed under the North Pole, and astronauts walked on the moon. Skilled surgeons replaced their patients' failing arteries with plastic tubing. Millions of people around the world simultaneously watched a historic event on television. The list of wonders seemed endless.

The reason science and technology proved so productive and influential was that, for the first time in history, they were effectively joined together on a massive scale. This union of "pure theoretical" science with "applied" science or "practical" technology had already made possible striking achievements in the late nineteenth century in some select fields, most notably organic chemistry, electricity, and preventive medicine. Generally, however, the separation of science and technology still predominated in the late 1930s. Most scientists were university professors, who were little interested in such practical matters as building better machines and inventing new products. Such problems were the concern of tinkering technicians and engineers, who were to a large extent trained on the job. Their accomplishments and discoveries owed more to careful observation and trial-and-error experimentation than to theoretical science.

During World War Two, however, scientists and technicians increasingly marched to the sound of the same drummer. Both scientific research and technical expertise began to be directed at difficult but highly practical military problems. The result was a number of spectacular breakthroughs, such as radar and the atomic bomb, which had immediate wartime applications. After the war, this close cooperation between pure science and applied technology continued with equal success. Indeed, the line between science and technology became harder and harder to draw.

The consequences of the new, intimate link between science and technology were enormous. Seventeenth-century propagandists for science, such as Francis Bacon, had predicted that scientific knowledge of nature would give human beings the power to control the physical world. With such control, they believed, it would be possible to create material abundance and genuine well-being. The successful union of science and technology created new industries and spurred rapid economic growth after 1945, making this prediction finally come true for the great majority of people in Europe and North America in the postwar era.

At the same time, however, the unprecedented success of science in controlling and changing the physical environment produced unexpected and unwanted side effects. Chemical fertilizers poisoned rivers in addition to producing bumper crops. A great good like the virtual elimination of malaria-carrying mosquitoes by DDT dramatically lowered the death rate in tropical lands, but it also contributed to a population explosion in those areas. The list of such unwelcome side effects became very long. By the late 1960s, concern about the undesirable results of technological change had brought into being a vigorous environmental movement. The ability of science and technology to control and alter nature was increasingly seen as a two-edged sword, which had to be wielded with great care and responsibility.

The Stimulus of World War Two

Just before the outbreak of World War Two, a young Irish scientist and Communist named John Desmond Bernal wrote a book entitled *The Social Function of Science.* Bernal argued that the central government should be the source of funds for scientific research and that these funds should be granted on the basis of the expected social and political benefits. Most scientists were horrified by Bernal's proposals, which were contradictory to their cherished ideals. Scientists were committed to designing their own research without regard for its immediate usefulness. As late as 1937, the great physicist Ernest Rutherford could state that the work he and his colleagues were doing in nuclear physics at Cambridge University had no conceivable practical value for anyone, and he expressed delight that such was the case. Nor did university scientists concern themselves with government grants, since many had independent incomes to help finance their still-inexpensive experiments.

The First Jet Engine   The marriage of pure science and technology produced inventions like the jet engine. The inventor, Frank Whittle, shows the engine to Dr. Alexander Wetmore, Secretary of the Smithsonian (left), as he accepts the gift from British Ambassador Sir Oliver Franks (right). *(Source: Bettmann/Hulton)*

Atomic Weapons   were the ultimate in state-directed scientific research. In this photo the awesome mushroom cloud of an American atomic bomb rises over the Pacific island of Bikini. *(Source: U.S. Dept. of Energy)*

The Second World War changed this pattern. Pure science lost its impractical innocence. Most leading university scientists went to work on top-secret projects to help their governments fight the war. The development of radar by British scientists was a particularly important outcome of this new kind of sharply focused research.

As early as 1934, the British Air Ministry set up a committee of scientists and engineers to study the problem of air defense systematically. A leading British expert's calculations on radio waves suggested that the idea of a "death ray" so powerful it could destroy an attacking enemy aircraft was nonsense, but that detection of enemy aircraft by radio waves was theoretically possible. Radio waves emitted at intervals by a transmitter on the ground would bounce off flying aircraft, and a companion receiver on the ground would hear this echo and detect the approaching plane. Experiments went forward, and by 1939 the British had installed a very primitive radar system along the southern and eastern coasts of England.

Immediately after the outbreak of war with Germany in September 1939, the British military enlisted leading academic scientists in an all-out effort to improve the radar system. The basic problem was developing a high-powered transmitter capable of sending very short wavelengths, which could be precisely focused in a beam sweeping the sky like a searchlight. In the summer of 1940, British physicists made the dramatic technical breakthrough that solved this problem of short-wave transmission. The new and radically improved radar system, which was quickly installed, played a key role in Britain's victory in the battle for air supremacy in the fall of 1940. During the war, many different types of radar were developed—for fighter planes, for bombers, for detection of submarines.

After 1945, war-born microwave technology generated endless applications, especially in telecommunications. Microwave transmission carried long-distance conversations, television programs, and messages to and from satellites.

The air war also greatly stimulated the development of jet aircraft and computers. Although the first jet engines were built in the mid-1930s, large-scale government-directed research did not begin until immediately before the war. The challenge was to build a new kind of engine—a jet engine—capable of burning the low-grade "leftovers" of petroleum refining, thereby helping to overcome the desperate shortage of aviation fuel. The task proved extremely difficult and expensive. Only toward the end of the war did fast, high-flying jet fighters become a reality. Quickly adopted for both military and peacetime purposes after the war, jet airplanes contributed to the enormous expansion of commercial aviation in the 1950s.

The problems of air defense also spurred further research on electronic computers, which had barely come into existence before 1939. Computers calculated the complex mathematical relationships between fast-moving planes and antiaircraft shells, to increase the likelihood of a hit.

Wartime needs led to many other major technical breakthroughs. Germany had little oil and was almost completely cut off from foreign supplies. But Germany's scientists and engineers found ways to turn coal into gasoline so that the German war machine did not sputter to a halt.

The most spectacular result of directed scientific research during the war was the atomic bomb. In August 1939, Albert Einstein wrote to President Franklin Roosevelt, stating that recent work in physics suggested that

it may become possible to set up a nuclear chain reaction in a large mass of uranium, by which vast amounts of power and large quantities of new radium-like elements would be generated. . . . This new phenomenon would also lead to the construction of bombs, and it is conceivable—though much less certain—that extremely powerful bombs of a new type may thus be constructed.[1]

This letter and ongoing experiments by nuclear physicists led to the top-secret Manhattan Project and the decision to build the atomic bomb.

The American government spared no expense to turn a theoretical possibility into a practical reality. A mammoth crash program went forward in several universities and special laboratories, the most important of which was the newly created laboratory at Los Alamos in the wilds of New Mexico. The Los Alamos laboratory was masterfully directed from 1942 by J. Robert Oppenheimer (1904–1967), a professor and theoretical physicist. Its sole objective was to design and build an atomic bomb. Toward that end Oppenheimer assembled a team of brilliant American and European scientists and managed to get them to cooperate effectively. After three years of intensive effort, the first atomic bomb was successfully tested in July 1945. In August 1945, two bombs were dropped on Hiroshima and Nagasaki, ending the war with Japan.

The atomic bomb showed the world both the awesome power and the heavy moral responsibilities of modern science and its high priests. As one of Oppenheimer's troubled colleagues exclaimed while he watched the first mushroom cloud rise over the American desert, "We are all sons-of-bitches now!"[2]

The Rise of Big Science

The spectacular results of directed research during World War Two inspired a new model for science—"Big Science." By combining theoretical work with sophisticated engineering in a large organization, Big Science could attack extremely difficult problems. Solution of these problems led to new and better products for consumers and to new and better weapons for the military. In any event, the assumption was that almost any conceivable technical goal might be attained. Big Science was extremely expensive. Indeed, its appetite for funds was so great that it could be financed only by governments and large corporations. Thus the ties between science and tax-paying society grew very close.

Science became so "big" largely because its equipment grew ever more complex and expensive.

The Apollo Program Astronauts Neil Armstrong, Michael Collins, and Edwin Aldrin, Jr., took off from Florida on July 16, 1969 in the Apollo spacecraft. Astronaut Armstrong was the first man to set foot on the moon, four days later, on July 20. The astronauts splashed down in the Pacific Ocean, and recovery was made by the U.S.S. *Hornet* on July 24. *(Source: National Aeronautics and Space Administration)*

Because many advances depended directly on better instruments, the trend toward bigness went on unabated. This trend was particularly pronounced in atomic physics, perhaps the most prestigious and influential area of modern science. When Rutherford first "split the atom" in 1919, his equipment cost only a few dollars. In the 1930s the price of an accelerator, or "atom smasher," reached $10,000, and the accelerators used in high-energy experiments while the atomic bomb was being built were in the $100,000 range. By 1960, however, when the western European nations pooled their resources in the European Council for Nuclear Research (CERN) to build an accelerator outside of Geneva—an accelerator with power in billions rather than millions of electron volts—the cost had jumped to $30 million. These big accelerators did an amazingly good job of prying atoms apart, and over two hundred different particles have been identified so far. Yet new answers produced new questions, and the logic of ever-more-sophisticated observations demanded ever-more-powerful and ever-more-costly accelerators in the postwar period.

Astronomers followed physicists in the ways of Big Science. Their new eye was the radio telescope, which picked up radio emissions rather than light. In the 1960s the largest of these costly radio telescopes sat atop a mountain and had a bowl a thousand feet wide to focus the radio signals from space. Aeronautical research and development also attained mammoth proportions. The cost of the Anglo-French *Concorde,* the first supersonic passenger airliner, went into the billions. Even ordinary science became big and expensive by historical standards. The least costly laboratory capable of doing useful research in either pure or applied science required around $200,000 a year in the 1960s.

Populous, victorious, and wealthy, the United States took the lead in Big Science after World War Two. Between 1945 and 1965, spending on scientific research and development in the United States grew five times as fast as the national income. By 1965 fully 3 percent of all income in the United States was spent on science. While large American corporations maintained impressive research laboratories, fully three-quarters of all funds spent on scientific research and development in the United States were coming from the government by 1965. It was generally accepted that government should finance science heavily. One wit pointed out that by the mid-1960s the "science policy" of the supposedly conservative Republican party in the

United States was almost identical to that of the supposedly revolutionary Communist party of the Soviet Union.

One of the reasons for the similarity was that science was not demobilized in either country after the war. Indeed, scientists remained a critical part of every major military establishment and, after 1945 as during World War Two, a large portion of all scientific research went for "defense." Jet bombers gave way to rockets, battleships were overtaken by submarines with nuclear warheads, and spy planes were replaced with spy satellites. All such new weapons demanded breakthroughs no less remarkable than those of radar and the first atomic bomb. After 1945 roughly one-quarter of all men and women trained in science and engineering in the West—and perhaps more in the Soviet Union—were employed full-time in the production of weapons to kill other humans.

Sophisticated science, lavish government spending, and military needs all came together in the space race of the 1960s—the most sensational example of Big Science in action after the creation of the atomic bomb. In 1957 the Russians used long-range rockets developed in their nuclear weapons program to put a satellite in orbit. In 1961 they sent the world's first cosmonaut circling the globe. Breaking with President Eisenhower's opposition to an expensive space program, President Kennedy made an all-out U.S. commitment to catch up with the Russians and land a manned spacecraft on the moon "before the decade was out." Harnessing pure science, applied technology, and up to $5 billion a year, the Apollo Program achieved its ambitious objective in 1969. Four more moon landings followed by 1972.

The rapid expansion of government-financed research in the United States attracted many of Europe's best scientists during the 1950s and 1960s. Thoughtful Europeans lamented this "brain drain." In his best seller *The American Challenge* (1967), the French journalist Jean-Jacques Servan-Schreiber warned that Europe was falling hopelessly behind the United States in science and technology. The only hope was to copy American patterns of research before the United States achieved an absolute stranglehold on computers, jet aircraft, atomic energy, and indeed most of the vital dynamic sectors of the late-twentieth-century economy.

In fact, a revitalized Europe was already responding to the American challenge. European countries

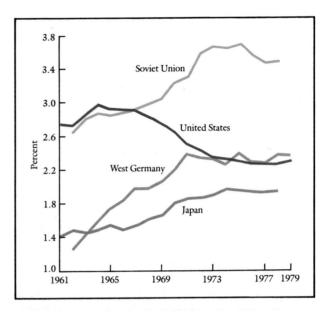

FIGURE 31.1 Research and Development Expenditures as a Percentage of GNP in the United States, Soviet Union, West Germany, and Japan, 1961–1979 While the United States spent less of its national income on research and development after the early 1960s, European nations and Japan spent more. This helped Europe and Japan narrow or even close the technological gap that had existed after the end of World War Two. *(Source: Data Resources, Inc.)*

were beginning to pool their efforts and spend more on science and engineering, as they concentrated on big projects like the *Concorde* supersonic passenger airliner and the peaceful uses of atomic energy. Thus European countries created their own Big Science. By 1974 many European nations were devoting a substantial percentage of their income to research and development and were in the process of achieving equality with the United States in many fields of scientific endeavor (Figure 31.1).

The Life of Scientists and Technologists

The rise of Big Science and of close ties between science and technology greatly altered the lives of scientists. The scientific community grew much larger than ever before: of all the scientists who have ever lived, nine out of ten are still alive today. The astonishing fact is that the number of scientists has been doubling every fifteen years for the past three centuries. There were, therefore, about four times as many scientists in 1975 as in 1945, just as there were a *million* times as many scientists as there were in 1670. Scientists, technologists, engineers, and medical specialists counted in modern society, in part because there were so many of them.

One important consequence of the bigness of science was its high degree of specialization. With close to a hundred thousand scientific journals being published by the 1970s, no one could possibly master a broad field like physics or medicine. Instead, a field like physics was constantly dividing and subdividing into new specialties and subdisciplines. The fifty or one hundred men and women who were truly abreast of the latest developments in a highly specialized field formed an international "invisible college." Cooperating and competing, communicating through special journals and conferences, the leading members of these invisible colleges kept the problems of the subdiscipline under constant attack. Thus intense specialization undoubtedly increased the rates at which both basic knowledge was acquired and practical applications were made.

Highly specialized modern scientists and technologists normally had to work as members of a team. The problems and equipment of Big Science were simply too complicated and expensive for a person to work effectively as an individual researcher. The collaborative "team" character of much of modern scientific research—members of invisible colleges were typically the leaders of such teams—completely changed the work and lifestyle of modern scientists. Old-fashioned, prewar scientists were like professional golfers—lonely individuals who had to make all the shots themselves. Modern scientists and technologists were more like players on American professional football teams. There were owners and directors, coaches and assistant coaches, overpaid stars and unsung heroes, veterans and rookies, kickoff specialists and substitutes, trainers and water boys.

If this parallel seems fanciful, consider the research group of Luis Alvarez at the high-energy physics Radiation Laboratory of the University of California at Berkeley in the late 1960s. This group consisted of more than two hundred people. At the top were Alvarez and about twenty Ph.D.'s, followed by twenty graduate research assistants and fourteen full-time engineers. Almost fifty people were categorized as "technical leadership"—computer programmers, equipment operators, and so on. Finally, there were more than a hundred "technical assistants"—primarily scanners who analyzed photographs showing the tracks of particles after various collisions. A laboratory like that of CERN outside Geneva resembled a small city of several thousand people—scientists, technicians, and every kind of support personnel. A great deal of modern science and technology went on, therefore, in large, well-defined bureaucratic organizations. The individual was very often a small cog in a great machine, a member of a scientific army.

The advent of large-scale scientific bureaucracies led to the emergence of a new group, science managers and research administrators. Such managers generally had scientific backgrounds, but their main tasks were scheduling research, managing people, and seeking money from politicians or financial committees of large corporations. This last function was particularly important, for there were limits to what even the wealthiest governments and corporations would spend for research. Competition for funds was always intense, even in the fat 1960s.

Many science managers were government bureaucrats. These managers doled out funds and "refereed" the scientific teams that were actually playing on the field. Was the *Concorde* supersonic jet too noisy to land in New York City? Did saccharin cause cancer, and should it be banned? The list of potential questions was endless. Beginning in the late 1960s, the number of such referees and the penalties they were imposing seemed to explode, driven forward by public alarm about undesirable side effects of technological advance. More generally, the growth of the scientific bureaucracy suggested how scientists and technologists permeated the entire society and many aspects of life.

Two other changes in the lives of scientists should be noted briefly. One was the difficulty of appraising an individual's contribution to a collaborative team effort. Who deserved the real credit (or blame) for a paper that listed twenty-five physicists as coauthors? Even in a field like chemistry, which remained relatively "small" in its research techniques, more than two-thirds of all papers had two or more authors by the 1970s. Questions of proper recognition within the team effort were thus very complicated and preoccupying to modern scientists.

A second, related change was that modern science became highly, even brutally, competitive. This competitiveness is well depicted in Nobel Prize winner James Watson's fascinating book *The Double Helix,* which tells how in 1953 Watson and an Englishman, Francis Crick, discovered the structure of DNA, the molecule of heredity. A brash young American Ph.D. in his twenties, Watson seemed almost obsessed by the idea that some other research team would find the solution first and thereby deprive him of the fame and fortune he desperately wanted. With so many thousands of like-minded researchers in the wealthy countries of the world, it was hardly surprising that scientific and technical knowledge rushed forward in the postwar era.

TOWARD A NEW SOCIETY

The prodigious expansion of science and technology greatly affected the peoples of the Western world. By creating new products and vastly improved methods of manufacturing and farming, it fueled rapid economic growth and rising standards of living. Moreover, especially in Europe, scientific and technological progress, combined with economic prosperity, went a long way toward creating a whole new society after World War Two.

This new society was given many catchy titles. Some called it the "technocratic society," a society of highly trained specialists and experts. For others, fascinated by the great increase in personal wealth, it was the "affluent society" or the "consumer society." For those struck by the profusion of government-provided social services, it was simply the "welfare state." For still others, it was the "permissive society," where established codes of conduct no longer prevailed. In fact, Western society in the postwar era was all of these: technocratic, affluent, welfare-oriented, and permissive. These characteristics reflected changes in the class structure and indicated undeniable social progress.

The Changing Class Structure

After 1945 European society became more mobile and more democratic. Old class barriers relaxed, and class distinctions became fuzzier.

Changes in the structure of the middle class, directly related to the expansion of science and technology, were particularly influential in the general drift toward a less rigid class structure. The model for the middle class in the nineteenth and early twentieth centuries was the independent, self-employed individual who owned a business or practiced a liberal profession like law or medicine. Many businesses and professional partnerships were tightly held family firms. Marriage into such a family often provided the best opportunity for an outsider to rise to the top. Ownership of property —usually inherited property—and strong family ties were often the keys to wealth and standing within the middle class.

This traditional pattern, which first changed in the United States and the Soviet Union (for very different reasons) before the Second World War, declined drastically in western Europe after 1945. A new breed of managers and experts rose to replace traditional property owners as the leaders of the middle class. Within large bureaucratic corporations and government, men and women increasingly advanced as individuals and on the basis of merit (and luck). Ability to serve the needs of a

The Double Helix The giant DNA molecule, which governs heredity in living things, has the form of a double helix, a kind of spiraling ladder with alternating sides of phosphate and sugar. James Watson and Francis Crick discovered the double helix structure of DNA, represented here by the model they are examining. *(Source: MRC Laboratory of Molecular Biology, University of Cambridge)*

A Modern Manager Despite considerable discrimination, women were increasingly found in the expanding middle class of salaried experts after World War Two, working in business, science, and technology. *(Source: Niépce-Rapho/Photo Researchers)*

large organization, which usually depended on special expertise, largely replaced inherited property and family connections in determining an individual's social position in the middle and upper middle class. Social mobility, both upward and downward, increased. At the same time, the middle class grew massively and became harder to define.

There were a number of reasons for these developments. Rapid industrial and technological expansion created in large corporations and government agencies a powerful demand for technologists and managers capable of responding effectively to an ever-more-complicated world. This growing army of specialists—the backbone of the new middle class—could be led effectively only by like-minded individuals, of whom only a few at best could come from the old property-owning families.

Second, the old propertied middle class lost control of many of its formerly family-owned businesses. Even very wealthy families had to call on the general investing public for capital, and heavy inheritance taxes forced sales of stock, further diluting family influence. Many small businesses (including family farms) simply passed out of existence, and their ex-owners joined the ranks of salaried employees. In Germany in 1950, for exam-

ple, self-employed people formed 33 percent of the labor force, and white-collar workers constituted 20 percent. By 1962 the percentages for these two groups were exactly reversed. Moreover, the wave of nationalization in western and eastern Europe after the Second World War automatically replaced capitalist owners with salaried managers and civil servants in state-owned companies.

Top managers and ranking civil servants therefore represented the model for a new middle class of salaried specialists. Well paid and highly trained, often with backgrounds in science or engineering or accounting, these experts increasingly came from all social classes, even the working class. Pragmatic and realistic, they were primarily concerned with efficiency and practical solutions to concrete problems. Generally, they were not very interested in the old ideological debates about capitalism and socialism, confidently assuming that their skills were indispensable in either system or any combination of the two.

Indeed, the new middle class of experts and managers was an international class, not much different in socialist eastern Europe than in capitalist western Europe and North America. Everywhere successful managers and technocrats passed on the opportunity for all-important advanced education to their children, but only in rare instances could they pass on the positions they had attained. Thus the new middle class, which was based largely on specialized skills and high levels of education, was more open, democratic, and insecure than the old propertied middle class.

The structure of the traditional lower classes also became more flexible and open. There was a mass exodus from farms and the countryside. One of the most traditional and least mobile groups in European society drastically declined: after 1945 the number of peasants declined by more than 50 percent in almost every European country. Meanwhile, because of rapid technological change, the industrial working class ceased to expand, stabilizing at slightly less than one-half of the labor force in wealthy advanced countries. Job opportunities for white-collar and service employees, however, expanded rapidly. Such employees bore a greater resemblance to the new middle class of salaried specialists than to industrial workers, who were better educated and more specialized. Developments within the lower classes contributed, therefore, to the breakdown of rigid social divisions.

Social Security Reforms and Rising Affluence

While the demands of modern technology and big bureaucracies broke down rigid class divisions, European governments, with their new and revitalized political leadership (see page 966), reduced class tensions with a series of social security reforms. Many of these reforms simply strengthened social security measures first pioneered in Bismarck's Germany before World War One. Unemployment and sickness benefits were increased and extended, as were retirement benefits and old-age pensions. Other programs were new.

Britain's Labour government took the lead immediately after the Second World War in establishing a comprehensive national health system; other European governments followed the British example. Depending on the system, patients either received completely free medical care or paid only a very small portion of the total cost.

Most countries also introduced family allowances—direct government grants to parents to help them raise their children. Lower-paid workers generally received the largest allowances, and the rate per child often kept increasing until the third or fourth child. These allowances helped many poor families make ends meet. Most European governments also gave maternity grants and built inexpensive public housing for low-income families and individuals. Other social welfare programs ranged from cash bonuses for getting married in Belgium and Switzerland to subsidized vacations for housewives in Sweden.

It would be wrong to think that the expansion of social security services after World War Two provided for every human need "from cradle to grave," as early advocates of the welfare state hoped and its critics feared. But these social reforms did provide a humane floor of well-being, below which very few individuals could fall in the advanced countries of northern and western Europe. (Social benefits were greatest in the wealthiest nations, such as Sweden, West Germany, and Britain, and less in poorer areas of southern and eastern Europe.)

These reforms also promoted greater social and economic equality. They were expensive, paid for in part by high taxes on the rich. In Britain, for example, where social security benefits for the population at large and taxes on the rich both became quite high, the top 5 percent of the population re-

ceived about 14 percent of national income after taxes in 1957, as opposed to fully 43 percent in 1913. Thus extensive welfare measures leveled society both by raising the floor and by lowering the ceiling.

The rising standard of living and the spread of standardized, mass-produced consumer goods also worked to level Western society. A hundred years ago, food and drink cost roughly two-thirds of the average family's income in western and northern Europe; by the mid-1960s, they took only about one-third to two-fifths of that family's income. Consumption of traditional staples like bread and potatoes actually declined almost everywhere in Europe after 1945; yet because incomes have risen rapidly, people eat more meat, fish, and dairy products. The goal of adequate and good food was attained almost universally in advanced countries.

But progress introduced new problems. People in Europe and North America were eating too much rather than too little, giving rise to an endless proliferation of diet foods and diet fads. Another problem was that modern consumers often appeared remarkably ignorant of basic nutrition. They stuffed themselves with candy, soft drinks, French fries, and spongy white bread, and frequently got poor value for their money. Finally, the traditional pleasures of eating good food well prepared suffered major declines in the postwar age of fast-food franchises and mass-produced burgers and standardized buns.

The phenomenal expansion of the automobile industry exemplified even more strikingly the emergence of the consumer society. In the United States, automobile ownership was commonplace far down the social scale by the mid-1920s, whereas only the rich could generally afford cars in Europe before the Second World War. In 1948 there were only five million cars in western Europe, and most ordinary people dreamed at most of stepping up from a bicycle to a motorcycle. With the development of cheaper, mass-produced cars, this situation changed rapidly. By 1957 the number of cars had increased to fifteen million, and automobiles had become a standard item of middle-class consumption. By 1965 the number of cars in western Europe had tripled again to forty-four million, and car ownership had come well within the range of better-paid workers.

Europeans took great pleasure in the products of the "gadget revolution" as well. Like Americans,

Sports Fans developed fierce tribal loyalties, finding comradeship and a sense of belonging cheering for their teams. Here Liverpool's famous rooting section goes wild with delight after its team clinches the English soccer championship in 1977. Soccer matches have occasionally degenerated into pitched battles between rival fans. *(Source: Wide World Photos)*

Europeans filled their houses and apartments with washing machines, vacuum cleaners, refrigerators, dishwashers, radios, TVs, and stereos. The purchase of these and other consumer goods was greatly facilitated by installment purchasing, which allowed people to buy on credit. Before World War Two, Europeans had rarely bought "on time." But with the expansion of social security safeguards, reducing the need to accumulate savings for hard times, ordinary people were increasingly willing to take on debt. This change had far-reaching consequences.

Household appliances became necessities for most families. Middle-class women had to do much of their own housework, for young girls avoided domestic service like the plague. Moreover, more women than ever before worked outside the home, and they needed machines to help do household chores as quickly as possible. The power tools of "do-it-yourself" work also became something of a necessity, for few dependable artisans were available for household repairs.

Leisure and recreation occupied an important place in consumer societies. Indeed, with incomes rising and the workweek shrinking from roughly forty-eight hours right after the war to about forty-one hours by the early 1970s, leisure became big business. In addition to ever-popular soccer matches and horse races, movies, and a growing addiction to television, individuals had at their disposal a vast range of commercialized hobbies, most of which could soak up a lot of cash. Newsstands were full of specialized magazines about everything from hunting and photography to knitting and antique collecting. Interest in "culture," as measured by attendance at concerts and exhibitions, also increased. Even so, the commercialization of leisure through standardized manufactured products was striking.

The most astonishing leisure-time development in the consumer society was the blossoming of mass travel and tourism. Before the Second World War, travel for pleasure and relaxation remained a rather aristocratic pastime. Most people had neither the time nor the money for it. But with month-long paid vacations required by law in most European countries, and widespread automobile ownership, beaches and ski resorts came within the reach of the middle class and many workers. At certain times of year, hordes of Europeans surged to the sea or the mountains, and woe to the traveler who had not made arrangements well in advance.

By the late 1960s packaged tours with cheap group flights and bargain hotel accommodations had made even distant lands easily accessible. One-fifth of West Germany's population traveled abroad each year. A French company, the Club Méditerranée, grew rich building imitation Tahitian paradises around the world. At Swedish nudist colonies on secluded West African beaches, secretaries and salespersons from Stockholm fleetingly worshiped the sun in the middle of the long northern winter. Truly, consumerism had come of age.

Renewed Discontent and the Student Revolt

For twenty years after 1945, Europeans were largely preoccupied with the possibilities of economic progress and consumerism. The more democratic class structure also helped to reduce social tension, and ideological conflict went out of style. In the late 1960s, however, sharp criticism and discontent re-emerged. It was a common complaint that Europeans were richer but neither happier nor better. Social conflicts began to appear once more.

Simmering discontent in eastern Europe was not hard to understand. The gradual improvement in the standard of living stood in stark contrast to the ongoing lack of freedom in political and intellectual life and made that lack of freedom all the more distasteful. As will be shown in the next chapter, such dissatisfaction found eloquent expression once again, despite the refinement of techniques of repression in eastern Europe and the willingness of the Soviet Union to crush reform efforts in Czechoslovakia with military might in 1968.

The reappearance of discontent in western Europe was not so easily explained. From the mid-1950s on, western European society was prosperous, democratic, and permissive. Yet this did not prevent growing hostility to the existing order among some children of the new society. Radical students in particular rejected the materialism of their parents and claimed that the new society was repressive and badly flawed. Though these criticisms and the movements they sparked were often ridiculed by the older generation, they reflected some real problems of youth, education, and a society of specialists. They deserve closer attention.

In contrast to the United States, high school and university educations in Europe were limited for centuries to a small elite. That elite consisted mainly of young men and women from the well-to-do classes, along with a sprinkling of scholarship students from humble origins. Whereas 22 percent of the American population was going on to some form of higher education in 1950, only 3 to 4 percent of western European youths were doing so. Moreover, European education was still directed toward traditional fields: literature, law, medicine, and pure science. Its basic goal was to pass on culture and pure science to an elite, and with the exception of law and medicine, applied training for specialists was not considered very important.

After World War Two, public education in western Europe began to change dramatically. Enrollments skyrocketed. By 1960 there were at least three times as many students going to some kind of university as there had been before the war, and the number continued to rise sharply until the 1970s. Holland had ten thousand university students in 1938 and a hundred thousand in 1960. In France 14 percent of young people went to a university in 1965, as opposed to 4.5 percent in 1950. With an increase in scholarships and a growing awareness that higher education was the key to success, European universities became more democratic, opening their doors to more students from the lower middle and lower classes. Finally, in response to the prodigious expansion of science and technology, the curriculum gradually changed. All sorts of new, "practical" fields—from computer science to business administration—appeared alongside the traditional liberal arts and sciences.

The rapid expansion of higher education created problems as well as opportunities for students. Classes were badly overcrowded, and there was little contact with professors. Competition for grades became intense. Moreover, although more "practical" areas of study were added, they were added less quickly than many students wanted. Thus many students felt that they were not getting the kind of education they needed for the modern world and that basic university reforms were absolutely necessary. The emergence of a distinctive "youth culture" also brought students into conflict with those symbols of the older generation and parental authority—professors and school officials.

These tensions within the exploding university population came to a head in the late 1960s and early 1970s. Following in the footsteps of their American counterparts, who pioneered with large-scale student protests in the mid-1960s, European university students rose to challenge their university administrations and even their governments.

The most far-reaching of these revolts occurred in France in 1968. It began at the stark new University of Nanterre in the gloomy industrial suburbs of Paris. Students demanded both changes in the curriculum and a real voice in running the university. The movement spread to the hallowed halls of the medieval Sorbonne in the heart of Paris. Students occupied buildings and took over the university. This takeover led to violent clashes with police, who were ordered in to break up a demonstration that was fast becoming an uprising.

The student radicals appealed to France's industrial workers for help. Rank-and-file workers ignored the advice of their cautious union officials, and a more or less spontaneous general strike spread across France in May 1968. It seemed certain that President De Gaulle's Fifth Republic would collapse. In fact, De Gaulle stiffened, declaring he was in favor of reforms but would oppose

"bedwetting." Securing the firm support of French army commanders in West Germany, he moved troops toward Paris and called for new elections. Thoroughly frightened by the protest-turned-upheaval and fearful that a successful revolution could lead only to an eventual Communist takeover, the masses of France voted for a return to law and order. De Gaulle and his party scored the biggest electoral victory in modern French history, and the mini-revolution collapsed.

Yet the proud De Gaulle and the confident, if old-fashioned, national political revival he represented had been cruelly mocked. In 1969 a tired and discouraged President De Gaulle resigned over a minor issue, and within a year he was dead. For much of the older generation in France, and indeed throughout western Europe, the student revolution of 1968 signaled the end of illusions and the end of an era. Social stability and material progress

Student Protest in Paris   These rock-throwing students in the Latin Quarter of Paris are trying to force education reforms or even to topple De Gaulle's government. Throughout May 1968 students clashed repeatedly with France's tough riot police in bloody street fighting. *(Source: Bruno Barbey/Magnum)*

had resulted in conflict and uncertainty. Under such conditions, all schemes for western European equality with the external superpowers—the United States and the Soviet Union—would have an air of unreality.

The student protest of the 1960s, which peaked in 1968 but echoed well into the 1970s, was due to more than overcrowded classrooms and outdated courses. It reflected a rebirth of romantic revolutionary idealism, which repudiated the quest for ever more consumer goods as stupid and destructive. Student radicalism was also related to the Vietnam War, which led many students in Europe and America to convince themselves that Western civilization was immoral and imperialistic. Finally, the students of the late 1960s were a completely new generation: they had never known anything but prosperity and tranquility, and they had grown bored with both.

The student revolt was also motivated by new perceptions about the new society of highly trained experts. Some reflective young people feared that universities would soon do nothing but turn out docile technocrats both to stock and to serve "the establishment." Others saw the class of highly trained specialists they expected to enter as the new exploited class in society. The remedy to this situation, both groups believed, was "participation"—the democratization of decision making *within* large, specialized bureaucratic organizations. Only in this way would such organizations serve real human needs and not merely exploit the individual and the environment. Thus the often unrealistic and undisciplined student radicals tried to answer a vital question: how was the complex new society of specialized experts to be made humane and responsive?

WOMEN AND THE FAMILY

The growing emancipation of women in Europe and North America was unquestionably one of the most important developments after the Second World War. This development gathered speed in the 1960s and reached a climax in the mid-1970s. Women demanded and won new rights. Having shared fully in the postwar education revolution, women were better educated than ever before. They took advantage of the need for trained experts in a more fluid society and moved into areas of employment formerly closed to them. Married women in particular became much more likely to work outside the home than they had been a few short years earlier. Women no longer had to fatalistically accept child bearing and child rearing, for if they wished they could use modern techniques of contraception to control the number and spacing of their offspring. In short, women became more equal and independent, less confined and stereotyped. A major transformation was in process.

The changing position of women altered the modern family. Since the emancipation of women is still incomplete, it is impossible to say for certain whether some major revolution has occurred within the family. Nevertheless, as women today consolidate and expand the breakthroughs of the 1960s and early 1970s, it seems clear that the family has experienced some fundamental reorientations. This becomes apparent if we examine women's traditional role in the home and then women's new roles outside the home in the postwar era.

Marriage and Motherhood

Before the Industrial Revolution, most men and women married late, and substantial numbers never married at all. Once a woman was married, though, she normally bore several children, of whom a third to a half would not survive to adulthood. Moreover, many women died in childbirth. With the growth of industry and urban society, people began to marry earlier, and fewer remained unmarried. As industrial development led to higher incomes and better diets, more children survived to adulthood, and population grew rapidly in the nineteenth century. By the late nineteenth century, contraception within marriage was spreading.

In the twentieth century, and especially after World War Two, these trends continued. In the postwar era, women continued to marry earlier. In Sweden, for example, the average age of first marriage dropped steadily from twenty-six in the early 1940s to twenty-three in the late 1960s. Moreover, more than nine out of ten women were marrying at least once, usually in their early twenties. Marriage was never more in vogue than in the generation after the Second World War. The triumph of romantic attraction over financial calculation seemed complete, and perhaps never before had young couples expected so much emotional satisfaction from matrimony.

After marrying early, the typical woman in Europe, the United States, and Canada had her children quickly. Whereas women in the more distant past very often had children as long as they were fertile, women in Europe and North America were having about 80 percent of their children before they were thirty. As for family size, the "baby boom" that lasted until the early 1960s made for fairly rapid population growth of 1 to 1.5 percent per year in many European countries. In the 1960s, however, the long-term decline in birthrates resumed. Surveys in northern and western Europe began to reveal that most women believed that two instead of three children were ideal.

Women must have 2.1 children on the average if total population is to remain constant over the long term. Indeed, the number of births fell so sharply in the 1960s that total population practically stopped growing in many European countries. By the mid-1970s more people were dying each year than were being born in Austria, East Germany, West Germany, and Luxembourg, where total numbers actually declined. The United States followed the same trend; the birthrate declined from twenty-five per thousand in 1957 to fifteen per thousand in 1973, and it recovered slightly thereafter only because the baby boomers were reaching child-bearing age, not because individual women were having more children. Since the American death rate has remained practically unchanged, the rate of population growth from natural increase (that is, excluding immigration) dropped by two-thirds, from 1.5 percent to 0.6 percent per year between the 1950s and the 1970s. The population of Africa, Asia, and Latin America was still growing very rapidly from natural increase, but that was certainly not true for most European countries and countries of predominately European ancestry.

The culmination of the trends toward early, almost-universal marriage and small family size in wealthy societies had revolutionary implications for women. An examination of these implications suggests why the emancipation of women—sooner or later—was almost assuredly built into the structure of modern life.

The main point is that motherhood occupied a much smaller portion of a woman's life than at the beginning of this century. The average woman's life expectancy at birth increased from about fifty years in 1900 to about seventy-five years in 1970. At the same time, women were increasingly compressing childbearing into the decade between their twentieth and thirtieth birthdays, instead of bearing children until they were in their late thirties. By the early 1970s about half of Western women, and more than half in some nations, were having their last baby by the age of twenty-six or twenty-seven. When the youngest child trooped off to kindergarten, the average mother still had more than forty years of life in front of her.

This was a momentous change. Throughout history, most married women had been defined to a considerable extent as mothers. Motherhood was very demanding: pregnancy followed pregnancy, and there were many children to nurse, guide, and bury. Now, however, the years devoted to having babies and caring for young children represented at most a seventh of the average woman's life. Motherhood had become a relatively short phase in most women's total life span. Perhaps a good deal of the frustration that many women felt in the 1960s and 1970s was due to the fact that their traditional role as mothers no longer absorbed the energies of a lifetime, and new roles in the male-dominated world outside the family were opening up slowly.

A related revolutionary change for women was that the age-old biological link between sexual intercourse and motherhood was severed. As is well known, beginning in the early 1960s many women chose to gain effective control over pregnancy with oral contraceptives and intrauterine devices. They no longer relied on undependable males and their undependable methods. Less well known are certain physiological facts, which help explain why many women in the advanced countries did elect to practice birth control at some point in their lives.

Women in the postwar era were capable of having children for many more years than their forebears. The age of *menarche*—the age at which girls begin to menstruate and become fertile—had dropped from about seventeen years in the early nineteenth century to about thirteen years by the 1970s. At the same time, the age at onset of menopause rose. At the beginning of the eighteenth century, menopause occurred at about age thirty-six, on average; it now occurred at about fifty. These physiological changes over time are poorly understood, but they were apparently due to better diets and living standards, which also substantially increased people's height and size. In any event, many modern women chose to separate their sexual lives from their awesome reproductive power, which had increased with the lengthening of the

Britain's Women on the March   After World War Two, more and more women entered the labor market as full-time workers. Although most Western women had full political rights by this time, they continued to struggle for economic rights, as these marchers through London's Piccadilly demonstrate. *(Source: Henri Cartier-Bresson/Magnum)*

time in which they were capable of bearing children. In doing so, these women became free to pursue sensual pleasure for its own sake. The consequences of this revolutionary development will continue to work themselves out for a long time.

Women at Work

For centuries before the Industrial Revolution, ordinary women were highly productive members of society. They often labored for years before marriage to accumulate the necessary dowry. Once married, women worked hard on farms and in home industries while bearing and caring for their large families. With the growth of modern industry and large cities, young women continued to work as wage earners. But once a poor woman married, she typically stopped working in a factory or a shop, struggling instead to earn money at home by practicing some low-paid craft as she looked after her children. In the middle classes, it was a rare and tough-minded woman who worked outside the home for wages, although charity work was socially acceptable.

Since the beginning of the twentieth century and especially after World War Two, the situation has changed dramatically once again. Opportunities for women of modest means to earn cash income within the home practically disappeared. Piano teachers, novelists, and part-time typists still worked at home as independent contractors, but the ever-greater complexity of the modern wage-based economy and its sophisticated technology meant that almost all would-be wage earners had to turn elsewhere. Moreover, motherhood took less and less time, so that the full-time mother-housewife had less and less economic value for families.

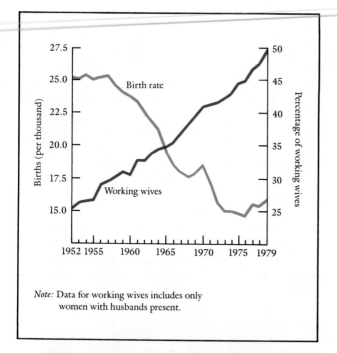

FIGURE 31.2 The Decline of the Birthrate and the Increase of Working Wives in the United States, 1952–1979 The challenge of working away from home encouraged American wives to prefer fewer children and helped to lower the birthrate.

clear that the rising employment of married women was a powerful force in the drive for women's equality and emancipation. Take the critical matter of widespread discrimination between men and women in pay, occupation, and advancement. The young unmarried woman of eighty years ago generally accepted such injustices. She thought of them as temporary nuisances and looked forward to marriage and motherhood for fulfillment. In the postwar era, a married wage earner in her thirties developed a totally different perspective. Employment became a permanent condition within which she, like her male counterpart, sought not only income but psychological satisfaction as well. Sexism and discrimination quickly became increasingly loathsome and evoked that sense of injustice that drives revolutions and reforms. The "movement" spread, winning converts among the young and newly awakened.

Rising employment for married women was a factor in the decline of the birthrate (Figure 31.2). Women who worked had significantly fewer children than women of the same age who did not. Moreover, survey research showed that young women who had worked and intended to work again revised downward the number of children they expected to have after the first lovable but time-consuming baby was born. One reason was obvious: raising a family while holding down a full-time job was a tremendous challenge and often resulted in the woman's being grossly overworked. The fatiguing, often frustrating multiple demands of job, motherhood, and marriage simply became more manageable with fewer children.

Another reason for the decline of the birthrate was that motherhood interrupted a woman's career. The majority of women in Western countries preferred or were forced to accept—interpretations varied—staying at home for a minimum of two or three years while their children were small. The longer the break in employment, the more a woman's career suffered. Women consistently earned less than men partly because they were employed less continuously and thus did not keep moving steadily up the bureaucratic ladders of large organizations.

Because most Western countries did little to help women in the problem of re-employment after their children were a little older, some women came to advocate the pattern of career and family typically found in communist eastern Europe. There, women were usually employed contin-

Thus the reduction of home-centered work and child care resulted in a sharp rise across Europe and North America in the number of married women who were full-time wage earners.

In communist countries, the trend went the furthest. In the Soviet Union, most married women worked outside the home; there women accounted for almost half of all employed persons in the postwar era. In noncommunist western Europe and North America, there was a good deal of variety, depending on whether married women had traditionally worked outside the home, as in France or Sweden, or stayed at home, as in Belgium and Switzerland. Nevertheless, the percentage of married women who worked rose sharply in all countries, from a range of roughly 20 to 25 percent in 1950 to a range of 35 to 60 percent in the 1970s. This rise was particularly dramatic in the United States, where married women were twice as likely to be employed in 1979 as they were in 1952.

The dramatic growth of employment among married women was a development whose ultimate effects are still unknown. Nevertheless, it seems

uously until they retired. There were no career-complicating interruptions for extended mothering. Instead, a woman in a communist country received as her right up to three months of maternity leave to care for her newborn infant and recover her strength. Then she returned to her job, leaving her baby in the care of a state-run nursery or, more frequently, a retired relative or neighbor. By the 1970s some western European countries were beginning to provide well-defined maternity leaves as part of their social security systems. The United States lagged far behind in this area.

What the increasing numbers of career-minded women with independent, self-assertive spirits meant for marriage and relations between the sexes was by no means clear. As we have seen, marriage remained an almost universal experience. More-over, the decline of informal village and neighborhood socializing with the advent of the automobile and suburban living made most wives and husbands more dependent than ever on their mates (and their children) for their emotional needs. Never had more been demanded from hearth and home.

The great increase in life expectancy for males and females by itself made marriage more stable, at least in one sense. The average couple was living together for forty years before the death of one dissolved the union, as opposed to less than twenty years together at the beginning of the century. And husbands were slowly getting the message that the old rule of leaving the dishes and diapers exclusively to wives needed rewriting, especially in two-income families. In short, the nuclear family

A Working Mother waves good-bye to her child in this scene from contemporary American life. Young couples seeking to own a large, elegant house, like the one shown here, almost always need the combined income of two wage earners. *(Source: Richard Hutchings/Photo Researchers)*

showed great strength, adapting itself once again to changing values and changing conditions.

At the same time, contrary trends clearly emerged in the late 1960s and carried over strongly into the 1970s and 1980s. Everywhere the divorce rate kept moving up: it doubled in the United States, for example, between 1970 and 1980. Nearly everywhere in Western countries, except in southern Europe, over one-quarter of marriages ended in divorce by the early 1980s; in Sweden the proportion was one in two. Studies of marriage showed that working women were considerably more likely to get divorced than nonworking women. The independent working woman could more easily afford to leave if dissatisfied, while the no-income career housewife was more nearly locked into her situation.

Beginning in the very late 1960s, the marriage rate also began to plunge in a number of Western countries, and it continued to decline throughout the 1970s before stabilizing in the 1980s. Both women and men married progressively later, and those who never married increased as a portion of the population. As the number of singles grew, there was also a considerable increase in the number of unmarried couples living together, reminiscent of patterns among the European working classes in the early days of industrialization. Some observers argued that young women and men were only postponing marriage because of less robust economic conditions. Others contended that marriage, after its long rise, was finally in retreat in the face of growing careerism and acceptance of new, less structured relations between (and within) the sexes. More fundamentally, falling birthrates, more married women in the workplace, later marriage, and increased divorce (and remarriage) rates were all related to the growing emancipation of women. They were all part of a complicated constellation of striking changes, which strongly suggested that a major break with the past had taken place in marriage patterns and family relationships.

SUMMARY

This chapter has examined the major postwar social changes that accompanied the political recovery and economic expansion discussed in Chapter 30. These social changes were profound. Science combined with technology, often under government

direction, to fulfill the loftiest hopes of its enthusiasts and achieve amazing success. The triumphs of applied science contributed not only to economic expansion but also to a more fluid, less antagonistic class structure, in which specialized education was the high road to advancement, regardless of the political system. Within the prosperous, increasingly technocratic society, women asserted themselves. Beginning in the 1960s, they moved increasingly into the labor market and gave birth to fewer children. In doing so, women began striking off in a new direction, a trend that has continued to this day. Their greater commitment to employment and their decision to raise fewer children—a social pattern in sharp contrast to that of the late 1940s and 1950s—foretold the more general break in Western history that occurred shortly thereafter, as will be shown in Chapter 32.

NOTES

1. Quoted in J. Ziman, *The Force of Knowledge: The Scientific Dimension of Society* (Cambridge: Cambridge University Press, 1976), p. 128.
2. Quoted in S. Toulmin, *The Twentieth Century: A Promethean Age*, ed. A. Bullock (London: Thames & Hudson, 1971), p. 294.

SUGGESTED READING

Ziman's volume cited in the Notes, which has an excellent bibliography, is a penetrating look at science by a leading physicist. C. P. Snow's widely discussed book, *The Two Cultures and the Scientific Revolution*, rev. ed. (1963), explores the gap between scientists and nonscientists. A. Toffler, *Future Shock* (1970), is an interesting but exaggerated best seller, which claims that many contemporary psychological problems are due to overly rapid technical and scientific development. J. Ellul, *The Technological Society* (1964), is also highly critical of technical progress, while D. S. Landes, *The Unbound Prometheus: Technological Change and Industrial Development in Western Europe from 1750 to the Present* (1969), remains enthusiastic. Two more stimulating works on technology are J. J. Servan-Schreiber, *The World Challenge* (1981), and H. Jacoby, *The Bureaucratization of the World* (1973). A. Bramwell, *Ecology in the Twentieth Century: A History* (1989), examines negative aspects of technical and industrial development.

In addition to studies cited in the Suggested Reading for Chapter 30, A. Simpson, *The New Europeans* (1968), is a good guide to contemporary Western society. Two engaging books on recent intellectual developments are J. Barzun, *The House of Intellect* (1959), and R. Stromberg, *After Everything: Western Intellectual History Since 1945* (1970). L. Wylie, *Village in the Vauclause,* rev. ed. (1964), and P. J. Hélias, *The Horse of Pride* (1980), provide fascinating pictures of life in the French village. A. Kriegel's *The French Communists* (1972) and *Eurocommunism* (1978) are also recommended. A. Touraine, *The May Movement* (1971), is sympathetic toward the French student revolt, while the noted sociologist R. Aron, in *The Elusive Revolution* (1969), is highly critical. F. Zweig, *The Worker in an Affluent Society* (1961), probes family life and economic circumstances in the British working class on the basis of extensive interviews. R. E. Tyrrell, ed., *The Future That Doesn't Work* (1977), is a polemical but absorbing attack on British socialism. W. Hollstein, *Europe in the Making* (1973), is a fervent plea to integrate Europe by a former top official of the Common Market. The magazines *Encounter, Commentary,* and *The Economist* often carry interesting articles on major social and political trends, as do *Time* and *Newsweek.*

E. Sullerot, *Women, Society and Change* (1971), is an outstanding introduction to women's evolving role. R. Patia, ed., *Women in the Modern World* (1967), compares women's situations in many countries. Two other influential books on women and their new awareness are S. de Beauvoir, *The Second Sex* (1962), and B. Friedan, *The Feminine Mystique* (1963). These may be compared with C. Lasch, *Haven in a Heartless World* (1977), and A. Cherlin, *Marriage, Divorce, Remarriage* (1981), which interpret changes in the American family. P. Robinson, *The Modernization of Sex* (1976), tells the fascinating story of the American investigators who helped change public attitudes by studying human sexual relations "scientifically."

On feminism in general, see B. Smith, *Changing Lives: Women in European History Since 1700* (1989), which provides a good overview and a current bibliography, and N. Cott, *The Grounding of Modern Feminism* (1987). The women's movement in Italy is considered in L. Birnbaum, *Liberazione de la Donna* (1986), which is written in English despite the Italian title. C. Duchen, *Feminism in France: From May '68 to Mitterrand* (1986), is also recommended. Good studies on British women include E. Wilson, *Only Halfway to Paradise: Women in Postwar Britain, 1945–1968* (1980), and M. Barrett, *Women's Opposition Today* (1980). C. Goldin, *Understanding the Gender Gap: An Economic History of American Women* (1989), provides a provocative economic analysis of women's issues.

32

The Recent Past, 1968 to the Present

*S*ometime during the late 1960s or early 1970s, the postwar era came to an end. With fits and starts, a new age opened, as postwar certitudes like domestic political stability, social harmony, and continuous economic improvement evaporated. In any event, that is how this historian reads the most recent past. Others may form different judgments, for we are simply too close to the postwar era to gain vital perspective on the period that has succeeded it. As Voltaire once said, "The man who ventures to write contemporary history must expect to be attacked for everything he has said and everything he has not said."[1]

Yet the historian must take a stand. We have already examined some indications of the end of the postwar era. Fundamental changes within the family, featuring new roles for women, gathered momentum in the late 1960s. The mini-revolution of 1968 was a fundamental turning point in recent French history, symptomatic of a general rebirth of political instability and even crisis in several leading nations. Above all, the astonishing postwar economic advance, unparalleled in its rapidity and consistency, came to an abrupt halt. Old, almost forgotten, problems like high unemployment, expensive energy, and international monetary instability suddenly re-emerged, and the buoyant self-confidence of the postwar era disappeared.

Finally, the end of the postwar era saw a gradual, groping march toward a new era in East-West relations, as renewed efforts to reduce cold war tensions and to liberalize Communist eastern Europe often dominated the headlines. These efforts achieved some success in the 1970s, and after renewed cold war competition in the early 1980s they reached fruition as the Soviet Union entered a period of sweeping change and communist rule collapsed in the satellite states of eastern Europe. The tremendous improvement in East-West relations provided a spectacular counterbalance to the long years of economic difficulties, which remained serious in the late 1980s, especially in eastern Europe.

In an attempt to make sense out of a turbulent recent past, which merges with an uncertain present, this chapter will focus on three questions of fundamental importance.

- First, why, after a generation, did the world economy shift into reverse gear, and what were some of the social consequences of that shift?
- Second, what were the most striking political developments within the nations of the Atlantic alliance? Specifically, how did West Germany take the initiative in trying to negotiate an enduring reconciliation with its communist neighbors, and why did the United States enter into a time of troubles before seeking to reassert its strength and leadership in the 1980s?
- Third, how did these changes interact with the evolution of the Soviet bloc?

Finally, the chapter will close with the astonishing changes of the Gorbachev era and with some reflections on the future.

THE TROUBLED ECONOMY

The energy crisis looms large in the sudden transition from almost automatic postwar growth to serious economic difficulties in the 1970s and 1980s. The first surge in oil prices in 1973 stunned the international economy, and the second surge in 1979 led to the deepest recession since the 1930s. The collapse of the postwar monetary system in 1971 and the rapid accumulation of international debts also caused heavy long-term damage. The social consequences of harder times were profound and many-sided.

Money and Oil

During the Second World War, British and American leaders were convinced that international financial disorder after 1918 had contributed mightily to economic problems, the Great Depression, and renewed global warfare. They were determined not to repeat their mistakes, and in the Bretton Woods Agreement of 1944 they laid the foundations for a new international monetary system, which proved instrumental in the unprecedented postwar boom.

The new system, operating through the World Bank and the International Monetary Fund, was based on the American dollar, which was supposed to be "as good as gold" because foreign governments could always exchange dollars for gold at $35 an ounce. The United States proceeded to make needed dollars readily available to the rest of the world, so readily that by early 1971 it had only $11 billion in gold left in Fort Knox and Europe had accumulated 50 billion American dollars. The result was a classic, long-overdue "run on the bank" in 1971, as foreigners panicked and raced to exchange their dollars for gold. President Richard Nixon was forced to stop the sale of American gold. The price of gold then soared on world markets, and the value of the dollar declined. Fixed rates of exchange were abandoned, and great uncertainty replaced postwar predictability in international trade and finance.

Even more serious was the dramatic reversal in the price and availability of energy. As described in Chapter 22, coal-fired steam engines broke the bottleneck of chronically inadequate energy in the late-eighteenth-century economy, making possible the Industrial Revolution and improved living standards in the nineteenth century. In the twentieth century, petroleum proved its worth, and the great postwar boom was fueled by cheap oil, especially in western Europe. Cheap oil from the Middle East permitted energy-intensive industries—automobiles, chemicals, and electric power—to expand rapidly and lead other sectors of the economy forward. More generally, cheap oil and cheap energy encouraged businesses to invest massively in machinery and improved technology. This investment enabled workers to produce more and allowed a steady rise in the standard of living without much inflation.

Saudi Riches   Saudi Arabia has enormous oil reserves, making it one of the most influential members of the Organization of Petroleum Exporting Countries and giving it one of the world's highest per capita incomes. Oil has also made rich men of Prince Fahd and King Khalid, shown here. *(Source: Robert Azzi/Woodfin Camp & Associates)*

In the 1950s and 1960s, the main oil-exporting countries, grouped together in the Arab-dominated Organization of Petroleum Exporting Countries (OPEC), had watched the price of crude oil decline consistently compared to the price of manufactured goods, as the Western oil companies vigorously expanded production and kept prices low to win users of coal to petroleum (Map 32.1). The Egyptian leader Nasser argued that Arab countries should manipulate oil prices to increase their revenues and also to strike at Israel and its Western allies. But Egypt lacked oil and Nasser failed. Colonel Muammar Khadafy of Libya proved more successful. He won important concessions from Western nations and oil companies in the early 1970s, and his example activated the OPEC countries. In 1971 OPEC for the first time presented a united front against the oil companies and obtained a solid price increase. The stage was set for the revolution in energy prices during the fourth Arab-Israeli war in October 1973.

The war began on the solemn Sabbath celebration of Yom Kippur, or the Day of Atonement, the holiest day in the Jewish calendar. Egypt and Syria launched a surprise attack on an unsuspecting Israel, breaking through defense positions and destroying a large part of the Israeli air force. In response to urgent pleas, the United States airlifted $2.2 billion of its most sophisticated weapons to Israel, which accepted a cease-fire after its successful counterattack had encircled much of the Egyptian army. Surprisingly, the Yom Kippur War eventually led to peace between Egypt and Israel. Egypt's initial military victories greatly enhanced the power and prestige of General Anwar Sadat (1918–1981), Nasser's successor. This advantage enabled the realistic Sadat to achieve in 1979 the negotiated settlement with Israel that he had long desired.

In the first days of the war, the Arab (and non-Arab) oil producers in OPEC placed an embargo on oil shipments to the United States and the Netherlands, in retaliation for their support of Israel. They also cut production and raised prices by 70 percent, ostensibly to prevent Europe from sharing oil with the United States. In reality, greed and a

MAP 32.1 OPEC and the World Oil Trade   Though much of the world depends on imported oil, Western Europe and Japan are OPEC's biggest customers. What major oil exporters remain outside of OPEC?

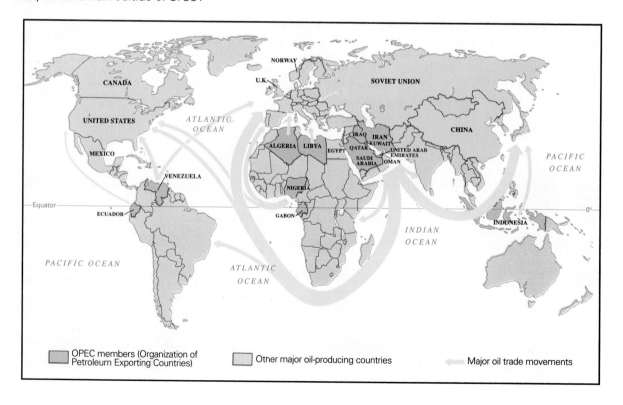

The Egyptian-Israeli Peace Treaty   of 1979 is celebrated by the men who made it possible: Egypt's President Anwar al-Sadat, U.S. President Jimmy Carter, and Israeli Prime Minister Menachem Begin. Egypt recognized Israel's right to exist and established normal diplomatic relations, while Israel agreed to withdraw from Egyptian territory occupied in the Six-Day War of 1967. *(Source: National Archives and Records Administration)*

desire for revenge against the West took over: a second increase in December, after the cease-fire, meant that crude oil prices quadrupled in less than a year. It was widely realized that OPEC's brutal action was economically destructive, but the world's major powers did nothing. The Soviet Union was a great oil exporter and benefited directly, while a cautious western Europe looked to the United States for leadership. But the United States was immobilized, its attention absorbed by the Watergate crisis (see page 1020). Thus governments, companies, and individuals were left to deal piecemeal and manage as best they could with the so-called oil shock—a "shock" that really turned out to be an earthquake.

Inflation, Debt, and Unemployment

Coming close on the heels of upheaval in the international monetary system, the price revolution in energy sources plunged the world into its worst economic decline since the 1930s. The energy-intensive industries that had driven the economy up in the 1950s and 1960s now dragged it down in the mid-1970s. Yet, while industrial output fell, soaring energy costs sent prices surging. "Stagflation"—the unexpected combination of economic stagnation and rapid inflation—developed to bedevil the public and baffle economists. Unemployment rose, while productivity and living standards declined.

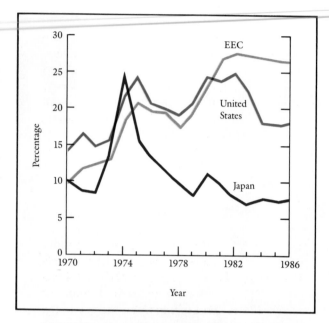

FIGURE 32.1 The Misery Index, 1970–1985 Combining rates of unemployment and inflation provided a simple but effective measure of economic hardship. This particular index represents the sum of two times the unemployment rate plus the inflation rate, reflecting the widespread belief that joblessness causes more suffering than higher prices. EEC = European Economic Community, or Common Market countries. *(Source: OECD data, as given in* The Economist, *June 15, 1985, p. 69.)*

But no cycle lasts forever, and by 1976 a modest recovery was in progress. People were learning to save energy, turning down thermostats, and buying smaller cars. Optimists argued that the challenge of redesigning lifestyles to cope with expensive energy actually represented a great opportunity.

Iran's Islamic revolution in 1978 and 1979 confounded these hopes, at least in the short run. Iranian oil production collapsed, OPEC again doubled the price of crude oil, and the world economy succumbed to its second oil shock. Once again, unemployment and inflation rose dramatically before another recovery began in 1982, driven by a reversal in oil prices, falling interest rates, and large U.S. trade and budget deficits. But the recovery was very uneven. In the summer of 1985, the unemployment rate in western Europe rose to its highest levels since the Great Depression. Fully nineteen million people were unemployed. Although unemployment declined somewhat in the late 1980s, large numbers of people remained out of work.

Many means were devised in the 1970s to measure the troubled economy, but perhaps none was more telling than the "misery index." First used with considerable effect by candidate Jimmy Carter in the 1976 U.S. presidential debates, the misery index combined rates of inflation and unemployment in a single, powerfully emotional number. Figure 32.1 presents a comparison of misery indexes for the United States and the Common Market countries between 1970 and 1986. As may be seen, "misery" increased on both sides of the Atlantic, but the increase was substantially greater in western Europe. This helps explain why these hard times—often referred to by Europeans simply as "the crisis"—probably had an even greater psychological impact on Europeans than on Americans.

Nor was the Soviet bloc spared. Both the Soviet Union and the satellite states of its eastern European empire did less and less well: annual rates of economic growth fell from 6 to 7 percent in the late 1960s to 2 to 3 percent in 1980. This performance was no worse than that of most Western countries, but it mocked the long-standing propaganda boast that communist countries would "catch and surpass the capitalistic West," a phrase that was quietly dropped in favor of less humorous slogans.

Debts and deficits piled up quickly in the troubled economy of the 1970s and 1980s. In the first place, the price hikes of 1973 required a massive global transfer of wealth to the OPEC countries from both rich and poor nations. Like individual consumers suddenly faced with a financial emergency, countries scrambled to borrow to pay their greatly increased fuel bills. Poor countries, especially, turned to the big private international banks. These banks received deposits—the so-called petrodollars—from OPEC members and lent them back out to poor countries so that these nations could pay their oil bills. This circular flow averted total collapse, but there was a high price to pay in the form of a rapid expansion of international debt.

Rich nations also went on a borrowing binge. Almost everywhere they ran up big debts to pay for imported oil and also to maintain social welfare services, as their economies declined and tax receipts fell. Western consumers also joined the race for ever-higher levels of debt. Borrowing to buy before prices rose seemed smart in the 1970s, and that attitude carried over into the 1980s. Like burgeoning government debt, a record-high level of consumer debt was a two-edged sword. It sustained current economic activity but quite possibly posed serious repayment problems, an appropriately ambiguous reflection of the troubled economy.

Some Social Consequences

The most pervasive consequences of recent economic stagnation were probably psychological and attitudinal. Optimism gave way to pessimism; romantic utopianism yielded to sober realism. This drastic change in mood—a complete surprise only to those who had never studied history—affected states, institutions, and individuals in countless ways.

To be sure, there were heartbreaking human tragedies—lost jobs, bankruptcies, and mental breakdowns. But, on the whole, the welfare system fashioned in the postwar era prevented mass suffering and degradation. Extended benefits for the unemployed, pensions for the aged, free medical care for the needy, surplus food and special allowances for parents with children—all these and a host of lesser supports did their part. The responsive, socially concerned national state undoubtedly contributed to the preservation of political stability and democracy in the face of economic difficulties, difficulties that might have brought revolution and dictatorship in earlier times.

The energetic response of governments to social needs helps explain the sharp increase in total government spending in most countries during the 1970s and 1980s. In 1982 western European governments spent an average of more than one-half of gross national income, as compared to only 37 percent fifteen years earlier. In the United States, the combined share of federal, state, and local government expenditures rose from 31 to 35 percent in the same years. The role of government in everyday life became more important.

In all countries, people were much more willing to see their governments increase spending than raise taxes. This imbalance contributed to the rapid growth of budget deficits, national debts, and inflation. By the late 1970s a powerful reaction to government's ever-increasing role set in, and Western governments were gradually forced to introduce austerity measures to slow the seemingly inexorable growth of public spending and the welfare state. The partially successful efforts of Margaret Thatcher in Britain and Ronald Reagan in the United States to limit the growth of social programs absorbed the attention of the English-speaking world, but François Mitterrand of France was the temporary exception who proved the general rule. After his election as president in 1981, Mitterrand led his Socialist party and Communist allies on a vast program of nationalization and public investment designed to spend France out of economic stagnation. By 1983 this attempt had clearly failed. Mitterrand's Socialist government was then compelled to impose a wide variety of austerity measures and to maintain those policies for the rest of the decade. The success of Thatcher, Reagan, and then Mitterrand in imposing antispending, antiwelfare policies led some observers to conclude, no doubt prematurely, that socialism had simply died in the West in the 1980s.

When governments were eventually forced to restrain spending, Big Science was often singled out for cuts, unless its ties to the military were very direct. The problems of CERN were a good example. Formed to pool western European efforts in high-energy particle physics (see page 992), CERN succeeded admirably in stealing the lead from the United States in this exciting but esoteric and uncommercial field. But the costs were truly enormous. In the 1980s CERN was increasingly attacked as an extravagant misallocation of scarce resources at a time when new fields, such as computers and genetic research, were bursting with scientific opportunities that offered mouth-watering commercial applications. More generally, tighter funding for Big Science accelerated the ongoing computer revolution. That revolution thrived on the diffusion of unprecedented computational and informational capacity to small research groups and private businesses, which were both cause and effect of the revolution itself.

Individuals felt the impact of austerity even earlier, for unlike governments they could not pay their bills by printing money and going ever further into debt. The energy crisis forced them to reexamine not only their fuel bills, but the whole pattern of self-indulgent materialism in the postwar era as well. The result was a leaner, tougher lifestyle, featuring more attention to nutrition and a passion for exercise. Correspondingly, there was less blind reliance on medical science for good health and a growing awareness that individuals must accept a large portion of the responsibility for illness and disease. More people began to realize that they could substantially increase their life spans simply by eating regular meals, sleeping seven or eight hours each night, exercising two or three times a week, maintaining moderate weight, forgoing smoking, and using alcohol only in moderation. A forty-five-year-old American male who practiced three or fewer of these habits could expect to live to be sixty-seven; one who adhered to five or six could expect to live eleven more years.

Economic troubles also strengthened existing trends within the family. Both men and women were encouraged to postpone marriage until they had put their careers on a firm foundation, so the age of marriage rose sharply for both sexes in many Western countries. Indeed, the very real threat of unemployment—or "underemployment" in a dead-end job—seemed to shape the outlook of a whole generation. The students of the 1980s were serious, practical, and often conservative. As one young woman at a French university told a reporter in 1985, "Jobs are the big worry now, so everyone wants to learn something practical."[2] In France, as elsewhere, it was an astonishing shift from the romantic visions and political activism of the late 1960s.

Harder times meant that ever-more women did work after they married. In the United States, 66 percent of all married women held jobs in 1986, as opposed to 55 percent in 1979 and 46 percent in 1973. New attitudes related to personal fulfillment were one reason for the continuing increase, especially for well-educated, upper-middle-class women. But for the vast majority of married women—the four-fifths who fell below the top 20 percent—economic necessity also played a major role.

Many wives in poor and middle-class families simply had to work, because after 1973 the average husband was earning less after the effects of continuous inflation were taken into account. The average inflation-adjusted wage for men in the United States declined to $26,000 in 1986, as opposed to $26,700 in 1979 and $28,600 in 1973. The per-

"The New Poor"   Economic crisis and prolonged unemployment in the early 1980s reduced many from modest affluence to harsh poverty, creating a class of new poor. This photograph captures that human tragedy. After two years of unemployment, this homeless French office worker must sleep each night in a makeshift shelter for the destitute. (Source: Dennis Stock/Magnum)

centage decline for the large group of American men with a high school degree or less education was substantially greater in these years.[3] As in the preindustrial era, the wife's labor provided the margin of survival for millions of hard-pressed families.

THE ATLANTIC ALLIANCE

Forged in the late 1940s to rebuild Europe and prevent possible Soviet expansion beyond the iron curtain, the Atlantic alliance—formally expressed in the North Atlantic Treaty Organization (NATO)—remained an enduring reality in the face of economic difficulties. But the alliance was neither static nor monolithic, and its evolution reflected major developments within the member states. Those in West Germany and the United States were of critical importance.

Germany's Eastern Initiative

The turning points of history are sometimes captured in dramatic moments rich in symbolism. So it was in December 1970, when West German Chancellor Willy Brandt flew to Poland for the signing of a historic treaty of reconciliation. Brandt laid a wreath at the tomb of the Polish unknown soldier and another at the monument commemorating the armed uprising of Warsaw's Jewish ghetto against occupying Nazi armies, after which the ghetto was totally destroyed and the Jewish survivors sent to the gas chambers. Standing before the ghetto memorial, a somber Brandt fell to his knees and knelt as if in prayer. "I wanted," Brandt said later, "to ask pardon in the name of our people for a million-fold crime which was committed in the misused name of the Germans."[4]

Brandt's gesture at the Warsaw ghetto memorial and the treaty with Poland were part of his policy of reconciliation with eastern Europe, which aimed at nothing less than a comprehensive peace settlement for central Europe and a new resolution of the "German question." That weighty question had first burst on the European scene with the modern nationalism of the French Revolution. How could fragmented Germany achieve political unity, and what role would a powerful, unified Germany play in the international order? "Resolved" in a certain fashion by Bismarck's wars of

unification, the question was posed again in the twentieth century when an aggressive Germany tried twice to conquer Europe. Agreed on crushing Hitler and de-Nazifying Germany during the Second World War, the wartime Allies then found themselves incapable of working together and imposing a general peace treaty on defeated Germany (see pages 960–962). Instead, Germany was divided into two antagonistic states by 1949, and the German question continued to fester as national unity disappeared.

The Federal Republic of Germany—commonly known as West Germany—was the larger of the two, with forty-five million inhabitants as opposed to eighteen million in East Germany. Formed out of the American, British, and French zones of occupation and based on freely expressed popular sovereignty, the Federal Republic claimed that the communist dictatorship installed by the Russians lacked free elections and hence all legal basis. While concentrating on completing its metamorphosis from defeated enemy to invaluable ally within NATO and the Common Market, West Germany also sought with some success to undermine the East German communist regime. Between 1949 and 1954, it welcomed with open arms 2.3 million East German refugees seeking political freedom and economic opportunity, and East Germany limped along while the Federal Republic boomed. But the building of the Berlin Wall in 1961 (see page 978) changed all that. It sealed the refugees' last escape route through West Berlin and allowed East Germany to stabilize and eventually become the world's most prosperous communist country.

As the popular socialist major of West Berlin, Willy Brandt understood the significance of the Berlin Wall and the lack of an energetic U.S. response to its construction. He saw the painful limitations of West Germany's official hard line when the Allies had, in fact, accepted the postwar status quo. Thus Brandt became convinced that a revitalized West Germany needed a new foreign policy, just as the German Social Democratic party he headed had abandoned doctrinaire Marxian socialism to become a broad-based opposition party after the Second World War. After a long battle and two bitter electoral defeats in the 1960s, Brandt became foreign minister in a coalition government in 1966 and won the chancellorship in 1969.

Brandt's victory marked the Federal Republic's political coming of age. First, it brought the Social Democrats to national power for the first time

Willy Brandt in Poland, 1970 Chancellor Brandt's gesture at the Warsaw memorial to the Jewish victims of Nazi terrorism was criticized by some West Germans but praised by many more. This picture reached an enormous audience, appearing in hundreds of newspapers in both the East and the West. *(Source: Bilderdienst Süddeutscher Verlag)*

since the 1920s and showed that genuine two-party political democracy had taken firm hold. Second, it was a graphic indication of West Germany's new-found liberalism and political tolerance, for the gravel-voiced Brandt was a very unconventional German. Illegitimate son of a poor, unwed shop-girl, and a fire-breathing socialist in his youth, Brandt had fled to Norway in the 1930s and had fought against Nazi Germany in the Second World War. Yet the electorate judged the man himself, turning a deaf ear to smears and innuendoes about treason and low birth. Third, Brandt showed that West Germany, postwar Europe's economic giant and political dwarf, was now both prepared and willing to launch major initiatives in European affairs.

The essence of Brandt's policy was to seek genuine peace and reconciliation with the communist East, as Adenauer had already done with France and the West. He negotiated treaties with the Soviet Union, Poland, and Czechoslovakia, which finally accepted existing state boundaries and the loss of eastern territory to Poland and the Soviet Union (see Map 30.1), in return for a mutual renunciation of force or the threat of force. Using the imaginative formula of "two German states within one German nation," Brandt's government also broke decisively with the past and entered into direct relations with East Germany, aiming for modest practical improvements rather than reunification, which at that point remained impractical.

Brandt constantly reiterated that none of these changes affected the respective military alliances of NATO and the Warsaw Pact. Yet, by boldly establishing "normal relations" with the communist East, West Germany seemed to turn another page not only on its ever-more-distant Nazi past, but on many cold war conflicts as well. Thus West Germany's eastern peace settlement contributed to a general reduction in East-West tensions, which included a limited agreement on nuclear arms control between the United States and the Soviet Union in 1972. And with the German question apparently resolved, West Germany had freed itself to assume without reservations a leading role in Europe.

Political Crisis in the United States

The late 1960s and early 1970s also marked the end of the postwar era in the United States. The natural leader of the Atlantic alliance fell into a long and self-destructive political crisis, which weakened the nation at home and abroad and echoed throughout the 1970s.

The crisis in the United States had numerous manifestations, ranging from apparently uncontrollable annual summer riots to brutal political assassinations, which struck down Martin Luther King and both President John F. Kennedy and his younger brother Robert. But the crisis first reached vast proportions in connection with President Johnson's leadership during the undeclared Vietnam War. Thus President Johnson, who wanted to go down in history as a master reformer and healer of old wounds (see page 980), left new ones as his most enduring legacy.

American involvement in Vietnam had its origins in the cold war and the ideology of containment (see page 963). From the late 1940s on, most Americans and their leaders viewed the world in terms of a constant struggle to stop the spread of communism, although they were not prepared to try to roll back communism where it already existed. As Europe began to revive and China established a communist government in 1949, efforts to contain communism shifted to Asia. The bloody Korean War (1950–1953) ended in stalemate, but the United States did succeed in preventing a communist government in South Korea. After the defeat of the French in Indochina in 1954, the Eisenhower administration refused to sign the Geneva accords that temporarily divided the country into two zones pending national unification by means of free elections. President Eisenhower then proceeded to acquiesce in the refusal of the anticommunist South Vietnamese government to accept the verdict of elections and provided it with military aid. President Kennedy greatly increased the number of American "military advisers," to sixteen thousand, and had the existing South Vietnamese leader deposed in 1963 when he refused to follow American directives.

After successfully portraying his opponent, Barry Goldwater, as a trigger-happy extremist in a nuclear age and resoundingly winning the 1964 election on a peace platform, President Johnson proceeded to expand the American role in the Vietnam conflict. As Johnson explained to his ambassador in Saigon, "I am not going to lose Vietnam. I am not going to be the President who saw Southeast Asia go the way China went."[5] American strategy was to "escalate" the war sufficiently to break the will of the North Vietnamese and their southern allies, the Vietcong, without resorting to "overkill" that might risk war with the entire communist bloc. Thus the South received massive military aid, American forces in South Vietnam gradually grew to a half-million men, and the United States bombed North Vietnam with ever-greater intensity. But there was no invasion of the North, nor were essential seaborne military supplies from the Soviet Union ever disrupted. In the end, the strategy of limited war backfired. It was the Americans themselves who grew weary, and the American leadership that cracked.

The undeclared war in Vietnam, fought nightly on American television, eventually divided the nation. Initial support was strong. The politicians, the media, and the population as a whole saw the war as part of a legitimate defense against communist totalitarianism in all poor countries. But in 1966 and 1967 influential opinion leaders like the *New York Times* and the *Washington Post* turned hostile, and the television networks soon followed. A growing number of critics denounced the war as an immoral and unsuccessful intrusion into a complex and distant civil war. There were major protests, often led by college students. Criticism reached a crescendo after the Vietcong "Tet Offensive" in January 1968. This, the Communists' first major attack with conventional weapons on major cities, failed militarily: the Vietcong suffered heavy losses and the attack did not spark a mass uprising. But U.S. critics of the Vietnam War interpreted the bloody combat as a decisive American defeat, clear proof that a Vietcong victory was inevitable. And although public opinion polls never showed more than 20 percent of the people supporting American withdrawal before that became the announced policy after the November 1968 elections, America's leaders now lost all heart. After an ambiguous defeat in the New Hampshire primary, President Johnson tacitly admitted defeat: he called for negotiations with North Vietnam and announced that he would not stand for re-election.

Elected by a razor-slim margin in 1968, President Richard Nixon sought to gradually disengage America from Vietnam and the accompanying national crisis. He restated the long-standing American objective of containment in Vietnam, of aiding the "South Vietnamese people to determine their own political future without outside interfer-

Nixon in China, 1972   Shown here toasting U.S.–China friendship with Chinese Premier Chou En-lai in Peking in February 1972, President Nixon took advantage of Chinese fears of the Soviet Union to establish good relations with Asia's Communist giant. Arriving after twenty-five years of mutual hostility, reconciliation with China was Nixon's finest achievement. *(Source: John Dominis, LIFE MAGAZINE © Time Inc. 1972)*

ence."[6] Using American military power more effectively, while simultaneously pursuing peace talks with the North Vietnamese, Nixon cut American forces in Vietnam from 550,000 to 24,000 in four years. The cost of the war dropped from $25 billion a year under Johnson to $3 billion under Nixon. Moreover, President Nixon launched a daring flank attack in diplomacy. He journeyed to China in 1972 and reached a spectacular if limited reconciliation with Communist China, which took advantage of China's growing fears of the Soviet Union and undermined North Vietnam's position. In January 1973, fortified by the overwhelming endorsement of the people in his 1972 electoral triumph, President Nixon and Secretary of State Henry Kissinger finally reached a peace agreement with North Vietnam. The agreement allowed remaining American forces to complete their withdrawal, while the United States reserved the right to resume bombing if the accords were broken. South Vietnamese forces seemed to hold their own, and the storm of crisis seemed past.

Instead, as the Arab oil embargo unhinged the international economy, the United States reaped the Watergate whirlwind. Like some other recent American presidents, Nixon authorized spying activities that went beyond the law. But in an atmosphere in which a huge series of secret government documents—later known as the "Pentagon Papers"—could be stolen and then given to the country's most influential newspaper for publication as part of its anti-Vietnam War campaign, Nixon went further than his predecessors. He authorized special units to use various illegal means to stop the leaking of government secrets to the press. One such group broke into the Democratic party headquarters in Washington's Watergate complex in June 1972 and was promptly arrested. Eventually, the media and the machinery of congressional investigation turned the break-in and later efforts to hush up the bungled job into a great moral issue. In 1974 a beleaguered Nixon was forced to resign in disgrace, as the political crisis in the United States reached its culmination.

The consequences of renewed political crisis during the Watergate affair were profound. First, the scandal resulted in a major shift of power away from the presidency toward Congress, especially in foreign affairs. Therefore, as American aid to South Vietnam diminished in 1973 and as an emboldened North Vietnam launched a general invasion against South Vietnamese armies in early 1974, first President Nixon and then President Gerald Ford stood by because Congress refused to permit any American response. After more than thirty-five years of battle, the Vietnamese Communists unified their country in 1975 as a totalitarian state—a second consequence of the U.S. crisis. Third, the belated fall of South Vietnam in the wake of Watergate shook America's postwar pride and confidence. Generally interpreted as a disastrous American military defeat, the Vietnam experience left the United States divided and uncertain. Only gradually did the country recover a sense of purpose in world affairs.

Détente or Cold War?

Brandt's Eastern initiatives and Nixon's phased withdrawal from Vietnam were part of many-sided Western efforts to reduce East-West tensions in the early 1970s. This policy of *détente*, or progressive relaxation of cold war tensions, reached its apogee with the Conference on Security and Cooperation in Europe, a thirty-five-nation summit that opened negotiations in Helsinki, Finland, in 1973 and concluded a final agreement in 1975. The Helsinki Conference included all European nations (except isolationist Albania), the United States, and Canada, and its Final Act contained certain elements of a general European peace treaty, like those signed at Vienna in 1815 and at Versailles in 1919. The Final Act formally stated that Europe's existing political frontiers, including those separating the two Germanies, could not be changed by force, and it provided for increased East-West economic and cultural relations as well. Thus the Atlantic alliance solemnly accepted the territorial status quo in eastern Europe, as well as the Soviet Union's gains from World War Two. In return for this major concession, the Soviet Union and its allies agreed to numerous provisions guaranteeing the human rights and political freedoms of their peoples. The Final Act was a compromise embodying Western concerns for human rights and Soviet preoccupations with military security and control of eastern Europe. Optimists saw a bright new day breaking in international relations.

These hopes gradually faded in the later 1970s. The Soviet Union and its allies often ignored the human rights provisions of the Helsinki agreement. Moreover, East-West political competition remained very much alive outside Europe. Many

Americans became convinced that the Soviet Union was taking advantage of détente, steadily building up its military might and pushing for political gains in Africa, Asia, and Latin America. Having been expelled from Egypt by Anwar Sadat after the 1973 war with Israel, the Soviets sought and won toeholds in South Yemen, Somalia, and later Ethiopia. Supporting guerrilla wars against the Portuguese in Angola and Mozambique, the Soviet Union was rewarded with Marxian regimes in both countries.

But it was in Afghanistan that Soviet action seemed most contrary to the spirit of détente. The Soviet Union had long been interested in its Islamic neighbor, and in April 1978 a pro-Soviet coup established a Marxian regime there. This new government soon made itself unpopular, and rebellion spread through the countryside. To preserve Communist rule, the Soviet Union in December 1979 suddenly airlifted crack troops to Kabul, the capital, and occupied Afghanistan with 100,000 men. Alarmed by the scale and precision of the Soviet invasion, many Americans feared that the oil-rich states of the Persian Gulf would be next and searched for an appropriate response.

President Carter tried to lead the Atlantic alliance beyond verbal condemnation, but among the European allies only Great Britain supported the American policy of economic sanctions. France, and especially West Germany, argued that the Soviets' deplorable action in Afghanistan should not be turned into an East-West confrontation and tried to salvage as much as possible of détente within Europe.

The alliance showed the same lack of concerted action when an independent trade union rose in Poland (see page 1027). After the declaration of martial law in Poland in December 1981, western Europe refused to follow the United States in imposing economic sanctions against Poland and the Soviet Union. Some observers concluded that the alliance had lost the will to think and act decisively in relations with the Soviet bloc. Others noted that occasional dramatic differences within the alliance reflected the fact that the Common Market and the United States had drifted apart and become economic rivals.

Yet, despite its very real difficulties, the Atlantic alliance, formed in the late 1940s to check Soviet expansion in Europe, endured and remained true to its original purpose in the 1980s. The U.S. military buildup launched by Jimmy Carter in his last years in office was accelerated by President Ronald Reagan, who was swept into office in the 1980 election by the wave of patriotism following an agonizing hostage crisis in Iran. The new American leadership was convinced that the military balance had tipped in favor of the Soviet Union. Increasing defense spending rapidly, the Reagan administration concentrated especially on nuclear arms and an expanded navy as keys to a resurgence of American power in the post-Vietnam era. Somewhat reluctantly, and in the face of large protest demonstrations, European governments agreed that NATO's forces had to be strengthened and that medium-range American cruise missiles with nuclear warheads should be installed on their soil, in response to the Soviet Union's vast arsenal of missiles targeted to destroy western Europe.

Thus the Atlantic alliance bent, but it did not break. In doing so, Western society gave indirect support to ongoing efforts to liberalize authoritarian communist states in eastern Europe, efforts that after repeated defeats finally burst through in spectacular fashion in the late 1980s. It is to this remarkable movement, which culminated in 1989 in the most promising achievement of the recent past, that we now turn.

THE SOVIET BLOC

Occasional differences within the NATO alliance on how to treat the Soviet bloc reflected not only shifts in Soviet conduct in foreign affairs, but also ambiguities in the course of developments within eastern Europe itself. On the one hand, attempts to liberalize the system had arisen in the 1950s, and the brutal totalitarianism of the Stalinist era was not re-established after Nikita Khrushchev fell from power in 1964. These changes encouraged Western hopes of gradual liberalization and of a more democratic, less threatening Soviet eastern Europe.

On the other hand, hard facts frequently intervened. The Soviet Union repeatedly demonstrated that it remained a harsh and aggressive dictatorship, a dictatorship that paid only lip service to egalitarian ideology and that was determined to uphold its rule throughout eastern Europe. Periodic efforts to achieve fundamental political change were inevitably doomed to failure, sooner or later. Or so it seemed to most Western experts into the middle of the 1980s.

And then Mikhail Gorbachev burst upon the scene. The new Soviet leader opened an era of reform that was as sweeping as it was unexpected. Many believed that Gorbachev would fall from power and that his reforms would fail in the Soviet Union. Such an outcome is clearly possible. Yet the scope of reform and then revolution in eastern Europe suggests that peoples there have indeed made a decisive breakthrough toward greater personal freedom and political democracy. Above all, reform in eastern Europe is based on powerful historical forces. It is not just the work of a single imaginative leader. It is also the result of long-standing campaigns to humanize communism and of a social transformation in the Soviet Union that has made rigid one-party dictatorship counterproductive and probably obsolete, as we shall now see.

The Czechoslovak Experiment

In the wake of Khrushchev's reforms in the Soviet Union (see pages 976–978), the 1960s brought modest liberalization and more consumer goods to eastern Europe, as well as somewhat greater national autonomy, especially in Poland and Rumania. Czechoslovakia moved more slowly, but in January 1968 it began making up for lost time. The reform elements in the Czechoslovak Communist party gained a majority and voted out the longtime Stalinist leader in favor of Alexander Dubček. The new government launched a series of major economic and political initiatives that fascinated observers around the world.

Educated in Moscow, Dubček was a dedicated Communist. But he and his allies within the party were also idealists who believed that they could reconcile genuine socialism with personal freedom and internal party democracy. Thus local decision making by trade unions, managers, and consumers replaced rigid bureaucratic planning. Censorship was relaxed, and mindless ideological conformity gave way to exciting free expression. People responded enthusiastically, and the reform program proved enormously popular. Czechoslovakia had been eastern Europe's only advanced industrial state before the Second World War, and Dubček was reviving traditions that were still deeply cherished.

Although Dubček remembered the lesson of Russian troops crushing the Hungarian revolution (see page 978) and constantly proclaimed his loy-

The End of Reform In August 1968 Soviet tanks rumbled into Prague to extinguish Czechoslovakian efforts to build a humane socialism. Here people watch the massive invasion from the sidewalks, knowing full well the suicidal danger of armed resistance. *(Source: Joseph Koudelka PP/Magnum)*

alty to the Warsaw Pact of communist states, the determination of the Czech reformers to build "socialism with a human face" frightened hard-line Communists. These fears were particularly strong in Poland and East Germany, where the leaders knew full well that they lacked popular support. Moreover, the Soviet Union feared that a liberalized Czechoslovakia would eventually be drawn to neutralism, or even to the democratic West. Thus the Eastern bloc countries launched a concerted campaign of intimidation against the Czech leaders, but Dubček's regime refused to knuckle under. The Soviet response was brutal. In August 1968, 500,000 Russian and allied eastern European troops suddenly occupied Czechoslovakia.

The Czechs made no attempt to resist militarily. The Soviets immediately arrested Dubček and the other top leaders and flew them to Moscow, where they were forced to surrender to Soviet demands. Gradually but inexorably, the reform program was abandoned and its supporters removed from office. Thus the Czechoslovak experiment in humanizing communism and making it serve the needs of ordinary citizens failed.

Shortly after the Czechoslovak invasion, Brezhnev declared the so-called Brezhnev Doctrine, according to which Soviet Russia and its allies had the right to intervene in any socialist country whenever they saw the need. Predictably, the occupation of Czechoslovakia raised a storm of protest. Many Communist parties in western Europe were harshly critical, partly out of conviction and partly to limit their electoral losses. But the occupation did not seriously alter ongoing Western efforts—most notably, those of West Germany's Willy Brandt—to secure better relations with the Eastern bloc countries. The reason was simple. The West considered Czechoslovakia to be part of Russia's sphere of influence, for better or worse. Thus the empire that Stalin had built remained solidly in place, and permanent changes in eastern Europe depended on developments in the Soviet Union.

The Soviet Union to 1985

The 1968 invasion of Czechoslovakia was the crucial event of the Brezhnev era, which really lasted beyond the aging leader's death in 1982, until the emergence in 1985 of Mikhail Gorbachev. The invasion demonstrated unmistakably the intense conservatism of Russia's ruling elite and its determination to maintain the status quo in the Soviet bloc.

Indeed, the aftermath of intervention in Czechoslovakia also brought a certain re-Stalinization of Soviet Russia. But now dictatorship was collective rather than personal, and coercion replaced uncontrolled terror. This compromise seemed to suit the leaders and a majority of the people, and the Soviet Union appeared stable in the 1970s and early 1980s.

A slowly rising standard of living for ordinary people contributed to stability, although the economic crisis of the 1970s markedly slowed the rate of improvement, and long lines and innumerable shortages persisted. The enduring differences between the life of the elite and the life of ordinary people also reinforced the system. Ambitious individuals still had tremendous incentive to do as the state wished, in order to gain access to special, well-stocked stores, attend special schools, and travel abroad.

Another source of stability was that ordinary Great Russians remained intensely nationalistic. Party leaders successfully identified themselves with this patriotism, stressing their role in saving the country during the Second World War and protecting it now from foreign foes, including eastern European "counter-revolutionaries." Moreover, the politically dominant Great Russians, who are concentrated in the central Russian heartland and in Siberia—formally designated as the Russian Federation—and who also hold through the Communist Party the commanding leadership positions in the non-Russian republics, constitute less than half of the total Soviet population. The Great Russians generally feared that greater freedom and open political competition might therefore result in demands for autonomy and even independence, not only by eastern European nationalities, but by the non-Russian nationalities of the smaller republics and the autonomous regions within the Soviet Union itself (Map 32.2). Thus liberalism and democracy generally appeared as alien political philosophies designed to undermine Russia's power and greatness.

The strength of the government was expressed in the re-Stalinization of culture and art. Free expression and open protest disappeared. In 1968, when a small group of dissenters appeared in Red Square

to protest the invasion of Czechoslovakia, they were arrested before they could unfurl their banners. This proved to be the high point of dissent, for in the 1970s Brezhnev and company made certain that Soviet intellectuals did not engage in public protest. Acts of open nonconformity and protest were severely punished, but with sophisticated, cunning methods.

Most frequently, dissidents were blacklisted and thus rendered unable to find a decent job, since the government was the only employer. This fate was enough to keep most in line. More determined but unrenowned protesters were quietly imprisoned in jails or mental institutions. Celebrated nonconformists such as Solzhenitsyn were permanently expelled from the country. Once again, Jews were persecuted as a "foreign" element, though some were eventually permitted to emigrate to Israel. As the distinguished Russian dissident historian Roy Medvedev explained in the mid-1970s,

The technology of repression has become more refined in recent years. Before, repression always went much farther than necessary. Stalin killed millions of people when arresting 1000 would have enabled him to control the people. Our leaders . . . found out eventually that you don't have to put people in prison or in a psychiatric hospital to silence them. There are other ways.[7]

Eliminating the worst aspects of Stalin's totalitarianism strengthened the regime, and rule by a self-perpetuating Communist elite in the Soviet Union appeared to be quite solid in the 1970s and early 1980s.

Yet beneath the dreary immobility of political life in the Brezhnev era the Soviet Union experienced profound changes. As a perceptive British journalist put it in 1986, "The country went through a social revolution while Brezhnev slept."[8] Three aspects of this revolution, which was seldom appreciated by Western observers at the time, were particularly significant.

First, the growth of the urban population, which had raced forward at breakneck speed in the Stalin years, continued rapidly in the 1960s and 1970s. In 1985 two-thirds of all Soviet citizens lived in cities, and a quarter lived in big cities (see Map 32.2). Of great significance, this expanding urban population lost its old peasant ways. As a result, it acquired more education, better job skills, and greater sophistication.

Second, the number of highly trained scientists,

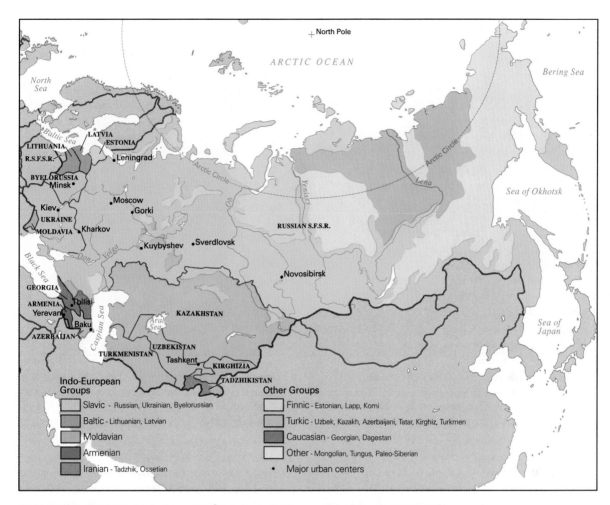

MAP 32.2 Soviet Peoples   One of the biggest challenges faced by Soviet leaders stems from the sheer size and diversity of the Soviet Union. Although the Great Russians dominate the Soviet Union and the Communist Party, they represent less than half the population. This map illustrates the potential for civic unrest spurred by resurgent nationalism among the different peoples of the Soviet Union.

managers, and specialists expanded prodigiously, jumping fourfold between 1960 and 1985. Thus the class of well-educated, pragmatic, and self-confident experts, which played such an important role in restructuring industrial societies after World War Two (see pages 995–997), developed rapidly in the Soviet Union. Moreover, leading Soviet scientists and technologists sought membership in the international "invisible college" of their disciplines, like their colleagues in the West. Correspondingly, they sought the intellectual freedom necessary to do significant work, and they often obtained it because their research had practical (and military) value.

Finally, education and freedom for experts in their special areas helped foster the growth of Soviet public opinion. Educated people read, discussed, and formed definite ideas about social questions. And if caution dictated conventional ideas (at least in public), many important issues could be approached and debated in "nonpolitical" terms. Developing definite ideas on such things as environmental pollution or urban transportation, educated urban people increasingly saw themselves as worthy of having a voice in society's decisions, even its political decisions. This, too, was part of the quiet transformation that set the stage for the reforms of the Gorbachev era.

The Rise of Solidarity This photograph shows the determination and mass action that allowed Polish workers to triumph in August 1980. Backed by a crowd of enthusiastic supporters, leader Lech Walesa announces the historic Gdansk Agreement to striking workers at the main gate of the Lenin Shipyards. (*Source: Jean Gaumy/Magnum*)

Solidarity in Poland

Before turning to those recent Soviet developments, we need to look at the growth of popular protest in the Soviet Union's satellite empire. In Poland, workers joined together en masse to fight peacefully for freedom and self-determination, while the world watched in amazement. Crushed in the short run but refusing to admit defeat, the Polish workers waged a long campaign that inspired and reflected a powerful reform current in eastern Europe.

Poland was an unruly satellite from the beginning. Stalin said that introducing communism to Poland was like putting a saddle on a cow. Efforts to saddle the cow—really a spirited stallion—led to widespread riots in 1956 (see pages 977–978). As a result, the Polish Communists dropped efforts to impose Soviet-style collectivization on the peasants and to break the Roman Catholic church. Most agricultural land remained in private hands as the Catholic church thrived. With an independent agriculture and a vigorous church, the Communists failed to monopolize society.

They also failed to manage the economy effectively. The 1960s saw little economic improvement. When the government suddenly announced large price increases right before Christmas in 1970, Poland's working class rose again in angry protest. Factories were occupied and strikers were shot, but a new Communist leader came to power nevertheless. The government then wagered that massive inflows of Western capital and technology, especially from a now-friendly West Germany, could produce a Polish "economic miracle" that would win popular support for the regime. Instead, bureaucratic incompetence coupled with worldwide recession put the economy into a nose dive by the mid-1970s. Workers, intellectuals, and the church became increasingly restive. Then the real "Polish miracle" occurred: Cardinal Karol Wojtyla, archbishop of Cracow, was elected pope in 1978. In June 1979 he returned for an astonishing pilgrimage across his native land. Preaching love of Christ and country and the "inalienable rights of man," Pope John Paul II electrified the Polish nation. The economic crisis became a spiritual crisis as well.

In August 1980, as scattered strikes to protest higher meat prices spread, the sixteen thousand workers at the gigantic Lenin Shipyards in Gdansk (formerly known as Danzig) laid down their tools and occupied the showpiece plant. As other workers along the Baltic coast joined "in solidarity," the strikers advanced truly revolutionary demands: the right to form free trade unions, the right to strike, freedom of speech, release of political prisoners, and economic reforms. After eighteen days of shipyard occupation, as families brought food to the gates and priests said mass daily amid huge overhead cranes, the government gave in and accepted the workers' demands in the Gdansk Agreement. In a state where the Communist party claimed to rule on behalf of the proletariat, a working-class revolt had won an unprecedented victory.

Led by a feisty Lenin Shipyards electrician and devout Catholic named Lech Walesa, the workers proceeded to organize their free and democratic trade union. They called it "Solidarity." Joined by intellectuals and supported by the Catholic church, Solidarity became the union of a nation. By March 1981 it had a membership of 9.5 million, of 12.5 million who were theoretically eligible. A full-time staff of forty thousand linked the union members together, as Solidarity published its own newspapers and cultural and intellectual freedom blossomed in Poland. Solidarity's leaders had tremendous well-organized support, and the threat of calling a nationwide strike gave them real power in ongoing negotiations with the Communist bosses.

But if Solidarity had power, it did not try to take power in 1981. History, the Brezhnev Doctrine, and virulent attacks from communist neighbors all guaranteed the intervention of the Red Army and a terrible blood bath if Polish Communists "lost control." Thus the Solidarity revolution remained a "self-limiting revolution," aiming at defending the cultural and trade-union freedoms won in the Gdansk Agreement without directly challenging the Communist monopoly of political power.

Solidarity's combination of strength and moderation postponed a showdown. The Soviet Union, already condemned worldwide for its invasion of Afghanistan, played a waiting game of threats and pressure. After a crisis in March 1981 that followed police beatings of Solidarity activists, Walesa settled for minor government concessions, and Solidarity again dropped plans for a massive general strike. It was a turning point. Criticism of Walesa's moder-

ate leadership and calls for local self-government in unions and factories grew. Solidarity lost its cohesiveness. The worsening economic crisis also encouraged grassroots radicalism and frustration: a hunger-march banner proclaimed that "A hungry nation can eat its rulers."[9] With an eye on Western public opinion, the Polish Communist leadership shrewdly denounced Solidarity for promoting economic collapse and provoking Russian invasion. In December 1981 the Communist leader General Jaruzelski suddenly struck in the dead of subfreezing night, proclaiming martial law and cutting all communications, arresting Solidarity's leaders and "saving" the nation.

Outlawed and driven underground, Solidarity fought successfully to maintain its organization and to voice the aspirations of the Polish masses after 1981. Part of the reason for the union's survival was the government's unwillingness (and probably its inability) to impose full-scale terror. Moreover, in schools and shops, in factories and offices, millions decided to continue acting as if they were free, even though they were not. Therefore, cultural and intellectual life remained extremely vigorous in spite of renewed repression. At the same time, the faltering Polish economy, battered by the global stagnation of the early 1980s and crippled by a disastrous brain drain after 1981, continued to deteriorate. Thus popular support for outlawed Solidarity remained strong and deep under martial law in the 1980s, preparing the way for its resurgence at the end of the decade.

The rise and survival of Solidarity showed again the fierce desire of millions of eastern Europeans for greater political liberty. The union's strength also demonstrated the enduring appeal of cultural freedom, trade-union rights, patriotic nationalism, and religious feeling. Not least, Solidarity's challenge encouraged fresh thinking in the Soviet Union, ever the key to lasting change in the Eastern bloc.

Reform in the Soviet Union

Fundamental change in Russian history has often come in short, intensive spurts, which contrast vividly with long periods of immobility. We have studied four of these spurts: the ambitious "westernization" of Peter the Great in the early eighteenth century (see pages 552–554), the Great Reforms connected with the freeing of the serfs in the mid-nineteenth century (see pages 806–808), the Russian Revolution of 1917 (see pages 875–882), and Stalin's wrenching "revolution from above" in the 1930s (see pages 925–933). To this select list of decisive transformations, we must now add the era of fundamental reforms launched by Mikhail Gorbachev in 1985. The ultimate fate of these ongoing reforms is still unclear. But they have already had a profound, probably irreversible impact. They have brought political and cultural liberalization in the Soviet Union, and they have permitted democracy and national self-determination to triumph spectacularly in the old satellite empire.

As we have seen, the Soviet Union's Communist elite seemed secure in the early 1980s, as far as any challenge from below was concerned. The long-established system of administrative controls continued to stretch downward from the central ministries and state committees to provincial cities, and from there to factories, neighborhoods, and villages. At each level of this massive state bureaucracy, the overlapping hierarchy of the Communist party, with its 17.5 million members, continued to watch over all decisions and manipulate every aspect of national life. Organized opposition was impossible, and average people simply left politics to the bosses.

Yet the massive state and party bureaucracy was a mixed blessing. It safeguarded the elite, but it also promoted apathy in the masses. Discouraging personal initiative and economic efficiency, it was also ill suited to secure the effective cooperation of the rapidly growing class of well-educated urban experts. Therefore, when the ailing Brezhnev finally died in 1982, his successor, the long-time chief of the secret police, Yuri Andropov, tried to invigorate the system. Andropov introduced modest reforms to improve economic performance and campaigned against worker absenteeism and high-level corruption. Relatively little came of these efforts, but they combined with a worsening economic situation to set the stage for the emergence in 1985 of Mikhail Gorbachev, the most vigorous Soviet leader in a generation.

Gorbachev was smart, charming, and tough. As long-time Soviet foreign minister Andrei Gromyko reportedly said, "This man has a nice smile, but he has got iron teeth."[10] In his first year in office, Gorbachev attacked corruption and incompetence in the upper reaches of the bureaucracy, and he consolidated his power by packing the top level of the party with his supporters. He attacked alcoholism and drunkenness, which were deadly scourges of Soviet society. More basically, he elaborated a whole series of reform policies designed to revive and even remake the vast Soviet Union.

The first set of reform policies was designed to transform and restructure the economy, which was falling ever further behind that of the West in the 1980s and failing to provide for the very real needs of the Soviet population. To accomplish this economic restructuring—this *perestroika*—Gorbachev and his supporters permitted freer prices, more independence for state enterprises, and the setting up of profit-seeking private cooperatives to provide personal services. These reforms initially produced some improvements, but shortages then grew as the economy stalled at an intermediate point between central planning and free-market mechanisms. By 1990 Gorbachev's timid economic initiatives had met with very little success, posing a serious threat to his leadership and the entire reform program.

Gorbachev's bold and far-reaching campaign "to tell it like it is" was much more successful. Very popular in a country where censorship, dull uniformity, and outright lies had long characterized public discourse, the newfound openness—the *glasnost*—of the government and the media marked an astonishing break with the past. A disaster like the Chernobyl nuclear accident, which devastated part of the Ukraine and showered Europe with radioactive fallout, was investigated and reported with honesty and painstaking thoroughness. The works of long-banned and vilified Russian émigré writers sold millions of copies in new editions, while denunciations of Stalin and his terror became standard fare in plays and movies. Thus openness in government pronouncements led rather quickly to something approaching free speech and free expression, a veritable cultural revolution.

Democratization was the third element of reform. Beginning as an attack on corruption in the Communist party and as an attempt to bring the class of educated experts into the decision-making process, it led to the first free elections in the Soviet Union since 1917. Gorbachev and the party remained in control, but a minority of critical independents were elected in April 1989 to a revitalized Congress of People's Deputies. Many top-ranking communists who ran unopposed saw themselves defeated as a majority of angry voters struck their names from the ballot. Millions of Soviets then watched the new congress for hours on television, as Gorbachev and his ministers saw their proposals debated and even rejected.

Democratization also encouraged demands for greater autonomy by non-Russian minorities, especially in the Baltic region and in the Caucasus. These demands certainly went beyond what Gorbachev had envisaged. In April 1989 troops with sharpened shovels charged into a rally of Georgian separatists in Tbilisi and left twenty dead. But whereas China's Communist leaders brutally massacred similar prodemocracy demonstrators in Beijing in June 1989 and reimposed rigid authoritarian rule, Gorbachev drew back from repression. Thus nationalist demands continued to grow in the non-Russian Soviet republics, an unexpected consequence of democratization.

Finally, the Soviet leader brought "new political thinking" to the field of foreign affairs. And he acted on it. He withdrew Soviet troops from Afghanistan, encouraged reform movements in Poland and Hungary, and sought to reduce East-West tensions. Of enormous historical importance, Gorbachev pledged to respect the political choices of the peoples of eastern Europe, and he thereby repudiated the Brezhnev Doctrine, which had arrogantly proclaimed the right of the Soviet Union and its allies to intervene at will in eastern Europe. By 1989 it seemed that, if Gorbachev held to his word, the tragic Soviet occupation of eastern Europe might well wither away, taking the long cold war with it.

THE REVOLUTIONS OF 1989

Instead, history accelerated, and 1989 brought a series of largely peaceful revolutions throughout eastern Europe (Map 32.3). These revolutions overturned existing communist regimes and ended the Communist party's monopoly of power. Revolutionary mass demonstrations led to the formation of provisional governments dedicated to democratic elections, human rights, and national rejuvenation. Watched on television in the Soviet Union and around the world, these stirring events marked the triumph and the transformation of the long-standing reform movement we have been considering in this chapter.

Solidarity and the Polish people again led the way. In 1988 widespread labor unrest, raging inflation, and the outlawed Solidarity's refusal to cooperate with the military government had brought Poland to the brink of economic collapse. Profiting from Gorbachev's tolerant attitude and skillfully mobilizing its forces, Solidarity pressured Poland's frustrated Communist leaders into another round of negotiations that might work out a sharing of power to resolve the political stalemate and the

Newly Elected President Mikhail Gorbachev vowed in his acceptance speech before the Supreme Soviet, the U.S.S.R.'s parliament, to assume "all responsibility" for the success or failure of perestroika. Previous parliaments were no more than tools of the Communist party, but this one has actively debated and sometimes opposed government programs. *(Source: Vlastimir Shone/Gamma-Liaison)*

economic crisis. The subsequent agreement legalized Solidarity again after eight long years. The agreement also declared that a large minority of representatives to the Polish parliament would be chosen by free elections in June 1989. The Communist party was still guaranteed a majority, but Solidarity won every single contested seat in an overwhelming victory. On July 4, 1989, Solidarity members jubilantly entered the 460-member Polish parliament, the first freely elected opposition in a communist country. A month later the editor of Solidarity's weekly newspaper was sworn in as the first noncommunist leader in eastern Europe since

Stalin used Soviet armies to impose his system there after the Second World War.

Hungary followed Poland. Hungary's Communist boss, János Kádár, had permitted liberalization of the rigid planned economy after the 1956 uprising, in exchange for political obedience and continued Communist control. In May 1988, in an effort to hang on to power by granting modest political concessions, the party replaced Kádár with a reform Communist. But growing popular resistance rejected piecemeal progress, forcing the Communist party to renounce one-party rule and schedule free elections for early 1990. Welcoming Western in-

MAP 32.3 Democratic Movements in Eastern Europe, 1989   With Gorbachev's repudiation of the Brezhnev Doctrine, the desire for freedom and democracy spread throughout Eastern Europe. Countries that had been satellites in the orbit of the Soviet Union began to set themselves free to establish their own place in the universe of free nations.

Celebrating on the Berlin Wall   In a year filled with powerful images, none was more dramatic or more hopeful than the opening of the Berlin Wall, symbol of the harsh division between Eastern and Western Europe. *(Source: Tom Haley/SIPA-PRESS)*

vestment and moving rapidly toward multiparty democracy, Hungarians gleefully tore down the barbed-wire "iron curtain" with Austria and opened their border to East German refugees.

As thousands of dissatisfied East Germans began pouring into Hungary, before going on to immediate resettlement in thriving West Germany, growing economic dislocation and huge candlelight demonstrations brought revolution in East Berlin. The Berlin Wall was opened, and people danced for joy atop that grim symbol of the prison state. East Germany's aging Communist leaders were swept aside and in some case arrested, as general elections were scheduled for March 1990. Subsequently, a conservative-liberal "Alliance for Germany," which was closely tied to West German Chancellor Helmut Kohl's Christian Democrats, defeated the East German Social Democrats in these elections. The Alliance for Germany quickly negotiated an economic union on favorable terms with Chancellor

Kohl, and by the summer of 1990 only certain political and military aspects of German unification remained unresolved, for these questions affected the security of the Soviet Union and the general balance of power in Europe. Communism also died in Czechoslovakia in December 1989, in an almost good-humored ousting of Communist bosses in ten short days.

Only in Romania was revolution violent and bloody. There the iron-fisted Communist dictator, Nicolae Ceauşescu, had long combined Stalinist brutality with stubborn independence from Moscow. Faced with mass protests, Ceauşescu, alone among eastern European bosses, ordered his ruthless security forces to slaughter thousands, thereby sparking a classic armed uprising. After Ceauşescu's forces were defeated, the tyrant and his wife were captured and executed by a military court. A coalition government emerged from the fighting, although the legacy of Ceauşescu's oppression left

In Bucharest's Palace Square, cranes remove the statue of Lenin that dominated the square during the dictatorship of Nicolae Ceauşescu. Despite Ceauşescu's vow that democratic reform would come to Romania "when pears grow on poplar trees," citizens joined in a mass revolt to topple the despot and his oppressive regime. *(Source: BI/Gamma-Liaison)*

a troubled country with an uncertain political future.

As the 1990s began, the revolutionary changes that Gorbachev had permitted, and even encouraged, had triumphed in all but two eastern European states—tiny Albania and the vast Soviet Union. The great question now became whether

the Soviet Union would follow its former satellites, and whether reform communism would give way there to a popular anticommunist revolution. Near civil war between Armenians and Azerbaijanis in the Caucasus, assertions of independence in the Baltic states, including Lithuania's bold declaration of national sovereignty, and growing dissatisfaction among the Great Russian masses were all parts of a fluid, unstable political situation. Increasingly, the reform-minded Gorbachev, the most creative world leader of the late twentieth century, stood as a besieged moderate, assailed by those who wanted revolutionary changes and by hard-line Communists who longed to reverse course and clamp down. Only time would tell how Gorbachev would meet this two-sided challenge and how far he would go in his reforms. Yet it seems probable that the Soviet Union, like the nations of eastern Europe, has already experienced irreversible movement in the direction of personal freedom and political democracy, a most surprising development that accords magnificently with the noblest traditions of Western society.

THE FUTURE IN PERSPECTIVE

What about the future? For centuries, astrologers and scientists, experts and ordinary people, have been trying to answer this question. Although it may seem that the study of what has been has little to say about what will be, the study of history over a long period is actually very useful in this regard. It helps put the future in perspective.

In 1931 a distinguished Harvard professor of genetics examined the prospects for the human race in an article read by millions. Among his predictions was that "in the year 2500 the population of the world should be about 3,500 millions, or about twice the figures of today."[11] In fact, the population of the world reached five billion in the 1980s and, outside the highly developed countries of Europe and North America, is still growing rapidly. The six-century projection of the learned expert was proved dead wrong in less than fifty years.

History is full of such erroneous predictions, a few of which we have mentioned in this book. Yet lack of success has not diminished the age-old desire to look into the future. Self-proclaimed experts even pretend that they have created a new science of futurology. With great pomposity they often act as if their hunches and guesses about future human developments are inescapable realities. Yet the study of history teaches healthy skepticism regarding such predictions, however scientific they may appear. Past results suggest that most such predictions will simply not come true, or not in the anticipated way. Thus history provides some psychological protection from the fantastic visions of modern astrologers.

This protection has been particularly valuable in recent years, because many recent projections into the future have been quite pessimistic, just as they were very optimistic in the 1950s and 1960s. Many people in the Western world have feared that conditions are going to get worse rather than better. For example, there have been fears that trade wars will permanently cripple the world economy, that pollution will destroy the environment, and that the traditional family will disappear. Until recently, many experts and politicians were predicting that the energy crisis—in the form of skyrocketing oil prices—meant disaster, in the form of lower standards of living at best and the collapse of civilization at worst. Then some of these same experts worried that the unexpected sharp decline in oil prices in the early 1980s would bankrupt both Third World oil producers, such as Mexico, and the large American banks that have lent them so much money. In fact, both the oil producers and the big banks muddled through and show few signs of collapsing. It is heartening to know that most such dire predictions do not prove true, just as the same knowledge of likely error is sobering in times of optimistic expectations.

One of the more frightening and pessimistic predictions recently in vogue has been that the northern nations of Europe and North America will increasingly find themselves locked in a life-and-death struggle with the poor, overpopulated southern nations of Africa, Asia, and South America. This North-South conflict, it has been predicted, will replace the old cold war struggle of East and West with a much more dangerous international class and race conflict of rich versus poor, white versus colored. Such, it is said, is the bitter legacy of Western imperialism.

As Map 32.4 shows, there is indeed an enormous gap between the very wealthy nations of noncommunist western Europe and North America and the very poor nations of much of Africa and Asia. Yet closer examination does not reveal a growing split between two sharply defined economic camps. On the contrary, there are five or six distinct categories of nations in terms of income level. The countries of eastern Europe form something of a middle-income group, despite their serious economic problems and long decades of communist dictatorship and mismanagement. So do the major oil-exporting states, which are still behind the wealthier

countries of western Europe. Poverty in parts of Latin America is severe, but as the map shows, standards of living are substantially higher there than in much of Africa and Asia, both of which encompass considerable variation.

When one considers differences in culture, religion, politics, and historical development, the supposed split between "rich" and "poor" nations breaks down still further. Thus a global class war between rich and poor appears unlikely in the foreseeable future. A more reasonable expectation is continuing pressure to reduce international economic differences through taxation and welfare measures, as has already occurred domestically in the wealthy nations. Such pressure may well bring at least modest success, for the wealthy nations generally realize that an exclusively Western (or "Northern") viewpoint on global issues is unrealistic and self-defeating. The true legacy of Western imperialism is one small world.

It is this that has made the nuclear arms race so ominous. Not only do the United States and the Soviet Union possess unbelievably destructive, ever-expanding nuclear arsenals, but Great Britain, France, China, and India all have "the bomb," and probably Israel and South Africa do as well. Other countries are equipped or desire to "go nuclear." Thus some gloomy experts have predicted that twenty or thirty states may have nuclear weapons in the near future. In a world plagued by local wars and ferocious regional conflicts, these experts have concluded that nuclear war is almost inevitable and have speculated that the human race is an "endangered species."

Such predictions and the undeniable seriousness of the arms race appear to have jolted Western populations out of their customary fatalism regarding nuclear weapons. Recent efforts to reduce or even halt the nuclear buildup in the Soviet Union and the NATO alliance have made some real progress. Above all, the Gorbachev era in the Soviet Union has opened the way to new thinking and genuine superpower cooperation on nuclear arms questions. An optimist can hope that comparable concern in non-Western areas may yet develop to help create the global political will necessary to control nuclear proliferation before it is too late.

MAP 32.4 Estimated GNP per Capita Income in the Early 1980s

Whatever does or does not happen, the study of history puts the future in perspective in other ways. We have seen that every age has its problems and challenges. Others before us have trod these paths of crisis and uncertainty. This knowledge helps save us from exaggerated self-pity in the face of our own predicaments.

Perhaps our Western heritage may even inspire us with pride and measured self-confidence. We stand, momentarily, at the end of the long procession of Western civilization winding through the ages. Sometimes the procession has wandered, or backtracked, or done terrible things. But it has also carried the efforts and sacrifices of generations of toiling, struggling ancestors. Through no effort of our own, we are the beneficiaries of those sacrifices and achievements. Now that it is our turn to carry the torch onward, we may remember these ties with our forebears.

To change the metaphor, we in the West are like a card player who has been dealt many good cards. Some of them are obvious, like our technical and scientific heritage or our commitments to human rights and the individual. Others are not so obvious, sometimes half-forgotten or even hidden up the sleeve. One thinks, for example, of the Christian Democrats, the moderate Catholic party, which emerged after World War Two to play such an important role in the western European renaissance. And in the almost miraculous victory of peaceful revolution in eastern Europe in 1989—in what the Czech playwright-turned-president Václav Havel called "the power of the powerless"—we see again the regenerative strength of the Western ideals of individual rights, representative government, and nationhood in the European homeland. We hold a good hand.

Our study of history, of mighty struggles and fearsome challenges, of shining achievements and tragic failures, gives a sense of what is the essence of life itself: the process of change over time. Again and again we have seen how peoples and societies evolve, influenced by ideas, human passions, and material conditions. As sure as anything is sure, this process of change over time will continue, as the future becomes the present and then the past. And students of history are better prepared to make sense of this unfolding process because they have already observed it. They know how change goes forward, on the basis of existing historical forces, and their projections will probably be as good as

The World in Modern Times, 1914 to the Present

	Politics	Science and Technology
1914	World War One, 1914–1918 *Lusitania* sunk, 1915 Easter Rebellion, 1916 U.S. declares war on Germany, 1917 Bolshevik Revolution, 1917–1918 Treaty of Versailles, 1919	Submarine warfare, 1915 Ernest Rutherford split the atom, 1919
1920	Mussolini seizes power, 1922 Forced collectivization in the Soviet Union, 1929 Stalin orders mass purges, ca 1929–1939 Hitler becomes chancellor of Germany, 1933 Rome-Berlin Axis, 1936 Nazi–Soviet Non-Agression Pact, 1939 World War Two begins, 1939	"Heroic age of physics," 1920s First major public broadcasts in Great Britain and the United States, 1920 Werner Heisenberg, "principle of uncertainty," 1927 Talking movies, 1930 First jet engines, ca 1935 Radar system in England, 1939
1940	Japan bombs Pearl Harbor, 1941 War in Europe ends, 1945 U.S. drops atomic bombs on Japan, 1945 United Nations, 1945 Cold war era begins, 1947 Collapse of colonial empires, 1947–1962 Israel established, 1948 Communist government in China, 1949 Korean War, 1950–1953 Civil war in Vietnam, 1954 "Peaceful coexistence," ca 1955–1957	J. Robert Oppenheimer, 1904–1967 First atomic bomb tested, 1945 James Watson and Francis Crick discover structure of DNA molecule, 1953 Russian satellite in orbit, 1957
1960	The Berlin Wall, 1961 United States in Vietnam, ca 1961–1973 *Détente,* 1970s Islamic Revolution in Iran, 1978–1979	European Council for Nuclear Research, 1960 Space race, 1960s Russian cosmonaut first to orbit globe, 1961 American astronaut first person on the moon, 1969
1980	Solidarity in Poland, 1980 *Glasnost* in the Soviet Union, 1985 Prodemocracy demonstrations in Beijing, 1989 Revolutions in Eastern Europe, 1989 Berlin Wall opened, 1989	

Economics and Society	Arts and Letters
Planned economies in Europe, 1914 Bread riots in Russia, 1917	Marcel Proust, *Remembrance of Things Past,* 1913–1927 "Modernism," ca 1905–1929 Oswald Spengler, *The Decline of the West,* 1918 Walter Gropius, the Bauhaus, ca 1919–1921
New Economic Policy in the Soviet Union, 1921 American stock market boom, 1928–1929 The Great Depression, 1929–1933 Roosevelt's "New Deal," 1933 National Recovery Administration, 1935 Mexico nationalizes petroleum industry, 1938	Modern existentialism, 1920s Dadaism in art, 1920s Virginia Woolf, *Jacob's Room,* 1922 James Joyce, *Ulysseus,* 1922 T. S. Eliot, *The Waste Land,* 1922 Surrealism in art, ca 1925 Erich Remarque, *All Quiet on the Western Front,* 1929 Pablo Picasso, *Guernica,* 1937
Bretton Woods Agreement, 1944 Marshall Plan, 1947 Organization of European Economic Cooperation, 1948 European economic progress, ca 1950–1969 European Coal and Steel Community, 1952 European Economic Community, 1957	Ludwig Mies van der Rohe, Lake Shore Apartments, 1948–1951 George Orwell, *1984,* 1949 Boris Pasternak, *Doctor Zhivago,* 1956
Collapse of postwar monetary system, 1971 OPEC oil price increase, 1973 Stagflation, 1970s	Alexander Solzhenitsyn, *One Day in the Life of Ivan Denisovitch,* 1962
Gorbachev implements perestroika, 1985 Economic crisis in Poland, 1988 Economic union between East and West Germany, 1989	

those of the futurologists. Students of history are also prepared for the new and unexpected in human development, for they have already seen great breakthroughs and revolutions. They have an understanding of how things really happen.

NOTES

1. Quoted in W. Laqueur, *Europe Since Hitler* (Baltimore: Penguin Books, 1972), p. 9.
2. *Wall Street Journal,* June 25, 1985, p. 1.
3. S. Rose and D. Fasenfest, *Family Income in the 1980s: New Pressures on Wives, Husbands and Young Adults* (Washington, D.C.: Economic Policy Institute, 1988), Working Paper No. 103, pp. 5–8.
4. Quoted in Kessing's Research Report, *Germany and East Europe Since 1945: From the Potsdam Agreement to Chancellor Brandt's "Ostpolitik"* (New York: Charles Scribner's Sons, 1973), pp. 284–285.
5. Quoted in S. E. Morison et al., *A Concise History of the American Republic* (New York: Oxford University Press, 1977), p. 735.
6. Richard Nixon, *Public Papers, 1969* (Washington, D.C.: U.S. Government Printing Office, 1971), p. 371.
7. Quoted in H. Smith, *The Russians* (New York: Quadrangle Books/New York Times, 1976), pp. 455–456.
8. M. Walker, *The Waking Giant: Gorbachev's Russia* (New York, Pantheon Books, 1987), p. 175.
9. T. G. Ash, *The Polish Revolution: Solidarity* (New York: Charles Scribner's Sons, 1983), p. 186.
10. Quoted in *Time,* January 6, 1986, p. 66.
11. E. M. East, in *Scientific Monthly,* April 1931; also in *Reader's Digest* 19 (May 1931): 151.

SUGGESTED READING

Many of the studies cited in the Suggested Reading for Chapters 30 and 31 are of value for the years since 1968 as well. Journalistic accounts in major newspapers and magazines are also invaluable tools for an understanding of recent developments. Among general works, W. Laqueur, *Europe Since Hitler,* rev. ed. (1982), and W. Keylor, *The Twentieth Century: An International History* (1984), are particularly helpful with their extensive, up-to-date bibliographies. The culture and politics of protest are provocatively analyzed in H. Hughes, *Sophisticated Rebels: The Political Culture of European Dissent, 1968–1987* (1988), and W. Hampton, *Guerrilla Minstrels:*

John Lennon, Joe Hill, Woodie Guthrie, Bob Dylan (1986). B. Jones, *The Making of Contemporary Europe* (1980), is a good brief account, while G. Parker, *The Logic of Unity* (1975), analyzes the forces working for and against European integration. D. Swann, *The Economics of the Common Market,* 5th ed. (1984), carries developments into the 1980s. L. Barzini, *The Europeans* (1983), draws engaging group portraits of the different European peoples today and is strongly recommended. On West Germany, H. Turner, *The Two Germanies Since 1945: East and West* (1987); L. Whetten, *Germany's Ostpolitik* (1971); and W. Patterson and G. Smith, eds., *The West German Model: Perspectives on a Stable State* (1981), are good introductions. Willy Brandt eloquently states his case for reconciliation with the East in *A Peace Policy for Europe* (1969). The spiritual dimension of West German recovery is probed by G. Grass in his world-famous novel *The Tin Drum* (1963), as well as in the novels of H. Böll. W. Laqueur, *The Germans* (1985), is a highly recommended contemporary report by a famous historian doubling as a journalist. P. Jenkins, *Mrs Thatcher's Revolution: The End of the Socialist Era* (1988), and D. Singer, *Is Socialism Doomed? The Meaning of Mitterrand* (1988), are provocative studies on Great Britain and France in the 1980s. Two outstanding works on the Vietnam War are N. Sheehan, *A Bright and Shining Lie: John Paul Vann and America in Vietnam* (1988), and A. Short, *The Origins of the Vietnam War* (1989).

Among the many books to come out of the Czechoslovak experience in 1968, three are particularly recommended: H. Schwartz, *Prague's 200 Days: The Struggle for Democracy in Czechoslovakia* (1969); I. Svitak, *The Czechoslovak Experiment, 1968–1969* (1971); and Z. Zeman, *Prague Spring* (1969). M. Kaufman, *Mad Dreams, Saving Graces: Poland, a Nation in Conspiracy* (1989), carries developments through the summer of 1989, while R. Leslie, *The History of Poland Since 1863* (1981), provides long-term perspective. T. Ash's book cited in the Notes is the best early study of Solidarity and it and more recent articles by Ash are highly recommended. It may be compared with a less sympathetic account by N. Ascherson, *The Polish August: The Self-limiting Revolution* (1982). A. Bramberg, ed., *Poland: Genesis of a Revolution* (1983), is a valuable collection of documents with extensive commentary.

On the Soviet Union, in addition to works cited in Chapter 30, D. Shipler, *Russia: Broken Idols, Solemn Dreams* (1983), is a solid report by an American journalist, while A. Shevchenko, *Breaking with Moscow* (1985), is the altogether fascinating autobiography of a top Russian diplomat who defected to the United States. A. De Porte, *Europe Between the Superpowers: The Enduring Balance* (1979), and J. Hough and M. Fainsod, *How the Soviet Union Is Governed* (1979), are major scholarly studies. M. Lewin, *The Gorbachev Phenomenon: A Historical Inter-*

pretation (1988), is excellent on the origins of the ongoing reforms, while Walker's *The Waking Giant,* cited in the Notes, is a fascinating eyewitness account of Soviet life in the mid-1980s. B. Eklof, *Soviet Briefing: Gorbachev and the Reform Period* (1989), focuses on 1987, a critical year. *The New York Times,* a great newspaper, provides excellent coverage of the revolutions of 1989 and of fast-breaking developments in eastern Europe and in the Soviet Union.

Among innumerable works on recent economic developments, L. Thurow, *The Zero-Sum Society* (1981), is an interesting example of early 1980s pessimism in the United States, and it may be compared with the engaging and informative work by J. Eatwell, *Whatever Happened to Britain? The Economics of Decline* (1982). W. Rostow, *The World Economy: History and Prospect* (1977), is a massive scholarly tome by a perennial optimist, and P. Hawkins, *The Next Economy* (1983), contains intelligent insights that merit consideration by the ordinary citizen. Three major intellectual works, which are rather somber in their projections, are R. Heilbroner, *An Inquiry into the Human Prospect* (1974), and J. Revel, *The Totalitarian Temptation* (1977) and *How Democracies Perish* (1983).

Chapter Opener Credits

Notes on the Illustrations

Pages 498–499: Charles Lebrun (1619–1690), who conceived and designed the series from which this tapestry—the July Tapestry—comes, was very influential in the arts in France during Louis XIV's reign. He became director of the Gobelins factory, where this tapestry was made in the late 17th century.

Page 503: Philippe de Champaigne (French, 1602–1674), *Cardinal Richelieu Swearing the Order of the Holy Ghost.*

Page 504: Antoine Coysevox (French, 1640–1730), *Louis XIV,* statue for the Town Hall of Paris, 1687–1689.

Page 508: "The Noble Is the Spider," from Jacques Lagniet, *Receuil des Proverbes,* 1657–1663.

Page 510: Nicholas Poussin (French, 1594–1665), *The Rape of the Sabine Women,* ca 1636–1637. Oil on canvas; 60⅞ x 82⅝ in. (46.160)

Page 517: Velazquez, *The Fable of Arachne (The Tapestry Weavers),* 1644–1648. Oil on canvas; 7′ 3″ x 9′ 6″. This painting represents a scene in Juan Alvarez's tapestry and carpet workshop in Madrid.

Page 525: Johannes Vermeer, known as Jan Vermeer van Delft (Dutch, 1632–1675), *Woman Holding a Balance,* ca 1664. Canvas; 16¾ x 15 in.

Page 527: Hiob Adriaensz Berckheyde, *The Old Stock Exchange, Amsterdam.* Canvas; 85 x 105 cm. (Inv. no. 1043)

Page 528: Pieter Claesz (Dutch, 1597–1660), *Still Life with Musical Instruments.*

Pages 532–533: Peter the Great brought architects and artists from the West to design and build his Summer Palace at Peterhof.

Page 544: J.C. Merk (or Merck) (d. 1730), *Prussian Riesengrenadier,* ca 1730. Plate 9 (Windsor 1260). Oil on canvas; 79½ x 39½ in.

Page 550: The Church of St. Basil (formerly the Cathedral of the Intercession), Moscow, 1555–1560, with 17th century additions.

Page 553: Etienne Falconnet (1716–1791), *The Bronze Horseman, St. Petersburg* (Leningrad), completed in 1783.

Page 555: The grand stairway of the Residenz at Würzburg (built by the powerful Schönborn family) was intended by its architect Balthasar Neumann (1678–1753) to allow a slow ascent to be able to take in gradually the ceiling painting by Giovanni Battista Tiepolo glorifying Bishop Schönborn, 1750–1753.

Pages 562–563: T. Malton, *Hall's Library at Margate,* aquatint, 1789.

Page 571: Louis XIV and Colbert visiting the Académie des Sciences, from C. Perrault's *Mémoires pour servir à l'histoire naturelle des animaux,* 1671.

Page 572: Frans Hals (Dutch, 1581/85–1666), *René Descartes,* 1649. Oil on panel, 19 x 14 cm.

Page 578: "Die Tafelrunde" is a copy by Joachim Tietze, Berlin, of the painting by Adolph von Menzel, 1850. The original belonged to the National Gallery, Berlin, and was destroyed in 1945.

Page 582: *Une Soirée chez Madame Geoffrin* by Anicet-Charles-Gabriel Lemonnier, (French, 1793–1824), depicts the first reading of Voltaire's "L'Orpheline de Chine" in 1755.

Page 586: V. Eriksen, *Catherine II on Horseback,* 1762.

Page 590: Marten Meytens (alternate spelling: Mijtens; Swedish-Austrian, 1695–1770), *Kaiseria Maria Theresie mit Familie.* Meytens was an active court painter; in 1759 he was made director of the Vienna Academy of Art.

Page 599: *Les Glaneuses* by Jean-François Millet (1814–1875), French genre and landscape painter of the Barbizon school. Oil on canvas; 21¼ x 26 in.

Page 604: Painting by Thomas Weaver, engraved by William Ward and published July 21, 1812. Mezzotint, 23⁷⁄₁₀ x 17⅘ in.

Page 615: Samuel Scott (English, 1702–1772), *Old East India Quay, London,* Victoria and Albert Museum. Samuel Scott was the most distinguished native English topographical view painter in the eighteenth century. Such painting was popularized in England by Canaletto during his residence there from 1746–1755.

Page 620: Frontispiece from a map of "the most Inhabited part of Virginia containing the whole province of Maryland with part of Pennsylvania, New Jersey and North Carolina drawn by Joshua Fry and Peter Jefferson in 1775," in Thomas Jeffrey's *America Atlas,* 1776, The British Library.

Page 622: Charles Willson Peale (American, 1741–1827), *General John Cadwalader, His First Wife Elizabeth and their Daughter Anne,* 1772. Philadelphia Museum of Art: The Cadwalader Collection, purchased with funds contributed by the Pew Memorial Trust & gift of the Cadwalader Family. Peale was primarily an artist, yet also a naturalist and inventor. He enjoyed the generous patronage of John Cadwalader.

Pages 626–627: P. Debucourt, *Celebrations in Les Halls on the birth of Dauphin, 21st January, 1782.*

Page 630: Jean-Baptiste Siméon Chardin (French, 1699–1779), *The Kitchen Maid,* ca 1738. Canvas; 18¼ x 14¾ in. (1952.5.38(117)) Chardin is now considered to be the most popular eighteenth century French artist. He was a realist in the manner of seventeenth-century Dutch masters.

Page 633: Attr. to Master of the Beguins (French, active ca 1650–1660), *Beggars at a Doorway.*

Page 640: Louis (or Antoine?) Le Nain (French, 1593–1648), *Famille de paysans dans un interieur,* ca 1640.

Page 647: "The Remarkable Effects of Vaccination," an anonymous nineteenth-century Russian cartoon in the Clements C. Fry Collection of Medical Prints and Drawings, Yale Medical Library.

Page 650: After M.E. Guignes, *Planting crosses at Embrun in May.* From *L'Illustration,* 1855 (1ᵉ semester), p. 309.

Page 651: W.W. Wheatley, "Dancing around the Church," 1848.

Page 653: From the City Temple, London.

Pages 658–659: After David, and probably the work

of a collaborator of David, *The Tennis Court Oath.* This is a slightly smaller painting than the famous pen drawing with sepia wash by David, 1791. It gives some idea of the intended color scheme of David's great project, which only remains as the famous drawing.

Page 664: John Trumbell (American, 1756–1843), *Signing of the Declaration of Independence,* 1786. Oil on canvas; 21⅛ x 31½ in. John Trumbell was considered to be one of the most significant American artists of his time.

Page 667: *Louis XVI and Benjamin Franklin,* France (Niderville, Lorraine). Probably by Charles Gabriel Sauvage, called Lemire (1741–1827). Biscuit porcelain, ca 1783–1785. H. 12⅝ in.

Page 672: A primitive but contemporary representation of the taking of the Bastille, by "Cholet" who was a participant in the attack.

Page 675: This was the first portrait of Mary Wollstonecraft, by an unknown artist, commissioned by William Roscoe.

Page 679: "Un Comité révolutionnaire sous la Terreur," after Alexandre Évariste Fragonard, French historical painter (1780–1850).

Page 682: Jacques-Louis David (French, 1748–1825), *Napoleon Crossing the Alps.* Oil on canvas.

Page 684: Francisco de Goya y Lucientes, *The Third of May, 1808* (1814–1815). Oil on canvas; 8′ 9″ x 11′ 3½″. Goya was known in the Spain of his day as a portraitist, history painter, and church painter.

Pages 690–691: William-Powell Frith (British, 1819–1909), *The Railway Station* (detail), completed 1862. Oil on canvas; 45¼ x 98¼ in.

Page 698: Engraving by Henry Beighton, 1717, of the atmospheric steam engine invented about 1705 by Thomas Newcomen, English blacksmith (1663–1729).

Page 701: Honoré Daumier (French, 1808–1879), *The Third-Class Carriage.* Oil on canvas. Daumier was both a caricaturist and a serious painter.

Page 712: From *Parliamentary Papers,* 1842, vol. XV.

Pages 718–719: Anton Ziegler, *Barricade in the Michaeler Square on the Night of 26 to 27 May 1848.* Oil on canvas; 68 x 55 cm.

Page 721: Isabey, *Congress of Vienna.* Royal Library, Windsor Castle, RL.21539.

Page 725: *Count Clemens von Metternich* (1773–1859) by Sir Thomas Lawrence, English painter (1769–1830).

Page 732: Left to right: K. Marx, F. Engels (rear), with Marx's daughters: Jenny, Eleanor, and Laura, photographed in the 1860s.

Page 734: John Constable (English, 1776–1837), *The Hay Wain.* Constable was one of the two great romantic painters of the period (Joseph Turner being the other), and was the first artist of importance to paint outdoors.

Page 737: Josef Danhauser (German, 1805–1845), *Liszt am Klavier,* 1840.

Page 739: Eugene Delacroix (French, 1798–1863),

Les Massacres de Scio. Delacroix was leader of the Romantic school. This dramatic interpretation of a contemporary event scandalized Paris Salon visitors in 1824.

Page 743: Eugene Delacroix (French, 1798–1863), *Liberty Leading the People,* 1830. Oil on canvas; 102½ x 128 in. Exhibited at the Paris Salon of 1831, the painting was acquired by the French Government.

Page 745: Honoré Daumier (French, 1808–1879), *Legislative Belly,* lithograph, 1834, 42 x 52.5 cm. Charles Deering Collection (1941.1258)

Pages 754–755: John O'Connor, *St. Pancras Hotel and Station from Pentonville Road.*

Page 758: "The Court for King Cholera," cartoon from *Punch,* XXIII (1852), 139.

Page 759: From Mayhew's *London Labour and the London Poor;* after a daguerrotype Beard.

Page 762: Cross-section of a Parisian house, about 1850, from Edmund Texier, *Tableauade Paris,* Paris, 1852, vol. I, p. 65.

Page 768: Paul-Emile Chabas (French, 1869–1937), *Un Coin de Table,* 1904. Oil on canvas. Bibliotheque des Arts Decoratifs.

Page 772: Pierre-Auguste Renoir (French, 1841–1919), *Le Moulin de la Galette a Montmartre,* 1876. 4′ 3½″ x 5′ 9″. Bequest of Gustave Caillabotte, 1894.

Page 775: Henri de Toulouse-Lautrec (French, 1864–1901), *At "A La Mie."* Oil on cardboard; 21 x 26¾ in. Purchased by S.A. Denio Fund and General Income for 1940.

Page 777: After a drawing by C. Koch, 1890.

Page 785: Hilaire Germain Edgar Degas (French, 1834–1917), *Les Repasseuses.*

Pages 788–789: Wall painting from the Town Hall and Civic Museum, Siena.

Page 792: Demolition of part of the Latin Quarter in 1860. Engraving from a drawing by Félix Thorigny.

Page 795: R. Legat, *Battle of Calatafim,* 1860.

Page 804: Thure de Thulstrup, *The Battle of Gettysburg,* from the CIVIL WAR, Gettysburg (Time-Life Books, Inc.). Courtesy, The Seventh Regiment Fund, Inc.

Page 807: Merchants of Nijni-Novgorod drinking tea. From *L'Illustration,* 29 August 1905.

Page 816: After Franz Schlegel, *Hussars of the 15th Regiment Dispersing Demonstrators in front of the Vienna Parliament Building, November 28, 1897.* Engraving.

Pages 822–823: Oil painting on glass, post 1780, by unknown Chinese artist.

Page 830: Townsend Harris, the American Consul, meeting with representatives of the Tokugawa Shogunate. Color on paper, 1857. Artist unknown. Tsuneo Tamba Collection, Yokohama.

Page 831: Scottish troops at the Great Sphinx at Giza, after helping to defeat Tarabi Pasha at the battle of Tel-el-Kebir, 1882.

Page 836: The intersection of Orchard and Hester Streets on New York City's Lower East Side, ca 1905. Oil over a photograph.

Page 841: A. Sutherland, *Battle of Omdurman,* September 2, 1898. Colored lithograph.

Page 844: From "The Graphic," November 9, 1895.

Page 849: Ichiyosai Kuniteru, *Tomioka raw-silk reeling factory,* ca 1875. Painted wood block. Tsuneo Tamba Collection, Yokohama.

Pages 856–857: John Nash (English), *Over the Top.*

Page 859: Anton von Werner (German, 1843–1915), *The Congress of Berlin,* 1878.

Page 862: After a watercolor by Willy Stöwer (German), *The German Fleet,* 1907.

Pages 890–891: Isaac Soyer (American, 1907–   ), *Employment Agency,* 1937. Oil on canvas; 34¼ x 45 in. Whitney Museum of American Art (Purchase 37.44). Photo: Geoffrey Clements, N.Y.

Page 898: Edvard Munch (Norwegian, 1863–1944), *The Dance of Life,* 1899.

Page 900: Frank Lloyd Wright (American architect, 1869–1959), Falling Water, Bear Run, Pennsylvania —perhaps the greatest modern house in America, 1936. The largely self-taught Wright was an exponent of what he called "organic architecture": the idea that a building should blend in with its setting and be harmonious with nature.

Page 903: Pablo Picasso (Spanish painter and sculptor, 1881–1973), *Guernica,* 1937. The original oil on canvas, 11′ 5½″ x 25′ 5¾″, is in the Museo del Prado, Madrid.

Page 925: French caricature by C. Leavdre, 1898.

Page 929: Arkady Aleksandrovich Plastov (Russian, 1893–1972), *Collective Farm Threshing,* 1949. Oil on canvas, 200 x 382 cm. Plastov's career was entirely in the Soviet era; his great paintings were calls to action—icons of socialism.

Page 945: The cartoon "Stepping Stones to Glory" by Sir David Low (1891–1963) appeared in the London *Evening Standard* on 8 July 1936.

Page 950: I. Toidze (Russian), *For the Motherland's Sake, Go Forward, Heroes,* 1942 poster.

Page 982: Detail from Diego Rivera's monumental fresco painting (8.59 x 12.87 m), *History of Mexico: From the Conquest to the Future,* 1929–30. From the West Wall, Stairway of the Palacio Nacional, Mexico City. In this detail, the priest Hidalgo presides over the cause of independence. In the center the Mexican eagle, symbol of nationality, holds the Aztec emblem of ceremonial war. Rivera was a painter, printmaker, sculptor, book illustrator, as well as a political activist.

Index

Nursing, of babies. *See* Breast-feeding
Nutrition: in 18th-century Europe, 639–641. *See also* Diet

Oath of the Tennis Court, 670
October Manifesto, 809
OEEC (Organization of European Economic Cooperation), 966–967, 969
Old Church Slavonic language, 547
Oldenbarneveldt, Jan van, 528
Old Regime, French, 669
Oleg, Varangian ruler, 547
Olivares, Count Gaspar de Guzman, 516
Omdurman, Battle of, 840
One Day in the Life of Ivan Denisovich (Solzhenitsyn), 977
On Liberty (Mill), 814
On the Origin of Species by the Means of Natural Selection (Darwin), 783
On the Revolutions of the Heavenly Spheres (Copernicus), 566
OPEC (Organization of Petroleum Exporting Countries), 1012(map), 1012–1013, 1014
Open-field agricultural system, 598–600
Opera House (Paris), 761
Opium trade, 828–829
Oppenheimer, J. Robert, 991
Organization of American States (OAS), 984
Organization of European Economic Cooperation (OEEC), 966–967, 969
Organization of Petroleum Exporting Countries (OPEC), 1012(map), 1012–1013, 1014
Organization of Work (Blanc), 730
Orient. *See* Asia
Orlov, Gregory, 585
Orphans. *See* Foundlings
Orwell, George, 899
O'Sullivan, John Louis, 729
Ottoman Empire, 538, 539(map); in Crimean War, 806; decline of, 858, 862; Congress of Berlin and, 862–863, 863(map); destruction of, 863, 863(map), 869
Ottoman Turks: Habsburg defeat of, 538–539; driven from Greece, 738
Overseas expansion: French, 508–509; Dutch, 528; Russian, 552–554, 808. *See also* Imperialism
Owen, Robert, 713–714, 819

Pacific, World War II in, 952–954, 953(map)
Paine, Thomas, 665
Painting. *See* Art
Pakistan, 973
Palaces: of Louis XIV, 506; baroque, 554–556; at Tuileries, 676; Crystal, 701; at Liège, 705–706
Palacký, Francis, 729, 748
Pale of Settlement, 834
Palestine, 887; independence granted to, 974; Jewish nation created in, 974
Palmerston, Lord, 751
Panama Canal, 826; United States' control over, 843
Pankhurst, Emmeline, 810

Papacy, unification of Italy and, 793
Papen, Franz von, 939, 940
Paris: salons in, during Enlightenment, 581–582, 583; hospital in, 645; 19th-century rebuilding of, 761, 763, 763(map); prostitution in, during 19th century, 774–775; Paris Commune and, 812, 817. *See also* France
Paris, Peace of: first (1814), 721; second (1815), 723
Paris Commune, 812, 817
Parlement of Paris, 577; absolutism and, 587, 588; renouncement of royal initiative, 669
Parliament (England): decline of absolutism and, 518, 519; restoration of monarchy and, 523; constitutional monarchy and cabinet government and, 523–524; liberal reform of, 738–742; social welfare measures and, 814; Irish nationalism and, 814–815
Parliament (Germany), 810, 811; under Bismarck, 798, 800–801
Parliament (Prussia), unification of Germany and, 797
Party Congress of 1927, 928
Passchendaele, battle at, 867, 869
Pasternak, Boris, 977
Pasteur, Louis, 760, 781
Pasteurization, 760
Paulette, 501–502
Peace of Paris: first (1814), 721; second (1815), 723
Peace of Utrecht, 513, 514(map), 618
Peace of Westphalia, 525
Pearl Harbor, Japanese attack on, 947
Peasants: eastern European, 534–537, 598–599; Russian, 551, 552, 553, 557, 560, 879, 927, 928; marriage of, in 18th century, 632; French, 677, 682; revolt in France, 677, 678; German, 19th-century migration of, 834; revolt in Russia, 879, 927; in Mussolini's Italy, 933. *See also* Common people; Serfdom
Peking, 850, 851; occupation by British and French, 829. *See also* Beijing
Penn, William, 523
Pentagon Papers, 1020
People, The (Michelet), 729
People's Budget, 814, 861–862
People's Charter, 741
Père Goriot, Le (Balzac), 784
Pereire, Émile, 708, 730
Pereire, Isaac, 708, 730
Perestroika, 1028–1029
Périer, Casimir, 744
Perry, Matthew, 829, 848
Persian Letters, The (Montesquieu), 576
Peru: silver mining in, 622; 19th-century migration to, 837
Pétain, Henri-Philippe, 874, 947, 952
Peter I (the Great), tsar of Russia, 506, 585; imitates Versailles, 506; reforms under, 552–554; builds St. Petersburg, 556–557, 560
Peter III, tsar of Russia, 584, 585
"Peterloo." *See* Battle of Peterloo
Petrograd, 876, 878. *See also* St. Petersburg
Petrograd Soviet, 877, 879

EIGHTH EDITION

Language Development
An Introduction

Robert E. Owens, Jr.
College of St. Rose

PEARSON

Boston   Columbus   Indianapolis   New York   San Francisco   Upper Saddle River
Amsterdam   Cape Town   Dubai   London   Madrid   Milan   Munich   Paris   Montreal   Toronto
Delhi   Mexico City   São Paulo   Sydney   Hong Kong   Seoul   Singapore   Taipei   Tokyo

Vice President and Editor in Chief: Jeffery W. Johnston
Executive Editor and Publisher: Stephen D. Dragin
Editorial Assistant: Jamie Bushell
Vice President, Director of Marketing: Margaret Waples
Marketing Manager: Weslie Sellinger
Senior Managing Editor: Pamela D. Bennett
Senior Project Manager: Linda Hillis Bayma
Senior Operations Supervisor: Matthew Ottenweller
Senior Art Director: Diane C. Lorenzo
Cover Designer: Jason Moore
Photo Researcher: Carol S. Sykes
Cover Image: SuperStock
Full-Service Project Management: Walsh & Associates, Inc.
Composition: S4Carlisle Publishing Services
Printer/Binder: Edwards Brothers Malloy
Cover Printer: Lehigh-Phoenix Color/Hagerstown
Text Font: Minion

Every effort has been made to provide accurate and current Internet information in this book. However, the Internet and information posted on it are constantly changing, so it is inevitable that some of the Internet addresses listed in this textbook will change.

Photo Credits: Catherine Wessel/CORBIS–NY, p. 2; Shutterstock, pp. 8, 36, 44, 110, 131, 146, 160, 195, 212, 226, 249, 367, 374, 384; BananaStock/Thinkstock Royalty Free, p. 27; Laima Druskis/PH College, pp. 41, 75; © Richard T. Nowitz/Bettmann/CORBIS All Rights Reserved, p. 56; Michal Heron/PH College, p. 68; Mike Good © Dorling Kindersley, p. 80; BananaStock/Superstock Royalty Free, p. 89; © Tom Stewart/CORBIS, p. 98; Elizabeth Hathon, p. 116; © Michael Honegger/Alamy, p. 178; Getty Images, Inc.–PhotoDisc, p. 186; © David Young-Wolff/PhotoEdit, p. 240; Annie Pickert/Pearson, pp. 268, 289; Dreamstime LLC–Royalty Free, p. 277; © Mary Kate Denny/PhotoEdit, p. 314; © Michael Keller/CORBIS, p. 329; Comstock Royalty Free Division, p. 351; Thinkstock, pp. 358, 380.

Library of Congress Cataloging-in-Publication Data
Owens, Robert E.
   Language development : an introduction / Robert E. Owens, Jr. — 8th ed.
     p. cm.
   Includes bibliographical references and index.
   ISBN-13: 978-0-13-258252-0
   ISBN-10: 0-13-258252-X
1. Language acquisition.   I. Title.
   P118.O93 2012
   401'.93—dc22

                           2010053085

10 9 8 7 6 5 4 3

www.pearsonhighered.com

ISBN-10:   0-13-258252-X
ISBN-13: 978-0-13-258252-0

"Say that again. I didn't hear you. I was listening to my toast."
Jessica Owens, age 4

To my granddaughter Cassidy,
who is reveling in this wonderful journey,
and to her brothers Dakota and Zavier.

Companion Website Feature

Jump-start your comprehension of how language develops by listening to engaging, interactive audio samples on the Companion Website at http://www.pearsonhighered.com/owens8e. From children to adults, you can expect to hear a range of language examples, including:

- Various dialectal speakers from across the United States
- Comprehensive interviews between adults and children, ranging in ages from 4 to 10 years
- Vocalizations of a 6-month-old child
- Single-syllable cooing of a 6-month-old child
- Vocalizations of 7-month-old child at bath time
- 8-month-old child
- 10-month-old child interacting with adult
- 12-month-old child interacting with mother
- 18-month-old child playing with mother
- 24-month-old child interacting with adult
- 28-month-old child playing with mother and grandfather
- 30-month-old twin males looking out window
- 34-month-old child talking with female adult
- 35-month-old child talking with female adult
- 36-month-old child celebrating birthday
- 38-month-old female pretending to talk on phone
- 45-month-old bilingual child discussing book with father
- 4-year-old female playing with dollhouse
- 4-year-old male building a puzzle
- 5-year-old male talking with female adult
- 5-year, 7-month-old male child
- 6-year-old female talking about her birthday and school
- 7-year-old introducing himself
- 9-year-old male talking to female adult
- 9-year-old talking about a scary experience
- 12-year-old female talking about school

Contents

3   *Neurological Bases of Speech and Language*   *57*

4   *Cognitive, Perceptual, and Motor Bases of Early Language and Speech*   *81*

9   *Preschool Development of Language Form*   *269*

Phew! That list even makes me tired. My hope is that you'll also find the new edition very useful.

Those of you who will one day become parents should appreciate the value of this text as a guideline to development. If you plan to work with children with disabilities and without you'll find that normal development can provide a model for evaluation and intervention. The developmental rationale can be used to decide on targets for training and to determine the overall remediation approach.

In recognition of the importance of the developmental rationale as a tool and of the changing perspectives in child language development, the eighth edition offers expanded coverage of preschool and school-age language development. Pragmatics receives increased attention, as does the conversational context within which most language development occurs. If you're a prospective speech-language pathologist, you will find these developmental progressions valuable when making decisions concerning materials to use with children with speech and language impairments. As consumers of educational and therapeutic products, you must be especially sensitive to the philosophy that governs the organization of such materials. Many materials claim to be developmental in design but are not. I recall opening one such book to find *please* and *thank you* as the first two utterances to be taught to a child with deafness. These words violate many of the characteristics of first words.

The experienced teacher, psychologist, or speech-language pathologist need not rely on such prepackaged materials if she or he has a good base in communication development. An understanding of the developmental process and the use of a problem-solving approach can be a powerful combination in the hands of a creative clinician.

With these considerations in mind, I have created what I hope to be a useful text for future parents, educators, psychologists, and speech-language pathologists.

New! CourseSmart eTextbook Available

CourseSmart is an exciting new choice for students looking to save money. As an alternative to purchasing the printed textbook, students can purchase an electronic version of the same content. With a CourseSmart eTextbook, students can search the text, make notes online, print out reading assignments that incorporate lecture notes, and bookmark important passages for later review. For more information, or to purchase access to the CourseSmart eTextbook, visit www.coursesmart.com.

Supplementary Materials: A Wealth of Resources for Students and Professors

Companion Website
Students will find numerous resources on the Companion Website for this text (http://www.pearsonhighered.com/owens8e), including Learning Objectives, Audio Samples, Practice Tests, Weblinks, and Flashcards.

Preface

There is no single way in which children learn to communicate. Each child follows an individual developmental pattern just as you did. Still, it is possible to describe a pattern of general communication development and of English specifically. This text attempts such descriptions and generalizations but emphasizes individual patterns, too.

New to This Edition

For those of you familiar with older editions, you'll find much has changed and, hopefully, much that you'll like. The changes in the eighth edition are as follows:

- Fewer chapters. I've reduced the overall size by two chapters without skimping on content.
- Totally revised Chapter 2. I've moved from a historic approach to a contemporary one. It was long past the time to retire both Skinner and Chomsky except as footnotes.
- Inclusion of research information in Chapter 2.
- Distribution of bilingual and dialectal development throughout the text rather than only in a separate stand-alone chapter. It seemed time to bring these speakers in out of the cold and put them where they belong in recognition of their importance and of the increase in bilingualism in the United States.
- Background information in Appendices. Several professors felt that necessary background information, especially in the preschool chapters, slowed the pace and added to already overcrowded chapters. I do know how to listen.
- Slimmed down Chapter 9. Preschool language form is more digestible now.
- A final farewell to good ol' Roger Brown. For too long, his research has dominated descriptions of preschool development, increasing the significance of his initial 14 morphemes beyond anything he ever intended. Instead I have tried to retain some of his overall vision but have blended in new constructionist research.
- A more constructionist perspective without relying completely on this theoretical work. That said, the constructionist emphasis on usage is extremely appealing as a description of children learning language rules one new word-based construction at a time.
- And of course, updated research. I spent over eight months just reading before I began to edit. For those compulsive types who count number of bibliographic entries, you'll find nearly 500 new references along with several retirements.

Instructor's Resource Manual/Test Bank and MyTest

Instructors will find a wealth of resources to support their course within the text itself. Each chapter within the Instructor's Resource Manual contains Main Points, Classroom Activities, and Suggested Supplemental Reading Materials. Test items located on MyTest include multiple choice, true/false, short answer, and essay questions, along with assessment software, allowing professors to create and customize exams and track student progress.

Acknowledgments

A volume of this scope must be the combined effort of many people fulfilling many roles, and this one is no exception.

My first thanks go to all those professionals and students, too numerous to mention, who have corresponded or conversed with me and offered criticism or suggestions for this edition. The overall organization of this text reflects the general organization of my own communication development course and that of professionals with whom I have been in contact.

The professional assistance of several people has been a godsend. Dr. Addie Haas, retired professor in the Communication Disorders Department at State University of New York at New Paltz, is a dear friend; a trusted confident; a good buddy; a fellow hiker; a skilled clinician; a source of information, ideas, and inspiration; and a helluva lot of fun. I will never forget our adventure "Down under." My department chair, Dr. Linda House, has created an environment at SUNY Geneseo in which I enjoy working. Irene Belyakov's suggestions, ideas, and, more importantly, her loving understanding have been a welcome source of encouragement. Linda Deats is always available to listen to my harebrained, half-baked ideas and to laugh with me at the many ridiculous things I do. For both Irene and Linda I wish a lifetime supply of lipstick and faux fur. Dr. Hugo Guo, a brilliant newly minted Ph.D., has also been a great help. He is a wealth of information and SUNY Buffalo is lucky to have added him to its already fine faculty. Finally, my dear friend Omid Mohamadi has kept me alert to new possibilities and given me a fresh perspective on the field of speech-language pathology. I look forward to more collaborations.

My thanks go also to the reviewers of this edition: Ahmed M. Abdelal, Bridgewater State College; Brenda L. Beverly, University of South Alabama; Thalia J. Coleman, Appalachian State University; and Cynthia Cress, University of Nebraska-Lincoln.

Several friends also offered encouragement and support. They are Dr. Robyn Goodman, Dr. Monica Schneider, Dr. Koomi Kim, Susan Norman, Fatima Rodriquez-Johnson, and my colleagues on the President's Commission on Diversity and Community. Thanks so much. I love you all.

I would like to express my love and appreciation to my children, Jason, Todd, and Jessica, who are as beautiful as young adults as they were as youngsters; and to my colleague at O and M Education, Moon Byung Choon.

Finally, a very special thanks to Kathryn Wind for her work in collecting additional samples of child speech for the Companion Website. She managed to collect several great new samples while being a full-time graduate student. I'm also indebted to the student researchers who helped me analyze over 175 language samples from which several research articles will flow. The now-graduated students are Katherine Allen, Lynda Feenaughty, Erin Filippini, Marc Johnson, Andrew Kanuck, Jessica Kroecker, Stephanie Loccisano, Katherine Lyle, Jordan Nieto, Catherine Sligar, Kathryn Wind, and Sara Young.

Language Development

An Introduction

1
The Territory

Before we can discuss language development, we need to agree on what language is and what it is not. Don't worry; as a user of language, you already know a great deal about it. This chapter will organize your knowledge and provide some labels for the many aspects of language you know. When you have completed this chapter, you should understand

- The difference between speech, language, and communication.
- The difference between nonlinguistic, paralinguistic, and metalinguistic aspects of communication.
- The main properties of language.
- The five components of language and their descriptions.
- A definition of a dialect and its relation to its parent language.
- The major factors that cause dialects to develop.
- Terms that will be useful later in the text:

antonym	linguistic competence	semantic features
bilingual	linguistic performance	semantics
bound morpheme	morpheme	sociolinguistic approach
code-switching	morphology	speech
communication	nonlinguistic cues	suprasegmental devices
communicative	paralinguistic codes	style shifting
competence	phoneme	synonym
deficit approach	phonology	syntax
dialect	pragmatics	vernacular
free morpheme	register	word knowledge
language	selection restrictions	world knowledge

Don't panic—introductory chapters usually contain a lot of terminology so that we can all "speak the same language" throughout the text.

To listen to language samples related to chapter content and to peruse other enhanced study aids, please see the Companion Website at www.pearsonhighered.com/owens8e

3

Language and the linguistic process are so complex that specialists devote their lives to investigating them. These specialists, called *linguists,* try to determine the language rules that individual people use to communicate. The linguist deduces the rules of language from the patterns demonstrated when we, as users of the language, communicate with one another. In a sense, each child is a linguist who must deduce the rules of his or her own native language. Two specialized areas of linguistics—psycholinguistics and sociolinguistics—combine the study of language with other disciplines. *Psycholinguistics* is the study of the way people acquire and process language. *Sociolinguistics* is the study of language, cultural, and situational influences. In developmental studies the sociolinguist focuses on caregiver–child interactions and on the early social uses of language.

Imagine encountering human language for the first time. Even if you had the most sophisticated computer-based code-breaking equipment, it would be impossible to figure out the many ways in which humans use language. For that task, you would need to decipher each of the 6,000 human languages and gain extensive knowledge of human interactions, emotions, and cultures. In other words, language is more than the sum of these parts. To understand language, we must consider it in the natural contexts in which it occurs (Kovarsky & Maxwell, 1997).

Language is the premier achievement of humans, and using it is something that all of us can do. Just imagine, the average adult English speaker produces about 150 words per minute, selecting each from somewhere between 30,000 and 60,000 alternatives, choosing from a myriad of English language grammatical structures, and making less than 0.1% errors! This becomes all the more amazing when you realize that the typical 4-year-old child has deciphered much of American English and already has well-developed speech, language, and communication skills. Truly remarkable given the complexity of the task!

You probably recall little of your own language acquisition. One statement is probably true: Unless you experienced difficulty and were enrolled in speech or language intervention, there was no formal instruction. Congratulations, you did most of it on your own. Now, we're going to attempt something almost as momentous . . . to explain it all!

To appreciate the task involved in language learning, you need to be familiar with some of the terminology that is commonly used in the field. All the terms introduced in this chapter and throughout the text are summarized for you in the Glossary. The remainder of this chapter is devoted to an explanation of these terms. First, we discuss this text in general. Then we distinguish three often confused terms—*speech, language,* and *communication*—and look at some special qualities of language itself. Finally, we'll examine dialects.

This Text and You

Although the full title of this text is *Language Development: An Introduction,* it is not a watered-down or cursory treatment of the topic. I have attempted to cover every timely, relevant, and important aspect of language development that might be of interest to the future speech-language pathologist, educator, psychologist, child development specialist, or parent. Of necessity, the material is complex and specific.

No doubt you've at least thumbed through this book. It may look overwhelming. It's not. I tell my own students that things are never as bleak as they seem at the beginning of the semester. Within the last 30 years, I have taken over 4,500 of my own students through this same material with a nearly 100% success rate. Let me try to help you find this material as rewarding to learn as it is to teach.

First, the text is organized into two sections. The first three chapters provide a background that includes terms, theories, and the brain and language. It's difficult to have to read this material when you really want to get to the development part, but all this background is necessary. The main topics of development are contained in the remaining chapters, which are organized sequentially from newborns through adults.

As with any text, there are a few simple rules that can make the learning experience more fruitful.

- Note the chapter objectives prior to reading the chapter and be alert for this information as you read.
- Read each chapter in small doses then let it sink in for a while.
- Find the chapter organization described at the end of each chapter's introduction. This will help you follow me through the material.
- Take brief notes as you read. Don't try to write everything down. Stop at natural divisions in the content and ask yourself what was most important. Visual learners may be helped by the process of writing.
- Review your notes when you stop reading and before you begin again the next time. This process will provide a review and some continuity.
- Try to read a little every day or every other day rather than neglecting the text until the night before the test. Cramming is not a good long-term learning strategy.
- Note the terms in the chapter objectives and try to define them as you read. Each one is printed in boldface in the body of the chapter. Please don't just thumb through or turn to the Glossary for a dictionary definition. The terms are relatively meaningless out of context. They need the structure of the other information. Context is very important.
- Try to answer the questions at the end of each chapter and on our Companion Website, www.pearsonhighered.com/owens8e, from your notes, or from your memory.
- I have tried to deemphasize linguists, authors, and researchers by placing all citations in parentheses. Unless your professor calls your attention to a specific person, she or he may not wish to emphasize these individuals either. It may be a waste of time to try to remember who said what about language development. "He said–she said" memorization can be very tedious. The exceptions, of course, are individuals mentioned specifically by name in lecture and in the text.
- Make ample use of the Companion Website: www.pearsonhighered.com/owens8e

I hope that these suggestions will help, although none is a guarantee.

Roll up your sleeves, set aside adequate time, and be prepared to be challenged. Actually, your task is relatively simple when compared to the toddler faced with deciphering the language she or he hears.

Speech, Language, and Communication

Child development professionals study the changes that occur in speech, language, and communication as children grow and develop. You might interpret these terms as having similar meanings or as being identical. Actually, they're very different and denote different aspects of development and use.

SPEECH

Speech[1] is a verbal means of communicating. Other ways of communicating include but are not limited to writing, drawing, and manual signing. The result of planning and executing specific motor sequences, speech is a process that requires very precise neuromuscular coordination. Each spoken language has specific sounds, or **phonemes,** and sound combinations that are characteristic of that language. In addition, speech involves other components, such as voice quality, intonation, and rate. These components enhance the meaning of the message.

A very complicated acoustic or sound event, speech is unlike any other environmental sound. Not even music achieves the level of complexity found in speech. Take a simple word such as *toe* and say it very slowly. The initial sound is an almost inhuman "tsch." This is followed by "o . . . w" in which your rounded mouth gradually tightens. Now say *toe* at normal speed and note how effortlessly this is done. Say it again and note how your brain integrates the signal as it comes in, creating the unified *toe*. You are a truly amazing being!

Speech is not the only means of face-to-face human communication. We also use gestures, facial expressions, and body posture to send messages. In face-to-face conversation, nonspeech means may carry up to 60% of the information.

Humans are not the only animals to make sounds; however, to my knowledge, no other species can match the variety and complexity of human speech sounds. These qualities are the result of the unique structures of the human vocal tract, a mechanism that is functional months before the first words are spoken. Children spend much of their first year experimenting with the vocal mechanism and producing a variety of sounds. Gradually, these sounds come to reflect the language of the child's environment.

LANGUAGE

Individual speech sounds are meaningless noises until some regularity is added. The relationship between individual sounds, meaningful sound units, and the combination of these units is specified by the rules of language. **Language** can be defined as a socially shared code or conventional system for representing concepts through the use of arbitrary symbols and rule-governed combinations of those symbols. English is a language, as is Spanish or Navajo. Each has its own unique symbols and rules for symbol combination. **Dialects** are subcategories of the parent language that use similar but not identical rules. All users of a language follow certain dialectal rules that differ from an idealized standard. For example, I sometimes find myself reverting to former dialectal usage in saying "*acrost* the street" and "open your **um**brella."

Languages are neither monolithic nor unchanging. Interactions between languages naturally occur in bilingual communities. Under certain circumstances, language mixing may result in a new form of both languages being used in that community (Backus, 1999).

Languages evolve, grow, and change. Those that do not become obsolete. Sometimes, for reasons other than linguistic ones, languages either flourish or wither. At present, for example, fewer than 100 individuals fluently speak Seneca, a western New York Native American language. The death of languages is not a rare event in the modern world. Languages face extinction as surely as plants and animals. When Kuzakura, an aged woman, died in western Brazil in 1988, the Umutina language died with her. It is estimated that as many as half the world's 6,000 languages are no longer learned by children. Many others are endangered. Most of these have less than a few thousand users. Only strong cultural and religious ties keep languages such as Yiddish and Pennsylvania Dutch viable. How long will they be secure?

---

[1]Words found in boldface in the text are defined in the Glossary at the end of the book.

This century may see the eradication of most languages. Sadly, it is doubtful that many of the 270 aboriginal languages of Australia—possibly some of the earth's oldest languages—will survive. The one that gave us the name for the cuddly "koala" is already gone. Of the 154 Native American languages now in use, nearly 120 are each spoken by less than a thousand individuals. Other endangered languages include OroWin, an Amazonian language with only three surviving speakers; Gullah, spoken by the descendents of African slaves on islands off the coast of South Carolina and Georgia; and Nushu, a southern Chinese language spoken only by women. The worldwide loss of languages is the result of government policy, dwindling indigenous populations, the movements of populations to cities, mass media, and noneducation of the young. The Internet is also a culprit in the demise of some languages. The need to converse in one language is fostering increasing use of English.

Each language is a unique vehicle for thought. For example, in many Native American languages, the Great Spirit is not a noun as in European languages but a *verb*. This concept of a supreme being is totally different from that of Europeans. As a speaker of English, can you even imagine it?

When we lose a language, we lose an essential part of the human fabric with its own unique perspective. A culture and possibly thousands of years of communication die with that language (Diamond, 1993). Study of that language may have unlocked secrets about universal language features, the origins of language, or the nature of thought. Within oral-only languages, the very nature of language itself is different. Words that have been passed on for generations acquire a sacredness, and speech is somehow connected to the Divine.

The death of a language is more than an intellectual or academic curiosity. After a week's immersion in Seneca, Mohawk, Onondaga, and other Iroquois languages, one man concluded:

> In the native world, these languages are more than collectible oddities, pressed flowers to be pulled from musty scrapbooks.
>
> These languages are the music that breathes life into our dances, the overflowing vessels that hold our culture and traditions. And most important, these languages are the conduits that carry our prayers to the Creator. . . .
>
> [W]e are struggling to reclaim what was stolen from us. Our languages are central to who we are as a native people.

"Come visit sometime," he offers. "I will bid you 'oolihelisdi'" (Coulson, 1999, p. 8A).

English is a Germanic variation of a much larger family of Indo-European languages as varied as Italian, Greek, Russian, Hindi, Urdu, Persian, and ancient Sanskrit. Although the Indo-European family is the largest family, as many as 30 others may exist, many much smaller.

Languages can grow as their respective cultures change. English has proven very adaptive, changing slowly through the addition of new words. Already the language with the largest number of words—approximately 700,000—English adds an estimated half dozen words per day. While many of these are scientific terms, they also include words popular on college campuses, such as *phat* (very cool), *herb* (geek), *cholo* (macho), and *dis* (scorn). English dictionaries have just recently added the following words: *24/7, bubba, blog, headbanger, gaydar, pumped (up), megaplex, racial profiling, slamming, brownfield, piercing, homeschool, netiquette,* and *sexting*. These words tell us much about our modern world.

Although most languages can be transmitted by speech, speech is not an essential feature of language. To some extent, the means of transmission influences processing and learning, although the underlying concepts of signing are similar to spoken languages (Emmorey, 1993; Lillo-Martin, 1991).

American Sign Language is not a mirror of American English but is a separate language with its own rules for symbol combinations. As in spoken languages, individually signed units are combined following linguistic rules. Approximately 50 sign languages are used worldwide, including one of the world's newest languages, Nicaraguan Sign Language, invented by children with deafness to fill a void in their education. On the other side of the earth in Al-sayyid, a Bedouin village in the Negev desert of Israel, another sign language has arisen without the influence of any other spoken or signed languages. Within this village approximately 150 individuals are deaf and use their language to communicate with each other and with hearing members of the community (Boswell, 2006).

Following is the American Speech-Language-Hearing Association definition of *language* (Committee on Language, 1983). The result of a committee decision, this definition has a little of everything, but it also is very thorough.

> Language is a complex and dynamic system of conventional symbols that is used in various modes for thought and communication.
>
> ■ Language evolves within specific historical, social, and cultural contexts.
> ■ Language, as rule-governed behavior, is described by at least five parameters—phonologic, morphologic, syntactic, semantic, and pragmatic.
> ■ Language learning and use are determined by the intervention of biological, cognitive, psychosocial, and environmental factors.
> ■ Effective use of language for communication requires a broad understanding of human interaction including such associated factors as nonverbal cues, motivation, and socio-cultural roles.

Languages exist because users have agreed on the symbols to be used and the rules to be followed. This agreement is demonstrated through language usage. Thus, languages exist by

Humans use language to communicate through a number of means, such as reading, writing, speaking, and listening.

virtue of social convention. Just as users agree to follow the rules of a language system, they can agree to change the rules. For example, the *eth* found as an ending on English verbs (ask*eth*) in the King James Version of the Bible has disappeared from use. New words can be added to a language; others fall into disuse. Words such as *DVD* and *blog* were uncommon just a few years ago. Users of one language can borrow words from another. For instance, despite the best efforts of the French government, its citizens seem to prefer the English word *jet* to the more difficult, though lyrical, *avion de reaction*.

English also has borrowed heavily from other languages while they have felt free to borrow in return. Here are a few English words taken from other languages:

- *Dope* (Dutch)
- *Immediate* (French)
- *Democracy* (Greek)
- *Tycoon* (Japanese)
- *Sofa* (Arabic)
- *Piano* (Italian)

In the process, meanings and words are changed slightly to conform to linguistic and cultural differences. More recently, English has incorporated words such as *tsunami* (Japanese), *barrio* (Spanish), *jihad* (Arabic), *sushi* (Japanese), and *schlep* (Yiddish).

Even strong, vibrant, firmly entrenched languages struggle against the embrace of the Internet and its accompanying English. Formal Spanish has given way to Cyber-Spanish with words such as *escapar* (escape) instead of *salir* and *un emilio* or *imail* (an email) instead of *un correo electronico*.

English has become the language of worldwide commerce and the Internet. Possibly a billion people speak English as a second language, most in Asia. As they learn English, these speakers are making it their own, modifying it slightly with the addition of words from their languages and incorporating their own intonational and structural patterns. In the near future, it may be more appropriate to think of English as a family of similar languages.

Braj Kachru, a professor in India, questions the very idea that English is inevitably linked to Western culture. He hypothesizes that English can be as adaptable to local culture as a musical instrument is to music. More succinctly put, English no longer belongs to The English. According to Professor Kachru (2005), the over 500 million Asian speakers of English should direct the language's course because the number of speakers in traditionally English-speaking countries is declining. The "Englishes" of the future may be hybrids or even new languages that may not be mutually understood by users from different cultures.

The socially shared code of English or any language allows the listener and speaker or writer and reader of the same language to exchange information. Internally, each uses the same code. The shared code is a device that enables each to represent an object, event, or relationship. Let's see how this is done. Close your eyes for a few seconds and concentrate on the word *ocean*. While your eyes were closed, you may have had a visual image of surf and sand. The concept was transmitted to you and decoded automatically. In a conversation, listener and speaker switch from encoding to decoding and back again without difficulty. Words, such as *ocean*, represent concepts stored in our brains.

Each user encodes and decodes according to his or her shared concept of a given object, event, or relationship; the actual object, event, or relationship does not need to be present. Let's assume that you encounter a priest. From past experience, you recognize his social role. Common elements of these experiences are *Catholic*, *male*, and *clergy*. As you pass, you draw on the appropriate symbol and encode, "Morning, Father." This representational process is presented in Figure 1.1. The word may also suggest a very different meaning, depending upon

FIGURE *1.1* *Symbol–Referent Relationship*

The concept is formed from the common elements of past experiences. The common elements of these experiences form the core of the concept. When a referent is experienced, it is interpreted in terms of the concept and the appropriate symbol applied.

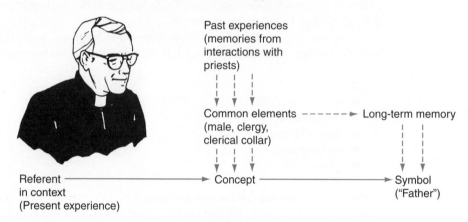

the experiences of each party. Let's assume for a moment that your biological father is an Episcopal minister. You see him on the street in clerical garb and say, "Good morning, Father." A passerby, unaware of your relationship, will assume something very different from the meaning that you and your father share. Coding is a factor of the speaker's and listener's shared meanings, the linguistic skills of each, and the context in which the exchange takes place.

Individual linguistic units communicate little in isolation. Most of the meaning or information is contained in the way symbols are combined. For example, "Teacher Jim a is" seems a meaningless jumble of words. By shifting a few words, however, we can create "Jim is a teacher." Another modification could produce "Is Jim a teacher?"—a very different sentence. Language rules specify a system of relationships among the parts. The rules for these relationships give language order and allow users to predict which units or symbols will be used. In addition, the rules permit language to be used creatively. Symbols and rules governing symbol combinations are used to create utterances.

Language should not be seen merely as a set of static rules. It is a process of use and modification within the context of communication. Language is a tool for social use.

COMMUNICATION

Both speech and language are parts of the larger process of communication. **Communication is the process participants use to exchange information and ideas, needs and desires.** The process is an active one that involves encoding, transmitting, and decoding the intended message. Figure 1.2 illustrates this process. It requires a sender and a receiver, and each must be alert to the informational needs of the other to ensure that messages are conveyed effectively and that intended meanings are preserved. For example, a speaker must identify a specific female, such as "Have you seen Catalina?" prior to using the pronoun *she*, as in "She was supposed to meet me." The probability of message distortion is very high, given the number of ways a message can be formed and the past experiences and perceptions of each participant. The degree to which a speaker is successful in communicating, measured by the appropriateness and

FIGURE *1.2* **Process of Communication**

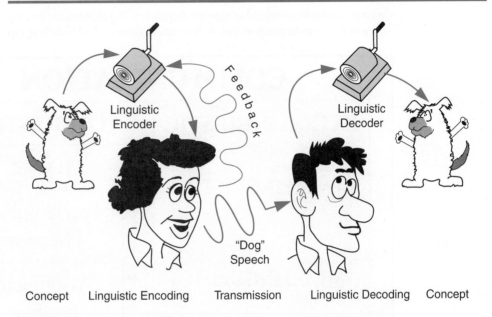

| Concept | Linguistic Encoding | Transmission | Linguistic Decoding | Concept |

effectiveness of the message, is called **communicative competence.** The competent communicator is able to conceive, formulate, modulate, and issue messages and to perceive the degree to which intended meanings are successfully conveyed.

Human communication is a complex, systematic, collaborative, context-bound tool for social action. Complexity can be demonstrated by the multifaceted and multifunctional aspects of the process. These include all aspects of communication and language plus additional mental processes, such as memory and planning, exercised within the cultural beliefs, situational variables, and social conventions of the individual participants. Although complex, the communication process represents a systematic pattern of behavior.

Conversations don't consist of disconnected, independent utterances. Instead, communication is collaborative. Partners actively coordinate construction of a joint dialogue as they negotiate to understand each other's meanings.

This process occurs within a specific cultural context that influences interpretation of linguistic units and speaker behaviors. The context is variable, changing minute by minute as the physical setting, partners, and topics change. I once introduced myself to a young Korean boy as *Bob*, unaware that *bob* means *rice* in Korean and that being someone's rice is an idiom for being his servant. Imagine how thrilled he was when I, his servant, subsequently hoisted him upon my shoulders as his mother and I headed down the street.

Finally, communication is a tool for social action. We accomplish things as we communicate. Let's eavesdrop on a conversation:

SPEAKER 1: Are you busy?
SPEAKER 2: No, not really.
SPEAKER 1: Well, if you could, please take a look at my lesson plan.
SPEAKER 2: Okay.

FIGURE *1.3* *Relationships of Speech, Language, and Communication*

Communication is accomplished through linguistic and paralinguistic codes and many means of transmission, such as speech, intonation, gestures, and body language.

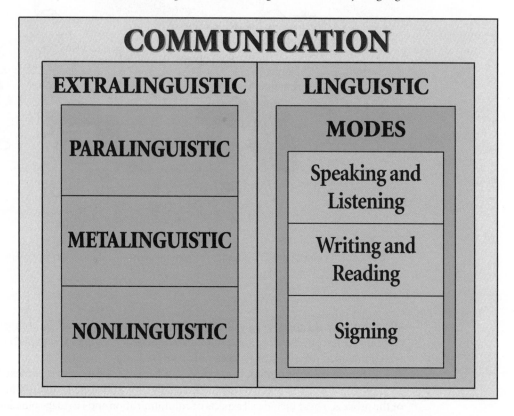

Speaker 1 used politeness to accomplish his goals. By prefacing his request with a question, he set up speaker 2 to respond more positively. His pre-request invited speaker 2 to respond in this way. That's why gran'ma told you you could catch more flies with sugar than with vinegar.

Speech and language are only a portion of communication. Figure 1.3 illustrates this relationship. Other aspects of communication that may enhance or change the linguistic code can be classified as paralinguistic, nonlinguistic, and metalinguistic. **Paralinguistic codes,** including intonation, stress or emphasis, speed or rate of delivery, and pause or hesitation, are superimposed on speech to signal attitude or emotion. All components of the signal are integrated to produce the meaning. *Intonation,* the use of pitch, is the most complex of all paralinguistic codes and is used to signal the mood of an utterance. For example, falling or rising pitch alone can signal the purpose of an utterance, as in the following example:

You're coming, aren't you. ↓ (Telling)
You're coming, aren't you? ↑ (Asking)

A rising pitch can change a statement into a question. Pitch can signal emphasis, asides, emotions, importance of the information conveyed, and the role and status of the speaker.

Stress is also employed for emphasis. Each of us remembers hearing, "You **will** clean your room!" to which you may have responded, "I **did** clean my room!" The *will* and *did* are emphasized.

Rate varies with the speaker's state of excitement, familiarity with the content, and perceived comprehension of the listener. In general, we tend to talk faster if we are more excited, more familiar with the information being conveyed, or more assured that our listener understands our message.

Pauses may be used to emphasize a portion of the message or to replace the message. Even young children recognize that a short maternal pause after a child's request usually signals a negative reply. Remember asking, "Can Chris sleep over tonight?" A long silence meant that your plans were doomed.

Pitch, rhythm, and pauses may be used to mark divisions between phrases and clauses. Combined with loudness and duration, pitch is used to give prominence to certain syllables and to new information.

Paralinguistic mechanisms are called **suprasegmental devices** because they can change the form and meaning of a sentence by acting across elements, or segments, of a sentence. As mentioned, a rising pitch can change a statement into a question without altering the arrangement of words. Similarly, "I did my homework" and "I *did* my homework" convey different emotions.

Nonlinguistic cues include gestures, body posture, facial expression, eye contact, head and body movement, and physical distance or proxemics. The effectiveness of these devices varies with users and between users. We all know someone who seems to gesture too much or to stand too close while communicating. Some nonlinguistic messages, such as a wink, a grimace, a pout, or folded arms, can convey the entire message.

As with language, nonlinguistic cues vary with the culture. Perfectly acceptable gestures in one culture may be considered offensive in another. Table 1.1 presents a list of common American gestures considered rude, offensive, or insulting in other cultures. Luckily, the smile is a universal signal for friendliness.

Metalinguistic skills are the abilities to talk about language, analyze it, think about it, judge it, and see it as an entity separate from its content. For example, learning to read and write depends on metalinguistic awareness of the component units of language—sounds, words, phrases, and sentences. Metalinguistic skills also are used to judge the correctness or appropriateness of the language we produce and receive, thus signaling the status of the transmission or the success of communication.

As you can see, like language, communication is very complex, yet it is almost impossible not to communicate. If you tried not to communicate, your behavior would communicate that you do not want to communicate.

When and how did human communication diverge from other primate communication? Unfortunately, speech doesn't leave any tangible evidence. Our best guess is that spoken language appeared around 50,000 to 100,000 years ago. The first "words" may have been imitations of animal sounds or may have accompanied emotion, such as crying, and actions, such as a grunt when attempting to move something heavy.

Although we can't answer the question more precisely, language itself may offer a place to begin an explanation. If we look at the characteristics of language, the first was that language is a social tool. If we take this further, we can conclude that language is a social means for achieving social ends based on shared understanding and purpose (Tomasello, 2008). Thus, human communication is fundamentally cooperative. Herein may be our answer.

The cooperative nature of human communication and the cooperative structure of human social interaction and culture are closely related. Early forms of communication were

TABLE *1.1* *Nonlinguistic Cues*

GESTURE	OTHER INTERPRETATIONS	COUNTRIES IN WHICH UNACCEPTABLE
Thumbs up		Australia, Nigeria, Islamic countries, such as Bangladesh
A-OK	Japan: *Money* France: Zero, worthless	Latin American countries
Victory or peace sign		England (if palm toward body)
Hailing a waiter (one finger raised)	Germany: *Two*	Japan
Beckoning curled finger		Yugoslavia, Malaysia, Indonesia, Australia
Tap forehead to signify "Smart"	Netherlands: *Crazy*	
Stop		Greece, West Africa
Hands in the pockets		Belgium, Indonesia, France, Finland, Japan, Sweden
Strong handshake	Middle East: Aggression	
Good-bye	Europe and Latin America: *No*	
Crossing legs and exposing sole of the foot		Southeast Asia
Nod head for agreement	Greece, Yugoslavia, Turkey, Iran, Bengal: *No*	

Source: Information from Axtell, R. E. (1991). *Gestures: The do's and taboos of body language around the world.* Baltimore, MD: Wiley & Sons.

most likely gestural in nature, including pointing and pantomiming (Tomasello, 2008). The co-operative nature of these gesture differs qualitatively from other primate communication, which is primarily requesting to fill immediate needs. In contrast, cooperative communication requires socio-cognitive skills of shared intentionality. While chimpanzees, with whom we share a common ancestor, do have and understand individual intentionality, they do not have the skills of shared intentionality, such as joint goals and joint attention, that are necessary for cooperative communication.

Early humans were probably driven to cooperate because of fear of hunger or the high risk of being eaten by predators (Bickerton, 2003). Thus, human cooperative communication resulted from a biological adaptation for collaborative activities; reciprocating could help survival.

Vocal communication probably emerged after conventionalized gestures. Most likely the earliest vocal accompaniments to gestures were emotional or added sound effects to some already meaningful action-based gestures or other actions. Some vocalizations may have accompanied specific acts such as mourning or imitated animal sounds. At some point, the vocalizations took on meaning of their own. Unlike ape communication, human vocalization is not context-bound or involuntary and this characteristic may be related to the need for vocal communication. While pointing works in context, we must rely on some other signal to communicate about something that is not present. In addition, vocal communication freed the hands for other purposes (Goldin-Meadow, 2005).

When we compare a gorilla skull to a Neanderthal skull from approximately 60,000 years ago, one striking difference can be noted in the vocal track of the early human. The reconfigured vocal track suggests that some consonant-like sounds were possible. More modern vocal tracks appear about 35,000 years ago. When compared to other primates, humans have more vertical teeth, more intricately muscled lips, a relatively smaller mouth, a greater closure of the oral cavity from the nasal, and a lower larynx or "voice box." All of these adaptations make speech as we know it possible. Most importantly, humans possess a large and highly specialized brain compared to their overall size.

It is the rules that enable us to communicate. Sounds can be combined, recombined, broken down, and combined another way to convey different meanings. A dog's bark cannot be manipulated in this way and is a relatively fixed form.

Grammar arose to express more complex relationships. This is especially important as communication moves from requesting to informing and information sharing (Tomasello, 2008).

Properties of Language

Linguists attempt to describe the properties or characteristics of language. In general, language is a social interactive tool that is both rule-governed and generative, or creative.

LANGUAGE IS A SOCIAL TOOL

It does little good to discuss language outside of the framework provided by communication. While language is not essential for communication, communication is certainly an essential and defining element of language.

As a shared code, language enables users to transmit ideas and desires to one another. In fact, language has but one purpose: to serve as the code for transmissions between people.

Overall, language reflects the collective thinking of its culture and, in turn, influences that thinking. In the United States, for example, certain words, such as *democracy*, reflect cultural meanings and emotions and, in turn, influence our concepts of other forms of government. The ancient Greek notion of democracy was somewhat different and influenced the Greeks' thinking similarly.

Likewise, at any given moment, language in use is influenced by what precedes it and influences what follows. The utterance "And how's my little girl feeling this morning?" only fits certain situations that define the appropriate language use. It would not be wise to use this utterance when meeting the Queen of England for the first time. In turn, the sick child to whom this is addressed has only limited options that she can use to respond. Responses such as, "Go directly to jail; do not pass 'Go' " and "Mister Speaker, I yield the floor to the distinguished senator from West Virginia," while perfectly correct sentences, just don't fit. The reason is that they do not continue the communication but, rather, cause it to break down.

To consider language without communication is to assume that language occurs in a vacuum. It is to remove the very *raison d'être* for language in the first place.

LANGUAGE IS A RULE-GOVERNED SYSTEM

The relationship between meaning and the symbols employed is an arbitrary one, but the arrangement of the symbols in relation to one another is nonarbitrary. This nonarbitrary organizational feature of language demonstrates the presence of underlying rules or patterns that occur repeatedly. These shared rule systems allow users of a language to comprehend and to create messages.

Language includes not only the rules but also the process of rule usage and the resulting product. For example, a sentence is made up of a noun plus a verb but that rule tells us nothing about the process by which you selected the noun and verb or the seemingly infinite number of possible combinations using these two categories.

A language user's underlying knowledge about the system of rules is called his or her **linguistic competence.** Even though the user can't state the rules, performance demonstrates adherence to them. The linguist observes human behavior in an attempt to determine these rules or operating principles.

If you have ever listened to an excited speaker or a heated argument, you know that speakers do not always observe the linguistic rules. In fact, much of what we, as mature speakers, say is ungrammatical. Imagine that you have just returned from the New Year's celebration at Times Square. You might say the following:

> Oh, wow, you should have . . . you wouldn't be-believe all the . . . never seen so many people. We were almost . . . ah, trampled. And when the ball came down . . . fell, all the . . . Talk about yelling . . . so much noise. We made a, the mistake of . . . can you imagine anything as dumb as . . . well, it was crazy to drive.

It's ungrammatical but still understandable.

Linguistic knowledge in actual usage is called **linguistic performance.** A user's linguistic competence must be deduced from his or her linguistic performance. You cannot measure linguistic competence directly.

There are many reasons for the discrepancy between competence and performance in normal language users. Some constraints are long-term, such as ethnic background, socioeconomic status, and region of the country. These account for dialects and regionalisms. We are all speakers of some dialectal variation, but most of us are still competent in the standard or ideal dialect. Dialectal speakers do not have a language disorder, just a difference. Other long-term constraints, such as intellectual disability and autism spectrum disorder, may result in a language disorder. Short-term constraints on nondisordered performance include physical state changes within the individual, such as intoxication, fatigue, distraction, and illness, and situational variations, such as the role, status, and personal relations of the speakers.

Even though much that is said is ungrammatical, native speakers have relatively little difficulty decoding messages. If a native speaker knows the words being used, he or she can apply the rules in order to understand almost any sentence encountered. In actual communication, comprehension is influenced by the intent of the speaker, the context, the available shared meanings, and the linguistic complexity of the utterance. Even kindergarteners know virtually all the rules of their language. Children learn the rules by actually using the language to encode and decode. The rules learned in school are the "finishing touches." A preschool child demonstrates by using words that he or she knows what a noun is long before he or she can define the term.

On one family trip, we passed the time with a word game. My 5-year-old daughter was asked to provide a noun. Immediately, she inquired, "What's that?" In my best teacher persona, I patiently explained that a noun was a person, place, or thing. She replied, "Oh." After some prodding, she stated, "Then my word is 'thing.' " Despite her inadequate understanding of the formal definition of a noun, my daughter had demonstrated for years in her everyday use that she knew how to use nouns.

A sentence such as "Chairs sourly young up swam" is ungrammatical. It violates the rules for word order. Native speakers notice that the words do not fall into predictable patterns. When rearranged, the sentence reads "Young chairs swam sourly up." This is now grammatical in terms of word order but meaningless; it doesn't make sense. Other rules allow language users to separate sense from nonsense and to determine the underlying meaning. Although "Dog bites man" and "Man bites dog" are very similar, in that each uses the same words, the meanings of the two sentences are very different. Only one will make a newspaper headline. Likewise, a single sentence may have two meanings. For example, the sentence "The shooting of the hunters was terrible" can be taken two ways: either they shot poorly or someone shot them. Language users must know several sets of rules to make sense of what they hear or read.

LANGUAGE IS GENERATIVE

Language is a generative system. The word *generative* has the same root as *generate*, which means to produce, create (as in *Genesis*), or bring into existence. Thus, language is a productive or creative tool. A knowledge of the rules permits speakers to generate meaningful utterances. From a finite number of words and word categories, such as nouns, and a finite set of rules, speakers can create an almost infinite number of sentences. This creativity occurs because

- Words can refer to more than one thing.
- These things can be called more than one name.
- Words can be combined in a variety of ways.

Think of all the possible sentences you could create by combining all the nouns and verbs you know. When this task is completed, you could modify each sentence by adding adverbs and adjectives, articles and prepositions, and by combining sentences or rearranging words to create questions.

The possibilities for creating new sentences are virtually endless. Consider the following novel sentence:

Large elephants danced gracefully beneath the street lights.

Even though you have probably never seen this utterance before, you understand its meaning because you know the linguistic rules. Try to create your own novel utterance. The process will seem difficult, and yet you form novel utterances every day and are not consciously aware of using any effort. In fact, much of what you said today was novel or new. You didn't learn those specific utterances. As a young child, you deduced the rules for forming these types of sentences. Of course, I do not mean to imply that sentences are never repeated. Polite social or ritualistic communication is often repetitious. How frequently have you said the following sentences?

How are you?
Thank you very much.
Can I, Mom, please?
See you soon.

These utterances aside, you can create whatever sentences you desire.

Children do not learn all possible word combinations. Instead, they learn rules that govern these combinations. Knowing the linguistic rules allows each language user to understand and create an infinite variety of sentences.

OTHER PROPERTIES

Human language is also *reflexive*, meaning we can use language to reflect on language, its correctness and effectiveness, and its qualities. Other animals cannot reflect on their own communication. Without this ability, this book would be impossible to produce.

An additional property of language is *displacement* or the ability to communicate beyond the immediate context. As far as we know, your dog's bark is not about something that he remembers of interest from last week. You, on the other hand, can discuss last week, or last year, or events in the dim past of history in which you were not a participant.

Although not always obvious from inside a language, the symbols used in a language are *arbitrary*, another property of language. There is, for example, nothing in the word "cat" that would suggest the animal to which it applies. Except for some words, such as "squash" and "cuckoo" that suggest a relationship between the sound and the action or thing to which a word refers, there is no naturally obvious relationship. The relationship is arbitrary.

Components of Language

A very complex system, language can best be explained by breaking it down into its functional components (Figure 1.4). Language can be divided into three major, although not necessarily equal, components: form, content, and use. Form includes syntax, morphology, and phonology, the components that connect sounds and symbols in order. Content encompasses meaning or semantics, and use is termed *pragmatics*. These five components—syntax, morphology, phonology, semantics, and pragmatics—are the basic rule systems found in language.

As each of us uses language, we code ideas (*semantics*); that is, we use a symbol—a sound, a word, and so forth—to stand for an event, object, or relationship. To communicate these ideas to others, we use certain forms, which include the appropriate sound units (*phonology*), the appropriate word order (*syntax*), and the appropriate words and word beginnings and endings (*morphology*) to clarify meaning more specifically. Speakers use these components to achieve certain communication ends, such as gaining information, greeting, or responding (*pragmatics*). Let's examine the five components of language in more detail.

SYNTAX

The form or structure of a sentence is governed by the rules of **syntax.** These rules specify word, phrase, and clause order; sentence organization; and the relationships between words, word classes, and other sentence elements. Syntax specifies which word combinations are acceptable, or grammatical, and which are not. For example, the syntax of English explains why "Maddi has thrown the ball" is a possible sentence, while "Maddi the ball has thrown" sounds awkward.

Sentences are organized according to their overall function; declaratives, for example, make statements, and interrogatives form questions. The main elements of a sentence are noun and verb phrases, each composed of various word classes (such as nouns, verbs, adjectives, and the like).

FIGURE *1.4* *Components of Language*

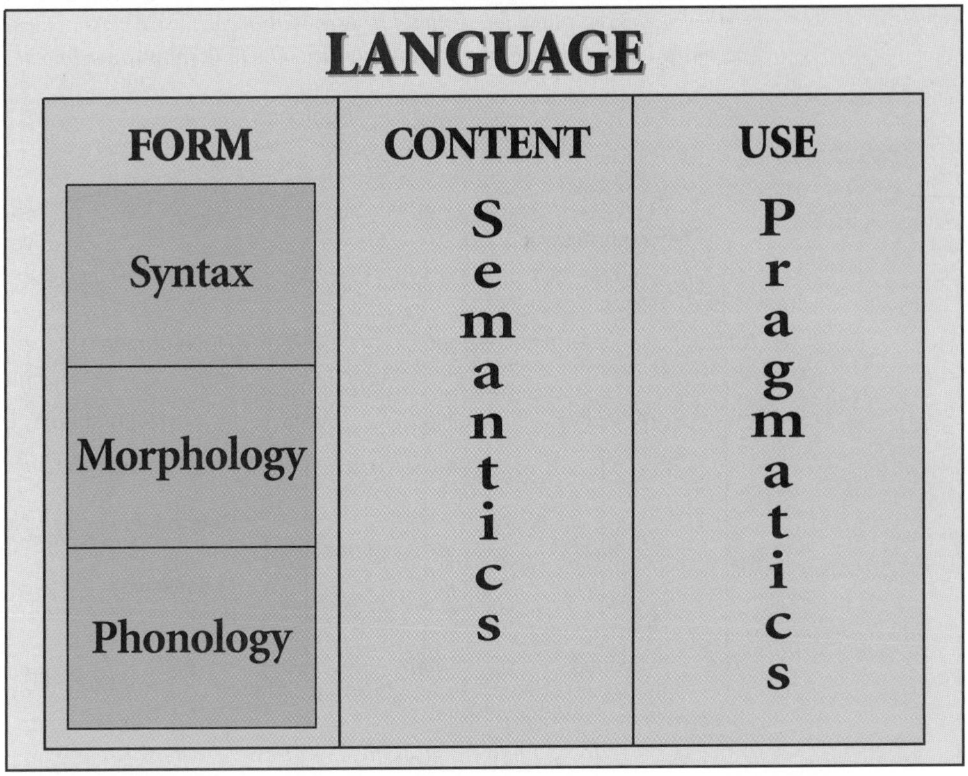

LANGUAGE		
FORM	**CONTENT**	**USE**
Syntax Morphology Phonology	Semantics	Pragmatics

Each sentence must contain a *noun phrase* and a *verb phrase*. The mandatory features of noun and verb phrases are a noun and a verb, respectively. The short biblical verse "Jesus wept" is a perfectly acceptable English sentence: It contains both a noun phrase and a verb phrase. The following, however, is not a complete sentence, even though it is much longer:

> The grandiose plan for the community's economic revival based upon political cooperation of the inner city and the more affluent suburban areas

This example contains no verb and thus no verb phrase; therefore, it does not qualify as a sentence.

Within the noun and verb phrases, certain word classes combine in predictable patterns. For example, articles such as *a*, *an*, and *the* appear before nouns, and adverbs such as *slowly* modify verbs. Some words may function in more than one word class. For example, the word *dance* may be a noun or a verb. Yet there is no confusion between the following sentences:

> The *dance* was attended by nearly all the students.
> The children will *dance* to earn money for charity.

The linguistic context of the sentence clarifies any ambiguity.

FIGURE *1.5* *Hierarchical Sentence Structure*

Within the noun and verb phrases, a number of different word classes can be arranged to form a variety of sentences. Many words could be used within each word class to form sentences such as "The young man ate his hamburger quickly" or "The mad racer drove his car recklessly."

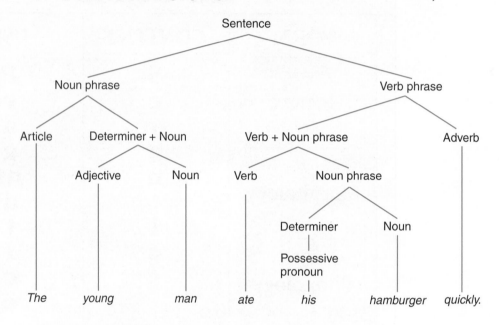

Syntax can be conceptualized as a tree diagram (Figure 1.5). Each noun phrase or verb phrase included in a sentence contains various word classes. In a given phrase, word classes may be deleted or added. As long as the noun and verb remain, a sentence is possible. This hierarchical structure permits boundless elaboration within the confines of the syntactic rules. Obviously, the tree diagram in Figure 1.5 has only limited use. Flexible use of language would require hundreds, if not thousands, of other possibilities. Children don't memorize diagrams; rather, they learn rules for ways of constructing them.

As language users, we sometimes get into difficulty when we must follow prescribed language rules. This usually occurs in writing. Spoken language is much more informal than writing and less constrained. In the nineteenth century, formal grammar guides were written, often prescribing rules used by the upper class. As a result, today we are saddled with the distinction in formal writing between *who* and *whom*, the incorrectness of using *since* to mean *because*, the inadmissibility of the split infinitive (*to finish quickly* is fine, but not *to quickly finish*), and the *not ending a sentence with a preposition* rule. Regarding the latter, Winston Churchill quipped, "That is the type of arrant pedantry up with which I shall not put." Grammatically, he's correct, but boy, is it awkward.

Languages can be divided roughly into those with so-called free word order and those with word-order rules. The Australian aboriginal language, Warlpiri, is relatively free. The same sentence may be expressed in several different word orders. Among word-order languages, rules fall into three classes based on the order of the subject, the verb, and the object. English is an example of the basic subject-verb-object (SVO) word order (*She eats cookies*). In contrast, Dutch, Korean, and Japanese have a basic verb-final form (SOV). The third type, represented by Irish, is verb-subject-object (VSO).

FIGURE *1.6* *Morpheme Classes and Examples*

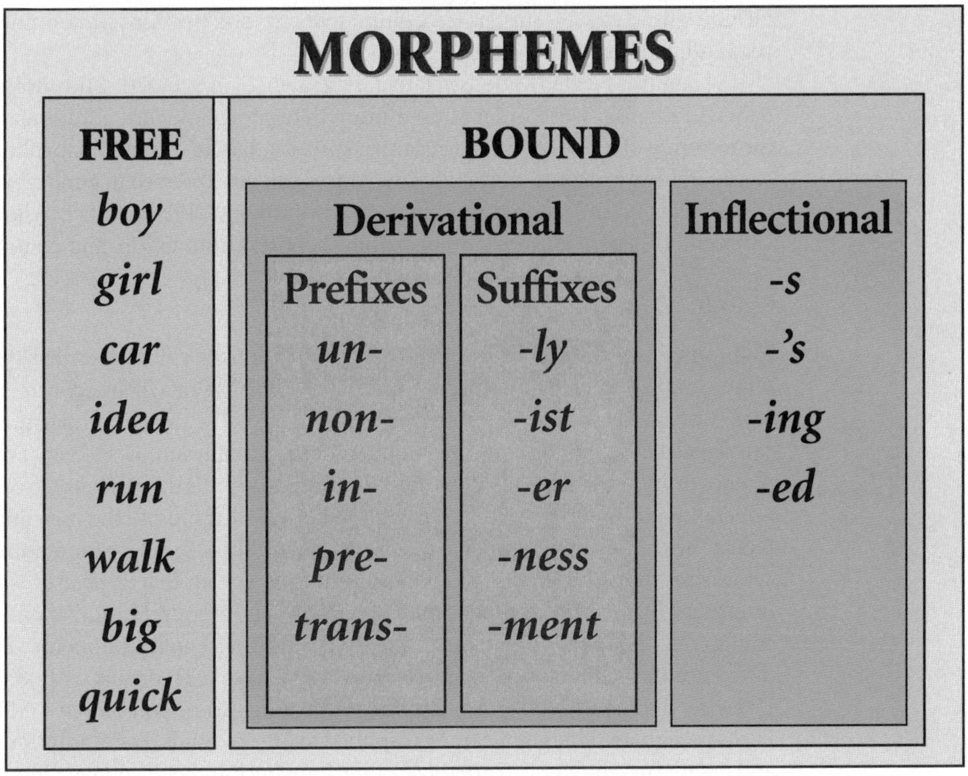

MORPHEMES			
FREE	**BOUND**		
	Derivational		**Inflectional**
boy	**Prefixes**	**Suffixes**	*-s*
girl	*un-*	*-ly*	*-'s*
car	*non-*	*-ist*	*-ing*
idea	*in-*	*-er*	*-ed*
run	*pre-*	*-ness*	
walk	*trans-*	*-ment*	
big			
quick			

MORPHOLOGY

Morphology is concerned with the internal organization of words. Words consist of one or more smaller units called *morphemes*. A **morpheme** is the smallest grammatical unit and is indivisible without violating the meaning or producing meaningless units. Therefore, *dog* is a single morpheme because *d* and *og* are meaningless alone. If we split the word into *do* and *g*, we have a similar situation, because there is nothing in *dog* that includes the meaning of *do*, and *g* is meaningless alone. Most words in English consist of one or two morphemes. In contrast, Mohawk, found in northern New York and southern Quebec, constructs words of several morphemes strung together.

Morphemes are of two varieties, free and bound (Figure 1.6). **Free morphemes** are independent and can stand alone. They form words or parts of words. Examples of free morphemes are *toy*, *big*, and *happy*. **Bound morphemes** are grammatical markers that cannot function independently. They must be attached to free morphemes or to other bound morphemes. Examples include *-s*, *-est*, *un-*, and *-ly*, meaning plural, most, negative, and manner, respectively. By combining the free and bound morphemes, we can create *toys*, *biggest*, and *unhappily*. Bound morphemes are attached to nouns, verbs, and adjectives. Furthermore, bound morphemes can be either *derivational* or *inflectional* in nature.

Derivational morphemes include both prefixes and suffixes. Prefixes precede the free morpheme and suffixes follow. Derivational morphemes change whole classes of words. For example, *-ly* may be added to an adjective to create an adverb, and *-ness* may be added to an adjective to create a noun: *mad, madly, madness*. Inflectional morphemes can be suffixes only. They change the state or increase the precision of the free morpheme. Inflectional morphemes include tense markers (such as *-ed*), plural markers, and the third person singular present-tense verb ending *-s* as in "she walk*s*."

Languages differ in their relative dependence on syntactic and morphological components. In English, word order is used more than morphological additions to convey much of the meaning of a sentence. Hungarian, in contrast, has an extensive morphological system and considerable word-order variability. Sentences can be expressed in almost every possible order. Chinese has no inflectional markings of any kind and still permits considerable word order variation. Listeners must rely on probability, context, intonation, and common sense.

PHONOLOGY

Phonology is the aspect of language concerned with the rules governing the structure, distribution, and sequencing of speech sounds and the shape of syllables. Each language employs a variety of speech sounds or phonemes. A phoneme is the smallest linguistic unit of sound that can signal a difference in meaning. Phonemes are actually families of very similar sounds. Allophones or individual members of these families of sounds differ slightly from one another, but not enough to sound like a different phoneme and thus modify the meaning of a word. If you repeat the /p/[2] sound ten times, each production will vary slightly for a number of physiological reasons. In addition, the /p/ sound in *pea* differs from that in *poor* or *soup* because each is influenced by the surrounding sounds. Even so, each /p/ sound is similar enough so as not to be confused with another phoneme. Thus /p/ is a distinct English phoneme. There is an obvious difference in the initial sounds in *pea* and *see* because each begins with a different phoneme. Likewise, the /d/ and /l/ sounds are different enough to be considered as different phonemes. Each can signal a different meaning if applied to other sounds. For example, the meanings of *dog* and *log* are very different, as are those of *dock* and *lock* and *pad* and *pal*. Phonemes are classified by their acoustic or sound properties, as well as by the way they are produced (how the airstream is modified) and their place of production (where along the vocal tract the modification occurs).

English has approximately 43 phonemes, give or take a few for dialectal variations (see Appendix A). Actually, the human speech mechanism can make approximately 600 possible sounds that languages could use. Let's create a new one for English! Say the word *butter* at normal speed and note the middle "tt" sound. It's not really a /t/ or a /d/, but somewhere in between with elements of both. If anything, it's a "td." Unfortunately, English doesn't recognize this difference. The Thai language does and treats this sound as a separate phoneme. In English, it's just a convenient way to pronounce words quickly. It's an allophone of /t/.

Phonological rules govern the distribution and sequencing of phonemes within a language. This organization is not the same as speech, which is the actual mechanical act of producing phonemes. Without the phonological rules, the distribution and sequencing of phonemes would be random.

Distributional rules describe which sounds can be employed in various positions in words. For example, in English the *ng* sound, which is found in *ring* and considered to be a single phoneme(/ŋ/), never appears at the beginning of an English word. In contrast, sequencing rules determine which sounds may appear in combination. The sequence /dn/, for example, may not appear back to back in the same syllable in English.

---

[2]Transcriptions of phonemes are placed within slashes, such as /p/. This book uses the notation of the International Phonetic Alphabet, as will be discussed in more detail in Appendix A.

Sequencing rules also address the sound modifications made when two phonemes appear next to each other. For example, the -*ed* in *jogged*, pronounced as /d/, is different from the -*ed* in *walked*, which is pronounced as /t/. On other occasions, the distributional and sequencing rules both apply. The combination /nd/, for example, may not begin a word but may appear elsewhere, as in *hand*. The word *stew* is perfectly acceptable in English. *Snew* is not an English word but would be acceptable; *sdew*, however, could never be acceptable because in English words cannot begin with sd.

SEMANTICS

Semantics is a system of rules governing the meaning or content of words and word combinations. Some units are mutually exclusive, such as *man* and *woman*; a human being is not usually classified as both. Other units overlap somewhat, such as *female*, *woman*, and *lady*. Not all females are women and even fewer could be called ladies. The actual words or symbols used represent not reality itself but our ideas or concepts about reality.

It is useful at this point to make a distinction between *world knowledge* and *word knowledge*. **World knowledge** refers to an individual's autobiographical and experiential understanding and memory of particular events. In contrast, **word knowledge** contains word and symbol definitions and is primarily verbal. Word knowledge forms each person's mental dictionary or thesaurus.

The two types of knowledge are related. Word knowledge is usually based, in part, on world knowledge. World knowledge is a generalized concept formed from several particular events. In part, your concept of *dog* has been formed from several encounters with different types of dogs. These events become somewhat generalized, or separated from the original context, and are, therefore, more broadly useful. With more experience, knowledge becomes less dependent upon particular events. The resultant generalized concepts form the base for semantic or word knowledge. As we mature, concepts in world knowledge may be formed without firsthand experience. Language meaning is based on what we, as individuals, know. This knowledge reflects not only the individual but the cultural interpretation placed on this knowledge.

As we converse with other users of the same language, we sharpen our concepts and bring them more to resemble similar concepts in others. In this way, we come to share definitions with others, thus making clear, concise, comprehensible communication possible.

Concept development results in increased validity, status, and accessibility. *Validity* is the amount of agreement between a language user's concept and the shared concept of the language community. *Status* refers to alternative referents: For example, *canine* can be substituted easily for the concept *dog*, and *dog* can be used to refer to the dry, hot, dog days of summer, to a dog-eared book, or to being dog-tired. *Accessibility* relates to the ease of retrieval from memory and use of the concept. In general, the more you know about the word and the more you use it, the easier it is to access.

Each word meaning contains two portions—semantic features and selection restrictions—drawn from the core concept. **Semantic features** are aspects of the meaning that characterize the word. For example, the semantic features of *mother* include parent and female. One of these features is shared with *father*, the other with *woman*, but neither word contains both features. **Selection restrictions** are based on these specific features and prohibit certain word combinations because they are meaningless or redundant. For example, *male mother* is meaningless because one word has the feature male and the other the feature female; *female mother* is redundant because biological mothers are female, at least for the foreseeable future.

In addition to an objective denotative meaning, there is a connotative meaning of subjective features or feelings. Thus, whereas the semantic knowledge of the features of *dog* may be similar, I may have encountered several large, vicious examples that you have not and may therefore be more fearful of dogs than you. Throughout life, language users acquire new features, delete old features, and reorganize the remainder to sharpen word meanings.

Word meanings are only a portion of semantics, however, and are not as important as the relationships between symbols. One important relationship is that of common or shared features. The more features two words share, the more alike they are. Words with almost identical features are **synonyms**. Some examples are *abuse* and *misuse*, *dark* and *dim*, *heat* and *warmth*, and *talk* and *speak*.

Antonyms are words that differ only in the opposite value of a single important feature. Examples include *up* and *down*, *big* and *little*, and *black* and *white*. (*Big* and *little*, for example, both describe size but are opposite extremes.)

Knowledge of semantic features provides a language user with a rich vocabulary of alternative words and meanings. To some extent, this knowledge is more important than the overall number of words in a language user's vocabulary. Because words may have alternative meanings, users must rely on additional cues for interpretation of messages.

Sentence meanings are more important than individual word meanings because sentences represent a meaning greater than the sum of the individual words. A sentence represents not only the words that form that sentence, but the relationships between those words. Mature language users generally recall the overall sentence meaning better than the sentence's specific form.

PRAGMATICS

When we use language to affect others or to relay information, we make use of pragmatics. **Pragmatics** is the study of language in context and concentrates on language as a communication tool that is used to achieve social ends. In other words, pragmatics is concerned with the way language is used to communicate rather than with the way language is structured.

Pragmatics consists of the following:

- Communication intentions and recognized ways of carrying them out.
- Conversational principles or rules.
- Types of discourse, such as narratives and jokes, and their construction.

More than in the other components of language, successful pragmatics requires understanding of the culture and of individuals.

In order to be valid, speech must involve the appropriate persons and circumstances, be complete and correctly executed by all participants, and contain the appropriate intentions of all participants. "May I have a donut, please" is valid only when speaking to a person who can actually get you one and in a place where donuts are found.

Sometimes the very act of saying something makes it so:

I *apologize* for my behavior.
I *christen* this ship the U.S.S. Schneider.
I now *pronounce* you husband and wife.

Again, certain conditions must be met before each is valid. When someone apologizes but is overjoyed by another's discomfort or when a child or nondesignated adult pronounces a couple husband and wife, the act is invalidated.

Not all speech performs an act. For example, saying "John should apologize for his behavior" doesn't make the apology. In this case, it is an expression of opinion.

Pragmatic rules govern a number of conversational interactions: sequential organization and coherence of conversations, repair of errors, role, and intentions. Organization and coherence of conversations include taking turns; opening, maintaining, and closing a conversation; establishing and maintaining a topic; and making relevant contributions to the conversation. Repair includes giving and receiving feedback and correcting conversational errors. The listener attempts to keep the speaker informed of the status of the communication. If the listener doesn't understand or is confused, he or she might assume a quizzical expression or say, "Huh?" Role skills include establishing and maintaining a role and switching linguistic codes for each role. In some conversations you are dominant, as with a small child, and in others you are not, as with your parents, and you adjust your language accordingly.

Conversation is governed by the "cooperation principle" (Grice, 1975): Conversational participants cooperate with each other. The four maxims of the cooperation principle relate to quantity, quality, relation, and manner. Quantity is the informativeness of each participant's contribution: No participant should provide too little or too much information. In addition, the quality of each contribution should be governed by truthfulness and based on sufficient evidence. The maxim of relation states that a contribution should be relevant to the topic of conversation. Finally, each participant should be reasonably direct in manner and avoid vagueness, ambiguity, and wordiness.

Three general categories of pragmatic rules concern

- Selection of the appropriate linguistic form.
- Use of language forms consistent with assumed rules.
- Use of ritualized forms.

Selection of form between "Gimme a cookie" and "May I have one, please" is influenced by contextual variables and the speaker's intention. One choice may work with a school friend, whereas the other is best with the teacher. Listener characteristics that influence speaker behaviors are gender, age, race, style, dialect, social status, and role.

Speech may be *direct* or *indirect*, reflected in the syntactic form. "Answer the phone" is a direct order or request to perform that act. On the other hand, an indirect syntactic form does not reflect the intention. For example, "Could you answer the phone?" is an indirect way of requesting. You know that the expected outcome is for you to answer the phone, not to answer the question with a "yes." Indirect forms are generally used for politeness.

Speech may also be *literal, nonliteral,* or both. In literal speech, the speaker means what she or he says. After a 10-mile hike, you might exclaim, "My feet really hurt," and no doubt they do. In contrast, nonliteral speech does not mean what the speaker has said. Upon discovering that transportation home has not arrived, the same tired hiker might state sarcastically, "Just what I need, more walking." Both literal and nonliteral meanings might be heard in the comment of a mother as she enters her child's messy room: "Mommy really likes it when kids pick up their room." She does like it, but she's also being sarcastic.

Roles in a conversation influence the choice of vocabulary and language form. For example, you might be very formal in your role as student presenter at a professional conference but very informal in the role of co-presenter with the other students when you celebrate your success later. In another example, your role as grandchild requires different language features than your role as a young parent, lover, or roommate.

The wheels of social interaction are "greased" by ritualized sequences, such as "How are you?" and "Wha's up?" These predictable forms ease social interactions and individual participation. We can all recall an occasion when we felt close to death and yet responded, "I'm fine! How are you?"—a response that has become ritualized in casual greetings.

FIGURE *1.7* **Model of Language**

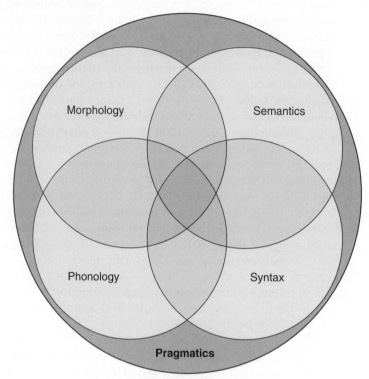

Functionalist Model

Pragmatics is the overall organizing
aspect of language.

RELATIONSHIP OF LANGUAGE COMPONENTS

The notion of language components may be artificial, merely an analytical device for linguists to use in discussing language. For example, some linguists emphasize the intimate relationship between semantics and syntax, rather than the structural independence of each. These linguists, called *emergentists*, stress the similarity and causal relationship between meanings and syntax, suggesting that grammar grows out of semantics.

That said, it may be helpful to think of the relationship between language components as presented in Figure 1.7, in which pragmatics is the organizing principle of language. In other words, language is heavily influenced by context. Context, both situational and linguistic, determines the language user's communication options. In addition, a need to communicate exists prior to the selection of content and form. It is only when the child desires a cookie and is in an appropriate context to receive one that he or she employs the rules of syntax, morphology, phonology, and semantics in order to form the request.

Obviously, the components of language are linked in some way. For example, the syntactic structure may require the morphological marker for past tense, which, in turn, changes phonetically to accommodate the affected word. In development, components may also influence one another in that changes in one may modify development in another.

*B*iracial children who learn both home languages simultaneously are able to become proficient in both languages by preschool age but then may shift dominance, sometimes losing the ability to be bilingual by teen or adult years.

Dialects

The United States is becoming an increasingly pluralistic society in which cultural and ethno-racial groups contribute to the whole but retain their essential character. One characteristic of these groups may be either language or dialect. Most groups continue to embrace their culture and, when non-English, their language.

It is conservatively projected that the population of people of color will increase in the United States to 63 million by 2030. At the same time, the white, non-Latino population will increase at a slower rate and will thus become a smaller proportion of the entire U.S. population. If current trends continue, white non-Latinos will be the largest *minority* by the year 2050.

At present, in the United States approximately one in four Americans identifies as other than white non-Hispanic. In the state of California and in a score of cities and several counties, people of color represent more than 50% of the population. This situation reflects traditional demographics and a population shift that is the result of recent immigration, internal migration, and natural increase.

Within the last twenty years, 80% of the legal immigrants to the United States have come from Asia and Latin America. Approximately 40% of all recent legal immigrants are Asian. As a result, there are over 12.5 million Asians and Asian Americans residing in the United States. Although this number represents only about 4% of the total U.S. population, it does not indicate the impact of Asians and Asian Americans on the country. Asians and Asian Americans tend to settle in coastal states, especially in the West, where they form large segments of the population. In addition, Asians and Asian Americans represent the fastest growing segment of the U.S. population. Approximately three-fourths of the legal Asian immigrants come from the five countries of Vietnam, the Philippines, Korea, China, and India. They represent several languages and dialects of those languages.

There are approximately 37 million Latinos in the United States. These include recent immigrants and several million who are Spanish-surnamed but identify with Latino culture to a lesser degree. Approximately 40% of all recent legal immigrants are Latino. These immigrants come primarily from Mexico and Central America, Cuba, and South America and speak various dialects of Spanish. Many U.S. citizens from Puerto Rico also move to the United States.

In addition, there are approximately 80,000 legal black immigrants per year from the Caribbean, South and Central America, and Africa. This group represents slightly less than 1% of the U.S. population. This minority represents a number of languages, as is evident from the many geographic areas of origin.

The exact number of illegal immigrants is unknown. Estimates range from 5 to 15 million, with a growth of approximately 500,000 per year.

The largest internal migration is and has been that of African Americans who number 35 million, or 11% of the U.S. population. Reversing the trend of the early- to mid-twentieth century, African Americans began returning to the South in the early 1970s. Many of these individuals speak regional and/or ethno-racial dialects, such as African American English.

To a smaller extent, Native Americans, totaling 2 million, or 0.7% of the U.S. population, have also experienced internal migration. At present, just over 20% of Native Americans live in Native Homelands or historic trust properties, compared to 90% in 1940. Their speech may reflect their native language or the specific dialect of American English they learned.

Currently, the 1.2 million Native Americans who are affiliated with some native community are divided among approximately 450 nations varying in size from the Cherokee nation of over 300,000 to groups of just a handful (Robinson-Zanatu, 1996). In addition to representing a variety of cultures, Native Americans speak over 200 different languages (Leap, 1993). Seventy-eight percent of Native Americans live in urban areas, creating an invisibility that usually is treated by those in the majority culture as of little consequence.

Birth rates differ across groups and also contribute to the changing demographics of the U.S. population. The majority white birth rate is 1.4, inadequate to maintain the relative proportion of whites in the United States. Birth rates for other populations are higher, for example, 1.7 for African Americans, 2.4 for Hispanic Americans, and 1.7 for Asian Americans (National Center for Health Statistics, 2006).

We cannot discuss language development adequately without considering dialectal variations, such as African American English and what we shall call Latino English and Asian English and their effect on the learning of American English and on the learner. To some extent languages are theoretical entities. The view of a monolithic, unchanging, immutable language does not fit reality. As mentioned, languages are fluid and changing.

Languages are especially changeable "around the edges, where they interact with other languages" (Backus, 1999). For example, in many bilingual communities, speakers develop new varieties of communication incorporating both languages, and these varieties function as the basic vernacular or everyday speech of the community.

Not all speakers of a language use the same language rules. Variations that characterize the language of a particular group are collectively called a dialect. A dialect is a language-rule system used by an identifiable group of people that varies in some way from an ideal language standard. Each of us is a dialectal speaker. Dialects usually differ in the frequency of use of certain structures rather than in the presence or absence of these structures. The ideal standard is rarely used except in formal writing, and the concept of a standard spoken language is practically a myth.

FIGURE *1.8* **The Relationship of the Idealized Standard Language and Its Dialects**

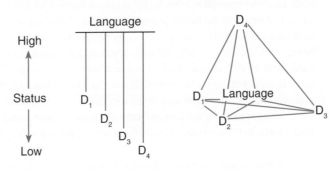

Because each dialect shares a common set of grammatical rules with the standard language, dialects of a language are theoretically mutually intelligible to all speakers of that language.

No dialect is better than any other, nor should a dialect be considered a deviant or inferior form of a language. To devalue a dialect or to presume that one dialect is better ultimately devalues individuals and cultures. Each dialect is a system of rules that should be viewed within its social context. A dialect is adequate to meet the demands of the speech community in which it is found. Thus, it's appropriate for its users. Like languages, dialects evolve over time to meet the needs of the communities in which they are used.

Despite the validity of all dialects, society places relative values on each one. The standard or a majority dialect becomes the "official" criterion. Majority speakers of the language determine what is acceptable, often assuming that their own dialect is the most appropriate. In a stratified society, such as that of the United States, some dialects are accorded higher status than others. But, in fact, the relative value of a dialect is not intrinsic; it represents only the listener's bias. Dialects are merely differences within a language.

The two ways of classifying dialects—the **deficit approach** and the **sociolinguistic approach**—are illustrated in Figure 1.8. In the diagram, dialects that are closer to the standard in the frequency of rule use are separated by less distance. Under the deficit approach, each dialect has a different relative status. Those closer to the idealized standard are considered to be better. Status is determined relative to the standard. The sociolinguistic approach views each dialect as an equally valid rule system. Each dialect is related to the others and to the ideal standard. No value is placed on a dialect.

RELATED FACTORS

Several factors are related to dialectal differences. These include (a) geography, (b) socioeconomic level, (c) race and ethnicity, (d) situation or context, (e) peer-group influences, and (f) first- or second-language learning. A child born and raised in Boston will not sound like a child from Charleston, South Carolina. In turn, a poor child and a wealthy preparatory school child from Charleston will not speak the same way. These differences are called *dialectal differences*. In general, the language of these children and their families reflects the environmental influences of the language spoken around them. No child learns dialect-free English.

The United States was established by settlers who spoke many different languages and several dialects of British English. Members of various ethnic groups chose to settle in specific geographic areas. Other individuals remained isolated by choice or by natural boundaries. In an age of less mobility, before there were national media, American English was free to evolve in several separate ways. A New York City dialect is very different from an Ozark dialect, yet both are close enough to Standard American English (SAE) to be identified as variants of SAE. As a child matures, he or she learns the dialect of the region. Each region has words and grammatical structures that differ slightly. What are *sack* and *pop* to the Midwestern American are *bag* and *soda* to the Middle Atlantic speaker. The Italian sandwich changes to *submarine, torpedo, hero, wedge, hoagie,* and *po'boy* as it moves about the United States. Within each region there is no confusion. Order a *milkshake* in Massachusetts and that's what you get—flavored milk that's been shaken. If you want ice cream in it, you need to ask for a *frappe*.

Some regions of the United States seem to be more prone to word invention or to novel use than others. In the southern Appalachian region, for example, you might encounter the following:

A man might raise enough corn to *bread* his family over the winter.
To do something without considering the consequences is to do it *unthoughtedly*.
Something totally destroyed would be torn to *flinderation*.
Long-lasting things are *lasty*.

Note that the form of each word follows generally accepted morphological marking rules, such as the *-ly* in *unthoughtedly*.

My daughter was given a vivid example of regional dialectal differences while conversing with a child from the Southern United States. Although she was white, the child's older half-brother was the product of a racially mixed marriage. Trying to figure out this situation, my daughter ventured the opinion, "Your brother is really *tan*." She was corrected quickly with, "No he ain't; he's *eleven*."

A second factor in dialectal differences is socioeconomic level. This factor relates to social class, educational and occupational level, home environment, and family interactional styles, including maternal teaching and child-rearing patterns. In general, people from lower socioeconomic groups use more restricted linguistic systems. Their word definitions often relate to one particular aspect of the underlying concept. Those from higher socioeconomic levels generally have more education and are more mobile. These factors generally contribute to the use of a dialect closer to the mainstream. For example, among African American children, boys from lower-income homes are more likely than middle-class African American boys or girls to use features of a dialect called African American English (AAE) (Washington & Craig, 1998). Worldwide, many lower-class or working-class English speakers change the final "ing" /ŋ/ to /n/, producing *workin'* for *working*.

Racial and ethnic differences are a third factor that contributes to dialect development. By choice or as a result of de facto segregation, racial and ethnic minorities can become isolated and a particular dialectal variation may evolve. It has been argued that the distinctive Brooklyn dialect reflects the strong influence of Irish upon American English. Yiddish influences have also affected the New York City dialect. The largest racial group in the United States with a characteristic dialect is African American. African American English is spoken by working-class African Americans, primarily in large industrial areas and in the rural South. Not all African Americans speak African American English.

Fourth, dialect is influenced by situational and contextual factors. All speakers alter their language in response to situational variables. These situationally influenced language variations are called **registers.** The selection of a register depends on the speaker's perception of the situation and the participants, attitude toward or knowledge of the topic, and intention or purpose. A casual, informal, or intimate register is called a **vernacular** variation. Informal American English uses more contractions (*isn't, can't*) and particles (get *up*, put *on*) than formal American English. The variation from formal to informal styles or the reverse is called **style shifting** and is practiced by all speakers. Regardless of the socioeconomic status of the speaker, style shifts seem to be in the same direction for similar situations. For example, in formal reading there is greater use of *-ing* (/ŋ/), while informal conversation is characterized by an increase in the use of *-in* (/n/). Most shifts are made unconsciously. Thus, we might read aloud "I am writing" but say in conversation "I'm writin'."

A fifth influence on language is peer group. In the United States, groups such as teens or lesbians and gay men have their own lexicons and idioms that are not understood by the society as a whole. Peer influence is particularly important during adolescence. Generally, the adolescent dialect is used only with peers. Linguists have labeled two strains of the current teen dialect as "mallspeak" and "texting." Minimalist and repetitive, the rather imprecise mallspeak is a spoken dialect that overuses words such as *like, y'know,* and *whatever*. In contrast, text messaging is another minimalist "code" used on cell phones. On chat lines and instant messaging, communicators use a shorthand including letters for words, such as "u" for "you" and "r" for "are," numbers for words, such as "4" for "for," phonetic spelling, such as "sum" for "some," and combinations, such as "sum1" for "someone" or "b4" for "before."

Finally, a dialect may reflect the primacy of another language. Speakers with a different native language often retain vestiges of that language. They typically **code switch** from one language to the other. The speaker's age and education and the social situation influence the efficacy of code switching.

AMERICAN ENGLISH DIALECTS

Standard American English (SAE) is an idealized version of American English that occurs rarely in conversation. It is the form of American English that is used in textbooks and on network newscasts. All of us speak a dialect of English or another language.

There are at least 10 regional dialects in the United States (presented in Figure 1.9): Eastern New England, New York City, Western Pennsylvania, Middle Atlantic, Appalachian, Southern, Central Midland, North Central, Southwest, and Northwest. In general, the variations are greatest on the East Coast and decrease to the West. Each geographic region has a dialect marked by distinct sound patterns, words and idioms, and syntactic and prosodic systems. Regional dialects are not monolithic. For example, within Southern American English, racial differences exist. This is further complicated by the use of Cajun/Creole American English in Louisiana (Oetting & Wimberly Garrity, 2006).

The major racial and ethnic dialects in the United States are African American English, Spanish-influenced or Latino English, and Asian English. In part, these dialects are influenced by geographic region and by socioeconomic factors. Spanish influences also differ depending on the country or area of origin. Colombian Spanish is very different from Puerto Rican Spanish. Asian English differs with the country of origin and the native language.

African American English

For the purposes of description, we shall consider African American English (AAE) to be the relatively uniform dialect used by African Americans in the inner cities of most large urban areas and in the rural South, when speaking casually. In short, it is the linguistic system used by working-class African American people within their speech community. As such, AAE shares many of the characteristics of Southern and working-class dialects. Obviously, not all African Americans speak the dialect. Even among speakers of AAE, a difference exists in the

FIGURE *1.9 Major American Geographic Dialects*

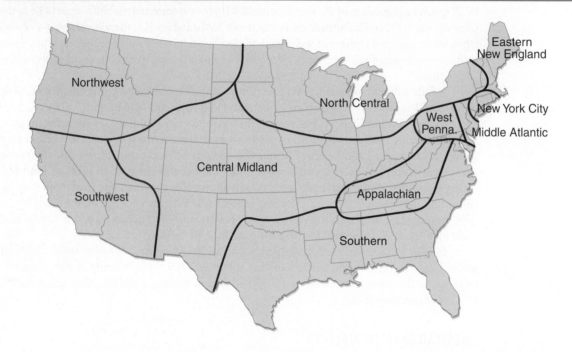

amount of dialectal features used by different individuals. Conversely, white speakers who live or work with speakers of AAE may use some of its features. It is also important to remember that there are variations of AAE that its speakers use for certain situations. As with other dialects, there is a formal–informal continuum. Individual differences may be related to age, geographic location, income, occupation, and education (Terrell & Terrell, 1993).

AAE is a systematic language rule system, not a deviant or improper form of English. Its linguistic variations from SAE are not errors. The linguistic differences between AAE and SAE are minimal. Most of the grammatical rules and underlying concepts are similar. Variations are the result of AAE's different and equally complex rule system. Although it shares features with other dialects, AAE has some features—such as the use of *be* in the habitual sense, as in "She *be* working there since 1985," and the triple negative, as in "Nobody don't got none"—that are primarily characteristic of AAE. Much of the sense of the dialect can also be found in its intonational patterns, speaking rate, and distinctive lexicon.

The major characteristics of AAE are listed in Appendix B. It is unlikely that any given individual who speaks AAE will exhibit all of these characteristics. The frequency of appearance of each feature will change with situational variations and over time.

Latino English

Within the United States, the largest ethnic population is Hispanic. Not all people with Spanish surnames speak Spanish; some do exclusively; and still others are **bilingual,** speaking both Spanish and English. The form of English spoken depends on the amount and type of Spanish spoken and the location within the United States. The two largest Hispanic groups in the United States are of Puerto Rican–Caribbean and Mexican–Central American origin. Although both groups speak Spanish, their Spanish dialectal differences influence their comprehension and production of American English. The dialect of American English spoken in the surrounding community also has an effect. As a result, the interference points may be very different for individual speakers. We will refer to these dialects collectively as *Latino English* (LE). Appendix B summarizes the major differences found between LE and SAE.

Asian English

Although we shall use the term *Asian English* (AE) throughout this text, it is clearly a misnomer because no such entity exists. It is merely a term that enables us to discuss the various dialects of Asian Americans as a group.

The most widely used languages in Asia are Mandarin Chinese, Cantonese Chinese, Filipino, Japanese, Khmer, Korean, Laotian, and Vietnamese. Of these, Mandarin Chinese has had the most pervasive influence on the evolution of the others. Indian and colonial European cultures, as well as others, have also influenced these languages. Each language has various dialects and features that distinguish it from the others. Thus, there is, in reality, no Asian English as a cohesive unit.

Nonetheless, the English of Asian language speakers has certain characteristics in common. These are listed in Appendix B. The omission of final consonants, for example, is prevalent in AE. In contrast to English, most Asian languages, with the exception of Korean, have open or vowel-final syllables.

Conclusion

LANGUAGE IS A SOCIAL TOOL consisting of a very complex system of symbols and rules for using those symbols. Native speakers of a language must be knowledgeable about the symbols employed and the acceptable usage rules, including concept, word, morpheme, and phoneme combinations.

Humans may be the only animals with a productive communication system that gives them the ability to represent reality symbolically without dependence on immediate context support. Although animals clearly communicate at some level, this communication is limited in topic and scope and usually is dependent on the context. For example, bees have an elaborate system of movements for conveying information, but it is extremely iconic (it looks like what it conveys) and unitopical (the topic is always where to find nectar). Whether higher mammals, such as chimpanzees and other primates, are capable of complex symbolic communication will be discussed in the next chapter. In any case, it is only after intensive, long-term training that these animals learn what the human infant acquires in a few short months with little or no training.

Dialectal differences can pose special problems for a language-learning child, especially when the child enters school. Yet children who speak with a dialect of American English seem to understand SAE. These young children, if motivated, follow a developmental sequence and learn a second language or dialect relatively easily. They already have a language rule system that enables them to understand other dialects and learn other languages. Although different from SAE, other dialectal systems are not deviant. The U.S. district court for eastern Michigan, in a ruling known as the *Ann Arbor decision* (Joiner, 1979), has ruled that AAE is a rule-governed linguistic system. Furthermore, educators must develop methods for teaching SAE to dialectal speakers.

Hopefully, this introductory chapter has given you an appreciation for the complexity of the topic we'll be discussing. Imagine the enormous task you faced as a newborn with the entirety of language acquisition before you. In the following chapters, I'll try to explain as clearly as I can how you did it. Along the way, you'll gain the knowledge to become an observant parent, guiding teacher, or competent speech-language pathologist.

Discussion

WELL, I DID WARN YOU! Yes, you're right; this is complicated and it can be confusing. It's good to reflect on what we've read at the end of each chapter and to ask ourselves "So what?"

The highlights in the chapter are the distinction between speech, language, and communication. Too many speech-language pathologists (SLPs) are still referred to as the "Speech Teacher" despite the fact that in school caseloads, the largest percentage of cases are now language impairments. If you told someone that you worked with language impairments, not speech, and he or she replied, "Aren't they the same thing?" how would you respond? Think about it. You have the ammunition from this chapter.

Other important aspects of this chapter include the characteristics of language. It's a social tool that's rule based, and those rules enable it to be used in a generative fashion. Language can also be characterized by its five areas: syntax, morphology, phonology, semantics, and pragmatics. Of these, pragmatics seems to be the organizing area because context determines the other four. All areas are interdependent, and changes in one area, either because of development or the dynamics of language use, will result in changes in the others.

This last item—the interdependence of the five areas of language—has important implications for development and also for intervention. When an SLP intervenes with a child or an adult with a language impairment, there may be unforeseen consequences. For example, working on writing with an adult with aphasia or language loss often due to stroke may have a beneficial and unintended effect on spoken language. Likewise, adding too many new words to a child's language lesson may increase phonological precision but slow the child's delivery and decrease sentence length. The effect will vary with the amount of change, the individual child, and the type and severity of the impairment.

As we travel through this text, note the changes that occur and the overall effect on communication. Where appropriate I will characterize change based on the five areas of language.

I know, I know . . . you sound fine, but everyone else has an accent! Not so fast. If nothing else, please take from this chapter that a standard American English really doesn't exist in your daily use of language. You speak a dialect . . . only I use the standard. I'm having fun with you. We all speak a dialect, especially me. The important thing to recognize is that no one dialect is better than any other. They are all rule-based variations. And they're all valid.

In the real world, however, some dialects are rewarded, while others are punished by the culture as a whole. Still, within a given community, a dialect that is punished by the larger society may be rewarded and may give status to its user. It is very difficult to separate a dialect from its culture.

Main Points

- Speech is a motor act and a mode of communication, but not the only one.

- Language is the code used in communication. More specifically, it is a set of symbols and the rules for using them.

- Communication is the act of transferring information between two or more people. Speech and language are two of the tools used to communicate.

- Characteristics of language. Language is . . .

  - A social tool

  - Rule governed

  - Generative

- Language has five parameters: syntax, morphology, phonology, semantics, and pragmatics.

- Pragmatics is considered by some sociolinguists to be the organizing principle of language that determines the other four aspects when communicating.

- We all speak a dialect of the language ideal.

- A dialect is a language-rule system spoken by an identifiable group of people that varies from the ideal language standard.

- The deficit approach to dialects assigns status based on the amount of variation from the standard. In contrast, the sociolinguistic approach recognizes all dialects as valid and related forms of a language with no relative status assigned.

- Factors related to dialectal differences are geography, socioeconomic level, race and ethnicity, situation or context, peer-group influences, and first- or second-language learning. Examples include African American English, Latino English, and "Asian English."

- Dialectal considerations affect education, employment, and perceived status.

Reflections

1. Speech, language, and communication are different aspects of the same process. Can you contrast all three?

2. Not all of the message is carried by the linguistic code. How do the other aspects of communication contribute?

3. Language is a social tool that is rule governed and generative. Explain these three properties of language.

4. Language consists of five interrelated components. Describe these components, as well as the units of morpheme and phoneme.

5. How do dialects relate to each other and to the parent language?

6. What factors contribute to the development of dialects? Relate these to the dialects found in the United States.

2

Describing Language

Models of language development help us understand the developmental process by bringing order to our descriptions of this process and providing answers to the questions *how* and *why.* Of the many linguistic theories proposed, we will examine the two main theoretical positions. Each contains a core of relevant information and reflects divergent views of language and child development.

Our knowledge of child language development is only as good as the research data that we possess. In turn, these data reflect the questions that researchers ask and the studies they design to answer these questions. When you have completed this chapter, you should understand

- The relationship of Generative or Nativist theories and Constructionist theories.
- The effect of the method of data collection on the resultant data.
- The effect of the sample size and variability on the resultant data.
- The issues of naturalness and representativeness.
- Collection and analysis procedures.
- The value of cross-language studies.
- The following terms:

Child directed speech
Constructionist approach
Generative approach
Emergentism
Nativist approach

To listen to language samples related to chapter content and to peruse other enhanced study aids, please see the Companion Website at www.pearsonhighered.com/owens8e

If you're like me, philosophical theories and arguments often result in a headache. My mind naturally looks for similarities rather than dissimilarities. I look for ways to unite rather than divide. Needless to say, trying to defend a notion that two theories are diametrically opposed has been always difficult. And yet, here we are in the present chapter, trying to explain the development and use of language from a theoretical point of view.

Linguistic theories are helpful in explaining the processes we'll describe in this text. For researchers, theories provide an explanation and also a framework for investigating language development and use. It is through these investigations that we collect the linguistic data from which this text is created. In this chapter, I will try to explain the primary theoretical approaches to the study of language. We will then explore how language data is gathered and explored. I'll try to do all this without inducing a headache on your part.

Linguistic Theory

The study of language and language development has interested inquiring persons for thousands of years. Psammetichus I, an Egyptian pharoah of the seventh century BCE with a difficult-to-pronounce name, supposedly conducted a child language study to determine the "natural" language of humans. Two children were raised with sheep and heard no human speech. Needless to say, they did not begin to speak Egyptian or anything else that approximated human language. Individuals as different as St. Augustine and Charles Darwin published narratives on language development. Several modern researchers have devoted their professional careers to the study of child development.

People study language development for a variety of reasons. First, interest in language development represents part of a larger concern for human development. People who specialize in early childhood education are eager to learn about this developmental process in order to facilitate child behavior change. Special educators and speech-language pathologists study child language to increase their insight into normal and other-than-normal processes. A second reason for studying language development is that it is interesting and can help us understand our own behavior. There is a slightly mystical quality to language. The developmental process has been called "mysterious" (Gleitman & Wanner, 1982) and "magic" (Bloom, 1983). As mature language users, we cannot state all the rules we use; yet, as children, we deciphered and learned these rules within a few years. Few of us can fully explain our own language development; it just seemed to happen. Finally, language-development studies can probe the relationship between language and thought. Language development is parallel to cognitive development. Hopefully, the study of language development may enable language users to understand the underlying mental processes to some degree.

Since language and language development are so complex, professionals are often at odds as to which approach provides the best description.

- The linguist is primarily concerned with describing language symbols and stating the rules these symbols follow to form language structures. The psycholinguist is interested in the psychological processes and constructs underlying language. The psychological mechanisms that let language users produce and comprehend language are of particular concern.
- The sociolinguist studies language rules and use as a function of role, socioeconomic level, and linguistic or cultural context. Dialectal differences and social-communicative interaction are important.

- The behavioral psychologist minimizes language form and emphasizes the behavioral context of language. The behaviorist is concerned with eliciting certain responses and determining how the number of these responses can be increased or decreased.
- The speech-language pathologist concentrates on disordered communication. Of greatest interest are the causes of disorder, the evaluation of the extent of the disorder, and the remediation process.

The study of how children learn language is like many other academic pursuits in that different theories that attempt to explain the phenomenon compete for acceptance. Occasionally one theory predominates, but generally portions of each are used to explain different aspects. Part of the problem in designing an overall theory is the complexity of both language and communication behavior. In the recent past, four theoretical approaches to language development have evolved, often in opposition to each other. These are behavioral, syntactic, semantic/cognitive, and sociolinguistic. Within the last decade, a new approach called Emergentism has become popular among linguists and answers some of the concerns expressed about the initial four. This chapter explores these approaches, examining their overall theories, limitations, and contributions. I've tried to give you the main points of each theory and to highlight the grains of truth in each. Look for similarities and contrasts. You might find it helpful to read each theory separately and allow time for processing before going on to the next.

NATURE VERSUS NURTURE

If you've had an introductory course in psychology or development, you have, no doubt, been introduced to the nature versus nurture debate. In its simplest terms, the discussion centers on whether some aspect of development occurs because it is an inherent part of being human, it's natural, or it occurs because of learning from the environment. Is someone a criminal because of his or her nature or because of the way in which he or she was raised? Is our destiny in our genes, in some aspect of being human, or do environment and learning mediate our biological inheritance?

This debate is alive and well in linguistics (Galasso, 2003). The way in which children acquire linguistic knowledge has been the focus of intense interest and debate in cognitive science for well over half a century (Bates & Goodman, 1999; Chomsky, 1957, 1965a; Crain & Lillo-Martin, 1999; Elman et al., 1996; Lindner & Hohenberger, 2009; MacWhinney, 2004). The two primary approaches representing nature and nurture are called generative or nativist and constructionist or empiricist respectively.

GENERATIVE APPROACH

The **Generative** or **Nativist approach** assumes that children are able to acquire language because they are born with innate rules or principles related to structures of human languages (Chomsky, 1965a, 1965b; de Villiers, 2001; Lenneberg, 1967; Wexler, 1998, 2003; Yang, 2002). Generativists assume that it is impossible for children to learn linguistic knowledge from the environment given that the input children hear is limited and full of errors and incomplete information (Chomsky, 1965a, 1965b). Even with these limitations, children are still able to acquire the linguistic knowledge quickly because of the guidance of innate linguistic hypotheses. Something innate or inborn guides a child's learning.

Beginning in the late 1950s, Noam Chomsky and others, working from the assumption that language is a universal human trait, tried to identify universal syntactic rules that applied to all human languages. These rules were assumed to be present in each human at birth in a location in the brain theoretically called the language acquisition device or LAD. Nativists then attempted to describe the syntactic rules that enabled adult language users to generate a seemingly endless number of sentences in their specific language.

It seemed only natural to apply the new adult linguistic models to child language acquisition. Known by various names, the resulting models basically assumed that children used the universal language rules found in their LADs to figure out the rules of the language to which they were exposed. In 1973, Roger Brown—we'll meet him later—reviewed and evaluated these models, concluding that none of them was totally satisfactory in explaining children's development of language. The basic problem was that the early Generativist theories were adult-based and there was no evidence that children used, or even needed, the adult-like linguistic categories and rules to acquire language. Many linguists concluded after looking at languages across different cultures that no single formal grammar was adequate to account for the acquisition process in all of the world's many languages (Slobin, 1973).

Several theorists suggested that, instead of syntax, a semantic-cognitive basis existed for children's early language (Bloom, 1973; Brown, 1973; Schlesinger, 1971; Slobin, 1970). Called the Semantic Revolution, the position held that the semantic-syntactic relations apparent in children's early language correspond rather closely to some of the categories of infant and toddler sensory-motor cognition. Instead of the subjects and verbs used by adults to produce sentences, children used meaning units, such as *Agents*, which caused action (*mommy, daddy*), *Actions* (*eat, throw*), and *Objects*, which received it (*cookie, ball*). These linguistic units that children know nonlinguistically might form the basis for a linguistic unit such as *Agent-Action-Object* (*Mommy eat cookie, Daddy throw ball*). Other combinations included *Possessor-Possessed* (*Mommy sock*) and *Object-Location* (*Key table*). Although these rules explained some child utterances, they failed to explain others that fit none or several categories. In addition, it was difficult to explain how children moved from these semantic-based rules to the more abstract syntactic rules of adults.

As a consequence, a group of theorists began to advocate a return to adult syntactic models (Baker & McCarthy, 1981; Hornstein & Lightfoot, 1981; Pinker, 1984). These linguists argued that the discontinuity of semantic and syntactic models of language learning posed genuine problems of explanation. They argued instead for a continuity assumption in which children operated with the same basic linguistic categories and rules as adults (Pinker, 1984). At this point, these theorists had returned to a linguistic nativism, which assumed that throughout their lives, all human beings possess the same basic linguistic competence, in the form of universal grammar (Chomsky, 1980). Unfortunately, there seems to be little evidence that children actually use abstract adult-like categories.

Generative grammar assumes that natural languages are like formal languages, such as mathematics. As such, natural languages are characterized by

■ A unified set of abstract algebraic rules that are meaningless themselves and insensitive to the meanings of the elements (words) they combine, and

■ A set of meaningful linguistic elements (words) that serve as variables in the rules (Tomasello, 2006).

To learn a language, each child begins with his or her innate universal grammar to abstract the structure of that language. Acquisition then consists of

■ Acquiring all the words, idioms, and constructions of that language, and

■ Linking the core structures of the particular language being learned to the universal grammar.

L anguage is acquired in the process of using it to communicate with others.

Being innate, universal grammar does not develop but is the same throughout a person's life span. In other words, there is a continuity in language acquisition and use. The assumption, therefore, is that when a child says "I'm eating a cookie," she has an adult-like understanding of the present progressive (*be* + *verbing*) form and can generate similar forms.

One problem for generative grammar is fixed and semi-fixed structures that are not based on abstract grammatical categories but on particular words or fixed expressions, such as *How do you do?* Words cannot be substituted nor other verbs substituted. A large portion of human linguistic competence involves the mastery of these routine expressions, plus idioms. Those learning English as a second language will experience difficulty with expressions in which the meanings are non-literal, such as *He's starting to get to me* and *Hang in there.* These expressions are not part of a core grammar that can generate grammatical rules. Instead, they seem to be memorized like words.

Constructionists would see these language structures as examples that structure emerges from use. Subsequently, a language community may conventionalize or adopt these linguistic structures from their language use.

CONSTRUCTIONIST APPROACH

In contrast to the Generative approach is the **Constructionist** or Empiricist **approach,** which argues that children learn linguistic knowledge from the environmental input to which they are exposed (Christiansen & Charter, 1999; Goldberg, 2006; MacWhinney, 2004; Reali & Christiansen, 2005; Tomasello, 2005). For this reason, this general approach is sometimes labeled "Interactionist." See Guo, Owen, & Tomblin (2010) for an excellent summary.

In short, according to this theoretical approach, children figure out the linguistic structures of the input language, assuming it contains sufficient information related to linguistic structures. As with Nativists, Constructionists are interested in language structure, but there is less theoretical commitment to language form and to ages of acquisition. To learn language, children rely on general cognitive mechanisms possessed (Abbot-Smith & Tomasello, 2006; Elman et al., 1996; Gomez, 2002; Tomasello, 2003). Note that this process is not accomplished by a specific language mechanism or language acquisition device but by general brain processes. Instead, Constructionists assume that language acquisition involves learning linguistic constructions from the input (Tomasello, 2000a, 2003).

In addition, the child is considered to be a contributing member in the learning process. The child and the language environment form a dynamic relationship. A child cues parents to provide the appropriate language that the child needs for language acquisition. A parent's adapted way of speaking to a child is termed **child directed speech** (CDS) and varies in many ways from speech to other adults.

One approach to language acquisition, sometimes termed **Emergentism**, views language as a structure arising from existing interacting patterns in the human brain rather than from language-specific structures, such as an LAD (Fausett, 1994; MacWhinney, 1998; Port & van Gelder, 1995). Although there is something innate in the human brain that makes language possible, that "something" did not necessarily evolve for language and language alone (Bates, 1997). For example, our brains seem to naturally seek patterns in incoming information. In this way, children find patterns in the language input they receive. In other words, language is most likely what we do with a brain that evolved to serve many varied and complex challenges (Tomasello & Call, 1997). A child's language emerges not from stipulated rules, but from the interaction of general cognitive mechanisms and the environment. The learning mechanisms found elsewhere in cognition are sufficient to bring about the emergence of complex language (Elman, 1999; MacWhinney, 2002; Sabbagh & Gelman, 2000). Although we are the only species capable of a fully grammatical language, we seem to have acquired language over time with a wide range of cognitive, perceptual, and social tools, none of which may have evolved for language alone (Bates, 1997).

One of the first theorists to propose how language learning occurs was B.F. Skinner, a well-known Behaviorist. In 1957, Skinner published *Verbal Behavior*, in which he assumed that learning language was similar to learning any behavior. In brief, he theorized that parents model language, young children imitate these models, and parents reinforce children for these imitations. Chomsky countered that

- Parents provide poor models when talking to each other,
- Children could not possibly learn all possible constructions by imitation, and
- That parents did not reinforce the grammatically correct constructions of young children.

Instead, according to Chomsky, children learned language rules by deciphering them from the utterances they heard. In order to do that, of course, children relied on innate structures found in the language acquisition device.

Later, sociolinguists countered that language acquisition follows a transactional model of child–caregiver give-and-take in which the child learns to understand the rules of dialogue, not of syntax or semantics. A communication base is established first, and language develops on this base to express verbally those intensions that the child previously expressed nonverbally. Social interactions and social relationships provide the needed framework that enables a child to decode and encode language form and content. Gradually, a child refines communication skills through repeated interactions. Contrary to the assertions of Chomsky, sociolinguists saw parent input to children to be highly selective. In turn, children selectively imitated those structures they were in the process of learning. Parents responded in conversational ways that served to reinforce a child's verbalization.

The Constructionist approach is a usage-based approach that sees language as composed of constructions or symbol units that combine form and meaning through the use of morphemes, words, idioms, and sentence frames (Goldberg, 1995). A central tenet is that language structure emerges from language use. The functions of language as a social tool are central to development. Language structures are irrelevant without a purpose. Rather than assuming that children have adult-like abstract linguistic knowledge, the usage-based approach suggests that children learn linguistic constructions gradually from the input in a gradual, piecemeal fashion (Guo et al., 2010).

The child hears a large number of word sequences with similar structures and begins to observe regularities in this input and to develop the word-specific constructions. For instance, a child may learn *He's* + *verb-ing* constructions from the word sequences like *He's eating, He's running, and He's jumping* and only use auxiliary '*is*' with the subject *He*. Likewise, a child might not use *Mommy* or *The dog* in place of *He* because the child has not learned that a lexical noun phrase may be used in the subject position. In other words, the child does not possess grammatical category abstractions such NP for the subject position. Later, using word-specific constructions, such as *He's* + *verb-ing, Mommy's verb-ing,* and *The dog's verb-ing,* the child will figure out that there are more abstract ways of representing these constructions and acquire a more abstract rule, such as *NP's Verb-ing.* Eventually, the child may learn the most abstract construction, such as *NP* + *be* + *Verb-ing.* Thus, different subjects and auxiliary be forms (e.g., am, is, are, was, were) can be used in this construction (Guo, 2011).

From a range of word-specific constructions, a child realizes that there are more abstract ways of representing these various constructions and acquires more abstract constructions. Even here correct production may be influenced by the frequency with which the child hears a particular grammatical construction (Bybee, 1995, 2002; Dąbrowska, 2000; Dąbrowska & Lieven, 2005). Remember that a variety of auxiliary or helping verbs (*am, is, are, was, were*) can fill the position between the noun and verb in the *Noun be verb-ing* construction.

As opposed to linguistic rules conceived by Generativist as abstract algebraic procedures for combining words and morphemes but not themselves contributing to meaning, Constructionist linguistic rules are themselves meaningful linguistic symbols (Tomasello, 2006). In other words, these patterns are meaningful units for communication. For example, *Noun be verb-ing* is used to communicate about an action occurring currently.

Because it is assumed that no universal grammar exists, usage-based theories do not have to explain the connection of such a grammar to language learning. Instead, children figure out their language from the regular and rule-based constructions of that language. As with all learning, they construct abstract categories and schemes from the concrete things they have learned. Children construct these abstractions gradually and in piecemeal fashion through two general cognitive processes:

- Intention-reading, by which they attempt to understand the communicative significance of an utterance, and
- Pattern-finding, by which they create the more abstract dimensions (Tomasello, 2006).

Linguistic input is crucial to this process.

Initially, children collect concrete pieces of language of many different shapes and sizes. Across these examples they generalize rules to construct more abstract linguistic constructions in their mind. These, in turn, underlie their ability to generate creative new utterances.

*D*ifferent theories have postulated how children learn language.

At the center of Constructionist theory is the grammatical construction, consisting of a unit of language comprised of multiple linguistic elements used together for a relatively coherent communicative function. Constructions vary in complexity, depending on the number of elements involved and their interrelations and in their abstractness.

CONCLUSION

Although we've only exposed the surface of these two theoretical approaches, you may be having some difficulty keeping the highlights of each separate. Table 2.1 presents the major elements of each theory.

Language Research and Analysis

Throughout this text, we will be discussing child language-development information that has been gathered from studies of child language. These data are difficult to collect and often require extraordinary procedures in order to ensure valid, reliable, and objective reporting.

In general, there are four goals of child language research (Bennett-Kaster, 1988):

1. To confirm general linguistic principles.
2. To discover principles of language development.
3. To clarify the relationship of language to developments in other areas, such as cognition.
4. To provide a more or less theoretical description of language development.

TABLE *2.1* **Comparison of Nativist and Constructionist Theories**

	NATIVIST	CONSTRUCTIONIST
Major focus	Language structure.	Language use.
Cognitive contribution	Specific neural structures dedicated to language enable humans to learn, process, and use language.	Language form and use result from complex human brains and the need to transmit messages in social interactions.
Language learning	Child learns language structure by learning specific language rules.	Child uses form that best accomplish the child's social goals. Through repeated use, child deduces rules.
Origins of language	Language is innate and thus universal language rules exist across languages.	Language universals do not exist. Instead, language evolved to meet social needs.
Role of environment	Child uses language input to deduce rules of the language.	Child and context have a dynamic relationship in which the child's behavior influences child directed speech tailored to the level required by the child to participate in social interactions.

The purpose and the researcher's theoretical predisposition will influence the type of data-collection procedure used. The researcher's behavioral, linguistic, cognitive, or eclectic theories will influence the specific language features studied and the overall study design. Research may be based on a model of language or language development that does not reflect the actual language hypotheses of children. Thus, the results might describe the child's fit or lack of fit to a model rather than the child's actual operating principles, hypotheses, or linguistic performance.

Just as there are different methods of collection, there are many considerations that influence the data gathered by these procedures. Let's briefly explore issues related to child language study, such as the method of study, the population and language sample size and variability, the naturalness and representativeness of the language sample, data collection, and data analysis. I shall refer frequently to two studies, those of Brown (1973) and Wells (1985). Other studies will be mentioned, as appropriate, without burdening the discussion with specific details of each. Cross-linguistic studies and data will also be discussed.

Issues in the Study of Child Language

While the notion of collecting and analyzing child language data may seem simple, in fact it is very complex. Several decisions must be made prior to data collection. The methods and procedures used can influence the resultant data and may unintentionally color the conclusions drawn from these data.

METHOD OF DATA COLLECTION

To a great extent the method of collection used is driven by the aspect of language being studied. Let's explore this briefly and the focus on expressive language. Three general areas of interest might include speech perception, language comprehension, and language production.

In general, speech perception studies are interested in speech discrimination of children, especially infants, and the ways in which these abilities may aid language learning. Recent advances in technology, especially digital recording and computers, have aided researchers in isolating, reproducing, and combining sounds for research (Gerken & Asline, 2005; Karmiloff & Karmiloff-Smith, 2001). Infants can even be tested while still in the womb for their responses to speech sounds in isolation and in connected speech. Responses may consist of moving or kicking. With older children and adults, speech perception is often tested with more specific responses, such as pointing. One new approach is called online or real-time research in which responses are paired with brain-imaging techniques, such as magnetic resonance imaging (MRI) to identify areas of the brain where perception occurs.

Language comprehension studies are interested in understanding. Subjects usually respond to structured procedures by looking, pointing, acting out, or following directions in response to a spoken or written stimulus. Of necessity, this type of research requires a standardized, structured experimental design to ensure that all subjects have the same input.

Expressive language studies can take a number of formats from very structured and experimental to more open-ended and observational. The primary difference is the degree of control the experimenter has over the context. We'll be primarily discussing expressive language studies in the following sections.

As mentioned, expressive language-development data are usually collected in two ways: spontaneous conversational sampling or natural observation and structured testing or experimental manipulation. Each method raises issues of appropriateness for the language feature being studied. Either one alone may be insufficient to describe a child's linguistic competence, that is, what he or she knows about language. Data yielded in one context may not appear in another. For example, in a study of pronouns in which I participated, children produced a wider variety in conversation and produced more advanced forms in more formal testing (Haas & Owens, 1985). Other researchers have also found that formal elicitation tasks, such as testing procedures, produce more advanced child language than conversational sampling (Eisenberg, 1997). Ideally, the linguist would employ both informal and formal or structured approaches, using the structured procedures to obtain more in-depth information on the data collected by the more broad-based naturalistic or informal procedures.

Some researchers prefer testing or experimental manipulation in order to control for some of the variables inherent in more naturalistic collection. Within a test or experimental procedure, various linguistic elements may be elicited using verbal and nonverbal stimuli in a structured presentation. Such control of the context, however, may result in rather narrow sampling.

Formal procedures enable researchers to gather data that may not be readily available using conversational or observational techniques. For example, it is difficult to assess children's comprehension or their metalinguistic skills without direct testing. Some hypotheses cannot be tested directly, however, so researchers must test indirectly or observe some features of language development.

Language and experimental factors must be manipulated with caution. One aspect of language can affect others, even though the researcher does not intend for this to happen. For example, among both children and adults, new information introduced into a conversation is consistently more phonologically accurate than older, shared information. Thus, pragmatics influences phonology.

Likewise, experimental factors can have unintended consequences. For example, a researcher may highlight an item in a picture in an attempt to ensure a child's accurate comment. Unfortunately, although the accuracy of the message is not increased when one item is marked, the amount of redundancy or inclusion of irrelevant information does increase (Lloyd & Banham, 1997).

In addition, testing and experimental tasks do not necessarily reflect a child's performance in everyday use. For example, in an experimental task, a child may rely on on-the-spot problem-solving techniques rather than on his or her own everyday operating theories and hypotheses (Karmiloff-Smith, 1986). In addition, noncompliance with testing or experimental procedures may not mean noncomprehension or lack of knowledge. Especially with preschoolers, incorrect responding may indicate a lack of attention or interest.

The results of testing can be especially suspect unless they are analyzed thoroughly. Test scores alone tell researchers nothing about performance on individual items. Two children may have the same score and very different responses. Scoring of individual items may be limited to a wrong-or-right dichotomy, with little analysis of the types of incorrect responses and the underlying processes that these answers may reflect. Testing contexts may provide more or fewer stimuli than are found in the real world, thus modifying the difficulty of the task for the child.

Language processing is not a single unitary operation as is often assumed in test construction, but consists of component operations, such as lexical or vocabulary access, syntactic decoding, and discourse processing, that are engaged at different times and with varying degrees depending on the linguistic task. So-called *offline test tasks*, as in fill-ins, or providing the missing word, measure only the endpoints of several linguistic processes.

During offline testing, components of the overall process are overlooked. For example, the process of guessing the missing word may be the reverse of what happens in conversation. Conscious guessing is too slow in conversation. Rather than context aiding in predicting the next word or phrase of the speaker, contextual information seems to provide a check that correct items have been uttered. Although such offline language collection techniques may tell us what children know, they tell us little about how children process or access language.

In contrast, *online tasks* attempt to measure operations at various points during processing and describe individual and integrative components (Shapiro, Swinney, & Borsky, 1998). For example, at what point in the cue "Mary has a blue dress and a red dress; she has two_____" does the child access the word *dresses*? We might be able to determine this information by the online technique of asking a child to paraphrase or answer yes/no questions after only limited information is presented. For example, if we say "Mary has a blue dress and a red dress," a child may access *dresses* based on *and* or *red* or *dress*. Online techniques would be interested in discovering at which point this occurred. Techniques can be much more elaborate than this simple example suggests. Although still in their infancy, online techniques are beginning to provide valuable linguistic-processing data.

In short, testing and experimental data may be very accurate but very limited. The results must be examined within the context of the specific tasks designed to elicit certain behaviors. A better measure is the consistency of use of a language feature across various tasks (Bennett-Kaster, 1988; Derwing & Baker, 1986).

Jerome Bruner, renowned child development specialist, began his career studying language in very controlled situations, analyzing discrete bits of language. The model was confining, and the language data felt artificial. He then began studying children at home, videotaping open-ended interactions with their families. As a result, his later data had a more authentic quality to it. Naturalistic studies, such as language samples, may yield very different data than experimental manipulations (Abu-Akel, Bailey, & Thum, 2004; Wilson, 2003).

Sampling spontaneous conversation is more naturalistic and, ideally, ensures analysis of real-life behaviors. Such collection is not without its problems. For example, the data collected may be affected by several variables, such as the amount of language, the intelligibility of a child, and the effect of the context. To date, linguists have not identified all the possible variables that can affect performance or the extent of their influence. As a result, certain linguistic elements may not be exhibited even when they are present in a child's repertoire. Some linguistic elements occur infrequently, such as passive-voice sentences, and others are optional, such as the use of pronouns. Usually, a single conversational sample is inadequate to demonstrate the full range of a child's communication abilities. It is difficult to estimate a child's competence or ability based on informal behavior. In addition, information on the child's production provides only a general estimate of comprehension.

Sampling techniques exist along a continuum from very unstructured, open-ended situations to more structured, restrictive ones in which the researcher attempts to control or manipulate one or more variables. For example, the researcher interested in narratives may want to elicit a particular variety, such as recounts, and directs a child to provide a story about something that happened to him or her. Pictures also might be used to elicit narratives. All such manipulations affect a child's language. For example, pretend play involving routine events facilitates communication with more topic maintenance and less miscommunication among children than in less familiar interactive situations (Short-Meyerson & Abbeduto, 1997).

Child language data may also be obtained from the CHILDES system of database transcripts. The system includes programs for computer analysis, methods of linguistic coding, and systems for linking these transcripts to digitized audio and video. A corpus of language samples is available along with studies from English and other languages. The Internet address for CHILDES is given at the end of the chapter.

Any given naturalistic situation may be insufficient for eliciting a child's systematic knowledge of language. Nor is there certainty that a given test situation will represent a child's naturally occurring communication. Thus, it is best to have data from a combination of collection procedures. In either case, the linguist is sampling the child's performance. The child's linguistic competence—what he or she knows about language—must be inferred from this performance.

SAMPLE SIZE AND VARIABILITY

The researcher must be concerned about two samples: the sample or group of children from whom data are collected and the sample of language data from each child. In both samples, the researcher must be concerned with size and variability. Too small a sample will restrict the conclusions that can be drawn about all children, and too large a sample may be unwieldy. The two samples, subjects and language, also interact, one influencing the other.

The number of children or subjects should be large enough to allow for individual differences and to enable group conclusions to be drawn. The overall design of the study will influence the number of subjects considered adequate. For example, it may be appropriate to follow a few children for a period of time, called a *longitudinal study,* but inappropriate to administer a one-time-only test to the same limited number of children. Other considerations will also influence the number of children studied. In a longitudinal study, for example, as many as 30% of the children may be lost because of family mobility, illness, or unwillingness to continue over a four- or five-year period. It might be better, therefore, to adopt an overlapping longitudinal design with two different age samples, each being observed for half the length of time that would have been needed in a longitudinal study.

Wells (1985), for example, sampled 128 children for two years each, using such an overlapping longitudinal model. In contrast, Roger Brown (1973) studied three children intensively for 10 to 16 months. Wells recorded each child for analysis for 27 minutes at three-month intervals throughout the study, collecting an average of 120 utterances on each occasion. In contrast, Brown averaged two hours of sampling each month. More recently, Hart and Risley (1995) collected monthly audio samples of parents and children in their homes for two years.

The sample of children should accurately reflect the diversity of the larger population from which they were drawn. In other words, the children sampled should represent all socioeconomic, racial and ethnic, and dialectal variations found in the total population, and in the same proportions found there. Other variables that may be important include size of family, birth order, presence of one or both parents in the home, presence of natural parents in the home, and amount of schooling. Some variables, such as socioeconomic status, may be difficult to determine, although parental education and employment seem to be important contributing factors. Mixed-race children may force the researcher to make decisions about racial self-identity that are not appropriate. Other variables, such as birth order, may be more important than more traditional variables, such as gender (Bennett-Kaster, 1988).

Research on the development of spoken language has focused largely on middle-class preschool children learning English. In contrast, lower-class children whose mothers have less education tend to be slower and less accurate than children of comparable age and vocabulary size whose mothers have more schooling. In general, these slower rates of language learning reflect children's disadvantaged backgrounds. This trend is also true for Latino preschool children learning Spanish as their first language (Hurtado, Marchman, & Fernald, 2007).

Characteristics of the tester, experimenter, or conversational partner are also important. In general, preschool children will perform better with a familiar adult. There is also some indication that children of color may perform better with adults with the same identity.

Some children found in the general population may be excluded when the study attempts to determine typical development. These may include children with known handicaps; bilingual children; twins, triplets, and other multiple births; and children in institutional care or full-time nursery school. Children may also be excluded who are likely to move during the course of the study or whose parents were deemed uncooperative or unreliable (Wells, 1985). For example, children with parents in the military are likely to move frequently, possibly prior to the completion of a longitudinal study. With each exclusion, the "normal" group becomes more restricted and, thus, less representative.

In order to draw group conclusions, subjects must be matched in some way. Although the most common way to group children is by age, such matching of subjects in language-development studies may be inappropriate (Pine & Lieven, 1990). Many language differences reflect developmental changes in other areas. Therefore, reliable age-independent measures of development, such as level of cognitive development, may be a better gauge of real developmental differences and may allow more appropriate comparisons of children's language development.

The problem of the appropriate amount of a child's language to sample becomes especially critical with low-incidence language features, such as passive sentences. Usually at least 100 utterances are needed in order to have an adequate sample, although the sample size depends on the purpose for which it is collected. High reliability on measures such as number of different words and mean utterance and sentence length in morphemes may require at least 175 complete and intelligible utterances (Gavin & Giles, 1996). Elements that occur less than once in 100 utterances may not occur within the typical sample of that length. In addition, a single occurrence is very weak evidence upon which to base an assumption that a child has acquired a linguistic feature. This assumption is strengthened, however, if a large proportion of the individuals being studied exhibit this linguistic element (Wells, 1985).

As mentioned, the amount of language collected will vary with the language feature being studied. Pragmatic aspects of language, which vary with the context, may require the inclusion of several contexts to provide an adequately varied sample. Such language uses as conversational openings, which occur only once in each conversation, would require varied contexts in order to enable a researcher to reach even tentative conclusions.

Resources such as personnel, time, and money are always limited. A researcher must decide on an appropriate sample size and an adequate level of analysis. In general, the larger the sample of children and/or speech, the fewer data it is possible to analyze. Conversely, the more detailed the analysis, the fewer children or the smaller the amount of speech it is possible to sample.

NATURALNESS AND REPRESENTATIVENESS OF THE DATA

Any sample should fulfill the twin requirements of naturalness and representativeness. Even testing should attempt to use familiar situations with a child in an attempt to meet these two requirements. A conversational sample will be more natural if the participants are free to move about and are uninhibited by the process of sample collection. A representative sample should include as many of the child's everyday experiences as possible. Unfortunately, little is known about the range and frequency of children's activities. To address this issue, Wells (1985) sampled randomly throughout the day for short periods.

Each day of collection, Wells collected 24 randomly scheduled samples of 90 seconds' duration each. Samples were scheduled so that four occurred within each of six equal time periods throughout the day. Eighteen of the 24 samples, totaling 27 minutes of recording, were needed for analysis. This allowed a possible 25% of the samples to be blank as a result of having been recorded while the child was beyond the range of the microphone. Two samples from each of the six time blocks were randomly chosen for transcription. After these had been transcribed, the process continued randomly with the remaining six samples until 120 intelligible utterances had been amassed. The remaining utterances were not transcribed for analysis. This procedure was followed once every three months for two years for each child.

As you can see, it is not always easy to obtain natural and representative language data. At least three potential factors may be problems. One problem is the *observer paradox*. Stated briefly, the absence of an observer may result in uninterpretable data, but the presence of an observer may influence the language obtained, so that it lacks spontaneity and naturalness.

The presence of an observer can also affect the type of sample collected. The behavior of the child and the conversational partner may be influenced by the presence of another person. For this reason, Wells (1985) collected samples on a tape recorder, with no observer present. The recorder was programmed to begin taping at randomly assigned times throughout the day. In contrast, Brown (1973) included two observers: one to keep a written transcript of the linguistic and nonlinguistic behaviors of the parent and child and the other to tend the tape recorder and to be a playmate for the child.

The absence of an observer may also complicate the process of determining the exact context of the language sample. At the end of each recording day, parents might be asked to identify contexts by the activity and participants present, although the reliability of such recalled information is doubtful (Wells, 1985). In addition, the immediate nonlinguistic context of each utterance cannot be reconstructed from audiotape alone. Digital audio and video recording may address this concern.

A second problem is a child's physical and emotional state at the time the information is collected. Usually, a child's caregiver is asked to comment on the typicalness of the child's performance.

A third problem relates to the context in which the sample is collected. Quantitative values—such as mean or average length of utterances (MLU) or the number of utterances within a given time, or the number of root words—vary widely across different communication situations and partners (Bornstein, Painter, & Park, 2002). For example, a play situation between a mother and child elicits more language than one in which a child plays alone. Productivity, or the amount of language, may be even more affected by a child's conversational partners than by different situations (Bornstein, Haynes, Painter, & Genevro, 2000).

Occasionally, information is collected in experimental or test-type situations. The rationale for collecting this type of data is that, through manipulation of the context, a linguist can obtain language features from a child that may not be elicited in conversation. Unfortunately, the language obtained is likely to be divorced from meaningful contexts in the child's experience and thus does not represent the child's use of language to communicate with familiar conversational partners in everyday contexts. Theoretically, the most representative sample should be elicited in the home for preschoolers and in the home or classroom for older children, with a parent, sibling, or teacher as the conversational partner.

Language samples should be representative in the two ways discussed previously. First, the population sample from which the language is collected should be representative of all aspects of the total population. Second, each child's language sample should be representative of his or her typical language performance. This is best ensured if the sample is collected in a variety of typical settings in which a child is engaged in everyday activities with his or her usual conversational partners.

COLLECTION PROCEDURES

Questions relative to collection of the language sample must of necessity concern the presence or absence of a researcher and the actual recording method. Wells (1985) attempted to minimize observer influences by having the child wear a microphone that transmitted to a tape recorder preprogrammed to record at frequent but irregular intervals throughout the day. Of course, there are problems with this process, such as the compactness and sensitivity of the microphone transmitter. In contrast, Brown (1973) used two researchers in the setting, while data were recorded on a tape recorder. This concern is somewhat addressed by the compactness of digital recording devices.

Several collection techniques exist, such as diary accounts, checklists, and parental reports, as well as direct and digitally recorded observation. The first three are alternatives to researcher observation and have been used effectively in the study of early semantic and morphologic growth (Marchman & Bates, 1994; Reznick & Goldfield, 1994). Such methods enable researchers to collect from more children because they are less time-consuming and have been pronounced reliable and valid while remaining highly representative (Marchman & Bates, 1994).

Electronic means of collection seem essential for microanalysis. Videorecording, while more intrusive, is better than audio alone, because it enables the researcher to observe the non-linguistic elements of the situation in addition to the linguistic elements. Although useful in some collecting, written transcription within the collection setting is the least desirable method for microanalysis. First, it is easy to miss short utterances. Second, it is nearly impossible to transcribe the language of both the child and the conversational partner because of the large number of utterances within a short period of time. Third, transcription within the conversational setting does not enable the researcher to return to a child's speech for missed or misinterpreted utterances.

The language sample should be transcribed from the recording as soon after it is collected as possible. Caregivers familiar with a child's language should be consulted to determine if the sample is typical of the child's performance.

Because transcription offers many opportunities for error, studies should ensure intra-transcriber reliability. This is not always easy to accomplish. Several factors contribute to transcription errors, including the type of speech sampled, the intelligibility of the child, the number of transcribers, the level of transcription comparison, and the experience of the transcriber(s) (Pye, Wilcox, & Siren, 1988). In general, the more defined the speech sampled, the better the intelligibility; the greater the number of transcribers, the larger the unit of comparison; and the more experienced the transcriber, the better the chance of having an accurate transcript. The type of speech sample may range from individual words to whole conversations. Larger units are more difficult to transcribe accurately. The use of more than one transcriber reduces the possibility of errors if the transcribers compare their transcriptions and resolve their differences in a consistent manner. Finally, lower levels of comparison, such as phonemes, increase the likelihood of error because of the precise nature of such units.

ANALYSIS PROCEDURES

Actual analysis may be ticklish, especially when trying to determine the bases for that analysis. For example, MLU is still the most common quantitative measure of language growth, although its value is questionable. In general, quantitative measures, such as numerical scores and MLU, are inadequate for describing language development in detail. Other quantitative values might include total number of words, number of words per clause, or clauses per sentence. Such values collapse data to a single figure. Breadth of behavior might be obtained by the number of different forms used by a child, such as number of different words and number of unique syntactic types (Hadley, 1999).

In contrast, qualitative research uses a variety of methods within natural situations or contexts to describe and interpret human communication. Given the interwoven character of communication and social interaction, it seems logical to study the two together. As a result, language is studied as a social tool used within the complex relationship of context and communication. Thus, qualitative research is holistic and emphasizes communication's synergistic nature.

By their nature, qualitative research methods change the units being studied. A single word or utterance cannot be analyzed as a separate entity but must be examined in the context of surrounding utterances, topics, or conversation or between partners.

It is also difficult to determine when a child or group of children actually knows or has mastered a language feature. The criteria for establishing that a child knows a word or a feature have not been preestablished. For example, with word knowledge, the researcher must have clear evidence that a child comprehends the word. In contrast, production criteria would probably be based on spontaneous use and consistent semantic intent. With young children, a researcher would also note consistent phonetic form and semantic intent, with decisions of knowledge not necessarily based on whether the form and meaning are related to an adult word.

Usually, mastery can be based on children using a feature in 90% of the obligatory locations or on 90% of the children using the feature consistently, but these percentages vary with individual researchers. Some researchers consider the average age for acquisition to be that point at which 50% of children use a language feature consistently. Of course, such measures are complicated by the complex nature of most language features and the extended period of time often needed for mastery. For example, forms such as correct use of *be* may take several years from first appearance to full, mature use.

An example of one real-life analysis difficulty may be illustrative. In a study of preschool pronoun development (Haas & Owens, 1985), a colleague and I were very surprised to find no errors in pronoun use in conversations among children even as young as 2. The children had adopted the rule *when in doubt, use a noun*. Thus, analysis that focused on pronouns only yielded no errors. When analysis expanded beyond pronouns, however, we found overuse of nouns.

Cross-Language Studies

Cross-language studies are usually undertaken in order to investigate universality, linguistic specificity, relative difficulty, or acquisitional principles (Berman, 1986). Studies of universality attempt to determine which aspects of language, such as nouns and verbs, appear in all languages.

One underlying question is the innateness and universality of linguistic processes. As you might imagine, Generativists are especially interested in this type of data.

Although yes/no questions are treated differently in different languages, the underlying processes may be universal. Positive questions, such as "Are you a dog?" are answered *yes* for a right or true proposition to express agreement and *no* for the opposite. In contrast, negative questions, such as "Aren't you a dog?" are answered in language-specific ways: as if the question is positive in English and Spanish, on the truthfulness or falseness in French and German, and on agreement or disagreement in Japanese, Chinese, Korean, and Navajo (Akiyama, 1992). In all of these languages, however, children begin as in English and Spanish, suggesting an underlying process exists.

Studies of linguistic specificity attempt to determine whether development is the result of universal cognitive development or unique linguistic knowledge. The development of spatial (location) and temporal (time) terms, for example, seems to be based on cognitive knowledge as well as on specific linguistic forms used to mark that knowledge. English uses *in* for containment and *on* for support. In contrast, Spanish uses *en* for both, and German uses *auf, an,* and *um* just for *on*. In Chalcatongo Mixtec, an Otomangucan language of Mexico, speakers use body parts for spatial terms, such as "The man is *animal-back* the house" for "The man is *on* the roof" and "The cat rug's *face*" for "The cat is *on* the rug" (Bowerman, 1993). While the concepts *in* and *on* seem very straightforward, linguistic expression differs greatly.

Relative difficulty studies look for language-development differences that may be explained by the ease or difficulty of learning structures and forms in different languages. For example, the passive sentence (e.g., *The boy was struck by the car*) form is very difficult in English and is mastered much later than the relatively easier form in Egyptian Arabic, Turkish, Sesotho, and Zulu (Demuth, 1990; Perera, 1994). These languages are very different from each other, a situation that raises many other questions. Unlike Turkish, for example, Sesotho, an African language, has a complex intonational system applied at the morphologic level (Demuth, 1993).

Finally, studies that investigate acquisitional principles try to find underlying language-learning strategies that children apply regardless of the language being acquired.

There are two basic methods of collecting cross-linguistic data. The first is to gather a range of studies completed in different languages, although these studies may differ in their aims and methods. While this method may be quicker, because the studies have already been completed, it may not be easy to draw conclusions from such a diverse collection. The second method is to use a similar design across subjects from different language groups. This method yields much more definitive data, with fewer complicating variables, but takes much more time and effort to organize, coordinate, and collect.

How can we compare language development across languages? MLU would vary with each language and with the inflectional or word-order nature of that language. Age comparisons ignore linguistic differences. Vocabulary greatly affects MLU, suggesting that vocabulary size might provide a better basis for crosslinguistic comparisons of grammatical development (Devescovi et al., 2005). In short, there is no one good method.

Conclusion

WITHIN THE LAST HALF CENTURY, linguists have proposed several theories of language acquisition. Over that time, many linguists did not adhere strictly to one theoretical construct but preferred to position themselves somewhere between. This apparent fence straddling reflects the complexity of language and language acquisition.

Complex topics such as language and language development require a great amount of study and research. If the data that result from such research are to be of value beyond the children from whom they were collected, researchers must consider a great variety of questions relative to the language features studied, the children selected, the amount of data, and the collection and analysis procedures. Describing child language development accurately is a difficult and time-consuming job.

Discussion

THERE IS MOST LIKELY a biological basis for language. Human brains are specialized for analyzing sequential information such as language. Language most likely reflects brain functioning.

An infant also has certain innate social and communicative abilities that enable the child to establish early communication with caregivers. In turn, these caregivers interact in such a way as to ensure the survival of the infant. It is within these interactions that the child is exposed to language, the source of the child's own language use.

From a well-established communication system and armed with certain cognitive skills, the infant begins to use the language of those around him or her. This language has many uses, most already established through gestures. In other words, the language is not just an imitation of the language that surrounds the child, but it also works for the child.

Without linguistic research, these data could not exist. Look at the references and you will get some idea of the range of this research. I have given you some of the issues in collection and analysis of linguistic data. Some of you may be interested in such research. We can always use new data, especially in other languages.

You may be interested in the research data collected by linguists and others who study child language. The Child Language Data Exchange System, or CHILDES, database contains information on child language, actual child language transcripts, and software tools for analysis. You can access this database at http://childes.psy.cmu.edu/.

Main Points

- Generativists or Nativists assume that children learn language with the aid of innate rules or principles related to the structure of human language.

- Generativists or Nativists characterize language as a set of abstract algebraic rules and a set of meaningful linguistic elements or words that children learn and then link back to language universals.

- Constructionists assume that children learn language from the input to which they are exposed using general brain processes.

- Constructionists believe language structure emerges from language use.

- Constructionists characterize language as a set of meaningful rules and a set of meaningful linguistic elements or words.

- Four goals of child language research are as follows:

  - To confirm general linguistic principles.

  - To discover principles of language development.

  - To clarify the relationship of language to development in other areas, such as cognition.

  - To provide a more or less theoretical description of language development.

- Research requires careful consideration of many variables including the method of data collection, sample size and variability, naturalness and representativeness of the data, and collection and analysis procedures.

- The goals of cross-language studies are as follows:

  - To determine what aspects of language are universal.

  - To determine whether development is the result of universal cognitive development or unique linguistic knowledge.

  - To identify underlying language-learning strategies.

Reflections

1. Explain the differences between the Generative/Nativist and Constructionist models of language with regard to the brain.

2. Explain the different ways in which a child is assumed to learn grammar in the Generative/Nativist and Constructionist theories.

3. Explain the two primary methods of data collection and the types of data generated by each.

4. Explain the way in which language sample and population sample size and variability affect the data collected.

5. Why are natural and representative language samples desired, and what are the potential problems that can interfere with collecting these types of samples?

6. How can the method of collection affect the language sample collected?

7. Discuss the issues related to analysis that may affect the results of language studies.

8. Discuss the primary areas of investigation undertaken in cross-language studies.

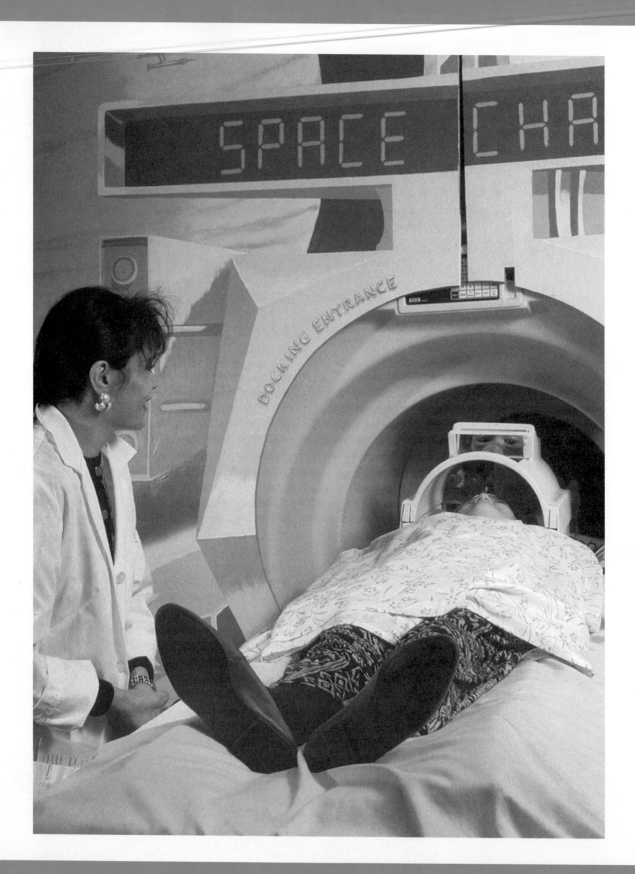

3

Neurological Bases of Speech and Language

OBJECTIVES

The brain is the only primary organ in the body concerned with processing linguistic information. The study of the manner and location of this processing is called **neurolinguistics.** In this chapter, you will learn about the structures and functions of the brain relative to language. When you have completed this chapter, you should understand

- Three basic brain functions.
- The major brain areas responsible for linguistic processing.
- The major theories of brain lateralization.
- The processes of language comprehension and production.
- The models that help explain linguistic processing.
- Information processing.
- The following terms:

angular gyrus	gyri	reticular formation
arcuate fasciculus	Heschl's area	sulci
Broca's area	information processing	supramarginal
central nervous	motor cortex	gyrus
system (CNS)	neurolinguistics	synapse
cerebrum	neuron	thalamus
corpus callosum	neuroscience	Theory of Mind
cortex	peripheral nervous	(ToM)
executive function	system	Wernicke's area
fissures	prefrontal cortex	working memory

Companion
Website

To listen to language samples related to chapter content and to peruse other enhanced study aids, please see the Companion Website at http://www.pearsonhighered.com/owens8e

Recently, I met a preschool child with whom I'd been acquainted previously. After we exchanged greetings, he eyed me suspiciously for several seconds. When I inquired if anything was wrong, he asked, "Do I remember you?" In our study of language, we might ask our brains the same question regarding incoming and outgoing messages because memory is a large portion of linguistic processing.

Neuroscience is the study of neuroanatomy or where structures are located and neurophysiology or how the brain functions. As sciences go, neuroscience is relatively new and relies extensively on the recent advances in neural or brain imaging. These include magnetic resonance imaging (MRI), positron emission tomography (PET), and computed tomography (CAT).

Neurolinguistics, as the name implies, is concerned with neurology and linguistics. More specifically, neurolinguistics is the study of the neuroanatomy, physiology, and biochemistry of language. Neurolinguists try to identify structures in the nervous system involved in language processing and to explain the process.

In this chapter, we will examine the main structures of the central nervous system, specifically those involved in processing language. We will also discuss the functioning of these structures and construct a model for language processing. Finally, we'll discuss two related topics, information processing and Theory of Mind.

Central Nervous System

Your nervous system consists of a brain, spinal cord, and all associated nerves and sense organs. The brain and spinal cord make up the **central nervous system** (CNS). Any neural tissue that exists outside the CNS is part of the **peripheral nervous system** (PNS), which conducts impulses either toward or away from the CNS. Nerves that conduct messages toward the brain are called *afferent* nerves and those that conduct information away are called *efferent* nerves. Your nervous system is responsible for monitoring your body's state by conducting messages from the senses and organs and responding to this information by conducting messages to the organs and muscles. These messages are transmitted through nerves.

Although we will concentrate on the CNS in this chapter, we should comment on the PNS before we move on. The PNS consists of 12 cranial and 31 spinal nerves that describe the location where these nerves articulate with or interact with the CNS. The cranial nerves are especially important for speech, language, and hearing and course between the brainstem and the face and neck.

The **neuron** or nerve cell is the basic unit of your nervous system. A nerve is a collection of neurons. There are approximately 100 billion neurons in your nervous system. Each neuron consists of three parts: a cell body, a single long *axon* that transmits impulses away from the cell body, and several branchy *dendrites* that receive impulses from other cells and transmit them to the cell body (see Figure 3.1). Axons vary greatly in length from 1 millimeter to 1 meter, a ratio of 1:1000. Neurons do not actually touch each other but are close enough to enable chemical-electrical impulses to "jump" the minuscule space, or **synapse,** between the axon of one neuron and the dendrites of the next. In short, the electrical charge of one neuron is changed by the release of neurotransmitters at its axon, which in turn affects the release of other neurotransmitters at the dendrite end of the second neuron. And it all happens instantaneously.

Most of your nervous system's neurons (approximately 85%) are concentrated in the CNS. At its lower end, your CNS contains the spinal cord, which transmits impulses between

FIGURE *3.1* **A Basic Neuron**

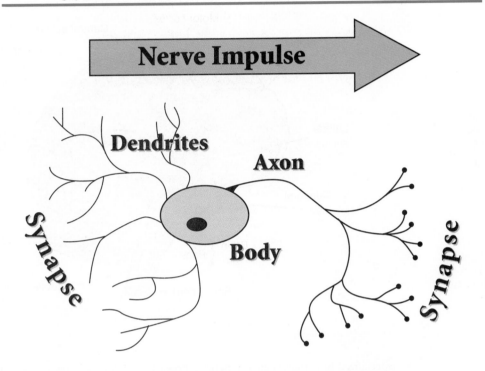

your brain and the peripheral nervous system. So important is the CNS to functioning that it is encased in bone and three membranous layers called the meninges. At the top of the spinal cord is the brainstem, consisting of the medulla oblongata, the pons, the thalamus, and the midbrain. These structures regulate involuntary functions, such as breathing and heart rate. Within the brainstem is a compact unit of neurons called the **reticular formation.** This body acts as an integrator of incoming auditory, visual, tactile, and other sensory inputs and as a filter to inhibit or facilitate sensory transmission. The **thalamus,** atop your brainstem, near the center of the brain, relays incoming sensory information (with the exception of smell) to the appropriate portion of the brain for analysis and prepares the brain to receive input. To the rear of the brainstem is the cerebellum, which controls equilibrium (Figure 3.2).

Primarily responsible for regulating motor and muscle activity by acting on the messages sent from "higher up," the cerebellum has little to do with the thought processes, analysis, and synthesis found in upper portions of the brain.

Atop the brainstem and the cerebellum is your **cerebrum** which is divided into left and right hemispheres. The largest portion of the brain, the cerebrum, weighs 40% of the brain's total. Most sensory and motor functions are *contralateral*, which means that each hemisphere is concerned with the opposite side of the body. With a few exceptions, the nerves from each side of the body cross to the opposite hemisphere somewhere along their course. Two exceptions to this crossover are vision and hearing. In vision, nerves from the left visual field of each eye, rather than from the left eye, pass to the right hemisphere, and those from the right visual field pass to the left hemisphere. Hearing is predominantly contralateral but not exclusively. More on this later. Your cerebral hemispheres are roughly symmetrical for most functions. For

FIGURE *3.2* *Schematic Lateral Surface of the Left Cerebral Hemisphere*

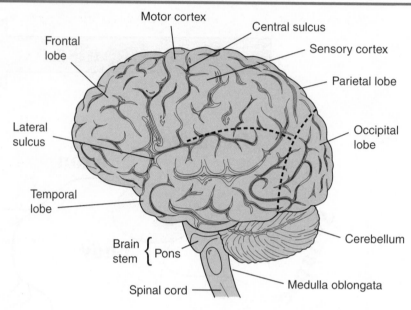

specialized functions, such as language, however, the hemispheres are asymmetrical, and processing is the primary responsibility of one or the other hemisphere.

Each hemisphere consists of white fibrous connective tracts covered by a gray **cortex** of primarily nerve cell bodies approximately one-fourth inch thick. The fiber tracts are of three types: association, projection, and transverse. Association fibers run between different areas within each hemisphere; projection fibers connect the cortex to the brainstem and below; and transverse fibers, as the name implies, connect the two hemispheres. The largest transverse tract is the **corpus callosum.** Your cortex has a wrinkled appearance caused by little hills called **gyri** and valleys called **fissures** or **sulci.** Each hemisphere is divided into four lobes labeled frontal, parietal, occipital, and temporal (Figure 3.2).

The central sulcus separates your frontal lobe from your parietal lobe. The most anterior or forward portion of the frontal lobe is called the **prefrontal cortex**, the newest portion of our brains to evolve. The prefrontal cortex is responsible for executive function, control, organization, and synthesis of sensory and motor information. **Executive function** tones or readies the brain and allocates resources and, as the name implies, is responsible, in part, for control over the entire operation. As in other mammals, large portions of your cortex are designated for sensory and motor functions. Immediately in front of the central sulcus is your **motor cortex,** a 2-centimeter-wide strip that controls motor movements. In general, the finer the movement, the larger the cortical area designated for it. In other words, your fingers have a proportionally greater cortical area devoted to motor control than does your trunk (Figure 3.3). Behind and parallel to the motor cortex and in the parietal lobe is your sensory cortex, which receives sensory input from your muscles, joints, bones, and skin. Other motor and sensory functions are found in specialized regions of your cortex. For example, the occipital lobe is primarily concerned with vision, and the temporal lobe processes auditory information. It is simplistic, however, to conceive of your brain as merely consisting of localized

FIGURE *3.3* **Schematic of Motor Cortex**

Parts of the body drawn to represent the portion of the motor cortex devoted to each.

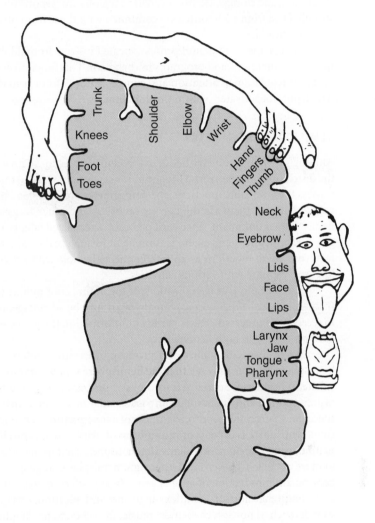

sensory and motor mechanisms because of the integration of sensory and motor information required for your body to function. Simply stated, your brain does not function based on separate, highly specialized areas. Rather, functions vary as portions of the brain interact (Frackowiak et al., 2004). In general, the higher or more complex the brain function, the more areas involved.

Three basic brain functions are regulation, processing, and formulation. The regulation function is responsible for the energy level and for the overall tone of your cortex. By maintaining the brain at a basic level of awareness and responsivity, this process, located in the reticular formation of the brainstem, aids the performance of the other two functions.

The individual thinker directs outcomes by both executive and self-regulating processes (Singer & Bashir, 1999). The executive function is a decision-making and planning control process through which you attend selectively, set goals, plan, and organize. The overlapping self-regulating process enables you to monitor, evaluate, and flexibly adjust behavior for successful performance.

The processing function, located in the rear of your cortex, controls information analysis, coding, and storage. Highly specialized regions are responsible for the processing of sensory stimuli. Data from each source are combined with those from other sensory sources for analysis and synthesis.

Finally, the formulation process, located in your frontal lobe, is responsible for the formation of intentions and programs for behavior. This function serves primarily to activate the brain for regulation of attention and concentration. Motor behaviors are planned and coordinated, but not activated, within this function.

HEMISPHERIC ASYMMETRY

Although there is symmetry between the hemispheres for many motor and sensory processes, the distribution of specialized functions is usually lateralized to one hemisphere. Although they possess these separate functions, the hemispheres are complementary, and information passes readily between them via the corpus callosum and other transverse bodies. Overall, neither hemisphere is dominant, since each possesses specialized talents and brings different skills to a given task. Neither hemisphere is competent to analyze data and program a response alone. In fact, your brain functions as an interconnected whole with activity throughout and differing levels of response with various activities.

Specialization, or lateralization, of the brain is not unique to humans, although the human brain may be the most asymmetrical. It may be advantageous for an organism to be able to receive and process a greater variety of information through specialization than to duplicate such processing in both hemispheres.

When a specific ability and primary processing centers are housed primarily in one hemisphere, we generally say that the hemisphere is *dominant* for that ability. The right hemisphere in humans is specialized for holistic processing through the simultaneous integration of information and is dominant in visuospatial processing, such as depth and orientation in space, and perception and recognition of faces, pictures, and photographs. In addition, the right hemisphere is capable of recognition of printed words but has difficulty decoding information using grapheme-phoneme (letter-sound) correspondence rules. (We'll discuss reading in more detail in Chapter 11.) Other right hemisphere language-related skills include comprehension and production of speech prosody and affect; metaphorical language and semantics; and comprehension of complex linguistic and ideational material and of environmental sounds, such as nonspeech sounds, music, melodies, tones, laughter, clicks, and buzzes. Interestingly, individuals who sign, whether deaf or hearing, have better memory for faces and objects than individuals who do not sign, suggesting that at least the visuospatial aspects of sign may be associated with the right hemisphere (Arnold & Murray, 1998). The left hemisphere is dominant for control of speech- and nonspeech-related oral movements and for mathematics and language processing.

The right hemisphere may play a role in some aspects of pragmatics, including the perception and expression of emotion in language, the ability to understand jokes, irony, and figurative language, and the ability to produce and comprehend coherent discourse (Joanette & Brownell, 1990). These aspects of language processing are especially difficult for adults with right-hemisphere injury. This data may not be specific for language because the right hemisphere also plays a greater role in processing emotion in nonverbal contexts and may represent more general information-processing differences between the two hemispheres.

In almost all humans, the left hemisphere is specialized for language in all modalities (oral, visual, and written), linear order perception, arithmetic calculations, and logical reasoning. Whereas the right hemisphere engages in holistic interpretation, the left is best at step-by-step processing. As such, the left hemisphere is adept at perceiving rapidly changing sequential information, such as the acoustic characteristics of phonemes in speech. Processing these phonemes for meaning, however, involves both hemispheres.

Not all human brains are organized as described. In general, almost all right-handers and approximately 60% of left-handers are left-hemisphere dominant for language. The remainder of left-handers, approximately 2% of the human population, are right-hemisphere dominant for language. A minuscule percentage of humans display bilateral linguistic performance, with no apparent dominant hemisphere. Thus, approximately 98% of humans are left-dominant for language. Women seem to be less left-dominant than men, having a slightly more even distribution between the hemispheres. In actuality, lateralization is probably a matter of degree, rather than the all-or-nothing patterns suggested.

BRAIN MATURATION

Language development is highly correlated with brain maturation and specialization. Whether this relationship is based on maturation of specific structures or on the development of particular cognitive abilities is unknown. (In Chapter 4 we'll discuss cognitive growth in the infant.) Two important aspects of brain maturation are weight and organization.

One overall index of neural development is gross brain weight, which changes most rapidly during the first two years of life, when the original weight of the brain at birth triples. Average brain weights are presented in Table 3.1. In addition, chemical changes occur and internal pathways become organized, connecting various portions of the brain. By age 12, the brain has usually reached its fully mature weight. The number of neurons does not change appreciably, but they increase in size as dendrites and axons grow to form a dense interconnected web. Disease, malnutrition, or sensory deprivation may result in less density and decreased functioning.

Most of the increase in functioning is the result of myelination, or the sheathing of the nervous system. In general, the myelined areas are the most fully developed and most rapidly transmit neural information. Myelination is controlled, in part, by sex-related hormones,

TABLE *3.1* *Gross Brain Weight of Child*

Age	Weight (Grams)	Percent of Adult Brain Weight
Birth	335	25
6 months	660	50
12 months	925	70
24 months	1065	80
5 years	1180	90
12 years	1320	100

Source: Information from Love & Webb (1986).

especially estrogen, which enhances the process. This fact may account for the more rapid early neurological development of girls. In general, sensory and motor tracts undergo myelination before higher functioning areas.

The brain is not simply growing. Microscopic "connections" are being made. Genes determine the basic wiring, and approximately half of the 80,000 genes in your cells are involved in the formation and operation of the CNS. It is experience, however, that determines the pathways. In the first month of life, synaptic firings may increase fifty-fold to over one thousand trillion. Use of these neural pathways stimulates and strengthens them, making subsequent use more efficient.

Language Processing

It is extremely difficult to identify the spot where language and speech reside in your brain. Processing areas often overlap. We are on safer ground to state that language is a complex process performed by many different interconnected areas of the brain, rather than located in a single area (Bates, 1997). The brain functions holistically, not as separate, individualistic, isolated units, and few operations are accomplished by one portion acting alone.

Recent advances in brain imaging have enabled researchers to monitor cerebral blood flow while a subject is conducting specific linguistic tasks (Raichle, 1994). Such online or "real-time" studies have helped researchers realize that linguistic processing, such as word retrieval and word and sentence comprehension, often relies on contributions from differing areas of the brain.

Position emission tomography (PET), a brain-imaging technique, has identified several regions of the brain that are active during speech-sound processing (Poeppel, 1996). Although there is greater activation in the left hemisphere during both perception and production, some right-hemisphere involvement also occurs (Toga, Frackowiak, & Mazziotta, 1996). In general, the frontal and temporal lobes are also more active than other regions in both perception and production, but there is no evidence for a single phonological processing center used in all phonological processing tasks (Bates, 1997).

The left insula, an area of cortex between temporal and frontal lobes, is found to be most active in speech production. The function of the insula is not fully understood, although it appears to be particularly important in motor feedback from the articulators. As in perception, there does not seem to be a speech production center. Even areas of the frontal lobe important for speech production are not speech-specific, but also participate in nonspeech tasks (Erhard, Kato, Strick, & Ugurbil, 1996). As a result, brain imagery results have fostered a theoretical move away from processing models based on exclusive sensory input and motor output channels of language processing (Goodglass & Wingfield, 1998).

In the 1960s and 1970s, many linguists assumed that language comprehension and production was linear in nature with processing proceeding in a sequential fashion. For example, comprehension was assumed to flow as follows:

$$phonetic \rightarrow phonological \rightarrow grammatical \rightarrow semantic$$

Production ran in the opposite direction. In other words, each process is unidirectional, and information from supposedly later analysis cannot influence the processing. For example, it does seem feasible that words would be selected independently of sentence frames and then put together like cars in a train. Research has demonstrated, however, that context can penetrate the earliest stages of word identification in comprehension and that speech sounds can affect sentence formation in production.

A more accurate representation of the comprehension process would be as follows:

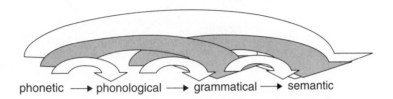

phonetic ⟶ phonological ⟶ grammatical ⟶ semantic

Linguistic processing, both comprehension and production, depends on your lexicon or personal dictionary of stored words and high usage phrases and on your stored linguistic rules. The systems for comprehension and production overlap partially. Brain-imaging techniques indicate that within-word perception occurs bilaterally in the posterior temporal lobe and that this area in the left hemisphere is also associated with both comprehension and production (Hickok, 2001).

Many parts of the brain are active in language processing. In addition, the number and location of these activated regions differ across individuals and vary with the task, based on the type of input and output, amount and kind of memory required, the relative level of difficulty and familiarity, attentional demands, and competition from other tasks. Although there is little evidence of a unitary language-processing area, some areas do seem to be more important than others, especially the frontal and temporal regions of the left hemisphere.

LANGUAGE COMPREHENSION

Comprehension consists of auditory processing and language decoding and involves many areas of the brain working together. Auditory processing is concerned with the nature of the incoming auditory signal, whereas decoding considers representational meaning and the underlying concepts. Processing begins with attending to incoming stimuli. Because it has a limited capacity to process incoming data, your brain must allocate this capacity by focusing its attention on certain stimuli while ignoring or inhibiting others. Think about what happens when you attend to someone talking to you while the TV is blaring in the background.

Auditory signals received in the brainstem are relayed to an area of each auditory cortex called **Heschl's area** or gyrus (Figure 3.4). Sixty percent of the signal is received at Heschl's gyrus from the ear on the opposite side of the body. Heschl's gyrus and the surrounding auditory areas separate the incoming information, differentiating significant linguistic information from nonsignificant noise. Linguistic information receives further processing. Linguistic input is sent to the left temporal lobe for processing, while paralinguistic input (intonation, stress, rhythm, rate) is directed to the right temporal lobe. Initial phonological analysis begins in Heschl's area and continues further along in the process (Frackowiak et al., 2004). Figure 3.5 presents receptive linguistic processing.

Although linguistic analysis is nearly instantaneous, long units such as sentences require the aid of memory in which the incoming information is held while analysis is accomplished. Called auditory working memory, it is most likely located in or near Broca's area in the left frontal lobe (Caplan, 2001; Fiebach, Schlesewsky, & Friedrici, 2001; Newman, Bavelier, & Neville, 2001). In addition, Broca's area may be responsible for your brain's attending to syntax, processing

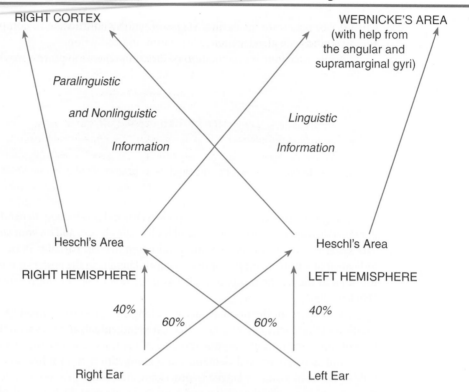

FIGURE 3.4 *Following the Path of Receptive Processing*

RIGHT CORTEX

WERNICKE'S AREA
(with help from
the angular and
supramarginal gyri)

Paralinguistic

and Nonlinguistic

Information

Linguistic

Information

Heschl's Area

Heschl's Area

RIGHT HEMISPHERE

LEFT HEMISPHERE

40%

40%

60%

60%

Right Ear

Left Ear

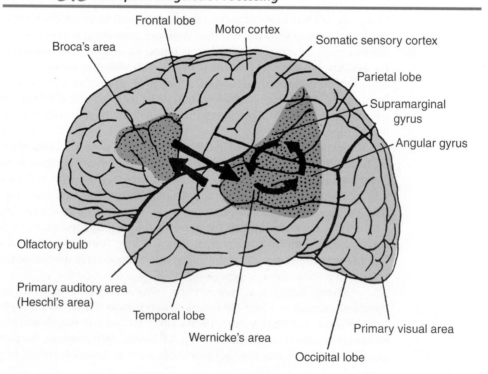

FIGURE 3.5 *Receptive Linguistic Processing*

Frontal lobe

Motor cortex

Broca's area

Somatic sensory cortex

Parietal lobe

Supramarginal
gyrus

Angular gyrus

Olfactory bulb

Primary auditory area
(Heschl's area)

Temporal lobe

Wernicke's area

Primary visual area

Occipital lobe

discrete units, such as single words or phrases, and further analysis of the phonological information passed along by Heschl's area.

While held in working memory, incoming information undergoes linguistic analysis in **Wernicke's area,** located in the left temporal lobe (Figure 3.5). Phonological and syntactic analysis is completed. All linguistic processing takes reasoning and planning, involving executive functions found in the frontal lobe (Bookheimer, 2002). Interestingly, well-rehearsed, automatic speech (*How ya doin'?*) seems to be processed and stored in the right hemisphere as whole units (Glezerman & Balkoski, 1999), freeing the left hemisphere for more complex analysis.

The **angular gyrus** and the **supramarginal gyrus** assist in linguistic processing, integrating visual, auditory, and tactile information with linguistic. The importance of these gyri and of multimodality input may be indicated by the relatively late myelination of these areas, occurring in adulthood, often after age 30. Although their functioning is not totally understood, the angular gyrus aids word recall, and the supramarginal gyrus is involved in processing longer syntactic units, such as sentences.

Written input is received in the visual cortex and transferred to the angular gyrus, where it may be integrated with auditory input. This information is then transmitted to Wernicke's area for analysis.

Semantic analysis of the now decoded message is distributed across the brain. The frontal lobe directs the process and evaluates the information coming from Wernicke's area where the semantic processing actually occurs. The right hemisphere is also involved in interpretation of figurative and abstract language processing in areas roughly corresponding to Broca's and Wernicke's areas (Bookheimer, 2002). Figurative language (Chapter 10) is non-literal as in *My dad hit the roof.* Abstract language represent ideas, intangibles, and concepts such as *beauty* and *love*.

Limited word-recognition and semantic decoding also occurs in the right hemisphere in addition to paralinguistic processing mentioned previously (Friederici, 2001; Goodglass, Lindfield, & Alexander, 2000). In addition, the right hemisphere may also work to suppress ambiguous or incompatible interpretations (Tompkins, Lehman-Blake, Baumgaertner, & Fassbinder, 2001).

Obviously, analysis for comprehension depends on memory storage of both words and concepts. The store of word meanings required for semantic interpretation is diffusely located, centered primarily in the temporal lobe, although conceptual memory is stored throughout the cortex. Prior to storage, incoming information is transmitted to the *hippocampus* in the left temporal lobe for consolidation.

Finally, pragmatic analysis involves the frontal lobe and integration of paralinguistic information from the right hemisphere. This includes executive function but also social awareness and reading intent.

Although your brain processes sequences of speech sounds approximately seven times faster than non-speech sounds, the speed of linguistic analysis varies with the linguistic and nonlinguistic complexity of the information and the speed of the incoming information. Each incoming message is processing at both a conversation-meaning and lexical-syntactic level with the conversational-meaning process given the very slight advantage of being activated milliseconds before the other (Brown, van Berkum, & Hagoort, 2000).

Let's take a look at sentence processing and different neurological mechanisms at work with two similar sentences. "Ann bumped into Kathy and fell over," in which it is assumed by most listeners that Ann fell, is processed much more rapidly than "Ann bumped into Kathy and she fell over," in which *she* is in doubt. If we measure brain activity using event-related potentials (ERPs), a measure of the electrical activity generated by the brain, we'll find that the first sentence is processed in a section of the brain used for syntactic processing and near Wernicke's area, while the second is processed in the parietal to right occipital area, used in semantic processing (Streb, Hemighausen, & Rösler, 2004).

*N*eurological impairment may require that a person find other means of communication.

LANGUAGE PRODUCTION

When we look at production, we find the same areas of the brain involved in integrated preparation and production of outgoing messages. Many functions are similar, although Broca's area is also responsible for programming the motor strip for speech. This suggests that motor production of speech may be important in development of phonological analysis (Bookheimer, 2002).

Production processes are located in the same general area of the brain as comprehension functions. The conceptual basis of a message forms in one of the many memory areas of the cortex. The underlying structure of the message is organized in Wernicke's area; the message is then transmitted through the **arcuate fasciculus,** a white fibrous tract underlying the angular gyrus, to **Broca's area,** in the frontal lobe (Figure 3.6). Like a computer, Broca's area is responsible for detailing and coordinating the programming for verbalizing the message. Signals are then passed to the regions of the motor cortex that activate the muscles responsible for respiration, phonation, resonation, and articulation.

The message is conceived abstractly and given specific form as it passes through the arcuate fasciculus. Writing follows a similar pathway, passing from Wernicke's area to the angular and supramarginal gyri. From here the message passes to an area similar to Broca's called *Exner's area* for activation of the muscles used for writing.

Using functional magnetic resonance imaging (fMRI) while participants either imitate or observe speech movements, researchers have found a common neural area for both tasks (Fridriksson et al., 2009). The greatest frontal lobe activity is in Broca's area in both tasks. Relatively less activity was observed in the left anterior insula, an area suggested to be important. While part of the cortex, the insula, are more interior to the brain as seen in Figure 3.7 on page 70. It would appear the cortical areas involved in the execution of speech movements are also used in the perception of the same movements in other speakers (Paulesu et al., 2003; Skipper, Nusbaum, & Small, 2005). In this way, portions of Broca's area support the auditory

FIGURE 3.6 *Productive Linguistic Processing*

Messages are transmitted from Wernicke's area to Broca's area via the white fibrous tract of the arcuate fasciculus.

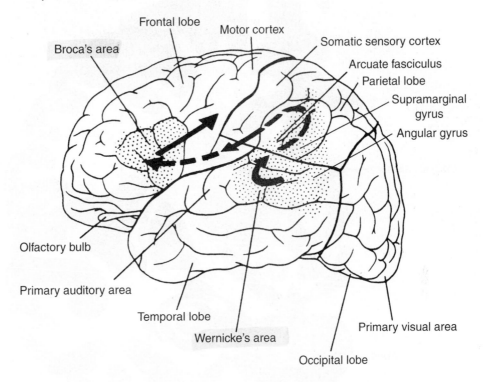

perception of speech. Interestingly, there is a right hemisphere area analogous to Broca's area which is also activated in both tasks, although at this time, its role is unclear.

Damage to any of these areas results in disruption of linguistic production, but with different effects. Injury to Wernicke's area usually disrupts both expressive and receptive language abilities. If damage occurs to the arcuate fasciculus, speech is unaffected except for repetitive movements, but the resultant speech may not make sense. Finally, damage to Broca's area results in speech difficulties, but writing and language comprehension may be relatively unaffected.

The actual processes are much more complex than our quick description suggests. Many areas have multiple or as yet unknown functions. Several models of brain functioning have attempted to fill this need.

MODELS OF LINGUISTIC PROCESSING

Several models help explain how cognitive processing in general and specific language processing occurs. The model that actually applies varies, depending on the task and the individual language user.

First, we should distinguish between structures and control processes. Structures are the fixed anatomical and physiological features of your CNS. Structures and their functions are

FIGURE *3.7* *Schematic of Left Insula*

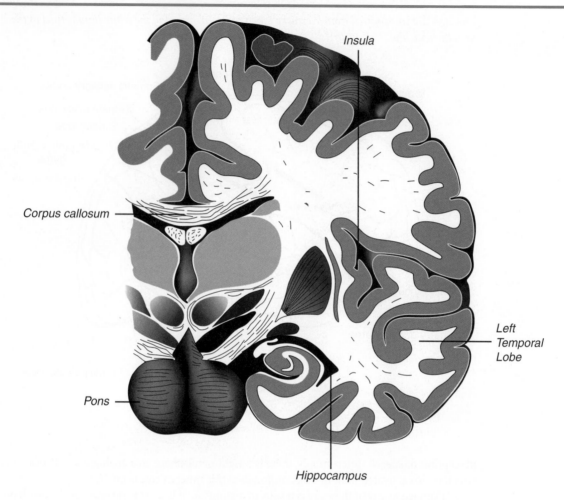

similar across most healthy brains. How these structures organize, analyze, and synthesize incoming linguistic information varies with the individual and with the task involved. The way information is processed represents the voluntary problem-solving strategies of each person, called **information processing**.

Information Processing

While the structures of your CNS probably vary little from mine, processes for dealing with incoming stimuli and formulating outgoing responses are more individualized. Although the exact nature of these cognitive processes is unknown, there is a relationship between measured intelligence and the speed of such information processing.

Qualitative differences may reflect operational or processing differences. For example, there may be differences between the automatic and effortful processing abilities. Automatic processes are those that are unintentional or that have become routinized and thus require very little of the available cognitive capacity. Automatic processing neither interferes with other tasks nor becomes more efficient with practice. Effortful processing, on the other hand, requires concentration and attention by your brain. For some, effortful processing is slower to develop and requires greater effort.

Both thought and language are processed by your brain's information processing system. This system includes cognitive processes involved in attention, perception, organization, memory, concept formation, problem-solving and transfer, and management or executive function (Groome, 1999) (Figure 3.8). Comprehension of a sentence involves integration of all these processes.

Attention Attention includes both awareness of a learning situation and active cognitive processing. As in Figure 3.8, the individual does not attend to all stimuli, thus stimulus D does not proceed. Attending can be divided into orientation and reaction. *Orientation* is the ability to sustain attention over time. Humans attend best when motivated and are especially attracted by high-intensity stimuli that are moving or undergoing change. In part, orientation is related to the individual's ability to determine the uniqueness of the stimulus. *Reaction* refers to the amount of time required for an individual to respond to a stimulus. In part, reaction time is a function of the individual's ability to select the relevant dimensions of a task to which to respond.

FIGURE *3.8* **Information-Processing Model**

Information processing contains the four steps of attention, discrimination, organization, and memory. The process is overseen by the Executive Function.

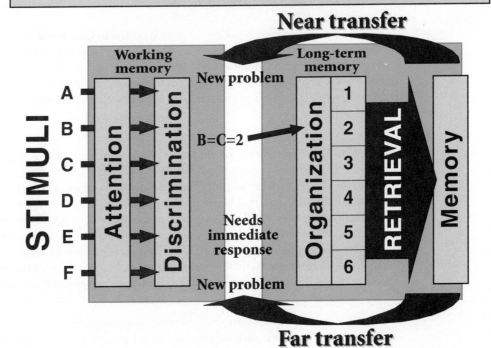

In general, less mature individuals are less efficient at attention allocation and have a more limited attentional capacity. These processes are relatively automatic for more mature individuals and require only minimal allocation of the available resources of the brain. Thus, children must allocate more of the limited resources of the brain at this level, leaving fewer resources available for higher level processes.

Discrimination   Discrimination is the ability to identify stimuli differing along some dimension. If an individual cannot identify the relevant characteristics, she or he will have difficulty comparing the new input with stored information. For example, in Figure 3.7, the brain decides that stimuli A and F are new problems. Stimuli B and C are similar and will be stored in bin 2. Finally, stimulus E demands an immediate response and the brain does so accordingly.

Discrimination, especially for language decoding, requires a special type of memory, called **working memory,** that holds the message during processing. Imagine trying to analyze a sentence if the first part has begun to fade from memory before the latter parts have been processed. Speech is fleeting. Once something is said, it disappears. Therefore, it is very important for decoding of spoken language that your brain be able to hold what was heard when it is no longer present. While held in working memory, a sentence can be scanned for words in your lexical storage and for syntactic structure and overall meaning. As with any task, each new sentence is not approached by the brain as a totally new problem; rather, linguistic experience seems to aid memory (Roberts & Gibson, 2002).

Working memory is involved in both processing and storage of information. Most likely, working memory consists of several related systems for language processing under the control of a central executive. The executive function supervises the organization and control of communication between the various systems and components. Other systems may include memory buffers for phonologic, semantic, and syntactic information that determine meaning and assign and analyze syntactic structure (Waters & Caplan, 2004). For example, the phonological buffer stores phonological information and allows for silent rehearsal prior to speaking (Baddeley, 1992, 2000).

As you might imagine, working memory is central to spoken and written language comprehension and to language acquisition and processing. Linguistic information is integrated and ambiguity resolved (Salthouse, 1990). As young children learn language, they rely on working memory to hold sentences during analysis to discover the linguistic properties. Among mature language users, verbal working memory allows synthesis and analysis with longer, more complex sentences.

Organization   The organization of incoming sensory information is important for later retrieval. Information is organized or "chunked" by category. Poor organization will quickly overload the storage capacity of your brain and hinder memory. It is theorized that memory capacity is fixed and, thus, that better memory results from better organization. The lack of chunking hinders later recall, because it is more difficult to remember unrelated bits of information. Two organizational strategies seem to predominate, mediational and associative. In mediational strategies, a symbol forms a link to some information. For example, an image might facilitate recall of an event. In associative strategies, one symbol is linked to another, as in such common linkages as "men and women" or "pins and needles."

Memory   Recall or memory is your ability to recall information that has been previously learned and stored. After linguistic analysis, information is forwarded for elaboration and association with other information. This organized information is then moved to more permanent storage via short-term memory (Groome, 1999). In the process, linguistic information is coded for both storage and retrieval. It is unclear whether each of the components of language—syntax, morphology, phonology, semantics, and pragmatics—has its own separate memory system for processing incoming and outgoing information.

Short-term memory is very limited, and most adults can hold fewer than ten items simultaneously (Baddeley, 1986). An incoming information is either discarded or held in short-term memory and rehearsed for more durable long-term memory.

Information is retained in long-term memory by rehearsal or repetition and organization. Encoding of information affects ease of retrieval. Memory is best when linguistic information is deep processed, which includes semantic interpretation and elaboration and relating to your prior experience and existing knowledge. Words may be stored in various locations based on meaning, word class, sound pattern, and various associational categories.

Every stimulus event has both a sensory impression or signal, which is inherent in the event, and an abstract or symbolic representation for that event. The signal is meaningful but nonlinguistic. For example, the sound of an engine may signal an automobile. In contrast, the abstract representation or word is linguistic in nature. Word retrieval from memory seems to proceed from semantic to phonological. In other words, the concept of the word is retrieved before the sound structure (Cutting & Ferriera, 1999).

Problem-Solving and Transfer Transfer or generalization is the ability to apply previously learned material in solving similar but novel problems. The greater the similarity between the two, the greater the transfer. When the two are very similar, generalization is called *near transfer*. When very dissimilar, it is called *far transfer*.

Other Processing

In addition to the steps in information processing, there are differing levels of processing. Explanations of these levels can help us understand linguistic processing and include *top-down/bottom-up*, *passive/active*, and *serial/parallel* processes.

Top-Down/Bottom-Up Processing At its most basic, "top" and "bottom" levels of cognitive processing exist. The bottom level is a somewhat shallow analysis of perceptual data that makes few demands on the brain. In contrast, top levels of processing include extraction and synthesis. These processes make higher demands on cognitive resources (Groome, 1999). Top-down and bottom-up processing differ with the level of informational input. Top-down processing is *conceptually driven,* or affected by your expectations concerning incoming information. In this way, the linguistic and nonlinguistic contexts enable you to predict the form and content of incoming linguistic information. Knowledge, both cognitive and semantic, is used to cue lower order functions to search for particular information. For example, when we hear "The cat caught a . . . ," we predict the next word. The initial syllable of the word may be all that is needed for confirmation (Gow & Gordon, 1993). The prediction is not confirmed when analysis indicates that the incoming information doesn't fit. At this point the system returns to the stimuli or data for reanalysis and interpretation.

Bottom-up processing is *data driven.* Analysis occurs at the levels of sound and syllable discrimination and proceeds upward to recognition and comprehension. For example, analysis of the word *mouse* would begin at the phoneme level with /m aʊ s/. Partially analyzed data from the perceptual level are passed upward and integrated with predictions from higher levels, which are moving down. Most likely, the two processes occur simultaneously in this way or are used for particular tasks.

Depending on the context, you may use both strategies simultaneously or rely more on one strategy. Incoming speech may be misinterpreted when a listener relies too heavily on words stored in his or her memory rather than on the incoming information. In one example, a small child on his first Halloween had been instructed to say the traditional "Trick or treat," his first exposure to these words. His parents were very surprised at the first house when he shouted "Chicken feet!" (Snyder, Dabasinskas, & O'Connor, 2002, p. 4.)

Passive/Active Processing   Passive and active processing are based on recognizing patterns of incoming information. In passive processing, incoming data are analyzed in fragments until enough information can be combined for you to recognize a pattern. This method is similar to bottom-up processing. The contrasting active process involves the use of a comparator strategy that matches input with either a previously stored or a generated pattern or mental model. World knowledge forms a basis. This model forms gradually from active engagement with the environment and helps each of us make sense of the world, anticipate or predict, and plan. In actual practice, both processes probably occur simultaneously.

Serial/Parallel Processing   The information-processing system can handle more than one task at a time. The different levels of processing may proceed either simultaneously and in parallel with each other or sequentially in a series of separate, autonomous processes (Pashler, 1997).

Processing varies with the speed and volume of information flow. Serial, or successive, processes are one-at-a-time in nature. Located in the left frontal and temporal lobes, successive processes analyze information at one level and then pass it on to the next level. For example, the incoming frequency, intensity, and duration of a signal are synthesized to determine the phonemic features. These features are bundled into phonemic characteristics, then syllables, words, and so on until the message is understood.

Parallel, or simultaneous, processing accesses multiple levels of analysis at the same time. Located in the occipital and parietal association areas and possibly in the right hemisphere, simultaneous processing deals with underlying meaning and relationships all at once.

In practice, the two processes occur together, with overall comprehension dependent on the one that most efficiently processes incoming information or outgoing signals. Although successive processing is more precise, it necessarily takes more of the brain's processing potential and is relatively slow. It is therefore quickly overwhelmed, so simultaneous processing must carry the bulk of the responsibility for comprehension. When the incoming rate slows, successive processing takes over again.

Imagine that your brain is writing out each message that enters, in the way you do when taking notes. If the lecturer goes slowly over important points, you can write every word or process successively. Since this situation is rare, however, you usually scramble to summarize what the lecturer has said, recording the overall meaning of the information. This situation is similar to the two functions of successive and simultaneous processing respectively.

Interestingly, signing, unlike speech, has a greater capacity to express information simultaneously (Emmorey, 1993). Although signs take longer to produce than words, only a minimal portion is needed to identify a sign. The visual nature of signs provides greater initial information, and few signs have similar initial shapes. Thus, confirmation is more rapid for signs than words.

*P*reschool children by about age 4 recognize that other people can have their own different knowledge and beliefs.

A LIMITED SYSTEM AND EXECUTIVE FUNCTION

The ability to process information is not limitless. In fact, only certain amounts of information can be analyzed and synthesized. This is seen when we multitask. Although it's relatively easy to hold a conversation while walking, it may be very difficult to receive and comprehend directions to a friend's house on your cell phone while typing an email. Language processing may be limited by the amount of incoming and stored language data, the demands of the task, and your available cognitive resources (Ellis Weismer & Hesketh, 1996; Just & Carpenter, 1992). As in any system, overloads decrease efficiency.

Overseeing the processing system is the brain's central executive or executive function that allocates and coordinates mental resources. Executive function determines cognitive strategies and activities needed for a task and monitors feedback and outcomes in order to reallocate resources if necessary.

Metacognition, or your knowledge of your own cognitive and memory processes, can facilitate encoding and retrieval and the use of problem-solving strategies. Decisions to execute these processes help you to manage their use and guide attending; to make decisions to attempt, continue, or abandon; and to monitor progress.

Theory of Mind

We have been discussing the brain, a physical structure that has both anatomical and physiological characteristics. In simple terms, we've been examining the equipment and how it works. This physical brain of yours is different from your mind, which includes your intellect and your consciousness. Words for the processes of your mind include thought, perception, memory, will, imagination, reason, and emotion. As you will see in the next chapter, your brain becomes functional during conception and the first few months of life. Development of your mind is a much longer process.

When you were born, you had no mental representations or images of anything in the outside world. In other words, objects that were not immediately available to your senses did not exist. This is why a young baby will not search for a toy when it is hidden, even right in front of her or him. From the infant's perspective, the toy no longer exists. The development of mental representations or images of objects is a gradual process that occurs throughout the first year of life as children interact with objects.

People, however, are not objects. People have consciousness. In addition to learning that like objects people have an independent existence, a child must learn that people have thoughts, beliefs, and feelings, and that these may or may not be the same as the child's. This knowledge is called **Theory of Mind (ToM).**

In this chapter, we have also discussed the processing of language. So far, however, we have focused on language form and content. What about intentions and their processing? That also involves Theory of Mind.

Although this may seem like double-talk, ToM is not a psychological theory like a theory of behavior (Eslea, 2002). ToM is the ability to understand the minds of other people and to comprehend and predict their behavior (Miller, 2006). It's called a theory because we can never really know someone else's mind; we can only guess, using our ToM to theorize what others know, think, or feel. In other words, we each theorize on the mind of other people. Did you ever say, "What could he have been thinking?" If so, you just verbalized Theory of Mind. ToM is not a single, unitary concept. Rather, it consists of several kinds of knowledge and skills (Miller, 2006).

So, how do we understand each other? We're only rarely explicitly aware. Instead, we use many signals to infer the intentions, desires, knowledge, and beliefs of others (Steen, 1997). In addition, we understand that these thoughts, states, and emotions of others are genuine and real for them, not just concepts. This inferential process is so automatic and so much a part of our comprehension and predictions about others that it only becomes obvious when something goes wrong.

Of interest for us is the relationship between linguistic abilities and the cognitive ability to understand others as intentional beings with their own beliefs and desires. After all, language provides us with a means for expressing and understanding meaning and intentionality. The relationship between ToM and language may be a dynamic one in which each contributes to the development of the other.

Although Theory of Mind may be an innate potential ability in humans, it requires social and interactional experience over several years to reach fully mature abilities. Even adults' abilities probably represent a continuum, varying from very complete and accurate to minimal. A mature ToM requires the ability to represent the emotions of others in a manner that differs from picking up these emotions directly (Steen, 1997).

In summary, Theory of Mind is concerned with the following:

- How brain activity produces the mind.
- How we gain an understanding that others also have minds.
- How we learn to recognize and form hypotheses about the different and separate beliefs, desires, mental states, and intentions in others.

We'll discuss more in the following chapters as we watch Theory of Mind develop in young children.

Conclusion

Language processing, both expressive and receptive, is located primarily in the left hemisphere of the brain in most adults. Anatomical differences between the hemispheres have been noted in the fetus, but specialization for language develops later in the maturing child. Although language-processing functions are situated anatomically within the brain, their exact location and function are not totally understood. The effects on these processes of past learning, problem-solving ability, memory, and language itself are also unclear. It is known, however, that cognition, or the ability to use the resources of the brain, is closely related to the overall language level of each individual.

When I was a child, we used to play "Button, button, who has the button," in which the child in the middle tried to guess which of the children in the circle around him or her held a button. Neurolinguistics can seem like this when we try to discern where language functions reside in the brain. Don't be troubled by the fact that functions may not be located exactly where we've said they are. The human brain is very flexible, and information is often storied in very diffuse areas.

Let's do a quick retracing. Comprehension goes from the ear to Heschl's area with 60% of the information crossing to the opposite hemisphere and 40% staying on the same side; then the two Heschl's areas divide linguistic from paralinguistic data, sending the linguistic to Wernicke's area in the left temporal lobe. Wernicke's area processes the linguistic information with aid from the angular and supramarginal gyri. What do they do? Easy to remember. *Supramarginal* starts with an "s," and so do *sequential* and *syntax*. The supramarginal gyrus processes units larger than words and the way they're joined together—syntax. The angular gyrus is left with word recall. Good!

Production is easier to remember. Wernicke's area formulates the message and sends it via the arcuate fasciculus to Broca's area in the frontal lobe. Broca's area is a computer that programs the motor strip, which in turn sends nerve impulses to the muscles of speech. Broca's area does not send nerve impulses directly to the muscles.

Just as the infant must learn to control its muscles, it must also learn to operate its brain. Different parts of the brain become more active during the first year and mature with myelination. As the child adds more and more information, he or she must learn to organize that information for access. Information processing helps us describe the process. For example, the child's lexicon, or personal dictionary, will eventually be organized by categories based on word meanings, rhymes, alliteration, opposites, and the like. With improved organization and repeated use, the brain's ability to remember increases, making greater language use possible.

Let me end with a granddaughter story of neurolinguistics. By the young age of 3½, Cassidy had discovered the usefulness of cognitive activity as a manipulative tool. She could sabotage any attempt to hurry her with "Waaaaaaaaaait, I'm thinking . . . I'm thinking." Although she may not have understood the process, she realized that those thoughts, ideas, and words came from somewhere.

Discussion

No discussion of neurolinguistics would be complete without the story of Alex, a young man born with a rare brain disorder known as Sturge-Weber syndrome, which resulted in seizure activity and severely limited blood supply to the left hemisphere of his brain

(Trudeau & Chadwick, 1997). As a result, the left hemisphere atrophied, while the right seemed normal. At age 8, when Alex's left hemisphere was removed as a last resort effort to stop his violent seizures, he was nonspeaking and seemingly unable to comprehend language.

Unexpectedly, at age 9, after recovery from surgery, Alex began to speak. Although at first beginning with single words and immature speech, his language began to grow rapidly. In a few months, Alex developed the language of a late preschooler. By age 16 and still improving, his language was equivalent to that of a 10- to 11-year-old.

The experience of Alex calls into question much that we have discussed in this chapter, in addition to the notion of a critical period or age—considered to be the preschool years—for language learning, after which such learning was believed to be extremely difficult. The brain of children is extremely "plastic," or malleable. In other words, functions such as language may be assumed by other areas of the brain whether in the course of normal development or as a result of injury.

As a practicing speech-language pathologist, educator, or psychologist, you will see many children with either brain injury or pathology. While it is important to know the area of injury, we cannot make assumptions about a client's language based on this information. Nor is the size of the damaged area directly related to the resultant deficits, if any. Nothing substitutes for a thorough assessment of speech, language, and communication. It is more important to thoroughly describe what a client can do than to be able to name the site of injury or to name the neurological condition.

Main Points

- It's difficult to pinpoint the neurological location of cognitive process. Most are diffusely located.

- The left temporal area is specialized for linguistic processing.

- Sound entering each ear is divided, and 60% crosses to Heschl's area on the other side of the brain while 40% is sent to Heschl's on the same side.

- Each Heschl's sends paralinguistic acoustic information to the right hemisphere and linguistic information to the left hemisphere.

- In the left hemisphere, incoming language is held briefly in Broca's area while processed by Wernicke's area with assistance from the supramarginal gyrus and the angular gyrus.

- Outgoing language is conceived in Wernicke's area, then transferred below the surface via the arcuate fasciculus to Broca's area, which programs the motor cortex to signal the muscles for speech.

- Information processing consists of four steps: attention, discrimination, organization, and memory.

- Theory of Mind is the gradually expanding ability to understand that other people have their own thoughts, beliefs, and feelings.

Reflections

1. Describe three basic brain functions: regulation, processing, and formulation. Explain how these functions, especially processing, relate to linguistic material.

2. In most humans the left hemisphere is dominant for linguistic processing. Can you name the major areas responsible for this processing?

3. Few theorists would argue with the notion of brain lateralization for language. Can you explain the major theories on how this lateralization occurs?

4. Explain briefly how language is processed relative to specific areas of the brain.

5. Describe information-processing theory and the several models of language comprehension and production processes associated with it.

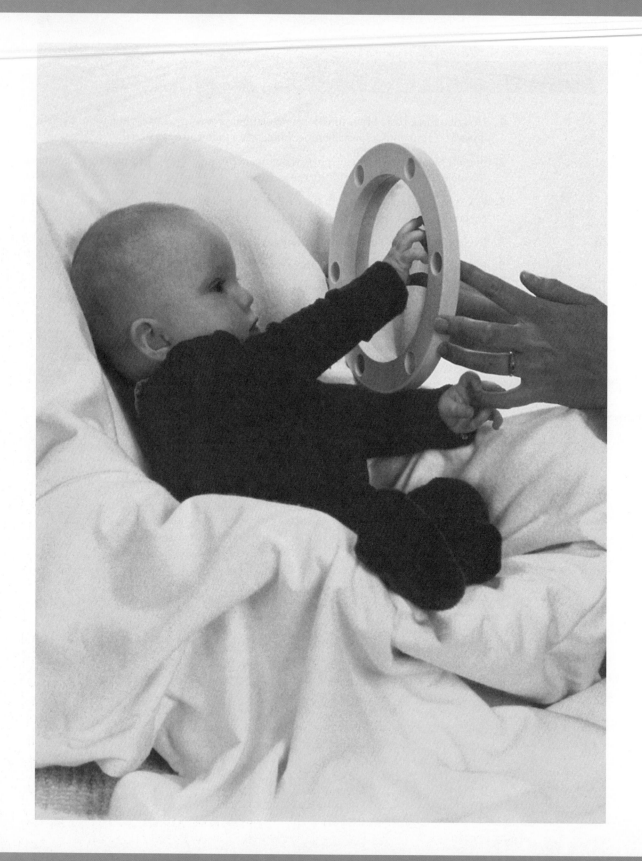

4

Cognitive, Perceptual, and Motor Bases of Early Language and Speech

OBJECTIVES

Congratulations, you've made it through the necessary background chapters. Now we're all using the same terms and are ready to begin discussing language development.

The use of symbols requires a certain level of cognitive or mental skill, as well as certain perceptual abilities and social and communication skills. Speech requires precise motor control. In this chapter, we shall explore both cognition and perception and relate them to the early development of symbols and speech. When you have completed this chapter, you should understand

- The relationship of cognition to language.
- The developmental characteristics of the sensory, perceptual, motor, and cognitive development.
- The sources of speech production.
- The major reflexes of the newborn relative to oral movement.
- The characteristics of babbling and reduplicated and variegated babbling.
- The aspects of the cognitive development that contribute to the ability to symbolize and represent.
- The contribution of memory and attention to early learning.
- The following terms:

accommodation	assimilation	echolalia
adaptation	babbling	equilibrium

To listen to language samples related to chapter content and to peruse other enhanced study aids, please see the Companion Website at www.pearsonhighered.com/owens8e

fully resonant nuclei (FRN)	organization	reduplicated babbling
habituation	phonetically consistent forms (PCFs)	reflexes
integrative rehearsal	phonotactic probability	rehearsal
jargon	phonotactic regularities	schemes
mental maps	quasi-resonant nuclei (QRN)	sensitive period
myelination		symbol
neonate		synaptogenesis
		variegated babbling

In the first three chapters, we touched on the relationship of cognition to language. Many (though not all) theorists would agree that the child's cognitive growth sets the pace for linguistic growth.

The purpose of this chapter is to examine early cognitive development for clues to the child's ability to use symbols and to speak. In addition, this chapter will add substance and developmental order to the cognitive information provided in Chapter 3.

An infant is not a passive creature but is actively engaged in his or her environment, organizing experiences into general classes and larger concepts. Of particular importance for students of language development is the means by which the child learns to represent and symbolize these ideas and concepts. The importance of this representational ability cannot be overemphasized. The ability to represent one thing with another is one of the most fundamental cognitive bases for language acquisition. For example, a child can use a piece of wood to represent a doll's chair. In a similar fashion, the word *chair* can also symbolize a chair.

In this chapter we will examine and try to explain early sensory, perceptual, motor, and cognitive development and their importance for language and speech development. Finally, we'll examine early learning. This developmental information and more are presented in Appendix C, Tables C.1 and C.2.

Neurological Development

The human brain seems wired for development of language, and most linguists agree that there is a biological basis for human language (Pinker, 1994). But biology alone is insufficient to explain the process. There is compelling evidence within brain maturation that suggests the importance of physiological changes within the infant for the development of language.

Brain development begins within 18 days of conception and continues for many years after birth. Although development begins early, the brain is one of the slowest organs to mature. Development is of two types, gross and micro. Gross development concerns the main neurological structures, while micro development is the organization of these structures.

All the brain's neurons are developed by the end of the second trimester—that's month six of pregnancy—but organization in the form of networks of neurons has barely begun. Initially, the brain overproduces neurons, and half or more are pruned back because they have not formed into networks. During the first six months of pregnancy, neurons multiply intensively. Beginning at about four months and continuing until birth, neurons migrate to form specialized areas of function. In the postnatal period, neurons experience *myelination* and *synaptogenesis,* or cells communicating with each other. Although physical brain organization is under genetic control, fetal development can be altered by environmental influences, such as maternal use of alcohol, nutrition, tobacco, and legal and illegal drugs; and disease, radiation, and toxins.

Cell differentiation within the brain of the fetus begins during the sixteenth week of gestation. During prenatal existence, growth occurs rapidly in the brainstem and in the primary motor and sensory cortices. After birth there is rapid growth in the cerebellum and in the cerebral hemispheres, especially in the visual receptor areas of the occipital lobe. The auditory receptor areas of the temporal lobes mature somewhat later than the visual receptor areas, possibly explaining the relatively early visual maturity of the infant compared to later-developing auditory maturity. The association tracts devoted to speech and language are relatively mature by late preschool, but some higher linguistic functioning areas are not fully mature until adulthood.

The primary anatomical asymmetry in the brain is found in the left temporal lobe. This area, enlarged even in the fetal brain, may account for the dominance of the left hemisphere in speech and language reception and production. This area continues to grow even larger in the mature brain and to myelinize at a slower rate than corresponding areas of the right hemisphere. The white fiber tract beneath the temporal lobe, called the *planum temporal,* is larger in the left hemisphere of about two-thirds of adults.

We don't know exactly when laterilization occurs. Lateralization of language in the left hemisphere may be progressive. In the infant brain, clear regions for specific abilities have not been delineated. A second and differing view holds that language may be fully lateralized from the start. Electrophysiological studies of infants have supported the idea that lateralization occurs long before the development of specific abilities. A third view assumes that much lateralization occurs during fetal development and that the environment contributes less to lateralization with age.

Whichever thesis we accept, there can be little disagreement on left-hemisphere dominance for most oral language processing in almost all adults. Let's explore the neural pathways and the processes involved.

When a baby is born, her or his brain is a jumble of neurons, many in stand-by, awaiting integration into something we call the mind. Although, thanks to genetics, some circuits or pathways are clearly defined at birth, others are waiting to establish their purpose through activation.

Even though approximately half of your genes—50,000 at last count—are concerned with the CNS, these only specify a tiny proportion of the pathways needed to be a fully functioning, thinking human. Activation of the brain means "connecting" neurons with other neurons by the firing of their synapses. You'll recall that neurons don't actually touch, but they do establish communication pathways or networks. Early experiences are crucial for most activation. The over 100 billion neurons will fire their synapses more than 100 trillion times by adulthood.

When these occur is extremely important. There appear to be both developmental and age limits on the brain's ability to create itself. Sensory areas mature in early childhood, while higher reasoning and language processing areas take until early adulthood. How do we know?

Thanks to the new imaging techniques mentioned in Chapter 3, researchers are now able to map brain activity as it occurs or "online" and also to follow infant development as different portions of the brain "turn on" or become more active with maturation. A correlation exists between neurological areas becoming active and cognitive functions known to reside in those areas.

Genes roughly determine where functions—such as hearing processing—will be located, but the fine details are determined by a baby's experiences. The sequence of brain activation is genetically programmed. The lower brain, tasked with basic bodily functioning, such as breathing, activates first. The cerebellum and basal ganglia, which control movement, are next.

At around two months of age, the motor cortex in the frontal lobe becomes more active. During this time, a child is gaining more control of volitional or voluntary motor behaviors, and many reflexive patterns are disappearing. Likewise, the visual cortex becomes more active at three months when a child gains a full-range focus, enabling her or him to focus on things close in or far distant. Activation of the limbic system, seat of emotion and memory, follows. The cerebral cortex where higher thinking resides is last.

During the second half of the first year, both the frontal cortex and the hippocampus, on the underside of the temporal lobe, become more active. This is not surprising given a child's increasing ability to remember stimuli and the initial associations between words and the entities to which they refer. In similar fashion, development of gestures, which require a child to plan for the desired response, appear at about eight months when the prefrontal cortex, responsible for forethought, becomes more active.

The experiences and interactions of an infant are helping him or her to organize the framework of the brain. Organization reflects experience. Incoming information changes the functioning of a baby's mind. A baby actively contributes to his or her own cognitive growth by observing, exploring, experimenting, and seeking information.

Early Cognitive Development

Theories of early cognitive development fall in and out of fashion. I shall try to weave my way through these explanations. From the preceding section, we recognize that various portions of the brain are becoming more active. I shall attempt to sketch how experiences influence cognitive development and aid brain organization.

It may be easiest to conceptualize development of the cognitive bases for language if we divide our discussion into four areas of development: sensation, perception, motor control, and cognition. We'll explore these areas in light of what we know about information processing from Chapter 3 and its four steps of attention, discrimination, organization, and memory. Then we'll finish by discussing early learning and the influence of cognition on early language development. Wow, that's a lot! So let's get started.

SENSATION

Sensation is the ability to register sensory information. All senses are functioning at birth and have been for some time. As a newborn, you possessed an impressive array of motor and sensory skills.

Touch is the first sense to develop in utero. From sensitivity in various regions of the body at eight weeks, sensation spreads to the entire body by week 14. Most pregnant women report that by gently stroking their enlarged "tummies" they can calm the fetus within. Pain receptors are formed by the twenty-sixth week.

A fetus is also sensitive to sounds very early and will startle to both sounds and movement at eight weeks. The inner ear is formed by 20 weeks postconception, and a fetus's hearing is functional at this point. While in utero, a fetus is exposed to many auditory stimuli, especially the sound of the mother's voice (DeCasper & Spence, 1986). For most newborns, mom's voice is their preferred environmental sound.

The middle and inner ears reach their adult size at 20 weeks of fetal development and are ready to function at birth. The auditory cortex is not mature, however, and the middle ear is filled with fluid. The immaturity of the cortex and the lack of internal coordination of the brain's hemispheres make it difficult for a newborn to integrate sounds. In addition, the middle ear is not as sensitive to sound as it will be within two weeks after birth, when the fluid is absorbed.

We have less information on the other senses, although we do know that fetuses can sense sweet and noxious tastes in their amniotic fluid. Sense of smell must also be activated while in utero because after birth a newborn prefers the scent of her or his mother over other scents and will turn toward its own amniotic fluid. We're not sure when vision becomes active.

Babies make little change in their sensory abilities with birth. Rather, the change is in the quantity and quality of sensation. Babies seem to love new stimulation. Ever-changing sensory experiences "nourish" their minds.

Newborns or **neonates** have difficulty controlling attention or concentrating mental activity. Either they cannot direct it willfully or they are captured by sensory stimuli and have difficulty breaking free. This is important because increased or decreased attention to a stimulus corresponds to an increase or decrease in the ease of remembering that stimulus (Adler, Gerhardstein, & Rovee-Collier, 1998).

A neonate is somewhat at the mercy of sensations, although he or she can shut out visual images by closing the eyes or averting gaze. If the level of stimulation is too low, an infant loses interest quickly. Attention is captured more easily by moderate stimulation. At a moderate level of stimulus strength, an infant's attention is maintained longer and more frequently. As the stimulus strength increases, such as becoming louder, so does attention, until a point is attained at which stimulus strength reaches an infant's tolerance threshold. A child will then avert his or her face, become restless, or cry for assistance.

Many of an infant's behavior-state changes reflect internal changes or intrinsic brain activities. For example, during the first month of life, an infant is frequently asleep or drowsy. Even so, external stimuli can influence the duration of these states. An infant is most receptive to external stimuli when alert but not overly active. Thus, the ability to attend is influenced by an infant's internal state. This changes quickly, and, within a few months, the level of external stimulation is a greater determinant of attending than an infant's state. By that time an infant is capable of maintaining a rather stable internal condition.

By 2 months of age an infant exhibits selective attending skills and can remain unresponsive to some background stimulus events. When presented with a stimulus repeatedly, an infant will react less strongly to each successive presentation. Becoming used to a stimulus, called **habituation,** is the result of patterns formed as stimuli occur repeatedly. An infant begins to expect the stimulus to occur. If the expectation is fulfilled, then the stimulus does not elicit a significant response. Thus, habituation enables an infant to attend to new stimuli without competition from older, less novel stimuli. Habituation requires sensory learning and perception.

PERCEPTION

Perception is using both sensory information and previous knowledge to make sense of incoming stimuli. The ability to discriminate differences in incoming information is a portion of perception, a process of gaining awareness of what is happening around us.

Of most interest for our study of language and speech development are auditory perceptual skills. In order for an infant's perceptual skills in these areas to grow and change, he or she must be exposed to stimulation from the environment. A child must hear speech over and over again. From birth, an infant is an active stimulus seeker who will even work to attain certain types of stimulation.

A newborn is capable of many types of auditory discrimination. For example, a newborn can discriminate between different sound durations and loudness levels, and different phonemes and consonants in short syllables (Bertoncini, Bijeljac-Babic, Blumstein, & Mehler, 1987; Davis & DeCasper, 1989; Moon, Bever, & Fifer, 1992). The ability to discriminate between phonemes evolves quickly. Newborns are also capable of discriminating different pitches or frequencies, especially in the human speech range. In fact, neonates respond to the human voice more often and with more vigor than to other environmental sounds. By 2 months, an infant is also able to discriminate frequency changes, such as high to low. Because intonational patterns are closely related to frequency shifts, we would expect to see this type of discrimination shortly thereafter, and this occurs by 7 months. At about the same time, infants are able to discriminate different words.

Visually, infants are able to perceive the somewhat blurry human face at birth and learn to direct their attention at faces very quickly. Within a few days, they can discriminate between different facial expressions. By 2 months, infants prefer an "average" face, probably because it matches an internalized concept of a face. When I had a beard—anything but "average"—infants often gave me very quizzical looks. By 3 months, infants can perceive facial differences. Between 5 and 8 months, children begin to perceive their own face, although they probably don't yet understand exactly who that vision in the mirror is (Legerstee, Anderson, & Schaffer, 1998).

Similarly, recognition of different facial expressions does not imply that an infant understands emotion. In any case, between 4 and 6 months, children respond more positively to a smile.

Some faces are more important than others. Within a few days of birth, infants can recognize their mother's face (Pascalis, deSchonen, Morton, Deruelle, & Fabre-Grener, 1995; Walton, Bower, & Bower, 1992). Although a stranger's face receives a longer study by an infant at 1 month, mom's face receives a more emotional response.

With increasing memory, a child moves from recognition of familiar faces, objects, and sounds to evocation of these. After repeated exposures, stimuli will elicit signs of recognition from a child. For example, the sight of the bottle might elicit sucking. With increased memory, a child is able to recall a stored image with only minimal stimulation. Thus, mother's footsteps may elicit her image for an infant. Within a child's memory, different aspects of a concept become linked, such as sight, sound, smell, feel, and a related sound sequence or word. Accessing one aspect of the concept opens all. Hearing the word *dog* triggers the concept. At some time around a child's first birthday, any stimulus may open the concept and elicit the symbol or name for a child. For example, seeing the dog or hearing a bark may enable a child to extract "Doggie!" By about 18 months, a toddler is able to evoke the word with no external stimulus. How that word forms requires some specific perception.

The Formation of Auditory Patterns

During the first year, a child lays down a perceptual framework for learning first words. An infant actively encodes the sound patterns of his or her native language, organizing these patterns into types and sequences. Although it was initially thought that these abilities were specific to humans, later research indicated that the ability to discriminate the sounds of human language is found in other mammals (Kuhl & Miller, 1978).

Since this discovery, the focus of study has shifted to the process by which children tune their perception to fit their native language. Learning about speech signals may begin as soon as the auditory system is functional. Thus, it's likely that an infant is learning something about the rhythms of its native language even while in utero. For example, French newborns seem to prefer listening to French, Japanese infants to Japanese, and so on.

Neonates prefer human speech to other nonlinguistic auditory stimuli. Although as neonates they are especially sensitive to intonation, by 3 months of age they seem to be more attentive to words (Ferry, Hespos, & Waxman, 2010).

Development of speech perception proceeds through the first year of life. Newborns are capable of detecting virtually every phoneme contrast used in human languages, something most adults can no longer perceive. The accuracy of a child's perceptual ability declines during the first year, as infants learn to lump together sounds that their language treats as equivalent, such as the /b/ and /v/ in Spanish (Polka & Werker, 1994). In other words, children spend much of the first year losing their ability to perceive contrasts that are not used in the speech around them. Thus, Japanese adults and older children find it very difficult to perceive the difference between "ra" and "la," although Japanese infants have no trouble at all.

As they are exposed to their native language, even newborns begin to recognize regularities, patterns that occur, some frequently, some less. This is part of the way in which our mind functions; it looks for patterns then forms concepts based on these patterns. The ability to detect patterns and to make generalizations is extremely important for later symbol and language rule learning (Marcus, 2001). Significant correlations exist between speech perception at 6 months of age and later word understanding, word production, and phrase understanding, thus indicating the importance of early phonetic perception in language acquisition (Tsao, Liu, & Kuhl, 2004).

Extracting and learning individual speech sounds from the speech stream is difficult, even though newborns are capable of discriminating *individual* phonemes. It is extremely problematic for a child to discern individual words and sounds in the ongoing, multiword utterances of adult speech. Yet by 5 months, most children respond to their own name and, within another month, respond to either *mommy* or *daddy* (Mandel, Jusczyk, & Pisoni, 1995; Tincoff & Jusczyk, 1999). These are frequently occurring words in a child's world. By 8 months, children begin to store the sound patterns for words, although meaning is not attached yet (Jusczyk & Hohne, 1997).

Between birth and 6 months of age, infants begin to show a preference for vowel sounds in their native language. Language-specific preference for consonants seems to occur later. An infant's perceptual ability is usually restricted to its native language's speech sounds by 8 to 10 months of age, about the time that most infants start to comprehend words. It's possible that *tuning in* to its own language sounds in order to comprehend requires an infant to *tune out* phonemes not used in that language (Bates, 1997).

Infants' decreasing ability to discriminate most sounds outside their native language results from experience (Best, 1995; Tsushima et al., 1994; Werker & Tees, 1994). As an aside, you can now appreciate why it is important for second-language learning to occur very early.

The period of 8 to 10 months is marked by changes in both perception and production. Timing may be related to brain developments that occur around the same time, including **synaptogenesis** or a burst in synaptic growth, changes in activity levels in the frontal lobes, and an increase in frontal control over other brain functions (Elman et al., 1996). In fact, the 8- to 10-month period includes dramatic changes in several cognitive and social domains, as noted in imitation of others and intentional communication, discussed later. In other words, speech and language development may to be linked to changes in other nonlinguistic factors.

Babies learn the prosodic patterns, syllable structure, and phonotactic organization of their native language and at this age use these skills to help break up and analyze the relative unbroken speech stream of mature speakers into recognizable words. Prosody is the flow of language. The prosodic pattern in English is characterized as stress-time, meaning that different syllables receive more stress and are held for a longer time while others receive less of both. Not all languages are so organized. For example, Japanese has short syllables with nearly equal stress and time. In English, 80% of words in conversation have stress on the initial syllable.

Young infants are sensitive to stress and to rising and falling intonational patterns. Even newborns are capable of discriminating different prosodic patterns and can recognize utterances in their native language from those in languages with different prosodic patterns (Mehler et al., 1988; Nazzi, Bertoncini, & Mehler, 1998). Stress patterns are one tool used by infants to determine word boundaries (Echols, Crowhurst, & Childers, 1997; Jusczyk, Houston, & Newsome, 1999; Morgan, 1994; Morgan & Saffran, 1995).

As noted, soon after birth, infants prefer their native languages to other languages (Moon, Cooper, & Fifer, 1993). Most likely, these preferences emerge from the infant's ability to detect language-specific prosodic or rhythm patterns. From early on, infants seem to be sensitive to the intonation of the language they hear. Even 2-month-olds tend to remember words better when presented with normal sentence intonation, than when they are presented with flat prosody (Mandel, Jusczyk, & Kemler Nelson, 1994). Stress or emphasis may also be important. Children tend to perceive and remember stressed syllables more readily than unstressed ones (Mandel, Jusczyk, & Pisoni, 1995).

By 5 months, infants can discriminate their own language from others with the same prosodic patterns (Bosch & Sebastián-Gallés, 1997; Nazzi, Jusczyk, & Johnson, 2000). Presumably, children use phonemes, frequent phoneme combinations, and syllable structure to reach this decision. For example, when 8-month-old children listen to long sound sequences such as "dabigogatanagotidabigo," they tend to pull out repeated sequences such as "dabigo" and to listen to these familiar sequences more than to other sequences (Saffran, Aslin, & Newport, 1996). By 9 months, children are using both the prosodic and these phonotactic clues to discern individual speech sounds within connected speech. Within two months, they are able to recognize allophones and to use these to aid in word boundary identification (Jusczyk, Houston, & Newsome, 1999).

Phonotactic organization consists of syllable structure and sound combinations. For example, /pt/ can appear at the end of both a syllable and a word in English but not at the beginning. In contrast, /fh/ and /vt/ are likely to occur across word boundaries, as in *calf hide* and *glove touches* respectively. Armed with this information, it's easier for a child to determine word boundaries.

Identifying word boundaries in continuous speech is relatively easy for adult listeners. For infants, however, this task can be very challenging because words are not consistently separated by pauses. Luckily, there are other types of information embedded in speech that mark word boundaries. These include **phonotactic regularities** and prosodic or flow patterns (Jusczyk et al., 1999; Mattys & Jusczyk, 2001). In fact, 8-month-old infants have been found to be sensitive to regularities in infant-directed speech (IDS) and can learn them quickly even in another language (Pelucchi, Hay, & Saffran, 2009).

Young language learners are especially sensitive to frequently occurring patterns in the language of their environment (Werker & Curtin, 2005). These patterns can be thought of as **phonotactic probabilities** or the likelihood that certain sounds, sound sequences, and syllable types will occur. For example, the likelihood of a word in English ending in /h/—not the letter but the sound—is zero. Nine-month-old infants have a listening preference for non-words composed of high phonotactic probabilities versus those with low phonotactic probabilities (Jusczyk, Luce, & Charles-Luce, 1994). In production, infants are better at saying frequent sequences (e.g., /kt/) than infrequent sequences (e.g., /gd/) (Edwards, Beckman, & Munson, 2004).

Phonotactic representations are also correlated with vocabulary growth. Children with smaller vocabularies have less robust phonological representations, making it more difficult for them to parse or divide words into their sounds and sound sequences. More specifically, vocabulary size seems to be related to young children's (26–32 months) ability to repeat phoneme combinations, especially in the initial position in non-words (Zamuner, 2009).

Of course, this doesn't explain how infants figure out these patterns in the first place. First, we need to recognize that an infant would not need complete knowledge of sound regularities. Instead, an infant would only need some word-like units with which to figure out regularities. For example, some words are heard as single words or in frequent word combinations

*P*arents help their infants explore the world and provide words for the experiences their children are having.

that would help a child identify those words (Bortfeld, Morgan, Golinkoff, & Rathbun, 2005; Brent & Siskind, 2001).

In short, infants are little statisticians, figuring out the probabilities of certain sound combinations in certain locations in words. Then they apply these probabilities to speech to figure out where word boundaries occur. One regularity available to infants is the probability between syllable sequences or the probability of one syllable type following another. Studies have demonstrated that infants are also sensitive to the probabilities of sound co-occurrences in speech (Aslin, Saffran, & Newport, 1998; Saffran, Aslin, & Newport, 1996).

In summary, infants and other mammals seem to start with an innate ability to hear speech sounds used in all human languages. Throughout the first year an infant tunes out irrelevant speech sounds and tunes into the phonological characteristics of his or her native language, but the infant will need oral motor control before he or she can talk.

MOTOR CONTROL

Motor control is muscle movement and the sensory feedback that informs the brain of the extent of that movement. Just discernable movement begins at seven weeks postconception with isolated limb movement evident two weeks later. Hand-to-face contact and body rotation are seen at ten weeks. This is when mothers-to-be often report feeling movement by the fetus.

A newborn or neonate is unable to control motor behavior smoothly and voluntarily. Instead, behaviors consist of twitches, jerks, and random movements, most of which involve automatic, involuntary motor patterns called **reflexes.** A newborn's primary oral reflexes, listed in Table 4.1, allow him or her to react to things in the world while learning to control his or her body. In addition, reflexes help to ensure survival by protecting vital systems. For example, the gag reflex protects the lungs from inhalation of ingested fluids.

TABLE *4.1*   *Selected Oral Reflexes of the Newborn*

REFLEX NAME	STIMULATION	RESPONSE
Phasic bite	Touching or rubbing the gums	Bite-release mouth pattern
Rooting	Stroking cheek at corner of mouth	Head turns toward side being stroked; mouth begins sucking movements
Sucking	Inserting finger or nipple into mouth	Rhythmic sucking

Although some reflexes, such as gagging, coughing, yawning, and sneezing, remain for life, most disappear or are modified by 6 months of age. This disappearance is related to the rapid rate of brain growth and to **myelination,** the development of a protective myelin sheath around the cranial nerves that facilitates neural functioning.

The oral reflexes of phasic bite and rooting are present at birth but disappear by 3 months of age. Phasic bite is a bite-release action that occurs when a newborn's gums receive tactile stimulation. Rooting results from tactile stimulation of the cheek near the mouth. In response, a newborn's lips, tongue, and jaw all move toward the area of stimulation. This reflex is often seen during nursing.

The reflex of most interest for speech development is the rhythmic suck-swallow pattern, which is first established at six months postconception, or three months before birth. At birth, sucking is primarily accomplished by up-and-down jaw action. Within a few weeks, the infant develops more lateral movement. Back-and-forth jaw movement appears at about 1 month. In order to suck, a neonate uncouples, or seals off, the nasal cavity from the oral cavity by raising the velum, or soft palate, and can then create a vacuum in the mouth by lowering the mandible or lower jaw, thus increasing the volume of the space.

To swallow, a neonate opens his or her mouth slightly and protrudes and then retracts the tongue. Although this action is greatly reduced by 3 months of age, it is not until around 3 years of age that independent swallowing without jaw movement appears. To complete a swallow, a neonate must also close off the larynx to protect the lungs. Pretty complicated, huh? More on the larynx later.

In the neonate, vocalization is controlled by the brainstem and pons, and development may coincide with maturation of portions of the facial and laryngeal areas of the motor cortex of the brain. Maturation of the pathways that link auditory and motor areas is not achieved until early in the second year and may be essential for imitation of sounds and speech intonation (Stark, 1986).

Newborns produce predominantly reflexive sounds, such as fussing and crying, and vegetative sounds, such as burping and swallowing. Reflexive sounds are primarily produced on exhalation and consist of relatively lengthy vowel-like sounds (Stark, 1986). In contrast, vegetative sounds are produced on inhalation and exhalation, are both consonant- and vowel-like, and are of brief duration. Production of both types decreases with maturation (Stark, Bernstein, & Demorest, 1993).

Initially, a newborn cries on both inhalation and exhalation, but there are many individual variations. The expiration phase of breathing gradually increases with crying. In general crying is most frequent before feeding and bed.

Crying helps a child become accustomed to airflow across the vocal folds and to modified breathing patterns. Because speech sounds originate at the level of the larynx, where the vocal folds are housed, this early stimulation is important. This breathing will further modify to the lengthened exhalations of speech.

Usually, other noncrying sounds accompany feeding or are produced in response to smiling or talking by the mother. These noncrying vowel-like sounds with brief consonantal elements have been characterized as **quasi-resonant nuclei (QRN).** QRNs contain phonation, or vibration of the vocal folds, but a child does not have sufficient control of the vocal mechanism to produce either consonants or full vowels. This is accomplished through resonation, or a modification of the vibratory pattern of the laryngeal tone through changes in the size and configuration of the vocal tract, which consists of the nasal cavity; the oral cavity, or mouth; and the pharynx, or throat. QRN are probably the result of opening the mouth less than an adult would when resonating a sound. Considerable air is emitted via the nasal cavity, and the resultant sounds range from partial nasal consonants, such as /m/ or /n/, to a nasalized vowel. Initially, production of these sounds is caused accidentally by chance movements of the vocal folds. QRN tend to be individual sounds rather than sound sequences. As these vocal behaviors increase, crying decreases.

The vocal tract of a neonate resembles that of nonhuman primates (Figure 4.1). The noncrying sounds tend to be nasalized because of the relative height of the larynx and the close proximity of the larynx and the vocal tract. During crying, the lower jaw and tongue are dropped and the soft palate and pharyngeal wall move rearward, resulting in the vowel-like quality of distress sounds. At other times, the tongue is in close proximity to or touching the soft palate. As a result, many of the comfort sounds have a nasal character.

By 2 months of age, an infant has developed oral muscle control to stop and start movement though tactile stimulation is still needed. This stage is characterized by laughter and

FIGURE *4.1* **Comparison of the Oral Structures of the Infant and Adult**

In part, the differences in the sounds of infants and adults can be explained by the physical differences of the two. In this schematic, the infant has been enlarged to the approximate size of an adult.

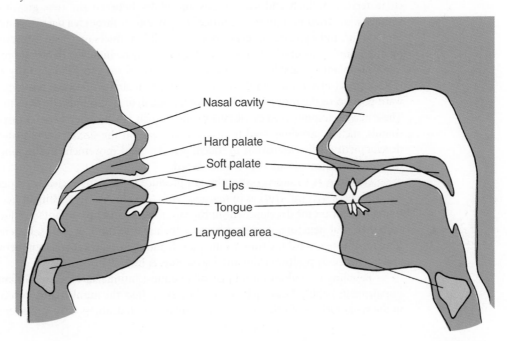

nondistress "gooing." Gooing consists of QRN in the same breath group with closure or near closure at the back of the mouth (Oller, 1978). Thus, an infant produces back consonant (/g, k, h/) and middle and back vowel sounds with incomplete resonance. See Appendix A for a description of speech-sound production and terminology.

An infant controls the timing of vocalizations and responsiveness. By 3 months of age, an infant vocalizes in response to the speech of others and is most responsive if his or her caregivers respond. During vocal turn-taking with a caregiver, 3-month-olds produce more speech-like syllabic vocalizations than isolated vowel sounds (Masataka, 1995). These are accompanied by index finger extensions, a possible early precursor to later developing gestures. These vocalizations continue throughout the first year and into the second even though verbalizations or words are added to a child's repertoire (Stark et al., 1993). By 16 weeks, sustained laughter emerges. At this age, my granddaughter Cassidy could get us all laughing infectiously.

By 4 months of age, an infant engages in up to four hours per day of nonnutritive sucking of fingers and objects and of examining its face and mouth. Neuromuscular control moves forward from the back of the oral cavity. With greater control of the tongue, an infant exhibits tongue cupping and strong tongue projection. If you have ever attempted to spoon-feed a 4- to 6-month-old, you will recall the difficulty of inserting the spoon because the infant protrudes the tongue. Food constantly reappears on the infant's lips and chin. In sucking, an infant is also able to use the intrinsic muscles of the tongue rather than a whole-jaw movement as before.

An infant's bite becomes more volitional, and he or she no longer relies on tactile stimulation. A child can place its lips around a spoon and use them to ingest the contents.

By 5 months, consonant-vowel (CV) syllable vocalizations, and to a lesser degree VC syllables, replace single phoneme, primarily vowel, vocalizations (Fagan, 2009). Although syllable and sound repetition is rare at this age, infants will repeat a few of their own sounds, usually vowels. Children are better at imitating tone and pitch signals. The sound units an infant produces at this age are called **babbling.** Babbling has a social element and an infant will vary the volume, pitch, and rate of babbling to attract attention. He or she will stop to listen to other sounds, especially mother's voice.

With maturity, longer sequences and prolonged individual sounds evolve. Production is characterized by high and low pitches and glides between the two, growling and gutteral sounds, some friction sounds—produced by passing air through a narrow constriction—nasal /m/ and /n/, and a greater variety of vowels. A child produces increasingly more complex combinations and units in which the vowel duration may be highly variable and often very long.

An infant is capable of resonating the laryngeal tone to produce **fully resonant nuclei (FRN),** vowel-like sounds similar to /a/. Constriction abilities become more mature in the forward portion of the mouth, and by 6 months labial, or lip, sounds (/b, p, w, m/) predominate. These may be accompanied by vibratory sounds, such as a "raspberry" or "Bronx cheer." Gutteral sounds, such as growling, tend to decrease. Increase in the size of the oral cavity and further development of discrimination to touch, pressure, and movement in the tongue tip and lips result in the increased variety of sounds heard.

Children as young as 6 months can produce at least three clearly recognizable vowels, "ee" (/i/) as in _see_, "ou" (/u/) as in _too_, and "ah" (//) as in _add_. Interestingly, because of the differing pace of motor development in the jaw, tongue, and lips, infants produce these sounds with their oral structures arranged in ways dissimilar to those of adults. In general, an infant's tongue is more toward the front of the mouth and there is less correlation between jaw height and tongue body position (Ménard, Davis, Boë, & Roy, 2010).

Babbling is random sound play of an almost infinite variety. Even infants with hearing impairments babble. Hearing loss does, however, affect the number and variety of consonants in the vocalizations of infants. In general, infants with deafness have a smaller repertoire than hearing infants, and a greater proportion of labial sounds and prolongable consonants such as nasals (/m, n, ŋ/), approximants (/w, j/), and fricatives (i.e., /f, v, s, z/).

During the babbling period, an infant experiments with sound production. Often the sounds produced differ from those in his or her native language. An infant has not acquired the phonological patterns of the surrounding language, such as sequencing and distribution of sounds. Despite these limitations, infants tend to produce sounds from the surrounding language more frequently than other speech sounds. The frequency of consonant appearance in babbling seems to be reflected in the order of later speech-sound acquisition in speech.

There is very little evidence that an infant's babbling is shaped gradually by selective reinforcement. Parents do not reinforce only those infant sounds used in their language. Social and vocal reinforcement has little effect except to increase the overall amount of babbling.

By approximately 6 months of age, an infant is able to pout and draw its lips in without moving the jaw. Within two more months, an infant can keep his or her lips closed while chewing and swallowing semiliquids. At the same time, chewing changes from vertical to a more rotary pattern, reflecting changes in tongue control. At 8 months, tongue control changes gradually to include more lateral, or sideways, movement. In addition, the tongue can remain elevated, independent of jaw movement. By 11 months, an infant has the neuromuscular control to elevate the tongue tip and to bite soft solid foods with some control. He or she can draw lips and cheeks in during chewing and close the lips when swallowing liquids.

As an infant demonstrates increasing versatility in oral movements, speech progresses to repetitive syllable production and takes on more of the qualities of the surrounding language. Babbling begins to change. Even though he or she still produces single-syllable sounds, an infant enters a brief stage of **reduplicated babbling** and begins to experiment with long strings of consonant-vowel (CV-CV) syllable repetitions or self-imitations, such as "ma-ma-ma." Reduplicated babbling often occurs when holding an object or while exploring the environment and is similar to the rhythmic pattern of hand movement in this activity (Stark et al., 1993). Development of back sounds, followed by true vowel sounds and consonant-vowel babbling, has been found in infants from different language environments.

At first a child's repertoire of consonants is restricted to plosives such as /p/, /b/, /t/, /d/, /g/, and /k/; nasals; and the approximant /j/. (See Appendix A for an explanation of speech sound symbols and their classification.) The phonemes are not mature and are produced slowly. In contrast, the resonant quality and timing of reduplicated babbling more closely approximate mature speech in which vowel duration is very brief. Initially, reduplicated babbling is self-stimulatory in nature and is not used when communicating with adults. Gradually, the child uses reduplicated babbling in more contexts.

Hearing ability appears to be very important in this imitative play, for at this point vocalizations of a child with deafness begin to decrease as does the range of consonants within babbling, especially after 8 months. Whereas a hearing child increasingly produces true consonants, a child with deafness is limited increasingly to /h/, /l/, and /r/ sound sequences. Although a child with deafness may continue to babble until school age, without intervention the repertoire probably will not expand.

A hearing child practices speech sounds for long periods each day, seeming to enjoy this new ability. If mother responds to these sounds, the infant is likely to repeat them. He or she may repeat "ma-ma" at mother's urging but doesn't realize that this sound stands for or represents *mother*. An infant learns very quickly, however, that this behavior can be used to gain attention.

A 6-month-old has some limited knowledge of speech. First, speech predicts the presence of humans. Second, the effects of speech on others vary along a predictable continuum. Finally, speech can fill a turn in conversational interactions. Beginning from this base, a child must discover what speech means.

Regardless of the language heard by an infant, vocalizations and later first words have similar phonological patterns. For example, plosives or stops (/p, b, t, d, k, g/), nasals (/m, n, h/), and approximants (/w, j/) constitute approximately 80% of the consonants in infant vocalizations and the first 50 words of English-speaking children. While the percentages differ, these same sounds often predominate in other non-English-speaking toddlers, such as Spanish-speaking Puerto Rican children, as well. The ratio of single consonants to consonant clusters—roughly 9:1—is also similar in babbling and the first 50 words. Finally, the ratio of CV to VC syllables is also similar at roughly 3:1 in both English and Spanish.

Infants whose parents speak to them in languages as different as Korean and English demonstrate similar consonant patterns in their reduplicated babbling (Lee, Davis, & MacNeilage, 2010). The infants' vowel patterns differ, however, and reflect the input language.

Some characteristics of babbling may be affected by the "parent" language (Levitt & Aydelott Utman, 1992). There is evidence that vowels reflect the parents' language in type and distribution. Syllable structure and the consonant repertoire are also affected.

At around 8 months, other changes occur in an infant's sound patterns. These include echolalia and variegated babbling. Between 8 and 12 months an infant begins to imitate the communication of others. Called echolalic speech, or **echolalia,** it is an immediate imitation of some other speaker. Initially, an infant imitates gestures and intonation, but by 8 months exhibits the identifiable pitch and contour patterns of his or her parent language.

Soon an infant begins to imitate sounds of others, but at first only those sounds he or she has produced spontaneously. Within a few months an infant will begin to use imitation to expand and modify his or her repertoire of speech sounds. Sounds that are not in the native language decrease in number. An infant will also imitate stressed syllables in certain often-used words. For example, a child may repeat "na-na" when mother says "banana," although he or she may not be associating the sound with the actual referent or thing to which it refers. The number of repeated single sounds and CV syllables increases during reduplicated babbling but appears to plateau immediately prior to the onset of variegated babbling (Fagan, 2009).

In **variegated babbling** adjacent and successive syllables are not identical. Sound sequences may also include VCV and CVC structures, although vowel and consonant sounds do not differ within these syllables. In addition, reduplicated babbling changes, becomes less self-stimulatory, and is used more in imitation games with adults. We should note that not all child language researchers report finding variegated babbling in children (Mitchell & Kent, 1990). Whatever the babbling, it has more of the intonation of speech.

During the first year, the average utterance is less than a second in duration and contains fewer than three sounds with no repetition. Interestingly, infant utterances do not become increasingly long and complex over time. Instead, they grow modestly from single sounds to CV syllables (Fagan, 2009). By their first words, infants tend to produce one- and two-syllable utterances (Fagan, 2009).

The Emergence of Speech Patterns

There is little evidence of any direct relationship between early babbling and the language spoken around an infant prior to 9 months (Boysson-Bardies & Vihman, 1991). The seemingly independent development of perception and speech development may be related to the different areas of the brain devoted to the two functions.

By 9 months of age, however, there is increasing evidence of a connection. Babbling changes first occur in intonational patterns. Called **jargon,** it consists of long strings of unintelligible sounds with adultlike prosodic and intonational patterns. Infants 7 to 10 months of age are sensitive to prosodic or rhythmic cues that help them segment speech into smaller perceptual units.

Mothers' speech to infants includes pauses at sentence boundaries, while mothers' speech to other adults often does not. Thus, a child is given cues to a grammatical unit of language.

A child's babbling gradually comes to resemble the prosodic pattern of the language to which he or she is exposed (Levitt, Utman, & Aydelott, 1993). Babbling patterns become shorter and phonetically more stable. The resultant jargon may sound like questions, commands, and statements. Many parents will swear at this point that their child is communicating in sentences, although the parents aren't exactly clear on what the child is saying. Apparently, the paralinguistic aspects of language are easier for the child to reproduce than the linguistic aspects.

Children's early intonation reflects the interaction of biological, affective, and linguistic influences (Snow, 2006). Although many modifications suggest the importance of linguistic input, the early expression of intonation in infants also points to the role of physiological changes and emotional experience.

Speech recognition and production pose numerous problems for an infant (Lively, Pisoni, & Goldinger, 1994).

- Auditory processing is complicated by the variety of speakers and contexts.
- The relationship of spoken words to their meanings is essentially arbitrary. There is a lack of any systematic relationship between the sounds in a word and the word's meaning. Acoustic and speech production similarity is unrelated to semantic similarity.
- An infant must learn to produce comprehensible speech without any direct instruction.
- The processes of learning to comprehend and to produce speech must be closely coordinated by an infant.

While comprehension involves placing input onto meaning, production involves generating output from a phonological representation in order to convey meaning. To make it even more difficult, this must all be accomplished within ongoing communication.

Phonological representations consist of phonemes and syllable structures of the native language that are stored in the brain after repeated exposure. As such, phonological representations of words form a stable template or pattern against which both input and output can be compared to see if it fits. In addition, phonological representations play a critical role in facilitating acoustic input, articulatory output, and meaning (Plaut & Kello, 1999).

As mentioned previously, prespeech sound making changes to reflect the input language. The CV pattern in early phonetic development has been found in both Indo-European languages, such as English, Arabic, and Hindi, and in non-Indo-European languages, such as Mandarin. By age 1, however, language-specific patterns, such as specific speech-sound combinations and frequency of occurrence are evident (Chen & Kent, 2005).

Many speech sounds will develop sound–meaning relationships. Called **phonetically consistent forms (PCFs),** these sounds function as words for an infant, even though they are not based on adult words. A PCF is a consistent prosodic and speech-sound pattern, such as "puda," created and used by a child to refer to an entity, such as the family cat. A child may develop a dozen PCFs before he or she speaks first words. PCFs are found across children regardless of the language they will later speak (Blake & deBoysson-Bardies, 1992).

PCFs may be a link between babbling and adultlike speech in that they are more limited than babbling but not as phonologically structured as adult speech. Characterized as meaningful babbling, PCFs display the active and creative role of a child as a language learner. A child does not use PCFs just because adult models are too difficult. Rather, he or she gets the idea that there can be sound–meaning relationships. Thus, the child demonstrates a recognition of linguistic regularities.

Before we move to cognition, it's worth noting that a child's ability to chew and to make sounds is not merely a reflection of the child's developing motor control. Instead, among typically developing infants from 9 to 22 months, lower jaw (mandible) motor control for production of early multisyllabic babbling is influenced by the interaction between linguistic and developing motor systems (Steeve & Moore, 2009). Variation in linguistic complexity changes motor organization to meet these demands. This same effect is noted with chewing and jaw movement. In other words, motor development is in part driven by the requirements of the task, such as babbling or chewing. In 9-month-olds, coordination of the muscles varies with the task. Coordination in babbling lags behind that for sucking and chewing (Steeve, Moore, Green, Reilly, & Ruark McMurtrey, 2008). For 15-month-olds, mandibular control is organized differently across speech and nonspeech tasks and these forms of motor control undergo continuing refinement into adulthood.

Newly acquired motor skills provide infants with practice prior to the use of similar behaviors in communication. In addition, the emergence of new motor skills changes infants' experience with objects and people in ways that are important for both general communicative development and the acquisition of language (Iverson, 2010). Without a doubt, speech production is a motor act, and there are links between oral-motor physiology, skill acquisition, and oral language (Green & Wilson, 2006; Nip, Green, & Marx, 2009; Thelen, 1991). Gestures, a basis for later language use, are also motor behaviors.

If we look at more general motor development, we find that repeated motor behaviors, such as arm movement, correlate with and precede development of reduplicated babbling (Eilers, Oller, et al., 1993). Repeated hand movement, such as banging a toy, offers multimodal feedback that, in turn, facilitates an infant's growing awareness of the relationship between movements and the resultant sound patterns. An infant engaged in rhythmic banging can feel the move, see the movement, and hear the sound, all occurring in synchrony. Infants are highly sensitive to this type of synchrony and to redundant cues and results (Gogate & Bahrick, 1998; Gogate, Bolzani, & Betancourt, 2006). It can be argued that when infants subsequently begin to babble, they are well prepared to recognize the contingent or related auditory feedback from their own sound production. This feedback allows them to monitor and adjust the vocal tract as they vary their sound production. As infants perform rhythmic arm movements, they have the opportunity to practice a skill that is a central characteristic of reduplicated babble.

COGNITION AND LANGUAGE DEVELOPMENT

Let's try to sift through cognitive development as it relates to the emergence of language. We'll begin with action schemes and the early integration of these motor patterns. This will lead to a discussion of imitation and exploration of the environment, especially objects. As infants begin to recognize patterns in behavior, they begin to anticipate the behaviors of others and to try to affect the outcomes of these behaviors through gestures and vocalizations. Then we'll briefly discuss object play and exploration and the concepts we believe infants form about objects and things in their environment.

Cognition consists of the mental activities involved in comprehension of information, including acquisition, organization and storage, memory, and use of knowledge. As you'll recall, cognition involves processes we call thought, learning, and problem solving to name a few.

We can notice cognition in several ways, such as brain-imaging technology and behavior change by an infant. For example, at around 4 to 5 months children begin to use the right hemisphere for facial recognition. Brain-imaging techniques can document this form of early hemispheric specialization. In a second example, by 6 months, infants are able to recognize faces from different angles. This behavior indicates that the child has stored enough information cognitively to be able to manipulate the visual image.

No doubt, biology plays a crucial role in determining development and enabling language, but such an explanation is insufficient (Elman et al., 1996). Most likely, both biology and experience are engaged in a complex interactive dance in which each contributes.

Although Nativists, led by Noam Chomsky, claimed that language is innate, he wasn't very clear what these biological foundations are. What does it mean when we say that human language is innate?

There are no obvious connections between our genome and language. If other aspects of the genome and human behavior hold true, then language rests on the interaction of large numbers of genes, each of which may not be specific to language alone. There is little evidence, however, for gene-determined hard-wiring of the circuitry of the brain. In other words, the human genome probably does not predetermine which neurons or nerve cells in the brain will communicate directly. Those "connections" are determined by experience. Still, genetics may contribute in two ways: brain structure and the timing of developmental events. These genetic contributions set the brain up for development but require environmental input.

Brain Structure

Cognitive structure can be specified at the neuron, local, and global levels (Elman, 1999). Individual neurons possess specific properties relative to their firing threshold and characteristics, the type of transmission produced or inhibited, and the nature of change after firing. Although there are a relatively small number of neuron types, they are not distributed randomly throughout the brain.

Local structure or architecture is the next higher level and describes differences in the number of layers of the cortex, density of cells, types of neurons, and the degree and nature of interconnectivity (Elman, 1999). At early stages of development, the cortex appears to display relatively little in the way of architectural differences. The much greater organization found in adults appears to result from development and environmental stimulation.

Last, global architecture refers to the way in which the various areas of the brain are connected together (Elman, 1999). While local architecture deals with the ways in which the circuitry is laid out, global architecture deals with connections between regions, especially inputs and outputs to subsystems, such as the primary sensory and motor areas.

Initially, the cortex appears to be relatively unorganized and to possess several organizational possibilities. Over time, however, a complex pattern of localized regions develops that is relatively consistent across individuals (Elman, 1999). The global architecture becomes similar, but this could not occur without external stimulation.

These different functional areas emerge during the time when neurons are produced in the first and second trimesters of pregnancy. At this time neural specification is not complete. Early specification of the cortex is accomplished by genetic mechanisms that signal axons to grow into their correct target region prior to beginning synapse formation (Alcamo, Chiriella, et al., 2008). The expression of genes can be disrupted by both mutations and prenatal environmental influences, such as drugs, alcohol, toxins, and inflammatory responses, resulting in long-term disturbance of both neuron differentiation and behavioral development (Stanwood & Levitt, 2007).

The early period of neural patterning is followed by an extended period of synapse formation, adjustment, and pruning or trimming back that typically lasts from the third trimester of gestation through puberty (Bourgeois, Goldman-Rakic, & Rakic, 1999; Huttenlocher & Dabholkar, 1997). Thousands of genes are responsible for synapse formation, plasticity or adaptability, and stabilization (Akins & Biederer, 2006; Sheng & Hoogenraad, 2007; Sudhof, 2008).

Experience is essential for the normally occurring regulation of synapse formation. Although cell specification and axon guidance are completed early and relatively rapidly by mid-gestation, the structure of functional areas, growth of dendritic "trees," and the peak formation of synapses are far more time-extensive processes, extending through the second and third years of life. This growth is highly dependent on stimulation. The slower growth of the cortex continues through puberty with the addition of myelin, dendritic growth, and a complex process of rerouting some synaptic connections.

Infants are capable of many complex cognitive behaviors.

No two human brains, even those of monozygotic or identical twins, are alike in every way. Instead, the cortex or surface of the upper brain is quite "plastic," meaning it is capable of reorganizing itself in a variety of ways. This is seen in children who sustain brain damage but recover seemingly lost abilities. These abilities are assumed by other portions of the cortex (Friedlander, Martin, & Wassenhove-McCarthy, 1991; Frost, 1990; Killackey, Chiaia, Bennett-Clarke, Eck, & Rhoades, 1994; O'Leary, 1993; Pallas & Sur, 1993; Sur, Pallas, & Roe, 1990). For example, studies using Magnetic Resonance Imaging (MRI) have shown that children with early brain lesions use a variety of alternative developmental pathways to preserve language functioning (Booth, MacWhinney, et al., 1999).

Developmental Timing

Timing refers both to when the brain is receptive to certain inputs and to changes in the brain itself as the result of learning. Although timing is sometimes under direct genetic control, it may also be indirect and the result of multiple interactions. As a result, the onset and sequencing of events in development represents both genetic and environmental effects.

Within the first two months postconception, the human brain begins to segment into specific regions. The patterning of the cortex into different functional areas begins as soon as the first neurons are produced. The timing of neuron growth and migration are controlled by genetic factors. Collectively, these events build the early plan for brain architecture. The cerebral cortex is organized to receive information from the environment by integrating information within and across different distinct functional areas and sending this information to other brain centers that generate a response.

Experience

Early life events exert a powerful influence on both the pattern of brain organization and behavioral development (see the excellent overview by Fox, Levitt, & Nelson, 2010). The foundations of brain architecture are established early in life by the interaction of genetic influences and environmental conditions and experiences (Friederici, 2006; Grossman, Churchill, et al., 2003; Hensch, 2005; Horn, 2004; Majdan & Shatz, 2006). Although genetics provides a "blueprint," environmental factors play a crucial role in coordinating both the timing and pattern of gene expression. For example, the ability to perceive a range of sound frequencies requires exposure to frequency variation in the environment, which later leads to language processing proficiency (Kuhl, 2004; Newport, Bavelier, & Neville, 2001; Weber-Fox & Neville, 2001). In this interaction, postnatal experiences drive the process of maturation while the ability of developmental processes to occur successfully is largely dependent on the prenatal establishment of basic brain architecture that provides the basis for receiving, interpreting, and acting on incoming information (Hammock & Levitt, 2006).

The role of environment and input to the brain is critical to the bias of neural formation in early life. Each sensory and cognitive system has a unique **sensitive period** (Daw, 1997). Depending on the ages of children, identical environmental input can have very different effects on cognitive development (Amedi, Stern, et al., 2007; Jones, 2000; Trachtenberg & Stryker, 2001; Tritsch, Yi, Gale, Glowatski, & Bergles, 2007).

During the sensitive period, portions of the brain become perceptually biased, making future modifications more difficult. For example, although 6-month-old infants can discriminate both human and monkey faces, only those exposed to monkey faces can readily discriminate between these faces at 9 months, while infants exposed to monkey faces and those not exposed can easily discriminate human faces (Pascalis, de Haan, & Nelson, 2002; Pascalis et al., 2005).

The types of experiences encountered in early development can have a profound effect on brain organization and development. In this way, sensitive periods represent a time during which an infant's capabilities can be modified and perhaps enhanced. The quality of experiences during these periods is extremely important. For example, typically developing children institutionalized at birth have IQs in the low 70s. If these children are placed in high-quality foster care before age 2, there are dramatic increases in IQ (Nelson, Zeanah, et al., 2007). A similar trend also occurs for language (Windsor, Glaze, Koga, & the BEIP Core Group, 2007), although the sensitive period is around 16 to 18 months.

Interestingly, circuits that process lower level linguistic information, such as speech sounds, mature earlier than those that process higher level information, such as syntax (Burkhalter, Bernardo, & Charles, 1993; Scherf, Behrmann, Humphreys, & Luna, 2007). High-level neural circuits that carry out sophisticated mental functions, such as syntactic processing, depend on the quality of the information they are provided by these lower level circuits. If low-level circuits are shaped by healthy experiences early in life, they provide high-level circuits with precise, high-quality information.

When a child hears speech sounds over and over, neurons in the auditory system stimulate "connections" in the child's auditory cortex in the temporal lobe. Over time, a child begins to construct auditory mental maps from the phonemes heard in the environment. This process is gradual, and sounds must be heard thousands of times before neurons are assigned. Distances and similarities between sounds are noted and recorded. Eventually, different clusters of neurons will respond to each phoneme, firing when the phoneme is heard.

This seemingly early "hardening" of low level circuits has an effect on language learning. For example, in general, adults are better at discriminating nonnative phoneme contrasts when they differ substantially from phonemes of their native language (Frieda, Walley, Flege, &

Sloane, 1999; Guion, Flege, Akahane-Yamada, & Pruitt, 2000; Kuhl, 2004). Adults are poorer at discriminating when the phonetic contrasts are similar to phonetic contrasts of their native language. In other words, the auditory system of adults is better capable of discriminating tones outside of the tonal environment in which the adult was raised. There is a perceptual bias in the adult neural network. All is not lost for those of you learning a second language because neurons seem to be constantly modifying connectivity, allowing learning from new environments to compete against already existing tendencies. So you can't use your brain's processing bias to excuse your poor grades in French 101!

Overall, changes in experience have a greater impact on younger brains than the same experience has on older more organized brains. Nevertheless, changes in the environment, especially those that are dramatic and pervasive, can alter neural connectivity and cognitive processing. This can be seen in deaf children who receive cochlear implants (Tomblin, Barker, Spencer, Zhang, & Gantz, 2005).

Early learning lays a foundation for later learning. Later development does not seem to be able to overcome the detrimental effects of early deprivation or poor neural development. On the other hand, in cases in which the early cognitive environment of infants is impoverished, early intervention has been shown to greatly improve cognitive, linguistic, and emotional capabilities (Ghera et al., 2009; Nelson et al., 2007; Windsor et al., 2007).

A controversial issue in the field of language development is whether language emergence and growth is dependent on specific language processes or on basic cognitive processes. For instance, during the first year, infants demonstrate general information processing abilities in memory, processing speed, attention, and representational competence that may account for language growth (Rose, Feldman, & Jankowski, 2004, 2005). Let's look at each of these areas briefly.

Memory

Memory is vital for acquiring all forms of knowledge, including language. Infants with better memory are more adept at encoding, storing, consolidating, and retrieving representations of objects and events, skills fundamental to language development. Infants with better recognition and recall memory are better able to link words with referents. In addition, infants with better working memory are able to hold more information while they segment the auditory stream into meaningful units, such as words and phrases. In another example, better visual *recognition memory* is related to better comprehension and gestural communication in toddlers and better receptive and expressive language in preschoolers (Heimann, Strid, et al., 2006; Rose, Feldman, Wallace, & Cohen, 1991; Thompson, Fagan, & Fulker, 1991). Better *recall memory* at 9 months is related to better gestural production at 14 months. Together, these two memory abilities, recognition memory and recall, also have predictive value. Better recognition and recall at 12 months predict better language skills at 36 months (Rose, Feldman, & Jankowski, 2009).

The first step in the long-term memory process is organization and storage of perceived information. Structuring or organizing incoming information is essential because a child is exchanging information with the physical environment continually and could easily overload his or her cognitive system. This underlying organization can be inferred from the similar way in which infants interact with objects of similar perceptual attributes. Although objects may have an infinite variety of characteristics, an infant has only a limited quantity of motor responses. Therefore, he or she generalizes and classifies objects into general response classes.

Organization is an attempt to bring systematic order to information. Organization is storing and representing knowledge. If long-term memory capacity is fixed, as assumed in information processing theory, increased organization must be related to more efficient processing. Through experience, the patterns become better organized, leaving more capacity for other information.

We cannot expect sophisticated memory from an infant. Some of the synaptic "connections" in the areas of the cortex responsible for long-term memory are not fully developed until middle childhood or even later (Bauer, 1996; Johnson, 1998; Rovee-Collier, 1999). Even so, memory is at work early in development. An infant becomes accustomed to its mother's voice while still in utero and can remember that sound after birth.

Information is placed in long-term storage and maintained by repetition, a process called **rehearsal.** Transferral to long-term memory requires a special type of rehearsal, called **integrative rehearsal,** in which new material is integrated into the structure of information already stored in long-term memory.

It has been posited that the structural components of memory do not change with age. Rather, substantial changes reflect modifications in the strategies children use to encode information. In other words, changes in memory performance are related to changes in long-term storage strategies. As children mature, they use different techniques to control information flow between parts of the system. For example, infants require more repetitive rehearsals than toddlers in order for information to be coded in long-term memory. As memory strategies change to accommodate increasing amounts of information, a child's ability to hold information increases. Cognitive development represents an increase in information processing capacity as a result of use of more efficient processing strategies (Case, 1992).

Over time, with repeated exposure, an infant becomes better able to retrieve the representation without the stimulus input. In addition, associations are made between the physical characteristics and the name of the stimulus. Mother's voice or the word "Mommy" may elicit the representation.

Finally, a child is able to retrieve the representation at will. A toddler can produce the word "Mommy" with no input stimulus, such as the presence of mother. As memory becomes less context-bound, a toddler is free to experiment and to use objects and symbols in novel ways. With increased memory, a young child is able to understand and produce more than one symbol at a time.

Processing Speed

Processing speed is related to performance on a wide variety of cognitive tasks. Obviously, faster processing speed enables operations to be performed more rapidly, and thus increases the capacity of working memory. We can assume that limitations in processing speed would make it difficult to keep up with speech input. This in turn would interfere with building internal representations of language essential for development (Leonard, Weismer, et al., 2007).

With maturation and repeated exposure to the environment, working memory, the memory needed to hold information while it is processed, expands and information processing becomes more automatic.

Attention

Attention includes the ability to engage, maintain, disengage, and shift focus. In general, infants with better attention are likely to acquire language more quickly. They are better able to follow the gaze of others, engage in joint or shared attention, and track referents or subjects of others' speech. During the first year, duration of looking, which may reflect more rapid encoding and/or greater facility at disengaging attention, and shift rate, which may reflect more active comparison of targets, change dramatically. In general, look durations become shorter and shift rates become faster (Colombo, Shaddy, Richman, Maikranz, & Blaga, 2004; Frick, Colombo, & Saxon, 1999; Rose, Feldman, & Jankowski, 2001).

There is a correlation between cognitive development and development of joint attention (Mundy, Block, et al., 2007). Joint or shared attention is found when two individuals, such as a mother and infant, attend to the same thing, such as a toy. The ability of an infant to focus on something while her or his mother discusses or manipulates it is important for learning and may be a precursor of focusing on a topic together in a conversation.

Representational Competence

Representational competence is the ability to extract commonalties from experiences and represent them abstractly or symbolically. Representational and symbolic abilities in which an infant establishes relations between words and referents is necessary for language development. These abilities are seen in infants' anticipation of future events, in object permanence, and symbolic play in which one object is used to represent another. These abilities all require an infant to represent things and locations not immediately available to the senses. Symbolic play and object permanence have long been associated with language development (Tamis-Lemonda, Shannon, Cabrera, & Lamb, 2004). Symbolic play is using an object for other than its intended purpose, such as a slipper being used as a pretend cellphone. Object permanence, seen when infants search for a missing object, is knowing that an object exists even when it is not readily visible. These representations are organized and stored in the brain for future use.

The basic unit of cognitive organization is a scheme or concept that underlies the ability to categorize or "chunk" information for storage and retrieval. Concepts are not distinctly separate entities but are linked to related stored information in complex webs called **mental maps.**

The perceptual data from each encounter with incoming information is compared to the concept, and if it fits, it is stored in that category. If the incoming information doesn't fit the concept, a new concept may need to be formed or the old concept altered in some way to fit or accommodate the new information. This change alters the category in turn. Readjusting categories is a form of learning based on environmental input.

The use of concepts frees cognitive resources for higher order functioning because each new example of the concept can be treated as familiar rather than novel. Concepts also reduce the infinite variety of sensations bombarding the brain into cognitively manageable data. For example, how many colors can you classify? You can perceive approximately 7 million (!) shades of color. Concepts such as yellow, blue, red, and the like simplify information processing and make organized storage possible. When we think or form an idea for communication, concepts are withdrawn from long-term memory and held in working memory while needed.

At a very early age an infant engages in cognitively evaluating and comparing stimuli. A face is insufficient to hold an infant's attention for long periods. Rather, an infant focuses on the contrast between the face and her or his internal representation of a face, called a concept or scheme. Stimulation is coming from both the stimulus and the scheme. These schemes provide an infant with an expectation of the properties of objects, events, and people in the environment.

The effect of language spoken to a child cannot be overemphasized. There is a direct correlation between the number of words heard by a child during early development and the cognitive abilities of that child even into the late preschool years (Hart & Risley, 1995). The more words a child hears, the faster she or he will learn language.

At about 7 months, an infant begins to "understand" one or two single words. Not only does he or she perceive different sequences of phonemes, but an infant associates them with entities in the environment. Incoming acoustic patterns are compared with stored sound traces and their associated meanings. Within another three months, he or she can recognize a familiar word within a phrase or a short sentence.

At 9 to 13 months, children "understand" words based on a combination of sound, nonlinguistic and paralinguistic cues, and context. In other words, in certain specific contexts children have limited comprehension of some phonemic sequences. The words are probably not comprehended outside of that context. The exceptions are the child's name and *no,* which most children seem to recognize. As a result of continued exposure to recurring sound patterns in context, a child learns these patterns in these situations.

Obviously, memory is important for retention and integration of input in order both to map or form a representation of the entire word connecting semantics and phonology and to retrieve that representation. Acoustic information, even just the initial sounds of a word, likely activates a semantic representation of the entire word, enabling an infant to derive some semantic information from the available input (Plaut & Kello, 1999). When the word is reliably distinguished from others, the semantic network activates the full meaning. While phonological representations of entire words probably build up gradually over time from sequences of acoustic input, semantic representations may begin forming with only one exposure to a word.

It is worth noting that information processing abilities cross different modalities (Rose, Feldman, & Jankowski, 2009). In other words, visual memory skills may represent underlying memory abilities that affect auditory memory (Visscher, Kaplan, Kahana, & Sekuler, 2007). This cross-modal transfer can be seen in other areas. For example, advances in symbolic play, using one object to represent another, suggest advances in linguistic representations, using words to represent objects.

LEARNING

Learning begins early. As mentioned, at 24 weeks postconception, a fetus habituates or becomes accustomed to repeated loud noise, such as a drum beat. This requires very limited working memory and recognition that repeated sounds are similar. While habituation does not seem to involve long-term memory and learning, response to mothers' voice does. Exposed to their mothers' voice while in utero, newborns express a preference for this sound. Children exposed to music in the last third of a pregnancy will also prefer this sound.

A child experiences the world as it is filtered or mediated by adults and older, more mature children. During interactions with the world, a child is engaged in cooperative dialogs with others who assist him or her. Cognitive processes adapted for a particular culture are transferred to a child. Language used by these "teachers" is crucial to cognitive change. Through these interactions with more mature members of the culture, a child develops skills and learns to think in a manner consistent with that culture. As such, a child serves a sort of apprenticeship, as his or her participation is guided through culturally relevant activities by a skilled partner.

Both the ability to learn new tasks and to retain this learning increases with age (Rovee-Collier, 1999). For example, a 2-month-old can retain previously learned motor skills for only a few days, while a 6-month-old can recall past learning for two weeks. By 12 months, memory has increased to eight weeks. The learning context is extremely important for retention, especially for very young infants. A behavior learned in the crib may not be recalled while on grandma's sofa. Also, as in adult learning, infant learning can be enhanced or reduced by the effect of subsequent learning.

Let's demonstrate this interaction through emotional learning. The neural pathways for emotion are established before birth; the rest is environmental. Reciprocal or shared emotional interactions strengthen the pathways. If the mother fails to respond repeatedly in a reciprocal way, her child can become confused and passive. Even at 1 month of age, infants learn the typical time it takes for Mom to respond to their cries and squeals.

You'll recall that, as an organism develops, its conceptual system changes. The system consists of organized patterns of reaction to stimuli called schemes or concepts. **Schemes** are a baby's cognitive structures used for processing incoming sensory information. An event is perceived in a certain way and organized or categorized according to common characteristics. This is an active process involving interpretation and classification. An individual's response to a given stimulus is based on his or her cognitive structures and ability to respond. With experience, schemes change and become more refined. In other words, the person learns. Let's take a closer look.

Cognitive development is not a quantitative accumulation of ideas and facts. It is a qualitative change in the process of thought. An individual organizes and stores material in qualitatively different ways as a result. Change occurs through a child's active involvement with the environment as mediated by a mature language user who interprets and facilitates interaction for a child. The motivation for cognitive change or learning is internal as a child attempts to reach a balance between new and previously held concepts or schemes.

All organisms adapt to changes in the environment. Such adaptations are cognitive as well as physical. Cognitive development is the result of organization and adaptation, two complementary processes (Piaget, 1954).

Organization and adaptation are two basic functions found in all organisms (Figure 4.2). **Organization** is the tendency to systematize or organize processes into systems. **Adaptation** is the function or tendency of all organisms to change in response to the environment. Adaptation occurs as a result of two related processes: assimilation and accommodation. We've discussed these processes before but without naming them.

Each organism is more effective in interacting with the environment if that organism is in equilibrium with the environment. **Equilibrium** is a state of cognitive balance, or harmony, between incoming stimuli and the organism's cognitive structures. Obviously, equilibrium is only momentary for any given stimulus, but nonetheless it is the state toward which all organisms supposedly strive. Equilibrium is the "driving force" of cognitive and other biological changes. Intelligence, or cognitive functioning, changes with each adaptation, or attempt to achieve equilibrium. The results occur in fairly predictable patterns in typically developing children.

Assimilation is the use of existing schemes to incorporate external stimuli (Figure 4.2). An attempt to deal with stimuli in terms of present cognitive structures, assimilation is the way an organism continually integrates new perceptual matter into existing patterns. For example, an Irish setter is similar enough to be incorporated into the dog category along with collies and German shepherds. The similarities are great enough to allow their assimilation. Without such categorization, we could make little sense of the environment. Not all stimuli fit into available schemes, however, and mental structures must be adapted to these stimuli.

Accommodation is a transformation process in response to external stimuli that do not fit into any available scheme and, therefore, cannot be assimilated (Figure 4.2). An individual has the option of modifying an existing scheme or developing a new one. The Irish setter could be included in the dog concept; an elephant is sufficiently different to require a new category. Once the organism has accommodated its schemes to the external stimulus, the new information is assimilated, or incorporated, into the new or modified scheme. Thus, the processes of assimilation and accommodation are complementary and mutually dependent. New or modified structures are created continually and then used to aid the organism's comprehension of the environment.

ROLE OF THE CAREGIVER

A baby's interaction with the environment is moderated by an adult or a more mature child who uses language to help explain and describe the child's experiences. While not directly teaching the child, this caregiver provides the opportunity for learning.

FIGURE *4.2* **Piaget's Cognitive Learning Process**

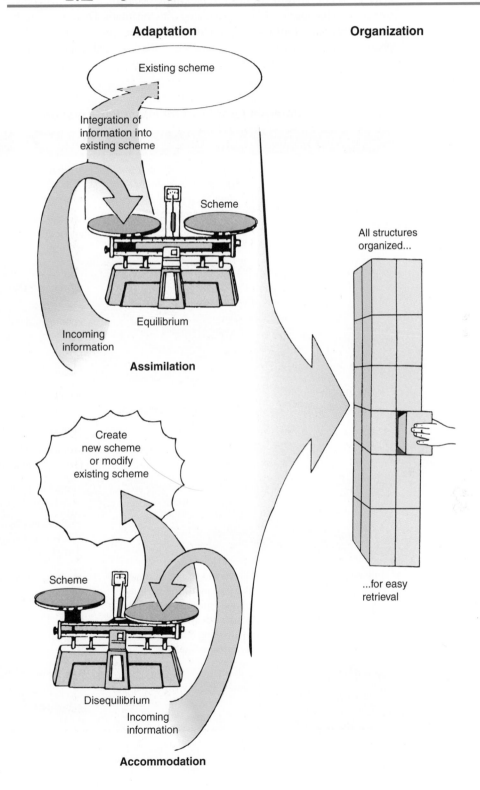

Adaptation

Existing scheme

Integration of information into existing scheme

Scheme

Equilibrium

Incoming information

Assimilation

Create new scheme or modify existing scheme

Scheme

Disequilibrium

Incoming information

Accommodation

Organization

All structures organized...

...for easy retrieval

The caregiver regulates not only the amount of stimulation but also the timing. Caregiver behavior is not random but fits into the child's behavior. By modifying his or her behavior, the caregiver maintains an interactional dialog with the infant. There are six techniques that mothers use to create opportunities for their children to participate (Schaffer, 1977). These techniques—phasing, adaptive, facilitative, elaborative, initiating, and control—are listed in Table 4.2.

TABLE *4.2* **Maternal Techniques for Infant Participation**

TECHNIQUES	BEHAVIORS	EXAMPLES
Phasing	Monitors infant behavior to determine when to slot her behavior for most impact; must know when to intervene to attain predictable outcome	Mother attains infant's attention to an object before using it in some way. Mother monitors infant's gaze and follows it for clues to infant interest.
Adaptive	Exhibits behaviors that enable infant to assimilate information more rapidly; maintains infant's attention and provides highly ordered, predictable input	Mother uses slower arm movements than with adults. Mother has more emphatic gestures and more exaggerated facial expressions than with adults. Mother's speech is simpler and more repetitive than with adults.
Facilitative	Structures routine and environment to ensure infant success	Mother holds toy so child can explore. Mother assists infant physically. Mother supplies needed materials for task completion.
Elaborative	Allows child to indicate an interest, then elaborates upon it; talks following the infant's activities and interests closely	Mother demonstrates play with object of infant's interest. Mother talks about infant's behavior as she performs (parallel talking).
Initiating	Directs infant's attention to objects, events, and persons; follows sequence of gaining infant's attention, directing it, and looking back to ensure that the infant is attending	Mother points to direct attention. Mother brings object into child's view.
Control	Tells infant what she is to do; pauses after key words that are emphasized and makes extensive use of gestures	Mother insists that infant eat. Mother stresses what she wants the infant to do.

Source: Information from Schaffer (1977).

The mother monitors her child's behavior continually and adapts her behavior accordingly. Her modifications enable the infant to enter the dialog as a partner. These mutual dialogs seem to reach their greatest frequency at around an infant age of 3 or 4 months (Cohen & Beckwith, 1975).

Conclusion

COGNITION PRECEDES LANGUAGE DEVELOPMENT. At this stage, a child expresses in his or her language only those relationships that are understood intellectually. It seems safe to assert that there are certain levels of cognitive functioning that must precede expressive language. It is also plausible that this relationship changes with maturation.

The child needs perceptual skills to discriminate the smallest units of speech and to process speech-sound sequences. Both skills require good auditory memory. At a linguistic-processing level, these sound sequences are matched with the entities and actions they represent, called referents. These representational abilities develop in the infant during the first two years of life through adaptation to, and organization of, incoming sensory stimuli.

Unfortunately, there are still many unanswered questions about this early relationship of cognition, or thought, and language. The mental processes involved in word–referent association and in the use of true symbols have not been adequately explained.

The cognitive basis of language is best illustrated in early semantic development. Much early expressive language development involves a child's learning how to express the meanings that he or she already knows. Stated somewhat differently, a child must develop a certain number of meanings before he or she can begin to confer information intentionally on the environment. By interacting with objects and persons in the environment, an infant forms primitive definitions that are later paired with the word and the referent. This relationship will be discussed in more detail in Chapters 6 and 7.

In the final analysis, the cognitive and perceptual bases for early language appear to be necessary for early language development but are not adequate for a full explanation of the process. This does not detract from the importance of early perceptual and cognitive development, but it begs for consideration of other factors. Language does not develop in a vacuum but, rather, within an environment of well-developed communication.

Sociolinguistic studies emphasize environmental influences, especially the social interactions between a child and its primary caregiver. It is possible that *event knowledge*, or the child's understanding of daily routines and events, rather than knowledge of objects, forms the conceptual foundation for language (Farrar, Friend, & Forbes, 1993). This possibility will be explored in Chapter 5.

Discussion

LANGUAGE DOESN'T JUST HAPPEN. A child needs certain cognitive perceptual, social, and communicative skills. In the future, you may work with children who lack the cognitive skills to use language. As a group, we might label these children as having mental retardation. A child might also lack perceptual skills. We might say these children have a severe learning disability. Other children may lack the motor skills for speech, such as those with cerebral palsy, or may have a sensory deficit, such as those who have deafness, but they may be able to develop language through some augmentative or alternative method of communication, such as pictures, sign, or the use of computers. As an SLP, teacher, or parent, you may need to decide whether to train cognitive skills with a child, or social or perceptual skills, or whether to go directly to communication and possible use of symbols. As a parent, teacher, or school psychologist, you may be a member of educational teams who must make these and other decisions.

Cognitive development may be thought of in terms of information processing. Recall how the four steps—attention, discrimination, organization, and memory—change during the first year. In addition, remember that infants learn through trial-and-error involvement with the environment. Finally, recall what children learn. They need to develop the skill to represent reality in their minds. More importantly, they must be able to recall the symbols that are used to represent that reality so that they can transmit these concepts to others. It is the development of that skill that we have addressed.

Main Points

- Sensory abilities change little at birth, but the level of stimulation greatly increases.

- Perception is the search for patterns in sensory information.

- Although newborns are capable of detecting every phoneme contrast found in human languages, this ability has been lost by 10 months as a child focuses on her or his native language.

- Motor speech production passes through babbling, reduplicated babbling, and variegated babbling on the way to first words. Other prespeech behaviors include jargon and echolalia.

- Genetics contributes to brain structure and developmental timing.

- During the first year, there are major cognitive changes in memory, processing speed, attention, and representational competence.

- Cognition and learning involve the formation of concepts or schemes and adaptation or the comparing of these schemes with incoming information. Adaptation consists of two subprocesses: assimilation in which incoming information confirms the scheme and accommodation in which the scheme must be modified to conform to incoming information.

- Learning consists of adaptation and organization.

- During the first year, memory moves from recognition to retrieval.

- Parents mediate the environment to help children make sense and be successful.

Reflections

1. List the newborn's sensation and motor skills.

2. Describe how sensation, perception, and cognition differ, and give the major changes in each during the first year of life.

3. What are concepts and categories, and how do they affect learning?

4. Describe the major changes in speech production in the first year.

5. What are the major learning developments in the first year of life, and how does cognition affect language development?

5

The Social and Communicative Bases of Early Language and Speech

OBJECTIVES

Language is acquired within the context of early conversations between a caregiver and a child. In this chapter we will describe the early interactions of these individuals and the contributions of each to the conversational context. In addition, we will explore the child's development of both communication skills and the intention to communicate and their relationship to theory of mind. When you have completed this chapter, you should understand

- The communication behaviors of the newborn.
- The importance of gaze coupling, ritualized behavior, and game playing.
- The development of gestures.
- The effects of baby talk, gaze, facial expression, facial presentation and head movement, and proxemics on the child's development.
- The importance of joint reference, joint action, and turn-taking on the development of communication.
- The following terms:

bracketing	joint action	referencing
clustering	mutual gaze	script
communication intention	protoconversation	social smile

To listen to language samples related to chapter content and to peruse other enhanced study aids, please see the Companion Website at www.pearsonhighered.com/owens8e

The word *infant* is derived from the Latin *infans*, which means "not speaking." In fact, terms such as *prelinguistic* and *nonverbal* are frequently used to describe infants. All these terms indicate a subtle prejudice that is reflected in the common assumption that it is the development of language and speech that lets children become communicating beings. This supposition does not reflect the actual behavior of infants, who communicate well before they have language. Actually, language is a communication tool whose development depends on the prior development of communication.

In Chapter 4 we discussed the cognitive and perceptual bases of language. Words and symbols have meaning only as they relate to these underlying cognitive representations. This process of associating words to meaning, however, does not occur in isolation. Although a child can, to some degree, understand the entities and relationships in the world by exploring on his or her own, this knowledge can be expanded and labeled only by interacting within a social environment.

Language is a social tool, and we must look to a child's interactive environment to understand its development. Simply put, children learn language to communicate better or to maintain better social contact. Use is the motivating factor.

The social context in which language occurs helps an infant understand that language. Both the nature of communication situations and the process of communicating aid linguistic development. As we shall see, context is employed heavily by the mother, or other caregivers, to augment verbal communication. Caregivers talk about objects that are immediately present in the environment. In addition, these communication exchanges have a predictable quality that also facilitates comprehension and learning. A child's knowledge of give-and-take exchanges and nonlinguistic signaling equip him or her to interpret or "crack the language code" used in such exchanges.

Language represents only a portion of a larger interactional pattern that reflects the way we socialize our children. In short, babies become human beings because that's the way they are treated. In the communication context, the caregiver assumes that the child is attempting to communicate meaningfully. Thus, in their early dialogs, the caregiver provides an opportunity for the child to take a conversational turn. Initially, any child response is treated as a meaningful turn. If the child gives no response, the caregiver proceeds with the next conversational turn. As the caregiver and child communicate, the child learns that people can exchange feelings and meanings.

In this chapter we will discuss infant–caregiver interactions almost exclusively. In middle-class American culture, the mother tends to be her infant's primary caregiver and, therefore, the primary socializing agent. Certainly, in some homes the father or a sibling fulfills the "mothering" function, but nearly all infant interactive studies have focused on the female parent. You should keep in mind that we will be discussing a "generic" mother–child duo and that many variations exist.

In working-class families, a mother's need to work, the family structure, and the neighborhood environment may result in older children becoming the primary caregivers. Studies indicate that these children behave in much the same way as middle-class mothers in their communication adaptations. Even so, these older children or mothers from either working-class families or different cultures may interact differently with their children than middle-class English-speaking mothers in the United States do.

There are many different ways to learn language. In some African cultures, a mother and child have less face-to-face interaction than in the United States. Instead, a mother spends the day reciting ritualized rhymes or songs. Through this process, her child learns that language is predictable. These interactions provide a culturally appropriate language-learning environment.

Within the middle-class American infant–caregiver exchange, an infant develops the essential skills for learning language. The dialog is one of mutual participation. The infant's contribution is as important as that of the caregiver. The caregiver integrates her or his behavior into the infant's behavior system, and both seem to adjust their behaviors to maintain an optimal level of interaction.

Although the content and intonation of these dialogs has been characterized as "baby talk," the dialog pattern is adult. Naturally, the roles taken by an infant and caregiver are different. The caregiver

- Has superior flexibility of timing and anticipates the infant's behavior.
- Has an intuitive curriculum and leads the infant's behavior slightly.
- Is able to monitor and code her changes of expression more rapidly than the infant.
- Can alternate among different means to attain the desired ends while the infant does not have the cognitive ability to assess situations and determine alternative strategies.
- Is more creative in introducing variations of her repetitive vocalizations each time.

Communication is maintained because a mother is socially sensitive to the effect of her behavior on the infant and tailors her speech to the task and to her child's abilities. Mothers learn this skill in order to sustain the exchange and to hold attention. In addition, the mother attributes meaning to the infant's behavior, enabling a dialog to occur. The mother acts as if she has a competent communication partner.

Much of this early dialog occurs in specific situations, or is situation-dependent. Within these situations, a mother attempts to provide more readily comprehensible segments. Daily routines also provide predictable patterns of behavior, which aid interpretation. As a result, an infant learns the conventions of conversation. It would be incorrect, however, to assume that a child does not influence the interaction. Mother and child engage as partners in a dialog.

In this chapter we will examine the behavior of both the caregiver and the infant in their early interactions. Of importance are the communication strategies that facilitate later speech and language development. The discussion will be developmental in nature and will concern, specifically, interaction and communication development in newborns and during the first year. Later in the chapter, we will explore adult communication strategies and interactional behaviors such as joint reference and joint action, game playing, and turn-taking. (See also Appendix C, Tables C.1 and C.2.)

Development of Communication: A Chronology

An infant's world is a world of people—people who do things for, to, and with the infant. In the process, an infant learns the conventions of communication into which he or she will eventually place linguistic elements. Every mother will verify the fact that her child began to communicate long before developing language. By the time a child begins to use words, he or she is already able to indicate intentions, and to elicit and interpret responses from others.

THE NEWBORN

Perceptual and cognitive abilities might suggest that a neonate is "prewired" for communication. For example, vision attains best focus at about 8 inches, where most infant–caregiver interactions occur. Within a few hours of birth, an infant can follow visually at this close range. During feeding, a mother's eyes are at a distance of almost 7½ inches exactly, and she gazes at her infant 70% of the time. The child is most likely, therefore, to look at and focus on its mother's face, especially the mother's eyes.

Visual preference is for the human face or a face pattern. Newborns prefer visual stimuli with angularity, light and shade, complexity, and curvature. The human face contains all these preferred parameters. Infants find the human face fascinating, and mothers attract as much interest as possible to their faces. Visual preferences suggest that the angles at the corners of the eyes and the dark-light contrast of the eye itself and the eyebrow might be particularly attractive. A caregiver interprets eye contact as a sign of interest or attention.

The importance of eye contact cannot be overstated. Parents of children with congenital blindness or children who avoid eye contact, such as those with autism spectrum disorder, may have difficulty relating to their children.

Undoubtedly, a newborn has been exposed in utero to sounds. He or she has also been hearing mother's somewhat muffled voice and experiencing the rhythmic movements that accompany mother's speech. In response to speech, adults make discrete and continuous synchronous movements at the phoneme, syllable, phrase, and sentence levels. This interactional synchronization, called *entrainment,* is also exhibited by a neonate within twenty minutes of birth. In contrast, a neonate will not produce synchronous movements to disconnected vowel sounds or to tapping. A newborn prefers acoustic patterns of her or his mother's speech.

A neonate's optimal hearing is within the frequency range of the human voice. As noted in Chapter 4, he or she is able to discriminate some parameters of voice and speech. A neonate has definite auditory preferences for the human voice over nonspeech sounds. Newborns also have a preference for their own mother's voice.

In fact, infants show a bias for listening to speech from birth (Vouloumanos & Werker, 2007). Genuine conversational speech seems to be an infant's preference. Interestingly, although neonates do not show a preference for nonsense speech over the vocalizations of rhesus monkeys, by 3 months, infants show a clear preference for human speech of several varieties (Vouloumanos, Hauser, Werker, & Martin, 2010).

Typically, a newborn will search for the human voice and demonstrate pleasure or mild surprise when finding the face that is the sound source. Upon sighting the face, a newborn's eyes widen, his or her face broadens, and he or she may tilt the head toward the source. Body tension increases, but the infant remains quietly inactive. Upon finding a nonhuman sound source, however, an infant does not demonstrate these recognition behaviors. When an infant responds, it is almost impossible for a caregiver not to become "hooked" on the infant.

A newborn will stop crying to attend to its mother's voice. In turn, the mother will stop doing almost anything to attend to her infant's voice. The selective attention of each partner and the ease of interacting predict later communication between the two.

A newborn's facial expressions demonstrate the high degree of maturity of the facial neuromuscular system, resulting in neonatal expressions resembling displeasure, fear, sorrow, anger, joy, and disgust. No experts attribute these actual emotional states to an infant, but caregivers act as if these emotions are present.

Infant head movements also have high signal value for a caregiver. The face and head become important for communication very early because of the relatively advanced maturational level of these structures compared to the rest of an infant's body. A newborn will turn its head to view a human face. Initially, the head and eyes move together. Three head positions, illustrated in Figure 5.1, are important because the caregiver interprets them as communication signals.

Newborns have individual personalities that affect the patterns of interaction. Differences may include an infant's general mood, intensity of activity and response, sensitivity to stimuli and adaptability to change, persistence, distractibility, and approach–withdraw. The best interaction is one in which there is a "good fit" between contextual demands and a child's temperament.

FIGURE *5.1* **Head Positions of Newborn**

TYPE	DESCRIPTION	RESULT FOR INFANT AND MATERNAL INTERPRETATION
Central	Faces mother or turns away slightly to either side	Infant: Can discern form Mother: Interprets as an approach or attending signal

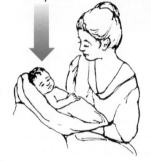

Peripheral	Turns head 15 to 90 degrees	Infant: Cannot discern mother's facial features so form perception lost; motion, speed, and direction perception maintained, so can monitor mother's head Mother: Signal of infant aversion or flight

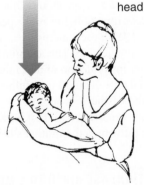

Loss of visual contact	Turns head more than 90 degrees or lowers head	Infant: Loss of motion, speed, and direction perception Mother: Termination of interaction; head lowering interpreted as more temporary

Source: Information from Stern (1977).

The newborn's visual focus is best at about 8 inches, and the mother's gaze during feeding is about 7½ inches.

A neonate also has a limited set of behaviors that will help him or her begin to communicate. In fact, newborns communicate unintentionally prior to birth, generally with kicks to express discomfort resulting from the mother's position.

An infant's state of wakefulness influences adults' behaviors. A caregiver learns the appropriate times to play with the neonate and to leave him or her alone. In other words, the caregiver learns the signals for engagement. The refinement of a baby's signals and responsiveness to a caregiver reinforce further communication.

A newborn's states are regulated by bodily processes such as ingestion, elimination, respiration, and hunger. The sleep–awake patterns of a caregiver and child provide shared periods for specific interactions. Under a caregiver's direction, the awake periods fill with specific action sequences such as feeding and dressing. With each successive awakening, a child's and caregiver's interactions become increasingly predictable. This common context aids infant interpretation and becomes the forum for later introduction of new information.

A mother appears to maintain an optimal state of infant wakefulness by holding her child in close proximity and by speaking. Both of these behaviors become more frequent in the first 2 weeks of an infant's life. A mother's behavior can bring an infant back to alertness or facilitate the shift to sleep. Thus, an infant's state influences the mother's behavior, which in turn influences the infant's state.

SOCIALIZATION AND EARLY COMMUNICATION: AGE BIRTH TO 6 MONTHS

Shortly after birth, an infant becomes actively involved in the interactive process with adults. By 1 month of age, an infant engages in interactional sequences. When awake and in the appropriate position with an adult, an infant will gaze at an adult's face and vocalize and respond to the mother's vocalizations and movements with movement and eye contact. As early as 6 weeks of age, infants are able to coordinate the amount of time spent gazing and will change their gaze patterns based on their partners' gaze (Crown, Feldstein, Jasnow, Beebe, & Jaffe, 2002).

As was noted, infants are especially responsive to their caregivers' voice and face. In fact, a young infant will attend to a human face to the exclusion of just about everything else. Within the first week of life, infants begin to make gross hand gestures, tongue protrusions, and mouth opening in response to similar behaviors. The caregiver treats this behavior as social in nature, embellishing it with communicational intent. By 1 month of age, an infant may make pitch and speech sound durations similar to those of a caregiver.

In addition, infants respond differentially to their mothers' face and voice. By as early as 2 weeks, an infant is able to distinguish its mother from a stranger. An infant will turn toward its mother and fix its gaze upon her mouth or eyes. The infant's facial expression will be one of interest or mild surprise, followed by a smile. At about 3 weeks of age, this smile of recognition is one of the first examples of a **social smile,** rather than one based on an infant's internal physical state. At around 3 to 6 weeks of age, infants smile in response to the human face and eye gaze; to the human voice (especially if high-pitched); and to tickling. The caregiver, of course, responds in kind.

A young infant is so tuned to the human face that at 3 weeks, he or she will even smile at an oval with two large dots for eyes but will not respond to the outline or to the eyes separately. This preference for eyes increases even more during the second month of life.

Visual responsiveness and memory are reflected in increased communication skills. Although a 2-month-old will search for its mother's voice, he or she will turn away from strange voices.

By the second month, certain people have become associated with particular behaviors. For example, an infant's mother becomes associated with feeding, and an infant will begin a sucking response upon seeing her. This recognition of familiar people, plus the infant's rapid boredom with other visual stimuli, signify an increase in visual memory. By 3 months of age, an infant can discriminate different people visually and respond accordingly.

This change is reflected in stages of smile development. At the end of the first month, an infant's smile becomes less automatic, but it is still unselective. During the third month, an infant smiles less at objects. In turn, his or her smile becomes more social and physically broader, with a crinkling around the eyes. This responsiveness is reflected in an infant's selective attention at 4 months of age to specific individuals and to joyful expressions longer than to angry ones. Often he or she will ignore feeding in order to concentrate on "people watching."

With maturity, infant cooing increases and is easily stimulated by attention and speech, and by toys moved in front of a baby. An infant coos when not distressed, and this behavior develops parallel to social smiling. By 2 months of age, cooing often occurs in bursts or episodes accompanying other expressions.

A 3-month-old infant's cognitive abilities are such that the expressionless human face alone does not have the stimulus power to hold his or her attention. The stimulus power of any one face resides in that face's similarity to, or difference from, the infant's internal facial schemes. If the mismatch is too great, such as a distorted face, an infant loses interest or gets upset.

To maintain attention, a caregiver must modify her behavior to provide the appropriate level of stimulation. She therefore exaggerates her facial expressions and voice and vocalizes more often. In turn, an infant responds to this new level of stimulation. "There is a progressive mutual modification in the child's and mother's behavior in that changes in the baby's development alter the mother's behavior and this, in turn, affects the baby" (Schaffer, 1977, p. 53). In this developmental dance, first one partner leads and then the other. An example of this meshing of infant behavior and caregiver expectations is an infant's sleep-awake cycle. Initially, an infant's sleep pattern is random: sleeping about two-thirds of the time, both day and night. By week 16 he or she sleeps about 10 hours at night, with time out for a feeding or two, and about 5 hours during the day. In this way the infant moves from an individual synchrony to an interpersonal one. As can be seen, both partners affect their mutual interaction. Infants affect caregivers and vice versa. Developmental changes affect the dynamic relationship between child and caregiver behaviors and the context.

At any given moment, a caregiver must determine the appropriate amount of stimulation based on an infant's level of attention. By 3 months, an infant can maintain a fairly constant internal state, so he or she can be attentive for longer periods. An infant's level of excitation is positively related to the level of incoming stimulation. If a caregiver provides too much stimulation, an infant overloads and turns away or becomes overexcited.

Maternal sensitivity to her infant is multifaceted and varies with the situation. In general, sensitivity permeates all the parent's behaviors with the infant and promotes rather than interrupts an exchange (van den Boom, 1997). Of most importance is timing of a mother's behaviors and the match between that behavior and the infant's behavior. In general, sensitive mothers vary their rate of noninterruptive speech based on their infant's rate of such behavior (Hane, Feldstein, & Dernetz, 2003). Mothers who are over- or underresponsive tend to undermine the attachment between themselves and their infants (Jafee, Beebe, Feldstein, Crown, & Jasnow, 2001).

Child temperament and parenting stress are especially important interactional factors (Noel, Peterson, & Jesso, 2008). Child temperament characteristics that aid social interaction are related to better narrative ability later. In contrast, high emotionality in children is related to poorer receptive vocabulary skills and shorter, less descriptive and less informative narratives. Negative child temperament factors might include a short attention span, easily aroused emotions, and high activity level (Coplan, Barber, & Lagace-Seguin, 1999).

Temperament influences children's language development and parent–child interactions from very early in life. For example, positive factors such as orienting toward a parent, easy soothability, and frequent smiling and laughter at 6 to 12 months of age are related to better receptive vocabulary at 21 months (Morales et al., 2000).

High parenting stress is related to children's poorer receptive and expressive vocabulary skills and adverse cognitive and behavioral outcomes. It is not stress itself that affects children but the affect of stress on parent–child interactions, which in turn affects children's development (Crnic & Low, 2002). For example, the amount of maternal physical stimulation is related to the interaction between infant temperament and mothers' reported parenting stress. In general, mothers of less frustrated infants provide more physical stimulation than mothers of easily frustrated infants under conditions of low or moderate stress. In contrast, mothers who reported high parenting stress provide low levels of physical stimulation regardless of child temperament. Parenting stress seems to affect children by impairing parent–child interactions and lowering maternal responsiveness (Calkins, Hungerford, & Dedmon, 2004).

Dialogs become more important and by the third month, handling has decreased by 30% from that at birth, but dialog has increased. Infants are full partners in this dialog, and their behavior is influenced by the communication behavior of their caregivers. A 12-week-old infant is twice as likely to revocalize if his or her caregiver responds verbally to the child's initial vocalization rather than responding with a touch, look, or smile. Similar revocalization patterns are also reported for 6-month-olds. There is a greater tendency for an infant's vocalizations to be followed by caregiver vocalizations, and those of the caregiver by the child's, than would be expected by chance. A caregiver may perceive her role as that of "replier" to the infant's vocalizations and prefer babbling that sounds like speech (Bloom & Lo, 1990).

This "conversational" turn-taking by adults with 3-month-olds benefits an infant's babbling and turn-taking (Bloom, 1988). As we have seen, babbling may become more speechlike and mature, containing syllables rather than individual sounds.

There appears to be a shift in the infant–caregiver vocalization pattern from simultaneous to sequential beginning at about 12 weeks (Ginsberg & Kilbourne, 1988). Prior to this, the infant produces vocalizations that overlap with those of its mother. Infants are more likely to initiate vocalizations when their mothers are vocalizing. In addition, both interactive partners make extensive use of smiles, head movements, and gestures. Although vocal exchanges are rather simple and contain little useful information, later, more complex messages will necessitate a turn-taking pattern rather than a concurrent one. At 12 to 18 weeks, there is a sharp increase in the alternating vocalization pattern, although concurrent vocalizations still occur more frequently. During alternating vocalization, both American and Japanese infants will pause as if awaiting a response (Masataka, 1993). If none is forthcoming, the child may revocalize.

Mothers begin to imitate their infants' coughing at 2 months of age. Initially, this behavior is performed to attract attention, but eventually an exchange emerges. By 4 months, an infant will initiate the exchange with a smile or a cough.

Eye gaze is also very important in these early dialogs. By 6 weeks of age, an infant is able to fix visually on its mother's eyes and hold the fixation, with eyes widening and brightening. An infant is more likely to begin and to continue looking if the caregiver is looking. In return, the caregiver's behavior becomes more social, and play interactions begin. At 3 months of age, an infant has a focal range that almost equals its mother's, and he or she becomes a true interactional partner in this modality.

Two types of gaze patterns have been identified. During joint or shared attending, gaze is directed at objects. Mothers monitor their infants' gaze and follow its orientation. **Mutual gaze,** or looking at each other, may signal intensified attention. At about 3 months, mutual gaze may be modified occasionally into *gaze coupling,* a turn-taking interaction of making and breaking eye contact. Mutual eye gaze may be important for the formation of attachment or bonding. Also called dyadic gaze, its rhythm of mother and infant looking at and looking away from each other's faces seems to be important in enabling infants to predict events and maternal behaviors (Beebe et al., 2008). Of particular importance is the relative lengths of time spent in mutual gaze and looking away and variations from that pattern. In general, both high-stress infants and high-stress mothers use more variation in their gaze patterns, making anticipation of each other's gaze patterns more difficult for both partners. High-stress mothers report more depression, anxiety, self-criticism, and traumatic childhood experiences.

Infant–caregiver bonding is determined by the quality of their interactions. Several factors influence bonding and an infant's subsequent feelings of security. The levels of maternal playfulness, sensitivity, encouragement, and pacing at 3 months have been found to be positively related to the security of attachment at 9 months.

During the first three months, a caregiver's responding teaches a child the signal value of specific behaviors. The infant learns the stimulus–response sequence. If he or she signals, the caregiver will respond. When the infant cries, the caregiver answers. Thus, the infant develops an expectation that he or she can change or control the environment. In addition, the child learns that signaling results in a predictable outcome. Possibly as high as 77% of infant crying episodes are followed by maternal responses, while only 6% are preceded by maternal contact. As a result of maternal responses, the cry becomes an infant's means of gaining contact with mother although this behavior doesn't seem purposeful yet.

Immediate positive parental responsiveness increases a child's motivation to communicate. If motivation is high, an infant will attempt more frequent and varied interactions. Motivation to communicate at 9 months is best indicated by earlier exploration behavior and displays of curiosity.

The degree of parental responsiveness varies with the culture, as does the amount of infant crying. In general, more mobile societies, such as hunter-gatherer cultures, exhibit little child crying. Carried by its mother in a sling, a child is often attended to before crying begins.

Mothers not only respond to their infants' cries but can identify the type of cry produced. Mothers can reliably rate their 3- to 4-month-olds' types of cries.

By 3 to 4 months, two additional response patterns have emerged: rituals and game-playing. These will be discussed in some detail later in this chapter. Rituals, such as feeding, provide a child with predictable patterns of behavior and speech. A child becomes upset if these rituals are changed or disrupted. Games, such as "peekaboo," "this little piggy," and "I'm gonna get you," have all the aspects of communication. There is an exchange of turns, rules for each turn, and particular slots for words and actions.

At 5 months the infant shows more deliberate imitation of movements and vocalizations. Facial imitation is most frequent at 4 to 6 months of age. By 6 to 8 months, however, hand and nonspeech imitation become most frequent for behaviors previously exhibited in the child's spontaneous behavior.

Between 3 and 6 months of age, the period of peak face-to-face play, an infant is exposed to tens of thousands of examples of facial emotions. In interactions with mother, a child mirrors mother's expression, and she, in turn, imitates the infant. The infant's repertoire of facial emotions is listed in Table 5.1.

As an infant approaches 6 months of age, this interest in toys and objects increases. Prior to this period, an infant is not greatly attracted to objects unless they are noise producing or made mobile and lively by an adult. This change reflects, in part, the development of eye–hand coordination, which is exhibited in reaching, grasping, and manipulation. From this point on, interactions increasingly include the infant, the caregiver, and some object.

Protoconversations

There are identifiable interactional phases in routines and game playing. Mothers and their 3-month-old infants exhibit initiation, mutual orientation, greeting, a play dialog, and disengagement, although any given exchange may not contain every phase. To initiate the exchange, a

TABLE *5.1*   *Infant Emotions*

EMOTION	DESCRIPTION	EMERGENCE
Interest	Brows knit or raised, mouth rounded, lips pursed	Present at birth
Distress	Eyes closed tightly, mouth square and angular (as in anger)	Present at birth
Disgust	Nose wrinkled, upper lip elevated, tongue protruded	Present at birth
Social smile	Corners of mouth raised, cheeks lifted, eyes twinkle; neonatal "half smile" and early startle may be precursors	4–6 weeks
Anger	Brows together and drawn downward, eyes set, mouth square	3–4 months
Sadness	Inner corners of brows raised, mouth turns down in corners, pout	3–4 months
Surprise	Brows raised, eyes widened, oval-shaped mouth	3–4 months
Fear	Brows level but drawn in and up, eyes widened, mouth retracted	5–7 weeks

Source: Information from work of Carroll Izard as reported by Trotter (1983).

mother smiles and talks to her infant. For its part, the infant vocalizes and smiles at mother when mother has paused too long. When one partner responds with a neutral or bright face, the mutual phase begins, and one partner speaks or vocalizes. The greeting consists of mutual smiles and eye gazes, with little body or hand movement. Turn-taking is seen in the play-dialog phase. The mother talks in a pattern of bursts interspersed with pauses, and the infant vocalizes during the pauses. Finally, disengagement occurs when one partner looks away. These interactional exchanges, called **protoconversations,** contain the initial elements of emerging conversation.

A 5-month-old also vocalizes to accompany different attitudes, such as pleasure and displeasure, satisfaction and anger, and eagerness. He or she will vocalize to other people and to a mirror image, as well as to toys and objects.

Both partners are active participants in protoconversational exchanges. The infant moves face, lips, tongue, arms, hands, and body toward the mother, whose behavior reflects that of the infant. In turn, the infant imitates the mother's movements. Frequently, the behaviors of the mother and infant appear to be so simultaneous as to constitute a single act. The infant frequently leads by initiating the behavior. Mother does not simply follow, however, but maintains a mutual exchange.

DEVELOPMENT OF INTENTIONALITY: AGE 7 TO 12 MONTHS

During the second six months of life, an infant begins to assert more control within the infant–caregiver interaction. He or she learns to communicate intentions more clearly and effectively. Each success motivates an infant to communicate more and to learn to communicate better. The primary modes for this expression are gestural and vocal.

By 7 months, an infant begins to respond differentially to his or her interactional partner, staying close to the caregiver, following her movements, and becoming distressed if she leaves. Even infant play with objects is influenced by maternal attending. Infants play with toys as long as their mothers look on, but when their mothers turn away, infants leave their toys 50% of the time and attempt to retrieve the lost attention. This maternal attachment is related to the predictability of the mother's behavior.

In recognition of an infant's interest in objects and increasing ability to follow conversational cues, the caregiver makes increasing reference to objects, events, and people. Increasingly, the infant demonstrates selective listening to familiar words and compliance with simple requests.

Infants imitate simple motor behaviors by 8 to 10 months, responding to requests to wave bye-bye. Infant responses to maternal verbal and nonverbal requests increase from 39.5% at 9 months to 52.0% at 11 months. Requests for action are answered one and a half times as frequently as requests for vocalization. By modifying forms and frequencies of reply, an infant gains considerable control over the communicative exchange.

Nine-month-olds can also follow maternal pointing and glancing. The infant cues on a combination of maternal head and eye orientation and on eye movement.

Visual orientation of both an infant and mother is usually accompanied by maternal naming to establish the topic of a protoconversation. The mother monitors her infant's glance for signs of interest. Mothers of 8- to 14-month-olds look at their infants so frequently that the responsibility for maintaining eye contact really rests with the child. This monitoring by the mother decreases as the child gets older.

Caregivers also monitor infant vocalizations. Parents of 8- to 12-month-olds can consistently recognize infant intonational patterns that convey request, frustration, greeting, and pleasant surprise.

Gaze and vocalization seem to be related. An infant's gaze is more likely to be initiated and maintained when its mother is vocalizing and/or gazing back, and, in turn, the mother is more likely to initiate and maintain vocalization when her infant is looking at her. Although mothers and 1-year-olds exhibit very little vocal overlap, they depart from their turn-taking behaviors when they laugh or join in chorus. The exchange is one of reciprocal actions, intonations, and gestures.

At around 1 year of age, children who have learned to coordinate gaze and vocalization look at their partners at the beginning of a vocal turn, possibly for reassurance. Only six months later, they tend to use a more adult pattern and to look at their partners at the end of a turn to signal a turn shift (D'Odorico, Cassibba, & Salerni, 1997).

The communication between infant and caregiver is closely related to the infant's resultant behavior state, and the child will show signs of distress when communication sequences end. The infant will vocalize and gesture for attention, then exhibit sadness or grimace.

Communication Intentions

At about 8 to 9 months, an infant begins to develop *intentionality* or goal directedness and the ability to share goals with others. Up to this point, the child has focused primarily on either objects or people. Outcomes were rarely predicted by the child.

The appearance of gestures signals a cognitive ability to plan and to coordinate that plan to achieve a desired goal rather than the trial-and-error behavior noted previously.

Intentionality is exhibited when a child begins to encode a message for someone else. For the first time, he or she considers the audience. A child may touch his or her mother, gain eye contact, then gesture toward an object. An explicit bid for attention is coupled with a signal, although the order may vary. Initially, a child's **communication intentions** are expressed primarily through gestures. Functions, such as requesting, interacting, and attracting attention, are first fulfilled by prelinguistic means and only later by language. The 9-month-old will use both gestures and vocalizations to accomplish several intentions.

Between 6 and 12 months, infants develop the vocal repertoire to regulate interactions with their caregivers. Emotional or nonintentional vocalizations differ from intentional ones, which are shorter with a lower overall frequency and a greater intensity (Papaeliou, Minadakis, & Cavouras, 2002). Differing pitch patterns in prelinguistic vocalizations of typically developing 10-month-old infants indicate that these vocalizations serve both as a means of purposeful communication when accompanied by nonvocal communicative behavior such as gestures and as a tool of thought when accompanied by explorative activities (Papaeliou & Trevarthen, 2006).

A three-stage sequence in the development of early communication functions includes perlocutionary, illocutionary, and locutionary levels (Bates, Camaioni, & Volterra, 1975). In Table 5.2, these stages are related to the infant's cognitive developments.

Perlocutionary Stage The perlocutionary stage begins at birth and continues into the second half-year of life. Throughout this stage, an infant fails to signal specific intentions beyond those behaviors that will sustain an interaction, such as cries, coos, and use of the face and body nonspecifically.

Initially, an infant's behavior is characterized by *attentional interactions* in which he or she attends to stimuli and responds to stimuli with diffuse undifferentiated behaviors, such as crying. Crying indicates general pain, discomfort, or need but does not identify the cause of the problem. Mother interprets her infant's behavior and responds differentially. Crying teaches an infant the value of behavior as a signal to communication partners.

The communication system becomes more effective as a caregiver learns to interpret a child's behavior. Interactions become more predictable. Gradually, an infant's greater cognitive

TABLE *5.2* **Development of Intentionality**

STAGE	AGE (MONTHS)	CHARACTERISTICS
Perlocutionary	0–8 (approx.)	Intention inferred by adults
		Attentional interactions
		■ No goal awareness ■ Attends to and responds to stimuli
		Contingency interactions
		■ Awareness of goal ■ Undifferentiated behavior to initiate or continue a stimulus, anticipates events, vocalizes for attention
Substage 1		Shows self
		Differentiated interactions
		■ Design, plan, and adjust behavior to achieve goal ■ Raise arms to be picked up, pull string to get object, look at adult and desired object
Illocutionary	8–12	Emergence of intentional communication
		Encoded interactions
		■ Coordinated plan to achieve goals ■ Gestures, brings objects to caregiver for help, climbs for desired objects
Substage 1		Shows objects
Substage 2		Displays a full range of gestures
		■ Conventional gestures: requesting, pointing or signaling notice, showing, giving, and protesting ■ Unconventional gestures: tantruming and showing off ■ Functional gestures
Locutionary	12+	Words accompany or replace gestures to express communication functions previously expressed in gestures alone or gestures plus vocalization
		Symbolic interactions

Sources: Information from Wetherby & Prizant (1989) and Bates et al. (1975).

ability will enable him to her to understand the outcome of behavior. Soon an infant will begin making deliberate attempts to share specific experiences with caregivers, fully expecting them to respond. Characterized by *contingency interactions,* behavior is directed toward initiating and sustaining interactions (Wetherby & Prizant, 1989). Affective signals, such as crying, will become more conventional and more directed toward and responsive to the communication context.

An infant calls attention to the environment by scanning and searching. The mother follows her infant's visual regard and provides a label or comment.

When aware of a child's desire to continue, a caregiver can sustain their "dialog." When more mature, the child will initiate a behavior and repeat it in order to sustain these interactions.

Toward the end of the perlocutionary period, infants become more interested in manipulating objects and begin to use gestures that demonstrate an understanding of object purpose or use and include such behaviors as bringing a cup to the lips or a telephone receiver to the ear. These gestures constitute a primitive form of naming. An infant demonstrates recognition that objects have stable characteristics and functions that necessitate specific behaviors. These early gestures are usually brief and incomplete. For example, a child may attempt to drink from an empty cup. In the early stages, sequences of events are also rare.

At this stage, an infant begins reaching for desired objects. For objects that are beyond its grasp, the infant's reach will later become a pointing gesture.

Illocutionary Stage   The second, or illocutionary, stage of communication development begins at 8 to 9 months of age. Within this stage an infant uses conventional gestures, vocalizations, or both to communicate different intentions. The emergence of intentional communication is reflected in gestures accompanied by eye contact with the child's communication partner, consistent sound and intonation to signal specific intentions, and persistent attempts to communicate. If not understood, a child may repeat the behaviors or modify them for the communication partner. In each behavior a child considers both the message and the partner's reception of it, thus exhibiting an intention to communicate.

Three sequential substages in the development of gestures have been noted. In the first substage, which begins prior to the illocutionary period, an infant exhibits or shows self. An infant hides its face, acts coy, raises the arms to be picked up, or plays peekaboo. Behavior becomes coordinated and regulated to achieve goals (Wetherby & Prizant, 1989).

In the second substage, an infant shows objects by extending them toward the caregiver but does not release them. A child draws attention to these objects as a way of sharing attention.

Finally, in the last substage, fully within the illocutionary stage, an infant displays a full range of gestures, including conventional means of showing, giving, pointing, and requesting (Figure 5.2). Other nonconventional gestures, such as having tantrums and showing off, are also present. In general, each infant develops its own style with nonconventional gestures. Finally, each infant develops one or more functional gestures or gestures that are shaped for specific meaning, such as touching the mouth repeatedly to signal *eat* or running to the door to signal *out*. My daughter would twist her legs around each other to signal *potty*.

The giving gesture, unlike showing, includes a release of the object. Frequently, giving follows a maternal request for the object. A favorite game becomes "the trade," in which the partners take turns passing an object between them.

Pointing may include the whole hand or only a finger with the arm extended. An infant makes only the minimal effort needed to convey the intention. Unlike requesting, pointing is not accompanied by movement of the upper trunk in the direction of the object. Pointing is a widespread, if not universal, pattern cross-culturally (Butterworth, 2003).

By 12 months of age, and possibly earlier, infant pointing to share with others, both attention to a referent and a specific attitude about that referent, is a full communicative act (Liszkowski, Carpenter, & Tomasello, 2007). This is seen in an infant's response to a communication partner's behavior. For example, if a partner responds by attending to something else with positive attitude, infants will repeat their pointing to redirect the partner's attention, showing an understanding of the partner's reference and active message repair. In contrast, when a partner identifies an infant's referent correctly but displays disinterest, an infant will not repeat pointing, and there is an overall decrease in pointing behavior. Finally, when the

FIGURE 5.2 *Infant Standardized Gestures*

Infants develop a set of standardized gestures in addition to nonstandardized and functional gestures.

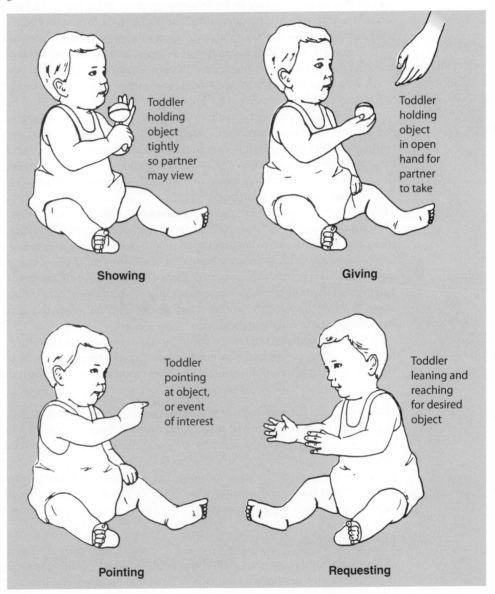

Toddler holding object tightly so partner may view

Showing

Toddler holding object in open hand for partner to take

Giving

Toddler pointing at object, or event of interest

Pointing

Toddler leaning and reaching for desired object

Requesting

partner attends to an infant's intended referent enthusiastically, infants do not attempt to repair the communication and there is an overall increase in gesturing.

Requesting is a whole-hand grasping reach toward a desired object or a giving gesture accompanied by a call for assistance. In its most mature form, each gesture contains a visual check to ensure that the communication partner is attending.

These initial gestures are used to signal two general communication functions: *protoimperatives*, such as requests, and *protodeclaratives*. Protoimperatives or requests generally request objects, participation, or actions (Bruner, 1983). An infant begins to realize with requests that she cannot be unreasonable or ask for something that she can do herself.

The acquisition of gestures by infants is reflected in maternal speech to these children. For example, the earlier infants produce imperative gestures, such as requesting, the more frequently their mothers talk about the infants' own states, using words such as *want, try,* and *need* (Slaughter, Peterson, & Carpenter, 2009). In turn, the mothers' talk about desires and intentions positively influences their infants' early developing communicative abilities.

Protodeclaratives, such as pointing or showing, have the goal of maintaining joint or shared attending. Thus, children communicate to share information as well as to request (Golinkoff, 1993). Nearly 30% of the communication episodes between presymbolic children and their caregivers are of this type. An infant will point in the presence of a communication partner but not when alone.

Initially, gestures appear without vocalizations, but the two are gradually paired. The prelinguistic vocalization patterns of infants vary based on intent. Social vocalizations, uttered apparently with the intention to communicate, and "private" speech, related to solitary activities, have differing pitch shapes or contours (Papaeliou & Trevarthen, 2006). Thus, prelinguistic vocalizations serve both as means of purposeful communication and as a tool of thought, functions later assumed by language.

Consistent vocal patterns, dubbed *phonetically consistent forms (PCFs)* in Chapter 4, accompany many gestures. PCFs occur with pauses that clearly mark boundaries, function as words for a child, are imitations of environmental sounds, and usually accompany events or actions in the environment. Other sounds are imitations of environmental sounds, such as a dog's bark or a car's engine. My granddaughter Cassidy started barking at about 7 months. Once an infant begins to use PCFs, mother will no longer accept other, less consistent vocalizations. PCFs are a transition to words in a highly creative developmental period when the child is also adept at employing gestures and intonation.

The appearance of intentional communication in the form of gestures requires a certain level of cognitive, as well as social, functioning. Person–object sequences, such as requests, in which a child signals an adult to obtain an object, begin at 8 to 10 months, along with a shift to more complex social interactions.

Locutionary Stage   The final stage of functional communication development is the locutionary stage, which begins with the first meaningful word. In these symbolic interactions, the child's intent becomes encoded in words that are used with or without gestures to accomplish the functions previously filled by gestures alone. For example, pointing develops, then vocalization within pointing, and finally verbalization or use of words. Words and gestures are used to refer to the same content. The gesture, which initially stands for the entire message, gradually becomes the context for more symbolic ways of communicating the message.

Comprehension

During the second six months, a child also begins to attach meaning to symbols. At 8 months, some infants may comprehend as many as 20 words (Fagan, 2009). Infants use two strategies, bracketing and clustering, to segregate speech directed at them (Goodsitt, Morgan, & Kuhl, 1993). **Bracketing** is the use of prosodic or rhythmic cues to detect divisions between clauses and phrases. Divisions are marked by maternal pauses, pitch changes, vowel lengthening, or by use of specific words. Although bracketing cues are helpful for identifying clauses and phrases, they are of little aid for deciphering words.

Clustering is the use of predictable phonotactic units within words. Each language permits only certain syllable and phoneme sequencing structures, so predictability is high within words. Between words, however, predictability is low, thus highlighting word-to-word transitions for infants.

Using a combination of these strategies, an infant is able to divide caregiver speech into manageable units. Predictable, familiar words and phrases become associated with familiar contexts, helping early meanings to form in the infant's brain.

Summary

During the first six months of life, an infant learns the rituals and processes of communication through interaction with his or her caregiver (Table 5.3). The caregiver treats the infant as a full conversational partner and acts as if the infant communicates meaningfully. The infant also

TABLE 5.3 *Infant Social and Communicative Development*

AGE	BEHAVIORS
Newborn	Vision best at 8 inches; prefers light–dark contrasts, angularity, complexity, curvature
	Hearing best in frequency range of human voice; prefers human voice; exhibits entrainment
	Facial expressions
1 week	"Self-imitation"; reflexive actions but treated as meaningful by caregiver
2 weeks	Distinguishing of caregiver's voice and face
3 weeks	Social smile
1 month	Short visual exchanges with caregiver; prefers human face to all else
2 months	Cooing
3 months	Face alone not enough to hold infant's attention: in response, mother exaggerates her facial movements
	More frequent dialogs; decrease of handling by 30%
	Revocalization likely if caregiver's verbal response immediately follows child's first vocalization
	Vocal turn-taking and concurrent vocalization
	Gaze coupling
	Rituals and games
	Face play
5 months	Purposeful facial imitation
	Vocalization to accompany attitude
6 months	Hand and nonspeech imitation
8 months	Gestures
9 months	Imitation of more complicated motor behaviors
	Following of maternal pointing
11 months	Response to about half of maternal verbal and nonverbal requests
12 months	Use of words to fill communicative functions established by gestures

learns that behavior can have an effect upon the environment. At first, the infant's communication is general and unspecified. During the second six months, he or she develops intentional communication, first gesturally, then vocally. When the infant begins to use meaningful speech, it is within this context of gestures and vocalizations.

Maternal Communication Behaviors

As we have noted, infants and caregivers engage in dialog soon after birth. It is a complex interaction between infant character/temperament and maternal speech. Both partners exert some control within this exchange. The infant sets the level of exchange because of limited abilities. The initial infant responses are rather rigid and fixed. Only gradually does the infant expand this behavioral repertoire.

The mother provides the framework and adjusts her behaviors to the information processing limitations of the infant. Mothers demonstrate a willingness to learn from and respond to an infant's behavior patterns. A mother's observation of her child's regular hunger rhythms, reflected in the child's readiness to nurse, and the mother's response to these rhythms instruct the infant on the nature of order.

Within a given exchange, both partners adjust their behavior continually to maintain an optimum level of stimulation. The mother maintains the infant's attention at a high level by her behavior. In response, the infant coos, smiles, and gazes alertly. Reinforced for her efforts, the mother tries even harder to maintain the infant's level of stimulation. Each party is responsive to the other. For example, the mother helps expand the infant's abilities by deliberately "messing up" more consistently than expected. By slightly exceeding the limits of the infant's behavior, the mother forces the infant to adjust to new stimuli.

The foundation for infant–caregiver face-to-face exchanges is in the modifications made by an adult to accommodate a child. The caregiver monitors the infant's state to determine the right time to begin an exchange, and then obtains the child's attention to optimize the interaction. Once the exchange begins, the adult modifies her or his behavior to maintain the child's interest.

Table 5.4 describes these behaviors and gives examples of each. Within the exchange, mothers make infantlike modifications such as exaggerated facial expressions, body movements, positioning, timing, touching, prolonged gaze, and baby talk. These modifications also occur in the behavior of other adults and older children as they interact with infants. Neither prior experience with infants nor prior learning seems to explain this adult behavior. Three factors appear important in influencing the initial interactions of a newborn and its mother: the medication used in delivery, the number of pregnancies, and the mother's socioeconomic and cultural background.

Most adults respond to the "babyness" of an infant, particularly the face, which they find irresistible. An infant's head is large in proportion to the body, with large eyes and round cheeks. In brief, a child looks cute. To this physical image an infant adds smiles, gazes, mouth opening, and tongue thrust. Infants with a facial deformity may elicit very different or negative responses.

In the following sections, we shall explore the modifications made by caregivers in response to their infants. This behavior varies with culture, class, and gender of an infant.

INFANT-ELICITED SOCIAL BEHAVIOR

Caregiver responses can be characterized as "infant-elicited social behaviors." They appear in response to infants but occur infrequently in adult-to-adult exchanges. These caregiver behaviors have exaggerated physical movement, usually slow or elongated in rate, and form a select,

TABLE *5.4* **Caregiver Foundations for Face-to-Face Communication**

BEHAVIOR	DESCRIPTION	EXAMPLES
Preparatory activities	Free infant from physiological state dominance	Reduce interference of hunger or fatigue Sooth or calm infant when upset
State-setting activities	Manipulate physical environment to optimize interaction	Move into infant's visual field Attain attention by modifying vocalizations
Maintenance of communication framework	Use of continuates by caregiver	Modulate speech, rhythmic tapping and patting, rhythmic body movements; provide infant with a focus of attention and action, a set of timing markers
Infantlike modifications of adult actions	Variation of caregiver activities in rate, intensity modulation, amplitude, and quality from those of adult–adult	Use baby talk—slowed and exaggerated Imitate baby movements—close, oriented straight ahead, parallel, and perpendicular to plane of infant

Source: Information from Tronick, Als, & Adamson (1979).

limited repertoire that is used frequently. The purpose of these modifications is to enhance recognition and discrimination by a child. The behaviors of one mother differ from those of another. Each caregiver develops his or her own style. Infant-elicited social behavior also consists of maternal adaptations in speech and language, gaze, facial expression, facial presentation and head movement, and proxemics.

Infant-Directed Speech (IDS)

The speech and language of adults and children to infants is systematically modified from that used in regular conversation. This adapted speech and language has been called infant-directed speech (IDS) or *motherese*. For our purposes, we shall use IDS to signify the speech and language addressed to infants (Table 5.5). We will use the term *motherese* or *parentese* later to denote speech and language used with toddlers. Use of IDS does not imply that mothers use forms such as *horsie* or *ni-night*. Parents do not use such "babyish" forms until a child is old enough to understand them.

Maternal input is very important for an infant's own communication development. For example, children who are deaf and exposed to maternal signing from birth achieve all linguistic milestones at or before the expected age for hearing children (Petitto & Marentette, 1990, 1991). In a second example, when Korean mothers speak to their infants, they use sounds that closely match their infant's production abilities as well as highlight perceptual differences between sounds (Lee, Davis, & MacNeilage, 2008). In this way infant-directed speech (IDS) may facilitate infant learning of phonological regularities of their native language.

TABLE 5.5 *Characteristics of Infant-directed Speech*

Short utterance length (mean utterance length as few as 2.6 morphemes) and simple syntax
Small core vocabulary, usually object centered
Topics limited to here and now
Heightened use of facial expressions and gestures
Frequent questioning and greeting
Treating of infant behaviors as meaningful: Mother awaits infant's turn and responds even to nonturns
Episodes of maternal utterances
Paralinguistic modifications of pitch and loudness
Frequent verbal rituals

IDS is characterized by short utterance length and simple syntax and use of a small core vocabulary. Mothers also paraphrase and repeat themselves. Topics are limited to the here and now. The mother's choice of content, type of information conveyed, and syntax appear to be heavily influenced by the context too. In addition, mothers use paralinguistic variations, such as intonation and pause, beyond those found in adult-to-adult speech. Employing more frequent facial expressions and gestures and an overall higher pitch, any one of us might engage in the following monolog:

> See the dog. (points, turns, looks, pauses)
> Big dog. (spreads arms, pauses)
> Nice dog. (pauses)
> Pet the dog. (pets, pauses)
> Can you pet dog? (pauses)
> Nice dog. Do you like dog? (pauses)
> Un-huh. Nice dog.

This little monolog contains most aspects of IDS.

Maternal speech prior to 6 months may contain fewer than 3 morphemes per utterance. This may increase to about 3.5 or more morphemes at 6 months. In part, this rise may reflect the increasingly complex communication of a mother and her infant. After one year, average maternal utterance length is reported to be between 2.8 and 3.5 morphemes. These lower values may represent maternal modeling in anticipation of an infant's speech. These adult-to-infant averages are well below the adult-to-adult average, which is around 8 morphemes. In addition, IDS is less complex structurally than adult-to-adult speech. In general, mothers who use more short sentences when their children are 9 months of age have toddlers with better receptive language abilities at 18 months (Murray, Johnson, & Peters, 1990). Such short, simple utterances can be found in IDS of many languages.

Mothers also use a considerable number of questions and greetings with their infants. These conversational devices may enable a mother to treat any infant response as a conversational turn, since both questions and greetings require a response. In turn, mothers respond to their infants' behaviors as a meaningful reply. Even an infant's burps, yawns, sneezes, coughs, coos, smiles, and laughs may receive a response from its mother. Over 20% of maternal utterances are greetings such as *hi* and *bye-bye* or acknowledgments such as *sure, uh-huh,* and *yeah.* This maternal response pattern does not occur with noncommunication like infant behaviors, such as arm flapping or bouncing.

Appropriate and consistent adult *responsivity* is very important in the emergence of early communication although the amount and type of responsivity varies greatly across caregiver–infant pairs. Communication results when the caregiver attributes meaning to a baby's behaviors. Consistently, mothers are able to identify what they perceive as communicatively important behaviors in their infants (Meadows, Elias, & Bain, 2000). Gradually, a child learns that his or her behavior results in consistent, predictable effects.

Caregivers spontaneously respond to 30% to 50% of infants' non-crying vocalizations. When adults fail to respond, 5-month-old infants will increase their vocalizing (Goldstein, Schwade, & Bornstein, 2009). Interestingly, those infants who respond most vigorously have the best language comprehension abilities at 13 months.

For its part, an infant responds selectively. Situational variations are important, and an infant is least likely to vocalize when engaged in activities such as being changed, fed, or rocked, or when its mother watches television or talks to another person. In contrast, some maternal nonvocal behaviors, such as touching, holding close, looking at, or smiling at an infant, increase the likelihood of infant vocalizations.

Maternal utterances often occur in strings of successive utterances referring to the same object, action, or event. These verbal episodes may facilitate understanding because speech is less difficult to understand if a string of utterances is produced referring to the same object. Information gained from preceding utterances assists comprehension of following ones. Most episodes with infants begin with object manipulation and a high proportion of naming by the mother. At the beginning of the episode, pauses between utterances are twice as long as pauses

Mothers are tuned to the conversational needs of their children and modify their behavior to maximize children's participation.

within the episode itself. Young children receive help with object reference and *episodic* boundaries. A typical episode might proceed as follows:

> (shakes doll) Here's baby! (pauses)
> Mommy has baby. (cuddles doll, pauses)
> Uh-huh, Betsy want baby? (surprised expression, pauses)
> Here's baby! (pauses)
> Oh, baby scare Betsy? (concerned expression, pauses)

High rates of redundancy also occur in IDS, and there is a great degree of semantic similarity between successive utterances. This high rate of syntactic and semantic redundancy increases the predictability and continuity of each episode. Mothers repeat one out of every six utterances immediately and exactly. These self-repetitions decrease as a child assumes increasing responsibility in the conversation.

Early content tends to be object centered and concerned with the here and now. For a mother, topics are generally limited to what her infant can see and hear. As a child's age approaches 6 months, mothers in the United States tend to use a more informational style and, as a result, talk more about the environment and the infant's behavior.

Within an episode, an infant and mother engage in a dialog in which the infant's new communication abilities can emerge. Certain elements appear over and over in the mother's speech and give her infant the opportunity to predict and engage in the dialog. These predictable maternal behaviors may aid the infant's comprehension, allow the infant to concentrate her or his attention, and provide models of the expected dialog.

One of the most common sequences is that of joint, or shared, reference. **Referencing** is the noting of a single object, action, or event and is signaled by a mother either following her infant's glance and commenting on the object of its focus, shaking an object, or exaggerating an action to attract her infant's attention.

In addition, mothers use paralinguistic variations, varying the manner of presentation. For their part, infants respond to intonation patterns before they comprehend language, preferring a high, variable pitch. Mothers use a broad range of pitch and loudness, although overall, their pitch is higher than in adult-to-adult conversations (Sachs, 1985). This pitch contour has been found in a number of languages. Conversational sequences may include instances of maternal falsetto or bass voice and of whispers or yells. Content words and syllables receive additional emphasis.

The mother also modifies her rhythm and timing. Vowel duration is longer than in adult-to-adult discourse. The mother also uses longer pauses between utterances. Signing mothers of children who have deafness maintain similar rhythms with their hands (Fernald, 1994). Japanese mothers use responding to alter the duration of their infant's vocalizations. The length of maternal pauses is reflected in the child's subsequent response (Masataka, 1993).

There are many similarities in intonation across parents from languages as different as Comanche, English, French, Italian, German, Japanese, Latvian, Mandarin Chinese, Sinhala, and Xhosa, a South African language. Parents use a higher pitch, greater variability in pitch, shorter utterances, and longer pauses when talking to their preverbal infants than when talking to other adults. In general, regardless of the language, mothers use a wider pitch range than fathers.

Parents who speak American English seem to have more extreme modifications in their speech than do parents in other languages, especially Asian languages. These differences may reflect the more open American style of communicating and the more reticent and respectful Asian style. Regardless of the language, infants seem to prefer the intonational patterns of IDS from a very young age (Cooper & Aslin, 1990).

In elicitation sequences with their infants, mothers use all the behaviors just mentioned in an attempt to get their infants to make sounds. Unlike games, elicitation sequences continue even when an infant does not respond. In such situations, the mother redoubles her efforts with increasing use of IDS. There is no fixed repertoire of behaviors, and mothers are very adaptable.

Mothers talk to their infants for several reasons. First, selected infant behaviors are treated as meaningful communication turns. For a 3-month-old infant, these behaviors include smiling, burping, sneezing, coughing, vocalizing, looking intently, and gaze shifting. Second, mothers talk about what they are doing. They employ baby talk, ask their infants' permission, and give reasons for their own actions. Finally, mothers also talk to their infants just for the fun of it. Three specific occurrences of "fun talking" are game playing, attempting to elicit infant vocalizations, and offering objects for play.

After speaking, a mother waits approximately 0.6 second, the average adult turn-switching pause. Next, she waits for the duration of an imaginary infant response and another turn switch. Since many maternal utterances are questions, the duration of an infant response is relatively easy for the mother to estimate. Thus, the infant is exposed to a mature time frame in which later discourse skills will develop.

Language development experts differ as to the purpose of IDS. First, a mother probably uses both repetition and variation to capture and maintain her infant's attention. Maternal patterns of repetition are found in nonverbal as well as verbal behaviors. Prosodic and intonational variations reach a peak at 4 to 6 months. This variety helps keep an infant alert and interested. As an infant gets older, mother introduces more vocal and verbal variety, and rhythm declines.

Second, simplified speech aids children in learning language. Because maternal modifications differ only slightly from what an infant already knows, stimuli provide an optimal level of training. Although mothers' responses to 2-month-old infants are stimulating and inject meaning into infants' expressions, it seems doubtful at this stage that verbal meaning has any influence on an infant.

Third, maternal modifications may maintain a child's responsiveness at an optimal level. A mother assumes that her infant is a communication partner. Thus, maternal speech modifications are an attempt to maintain the conversation despite the conversational limitations of the infant. With a 3-month-old infant, the mother structures the sequence so that any infant response can be treated as a reply.

Fourth, maternal modifications maintain a conversation in order to provide a context for teaching language use. The mother's modifications are highly correlated with the level of her infant's performance.

Finally, maternal adaptations may reflect evolutionary developments in the human species (Fernald, 1994). The long period of offspring dependency found in humans may necessitate the use of such adaptations as an important part of nurturing and survival of the infant.

In a final analysis, IDS adaptations fulfill three functions. First, the mother's speech modifications gain and hold the infant's attention. Second, the modifications aid in the establishment of emotional bonds. Third, maternal speech characteristics enable communication to occur at the earliest opportunity.

Gaze

A mother modifies her typical gaze pattern, as well as her speech, when she interacts with her infant. Mature adult gaze patterns, which rarely last more than a few seconds, can evoke strong feelings if extended. In a conversational exchange, mature speakers look away as they begin to speak and check back only occasionally. When a mother gazes at her infant, however, she may remain in eye contact for more than thirty seconds. During play, maternal gazing may occur up to 70% of the time simultaneous with vocalization.

A mother also monitors her infant's gaze, adjusting her conversational topic accordingly. Gradually, an infant's gaze behavior comes to follow its mother's pointing or naming, although the infant is still free to gaze where it chooses. Caregivers also learn that their infant will look into their faces for interpretation of novel events.

Maternal gaze modifications help maintain an infant's interest and focus attention on mother's face. A mother's monitoring of her infant's gaze enables them to establish joint reference to be discussed later.

Facial Expression

Mothers use facial expression skillfully to complement their talking. Facial expressions can fulfill a number of conversational functions, including initiation, maintenance and modulation of the exchange, termination, and avoidance of interaction. Mock surprise is frequently used to initiate, invite, or signal readiness. In this expression, a mother's eyes open wide and her eyebrows rise, her mouth opens, her head tilts, and she intones an "o-o-o" or "ah-h-h." Owing to the brevity of most interactional exchanges, a mother may use mock surprise every 10 to 15 seconds.

An exchange can be maintained or modulated by a smile or an expression of concern. Similar to adult exchanges, a smile signals that communication is proceeding without difficulty. An expression of concern signals communication distress and a willingness to refocus the exchange.

Termination is signaled by a frown, accompanying head aversion, and gaze breaking. Occasionally, the frown is accompanied by a vocalization with decreased volume and dropping pitch.

Finally, avoidance of a social interaction can also be signaled by turning away, but with a neutral or expressionless face. There is little in a mother's face, therefore, to hold her infant's attention.

Naturally, a mother's repertoire includes a full range of facial expressions. Mothers use these expressions to maintain their infants' attention and to aid comprehension.

Facial Presentation and Head Movement

Mothers use a large repertoire of head movements to help transmit their messages, including nodding and wagging, averting, and cocking to one side. The sudden appearance of the face, as in "peekaboo," is used to capture and hold a child's attention. In a variation of this procedure, a mother lowers her face and then returns to a full-face gaze accompanied by a vocalization. Many games, such as "I'm gonna get you" and "raspberries on your tummy," are accomplished by a full-face presentation. Frequently, a mother also exhibits mock surprise.

Proxemics

Proxemics, or the communicative use of interpersonal space, is a powerful interactional tool. Each person has a psychological envelope of personal space that can be violated only in the most intimate situations. When communicating with her infant, however, a mother acts as if this space does not exist and communicates from a very close distance. As an infant gets older, the American mother communicates more and more from a distance. The resultant decrease in touching is accompanied by increased eye contact.

CULTURAL, SOCIOECONOMIC, AND GENDER DIFFERENCES

The interactional patterns just described reflect the infant–caregiver behaviors found in middle-class American culture. In other cultures, a caregiver provides different types of linguistic input. For example, extended families, common in many cultures, offer multiple caregivers.

In general, maternal responsiveness is determined by an interplay of the maturational level of the infant and culture-specific interactional patterns (Kärtner, Keller, & Yovsi, 2010).

Differences in the interactions of mothers and infants may reflect cultural differences, especially as regards the assumed intentionality of infants to communicate (Toda, Fogel, & Kawai, 1990). Mothers in the United States are more information oriented than mothers in Japan. U.S. mothers are more chatty and use more questions, especially of the yes/no type, as well as more grammatically correct utterances with their 3-month-olds. In contrast, Japanese mothers are more emotion oriented and use more nonsense, onomatopoetic, and environmental sounds, more baby talk, and more babies' names. These differences may reflect each society's assumptions about infants and adult-to-adult cultural styles of talking. In the United States styles are direct and emphasize individual expression. Styles in Japan are more intuitive and indirect and emphasize empathy and conformity.

Japanese mothers also vocalize less with their 3-month-old infants but offer, in turn, more physical contact than do mothers in the United States. This difference is also reflected in more frequent nonverbal responding by Japanese mothers and more frequent verbal responding by U.S. mothers. The types of utterances to which mothers are most likely to respond also differ. U.S. mothers are more likely to respond to their 3-month-old's positive cooing and comfort sounds, while Japanese mothers are more likely to respond to discomfort or fussing sounds. In response, Japanese mothers try to soothe their infants with speech. U.S. mothers are more likely to talk to maintain attention while Japanese mothers talk more within vocal activities to elicit vocalizations.

Mothers make use of pitch very early. In English, a rising contour is used to gain an infant's attention. This pattern is not universal. For example, mothers speaking Thai to their infants use a falling pitch pattern, and those speaking Quiche Mayan, a native Mexican language, use a flat or falling contour. Maternal speech patterns are acquired behaviors, reflecting the culture in which the mother was raised.

Within North American culture, race, education, and socioeconomic class each influence maternal behaviors toward a child. For example, although inner-city, lower-class African American mothers reportedly engage in vocal behavior at about the same rate as middle-class African American mothers, data reveal other more subtle differences (Hammer & Weiss, 1999). Middle-class mothers incorporate language goals more frequently in their play with their infants. In response, middle-class African American infants initiate verbal play more frequently and produce twice as many vocalizations as lower-class infants.

While middle-class North American mothers ask more questions, seemingly to stimulate language growth, mothers from lower socioeconomic classes use more imperatives or directives. Similarly, better educated mothers are more verbal. Siblings and peers are more important in the infant socialization process within the homes of minority and lower socioeconomic class families, possibly accounting for the decreased talking by the mother.

Within some groups, children may be expected to learn language through observation, not interaction. In one Piedmont, South Carolina, African American community, infants are not viewed as capable of intentional behavior, so their vocalizations are often ignored.

Cultural and socioeconomic differences are not maladaptive. Quite the contrary, they reflect the values and beliefs of an ethnic or other recognizable group. It is not known which aspects of maternal adaptation are most important for a child's communication development. It would be inappropriate, therefore, to suggest that one culture's maternal practices are better than another.

Differences also reflect the gender of the infant. In general, mothers tend to maintain closer proximity to their daughters than to their sons, at least until the age of 4 years. This gender difference is reflected in other ways. At 2 years of age, female infants receive more questions, male infants more directives. With female infants, mothers are more repetitive, acknowledge more child answers, and take more turns. In short, more maternal utterances of a longer length are addressed to daughters than to sons. This difference is not related to the child's linguistic behavior, there being very few if any gender differences in children's language performance at this age.

Interactions Between Infant and Caregiver

Some interactional behaviors are of particular interest for language development. These behaviors, which we will examine in detail, are joint reference, joint action, turn-taking, and situational behaviors.

JOINT REFERENCE

As mentioned previously, *reference* is the ability to differentiate one entity from many and to note its presence. The term *joint reference* presupposes that two or more individuals share a common focus on one entity. In part, early identification of children with autism spectrum disorder is based on a seeming inability to engage in joint reference.

Joint reference is particularly important for language development, because it is within this context that infants develop gestural, vocal, and verbal signals of directly attending or signaling notice. Many words, such as *look,* serve a notice function. A child calls attention to an object, event, or action in the environment by naming it, thus conveying the focus of his or her attention to a conversational partner.

There appear to be three aspects of early joint referencing: indicating, deixis, and naming. *Indicating* can take a gestural, postural, or vocal form. At an early age, the infant and mother engage in a system to ensure joint selective attention. For example, a mother will shake an object before her infant to attract the infant's attention to it. These routines are used to attain eye contact, the first step in establishing joint reference. As an infant matures, indicating behaviors change. As other forms develop, a gesture may carry less of the message content. In its turn, the gesture becomes the context for other content. A reaching gesture changes from an actual reach to a mere indication of a reach. Finally, indicating methods become more standardized, more recognizable by others.

Deixis is the use of spatial, temporal, and interpersonal features of the content to aid joint reference and is found in words such as *here, there, this, that, before, after, you,* and *me.* The listener must convert deictic aspects to her or his own perspective.

The third aspect of referencing is *naming.* Infants are able to associate names with their referents prior to developing the ability to produce names.

Development of Joint Reference

Four phases in the development of joint reference have been identified (Table 5.6). The first phase, lasting for the first six months of life, is characterized by mastery of joint attention. An infant learns to look at objects and events in the environment in tandem with mother and to maintain eye contact. Maternal encouragement of attending by her infant is positively related to later language development (Karrass, Braungart-Rieker, Mullins, & Lefever, 2002).

TABLE 5.6 *Development of Joint Reference*

PHASE	AGE	DEVELOPMENT
Phase I:	4–6 wks.	Caregiver places object in child's field of vision, shakes object, says "Look"
Mastering	8 wks.	Infant visually follows caregiver's movements
Joint	12 wks.	Infant attends to utterances addressed to her
Attention	4 mos.	Infant follows caregiver's line of regard and response quickens with caregiver's "Look"
	6 mos.	Infant may respond to object or event name and/or intonational pattern to establish joint reference
Phase II: *Intention to Communicate*	7 mos.	Infant establishes joint reference by pointing to or showing objects or events but without looking at adult for confirmation
	8 mos.	"Reach-for-real" and "reach-for-signal" with gaze shift between object and caregiver
Phase III: *Gestures and Vocalization*	8–12 mos.	Reaching or requesting, pointing and showing ■ Protoimperatives and protodeclaratives ■ Gesture only becomes gesture plus vocalization
Phase IV: *Naming and Topicalization*	12 mos.	Joint reference established more within the structure of dialogs. ■ Child assumes more control and parental questioning decreases

Source: Information from Bruner (1975, 1977), Lewis & Freedle (1973), Ryan (1974), Scaife & Bruner (1975).

Initially, a mother interests her infant by using direct face-to-face techniques. She does not use objects until her infant is 4 to 6 weeks old. At this point, the mother elects to bring the object into the infant's field of vision or to follow the child's gaze. Both strategies are accompanied by shaking or moving of the object and talking, frequently using the infant's name or phrases such as "Oh, look." The mother's comments on the object of their joint attention become routine. As a result, interactional expectations are established by the infant, although initially these routines mean little.

The number of conversational partners influences joint attention. In multi-child contexts, mothers engaged in joint attention more with each child than with both. While this results in mothers engaging in less joint attention with each child individually than they would in a mother–child context, the multi-child context appears to be a positive language learning environment when measured by the size of the toddler's vocabulary (Benigno, Clark, & Farrar, 2007).

An infant's understanding develops slowly. By 8 weeks an infant is able to follow his or her mother's movements visually. At 3 months infants can distinguish and attend to utterances addressed to them. A 4-month-old infant is able to follow its mother's line of regard or pointing. Within a short time, the infant's response quickens with mother's directives, such as "Look!" When my little friend Natalia was an infant, her Spanish-speaking mother Catalina continually directed her baby's attention with "Mira!" (look). Later, mothers use object or event names to establish joint reference. By 6 months a mother's intonational pattern signals her infant to shift attention, although the mother and infant use a number of cues to regulate reference.

The second phase is characterized by the beginning of intentional communication. An infant's heightened interest in objects is accompanied by reaching. With the onset of reaching, objects become the focus of attention and face-to-face contact decreases from 80% to 15% of infant–mother contact time.

Initially, an infant's reach is solely a reach and is not intended to communicate any other meaning. The infant does not look toward mother to see if she has received the message. Instead, the infant orients toward either the object or mother. By 8 months the reach is less exigent, and the infant begins to look at mother while reaching. At this point, the infant has two reaches, a "reach-for-real" and a "reach-for-signal," indicating that he or she expects maternal assistance. The infant's reach-for-signal becomes a gesture. He or she shifts gaze from the object to mother and back again. Mother responds with the object or with encouragement of an even greater effort.

There are also thematic changes in mothers' speech to their infants at 5 to 7 months. Mothers move from a social mode, in which they discuss feelings and states, to an activity mode, in which they discuss both their baby's activities and events outside the immediate context. The concentration is on objects.

In the next phase an infant begins to point and to vocalize. Gradually, the full-hand reaching grasp becomes a finger point. The pointing behavior becomes separated from the intention to obtain an object. In response, a mother asks questions and incorporates the child's pointing and interests into the dialog.

Mothers' comments based on the child's action or interest at 9 months seem related to better language comprehension by children later (Rollins, 2003). Such behaviors indicate that a mother is sensitive to the focus of her child's attention.

Finally, in the last phase an infant masters naming and topicalizing. With this change in a child's behavior there is a corresponding increase in its mother's use of nouns. Increasingly, exchanges involve objects. Initially, the mother provides object and event labels. This strategy is modified when the child begins to talk. The mother attempts to get the child to look, to point, and to verbalize within the ongoing dialog. She uses object-related questions, such as "What do you want?" to elicit these verbalizations. As the child assumes more control of the dialog, the mother's questioning decreases.

Theory of Mind

You may recall that Theory of Mind is the understanding of the mental states and behaviors of others. Although Theory of Mind develops over several years, we may see its beginning in the joint attention or joint reference of infants (Miller, 2006). The capacity to coordinate one's attention with a partner is a critical first step in learning to comprehend and predict the thoughts and actions of other people (Tomasello, 1992b). When a child shares the experience of attending with its mother, he or she comes to understand that others intend for such sharing to occur. Through words and gestures, a mother singles out objects events and actions for attention and specifies aspects for special recognition. Within this context of sharing, a child begins to appreciate intentional communication.

Summary

The reference function, established months before meaningful language appears, is the vehicle for the development of naming and establishing a topic. More important, joint reference provides one of the earliest opportunities for the infant to engage in a truly communicative act of sharing information. Specific speech and language skills develop as more precise means to transmit the signal to a communication partner.

JOINT ACTION

Throughout the first year of life, a caregiver and infant develop shared behaviors in familiar contexts. These routinized actions, called **joint action,** provide a structure within which language can be analyzed. Routinized activities, such as game playing and daily routines, let a child encounter rules within a pleasurable experience. From game playing and routines, a child learns turn-taking and conversational skills.

These social interactions are among the most crucial infant learning and participating experiences. Within these joint action sequences, an infant begins to learn the conventions of human communication. Crying patterns become dialog patterns.

An infant's initial crying is gradually modified into recognizable signals by its mother's repeated response. Crying shifts from a demand mode to an anticipatory request mode. As a mother responds to her infant's demand cry, she establishes an expectation within her infant. The resultant request cry is less insistent. The infant pauses in anticipation of her mother's response. This shift is a forerunner of early dialogs in which a behavior or a vocalization is followed by a response.

Early examples of dialogs can be found in the anticipatory body games of infant and mother, such as "peekaboo" and "I'm gonna get you." Gradually, the infant's and mother's play evolves into an exchange in which the partners shift roles. For example, when passing an object back and forth, each partner plays the passer and the recipient in turn. Exchange, rather than possession, becomes the goal. Within these exchange games, an infant learns to shift roles, take turns, and coordinate signaling and acting. Role-shifting and turn-taking become so important that an infant will react with frustration, often accompanied by gestures and vocalizations, if the turn is delayed. In coordinating his or her signals and actions, an infant learns to look at mother's face in anticipation of the mother's signals.

Over time, a reciprocal mode of interaction replaces the exchange mode. With the reciprocal mode, activities revolve around a joint task format, such as play with an object, rather than a turn-taking format.

Game Playing

Infants and caregivers engage in play almost from birth. Each mother and infant develop a unique set of games of their own. As each mother becomes familiar with her infant's abilities and interests, she creates interpersonal games. These games, in turn, become ritualized exchanges.

The most striking feature is the consistency of each mother's behavior both within and between these play sequences, especially the repetitiveness of a mother's vocal and nonvocal behaviors. Approximately one-third to two-thirds of maternal behavior directed toward an infant occurs in *runs,* or strings of behavior related to a single topic. This form of stimulation may be optimal for holding an infant's attention.

Early face-to-face play occurs in alternating cycles of arousal. An infant is aroused by maternal stimulation. A strong positive correlation exists between the sensory modality of a mother's stimulation and her infant's responses. For example, if a mother stimulates vocally, her child is likely to respond vocally.

An infant as young as 6 weeks old can initiate games by modifying its internal state of alertness. By 13 weeks an infant has adopted a true role in social games and thus signals readiness to begin play. When the mother approaches with a still face, her infant initiates the interaction by performing its repertoire of facial expressions and body movements. If the infant fails to get a response, it turns away. This behavior is modified, in turn, to independent exploration play by 23 weeks.

Over time, an infant's vocalizations accompanying game playing change and reflect the changes seen in overall language development (Rome-Flanders & Cronk, 1995). The percentage of vocalizations and single syllables gives way to jargon and phonetically consistent forms (PCFs), which in turn are pushed aside for single words and multiword expressions. Although vocalizations decrease as a percentage of overall communication, the overall amount of vocalizing remains constant. It is possible that these sounds signal an availability to play and a willingness to participate.

Mothers adjust gradually to these developmental changes and to changes in their infant's internal state. First, a mother adjusts her timing to her infant's arousal to find the appropriate slot for her behavior. By modifying her timing, a mother attempts to alter the interactional pattern, to prolong the interactions, or to elicit a response from the infant. Second, a mother attempts to maintain a moderate level of infant arousal, an optimal state for learning. In turn, the mother is reinforced by her infant's responsiveness. Finally, a mother maintains a balance between her agenda and her infant's behavior. For example, when the infant does not interact for a period of 5 to 10 seconds, the mother responds with her bag of tricks. She makes faces, smiles, protrudes her tongue, moves her limbs, or vocalizes. In so doing, she is careful to leave an opportunity or slot for the infant to respond.

One very popular infant–mother game is "copycat" in which a mother's imitative behavior is dependent on her infant's. The importance of this particular game for later imitation by the infant cannot be overemphasized.

Maternal imitation is not an exact imitation, however, and a mother pulls her child in the direction of the mother's agenda. First, the mother may maximize the imitation by exaggerating her infant's behavior and thus calling attention to it. Second, she may minimize the imitation to a short, quick flash, used to draw her infant back to the mother's ongoing behavior. Third, the mother may perform a modulating imitation such as responding with a mellowed version of the infant's behavior. For example, the mother may perform mellow crying in imitation of the child's wail. This may have a calming effect on the child.

In contrast, infant behaviors that can be interpreted as having communicative intent receive a conversational response. For example, mothers do not usually imitate prespeech or small hand movements such as pointing. Instead, they reply to these with IDS.

Early play consists primarily of social behaviors. During the first six months, the focus of play is social; there are no specific game rules. Social play is usually spontaneous and occurs frequently during routines. Once play begins, all other tasks end.

During the second six months of life, object play increases. Object play is almost nonexistent at 3 months of age. By 6 months, play often begins with the body but is repeated with a toy. Increasingly, infant and mother participate in a ritualized give-and-take of objects as infant possession time decreases steadily from 30 to 10 seconds over the next four months. By 11 months the child does not need coaxing before releasing an object. Another popular infant game is "retrieve," in which the child drops an object in anticipation that mother will return it. Infants in all cultures seem to enjoy the shared anticipation and the predictable sequence under their own control. Games allow for lots of shared meaningful communication at a nonverbal level. Throughout the first year, play demonstrates many of the characteristics of later conversation.

Sequence of Social Play

In a typical social play period, the "game" begins with a greeting when the partners catch each other's glance. This initiation is followed by a moment of mutual gaze. If either partner breaks the gaze pattern, play ceases momentarily. Maintenance of the gaze signals readiness and is usually followed by a maternal mock surprise, in which she raises her eyebrows, widens her eyes, opens her mouth, and repositions her head. Her infant responds with wide eyes, an open mouth, a smile, and head reorientation. The infant may wag its head or approach mother's face, but the result is a full-face positioning. Play begins.

This initial exchange in play is actually a greeting. The exchange, which may last for only a second, accomplishes two things. First, all other activities stop; second, there is a reorientation to a face-to-face position, in which signals will be most visible. Often the infant is not prepared, and there are false starts.

Two episodes of the play sequence that may occur several times per minute are *engagement* and *time out*. Episodes of engagement are variable-length sequences of social behaviors separated by clearly marked pauses. Each sequence begins with a greeting that is less full than the initial greeting. Within each episode, the rate of caregiver verbal and nonverbal behaviors is relatively constant. These behaviors occur in discrete bursts within each episode. The mother keeps most of her behaviors under half a second in duration.

Tempo can be used to soothe or arouse the infant. For example, the mother increases her rate to exceed that of a fussy child, then gradually slows in order to soothe her infant. Although the rate of maternal behaviors within an episode is constant, the tempo between episodes may vary considerably. For example, the excitement caused by "I'm gonna get you" is due to changes in tempo.

Generally, each episode has one major purpose: to establish attention, to maintain attention, or to enter into play. Within each episode, therefore, the mother's behavior is fairly predictable for her infant. These maternal consistencies, accompanied by slight variations, are ideal for gaining and maintaining the infant's attention.

Maternal behaviors often occur in repetitive runs within each episode. The average run is three or more units in length. For example, the mother may introduce a topic and then vary it systematically, as in the following sequences:

You're so big, aren't you?
So big.
Oh, so big.

No, we can't do that.
No, not that.
Oh, no.

These repetitions have enormous instructional potential. They expand the infant's range of experience and maintain her or his attention.

Episodes of time out consist of rests used to readjust the interaction. Time out, usually lasting for 3 seconds or longer, occurs when the infant signals, often by fussing or averting the gaze, that he or she is no longer excited. Time out provides an opportunity to retune the interaction. The mother changes the focus of the interaction by glancing away or at some other infant body part or by sitting quietly.

Routines

Communication can be dynamic, complex, and difficult to predict. At first, it must seem to an infant that the behaviors of others are random and unrelated. This is not the best learning environment. In contrast, routines, such as bathing or dressing, offer conventionalized, predictable contexts in which caregivers provide order. An infant can rely on the order and on caregiver cues. The frequency of routines increases throughout the infant's first year.

Routines provide **scripts** that have "slots" for the infant's behavior and aid meaningful interpretation of the event. Just as a fast-food restaurant has a script that constrains adult behavior, dressing and feeding also have similar scripts for an infant. Gradually, the infant learns a script, and this, in turn, eases participation. The more you know the script, the more energy you can devote to differing aspects of participation. By providing a framework, scripts reduce the cognitive energy needed to participate and to make sense.

Infants' event knowledge, which is one of the conceptual foundations of later language development, is gained within familiar daily routines and events. Event knowledge includes information on the actors, actions, props, causality, and temporal aspects of an event. Later, this knowledge is translated into the semantic categories of early speech.

In fact, much of the content of a child's language may come from these daily interactions. When children begin to talk, they display greater semantic complexity and range, longer utterances, and more unique words in these familiar situations (Farrar et al., 1993).

Summary

Although each infant–caregiver pair evolves different patterns of interaction, there are similarities that are important for later communication development. These include the "process" of shared communication, the mutual topic–comment, routines, and learning to anticipate partner behavior change. Play is particularly relevant to language acquisition. First, play usually occurs in a highly restricted and well-understood *semantic domain*. Games such as "peekaboo" and "I'm gonna get you" have a restricted format, limited semantic elements (*hands, face, cover, uncover*), and a highly constrained set of semantic relations (*hands, cover, face*). Mother is frequently the agent of some action upon an object (*mommy roll ball*).

Second, play has a well-defined task structure. The order of events enables the child to predict. Later, the rules of language will provide similar boundaries.

Third, play has a role structure similar to that of conversation. We might call these *plays* and *audience*. The infant learns to recognize and to play various roles. In addition, she or he learns that roles have a property of reversibility.

TURN-TAKING

Most of the interactional behaviors discussed so far have contained an element of turn-taking. The infant's development of this skill is essential for development of later conversational skills.

In very early feeding sessions, turn-taking occurs as a mother fits her behavior into her infant's rhythms. For example, initially, mothers jiggle the nipple to increase or to elicit feeding. Infants respond by decreasing their sucking behavior. Within two weeks mothers learn to cease their jiggling to elicit sucking. The resultant cycle becomes one in which an infant pause is followed by a jiggle. The jiggling stops. After a short delay, an infant begins to suck. Thus, early feeding behaviors represent a pattern of turn-taking.

Most early infant and mother turns last for less than one second. The pattern is like a dance in which the partners know the steps and the music and can dance accordingly. As a result, sequences of infant–mother behavior emerge.

Even body games, such as tickling, lifting, and bouncing, contain pauses for infant responses. The pauses are initially short, but they lengthen as an infant gains the ability to respond more fully. This gradual pause lengthening is also found in the maternal responses of Japanese mothers (Masataka, 1993). At 3 to 6 months of age, the infant responds or attends quietly. Gaze, facial expression, body movement, or vocalization can all fill a turn. A lack of maternal pauses can result in overstimulation and a less responsive infant.

A set of conversational behaviors evolves from these infant turn-filling behaviors, such as the development of reciprocal and alternating patterns of vocalizations called *protoconversations.* Gestures and, later, words will develop to fill an infant's turn as true conversations develop.

SITUATIONAL VARIATIONS

Mothers use a variety of naturally occurring situations to facilitate language and communication development. Prelinguistic behaviors may be situationally bound, even at an early age. Certain infant–mother situations occur frequently. Eight interactional situations accounted for almost all locational activities of the 3-month-old infant. From most to least frequent, these situations are mother's lap, crib/bed, infant seat, table/tub, couch/sofa, playpen, floor, and jumper/swing. Of developmental importance is the frequency of vocalization within each situation.

Within each situation, certain infant–mother behaviors occur regularly. This regularity is the basis for a child's development of meaning, which emerges from nonrandom action sequences, especially vocalization sequences associated with different "situational" locations. For example, the infant is usually placed in the crib to sleep. Therefore, the mother neither responds nor initiates vocalizations. On the other hand, at the table or in the tub, the infant is subjected to many vocalizations and nonrandom maternal behaviors. Situations provide a context within which the child can process the nonrandom content. These nonrandom behaviors of a parent form an early meaning base.

Conclusion

SYMBOLIC COMMUNICATION IN THE FORM of spoken language develops within the context of a very early communication system that is integrated and nonspeech in nature. Presymbolic communication enables a child to learn language. Over the first year, an infant's early behaviors acquire intentionality and serve several communication functions.

A child's initial behavior communicates little, if anything, beyond the immediate behavior itself. Infant behaviors are not as significant overall as a mother's response to these behaviors. Mothers perceive their infants as persons and interpret their baby's behavior as communicative, verbal, and meaningful.

Humans are social animals who live generally within a social network. An infant is dependent on others, especially mother. The mother is controlled to a great extent by the infant's biological needs. In addition, the infant is adaptable to the social world. The mother is very responsive to the infant's behavior and mindful of the infant's current abilities. She accommodates quickly to infant behavior changes, but her own behavior always has a direction. In general, the mother modifies her behavior by simplifying her speech, by increasing the amount and quality of her nonverbal communication, and by relying heavily on the context. She gives linguistic input while providing an opportunity or turn in which the infant can respond.

Both semantic structure and pragmatic functions are derived by an infant from social interaction. A child infers meaning from mother's vocalizations and nonrandom behaviors in interactional situations. Word relationships are learned through joint action routines, such as games, in which a child takes a particular role within the interaction.

The reference function derives from joint attention. A mother and child attend jointly to a rather limited array of objects they share in common. These form the initial concepts that are later expressed in words by the child. In addition to reference, other communication functions, such as requesting and giving, are also expressed preverbally.

Intentions or language uses develop as a result of a mother's responsiveness to her child's earliest interactional behaviors. As the infant learns to control the behavior of others, he or she begins to modify and regularize signals in order to communicate more specifically. The particular words that an infant later uses expressively will be determined by pragmatic factors, such as the intentions these words express. An infant will use those words that are most accurate for expressing its intentions.

Social communication is found in mother–infant discourse over the first year of life. In turn, communication skills developed within the infant–mother duo provide a basis for the infant's learning of the linguistic code.

It may not be glaringly obvious, but in both Chapters 4 and 5, we have addressed the *how* of language development but not the *why*. There is a simple explanation for this omission: We don't know why children develop language.

Although behaviors that a child learns may lead to language, we cannot conclude that a child learned them for that reason (Locke, 1996). An infant does not understand the long-term consequences of its learning, nor is it storing away knowledge for an unknown future. Even if a young infant did sense a need for attaining linguistic competence, he or she is incapable of planning for this eventuality.

The social and communicative bases for language development can be used to explain, in part, the motivation for learning language. A child and caregiver establish strong communicative bonds. Because of the enjoyment or reinforcement each partner receives from these communicative interactions, he or she is desirous of even more communication. The frustration of being misinterpreted and the joy of being understood are strong motivators for both the child and caregivers to modify their language. The infant attempts to learn the code used by the caregiver, who, in turn, simplifies that code to enhance the infant's comprehension. The outcome for the infant is that he or she understands and uses more language within communicative interactions as an attempt to participate even more.

Discussion

WITHIN A DISCUSSION OF THE SOCIAL and communicative bases of language, we get to the motivation for learning language in the first place. Language is learned within well-established communication. Learning language makes the learner a better communicator.

Most importantly, children become communicators because we treat them that way. We expect them to communicate. If an SLP or teacher doesn't expect his or her clients to communicate, they won't. Not to expect better performance is to give up.

Babies seem prewired for communication, but it is what caregivers—primarily the mother—do with this "predisposition" that is important. Recall how the child progresses to gestures, the first signs of intention to communicate, and how words fulfill the intentions expressed through these gestures. Remember the early learning within joint action routines and game playing that teaches the child about predictability in interactions and about turn-taking. Think of all the things an infant can do socially. And don't forget all the intentional communication expressed through the child's gestures. The first word is merely the icing on the cake.

Sadly, some children will not obtain a strong social and communicative base for language. This may be due to environmental or individual factors or both. Children in abusive or neglectful homes may fail to bond with a parent or may become fearful of sound making. Other children, such as those with autism, may fail to bond with and respond to their caretakers because of a seeming inability to relate to other humans in a way that differs from the way in which the child relates to objects. Whether the factors are environmental or individual, the result may be impaired language and communication.

Main Points

- Children become communicators because we treat them that way.

- Language is acquired to fill the intentions initially expressed in gestures.

- There is a mutual modification in the behavior of the infant and the mother, in that changes in the baby's behavior result in changes in the mother's, which in turn affect the infant.

- Newborns seem to prefer the human face and voice over other stimuli.

- Of particular importance for later communication are the early patterns of gaze coupling, turn-taking, stimulus-response bonds, routines, and games. Routines teach the child that behavior is predictable and facilitate a child's participation, while games have many of the attributes of conversations.

- Intentions go through stages of development: perlocutionary, illocutionary, and locutionary. During the illocutionary a child learns to signal intent via gestures, first showing itself, then showing, and finally with an array of gestures. Initially, each gesture is silent, then vocalization is added, and finally a word or verbalization accompanies the gesture.

- Mothers modify their behavior to facilitate interactions.

- Cultural differences exist and signify only difference. There are many ways to help children acquire language.

- Of particular importance for early communication are joint or shared reference and joint action.

Reflections

1. Discuss the abilities and behaviors of the newborn that suggest prewiring for communication.

2. Describe the aspects of conversation found in gaze coupling, ritualized behaviors, and game playing.

3. Why are gestures particularly important? Describe the sequence of gestural development.

4. What communicative behaviors does the infant elicit from the mother, and what is the effect of each on communication?

5. Explain why three interactions—joint reference, joint actions, and turn-taking—are particularly important for the development of early communication, and trace briefly the development of each.

6. Explain the cultural and socioeconomic differences found in the interactions of caregivers and infants.

6

Language-Learning and Teaching Processes and Young Children

It's difficult to explain language learning without discussing children's learning strategies and parents' teaching techniques. Although the relationship is not one of pupil and teacher, many of the elements of that relationship exist in a more subtle form.

Learning language is not just a process of accumulating language structures and content. Children use certain strategies to comprehend the language they hear and to form hypotheses about the underlying language rules. Caregivers also aid linguistic analysis by modifying the speech stream directed at children. When you have completed this chapter, you should understand

- The relationship between comprehension, production, and cognition.
- The role of selective imitation and formulas.
- Universal language-learning principles.
- The characteristics of motherese or parentese.
- The types of parental prompting.
- The effects of parental expansion, extension, and imitation.
- The use of parental turnabouts.
- The importance of play.

To listen to language samples related to chapter content and to peruse other enhanced study aids, please see the Companion Website at www.pearsonhighered.com/owens8e

■ The effects of cultural variation on the language-learning process.
■ The following terms:

analogy	formula	motherese
bootstrapping	functionally based	pattern-finding
contingent query	distributional	reformulation
entrenchment	analysis	request for clarification
preemption	hypothesis-testing	schematization
evocative utterances	utterances	selective imitation
expansion	intention-reading	turnabout
extension	interrogative utterances	

In Chapters 4 and 5 we discussed the bases for language development. These bases are inadequate, however, as an explanation of the extremely complicated process of language learning. Language development is not haphazard. Although large, general changes occur in an orderly, predictable fashion, there is great individual variation that reflects underlying language-learning strategies, linguistic complexity, and cognitive-conceptual growth.

Even though adults do not attempt to teach language directly to children developing typically, we do adapt our language input to a child's level of attention and comprehension. In the process, we provide models of simplified language. We also tend to react to a child's utterances in a way that increases the chance that he or she will repeat the structures later. This reinforcement is not direct but instead includes such indirect behaviors as repeating and responding to a child's utterances. It is also important to remember the context of most language-learning exchanges. As you already know, children engage in conversations with their caregivers throughout the day while engaged in activities and routines that form the backdrop for communication.

In this chapter we examine issues related to language learning. We begin by exploring the relationship between comprehension, production, and cognitive growth. In addition, child language-learning strategies and adult teaching strategies are explored. Finally, we discuss the conversational context in which a child's language develops and the maternal strategies for maintaining a conversation. Naturally, the strategies used by both a child and an adult differ with their culture, the language being learned, and the language maturity of the child.

Comprehension, Production, and Cognitive Growth

There is a strong link between comprehension, production, and cognition. A child's cognitive conceptual development is the primary tool for comprehension. The properties of individual languages also affect development.

COGNITION AND LANGUAGE

Cognitive skills and language abilities are associated; they develop in parallel fashion. New and increased cognitive ability may enable a child to function differently, but it does not cause language change. Rather, cognition and language are strongly related with underlying factors. For example, cognitive development in infants and toddlers is strongly related to increased memory and to the ability to acquire symbols in many areas, including language and gestures. First words and recognitory gestures, such as sniffing flowers, appear at about the same age. At times, evidence of the correlation between language and cognition is strong, especially during the first two years of life.

Language skills seem to be closely related to specific cognitive skills. For example, a significant difference in the cognitive levels of play exists between children who use no words and those who use single words. Children who do not produce words are more likely to play with toys such as blocks, while children who produce single words are more likely to play with "animate" objects, such as dolls or action figures. The play of children beginning to combine words consists of combining two or more play sequences and/or performing the same action on a sequence of entities.

Cognitive growth may have an especially important influence on early word combinations. Many of the principles of cognitive learning can also be applied to language learning, such as

- Selectively attending to perceptually important stimuli.
- Discriminating stimuli along different dimensions.
- Remembering stimuli.
- Classifying stimuli according to the results of the discriminations.

These principles correspond to the steps taken in information processing presented in Chapter 3.

Children are active learners, forming hypotheses based on patterns in the incoming language stream. Data are tested and incorporated into the system or used to reorganize the system. As a child's mind stores bits of information, she or he tries to organize them based on perceived relationships.

Organization of longer utterances requires better short-term memory and knowledge of syntactic patterns and word classes. Hierarchical word-order organization develops similar to that in Figure 1.5, and individual words become "slot fillers" for various word classes.

Development of many grammatical constructions also reflect cognitive development. For example, reversibility, or the ability to trace a process backward, is strongly related to acquisition of *before* and *after, because,* and *why.* In order to respond to a *why* question, a child must be able to use *because* and reverse the order of events.

ADULT:	*Why* are you wet?	RESULT:	Event$_2$
CHILD:	*Because* I spilled my apple juice.	CAUSE:	Event$_1$

Knowledge structures of two types are assumed to guide word acquisition: *event-based knowledge* and *taxonomic knowledge* (Sell, 1992). Event-based knowledge consists of sequences of events or routines, such as a birthday party, that are temporal or causal in nature and organized toward a goal. These sequences of events contain actors, roles, props, and options or alternatives. A child uses this knowledge to form *scripts* or sets of expectations that aid memory, enhance comprehension, and give the individual child a knowledge base for interpreting events.

Taxonomic knowledge consists of categories and classes of words. New words are compared categorically and organized for retrieval.

Event-based or "world" knowledge influences vocabulary acquisition and may be the basis for taxonomic or "word" knowledge. Words are learned within a social context; their meaning is found in a child's representation of events.

Early words are first comprehended and produced in the context of everyday events. From repeated use, the words themselves become cues for the event. For example, the words *bath* and *soap* become cues for bathing, while *cookie* and *juice* represent snack. As the child acquires more words, *cookie, cracker, milk,* and *juice* become *things I eat,* which later evolves into the category *food.* Preschoolers rely on event-based knowledge, while kindergarteners use more categorical script-related groupings such as *things I eat.* By age 7 to 10, children are using taxonomic categories, such as *food* (Sell, 1992).

Comprehension and Production

The exact developmental relationship between language comprehension and production is unclear. In comprehension, a child uses both linguistic and conceptual input plus his or her memory. In contrast, production also uses linguistic and conceptual input but relies on linguistic knowledge alone for encoding.

Comprehension prior to production was previously considered a universal of language acquisition. Data from young Thai children suggests, however, that they may employ a distributional (location and frequency) strategy for production of certain language forms before they comprehend these forms (Carpenter, 1991). In other words, they produce frequently used words that appear in the same linguistic location repeatedly. This may be only one of several strategies used by all children.

The comprehension–production relationship is a dynamic one that changes with a child's developmental level and with each aspect of language. In other words, the relationship between comprehension and production changes because of different rates of development and different linguistic demands.

The comprehension of presymbolic infants is difficult to determine. An infant may look where mother looks, act on objects that mother references, and imitate the actions of others. Thus, measurement by researchers is complicated by the infant's strategies and the interactive cooperation of the caregiver who interprets the child's behavior as meaningful.

In early phonological development, the relationship is easier to discern. Infant perception of speech-sound differences greatly precedes expression. A child can perceive speech sounds very early. Intonational patterns are also discriminated early, at around 8 months of age.

Infant acoustic-phonetic comprehension of first words may be less specific (Walley, 1993). Initially, recognition and comprehension are holistic, such as grossly discriminating *dog* from *cookie.* Rather quickly, however, an infant acquires the detailed perceptual skill needed for more subtle distinctions, such as *hot* and *hit.* Over 50% of the most common monosyllabic words spoken by 1- to 3-year-olds have three or more other words that differ by only one phoneme (Dollaghan, 1994).

Comprehension and production of first words pose different problems. Obviously, a child does not fully comprehend the word before he or she produces it. Full comprehension would require a greater linguistic and experiential background than that of a year-old infant. Instead, event-based knowledge is used by toddlers or 12- to 24-month-olds to form responses (Paul, 1990). For example, when a caregiver says, "Let's read a book," and hands one to a child, the child responds by opening the book, which is part of the book script. In fact, up through age 2, comprehension is highly context-dependent (Striano, Rochat, & Legerstee, 2003). Most speech addressed to a toddler is associated with that immediate nonlinguistic context. In fact, adults may overestimate a child's comprehension unless they consider all the paralinguistic and situational cues. Later, preschoolers focus on linguistic factors to gain the information needed. Event knowledge continues to be important, however, even for adults, and comprehension is easiest within familiar events.

Even though a symbol signifies a particular referent, the meaning of the symbol goes beyond that referent. True meaning refers to a concept, not to individual examples.

After a mother labels an entity, her child forms hypotheses about its nature. In turn, the child tests these hypotheses by applying the label. The mother monitors the child's output to check the accuracy of fit between her and the child's underlying concepts. The mother improves

TABLE *6.1* **Comprehension and Production of Single Words by Syntactic Category**

	COMPREHENSION (FIRST 100 WORDS)	PRODUCTION (FIRST 50 WORDS)
Nominals (Nouns)		
Specific	17%	11%
General	39%	50%
Action	36%	19%
Modifiers	3%	10%
Personal-social	5%	10%

Source: Information from Benedict (1979).

the child's accuracy by providing evaluative feedback. Hence, the child's comprehension and production are fine-tuned essentially at the same time.

Within the first 50 words, comprehension seems to precede production. As a group, children understand approximately 50 words before they are able to produce 10, although the range of comprehended words varies greatly across children. The distribution of syntactic types also varies between comprehension and production (Table 6.1). As children mature, the distribution changes.

In summary, the ability to comprehend words develops gradually, and initially is highly context-dependent. Symbolic comprehension continues to develop through the second year of life (Striano et al., 2003).

If comprehension precedes production, we would expect a child to understand word combinations before using multiword utterances. Here the nonlinguistic context is an essential comprehension aid. In addition, comprehension of a simple sentence depends on recognition of highly meaningful words within it. A child need not know syntax if he or she knows the meanings of these words separately. The nonlinguistic context provides additional relational information. Yet, children seem to respond best to verbal commands that are slightly above their production level, suggesting comprehension above their level of production.

Toddlers rely on basic semantic relations, use of objects, and routines for comprehension. Two strategies may be used with objects, *do-what-you-usually-do* and *act-on-the-object-in-the-way-mentioned*. Using the first strategy, balls would be rolled, thrown, dropped, or passed back and forth, no matter what the child heard. Young preschoolers use this "probable event" strategy. If there is no obvious probable action, a child may respond randomly or use basic syntactic relationships for comprehension. With the second strategy, noting the action, the child would throw the ball whether the caregiver said, "Now, you *throw* the ball," or "Remember how Johnny *throws* the ball in the baseball game?" Event knowledge is still very important. Verb comprehension may be acquired one verb at a time, moving from general verbs, such as *do,* to more specific verbs, such as *eat* and *sit.* By 28 months, he or she can use word order for limited comprehension.

By late preschool, children learning English use word order consistently for comprehension, although they may still revert to event knowledge. Children who overrely on word order may ignore such terms as *before* and *after.* It is not until age 5 or 6 that children begin to rely consistently on syntactic and morphologic interpretation. By age 7 to 9, children are using language to acquire more language, such as word definitions, and are more sensitive to phrases and subordinate clauses and to connectors, such as *before, after, during,* and *while.*

LESS IS MORE

A child changes throughout the period that he or she is learning language. It would seem logical to suppose that a child's brain would undergo change during this learning (Elman, 1999). One developmental change occurs in *working memory* and attention. Working memory is relatively short-lived and holds information, such as this sentence, while your brain processes the information. Both working memory and attention are initially limited and increase over time.

Although these abilities are very limited at first, that may actually be an advantage for learning language (Elman, 1999). Short, simple sentences will be easier to process, and they provide a starting point for discovering words, categories of words, and grammatical patterns in the environment. Once this information has been induced, it provides a basis for moving on. As working memory improves, it can deal with increasingly complex input and, in the process, help a child refine his or her knowledge.

When we view the problem of learning language from this perspective, such maturational limitations are really a plus. Deconstructing the language code and mastering it is an extremely complex process. Beginning small is a good place to start. It seems logical that a child might need cues to help discover grammar. That's why Chomsky and his followers theorized that the child was aided by the language acquisition device (LAD). Each child, they reasoned, was prewired to know certain language concepts, such as the formation of a sentence. Instead, Emergentists suggest that the timing of memory and other cognitive developments have the effect of limiting language processing in exactly the right way to enable a child's brain to solve this problem (Elman, 1999).

Although it seems counterintuitive from an adult perspective, some problems, such as learning language, may be best solved by starting small. We might call this the "less is more" hypothesis (Newport, 1988, 1990).

Maybe we can illustrate how limited resources can affect the process by looking at young language learners in comparison to older ones. It is well-documented that late learners of a language, either a first or second one, exhibit poorer performance relative to early or native learners. While learning language, groups of young and old children make similar numbers of errors, but the types of errors differ. Late learners make more morphological mistakes and rely more heavily on fixed forms in which internal morphological elements are frozen in place and therefore often used inappropriately. For example, *I don't* and *you don't* may result in *he don't*. Similarly, a late learner may rely on *drink-drank-drunk* to produce *think-thank-thunk* or *link-lank-lunk*. In contrast, young native learners make more errors of omission.

These differing error patterns may be based on differing ability to analyze the structure of language utterances, with younger learners having an advantage (Newport, 1988, 1990). Although the young learner is handicapped by short-term memory, this reduces the space that can be examined by the child. In contrast, the late language learner's greater storage and computational skills work to his or her disadvantage, because the form-meaning (ed = past) relationships that underlie morphology are huge and present a formidable challenge when tackled all at once.

Summary

During the preschool years, the relationship between comprehension, production, and cognition changes as the child matures. In general, linguistic developments parallel much of the cognitive growth of the preschool child, although this is not a one-to-one relationship. A young child's brain, however, does seem to be uniquely suited for the task of unraveling language and reconstructing it again in his or her own form.

Child Learning Strategies

Although there are many variations in the way in which children learn language, there are ample similarities. These suggest underlying strategies that differ with the language level of a child. In the following section, we consider the language-learning strategies most frequently associated with toddlers and preschoolers.

TODDLER LANGUAGE-LEARNING STRATEGIES

To assume that toddlers, children ages 12 to 24 months, merely speak what they hear is to oversimplify the acquisition of language. A child must use certain learning methods to sort out relevant and irrelevant information in adult and sibling conversations. A child must decide which utterances are good examples of the language for accomplishing his or her communication goals and must hypothesize about their underlying meanings and structures.

Receptive Strategies: When Is a Word a Word?

As toddlers mature, they become increasingly adept at acquiring new words under conditions that are not always ideal (Baldwin, 1993). Although 14- to 15-month-olds experience difficulty establishing stable symbol-referent associations even with caregiver assistance, 18- to 19-month-olds are able to establish these links even when the caregiver names entities to which the toddler is not attending.

Before children can recognize words, they must gain a sense of how sounds go together to form syllables of the native language (Jusczyk, 1999). Infants may use lexical, syntactic, phonological, and stress-pattern cues in combination to break the speech stream they hear and aid interpretation. These cues are probably used flexibly depending on what's available in any given situation (Sanders & Neville, 2000). For example, English words can begin with a consonant blend, such as *bl* or *str*; Korean words cannot. Armed with these phonological structures gained by listening to speech, the child can more easily locate word boundaries. As a result, the seemingly endless speech flow becomes a series of distinct but, for now, meaningless words. For example, 6- to 10-month-old children reared in English-speaking homes begin to develop a bias in favor of words with the English pattern of emphasis on the first syllable, such as *mommy, daddy, doggie,* and *baby*. By 11 months, infants are sensitive to word boundaries and phonological characteristics of their native language (Myers et al., 1996; Shafer, Shucard, Shucard, & Gerken, 1998).

Although adults modify their speech to highlight word and sentence boundaries and to hold a child's attention, and although words usually pertain to semantic and pragmatic concepts previously established, these explanations alone are insufficient for describing how toddlers learn words. What do children bring to the task? What assumptions do children make about language they encounter? Although linguists don't really know, they can infer from the language behavior of toddlers that certain lexical principles or assumptions are being used.

Three assumptions of toddlers seem fundamental:

- People use words to refer to entities.
- Words are extendable.
- A given word refers to the whole entity, not its parts. (Golinkoff, Mervis, & Hirsh-Pasek, 1994)

The first or *reference principle* assumes that people refer. Words do not just "go with" but actually "stand for" entities to which they refer. Therefore, a toddler must be able to determine the speaker's intention to refer, the linguistic patterns used, and the entities to which they refer. A subprinciple, the *mutual exclusivity assumption,* guides initial word learning by presupposing that each referent has a unique symbol. In other words, a referent cannot be both a *cup* and a *spoon.* Eventually, as a child gains multiple referents for some words, this assumption will be overridden (Markman, 1992; Merriman & Bowman, 1989).

As you will recall from Chapter 1, words are symbols that represent concepts, not specific referents. Using the second or *extendability principle,* an infant assumes that there is some similarity, such as shared perceptual attributes, that enables use of one symbol for more than one referent. Thus, *cup* can refer to the child's cup and to those that the child perceives to be similar, such as other child cups.

There is still some ambiguity, however, because the word *doggie* could refer to the dog's fur, color, bark, four legs, or any number of similarities. The third or *whole-object principle* assumes that a label refers to a whole entity rather than to a part or attribute. In fact, object parts are rare in toddler lexicons (Mervis, 1990). Mothers aid this assumption of their children by providing basic-level terms (*table*) before more restricted terms (*leg, top, drawer*). Basic-level terms are often accompanied by pointing, while more restricted terms often require additional explanation or information. Thus, parental teaching strategies seem to match children's learning preferences.

Three additional assumptions may be needed for the toddler to form hypothetical definitions quickly and to use syntactic information. These are

- Categorical assumption.
- Novel name-nameless assumption.
- Conventionality assumption (Golinkoff et al., 1994; Markman, 1992).

The *categorical assumption* is used by children as young as 18 months to extend a label to related entities. Classification is based not just on perceptual attributes, but on function, world knowledge, and communication characteristics, such as shortness of length and commonality. Unlike the extendability principle, which would apply *cup* to a limited sample, the categorical assumption goes beyond basic-level referents of the same kind to categories of entities. In this case, *cup* may be extended to all objects that hold liquid.

The *novel name-nameless assumption* enables a child to link a symbol and referent after only a few exposures. In short, a child assumes that novel symbols are linked to previously unnamed referents. Use of this assumption seems to correspond to the vocabulary spurt experienced by many children at around 18 months (Mervis & Bertrand, 1993). Caregivers aid the child by naming and pointing to, holding, or manipulating novel objects to further specify the referent (Masur, 1997). As children mature, they rely less on these gestural assists and more on the caregivers' language (Namy & Waxman, 1998).

Finally, the *conventionality assumption* leads a child to expect meanings to be expressed by others in consistent conventional forms. In other words, caregivers don't change the word's meaning with each use. A car is consistently called by that name. Conversely, because a child wishes to be understood, he or she is motivated to produce the forms used by the language community.

We are not certain that children actually use these principles or make these assumptions. Toddlers employ these or similar principles, however, in order to make sense of the speech stream directed at them. It cannot be overemphasized that this learning process is an active one (Tomasello, Strosberg, & Akhtar, 1996). Children actively attempt to understand adult language and to make word-referent associations.

Expressive Strategies

Young children use at least four expressive strategies to gain linguistic knowledge. These are evocative utterances, hypothesis testing, interrogative utterances, and selective imitation (McLean & Snyder-McLean, 1978). **Evocative utterances** are statements a child makes naming entities. After a child names, an adult usually gives evaluative feedback that confirms or negates the child's selection of exemplars. As a result, the child either maintains or modifies his or her meaning. As you might expect, there is a positive relationship between the amount of verbal input from adults at 20 months and vocabulary size and average utterance length of the child at 24 months. Children are more verbal in homes in which parents are more verbal.

Hypothesis-testing and **interrogative utterances** are more direct methods of acquiring linguistic knowledge. When seeking confirmation of a word meaning, the child may say a word or word combination with rising intonation, such as "doggie ↑" or "baby eat ↑." A responding adult either confirms or denies the child's hypothesis. When unaware of an entity label, a child uses an interrogative utterance, such as "What?" "That?" or "Wassat?" These requests for information are even found in the pointing and vocalizing behaviors of infants prior to first words. At 24 months there is a positive correlation between the number of interrogative utterances used by children and their vocabulary size.

The last strategy, imitation, is selective. Children do not imitate indiscriminately. They are actively selecting. Table 6.2 contains examples of selective imitation. Note that the ends of utterances seem to have particular perceptual importance for children.

Role of Selective Imitation   **Selective imitation** is used in the acquisition of words, morphology, and syntactic-semantic structures (Perez-Pereira, 1994; Speidel & Herreshoff, 1989). In general, imitation is defined as a whole or partial repetition of an utterance of another speaker within no more than three successive child utterances. Approximately 20% of what toddlers say is an imitation of other speakers, although there are widespread differences across children, reflecting use or situational variations. For example, the amount of child imitation seems to reflect the amount of maternal imitation of her child.

Usually, imitations are slightly more mature than the production capacities of a child, indicating selective imitation's use as a learning strategy. The role of imitation as a strategy is

TABLE 6.2 *Examples of Selective Imitation*

ADULT:	Daddy home.
CHILD:	Daddy home.
ADULT:	The doggie is sick.
CHILD:	Doggie sick.
ADULT:	You want the baby?
CHILD:	No.
ADULT:	Okay, mommy want baby.
CHILD:	Want baby.
ADULT:	Want Mommy to throw ball?
CHILD:	No.
ADULT:	What then?
CHILD:	Throw ball.

very complex. For example, imitation of others is important for vocabulary growth, while self-imitation seems to be important for the transition from single-word to multiword language production (Veneziano, Sinclair, & Berthoud, 1990).

The use of selective imitation as a learning strategy may also vary with individual children, although the overall amount decreases with age, especially after age 2. It appears that imitation's usefulness as a language-learning strategy decreases as language becomes more complex.

At the single-word level, selective imitation seems particularly important for vocabulary growth, although conceptual development is certainly central as well. Although the presence of the referent increases the likelihood of imitation, a child's ability to repeat an utterance depends on his or her understanding of its meaning.

Many imitations and much early vocabulary growth take place within the context of daily routines, which may contain predictable or repetitious language. Imitations may appear later in an altered form. For example, when a child goes to the door, his mother may say, "Do you want to go out?" When next the child goes to the door, he may say, "Out." The word is the same, but the intent has changed.

It has been suggested that imitation may also serve a conversational role, enabling a child to relate his or her utterances to those of more mature language users. In the following exchange, note how the child uses imitation to tie utterances to those of the adult:

PARENT:	See Johnny ride his bike?
CHILD:	Ride bike. Bike fall.
PARENT:	No. He won't fall.
CHILD:	No fall. No go boom.

The form of the imitation may be determined by the child's intent.

Note in the example how the child proceeds from repetitious utterances (*Ride bike*) to semantically diverse ones (*No go boom*). In the revisions, the child alters the preceding utterance (*No. He won't fall.*) in order to maintain both the conversational and semantic relations and to sustain the topic. Children use two strategies of revision: *focus operations* and *substitution operations*. Focus operations, which predominate until about age 3, require only minimal linguistic skills. The child focuses on one or more words and repeats them. For example, when the caregiver says, "Baby's going to sleep in her bed," the child might say, "Sleep bed."

In a substitution operation, the child repeats only a portion of the utterance but replaces words. For example, in response to "Baby's going to sleep in her bed," the child might say, "Sleep blanket." The topic is maintained, but the structure is changed. This behavior increases with age and resembles the conversational replies found in the more mature language use seen below:

ADULT$_1$:	I'm going to put the baby down for a nap.
ADULT$_2$ (Reply):	Better cover her; it's chilly.

The high degree of creativity found in preschool language may, in fact, reflect this substitution process. A high percentage of preschool children's novel utterances differ only slightly from utterances produced previously. For example, a child says, "Where's Anna's plate?" Previously, she had said "Where's Anna's **W**?" and "Where's **mommy's** plate?" (Lieven, Behrens, Speares, & Tomasello, 2003, p. 340).

It is assumed that a language-learning child must store enough adult examples to allow him or her to abstract the linguistic relationship involved and to form a hypothesis. As children become more proficient with a structure in spontaneous speech, their imitation of it decreases.

Although the exact role of imitation in language acquisition is unclear, it appears that children most frequently selectively imitate items that they are in the process of learning or that have recently appeared. As such, imitation may serve young children as a modeling and stabilizing process for new structures. Imitation would thus reflect a child's developmental level and the teaching strategies of the adults around him or her.

Role of Formulas   A verbal routine or unanalyzed chunk of language often used in everyday conversation is called a **formula.** As memorized units, formulas function often as an entire utterance. For example, I knew a young child who continually ended all interactions with "See ya, bye!" None of the words are used separately in other expressions. Children's use of formulas is reported in several languages (Hickey, 1993; Perez-Pereira, 1994; Plunkett, 1993). Although they are a form of deferred imitation, formulas have a purpose well beyond a repetitive one.

Use of formulas may represent a whole-to-parts learning strategy for some children (Hickey, 1993; Pine, 1990; Pine & Lieven, 1990). Newly acquired forms learned as formulas gradually progress from unit learning to parts learning as a child analyzes the formula into its individual symbols (Elbers, 1990). Segmentation, or the analysis of formulas into their parts, coincides with the vocabulary spurt noted in children at approximately 20 months (Plunkett, 1993).

Unfortunately, some children—discussed in more detail in Chapter 7—use formulas with little or no analysis of the individual parts. Unlike segmentation, this is a nonproductive language-learning strategy. Thus, while formulas aid initial vocabulary growth, their nonsegmentation may constrain development.

Summary   Selective imitations and formulas function much as routines, providing a known "scaffolding" for a child and reducing the language-processing load. Both aid linguistic analysis and are used meaningfully in conversation. Other strategies, such as the use of evocative, interrogative, and hypothesis-testing utterances, enable a child to further participate in conversation and to explore and test new words and structures.

PRESCHOOL LANGUAGE-LEARNING STRATEGIES

Obviously, the usefulness of selective imitation will be limited as a child begins to acquire structures of more than a few words. This inefficiency of imitation accounts for the rapid decline of its use at between 24 and 30 months of age, suggesting the use of other learning strategies.

In general, children use what they know about language to help them decipher what they don't know. For example, they may use semantics to decode syntax or syntax and context to figure out word meanings. This process is called **bootstrapping.** "To pull yourself up by your bootstraps" is an old American English idiom meaning to use the resources at hand to better yourself. This is what a child does when he or she uses knowledge in one area to enhance performance in another.

Using *semantic bootstrapping,* young language-learning children analyze syntax based on semantic structures. Persons and things become nouns, actions morph into verbs, attributes to adjectives, and spatial relations and directions form adverbs and prepositions.

In similar fashion, syntactic structures can be used to deduce word meanings (Gleitman, 1993). You may use this practice when you read an unknown word in text. This process is called *syntactic bootstrapping.* Relationships between words can aid in identification of parts of speech and their use. In practice, semantic and syntactic bootstrapping are complementary processes.

Certain distinctions are learned before others. For example, one-time actions, such as *fall* and *break,* are likely to appear first in past tense, while ongoing durative actions, such as *eat* and *play,* appear in the present tense. Regardless of the language, changes in question form generally occur in yes/no questions prior to *wh-* questions. Within *wh-* questions, those that ask *what* and *where* appear first, while *why* and *when* questions appear later. This is true in languages as different as Korean, Tamil, and English and reflect both cognitive and linguistic factors.

Children in the initial stage of language development also talk about the same general types of things. Utterances consist of animate or action-causing subjects (*mommy, baby, dog*) called *agents* and inanimate or action-receiving objects (*ball, juice, cookie*) called *objects*. Only later do children use inanimate subjects (**Ball** fall) and animate objects (Kiss **baby**). Syntactic rules are learned gradually. Initially, the rule may be unanalyzed and used in situation-specific instances. Use will generally proceed sporadically until a child masters the rule.

We can assume that children begin by learning the basic sentence type, which in English is subject-verb-object. Although adults may use this sentence type only 40 to 60% of the time, children probably assume that this order represents the basic order. Additional intonational and situational cues may help differentiate those utterances that vary from the basic sentence type.

Most likely, young children determine the syntactic rules by using cues provided by the meaning of an adult's utterance. Mothers aid in this process by talking primarily about the present context.

Using knowledge of semantics, a preschooler attempts to *pay attention to how and where semantic distinctions are marked* syntactically. This varies across languages. For example, consonants and the inside of words are important in modern Hebrew, stems and word endings are important in Hungarian, and word and phrase order and relationships are important in English.

In addition to learning words, meanings, and word order, a child learns the classes in which words belong, such as nouns and verbs. Language rules apply to word classes, not to individual words. Most likely a child hypothesizes that words are similar and thus belong together because of the way they are treated linguistically. For example, a child hears certain words in English receive -*ed* and -*ing* markers and begins to "chunk" these words together into what adults call *verbs*. As the child discriminates similarities, words treated in the same manner are organized and linked together. New members are added as they meet the same criteria. Although this explanation is somewhat simplified, it adequately describes an active process by the child that corresponds to our knowledge of information processing and hypothesis building.

Initially, children rely on a few rigid syntactic formulas. In English, children become dependent on the subject-verb-object (SVO) (*Mommy is eating a cookie*) sentence form. Later, they learn other forms and develop a flexible system that is adaptable to different discourse situations. This evolution from rigid to flexible systems has been reported in the development of languages as different as English, Chinese, French, modern Hebrew, Hungarian, and Turkish.

Children's grammatical errors do not necessarily reflect a lack of either knowledge or development. Even some children with little knowledge of a grammatical structure may make few errors with that structure because they attempt to produce it infrequently (Rispoli, 2005). Other children—we might call them risk-takers—attempt repeatedly to produce these structures with the result that they make frequent errors.

From a cross-linguistic perspective, the development of syntactic and morphological features seems to progress through three phases. First, use of the language feature is context based and dependent on extralinguistic cues. Second, a child relates meanings to forms such as word order such as "A acts on B," as in *Mommy eats soup*. In the third phase, a child acquires mature use of the language feature based on internalized rules.

TABLE *6.3* *Universal Language-Learning Principles*

1. Pay attention to the ends of words.

2. Phonological forms of words can be systematically modified.

3. Pay attention to the order of words and morphemes.

4. Avoid interruption and rearrangement of linguistic units.

5. Underlying semantic relations should be marked overtly and clearly.

6. Avoid exceptions.

7. The use of grammatical markers should make semantic sense.

Source: Information from Slobin (1978).

Universal Language-Learning Principles

There are patterns of development that suggest underlying universal syntax learning strategies and operational principles of children (see Table 6.3) (Slobin, 1978). Although we do not know the exact strategies children use, we can infer their presence from consistent behaviors of young children learning different languages. The following sections address some of these principles. A caution: The following sections require a lot of thought. Go slow; pause often to digest.

Pay Attention to the Ends of Words Across languages, the same semantic notion, such as a verb tense or spatial relation, may be produced linguistically at very different ages. If we assume that the underlying concept can be acquired cognitively by children at the same age, then differences in age of production must reflect language differences. In general, children acquire linguistic markers that occur at the ends of words, such as the English *-s, -er, -ed,* before those that appear at the beginnings of words, as in *un-, dis-, in-*. Similarly, English verb endings, such as *-ing,* are acquired before auxiliary or helping verbs, such as *is,* that precede the verb (*is eating*). A corollary could be stated as follows: *For any given semantic notion, suffixes or post-positions will be acquired earlier than will prefixes or pre-positions.* For example, the comparative *-er* (*costlier*) and superlative *-est* (*costliest*) endings are acquired before the alternative *more* (*more costly*) and *most* (*most costly*) markers. The child is thus more likely to learn *sweeter* than *more sweet*.

Many new or expanded grammatical structures initially occur at the end of sentences, suggesting that the final position in longer structures is also important for learning. Initial word order in children's questions may also reflect attention to the ends of adult utterances. For example, after hearing a parent say, "I don't know where it is," a child may later produce the question form "Where it is?"

Phonological Forms Can Be Systematically Modified Through experimentation, the child learns to vary pronunciation. Gradually, the child recognizes that various sound changes, consistent across several words, such as the final /t/ sound on *walked* and *talked,* can reflect underlying meaning changes.

Pay Attention to the Order of Words and Morphemes The standard order of morphemes used in adult utterances is preserved in child speech. Thus, a child produces "charm*ingly*," not "charm*lying*."

*C*onversations with adults afford preschoolers chances to make verbal contributions, learn when to speak, and develop cohesiveness between speaker and listener.

In English, general word order (SVO) is maintained by preschoolers also. This ordering leads to another universal corollary: *Word order in child speech reflects word order in adult forms of the language.* This seems to be especially true in languages such as English, in which word order is important for underlying meaning.

A second universal corollary states that *in early stages of development, sentences that do not have standard word order will be interpreted using standard word order.* Two following examples from English relate to passive sentences and ordering of events. In the first example, English-speaking preschoolers interpret passive sentences as if they represent the common agent-action-object form. The child will therefore interpret "The cat is chased by the dog" as "The cat chased the dog." In a second example, 3-year-old children will ignore the conjunctions *before* and *after* in compound sentences, interpreting the order of the clauses as an order of occurrence. In other words, clause 1 occurred first, then clause 2. For example, the sentence "We'll go to Grandma's after the movie" may be interpreted as "Grandma's, then movie."

Avoid Interruption and Rearrangement of Linguistic Units

As mentioned, in English, children learn the subject-verb-object form early. Interruption and rearrangement of this form place a strain on a child's processing, especially with sentences that require a child to retain large amounts of information.

A related universal corollary states that *structures requiring rearrangement of elements will first appear in nonrearranged form.* In other words, a form in English that differs from the predominant subject-verb-object format will first appear in the subject-verb-object form. In some children's speech, the auxiliary or helping verb in questions (What *are* you eating?) appears originally in a noninverted form (What you *are* eating?), keeping the verb "is eating" together.

A second related corollary states that *discontinuous morphemes are reduced to, or replaced by, continuous morphemes whenever possible.* In English, this universal is demonstrated again in the progressive verb form, consisting of the auxiliary verb "be" plus a main verb with the inflection -*ing* (*is eating*), which appears initially in children's speech without the auxiliary verb, as in "I eating ice cream."

There is a tendency, states a third axiom, to *preserve the structure of the sentence as a closed entity by sentence-external placement of new linguistic forms.* In other words, new structures may be tacked on to the beginning or end of the sentence prior to moving within it. For example, in English early negatives are attached to the beginning (*No* eat soup) and, occasionally, to the end of a sentence. Only later does the negative move into the sentence, as in "I *no* eat soup." Initial subordinate clauses and infinitive phrases are attached at the end of the sentence first and develop within the sentence later.

Finally, a fourth universal corollary states that *the greater the separation between related parts of a sentence, the more difficult it is for the child to process adequately.* A sentence containing a phrase or clause is more difficult to interpret if the phrase or clause interrupts the subject-verb-object (SVO) format. A sentence such as "I saw the man *who fell down*" is easier for preschoolers to interpret than "The man *who fell down* ran away." In a sentence such as "The girl who stole the horse ran away," a young child is likely to interpret it as "The girl stole the horse and the horse ran away."

To produce complicated sentences, a preschooler must take some risks (Dale & Crain-Thoreson, 1993). As mentioned, not all children are language risk takers.

Underlying Semantic Relations Should Be Marked Overtly and Clearly
As a child listens to and attempts to interpret speech, obvious, consistent morphological markers may help. To some extent, children demonstrate the importance of these markers in their own speech. For example, small functor words (*the, of, and*) and other morphological markers may receive more emphasis in child speech than in adult speech.

Not all languages are the same in their use of morphological markers. Both the Tamil and Turkish morphological systems are learned early because of their regularity and clarity of marking. Each affix encodes only one feature, and, by age 2, most children are using them correctly. Compare this to English, in which three phonological forms (/s, z, ə z/) are used for plural (*three dogs*), third person singular (*he walks*), and possessive (*daddy's key*) marking.

A related universal corollary states that *a child will begin to mark a semantic notion earlier if its morphological structure is more obvious perceptually.* The development of the passive (*The boy was hit by the girl.*) is illustrative. The concept of the passive form is not difficult for children to learn, but in English the linguistic structure is. Egyptian Arabic-speaking children learn the passive prefix *it-* rather early. In English, a passive sentence requires several syntactic changes and may not be acquired fully until adolescence.

A second universal states that *there is a preference for marking even unmarked members of a semantic category.* This preference may account for some of the overextensions in English. Overextension is when a language feature, such as a morphological ending, is used where it is not required. For example, the clear -*ed* past-tense marker may be used with irregular verbs (*wented*) that may appear to a child to have no marking (*went*). Preference for marking may also be seen with the plural as in *mans* and *feets*.

When a child first learns a linguistic entity that can be contracted or deleted, contractions or deletions tend not to be used. In other words, initially a child will use the full form of contractible or deletable forms. In English, young children may respond with "I will" when asked to imitate "I'll" in a sentence. Similarly, the verb *to be* first appears as "he is," although adults use "*he's*" more frequently. In an imitation task, children may replace optionally deleted forms that are not present in the model sentence. For example, when repeating "She's not eating but he is," a child might say, "She *is* not eating but he is *eating*." It's no surprise, therefore, that for young children *it is easier to understand a complex sentence in which material usually deleted is not deleted.*

Avoid Exceptions   You used this strategy when you learned French or Spanish in high school! There is also a tendency among children to overgeneralize linguistic rules and to avoid exceptions to these rules. As a group, the rules for a larger class, such as past tense (*walked, jumped, asked*), are learned before those for a subclass, such as irregular past tense (*ate, drank, thought*). Thus, the stages of linguistic marking of semantic notions are as follows (Marchman & Bates, 1994; Marcus et al., 1992):

1. No marking (walk).
2. Appropriate marking in a small number of cases (walk*ed*).
3. *Overgeneralization of marking* although limited and with a small number of examples (eat*ed*).
4. Adultlike system (walk*ed*, ate).

For example, initially there is no marking of the English past tense. Next, some irregular past-tense verbs, such as *came* and *fell*, are formed correctly, but the regular past *-ed* is not used. Once learned, the regular past is overextended to irregular verbs, as in *comed* and *falled*, in an attempt to introduce regularity. Finally, full adult usage is acquired.

A second developmental universal states that *rules for larger classes are learned before rules for subdivisions, and general rules are learned before exceptions.* Most plural nouns, for example, can use the word *many* to indicate quantity, such as *many cookies* or *many blocks.* Children learn this rule quickly. Mass nouns, a smaller class—liquids or granular substances, such as *sand* or *water*—require *much.* It takes children longer to learn to use *much* with the appropriate nouns.

Overextension of morphological or syntactic rules may be related to an increase in number of examples learned to which the rule applies (Marchman & Bates, 1994). Initial learning, most probably by rote memorization, continues until such time as the number is large enough for a child to synthesize a general rule (Plunkett & Marchman, 1993). Overextension begins at this point.

Grammatical Markers Should Make Semantic Sense   Overextension of rules, when it occurs, is usually limited to the appropriate semantic category. Inflectional markers, such as *-s, -ed,* or *-ing,* and words, such as *a, the,* or *at,* are applied within certain grammatical classes. Thus, the *-ed* morphological marker is applied to words in the verb class. Smaller, less important words, called functors, are substituted for functors from the same class. For example, a child may use *in,* a preposition, incorrectly in place of *at,* another preposition, but he or she will not substitute *the* for *at,* because *the* is not a preposition. One corollary of this principle states that *the choice of the functor word is always within the given functor class and subcategory.*

A second corollary states that *when selecting an appropriate marker from among a group performing the same semantic function, the child tends to rely on a single form.* For example, the selection of the /s/, /z/, or /ɔ z/ phonological form of the plural is based on the ending consonant of the stem word as in *cats*/s/, *dogs*/z/, and *wishes*/ɔ z/. Initially, a child relies on only one form of the plural where possible.

Summary It must be stressed these principles are theories that attempt to explain the order of acquisition. A child has certain concepts, based on cognitive growth, that are expressed through the linguistic system. Using certain principles of acquisition, a child scans the language code to discover the means of comprehension and production.

CHILDREN'S PROCESSES OF LANGUAGE ACQUISITION

As we'll see in the following discussion, and then again in Chapter 9, children's early linguistic representations are highly concrete and specific pieces of language are not in abstract categories and rules (Savage, Lieven, Theakston, & Tomasello, 2003). From these often word-specific constructions, children's thinking gradually grows more abstract as they encounter more and more examples. Frequency of use and probability in the language that surrounds children are important factors.

When confronting all the language data around them, children may use two general cognitive processes (Tomasello, 2003): intention-reading and pattern-finding, mentioned in Chapter 4. **Intention-reading** is a uniquely human social cognitive skill for understanding language behavior of others. **Pattern-finding** is a cognitive skill we share with other primates that enables us to find common threads in disparate information, such as seeking underlying rules for language. More specific process may explain how learn symbols and categories and the ways in which those categories relate.

Intention Reading

Cultural learning is basic to language learning and can be explained simply as the ability to do things the way that other people do. In order to learn from those in the culture, a child must determine the intentions of others. In human linguistic communication, the fundamental unit of intent is the utterance. As a child is attempting to comprehend the communicative intention of an utterance, he or she may also be attempting to comprehend the functional roles being played by its various components of the utterance. Identifying these roles is only possible if the child has some understanding of the adult's overall communicative intent and discovering how each component contributes. In this way, a child learns the communicative function of words, phrases, and utterance units that will enhance pattern-finding.

Pattern-Finding

It is believed by some linguists that children use several techniques in pattern-finding, among them (Tomasello, 2003):

- **Schematization** and **Analogy,** which account for how children create abstract syntactic constructions from concrete pieces of language they have heard.
- **Entrenchment** and **Preemption,** which account for how children confine these abstractions to those of their linguistic community.
- **Functionally Based Distributional Analysis,** which accounts for how children form linguistic categories, such as nouns and verbs.

Let's look at each briefly.

Schematization and Analogy Young children hear and use the same utterances repeated over and over, sometimes *ad nauseum,* but with systematic variation. Common expressions are

Where's the X?, I wanna X, Let's X, Can you X?, Gimme X, and *I'm Xing it* (Tomasello, 2003). In short, a child learns these recurrent concrete pieces of language or schemes for specific functions and individual words to fill the slots in each. For example, Gimme X is a common way to request something, but the thing being requested changes across situations. Although the slot for X is somewhat open, it is constrained by the function of the utterance.

If a child understands the relationship across schemes, such as *X is Y-ing the Z* and the *A is B-ing the C,* then a child sees that X and A play analogous roles, as do C and Z. In this way, different constructions develop their own syntactic roles. This first occurs with each construction, so roles may include *eater* and *thing eaten,* then by use of analogy become more abstract. Word order and morphological markers may aid this process.

Entrenchment and Preemption When we do something in the same way successfully several times, that way of doing it becomes habitual. That's entrenchment. Preemption is the notion that if someone communicates to me using one form, rather than another, there was a reason for that choice related to the speaker's specific communicative intention. This motivates a listener to search for that reason and distinguish the two forms and their appropriate communicative contexts. Using both processes together, a child inspects different possible forms expressing different communicative intentions.

Functionally Based Distributional Analysis Over time, concrete linguistic items, such as words or phrases that serve the same communicative function, are grouped together into a category. Thus, noun and verb are categories based on the functions that different words of each type serve within differing constructions. These categories are based on usage in that nouns are defined by what nouns do.

Production

A child's language production consists of constructing utterances out of various already learned pieces of language in a way appropriate to the communication context. This requires a child to focus on both an utterance's form and its function or intent. In other words, a child does not put together utterances from scratch, one morpheme at a time, but rather, pieces together the utterance from a ragtag assortment of different pre-existing linguistic units (Tomasello, 2003).

This can be seen in the production of preschool children in which as little as one-third of their utterances may be novel and of these three-quarters may consist of repetitions of some previously used utterance within the last week or so (Lieven et al., 2003). The small number of novel multiword utterances will most likely involve combinations of "fill-ins" and "add-ons" to already well-established constructions.

It would seem, then, that a child has three basic options for producing an utterance on a specific occasion (Lieven et al., 2003):

- Retrieve a functionally appropriate concrete expression and just say it as it had been heard.
- Retrieve an utterance-level construction and simultaneously "tweak" it to fit the current communicative situation.
- Produce an utterance by combining word and phrase schemes without using an utterance-level construction based on the context.

In this way, a child cobbles together a situationally appropriate utterance from pieces of language of various shapes, sizes, and degrees of abstraction rather than gluing together words and morphemes following countless abstract language rules.

Adult Conversational Teaching Techniques

Adults engage in very little direct language teaching, but they do facilitate their children's language acquisition. Although very little time is spent in direct instruction, many caregiving and experiential activities relate to language acquisition. Obviously, these parental techniques vary with the language maturity of a child and the culture and language involved. While several parental factors may affect children's language development, the level of maternal education seems to be most highly correlated (Dollaghan et al., 1999).

ADULT SPEECH TO TODDLERS

The affect of a parent's behavior on her child's language acquisition varies with the age of the child (Masur, Flynn, & Eichorst, 2005). Around a child's first birthday, nonverbal adult behavior seems to influence an infant's vocabulary growth in a positive way. In contrast, maternal verbal behavior is more important for a child's vocabulary growth during the 13- to 17-month ages, especially verbal responses to her child and her supportive directions. These changes reflect a child's increasing ability to comprehend and use verbal information. Intrusive verbal directions by the mother negatively influence vocabulary growth.

Throughout the first two years of life, parents talk with their children, label objects and events, and respond to their children's communication. It would be simplistic, however, to assume that a child just applies the labels heard to his or her pre-existing internal concepts. Meaning is also derived from the communication process (Levy & Nelson, 1994). Initially, words are constrained by the conversational context, but later a child encounters words in other contexts and gradually modifies their meaning. Within the conversational context, parents aid acquisition by engaging in modeling, cueing, prompting, and responding behaviors that affect the linguistic behaviors of their children.

Modeling: Motherese (Parentese)

Children's speech occurs in conversation and generally serves to maintain the exchange. As noted previously, communication behavior is well established by the time a child begins to speak. Almost from birth, a child encounters a facilitative verbal environment that enables him or her to participate as a conversational partner.

As a child's communication behaviors develop, its mother unconsciously modifies her own behaviors so that she requires more child participation. For example, the mother may not accept babbled responses once her child begins to use single words. Instead, she may respond to babbling with "What's that?"—a request for a restatement. Once the child is able to verbalize, the mother "ups the ante" and withholds the names of objects or repeatedly asks the name until the child replies with a word.

Word learning depends on the establishment of joint reference, as noted in Chapter 5. Mothers are very effective at following their child's line of regard, then labeling the object of the child's attention. The more time allotted to such joint attending, the larger a child's vocabulary as a toddler (Akhtar, Dunham, & Dunham, 1991). In short, a child is more likely to learn a symbol when focused on the referent as he or she is during joint attending. As might be expected, mismatches between the focus of a child's attending and the adult's labeling of that focus occur frequently. When this occurs, the caregiver attempts to redirect the child both nonverbally and verbally (Baldwin, 1993). As a result, 18-month-old toddlers may learn some words from only one exposure.

First words are learned within interactive contexts. Those structures modeled most frequently by mothers are most likely to be used by their children. Data from both English and Modern Hebrew demonstrate that nearly all the utterances of young children mirror patterns used by their mothers.

Initially, mothers provide object names, but within a short time they begin to request these names from children. By the middle of the second year, mothers are labeling and requesting at approximately equal rates, and dialog is fully established. This dialog becomes the framework for a new routine. The mother begins to shape the child's speech by distinguishing more sharply between acceptable and unacceptable responses. The child's verbalizations are often responses that fill specific slots within the dialog, such as answering a question. Within the dialog, the mother provides consistency that aids her toddler's learning, including the repetition rate, the rate of confirmation, and the probability of reciprocating.

At age 1, infants are alert to the subtle stress placed on new words by adults and that this stress aids word learning (Curtin, 2009). Two-year-olds recognize early on that adults use prosodic features, such as pitch, duration, and loudness to indicate new referents (Grassmann & Tomasello, 2007). Toddlers use this information in word learning.

In addition, mothers make other speech modifications that, taken together, are called **motherese** or *parentese*. The characteristics of motherese are listed in Table 6.4. Compared to adult–adult speech, motherese exhibits (a) greater pitch range, especially at the higher end; (b) lexical simplification characterized by the diminutive ("doggie") and syllable reduplication

TABLE *6.4 Characteristics of Motherese Compared to Adult-to-Adult Speech*

Paralinguistic
Slower speech with longer pauses between utterances and after content words
Higher overall pitch; greater pitch range
Exaggerated intonation and stress
More varied loudness pattern
Fewer dysfluencies (one dysfluency per 1,000 words versus 4.5 per 1,000 for adult–adult)
Fewer words per minute

Lexical
More restricted vocabulary
Three times as much paraphrasing
More concrete reference to here and now

Semantic
More limited range of semantic functions
More contextual support

Syntactic
Fewer broken or run-on sentences
Shorter, less complex sentences (approximately 50% are single words or short declaratives)
More well-formed and intelligible sentences
Fewer complex utterances
More imperatives and questions (approximately 60% of utterances)

Conversational
Fewer utterances per conversation
More repetitions (approximately 16% of utterances are repeated within three turns)

(consonant-verb syllable repetition); (c) shorter, less complex utterances; (d) less dysfluency; (e) more paraphrasing and repetition; (f) limited, concrete vocabulary and a restricted set of semantic relations; (g) more contextual support; and (h) more directives and questions.

As you know from Chapter 5, mothers use short utterances when conversing with their infants. Interestingly, they use even shorter, less adult utterances with toddlers. The lowering of a mother's MLU, beginning months prior to her child's first words, is positively related to better receptive language skills by her child at 18 months of age, although there seems to be no measurable effect on expressive language (Murray et al., 1990). Mothers aid their baby's *bootstrapping*, mentioned previously, by maintaining semantic-syntactic consistency (Rondal & Cession, 1990). For example, in utterances addressed to children, mothers use agents or action-causers (*mommy, daddy, boy, dog*) as subjects almost exclusively. Maternal behavior makes it easier for her child to decipher the syntax of mother's utterances.

As her child's language matures, a mother's speech directed to a child likewise changes. Motherese seems well-tuned to the child's language level.

The amount of maternal speech, of partial repetitions of a child, of gestures accompanying speech, and of initiated statements commenting on her child's activity or eliciting attention vary with a child's overall language level. The dependence on nonlinguistic contextual cues, such as gestures, decreases with an increase in a child's linguistic abilities. These dynamic elements appear to be strongly related to a child's subsequent development. At age 2, the amount of shared attention and maternal gestures and relevant comments are positively correlated with a child's verbal learning a year later (Schmidt & Lawson, 2002). Clearly, adult input is extremely important.

Slow at first, the rate of both mother's and child's linguistic change increases with age. The length and complexity of a mother's utterances change most between 20 and 27 months, when her child's language changes most rapidly. In contrast, there seems to be little or no change in the structural complexity of motherese between 8 and 18 months. During this period there is also little corresponding change in the complexity of child speech, the changes consisting primarily of the addition of single words.

Mothers fine-tune their language input to their children based primarily on the children's comprehension level. Other factors that influence the level of a mother's language are the conversational situation, the content, and her intent. Overall, adults will simplify their input if the child does not seem to comprehend.

The amount of parental labeling or naming in both English and French varies with the age and development of a child. A positive relationship exists between the amount of adult labeling with young children and a child's subsequent vocabulary growth (Poulin-Dubois, Graham, & Sippola, 1995). As the use of noun labels decreases with development, nouns are replaced by verbs describing the action performed by the object (Schmidt, 1996).

Conversational input by mothers provides useful data for children to create early meanings for non-object terms, such as color, number, and time (Tare, Shatz, & Gilbertson, 2008). Non-object terms pose a challenge for word learning by children because of the non-obvious word-referent relationship when compared to object names.

Undoubtedly, a child's characteristics have an influence on the language input to which a child is exposed. The toys that a child plays with also influence the amount and types of language produced by an adult. In general, toys that encourage role play, such as dolls, elicit more language of a greater variety from parents.

Adults simplify their language in order to be understood. Apparently, however, adults are not conscious of their modifications, nor are they consciously attempting to teach language. Adult-to-child speech seems to be modified in response to the amount of child feedback and participation. Not only is much of the speech addressed to a child adapted for the child's linguistic level, but speech that is not adapted may be simply ignored or not processed by children. In other words, children play an active role in selecting the utterances to which they will attend. A lack of response is important, for it informs a parent there has been a breakdown in communication that, in turn, necessitates linguistic changes by that parent. Although the exact nature of child feedback is unknown, children seem to be the key to adult linguistic changes.

The pragmatic aspects of a mother's speech may be related to the talking style of her child. Mothers of children who name frequently use more descriptive words and fewer directions. In addition, these mothers use more utterances within a given situation than mothers of children who name less.

The nonlinguistic context is also critical. In order to use motherese, it's necessary for an adult to see a child. In fact, these maternal linguistic modifications are different when her child is absent.

Despite linguistic inadequacies, children can participate effectively because of their mothers' ability to maintain the conversation. The steady, rhythmic flow of the dialog depends on the structural similarity of a mother's and child's utterances and on the correspondence of a mother's speech to events in the environment. She enables her child to participate through her use of turn-passing devices such as questions. She does not use turn-grabbing or turn-keeping behaviors, such as "well . . . ," "but . . . ," or pause fillers.

Mothers maintain control, however, and the dialog is much less symmetrical than it may appear. They maintain the interaction by inferring their children's communication intentions, compensating for the children's communication failures, and providing feedback. After her child reaches age 2, the mother slowly relinquishes her control.

Within the interactional sequence, a mother analyzes, synthesizes, and abstracts language structures for her child. Through word substitutions, she aids her child's learning of language form. A sequence might be as follows:

CHILD: She running.
MOTHER: She's running fast. Oh, she's tired. Now she's running slowly. She's
           stopping. She's jumping slowly. Now she's jumping quickly.

Note how the mother uses the same forms repeatedly. As a result, her child is not a lone linguist attempting to learn the language code; much of analysis, synthesis, and abstraction is performed by the mother.

Fathers and Other Caregivers   Despite the name *motherese,* these speech modifications are not limited to mothers. Fathers and other caregivers modify their speech in very similar ways. In fact, fathers seem to provide even more examples of simplified adult speech than mothers.

The range of vocabulary used by fathers and mothers with their young language-learning children is similar, but fathers use fewer common words. In this way, fathers are more demanding than mothers.

Although fathers make modifications similar to those of mothers, they are less successful in communicating with toddlers, as measured by the amount of communication breakdown (Tomasello, Conti-Ramsden, & Ewert, 1990). Fathers use more requests for clarification than mothers. In addition, the form of these requests is more nonspecific ("What?") than those of mothers ("You want what?"). Fathers also acknowledge their children's utterances less frequently ("Um-hm," "Yeah," "Okay"). In return, children tend to persist less in conversation with their fathers than with their mothers. It is possible that fathers serve as a bridge for their children between communication with the mother and with other adults. The child learns how to communicate with those less familiar with his or her style and manner.

Even children as young as 4 years of age make language and speech modifications when addressing younger language-learning children. Adult and peer language modifications differ somewhat. In general, peer speech to toddlers is less complex and shorter and contains more repetition than adult-to-toddler speech, although peers elicit fewer language responses than parents. Peer interaction may provide a "proving ground" where younger children can try new linguistic structures.

Children enrolled in daycare centers and preschools also encounter a variety of motherese that varies with the size of the group and the age of the children (Scopesi & Pellegrino, 1990). In general, the larger the group of children, the less individual adaptation by an adult. Larger groups force teachers to concentrate on keeping attention and control. While use of behavior and turn-taking control techniques by teachers results in little toddler language production, use of child-centered strategies, such as adopting a child's topics and waiting for child initiations, and interaction-promoting behaviors result in high levels of talkativeness by toddlers (Girolametto & Weitzman, 2002; Girolametto, Weitzman, van Lieshout, & Duff, 2000). There are clear language-learning advantages for children attending preschool when the curriculum emphasizes language and literacy (Craig, Connor, & Washington, 2003).

The presence of older siblings may also influence the language a younger child hears and produces. For example, an older child will usually respond to more of a parent's questions, thereby reducing the number of responses made by a younger child. The younger child will often respond by imitating the older sibling. In this situation, the mother uses fewer rephrased questions, fewer questions with hints and answers, and fewer questions when the older child is present. In addition, the mother uses more direct repetitions of questions.

Summary   Parents who use a more conversational style with less direct instructing are more likely to have children who learn language more quickly. In other words, children benefit more from language input when parents are more concerned with understanding and participation and less so with teaching.

The exact effect of motherese on language acquisition is unknown. The modifications made by mothers may aid language acquisition by bringing maternal utterances into the "processing range" of a child. If nothing else, they increase a mother's chances of getting a response from her child. Since we find similar modifications in many cultures, we can assume that, at least, they somehow facilitate communication between adults and children.

The modifications of motherese seem to be maximally effective with the 18- to 21-month-old child. The child attends selectively, focusing on the best examples of various structures.

Prompting

Prompting includes any parental behaviors that require a toddler's response. Three common types are fill-ins, elicited imitations, and questions. In fill-ins, the parent says "This is a. . . ." No response or an incorrect response from the child will usually result in additional prompts and recueing.

In elicited imitations, the parent cues with "Say X." Young language-learning children respond to slightly over half of the elicited imitations addressed to them.

Questions may be of the confirmational yes/no type, such as "Is this a ball?" or of the *wh-* variety, such as "What's that?" or "Where's doggie?" Unanswered or incorrectly answered questions are usually reformulated by the adult. Approximately 20 to 50% of mothers' utterances to young language-learning children are questions. The individual range varies greatly.

In general, these three types of maternal language-teaching utterances have a shorter average length than the majority of the utterances addressed to the child. Maternal yes/no interrogatives, such as "Are we going home?" appear to correlate with child language-development gains in syntactic complexity, while intonational interrogatives, such as "You going home?" correlate with gains in a child's pragmatic ability. In contrast, maternal directives, such as "go get your coat," seem to correlate highly with child gains in utterance length and semantic-syntactic complexity but may slow vocabulary growth.

Parents employ an interesting technique to give their toddler an opportunity to produce two related single-word utterances. After a child produces a single-word utterance, his or her parent uses questions to aid the child in producing other elements of a longer utterance. The parent concludes by repeating the whole utterance. The following exchange is an example of this strategy:

Child:	Daddy.
Adult:	Uh-huh. What's Daddy doing?
Child:	Eat.
Adult:	Yeah, *Daddy eat* cookie.

Prompting and cueing are effective teaching techniques and their effectiveness has been demonstrated with children with language disorders.

Responding Behaviors

Parents do not directly reinforce the syntactic correctness of toddler's utterances as in "good talking" or "you're such a big girl." In fact, less than 10% of children's utterances are followed by verbal approval. Generally, such reinforcement is given for truthfulness and politeness, not for the correctness of the syntax.

Feedback by parents, however, does follow their children's language production and varies with its correctness (Furrow, Baillie, McLaren, & Moore, 1993; Moerk, 1991). Imitation, topic changes, acknowledgments, or no response are more frequent following grammatically correct child utterances, while reformulations, expansions of the child's utterance, and requests for clarification are more likely following ungrammatical utterances. Different responses may signal a child as to the acceptability of the utterance. For example, Japanese mothers facilitate their infants' transition between sounds and words by repeating poorly formed child words correctly, thus signaling errors for the child and providing an alternative (Otomo, 2001). Let's look at some of the strategies used by English-speaking moms in the United States.

Let's assume that a 30-month-old says to you, "Gran'ma car, go zoo, 'morrow with Nuncle Juan." You might reply, "Yes, tomorrow Uncle Juan and you are going to the zoo in grandmother's car." What you just did is called a **reformulation** or a recast utterance. Your goal is not to teach but to understand the child. That said, what is the effect on the child?

As in the example, children's truncated or ungrammatical utterances can leave caregivers wondering what exactly a child means, so adults frequently check their own understanding against the child's meaning. An adult does this, as you did above, by reformulating the child's utterance into what the adult thinks the child meant to say. In the process, the adult locates the error or errors and embeds a correction. As a result, the child hears a more conventional form for expressing his or her meaning.

With preschoolers, adults reformulate more frequently than they imitate error-free utterances (Chouinard & Clark, 2003). As mentioned previously, imitation among both children and adults decreases markedly as the child passes from toddler to preschooler. In a similar fashion, reformulations decrease as a child passes through the preschool years (Chouinard & Clark, 2003).

We assume from their behavior that children understand reformulations to be corrections. For their part, children either repeat the reformulation, acknowledge the correction with *yeah* or *uh-huh* and continue the conversation, or reject the reformulation because the adult has misunderstood the child's meaning. Reformulation is a great teaching tool because of its immediacy, timeliness, and the attending of the child.

The type of reformulation used by the mother may have an effect on the particular form being learned (Farrar, 1990). For example, reformulating the child's previous utterance by adding, substituting, or moving a morpheme may aid learning of plurals and progressives (is eat*ing*) but has less effect on the past tense or the verb *to be,* which seem to benefit from removal of morphemes and restatement of correct forms.

Some responding behaviors seem to have reinforcing value. Approximately 30% of mothers' responses to 18- to 24-month-old children consist of expansions. An **expansion** is a more mature version of a child's utterance in which the word order is preserved. For example, if a child says "Mommy eat," mother might respond with "Mommy is eating her lunch." The mother assumes that the child intends to communicate a certain meaning. As a child's average utterance length increases beyond two words, the number of expansions by the mother decreases. Approximately one-fifth of a 2-year-old's ill-formed utterances are expanded by the mother into syntactically more correct versions.

Children seem to perceive expansions as a cue to imitate. Nearly a third of adult expansions are in turn imitated by the child. These imitations are likely to be more linguistically correct than the child's original utterance. Let's see how it works:

CHILD:	Block fall.
ADULT:	Um-hm, blocks fall *down.*
CHILD:	Block fall down.

Hopefully, spontaneous productions follow, and rules are generalized to conversational use. As spontaneous production of structures occurs, imitation of these structures decreases. Expansion adds meaning to a child's utterance at a time when the child is attending to a topic he or she has established. In addition, expansion provides evaluative feedback. Expansions continue the topic of conversation and encourage a child to take his or her turn and, thus, to maintain the dialog.

Right now expansion and reformulation probably seem like the same thing. Let's sort it out. Expansions, used primarily with younger children, maintain the child's word order while providing a more mature form of the child's utterance. While both expansion and reformulation seek to preserve the child's meaning, reformulation is a strategy for older children who are beginning to create truly complicated sentences. Think of reformulation as the next step in caregiver teaching after expansion. Reformulations go beyond a mere expansion and can involve considerable rearrangement of the sentence elements while preserving the child's meaning as you did in the example.

Extension, a comment or reply to a child's utterance, may be even more helpful. For example, when a child says "Doggie eat," the partner replies, "Doggie is hungry." Thus, extension provides more semantic information. Its value lies in its conversational nature, which provides positive feedback, and in both its *semantic* and *pragmatic contingency.* A semantically contingent utterance is one that retains the focus or topic of the previous utterance. A pragmatically contingent utterance concurs with the intent of the previous utterance; that is, topics invite comments, questions invite answers, requests invite responses, and so on. In short, both types of contingency maintain the conversational flow, which is inherently rewarding to almost all children.

Finally, parents imitate their toddler's speech. In conversations between adults and preschool children, adults repeat to establish that they have understood and children repeat to ratify what adults have said (Clark & Bernicot, 2008). For both adults and children, repetition signals attention to the other's utterances, and places the repeated information repeated in common ground. With 2-year-old children, adults combine their repeats with new information. Children then re-repeat the original form about 20% of the time. With older preschool children, adults check on intentions but less frequently, and only occasionally check on form. Older children also re-repeat, but, like adults, add further information.

All three responding behaviors—expansion, extension, and imitation—result in greater amounts of child imitation than adult topic initiation or nonimitative behaviors. Hence, expansion, extension, and imitation appear to be valuable language-teaching devices. Each reinforces a child's utterance, and expansion and extension also provide models of more mature language. Maternal extending correlates significantly with changes in the length of a child's utterances. The adult utterance is semantically contingent upon the preceding child utterance. This characteristic decreases the linguistic processing load on a child because the adult utterance is close to the child's utterance in form and content. Parents do not consciously devise these teaching strategies; rather, they evolve within child–caregiver conversations.

ADULT CONVERSATIONS WITH PRESCHOOLERS

As noted in Chapter 5, caregivers' altered behavior enables infants to engage in successful communication as early as possible. This process continues in the preschool years. Mothers provide opportunities for their children to make verbal contributions, draw them into conversations and provide a well-cued framework for the exchange, show their children when to speak, and thereby develop cohesiveness between the speaker and the listener. Mothers ask children to comment on objects and events within their experience. They also expand information by talking about the same object or event in different ways or by adding new ideas and elaborating on them. These maternal modifications appear to be correlated with advances in the child's language abilities.

What Children Hear

To understand how children acquire language, we need to know something about the language they hear, primarily from their mothers. For example, English-speaking 2- to 3-year-old children hear approximately 5,000 to 7,000 utterances each day, between a quarter and a third of these being questions (e.g., *Where's your crayon?*) and approximately a quarter are imperatives (e.g., *Stop that; Come here*) (Cameron-Faulkner, Lieven, & Tomasello, 2003).

Almost 80% of mother utterances are full adult sentences. The rest are phrases, most often a noun phrase (e.g., *the big dog, her little pony, the girl in the car*) or prepositional phrase (e.g., *on the phone, at school, with grandma*). About a quarter of the mothers' utterances use the copula or verb *be* (e.g., *am, is, are, was, were*) as the main verb (e.g., *I'm busy now; Mommy's sick today; The doggies are hungry*). Interestingly, only about 15% of the mother utterances had the *subject-verb-object* (SVO) sentence form characteristic of English, and over 80% of these had a pronoun subject (*I, you, he, she, it, we, they*).

Further analysis indicates highly frequent patterns or frames in the mother utterances, some of which are repeated as many as 40 times per day (Cameron-Faulkner et al., 2003). Most of these patterns consisted of two words or morphemes. Approximately 45% of all maternal utterances begin with one of the following words: *what, that, it, you, are/aren't, do/does/did/don't, I, is, shall, a, can/can't, where, there, who, come, look,* and *let's*. In turn, the children used many of these same word-based utterance frames in their own speech.

Although a language-learning child is thus faced with the formidable task of acquiring perhaps hundreds of different sentence and phrase constructions based on input, the appearance of these constructions in the speech of their mothers is not random. Acquisition is made a little easier by mothers. The majority of the utterances a child hears are highly repetitive word-based frames that they experience sometimes hundreds of times every day.

Mothers of 3- to 4-year-olds use many techniques to encourage communication. For example, mothers begin twice as many utterances with words such as *well* and *now* as their children do. These signals, plus varied intonation, are used with responses and help a child understand by signaling that a response is coming. In addition, mothers use a high proportion of redundant utterances to acknowledge and reassure children as in the following:

CHILD: Want cookie.
MOTHER: You want a cookie? Well, let's see. You want a chocolate cookie?
CHILD: Yeah, chocolate.
MOTHER: Okay, one chocolate cookie for Stacy.

A mother frequently acknowledges with "good" or "that's it." This response fills a minimal turn and adds little additional information, but encourages her child without being overly disruptive to the child's speech stream. Maternal repetition of her child's utterance seems to be for the purposes of emphasis and reassurance.

Clearly in control, mothers are not equally helpful in all areas of language. For example, mothers are not as facilitative with turn-taking as they are with other pragmatic skills. Control of the conversation seems more important to mothers than facilitation. As a child gets older, mother uses more imperatives.

As the dominant conversational partner throughout the preschool years, mothers interrupt their children much more than their children interrupt them. When interrupting, mothers usually omit the politeness markers, such as *excuse me,* seen in adult–adult dialog. The frequency of these interruptions decreases with a child's maturity level. When interrupted, children usually cease talking and then reintroduce the topic. In contrast, mothers usually continue to talk when interrupted by their children and do not reintroduce the topic as often. These actions teach a child to negotiate conversations with others.

Naturally, teaching methods change as a child matures. Expansion of her child's utterances is not as effective a teaching tool with the preschool child as it is with the toddler. Instead, a mother's expansion of her own prior utterances may be more important. This expansion is characterized by a maternal self-repetition followed by an expansion, such as "Want big cookie? Does Maury want a big cookie?" Thus, the mother assists the child in finding the structural similarity by a comparison of adjacent utterances.

Mothers also continue to facilitate the structure and cohesiveness of conversations by maintaining and reintroducing the topic. With increasing age, a typical child takes a greater number of turns on each topic, although the number of turns is still low by adult standards and does not change radically until school age.

Maternal speech to 30-month-olds benefits syntactic learning by providing language-advancing data and by eliciting conversation (Hoff-Ginsberg, 1990). From a mother's point of view, it seems more important to engage her child in conversation than to elicit advanced syntactic forms from the child. Conversation keeps a child's attention on language input and motivates the child to participate.

The mother sustains her child's interest by the use of mild encouragement ("Oh, that's nice") and praise ("What a lovely picture"). Generally, such elicitation and feedback on the quality of a child's language productions does little to contribute to development beyond keeping her child involved.

The effects of conversation appear to be structure-specific. As might be expected, questions contribute to the development of auxiliary or helping verbs and the verb *to be*, because these words are prominently placed at the beginning of the sentence, as in "*Did* you eat the cookies?" and "*Is* he happy or sad?" (Richards, 1990; Richards & Robinson, 1993). Mothers also use yes/no questions to reformulate their children's utterances. For example, when the child says "Mommy eating," the adult might reply in a teasing way "*Is* mommy eating?"

Mothers invite child utterances, primarily through the use of questions, often followed by self-responses. This form of modeling is an effective teaching tool. For example, she might ask, "What color should we use?" followed by "I pick red." In turn, her child may respond "I pick green."

Shared knowledge of events or routines is still important and provides scaffolding for new structures (Lucariello, 1990). Scripts that emerge from these shared events, such as going to the park or riding in the car, concentrate a child's attention, provide models, create formats, and limit a child's linguistic options, thus decreasing the amount of child cognitive processing and supporting the topic of conversation. This scaffolding is particularly important when discussing either nonpresent referents or topics. Approximately 85% of 24- to 29-month-old children's information-providing utterances on nonpresent topics occur in such scripted contexts.

Turnabouts

The turn-taking goals of adult–adult and adult–child conversations differ. In adult–adult conversations, the participants try to obtain a turn, whereas the adult goal in adult–child conversations is to get the child to take her or his turn. As with a younger child, mothers rely heavily on the questioning technique of elicitation. One variant of this technique is a **turnabout,** an utterance that both responds to the previous utterance and, in turn, requires a response. Thus, a turnabout fills a mother's turn and then requires a turn by her child. By using turnabouts, a mother creates a series of successful turns that resemble conversational dialog. Here's an example:

CHILD:	We had pizza.
ADULT:	Pizza! Hmmm, I bet you went to a _____
CHILD:	Birthday party!
ADULT:	I love birthday parties. Whose party was it?

Generally, a turnabout consists of some type of response to, or statement about, a child's utterance and a request for information, clarification, or confirmation that serves as a cue to the child. The mother often initiates a topic or an exchange with a question, thus gaining control. If asked a question, she regains control by responding with another question. Resultant dialogs consist of three successive utterances: the mother's first question, the child's response, and the mother's confirmation, which may include another question. For example, the mother might say, "Can you tell me what this is?" and then respond to the child's answer with "Um-hum, and what does it do?" Thus, the mother is now back in control. In general, the child is less likely to respond to the mother without a turnabout.

Repeatedly hearing a caregiver's questions can have a beneficial effect on a preschooler's development of more adultlike questions (Valian & Casey, 2003). Corrective feedback also facilitates development of some syntactic structures.

There are several types of turnabouts, shown with examples in Table 6.5. One type, the **request for clarification** or **contingent query,** is used by both adults and children to gain information that initially was not clearly transmitted or received. Its use requires that both the listener and the speaker attend to prior discourse. Thus, its use may be related to the development of the ability to refer to what has come before. In addition, children receive little negative feedback

TABLE *6.5* **Turnabouts**

Type	Example
Wh- question	When did that happen?
Yes/no question	Does he scratch a lot?
Tag question	I bet he doesn't like fleas, does he?
Request for clarification	
General	What?
	Huh?
Specific	What does your dog have?
Confirming	Fleas?
	Does he have fleas?
Correction	Fleas! (With an expectant tone)
I wonder statement	I wonder where he got them.
Fill-in	Fleas make you . . .
Expansion with (yes/no) turnabout	Your dog has fleas. Did you give him a bath?
Extension with (*wh-*) turnabout	My dog had fleas once. Yukk! What did you do?

Source: Information from Kaye & Charney (1981).

via contingent queries. Parental requests for clarification are just as likely to be attempts to clarify genuine misunderstandings and miscommunications as to correct production errors.

Children aged 3 to 5½ are able to produce and respond effectively to contingent queries from both adults and peers, although younger children are more effective in their use with adults.

With 2- to 3-year-olds, mothers employ yes/no questions in turnabouts most frequently. This form requires a confirmation and is easy for children as young as 18 months to process. If a child does not respond appropriately, the conversational expectations of the mother are not fulfilled, and she will ask fewer contingent queries. It is clear that once again the caregiver's conversational behaviors reflect the feedback she receives from the child.

Importance of Play

It is easy to forget that much of a child's language develops within the context of play with an adult or with other children. Play can be an ideal vehicle for language acquisition for a number of reasons:

- Play is not goal oriented, so it removes pressure and frustration from the interactive process. It's fun.
- Attention and focus are shared by the interactive partners, so topics are shared.
- Games have structure and variations in the order of elements, as does grammar.
- Games, like conversations, contain turn-taking.

TABLE 6.6 *Cognition, Play, and Language*

Approx. Age (mos.)	Cognitive Development	Play Development	Language Development
Below 12	Association of events with habitual actions	Recognition of objects and functional use	Presymbolic communication
12–15	Global representation of events	Self-pretend: Meaningful actions used playfully	Single words for global referent
15–21	Analysis of represented objects or events	Differentiated pretend play with dolls and other activities. Decentered play with reference to others	Reference to a range of entities, parts, and states
21–24	Juxtaposition of symbolic elements	Pretend combinations	Simple language combinations
24–26	Complete event stored with organized component parts	Planning and storage of symbolic goal while trying to accomplish. Combinatorial play episodes with two themes	Store message while parts organized

Source: Information from Bretherton (1984).

In languages as different as English and Japanese, levels of play and language development appear to be similar (Ogura, 1991). Play and language develop interdependently and demonstrate underlying cognitive developments. This relationship is presented in Table 6.6.

Initially, both play and language are very concrete and depend on the here and now. With cognition maturity, however, they both become less concrete. At about the time that children begin to combine symbols, they begin to play symbolically in which one play object, such as a shoe, is used for another, such as a telephone. In like fashion, symbols represent concepts.

Children often attempt to involve their parents in this pretend play. As playmates, parents can show by example how to play. Often, parents contribute running narratives of the play as it progresses and provide children with the basic problem–resolution narrative or story model. Even 2-year-olds can learn the basic problem–resolution format, as in "The doggie barked, so Mommy let her go outside." In general, the number of sequences in children's play is related to the syntactic complexity of their speech.

Thematic role playing and accompanying linguistic style changes begin at around age 3. By this age, children possess generalized sequential scripts of many familiar situations. At first, a child's role represents himself or herself. Later roles are projected on other persons and dolls.

By age 4 a child is able to role-play a baby, using a higher pitch, phonetic substitutions, shorter and simpler utterances, and more references to self. At about this time, a child begins to role-play "Mom and Dad" differently. In general, mothers are portrayed as more polite, using more indirect requests, with a higher pitch and longer utterances. Role-played fathers make more commands and give less explanation for their behavior. Prosodic and rhythmic devices are the first stylistic variations used by children, followed by appropriate content and then syntactic regularities.

In social play with others, language is used explicitly to convey meaning because of the different realistic and imaginary meanings of props ("This'll be a phone") and roles ("You be the daddy"). Language is used to clarify ("You can't say that if you're the baby") and negotiate ("Okay, you can say it if you want to"). Play themes consist of sequential episodes whose organization increases with a child's age.

The language used in play is influenced by the participants and the play context. In general, preschoolers prefer same-gender pairs with no adult present. While children of both genders prefer replica play, such as dolls, a pretend store, or dress-up, boys also prefer play with blocks and things that can be used to build.

Initially, preschoolers prefer very functionally explicit props, such as a phone, car, or cup. As children mature and participate in more frequent imaginative play, they use more ambiguous props, such as blocks or stones, that can represent other entities. Remember making a meal from dishes and rocks or mud?

Although a preschool child is too young for team games and is not cognitively ready to follow game rules, he or she does enjoy group activities. Language learning is enhanced by the songs, rhymes, and finger plays common among children in daycare or preschool. Within play, a child and a communication partner can participate in a dialog free of the pressures of "real" communication. In addition, the child is free to experiment with different communication styles and roles . . . after all, this is play!

Variations on a Theme

We would be doing both children and mothers a disservice if we failed to note that there are many differences in both conversational partners. Let's examine the individual differences of both and the cultural differences that primarily influence the behavior of mothers.

INDIVIDUAL CHILD DIFFERENCES

Children vary not only in the rate of language development but also in the route. Preschoolers developing typically may exhibit as much as two years variation in language development. Individual developmental differences are related to differences in intellect, personality, and learning style; ethnicity and the language of the home; socioeconomic status; family structure; and birth order. In general, these relationships are very complex, not simply cause and effect. Some factors, such as intelligence, may be much stronger than others. Socioeconomic factors alone, for example, may have little overall effect on rate of language development. There may be more differences within socioeconomic classes than between them.

Birth order or position in the family has a significant effect on early language development. Single children have a greater opportunity to communicate with adults than do children with several siblings and thus develop language more quickly. Twins who spend a great deal of time talking to each other may have multiple phonological errors (Dodd & McEvoy, 1994).

The learning style of a child also affects language learning to some extent. In general, an active, outgoing child is more likely to learn language more rapidly than a placid, retiring child. The former is more inclined to join in and to communicate with whatever means are available, fostering learning the language code.

*C*ultural factors can reflect differences in the role or status of children, caregiving, and beliefs about how children learn language.

Individual styles of learning are evident very early (Hampson & Nelson, 1993). Different types of maternal stimulation also affect children in diverse ways. Some toddlers attend to symbols while others prefer paralinguistic and nonlinguistic elements. Maternal behaviors may be in response to these differences rather than a cause of them as is often assumed.

Considering solely the rate of language learning may be misleading without accompanying information on the route. For example, some children exhibit advances in expressive language use, while others who seem somewhat delayed in this area exhibit superior comprehension skills.

CULTURAL AND SOCIAL DIFFERENCES

Obviously, not all children receive the sort of "idealized" language input reported in this chapter. In addition, mothers in non-Western cultures or nonmajority U.S. cultures use other equally valid techniques to gain and hold children's attention and facilitate learning.

In middle-class American English-speaking families, parental behaviors differ based on the number and gender of the children and perceived differences in the children's abilities, and in two- or single-parent households. For example, the conversations of mothers with their twins are five times longer and elicit more turns from all speakers than conversations between mothers and a single child (Barton & Strosberg, 1997). Similar findings are reported for conversations between a mother, her infant, and an older sibling.

Mothers of premature children may continue to use linguistic strategies more appropriate for younger children even when their children are age 4 (Donahue & Pearl, 1995). In contrast, mothers of late-talking toddlers seem to use the same conversational cues as mothers of toddlers developing typically, although both highly controlling mothers and their late-talking children appear to have less conversational synchrony as measured by semantic relatedness and amount of responding (Rescorla & Fechnay, 1996).

Parenting style affects a toddler's pragmatics and to a lesser degree, grammar (Taylor, Donovan, Miles, & Leavitt, 2009). Mothers who used more negative control, characterized by high levels of prohibitions (*Don't! No!*) and commands, had children with poorer language skills than mothers who used high levels of guidance or control alone but without the negativity.

When studies control for the effects of socioeconomic level, preschoolers from single-parent homes appear to have better receptive and expressive language and to have fewer communication problems, especially when compared to children from households with married, working parents (Haaf, 1996). This difference may reflect the more intensive, one-on-one communication between the single parent and the children in these homes. In the absence of another adult, a single parent may spend more time talking to a child.

Socioeconomic and cultural factors result in many different child–caregiver interactive patterns. Among lower class families, the lack of resources may restrict opportunities for children, and parental work schedules may limit parent–child interactions.

Children living in poverty face heightened risks to their cognitive development compared to non-poor children (Bradley & Corwyn, 2002; Smith, Brooks-Gunn, & Klebanov, 1997). For example, the vocabularies of children from lower socioeconomic backgrounds develop more slowly than those of children from higher socioeconomic backgrounds (Rescorla & Alley, 2001). Poorer development seems especially true for children exposed to chronic poverty early in life (Duncan & Brooks-Gunn, 2000; NICHD Early Child Care Research Network, 2005). Children from low socioeconomic families may be at-risk for language development problems because of poor health and poor education. Poverty also affects children's development by increasing family stressors, creating psychological distress, and impairing the quality of parent–child interactions (McLoyd, 1998). Although socioeconomic status affects expressive and receptive language performance, it does not seem to influence working memory abilities (Engel, Santos, & Gathercole, 2008).

On any given day, approximately 750,000 individuals are homeless in the United States (U.S. Dept. of Housing and Urban Development, 2008). Of these about 40% are families (National Coalition for the Homeless, 1999). Language, learning, and cognitive delays are common in preschool children.

Data from mothers and children in homeless shelters is complicated by factors such as poverty, health issues, and race and ethnicity. Nonetheless, we find that both children and mothers in homeless shelters exhibit deficits or delays in at least one of the following: auditory comprehension, verbal expression, reading, and writing (O'Neill-Pirozzi, 2003).

In the Deaf culture, among parents and children who are both deaf and for whom American Sign Language is the primary means of communication, motherese is conveyed by sign and facial expression. Use of sign can present a potential problem because facial expression marks both affect and grammatical structures, such as questions. With only limited use of paralinguistic cues, such as higher pitch and exaggerated intonation and stress, a mother's nonvocal facial expression takes on added importance as a conveyer of her intentions and as a device to hold a child's interest. Prior to a child's second birthday mothers of children with deafness use facial expression primarily for emotion. There is a shift to more grammatical uses after that point (Reilly & Bellugi, 1996).

Cultural differences may reflect three related factors:

1. The role or status of children.
2. The social organization of caregiving.
3. Folk beliefs about how children learn language.

We must also be careful not to assume that the way middle-class mothers in the United States interact with their children is the only way or the most correct way. In general, interactive patterns between children and their caregivers have evolved to fulfill the special needs of the populations and cultures in which they occur.

In the middle-class American family, the child is held in relatively high regard. This is also true among the Kaluli people of New Guinea. In contrast, the relatively lower standing of children reported in western Samoa and among some African Americans in rural Louisiana results in an expectation that children are to speak only when invited to do so (Ochs, 1982). It is important to remember that low status does not mean a lack of affection for children. Within these same rural southern African American communities, a child is not expected to initiate conversation but to respond to adult questions in the shortest possible form. A child is not expected to perform for adults, and most of a child's requests for information are ignored. What expansion exists is an expansion by adults of their own utterances, not those of the child. It is believed in this culture that children learn by observation, not interaction.

Middle-class American mothers talk *with* their children, not *at* them. Many maternal utterances consist of comments on topics established by a child through word or action. This tendency to follow a child's conversational lead is evidenced in maternal expansion and extension of the child's utterances. Although these semantically related maternal utterances can enhance language acquisition, it has not been proven that they are crucial to the process. While Chinese and Western mothers both interpret babbling as meaningful, talk about what their children are doing, do not overtly correct, and recognize that their infants understand some words prior to speaking, Chinese mothers use less expansion and conversational prompting and more direct teaching of language (Johnson & Wong, 2002).

Not all cultures value verbal precocity in children or demonstrate the adult modifications seen in motherese. Among the Kipsigis of Kenya and rural African Americans in Louisiana, for example, comprehension is more important than verbal production in young children; many of the utterances directed to them consist of directives and explanations. Kaluli parents and Samoan parents rarely follow their children's conversational leads. Language acquisition does not seem to be slowed or delayed in any way.

Mothers may use other strategies that seem equally effective to those described in this chapter. For example, Kaluli mothers mentioned previously and some Mexican American mothers provide models of appropriate language for specific situations and direct their young children to imitate these models. In situations with other adults, children are directed by their mothers in the appropriate responses. This recycling of appropriate utterances for recurring situations is a language-learning device. Like semantically related adult utterances found in middle-class American homes, these predictable situational responses may be highly comprehensible to a child without complete grammatical knowledge (Snow, 1986).

The expectation of a quiet child does not necessarily reflect children's low status. Within the Apache nation, it is a societal norm to value silence from all people. In general, Japanese parents also encourage less talking by their children, although children are held in very high regard. Nonverbal behavior is more important in Japan than in the United States, and

Japanese parents anticipate their children's needs more often, so children have fewer reasons to communicate.

The second factor, social organization of caregiving, also varies widely and reflects economic organization and kinship groupings. In some cultures, such as that of western Samoa, older siblings are more responsible for caregiving than in middle-class American homes. This arrangement is also characteristic of many inner-city households in the United States. There is no evidence, however, that children raised by older siblings learn language more slowly than those raised by adults.

Finally, folk "wisdom" on language acquisition affects the language addressed to a child. The Kipsigis of Kenya believe that a child will learn by himself or herself. Thus, there is no baby talk or motherese. A child is encouraged to participate in conversation through imitation of its mother's model of adult speech. The Kaluli of New Guinea also require imitation from a child in certain social rituals, even though the child may not understand what he or she is saying.

Among both middle- and lower-class African American families, a general belief exists that children learn language by listening and watching, thus there is little need to adapt adult behaviors for a child (Scheffner Hammer & Weiss, 2000). Even so, middle-class African American mothers seem to have a "teaching agenda" that emphasizes production of language by their children. In general, these middle-class mothers include more language in their child play and use a wider range of words with their children than lower-class mothers (Scheffner Hammer & Weiss, 1999). As a consequence, middle-class African American infants initiate more verbal play and produce twice as many vocalizations as lower-class infants. In contrast, lower-class mothers have a very limited teaching agenda and interact less with their children.

Cultural differences are evident in the maternal behavior of Japanese and North American middle-class mothers. While American mothers talk more with their children and encourage them to respond, Japanese mothers engage in more rocking, carrying, and "lulling." In responding to their infants, American mothers use more facial and vocal behaviors, while Japanese mothers are more nonverbal, responding with touch. With toddlers, Japanese mothers employ more vocalizations similar to the American English *uh-huh,* which is not surprising given the importance of *omoiyari,* maintenance of harmony, in that culture.

The intentions of American mothers are providing information and directing. In contrast, the Japanese mother exhibits fewer of these behaviors, preferring to use nonsense words, sound play, and emphatic routines, such as discussing feelings. Her productions are usually very easy for her child to imitate.

In general, Japanese mothers are less likely to talk about objects; when they do, it is often without the use of the object's name, used more frequently in the United States. Although both American and Japanese mothers use questions frequently, American mothers use them more in the context of labeling. It is not surprising, therefore, that American toddlers have larger noun vocabularies while Japanese toddlers have more social expressions (Fernald & Morikawa, 1993).

Still, similarities exist across languages. Both American and Japanese mothers use linguistically simple forms when addressing young language-learning children, repeat frequently, and use intonation to engage the infant (Fernald & Morikawa, 1993). The common motivation for these changes seems to be an intuitive sense of the developmental level of the child.

Early book-reading by mothers to infants and toddlers is important for children's language and cognition in the preschool years (Raikes et al., 2006). In general, mothers read more to firstborn and female toddlers, and mothers with higher verbal ability and education read more than other mothers. Among low-income mothers, white non-Latina mothers read more than African American and Latina mothers.

Children are not limited to direct language input and can acquire language-based knowledge by drawing upon a range of experiences. They can also learn language by indirect means, such as conversational exchanges between other individuals. Children can learn language from speech that is not addressed to them.

Television can also provide some very limited input. Unlike conversations, television is passive and does not require a response. In addition, the language provided by television is not related to ongoing events within a child's interactive context. Although having adults read to a child positively affects the size of the expressive vocabulary of English- and Spanish-speaking preschoolers, watching television does not have this beneficial effect (Patterson, 2002).

Even with all this variation, children still learn their native languages at about the same rate as middle-class American children. In general, in the United States, most adults treat a child as a communication partner. The language-learning American child is raised primarily by his or her parent(s) or paid professionals or paraprofessionals who model and elicit language. Even within the United States, however, there is no definitive pattern.

Of most importance among children in the United States are maternal stimulation and the overall quality of the home. For example, among African American families, a strong correlation exists between maternal sensitivity, responsiveness, stimulation, and elaborativeness and a child's cognitive and communicative skills at age 1 (Wallace, Roberts, & Lodder, 1998). Although socioeconomic differences exist within the African American community, there is strong evidence of these maternal behaviors among all African American mothers.

Conclusion

L ANGUAGE LEARNING IS A COMPLEX process that involves linguistic processing and child and adult language-learning strategies. Different cultures exhibit different strategies.

Comprehension and imitation by a toddler seem to be particularly important. Both appear to be at the cutting edge of language development, although the exact relationship is unknown and seems to change with a child's functioning level.

We do not know the exact language-learning strategies used by young children. These strategies and their underlying cognitive abilities are inferred from children's behaviors. Consistency in a child's language suggests the presence of underlying rule systems. At present, linguists are unsure of the process of rule construction. Undoubtedly, though, comprehension and production are interrelated. This dynamic relationship changes with the level of development and with the structure being learned. The order of acquisition of structures for expressing complex relationships reflects a child's cognitive growth. A child must understand the concept of the relationship and the linguistic forms used to express that relationship before he or she can use this relationship in his or her own language.

Environmental influences strongly affect language development. Adult modeling and responding behaviors are very important, especially for toddlers. Adult–child language provides a simplified model. Certain responding behaviors also reinforce a child's communication attempts.

Although a direct teaching explanation of language development is inadequate, there is a strong indication that modeling, imitation, and reinforcement are central to the learning process. Those elements of maternal speech that change to reflect a child's overall language level seem to be most significant for later language development. The process is much more subtle than that employed in the more direct language training seen in therapeutic intervention.

Although diminished with a child's age, the role of significant caregivers in language development is still critical with preschoolers. Caregivers continue to manipulate the conversational context to maximize language learning by a child. This context and play are important sources of language modeling and use for preschool children.

Discussion

IN THIS CHAPTER, WE'VE SEEN how children approach the learning of language, how they decide what a word is, how they try to decipher the sequential code by applying certain rules to breaking down language, and how they are helped by the environment. If you assume that you are in another culture in which English is never used, you begin to appreciate what the child and caregivers do in order to be understood and to help the child's learning. Look at the child learning strategies again. Wow, what a great way to try to understand language and to attempt to use it! Now look at the adult teaching strategies. We could only hope that those speakers of that other language would be so kind as to use some of these strategies with us until we understand their language.

It is important to recall that caregivers do not decide to teach language. The so-called teaching strategies mostly flow from a desire to be understood. Are they all applicable to intervention with the child with a language impairment? Each SLP and teacher must decide for himself or herself how to best use this developmental knowledge.

We must also remember that, just as language is culturally based, so are the teaching strategies demonstrated by middle-class mothers in the United States. The French-speaking Haitian mother of a toddler or preschooler with a language impairment may interact very differently. Again the SLP must decide if the mother's interactions are appropriate given her culture and the severity of the child's impairment. The goal is not to create a carbon copy of the middle-class American mother. Remember that even mothers who exhibit the best motherese can have children with language problems. All professional interactions must be mindful of and sensitive to cultural variability.

Main Points

- In *very general* terms, children's early language follows a pattern in which they "know" something, then comprehend its name, and finally produce the name.

- Several assumptions by an infant may be behind learning a word, including the following:

  - People use words to refer to entities.

  - Words are extendable.

- A word refers to the whole entity, not the parts.
- Names refer to categories of things.
- Novel names refer to previously nameless entities.
- Adults refer to entities in consistent conventional ways.

- Expressive strategies of toddlers include evocative utterances, hypothesis testing, interrogative utterances, and selective imitation.

- Selective imitation is at the growing or developing edge of a child's language and helps stabilize new forms.

- Bootstrapping, a strategy of preschoolers, is using what you know, such as semantic categories, to figure out what you don't, such as syntactic units.

- Preschooler learning principles are as follows:
  - Pay attention to the ends of words.
  - Phonological forms can be systematically modified.
  - Pay attention to the order of words and morphemes.
  - Avoid interruptions and rearrangement of linguistic units.
  - Underlying semantic relations should be marked overtly and clearly.
  - Avoid exceptions.
  - Grammatical markers should make semantic sense.

- Adult speech to toddlers includes modeling (motherese or parentese), prompting, and responding (reformulations, expansions, extensions, and imitations) that collectively facilitate language learning.

- Adult speech to preschoolers includes turnabouts that facilitate the child's turn in a conversation by prompting the child's next response.

- Play is an important area for language growth and trial.

- Cultural differences vary widely but contribute to a child's language learning.

Reflections

1. Describe the complex relationship between comprehension and production as it relates to the young language-learning child.

2. After noting similarities in children's structures in several languages, Slobin proposed a set of universal principles of language learning. State the main principles, and give an example of each.

3. Describe the role of imitation for toddlers and the development from repetitious utterances to semantically diverse ones.

4. Mothers and fathers talk very differently to their young child than they do to other adults. What are the characteristics of motherese or parentese?

5. List the various types of prompts parents use to encourage their children to speak.

6. Although parents may not directly reinforce their young language-learning children, they do expand, extend, and imitate. Describe the differences between these three behaviors, and explain the effects of these behaviors on the child.

7. What is a turnabout, and how is it used by caregivers?

8. Describe the importance of play for language development.

9. Children in the United States and in other cultures receive a variety of linguistic inputs and are expected to communicate in numerous ways. What are the factors that affect parent–child interaction? What effects do these factors have on language development?

7

First Words and Word Combinations in Toddler Talk

C hildren's initial language consists of more than the mere accumulation of single words. As with all language, children's initial attempts reflect patterns of production. When you have completed this chapter, you should understand

- The most frequent categories and syllable constructions in first words.
- The intentions of early vocalizations/verbalizations.
- The bases for early concept development.
- The bases for extensions and overextensions.
- The two-word combination patterns.
- The common phonological rules of toddlers.
- The following terms:

associative complex hypothesis	item-based construction	presupposition
consonant/cluster reduction	language socialization	prototypic complex hypothesis
fast mapping	lexicon	reduplication
functional-core hypothesis	neighborhood density	semantic-feature hypothesis
holophrase	open syllable	underextension
initial mapping	otitis media	word combination
	overextension	
	phonotactic probability	
	pivot schema	

To listen to language samples related to chapter content and to peruse other enhanced study aids, please see the Companion Website at www.pearsonhighered.com/owens8e

This is it—finally—the place where language is said to begin. But don't expect a change overnight. Words will appear gradually and may be mixed with jargon in long, incomprehensible strings. The child is still experimenting with sounds. Speech may be suddenly interrupted by shrieks or a series of babbles. As a result, a child may talk a great deal without seeming to say much. (In that way, children resemble some adults I know.) One sound pattern may represent several concepts, or inconsistent production may result in several sound patterns for one word. Words may be changed by deletion of syllables or modification of stress patterns. Whole phrases may be used as single words. If it sounds confusing, it is; but what a wonderful time for the excited family. Before we begin our discussion of language, let's quickly explore the life of toddlers, those little folks who will utter their first words. (See Appendix C, Table C.3 for more information.)

With a beginning realization of self and a new (albeit shaky) method of locomotion called walking, an infant begins the second year of life. During that year he or she will change from a dependent infant to a more independent toddler. Newly acquired walking skills and increased linguistic abilities give him or her mobility and tools to explore.

Much of the second year is spent perfecting and varying walking skills. There is a deceleration in bodily growth rate. Brain growth also decelerates, and head size increases only slightly.

By 15 months, a toddler is experimenting with different forms of walking, such as running and dawdling. Favorite games are hiding or being chased. At 18 months, a toddler is able to walk backward and to stop smoothly but is not able to turn corners very well. Walking is still not perfected, and there is a rolling, "drunken sailor" quality to these movements. Within six months, he or she progresses to a stable walking rhythm. A 2-year-old is able to walk on tiptoes, stand on one foot with assistance, jump with both feet, and bend at the waist to retrieve an object on the floor.

New mobility, plus increasing control over his or her fine-motor abilities, gives a toddler new freedom to explore. If allowed by his parents, a toddler will get into everything and initiate active and systematic exploration. As a toddler, my brother went through the house dumping a liberal mound of baby powder into each opened drawer just after my mother had completed cleaning.

Most of a toddler's play and exploration is solitary and nonsocial. He or she demonstrates an interest in small objects. A favorite game is carrying objects and handing them to others. During the entire second year, toddlers test objects' qualities by touching, pushing, pulling, and lifting. A toddler enjoys exploring new sights, sounds, and textures.

Increased fine-motor skills and a longer attention span enable a toddler to look at books. By 18 months, a child recognizes pictures of common objects. Six months later, he or she pretends to read books and has the fine-motor skills to turn pages one at a time. A toddler is also capable of holding a crayon and scribbling.

Toys are used increasingly in play. By 18 months, a toddler plays appropriately with toy phones, dishes, and tools. He or she likes dress-up play. Dolls and stuffed animals become more important. My own children loved to pound pegs through a wooden toy workbench and to stack objects. The toddler often repeats daily routines with toys and demonstrates short sequences of role playing at age 2. My son Jason loved to imitate his mother's morning ritual in the bathtub. Toddlers will play near but not usually with other children.

Much of the social interaction of the second year involves a toddler's attempts to be in the spotlight. Having learned to influence others, a toddler will do almost anything for attention. The 15-month-old gains attention by "dancing" to music and becomes more adept at imitating hand movements, such as clapping and waving. At around 18 months, a toddler begins to imitate the family's housework. One of my nieces became quite domestic at this age.

Increasing self-awareness and the ability to influence others are reflected in a toddler's growing noncompliance. At 16 months, a toddler begins to assert some independence by ignoring or dawdling in response to parental requests. By 21 months, this behavior has evolved into a very defiant "no." The child frequently says "no" even when he or she means *yes*. One little friend, Dean, shouted "no" for *no* and "no" with up-and-down head nodding for *yes*.

A 2-year-old has many self-help skills. For example, the 2-year-old can usually place food on a spoon and feed himself or herself, undress except for untying shoelaces, wash, turn on simple devices, open easy doors, and straighten a bed. When the child needs help, he or she knows how to request it.

The actual point at which language is said to begin is arbitrary and depends on your definition of *language*. For our purposes, we shall assume that language begins at around the first birthday with the appearance of the first word. To be considered a true word, (1) the child's utterance must have a phonetic relationship to some adult word, (2) the child must use the word consistently, and (3) the word must occur in the presence of a referent, thus implying an underlying concept or meaning. Therefore, a babbled "dada" would not qualify because there is no referent. Likewise, phonetically consistent forms do not approximate recognizable adult words. (See Chapter 4 for a description of PCFs.)

The emergence of first words or verbalizations does not signal the end of babbling, jargon, and PCFs. All three continue to be produced by the child throughout the second year of life (Robb, Bauer, & Tyler, 1994). Individual children exhibit very different patterns of vocalization-verbalization use. Children with slow or delayed early language development may be predisposed for slower language acquisition later and a slower rate of literacy development (Rescorla, 2002). Words emerge slowly and often are accompanied by gestures. Note that babbling and jargon also continue to occur.

Language development in the second year consists of vocabulary growth and word combinations. Vocabulary growth is slow during the first few months. Phrases frequently used by adults in a child's environment may be repeated as single words. For example, many children say "Wassat?" and "Go-bye." A favorite of the 18-month-old is the *name game* in which a toddler touches an object, queries "Wassat?" and awaits a reply. Each toddler has his or her own **lexicon,** or personal dictionary, with words that reflect, in part, the child's environment.

During the second half of the second year, toddlers begin to combine words and to increase the rate of vocabulary growth. The early word combinations appear to follow predictable patterns, and the toddler is likely to produce phrases such as "More cookie," "Daddy eat," "No night-night," and so on. Within a few months, short-term memory has increased so that the child can attempt a few longer constructions, such as "Daddy eat cookie." Vocabulary also increases rapidly. At age 2 the toddler has an expressive vocabulary of about 150 to 300 words.

A continuity exists between prelinguistic and linguistic skills. Early gesture use is important for communication and also for communication development. Better gesture and object use at 12 months predicts better vocabulary at 24 months (Bavin et al., 2008). In addition, use of conventional gestures at 14 months is positively related to receptive language and vocabulary size more than two years later (Rowe, Özçaliskan, & Goldin-Meadow, 2008). In addition, acts for joint attention at 14 months and the number of different consonants at 19 months are positively related to expressive language at 3 years (Watt, Wetherby, & Shumway, 2006).

Table 7.1 presents a conversation between a 22-month-old toddler and her mother. The child's average utterance length is short—only 1.9 morphemes in the entire sample from which this portion is taken—as is the mother's. Not that the mother makes extensive use of imitation, expansion and extension.

At first reading, it is obvious that the conversation in Table 7.1 is very concrete and concerned with the task of coloring. There is no great variety in the words used, and the child

TABLE *7.1* *Toddler Language Sample*

What do you see?

1. Birthday cake Kelly house.
   A birthday cake at Kelly's house? What else was at Kelly's house?

2. Birthday cake mommy.
   Mommy had a birthday cake. What else did you have?

3. Kelly house.
   Kelly's house. Oh, look.

4. Color on the table.
   The man colored on the table. Well, that's all right. What are you making?

5. Doggie.
   Are you making a doggie?

6. Okay.
   All right. Oh, that's nice, T.

7. Where more doggie there?
   Is there another doggie underneath?

8. Yeah.
   Where can you find the picture? Is that what you're looking for, the picture of the doggie? Where's the doggie?

9. A doggie.

10. Color a doggie.
    Okay, you color the doggie.

11. Mommy color crayon.
    Mommy has crayons. Mommy's coloring. What's mommy making?

12. Doggie.
    A doggie?

13. Okay.
    All right, I'll make a doggie. Is this the doggie's tail?

14. The doggie's tail.
    Doggie's tail.

15. More.
    More doggie?

16. Okay.
    Can T. color? Hum?

17. More doggie there.

18. More doggie daddy.
    More doggie daddy?

19. Wants a more doggie.

20. More doggie.

21. Put more doggie there.

repeats these words frequently. The child engages in turn-taking and is very responsive. Many of the child's utterances, such as 9 and 14, are whole or partial imitations. The child has a wide range of intentions. Within this segment, she answers (1, 2, 3, 5, 8, 12) and asks questions (7), replies to her mother's utterances (4, 6, 13, 16), makes declarations (10, 18), gives directions to her mother (11, 17, 21), and makes demands (15, 19, 20).

Before you begin this chapter, take a few minutes to think about a 12- to 18-month-old child and what he or she knows. Jot down a short list of 10 to 20 words that he or she might say. Try it; you'll be surprised how much you already know. Much of a child's pronunciation will not mirror adult speech. For that reason, you might want to write possible child pronunciations after applicable words. For example, *water,* an early word for many children, will probably be spoken as "wawa."

Once you have completed your list, imagine how these words might be used in conversation. Examine your list for patterns. You probably know more about language development than you realize. What types of words—nouns, verbs, and so on—predominate? What speech sounds are used most frequently? What syllabic constructions—CV, VC, CVCV-reduplicated, CVCV, CVC, and so on—are most frequent?

It is also important to consider the contexts in which first words occur. A child's first words occur as requests for information, or for objects or aid, or as comments. Intentions, previously expressed through gestures and vocalizations, are now expressed through words. There is carryover of pragmatic functions from presymbolic to symbolic communication.

Keep your list handy. As we progress through this chapter, you may be surprised by the accuracy of your responses.

Single-Word Utterances

A toddler's first meaningful speech consists of single-word utterances, such as "doggie," or single-word approximations of frequently used adult phrases, such as "thank you" ("anku") or "what's that?" ("wassat?"). At this point, "words" are phonetic approximations of adult words that a child consistently uses to refer to a particular situation or object. The meaning of the word may be very restricted at first and may apply to only one particular referent or thing to which it refers. For example, "doggie" (usually "goggie" or "doddie") may refer only to the family's pet but not to other dogs. As a result of linguistic and "world" experience, a child will gradually modify the definition, and, at some point, it will be close to the generally accepted notion of the word's meaning. Remember that a word signifies a referent but that the referent is not the meaning of the word. Meaning is found in language users' concepts or mental images, not in individual examples.

In general, a toddler talks about the world he or she knows and will not comment on inflation, unemployment, politics, or international relations. Instead, a toddler may request toys, call people, name pets, reject food, ask for help with clothing, and discuss familiar actions or routines. My own children began speaking with words such as *mama, dada, pepa* (the dog), *all gone,* and *bye-bye.* Single words are used to make requests, comments, inquiries, and so on.

A child seems to begin speaking by attempting to learn whole adult utterances that represent various communicative purposes. If the latter is true that early utterances represent partial learning of longer, more complex adult utterances and the child's first productions correspond to adult expressions (Tomasello, 2006).

Many linguists believe children's early one-word utterances represent **holophrases** that convey a holistic communicative intention. Functionally speaking, children's early one-word utterances are semantic-pragmatic packages or holophrastic expressions that express a single communicative intention (Tomasello, 2006). Usually, these intentions are the same as those of the adult expressions from which they were learned (Barrett, 1982; Ninio, 1992). Many of children's early holophrases are individualistic and will evolve and change over time.

The reason children respond with one-word or one phrase (e.g., *Wassat?*) expressions is unknown. Most likely the child only attends to a part of the adult expression, or because of limited working memory, the child can process only one word or phrase at a time.

Regardless of the language a child is acquiring, early words are used to

- Request or indicate the existence of an object by naming it with a requesting or neutral intonation.
- Request or describe the recurrence of objects or events, using words such as *more, 'gain,* and *'nother.*
- Request or describe changing events involving objects by *up, down, on, off, in, out, open,* and *close.*
- Request or describe the actions of others with words such as *eat, kick, ride,* and *fall.*
- Comment on the location of objects and people with words such as *bed, car,* and *outside.*
- Ask some basic questions such as *What?, What that?,* and *Where mommy?*
- Attribute a property to an object such as *big, hot,* and *dirty.*
- Use utterancess to mark specific social events and situations or perform some act, as with *hi, bye, and no* (Tomasello, 2006).

Longer utterances are learned as a means of further clarifying the intention. While a young child may say "Doggie" to mean both *See doggie* and *Want doggie,* an older child will clarify these intentions with the addition of "See" and "Want."

Important for later language development is what parts of adult expressions children choose for their holophrases. This is dependent, of course, on the language being learned and the talking style of the adults in a child's life. For example, English has inherited short verb phrases from German that include a verb particle such as *take off, pick up, put on,* and *get down*. English-speaking children often learn the particle (e.g., *off, up, on, down*) early and will subsequently have to learn the entire phrase. In Korean and Mandarin Chinese, which do not have verb particles, children learn fully adult verbs from the onset because this is what adults speak to them (Gopnik & Choi, 1995; Tardiff, 1996). Let's explore some qualities of single-word utterances together.

PRAGMATICS

In order to explain early child language fully, we must consider the uses to which these utterances are put. As we noted in Chapter 5, communication is well established before the first word appears. Words are acquired within the established communication system of a child and caregiver.

Both the repetitiveness of certain daily routines, both verbal and nonverbal, and a mother's willingness to assign meaningful intent to her child's speech aid language development. Parent responses also foster word–meaning associations by providing feedback to a child that the intended meaning was or was not comprehended.

In addition, the intentions of a child's early utterances are also important. Early words develop to fulfill the intentions originally conveyed by gestures. Novel words may be learned through actual use by a child in conversation (Nelson, 1991; Nelson, Hampson, & Shaw, 1993). A child may say a word in a context where it "sounds right based on what the child has heard." The responses of others confirm or deny the child's production.

There is a strong relationship between first words and the frequency of maternal use of these words (Harris, Barrett, Jones, & Brookes, 1988). Many words are used in the same context in which the mother used them previously, such as "bye-bye" while waving and "choo-choo" while playing with a toy train. Not all words are used this way, however, and a significant number are also used to name or label entities or to request something.

Before we continue, return to the fictitious list of first words you generated at the beginning of this chapter. Pause for a moment and consider how these words might be used socially, that is, to attain information, fulfill needs, provide information, and so on. Now, let's see how well you did.

Development of Intent

In Chapter 5 we examined the illocutionary functions or intentions of early gestures. Initially, intentions are signaled by gestures only. To these a child adds vocalizations and then words or verbalizations. Many early words, however, can be interpreted only with consideration of the accompanying gesture. Gradually, a child learns to express intentions more through words and grammar, although gestures remain important, even for adults.

Gestures   By the time a child begins producing words, he or she has typically been communicating with others through gestures and sounds for months. A child's first linguistic productions are learned and used in the context of this nonlinguistic communication and for the same basic intentions or purposes. The primary intentions expressed are declarations or statements and requests for objects, with requests for information or questions coming shortly thereafter. A child's first declarations are usually about a shared referent or focusing the listener's attention on a new one.

The child's utterances have conventional intonational patterns indicating requests, comments, or questions, the same intentions as the adults' more complex utterances. This would indicate that a child is not attempting to learn isolated words, but to communicate an entire adult utterance (Tomasello, 2006).

During the second year, gestures and words become more coordinated for specific intentions. Reaching increasingly signals a request or demand, while pointing signals a declaration or a reference to something in the environment (Franco & Butterworth, 1996).

Symbolic gestures, such as panting like a dog, appear at about the same time as first words and develop in parallel for several months (Acredolo & Goodwyn, 1990). Children will continue to use gestures for several communication purposes and as a backup for speech or as an assist for words that are lacking (Caselli, 1990).

Obviously, not all children are alike. Some rely more on gestures, while others prefer speech, although almost all toddlers use gestures spontaneously with speech and sound making (Morford & Goldin-Meadow, 1992). In addition, young toddlers may rely on caregiver gestures for comprehension.

Vocabulary production in 18- to 28-month-olds appears to be related to the child's ability to make functional gestures (Thal, Tobias, & Morrison, 1991). Functional gestures depict objects through actions demonstrating the object's function, such as pretending to eat from an empty spoon.

In similar fashion, the development of multiword utterances seems to be correlated with the production of gestural combinations. The lengths of "utterances" in both words and gestures are similar.

From age 12 to 18 months, a child increasingly gestures and verbalizes while looking at her or his communication partner. This may be an important transition to the ability to consider both the topic and the listener simultaneously.

In addition, there is a subtle shift that occurs when a child looks at the partner. Initially, a child looks at her or his conversational partner after both pointing and reaching. Gradually, the child changes so that the look occurs before the pointing gesture, indicating knowledge of the need to have a listener's intention before referring to something, and following reaching as a check on transmission.

Gestures can be both a source of semantic knowledge and an expression of that knowledge, especially at a time when oral language skills are limited (Capone, 2007). Both infants and toddlers may use gestures to compensate for limitations in articulation and phonology. Gestures may be an efficient means of communicating knowledge or they may facilitate word retrieval at a time when word knowledge is still evolving and weak (Goldin-Meadow & Wagner, 2005). By offering a visual representation of the word, gestures may free cognitive resources for other tasks (Goldin-Meadow, Nusbaum, Kelly, & Wagner, 2001).

From infancy, gestures both supplement and predict speech (Capone & McGregor, 2004). Infants in the one-word stage communicate with deictic gestures, such as pointing or requesting, and some iconic gestures that function as words not yet spoken by the child, such as moving their arms to indicate a bird's flight (Acredolo & Goodwyn, 1988, 1996). Pointing and other deictic gestures precede first words, and when first words emerge, pointing gestures and some single iconic gestures are used to communicate. Iconic gestures convey meaning through the form, action, or spatial position of the body and are often hand movements (Goldin-Meadow, 2003; McNeil, 1992). In general, toddlers use deictic gestures more often than iconic ones.

A high proportion of toddlers use gestures to communicate. A toddler's gesture-speech combinations can be characterized as either reinforcing or supplemental combinations. Reinforcing combinations convey matching information, such as pointing at dog while saying "Dog." Supplemental combinations convey different information from speech and gesture, such as using a requesting gesture while saying "Juice." Supplemental combinations are positively correlated with expressive language skills (Capirci, Iverson, Pizzuto, & Volterra, 1996; Morford & Goldin-Meadow, 1992). The semantic relations expressed in gesture–speech combinations, such as saying "Daddy" while pointing to his coat precede those same semantic relations heard in spoken word combinations, as in "Daddy coat" (Özçalişkan & Goldin-Meadow, 2005). These gesture-speech combinations suggest that early semantic relations are established sooner than speech alone would suggest.

Both gestures and language are served by the same regions of the brain. Motor control areas of the brain are activated during language tasks that do not involve speech. Nonetheless, there are patterns of joint activation between areas for the hand and the mouth. In other words, when language is activated, motor control areas for both speech and gesture are readied for production.

Gestures and Joint Attending   When infants point, we assume that they themselves intend for their partner to attend to a referent. Some development experts, however, contend that what the infant is really doing is not referring to the object at all but actually attempting to get an emotional reaction to him- or herself from the adult (Moore & D'Entremont, 2001). Theoretical debates about infant pointing and prelinguistic communication center on whether young infants are attempting to influence the intentional/mental states of others by causing them to *know* something or whether infants are simply aiming to achieve certain behavioral effects in others by causing them to *do* something (Liszkowski, 2005, 2006; Moore & D'Entremont, 2001; Tomasello, Carpenter, Call, Behne, & Moll, 2005).

When an adult responds to an infant's point with an emotion but ignores the referent, the infant shows signs of dissatisfaction by repeating the point in an attempt to redirect the adult's attention. If the adult continues to ignore the infant's intent, then over time the infant will point less often (Liszkowski, Carpenter, Henning, Striano, & Tomasello, 2004). When the adult correctly identifies the intended referent, infants simply continue sharing attention and interest, but when

*L*ike gestures, first words are often acquired within everyday routines between children and their caregivers.

the adult identifies the incorrect referent, the infant repeats pointing to the intended referent in an attempt to direct attention (Liszkowski, Carpenter, & Tomasello, 2007). In these ways in both their comprehension and production of pointing gestures, 12- to 14-month-olds demonstrate an understanding of both pointing and naming as intentional acts whose purpose is to induce the partner to attend to some entity within a joint-attention context. This process involves much more than simply gaze or point following or gaining attention to oneself. It involves a communicator's intention to direct a partner's attention to a particular referent so that the partner, by identifying this intended referent, will make the needed relevance inferences and comprehend the communicator's overall social intention. These two motives are distinctly different.

It is entirely possible that when a young infant points for an adult she or he is in some sense trying to influence the adult's intentional/mental states while at the same time engaging in uniquely human skills and motivations for cooperation and shared intentionality, which enables joint intentions and joint attention to occur (Tomasello, Carpenter, & Liszkowski, 2007). This suggests that early verbal communication and gestures share a common social-cognitive, social-motivational basis of shared intentionality.

Infants possess the basic social-cognitive and social-motivational skills for engaging in human-style cooperative communication by around 12 to 14 months of age. What they possess is an understanding about

- The choices people make in their intentions and attention.
- Why people make these choices.
- What knowledge they do and do not share with others based on what they have experienced together with them in joint attention interactions.
- The basic cooperative motives.

From their earliest communicative pointing, infants' intention is to direct others' attention to some entity, suggesting a process of influencing the minds of others. Infants understand from very early that one achieves one's social intention mainly by making others aware of it, indicating a clear understanding of the mental states of others (Tomasello et al., 2007).

What seems to be important here is a notion of shared intentionality, although individual intentionality is necessary as well. The comprehension and use of linguistic symbols, in flexible and communicatively appropriate ways, depend on an infant's understanding of others as intentional agents with whom one can share experience.

The social-cognitive basis for cooperative verbal communication is mainly joint attention, which requires the ability to know things mutually with others, and the communicative intention that derives from skills of joint attention, the intention that we know something together (Tomasello et al., 2007). Even in more traditional societies, such as in rural Nigeria, there is a relationship between toddlers' ability to establish joint reference and language development (Childers, Vaughan, & Burquest, 2007).

The social-motivational part comprises the cooperative motives of helping by informing and sharing emotions and attitudes in a communicative context. These cooperative motives are mutually assumed by both the infant and the infant's partner.

Sound and Word Making   There appears to be a pattern in young children's vocalizations and gestures. As you'll recall, children add sounds or vocalizations to gestures and then replace these with words or verbalizations. Gradually, intent moves from being expressed primarily through the gesture to being more language dependent. Early, more general vocal-gestural intentions are presented in Table 7.2. Similar, more specific intentions will be expressed through speech and gestures or speech alone in the second year of life.

TABLE *7.2* *Vocal-Gestural Intentions*

Vocal-Gestural Intentions	Child's Utterance	Child's Nonlinguistic Behavior
Requesting action	Word or marked prosodic pattern	Attends to object or event; addresses adult; awaits response; most often performs gesture
Protesting	Word or marked prosodic pattern	Attends to adult; addresses adult; resists or denies adult's action
Requesting answer	Word	Addresses adult; awaits response; may make gesture
Labeling	Word	Attends to object or event; does not address adult; does not await response
Answering	Word	Attends to preceding adult utterance; addresses adult
Greeting	Word	Attends to adult or object
Repeating	Word or prosodic pattern	Attends to preceding adult utterance may not address adult; does not await response
Practicing	Word or prosodic pattern	Attends to no specific object or event; does not address adult; does not await response
Calling	Word (with marked prosodic contour)	Addresses adult by uttering adult's name loudly; awaits response

Source: Information from Dore (1975).

As stated, first words fulfill the intentions previously expressed through gestures and vocalizations. Initially, very different verbal forms may develop to express each intention. Specific words or sounds may be used with each intention. As words increase and intentions diversify, words and utterances become more flexible and multifunctional. The disappearance of specific symbol–intention relationships usually occurs from 16 to 24 months, corresponding to the beginning of multiword combinations.

Six pragmatic categories describe the general purposes of language: control, representational, expressive, social, tutorial, and procedural (Wells, 1985) (see Table 7.2). Speakers use the control function to make demands and requests, to protest, and to direct others. The representational function is used to discuss entities and events and to ask for information. In contrast, the expressive function is not necessarily for an audience. A child may use language to accompany play, to exclaim, or to express feelings and attitudes. The social function includes greetings, farewells, and talk routines. For young children, the tutorial function consists mostly of practice with language forms. Finally, the procedural function is used to maintain communication by directing attention or by requesting additional or misinterpreted information.

Vocal-gestural acts fulfill aspects of all these categories. Table 7.3 illustrates the relationship of vocal-gesture intentions to later ones and offers examples of each.

Along with the development of single words and word combinations, the child continues to develop sound patterns for specific intentions. These patterns appear in both relatively nontonal languages, such as English, and tonal languages, such as Latvian, Thai, and Lao, that have varied intonational patterns. Used most often by 2-year-olds in dialogs rather than in monologs, these patterns are not the same as those found in adult speech.

First, children develop a flat or level contour for naming or labeling. Between 13 and 15 months, children develop a rising contour to express requesting, attention getting, and

TABLE *7.3* *Early Intentions*

Broad Pragmatic Categories (Wells, 1985)	Vocal-Gestural Intentions (Dore, 1974)	Early Verbal Intentions (Owens, 1978; Wells, 1985)	Examples
Control	Requesting action	Wanting demands	*Cookie* (Reach)
		Direct request/commanding	*Help* (Hand object to or struggle)
	Protesting	Protesting	*No* (Push away or uncooperative)
Representational	Requesting answer	Content questioning	*Wassat?* (Point)
	Labeling	Naming/labeling	*Doggie* (Point)
		Statement/declaring	*Eat* (Commenting on dog barking)
	Answering	Answering	*Horsie* (in response to question)
		Reply	*Eat* (in response to "The doggie's hungry")
Expressive		Exclaiming	Squeal when picked up
		Verbal accompaniment to action	*Uh-oh* (With spill)
		Expressing state or attitude	*Tired*
Social	Greetings	Greeting/farewell	*Hi*
			Bye-bye
Tutorial	Repeating/practicing	Repeating/practicing	*Cookie, cookie, cookie*
Procedural	Calling	Calling	*Mommy*

*This table represents a combination of the work of several researchers and an attempt to remain true to the intended purposes of child speech.

curiosity and a high falling contour, which begins with a high pitch that drops to a lower one, to signal surprise, recognition, insistence, or greeting. Next, children use a high rising and a high rising-falling contour to signal playful anticipation and emphatic stress, respectively. Finally, at around 18 months, children use a falling-rising and a rising-falling contour for warnings and playfulness, respectively.

By 15 months, most children are naming or labeling favorite toys and foods and household pets, exclaiming, and calling to attract attention. Within another three months, the average child adds wanting demands (*I want. . . .*). By 2 years of age, most children have added verbal requesting or commanding, content questioning, unsolicited statements or declarations, verbal accompaniments to play (*Whee!*), and expressions of states and attitudes, most frequently, "I tired" (Wells, 1985). Other early intentions include protesting (*no*), answering, greeting, and practice or repeating.

As children mature, the frequency of different intentions changes (Wells, 1985). At 15 months, over 75% of all utterances are representational, expressive, and procedural, with naming/labeling and calling predominating. By 21 months and rapidly approaching the dreaded "terrible twos," control functions increase markedly, while expressive functions are reduced by nearly half. Throughout this period, social and tutorial functions occur infrequently. Some early intentions, such as wanting demands, naming/labeling, calling, and practice, decrease rapidly as a percentage of overall intentions from 24 to 36 months. Other relatively later-developing intentions, such as direct requesting/commanding and statement/declaration, gradually increase.

During the one-word stage, my own sons gave a striking exhibition of requesting/commanding. Both boys had stayed with their grandmother during their mother's hospitalization for their sister's birth. During "Gran'ma's" visit, they learned to chase two particularly pesky stray dogs with "Skat!" Later, when in a room alone with their newly arrived, sleeping sister, the two boys looked through the bars of her crib and commanded "Skat! Skat!" Fortunately, she didn't follow orders well even then.

Initially, speech emerges to accompany action, such as requests possibly meaning *notice me*. A child's first words may accompany pointing and be used to display a wish or to express displeasure. A child may draw attention first (*Mommy*), then make a request (*up*) or use *look* for control or *there* to complete a task. As he or she matures, a child may attend to an object and the action associated with it. Thus, the child may use *eat* when referring to a cookie being eaten. Later, he or she notes object relations or comments on the event, such as asking for a repetition with *again* and *more*. Thus, the child is not just acquiring a stack of word meanings. Rather, the child is making meanings known to a conversational partner by using them to build a communication system with that partner.

With two-word speech content can be communicated more completely without as much dependence on nonlinguistic channels. It is important to remember, however, that grammatical form is not the determiner of communication function. A single intention can be realized in a variety of grammatical forms. A child can express a request with "Gimme cookie," "Cookie me," or "Cookie please." Conversely, one form can serve a variety of intentions. For example, an utterance such as "Daddy throw" can serve as a descriptor of an event, a request for action, or even a request for information (question).

At around age 2, even as the number of intentions increases, a child begins to combine multiple intentions within a single utterance. For example, on spying some fresh-baked cookies, the child might say, "Mommy, cookies hot?" Even though she is attempting to attain information, she may also be hoping to attain a cookie. Thus, we have a request for information and a request for an entity within the same utterance.

Conversational Abilities

Even at the single-word stage, a child has some knowledge of the information to be included in a conversation, giving evidence of **presupposition**—that is, the assumption that the listener knows or does not know certain information that a child, as speaker, must include or delete from the conversation. For example, as an adult, when you are asked, "How do you want your steak?" you might reply, "Medium rare." There is no need to repeat the redundant information, "I would like my steak. . . ." You omit the redundant information because you presuppose that your listener shares this information with you already. In contrast, you would call your listener's attention to new, different, or changing circumstances that may be unknown to the listener ("Did you know that. . . ?" "Well, let me tell you about . . .").

Toddlers seem to follow certain rules for presupposition:

1. An object not in the child's possession should be labeled.
2. An object in the child's possession, but undergoing change, as in being eaten, should be encoded by the action or change.
3. Once encoded, an object or action/state change becomes more certain. If the child continues, she or he will encode some other aspect, such as location.

The order of successive single-word utterances ("Doggie. Eat.") reflects these rules. This may explain, in part, the variable order of successive single-word utterances. Sometimes "Eat. Doggie." is perfectly fine. With the onset of two-word utterances, a child learns some word-order rules that may override informational structure. Because children often encode things in the immediate context, it is relatively easy for adults to interpret an utterance in a manner similar to that of a child.

INITIAL LEXICONS

Initial individual vocabularies or *lexicons* may contain some of the common words listed in Table 7.4. Although there are many variations in pronunciation, some of the most frequent forms are included in parentheses. (See Appendix A for an explanation of the International

TABLE *7.4* **Representative List of Early Words**

juice (/dus/)	mama	all gone (/ɔdɔn/)
cookie (/tʊti/)	dada	more (/mɔ/)
baby (/bibi/)	doggie (/dɔdi/)	no
bye-bye	kitty (/tldi/)	up
ball (/bɔ/)	that (/da/)	eat
hi	dirty (/dɔti/)	go (/d oʊ/)
car (/tɔ/)	hot	do
water (/wʌwʌ/)	shoe (/su/)	milk (/mʌk/)
eye	hat	
nose (/n oʊ/)		

Phonetic Alphabet.) How does this sample compare with the one you devised earlier? As we note patterns in early speech, check them against your list.

An analysis of first words indicates that over half consist of a single CV syllable with the remainder split between single vowels and two CV syllables (CVCV) (Fagan, 2009). Non-word vocalizations are similar in structure. The overwhelming majority of words and non-words contained three or fewer sounds each. For example, in our list in Table 7.4 we find CV words, such as *no* and *car* (/tɔ/); CVCV-reduplicated words, such as *mama, dada,* and *water* (/wʌwʌ/); and CVCV words, such as *doggie* (/dɔdi/). How does your list compare? There are very few CVC words, and many of these will be modified in production. The final consonant may be omitted to form CV or followed by a vowel-like sound approximating a CVCV construction. For example, a word such as *hat* might be produced as *hat-a* (/hatʌ/) similar to a CVCV construction. Front consonants, such as /p, b, d, t, m, w, and n/, and back consonants, such as /g, k/, and /h/, predominate. No consonant clusters, such as /tr/, /sl/, or /str/, appear. Clusters are too difficult to produce at this age.

The first words of Spanish-speaking children also demonstrate some of the same characteristics. CV, VC, and CVCV syllable structures predominate (Jackson-Maldonado, Thal, Marchman, Bates, & Gutierrez-Clellan, 1993). The phonemes /p, b, m/ and /n/ are also used frequently, plus /g/ and /k/. As a group, these sounds can be found in 70% of the most frequent words of Spanish-speaking children.

A child's first lexicon includes several categories of words. The most frequent words among a child's first 10 words generally name animals, foods, and toys. First words usually apply to a midlevel of generality (*dog*) and only much later to specific types (*spaniel, boxer*) and larger categories (*animal*). Even at this midlevel, however, a child uses the word at first to mark a specific object or event rather than a category. The list in Table 7.4 contains animals (*doggie* and *kitty*), foods (*juice* and *cookie*), and toys (*ball*). How about your own list?

Initial lexical growth is slow, and a child may appear to plateau for short periods. Some words are lost as a child's interests change and production abilities improve. In addition, a child may continue to use a large number of vocalizations that are consistent but fail to meet the "word" criterion. At the center of a child's lexicon is a small core of high-usage words. The lexical growth rate continues to accelerate as a child nears the 50-word mark. Eighteen-month-old infants are capable of learning new word-referent associations with as few as three exposures (Houston-Price, Plunkett, & Haris, 2005). The second half of the second year is one of tremendous vocabulary expansion, although there is much individual variation. In general, girls seem to begin to acquire words earlier and have a faster initial trajectory (Bauer, Goldfield, & Reznick, 2002).

By 18 months of age, the toddler will have a lexicon of approximately 50 words. Nouns (*milk, dog, car, mama, dada*) predominate, often accounting for over 60% of a child's lexicon. Most entries are persons and animals within the environment or objects the child can manipulate. Not all noun types are represented; individual objects and beings are most frequent. There are no collections, such as *forest,* or abstractions, such as *joy.*

Again, many of these characteristics are also found in the first words of Spanish-speaking toddlers. *Mama* and *papa* are popular, along with labels for toys, body parts, foods, the names of people, *more* (*mas*), and *yes/no* (*sí/no*) (Jackson-Maldonado et al., 1993).

Between 18 and 24 months, most children experience a "vocabulary spurt," especially in receptive vocabulary (Harris, Yeeles, Chasin, & Oakley, 1995; Mervis & Bertrand, 1995). Words that are learned only in specific contexts and those that are relatively context-free tend to retain these characteristics. Specific words learned are determined by a combination of factors, including their relevance for the child and the cultural significance of the referent (Anglin, 1995a).

Growth in the overall size of a child's lexicon does not follow a smooth trend. After children have acquired about 100 words, most, but not all, experience a rapid rise in the rate of acquisition, called the "vocabulary spurt" (Bates & Carnevale, 1993; Bloom, 1993). The actual timing of the spurt may be dependent on the rate of cognitive development (Mervis & Bertrand, 1995). The cause of and the reason for the timing is unknown but may be related to one of the following:

- Development of more articulation control. Once a child has overcome difficulty producing certain phonological forms, she or he is free to produce words that had been too difficult before.
- The role of syntactic patterns. Once a child learns certain syntactic frames used by parents, such as *This is X, Here's the X,* or *Show me your X,* a child can quickly pick up a large quantity of words to fill the "slot" within that frame.
- Underlying growth in cognitive capacities.
- Learning and using words.

In all cases, the vocabulary spurt can be viewed as arising from the dynamic pairing of the semantic learning with quickly developing phonological advances, a system of syntactic patterns, or cognitive advances (MacWhinney, 1998).

Lexically precocious 2-year-old children—those with larger vocabularies—are also grammatically precocious, with a greater range of grammatical structures and more advanced combinatorial skills (McGregor, Sheng, & Smith, 2005). In general, among 2-year-olds, grammatical development is more closely associated with lexicon size than with chronological age.

Nouns Predominate

The proportion of nouns and verbs in a child's lexicon changes with development (Bates et al., 1994; Marchman & Bates, 1991). There is an initial increase in nouns until a child has acquired approximately 100 words. At this point, verbs begin a slow proportional rise with a proportional decrease in nouns. Other word classes, such as prepositions, do not increase proportionally until after acquisition of approximately 400 words, but that won't take long.

Regardless of the language spoken, children's early vocabularies contain relatively greater proportions of nouns than other word classes (Bornstein et al., 2004). In early lexical development, children speaking all languages seem to have a predisposition to learn nouns (Ogura et al., 2006).

As vocabulary growth and grammar emerge, the proportion of verbs increases substantially, reflecting the properties of the input language. For example, the proportional increase, then decrease, in nouns is also found in the lexicons of Spanish-speaking toddlers (Jackson-Maldonado et al., 1993).

Although nouns also predominate in the initial words of Korean children, an earlier and proportionally higher use of verbs may reflect both the maternal tendency to use single-word verbs and to use activity-oriented utterances, and the SOV organization of the Korean language that places verbs in a prominent position at the end of the sentence (Gopnik & Choi, 1990; Kim, McGregor, & Thompson, 2000). In fact, Korean children exhibit their own "verb spurt" not seen in English (Choi & Gopnik, 1995).

There are several possible explanations for the early predominance of nouns in the speech of toddlers learning American English.

- A child may already have a concept of objects from time spent in social interaction around objects and in object exploration.
- Nouns are *perceptually/conceptually distinct.* The "things" that nouns represent are more perceptually cohesive than events or actions, in which perceptual elements are scattered.

■ The *linguistic predictability* of nouns makes them easier to use and accounts for their early predominance. Nouns represent specific items and events and thus relate to each other and to other words in specific, predictable ways. For example, they can be *on* or *in,* or other objects can be *on* or *in* them. Some are *eaten*; others *thrown.*

■ The frequency of adult use, adult word order, the limited morphological adaptations of nouns, and adult teaching patterns seem to affect children's production. Learning may be made easier by clear parental labelling within context. Maternal naming of objects is most frequent about the time that the first word appears. After that time there is a subtle shift to more action words (Schmidt, 1996).

Although word order varies across languages, nouns still form a substantial part of most initial lexicons. Mothers may modify word order to place nouns in more prominent positions. For example, Turkish mothers even violate the SOV order to place nouns last (Aslin, 1992). These changes are reflected in children's initial lexicons. Mandarin caregivers, on the other hand, emphasize verbs over nouns, with a resultant higher proportion of verbs in the initial lexicon of Mandarin-speaking toddlers (Tardif, Shatz, & Naigles, 1997). Likewise, the noun bias of English is not seen in maternal speech in Ngas, a Nigerian language. Mothers use proportionally more verbs (Childers et al., 2007).

In English, nouns have fewer morphological adaptations than verbs or other parts of speech, only the addition of the plural *-s* (Goldfield, 1993). Hence, a child hears the root word more. Although this distinction is not true for all languages, still, initial lexicons tend to be dominated by nouns.

The frequency of nouns in adult-to-adult speech is low, but nouns occur more frequently in adult-to-child speech, receive more stress than other words, are often in the final position in utterances, and have few morphological markers (Goldfield, 1993; Nelson et al., 1993). The proportion of nouns in adult-to-child speech varies with the context and the child's developmental level (Barrett, Harris, & Chasin, 1991; Goldfield, 1993). Nouns are also more frequent in toy play and in short maternal utterances. Verbs are more frequent in non-toy or social play and in conversations.

It is important to note that object-naming games found in American English—"What's that"—are culture based and not found in all cultures (Tomasello & Cale Kruger, 1992). American mothers also prompt their childern to produce nouns more frequently than verbs, which they prompt their children to produce as an action rather than as a word (Goldfield, 2000). While English-speaking mothers of toddlers use more nouns and focus on objects, Korean mothers use more balance between nouns and verbs and focus on both objects and actions especially in toy play (Choi, 2000). Experimental data suggest that for 16- to 18-month-old toddlers, learning words primes the child's lexical or "personal dictionary" system to learn even more words (Gershkoff-Stowe & Hahn, 2007). In other words, vocabulary development may consist of a process of continually fine-tuning the lexical or vocabulary system in order to increase storage and accessibility to information. The lexical system is enhanced through use.

It's easy to see that the effect of frequency of parental input on word learning is not straight-forward. Instead, there is a complex interaction with the type of word, receptive and expressive language of the child, and developmental stage (Goodman, Dale, & Li, 2008). In general, among 8- to 30-month-old children, the frequency of parental input correlates significantly only with the age of acquisition only for common nouns.

Individual children exist along a continuum from a referential style in which they use many nouns ("noun lovers") to an expressive style in which they use few ("noun leavers"), preferring interactional and functional words, such as *hi, bye-bye,* and *no.* Children with a referential learning style tend to elaborate the noun portion or noun phrase of their sentences, whereas those with an expressive style prefer to elaborate the verb phrase.

Children with a high proportion of nouns—70% or more—exhibit a rapid increase in the number of words in their lexicons between 14 and 18 months of age. In contrast, children whose lexicons have more balance between nouns and other word types tend to have a more gradual increase in word acquisition. These differences have been found among toddlers in both English and Italian and may indicate two acquisition strategies: (1) naming "things" and (2) encoding a broad range of experiences (D'Odorico, Carubbi, Salerni, & Calvo, 2001; Goldfield & Reznick, 1990).

More than just a high or low proportion of nouns, the referential-expressive continuum represents a difference in learning style that affects language development. Children with a referential style seem to have more adult contacts, use more single words, and employ an analytic, or bottom-up, strategy in which they gradually build longer utterances from individual words (Hampson, 1989). In contrast, children with an expressive style have more peer contacts, attempt to produce longer units, and employ a holistic, or top-down, strategy in which longer utterances are broken into their parts. Although the referential style is usually associated with a faster rate of development, other factors, such as gender, birth order, and social class, seem to be more important (Bates et al., 1994; Lieven & Pine, 1990).

Most children begin language acquisition by learning some adult expressions holistically, such as *I-wanna-do-it, Lemme-see,* and *Where-the-doggie* (Pine & Lieven, 1993). This pattern characterizes the speech of some children, such as later-born children who observe siblings, more than others (Barton & Tomasello, 1994; Bates, Bretherton, & Snyder, 1988). Children who have an overdependence on this strategy, characterized as "swallowing language whole" or using memorized *formulas,* may be at a real disadvantage in learning language. In order to extract productive linguistic elements that can be used appropriately in other utterances in the future, a child must engage in a process of segmenting or dividing utterances—analyzing, if you will—to determine which components of speech input can be recombined with others to form novel utterances. I'm a good example of using formulas. When I go to a country in which I do not speak the language, I memorize a few phrases. This means that I cannot take the phrases apart and form original utterances.

Here Come the Verbs   Twenty-month-olds understand meaning distinctions among several word categories, such as nouns and adjectives (Hall, Corrigall, Rhemtulla, Donegan, & Xu, 2008). Modifiers and verblike words, such as *down,* appear soon after the first word. True verbs, such as *eat* and *play,* occur later. Verbs and other words serve a relational function; they bring together items or events. Unlike objects, actions are not permanent, and verbs may not be accompanied by any consistent maternal gesturing. Thus, a child learning language is less able to guess their meanings after only a brief opportunity to make the symbol–referent connection.

There are several challenges in learning a verb (Hirsh-Pasek & Golinkoff, 2006). First, to correctly establish a verb's meaning, a child needs to find the underlying concept. The concepts that verbs refer to are abstract and hard to determine from the physical environment. For example, verbs differ greatly depending on who is performing the action. An out-of-shape and not-too-coordinated man looks very different from a ballerina although both actions are *dance.* Some verbs describe momentary actions, such as *throw,* while others have more duration, such as *play.* In addition, some nouns can be verbs, as with *skate,* while others cannot, as with *car.*

Before children can learn the meaning of a verb, they need to determine which words are the verbs. First, a child must identify a verb in the speech stream. Although 7.5-month-olds can segment nouns from fluent speech, only 13.5-month-olds succeed with verbs. Children may be helped by the way in which English sentences are formed. Subject-verb-object form may help if children can more readily identify nouns or pronouns. For example, Mommy + X + (food), as in *Mommy eat cookie* or *Mommy eat apple,* may provide a format within which the child can identify the action.

Verb learning presents a different situation than noun learning. As many as 60% of the verbs in maternal speech refer to future action. This order of word followed by the action, as in "Mommy's going to roll the ball" before she does, seems to facilitate comprehension and production for 15- to 21-month-olds (Tomasello & Cale Kruger, 1992). The reverse process, action followed by the verb, seems to facilitate production only. In contrast, noun learning is best in an ongoing condition, in which a child can focus on an adult and still maintain the object within sight.

Nouns seem to enjoy a natural advantage even among 3- to 5-year-olds. In supposedly verb-friendly languages such as Chinese and Japanese, children require both grammatical or sentence support and pragmatic or usage support to learn verbs, while English-speaking children require only grammatical support (Imai et al., 2008).

With vocabulary growth and the emergence of grammar, the proportion of verbs increases substantially. This is true for parental speech too. For example, when children begin to combine words, Japanese mothers shift away from a dominance of nouns in their toy play with their children (Ogura, Dale, Yamashita, Murase, & Mahieu, 2006).

MEANING OF SINGLE-WORD UTTERANCES

A toddler initially uses language to discuss objects, events, and relations that are present. She or he has spent a year or more organizing the world, making sense of, or giving meaning to, experiences. A word refers to a stored concept rather than to an actual entity. A child's exact word meaning—what is mapped on the word—is unknown. Early lexicons until about 18 months of age seem to follow a principle of mutual exclusivity mentioned in Chapter 6. Stated simply, *if the word means X, it can't mean Y or Z.*

The child may use two different processes to form internal representations. Some symbols may be context-bound, or attached to a certain event, and, thus, only used in that context. Over time many of these word definitions will become decontextualized. Other words may be used to designate entities, actions, and relationships in several contexts. The definitions may broaden with maturity. In general, context-bound words are less likely to appear as the child approaches age 2 (Barrett et al., 1991).

The child's communication partner generally interprets the child's utterance with reference to the ongoing activity and to the child's nonlinguistic behavior. Adults often paraphrase the child's utterance as a full sentence, thereby implying that the child encoded the full thought. This assumption is probably erroneous. The child is operating with several constraints of attention, memory, and knowledge. In particular, the child has difficulty with the organization of information for storage and retrieval.

Word knowledge may be derived from multisensory experiences (Barsalou, Simmons, Barbey, & Wilson, 2003). These experiences are then integrated into meaningful units and the pattern of activation is stored in long-term memory. More specifically, sensory neurons activated during an initial exposure to a word and its referent are reactivated during subsequent experiences to enrich the word's representation. For example, early object representations may be formed by the word, object parts, and object function (Chaigneau & Barsalou, in press).

Where Do Meanings Come From?

Children are sensitive to differing aspects of word learning within the first year of life. By the second half of the first year, infants are reliably pairing arbitrary sounds with meanings, a process called *mapping sounds onto meanings.* For example, 6-month-old infants can pair the word "mommy" with videos of their mothers (Tincoff & Jusczyk, 1999). By 10 months infants have up to 10 words in their comprehension vocabulary (Fenson et al., 1994). Around their first birthday, infants recognize that words refer to commonalities across categories of objects, such as different type of cups, can extend them to new exemplars, and can retain new labels for up to 24 hours (Schafer, 2005; Waxman & Booth, 2003).

Word learning, whether in children or adults, is unlike most other kinds of learning. Much of human and animal learning is associative, meaning it is learned by relationships of time or location and perfected through repetition. Word learning, however, seems to be more than just associations formed between repeated pairings of an object with a name (Baldwin, 1991; Bloom, 2000; Tomasello, 1992b).

As the building blocks of language, words have a social as well as cognitive quality to them. If we accept this fact, we might assume that even the earliest word learning reflects sensitivity to the social intentions of the speaker. Although this seems to be true for older children (12-, 18-, and 24-month-olds), 10-month-olds seem to learn new labels by relying on the perceptual attributes of an object instead of social cues provided by a speaker (Pruden, Hirsh-Pasek, Michnick Golinkoff, & Hennon, 2006). This despite the fact—as we know—that infants are sensitive to social information much earlier.

Social sensitivity seems to become more important for word learning as children begin to produce words and is online by 12 to 18 months of age (Gergley, Nadasdy, Csibra, & Biro, 1995). In word learning, they attend both to social information, such as eye gaze, and to a speaker's intent (Hollich, Hirsh-Pasek, & Michnick Golinkoff, 2000). As a result, children rapidly increase their vocabularies. In fact, the ability to detect and use a speaker's intention may be necessary for word learning (Baldwin & Tomasello, 1998). For example, 18-month-olds seem to learn a name for a novel object only when the speaker's intent to name it is clear (Baldwin et al., 1996). If a speaker fails to look toward an object, the word usually does not enter a child's vocabulary. Although the ability to use social signals is still fragile at 18 months, children become word-learning experts by 24 months (Hollich et al., 2000; Moore, Angelopoulos, & Bennett, 1999).

Concept Formation

When a toddler uses the word *dog* for a horse but not for a poodle, it is difficult to determine the concept of *dog* that underlies the child's word. Adults might conclude that the child is using perceptual characteristics, such as four legs and a tail. In truth, we don't know.

Several hypotheses have been proposed to explain concept formation and word learning. Among these are the following:

- The **semantic-feature hypothesis** proposes that a child establishes meaning by combining features that are present and perceivable in the environment, such as shape, size, movement, taste, smell, and sound. A child's definition of *doggie,* therefore, may include features such as four legs, fur, barking, and a tail. When she or he encounters a new example of the concept *doggie,* or one that is close, such as a bear, a child must apply the perceptual attribute criteria to determine the name of this new being. As children mature, they add or delete features, and the concept becomes more specific, thus more closely resembling the generally accepted meaning.
- The **functional-core hypothesis** focuses on motion features rather than static perceptual features. Concept formation begins with the formation of a function or use meaning. In other words, the meaning of *spoon* is in its use. If you ask a young child "What's an apple?" the child might respond, "Something you eat." Children's definitions do have a strong element of function or action but not all words are so easily defined.

- ■ The **associative** and **prototypic complexes hypotheses** say either (1) that each successive use of a word shares some feature or is associated with a core concept or (2) that the child's underlying concept includes a central reference or prototype respectively. In the latter, the closer a new referent is to the prototype, the more likely it is to be labeled with that name. Figure 7.1 presents a possible prototypic definition. The degree to which a particular example is considered to be prototypic of the concept is related to the number of features the example has in common with other referents of the concept. Older children and adults seem to analyze a concept into its essential features, which are used to determine "goodness-of-fit" of new examples.

The short answer to "How do children organize their definitions and on what are they based?" is that we have no idea. It may be all or none of the above theories, and it may vary by word and across child.

Extension: Under, Over, and Otherwise

A child's receptive vocabulary precedes her or his expressive vocabulary. Although there is wide individual variation, the receptive vocabulary may be four times the size of the expressive vocabulary between ages 12 to 18 months. A child who understands *motorcycle, bike, truck, plane,* and *helicopter* may label all of them *car.*

Usually, a child's meaning encompasses a small portion of the fuller adult definition. For example, a child might hear a mature speaker say "No touch—hot!" as the child approaches the stove. Subsequently, the child may use the phrase as a general prohibition meaning "Don't do it!"

Formation of a link between a particular referent and a new name is called **fast** or **initial mapping,** and it is typically quick, sketchy, and tentative. Most learning occurs after this initial

FIGURE *7.1* **Possible Prototypic Concept of Furniture**

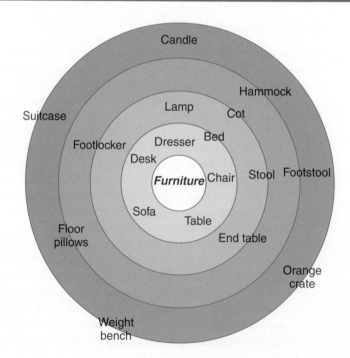

mapping as a child is exposed repeatedly to new instances of a word. Gradually, the word is freed from aspects of the initial context that may be irrelevant to the meaning.

In the process of refining meanings, children form hypotheses about underlying concepts and extend current meanings to include new examples. Through this extension process, a child gains knowledge from both examples and nonexamples of the concept.

Concepts may be very restricted or widely extended. Overly restricted meanings are called **underextensions.** Using "cup" for only "my child cup" is an example of underextension. In contrast, **overextensions** are meanings that are too broad when compared to the adult meaning. Calling all men "Daddy" is an example of overextension. Toddlers seem to overextend both receptively and expressively possibly because they fail to differentiate between basic concepts (*dog*) and conceptual categories (*pet*) (Storkel, 2002).

A child receives both implicit and explicit feedback about extensions of both types. Implicit feedback can be found in the naming practices of others, to which a child attends. In contrast, explicit feedback includes direct correction or confirmation of a child's extensions by more mature language users. As a child extends the meaning of *cup* from "my child cup," he or she may include bowls and pots in addition to coffee mugs and tea cups. In the course of daily events, more mature speakers will call bowls and pots by their accepted names and correct the child's attempts more directly.

Over time, words develop a "confirmed core" and a peripheral area of potential generalization. As long as a child sticks closely to the confirmed core, she or he will tend to undergeneralize a word. In the center are the best instances that display the maximum match. At the periphery, however, are instances that are less clear and compete with closely related words. Overgeneralizations occur when a child must communicate about objects that are not inside any confirmed core.

Underextensions are common in both receptive and expressive language. In contrast, overextension is usually limited to expressive language, although there is considerable individual variation. At this early stage of acquisition, toddlers comprehend many more words than they produce.

Overextensions are common among toddlers in all languages, including those acquiring American Sign Language (Siedlecki & Bonvillian, 1998). A lack of specific words in the child's lexicon may account for the behavior. The child may not know what else to call something, so he or she uses a word already known.

Most overextensions fall into three general types:

- Categorical overinclusions occur when a child uses a word to label a referent in a related category, such as saying *baby* for all children, *hot* for hot and cold, or *dada* for both parents. The largest number of overinclusions are with people.
- Analogical overextensions include the use of a word to label a referent based on inferred perceptual, functional, or affective similarity, such as saying *ball* to refer to round objects or *comb* to label a centipede.
- Predicate statements occur when a child notes the relationship between an object and some absent person, object, property, or state, such as saying "doll" when seeing the empty bed or "door" when requesting adult assistance with opening or closing some object. Types of predicate overextensions are shown in Table 7.5.

When we examine extensions of the first 75 words, perceptual similarity seems to account for nearly 60% of both. Most perceptual similarities seem to be visual. Action or functional similarity accounts for about 25% of children's extensions. Thematic or contextual association of an object with the event in which it is used, as when a child uses the word *nap* when referring to a blanket, seems to account for only about 12% of extensions. Finally, a very small number of

TABLE *7.5 Predicate Overextensions*

STATEMENT TYPE	EXAMPLE
Former or unusual state	*Cookie* for empty plate
Anticipations	*Key* while standing in front of door
Elements	*Water* for turned-off hose
Specific activity	*Peepee* for toilet
Pretending	*Nap* while pretending to sleep

Source: Information from Thomson & Chapman (1977).

extensions are based on affective or emotional similarity. More than half of these extensions involve prohibitive or frightening words, such as *hot* or *bad*.

The majority of children use words correctly, often for generalized referents rather than for a single referent. Within one month of acquisition, more than three-fourths of words are generalized. Of the remainder, most are names for specific entities, such as *Mama*. Words acquired during initial lexical growth are more likely to be both under- and overgeneralized than words acquired later. Overextension does not occur immediately, but rather during the rapid vocabulary growth that accompanies early multiword utterances.

As many as a third of the first 75 words may be overextended. Some categories, such as letters, vehicles, and clothing, are overextended at a greater rate than others. Many children overextend words such as *car, truck, shoe, hat, dada, baby, apple, cheese, ball, dog,* and *hot*.

In summary, it appears that extensions of all types are an aspect of the word-acquisition process. As a child begins to use the acceptable adult meaning, adults become unwilling to accept the child's overinclusiveness and overextending decreases.

Early Multiword Combinations

When children begin to combine words into longer utterances at about 18 months of age, they do so in predictable patterns that appear to be universal. With increasing memory and processing skills, a child is able to produce longer utterances by recombining some of these early patterns. Language learning in much of the latter half of the second year involves these combinations. It is important to keep in mind, however, that the child still produces a great many single-word utterances and continues to babble and use jargon.

Why does a young child produce short utterances? I'll spare you the long, complicated answer. In short, children's language production is similar to that of adults, meaning that it is a complex interaction of syntactic knowledge, limited cognitive resources, especially working memory, a child's communicative goals, and the structure of the conversation (Valian & Aubry, 2005).

TRANSITION: EARLY WORD COMBINATIONS

Prior to the appearance of two-word utterances is a period in which a child produces sequences of words, sounds, and gestures in seeming combination and in a variety of forms. In any gesture-rich culture, such as Italy, children may make early transitional combinations of a word plus a representational gesture, such as putting a fist to the ear to signal *telephone* or flapping the arms for *bird* (Capirci et al., 1996). A larger number of such combinations is related to greater verbal production in the later multiword stage.

The types of gesture-speech combinations a child produces during the early verbal stages of language development change with the child's changing cognitive and language skills (Özçaliskan & Goldin-Meadow, 2005). While children and their caregivers produce the same types of gestures and in approximately the same distribution, children differ from caregivers in the way they use gestures accompanying speech. Although caregivers' use of reinforcing (*ball* + point at ball), disambiguating (*that one* + point at ball), and supplementary gesture-word combinations (*push* + point at ball) does not increase during the second year of life, children's use does as they mature. Two element gestural-verbal combinations, such as pointing at a car and saying "Go," increase as a child approaches the production of two-word utterances (McEachern & Haynes, 2004).

A second transitional form consists of a CV syllable preceding or following a word. The phonology of the extra syllable is inconsistent and has no referent while the word is more consistent. For example, the child might say the following on several different occasions:

ma baby
te baby
bu baby

Other phonological forms may be more consistent but still have no referent. For example, another variation consists of a word plus a preceding or following sound in which the word varies while the vocalization is stable. Examples of these forms are as follows:

beda cookie
beda baby
beda doggie

A third transitional form consists of reduplications of a single-word utterance, such as "Doggie doggie."

At this point in my language development class, someone always asks about early word combintions such as *all gone*. So let's briefly discuss these seeming combinations that actually consist of two words learned as a single unit. "Daddybob" was a favorite of my children. Usually, a child does not use the two single-unit words independently as words nor in combination with others. Common exambles of single-unit words include:

all-gone
go-bye
so-big
go-potty

Because the words almost always appear together, linguists don's consider these combinations to be true two-words utterances. That's coming up next.

MULTIWORD UTTERANCES

Children progress naturally from one-word utterances to two-word ones. At about 18 months of age, many children begin combining words or holophrases. There is continuity in language development, so it is not surprising that children's earliest multiword utterances are produced to talk about many of the same kinds of things they talked about previously in their one-word holophrases. These multiword utterances come in three varieties:

- Word combinations.
- Pivot schemas.
- Item-based constructions. (Tomasello, 2003)

Let's look at each in turn. Examples are presented in Table 7.6.

Word combinations consist of roughly equivalent words that divide an experience into multiple units. For example, a child has learned to label a dog and a bed and then spies the family dog on her bed and says, "Doggie bed." Initially, these utterances may be expressed as successive single-word utterances with a pause between them and a drop in voice on each. This may be a transition to word combinations in which there is little pause and a drop in voice only on the last word.

Pivot schemas show a more systematic pattern. Often one word or phrase, such as *want* or *more*) seems to structure the utterance by determining the intent of the utterance as a whole, such as a demand. Often there is an intonational pattern, such as an insistent sound to the utterance, that also signals the intent. Other words, such as *cookie,* or phrases, such as *go-bye,* simply fill-in-the-blank or slot, so to speak, as in *More cookie* or *Want go-bye.* In many of these early utterances one event-word is used with a wide variety of object labels as in *More cookie, More juice,* and *More apple.*

Use of pivot schemas is a widespread and productive strategy for producing many two-word utterances from a limited set of constructions. When 22-month-olds are taught a novel name for an object, they seem to know immediately how to combine that word with pivot-type words in their vocabularies, indicating that they also have the rudiments of grammatical classes for words that will fit into the slot in the pivot schemas (Tomasello, Akhtar, Dodson, & Rekau, 1997).

TABLE *7.6 Multiword Utterance Patterns*

PATTERN	EXPLANATION	EXAMPLES
Word combinations	Equivalent words that encode an experience, sometimes as two successive one-word utterances.	Water hot Wave bye Drink cup
Pivot schema	One word or phrase structures the utterance by determining intent. Several words may fill the "slot," as in "Want + 'things I want.'"	Throw ball, Throw block, Throw airplane More juice, More cookie, More bottle Want blanket, Want up, Want out
Item-based constructions	Seem to follow word-order rules for specific rules. May contain morphological markers.	Baby eat, Hug baby, Baby's bed Daddy driving, Drive car, Drive to gran'ma'.

Don't think of these as categories such as nouns and verbs. More likely, the categories reflect "things I want" or "things that disappear." In fact, pivot schemas do not appear to have any internal grammar. For example, "No juice" and "Juice no" seem to have the same meaning.

There is consistency, however, most likely reflecting the word order children have heard most often in adult speech. Thus, English-speaking toddlers are likely to say "No juice" while Korean-speaking ones are likely to say "Juice no." In other words, a child does not seem to be following his or her own deduced word-order rules.

Interestingly, and this is an important distinction, novel words used in pivot schemas are not used creatively to make other constructions. For example, if a child is taught a novel nonsense action word such as *meeking* in the construction "Look meeking. That is called meeking," the child will not subsequently make novel two-word utterances using *meeking* as an action verb, such as "Mommy meeking" (Tomasello et al., 1997). We can conclude that at this point in development, each pivot schema is its own grammatical island, and a child does not have the grammar of the language.

Under communication pressure, such as being hurried or not knowing the correct word, a child may create utterances that seem unusual to adults . . . and make us smile! For example, a toddler might say "I brooming" as she sweeps or "That a flying" when referring to a helicopter.

We find similar constructions in the initial phase of children learning English as a second language. Many children will learn what are called "carrier phrases" or high-usage phrases into which many words can be inserted.

Item-based constructions, on the other hand, do seem to be following word-order rules with specific words. There certainly is sufficient evidence that young children comprehend word order with familiar verbs (Hirsh-Pasek & Golinkoff, 1991, 1996). A child's word-specific, word-ordered constructions seem to be dependent upon how a child has heard a particular word being used. For example, some verbs may be used in only one type of (e.g., *Cut__*), while others were used in more complex forms of several different types (e.g., *Draw__*, *Draw__on__*, *Draw__for__*, *__draw on__*)(Tomasello, 1992a).

Within a specific word's development, there is great continuity. New uses almost always replicated previous uses and then make some small addition or modification. For example, a child may say "Doggie bed" and later produce "Doggie's bed." In fact, the best predictor of this child's use of a given word is not use of similar words on that day but use of the same word on immediately preceding days (Lieven, Pine, & Baldwin, 1997; Pine & Lieven, 1993; Pine, Lieven, & Rowland, 1998). This seems true for children speaking languages as dissimilar as Inuktitut, Dutch, Hebrew, Spanish, Italian, Portuguese, Catalan, and Russian (Allen, 1996; Behrens, 1998; Berman, 1982; Gathercole, Sebastián, & Soto, 1999; Pizutto & Caselli, 1992; Rubino & Pine, 1998; Serrat, 1997; Stoll, 1998).

In general, words such as verbs and their place in word-ordered constructions seem to be learned one verb at a time until children begin to generalize language rules after age 3. In this way, children's syntactic structures are at best relatively independent from each other and dependent on certain words, especially verbs.

Unlike pivot schemas, item-based constructions contain morphological markers (*-ing, -s, -ed*), prepositions (*in, on, to*), and word order to indicate syntactic classes of words that are treated in certain ways. For example, only nouns receive a plural *-s* marker and follow prepositions. These syntactic structures are not generalized. Instead, they are learned and applied word-by-word after hearing similar words used in the same way by adults (Tomasello, 2003).

The toddler is faced with a formidable task trying to form schemes of abstract syntactic rules. It is not surprising, therefore, that this would be accomplished one word at a time.

*F*or toddlers, their primary conversational partners are parents and siblings.

Social-Cognitive Skills and Multiword Utterances

Children construct multiword utterances from the language they hear around them. The ability to do this rests on a child's underlying social-cognitive skills. To accomplish this task, children must be able to do the following:

- Plan and create a multiple-step procedure toward a single goal.
- Form abstractions across individual items.
- Create item-based constructions (Tomasello, 2003).

Let's discuss each one briefly.

Planning and creating a multi-step path to accomplish a goal is seen in the problem-solving behaviors of 14- to 18-month-old toddlers. A toddler forms "mental combinations" (Piaget, 1952) of the steps required to succeed. For example, if a toy is unreachable, a toddler will make a plan and attempt it to retrieve the toy. In addition, toddlers are able to copy sequences of behavior from others. For example, 14-month-old children are able to imitate two- and three-step physical sequences in the correct order in order to assemble a complex toy (Bauer, 1996).

We see toddlers' ability to form abstractions across items in their play. Certain actions, such as pushing can be performed on several different objects. For example, pushing can be performed on toy cars, balls, the baby stroller, and to mom's dismay, any food on the highchair tray. This skill would seem to be exactly the kind of cognitive ability needed to create a pivot schema across different utterances, yielding *Push X*. The X may be categorized by the child as "pushable things."

Children engage in nonlinguistic activities involving clear and generalized roles, such as using objects in specific ways or building with blocks that may lead to creating item-based constructions. Unfortunately, there is nothing in nonlinguistic activities that corresponds to *second-order symbols* (Tomasello, 1992b), such as syntactic and morphological markers. More specifically, meaning is in words, and many grammatical functions are piggybacked on these words. Syntactic constructions are dependent of the semantic elements contained in the words, thus the term second-order symbols. As children hear a word such as *push* used over and over again, presumably they construct a schema that *push* is structured so that a *pusher* precedes it and a *pushee* follows, regardless of the specific identity of each entity (Tomasello, 2003).

Phonological Learning

Phonological development has a strong influence on the first words a child produces. In general, a child will avoid words that he or she cannot pronounce. New words are added when a child develops a "phonological template" or format for those words. For example, when a child acquires a CVC template for final plosive sounds, he or she may add *top, pop, cat, dog, bike,* and *cake* to name a few but still not produce *car, knife,* or *bath.* Conversely, lexical or vocabulary development will have a strong influence on the sounds that a child produces. A child's "favorite phonemes" are usually taken from the sounds present in his or her first and favorite words. A child then attempts these sounds in other words. Think of these favorite words and sounds as a kind of language acquisition basecamp (Bates, 1997). Our little language explorer traverses the world of words and sounds but never loses sight of home.

In the second year, a child faces the task of matching up articulations to auditions, or what he or she says with what he or she hears or has heard. Gaining control of articulation is a major challenge for the 2-year-old. When we break the task down, we find that a child must go from present or stored auditory features to articulation while encoding the sequence and rhythm of each syllable in the word. Just as learning auditory sequences requires memory, the learning of articulatory sequences involves rehearsal and memory (MacWhinney, 1998).

As many as three different representations or maps may be involved in learning a word: auditory, conceptual, and articulatory (Miikkulainen & Dyer, 1991). Word learning involves the association of elements of all three maps. The important feature of the auditory map may be syllabic units, rather than separate consonant and vowel phonemes, given the importance of syllables in early child language (Bijeljac, Bertoncini, & Mehler, 1993; Jusczyk, Jusczyk, Kennedy, Schomberg, & Koenig, 1995). Even 4-month-olds can recognize individual syllables and remember syllable sequences.

AUDITORY MAPS

The learning of a word is an association between a pattern on the auditory map and a pattern on the concept map, between the way a word sounds and its meaning (Hebb, 1949; Kandel & Hawkins, 1992; Naigles & Gelman, 1995; Reznick, 1990). When a child hears a word and sees an object simultaneously, an association is formed. Most likely, at this early juncture, many elements of the two maps are not interconnected (Shrager & Johnson, 1995). Tentative associations are maintained until additional neural connections can be established. If an initial association is not supported by repeated exposure, the word will be forgotten.

As mentioned, the phonological system of humans is a paired system of incoming and outgoing lexicons (personal dictionaries) (Baker, Croot, McLeod, & Paul, 2001). On the incoming side is the child's knowledge base of stored information about words based on language input and application of the child's phonological codes or learned patterns. Outgoing signals are stored in a parallel branch of the system. Remember that there are also semantic avenues for storage that overlap these phonological ones, thus increasing the efficiency of the entire storage system.

Speech perception is based on the child's use of these learned phonological codes to help hold incoming information in working memory while it's analyzed (Nittrouer, 2002). Words are recognized and placed in long-term memory using these same codes. Although word boundaries often are difficult to determine in connected speech (*Jeat? = Did you eat?*), children, as we know, learn to discern recognizable sound patterns and use these to break down the incoming speech stream.

Production may be stimulated by either side of the phonological system (Baker et al., 2001). For example, in imitation, a child is stimulated by the incoming speech model. In more spontaneous speech, a child relies on the stored lexical items on the outgoing side (Hewlett, 1990).

To discuss early lexical development we must consider both the phonological character of the words acquired and a child's emerging phonological system. Lexical characteristics that influence linguistic processing are the word's frequency of use, the **neighborhood density,** and the **phonotactic probability** (Storkel & Morrisette, 2002).

- Frequently used words would be recognized by the child more quickly and accurately and produced more rapidly than infrequent ones. On the other hand, high density or lots of neighbors can result in more confusion and slower, less accurate recognition and production (Vitevitch, 2002; Vitevitch, Luce, & Pisoni, 1999).
- Neighborhood density is the number of possible words that differ by one phoneme. For example, there are very few words in the neighborhood with *the,* thus density is low. Neighbors that differ by one phoneme include *they, thee, though,* and *thou.* All things being equal, which they never are, words in less dense neighborhoods are easier to learn.
- Phonotactic probability is the likelihood of a sound pattern occurring. Sound pattern probability is established for the child through experience. Each time a sound sequence is encountered, a connection is formed in the child's mind between the sounds produced. Common sound sequences (/st-, bl-, -ts/) are perceived and produced more quickly than less common ones (/skw-, -lf/) (Levelt & Wheeldon, 1994; Vitevitch & Luce, 1999), although it will be years before some consonant sequences are mastered. These stored patterns are used to divide the speech stream into separate words. For example, a /bl/-blend is likely to signal the beginning of a word, and either an /nd/-blend or /ŋ/ the end.

Although phonological representation in adults is generally assumed to relate to phoneme information, young children seem to operate with more holistic or whole word representations. A component of phonological development is a transition from holistic to segmental storage of phonological information, that while very individualistic depending on age and vocabulary size, begins at about the time when toddlers combine words (Vogel Sosa & Stoel-Gammon, 2006).

Infants attend more readily to frequently occurring words. Because they have few stored words—their *neighborhoods* are sparsely populated—children tend to use global or whole-word recognition strategies. Phonotactic probability emerges at about 9 months as the child learns the likelihood of sound patterns occurring in the speech of others in the environment.

Early language learning is pattern learning, and only certain sound patterns are permissible within each language. As mentioned, children enter the phonological system at the whole-word or global level when they begin to speak (Beckman & Edwards, 2000). Words are not built phoneme by phoneme but are perceived, learned, and produced as whole-sound-patterned units.

ARTICULATORY MAPS

As mentioned, language learning may be both implicit and explicit, reflecting the parallel receptive and expressive phonological systems previously discussed (Velleman & Vihman, 2002). Implicit learning is incidental and unintentional, including mere exposure to the language. Through exposure, an infant gains an expectation for the frequency of occurrence of different phonological patterns, gradually gaining a sense of the language norm. In explicit learning, a child attempts to replicate an adult word heard previously.

A child's initial exposure to rhythmic patterns occurs while still in the womb. An infant gradually becomes familiar with the rhythmic patterns of language by 4 months and with recurring sound distribution patterns by 7 to 8 months. This sound pattern sensitivity occurs at about the same time as a child's production of reduplicated babbling. For the child, this may be the first actual link between the perception and execution portions of his or her phonological system. Theoretically, once so alerted to CVCV patterns in his or her own production, an infant would attend more to these patterns in the speech of others. Gradually, different word shape patterns, such as CV, VC, CVCV, and CVC, evolve from motor practice and the perceived speech of other speakers in the environment. Later, these accessible forms become the templates for a child's first words. In other words, a child unconsciously matches adult words to the phonological patterns that he or she has formed. For example, the adult word *bottle* is fit into the child's CVCV-reduplicated template to form *baba*.

Studies in development of English, French, Japanese, Finnish, Swedish, and Welsh find that first words are similar in form to the child's concurrent babbling (McCune & Vihman, 2001; Vihman & Velleman, 2000). In general, the words match adult forms, but sounds or patterns that do not fit the child's templates or are difficult to produce are omitted. Sound substitutions are rare.

Toddlers seem to adopt a "frame-and-slot" strategy in which they acquire certain templates or frames, and words selected for expression are similar enough in number of syllables, consonants and location, and syllable stress to fit these frames. Thus, a child integrates words and phrases from the environment with his or her own vocal patterns. This process may account for the large percentage of first words of children that contain similar sounds, sound combinations, and syllable shapes (Coady & Aslin, 2003).

As more words are produced, children demonstrate a bias toward consistency over precision by trying to match adult words to the previously existing templates and sound patterns. Words may be produced correctly at first but later modified to fit a child's templates.

A child's repertoire of individual speech sounds is also important in first word production. In general, the greater the number of consonants produced at 9 months, the larger a child's lexicon at 16 months (McCune & Vihman, 2001).

Different children exhibit different "favorite sounds" and use these, in part, in selecting the first words that they will produce. Although there is a wide range of individual differences, certain language-based phonetic tendencies are seen in most children, including a preference for monosyllables over longer strings, and stops (/p, b, t, d, k, g/) over other consonants. Preferences for particular speech sounds at age 1 year do not correspond to mastery of these same speech sounds at age 3 years. Relationships are more subtle. In general, the greater the proportion of true consonants in babbling and true words at age 1, the more advanced the phonological development of a child at age 3 (Vihman & Greenlee, 1987).

Phonological experimentation may exist along a continuum from those children who are very cautious or systematic to those who are more adventurous. More systematic children operate with strong phonetic and structural constraints that are relaxed gradually. In contrast, adventurous speakers have a loose, variable phonological organization and attempt words well beyond their capabilities. This variability at age 1 tends to result in inconsistent production of sounds at age 3 (Vihman & Greenlee, 1987).

Conclusion

A child learning language auditorily—as almost all of us have done—must map or form both the auditory features and the semantics or concept of a word in parallel (Naigles & Gelman, 1995; Reznick, 1990). A child already possesses fairly well-structured knowledge of the basic objects in the immediate environment (*mommy, daddy, dog, ball,* and so on) and particular activities (*bathe, eat, fall,* and the like). It is difficult to measure the size of a child's comprehension vocabulary preceding first word production, but it is probably around twenty words.

With the production of words, a child needs phonological consistency to transmit messages. After the onset of meaningful speech, there is much individual variation in the pattern and rate of speech-sound growth and in the syllable structure of the words acquired.

SINGLE-WORD UTTERANCE PATTERNS

As noted previously, nearly all of the initial words are monosyllabic CV or CVCV constructions. Labial (/p, b, m, w/) and alveolar consonants (/t, d/), mostly plosives (/p, b, t, d, g, k/), predominate, but there are occasional fricatives (/s, f/) and nasals (/m, n/). Vowel production varies widely among children and within each child, but the basic triangle of /a/, /i/, and /u/ is probably established early. Within a given word, the consonants tend to be the same or noncontrasting, such as *baby, mama, daddy, dawdie* (*doggie*). It is the vowels that initially vary. Consonant contrasts or differences occur more frequently in CVC constructions, such as *cup.*

The order of appearance of the first sounds that children acquire—/m/, /w/, /b/, /p/—cannot be explained by the frequency of their appearance in English. Although not the most frequently appearing English sounds, /m/, /w/, and /p/ are the simplest consonants to produce. The /b/ is relatively more complex, although relatively easy to perceive.

PHONOLOGICAL PROCESSES

Phonological processes are systematic procedures used by children to make adult words pronounceable. They enable children to produce an approximation of an adult model. In other words, for a child, phonological processes are a way of getting from an auditory model to speech production. As noted, for example, a child may adopt a CV strategy for CVC words, producing /kʌ/ for *cup* (/kʌp/).

Early phonological processes appear to be word-specific. There is a slow expansion and change in a child's phonological system as rules are created and new words are modified to fit a child's existing sound patterns.

Children's phonological processes exhibit tremendous individual variation for several reasons (Ingram, 1986). First, the entire system of each child is constantly changing. Initially, a child may have one phonemic form for several adult words or several forms for the same word. Thus, *baba* may be used for *baby, bottle,* and *rabbit,* or both *doddie* and *goggie* may be used for *doggie.* Gradually, a child develops processes that enable him or her to distinguish between similar adult words. For example, a child with the rule CV = /d/V may produce both *no* and *go* as *do* (/dou/). The word *key* becomes *dee* (/di/). Over time, the consonant will broaden to allow for more diverse sound production.

Second, some words are produced consistently, while others vary greatly. Within a given word, there may be trade-offs: The acquisition of one part of a word may, in turn, distort another part, which the child produced correctly in the past.

Third, phonological variation may be the result of toddlers' use of differing phonological production processes, such as reduplication, diminutives, assimilation, CVCV construction, open syllables, and consonant cluster reductions (Table 7.7). **Reduplication** occurs when a child attempts a polysyllabic word (*daddy*) but is unable to produce one syllable correctly. The child compensates by repeating the other syllable (*dada*).

The diminutive is formed by adding the vowel /i/, written as *ie, y,* or *ee* to a CVC word, as in *doggie* for *dog* and *fishy* for *fish,* in an attempt to produce a CVCV word. In assimilation, a child does not change the syllables to become the same, that's reduplication, but changes the consonants only. So the word doggie often becomes dawdie (/dɔdi/) or gawgie (/gɔgi/).

Multisyllabic words or words with final consonants are frequently produced in a CV multisyllable form. For example, *teddybear* becomes /tedibɛ/ (CVCVCV). **Open syllables**—those that end in a vowel—predominate. Closed syllables—those that end in a consonant—occur only at the ends of early words.

Consonant/cluster reduction results in single-consonant production, as in *poon* for *spoon.* Differences exist across languages as to which sound—first or second—is usually omitted. Differences reflect the different sound combinations allowable in each language and that language's rules for syllabification (Lleó & Prinz, 1996). Other phonological processes of preschool children are found in Chapter 9.

A child produces those parts of words that are perceptually most salient or noticeable. Auditory saliency is related to relatively low pitch, loudness, and long duration. For similar reasons, children often delete weak syllables, resulting in *nana* for *banana.*

Fourth, variation may reflect multiple processes within the same word. The result may only vaguely resemble the target word. For example, *tee* may be used for *treat.* In this example, a child has deleted the final consonant and simplified the consonant cluster. In similar fashion, suppose that a child has one rule that says that clusters reduce to a front consonant, a second

TABLE *7.7* **Common Phonological Rules of Toddlers**

TYPE	EXAMPLES
Reduplication (CVCV)	*Water* becomes *wawa* (/wɑwɑ/) *Mommy* becomes *mama* (/mɑmɑ/) *Baby* becomes *bebie* (/bibi/)
Assimilation	*Dog* becomes *gog* (/gɔg/) *Candy* becomes *cacie* (/kæki/)
CVCV construction	*Horse* becomes *hawsie* (/hɔsi/) *Duck* becomes *ducky* (/dʌki/)
Open syllables	*Blanket* becomes *bakie* (/bæki/) *Bottle* becomes *baba* (/bɑbɑ/)
Cluster reduction	*Stop* becomes *top* (/tɑp/) *Tree* becomes *tee* (/ti/)

that all initial sounds are voiced, and a third that words with a closed syllable ending receive a final vowel. If the target word is *treat,* it might change as follows:

Target	Treat
Apply rule 1 (cluster = front C)	Peat
Apply rule 2 (initial C = voiced)	Beat
Apply rule 3 (CVC = CVCV)	Beatie (/biti/)

Of course, this is neither a conscious nor a step-by-step process for the child. The child reduces the complexity of the adult model to a form he or she can produce.

A child may even produce the same form for two different words. She or he may interpret adult words as having portions to which different rules apply. For example, suppose that the child produces both *spoon* and *pudding* as *poo* (/pu/). Let's see how this could happen. Assume that consonant clusters, such as *sp,* may be reduced to the plosive sound only and that final consonants, such as *n,* omitted. Thus, *spoon* becomes *poo.* If the child also omits unfamiliar sounds, such as *-ing, pudding* would become *pud,* which, in turn, with omission of the final consonant, just as in *spoon,* might be reduced to *poo,* too (/pu/).

Finally, individual phonological variation may reflect each child's phonological preferences as well. Such preferences might involve different articulatory patterns, classes of sounds, syllable structures, and location in words. Favorite words may conform to the child's production patterns. As the child learns different phonological patterns, he or she applies them to the production of words.

The most frequent phonological process found in children under 30 months of age is consonant cluster reduction, although there is a dramatic drop in the use of this process after 26 months (Preisser, Hodson, & Paden, 1988). Overall, syllabic phonological processes decrease rapidly just prior to the second birthday.

LEARNING UNITS AND EXTENSION

Most likely, individual speech sounds are not the units of development. Rather, as mentioned, the whole word functions as a phonetic unit. Only later does a child become aware of speech-sound contrasts. The child's "word" is a representation of its adult model. The primacy of words over individual phonemes may be reflected in the wide variation in pronunciation across individual words, and the movement of sounds within but not between words.

A child's earliest words are very limited in the number and type of syllables and phonemes. These restraints are gradually relaxed, resulting in greater structural complexity and phonetic diversity. In this progression, a child frequently generalizes from one word to another. Thus, phonological development occurs with changes in the pronunciation of individual words. Some changes result in improved identification of structures and sounds, others in new skills of production, and still others in the application of new phonological rules governing production.

While constructing his or her own phonological system, a child will extend rule hypotheses to other words. As a result, some child "words" will change to versions that are closer to an adult pronunciation, and others will become more unlike this model. In these cases, the rules have been overextended. These changes reflect the acquisition of underlying phonological rules rather than word-by-word or sound-by-sound development.

It appears, then, that a child's first language is governed by phonological rules in addition to those for pragmatics, semantics, and syntax. The child invents and applies a succession of phonological rules reflecting increasing phonological organization via a problem-solving, hypothesis-forming process.

Individual Differences

Individual variation occurs both within and across components of early language. For example, some children acquire vocabulary or grammatical structures faster than other children, while at the same time there may be differences within the same child between these two areas of language development. This has set off considerable linguistic debate about the nature of the underlying cognitive mechanisms. Do different areas of language depend on different cognitive mechanisms or different aspects of similar ones? For example, while the underlying memory systems may be similar, the methods of representing lexical and syntactic information may differ.

Among toddlers, the level of grammatical complexity reflects vocabulary growth more than does the age of the child (Thal, Bates, Goodman, & Jahn-Samilo, 1997). It would seem that a certain level of vocabulary is necessary for the emergence of word combining and later grammatical development. Termed *lexical bootstrapping,* this notion suggests that vocabulary is the foundation for grammar. In contrast, *syntactic bootstrapping* posits that young children can use syntactic knowledge, such as the kinds of words that appear in certain parts of a sentence, to narrow down word meaning (Gleitman, 1990). These processes imply closely interlinked acquisition mechanisms for the early lexicon and syntax. Longitudinal twin studies provide evidence of both types of bootstrapping operating in 3-year-olds (Dionne, Dale, Boivin, & Plomin, 2003).

We could even suggest *phonological bootstrapping* in which prosody, phoneme, and syllable information in speech are used by a child to determine both (Morgan & Demuth, 1996). It is even possible that phonological working memory that enables people to hold strings of speech sounds facilitates both vocabulary acquisition and syntactic processing by serving a similar function for larger linguistic units (Baddeley, Gathercole, & Papagno, 1998).

Several additional factors may influence early language acquisition, including overall health, cognitive functioning, environment of the home, middle ear infections or **otitis media,** motor speech problems, socioeconomic status, exposure to television, and international adoption and second language learning. Some of these have been discussed previously.

Typically developing 16-year-olds enjoy normal friendships, whereas children with either language impairment or delay are more likely to exhibit poorer quality interactions (Durkin & Conti-Ramsden, 2007). Toddlers with language delays exhibit more social withdrawal than do typically developing toddlers (Rescorla, Ross, & McClure, 2007).

Otitis media can negatively affect early language development. Fortunately, these negative consequences on both language comprehension and production appear to be resolved by the age of 7 and no lingering effects are seen (Zumach, Gerrits, Chenault, & Anteunis, 2010).

Early, chronic exposure to television may have a negative impact on development of children. Both the quantity and quality of parent–child interaction decreased in the presence of background television (Kirkorian, Pempek, Murphy, Schmidt, & Anderson, 2009). Background TV significantly reduces toy play episode length and focused attention during play of toddlers and young preschool children even when they pay little overt attention to it (Schmidt, Pempek, Kirkorian, Frankenfield Lund, & Anderson, 2008).

BILINGUALISM

The prevalence of bilingualism reflects the cultural mixing within a nation. In an isolated country, such as Iceland, the rather homogeneous nature of the culture is reflected in the scarcity of bilingualism. In the United States, approximately 20% of the population is bilingual, mostly speaking Spanish and English. Other countries may have large bilingual populations because of a large, influential neighbor with a different language, because the official language differs from the indigenous one, or because of a large immigrant population. In the United States, dual-language children are usually treated as different because the majority culture is monolingual. Worldwide, however, dual or multilingual children are probably as numerous as monolingual ones (Tucker, 1998). In fact, bilingual children seem to have metalinguistic advantages over monolingual children (Bialystock, 2001).

True balanced bilingualism, or equal proficiency in two languages, is rare. Nonbalanced bilingualism, in which an individual has obtained a higher level of proficiency in one of the languages, is more common. The language in which the individual is more proficient may not be the native language, which can recede if devalued or used infrequently (Hakuta, 1987).

It is also possible for a person to be semiproficient or semilingual in both languages. This situation may occur for any number of reasons explained later in the chapter.

Decreased proficiency may reflect mixed input. Children who hear "Spanglish" (Spanish + English) in south Florida and in the southwestern United States or "Franglais" (French + English) in parts of Quebec province can be expected to have more mixing in their own language. Examples of Spanglish among Miami adolescents include *chileado* (chilling out), *coolismo* (ultra-cool or way cool), *eskipeando* (skipping class), *friquado* (freak out), and *¡Que wow!* More detrimental to the learning of either language is the mixing of syntax as in *¿Como puedo ayudarlo?* literally *How can I help you?*, following English word order—in place of the Spanish *¿Que desea?*

In the United States, speakers of English are in a privileged position in which English is widely used, valued, and has institutional support; therefore, it has attained a higher status. Speakers of English form a majority ethnolinguistic community. On the other hand, speakers of Spanish or Tagalog, a Filipino language, each represent a minority ethnolinguistic community whose language is given less support, reflecting its less valued status. These relative status differentials differ across communities. For example, in Miami's Little Havana, Spanish has a relatively higher status than it enjoys in other parts of the Southern United States, yet in much of the United States, Spanish enjoys relatively higher minority status than Urdu, a Pakistani language, which has many fewer speakers. In a second example, Canada is officially a bilingual country of two majority languages, although English has relatively higher status in most parts of the country. In Quebec, however, the relative differential is reversed.

There is a not-so-subtle prejudice against other languages in the general U.S. culture, and American English speakers may respond to these languages stereotypically. Unfortunately, recognition of this prejudice can even be seen in the speech of bilingual adults. For example, when speaking Spanish with an Anglo, Hispanic adults tend to Americanize Spanish words, but they do not do so with an Hispanic audience.

Bilingual Language Learning

It has long been assumed that bilingual children are at a disadvantage when learning language and that their progress in one or both languages is delayed. Several factors account for the variability across children in second-language acquisition. These include the age at which a child receives input in each language, the environment in which the language occurs, the community support and social prestige of each language, differences and similarities in the languages, and individual factors such as motivation and language-learning aptitude (Kohnert & Goldstein, 2005).

A child who learns two languages also learns two cultures, a double learning task, especially if the languages and cultures are very dissimilar. Both languages and cultures are learned through interactions with caregivers and others. Language is central to the process of learning culture, and cultural patterns teach children the appropriate way to communicate. The intertwined nature of the process is called **language socialization** (Genesee, Paradis, & Crago, 2004).

Simulataneous Acquisition   Simultaneous acquisition is the development of two languages prior to age 3. Simultaneous bilingual acquisition can be characterized by initial language mixing, followed by a slow separation and increasing awareness of the differences. In final separation of the phonological and grammatical systems there may be enduring influence of the dominant system in vocabulary and idioms.

In spite of the bilingual linguistic load, the child acquires both languages at a rate comparable to that of monolingual children (Oller, Eilers, Urbano, & Cobo-Lewis, 1997). There is little difference in the size and diversity of the lexicons of monolingual and bilingual toddlers, and later syntactic and reading development in both languages appears typical (Abu-Rabia & Siegel, 2002; Junker & Stockman, 2002; Peña, Bedore, & Rappazzo, 2003). The degree of dissimilarity between the two languages does not appear to affect the rate of acquisition. The key to development is the consistent use of the two languages within their primary-use environments.

As you know, the connections between cognition and language are complex and multidimensional. A young child learning two languages simultaneously must be able not only to discriminate speech sounds but to remember language-related information.

Infants exposed to two languages simultaneously are able to discriminate words in both languages at the same age as children exposed to only one language can discriminate words in that language (Polka & Sundara, 2003). Similarly, the babbling of 10- to 12-month-olds reflects the language or languages to which they have been exposed (Maneva & Genesee, 2002).

There seem to be three stages in the simultaneous acquisition of two languages in young children. During the first stage, a child has two separate lexical systems, reflecting the child's capacity to differentiate between the two languages prior to speaking (Pearson, Fernandez, & Oller, 1995; Petitto et al., 2001). Vocabulary words rarely overlap (Genesee, Nicoladis, & Paradis, 1995). A child learns one word from either language for each referent. When there is an overlap, the child does not treat the words as equals. Some words are treated as corresponding, although they are not considered so by adults. This is similar to the early meaning differences found between adult words and words of a monolingual child. Initially, words from both languages are combined indiscriminately. Rather than signifying a mixing of the two languages, such things as the use of words from both languages may be an example of overextension. A child uses whatever vocabulary he or she has available. Mixing of grammatical elements may reflect a lack of development of structures in one of the languages, possibly because these structures are too difficult at present.

In the initial stage of simultaneous bilingual development, children may actually have two different language systems that they are able to use in different contexts or in functionally different ways (Genesee, 1989). Thus, a child may use one system with adults of one language and one with adults of the other.

Although a child may store some words in only one language, approximately 30% of bilingual toddlers' vocabularies consist of word equivalents from both languages. In other words, a toddler has two words for the same referent, such as *gato* in Spanish and *cat* in English (Nicoladis & Genesee, 1996; Nicoladis & Secco, 2000; Pearson et al., 1995; Quay, 1995). Thus, at least in part, bilingual children establish two vocabularies from the beginning.

Although monolingual toddlers can learn minimally different words (e.g., *bih* and *dih*) by 17 months of age, bilingual toddlers take until 20 months (Fennell, Byers-Heinlein, & Werker, 2007). This may indicate that bilingual children's use of phonemic information versus whole word learning develops later, possibly due to the increased burden of learning two languages. Even so, this delay is minimal and may be helpful in bilingual word learning.

In the second stage, a child has two distinct lexicons but applies the same syntactic rules to both. This lexical generalization process is difficult and occurs slowly. A child must separate a word from its specific context and identify it with the corresponding word in the other language if one exists. Each word tends to remain tied to the particular context in which it was learned, and corresponding words are not usually learned simultaneously. The child is able to move between the two lexicons and to translate words freely. Unfortunately, this flexibility is not found at the syntactic level. The nonparallel sequence of syntactic learning reflects the difference in linguistic difficulty of particular syntactic structures within the two languages. In general, a child learns structures common to both languages first, the simpler constructions before the more complex. Thus, if a construction is more complex in one language, it will be learned first in the other language in its simpler form.

Finally, in the third stage, a child correctly produces lexical and syntactic structures from each language. Although there is still a great deal of interference, it is mostly confined to the syntactic level.

Although as preschoolers children make grammatical errors, there is little evidence of reliance on only one language (Paradis, Nicoladis, & Genesee, 2000). This does not mean that influence by either language is nonexistent. Nor do the languages develop in perfect synchrony. Language dominance, the language in which a child has relatively more proficiency, is dependent on the amount of input a child receives in that language.

All children acquiring two languages simultaneously exhibit some code-mixing, which can include both small units—such as sounds, morphemes, and words—and large units—such as phrases and clauses. Studies involving various combinations of two languages being learned simultaneously indicate that children's code-mixing is systematic and conforms to the grammatical rules of the two languages (Allen, Genesee, Fish, & Crago, 2002; Genesee & Sauve, 2000; Lanza, 1997; Meisel, 1994). Individual differences across children include the amount and type of mixing.

As few as 2% of bilingual preschoolers' utterances may contain some mixing. In general, mixes are used when a child lacks an appropriate word in one language or when the mixed entry is a more salient word to the child. The child's mixing seems to result from a mixed adult input. For Spanish-speaking children in the United States, mixing consists primarily of inserting English nouns into Spanish utterances. The structural consistency of the utterance is maintained.

To decrease interference, a child may try to keep the two languages as separate as possible, associating each with a particular person (Redlinger & Park, 1980). As a child becomes more familiar with the syntactic differences, the tendency to label people with a certain language decreases. A child becomes truly bilingual and can manage two separate languages at about age 7.

Bilingual children may develop separate language systems that are interdependent (Paradis, 2001; Paradis & Genesee, 1996). *Interdependence* is seen in the processes of transfer, deceleration, and acceleration in bilingual language acquisition. In transfer, speech sounds specific to one language will transfer to productions of the other language. Transfer has been found to occur in a bidirectional manner. Each language influences the other.

Deceleration occurs when phonological development emerges at a slower rate in bilingual children than in monolingual children. Interaction between the two languages may interfere with acquisition of some linguistic features and thus result in poorer linguistic skills in bilinguals compared with monolinguals (Gildersleeve-Neumann, Kester, Davis, & Peña, 2008; Goldstein & Washington, 2001). At the same time, some aspects of language may be accelerated because interaction between the two languages of bilingual children aids in the acquisition process and thus results in superior linguistic skills in bilinguals compared with monolinguals (Gawlitzek-Maiwald & Tracy, 1996; Kehoe, Trujillo, & Lleó, 2001; Lleó, Kuchenbrandt, Kehoe, & Trujillo, 2003). The effects of interdependence will vary with the two languages, specific language features, and the age of the child (Fabiano-Smith & Goldstein, 2010).

Simultaneous bilingual children who may be proficient in both languages as preschoolers often shift dominance to the majority language, typically the language used in school. If the trend continues, a child may not be bilingual as a teen or adult.

The truly bilingual person possesses a dual system simultaneously available during processing. In addition, semantic input may be processed in each language regardless of the language of input. Most information is processed at the semantic level, because the interpretation of surface syntax requires much greater proficiency.

My Colombian "granddaughter" Natalia, a very bright preschooler, came to the United States when she was 5 months old with her bilingual Spanish-English, college-educated parents. At home, her parents and their friends spoke Spanish. When she began attending an English-only daycare around age 1, her parents were advised to stop speaking Spanish at home. Luckily, they ignored the recommendation.

At first, Natalia spoke very little at daycare, and, when she did begin to use English, it was often mixed with Spanish. At home her parents continued to speak to her in Spanish. When Natalia was 30 months old, her grandmother (who speaks limited but serviceable English) and her great-grandmother (who speaks only Spanish) came from Bogota for a visit. To my sheer delight, Natalia conversed easily with her great-grandmother in Spanish, switched to English for me, and negotiated Spanish and English with her grandmother. If speaking in English when her grandmother became confused, Natalia smoothly transitioned to Spanish for an explanation, then back to English.

Cross-Language Adoptions: A Special Case

International adoptions account for approximately 10% of all adoptions in the United States, or nearly 13,000 adoptions per year, most from China, Russia, and Guatemala (U.S. Department of State, 2009). Up to 88% of these children were initially raised in orphanages, which in itself may pose special challenges for the infant.

Children raised in developing world orphanages show substantial language delays, with some not yet producing intelligible words in their native language at 30 months of age (Windsor, Glaze, & Koga, 2007). Foster care after the substantial language delays associated with institutionalization or the presence of a preferred caregiver in an institution can facilitate language growth.

These children usually demonstrate a unique language developmental pattern (Glennen, 2002). Adoptive families rarely speak a child's birth language. Thus, a child experiences attrition of the native language (L_1) while learning the new adoptive language (L_2). In fact, L_1 atrophies very quickly. For example, even in rather late adoptions, such as 4- to 8-year-old Russian-speaking children, most of the expressive language is lost within three to six months (Gindis, 1999).

Rapid switching from one language to another is difficult even for an infant. Remember, an infant as early as 10 months of age is able to recognize language patterns in L_1. If adopted after that age, a child must learn to discriminate patterns in the new language. Initially, adopted infants lag behind native English-speaking children, but follow the same developmental pattern (Glennen & Masters, 2002). If adopted as infants or toddlers, most children will exhibit the same language abilities as monolingual English-speaking preschoolers after as little as two years (Roberts, Pollock et al., 2005).

Internationally adopted infants with delays in prelinguistic and vocabulary comprehension measures in their native language are likely to have slow language development initially. Although receptive language and articulation are well developed by age 2, expressive language is still emerging (Glennen, 2007).

Conclusion

LANGUAGE ACQUISITION OFFERS AN informative look into the organizational world of the young child. In order to understand this world, adults have categorized and subdivided children's language in adult terms in the past. This implies that children conceptualize the world and language as an adult does, and that children's motivation or communicative intent to use language is also adultlike. Actually, we don't know a child's meanings or purposes. We cannot assume that the salient features of an event that we might encode also have meaning for a child. In fact, the intentions and semantic knowledge attributed to toddlers may be describing merely the products of the child's language and not what the child actually knows. For example, the "boy" in "boy push truck" may be, for the child, simply the first perceived element in an event rather than the word-combination patterns I've suggested.

A child's utterances are the result of a complex process that begins with the referents involved. In single-word utterances, a child's selection of lexical items seems to be strongly influenced by the pragmatic aspects of the communication context and by the concepts she or he can encode. Many words represent a child's very limited repertoire of phonetic elements. In addition, longer utterances follow simple ordering rules that express meaning. This rule system is independent of pragmatic rules and intentions but is strongly influenced by both in actual use.

During the second year of life, a child becomes more efficient in regulating social interactions through language; communication becomes more easily interpretable. By 24 months, a child can truly engage in conversations, initiating and maintaining topics, requesting information, and predicting and describing states and qualities. He or she is more independent, secure, and autonomous and takes greater responsibility for communication interactions.

Although a child's language is different from an adult's, it is nonetheless a valid symbolic system for that child. It works for him or her within his or her world. First language acquisition is an important initial step in language development. Many of the relations a child has learned to express via a combination of gestures, vocalizations, single words, and word order are now ready for more adultlike linguistic forms.

Discussion

FINALLY, THE FINAL WORD ON FIRST WORDS! But don't worry, there's lots of book left. Were you surprised by how much you already knew about first words? If you went to the trouble to create your own fictitious list as I suggested, undoubtedly you had many of the same words as I did. If you had other words, most probably you still had the same characteristics I outlined for sounds and syllable structure. Were you surprised to discover that there were similarities across languages?

Remember that toddlers talk about what they know. Their choice of words is also constrained by each toddler's phonological repertoire, context, and culture. It only seems logical that the child's definitions would be different from your own, if for no other reason than that you have had so much more experience. What about the child with very little experience? What does he or she talk about? Sometimes children with severe handicapping conditions are sheltered from the world by well-meaning caregivers. Might the job of an SLP, psychologist, or teacher include experiential enhancement?

Because learning a word is more than just saying it, early meanings are very important. Likewise, early pragmatic skills such as intentions, turn-taking, and presupposition are critical. Phonological development will continue to be entwined with lexical and grammatical development for at least three years. For example, children who have difficulty with the /s/ may postpone production of the grammatical markers for plural (cats), possessive (cat's), or third person singular (he walks).

Main Points

- Words are acquired to fulfill intentions within the well-established communication system of child and caregiver.

- First words can express a wide range of intentions.

- First words have predictable sound (/p, b, d, t, g, k, h, m, w, n/) and syllable (VC, CV, CVCV-reduplicated, CVCV) patterns.

- Nouns predominate in the first 50 words.

- Some children analyze communication into words while others prefer to use whole phrases (formulas).

- Word meanings may be based on static attributes or functions of the referent or may be constructed with a best example of the meaning at the core.

- Words are initially fast mapped, formed in a fast, sketchy, tentative way, and may underextend or overextend the adult meaning.

- Early multiword utterances follow predictable patterns represented by word combinations, pivot schemas, and item-based constructions.

- The relationship of phonology and semantics is dynamic, and children avoid words they cannot pronounce, even when they know the word.

- Phonological patterns include reduplication, assimilation, CVCV constructions, open syllables, and cluster reduction.

- Bilingual children learning two languages simultaneously are not at a developmental disadvantage.

Reflections

1. List the most frequent categories of first words, and give some explanation for the things children talk about. Describe the syllable structure of first words.

2. Describe the various intentions toddlers express in their early vocalizations and verbalizations.

3. Compare the three hypotheses that have been advanced as explanations of early concept formation: semantic-feature, functional-core, and prototypic complex.

4. Children extend early words to novel examples. Describe the bases for most over- and underextensions, and explain the possible uses of extensions by children.

5. List the three patterns that children seem to follow when they begin to combine words, and give examples of each.

6. Three common phonological rules of toddlers are reduplication, open syllables, and consonant-cluster reduction. Explain each and give an example.

7. Explain the three stages of a young child's simultaneous development of two languages.

8

Preschool Pragmatic and Semantic Development

OBJECTIVES

Preschool language development is characterized by rapid changes in the use, content, and form of language. Children become real conversational partners and use their language to create context. In addition to learning new words, children learn the meaning of word relationships. When you have completed this chapter, you should understand

- Conversational abilities of the preschool child.
- Narrative development.
- Lexical growth.
- Development of relational terms.
- Impact of development of Theory of Mind (ToM).
- Interrelatedness of language development.
- The following terms:

agent	ellipsis	narrative level
anaphoric reference	event structure	patient
archiform	fast or initial mapping	register
centering	free alternation	semantic case
chaining	interlanguage	topic
deixis	narrative	

To listen to language samples related to chapter content and to peruse other enhanced study aids, please see the Companion Website at www.pearsonhighered.com/owens8e

The speed and diversity of language development during the preschool years are exciting. Within a few short years, a child moves from using simple multi-word utterances to using sentences that approach adultlike form. This development is multidimensional and reflects a child's cognitive and socioemotional growth.

All aspects of language are related, and changes in one part of this complex system affect others. For example, increased vocabulary enables the preschooler to express a wider range of intentions.

In this chapter we will highlight the major preschool achievements within pragmatics and semantics. First, we'll explore the overall development of preschoolers. This information and more are presented in Appendix C, Table C.4. Next, we'll examine the social context of language development and the use of language within that context. Special attention will be given to conversational abilities and narrative development. Then we will explore semantic development, especially vocabulary and relational terms. These changes will be discussed as they relate to cognitive development. Last, we'll describe the effect of Theory of Mind and how semantics and pragmatics affect language form.

Preschool Development

By age 3, a child has perfected walking on flat surfaces. He or she can run well, climb stairs without assistance, and balance on one foot.

Fine-motor abilities continue to develop slowly. The 3-year-old can dress except for shoe-tying and can use a knife for spreading but not cutting. He or she explores by dismantling or dismembering household objects or favorite toys. Although scribbling has developed into more representational drawing, a single "drawing" may represent many very different things. He or she uses toys in imaginative ways and exhibits much make-believe play. Unlike 2-year-olds, a child of 3 is likely to play in groups with other children and to share toys and take turns. Play is often accompanied by sounds and words as the child explains actions, makes environmental noises, or takes various roles.

Speech and language are used in many other ways, and there is a tremendous relative growth in vocabulary. A 3-year-old uses an expressive vocabulary of 900 to 1,000 words and employs about 12,000 individual words per day.

Two aspects of the linguistic environment more readily reflected in speech of this age group are adult intonation and swearing. I recall eavesdropping on my 3-year-old daughter Jessica as she imitated my disciplining. Every family also has at least one embarrassing story about a swearing incident at Grandma's house or in a crowded shopping mall. Our most embarrassing tale involved an alphabet game in which children were saying words that began with certain sounds.

The motor skills of a 4-year-old reflect the increased control of independent movements of the right and left sides. A child of 4 can hop on one foot for a short period and can ascend and descend steps with alternating foot movements. Hand preference is also more pronounced, and children are able to copy simple block letters with the dominant hand. At age 4, my granddaughter Cassidy was writing letters and incorporating them into her own brand of "writing." She even pretended to read her compositions although the story changed each time. Letters proceeded from left to right but were often mixed into drawings, too.

Increased memory helps a preschooler recount the past and remember short stories. This memory and recall are aided by a child's increased language skills. A child also demonstrates categorization skills that seem to indicate more advanced procedures for storage of learned information. Many 4-year-olds can name the primary colors and label some coins. Although a child can count to 5 or higher by rote, he or she has a notion of quantity only through 3.

Socially, most 4-year-olds play well in groups and cooperate well with others. Although there is still a lot of object play, role play becomes increasingly frequent. Living several hours' drive apart, my granddaughter Cassidy and I would often take different roles on the phone as we played variations on a favorite movie or book.

The ability to carry a role through story play is reflected in the 4-year-old's language. The child can tell simple stories of his or her own or others' authorship. Increased language skills enable the child to form more complex sentences. Vocabulary has increased to 1,500 to 1,600 words, with approximately 15,000 used each day.

In general, 4-year-olds are very social beings who have the linguistic skills and the short-term memory to be good, if somewhat limited, conversationalists. My daughter Jessica, now an adult, teasingly asked a 4-year-old for a date. He responded, "No, I'm not grown up yet, but we could go to dinner as a family." Four-year-olds are very anxious to exhibit their knowledge and abilities.

Pragmatic Development

In general, children learn language within a conversational context. For most children, the chief conversational partner is an adult, usually a parent. As children broaden their social networks to include those beyond the immediate family, they modify their self-esteem and self-image and become more aware of social standards. Their language reflects this larger network and the need for increased communicative clarity and perspective.

During the preschool years, a child acquires many conversational skills. Still, much of a child's conversation concerns the immediate context, and he or she has much to learn about the conventional routines of conversation. Even though a child has learned to take turns, conversations are short and the number of turns is very limited. These skills will be refined during the school years. Notice how creatively the children in Box 8.1 use language within a routine situation.

A longer dialogue is presented in Table 8.1. This conversation was collected in the home and is also a conversation between a child and her mother. The two are engaged in role play with a child's sink, table, and dishes. The mother's speech is complicated by her taking two roles: that of the baby, Michelle, and that of another person in the situation. The child plays herself as the mother of Michelle. The adult uses turnabouts to a greater extent than the mother in the first segment. Expansion is very limited and occurs only after child utterance 24. The child is 32 months old, and her MLU from the larger sample is approximately 3.3. In general, the child

---

BOX *8.1*

Imaginative Conversation of Two 60-Month-Old Children

J: Let's play house. Okay? This is mine. You're the father and I'm the mother. (To baby) Oh, sweetie. You want me to wash you? (To T) I have to wash her. I'll play with my baby.

T: Pretend this is her liver and the kidney of the . . .

J: (Interrupting) This is our baby's!

T: . . . of the, of the yucky bacon.

J: You're disgusting.

T: Okay. I'm cutting up the liver.

TABLE 8.1 *Early Preschool Language Sample*

1. She wants some coffee.
    Oh, well, do you have a cup? Where's it at?

2. I don't know where in here.
    Well, just find a cup for her. This is her cereal.

3. Don't know where is it.
    Well, she can't have coffee.

4. Can't have coffee.

5. What's that?
    Coffee.

6. She have coffee?
    Okay. Do you want to feed her and I'll finish ironing?

7. Yeah.
    Okay. Boy, this iron gets hot.

8. What do you do?
    I burned myself.

9. Oh.
    I got burned.

10. Oh, let me . . .

11. No, it's not hot.
    Pshew.

12. It's coldy.

13. I touch it.
    Oh, I think it's hot. Feel it.

14. It's coldy.
    I think it's hot. Okay, the ironing's finished. What are you feeding her?

15. The apple.

16. Michelle eat cereal.
    Gee, okay.

17. She wants some, some, some coffee.
    Oops.

18. That's her coffee.
    Okay, I'll pour some more. Oh, my goodness.

19. It's hot.
    I better put this back on the stove, don't you think?

20. Yeah, don't think.
    Where's the milk?

(Continues)

TABLE *8.1 continued*

21. In the refrigerator.
    Okay, let me get some milk. There, got her bottle ready for you.

22. All right.
    Okay.

23. She eated it alldone.

24. She has to go sleep.
    She has to go to sleep. Well well, you better wipe her face.

25. Oh.
    Gee, J., you don't know what you're doing, do you?

26. Yeah.
    Oh, come here, Michelle. Oh, she's still hungry. Can you feed her some more?

27. She wants one that's good.
    Oh.

28. I fix.
    What are you fixing now?

29. I fixing her cereal.
    Oh, the poor little baby's so hungry. Don't you ever feed her?

30. Yeah.
    I think you need to buy her . . .

31. She want some bottle.
    Okay, you color doggie on this.

is very responsive. As might be expected, this preschooler's greater output of language compared to the toddler in Table 7.1 also demonstrates many more language features. Both children have much variety in their language and initiate and respond to conversation.

Much of a preschooler's conversation still occurs within the mother–child dialog. This linguistic environment has a significant influence on language learning. Even though a child is becoming a fuller conversational participant, mother is still very much in control, creating and maintaining the dialog. This conversational asymmetry continues throughout the preschool period.

Conversational formats and routines provide a scaffolding or support for a preschooler that frees cognitive processing for more linguistic exploration and experimentation. In part, scaffolding and a child's increased cognitive abilities and knowledge enable her or him to talk about nonpresent referents. This more decontextualized language emerges around 18 to 24 months. When a mother discusses past or future events, she tends to rely on their shared knowledge of known, routinized, or scripted events, such as going to McDonald's or to a birthday party. This event knowledge is the topic over 50% of the time. With their 2- to 2½-year-olds, mothers talk about specific past events, such as going to the zoo, and future routine events, such as the upcoming bathtime (Lucariello, 1990).

In addition to conversation, a preschool child engages in monologues. These self-conversations, with no desire to involve others, may account for 20 to 30% of the utterances of 4-year-olds (Schober-Peterson & Johnson, 1991). Although 3-year-olds use monologues in all types of activities when alone, 4-year-olds are more selective and are most likely to use "private speech" only in sustained, focused goal-directed activities such as drawing a picture (Winsler, Carlton, & Barry, 2000).

The presleep monologs of many children are rich with songs, sounds, nonsense words, bits of chitchat, verbal fantasies, and expressions of feelings. Some children engage in presleep self-dialog in which they take both parts.

Gradually, a child's monologues become more social. First, a preschooler engages in them when others are nearby; later he or she will share a topic with a listener, as when telling a story.

In general, throughout the preschool years, audible monologue behavior declines with age, but inaudible self-talk increases. Self-talk decreases after age 10 but doesn't disappear. As adults, most of us still talk to ourselves occasionally, especially when we believe we are alone.

In the following sections, we shall explore the conversational context of preschool language development and a child's conversational abilities and describe the development of narration or storytelling.

THE CONVERSATIONAL CONTEXT

In general, a 2-year-old is able to respond to his or her conversational partner and to engage in short dialogs of a few turns on a given topic. The child can also introduce or change the topic of discussion although he or she is limited in the choice of topics available. In addition, a 2-year-old has limited conversational skills, although he or she learned turn-taking as an infant. Within mother–child conversations, a child learns to maintain a conversational flow and to take the listener's perspective. The preschooler is aided by mother's facilitative behaviors mentioned in Chapter 6. In general, mother and child each engage in roughly 30% opening or initiating and 60% responding behaviors. Initiating behaviors include introductions of a new topic, referrals to a previous one for the purpose of shifting the topic, and deliberate invitations for the partner to respond, such as a question. Responding behaviors include acknowledgments (*I see, uh-huh*), yes/no responses, answers, repetitions, sustaining or reformulated responses, and extensions/replies. Mothers maneuver the conversation by inviting verbal responses.

Child Conversational Skills

When initiating conversations with peers, preschool children mention a person—most often the listener—over 70% of the time with a particular interest in mental states (*think, feel, remember*). This behavior suggests that preschoolers are using their developing Theory of Mind (ToM) in finding common ground with peers (O'Neill, Main, & Ziemski, 2009). Theory of Mind will be discussed in detail in a later section of this chapter, but for now recall the ToM is realizing that others have their own perspective.

A young child is good at introducing topics in which he or she is interested but has difficulty sustaining that topic beyond one or two turns. Frequent introduction of topics results in few contingent responses by the child. Contingent speech is influenced by and dependent on the preceding utterance of the partner, as when one speaker replies to the other. Fewer than 20% of a young preschooler's responses may be relevant to the partner's previous utterance. This percentage increases with a child's age.

Taking a turn or building a bridge for the next and previous speaker's turns is especially difficult. By age 3, a child can engage in longer dialogs beyond a few turns, although spontaneous speech is still easier than the contingent or connected speech found in more mature conversations. With increased age, a preschooler gains the ability to maintain a topic, which in turn results in fewer new topics being introduced within a given conversation.

Nearly 50% of 5-year-olds can sustain certain topics through about a dozen turns. Whether they do depends on the topic, the partner, and the intention of the child. The number of utterances within a single turn also varies with a child's intention (Logan, 2003). Multi-utterance turns containing longer, more complex utterances typically serve an assertive function. Note the increase in utterances per turn as the child in Box 8.2 tries to influence her partner's behavior.

Preschool children's reactions to explanatory and non-explanatory adult information confirm that young children are motivated to actively seek causal information and to use specific conversational strategies in doing so (Frazier, Gelman, & Wellman, 2009). In general, children are more likely to agree and to ask follow-up questions in response to adult explanations and are more likely to re-ask their original question and provide their own explanation following non-explanations.

There is a large increase in the amount of verbal responding between ages 24 and 30 months. A 30-month-old is, in addition, very successful at engaging her listener's attention and responding to listener feedback. For many children, there is an increase in overall talkativeness at around 36 months of age. Many 3-year-olds and even more 4-year-olds chatter away seemingly nonstop. The largest proportion of the speech is socially directed.

A 2-year-old considers the conversational partner only in small measure by providing descriptive details to aid comprehension. He or she uses pronouns, however, without previously identifying the entity to which they refer, as in initiating a conversation with "I not like *it.*" Between ages 3 and 4, a child seems to gain a better awareness of the social aspects of conversation. In general, utterances addressed to conversational partners are clear, well formed, and well adapted for the listener. By age 4, a child demonstrates a form of motherese when addressing very young children. This use of register or style is evidence of a growing awareness of conversational roles.

BOX *8.2*

Increased Utterances for Control

THE 52-MONTH-OLD CHILD is trying to get the adult to capture some ducks for petting.

> CHILD: If we be quiet maybe they'll come up. And if we pretend we're statues maybe they'll come up and try to peck us. And then we can grab them.
>
> ADULT: I don't think that's going to work.
>
> CHILD: I think it is. It might if we stay here for a long time. They'll come peck us, then we can stick out our hands and grab 'em like that.
>
> ADULT: I don't think it is. They're tricky.
>
> CHILD: I think you should go down there and put one on a rope. And then you can tie it in the garage and then we can pet it and … hold it for a long time. And they won't be able to get away.

And later …

> CHILD: Maybe, maybe if we're more quieter and we do it together, we can get 'em. Over there, maybe, if we hold a rock. Let's right up here and maybe when they come up here they can pick it. And we c-can get a leash, then we can grab them when they come near us. And then we'll have one and then we can tie it around the house and the garage. And everyone can see it … when they come here.

Becoming more aware of the listener's shared assumptions or presuppositions, a 3- to 4-year-old child uses more *elliptical* responses that omit shared information. The child need not repeat shared knowledge contained in the partner's questions. If his mother asks, "What are you doing?" the preschooler's elliptical response, "Playing," omits the *I am* as redundant information.

A 2-year-old's language is used in imaginative ways and in expression of feeling, often "I'm tired." Both increase with age. By age 4, a child uses twice as many utterances as a child of 3, discussing feelings and emotions. My children constantly amazed me with their affective responses. Once at Christmas, my 4-year-old son Todd comforted an elderly recently widowed neighbor by stating, "I hope our lights will make you happy."

There is also a related shift in verb usage with less use of *go* and *do*. By age 5, a child uses *be* and *do* predominantly. This change indicates that the child is speaking more about state, attitude, or feeling and less about action.

A preschool child appears to be aware of the conventions of turn-taking but does not use as many turnabout behaviors as adults. Although simultaneous vocalizations are common among infants and their mothers, by age 2 simultaneous talking has decreased significantly and the more mature alternating pattern found in conversations is predominant (Elias & Broerse, 1996). Conversational turn-taking between mothers and their 2- to 2½-year-old children is very smooth. Less than 5% of the turns of either participant are interrupted by the other partner. As a 3-year-old becomes more aware of the social aspects of discourse, he or she acknowledges the partner's turn with fillers, such as *yeah* and *uh-huh*. Preschool children learning languages as different as Japanese and English find it easier to follow maternal linguistic cues to turn-taking, such as questions, than paralinguistic or phonetic cues (Miura, 1993).

Throughout the preschool period, about 60% of child–partner exchanges are characterized by a child's attempts to control the partner's behavior or to relay information. Preschool boys are more likely than girls to use the word *no* to correct or prohibit a peer's behavior (Nohara, 1996). Girls use *no* more to reject or deny a playmate's proposition or suggestion. By kindergarten age, a child is able to cloak intentions more skillfully and to use indirect requests. The exchange of information has gained in importance throughout the preschool years, however, and by age 4 is clearly the most important function, accounting for nearly 40% of these exchanges. Other exchanges serve functions such as establishing and maintaining social relations, teaching, managing and correcting communication, expressing feelings, and talking to self.

Register   By age 4, children can assume various roles, especially in their play. Roles require different styles of speaking called **registers.** *Motherese,* discussed in Chapter 6, is a register. Children as young as age 4 demonstrate use of register when they use a form of motherese to address younger children.

Competence with different registers varies with age and experience (Anderson, 1992). The ability to play various family roles, such as mother or baby, appears early in play. Roles outside the family require more skill, possibly even technical-sounding jargon, as when playing a nurse, teacher, or auto mechanic. My then-5-year-old daughter loved to play hair salon, using all the terms that accompanied that activity and using me as the customer. Younger children prefer familiar roles.

Pitch and loudness levels are the first variations used by preschoolers to denote differing roles (Anderson, 1992). Often, louder voices are used for adult males. Later variations include the average or mean length of the utterances and the choice of topics and vocabulary.

There are some gender differences. Girls assume more roles, speak more, and modify their register more to fit the roles. Due to socialization, boys may be more conscious of assuming gender roles that might be interpreted as inappropriate (Anderson, 1992).

One aspect of register is politeness, achieved by using polite words (*please, thank you*), a softer tone of voice, and more indirect requests (*May I have a cookie please?* instead of *Gimme a cookie*). Use of these devices varies with the conversational partner and with the age of a child. For example, 2- to 5-year-olds use more commands with other preschoolers and more permission requests (*Can I . . . , May I . . .*) with older children and adults. Imperatives (*sit down, come over here*) also may be used with superiors, and their compliance, followed by a younger child's sly smile, indicates that the child knows she or he has scored a coup. Although even 2-year-olds are capable of using *please* and a softer tone, it is not until age 5 that children recognize that indirect requests are more polite (McCloskey, 1986). This recognition occurs in other languages with indirect forms, such as Italian, at about the same age.

Conversational Repair Young children use questions and contingent queries (requests for clarification) ("What?," "Huh?," "I don't understand"), to initiate or continue an exchange, but not to the extent that adults do when addressing young children. Approximately one-fourth of the requests for clarification of 2-year-olds are nonverbal, such as showing a confused expression. As preschoolers mature, nonverbal methods decrease as the primary means of communicating confusion.

Approximately one-third of preschoolers' clarification requests seek general or nonspecific information ("What?" "Huh?"). A child may lack the ability to state what is desired, however, in part because he or she has difficulty determining what is misunderstood. It is not until mid-elementary school that a child develops the ability to make well-informed specific requests for clarification.

Although 2½-year-olds are able to respond to requests for clarification, they do not respond consistently and do not resolve the breakdown 36% of the time when they do (Shatz & O'Reilly, 1990). Young preschoolers have more success with requests for clarification that follow their own requests for action ("Throw the ball at Tobey") rather than to those that follow their assertions or declarations ("I saw a rhinohorserus"). From a purely selfish point of view, they want their requests comprehended correctly.

A preschooler is not always successful in getting the message clarified because of difficulty detecting ambiguity. Usually, a preschooler is unable to reformulate the message in response to a facial expression of noncomprehension and must be specifically requested to clarify. The most common clarification strategy among preschoolers is a simple repetition, especially if the request is a nonspecific "Huh?" or "What?" The abilities to clarify and to organize information more systematically also do not develop until mid-elementary school. Children as young as 3 do seem to be able to recognize the need to clarify their own gestures, however, and can modify their behavior accordingly (O'Neill & Topolovec, 2000).

If you've listened to a 2½-year-old speak, you know that her or his production is not smooth. Rather, there are revisions and pauses or "stalls" as the child changes the sentence form or searches for the correct word (Rispoli & Hadley, 2001). Understanding children's revisions may be crucial to our knowledge of how sentence production is regulated or monitored.

In monitoring, the intended message is compared with the actual sentence output. In other words, a central monitoring mechanism in the brain receives input from both the produced language and the internal representation. Some revisions, such as phonological ones, may occur as the speech is being produced, while others, such as matching intent with the produced utterance, may take longer and await the entire utterance before making a judgment (Hartsuiker & Kolk, 2001; Oomen & Postma, 2001).

Stalls add or change nothing to the linguistic structure being produced. These pauses or interruptions include

- Long silent pauses.
- Pauses filled with *um* or *uh*.
- Repetitions of material already produced while a child picks up the lost thread of what he or she was about to say (Rispoli, Hadley, & Holt, 2008).

It is possible that stalls result from the differing processing rates between higher level linguistic processing and lower level and quicker speech processing. When a slowdown occurs at a higher level and an individual has already begun to speak, he or she is forced to stall. The sources of stalls are heterogeneous and may result from planning problems that leave a speaker temporarily with nothing to articulate, from an inability to rapidly retrieve a lexical item, or from covert speech repairs.

Developmental changes in revision rate seem to reflect changes in the children's ability to monitor their language production (Rispoli et al., 2008). For example, at 27 months of age, revisions occurred in approximately 1% of children's sentences, the equivalent of one revised sentence in every 100 active declarative sentences, and increased with age. Interestingly, no comparable change is seen in pauses or stalls, which are approximately of 9 to 10 stalls per 100 sentences from age 27 to 33 months, although much individual variation exists. Stall rates increase significantly with a sentence's length, whereas revision rate remains constant. It's possible that many short utterances contain rote or memorized phrases, such as *How are you?* or *See you later,* that bypass encoding and monitoring processes used more extensively in longer utterances. In other words, stalls and revisions are different phenomenon representing differing processes.

Two-and-a-half-year-old bilingual children are capable of repairing communication breakdowns by switching languages to match that of their partner (Comeau, Genesee, & Mendelson, 2007). Interestingly, they avoided this repair strategy when attempting to repair breakdowns that are not based on language differences. This behavior indicates that even very young bilingual children are capable of identifying their language choice as a cause of a communication breakdowns and that they can differentiate these types of breakdown from others.

Topic Introduction, Maintenance, and Closure A **topic** can be defined as the content about which we speak. Topics are identified by name as they are introduced. You might say, "I had escargot last night," in an attempt to establish the topic of eating snails. I might reply, "Oh, did you like them?" Now, we are sharing a topic. My reply was an agreement to accept the topic. Not all topics are as direct. For example, the utterance "Well, what did you think of the rally last night?" might be used to establish several different topics, depending upon the manner in which it is stated.

In a larger sense, a topic is the cohesion in a conversation. Through skillful manipulation of the topic, we as participants can make a conversation successful or unsuccessful. For example, the topic of professional sports will work in conversation with many adult males; needlepoint, French cuisine, and American folk art may not. There are conversational partners, however, who could converse on any of these topics for hours.

Once introduced by identification, the topic is maintained by each conversational partner's commenting with additional information; altering the focus of the topic, called *shading*; or requesting more information. The topic is changed by introducing a new one, reintroducing a previous one, or ending the conversation. Obviously, topic development evolves in the context of conversations.

At first, an infant attracts attention to self as the topic. By age 1, an infant is highly skilled at initiating a topic by a combination of glances, gestures, vocalizations, and verbalizations, although he or she is limited to topics about items that are physically present. At this age topics typically are maintained for only one or two turns. Only about half of the utterances of children below age 2 are on the established topic. Child utterances on the topic usually consist of imitations of the adult or of new related information. Extended topic maintenance beyond a turn or two seems to be possible only within well-established routines. These routines, such as bathing or dressing, provide a structure for the discourse, thus relieving a young child of the (for now) nearly impossible task of conversational planning.

By age 2, a child is capable of maintaining a topic in adjacent pairs of utterances. These utterances follow a pattern, such as question/answer. A mature language partner usually offers the toddler choices, as in "Do you like candy or ice cream best?"; asks questions; or makes commands or offers. In this way, the mature partner interprets events for the child and scaffolds or structures the conversation for coherence.

Between ages 2 and 3, a child gains a limited ability to maintain coherent topics. By age 3½, about three-fourths of a child's utterances are on the established topic. Topics may last through more turns when children are enacting familiar scenarios or engaging in sociodramatic play, describing a physically present object or an ongoing event, and problem solving. Shorter topics may occur when capturing someone's attention, establishing a play situation, and ensuring cooperation while assigning toys or roles. Notice the rapid topic change in the conversation in Box 8.3.

Repetition is one tactic used by preschoolers to remain on a topic. In the following conversation, the child imitates the adult skillfully:

ADULT: Later, we'll go to the store for daddy's birthday present.
CHILD: Go store for daddy's present.
ADULT: Um-hum, should we get him a new electric razor?
CHILD: Yeah, new razor.

BOX 8.3

Rapid Topic Change

DANNY IS 40 MONTHS and Matthew is 34 months.

D: What do you want for dessert? The cake is devil's food.
M: I would pick my cup.
D: Let's play with this. What is it? A puppet? A puppet!
M: I'm pooped. I'm a lion.
D: Oh.
M: I could be a wolf. I could be a wolf. Gr-r-r. I have to eat that food.
D: I'll knife the wolf. You're dead.
M: No.
D: It's my jello. Look at these toys. Let's pick them up.
M: Oh, the mirror. I see you.
D: Here's a spoon.
M: Let's be cowboys.

Even 5-year-olds continue to use frequent repetition to acknowledge, provide cohesion, and fill turns. Still, topics change quickly, and 5-year-olds may discuss as many as 50 different topics within 15 minutes.

Presuppositional: Adaptation to the Listener's Knowledge

Presupposition, as we mentioned earlier, is the process whereby a speaker makes background assumptions about a listener's knowledge. This occurs on several levels. The speaker needs to be aware of the listener's word meanings and knowledge of the social context and conversational topic. You and I can't have a meaningful conversation if you don't understand either the words I'm using or the topic. Every one of us has had to stop a speaker—usually someone close to us—at some time and say, "I don't have any idea what you're talking about." We were unable to identify the topic.

In general, a preschool child becomes increasingly adept at knowing what information to include, how to arrange it, and which particular lexical items and linguistic forms to use. This ability emerges gradually on a usage-by-usage basis rather than as a single linguistic form. Nonetheless, some linguistic forms are used as presuppositional tools. These include articles, demonstratives, pronouns, proper nouns, some verbs, *wh-* questions, and forms of address. The definite article (*the*), pronouns, demonstratives (*this, that, these, those*), and proper names refer to specific entities that, it is presupposed, both the speaker and the listener can identify.

The form of address used is based on presuppositions relative to the social situation. As speakers, we address only certain people as *dear* or *honey* or by their nicknames. These forms are not used with strangers or with people in positions of authority over us. I remember that when I was a child my grandmother and her sisters used nicknames to relate to each other, but we children were forbidden to follow this practice.

The choice of topic itself is based on an assumption of participant knowledge or at least interest. Once the topic is introduced, each participant generally presupposes that the other knows what the topic is, so there is no need to keep restating it. New topics or information are generally introduced in the final position or near the end of a sentence, marked with the indefinite article *a* or *an,* and emphasized to signal the listener, as in "Did you buy a car?"

Acquiring presuppositional skills requires learning to use many linguistic devices. Thus, the acquisition process extends well into school age.

Prior to age 3, most children do not understand the effect of not providing enough information for their listener. By age 3, however, they are generally able to determine the amount of information a listener needs. Children usually mention the most informative items first, as in the following example:

ADULT: What happened yesterday?
CHILD: I went to the doctor and got a needle. (Rather than "I got up, had breakfast, then brushed my teeth, and . . .")

Three-year-olds are able to adjust their answers based on decisions of what the listener knows and does not know. Thus, the more knowledgeable listener receives even more information and more elaborate descriptions while receiving less redundant information.

Most 3-year-olds also can distinguish between definite (*the*) and indefinite (*a, an*) articles. At this age, they use the articles with approximately 85% accuracy. If a preschooler makes errors in usage, it is usually because he or she has assumed erroneously that the listener shares the referent. For example, the child might say, "I liked *the* popsicles," the definite article being used without first introducing the referent. Are we discussing popsicles taken from the freezer or bought from a vendor? When? Where? This same error of assuming a shared referent is also evident in the use of pronouns. For example, the topic in "I liked it" is difficult to determine. Even older preschool children may point to the referent rather than identify it verbally, presupposing that the listener understands. The referent may be even more ambiguous if it is not present.

Some verbs, such as *know* and *remember,* when used before a *that + clause* construction, presuppose the truthfulness of the clause that follows. In the following sentences, the speaker is conveying a belief in the truthfulness of the ending clause:

> I know that you have a red dress.
> I remember that the cat was asleep in this chair.

Not all verbs presuppose the truth of the following clause, as in the case of "I think. . . ." In this instance, the speaker is not as certain as when he says, "I know. . . ."

Verbs such as *know, think, forget,* and *remember* are used correctly as presuppositional tools by age 4. Prior to age 4 children use *think* and *know* to regulate an interaction (*You know how*) not to refer to a mental state (*I know my letters*). At about age 3½ my granddaughter would ponder great thoughts then say things like "I think that you look a little darker" (to a suntanned Asian friend) or "I feel like playing Shrek." Children's use of these words reflects that of their mothers (Furrow, Moore, Davidge, & Chiasson, 1992). By age 5 or 6, a child understands the use of other verbs, such as *wish, guess,* and *pretend* (Moore, Harris, & Patriquin, 1993). These verbs presuppose that the following clause is false. Thus, when I say, "I wish I had a pony," it is assumed that I do not. Verbs such as *say, whisper,* and *believe* are not comprehended by most children until age 7 (Moore et al., 1993).

Questions are used to gain more information about a presupposed fact. In the example "What are you eating?" it is presupposed that the listener is eating. In "Where is the party?" the speaker presupposes that there is one and that the listener knows its location.

The presuppositions that accompany *wh-* questions seem to be learned with each *wh-* word. Children seem to be able to respond to specific *wh-* words even when they use these words infrequently in their own speech.

The use of devices, such as word order, stress, and ellipsis, changes with age. In early two-word combinations, toddlers place new information first, as in "Doggie eat," establishing *doggie* as the topic. This practice declines with longer, more adultlike utterances in favor of the more widely used last position, as in "Wasn't that a great picnic?" establishing *picnic* as the topic. Children also use stress at the two-word stage to mark new information for the listener. With age, a child becomes even more reliable in his use of this device.

Ellipsis is used more selectively and with greater sophistication as the child's language and conversations become more complex. Through **ellipsis,** mentioned previously, the speaker omits redundant information that has been previously stated, thereby assuming that the listener knows this information. For example, in response to "Who is baking cookies?" the speaker says, "I am," leaving out the redundant information "baking cookies."

Directives and Requests The purpose of directives and requests is to get others to do things for the speaker. The form can be direct or indirect, conventional, or nonconventional. Examples include:

> Stop that! (direct)
> Could you get the phone? (indirect, conventional)
> Phew, it's hot in here. (indirect, nonconventional)

*P*reschool children can express an ever-expanding set of intentions and can play a variety of language roles.

In the first example, the goal is clearly stated or direct. In the second, the form appears to be a question, although the speaker is not really interested in whether the listener has the ability to perform the task; the ability is assumed. The form is conventional and polite. Finally, in the third, an indirect nonconventional form, the goal is not mentioned and cannot be identified by strict syntactic interpretation. It's unconventional because it's not the typical way in which we ask to turn on the air conditioner.

By 2 years of age, a child is able to use some attention-getting words with gestures and rising intonation; however, he or she is often unsuccessful at gaining attention. A child tends to rely on less specific attention-getting forms, such as "Hey," frequently ignored by adults. Request words such as *more, want,* and *mine,* problem statements such as *I'm tired* and *I'm hungry,* and verbal routines are common. Two early directive types are the need statement ("Want/need . . .") and the imperative ("Give me . . ."). Few, if any, indirect forms are used. The child refers to the desired action or object. These requests become clearer with age, and the child identifies all elements of the request, not just what is desired.

Two- to 3-year-olds make politeness distinctions based on the age or size, familiarity, role, territory, and rights of the listener. Often young children will use *please* in a request, especially if the listener is older or bigger, less familiar, in a dominant role, or possessor of an object or privilege desired.

Action requests, especially indirect ones, addressed to a child are likely to be answered with the action even when information is sought. Thus, when Grandma says, "Can you sing?" and is seeking a simple "yes" response, she may get a tuneful rendition that she didn't really want. Interpretation seems to be based on past experience and on a child's knowledge of object uses and locations, activity structures, and roles.

At age 3, a child begins to use some modal auxiliary verbs in indirect requests ("*Could* you give me a . . . ?"), permissive directives ("*Can/may* I have a . . . ?"), and question directives ("*May*

I have a . . . ?"). Modals are auxiliary or helping verbs that express the speaker's attitude toward the main verb and include *may, might, must, could, should,* and so on. These forms reflect syntactic developments and a child's increasing skill at modifying language to reflect the social situation. These changes, especially the use of auxiliary verbs within interrogatives, enhance a child's skill at politeness and the use of requests. Auxiliary verb development will be discussed in Chapter 9.

A 4-year-old is more skilled with indirect forms although still unsuccessful more than half of the time at getting someone else's attention. Only about 6% of all the requests by 42- to 52-month-olds are indirect in nature, although there is a sharp increase in the use of this form at around age 4½. At around age 4, a child becomes more aware of his or her partner's point of view and role, and of the appropriate form of request and politeness required. Examples include "Why don't you . . ." and "Don't forget to. . . ." The child also offers more explanations and justifications for requests. In addition, a 4-year-old is able to respond correctly to forms such as "You should . . . ," "Please . . . ," and "I'll be happy if you . . ." (Carrell, 1981).

A desired goal may be totally masked in a 5-year-old's directive. For example, as my daughter sped to a nearly missed appointment, my 54-month-old granddaughter asked, "Is there a speed limit on this road?" Sufficiently chastised, her mom slowed accordingly. The form of the request may be very different from a child's actual intention. For example, desiring a glass of juice, a child might say, "Now, you be the mommy and make breakfast." Such inferred requests or other nonconventional forms are very infrequent, however, even in the language of 5-year-olds. In general, children rely on conventional forms and the use of markers such as *please.*

Five-year-olds continue to increase use of explanations and justifications, especially when there is a chance of noncompliance by the listener. Often the justifications are self-contained statements, such as "I need it" or "I want it," but they may refer to rights, reasons, causes, or norms. Justifications are initially found in children's attempts to stop an activity. My daughter gained neighborhood notoriety for her very precise "Stop it, because I do not like it!"

Although she or he has made tremendous gains, a preschooler is still rather ineffectual in making requests or in giving directives. He or she needs to become more efficient at gaining a potential listener's attention, more effective in stating the goal, more aware of social role, more persuasive, and more creative in forming requests. The increased complexity of a school-age child's social interactions and the new demands of the school environment require greater facility with directive and request forms.

Deixis   In ancient Greek, **deixis** means indicating or pointing. Deictic terms may be used to direct attention, to make spatial contrasts, and to denote times or participants in a conversation from the speaker's point of view. It is not easy for young children to adopt the perspective of another conversational participant. Thus, correct use of these terms indicates a child's pragmatic and cognitive growth. In this section, we discuss the development of *here/there, this/that,* and personal pronouns. As many as 30% of 7-year-olds may have difficulty comprehending some of these deictic contrasts, even those used in their own speech production.

The development of *this, that, here,* and *there* illustrates the difficulties inherent in learning these terms. Mothers use *that* and *there* more frequently than the other two, although children use all four equally. Mothers use these terms most frequently in directing their child's attention. It is not surprising, then, that children use *that* and *there* for directing attention. *There* is also used to note completion. ("There, I finished.")

Later, children use *this* and *here* for directing attention but make little differentiation based on the location of the object of interest. In mature use *this* is near; *that* is far. A child's comprehension is aided by the gestures used by adults.

Gradually, children begin to realize that these terms denote a contrast in location relative to the speaker. Adult gestures are no longer depended on for interpretation. Children still experience difficulty with the actual size of the area covered by terms such as *here*. This is made more difficult by the fact that *here* can be used for a variety of references, from "Come *here*," meaning this very spot, to "We have an environmental problem *here*," meaning on the entire earth.

There are three problems in the acquisition of deictic terms: point of reference, shifting reference, and shifting boundaries. The point of reference is generally the speaker. Hence, when you say the term *here*, you are speaking of a proximal or near area. The child must learn that the speaker is the point of reference. This introduces a potential problem, since each new speaker creates a new reference point. Terms that shift most frequently seem to be the hardest to learn.

The boundaries of *this/that* and *here/there* shift with the context and are not generally stated by the speaker. For example, the term *here* has very different boundaries in the following two sentences:

Put your money here, please.
We have a democratic form of government here.

In general, proximal terms, such as *this* and *here*, are usually easier to learn than distal terms, such as *that* and *there*. At least one deictic term—*here, there, this,* or *that*—is usually present in the first 50-word lexicon of most children.

Some pronoun contrasts develop prior to spatial deictic terms, such as *here* and *there*. The contrasts *I/you* and *my/your* develop relatively early, typically by age 2½. These terms may be easier to learn than spatial contrasts because of the relatively distinct boundaries. These pronoun meanings are integral to the concept of person.

Learning of deictic terms has three phases. In the initial phase, there is no contrast between the different dimensions. As previously discussed, terms such as *here* and *there* are used for directing attention or for referencing. In other words, deictic terms are used nondeictically. Among 2½-year-olds, deictic words seem to be used indiscriminately, with a gesture to indicate meaning. Because there are no definitive boundaries between terms such as *here* and *there*, it is difficult to determine a child's concept. As late as age 4, some children exhibit no difference between the use of *this* and *that*. Children seem to prefer to use themselves or a near point as reference.

Gradually, children develop a partial contrast. A child frequently uses the proximal term (*this, here*) correctly but overuses it for the nonproximal (*that, there*). An alternative pattern is characterized by correct child use only in reference to self or to some inconsistent point.

Finally, a child masters the full deictic contrast. The age of mastery differs for the various contrasts, and some children continue to produce deictic errors into early school age. In general, mastery of *here/there* precedes mastery of *this/that*, possibly because the latter pair contains the notion of *here/there*. Mastery of the full adult system of deixis requires several years.

Intentions

As might be expected from the preceding sections, a preschool child's comprehension and production of intentions increases. Although preschoolers become increasingly skilled in comprehending the intentions of others, even 5-year-olds must still rely on gestures for some interpretation (Kelly, 2001). By about 30 months, the relative frequency of the six large pragmatic categories—representational, control, expressive, procedural, social, and tutorial, found in Table 7.3—stabilizes throughout the rest of the preschool period. The control and representational functions account for 70% of all child utterances. Among 30-month-olds, statements or assertions may outnumber direct requests by as much as three to one (Golinkoff, 1993). Table 8.2 lists the major intentions mastered by preschoolers. Developmental trends are presented in Figures 8.1 and 8.2.

The representational category is dominated by the *statement* function, which gradually increases to 50% of all representational utterances and roughly 20% of all utterances by age 5. The earlier dominance of *naming* in toddler language no longer exists, and these utterances, as might be expected, account for very few representational utterances by age 5. Other representational functions used by at least 90% of 5-year-olds include *content questions* ("What . . . ?" "Where . . . ?"), *content responses* or answers, and *yes/no questions* ("Is this a cheeseburger?").

Within the control function, there is great diversity. The *wanting* function that dominated in toddler language decreases rapidly after 24 months of age. In contrast, *direct requesting* continues a slow increase until around 39 months, when its frequency levels off at 25% of all control utterances but remains the dominant control function throughout the preschool years. Other control intentions used by at least 90% of 5-year-olds include *prohibition* ("Don't do that"), *intention* ("I'm going to put it in"), *request permission* ("Can I have one?"), *suggestion* ("Should we have ice cream?"), *physical justification* ("I can't 'cause the dollie's there"), offer ("Do you want this one?"), and *indirect request* ("Will you pour the juice?").

Expressive functions used by at least 90% of 5-year-olds include *exclamation, expressive state,* and *verbal accompaniment,* all noted previously in toddler language (Table 7.3). Procedural functions used by at least 90% of 5-year-olds include *call, contingent query,* and *elicited repetition,* in which a child repeats the speaker's utterance with a rising intonation ("Daddy will be home soon?"↑). Finally, the *social* and *tutorial* functions together account for less than 4% of the child's utterances at age 5.

TABLE *8.2* *Intentions Exhibited by 90% of Children*

INTENTION	AGE AT WHICH 90% OF CHILDREN USE INTENTION (IN MONTHS)
Exclamation and call	18
Ostention (naming)	21
Wanting, direct request, and statement	24
Content question	30
Prohibition, intention, content response, expressive state, and elicited repetition	33
Yes/no question, verbal accompaniment, and contingent query	36
Request permission	45
Suggestion	48
Physical justification	54
Offer an indirect request	57

Source: Information from Wells (1985).

FIGURE *8.1* *Communication Functions as a Percentage of All Utterances*

Note that the Representational and Control functions predominate throughout the preschool years, accounting for approximately 65% of all utterances by age 5 years. The Representational function includes statements and questions. Within the Control function are demands, requests, and statements of prohibition.

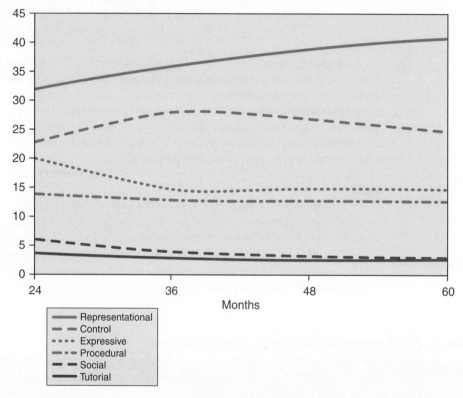

Source: Information from Wells (1985).

NARRATIVES

Oral narratives or stories are an uninterrupted stream of language modified by the speaker to capture and hold the listener's interest. Unlike a conversation, the narrator maintains a social monolog throughout, producing language relevant to the overall narrative while presupposing the information needed by the listener. **Narratives** include self-generated stories; telling of familiar tales; retelling of books, movies, or television shows; and recounting of personal experiences. Most adult conversations include narratives of this latter type, possibly beginning with "You'll never believe what happened to me. . . ." Common in the conversations of preschoolers, narratives aid children in constructing their own autonomous selves as portrayed in their stories (Wiley, Rose, Burger, & Miller, 1998).

Although conversation and narratives share many elements, such as a sense of purpose, relevant information, clear and orderly exchange of information, repair, and the ability to assume the perspective of the listener, they differ in very significant ways. Conversations are dialogs, while narratives are essentially decontextualized monologs. *Decontextualization* means

FIGURE *8.2* **Most Common Intentions as a Percentage of All Utterances**

Ostension or naming predominates at age 2 years but quickly decreases. Wanting also decreases as Direct Requests increase to fill the Control function. While other intentions change some between ages 24 and 60 months, the largest change is seen in the increase in Statements, which are nearly 20% of all utterances by age 5 years.

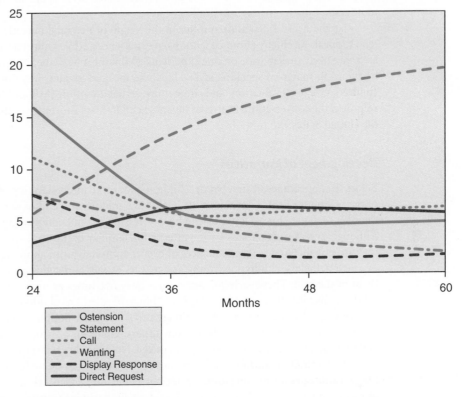

Months

—— Ostension
— — Statement
•••• Call
—•— Wanting
— — Display Response
—— Direct Request

Source: Information from Wells (1985).

that the language does not center on some immediate experience within the context. Instead, language creates the context of a narrative.

Narratives contain organizational patterns not found in conversation. In order to share the experience, the speaker must present an explicit, topic-centered discussion that clearly states the relationships between events. Thus, events are linked to one another in a predictable manner.

Narratives usually concern people, animals, or imaginary characters engaged in events. Conversations usually involve activities in the immediate context.

Other differences include the narrative use of extended units of story text; introductory and organizing sequences that lead to a narrative conclusion; and the relatively passive role of the listener, who provides only minimal informational support in our culture. The narrative speaker is responsible for organizing and providing all of the information in an organized whole. It is not surprising, therefore, that narratives are found more frequently in the communication of more mature speakers.

Possibly even more than conversations, narratives reflect the cultures from which they emerge. Within the United States, middle-class children are encouraged to elaborate on their own experiences and to express opinions on these experiences. In contrast, working-class children are also encouraged to tell personal narratives but are not automatically given the right to express their own views or opinions (Wiley et al., 1998).

In talking about a book with their mothers and subsequent independent retelling of the story, older preschool children's story retelling skills are related to the extent to which mothers encouraged their active participation during joint book reading (Kang, Kim, & Alexander Pan, 2009). Children's responsive is closely associated with types of talking used by their mothers.

Japanese and U.S. children differ in the length of personal narratives. Japanese children tend to speak succinctly about collections of experiences, while children from the United States are more likely to elaborate on one experience (Minami & McCabe, 1991). A possible link may be found in maternal speaking styles. Japanese mothers request less information from their children, give less evaluation, and show more verbal attention (Minami & McCabe, 1995). In response, the conversational turns of Japanese children are shorter than those of children from the United States.

Development of Narratives

Before the appearance of first words, children have some understanding of familiar events and of the positions of some actions at the beginning, middle, and end of sequences. For example, there's a sequence for taking a bath with undressing at the beginning and drying at the end. Although 2-year-olds possess basic patterns for familiar events and sequences, called *scripts*, they are not able to describe sequences of events accurately until about age 4.

Nonetheless, children as young as age 2 to 3½ talk about things that have happened to them in the past. These early *protonarratives* have five times as much evaluative information ("I didn't like it," "It was yukky," "I cried," "I hate needles") as children's regular conversation. Between ages 2 and 2½, the number of these protonarratives doubles, and children begin to sequence events with very little help from others. Children also begin to tell self-generated, *fictional* narratives between 2 and 3 years of age. Note the short narrative in Box 8.4.

The overall organization of a narrative is called the **narrative level.** In general, children use two strategies for organization: centering and chaining. **Centering** is the linking of entities to form a story nucleus. Links may be based on similarity of features. **Chaining** consists of a sequence of events that share attributes and lead directly from one to another.

Most of the stories of 2-year-olds are organized by centering. The stories usually center on certain highlights in a child's life and may have a vague plot. Frequently, children tell of events that they find disruptive or extraordinary. Considering the listener only minimally, a preschooler demonstrates little need to introduce, to explore with, or to orient the audience. Thus, these stories often lack easily identifiable beginnings, middles, and ends.

By age 3, however, nearly half of children use both centering and chaining. This percentage increases, and by age 5, nearly three-fourths of the children use both strategies.

BOX 8.4

A Short Narrative by a 52-Month-Old Child

THE JOKE IS ... UM ... I did it this morning on daddy. I said, "Daddy, I pulled my teeth out." He said um, "Where is it?" And then I said, "April Fools!" It's April Fools Day.

Initially, identification of the participants, time, and location may be nonexistent or minimal. Although these elements improve with maturity, even children of 3½ may not identify all story participants (Peterson, 1990). In part, this may result from the fact that most self-generated stories involve individuals well known to the child and to most listeners, thus there is no need to identify them. A sense of time frame is also vague or nonexistent initially but improves with the use of terms such as *yesterday* or *last year,* even though these terms may be used inaccurately. Location is more commonly identified, especially when the narrative events occurred in the home. With maturity, preschool children become better able to identify out-of-home locations.

The organizational strategies of 2-year-olds represent centering *heaps,* sets of unrelated statements about a central stimulus, consisting of one sentence added to another. Although there is no overall organizational pattern, there may be a similarity in the grammatical structure of the sentences:

> The doggie go "woof." The cow go "moo." The man ride tractor—"Bpt-bpt-bpt."

There is no story line, no sequencing, and no cause and effect. The sentences may be moved anywhere in the text without changing the overall meaning. Heaps may also be used to describe a scene.

Somewhat later, preschoolers begin to tell narratives characterized as centering *sequences.* These include events linked on the basis of similar attributes or events that create a simple but meaningful focus for a story. The organization is additive, not temporal or time based, and sentences may be moved without altering the narrative:

> I ate a hamburger (Mimes eating). Mommy threw the ball, like this. Daddy taked me swimming (Moves hand, acts silly). I had two sodas.

In these early stories, there is a dominance of performance and qualities, such as movement, sound production, and prosody. Gradually, between ages 3 and 7 years, children's narratives increase in the use of prose and plots.

Temporal, or time-based, event chains emerge between ages 3 and 5 years. In these narratives, events follow a logical sequence. *Primitive temporal narratives* are organized around a center with complementary events:

> We went to the parade. There was a big elephant. And tanks (Moves arm like turret). The drum was loud. There was a clown in a little car (Hand gestures "little"). And I got a balloon. And we went home.

Although there is sequencing, there is no plot and no cause and effect or causality.

Narratives are event descriptions based on underlying event scripts. Event description, such as explaining how to make cookies, involves more than just describing single events in a sequential order. To describe the sets of sequences that form the total event, the speaker must be able to describe single events and event combinations and relationships and to indicate the significance of each event within the overall **event structure.** For example, the event structure for a day at the beach involves event sequences for getting ready, preparing the picnic, riding in the car, finding a spot on the beach, and so on.

Descriptions of entire events are based on a framework of scripts. Scripts based on actual events form an individual's expectations about sequences and impose order on event information. These familiar activity sequences or scripts consist of ordered events within routine or high-frequency activities. As such, scripts influence interpretation and telling of events and narratives. By age 3, children are able to describe chains of events within familiar activities, such as a birthday party. Theoretically, scripts are similar across members of the same culture based on their common experiences.

The speaker must have knowledge of both single events and connected sequences, the linguistic knowledge of the method for describing events, and the linguistic and cognitive skill to consider the listener's perspective. Linguistic devices that speakers use include marking of beginnings and endings, marking of aspect, and modal auxiliary verbs. Beginnings can be marked by words or phrases such as *once upon a time, guess what happened to me, let's start at the beginning,* and so on. Endings include *the end, all done,* and *and that's how it happened.* Aspect and modal auxiliary verbs will be explained in detail in Chapter 9. Let's just say that aspect has to do with referencing time from inside the narrative and modal auxilary or helping verbs express mood or attitude as in *could* versus *should.*

The elements of event knowledge are seen in the narratives of 4-year-olds. Underlying every story is an *event chain.* Events include actions, physical states such as possession and attribution, and mental states such as emotions, dispositions, thoughts, and intentions that may be causally linked as motivations, enablements, initiations, and resultants in the chain.

Narratives characterized as *unfocused temporal chains* lead directly from one event to another while other attributes—characters, settings, and actions—shift. This is the first level of chaining, and the links are concrete. As a result of the shifting focus, unfocused chains have no centers:

> The man got in the boat. He rowed. A big storm knocked over the trees—whish-sh, boom. The doggie had to swim. Fishies jumped out of the water. He had warm milk. And then he went to bed.

Temporal chains frequently include third-person pronouns (*he, she, it*); past-tense verbs; temporal conjunctions such as *and, then,* and *and then*; and a definite beginning and ending.

Focused temporal or causal chains generally center on a main character who goes through a series of perceptually linked, concrete events:

> There is this horsie. He eats—munch, munch—hay for breakfast. He runs out of the barn. Then he plays in the sun. He rolls in the warm grass. He comes in for dinner. He sleeps in a bed (Mimes sleep).

Causal chains, in which one event causes or has caused another, are infrequent until age 5 and will be discussed later.

By the time children begin school, most have acquired the basic elements of narratives and can recount sequentially familiar or significant events. These narratives form much of the content of the conversations later encountered in older children and adults.

THEORY OF MIND

As you may recall, Theory of Mind (ToM) is the ability to attribute and infer mental states in other people (wishes, beliefs, knowledge, or emotions). There is a close relationship between ToM and communicative abilities (Astington, 2003; Hughes & Dunn, 1998; Welch-Ross, 1997). In short, the capacity to consider mental states in others seems to be a key factor that regulates communicative exchanges. Still, the nature of the relationship is not completely understood. For example, early linguistic development seems to have a role in children's subsequent development of ToM (Astington & Jenkins, 1999; Lohmann & Tomasello, 2003).

*T*he development of narratives, as well as more complicated aspects of semantic development, are generally accomplished by age 5.

In contrast, other studies suggest that the development of ToM facilitates both interpersonal relationships and communicative interchanges (Slomkowski & Dunn, 1996; Welch-Ross, 1997). These findings suggest that as children grow in their ability to establish relationships between their own mental concepts and those of others, they are more able to understand conversations as a "meeting of the minds" in which being aware of your partner's intentions and informational needs is essential.

In general, older children with more mature ToM abilities take part in sophisticated pretend play more frequently, use more mental state terms (*sad, angry*) in their everyday conversations, and are considered by their teachers as having more developed social and interactive abilities (Astington & Jenkins, 1995; Hughes & Dunn, 1998; Lalonde & Chandler, 1995; Slomkowski & Dunn, 1996). Although it is difficult to determine whether ToM abilities cause better communication or the opposite, it is clear that both require similar sociocognitive abilities.

Apologies are an interesting example of how children become more attuned to their listener. Children are exposed to apology terms primarily through apologies directed to them and also to a lesser degree through talk about apologies. Before age 2, apologies are rare. Parents play a roll in acquisition in apologetic behavior. As children move through the preschool years into early elementary school, there is a decrease in directly elicited apologies by parents (*Tell John you're sorry*) and an increase in indirectly elicited ones (*How do you think John feels?*). With age children's apologies also became more elaborate (Ely & Berko Gleason, 2006).

Children cannot comprehend the desires or emotions of others until they are aware of their own. Thus, self-awareness develops in parallel with ToM (Eslea, 2002). First, at about 18 months, children learn to recognize themselves and then, about six months later, to express their own emotional states. Ever notice a toddler attempting to "hide" by covering his or her eyes? The child has not made a distinction between self and others. Here's another example from a telephone conversation with a 3-year-old (Eslea, 2002):

ADULT: What have you been doing today?
CHILD: Playing with this.
ADULT: Oh, right. What is it?
CHILD: THIS!!!

It's common for children at this age to fail to realize that other people cannot always see what they can see.

At age 2 children are able to express their own emotions verbally, and to begin in pretend play to recognize emotions in others. Most 4-year-olds can relate the emotions of others to desires or intentions and can understand that others may have a different perspective on the world from their own (Eslea, 2002). The development of Theory of Mind has profound importance for the development of language, cognition, and social understanding. The understanding that others have knowledge and beliefs different from your own is a major developmental breakthrough.

There is an important change in social cognition in the late preschool years (Wellman, 2002; Wellman & Liu, 2004). Between the ages of 3 and 5 years, children move from an initial incapacity for differentiating between different points of view, through a capacity for making general judgments about what their partners know or do not, to a capacity for taking into account that ignorance or a lack of information may lead to false beliefs by others (Wellman & Liu, 2004). Understanding of false belief seems to be the most powerful predictor of changes in older preschool children's development of communicative competence (Resches & Pérez Pereira, 2007).

As children become more aware of the thoughts and emotions of others, their narrative portrayals change. At age 3, they represent characters in their stories almost exclusively as actors and describe them by physical and external characteristics. By age 4, characters begin to exhibit rudimentary mental states, which are expanded by age 5 (Nicolopoulou & Richner, 2007).

In general, the language of preschool children with poorer ToM abilities is more ambiguous or incomplete and poorly adapted to the listener's previous knowledge and informational needs. In contrast, children with higher ToM abilities offer clear, simple directions and precise descriptions that are better adapted and more relevant to the aims of the task, the listener's needs, and their own role in the communication task (Resches & Pérez Pereira, 2007). Comments and questions are used to check on the information held by and point of view of the listener. In addition, those children with higher ToM abilities were better in determining their listeners' misunderstandings or lack of understanding and more efficient in repairing them, often with reformulated information rather than simple repetition.

Exhibition of ToM in 4-year-olds corresponds with activation of the anterior medial portion of the frontal lobe and the juncture of the temporal and parietal lobes in the right hemisphere (Figure 8.3) (Sabbagh, Bowman, Evraire, & Ito, 2009). While the right temporoparietal junction in preschool and early elementary children seems to be activated for interpretation of both thought and movement by others, by age 11 this area of the brain seems involved primarily in interpretation of others' thoughts (Saxe, Whitfield-Gabrieli, Scholz, & Pelphrey, 2009).

Maternal speaking style has the potential to promote or hinder children's understanding of the mind and subsequent development of ToM. For example, among 3-year-olds, the nonpreschool children perform significantly better on mental verb (*think, know, remember*) comprehension task than children in preschool and use fewer mental state statements and more questions, fewer first-person utterances (*I, me*) and more second-person utterances (*you*), and less use of the verb *think* in its "very certain" form (*I think this so you should*) less often. Greater understanding of the mind was positively associated to maternal mental verb questions (*What*

FIGURE *8.3* **Right Hemisphere and Theory of Mind**

Areas of the right hemisphere activated in 4-year-olds and believed to be associated with emergence of Theory of Mind (ToM). Information drawn from Sabbagh et al. (2009).

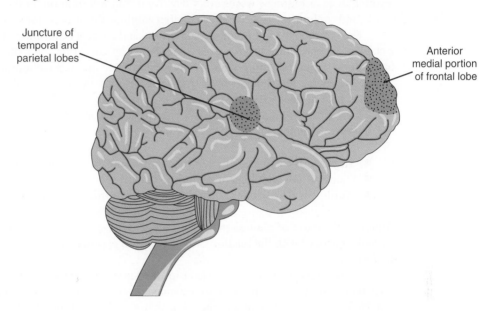

Juncture of temporal and parietal lobes

Anterior medial portion of frontal lobe

do you think?) and single-clause utterances and negatively associated with maternal statements (Howard, Mayeux, & Naigles, 2008).

SUMMARY

Although there is a considerable difference among families and across cultures in the overall amount of talking, there are certain overall patterns. To some extent, the amount of talking is a function of the energy level of a child and his or her conversational partners. Therefore, the largest proportion of talking occurs in the morning shortly after breakfast. The amount of talking is also related to the activity in progress. Most preschool speech accompanies solitary play or play with others or occurs within activities devoted primarily to conversation. The amount of talking within these latter activities increases throughout the preschool years. In contrast, relatively less talking occurs while either game or role playing, looking at books or television, or doing chores. In general, preschool boys play more alone, talking to themselves and calling bystanders to notice this play. In contrast, girls engage more in household activities and play and are drawn into talk while organizing the task at hand.

Throughout the preschool years, a child learns to become a truer conversational partner, using a greater variety of forms to attain desired ends. In addition, a child expands presuppositional skills and is better able to take the perspective of the other participant. Although he or she can take conversational turns without being prompted with a question, a child still tends to make more coherent contributions to the conversation if discussing an ongoing activity in which engaged at the time. A child is more aware of social roles at age 5 than at age 2 and can adjust his or her speech for younger children or for role playing, but lacks many of the subtleties of older children and adults. As he or she begins to attend school, a child will be under increasing pressure by both teachers and peers to use language even more effectively.

Semantic Development

When we think about word learning in an abstract way, it seems impossibly difficult. Imagine learning three or four new words every day. Try it. You will soon tire of the task, forget some words, and confuse others. Yet, young children continue this process for years.

The preschool period is one of rapid lexical and concept acquisition. It is estimated that a child adds approximately five words to his or her lexicon or personal dictionary every day between the ages of 1½ and 6 years. Word meanings are inferred without direct teaching by adults. In general, preschoolers with larger vocabularies are more popular with their peers (Gertner, Rice, & Hadley, 1994).

Several factors influence children's knowledge of words between 16 and 30 months of age. In general, children know

- More words composed of low-probability sounds and sound pairs.
- Shorter words with high neighborhood density.
- Words that were semantically related to other words. (Storkel, 2009)

Although the effect of phonology is constant across age, the effect of lexical and semantic variables changed with the relation of new words to existing words becoming more important with age.

At age 2, several processes seem to be involved in word learning: word frequency, word segmentation, fast mapping, and a longer, extended process whereby the word meaning is fleshed out (Hoff & Naigles, 2002; Huttenlocher, Haight, Bryk, Seltzer, & Lyons, 1991). For example, there is a strong relationship between the frequency of mothers' use of content words at 16 months and the age at which a child produces a word. More frequent words are produced earlier.

Word segmentation or dividing words into phonemes and morphemes is simplified when mothers place words in highly salient or easily noticeable or important positions, such as the final position in an utterance (Aslin, 1999; Choi, 2000; Choi & Gopnik, 1995; Shady & Gerken, 1999; Smiley & Huttenlocher, 1995; Tardif et al., 1997). For example, mothers use the final position to highlight new or unfamiliar words (Cleave & Kay-Raining Bird, 2006; Fernald & Mazzie, 1991). In addition, mothers place unfamiliar nouns in shorter utterance than familiar nouns.

Fast mapping is the initial word-referent relationship or word "meaning" created by a child based on limited exposure to a word (Bedore & Leonard, 2000; Houston-Price et al., 2005; Kay-Raining Bird & Chapman, 1998; Merriman, Marazita, & Jarvis, 1995).

It is possible that a preschool child employs **initial- or fast-mapping** strategy that enables him or her to infer a connection between a word and its referent or entity referred to after only one exposure. Initial acquisition is receptive in nature. Obviously, only a small portion of the overall meaning goes into a child's memory after only one exposure. The actual information is affected by both the world and word knowledge of a preschooler. Not all words are learned with the same ease. In general, nouns seem to be easier to fast map than verbs.

Words may be fast-mapped using one or more of the following strategies (Storkel, 2001):

- The range of possible meanings may be constrained by the situation and also by the meanings already possessed by a child (Golinkoff et al., 1994; Waxman & Kosowski, 1990). Using reasoning similar to the novel name–no name strategy mentioned in Chapter 6, a child would reason that the definition cannot be the same as one already possessed.

■ An associational strategy might be used in which the regularities in the language, such as word order and bound morphemes, give him or her clues as to the meaning (Samuelson & Smith, 1998; Schafer & Plunkett, 1998).

■ A child may use phonotactic probability or the likelihood of occurrence of different sound sequences to aid rapid recall of newly learned words (Storkel, 2002, 2003).

On one family vacation, my 54-month-old granddaughter commented on my partner's broken "arm." I corrected her with the word *wrist* and offered an explanation. After a few seconds, she added, "I have another wrist," while pointing at her ankle. She had overextended the meaning based on a quick analysis of the physical function of a wrist.

Fast mapping may be the first in a two-step process of lexical acquisition. First, the child roughs out a tentative definition connecting the word and available information. This step may be followed by an extended phase in which a child gradually refines the definition with new information acquired on subsequent encounters. Retrieval may be affected by the nature of the referent, the frequency of exposure to the word, the form and content of the utterance in which it occurs, and the context.

Fuller word meanings are derived from use by both a child and others. Mothers place words in a variety of syntactic forms. For example, greater variety of sentences into which a word is used by mothers is highly correlated with future use of that verb by their children (Naigles & Hoff-Ginsberg, 1998). Similarly, among 2-year-old children, longer maternal utterances are correlated with larger child vocabularies ten weeks later (Hoff & Naigles, 2002).

Most likely, young children learn single words as unique units, each with its own meaning, probably unrelated to other word meanings. Although these word meanings lack relationship, the system is simple and easy to use.

Children may use two operating principles to establish meanings: *contrast* and *conventionality* (Clark, 1990). Contrast is the assumption that every form—morpheme, word, syntactic structure—contrasts to every other in meaning. A speaker chooses a form because it means something other than what some other expression means. In other words, it contrasts to other options. Conventionality is the expectation that certain forms will be used to convey certain meanings, such as *-ing* to convey action.

Taken together, the two principles predict that, whenever possible, children will use established forms with conventional meanings that contrast clearly to other forms. Difficulty occurs when a well-established form has a meaning similar to that of a newly learned form. Thus, it may be easier for children to form unrelated unique meanings initially.

New word meanings come from both linguistic and nonlinguistic contexts (Au, 1990) and from the surrounding syntactic structure (Naigles, 1990). Let's assume that a child hears the following sentence: "Bring me the *chromium* tray, not the red one" (Gathercole, 1989, p. 694). He or she might proceed through the following steps to differentiate the meaning:

1. Assume that Mommy is trying to communicate with me.
2. Unknown word used in reference to trays as descriptor.
3. Only observable difference between the trays is color.
4. Chromium must be a color.
5. One tray is red.
6. Must not have wanted red tray or would have asked for it.
7. Therefore, must want other than red tray, which is chromium in color.

Preschoolers' noun definitions often include physical properties, such as shape, size, and color; functional properties or what the entity does; use properties; and locational properties, such as *on trees* or *at the beach*. Often missing are superordinate categories, as in *a car is a vehicle*; relationships to other entities, as in *a mouse is much smaller than a cat*; internal constituents, as in *an apple has seeds inside*; origins, as in *hatch from eggs*; and metaphorical uses, as in *suspicious things are called "fishy."* Adult and older school-age children's definitions contain all these elements.

Preschool verb definitions also differ from those of adults or older children. A preschooler can explain who or what does the action, to what or whom it's done, and where, when, and with what it's done. Usually missing is how and why it's done and a description of the process found in full adult definitions. In languages as different as Korean and English, it appears that preschool children learn novel verbs by noticing the differences, especially the objects used with each verb (Childers & Paik, 2009).

Verbs may be initially mapped based on the number and type of morphological ending applied (Bedore & Leonard, 2000; Behrend, Harris, & Cartwright, 1995). The number of verb endings varies across languages from English, with very few—making fast mapping of verbs easy—to languages such as Spanish that have many verb inflections. Children tend to use the *-ing* ending on action verbs and *-ed* on verbs denoting results of events. In order to generalize verb meanings, a child must be able to extend the verb to other outcomes and manners of action (Forbes & Poulin-DuBois, 1997).

When gaps exist in preschoolers' vocabularies either because they've forgotten or never knew a word, children invent words. For example, verbs might be created from nouns to produce the following:

> I'm *spooning* my cocoa. (Stirring)
> You *sugared* your coffee. (Sweetened)

In the preschoolers' defense, English allows this practice with some nouns, as in *paddling a canoe, shoeing a horse,* and *suiting up,* to name a few. Production of invented words seems to follow from children's construction of compound words from two or more known single ones, as in *doghouse, birdhouse,* and *fish-house* (aquarium). In both cases, production demonstrates recognition of word formulation.

Most invented words reflect adult practices, so *fisherman* and *policeman* may be reflected in *cookerman* (chef) and *pianoman* (pianist), or overgeneralization, so *house-houses* may be extended to *mouse-mouses*.

Late preschool children sometimes invent compound words that are unique in form, such as *drive-trucker*. These may reflect a child's greater familiarity with the verb-object (*drive trucker*) word order when trying to produce the complex object-verb-er (*truckdriver*) order (Murphy & Nicoladis, 2006).

Although vocabulary growth between ages 1 and 3 years is positively related to the diversity of words in the mother's speech and to maternal language and literacy skills, it is not related to the overall amount of maternal talkativeness (Pan, Rowe, Singer, & Snow, 2005).

Children also expand their vocabularies through parental storybook reading. Especially helpful for children are discussions with the reader that accompany the narrative (Senechal, 1997). Even low levels of language participation, such as naming and describing, as well as reasoning and making inferences, can have a positive effect on the child's subsequent language use (van Kleeck, Gillam, Hamilton, & McGrath, 1997).

As a child's lexicon expands, the need for better cognitive organization increases and some semantic networks or interrelationships are formed. Relationships may consist of words for referents found in the same context, such as *spoon, bowl, cup,* and *table,* or word associations, such as *stop and go, rise and shine,* and *red, white, and blue.* Preschoolers demonstrate these relationships in their inappropriate use of words and in word substitutions, such as using *spoon* to refer to a fork.

RELATIONAL TERMS

The acquisition of relational terms, such as those for location and time, is a complex process. In general, the order of acquisition is influenced by the syntactic complexity, the amount of adult usage in a child's environment, and the underlying cognitive concept. We shall briefly consider interrogatives or questions, temporal relations, physical relations, locational prepositions, and kinship terms.

Interrogatives

Children's responses to different types of questions and their production of these same types have a similar order of development. Early question forms include *what* and *where,* followed by *who, whose,* and *which,* and finally by *when, how,* and *why.* Most of the later forms involve concepts of cause, manner, or time. Their late appearance can be traced to the late development of these concepts. In other words, a child must have a concept of time in order to comprehend or to answer *when* questions. Occasionally, however, a preschoolar responds to or asks questions without fully understanding the underlying meaning. Children seem to be employing the following answering strategy: If the word meaning is unknown, answer on the basis of the verb. Unaware of the meaning of *when,* the child might respond to "When are you going to eat?" with "A cookie!"

Semantic features of the verb are particularly important for certain types of child answers. For example, the verb *touch* is more likely to elicit a response focusing on what was touched, where it was touched, and for what reason regardless of the question. Other verbs elicit different responses, with little regard for the *wh-* question form employed. Preschool children rely heavily on contextual information when answering questions and become increasingly better at integrating this information with linguistic cues (Ryder & Leinonen, 2003).

Even young school-age children have difficulty answering some forms of *wh-* questions that they seem to comprehend. Recognition of the general type of information requested may precede the ability to give acceptable and accurate answers.

Causal, or "why"-type, questions may be especially difficult for a preschool child because of the reverse-order thinking required in the response. The 3-year-old child experiences difficulty reversing the order of sequential events. Yet it is this type of response that is required for the *why* interrogative. For example, "Why did you hit Randy?" requires a response explaining the events that preceded the fist fight. It is not unusual to hear a 3-year-old respond " 'Cause he hit me back," a consequence, demonstrating an inability to reverse the order.

Temporal Relations

Temporal terms such as *when, before, since,* and *while* can convey information on the order, duration, and simultaneity of events. The order of acquisition of these terms is related to their use and to the concept each represents. In general, words of order, such as *after* and *before,* precede words of duration, such as *since* and *until.* These, in turn, precede terms of simultaneity, such as *while.* This hierarchy reflects a sequence of cognitive development.

Preschool children gain a sense of order before they have a sense of duration. Five-year-olds understand *before* and *after* better than simultaneous terms such as *at the same time* (see Table 8.3).

Temporal terms are initially produced as prepositions and then as conjunctions joining clauses. Thus, the child will produce a sentence such as "You go *after* me" before he says, "You can go home *after* we eat dinner." It is not uncommon for even 6½-year-olds to have difficulty with some of the syntactic structures used with *before* and *after* to link clauses.

When the meaning of a temporal term is unknown, the preschool child tends to rely on the order of mention. Employing this strategy, a 3-year-old will interpret the following sentences as all having the same meaning:

Before you go to school, stop at the store.
Go to school before you stop at the store.
After you go to school, stop at the store.
Go to school after you stop at the store.

In the first and last examples, note that the desired order of occurrence of events is the reverse of the word order stated.

A second interpretive strategy used by older preschool and some school-aged children reflects a syntactic approach. The child adopts a strategy in which the main clause becomes the first event. For example, the sentence "After arriving home, *Oz bought a paper*" would be interpreted as "Oz bought a paper, then he arrived home." Main and subordinate clauses are discussed in more detail in Chapter 9.

When all else fails, a child relies on knowledge of real-life sequences. For example, you wake up before eating breakfast. This strategy of comprehension works as long as the utterance conforms to a child's experiential base.

Preschoolers generally do not follow multiple directions well, as in "First do X, then Y, and then Z." Children 3½ to 5 years of age often omit one of the steps. This behavior may

TABLE *8.3* *Summary of Comprehension of Locational and Temporal Relationships*

AGE (MONTHS)	RELATIONSHIPS UNDERSTOOD
24	Locational prepositions *in* and *on*
36	Locational preposition *under*
40	Locational preposition *next to*
48 (approx.)	Locational prepositions *behind, in back of,* and *in front of,* difficulty with *above, below,* and *at the bottom of*; kinship terms *mother, father, sister,* and *brother* (last two are nonredprocating)
60	Temporal terms *before* and *after*
60+ (school-age)	Additional locational prepositions in temporal expressions, such as *in a week*; most major kinship terms by age 10; more precise locational directives reference the body (*left* and *right*)

be more common than order reversal and may reflect the limited short-term memory and cognitive-processing capacity of preschool children.

Physical Relations

Relational terms such as *thick/thin, fat/skinny, more/less,* and *same/different* are frequently difficult for preschool children to learn. In general, a child first learns that the terms are opposites, then the dimensions to which each term refers. The order of acquisition may be based on semantic–syntactic relations and the cognitive relations expressed. Terms such as *big* and *little* refer to general size on any dimension and would be acquired before more specific terms, such as *deep* and *shallow,* which refer physically to bodies of water. In other words, less specific terms are usually learned first.

The positive member, such as *big* or *long,* of each relational pair, as in *big/little* and *long/short,* represents the presence of the entity that it describes (size and length, respectively) and is learned first. The presence of size is *big,* the positive term. The negative aspect or the absence of size is *little.* A general order of acquisition is presented in Table 8.4.

The child seems to learn by accumulating individual examples of each term. Hence, understanding may be restricted to specific objects even if it appears to be more adultlike.

Learning and interpretation of descriptive terms is dependent on context. For example, 2-year-olds understand *big* and *little* used in comparing the size of two objects or judging an object's size for a particular task. It is more difficult for a child to recall the size of a nonpresent entity. This changes, of course, as memory improves.

Terms such as *more/less* and *same/different* pose a different problem for a preschool child. There may be an underlying concept for *more/less* in which a young preschool child interprets both terms to mean amount. When presented with a selection task, preschoolers tend to pick the larger grouping, whether cued with *more* or with *less.*

Conceptual development seems equally important for the acquisition of *same* and *different.* The ability to make same/different judgments seems to be related to development of *conservation,* the ability to attend to more than one perceptual dimension without relying strictly on physical evidence. Without this ability, young preschoolers experience difficulty making same/different distinctions.

TABLE *8.4 Order of Acquisition of Physical Relationships*

Hard/soft
Big/little, heavy/light
Tall/short, long/short
Large/small
High/low
Thick/thin
Wide/narrow
Deep/shallow

Locational Prepositions

A child understands different spatial relations before beginning to speak about them. The exact nature of that comprehension is unknown, since a child as old as 3½ still relies on gestures to convey much locational meaning. The first English prepositions, *in, on,* and *to* appear at around 2 years of age. When a child does not comprehend these prepositions, he or she seems to follow these interpretive strategies: *If it's a container, something belongs inside* and *if it's a supporting surface, something belongs on it.* Thus, children may respond in relation to the objects mentioned rather than the prepositions used. Other possible interpretive cues may be the word order of adult utterances and the context. Using these rules, children respond in predictable ways.

Children 18 months of age seem to base their hypotheses about word meanings on these strategies. As a result, they act as if they understand *in* all the time, *on* with surfaces but not containers, and *under* not at all. By age 3, most children have figured out the meanings of all three prepositions. When 3- and 4-year-olds are faced with more complex prepositions such as *above, below, in front of,* or *at the bottom of,* however, they tend to revert to these strategies again.

Terms such as *next to* or *in front of* offer special problems. For example, *next to* includes, but is not limited to, *in front of, behind,* and so on. In turn, these terms differ in relation to the locations to which they refer. With fronted objects, such as a chair or a digital monitor, locational terms take their reference from the object. For example, *in front of the TV* means *in front of the screen.* With nonfronted objects, such as a saucer, the term takes its location from the speaker's perspective. Interpretation requires a certain level of social skill on the part of the listener, who must be able to adopt the perspective of the speaker. *Next to* is usually learned at about 40 months, followed by *behind, in back of,* and *in front of* around age 4 (see Table 8.3). Children seem to use fronting and the height of the object as cues for initial interpretation.

A 3-year-old child interprets most prepositions of movement to mean *toward.* Hence, the child at first favors *to* over *from, into* over *out of,* and *onto* over *off.* Terms that signal movement *toward* are easier than their opposites.

Syntactic form may also affect acquisition. Prior to age 4, *in, on,* and *over* often are used predominantly as prepositions for object location while *up, down,* and *off* are used both as locational prepositions and verb particles. A *verb particle* is a multiword grammatical unit that functions as a verb, such as *stand up, sit down,* and *take off.* Thus, there is opportunity for confusion and a lack of consistency.

Kinship Terms

A preschooler gains very limited knowledge of kinship terms that refer to family members, such as *dad, sister,* and *brother.* At first a child treats the term as part of the person's name. For a while, my children called me "daddybob." In this stage a child does not possess the components of the kinship term. Initially, for a child, terms are related to specific individuals and to a child's personal experience.

Next, a child gains some features of the definition of the person but not of the relationship. For example, "A grandmother is someone who smells like flowers and wears funny underwear" (an actual child's definition).

A child gains a few of the less complex relationships first (Table 8.5). Complexity may be thought of as the number of shared features. For example, *father* has the features *male* and *parent,* but *aunt,* a more complex term, has *female, sister,* and *parent* of whom she's the sister.

TABLE 8.5 *Order of Acquisition of Kinship Terms*

Mother, father, sister, brother
Son, daughter, grandfather, grandmother, parent
Uncle, aunt, cousin, nephew, niece

After *Mommy* and *Daddy,* the child learns *brother* and *sister.* Roughly, the meanings are *brother = related boy* and *sister = related girl.* By age 4, a child may understand what a brother or sister is but doesn't realize that he or she can also be a brother or sister to someone else. In other words, the term is not used reciprocally. Eventually, a child will understand all features of the kinship terms and reciprocity. Most of the major kinship terms are understood by age 10.

CONCLUSION

In development, there seems to be a constant interchange between semantic and syntactic development that we would expect if words and grammar are two aspects of the language system. Grammatical growth is more closely related to vocabulary growth than to chronolgical age.

There seem to be strong genetic correlations between lexical and syntactical growth from 2 to 3 years of age (Dionne et al., 2003). This data and that from older preschoolers would suggest a common cognitive mechanism for language development. This does not negate the importance of environmental factors in determining language development. It would appear that both genetic and environmental factors underlie development and account for many of the individual differences across a wide range of linguistic skills (Hayiou-Thomas et al., 2006).

Semantic and Pragmatic Influence on Syntactic Development

Aspects of language do not act independently, and development in one area influences the others. More correctly, the aspects of language develop together. In the next chapter, we'll be discussing preschool development of language form, especially syntax. This does not occur independently from semantics and pragmatics. Let's briefly discuss the influence of semantics and pragmatics on syntax.

SEMANTICS

A central task in learning language acquisition is differentiating how different roles in an event are indicated. In other words, children need both to comprehend and produce the *who-does-what-to-whom* of the event. Languages indicate the **semantic case** or category, such as **agent** (who) and the **patient** (whom) and their relation, in different ways, including word order and morphological markers. In general, languages differ along a continuum in which highly word-ordered languages, such as English, have fewer morphological markers, and those with a freer word order, such as Italian, have more markers. Given the characteristics, English-speaking language-learning children rely on several cues, including the following:

- Order of the participants, which is typically agent before patient.
- Morphological marking of semantic case marking on pronouns indicating the participants, such as *I, he, she* vs. *my, him, her.*
- Animacy or the animate nature of agents who cause actions, as in **Mommy** *throw ball.*
- Stress or emphasis.
- Special markers, such as the passive agent-marker *by* in as in *The boy was kicked by the horse.*

Several cross-linguistic studies have demonstrated that in their spontaneous speech, children learning many different languages generally conform to adult usage, even though word order seems to provide the most information initially (Chan, Lieven, & Tomasello, 2009). In English, children will primarily depend on word order to both comprehend and produce sentences.

Interestingly, when English-speaking children as young as 2 are asked to act out an utterance such as "The spoon kicked the horse," they use word-order cues to interpret the sentence even though the more likely real-world scenario is just the opposite. When presented with the same utterance, Italian-speaking children ignore word order and make the horse kick the spoon, because word order is quite variable in Italian. Instead the children use semantic plausibility, which in this case is that the animate entity would do the kicking.

Probably, the most discussion of case marking in English has centered around pronoun case errors, such as **Me** *go* and **Her** *eating.* About 50% of English-speaking 2- to 4-year-olds make such pronoun errors, especially substituting patient for agent (**Me** *do it*) but rarely the reverse (*Mommy spank* **I**). If we examine the most common errors, *her* for *she* and *me* for *I,* we see some interesting phenomena. The female third-person singular pronoun is *she* (subjective), *her* (objective), *her* (possessive), and *herself* (reflexive). We might expect, therefore, that children would seek some regularity and substitute *her* for *she* (Rispoli, 1994b, 1998). This would follow the phonological regularity found in the first sound of the masculine pronouns *he-him-his-himself* and the third-person plural *they-them-their-themselves.* In other words, errors may be based on both semantic and phonological factors, although no one is certain.

PRAGMATICS

Unlike semantic cases, syntactic roles such as noun and verb are more abstract. While agent-action-object (*Mommy eat cookie*) can be interpreted based on semantic order, syntactic roles of noun-verb-noun (*Mommy eat cookie*) offer less guidance, especially because the two nouns are not morphologically marked in different ways in English. A noun is traditionally defined as a "person, place, or thing" and a verb as an "action word." But nouns can indicate actions, as in the words *discussion* or *biking,* and verbs can indicate non-actions, such as *feel* and *be.* In some cases, even markers, such as use of articles and plural *-s* with nouns (*the cats*) are not appropriate with some proper nouns (*the Mr. Smiths* or the *New York Cities*).

In fact, it is the communicative function—that's pragmatics!—of the words that defines their use. More specifically, articles used with nouns help the listener to locate a referent in actual or conceptual space and verb tense markers help the listener locate a process in actual or conceptual time (Langacker, 1991). In fact, young children use adult nouns early in development to refer to non-object entities such as *kiss, lunch,* and *night* and verbs for non-actions such as *like, feel, want,* and *be* (Nelson et al., 1993). Young children also learn many words that can used as both nouns and verbs, such as *bite, brush, call, drink, help, hug, kiss,* and *walk* (Nelson, 1995).

Instead of understanding abstract syntactic categories such as noun and verb, preschoolers initially understand particular kinds of words based on what those words can and cannot do communicatively. Taught a nonsense word in a format "Look! A wuggie," 2-year-old-children are immediately able to combine the word with verbs (*Hug wuggie*) and to make it plural (*Wuggies*) even though they had never heard these utterances before (Tomasello et al., 1997).

The distinction between nouns and pronouns very clearly illustrates the role of pragmatics in development of syntax. Learning the English pronominal system is a very complex process. Although a pronoun is a simple device that enables one word to be the equivalent of one or several other words, the listener must understand these equivalences. Typically, speakers use **anaphoric reference,** or referral to what has come before. We can thus decipher *his* and *it* in the sentence, "The boy was watching *his* television when *it* caught fire."

A conversational device, pronouns provide cohesion between old and new information. New information is first identified by name. Then, once identified, it becomes old information and can be referred to by a pronoun. The pronoun refers to what came before or makes anaphoric reference to it. As a kind of "shorthand," pronouns facilitate integration of all the complex semantic information in a conversation (Yang, Gordon, Hendrick, Wu, & Chou, 2001). When there is possible confusion, preschool children often use pronominal apposition, as in "My mother, she. . . ." Unless it is a dialectal characteristic, pronominal apposition begins to disappear by school age.

Language Development Differences and Delays

Several factors, such as a child's health, the quality of parent–child interactions, or introduction of a second language, may lead to development that does not follow the outline of this chapter. Let's discuss these briefly.

LANGUAGE DEVELOPMENT DIFFERENCES

In general, language development differences that are not causes of concern fall into two broad categories, bilingualism and dialectal differences. It is important to stress that these differences are just that. They are differences and not disorders. That is not to say that they do not mask disorders. While a full discussion of language disorders is beyond the scope of this text, suffice it to say that a language disorder would show up in both the native language and in the second language, which in this case is American English. In the previous chapter, we discussed simultaneous development of two languages. Here we shall discuss sequential or successive development. We will also explore dialectal development, focusing on African American English.

Successive Acquisition

Most bilingual children develop one language (L$_1$), such as Spanish, at home and a second (L$_2$), such as American English, with peers or in school, usually after age 3. Children who begin learning English at age 5 master comprehension before expression, although English dominance does not occur until middle school (Kohnert & Bates, 2002). Although humans are capable of acquiring a second language at any age, by the late teens it is difficult for a speaker to acquire native-speaker pronunciation characteristics in a second language. In part, this difficulty may reflect the tendency of mature speakers to use the discourse-processing strategies of their native language to interpret the second language (Tao & Healy, 1996). Speakers who learned English later in life tended to rely on stress patterns from their native language to interpret English and used English syntax relatively less (Sanders, Neville, & Woldorff, 2002).

The age of arrival in an English-speaking country seems to be critical for second-language learning, especially for East Asians (Jia, Aaronson, & Wu, 2002). For example, Chinese-speaking children who come to the United States before age 9 switch their language preference to English within a year and become more proficient in English than in Chinese (Jia & Aaronson, 2003). Children who immigrate after age 9 usually maintain a preference for Chinese and become less proficient in English than in Chinese. Age of arrival is less of a factor for children immigrating from Europe and may reflect the relative similarity of European language and culture with that of the United States or Canada when compared to East Asian language and culture.

Although young children do not necessarily acquire L_2 faster or more easily than adults, they eventually outperform these adults in L_2. In addition, children are less susceptible than adults to interference from L_1.

Early exposure to L_2 may result in a delay in L_1 before it is mature. In turn, competence in L_2 may be a function of relative maturity in L_1. The result may be *semilingualism,* a failure to reach proficiency in either language. In contrast, children learning a second language at school age have acquired some metalinguistic skills that may facilitate L_2 learning (Schiff-Meyers, 1992). There are trade-offs between age and second-language learning.

Success in nonsimultaneous language acquisition is more closely related to a learner's attitude toward and identity with users of the language being acquired, and his or her positive attitude toward the first language and culture. Need is another strong motivating factor. Interestingly, within limits, intelligence seems to have little effect. Most children acquire a second language rapidly, although the strategies used differ with age, a child's linguistic knowledge, and the nature of the two languages. The more a child's learning style matches the teaching style the better the development of L_2. Children tend to learn in immediate contexts through sensory activity, while adults prefer explicit rule training. Such home factors as literacy and a positive attitude toward both languages are also very important (Hamayan & Damico, 1991).

When children learn two languages successively, they seem to go through easily recognizable stages. In the first stage, a child uses L_1 in the L_2 or English environment even though everyone else is speaking English. A child may persist in this behavior but rapidly realizes that it doesn't work.

A second, nonverbal stage, lasting a few weeks or months, follows, during which a child gains receptive knowledge but says very little in English. Communication is primarily by gesture.

When a child begins to speak, he or she usually uses single words or short phrases or relies on high-usage phrases, such as "Okay," "I don't know," and "What's happening?" Gradually, a child begins to produce original phrases and sentences.

During this stage, a child assumes that what is being said is relevant to the situation or to what the speaker is experiencing. A child scans for recurring linguistic patterns. The social strategy is to join the group and act as if he or she knows what is being communicated. A child tries to use the few phrases and words that give the impression of being able to speak the second language.

Speakers seem to adopt one of two strategies: other-directed or inner-directed. Those choosing the other-directed strategy approach the language-learning task as an interpersonal one. The goal is to get the message across in any way possible. In contrast, those who choose an inner-directed strategy approach the task as an intrapersonal one. Focus is less on communication and more on breaking the language code. Inner-directed individuals may appear to be rather quiet and withdrawn. Actually, they are engaging in "private" speech in which they repeat the utterances of others, recall and practice phrases, create new utterances, modify and expand existing utterances, and rehearse for future social performance (Saville-Troike, 1988).

Communication becomes the goal. A child's strategies include using to the utmost the linguistic units he or she understands and working on overall communication, while saving the details for later. A child begins talking with whatever units he or she can produce and comprehend.

In a final stage, a child can use English creatively in conversation. This may take three to five years. It may be several more years before a child is capable of thinking and learning in English. Factors that influence the transition are a child's intelligence, the similarity or dissimilarity of the two languages, and the amount of exposure to L_2.

During the period of transition, a child may use **interlanguage,** in which the grammar and pronunciation of L_2 is influenced by L_1. This is a natural part of the language-learning process. Errors frequently occur with morphological endings and short, unstressed words such as auxiliary verbs, pronouns, and prepositions. Because L_2 learners rely on their first language to guide them in learning English, speakers of the same L_1 often have the same accent and make similar grammatical mistakes. The L_1 phonological system will affect L_2 pronunciation. For example, many Asian languages do not have the /r/ and /I/ sounds. For L_2 speakers of English, these sounds maybe omitted or misarticulated.

Contrary to common opinion, L_1 and L_2 are not always negatively influencing each other. L_1 can actually form the foundation for L_2. Certain language processes are basic, and knowledge in L_1 can be transferred to L_2. For example, nouns are treated the same way in most languages. Although negative interference can occur, fewer than 5% of the errors in the second language are traceable to this source.

Since the child already has one linguistic system, he or she has an acoustic-perceptual system, an articulatory repertoire, and a cognitive-semantic base from which to begin acquiring a second language. Therefore, errors, although similar, are more limited than in first-language acquisition. Errors cannot be predicted based on the linguistic form of the two languages. The effects of either language upon the other vary with each child, and interference appears to be minimal. Unlike many older learners, children do not use their knowledge of L_1 to formulate utterances in L_2. Instead, they treat the new language as an independent system and gradually construct it from the speech they hear.

Typically, one language continues to develop to adult norms, while the other achieves a somewhat lower level. The growth of both L_1 and L_2 is dependent upon many factors. For example, children in the United States who speak Hmong stabilize their development of this language at some point below full maturation while continuing to develop English dynamically (Kan & Kohnert, 2005). Use determines which language becomes dominant.

In general, second-language learning by young children mirrors first-language learning. At first, a child begins with single words or common short phrases and then moves to short sentences and morphological markers. Semantic relations are expressed first by order and then with morphological markers. Sentence alterations, such as negation and interrogation, follow acquisition patterns similar to those found in first-language learning. The errors made by a child learning English as a second language are also similar to those made by those learning English first.

Common differences noted in L_2 learning include omission and overextension of morphological inflections, double marking, misordering of sentence constituents, and the use of archiforms and free alternation. An **archiform** is one member of a word class used exclusively, such as *that* for all demonstratives. As more members of a class are acquired, perhaps *this, these,* and *those,* the child may vary usage among the members without concern for the different meanings; this is called **free alternation.**

Phonologic development also follows a similar pattern in first and second languages. The phonological system from the first language forms a foundation for the second. Gradually the two phonologic systems become differentiated. Bilingual Spanish-English children have the same phonological skills in phoneme and syllable production in both Spanish and English as predominantly Spanish-speaking and predominantly English-speaking children respectively (Goldstein, Fabiano, & Swasey Washington, 2005).

Although a school-age child may have no conversational difficulties, he or she may experience problems with the decontextualized language of the classroom. It may take six to seven years to obtain cognitive-academic proficiency in L_2.

Development of African American English

You will recall that African American English is a dialect spoken by many lower-class African Americans in the urban North and rural South and by others who live in close proximity to these populations. The dialectal characteristics presented in Appendix A develop gradually through the preschool and school-age years.

Throughout this book we are concentrating on the "generic" child, most typically white and middle class. Some working-class African American children do not acquire language within a similar social context. Urban African American children may pass through three stages of language acquisition. First, they learn the basics of language at home; then, from ages 5 to 15, they learn a local vernacular dialect from their peers; and, finally, they develop the more standard AAE dialect. It should be remembered, however, that even among heavily dialectal speakers of AAE, only about 20% of words are affected (Craig & Washington, 2002). In addition, some children who use African American English begin to dialect shift to the mainstream dialect as early as preschool (McDonald Connor & Craig, 2006).

Southern, rural, working-class African American children are not encouraged to communicate conversationally or to ask questions. In some southeastern Appalachian working-class towns, children are addressed indirectly and are not expected to provide information. Children are exposed to a wide variety of language through extended families and neighbors who tease and verbally challenge toddlers. The children often begin to speak by imitating the ending phrases of these speakers. Children who try to interrupt adult conversation may be scolded for their speech inaccuracies or for their less mature language. Within other regions, language stimulation may appear in other forms, such as rhymes, songs, or stories. In general, the mothers of these children do not feel obligated to teach language. Development differs in the demands for communication placed on the child. Therefore, children differ in their expectations of appropriate communication behavior.

LANGUAGE DEVELOPMENT DELAYS

Several factors seem to predict later speech and language impairments among preschool children. In general, these include

- Male gender.
- Ongoing hearing problems.
- A more reactive temperament, consisting of responding negatively to frustration, such as having tantrums.

Factors that could potentially moderate impairment include

- A more persistent and more sociable temperament.
- Higher levels of maternal psychological well-being (Harrison & McLeod, 2010).

Significant predictors of late language emergence (LLE) at 24 months of age also include family history of LLE and early neurobiological growth (Zubrick, Taylor, Rice, & Slegers, 2007). These factors suggest a strong role for neurobiological and genetic mechanisms of the onset of LLE. In addition, these factors operate across a wide range of maternal and family characteristics, such as parental educational levels, socioeconomic resources, parental mental health, parenting practices, or family functioning.

Delayed language development often predicts a long period growth difference, particularly for syntax and morphology. Children with a history of LLE at 24 months perform below typical children at age 7 in both speech and language production (Rice, Taylor, & Zubrick, 2008). Even in late adolescence, children with slow language development at 24 to 31 months have weakness in both spoken and written language-related skills (Rescorla, 2009).

Conclusion

BY KINDERGARTEN, A CHILD IS ABLE to uphold his or her end of the conversation. Although a preschooler does not have the range of intentions and subtle conversational abilities or vocabulary of a school-age child, he or she can participate and make valuable conversational contributions. As a child matures socially and cognitively, communication skills and language reflect these developments.

Within a conversational context, a preschool child has progressed from two-, three-, and four-word sentences to longer utterances that reflect adultlike form and content rules. Caregivers continue to treat a child as a conversational partner, and a child's contribution increases in meaningfulness in addition to skill of formation. Increased vocabulary and relational terms enable a child to sustain a conversation on limited topics and to relate action narratives of past and imagined events.

Adults, especially parents, are still the primary conversational partners, although others, such as preschool or daycare friends or siblings, are becoming more important. As a child plays with other children and interacts with adults, he or she learns to modify language for the listener and becomes more flexible. This aspect of language will change greatly throughout the school years.

Discussion

ALTHOUGH TURN-TAKING DEVELOPS EARLY, it is a big jump from taking turns to becoming a good conversational partner. A preschool child is learning to begin and end conversations, to introduce, maintain, and change topics, and to decide on the right amount of information to provide. In addition, he or she is introducing narratives into the conversation, recalling past events for the conversational partner. It will be many years before conversational and narrative skills reach that of an adult, but we have a strong beginning.

New words and word relationships are also being added to a preschooler's expanding vocabulary. Relational terms such as *better than* and *in front of* and those for temporal relationships are especially difficult. Terms, such as conjunctions (*and, because, so*), that link sentence elements will also take more time to develop. These and other terms will be added to the child's lexical storage over the next few years.

At the end of the chapter, we discussed the development of pronouns. The importance of that development for us is in its illustration of the interdependence of the different areas of language. Pronouns might seem simple, but little in language development really is, and all aspects of development are interrelated.

In practice, the SLP cannot ignore these aspects of language. To program only for a child's language form is to miss the importance of that form's use within the environment. Training structures for which the child has no use is ensuring that the structures will not generalize. Training language form with words that are meaningless to a child also weakens the impact of intervention.

Main Points

- Preschool conversational advances include increasing use of registers or styles of talking after age 4, limited conversational repair, rapid topic shifts with two to three turns on a topic, increased consideration of the listener and use of presupposition, some forms of indirect request, and deictic terms.

- The number of different intentions expressed by preschoolers increases and the frequency changes, most notably in a big increase in representational uses and a decline in the use of tutorial uses, especially imitation.

- The overall organization of narratives moves from centering to chaining. Temporal chains appear at age 3 and causal chains by age 5.

- A child learns two to three new words each day by first fast mapping the meaning, then slowly refining it over time.

- New words include relational terms such as interrogative words, temporal terms, physical descriptors, locational prepositions, and kinship terms. All will influence the development of syntax.

- Development of Theory of Mind (ToM) greatly enhances the conversational skills of preshool children.

- An interrelatedness exists with the different aspects of language. This is demonstrated by the effect of both semantics and pragmatics on syntax.

Reflections

1. Briefly describe the conversational skills of the preschool child.

2. Describe the development of preschool narratives.

3. Explain the process of vocabulary expansion among preschool children.

4. Summarize the development of relational terms. Explain the principles in operation.

5. Describe the major changes in Theory of Mind seen in preschool children.

6. Explain the influence of semantics and pragmatics on syntactic development.

9

Preschool Development of Language Form

OBJECTIVES

The preschool years are a time of tremendous growth in all aspects of language, especially language form. From two- and three-word utterances, a child progresses to sentences that approximate adult language in their complexity. When you have completed this chapter, you should understand

- The major characteristics of syntactic development.
- Preschool morphological development.
- The acquisition order for negative and interrogative sentences.
- The differences between embedding and conjoining and their acquisitional order.
- The major phonological processes observed in preschool children.
- The following terms:

aspect	mean length of	phrase
copula	utterance (MLU)	sibilants
epenthesis	modal auxiliary	tense

To listen to language samples related to chapter content and to peruse other enhanced study aids, please see the Companion Website at www.pearsonhighered.com/owens8e

Much of adult morphology, syntax, and phonology has appeared by the time a child goes to kindergarten. This chapter will explain this process and help you understand the course and method of these incredible changes.

Children observe patterns of language use in the environment and gradually—sometimes one verb at a time—form hypotheses about the underlying rules. These hypotheses are then tested in the child's speech. Over time, the child's rules change to reflect cognitive and social maturity and greater sophistication in producing and using the linguistic code in conversation. The speed of change varies across linguistic features. Many months or years may be required before the child has complete control of a linguistic element in all contexts. I still make mistakes. How about you?

In this chapter, we'll first relate development of language form to what we learned about semantics in the last chapter. Then we'll discuss development of language form and attempt to relate developments in one area of language to those in others.

Given the amount of development that occurs in language form during preschool years, this chapter is long and complicated. I've tried to shorten it by placing background material in Appendix E. If you don't know a phrase from a clause or never thought about how you form a question syntactically, you might want to read Appendix E before you go any further. If you need further input, ask your professor to suggest a good basic grammar text. Several websites might also be helpful, including

> http://en.wikipedia.org/wiki/English_grammar
> http://grammar.about.com/od/basicsentencegrammar/a/basicstructures.htm
> www.grammar.cl/Notes.htm

The Semantic–Syntactic Connection

The exact manner through which children acquire grammar is unknown. Different decision criteria may be used depending on the individual sentence, such as information concerning subsequences of words and the individual words themselves (Allen & Seidenberg, 1999).

Variations in rules and use patterns have even caused some linguists to question the very notion that acquisition of syntax involves rule learning (Bybee, 2002). For example, brain imaging has shown that regular and irregular forms of language rules, as in regular past-tense *walked* and irregular *went,* are processed in different parts of the brain, suggesting that they are not linked as a single rule system (Jaeger, Lockwood, Kemmerer, Van Valin, & Murphy, 1996; Kawamoto, 1994; Weyerts, Penke, Dohrn, Clahsen, & Münte, 1996).

In the brain, irregular forms may be associated more closely with semantic information or meaning rather than with morphology. In other words, because we don't seem to access *went* by combining *go* and *-ed,* we might access it directly by a semantic route.

The relationship also flows in the other direction. Individual word learning certainly depends on a word's meaning but also on the role that the word plays in sentences and the ways in which the word is combined with others. Stated another way, word learning is related to syntactic knowledge. It seems logical that children would use all types of information whenever they are reliable (MacWhinney, 1998).

Certain types of words, such as nouns and verbs, are treated in distinct ways in sentences. Evidence suggests that children make assumptions about words and that caregivers, usually un-intentionally, use conversational strategies that support these assumptions (Hall, Quartz, &

Persoage, 2000; Imai & Haryu, 2001; Mintz & Gleitman, 2002; Waxman & Markow, 1999). For example, from adult use a child might correctly assume the following:

if . . . this is an X	must be . . . noun
. . . this is X	. . . proper noun
. . . this is an X one	. . . adjective

When a new word is learned, a child tentatively assigns it to a syntactic category.

By noting how the word is used by others, a child confirms the category assignment or makes appropriate changes in category status. For example, when children as young as 20 months are given a human and a nonhuman figure and asked either to "Show me the X" or to "Show me X," they point to the nonhuman and human figures respectively, demonstrating that syntactic context—the use of the definite article *the*—is a guide to word learning. Similar results have been demonstrated with other syntactic constructions (Landau, Smith, & Jones, 1992).

When caregivers read to preschool children, they treat words differently (Hall, Burns, & Pawluski, 2003). Nouns and proper nouns are introduced with little explanation (i.e., *This is an X*). On the other hand, adjectives are introduced and then described or contrasted with other meanings (i.e., *This is an X one. That means . . .*). In this way caregivers help a child acquire words, their meanings, and syntactic category.

Although nouns are the most easily identifiable word class, words such as "justice" and "love" are so clearly not persons, places, or things that their membership as nouns can only be inferred by their syntactic use as nouns. Thus, both syntactic and semantic factors play a major role in the emergence of language form (MacWhinney, 1998).

Sentence processing involves more than just storage of a sequence of words or sounds. The brain predicts the next word in the sentence based on syntactic patterns and grammatical and pragmatic cues (Elman, 1993). Meaning is found in the individual words and in their combination.

In production, word combinations depend not only on semantics, syntax, and sentence frames, but also templates into which only certain words are acceptable. For example, children sometimes confuse *pour* and *fill*, resulting in "I poured the tub with water" instead of "I poured water into the tub," and "I filled water into the tub" instead of "I filled the tub with water" (Bowerman, 1988). Correct production requires a child to deduce the pattern "V N with N" for words with the semantic features of *fill*, *stuff*, and *cover* and the pattern "V N into N" for words with the semantic features *pour*, *dump*, and *empty*.

Syntactic and Morphologic Development

Before we begin wading through preschool syntactic and morphologic development, we say something about the way the material will be organized in the following sections. Some changes in preschool language development correspond to increases in a child's average utterance length, measured in morphemes. This value, the **mean length of utterance (MLU),** is a moderate predictor of the complexity of the language of young English-speaking children (Blake, Quartaro, & Onorati, 1993). Up to an MLU of 4.0, increases in MLU correspond to increases in utterance complexity. Above 4.0, growth in utterance length slows considerably and individual variation increases, resulting in MLU becoming a less reliable measure as seen in Figure 9.1.

At best, MLU is a crude measure that is sensitive only to those language developments that increase utterance length. For example, the movement of elements within the utterance may result in more mature utterances but will not increase the MLU. Although there is a positive correlation

FIGURE *9.1* *Changes in MLU with Age in Months*

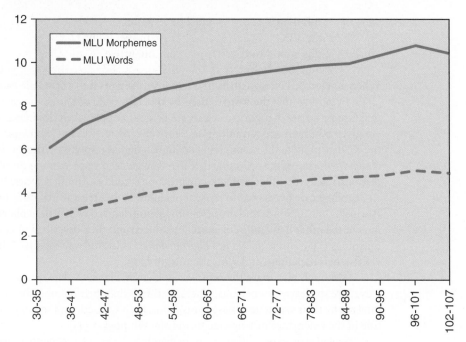

Source: Information from Rice et al. (2010).

between MLU and age, MLU may vary widely for children with the same chronological age. It is also important to note that although MLU is a rough estimate of language complexity for English-speaking preschoolers, it is not so for users of other languages, such as modern Hebrew, in which complexity does not necessarily result in longer utterances (Dromi & Berman, 1982).

Having said all that, MLU can still help us to conceptualize development. From age 18 months to 5 years, MLU increases by approximately 1.2 morphemes per year, although there is some indication of a decreased rate after 42 months (Scarborough, Wyckoff, & Davidson, 1986). Although much of the work on MLU, suggesting stages of development, has been discredited, mean utterance length may help us to conceptualize development. In addition, MLU is one of the quantitative values used by speech-language pathologists to describe the language development of children with potential language disorders. Appendix D presents the manner in which MLU is typically calculated in such diagnostics.

Patterns in Preschool Language Development

Preschool children are not little automatons, each following in exact lockstep stages of development. Instead, each child is listening to the language of his or her environment and trying to figure out how to say what he or she wants to say. Still, there are some patterns that are now becoming clear. These are as follows (Tomasello, 2006):

■ Most children below age 3 in both production and comprehension do not fully understand the subject-verb-object word order.

- Many sentence types used by children after age 3 are learned with specific verbs and only generalize to language rules later in development. In other words, rules may be learned one word at a time. At some point after their third birthday, children seem to reorganize their knowledge of these independently learned patterns and to extract more abstract rules or schemes.
- Children gradually begin to form abstract utterance-level constructions by creating analogies among utterances. Children try to categorize whole utterances and other linguistic constructions on the basis of the functional interrelations among the components. For example, in the utterances *Donte is pushing the swing* and *Mommy is planting the flowers,* there is a basic relational pattern of *A is B-ing the C* in which each letter plays a role first based on function, as in *A* causes an action, to more abstract syntactic roles.
- One major reason children show certain syntactic patterns in their language is because these are the patterns they hear in the language around them. Initially, children learn verbs for the constructions in which they have heard them. While this is the case at the earliest stages of development, it is less true after age 3 when children begin making more syntactic abstractions.

Armed with these generalizations, let's get started.

Bound Morphemes

English is a morphologically poor language when it comes to bound morphemes. If you know Spanish, Italian, or French, think of all the verb endings you had to learn. In English there are few, but let's explore the preschool ones that develop.

In general, morphological learning is characterized by what's termed *U-shaped* developmental growth that seems to signal underlying changes in linguistic representations and processes. Before we begin, we need to clarify that the "U" shape represents correct production and comprehension, meaning at first it seems that a child has learned it correctly, but then the child makes more errors, and finally, correct use returns. Initial use of the bound morpheme may be limited to specific words heard frequently in the child-directed speech of adults. The errors come as a child tries to extend use of the morpheme to words the child has not heard used by others or to infrequently heard words. Gradually, a child begins to abstract a scheme or rule for use of the morpheme.

Morphological learning may be made more difficult in English for several reasons (Tomasello, 2006):

- Bound morphemes are phonologically reduced and unstressed monosyllabic bits of language.
- In general, bound morphemes carry very little concrete semantic information and may be redundant.
- Many grammatical morphemes or at least their phonological forms are multifunctional.

Redundancy can be seen with several bound morphemes. For example, when we say *two kittens,* the number two tells us we mean plural, so the plural *-s* is redundant. This isn't always the case, as in I'll have some cake (a piece) and I'll have some cakes (several). But of course this just confuses the issue for a language learner!

The multifunctional quality of some morphemes can be seen in the overworked /s/, /z/, /əz/ markers that can be used for plural (*two cakes,* /s/; *two cards,* /z/; *two cages,* /əz/), possessive (*cat's,* /s/; *dog's,* /z/; *witch's,* /əz/), and third person *-s* (*she kicks,* /s/; *it turns,* /z/; *he kisses,* /əz/). When we compare children's use of the third person present *-s* to the past *-ed,* which is not used to mark any other early morphological distinction, we see the confusion arising from the use of *-s* to also mark plural and possessive. Although all 6-year-old children comprehend *-ed,* it is not until age 7 that all children comprehended *-s* (Beyer & Hudson Kam, 2009). Obviously semantic and phonological distinctions must be explored before a child can use bound morphemes effectively.

Mom's help with some of these grammatical morphemes through the use of recast or reformulated utterances are mentioned in Chapter 7 (Farrar, 1990, 1992). Thus, mothers provide a child with an immediate comparison of her or his own immature utterance and the corresponding adult form.

As mentioned, a child may also learn a morphologic marker only in specific sentence forms with particular words before going on to learn the general morphologic rule (Wilson, 2003). Even as adults, many of us are not aware of morphological differences, such as the difference between *data* and *datum* or between *uninterested* and *disinterested.*

At an MLU of 2.0 to 2.5, which usually begins around the second birthday, bound morphemes begin to appear. Their development is very gradual, and considerable individual variation exists. These and other morphemes may first be learned in specific constructions involving particular words. Most are not fully mastered (used correctly 90% of the time) until much later. Bound morphemes discussed are presented in Table 9.1.

TABLE *9.1* **Bound Morphemes Acquired in the Preschool Years**

MORPHEME	EXAMPLE	AGE OF MASTERY* (IN MONTHS)
Present progressive *-ing* (no auxiliary verb)	Mommy driv*ing.*	19–28
Regular plural *-s*	Kitties eat my ice cream. Forms: /s/, /z/, and /Iz/ *Cats* (/kæts/) *Dogs* (/dɔgz/) *Classes* (/klæsəz/), *wishes* (/wIʃIz/)	27–33
Possessive *'s*	Mommy*'s* balloon broke. Forms: /s/, /z/, and /Iz/ as in regular plural	26–40
Regular past *-ed*	Mommy pull*ed* the wagon. Forms: /d/, /t/, and /Id/ *Pulled* (/pʊld/) *Walked* (/wɔkt/) *Glided* (/gaIdid/)	26–48
Regular third person *-s*	Kathy hits. Forms : /s/, /z/, and /Iz/ as in regular plural	26–46

*Used correctly 90% of the time in obligatory contexts.

PROGRESSIVE *-ing*

The progressive verb tense is used in English to indicate an activity that is currently or was recently in progress and is of temporary duration, such as I *am swimming.* The progressive form consists of the auxiliary or helping verb *to be* (*am, is, are, was, were*), the main verb, and the *-ing* verb ending. Children initially express this verb tense as *present* progressive, which means the action is happening now, but with only the *-ing* ending. For example, a child might say "Doggie swimming" or "Mommy eating." The progressive verb tense without the auxiliary is the earliest verb inflection acquired in English and is mastered early for most verbs used by young children.

The progressive can be used with action verbs in English but not with verbs of state, such as *need, know,* and *like.* Young children learn this distinction early, and few overgeneralization errors result. (*I am knowing you, He is needing help.*) A child probably learns the rule one verb at a time by applying it to individual verbs to determine whether they are "*-ing*able." Later children abandon this strategy as too cumbersome and adopt an *-ing* rule.

State verbs are not capable of expressing the present progressive meaning of temporary duration. When a child says "I eating," it is assumed that she'll stop soon. The action is temporary. On the other hand, adults don't say "I am knowing" because with *know* or other verbs, such as *possess* and *love,* it is assumed that this state is of some duration.

Early learning may also reflect that there are no irregular progressive forms, resulting in less confusion for a child. Forms that are overgeneralized by children, such as the regular past-tense *-ed,* have both regular (*walked*) and irregular (*ate*) forms. You may recall the preschool learning principles in Chapter 6. Development of progressive *-ing* demonstrates a child's focus on the ends of words and avoidance of exception.

REGULAR PLURAL *-s*

In English there is no morpheme to indicate the singular form of a noun; thus, a singular noun is called *uninflected* or *unmarked.* The regular form of the plural, marked in writing by *-s,* is acquired orally prior to age 3. Learning of irregular forms, such as *feet* and *mice,* takes considerably longer and largely depends on how frequently these forms are used in a preschooler's environment.

The regular plural appears in short phrases first, then in short sentences, and finally in longer sentences. A U-shaped learning curve can be seen with the regular plural. Initially, there is no difference between the singular and plural, and a number or the word *more* may be used to mark the plural such as "Two puppy" or "More puppy" to indicate plural. Next, the plural marker will be used for selected instances, probably on plural words that are used frequently by adults. Then the plural generalizes to other instances, some of which are inappropriate. Thus, we get such delightful forms as *foots* and *mouses.* Finally, the regular and irregular plural are differentiated.

The amount of overgeneralization to irregular forms is relatively low, suggesting that children prefer the correct form to an overgeneralized rule (Marcus, 1995). When deciding between the singular and plural forms, young children seem to rely on all linguistic information—form, content, and use—as if unable to rely on any one form alone (Prasada & Ferenz, 2002).

Acquiring the English plural involves phonological learning as well. If a word ends in a voiced consonant (see Appendix A for an explanation), the voiced plural marker /z/ is used, as in *beds* (/bɛdz/). In contrast, voiceless consonants are followed by the voiceless /s/, as in *bets* (/bɛts/). These rules do not apply if the final consonant is similar to the /s/ and /z/. The /s/, /z/, /ʃ/, /ʒ/, /tʃ/, and /dʒ/ are called *sibilant sounds,* or **sibilants.** If a word ends in a sibilant, the plural marker is /Iz/ or /əz/, as in *bridges* (/brIdʒIz/). The child may be age 3½ or beyond before these phonological rules are acquired. This distinction is especially difficult for children with hearing or perceptual impairments because of the relatively high frequency, low intensity, and the complexity of sibilant sounds.

POSSESSIVE -*'s* OR -*s'*

The possessive is originally marked with word order and stress; the use of the possessive marker (*'s* or *s'*) is mastered relatively late. Initially, the possessive is attached only to single animate nouns, such as *Mommy* or *doggie,* to form *Mommy's* or *doggie's.* The earliest entities marked for possession are alienable objects, such as clothing, rather than inalienable entities, such as body parts. The morphological form is mastered by age 3. Phonological mastery takes much longer, however, and is similar in use to the rules for the plurals /s/, /z/, and /Iz/.

The most common forms in early marking of possession are *(It's) X's____, That's X's/my____,* and *This is X's/your____.* Similar constructions are found in Korean, although the two languages differ greatly (Clancy, 2000).

REGULAR PAST -*ed*

Few, if any, regular past inflected verbs (*walked, jumped*) appear at the single-word level. Once a child learns the regular past-tense rule, however, it is overgeneralized to previously acquired irregular past-tense verbs, producing forms such as *comed, eated,* and *falled.* Although the regular -*ed* suffix overgeneralizes to irregular verbs, the reverse does not seem to occur, even in languages with extensive verb inflection such as Spanish (Clahsen, Aveledo, & Roca, 2002). Like other morphemes, the regular past has several phonological variations. The voiced /d/ follows voiced consonants, as in *begged* (/bɛgd/), and the unvoiced /t/ follows unvoiced consonants, as in *walked* (/wɔkt/). The third variation, /Id/ or /əd/, follows words ending in /t/ or /d/, such as *sighted* (/saItId/). The /əd/ or /Id/ form, acquired later than the voiced–voiceless /d–t/ distinction, only occasionally overgeneralizes to irregular verbs ending in /t/ or /d/, such as *heard, told,* and *hurt.*

Some children have an extended period of weeks or months during which both the correct form and the overgeneralized form of certain verbs coexist (Marcus et al., 1992). When a child overgeneralizes and produces *goed,* the language system itself contains a mechanism for eventual recovery (MacWhinney, 1998). In the competition between *went* and *goed, went* will be solidified over time because of its repeated occurrence in the speech of others. Meanwhile, the only thing going for *goed* is that it follows the -*ed* rule for regular past. A child learns to block overgeneralization by assuming that there is only one way of saying past *go.* The solution to the problem emerges from the competition between alternative expressions. When use in the environment does not agree with a child's use, the environmental input dominates and the child recovers from the overgeneralization.

REGULAR THIRD PERSON SINGULAR -*s*

The person marker on the verb is governed by the person (*I, you, he/she*) and number (*I, we*) of the subject of the sentence. In English, the only present-tense marker is an -*s* on the third person singular verb, as in "That dog bark*s* too much" or "She run*s* quickly." All other forms are uninflected or unmarked, as in *I run, you dance, we sit,* and *they laugh.* Only a few English verbs, such as *say, do,* and *have,* are irregular. Although the regular and irregular forms appear early, they are not mastered until 3½ to 4 years of age, and there is a long period of inconsistent use. For young children, use of person and number markers, such as third person -*s,* may be affected by qualities of the noun, such as being animate or having life (Barker, Nicol, & Garrett, 2001).

For example, a dog is animate, so the child may use the morphologic marker (*Dog eats*), but a candle is not, so the child may omit the marker (*Candle melt*).

Until it stabilizes, use of the third person singular morpheme *-s* is somewhat dependent on the phonological complexity of the verb stem to which it is attached (Song, Sundara, & Demuth, 2009). In general, children produce third person singular morphemes more accurately in verbs with phonologically simple vowel endings (e.g., see<u>s</u>) as compared with complex consonant endings (e.g., nee<u>ds</u>). Children also produce *-s* more accurately in the final position in utterances compared to positions internal to an utterance.

Omission with new verbs may be influenced by adult questions in which the inflection has been transferred to the auxiliary verb as in the following:

ADULT: Where does it sweep?
CHILD: It sweep here.

Familiar verbs, such as *eat* and *go,* are not affected by such questions and will appear in a child's answer as *eats* and *goes* (Theakston, Lieven, & Tomasello, 2003).

Development of full understanding of third person *-s* may take even longer than correct production. Speakers of mainstream American English do not rely on the third person marker alone for either comprehension of tense (*cuts/cut*) or verb–noun distinctions (*the penguin dresses/the penguin dress*) until age 5 and not reliably until age 6 (de Villiers & Johnson, 2007). In contrast, African American English (AAE)–speaking children do not seem to use the information in the third person *-s* at all. This might be expected because the third person marker is rarely used by speakers of AAE.

NOUN AND ADJECTIVE SUFFIXES

During the preschool years, a child begins to acquire a few additional suffixes for nouns and adjectives. These include the adjectival comparative *-er* and the superlative *-est.* By adding these to descriptive adjectives, a child can create forms such as *smaller* or *biggest.* Children

Some morphologic developments begin around age 2 and continue well into the school-age years.

understand the superlative by about 3½ years of age; the comparative somewhat later, at age 5. Correct production follows. Specific forms, such as *better* or *best,* which are exceptions to the rule, usually take longer to master.

The derivational noun suffix *-er,* added to a verb to form the name of the person who performs the action, is also understood by age 5 and mastered in production soon after. For example, the person who *teaches* is a *teacher;* the one who *hits* is a *hitter,* and so on. One reason for the late appearance of this marker may be its ambiguous nature. The *-er* is used for both the comparative (*bigger*) and for noun derivation (*teacher*). In addition, several other derivational noun suffixes, such as *-man, -person,* and *-ist,* can also be used to designate the person who performs an action. Two-year-olds tend to rely on the *-man* suffix, often emphasizing it, as in *fisher**man,*** which contains both the *-er* and the *-man.* Other more creative examples are *busman, storewomen,* and *dancerman.*

DETERMINANTS OF ACQUISITION ORDER

The cognitive relationship between the semantic and syntactic complexity of these morphemes and the frequency of use in adult speech help explain development. The role of English syntactic and semantic complexity becomes evident when we note the order of acquisition in other languages. For example, the concept underlying plural—one and more than one—is quite simple and is learned as early as age 1 by some children. In Egyptian Arabic, plural marking is very complex, and there are many exceptions to the plural rule. Compared to English-speaking preschoolers, many Egyptian teenagers still have difficulty with the plural.

Initial morphological development of verb markers may be related to the underlying semantic aspects of the verb. The child begins by developing a few protoform verbs that are general and nonspecific, such as *do, go,* and *make.* Once these general forms are developed, the verb markers for these forms appear quickly, suggesting that initial morphological learning may be on a word-by-word basis. In contrast, more specific verbs may be unmarked.

The underlying temporal concept of the verb also seems to be a factor in morphologic learning. For example, the present progressive *-ing* first appears on verbs that display a discrete end with no obvious result, such as *drive,* but not on verbs that describe a discrete event, such as *break, hit,* or *drop.* In contrast, the past-tense marker is more likely to appear on verbs that describe a discrete event that express a result (Li & Shirai, 2000). Thus, initially a child is more likely to say "Daddy is *driving* the car" and "I *dropped* my cup."

What appears to be working here is something called lexical aspect, defined as the temporal or time properties of situations referred to by items in a sentence. The types of verbs in question differ in whether the situation has an inherent endpoint. Accomplishments, such as *broke,* express a change of state or location. Activities, such as *playing,* do not. These are two examples of lexical aspect. Others include whether the verb implies a dynamic of changing situation, a continuing or singular incident and whether the action is complete or incomplete (Smith, 1997). For example, one study of 2- to 3-year-olds found that children's imitation of verb tenses differed based on the accomplishment *versus* activity nature of the verb (Johnson & Fey, 2006).

Morphological learning requires that a child correctly segment words into morphemes and correctly categorize words into semantic classes. If a child undersegments, she or he won't break the word or phrase into enough morphemes. The result is creations such as "He *throw-uped* at the party" or "I like *jump-roping.*" Most of us learned the alphabet as ". . . J, K, Elemeno, P, Q, . . . ," another good example of undersegmenting. In oversegmenting, the child uses too many morphemes, as in "Daddy, you're *interring-upt* me!" and my son Todd referring to grown-ups as *dolts,* having oversegmented *adult* into the article *a* and *dolt.* Judging from some of the adults I know, maybe my son was more observant than we gave him credit for being! I've met my share of *dolts*! Two other examples are illustrative. Upon being told her behavior was "inappropriate," a friend's child replied, "No, I'm out of propriate." Last, another friend told of weeks of planning for a trip to Seattle only to find her daughter despondent after three days there. When asked, her daughter pleaded, "I want to see Attle."

Morphemes are not treated the same way by all language-learning children. In polymorphemic languages such as Mohawk, a northern New York and southern Quebec Native language in which words consist of many morphemes, children initially divide words by syllables rather than morphemes. Thus, children are more likely to note and produce stressed syllables than morphemes.

Morphological rules in English apply to classes of words. Hence, *-ing* is used only with action verbs. If the child miscategorizes a word, errors may result. He or she may use inappropriate morphological prefixes and suffixes, as in the following:

> I'm *jellying* my bread. (Using a noun as a verb, although we do say "buttering my bread")
> I got *manys*. (Using a pronoun as a noun)
> He runs *fastly*. (Using an adjective as an adverb)

Often these errors reflect a child's limited descriptive vocabulary. One of my favorites came from my son Jason who, after a fitful sleep, announced, "I hate *nightmaring*." Overgeneralization occurs when a child applies a category rule to subcategories, such as the regular past *-ed* on irregular verbs. Other examples include the following:

> I saw too many *polices*. (Using the plural *-s* inappropriately on a mass noun)
> I am *hating* her. (Using the present progressive *-ing* inappropriately on a state verb)

In another example, a child may apply a limited morpheme to other words, as in *unsad* and *unbig*. Many of the humorous utterances that young children produce reflect errors in segmentation or categorization.

Morphologic rule learning reflects phonologic and semantic rule learning as well. Morphologic rules are learned at an early age, beginning with rules that apply to specific words and continuing through sound-sequence rules. Initial learning may occur on a case-by-case basis. Higher-order rules require more complex integrative learning. Through lexical generalizations, the child learns that a concept may have more than one form and that forms originally construed to be morphologically distinct, such as *more big* and *bigger,* are actually alternatives of the same concept.

Later, morphophonemic rules are required to account for commonalities. For example, the /f/ sound turns to /v/ preceding a plural, as in *knife/knives* and *wolf/wolves.* This rule is not true for all words ending in /f/, such as *cough* or *laugh.* Remember, a preschooler is learning these orally, not in written form. The child recognizes regularity but still must sort out the exceptions. Each of us has heard a small child say a word such as *knifes* (/naIfs/) during this phase.

Phonological variations may influence early morphological use. A child may not recognize the common morpheme beneath variations. For example, a child may not realize that the ending sound on *cats, dogs,* and *bridges* signals the same morphologic change, pluralization. Morpheme recognition is easier if the semantic and phonologic variations are minimal, as with *big–bigger–biggest,* rather than *good–better–best.*

In addition to phonologic considerations, the underlying semantic concept may influence morphologic development. For example, cognitive and semantic distinctions may be reflected in the order of acquisition of auxiliary verbs. Initially, the child learns auxiliary verbs concerned with the agent in actual events (*do, have, will*), then with the agent as potential doer (*can, have got to, have to, must, should, had better*), then with a likelihood of events (*might, may*), and finally with inferences about events not experienced (*could*). Thus, a child progresses from a concrete action orientation to a more abstract reference.

Early morphologic development focuses on more concrete relationships, such as plural and possession. Abstract relationships such as person and number markers on the verb tend to take longer to master. The progression from concrete to abstract is also reflected in a developing child's cognitive processing.

Check out the speech and language of a 29-month-old on the website. Note the morphologic endings, and the use of past tense. Take some time to relax your brain. This is difficult information. Just listen for a while.

Phrase Development

Phrases are units of syntax that are used in the construction of longer units, such as sentences. In short, a **phrase** is a group of words that functions as a single distinct syntactic unit that is less than a sentence and does not contain both the subject (noun, pronoun) and the predicate (verb). As such, phrases fill syntactic functions in the sentence, such as noun, verb, or adverb and so on. For example, in the sentence *She was here*, "here" is an adverb. I could also say *She was at our summer cottage.* In this case, "at our summer cottage" serves the adverb function. Similarly, in the sentence *Almost everyone on our flight became ill*, "Almost everyone on our flight" serves a noun function, and we could replace it with a pronoun to say *They became ill.*

As units of syntax, phrases usually develop within sentences. It seems prudent, however, to pull them out and separately discuss how they develop.

NOUN PHRASE DEVELOPMENT

Noun phrases (NPs) make reference to things in various ways (*your big dog; Derek, my brother; the girl who fell down*). In this way, NPs act as the noun or serve the function in a sentence. NPs can have many elements and become quite complicated. All the elements of a NP are presented in Table 9.2. As you can imagine, it will take several years before a child is able to use all of these easily.

NP elaborations begin when children begin to combine words but this usually occurs when nouns are in isolation rather than in a longer utterance. The list of early modifiers is generally small (*big, yukky, my*) and only gradually expands as new words are learned. Multiple modifiers are rare.

Children seem to acquire a general rule that adjectives precede nouns in English very early. Around age 2, children also learn that adjectives and articles do not precede pronouns and proper nouns (P. Bloom, 1990a). It is not acceptable in most situations for mature English speakers to say *little he* or *the Juan*. Of course, children can still make mistakes as they acquire new words.

By age 3, most children produce NP elaboration with the addition of each of the major elements—Determiner, Adjective, and Post-noun Modifier—except Initiator (Allen et al., in press). Although the specific elements used by children differ, most children are using articles, possessive pronouns, and adjectives. Words seen frequently include demonstratives *this, that, these,* and *those;* articles *a* and *the;* and words such as *some, other, more,* and *another.* The most frequent NP elaborations involve one element before the noun as in "*A girl eated my cookie.*"

Gradually, a child learns the order of different NP elements. As a mature user, you inituitively know that *my big red candy apple* is correct but *red big candy my apple* is not.

TABLE *9.2* *Elements of the Noun Phrase*

INITIATOR	+ DETERMINER	+ ADJECTIVE	+ NOUN	+ MODIFIER
Only, a few of, just, at least, less than, nearly, especially, partially, even, merely, almost	Quantifier: *All, both, half, no, one-tenth, some, any, either, each, every, twice, triple* Article: *The, a, an* Possessive: *My, your, his, her, its, our, your, their* Demonstratives: *This, that, these, those* Numerical term: *One, two, thirty, one thousand*	Possessive Nouns: *Mommy's, children's* Ordinal: *First, next, next to last, last, final, second* Adjective: *Blue, big, little, fat, old, fast, circular, challenging* Descriptor: *Shopping* (center), *baseball* (game), *hot dog* (stand)	Pronoun: *I, you, he, she, it, we, you, they, mine, yours, his, hers, its, ours, theirs* Noun: *Boys, dog, feet, sheep, men and women, city of New York, Port of Chicago, leap of faith, matter of conscience*	Prepositional Phrase: *On the car, in box, in the gray flannel suit* Adjectival: *Next door, pictured by Renoir, eaten by Martians, loved by her friends* Adverb: *Here, there* Embedded clause: *Who went with you, that you saw*
Examples: *Nearly* . . . . *Almost all of* . . . . *Nearly*	*all the one* *hundred* . . . . *her thirty* . . . . *half of your*	*old college* . . . . *former* . . . . *brother's* *old baseball*	*alumni* . . . . *clients* *uniforms*	*attending the* *event* *in the closet*

Although 3-year-olds seem to understand that pre-noun adjectives (**big** *dog*) restrict or modify the noun, they do not seem to have the same understanding of post-noun modifiers (*dog* **in the car**). Nonetheless, the first post-noun modification appears around the third birthday with adverb words, as in "That one *there*" and "This *here*."

By age 4, a child has added quantifiers, demonstratives, and post-noun prepositional phrases (Allen et al., in press). These are presented in Table 9.2. Embedded clauses appear in the post-noun position shortly thereafter but are not widely used by most children until school age. Development of clausal embedding will be discussed later.

Articles *a* and *the*

The articles *the* and *a* appear before age 2 but take some time to master. Initially used interchangeably, it is sometimes difficult to ascertain from a child's pronunciation which article is being used. For adults, the indefinite article *a* is used for nonspecific reference—*a cat* doesn't specify which one—and the definite *the* denotes specific reference. Pragmatic considerations also influence article use. New information is generally marked with *a*, whereas old information is signaled by *the* + noun or use of a pronoun. Of most importance when choosing the appropriate article or use of a pronoun is the speaker's assessment of the knowledge and expectations of the listener as based on their shared perceptual, previously shared experience, and the immediately preceding discourse.

Correct use of articles and adjectives develops gradually during preschool and kindergarten, possibly as individual words enter a child's lexicon or personal dictionary (Kemp, Lieven, & Tomasello, 2005). Pragmatic correctness, such as use of articles to mark new and old information, usually comes later than meaning knowledge. Although there are some language differences, Dutch, English, and French 2- to 3-year-old children show a relatively adult-like pattern of association for the distinctions of indefinite/definite and new information/old information (Rozendaal & Baker, 2008). The pragmatic distinction between shared and not shared information appears later.

Initially, the indefinite article *a* tends to predominate. Gradually, children come to use the definite article *the* more frequently. Although most preschoolers follow a similar path in development of articles, the rate varies considerably (Abu-Akel et al., 2004).

By 36 months, 90% of children use *a* and *the* correctly, although they tend to overuse the definite article (*the*). This overuse, discussed under presuppositional skills in Chapter 8, may reflect a child's egocentric assumption that the listener knows more than he or she does. By age 4, a child is more capable of making complicated inferences about the listener's needs. In addition, the 4-year-old knows to use *some* and *any* rather than *a* and *the* with nouns, such as *sand, water,* and *salt,* called *mass nouns* because the name denotes no specific quantity. Some children, especially those with language impairments, will continue to overuse the definite article well into elementary school. Many East Asian languages do not contain articles, so you can imagine the difficulties inherent in learning English.

VERB PHRASE DEVELOPMENT

A verb is a syntactic element that expresses existence (*I **am***), action (*She **is jumping***), or occurrence (*We **thought** of you instantly*). A verb phrase (VP) is a construction that includes the verb and all that follows, including noun phrases. The elements of verb phrases are presented in Table 9.3. Before you begin to read this discussion, you might want to review Appendix E and the discussion on verbs. You might also find this website handy:

>   *www.examples-help.org.uk/parts-of-speech/verb-tenses.htm*

In short, VPs say something about people, things, places, and events (*is happy, eats, planted the tree*).

Many verbs appear in the single-word phase of development. At this time, both *transitive* and *intransitive* verbs are produced, but a child does not observe the adult rules for each.

Early in development, children spontaneously produce simple transitive verbs or phrases to describe activities people perform with objects. The main verbs young children use most frequently in these constructions are *break, bring, cut, do, draw, drop, eat, find, get, have, help, hurt, make, open, play, push, put, read, ride, say, take, throw,* and *want.* The primary commonality in intransitive verbs is that they are used for a single participant and action. The most common verbs used in these constructions are *break, come, cry, fall, go, hurt, jump, laugh, open, play, run, see, sing, sit, sleep, stop,* and *swim* (Tomasello, 2003). Note that some words appear on both lists.

A strong correlation exists between the variety of maternal verb usage and a child's development of verbs. The child seems initially to learn verbs as individual items rather than a verb as a member of a category of words. As the child acquires each new verb, he or she observes similarities of syntactic use across items and uses these similarities to predict novel combinations.

A 30-month-old child uses many of the morphological modifications discussed previously, and quickly learns the present progressive *-ing* marker.

Characteristics of a verb can influence the ways in which children learn and use them. For example, children prefer to use past tense with words such as *broke* and *made,* which they consider to be accomplished, complete, and whole. In contrast, children prefer to use present tense or progressive for events considered to activities that last and unfold, such as *playing* or *riding* (Clark, 1996; Tomasello, 1992a, 2003). Interestingly, this is the pattern they hear in child directed speech of adults (Shirai & Anderson, 1995).

TABLE 9.3 *Elements of the Verb Phrase*

MODAL AUXILIARY +	PERFECTIVE AUXILIARY +	VERB *TO BE* +	NEGATIVE* +	PASSIVE +	VERB +	PREPOSITIONAL PHRASE, NOUN PHRASE, NOUN COMPLEMENT, ADVERBIAL PHRASE
May, can, shall, will, must, might, should, would, could	*Have, has, had*	*Am, is, are, was, were, be, been*	*Not*	*Been, being*	*Run, walk, eat, throw, see, write*	*On the floor, the ball, our old friend, a doctor, on time, late*

Examples:
Transitive (may have direct object)
May . . . . have . . . . wanted . . . . a cookie
Should . . . . not . . . . throw . . . . the ball
in the house

Intransitive (does not take direct object)
Might . . . . have . . . . been . . . . walking . . . . . . to the inn
Could . . . . not . . . . talk . . . . with you

Equative (verb *to be* as main verb)
. . . . . is . . . . not . . . . a doctor
. . . . . was . . . . late
. . . . . were . . . . on the sofa
May . . . . be ill

*When modal auxiliaries are used, the negative is placed between the modal and other auxiliary forms, for example, *might not have been going.*

Auxiliary or helping verbs *can, do,* and *will/would* first appear in their negative form (*can't, don't, won't*) at 30 months, when MLU is approximately 2.5. Sadly, every parent can attest to the appearance of forms of negatives ("I won't eat it!").

True auxiliary or helping verbs appear later, including *be, can, do,* and *will*. The verb *to be* may not correctly reflect the verb tense or the number and person of the subject, given its many forms. Thus, a 31- to 34-month-old child may produce "He *am* going," "You *is* running," and so on, although initially she or he will probably overuse *is*. At this age, a child may also begin to overextend the regular past *-ed* marker to irregular verbs, thus producing *eated, goed,* and so on. A sentence may be doubly marked for the past, producing sentences such as "I *did*n't throw*ed* it."

Irregular past-tense verbs, those that do not use the *-ed* ending, such as *ate, wrote,* and *drank,* are a small but frequently used class of words in English. Not all of the approximately 200 irregular verbs in English occur with the same frequency. A small subset of these verbs appears in single-word utterances or by age 2, probably learned individually. For many children, these include *came, fell, broke, sat,* and *went*. Table 9.4 presents the ages at which 80% of preschoolers correctly use certain irregular verbs (Shipley, Maddox, & Driver, 1991). Given the lack of rules for irregular past-tense verbs, it's surprising that preschool children actually make

TABLE *9.4* *Age of Development of Irregular Past-Tense Verbs*

AGE (IN YEARS)*	VERB
3–3½	Hit
	Hurt
3½–4	Went
4–4½	Saw
4½–5	Gave
	Ate

*Age at which 80% of children use verb correctly in sentence completion task.
Source: Information from Shipley, Maddox, & Driver (1991).

so few errors (Xu & Pinker, 1995). Most errors seem to be based on attempts to generalize from existing irregular verbs as in *sing/sang* influencing *bring* to create *brang*. In similar fashion, knowledge of *drink, drank, drunk* may result in *think, thank, thunk*. Many irregular verbs are not learned until school age.

By 40 months the modal auxiliaries *could, would, should, must,* and *might* appear in negatives and interrogatives or questions. Semantically, **modal auxiliaries** are used to express moods or attitudes such as ability (*can*), permission (*may*), intent (*will*), possibility (*might*), and obligation (*must*). Wide variation exists in the acquisition of auxiliary verbs. Table 9.5 presents the ages by which 50% of children begin to use selected auxiliary verbs. Most children use the auxiliaries *do, have,* and *will* by 42 months.

By 46 months a child has usually mastered both the regular and the irregular past tense in most contexts, as well as other morphemic inflections, such as the third person singular -*s* and the copula or verb *to be* as a main verb. Many verb forms are still to be mastered, past-tense modals and auxiliaries, many irregular past verbs, and the passive voice.

TABLE *9.5* *Auxiliary Verb Use by 50% of Children*

AGE (IN MONTHS)	AUXILIARY VERB
27	*Do* *Have + V-en*
30	*Can* *Be + V-ing* *Will*
33	*Be going to*
36	*Have got to*
39	*Shall*
42	*Could*

Source: Information from Wells (1979).

Time and Reference

In English, time and reference to that time are marked by both verb tense and aspect. **Tense,** such as past or future, relates the speech time, which is in the present, to the event time, or the time when the event occurs. **Aspect** concerns the dynamics of the event relative to its completion, repetition, or continuing duration. A child's acquisition of tense and aspect reflects both cognitive and linguistic development.

Not all languages use tense and aspect. For example, Mandarin Chinese uses only aspect, and modern Hebrew uses only tense. The development of the linguistic markers for tense and aspect depends on the relative difficulty of acquiring these markers. In English, tense and aspect, which are intertwined, are acquired later than in Japanese, in which there are distinct suffixes for each.

Children's sense of time and reference to it go through phases of development during the preschool years. These are noted in Table 9.6. Initially, a child talks about things that are occurring now (A). The event time is the same as the speech time. There is no tense or aspect marking. This form is seen in children's use for requests ("Want juice") and to comment ("Doggie run").

Between the age of 18 months and 3 years (B), children speak about the past or present, although the reference point is always in the present. Aspect markers are not combined with tense. Children can distinguish past from nonpast, complete actions from noncomplete, continuative from noncontinuative, and future from nonfuture.

TABLE **9.6** *Development of Production of Time and Reference*

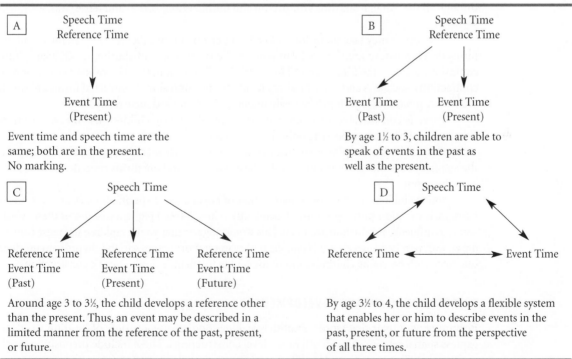

Source: Information from Weist (1986).

Around age 3 to 3½, a child gains a sense of reference other than the present (C). This occurs at about the same age in very different languages. The notion of referent points can be seen with the following two examples:

Kim drove yesterday.
We had hoped to go yesterday.

In the first, the action was completed in the past but we are describing it from the reference point of the present. In the second, the event is clearly in the past but the reference is some time even earlier, prior to yesterday. Initially, children use adverbs of time such as *yesterday* and *tomorrow*. Only later do they use terms such as *before* and *after*.

Finally, between age 3½ and 4 (D), a child acquires a flexible reference system. This development allows free reference to different points in time. For example, the child might say, "Yesterday, Gran'ma asked, 'Would you like to go to the zoo next week?'" A flexible reference system evolves at about the same time that the child acquires the cognitive skills to arrange things in a series and to reverse this sequential order.

Special Case of the Verb *to be*

The verb *to be* (*am, is, are, was, were*) may serve as a main verb or as an auxiliary, or helping, verb. As a main verb, it is called the **copula** and is followed by a noun, an adjective, or some adverbs or prepositional phrases. For example, in the sentences "He *is* a teacher," "I *am* sick," and "They *are* late," the verb *to be* is the only verb and hence the main verb or copula. All of these sentences contain the copula, followed by a noun, *teacher*; an adjective, *sick*; and an adverb, *late*, respectively.

The copula is not fully mastered until around age 4. It takes some time before a child sorts through all the copular variations for person and number (*am, is, are*) and tense (*was, were, will be, been*).

The copula may take many forms to reflect person and number. In general, the *is* and *are* forms develop before *am*. The *is* form tends to be overused, contributing to singular–plural confusion, such as "He *is* fast" and "They *is* big" or "We *is* hungry." The overgeneralization of contractions, such as *'s* and *'re*, also seems to add to the confusion. Contracted forms are short, often unemphasized, and therefore easily undetected when used incorrectly.

There is considerable variation with *it's*. Initially, young children use *it's* and *it* interchangeably, the copula appearing only very gradually.

The auxiliary or helping verb *to be* develops more slowly than the copula. Like the copula, the auxiliary *be* is mastered around age 4. The auxiliary *is* and *are* forms precede the *am* form, as in the copula.

Young children seem to form their notion of *be* on a word-specific (*am, is, are, was, were*) basis, each variation forming semi-independently (Guo, 2009). Frequency of use of these words seems to influence production accuracy. This would suggest that young children use tense (*am, is, are* vs. *was, were*) and agreement (*I am, she is, they were*) morphemes variably. In order to produce utterance with *be*, young children seem to use highly frequent/lexically specific constructions.

PREPOSITIONAL PHRASE DEVELOPMENT

Beginning with their first words, English-speaking toddlers use a variety of location words to express spatial relationships in utterance-level constructions. These include prepositions such as *down, in, off, on, out, to, under,* and *up,* and *verb + particle* constructions, such as *get X down, pick X up,* and *wipe X off,* a holdover from English's German roots. The earliest prepositions are

---

BOX 9.1

Examples of Prepositions and Prepositional Phrases of Preschoolers

---

27 months:	Come **on.**
	Granpa's **in woods.**
36 months:	I'm pouring it **in.**
41 months:	Hi dad, yell **at him** to come back.
42 months:	It's time **for my baby** to go **to bed.**
52 months:	He's doing it **with his feet.**
56 months:	Now it's time **for them** to go **to the store with mommy.**

---

typically *in, on,* and *to* (Allen et al., in press). More complex structures might include structures such as *Draw star on me* and *Peoples on their boat* within a few months (Tomasello, 1992b). By age 3, most children have sufficient flexibility to talk explicitly about location event with three participants as in *Mommy put cereal in my bowl.* Notice that the prepositional phrase is at the end of the sentence, which is common in early use. Examples of preschool prepositional phrases are presented in Box 9.1. Development will continue into school age as a child adds ever more complicated prepositional relations and temporal and figurative uses. A full list of prepositions is included in Appendix E.

INFINITIVE PHRASE DEVELOPMENT

Between 2 and 3 years of age, children begin to acquire infinitives. The most frequent error is omission of "to." These errors seem to be related to different verbs that precede the infinitive, as in "going to" and the frequency with which these verbs are heard by a child (Kirjavainen, Theakston, & Lieven, 2009). At around age 2½ a child develops semi-infinitives such as *gonna* and *wanna.* Occasionally, these forms are followed by a verb, as in "I want (or *wanna*) eat cookie," but at this age, they usually are used alone, as in "I wanna." The word *to* is first used at about this time, but as a preposition indicating "direction toward," as in "I walked *to* the store," not as an infinitive. By age 3, forms such as *gonna, wanna, gotta, hafta,* and *sposta* are being used regularly preceding verbs to form infinitive phrases, usually in the object position of the sentence, as in "I want *to eat.*" Examples include "I got*ta go*" and "I wan*na play.*" The *gotta* and *wanna* and the infinitives *(to) go* and *(to) play* share the same subject. As in the examples, almost all of the initial infinitives follow a pattern of *I* + present tense *gotta, hafta,* and so on (Diessel & Tomasello, 2001). Negatives are rare.

From age 2 to 5, infinitive phrases change in several ways (Tomasello, 2003). First, single nouns and third person pronouns *(he, she, it)* are used in place of *I* (*He wants to eat now; Mommy want to drink that*). Second, negative infinitives appear (*I don't like to eat mustard*). Third, a wider range of verbs, such as *remember* and *forget* are used prior to the infinitive phrase (*I forgot to buy candy*). Fourth, other tenses are used as noted in the previous example. Fifth, children learned more complex constructions with a noun phrase between the two verbs (*I want mommy to do it*). Finally, children develop *wh-* infinitives, such as *I forget when to go to school.*

More complex infinitives typically appear, usually at the ends of sentences. For example, the child develops *wh-* infinitives, such as "I know *how to do it*" and "Show me *where to put it.*" The child also begins to use unmarked infinitive phrases—those without *to*—following verbs such as *help, make,* and *watch,* as in "She can help me *pick these up.*" This form is more difficult for a child because the infinitive is not clearly marked. Infinitives are initially learned and used

BOX 9.2

Examples of Embedded Infinitive Phrases of Preschoolers

24 months:	He **gonna get** this.
37 months:	I'm **gonna clean** my room up.
39 months:	Mom. I want **to watch** Shrek.
	It's **gotta go** in here.
53 months:	That's where his shoes are supposed **to go**.
	Sissy knows how **to play** a game.
59 months:	We're **gonna make** pizza together.
60 months:	There's nothing else I do **to help** my friends.

with a small set of verbs, such as *see, look, know, think, say,* and *tell,* as in "I want *to see it*" or "I don't have *to tell you*."

Around 3½, a child begins to use infinitives with nouns other than the subject. For example, a child may say "This is the right way *to do it*" or "I got this *to give to you*." Most children with MLUs above 4.5 continue to use simple but true infinitives with the same subject as the verb. Examples of the infinitive of preschoolers are presented in Box 9.2.

GERUND PHRASE DEVELOPMENT

In general, gerund development follows that of infinitives. Gerunds appear after age 4. They first appear in the object position at the end of the sentence. These forms are used infrequently. The most common forms of gerunds are *See X verb-ing* and *Watch X verb-ing*.

Sentence Development

In general, preschool sentence development can be gauged by an increase in the number of sentence elements and in the diversity of sentence forms. Description of this process becomes increasingly difficult, as complexity reflects internal movement of elements and diversity results in many forms, each occurring only infrequently. Increases in the number of elements usually occur in declaratives before occurring in other sentence types. The emergence of adult forms takes some time. The majority of English-speaking children, however, possess these basic sentence types by age 5.

Before reading further, you might want to consult Appendix E, especially on the making of negative and interrogative sentences. The development of each is included in Table 9.7.

DECLARATIVE-SENTENCE FORM

Declarative sentences or statements gradually increase in complexity and in number of elements or constituents throughout the preschool years. A child develops the basic *subject + verb + object* sentence format by about 30 months.

By an MLU of 2.5–3.0 or about 33 months, a child has added the auxiliary verb forms *do, have, can, be,* and *will.* The *subject + auxiliary + verb + object* form ("Mommy *is* eating ice

*O*lder preschool children are able to express complicated relationships about location and talk about the past, present, and future.

cream"; "I'*ll* drive that") appears before forms such as "*will* be." Declaratives with double auxiliaries, as in "You *will have* to do it," appear around 3½.

Finally, close to age 4, a child acquires indirect objects. The *subject* + *verb* + *indirect object* + *object* form ("He gave *me* the ball") appears prior to the *subject* + *verb* + *object* + *to* + *indirect object* form ("He gave the ball *to me*"). Thus, by age 5, a child is capable of saying "She could have given a gift to me." Impressive! But you won't hear it often.

Indirect objects occur in three forms in English, *to* + *object* (*I gave it to mommy*), *for* + *object* (*We bought it for daddy*), and double-object (*I bringed mommy flowers*). Although many verbs, such as *bring, give,* and *offer,* can occur in the *to*+*object* and double-object format, a great many are *to*+*object* only (*donate*) or double-object only (*cost, deny, fine*). The verbs young children use most frequently in the double-object format are *being, buy, find, get, give, make, read, send, show, take,* and *tell* (Campbell & Tomasello, 2001).

INTERROGATIVE-SENTENCE FORM

Through the use of intonation, children learn to ask questions very early. By age 4, the child, according to many parents, seems to do nothing else but ask questions. Questioning is a unique example of using language to gain information about language and about the world in general. I recall my own sense of loss when I replied "I used to" to my 4-year-old daughter's query "Do you ever talk to the trees?"

Questions are prevalent in the speech adults address to children. Although the amount of questioning doesn't change much in the first 18 months for each parent–child pair, the types of questions and the topics do. At first, questions are used to comment on where the child is gazing (*Are you looking at a birdie?*) or to direct the child's attention to the mother's activity

TABLE 9.7 *Acquisition of Sentence Forms**

AGE (IN MONTHS)	MLU	DECLARATIVE	NEGATIVE	INTERROGATIVE	EMBEDDING	CONJOINING
12–22	MLU: 1–1.5	Agent + action; Action + object	Single word—*no, all gone, gone*; *negative* + X	*Yes/no* asked with rising intonation on a single word; *what* and *where*		Serial naming without *and*
22–26	MLU 1.5–2.0	Subj. + verb + obj. appears	*No* and *not* used interchangeably	*That X?* *What* + NP + (doing)?	*In* and *on* appear	*And* appears
27–28	MLU: 2.0–2.25	Subj. + copula + complement appears		*Where* + NP + (going)?		
28–30	MLU: 2.25–2.5	Basic subject-verb-object used by most children	*No, not, don't,* and *can't* used interchangeably	*What* or *where* + subj. + pred. Earliest inversion appears	*Gonna, wanna, gotta,* etc. appear	
31–32	MLU: 2.5–2.75	Subj. + aux. + verb + obj. appears; auxiliary verb forms *can, do, have, will,* and *be* appear	negative element placed between subject and predicate	with copula in *What/where* + copula + subj.		*But, so, or,* and *if* appear
33–34	MLU: 2.75–3.0	Auxiliary verb appears with copula in subj. + aux. + copula + X	*Won't* appears	Auxiliary verbs *do, can,* and *will* begin to appear in questions; inversion of subject and auxiliary verb appears in yes/no questions		
35–37	MLU: 3.0–3.5		Negative appears with auxiliary verbs (subj. + aux. + neg. + verb)	Inversion of auxiliary verb and subject in *wh-* questions	Object noun-phrase complements appear with verbs such as *think, guess,* and *show;* embedded *wh-* questions	Clausal conjoining with *and* appears (most children cannot produce this form until age 4); *because* appears

38–40	MLU: 3.5–3.75	Double auxiliary verbs appear in subj. + aux. + aux. + verb + X	Adds *isn't*, *aren't*, *doesn't*, and *didn't*	Inversion of copula and subject in yes/no questions; adds *do* to yes/no questions; adds *when* and *how*	Infinitive phrases appear at the ends of sentences	
41–46	MLU: 3.75–4.5	Indirect object appears in subj. + aux. + verb + ind. obj. + obj.	Adds *wasn't*, *wouldn't*, *couldn't*, and *shouldn't*; negative appears with copula in subj. + copula + neg.	Adds modals; stabilizes inverted auxiliary; some adult-like tag questions appear	Relative clauses appear in object position; multiple embedding appear by late stage V; infinitive phrases with same subject as the main verb	Clausal conjoining with *if* appears; three-clause declaratives appear
47+	MLU: 4.5+		Adds indefinite forms *nobody, no one, none,* and *nothing*; has difficulty with double negatives	Questions other than one-word *why* questions appear; negative interrogatives beyond age 5	Gerunds appear; relative clauses attached to the subject; embedding and conjoining appear within same sentence above an MLU of 5.0	Clausal conjoining with *because* appears with *when, but,* and *so* beyond an MLU of 5.0; embedding and conjoining appear within the same sentence above an MLU of 5.0

*Based on approximately 50% of children using a structure.

(*What's mommy doing?*). By 18 months, the questions are mostly tutorial or genuine requests for information.

Children begin to ask questions at the one-word level through the use of rising intonation (*Doggie?* ↑), through some variation of *what* (*Wha? Tha?* or *Wassat?*), or through phonetically consistent forms. There appear to be three phases of question development in young children (Table 9.7). The first phase, which corresponds to an MLU of 1.75 to 2.25, is characterized by the following three types of question form:

Nucleus + intonation	That horsie?
What + noun phrase + (*doing*)	What that?
	What doggie (doing)?
Where + noun phrase + (*going*)	Where ball?
	Where man (go)?

These questions are confined to a few routines in which a child requests the names of objects, actions, or locations. The child neither comprehends nor asks other *wh-* questions, although *why* may be used alone (*why?*) as a turn filler to keep the conversation going. *What* and *where* may appear early because they relate to the child's immediate environment. *What* is used to gain labels; *where,* to locate objects. In addition, both are heavily used by parents to encourage a child's speech and are related to the early semantic categories of nomination and location.

When his or her MLU is 2.25 to 2.75, around 30 to 32 months, a child continues to ask *what* and *where* questions but uses both a subject and a predicate, as in "What doggie eat?" and "Where Johnnie go?" Other questions, such as the yes/no type, may still be identified by rising intonation alone, as in "Daddy go work?" ↑.

Subject-verb inversion occurs at the end of this phase in *wh-* interrogatives with the copula (*wh-* + *copula* + *subject* as in *Where is daddy?*). The first *wh-* words used in this construction are *what* and *where.*

At an MLU of 2.75 to 3.5 or 33 to 37 months, a child begins to invert subjects and auxiliary verbs. During this phase a child also is acquiring the auxiliary verb in other sentence types, although some errors will persist. Here are two examples of noninversion by a 34- and 53-month-old child respectively, "What we can do?" and "We going on a froggy hunt?" At about the same time or shortly after, a child begins to invert within *wh-* and yes/no copular and *do* addition interrogative constructions (Santelmann, Berk, Austin, Somashekar, & Lust, 2002).

In *wh-* questions, the type of *wh-* word may influence whether the auxiliary is inverted. In general, the earlier the *wh-* word is acquired, the more likely the verb is to be inverted. Hence, a child would be more likely to invert the verb in *what* (*What is daddy doing?*) questions than in *Why* (*Why are we going?*) questions. Correct inversion of the subject and the auxiliary verb also varies with specific verbs (Rowland, Pine, Lieven, & Theakston, 2005). For example, *are, have, do,* and modal auxiliary verbs were significantly more difficult for children to invert than auxiliary verbs *is* and *has.*

To add to your confusion, noninverted questions such as "He's eating clams?" or "He's eating what?" are acceptable in some contexts. Say these sentences out loud and you'll note that you would use these to obtain clarification of a previous statement or an indication of surprise, as in the following exchange:

SPEAKER 1: *I just saw Mike at the Fish Shack eating clams!*
SPEAKER 2: *He was eating what?*

Contrast this with inverted interrogatives, such as "What was Mike eating?"

The acquisition of auxiliary *do* and modal auxiliaries is complex. Modal auxiliaries in declaratives appear after the subject and internal to the sentence, as in "Derek *can* run quickly." In contrast, in most questions auxiliaries occur in an inverted subject–verb form before the subject, as in "Where *can* we go?" or "*Can* we eat now?" The exception occurs when the *wh-* word is the subject of the sentence, as in "Who *can* go with her?"

To add to the confusion, the auxiliary *do* usually does not occur in positive declarative sentences except for emphasis, as in "I love roller coasters" contrasted with "I *do* love roller coasters." The auxiliary *do* tends to occur in its positive form only in interrogatives, as in "*Does* she run track?" The negative *do,* on the other hand, can occur in both declaratives, as in "He *doesn't* eat dairy products," and in interrogatives, as in "*Doesn't* she want to go?"

It should be obvious why it takes English-speaking children time to master many of these rules, especially those governing interrogatives. Most preschool children will produce interrogatives with errors at the same time that they produce correct interrogatives for a relatively long period of time. In general, we can say that

- Error rates in *wh-* questions vary with the specific *wh-* word used. For example, most children make more errors in *why* questions.
- Errors occur with some auxiliaries more than others. For example, in both declaratives and interrogatives of children ages 34 to 42 months, *can* tends to be produced correctly most often, followed by *will* and then *does* (Rowland & Theakston, 2009). This order may reflect the additional knowledge regarding how to mark tense, person, and number required to allow correct use of *do.*
- Higher error rates tend to occur in negative questions.

At all ages, performance in declaratives is significantly better than in questions. Taken together, these trends suggest a complex interaction among sentence type, negative–positive polarity, and type of auxiliary verb.

Children seem to understand the relation between positive and negative forms of auxiliary *can, will,* and *does* in declaratives by age 3. Although children seem to recognize the relationship, this alone is not sufficient to ensure correct use of negative forms in questions. Negative interrogatives pose particular problems for children in the earliest stages of auxiliary acquisition. For example, there are very low levels of correct use in negative questions at 35 months. By 41 months, however, this difference is negligible (Rowland & Theakston, 2009).

To some extent, input from adults seems to affect acquisition order, although this alone does not explain the process. For example, adult yes/no questions starting with *can* are more frequent than questions beginning with *will* and *does.* Although all forms of *do (do, does, did)* occur at a high frequency in yes/no questions, this does not appear to be reflected in high levels of accurate use of *does,* suggesting a lack of generalizing across auxiliary forms.

When children produce auxiliary verb substitutions in interrogatives, they predominantly use either *can* or *is* in the inverted position. These two auxiliaries are very frequent in yes/no questions of mothers. This suggests that children rely on high-frequency forms in their own production of questions but combine these high-frequency auxiliaries with different subjects.

Auxiliary substitution errors might arise for two reasons.

- Children lack syntactic knowledge and have not learned how to produce declaratives and/or interrogatives correctly with some auxiliaries, and, therefore make substitution errors more often with forms with which they are less familiar.
- Children lack semantic knowledge and do not understand the meaning of more subtle distinctions between some auxiliaries.

At 35 months, nearly half of the substitution errors are double marking. The resultant utterances include two auxiliary verbs, as in "*Is* the boy *doesn't* ride his bike?" or "*Is* the girl *will* jump over it?"

By 40 months, most children attain the basic adult question form. In addition, *who, when,* and *how* interrogatives appear, although the child still has some difficulty with the temporal or time aspects of the last two. Examples of child questions are presented in Box 9.3.

The general order of acquisition of *wh-* question types is determined primarily by the frequency of use by caregivers and to a lesser degree by the elements in the declarative form of the sentence that each *wh-* word replaces (Rowland, Pine, Lieven, & Theakston, 2003). Words such as *what, where,* and *who* are pronoun forms for the sentence elements they replace. For example, in the sentence "Mother is eating ice cream," we can substitute *what* for *ice cream.* The resultant question is "What is mother eating?" In contrast, words such as *how* and *when* are used to ask for semantic relations within the sentence. These semantic relations are more difficult than simple noun substitutions; they develop later and usually cannot be replaced by a single word. The late development of *why* interrogatives can be explained in similar fashion. Unlike the other *wh-* types, *why* interrogatives affect the entire clause rather than sentence elements or relationships.

The ability to respond to *wh-* questions is also related to semantics and to the immediate context. In general, preschool children are more successful in giving appropriate and accurate responses when the question refers to objects, persons, and events in the immediate setting. Recognition of the type of information sought, such as an object or a location, seems to precede the ability to respond with the specific information requested, such as the name of the object or location.

Between an MLU of 3.75 to 4.5 interrogative development is mainly concerned with tensing and modals. In addition, the almost 4-year-old child stabilizes the use of the inverted auxiliary.

BOX 9.3

Examples of Interrogative Sentences of Preschoolers

26 months:	Want on?
30 months:	What is that thing?
	Where's my sticker book?
42 months:	Chalk used to be here but where did it go? (Conjoining)
46 months:	Does yours smell like this?
	Does this go this way?
50 months:	How do you put these on?
	Let's show the women that's in here, okay? (Immature tag with embedded clause)
	Can I have a little bit, too?
61 months:	Why are you gonna be back in a little while? (Embedded phrases)
64 months:	Do you know what person this is? (Embedded clause)
	What happens if we break this? (Conjoining)
	Looks like soap, doesn't it? (Mature tag)
	I wonder what that is? (Embedded clause)

Mature tag questions appear at this relatively late point due to their relative complexity and infrequent usage in American English. Less complex forms—using tags such as *okay, huh,* and *aye,* as in "I do this, okay?"—develop earlier. These forms are more commonly used among English-speaking populations of Canada and Australia in sentences such as "Nice day, aye?"

Three phases have been identified in the development of tag questions. At first, grammatically simple tag forms, such as *okay* and *right,* are used. Truer tags are added later, but with no negation of the proposition (Weeks, 1992). For example, the child might ask, "You like cookies, *do* you?" Finally, the full adult tag, as in "You like cookies, *don't you*?" or "You don't like cookies, *do you*?" is acquired during early school age. Mature tags require complex syntax, so simple tags predominate until age 5.

American English–speaking children acquire the adult form of tag questions later than do British and Australian children because of its infrequent use in American English. Canadian children may also be somewhat late in mastering the full adult form because of the colloquial use of *aye,* as in "You bought a new jacket, *aye*? Just right for this snow, *aye*?" I usually tease my Canadian students that it is impossible for them to make a declaration because they always attach *aye* to the end of every sentence. (Which, of course, they don't.)

Negative interrogatives appear after age 5. In general, negative interrogatives, such as "Aren't you going?" are first acquired almost exclusively in the uninverted form, as in "You aren't going?"

IMPERATIVE-SENTENCE FORM

Adult imperative sentences appear around age 2½. In the imperative form the speaker requests, demands, asks, insists, commands, and so on that the listener perform some act. The verb is uninflected and the subject, *you,* is understood and therefore omitted. Examples include the following:

> Gimme a cookie, please.
> Throw the ball to me.
> Pass the peas, please.

It is somewhat difficult to recognize the imperative in English because there are no morphologic markers. Younger children will produce early forms that mirror imperative sentence form, such as "Eat cookie." These are not true imperatives, however, because young children often omit the subject from sentences clearly intended to be declarative. Instead, these omissions reflect cognitive processing limitations. This is not meant to imply that toddlers cannot demand of or command others. Even at a prelinguistic level, infants are very adept at expressing their needs. At age 18 months, my granddaughter had the presence to demand "Juice NOW."

NEGATIVE-SENTENCE FORM

Five adult forms of the negative exist in English: (1) *not* and *-n't* attached to the verb; (2) negative words, such as *nobody* and *nothing*; (3) the determiner *no* used before nouns or nounlike words, as in "*No* cookies for you"; (4) negative adverbs, such as *never* and *nowhere*; and (5) negative prefixes, such as *un-, dis-,* and *non-*. The different forms develop at different times.

The earliest negative to appear is the single-word form *no,* which is frequently found within the first 50 words. Syntactic negation appears in two-word utterances. The negative element appears prior to the verb, as in "No eat ice cream," and utterances such as "No Daddy go bye-bye" appear less frequently. The full *negative + sentence nucleus* form is usually seen in rejection of a proposed or current course of action. For example, if the father were in the process of leaving and the child objected, he or she might state, "No Daddy go bye-bye."

The specific negative element(s) the child uses seems to reflect parental use with the child. Some parents prefer to control behavior with *no*; others employ *don't*. In general, children prefer to use certain forms to fulfill specific intentions. Since this is an individual preference, there is great variety. Examples of negative sentences from several different children are presented in Box 9.4.

There seem to be three periods of syntactic development of negation (Table 9.7). The first period, just discussed, occurs up to an MLU of 2.25. In the second period, around age 30 months, the negative structure is placed between the subject and the predicate or main verb. A child uses the contractions *can't, don't, no,* and *not* interchangeably. The child does not differentiate these forms, and their positive elements, *can* and *do,* appear only later. Hence, the sentences "I don't eat it" and "I can't eat it" may mean the same thing. *Won't* appears shortly thereafter and, for a brief period, may also be used interchangeably with *no, not, don't,* and *can't.*

In the final period, an MLU of 2.75 to 3.5, a 3-year-old child develops other auxiliary forms. The child develops the positive elements *can, do, does, did, will,* and *be,* which is used with *not* followed by a main verb, as in "She *cannot go.*" Contracted forms also continue to occur in *don't, can't,* and *won't.* It will be some time, however, before the child correctly uses all the morphologic markers for person, number, and tense with auxiliary verbs. Because use of auxiliaries is a relatively new behavior for the child, he or she may continue to make errors, such as double tense markers, as in "I didn't did it."

By an MLU of 3.5 to 3.75 or 38 to 40 months of age, a child's negative contractions include *isn't, aren't, doesn't,* and *didn't.* This development of negative forms continues with the addition of the past tense of *be* (*wasn't*) and modals such as *wouldn't, couldn't,* and *shouldn't.* These forms appear infrequently at first.

Four-year-olds comprehend many negatives, especially with descriptive terms, such as *big,* to mean the opposite, thus, "He's not big; he's little." Not all negatives can be interpreted in

---

BOX *9.4*

Examples of Negative Sentences of Preschoolers

27 months:	I **not** make mess.
42 months:	I'm **not nothing** of yours (Double negative, but then a self-correction);
	I'm **not having anything** of yours.
52 months:	I think he's **never** probably done it before.
57 months:	But I **can't** tell you when I'm back from vacation.

Negative conversation between 54-month-old E and 32-month-old B.

B: Look what I found. A mitten. I found a mitten.
E: That's **not** a mitten.
B: What is it?
E: He's a puppet.
B: Puppet. And that's a puppet. That's a puppet.
E: This is **not** a puppet. This is a big soft worm.
B: Throw it on the floor. I **don't** want it.

this manner. For example, "He's not walking" has no opposite and could mean that he's crawling, running, rollerblading, biking, or driving, to name just a few possibilities. Even though children have a preference for a strong negative interpretation, they are capable of using semantic characteristics of objects, aspects of the verb, and experience to modify their interpretations (Morris, 2003).

It would be incorrect to assume that children master the negative within the preschool period. Negative interrogatives do not appear until after age 5. In addition, indefinite forms, such as *nobody, no one, none,* and *nothing,* prove troublesome even for some adults. It is not uncommon to hear

> I *don't* want *none.*
> *Nobody don't* like me.
> I *ain't* scared of *nothing.*
> I *didn't* get *no* cookies.

Some of these double negatives occur so frequently in the speech of children and some adults that they almost seem acceptable.

SUBORDINATE CLAUSE DEVELOPMENT

Subordinate or dependent clauses, discussed in more detail in Appendix E, are used by language users to combine clauses in a certain way that forms a complex sentence. Among preschool children we see two types primarily, object-noun-phrase complements and relative clauses. Clausal object-noun-phrase complements first appear around age 3. These subordinate clauses generally have the form of simple sentences, as in

> I know *that you can do it.*
> I think *that I like stew.*

At first, the basic *I know* format first appears alone meaning something akin to *maybe.* Other pronouns and verb tensing appear only rarely (Diessel & Tomasello, 2001). The *I know* fixed phrase is then pieced with a subordinate clause.

In general, the subordinate clause fills an object role for verbs, such as *think, guess, see, say, wish, know, hope, like, let, remember, forget, look,* and *show.* The verb in the main clause is most often *think,* as in "I think that I saw a cat." Above an MLU of 4.5, the child may omit the conjunction *that.* Other examples are presented in Box 9.5.

A second type of embedding occurs with the attention-getting verbs like *Look* and *See,* followed by a clause. This type is almost exclusively imperative. Both the *I know* and *Look/See* formats suggest that initially a child's learning may be word-specific rather than representing adult-like understanding.

Later subordinating words in embedded *wh-* complements include *wh-* words such as *what, where,* and *when,* with *what* being used most frequently. Since this form appears at about the same time that the child begins to acquire the adult interrogative form, some initial confusion may exist. Resultant forms may include

> I know *what is that.*
> Tell me *where does the smoke go.*

Other examples are presented in Box 9.5.

BOX 9.5

Examples of Embedded Noun-Phrase Complement Clauses of Preschoolers

32 months:	Oh, look **what I found.**
52 months:	Sometimes I forget **what animals they are.**
	I think **the problem is the duckies don't like coming here.**
54 months:	Actually, I'm pretending **it's paint.**
59 months:	I think **that's funny.**
	You know **what I'm going to be when I grow up?**
	(Embedding and conjoining)
60 months:	You know **how people leave out something sometimes.**
	I remember **that I fell down outside.**
	I don't know **where mom put it,** but I think **it's in my room.**
	(Multiple embedding)

Almost all of children's initial relative clauses are the same two forms (Diessel & Tomasello, 2001):

Here's the X that verbs
That's the X that verb-s

The main clause basically introduces a new topic using *Here/That* plus *is*. The complex relative clause construction is based in a simpler set of word-specific or item-based constructions.

Many early relative clauses modify empty or nonspecific nouns—*one, kind, thing, place, way*—to form sentences such as "This is the one (*that*) *I want*" or "This is the way (*that*) *I do it.*" In these examples, the object of the sentence is *one* or *way,* and the subordinate clause specifies *which one* or *which way.* Later, relative clauses are used to modify common nouns, as in "Chien Ping has the book (that) I bought."

Full relative clauses appear close to the fourth birthday, although partial forms may appear earlier. They develop gradually, accounting for less than 15% of the two-clause utterances of 5-year-olds. As with other types of embedding, expansion begins at the end of the sentence, as in the following:

This is the kind *what I like.*
This is the toy *that I want.*

In these examples, the relative clause is attached to and modifies the object of the sentence. Some examples of relative clauses attached to the subject include

The one *that you have* is big.
The boy *who lives in that house* is a brat.

Relative clauses attached to the subject do not develop until after 5 years of age, although these forms are still rare by age 7. Examples are presented in Box 9.6.

Many connective words used to join clauses are first learned in nonconnective contexts. For example, *what* and *where* appear in interrogatives prior to their use as relative pronouns.

> ### BOX 9.6
>
> **Examples of Embedded Relative Clauses of Preschoolers**
>
> | | |
> |---|---|
> | 41 months: | That's all the kites **I bought.** |
> | 52 months: | I love birdies **that do tricks.** |
> | 53 months: | Well, there's other things **that go in it.** |
> | 54 months: | That's a pretty necklace **that you have on.** |
> | | This is **where we get it out from.** |
> | 60 months: | That's one of God's things **that he doesn't like.** |

The connective *when* is an exception. *When* is used as a connector to mark temporal relations before the *when* question form develops. Thus, children are likely to produce "I don't know *when* he went" before "*When* did he leave?" Most preschool errors involve use of the wrong relative pronoun as in the following examples (McKee, McDaniel, & Snedeker, 1998, p. 587):

> The potato what she's rolling.
> Those plates why the elephants are eating them.
> The chairs who are flying.

Mature English speakers can omit some relative pronouns, such as *that,* without changing the meaning of the sentence. At first, a preschool child needs these pronouns in order to interpret the sentence. By age 4, however, she or he can comprehend a sentence that omits the relational word. Most children begin to omit some relative pronouns in production soon after, although this form is rare in the speech of preschool children:

> This is the candy *that* Hasan likes. (relative pronoun present)
> This is the candy Hasan likes. (relative pronoun omitted)

Most 4-year-old children can produce multiple embeddings within a single sentence, although such forms are rare even throughout the early school years. For example, a child may combine a subordinate clause (italicized) with an infinitive (underlined) to produce

> I think *we g*<u>*otta go home now*</u>.

Later forms also include conjoined clauses and embedding in the same sentence.

COMPOUND SENTENCE DEVELOPMENT

Most children have appropriate production of *and* to list entities (*dogs and cats and . . .*) between 25 and 27 months of age. Cognitively, children are able to form collections of things. Around age 3, individual sentences within an ordered series may begin with *and,* as in the following:

> And I petted the dog. And he barked. And I runned home.

In this example, *and* fills a temporal function meaning *and then.*

At an MLU of approximately 3.5, the conjunction *because* appears, either alone or attached to a single clause, as in the following examples:

ADULT: Scott, why did you do that?
CHILD: Because.
ADULT: Scott, why did you do that?
CHILD: Because Roger did.

Utterances with *because* are particularly interesting, demonstrating an inability by young children to give reverse order. Since a 3- or 4-year-old child has difficulty recounting events nonsequentially, she or he will respond to questions with a result response rather than a causal one (see the discussion of 4-year-olds in Chapter 8). In response to "Why did you fall off your bicycle?" the child is likely to respond, "'Cause I hurt my leg"—a result, not a cause.

The first clausal conjoining occurs with the conjunction *and* around age 3½ (Table 9.7). For example, a child might say, "I went to the party *and* Jimmie hit me." It is not until closer to age 4, however, that most children can use this form. In general, *and* is used as the all-purpose conjunction, as in the following:

We left *and* mommy called. (meaning *when*)
We had a party *and* we saw a movie. (meaning *then*)
She went home *and* they had a fight. (meaning *because*)

Depending on the child, *and* may be used five to 20 times as frequently as the next most common conjunction in the child's repertoire. Even in the narratives of 5-year-olds and school-age children, *and* is the predominant connector of clauses.

Clausal conjoining with *if* appears shortly after *and,* followed quickly by *because,* and *when, but,* and *so* even later. Most children are capable of conjoining clauses with *if* during this latter period. These are not usually complicated sentences; they are more likely to be of the "I can *if* I want to" form.

Initially, the causal relationship may be signaled by *that's why,* as in "They were running; that's why they broke the window." Note that the order of the clauses is as they happened and not the reverse we would find if the child had used *because.* The order of conjunction acquisition reported for American English seems to be true for other languages as well and may reflect the underlying cognitive relationship.

The conjunctions *because* and *so* are initially used to mark psychological causality or statements of people's intentions. For example, use of *because* might explain "He hit me *because he's mean*" rather than "The bridge fell *because the truck was too heavy.*" If the child was to discuss the bridge falling, he or she might explain, "The bridge fell *because it was tired,*" using feeling or intention to explain the event. Increasingly, children recount the past as they become older, and, as noted, narratives become more causally related. With this recounting, there is a greater necessity to discuss the intentions preceding behaviors, as in Box 9.7.

At around age 4, a child may begin to exhibit conjoining and embedding of both phrases and clauses within the same sentence. Most children are using this type of structure, although sparingly, by age 5. Such multiple embedding might result in the following:

Sally wants <u>to stay</u> <u>on the sand</u> and Carrie is scared <u>of crabs</u>.
      <u>Inf. Ph. Prep. Ph.</u>   <u>Prep. Ph.</u>
      Independent Clause   Independent Clause

BOX 9.7

Examples of Conjoining Clauses of Preschoolers

---

32 months:	I'm gonna see **if** I can turn the light off.
46 months:	The first time **when** I went one wave catched me.
52 months:	Maybe both of us can try and run down there **and** try to catch one.
	If he would've been a person **then** he would have been able to scratch himself like that.
	And shut the cage door **so** they can't get out.
	I don't know *what's gonna happen* **but** I think *it's gonna work.* (*Embedding* and **conjoining** of clauses)
57 months:	We better let this stay out **when** I need to go on vacation.
60 months:	And Colin said *he won't lie* **but** then he did lie. (*Embedding* and **conjoining** of clauses)
	I had something for you **but** I don't know *where it is.* (*Embedding* and **conjoining** of clauses)
	We went to Pizza Hut **but** we were going to the movies **so** we didn't know *what happened.* (*Embedding* and three-clause **conjoining**)

Three-clause sentences, both embedded and conjoined, appear at about the same age. The child might join three main clauses, as in the following:

> *Julio flew his kite, I ate a hot dog,* and *papa took a nap.*

Another variation might include the embedding and conjoining of three clauses, as in the following:

> <u>I saw Spider-Man,</u> and <u>Clarita saw the one</u> <u>that had that other guy</u>.
>   Indep. Clause   Indep. Clause   Dependent Clause

By age 4½ to 5, multiple embeddings and three-clause sentences may account for about 11% of all child utterances.

Pragmatic and semantic factors seem to affect conjoining as well. Clausal conjoining occurs when two referents must be clearly distinguished for the listener. A child encodes only what he or she presupposes the listener needs to interpret the sentence.

Although the form of compound sentences is temporal, *clause + conjunction + clause,* the semantic relations between the clauses, as expressed in the conjunction, form a hierarchy that affects the order of acquisition: additive, temporal, causal, or contrastive. Initial clausal conjoining is additive; no relationship is expressed, as in "Irene went on the hike and Robyn was at Grandma's." Next, conjoining is used to express either simultaneous or sequential events, as in "Diego went to school and he went shopping after dinner." Causal relationships with *and* and *that's why* appear first, as in "*X and* [led to] *Y.*" Later *because* is used. Finally, the child expresses a contrasting relationship, usually with the use of *but.* The late appearance of the conjunction *but* in clausal conjoining is probably related to the complex nature of such propositions. The expectation that is set up in the first clause is not confirmed in the second, as in "I went to the zoo, but I didn't see any tapirs."

SUMMARY

The syntactic development of the preschool child is rapid and very complex. The interrelatedness of both syntactic structure and syntactic development makes it difficult to describe patterns of development. In general, the preschool child tries to discover and employ syntactic regularity. Note the conversation in Table 9.8.

As in many aspects of learning, syntactic acquisition is facilitated by practice (Keren-Portnoy, 2006). Early learning facilitates subsequent learning. The language-learning principles discussed in detail in Chapter 6 are evident in the acquisition process.

As you will note when you talk with young children, their sentences are often disruptive and filled with false starts and revisions. These behaviors indicate similar aspects of development. First, disruptions tend to occur in the longest, most complex sentences, indicating that these sentences are at the leading or growing edge of the child's language, much as imitation was earlier (Rispoli & Hadley, 2001). In these sentences, a child is at increased risk for difficulties.

As a child's language develops, the rate of disruptions followed by revision also increases (Rispoli, 2003). Revision involves self-monitoring and rapid replacement of words and structures with linguistic alternatives. Thus, increasing revision demonstrates more skill not less.

TABLE *9.8 Late Preschool Language Sample*

1.	Oh, this almost looks like the other one.
2.	See? But it has the same hat.
3.	Hey, I'm gonna put the sticker right here, okay?
4.	Put your stickers right here. So we can pretend these are the TVs.
5.	Okay. I'm making dinner.
6.	Oh, onions. Oh.
7.	Oh, let me toast it. No way.
8.	I'm gonna cook, okay?
9.	While you do your stuff, okay? I'm toasting. I'm making a piece of bread.
10.	I'm eating this bread.
11.	Good bread.
12.	I think I'm gonna go to work soon.
13.	Get this orange out of here. Honey . . .
14.	What?

TABLE *9.8* **Continued**

15. Let's get married now.

16. Just a place to get married . . . under the table.
    We have to have our toast under. . . . You be married too. Don't touch me.

17. Mine.
    No, you can touch me, you can touch me. I just kidding. . . .

18. I know you just kidding.
    Why'd you say "bye"?

19. Because.

20. I said "bye." . . .
    Here have a piece of bread.

21. I said "bye" just because . . . I said "bye" 'cause I had to go to work and you won't let me.

22. That's why.
    Go to work, honey.

23. Mmmm.

24. It got real leaves.

25. This is a real leaves.

26. They're real leaves, you know?

27. See?
    What? 'Cause they come off?

28. Uh-huh.

29. Wanna see?
    Don't do it. You'll break their toys.

30. Mmmm, bye, I'm going to work.
    Bye-bye. Pretend you came back with that hat on from work and I made you a piece of bread and put a piece of bread.

31. And I won't eat it.
    Okay. When you came back from work, I'll give you a piece of bread.

32. Okay, then I won't eat it.

33. Bye.
    Bye-bye, hon.

Phonemic and Phonologic Development

As mentioned, many of the morphologic and syntactic changes in the preschool years are related to phonologic development and reflect the child's underlying phonologic rule system. In addition to developing speech sounds, a preschool child is also developing phonologic rules that govern sound distribution and sequencing.

As with other aspects of language, a child's phonologic development progresses through a long period of language decoding and hypothesis building. The child uses many rule forms that will be discarded or modified later. These rules reflect natural processes that act to simplify adult forms of speech for young children. Much of a child's morphologic production will depend on her or his ability to perceive and produce phonologic units. During the preschool years, as a child acquires speech sounds and a phonologic system, she or he develops the ability to determine and signal differences in meaning through speech sounds. It appears that perception of speech sounds precedes production but that the two aspects are not parallel.

SPEECH-SOUND ACQUISITION

Speech is a very complicated acoustic event. No other meaningful environmental sounds, not even music, achieve its level of complexity. In perception of fluent connected speech, listeners use many different parts of the phonemic context to decode the signal. If we separate the /t/ in *tea* (/ti/) from the /i/ it sounds like a very short "tsch." Yet, our brain is able to integrate the signal as it comes in, creating the unified perception of *tea*. To further complicate this process, the /t/ in *tea* is very different from the /t/ in *toe*, but we are able to perceive the same sound across these different phonemic contexts.

Several studies have attempted to establish an order of phoneme acquisition by young children. Comparing the results of these studies (Figure 9.2), we can make the following statements:

1. As a group, vowels are acquired before consonants. English vowels are acquired by age 3.
2. As a group, the nasals are acquired first, followed by the plosives, approximants, lateral approximants, fricatives, and affricatives.
3. As a group, the glottals are acquired first, followed by the bilabials, velars, alveolars and post-alveolars, dentals and labiodentals, and palatals.
4. Sounds are first acquired in the initial position in words.
5. Consonant clusters and blends are not acquired until age 7 or 8, although some clusters appear as early as age 4. These early clusters include /s/ + nasal, /s/ + approximant, /s/ + stop, and stop + approximant in the initial position and nasal + stop in the final position.
6. There are great individual differences, and the age of acquisition for some sounds may vary by as much as three years.

Most 3-year-olds have mastered the vowel sounds and the consonants /p/, /m/, /h/, /n/, /w/, /b/, /k/, /g/, and /d/. There is much individual variation in speech-sound development, however, and at least 50% of 3-year-olds are also proficient in their use of /t/, /ŋ/, /f/, /j/, /r/, /l/, and /s/ (Figure 9.2). By age 4, most children have added /t/, /ŋ/, /f/, and /j/. At least 50% of all 4-year-olds can produce /r/, /l/, /s/, /tʃ/, /ʃ/, and /z/ (Figure 9.2). By the fifth birthday, most children add /ɹ/, /l/, /s/, /tʃ/, /ʃ/, /z/, /dʒ/, and /v/. At least 50% can also produce the /ð/ ("th" in "*there*") sound correctly (Figure 9.2). Five-year-olds still have difficulty with a few consonant sounds and with consonant blends, as in "*street*" or "*clean*."

Although there is considerable agreement across languages as diverse as English and Cantonese on the order of consonant development, no universal ordering exists. Rather, consonant development is the result of a complex interplay of biological factors and such factors as each sound's articulatory difficulty, frequency of occurrence in a language, and functional load or the relative importance of a phoneme in contrast to other phonemes. For example, the

FIGURE *9.2* *Average Age of Acquisition of English Consonants*

Compiled from Olmstead (1971) and Sander (1972), representing the ages at which 50% of English-speaking children can produce a sound correctly in all positions in conversation and formal testing.

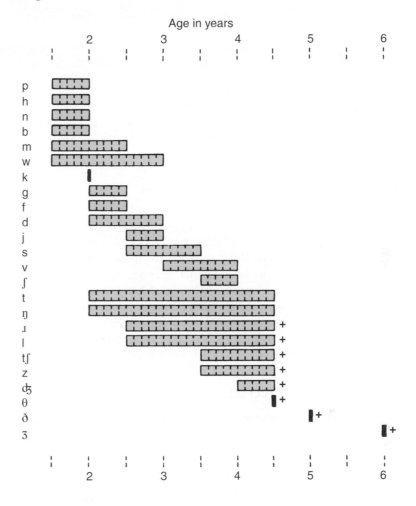

voiced "th" or /ð/ phoneme (*this, that*) in English could be replaced with /d/ in all instances with very little confusion, so the functional load is low. In contrast, the /w/ phoneme in English is used in a variety of phonemic contexts and would be difficult to replace, thus its functional load is high. Functional load seems to be particularly important for the acquisition of American English consonants, while frequency is more important in the acquisition of Cantonese (Stokes & Surendran, 2005).

Still, surprising similarity exists in speech-sound acquisition across languages (Amayreh & Dyson, 1998; Paulson, 1991; So & Dodd, 1995). The specific use patterns of different languages influence both the order and speed of acquisition. The acquisitional order of phonemes common to several languages is presented in Table 9.9. Although all English

TABLE *9.9* *Acquisitional Order of Consonant Sounds Across Languages*

AGE	ENGLISH	SPANISH	CANTONESE	ARABIC
By 3 years	t, d, k, f, m, n, w	k, m, n, j	t, n, p, j, m, w	t, k, f, m, n, w
3–4	j, s	d, f, t	k	d
4–5		w	f, s	
5–6		s		s
6+				j

This data is the compilation of a liberal interpretation of several studies, often with differing criteria. Differences reflect the slight variation in phoneme production in different languages and the use patterns within each language. Only phonemes used in all four languages are presented. Despite some glaring differences, there is considerable similarity across languages.

Sources: Information from Amayreh & Dyson (1998); Paulson (1991); Smit, Hand, Freilinger, Bernthal, & Bird (1990); So & Dodd (1995).

consonants are acquired by age 8, some Arabic consonants are not acquired until later in their standard form, although more casual forms are acquired earlier (Amayreh, 2003).

Compared to monolingual Spanish and monolingual English preschoolers, the speech sound development of bilingual 3 to 4-year-olds is slower and shows the effects of transfer from Spanish to English (Fabiano-Smith & Goldstein, 2010). The frequency of use of the sound does not predict acquisition of either similar or dissimilar sounds indicating both separation and interaction between the bilingual children's two languages (Paradis & Genesee, 1996).

PHONOLOGIC PROCESSES

We will discuss only the phonologic processes most common of the preschool child (Table 9.10). Most of these processes, introduced in Chapter 7, are discarded or modified by age 4.

Syllable Structure Processes

Once a child begins babbling, the basic speech unit used is the CV syllable. During the preschool years, the child frequently attempts to simplify production by reducing words to this form or to the CVCV structure.

The most basic form of this process affects the final consonant. The final consonant may be deleted or followed by a vowel. Final-consonant processes usually disappear by age 3 (Grunwell, 1981).

In addition, a child may delete unstressed syllables to produce, for example, *way* for *away.* Initially, any unstressed syllable may be eliminated, although over time a child typically adopts a pattern of deleting only initial unstressed syllables. Syllable reduction may be more complex than simply deleting the unstressed syllable and may reflect the interaction of syllable stress, location within the word, and phrase boundaries (Snow, 1998). This deletion process continues until age 4. Development of syllables, word shapes, and consonant cluster types are presented in Table 9.11.

TABLE *9.10* *Phonologic Processes of Preschool Children*

PROCESSES	EXAMPLES
Syllable structure	
Deletion of final consonants	*cu* (/kʌ/) for *cup*
Deletion of unstressed syllables	*nana* for *banana*
Reduplication	*mama, dada, wawa* (water)
Reduction of clusters	/s/ + consonant (*stop*) = delete /s/ (*top*)
Assimilation	
Contiguous	
Between consonants	*beds* (/bɛdz/), *bets* (/bɛts/)
Regressive VC (vowel alters toward some feature of C)	nasalization of vowels: *can*
Noncontiguous	
Back assimilation	*dog* becomes *gog*
	dark becomes *gawk*
Substitution	
Obstruants (plosives, fricatives, and affricatives)	
Stopping: replace sound with a plosive	*this* becomes *dis*
Fronting: replace palatals and velars (/k/ and /g/) with alveolars (/t/ and /d/)	*Kenny* becomes *Tenny*
	go becomes *do*
Nasals	
Fronting (/ŋ/ becomes /n/)	*something* becomes *somethin*
Approximants replaced by	
Plosive	*yellow* becomes *yedow*
Glide	*rabbit* becomes *wabbit*
Another approximant	*girl* becomes *gaul* (/gɔl/)
Vowels	
Neutralization: vowels reduced to /ə/ or /a/	*want to* becomes *wanna*
Deletion of sounds	*balloon* becomes *ba-oon*

Source: Information from Ingram (1976).

Reduplication is a third process for simplifying syllable structure in which one syllable becomes the same as another in the word, resulting in the reduplicated structure, as in *wawa* for *water*. This process disappears for most children before 30 months of age (Grunwell, 1981). The final syllable is usually deleted or changed. Otherwise, the clearly stressed syllable is most often reproduced. The final position is not particularly important for preschoolers unless it is preceded by an *un*stressed syllable, as in *elephant* or *ambulance.*

Finally, preschoolers reduce or simplify consonant clusters, usually by deleting one consonant. Unlike some Asian languages, English has a large variety of clusters that can make production of many words difficult for young children. Cluster reduction is also one of the most common phonologic processes seen in the speech of Spanish-speaking Puerto Rican

TABLE *9.11* *Phonologic Development*

AGE IN MONTHS	SYLLABLE STRUCTURE	NUMBER OF SYLLABLES
24	CV, VC CVC	2
36	CV, VC, CVC, CC___, ___CC	2
48	CV, VC, CVC, CC___, ___CC, CC___CC	3
60	CV, VC, CVC, CC___, ___CC, CC___CC	3+

Source: Information from Shriberg (1993).

preschoolers (Goldstein & Iglesias, 1996). While deletions differ based on the parent language and the individual child, we can predict with some certainty how preschoolers will simplify many clusters. The following are a few examples from English:

Cluster	*Deletion*	*Example*
/s/ + plosive	/s/	*stop* becomes *top*
plosive or fricative	liquid or glide	*bring* becomes *bing*
+ liquid or glide	*swim* becomes *sim*	

A child may also exhibit **epenthesis,** or vowel insertion, producing both consonants with a vowel between them. Thus, *tree* becomes *teree.* This vowel-insertion process is infrequent. The specific strategy used and the speed of consonant cluster development vary with the sounds involved (Vihman & Greenlee, 1987).

Nasal clusters are more complex. If a nasal (/m, n, ŋ/) plus a plosive or fricative is reduced, younger children will delete the nasal. Thus, *bump* becomes *bup.* Older preschoolers will delete the plosive if it is voiced (/b, d, g/). Employing this rule, the older child reduces *mend* to *men.*

Clusters emerge in the speech of children at around age 2 (Lleó & Prinz, 1996). Emergence is probably related to having more mature motor control and to experiencing a spurt in vocabulary that necessitates more specific production as a means of distinguishing different words. Although most 2-year-olds can produce consonant clusters, few do so correctly (McLeod, van Doorn, & Reed, 2001a). Individual differences reflect the sounds, types of clusters, and the locations within words. Development is slow, and by 30 months only half of children are producing some clusters correctly.

Children's earliest attempts to produce clusters are inconsistent (McLeod, van Doorn, & Reed, 2001b). Over time, nonpermissible combinations, such as /pw/, give way to permissible ones (Watson & Scukanec, 1997), usually in the final position in words first. By age 3, children are producing final clusters, such as /nd, ts, nz, ŋk, ps/ and /nts/. Word-initial clusters may offer a greater challenge because of the greater variety. As a group, s-blends in the initial position (/sp, sk, sm/) are mastered before blends with /l/ and /r/ (/pl, gl, br, kr/), which, in turn, precede three-consonant blends (/skw, spl, θr/) (Smit, Hand, Freilinger, Bernthal, & Bird, 1990).

Most children stop using the cluster-reduction strategy by age 4. Consonant clusters are mastered by age 6 or 7 (Smit et al., 1990).

Assimilation Processes

Assimilation processes simplify production by producing different sounds in the same way. In general, one sound becomes similar to another in the same word. Assimilation processes may be contiguous or noncontiguous and progressive or regressive. Contiguous assimilation occurs when the two elements are next to each other; noncontiguous assimilation, when apart. Progressive assimilation occurs when the affected element follows the element that influences it; regressive assimilation, when the affected element precedes. For example, children generally produce two varieties of *doggie.* One, *doddie,* exemplifies progressive assimilation, while the other, *goggie,* is regressive.

Regressive contiguous assimilation is exhibited in both CV and VC syllables. The consonant in CV structures may be affected by the voicing of the vowel, as when the voiceless *t* in *top* is produced as a voiced *d,* resulting in *dop.* In regressive VC assimilation, the vowel alters toward some feature of the consonant, as in the nasalized vowels in *can* and *ham.* Progressive contiguous assimilation is much less common.

The most common type of noncontiguous assimilation is back assimilation, in which one consonant is modified toward another that is produced farther back in the oral cavity. The *d* in *dark,* for example, may become a *g* to produce *gawk* (/gɔk/) to conform with the back consonant /k/.

Substitution Processes

Many preschoolers substitute sounds in their speech. These substitutions are not random and usually are in only one direction. The /w/ is often substituted for /ɹ/, for example, but only rarely does the opposite occur. In addition, when a child masters a phoneme, it does not overgeneralize to words in which the substituted sound is the correct sound. For example, the child may say *wabbit* until mastering /ɹ/. Although the child can now produce *rabbit,* the /ɹ/ does not overgeneralize to the /w/ in *what* and *wanna,* in which /w/ is correct.

Sound-for-sound substitutions are usually articulatory in nature. Phonological processes, on the other hand, involve substitutions of classes of sounds, such as all or most back consonants.

Types of substitutions processes can be described according to the manner of production of the target sound. For example, obstruant sounds, which include fricatives and affricates, may experience *stopping,* in which a plosive is substituted. Stopping is most common in the initial position in words, as in *dat* for *that* or *dis* for *this.* This process decreases gradually as the child masters fricatives, although stopping with *th* sounds (/ð, θ/) may persist until early school age. Early production of nasal sounds may also be accompanied by stopping. This denasalization, similar to "head cold" speech, substitutes a plosive from a similar position in the oral cavity for a nasal (*Sam* becomes *Sab*).

Another frequent process is *fronting,* a tendency to replace palatals and velars with alveolar sounds. Thus, /t/ and /d/ are substituted for /k/ and /g/, producing *tan* for *can* and *dun* for *gun.* Slightly fewer than 25% of 3-year-olds demonstrate fronting. This percentage decreases rapidly, so that by age 4½ fewer than 4% of children still exhibit this behavior. Fronting is also evident in nasal sounds. The /n/ may be substituted for /ŋ/, as in *sinin* for *singing.*

Although approximants /l/ and /ɹ/ may also experience stopping initially, they are usually replaced by another approximant. Another process, *gliding,* in which /j/ or /w/ replaces /l/ or /ɹ/, may last for several years. I recall one example of gliding that occurred after I had broken my leg in a bicycling accident. Out of concern, my son Jason inquired, "How your yid?" (leg). This process was also evident in his production of "little" (/jɪdə/) and most other words with /l/. Not only does this demonstrate gliding on the /l/; the /g/ is fronted as well.

Multiple Processes

In actual practice, it may be difficult to decipher the phonologic processes a young child is using. Often, several processes will be functioning at once. For instance, my children all called our family dog "Peepa" (/pipə/). Her real name was Prisca (/pɹɪskə/). We see reduction of the *pr* cluster (in a *stop + liquid* cluster, the liquid is deleted). The second cluster, *sc*, also experiences reduction; but even more importantly, it demonstrates progressive noncontiguous assimilation, becoming a /p/. Finally, the first vowel, /I/, is replaced by /i/, which may be the result of the vowel's altering toward some feature of /p/, another assimilation effect. Whew! And that's only one word!

Perception and Production

Speech-sound perceptual skills in conversations develop relatively late. Although 3- and 4-year-olds can be taught to separate the sounds in words, these skills are very limited. Children do not perform well when asked to make judgments of the appropriateness of sounds. For instance, when K.C., the child of a friend, was in kindergarten, he drew a painting with streaks of bright color and put a big *W* on it. His mother was delighted. "Is that 'W' for 'Whalen'?" (his last name). He looked at her with scorn. "No silly, wainbow!"

Preschool children probably do not perceive spoken language as containing phoneme size units. Yet they seem able to make different speech sounds. Children may know that words are different or similar before they know the basis of those differences and similarities. Through slow evolution from relatively pure sound play, speech sounds gradually change into more deliberate productions that focus on phonological segments and their relationships.

Another important factor in perception and production is phonological working memory. Preschoolers with good phonological memory skills tend to produce language that contains more grammatic complexity, a richer array of words, and longer utterances than preschoolers with poor memory skills (Adams & Gathercole, 1995).

Summary

The preschool child follows a set of phonologic processes that provide for consistent speech performance. Gradually, these processes change and evolve as the child develops better production skills. The mastery of American English speech sounds is presented in Figure 9.2. Because a child's perception does not mirror that of an adult, initial production also differs.

It may be that a child has two representations, or models, of production: the adult model and his or her own. The child considers the adult model to be the correct one and monitors both productions for comparison.

During the preschool years, a child also acquires much of his or her speech sound inventory but does not master all English speech sounds until about age 7. In addition, there are many phonological rules related to morphological acquisition that are not mastered until school age.

Even at age 3, however, there are wide differences in rate of development, phonological processes used, and phonological organization. The processes of assimilation, and of consonant and syllable deletion, are very common. Use of cluster reduction is determined, at least in part, by the sounds involved.

It's important to recall that all aspects of language and language development are intertwined and interdependent. Development in one area affects all the others. For example, among some two-year-olds the accuracy of phonemic production decreases as word combinations become more complex (Nelson & Bauer, 1991).

Conclusion

BY AGE 5, A CHILD uses most of the major varieties of the English sentence, many morphological suffixes, and most English sounds and syllables. Language forms that will be mastered within the school years and adulthood have already begun to be acquired. The order of acquisition of language form reflects patterns of underlying cognitive and social growth, learning strategies, and linguistic complexity. Resultant forms often reflect the use environment and the child's attempt to simplify complex forms. Complicated syntactic structures may be acquired on a word-specific basis until a child deduces the underlying rule.

During the school years, knowledge of language use increases, and use begins to influence form more decisively. Having acquired much of the *what* of language form during the preschool years, the child turns to the *how* of language use.

Discussion

LONG CHAPTER? CONGRATULATIONS FOR FINISHING. Language form is the area of language development expanding most rapidly during the preschool years.

Notice the interdependence of suffixes with phonologic rules. It's difficult to separate the two. Many morphemes, such as the verb *to be,* take a long time to be mastered by children.

Sentence development is a long process too. Believe it or not, we have just skimmed the surface. Take a look at Table 9.7 again. I tell my own students not to worry about what happens when. That will come to you with time. Instead, try to understand the sequence. What comes first? What next? Why? Look for similar developments, especially with auxiliary verbs, across sentence types. Begin to see patterns.

Finally, with phonological rules, remember that these are processes used by children to simplify words that they cannot pronounce. In this way they are like the shortened versions of adult sentences that children produce. Assume that the basic building block is CV and that the easiest words are CV and CVCV-reduplicated, and everything else makes sense.

Can you imagine trying to decide what to teach a preschool child with language impairment? So many possibilities exist. Luckily, preschool teachers will have SLPs to help them decide. SLPs will use a myriad of testing and sampling procedures, plus a strong dose of clinical intuition in deciding the best language features to target.

With time, the development of language form by preschoolers will become easier for you, and you'll find yourself listening to children and trying to determine which structures they do and do not have. Pity your poor nieces and nephews, not to mention your own children, and your friends who must listen to you describe development of copula!

Main Points

- Semantic and syntactic development are interdependent.

- Much of preschool syntactic and morphologic development can be described with MLU.

- Morphologic learning is influenced by the difficulty of the underlying concept, the grammatical and pragmatic functions, and the phonological variations.

- Noun phrases rarely go beyond article + adjective + noun, although children can do more.

- Verb phrases increase with added auxiliary or helping verbs and use of phrases.

- Sentences become more adult-like through the preschool years.

  - Declaratives add first one, then two, auxiliary verbs, and then indirect objects.

  - Negative forms develop as the negative element moves from the first position (*No night-night*) to a position between the subject and verb (*Mommy no eat cookie*). Other negative forms are added (*couldn't, shouldn't*) and later indefinite forms (*nobody*), resulting in double negatives (*Nobody don't*).

  - Interrogatives also become more adult-like at about 29 to 32 months of age with the inversion of the subject and auxiliary verb or the subject and the copula. Various *wh-* words are added throughout the preschool years, beginning with *what* and *where* and ending with *when, how,* and *why*.

  - Embedded clauses first fill the object function in a sentence (*I know **what you did***), then modify the object (*I like the one **you have***), and finally, modify the subject (*The boy **who hit me** is mean*).

  - Although some conjunctions develop early, conjoining does not occur until age 3½ and will continue a slow development into early adolescence as new conjunctions are added.

  - Syntactic structures seem to be learned in a word-specific way. Thus, children learn to embed clauses following *I know* before they generalize to other verbs and pronouns and begin to form a rule.

- Clausal conjoining and embedding occur in the same sentence late in preschool but only rarely.

- Most speech sounds are acquired by age 5, although some consonant blends will remain difficult.

- Most phonological processes will disappear but include deletion of final consonants and unstressed syllables, reduplication, reduction of consonant clusters, assimilation, and substitution.

Reflections

1. Several general patterns of language development were presented in the chapter. State and explain each.

2. Preschool morphological development mainly concerns bound suffixes. Explain the factors that influence their development.

3. Several phrase types develop during the preschool years. Describe the development of noun and verb phrases.

4. Describe the acquisition order of negative and interrogative sentence types.

5. Much of development can be explained by word-specific or item-based development. Give examples of this development in embedding of subordinate clauses.

6. Describe the major phonological processes found among preschool children.

10

Early School-Age Language Development

OBJECTIVES

The school-age years are a very creative period for language development. Emphasis shifts from language form to content and use. The adult speaker is versatile and able to express a wide range of intentions. Much of language form is refined during school-age and adult development. Along with increased vocabulary and use, the child and adult master the fine points of American English form. When you have completed this chapter, you should understand

- The conversational abilities of school-age children.
- Language differences between genders.
- Story grammar development.
- The syntagmatic-paradigmatic shift.
- Development of figurative language.
- The different types of passive sentences and their development.
- The continued development of embedding and conjoining and possible reasons for the sequence of conjunction development.
- Morphophonemic changes.
- Metalinguistic abilities.
- The following terms:

account	metaphoric	recount
decentration	transparency	story
eventcast	morphophonemic	story grammar
metalinguistic	nonegocentrism	

To listen to language samples related to chapter content and to peruse other enhanced study aids, please see the Companion Website at www.pearsonhighered.com/owens8e

The preschool years have been viewed as the critical period for language learning. Although the early years are extremely important, there is little empirical support for the critical-period notion.

In fact, throughout early school-age years there is an increase in the size and complexity of the child's linguistic repertoire and in the use of that repertoire within the context of conversation and narration. The early school-age period is one of tremendous linguistic creativity filled with rhymes, songs, word games, and those special oaths and incantations passed along on the "underground" from child to child. Each small gang of children attempts to adopt its own special secret language. Children learn to pun and to find humor in word play. Special terms are invented, such as *bad* or *phat,* which means "really good," and *geek* to note those to be excluded. There are also oaths children consider to be as binding as any adult legal code:

> *Finders keepers.*
> *Cross your heart.*
> *Dibs* or *call it.*
> *No call backs.*
> *Pinky swear.*

For those who break the rules or who, for some other reason, earn a child's enmity, there is that special area of school-age cruelty, the taunt or tease:

> *Fatty, fatty, two-by-four . . .*
> *Hey, metal mouth.*
> *Liar, liar, pants on fire.*

The list of taunts, which are often based on physical characteristics, can go on for longer than any of us care to recall.

In its literary forms, the creative language of school-age children can be heard in camp songs, nursery rhymes, jump-rope rhymes, and jokes or read in graffiti. Those of us who grew up in inner-city areas experienced an especially rich heritage of urban rhymes and rumors, not to mention graffiti, such as my favorite paraphrase of Descartes, penned by two different adolescent scholars, the second in response to the first:

> I think, therefore, I am . . .
> . . . a figment of my own imagination.

Such creativity is mirrored in overall language development.

The early school-age years are characterized by growth in all aspects of language, although the development of pragmatics and semantics seems to be the most prevalent (Table 10.1). In addition to mastering new forms, the child learns to use these and existing structures to communicate more effectively. Overall, language development slows, but individual differences are great. A lexical difference as great as 6,000 words may separate average from poor students (Scott, Nippold, Norris, & Johnson, 1992).

Much of the syntactic development in the school years is intrasentential, at the noun- and verb-phrase level. Other development involves the refinement of features learned earlier. The child continues to operate from his or her own mini-theories about language, which are correct for some situations but not all. These theories become broadened, refined, and more flexible as they blend with the language-use skills that the child continues to acquire.

TABLE *10.1* **Summary of School-Age Children's Pragmatic and Semantic Development**

AGE IN YEARS	PRAGMATIC	SEMANTIC
5	■ Uses mostly direct requests ■ Repeats for repair ■ Begins to use gender topics	
6	■ Repeats with elaboration for repair ■ Uses adverbial conjuncts *now, then, so, though*; disjuncts rare	
7	■ Uses and understands most deictic terms ■ Narrative plots have beginning, end, problem, and resolution	■ Uses *left/right, back/front* ■ Shifts from single-word to multiword definitions
8	■ Sustains concrete topics ■ Recognizes nonliteral meanings in indirect requests ■ Begins considering others' intentions	
9	■ Sustains topics through several turns ■ Addresses perceived source of breakdown in repair ■ Produces all elements of story grammar	■ Has generally completed most of syntagmatic-paradigmatic shift ■ Begins to interpret psychological states described with physical terms (*cold, blue*) but misinterprets
10		■ Comprehends *in* and *on* used for temporal relations ■ Comprehends most familial terms
11	■ Sustains abstract topics ■ 20% of narrative sentences still begin with *and*	■ Creates abstract definitions ■ Has all elements of conventional adult definitions ■ Understands psychological states described with physical terms
12	■ Uses adverbial conjuncts (4/100 utterances) *otherwise, anyway, therefore,* and *however,* disjuncts *really* and *probably*	

While many rules are learned during the preschool years, many exceptions are discovered during the school years. With a more flexible language system at hand, the child learns to be more economical in its use and to avoid redundancy such as the double negative (*Nobody don't . . .*).

Metalinguistic ability, the awareness that enables a language user to think about and reflect on language, also becomes well developed during the school-age period. This ability to think about language in the abstract is reflected in the development of writing and reading skills.

In this chapter, we'll first examine the early school-age child. This information and more is presented in Appendix C, Tables C.4 and C.5. After this, we'll discuss pragmatic and semantic development followed by a description of development of language form.

The Early School-Age Child

By the fifth birthday, a child has a good sense of self, possessing a good awareness of the body and how to use it. A 5-year-old knows her or his own left and right but can't transfer them to others. Although a child has a hand preference, each hand can be employed independently for tasks such as dressing and cutting meat with a knife. Small-muscle control enables the child to draw recognizable pictures, to color within the lines, and to copy short words.

The 5-year-old has a good sense of time and understands words such as *yesterday, today,* and *tomorrow.* This, in turn, influences the child's understanding of cause and effect and comprehension of terms such as *before* and *after.*

Although the 5-year-old has good physical reasoning abilities, he or she still believes in magic as an explanation for much that happens. When my son Todd turned 5, he asked for a magic kit. Mom and Dad complied. After opening it, he turned to us for a demonstration. We dutifully explained each trick and showed him how it was done. When we finished, he cried in a very disillusioned voice, "No, no, I wanted *real* magic."

Five-year-olds use very adultlike language, although many of the more subtle syntactic structures are missing. In addition, the child has not acquired some of the pragmatic skills needed to be a truly effective communicator. Expressive vocabulary has grown to about 2,200 words. Word definitions still lack the fullness of adult meanings, however, and this aspect continues to be refined throughout life.

Although there are still many aspects of speech, language, and communication to be mastered, the 5-year-old has made spectacular progress in only a few years. The child of 5 is able to use language to converse and to entertain. He or she can tell stories, has a budding sense of humor, and can tease and discuss emotions. Over the next few years, language development will slow and begin to stabilize but will be nonetheless significant.

In the first six years of school, the child develops cognitive and communicative skills that by age 12 almost equal those of the adult. Increasingly, a child becomes less home centered, as school and age peers become more important.

Physically, the school-age child gains greater coordination of gross- and fine-motor movements. Throughout the period, physical coordination enables the child to perform more motor acts at one time and therefore to enjoy sports and coordinated games. With more mature motor skills, he or she gains more self-help skills and increased independence.

Cognitive skills change markedly during the first six years of school. The brain is nearly adult in size by age 8, but development is not complete. Intrabrain pathways must be better developed. Brain weight changes little; growth is internal. During the first six years of school, a child's mental abilities mature from concrete problem solving, requiring sensory input, to abstract thought. Four major cognitive developments in the period from ages 7 to 11 are inferred reality, decentration, transformational thought, and reversible mental operations. *Inferred reality* is an inference about a physical problem based not only on perceived appearances but also on internal information. For example, a preschooler bases his judgment of a container's volume on its height alone. A school-age child bases conclusions on all physical characteristics and on her knowledge of the volume of liquid poured into the container. *Decentration* is the ability to consider several aspects of a physical problem at once. *Transformational thought* refers to the ability to view a physical problem as existing in time and to anticipate future consequences effectively. Finally, *reversible mental operations* enable a child to recognize that change can be undone or reversed.

A school-age child is also a very social being, and peers, especially same-gender peers, become very important. This can be a trying period for parents, as children begin to establish an identity separate from their family. One afternoon my son Todd stormed into the house from his friend's house and demanded to know "the truth." "There's one thing you'll never tell me," he challenged. Fearing the worst, I suggested that he ask anyway. What a relief when he shot back, "Is there a real Easter Bunny?" With this peer socialization comes a less egocentric perspective. As Theory of Mind continues to develop, a child begins to realize that his or her own reality is not the only one.

The child also learns to manipulate and influence others, especially through the use of language. During the early school-age years, the child refines the conversational skills needed to be a truly effective communicator. This communication development reflects the child's growing appreciation for the perspective of others.

In addition, the child's vocabulary continues to grow. A first-grader has an expressive vocabulary of approximately 2,600 words but may understand as many as 8,000 to 10,000 root English words and 14,000 when various derivations are included (Anglin, 1993). Aided by school, this receptive vocabulary expands to an understanding of approximately 50,000 words by sixth grade. Multiple word meanings are also acquired.

In part, the school-age child's relatively slower language growth compared to the preschooler's reflects the systematic development and stabilization of word-formation and sentence-structuring rules. In short, the school years are a period of stabilization of rules previously learned and the addition of new rules. Let's explore this development together.

Pragmatic Development

The area of most dramatic linguistic growth during the school-age and adult years is language use, or pragmatics (Table 10.1). It is in pragmatics that we see the interaction of language and socialization.

Although environment is important, twin studies indicate that over half of the variance in young school-age children's conversational language skills may be accounted for by genetic effects (DeThorne et al., 2008). The association between early language and reading in late elementary school also is underpinned by common environmental and genetic influences (Harlaar, Hayiou-Thomas, Dale, & Plomin, 2008).

A preschool child does not have the skill of a masterful adult storyteller or even of a junior high student who wants something. No adult is fooled by the adolescent's compliment, "Gee, Mom, those are the best-looking cookies you've ever made," but both parties understand the request, however indirect it may be.

Preschool children frequently begin a conversation assuming that *here* for them is *here* for everyone or without announcing the topic. Once, in imaginative play, my preschool daughter shifted characters on me with no announcement. As the Daddy, I was being told to go to my room! When I balked, she informed me that now I was a child—an abrupt demotion. It had not occurred to her to prepare me for this shift in conversation.

The demands of the classroom require major changes in the way a child uses language. Very different rules for talking apply between the classroom and conversation. A child must negotiate a turn by seeking recognition from the teacher and responding in a highly specific manner to questions, which may represent over half the teacher's utterances. "Text-related" or ideational language becomes relatively more important than social, interpersonal language. A child is held highly accountable for responses and is required to use precise word meanings. A child who comes to school with different language skills and expectations may suffer as a consequence.

Throughout the school years, the cognitive processes of nonegocentrism and decentration increase and combine to enable a child to become a more effective communicator. **Nonegocentrism** is the ability to take the perspective of another person. In general, as the communication task becomes more complex or difficult, a child is less able to take a partner's perspective. Thus, as a child gains greater facility with language structure, he or she can concentrate more on the audience.

Decentration, mentioned earlier, is the process of moving from rigid, one-dimensional descriptions of objects and events to coordinated, multiattributional ones, allowing both speaker and listener to recognize that there are many dimensions and perspectives to any given topic. In general, younger children's descriptions are more personal and do not consider the information available to the listener. Their accuracy depends on what is being conveyed, with abstract information being communicated least accurately by children.

In this section, we first shall consider two aspects of language use: narratives and conversations.

NARRATIVES

Narratives reflect the storyteller's experience and, as such, are sense-making tools. The scripts formed by experiences are the foundations for narratives. In turn, the ability to relate well-formed narratives affects the judgments others make about a speaker's communicative competence. As a consequence, narratives help children maintain a positive self-image and a group identification within their families and communities.

Five- and 6-year-olds produce many different types of narratives. Anecdotal narratives of a personal nature predominate, possibly accounting for as many as 70% of all narratives at this age. In contrast, fantasy stories are relatively rare.

Children learn about narratives within their homes and their language communities. Emerging narratives reflect different cultures. Although every society allows children to hear and produce at least four basic narrative types, the distribution, frequency, and degree of elaboration of these types vary greatly. The four genres include

- The **recount** tells about past experiences in which a child participated or observed or about which a child read and is usually requested by an adult.
- The **eventcast** is an explanation of some current or anticipated event and may be used to direct others in imaginative play sequences, as in *You're the daddy; and you pretend to get dressed; you're going to take the baby to the zoo.*
- **Accounts** are highly individualized spontaneous narratives in which children share their experiences ("You know what?") and thus are not reporting information requested by adults.
- **Stories,** although fictionalized and with seemingly endless content variation, have a known and anticipated pattern or structure in which the main character must overcome some problem or challenge.

In middle- and upper-class school-oriented families in the United States, the earliest narratives are eventcasts that occur during nurturing activities, such as play, and reading. Within these activities, caregivers share also many accounts and stories. By age 3, children are expected to appreciate and use all forms of narration. Parents invite children to give recounts. These invitations decrease as the child gets older.

By the time most children in the United States begin school, they are familiar with all four forms of narration. In the classroom, children are expected to use these forms. This expectation may be unrealistic given the experiences of some children. For example, Chinese American children are encouraged to give accounts within their families, but not outside the immediate household. The majority culture teacher may have very different expectations.

In some white working-class Southern communities, children's recounts are tightly controlled by the interrogator and seem to be the predominant form during the preschool years. Accounts do not begin until children attend school. In these same communities, children and young adults also tell few stories, a form predominantly used by older, higher-status adults.

In contrast, Southern African American working-class children produce mostly accounts or eventcasts and have minimal experience with recounts. This may relate to the difficulty children in this environment have gaining adult attention mentioned in Chapter 6.

Development of Narratives

Most 6-year-olds can convey a simple story or recount a movie or television show, often in the form of long, rambling sequential accounts. During the school-age period, these narratives undergo several changes, primarily in their internal structure.

As noted in Chapter 8, children gradually learn to link events in linear fashion and, only later, with causal connectives. Generally, by age 6, children's narratives become causally coherent. These narratives require a child to manipulate content, plot, and causal structure. Even so, the conjunction *and* continues to be used as frequently in the narratives of 9-year-olds as it was in those of preschoolers. The purpose seems to be cohesion (*And then . . . And then . . .*) rather than conjoining (clause + *and* + clause).

Causality involves descriptions of intentions, emotions, and thoughts and the use of connectives, such as *because, as a result of,* and *since,* to name a few. To some degree, use of causality requires the speaker to be able to go forward and backward in time. While 2- and 3-year-olds can sequence in a forward direction, they have great difficulty with the reverse. The stories of these preschoolers consist predominantly of actions.

Although 2- and 3-year-olds have mastered some causal expressions, they are unable to construct coherent causal narratives. Causality can be seen, however, in 2- and 3-year-olds' use of plans, scripts, and descriptions of their own behavior and thoughts. A *plan* is a means, or series of actions, intended to accomplish a specified end. Thus, a plan is an intention or a model of causality (*If . . . then . . .*). *Scripts* are dialogs that accompany familiar routines in the child's everyday environment. Children incorporate these into their narratives. By age 2½, a child has acquired the words to describe perceptions (*see, hear*), physical states (*tired, hungry*), emotions (*love, hate*), needs, thoughts (*know*), and judgments (*naughty*).

Between ages 2 and 10, children's stories begin to contain more mental states and more initiations and motivations as causal links. Initially, psychological causality, such as motives, is more frequently used than physical causality or the connection between events. At around age 4, children's stories begin to contain more explicit physical and mental states. By age 6, children describe motives for actions.

In mature narratives, the center develops as the story progresses. Each incident complements the center, follows from previous incidents, forms a chain, and adds some new aspect to the theme. Causal relationships move toward the ending of the initial situation called the *climax*:

> There was a girl named Ann. And she got lost in the city. She was scared. She looked and looked but couldn't find her mommy and daddy. She slept in a cardboard box by the corner. And one day the box got blowed over and a police lady found her sleeping. She took her home to her mommy and daddy.

Mature narratives may consist of a single episode, as above, or of several episodes. An episode contains a statement of the problem or challenge, and all elements of the plot are directed toward its solution.

Although 4- and 5-year-olds include many elements of narration, such as plans and scripts, in their conversations, they lack the linguistic skill to weave a coherent narrative. Between ages 5 and 7, plots emerge. Gradually, these simple plots are elaborated into a series of problems and solutions or are embellished from within.

Both adults and children prefer stories directed toward a goal, such as the overcoming of an obstacle or problem. Narratives of a 7-year-old typically involve a beginning, a problem, a plan to overcome the problem, and a resolution.

The development of causal chains is a very gradual process. Initially, the narrative may be truncated so that the problem is solved, but it is unclear how this happened. This occurs in the following:

> And there was this bad guy with a—"k-k-k-k" (gun noise)—death ray. And he was gonna blow up the city. So, the Power Rangers snuck in to his house and stopped him. The end.

In another early form, the problem is resolved without the intervention of the characters in the story. A common device is to have the main character awaken from a dream, resulting in the disappearance of the problem:

> . . . He was in the middle of all these hungry lions. And he lost his gun. He couldn't get away. And then he woke up. Wasn't that funny?

By second grade, a child uses beginning and ending markers in fictional narratives (*once upon a time, lived happily ever after, the end*) and evaluative markers (*that was a good one*). Throughout elementary school, use of both beginning and ending markers increases. Evaluative markers also occur more frequently and increase in use even more (Ukrainetz et al., 2005). Story length increases and becomes more complex with the aid of syntactic devices such as conjunctions (*and, then*), locatives (*in, on, under, next to, in front of*), dialog, comparatives (*bigger than, almost as big as, littlest*), adjectives, and causal statements. Although disquieting events, such as getting a needle or losing a toy, are still central to the theme, characters tend to remain constant throughout the narrative. Distinct episodes have been replaced by a multiepisodic chronology, although the plot is still not fully developed.

The sense of plot in fictional narratives is increasingly clear after age 8. Definite character-generated resolution of the central problem is present. The narrative presentation relies largely on language rather than on the child's accompanying use of actions and vocalizations. Like a good storyteller, a child manipulates the text and the audience to maintain attention.

In general, older children's narratives are characterized by the following:

1. Fewer unresolved problems and unprepared resolutions.
2. Less extraneous detail.
3. More overt marking of changes in time and place.
4. More introduction, including setting and character information.
5. Greater concern for motivation and internal reactions.
6. More complex episode structure.
7. Closer adherence to the story grammar model.

These changes represent a child's growing awareness of story structure and increasing understanding of the needs of the audience.

Two later developing narrative abilities are drawing inferences and summarizing. Even 10-year-olds have difficulty making inferences from a narrative. Summarizing may involve (1) comprehending propositions, (2) establishing connectives between these propositions, (3) identifying the structure of the story, (4) remembering information, (5) selecting information for summarizing, and (6) formulating a concise, coherent representation (Johnson, 1983). The last two skills are refined in the upper elementary grades.

Story Grammar Development Like much in language, narratives are organized in predictable, rule-governed ways that differ with culture. The structure of the narrative consists of various components and the rules underlying the relationships of these components. Components and rules, collectively called a **story grammar,** form a narrative framework, the internal structure of a story.

Formed from reading and listening to stories and from participating in conversations, story grammars can aid information and narrative processing, as well as narrative interpretation and memory. Like a script, components may help the listener anticipate content. The competent storyteller constructs the story and the flow of information to maximize comprehension.

The typical story in English involves an animate or inanimate protagonist in a particular setting who faces some challenge to which he or she responds. The character makes one or more attempts to meet the challenge and, as a consequence, succeeds or fails. The story usually ends with the character's emotional response to the outcome. This brief outline contains the main components of a story grammar in English.

A story grammar in English and most Western languages consists of the setting plus the episode structure (*story grammar = setting + episode structure*). Each story begins with an introduction contained in the setting, as in "A long, long time ago, in a far off galaxy . . ." or "You'll never guess what happened on the way to work this morning; I was crossing Main Street. . . ." An episode in English consists of an initiating event, an internal response, a plan, an attempt, a consequence, and a reaction. Each component is described in Table 10.2. While only 50% of kindergarten children can retell narratives with well-formed episodes, this percentage increases to 78% by sixth grade. Like clauses, episodes may be linked additively (*and*), temporally (*and then, next*), causally (*because*), or in a mixed fashion. A story may consist of one or more interrelated episodes.

There appears to be a sequence of stages in the development of story grammars. Certain structural patterns appear early and persist, while others are rather late in developing. The resultant narratives can be described as *descriptive sequences, action sequences, reaction sequences, abbreviated episodes, complete episodes, complex episodes,* and *interactive episodes.* The structural qualities of each type of story grammar are listed in Table 10.3.

Descriptive sequences consist of descriptions of characters, surroundings, and habitual actions. There are no causal or temporal links. The entire story consists of setting statements:

> There was this magician. He had a big hat like this. He turned elephants into mice. And he had birds in his coat. The end.

This type of structure is characteristic of the initial narratives of preschool children, described earlier as *heaps.*

Action sequences have a chronological order for actions but no causal relations. The story consists of a setting statement and various action attempts:

> We got up early on Christmas morning. We lighted the tree. We opened gifts. Mommy made cinnamon buns. Then we played with the toys.

This type of story grammar is the type seen in early sequential and temporal chain narratives of preschool children.

TABLE *10.2* *Story Grammar Components*

COMPONENT	DESCRIPTION	EXAMPLE
Setting statement	Introduce the characters; describe their habitual actions and the social, physical and/or temporal contexts; introduce the protagonist.	There was this boy and
Initiating event	Event that induces the character(s) to act through some natural act, such as an earthquake; a notion to seek something, such as treasure; or the action of one of the characters, such as arresting someone.	. . . he got kidnapped by these pirates.
Internal response	Characters' reactions, such as emotional responses, thoughts, or intentions, to the initiating events. Internal responses provide some motivation for the characters.	He missed his dog.
Internal plan	Indicates the characters' strategies for attaining their goal(s). Young children rarely include this element.	So he decided to escape.
Attempt	Overt action(s) of the characters to bring about some consequence, such as to attain their goal(s).	When they were all eating, he cut the ropes and
Direct consequence	Characters' success or failure at attaining their goal(s) as a result of the attempt.	. . . he got away.
Reaction	Characters' emotional response, thought, or actions to the outcome or preceding chain of events.	And he lived on an island with his dog. And they played in the sand every day.

TABLE *10.3* *Structural Properties of Narratives*

STRUCTURAL PATTERN	STRUCTURAL PROPERTIES
Descriptive sequence	Setting statements (S) (S) (S)
Action sequence	Setting statement (S) + Attempts (A) (A) (A)
Reaction sequence	Setting statement (S), Initiating event (IE) + Attempts (A) (A) (A)
Abbreviated episode	Setting statement (S), Initiating event (IE) or Internal response (IR) + Direct consequence (DC)
Complete episode	Setting statement (S); Two of the following: Initiating event (IE), Internal response (IR), or Attempt (A); + Direct consequence (DC)
Complex episode	Multiple episodes Setting statement (S); Two of the following: Initiating event (IE$_1$), Internal response (IR$_1$), or Attempt (A$_1$); Direct consequence (DC$_1$); followed by another episode Expanded complete episode Setting statement (S), Initiating event (IE), Internal response (IR), Internal plan (IP), Attempt (A), Direct consequence (DC), and Reaction (R)
Interactive episode	Two separate but parallel episodes that influence each other

Reaction sequences consist of a series of events in which changes cause other changes with no goal-directed behaviors. The sequence consists of a setting, an initiating event, and action attempts:

> There was a little puppy. He smelled a kittie. The kittie scratched the puppy. The puppy ran away. He smelled a girl. The girl took the puppy home and gave the pu . . . him milk. And that's the end.

In contrast, *abbreviated episodes* contain an implicit or explicit goal. At this level, the story may contain either an event statement and a consequence or an internal response and a consequence:

> This girl hated spinach. And she had a big plate of it. And she fed the spinach to the dog under the table. After her plate was all clean, she got a big dessert. That's all.

Although the character's behavior is purposeful, it is usually not premeditated or planned; instead, the characters react. Reaction sequences and abbreviated episodes are characteristic of the narratives of school-age children until approximately age 9.

Complete episodes contain an entire goal-oriented behavioral sequence consisting of a consequence statement and two of the following: initiating event, internal response, and attempt:

> Once this man went hunting. He woke up a big bear. The bear chased him up a tree and climbed up. To get away, the man waved at a helicopter. The helicopter gave the man a rope. He climbed up and got away from the bear. The end.

Complex episodes are expansions of the complete episode or contain multiple episodes:

> Spiderman saw a bank robber. He jumped down and captured one of them with a punch. And he called the police. One bank robber got away in his truck. Spiderman ran after the truck. He threw his net over the truck and got the bank robber. And that was the end of the bank robbers.

Finally, *interactive episodes* contain two characters who have separate goals and actions that influence the behavior of each other:

> Mary decided to build a doghouse. She bought all the wood she needed. Her cat got jealous. Mary cut all the wood and hammered it. The cat rubbed her leg and meowed. Mary was too busy to stop and she painted it. The cat meowed more. When Mary was all done, she let the dog go to sleep. And then she hugged the kitty too.

Complete, complex, and interactive story grammars are seen in the narratives of mid- and late-elementary school children, adolescents, and adults. Most children produce all the elements of story grammar, although not necessarily in the same narrative, by age 9 or 10.

Narrative Differences

As might be expected, not all children of a given age exhibit the same levels of narrative competence. The narratives of underachieving children may be shorter, have less internal organization and cohesion, and contain fewer story grammar components and less sentence complexity (Hayes, Norris, & Flaitz, 1998).

Narration varies with the context or situation and with the culture of the speaker. Situational variables may influence the type of storytelling as much as the developmental level of the narrator. Constraints include the type and size of the audience, the goal, time allotment, and competition for the floor (Scott et al., 1992). The more familiar the audience, the longer the clauses and the more use of embedded clauses.

Narratives of children in the United States reflect cultural differences (McCabe & Bliss, 2003), which are summarized in Table 10.4. For example, in comparison to the sequentially organized narratives of European American children, the stories of African American children seem less focused and less organized. This reflects the expectation of African Americans for the telling of more rambling, multi-event tales that are performed for the enjoyment of the listeners.

By comparison, the narratives of Japanese American children seem concise. This reflects the cultural expectation of *omoiyari* or empathy. The storyteller is expected to get to the point and not to be too garrulous, which would be disrespectful of the listener.

Finally, in Mexican American homes, completing a narrative is secondary to conversational interaction. In other words, the process of telling is more important than the product. Often a main event in the home, narratives frequently are told by children while meals are being prepared. The mother maintains the exchange and facilitates the process but is not intent on obtaining a narrative of sequential events.

Linguistic differences will account for differing methods of introducing new elements, referring to old information, and providing cohesion. Still, we find that narratives become increasingly more complex and more coherent in all languages. More characters and dialog and multiple and complex episodes are used. Across languages, the number of characters varies with the style and purpose of the narrative (Guttierrez-Clellan & Heinrichs-Ramos, 1993).

The narratives of some African American children, especially girls, have a distinct structure that differs from the story grammar model presented previously. Characterized as *topic-associating*, these narratives consist of theme-related incidents that make an implicit point, such as the need to help your baby brother or to avoid someone. These narratives often lack clear indicators of characters, place, or shifts in time (Michaels, 1981, 1991).

As Spanish-speaking children mature, their narratives become more detailed and contain longer sentences with more embedding, a higher proportion of grammatically acceptable sentences, and more complete episodes, more embedding, although overall story length increases little (Guttierrez-Clellan & McGrath, 1991; Muñoz, Gillam, Peña, & Gulley-Faehnle, 2003). These narratives exhibit an increase in cohesion, ellipsis, and more accurate reference and a decrease in ambiguities and redundancies with age (Guttierrez-Clellan & Heinrichs-Ramos, 1993). Cohesion is achieved through the use of articles and nouns (*un niño/a boy*), pronouns (*ella/she*), ellipsis (*El fue a la tienda, cogio un poco de comida/he went to the store, got some food*) and demonstratives (*este/this*). In fact, ellipsis may be even more pronounced than in English because Spanish verb endings indicate person, eliminating the need for pronouns. For example, *hablo* means *I speak*, the "o" signaling the first person singular pronoun. The increasing use of ellipsis with locations is consistent with that noted in the narratives of English-speaking children. Props in Spanish narratives are usually referenced by name as in English, as "He put on *his coat.*"

Italian-speaking children also use nouns to introduce new information. Although pronouns and inflected verbs are also used, school-age Italian-speaking children rely more on nouns, thus reducing ambiguity on the part of the listener (Orsolini, Rossi, & Pontecorvo, 1996).

Across languages such as English, German, French, and Mandarin, clear marking of new information in the form of a noun does not emerge until age 7 (Hickman, Hendriks, Roland, & Liang, 1996). Because languages differ in form, it might be expected that the development of sentence structure to indicate newness would also differ. For example, in English, new information is often placed at the end of the sentence, but this practice does not emerge fully until adulthood. In contrast, use of sentence structure to introduce newness is used more frequently by French-speaking children. An interplay exists between discourse factors governing information flow, cognition relative to narrative complexity, and language-specific forms.

TABLE 10.4 *Typical Features of Children's Narratives*

FEATURES	EUROPEAN AMERICAN	AFRICAN AMERICAN	SPANISH-SPEAKING MEXICAN AMERICAN	JAPANESE AMERICAN
Focus	Single experience of child	May contain several experiences; preference for lengthy narratives that are expected and enjoyed	Frequent mention of family members as reference to who narrator is and where; frequent code switching and when events occurred	Preference for concise narratives; poor behavior to concentrate on self too much
Events	Told in simple past and in chronological sequence by age 5	Occasionally combine numerous experiences into single narrative	De-emphasize sequencing, emphasize flow of conversation; less emphasis on past events	Frequently several experiences in one narrative rather than elaborating on event
Resolution	Problem or goal resolved or not by end of narrative	May or may not be resolution	Often resolution but not as important as in European American narratives	Concise, get to the point readily; make every effort to be understood
Organization	Topic-centered, setting explained, sequence of actions, culminating in high point or crisis that is evaluated, resolution, and relationship to present conversation	Both topic-centered and thematic (topic-associating) formats with several experiences related by a theme; each experience may have different tempo and tone	Conversation-focused; emphasis more on relationships; emphasis on habitual activities (*we ran* vs. *we were running*)	Sequential although adults favor nonsequential format; value implication rather than explication; omission of pronouns

Source: Information from McCabe & Bliss (2003).

Dialog is increasingly used within narratives as children mature. As in English, children developing other languages, such as Turkish, gain increasing ability to relate conversations by adopting different roles within their narratives, switching from character to narrator and back again (Ozyurek, 1996).

CONVERSATIONAL ABILITIES

Successful communication rests on the participants' knowledge of people, relationships, and events. Participants must be actively involved, asking and answering questions, making voluntary replies and statements, and being sensitive to the contributions of others. They collaborate to ensure mutual understanding. Great individual variability exists, and some 7-year-olds are more adept than the least effective adults (Anderson, Clark, & Mullin, 1994).

The most successful communicators use questions to probe before introducing a possibly unfamiliar topic. Although the number of questions does not increase with age, more successful communicators use more questions and have more answered than do the least successful. In addition, regardless of age, more successful school-age communicators are quick to recognize communication breakdown and to offer further explanation or to repair (Anderson et al., 1994).

Adults still exercise control over much of the conversation of a young school-age child by asking questions. Role, power, and control relationships are evident in children's responses. In general, responses to adult queries by first-graders are brief, simple, and appropriate, with little elaboration. In contrast, responses to peer questions are more complex and more varied.

In peer interaction among young school-age children, approximately 60% of the utterances are effective, measured by the clarity and structural completeness of the utterance sent, the clarity of reference and relevance to the situation, the form of the utterance, and the requirement for and maintenance of attention. Social perspective-taking, the ability to understand and adopt varying points of view, is necessary for successful communication and is used to persuade, comfort, and to be polite (Bliss, 1992). The largest gains in social perspective-taking and subsequent tailoring of individualized messages occur in middle childhood (ages 7 to 9). As you well know, however, even adults don't always behave in a partner-oriented way and often fail to consider the perspectives of others (Buhl, 2002).

In the following section, we'll explore many of the important conversational changes seen in childhood. These will include language uses; speaking style; topic introduction and maintenance; and use of indirect requests, conversational repair, and deictic terms.

Language Uses

Almost from the time a child begins to speak, he or she is able to provide information and to discuss topics briefly. Language functions increase greatly with the demands of the classroom. Children are required to explain, express, describe, direct, report, reason, imagine, hypothesize, persuade, infer cause, and predict outcomes. New vocabulary and syntactic forms accompany these functions. For example, hypothesizing uses *how about . . . , what if . . . ,* and so on, while persuading uses *yes but, on the other hand, because if . . . then . . . ,* and the like.

Because of cultural difference, the expectations of the classroom teacher may differ from that of a child. For example, majority English-speaking teachers may prefer individual recitation, while children from populations such as the native Canadian Inuit participate best within cooperative group interactions, the cultural norm (Crago, Eriks-Brophy, Pesco, & McAlpine, 1997). The reluctance of Inuit children to respond individually may be misinterpreted by the teacher as being uncooperative. Similarly, Algonquin narration is a cooperative group effort that may not be appreciated by the teacher demanding individual storytelling. In addition, the teacher's stopping of a narrative to correct grammar may violate the function of narratives in Algonquin culture, which is to amuse or tell a troubling experience.

Speaking Style

The style-switching behavior reported for 4-year-olds is even more pronounced by age 8. When speaking with peers, a child makes more nonlinguistic noises and exact repetitions and engages in more ritualized play. With adults, a child uses different codes for his parents and for those outside the family. In general, parents are the recipients of more demands and whining, and of shorter, less conversational narratives.

Topic Introduction and Maintenance

A school-age child is able to introduce a topic into the conversation, sustain it through several turns, and close or switch the topic. These skills develop only gradually throughout elementary school and contrast sharply to preschool performance. The 3-year-old, for example, sustains the topic only 20% of the time if the partner's preceding utterance was a topic-sharing response to one of the child's prior utterances. In other words, topics change rapidly. Four-year-olds can remain on topic when explaining how a toy works but still cannot sustain dialog.

In general, the proportion of introduced topics maintained in subsequent turns increases with age, with the most change occurring from late elementary school to adulthood. A related decrease in the number of different topics introduced or reintroduced occurs during this same period. Thus, there is a growing adherence to the concept of relevance in a conversation. An 8-year-old's topics tend to be concrete. Sustained abstract discussions emerge around age 11.

Peer interaction supplies chances for middle-childhood-aged children to make gains in social perspective taking and tailoring of individual messages.

Indirect Requests

One verbal strategy adults use widely is the indirect request that does not refer directly to what the speaker wants. For example, "The sun sure is a scorcher today" may be an indirect request for a drink. Development of indirect requests is particularly noteworthy because such requests represent a growing awareness of the importance of both socially appropriate requests and the communication context.

Indirect requests are first produced in the preschool years. The proportion of indirect to direct requests increases between ages 3 and 5. This proportion does not change markedly between ages 5 and 6, although the internal structure of requests develops. In general, the 5-year-old is successful at directly asking, commanding, and forbidding. By age 7, he or she has acquired greater facility with indirect forms. Flexibility in indirect request forms increases with age. For example, the proportion of hints—"That's a beautiful jacket, and it would go so well with my tan"—increases from childhood through adulthood.

A school-age child seems to be following two rules: Be brief and be devious (or avoid being demanding). More creative and more aware of social roles than the preschooler, a school-age child knows that overpoliteness is inappropriate. As with preschoolers, however, an 8-year-old is more polite to adults and to those perceived as uncooperative than he or she is to his or her peers.

After age 8, a change occurs in a child's awareness of others, and he or she increasingly takes their intentions into consideration. While a younger child acts as if expecting compliance, an 8-year-old may signify the possibility of something else. In general, an 8-year-old is more polite when not from the listener's peer group, when interrupting the listener's activities, and when the task requested is difficult. Although a child's use of requests is similar to that of adults, he or she still has some difficulty with indirect requests and may interpret them literally. It's not until adolescence that a child approaches adult proficiency.

A preschool child has difficulty understanding many forms of indirect request. Although 6-year-olds generally respond best to literal meanings, 8-year-olds and adults recognize most nonliteral requests for action as well. For example, the 6-year-old who is asked "Can you pass the cup?" may respond "Yes" but not follow through, treating the request as a question.

More mature language users consider the context more fully and deduce that these questions are indirect requests for action. Decisions about the nature of a request—for information or compliance—can be difficult. By age 11, children are able to use the utterance and context to infer the speaker's intent accurately (Abbeduto, Nuccio, Al-Mabuk, Rotto, & Maas, 1992).

There seems to be a general developmental pattern to the comprehension of indirect requests. As a child matures, comprehension of most types of indirect request increases. Interrogative forms, such as *shouldn't you?* and *should you?* are more difficult than declarative forms, such as *you shouldn't* and *you should.* Negative forms, such as *please don't* and *you shouldn't,* are more difficult for 4- to 7-year-olds than positive forms, such as *please do* and *you should.* Polarity is a strong factor, especially when it differs from the literal meaning. *Shouldn't you?* for example, is in a negative form but is a prod for positive action, as in "Shouldn't you leave?" In contrast, *Must you?* although positive in form, conveys caution or cessation, as in "Must you stop now?" These levels of relative difficulty change little from childhood to adulthood and reflect the same comprehension difficulties experienced by adults.

In part, development of comprehension also reflects the words used. Four- and 5-year-olds understand most simple indirect requests containing *can* and *will* but have difficulty with others, such as *must* and *should.*

Conversational Repair

More mindful of the listener's needs, a school-age child attempts to clarify the conversation through a variety of strategies. Rather than merely repeating, as most 3- to 5-year-olds do, a 6-year-old may elaborate some elements in the repetition, thus providing more information. Until age 9, however, the predominant repair strategy is repetition. In contrast, a 9-year-old clearly provides additional input for the listener. Although not as proficient as adults, 9-year-olds are capable of addressing the perceived source of a breakdown in communication by defining their terms, providing more background context, and talking about the process of conversational repair.

Deictic Terms

By school age, most children can produce deictic terms (*here, there*) correctly. By about age 7, a child should be able to produce and comprehend both singular and plural *demonstratives* (*this, that, these, those*) or words that indicate to which object or event the speaker is referring. Children under age 7 do not incorporate all semantic features of demonstratives. First, a child must understand that *this* and *that* are pronouns when used alone, as in "See *that*," and articles when followed by a noun, as in "*That* one's big." Second, a child must comprehend the feature of more or less far, that is, of distance. Third, a child must realize that the speaker is the referent, the deictic aspect of demonstratives. The last two features overlap with those of *here* and *there.*

An initial strategy for the production of deictic verbs, such as *bring* and *take,* is to use them with locational terms for directionality, as in *bring it here* or *bring it there.* The causal meaning of the verb—it causes something to happen—is acquired first. Later, a child learns the deictic meaning.

SUMMARY

As a child gains greater facility with the form and content aspects of language, he or she is able to concentrate more on language use in narratives and in conversational give-and-take. As he or she develops, a child requires less and less of his or her limited-capacity system for planning and encoding the message. More capacity is therefore available for adapting messages to specific audiences and situations. Gradually, a child is able to reallocate these limited resources and so to increase the effectiveness of his or her communication system.

Semantic Development

During the school-age period and adult years, an individual increases the size of his or her vocabulary and the specificity of definition. Gradually, a child acquires an abstract knowledge of meaning that is independent of particular contexts or individual interpretations. In the process, she or he reorganizes the semantic aspects of language (Table 10.1). The new organization is reflected in the way the child uses words. One outgrowth is the creative or figurative use of language for effect. This entire process of semantic growth, beginning in the early school years, may be related to an overall change in cognitive processing.

VOCABULARY GROWTH

School-age and adult years are a period of continued growth in the understanding of words and relationships. It is estimated that, by graduation from high school, a young adult may understand as many as 80,000 words. The expressive vocabulary may be considerably smaller. Actually, this number of words is increased with the addition of morphological prefixes and suffixes that change word meanings (Anglin, 1995b). Elementary school children appear to store words based on root words (e.g., *day*) and morphological variations (e.g., *days, daily*) (Rabin & Deacon, 2008). Many words are added from context, often while reading, especially after fourth grade.

Adding lexical items are only a portion of the change. Vocabulary growth is not the same as semantic sophistication or depth of understanding. While new words may increase the size of the child's lexicon, real change comes in interrelated semantic concepts, semantic classes, synonyms, homonyms, and antonyms. These are all part of a child's understanding of a word.

More than other areas of language, development of semantics varies widely with educational level, socioeconomic status, gender, age, and cultural background. In general, middle-class urban youngsters have more complete definitions than working-class rural children (Walker, 2001). Definitional skill is highly correlated with involvement in an academic culture. As a result, some working-class fourth-graders outperform their parents in providing oral definitions (Kurland & Snow, 1997).

During school-age and adult years, there are two types of increases in word meanings. First, a child adds features to the definition that are common to the adult definition. In other words, a child *slowmaps* word definitions beyond the functional and physical properties that are core aspects of the definitions of children as old as 5 (McGregor, Friedman, Reilly, & Newman, 2002). Second, a child brings together all the definitions that can fit a single word. The multiple meanings of school-age children and the less flexible semantic systems of younger children are illustrated in the following closing retort of an argument between my two nieces, Michelle, then 11, and Katie, age 7:

> MICHELLE: Well, when I have children, I hope they don't get any of your genes.
> KATIE (after a short pause):   No, and they won't get any of my sneakers, either.

Definitional skills—the ability to provide definitions of words—are related to the acquisition of metalinguistics, which is discussed at the end of the chapter. Both increase as a function of age and educational level (Benelli et al., 2006).

Between the ages of 7 and 11, there are significant increases in comprehension of spatial, temporal, familial, disjunctive, and logical relationships. A child acquires many dictionary-like and multiple meanings during this period. The rate of growth slows and stabilizes during the teen years.

New words may reflect the cognitive and linguistic activities of education, such as *remember, doubt, conclude, assert, interpret,* and *predict.* Others, such as connectives—*but, although, however*—are used for narratives and in reading and writing. Full understanding of most connectives occurs gradually, and some are still not mastered by eighth grade. Finally, as the child attempts to be more precise, he or she adds adverbs of magnitude, such as *slightly, somewhat,* and *unusually.* Acquisition of these terms continues into adulthood.

Semantic constraints may delay full mature use of even seemingly simple words such as *in, on,* and *at.* Many prepositions can mark locative, temporal, and figurative relationships. For example, prepositions such as *in* and *on* represent periodicity of duration, whereas *at* represents a moment in time. Although *in* and *on* are acquired at age 2 to mark location, they are also used for periods of time, such as days (*on Monday*) or parts of days (*in the morning*), or for months (*in May*). In contrast, *at,* another locational preposition, is used for specific moments (*at midnight, at 9:15*). The temporal concept of periodicity develops much later than the locative—not until about age 10. A child is into teenage years before he or she can explain the periodicity/moment distinction.

In the early years of elementary school, a change occurs in the use of spatial relational terms. There is a decrease in the use of nonspecific and general terms and a corresponding increase in the use of specific spatial terms from ages 4 to 7. For example, usage shifts gradually from nonspecific deictic terms, based on the speaker's perspective (*here, there*), through environmental-based terms (*away from the window, toward the door*), to spatial terms (*top, up, left*). Increasing precision of use continues into adulthood.

These new relations also require new, more complex syntactic structures. Although *first* and *last* can be applied to single words, newly acquired *before* and *after* are clausal or phrasal connectives requiring a more complex structure.

As discussed in Chapter 7, words refer to concepts. As he or she matures, a child acquires more features of the concept. Some instances are more typical than others and are easier for children to learn. In general, a child's definition is less well delineated and relies more on perceptual knowledge. In contrast, adult definitions reflect both perceptual attributes and functions.

A child's ability to define words may progress in two ways during the early school years. First, a child progresses conceptually from definitions based on individual experience to more socially shared meaning. Second, he or she moves syntactically from single-word action definitions to sentences expressing complex relationships. This shift in form occurs at around second grade. Similar shifts in definition content occur throughout grade school. Supplying precise semantic content seems to develop prior to using correct syntactic form to provide a definition (Johnson & Anglin, 1995).

As a school-age child's definitions gradually become more literate or dictionary-like, they share certain characteristics. The definitions become more explicit. Around age 11, a child acquires all the elements of the conventional adult definition. The developmental sequence of elements of definitions is presented in Table 10.5. A preschooler's individual, experientially based definition thus shifts to the more conventional, socially shared one of older children and adults.

Vocabulary knowledge is highly correlated with general linguistic competence. A relationship may exist between stored word knowledge and comprehension of discourse. Throughout the school years, the child becomes better at deducing word meaning from context. Older elementary school children seem to rely on syntax for clues to word meaning, but far from relying on the narrow sentence use, eleven-year-olds abstract and synthesize meaning to form a definition (Marinellie, 2010).

CONCEPTUAL CHANGE

Adults organize language, especially object concepts in various ways. Two prominent organizational schemes are taxonomies and themes. Taxonomies are categories of objects that share a common essence, such as trees or tools. Although objects in a category likely share similar

TABLE *10.5* **Developmental Sequence of Definitions**

Elements Required	Example
Noun phrase$_1$ . . .	*Dogs* have yukky breath.
NP$_1$ is . . .	*Dogs are* always barking and breathing.
NP$_1$ is NP$_2$ . . .	*Dogs are things* with four legs, a tail, bad breath, and barking.
NP$_1$ is NP$_2$ (superordinate category)	*Dogs are animals* that usually live in people's houses.

perceptual features, mature taxonomic knowledge includes other aspects such as functional use or biological essence (Carey, 1988, 1991; Medin & Ortony, 1989; Springer & Keil, 1991). Objects related by themes are bound by an event. For example, gifts, a birthday cake, and party hats are part of a birthday party scheme. Objects are related based on space, such as cake and presents in the same room; cause, such as candles and the birthday child to blow them out; and function, such as knife and cake (Lin & Murphy, 2001). Although mature definitions contain both taxonomic and thematic information, taxonomic knowledge is more readily accessible for both children and adults (Whitmore, Shore, & Hull Smith, 2004).

It appears that both thematic and taxonomic relations are present from an early age. In young children, more abstract taxonomic relations are more fragile than thematic ones in their mental representation. For example, a category such as tools includes objects that look very dissimilar and have several different functions. The fragility of these categories may result in a reliance on more thematic organization when demands are high. As a result, preschoolers switch between organizational strategies depending on the task and context (Blaye & Bonthoux, 2001; Nguyen & Murphy, 2003; Osborne & Calhoun, 1998; Walsh, Richardson, & Faulkner, 1993; Waxman & Namy, 1997). By age 6, children organize concepts in ways similar to adults, and this organization is based on more than physical similarity (Hashimoto, McGregor, & Graham, 2007). Within two years, categorical relations seem to be the preferred method of organization. Over time and with more encounters with the word, thematic knowledge gradually increases (Chaffin, Morris, & Seeley, 2001).

Education may play a part as well. For example, uneducated adults seem to rely less on taxonomic organization than do children who have completed grade school. With development and education, taxonomic structures strengthen and are less affected by the task or context. Taxonomic organization is promoted by compare and contrast activities in the classroom and by exercises requiring synonyms and antonyms. Likewise, verbal definitions may increase categorical knowledge because definitions often begin with categorical affiliation, as in "An apple is a fruit."

RELATED COGNITIVE PROCESSING

During the school years, there appears to be a change in cognitive processing, storage, and retrieval that reflects a shift in categorization. The initial change occurs in elementary school, with a shift from concrete to abstract during adolescence. The increasing reliance on linguistic categorization allows the child to process greater amounts of linguistic information.

Several factors affect vocabulary acquisition. First, both children and adults use a strategy of "chunking" semantically related information into categories for remembering. Thus, seventh-graders rely more on chunking for recall than do first-graders. Second, the use of semantic relations resolves word ambiguities. For example, *there, their,* and *they're* sound very similar and could be confused, except for the very different semantic relations they represent. Third, categorical structures are stored hierarchically. Fourth, facilitative neural networks connect related word-concept structures. Thus new vocabulary acquisitions are associated with previous knowledge.

Individuals may use several levels of linguistic processing simultaneously:

Surface—syntactic rules and phonetic strings
Deep—semantic categories and relations
Contextual—situation or image

The mode or modes of processing relied on reflect the properties of the sentence and the maturation of the processor.

During early school years, children show a shift in linguistic processing from reliance on surface to reliance on deep strategies. This shift may mirror gradually decreasing cognitive reliance on visual input for memory and recall, a gradual change from visual encoding by preschoolers to overt naming as the dominant memory process of school-age children. Kindergarteners also employ a naming strategy to enhance recall. Dependence on visual input for recall does not appear to lessen greatly until approximately age 9.

The processing shift may also reflect a child's increasing ability to integrate situational nonlinguistic information with linguistic information. These abilities are needed for effective daily communication. An example is the use of stress or emphasis in sentence decoding. There is a progression in the ability to use stress cues throughout elementary school and into the teenage years. As adults, we may use the following sequence of processing strategies:

1. Segment the message into the underlying sentences.
2. Mark the relations between the underlying sentences.
3. Determine the semantic relations of the lexical items.
4. Determine the semantic probabilities of co-occurrence.
5. Label the functions and properties of specific lexical items.

Children may begin to employ these strategies as early as age 5.

FIGURATIVE LANGUAGE

A school-age child also develops figurative language, which enables use of language in a truly creative way. Figurative language is words used in an imaginative sense, rather than a literal one, to create an imaginative or emotional impression. Figurative language enriches and enlivens our communication and is used to convey information that may be inexpressible or less effectively expressed in literal language. Use is indicative of higher language functions and correlates with adolescent literacy skills (Dean Qualls, O'Brien, Blood, & Scheffner Hammer, 2003). Conversation, classroom teaching, and reading use figurative expressions frequently (Nippold, 1991).

Preschool children do not understand the nonliteral meanings of sarcasm and irony. Sarcasm is directed at a target, usually another person, "*Those* are nice shoes," indicating dislike. A preschooler is likely to reply, "Thanks, my mommy got 'em for me." Irony is not directed specifically as in "Great weather" when it is pouring rain. Although 5- to 6-year-olds are beginning to understand that the nonliteral meanings of sarcasm and irony do not distinguish the speaker's intention. It is not until age 9 or 10 that children become more accurate at understanding a speaker's intention, rating sarcastic criticism as more "mean" than irony (Glenwright & Pexman, 2010).

The primary types of figurative language include idioms, metonyms, metaphors, similes, and proverbs. Idioms are short expressions that cannot be analyzed grammatically. These colorful terms are not learned as part of a rule system and cannot be interpreted literally. They are acquired through continual use, and their meanings are inferred from context. For example, *hit the road* does not mean to strike a sharp blow to the asphalt but, rather, to leave. Table 10.6 presents some American English idioms.

Metaphorically transparent idioms are easier for children and adults to interpret than metaphorically opaque ones. **Metaphoric transparency,** or the extent of the literal–figurative relationship, directly affects ease of interpretation. Idioms, such as *hold your tongue,* have closely related literal and figurative meanings or are metaphorically transparent, because the meanings relate to speaking and to the tongue. In contrast, *beat around the bush* and *kick the bucket* do not have closely related meanings and are therefore metaphorically opaque. Even adults find less literal idioms difficult to interpret (Cronk, Lima, & Schweigert, 1993).

TABLE *10.6* *Common American English Idioms*

strike a bargain	jump the gun	superior *to* (better *than*)
hit the road	break a date	in search *of* (search *for*)
take a cab	hop a plane	throw a party
robbed blind	do lunch	off the wall
in the pink	on a lark	

Regional and cultural differences affect idiom understanding. Although high-use idioms, such as *to put their heads together,* are easy for all American English-speaking children, low-use idioms, such as *to paper over the cracks,* are more easily understood by children who represent the majority culture (Qualls & Harris, 1999).

Metonyms are figures of speech in which an individual example stands in for a whole category of things, such as "All hands on deck," in which *hands* stands for sailors. Similarly, the word "Washington" may be used to represent the U.S. government. In this case, we might say "Washington is in crisis." The utterance does not mean that everyone in the capital is panicked.

Metaphors and similes are figures of speech that compare actual entities with a descriptive image. In a metaphor, a comparison is implied, such as "She kept a *hawk-eyed* surveillance." In contrast, a simile is an explicit comparison, usually introduced by *like* or *as,* such as "He ran *like a frightened rabbit.*" To form a metaphor or a simile, the speaker must perceive a resemblance between two separate elements. The basis of the similarity is not literally true.

Preschool children produce many inventive figures of speech, such as the following examples (Gardner & Winner, 1979):

A bald man is described as having a "barefoot" head.
A stop sign is described as a "candy cane."
A folded potato chip is described as a "cowboy hat."

I recall my daughter Jessica's description of the Lincoln Memorial, with its many columns, as "Lincoln's crib." My son Jason referred to his bruise as a "rotten spot." One of my students reported her daughter crying because she had hurt her "foot thumb" or big toe. The same child requested "ear gloves" or earmuffs for her cold ears. Heather Leary, a student's child, upon seeing snow for the first time, described it as "white rain like bubbles," a rather poetic image. These early figures of speech are usually based on physical resemblance or on similarities of use or function. They appear to be an extension of, or an accompaniment to, symbolic play. Children as young as age 3 can produce intentional, appropriate, descriptive metaphors (Gottfried, 1997). There is significant development of metaphorical expressions in later preschool years.

A young child's creative descriptions do not imply that he or she can use figurative language. Rather, this linguistic creativity usually results from not knowing the correct word to use.

Metaphors become less frequent, if more appropriate, in spontaneous speech after age 6. Two possible reasons for this decline are, first, that the child now has a basic vocabulary and is less pressured to stretch his or her vocabulary to express new meanings and, second, that the rule-guided linguistic training of school leaves little room for such creativity. The remaining figures of speech, although less numerous, are more adultlike. The decline in what children produce spontaneously, however, does not reflect a decline in what they are capable of producing. Both the quantity and quality of metaphors in creative writing increases in later elementary school.

Comprehension of figurative language increases with age. Some idioms are comprehended during late preschool (Abkarian, Jones, & West, 1992). Even at age 7, however, comprehension seems to be context-dependent, and production by the child lags well behind (Levorato & Cacciari, 1992). The 5- to 7-year-old avoids crossing from physical into psychological domains and prefers to associate two terms rather than equating them. Child interpretation thus alters the relationship. For example, "She is a cold person" may be interpreted as "She lives at the North Pole." In contrast, the 8- to 9-year-old is beginning to appreciate the psychological process. A child still misinterprets the metaphor, however, because he or she does not fully understand the psychological dimension.

In contrast, the older school-age child is able to make metaphoric matches across several sensory domains. For example, colors can be used to describe psychological states, as in "I feel *blue.*"

Proverbs are short, popular sayings that embody a generally accepted truth, useful thought, or advice. Often quite picturesque, proverbs are very difficult for young school-age children to comprehend. Examples of proverbs follow:

> Don't put the cart before the horse.
> A new broom sweeps clean.
> You can't have your cake and eat it, too.
> Look before you leap.

The 6-, 7-, or 8-year-old child interprets proverbs quite literally. Development of comprehension continues throughout adolescence and adulthood.

The ability to comprehend proverbs is strongly correlated with perceptual analogical reasoning ability. Analogical reasoning problems follow the format "———— is to ———— as ———— is to ————." In similar fashion, a child attempting to comprehend a proverb must understand the underlying relationships between the proverb and the context. Both figurative language comprehension and analogical reasoning are strongly related to receptive vocabulary development, underscoring the semantic link between these skills.

Accuracy in interpreting idioms and proverbs slowly increases throughout late childhood and adolescence. Although 5-year-olds interpret most figurative expressions literally, even they can interpret some idioms in context. When compared to adults, however, children's understanding of idioms is less sophisticated, more concrete and incomplete (Nippold & Duthie, 2003).

Idiom learning is closely associated with familiarity and with reading and listening comprehension skills (Nippold, Moran, & Schwarz, 2001). Of course, development of individual figurative expressions varies widely and depends, among other things, on world knowledge, learning context, and metaphoric transparency.

World knowledge is related to a general ability to interpret figurative expressions. For example, *smooth sailing* and *fishing for a compliment* have more meaning if you've sailed or fished.

Figurative expressions are easier for adolescents to comprehend in context than in isolation, possibly because figurative language is learned in context. Frequency of exposure, in contrast, has only a minor effect (Levorato & Cacciari, 1992).

A figurative expression may be learned and stored as a large single lexical item—just as a word is learned and stored—rather than as individual words within the expression. As with single words, the meanings of figurative expressions are inferred from repeated exposure to these expressions in different contexts. For example, after the election, Grandpa says of the side with the poor showing, "They better *throw in the towel.*" After working hard at her job, Mom sighs exhaustedly and says, "I'm *throwing in the towel.*" Soon the child infers that the expression means something akin to *quitting in defeat.* This task is an analytical one in which a child must actively think about the meaning of the expression in context and perceive the metaphoric comparisons.

The figurative and literal interpretations of figurative language may be processed in simultaneous but separate processes (Cronk & Schweigert, 1992). The figurative meaning most likely is stored in the child's lexicon as a single unit. The less frequently the expression is accessed, the more difficult it is to locate.

With interpreting, the literal process occurs as it would with any incoming signal. Meanwhile, lexical figurative analysis of the entire expression occurs. If the context supports the figurative interpretation, literal interpretation is interrupted and does not proceed (Needham, 1992).

Syntactic and Morphologic Development

Among school-age children, language productivity and syntactic complexity are strongly influenced by the type of speaking task and familiarity with the topic (Nippold, 2009). Language development consists of simultaneous expansion of existing syntactic forms and acquisition of new forms (Table 10.7). A child continues with internal sentence expansion by elaborating the noun and verb phrases. Conjoining and embedding functions also expand. Additional structures include the passive form. During the school-age years, adolescence, and early adulthood, syntactic development is characterized by gradual increases in the length and complexity of utterances produced in spoken and written communication (Nippold, 2007).

Both language productivity and syntactic complexity were greater when children talk in an expository genre than in a conversational genre (Nippold, 2009). In addition, during conversation, syntactic complexity is greater when they talk about an area of expertise, such as chess, compared with other topics. Further, children produce substantially greater amounts of language and higher levels of syntactic complexity during an explanation task ("What is a simultaneous match?") compared with either conversation about their expertise ("Why do you enjoy chess?") or general conversation.

Although a child has achieved basic sentence competence by age 5, fewer than 50% of first-graders can produce correct pronouns, "cause" clauses, and gerunds. Fewer than 20% can produce *if* and *so* clauses and participles. You will recall that gerunds are verbs to which *-ing* has been added to produce a form that fulfills a noun function. For example,

> He enjoys *fishing.*
> *Running* is his favorite exercise.

In participles, the same form fills an adjectival role, as in

> We bought *fishing* equipment.
> Do you like your new *running* shoes?

Participial phrases also contain other adjectives ending in *-ed* (*bearded* scholar), *-t* (*unkept* house), and *-en* (*broken* arrow).

TABLE *10.7* **Summary of School-Age Child's Development of Language Form**

Age in Years	Syntax/Morphology	Phonology
5	▪ Produces short passives with *lost*, *left*, and *broken*	
6	▪ Comprehends parallel embedding, imperative commands, *-man* and *-er* suffix ▪ Uses many plural nouns	▪ Identifies syllables ▪ Masters rule for /s/, /z/, and /əz/ pluralization ▪ Is able to manipulate sound units to rhyme and produce stems
7	▪ Comprehends *because* ▪ Follows adult ordering of adjectives	▪ Recognizes unacceptable sound sequences
8	▪ Uses full passives (80% of children) ▪ Uses *-er* suffix to mark initiator of an action (*teacher*) ▪ Is able to judge grammatical correctness separate from semantics	▪ Is able to produce all American English sounds and blends
9	▪ Comprehends and uses *tell* and *promise*	
10	▪ Comprehends and uses *ask* ▪ Comprehends *because* consistently ▪ Uses pronouns to refer to elements outside immediate sentence ▪ Understands difference between *definitely, probably,* and *possibly*	
11	▪ Comprehends *if* and *though* ▪ Creates *much* with mass nouns ▪ Uses *-er* for instrument (*eraser*)	
12		▪ Uses stress contrasts

MORPHOLOGIC DEVELOPMENT

Learning to use a morphological rule begins with the hypothesis that a small set of words are treated in a certain way grammatically. The first uses of a morphological marker are probably the result of memorization acquired one word at a time. This is followed by morphological generalizations about phonological marking (/d, t/) and meaning (past tense). Gradually, a child forms a rule.

There is individual variation. For example, although 6-year-old children from low- and middle-income backgrounds who speak African American English have patterns for marking past tense that differ for non-AAE-speaking children, these patterns do not conform to that found in children with language impairment (Oetting & Pruitt, 2009).

While some inflectional suffixes are refined during the school-age years, the main developments occur in the addition of inflectional prefixes (*un-, dis-, non-, ir-*) and derivational suffixes (Nagy, Diakidoy, & Anderson, 1991). The development of inflectional prefixes is very gradual and protracted, continuing into adulthood. I, for one, know that *flammable* written on a truck means *keep your distance*, but I'm easily confused by *inflammable*. Compare these to *appropriate* and *inappropriate*.

Derivational suffixes—those that change word classes—are a much larger set of word parts and are usually used to change the part of speech of the base word. Many inflectional suffixes appear during the preschool years on a word-by-word basis. As a group, derivational suffixes have a smaller range of use and many irregularities. Refer to Figure 1.6 for a list of derivational suffixes. Often, use is very restricted, as in the use of *-hood* or *-ment*. For example, *-ment* changes the verb *attach* to the noun *attachment* but cannot be used with common verbs, such as *talk, eat, drink,* and *sit*. To make it all the more confusing, over 80% of English words with derivational suffixes do not even mean what the parts suggest. Despite this fact, knowledge of derivational suffix meaning is a significant factor in interpreting novel words (Lewis & Windsor, 1996).

Derivational suffixes are first learned orally, although reading strengthens learning, especially for more complex forms. A very limited general order of school-age acquisition is *-er, -y,* noun compounds, and *-ly*. Mastery continues into late adolescence. The *-y* marker used to form adjectives such as *sticky* and *fluffy* is not fully acquired until age 11, and the *-ly* marker used to form adverbs such as *quickly* is mastered only in adolescence.

Difficulty in learning is related to *morphophonemic processes,* discussed later in the chapter, and to semantic distinctions. For example, the *-er* suffix has several semantic uses and is initially acquired to mark the initiator of some action, such as paint*er* for the person who paints and teach*er* for the person who teaches. Although this suffix may appear in late preschool with some specific words, children are not able to use it generatively to create words until age 8.

A second *-er* used to mark the instrument for accomplishing some action is acquired even later, around age 11. Examples of the instrumental *-er* include cleaning the shower with a clean*er* or erasing with an eras*er*. Again, early learning is on a word-by-word basis. In part, the late development of the instrumental *-er* can be explained by the child's use of other more common words in place of the "verb + er" form, such as the more appropriate *stove* for *cooker* and *shovel* for *digger*. Other words have no non-*er* equivalent.

A third type of *-er* ending is used in the comparative, as in *tall**er***. Young elementary school children show no preference for either the *adjective + er* (*bigger*) or the *more adjective* (*more big*) form of the comparative, using each indiscriminately (Graziano-King & Smith Cairns, 2005). During mid-elementary school, they prefer the *adjective + er* form. Finally, by adulthood, English speakers follow more rule-based usage (see Box 10.1).

Although only a few hundred word definitions are taught directly, children generalize their morphologic knowledge to new words for semantic decoding. This process becomes increasingly important with maturity as less frequently used words are encountered more.

BOX **10.1**

Examples of Morphology

Comparative and Superlative

59 months	He might think of something funn*er*.
62 months	This is a bigg*est* one here.
73 months	I don't like school, 'cause it's *more fun* at home.

NOUN- AND VERB-PHRASE DEVELOPMENT

Children of 5 to 7 years use most elements of noun and verb phrases but frequently omit these elements, even when they are required. Even at age 7, they may omit some elements (. . . *some of cake*) but expand others redundantly (*Nico, who is more bigger than you* . . .). The rhythm of a sentence seems to be more salient, and children often miss small, unstressed functor words. In addition, school-age children still have difficulty with some prepositions, verb tensing and modality, and plurals. Unique instances or rule exceptions, such as irregular past and plural, are particularly difficult.

Noun Phrases

Within the noun phrase, development continues with additional modifiers and mastery of the pronoun system. At 60 months, children add the Adjective element descriptor in which a noun serves as a modifier (e.g., *the penguin school, the pumpkin patch*). This element is in addition to articles (e.g., *the, a*), possessive pronouns (e.g., *his, her, my*), and adjectives (e.g., *big, little*), quantifiers (e.g., *many, some*), demonstratives (e.g., *this, that*), and post-noun prepositional phrases (e.g., *at school*) (Allen et al., 2010). The predominant forms are

> Article + Adjective + Noun (*a pink coat, the coolest playground*)
> Article + Descriptor + Noun (*the pumpkin patch, the party stuff*)
> Article + Noun + Prepositional phrase (*a house for your little daughter*)

Most children produce three-element NPs only. Examples of NPs are presented in Box 10.2.

BOX 10.2

Examples of Noun Phrases

---

60 months

Article + Adjective + Noun	*a little daughter, a good cat*
Article + Descriptor + Noun	*a bear workshop, the party stuff, the goat sound, the brake station*
Article + Noun + Prepositional phrase	*a picture of Damien, the bottom of it*

72 months

Article + Adjective + Adjective + Noun	*a little furry spot*
Article + Adjective + Descriptor + Noun	*a big kid room, the little baby chicks*
Article + Adjective + Noun + Prepositional phrase	*a big cloud of dust, a red mark on his stomach*
Article + Adjective + Noun + Embedded clause	*the new one I like*
Article + Adjective + Noun + Adverb	*a little heart right here*

Source: Information from Allen et al. (2010)

The post-noun embedded clause is added by 72 months. There also are changes in three-element elaborated noun phrases (ENPs). At this age, most children are producing four-element NPs, although no form predominates (Allen et al., 2010).

At 84 months, children add numerical terms to the Determiner category. The *Initiator category,* the possessive noun and ordinal elements of *Adjective category,* and the post-noun *Modifier* elements of adjectival and adverbial are not used by most children or are used infrequently.

With pronouns, a child learns to differentiate better between subject pronouns, such as *I, he, she, we,* and *they,* and object pronouns, such as *me, him, her, us,* and *them,* and to use reflexives, such as *myself, himself, herself,* and *ourselves.* In addition, a child learns to carry pronouns across sentences and to analyze a sentence to determine to which noun a pronoun refers. For example, a child must perform some complex analysis in order to interpret the following sentences:

Mary's mother was very sick. Mary knew that *she* must obtain a doctor for *her.*

The child must be able to hold more than one dimension of the noun phrase or of an entire clause and to comprehend or use a pronoun in its place. This procedure is demonstrated in the following sentences:

The earth began to tremble shortly before rush hour, reaching full force 40 minutes later. *It* was devastating.

By age 10, a child is able to use pronouns to make this type of reference outside the immediate sentence.

Adjective ordering also becomes evident within the noun phrase. In English, multiple properties are generally described by a string of sequentially ordered adjectives. As noted in Table 9.2, different semantic classes of adjectives have definite positions based on a complex rule system. During school age, the most evident change comes in the addition of post-noun modifiers in the form of embedded phrases (The blond girl *by the window . . .*) and clauses (The blond girl *who is standing by the window . . .*).

Even 3-year-olds display the same ordering preference as adults for the first adjective in a sequence. A child does not show adult-type ordering for the other adjectives until school age. Earlier ordering preferences may reflect an imitative strategy rather than the analytical approach of adults. The period from ages 5 to 7 marks a phase of improved cognitive ability to discriminate perceptual attributes and their relationships expressed in adjectives.

The distinction between mass and count nouns and their quantifiers is acquired only slowly throughout the school years. Mass nouns refer to homogeneous, nonindividual substances, such as *water, sand,* and *sugar.* Count nouns refer to heterogeneous, individual objects, such as *cup, bicycle,* and *house.* Mass nouns take quantifying modifiers, such as *much* and *little,* as in *much sand,* while count nouns take quantifiers, such as *many* and *few,* as in *many cups.* Try the reverse, *much cups.* It sounds awkward. Prior to learning the distinction, a child discovers a way around the quantifier difference by using *lots of* with both types of nouns.

Children must also learn to use the determiner (*this, that*) with count nouns and not with mass nouns. By early elementary school, the child has learned the correct noun forms of most mass and count nouns, so words like *monies* and *mens* are more characteristic of preschool language. *Many* then appears with plural count nouns, as in "many houses." *Much* is usually learned by late elementary school, although adolescents still make errors.

Verb Phrases

Verbs appear to offer greater difficulty for school-age children than nouns. These difficulties may be related to varied syntactic marking. For example, verb action can be reversed in three ways:

1. Use of the prefix *un-*: "She is tying her shoe. She is *un*tying her shoe."
2. Use of a particle following the verb: "Pull *on* your boots. Pull *off* your boots."
3. Use of separate lexical items: "She *opened* the door. She *closed* the door."

Certain forms may be used only with specific verbs. A child's resultant confusion produces sentences such as these (Bowerman, 1981):

> I had to untake the sewing. (take out the stitches)
> I'll get it after it's plugged out. (unplugged)

The difficulty of learning how to state underlying verb relationships may account for the greater amount of time needed for acquisition of verbs compared to common nouns.

During the school years, a child adds verb tenses, such as the perfect [*have + be + verb*(*en/ed*) as in *has been eaten,* or *have + verb*(*en/ed*) as in *has finished*], additional irregular past-tense verbs (see Table 10.8), and modal auxiliary verbs or modals.

Modals express a semantic notion of possibility, obligation, permission, intention, validity, truth, and functionality. Some modal auxiliaries appear in preschool. In addition, school-age children and adults also express the notion of modality in adverbs (*possibly, maybe*), adjectives (*possible, likely*), nouns (*possibility, likelihood*), verbs (*believe, doubt*), and suffixes (*-able*). Not all forms of modality develop simultaneously, and the process is a lengthy one. In general, the possibility, obligation, permission, and intention forms develop before the validity, truth, and functionality forms. Even 12-year-olds do not have an adult sense of modality.

TABLE *10.8* *School-Age Development of Irregular Verbs*

AGE	VERBS
5-0 to 5-5	*took, fell, broke, found*
5-6 to 5-11	*came, made, threw, sat*
6-0 to 6-5	*ran, flew, wore, wrote, cut, fed, drove, bit*
6-6 to 6-11	*blew, read, shot, rode*
7-0 to 7-5	*drank*
7-6 to 7-11	*hid, rang, slept, drew, dug, swam*
8-0 to 8-5	*left, caught, slid, hung*
8-6 to 8-11	*sent, shook, built*

Note: Nine words did not reach criterion by 8-5 through 8-11 years. These were *bent, chose, fought, held, sang, sank, stood, swang,* and *swept.*
Source: Information from Shipley, Maddox, & Driver (1991).

Adverbs of likelihood, such as *definitely, probably,* and *possibly,* can pose a problem even for school-age children. In general, preschoolers don't understand the distinction between the terms. By fourth grade, however, most children know the difference. The terms are not learned at the same time; *definitely* is learned first and understood best by most children (Hoffner, Cantor, & Badzinski, 1990). And of course preschool language is filled with *really* and *actually.*

Even within a form, such as the word *will,* different functions develop at different rates. Cognitively, *will-do* (I will go) seems to develop before *will-happen* ("It will take some effort"). This is true in languages as different as English, Greek, and Turkish.

SENTENCE TYPES

In general, comprehension of linguistic relationships expressed in sentences improves throughout the school years (Table 10.7). The comparative relationship, as in **as big as,** *smaller* **than,** and **more fun than,** is the easiest one for young school-age children to interpret. The cognitive skills needed for comparative relationships develop during the preschool years but must await linguistic development. Other sentential relations, such as passive, are more difficult for school-age children to interpret.

Syntax does not fully represent the organization of a spoken sentence. Prosody—rate and pausing—seems to aid mature listeners by segmenting linguistic units, just as it helps language-learning children (Gerken, 1996). When speakers pause at inappropriate boundaries, they interfere with their listeners' syntactic processing (Speer, Kjelgaard, & Dobroth, 1996). It is possible that the rhythmic outline of a sentence forms a frame in auditory working memory into which the syntactic elements are placed for analysis. In fact, prosodic information can aid older children and adults in identifying sentence elements, even when these elements are jumbled or misplaced (Nagel, Shapiro, Tuller, & Nawy, 1996).

Sentence production continues to expand during school-age through adult years across individuals at all socioeconomic levels and of all racial/ethnic groups (Craig, Washington, & Thompson-Porter, 1998). In both English and Spanish, sentences become longer with the addition of more words, embedded phrases, and embedded clauses. As might be expected, in both English and Spanish, children with low school achievement have less complex syntax (Guttierrez-Clellen, 1998).

Passive Sentences

Passive sentences are troublesome, both receptively and expressively, for English-speaking children in large part because of the syntactic form. The passive form is acquired earlier in non-Indo-European languages, such as Inuktitut (Allen & Crago, 1996); Sesotho (Demuth, 1989, 1990), a West African language; Zulu; and Quiche Mayan, a native Mexican language. In English passive sentences, the agent or cause of action and the patient or recipient are reversed, so in "Deshon was pushed by Trevor," we focus on Deshon and not on Trevor's act. In another variation, an instrument used to complete an action, as in *ball,* becomes the focus in "The ball was thrown by mommy." American English-speaking adults use the passive form infrequently. As you might imagine, then, 5-year-old children rarely produce full passive sentences.

Children do not truly comprehend some forms of passive sentences until about age 5½. Prior to this age, children use extralinguistic strategies, such as contextual support, to interpret passive sentences. Children may also rely on action verbs for interpretation.

An additional clue for passive interpretation may be the presence of a preposition. In general, young school-age children interpret a sentence as passive when *from* or *by* is present and as active when *to* is used. Thus, "The picture was painted *by* Mary" is passive, and "The picture was given *to* John" is active.

Production of passives begins in the late preschool years with short sentences containing noun + *be/get* + verb(*-en/-ed*), such as "It got broken" or "It was crushed." In these early passives, the noun or pronoun subject is almost always inanimate. These forms may be based on the adjective form of the copula, as in "He was sad." Verbs of state, such as *lost, left,* and *broken,* tend to predominate in these short passives. Later, a child uses action verbs, such as *killed, hit,* and *crashed,* in both short and full passives (*He got hit*).

In fact, children form passives with *get* and *be* quite distinctively (Budwig, 1990.) For example, *got* is most often used when an animate patient is negatively affected by a non-agent, as in "I got sick from the party." On the other hand, *be* is used when an inanimate entity undergoes a neutral change of state, as in "The hamburgers was cooked on the grill."

Although use of the past-tense *-ed* (He *kicked* the ball) is acquired by most children by age 4, development of the participles *-ed* (He was *kicked* by his friend) and *-en* (We were *beaten* by East High School) used in passive sentences takes until school-age to be mastered (Redmond, 2003). Commission errors—applying the morphological marker where it is not needed (He was *cutted* by the axe. It was *boughten* by her.)—may persist into early adolescence.

Approximately 80% of 7½- to 8-year-olds produce full passive sentences. In general, a full passive contains some form of *be* or *got,* a verb with past-tense marker, and a preposition followed by a noun phrase as in "The window *was broken by Diego.*" Some passive forms do not appear until 11 years of age.

Passives may be of three general types: *reversible, instrumental nonreversible,* and *agentive nonreversible.* In the reversible type, either noun could be the actor or the object: "The dog was chased by the cat" could be reversed to read "The cat was chased by the dog." In the nonreversible type, the nouns cannot be reversed. The two nonreversible passives include one in which the subject is an inanimate instrument, such as *ball,* and another in which the subject is an agent, such as *boy.* An example of the instrumental type is "The window was broken by the ball." In the agentive type, "The window was broken by the boy." Both are nonreversible since we could not say "The ball/boy was broken by the window." These semantic distinctions appear to be important for development of the passive form.

As a group, children use about an equal number of reversible and nonreversible passives. Prior to age 4, children produce more reversible passives and with considerable word-order confusion. Children say "The boy is chased by the girl" when in fact the boy is in pursuit. This confusion is reflected in sentence interpretation as well. Only about 50% of 5-year-olds can correctly interpret reversible passives.

A marked increase in nonreversible passive production occurs just prior to age 8. The type of nonreversible passive that is most prominent changes with age. Agentive nonreversibles appear at age 9. Instrumental nonreversible passives are the most frequent nonreversibles for 11- to 13-year-olds. For this age group, semantic distinctions are also signaled by preposition use. Reversible passives use *by,* whereas nonreversibles use *with.* Adults may use either *by* or *with* in the instrumental nonreversible type. Both children and adults use *by* with the agentive nonreversible passive. Children's passives thus seem to be semantically different from those of adults and reflect a lengthy period of acquisition.

BOX 10.3

Examples of Embedding and Conjoining

61 months	I think *I don't know what this is*. (Multiple embedded clauses)
	The frog could just gulp you up you know cause look how big it is. (Clausal conjoining and embedding)
64 months	Nicky said it wasn't real but mommy said it was because she tried to hit it and she broke it. (Embedded and conjoined clauses)
72 months	I got hit *in the eye with a baseball bat from the gym*. (Multiple prepositional phrases embedded)
73 months	The people *across the street* are going too. (Post-noun modifier)

Conjoining

A child's repertoire of embedded and conjoined forms increases throughout the school years. Syntactic rules for both forms are observed more frequently. Examples are presented in Box 10.3. Clausal conjoining expands with the use of the following conjunctions:

Type	*Examples*
Causal	*because, so, therefore*
Conditional	*if*
Disjunctive	*but, or, although*
Temporal	*when, before, after, then*

The conjunction of choice for narration, however, remains *and*. Between 50 and 80% of the narrative sentences of school-age children begin with *and* (Scott, 1987). This percentage decreases as children mature. By 11 to 14 years of age, only approximately 20% of narrative sentences begin with *and*. This percentage decreases to 5% under the somewhat more formal constraints of writing.

Other conjunctions are more frequently used for clausal conjoining. Up to age 12, *because* and *when* predominate, with *if* and *in order to* also used frequently.

Even though *if, so,* and *because* are produced relatively early in the late preschool years, full understanding does not develop until much later. Semantic concepts of time and pragmatic aspects of propositional truth may affect comprehension.

Learning to understand and use *because* is not an easy task. To understand a sentence with *because,* a child must comprehend not only the relationship between two events, but also their temporal sequence. This sequence is not the same as the order presented in the sentence. In "I went because I was asked," the speaker was invited before he or she actually left, although the linguistic ordering is the reverse. At first, a child tends to confuse *because* with *and* and *then,* using them all in a similar fashion. In both comprehension and production, the preschool child appears to follow an order-of-mention strategy. Although the causal relationship appears to be understood prior to age seven, knowledge of the ordering role of *because* seems to be weak.

True comprehension of *because* does not seem to develop until age 7. Consistently correct comprehension of *because* sentences may not occur until around age 10 or 11.

The long developmental period for conjunctions may be related to an interesting finding. Experimental results suggest that semantic understanding of the relations expressed by conjunctions continues to develop long after children begin to use these terms correctly in their speech (Cain, Patson, & Andrews, 2005).

Pragmatic factors may also affect the development of conjunctions. Children are more accurate at judging the speaker's meaning if the speaker expresses belief in the truthfulness of the utterance and if the two clauses are related positively. The conjunction *because* expresses both strong belief and a positive relationship. Other conjunctions express different relations. For example, both *because* and *although* presuppose that the speaker believes the two expressed propositions to be true:

> It is a block because it is cubical.
> It is a block, although it is made of metal.

In contrast, *unless* and *if* presuppose speaker uncertainty about at least one of the propositions:

> It is a block unless it is round.
> It is a block if it is wooden.

Similarly, *because* and *if* express a positive relationship between the two clauses, while *although* and *unless* express a negative relationship. *Although* expresses an exception or an illogical relationship. *Unless* requires that the truth of one proposition be denied in order for the relationship to be logical. Figure 10.1 expresses these concepts. In general, the more positive the relationship, the easier it is to comprehend the conjunction. Thus *because* is learned before *if* and *although,* which in turn are followed by *unless.* Even fifth-graders may have difficulty understanding *unless.* Younger children do not understand the appropriate pragmatic cues for disbelief and uncertainty. Therefore, they rely on syntactic cues.

Embedding

By 5 years of age, most children can easily produce sentences containing all types of subordinate clauses (Diessel, 2004). From this point on, development focuses on

- Increased efficiency with which complex structures are accessed.
- Multiple and embedded subordinate clauses.
- Integration of these utterances into organized and sustained discourse (Bates, 2003; Berman & Verhoeven, 2002; Nippold, Hesketh, Duthie, & Mansfield, 2005; Nippold, Mansfield, & Billow, 2007; Verhoeven et al., 2002).

FIGURE *10.1* **Concepts Expressed by Conjunctions**

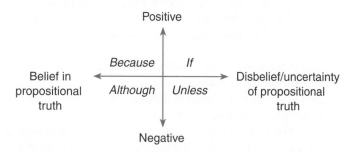

Source: Information from Wing & Scholnick (1981).

Developmental changes in syntactic complexity are influenced in part by intellectual stimulation and expanded knowledge. For example, academically stronger children produce longer sentences with greater amounts of subordination in both speaking and writing than do academically weaker ones. We could go so far as to say that "complex thought is driving the development of complex language" (Nippold et al., 2005, p. 1048).

The percentage of embedded sentences increases steadily to 20 to 30% in children's narratives throughout the school years. Relative pronoun use is expanded with the addition of *whose, whom,* and *in which.* Multiple embeddings also increase with maturity and are one of the most significant differences between the narrative syntactic structure of 6- to 8-year-olds and 10- to 12-year-olds.

Although school-age clausal embeddings include relative pronoun deletions and center or subject-relative clause embedding, these forms are rarely produced prior to age 7. Examples of each of these forms include the following:

> I'm engaged to someone (*whom*) you know. (Relative pronoun deletion)
> The book (*that*) *Reggie read* was exciting. (Center or subject-relative clause embedding)

Center embedding is particularly difficult for young school-age children.

Semantic role is an important factor in interpretation. If the object of a center embedding is inanimate, it is less likely to be misinterpreted than an animate object is. In the following, *window* cannot *run,* so there is no confusion in the first sentence, but the second may be misinterpreted:

> The boy who broke the window ran away. (Interpreted correctly)
> The boy who hit the girl ran away. (Could be interpreted by a child to mean that the girl ran away)

Faced with confusion, a child resorts to a *subject + verb + object* interpretation strategy.

Comprehension of embedded clauses also seems to be based on the place and manner of the embedding. Embeddings may occur at the end of a sentence or in the center. The two clauses may be parallel, in which both share the same subject or object, or nonparallel, in which they do not:

> The *boy who* lives next door gave me a present. (Parallel central embedding: The same subject—*boy*—serves both clauses)
> He gave me a *present that* I didn't like. (Parallel ending embedding: The same object—*present*—serves both clauses)
> He gave me the *present that* is on the table. (Nonparallel ending embedding: The object of one—*present*—is the subject of the other)
> The *dog that* was chased by the boy is angry. (Nonparallel central embedding: The subject of the main clause—*dog*—is the object of the embedded clause)

This order is the general developmental sequence from easiest to most difficult. The relative difficulty of center embedded clauses may be due to limitation in auditory working memory (R. Lewis, 1996). As a child matures, auditory working memory is able to hold more items for longer periods of time.

Working memory is significantly involved in school-age children's comprehension of complex sentences (Montgomery, Magimairaj, & O'Malley, 2008). Simple sentence comprehension does not seem to require extensive use of working memory. Of most importance for comprehension of complex sentences are both processing speed and control and allocation of attention.

First-graders rely heavily on word order for interpretation and are confused by semantic class reversals between subject and object class. By seventh grade, a child has little difficulty interpreting these sentences and relies primarily on grammatical cues. This change probably reflects a child's underlying cognitive development.

SUMMARY

During the school-age years, a child adds new morphologic and syntactic structures and expands and refines existing forms. These developments enable expression of increasingly complex relationships and use of more creative language. Underlying semantic concepts are often the key to this complex learning.

Phonologic Development

During the early school years, a child completes the phonetic inventory (Table 10.7). By age 8 he or she can produce all English speech sounds competently. Sounds in longer words or blends may still be difficult. The acquisition of sounds, however, is only one aspect of a child's phonological competence.

By age 5, a child can identify syllables. Very few 4-year-olds are able to identify these units. A 4-year-old child is able to decide if a sound sequence conforms to the phonological rules of English. He or she will repeat words that contain possible sequences, even when the words are not real, but will modify impermissible sequences when repeating them in order to produce sequences more like English. A 7-year-old tends to replace the meaningless words with actual words. These changes most likely reflect the child's increasing metalinguistic skills, which will be discussed later.

MORPHOPHONEMIC DEVELOPMENT

Morphophonemic changes are phonological or sound modifications that result when morphemes are placed together. For example, the final /k/ in *electric* changes to a /s/ in *electricity*. Several rules for morphophonemic change are learned gradually throughout elementary school.

One rule, usually learned by first grade, pertains to the regular plural -*s* mentioned in Chapter 9. The 5- to 6-year-old has learned the rule for /s/ and /z/ but not for /əz/ in all cases. Even in third grade nouns ending in -*sk* and -*st* clusters may be difficult for some students to pluralize. Is the plural of *desk* /desk**s**/ or /desk**əz**/?

During the school years, a child also learns the rules for vowel shifting. For example, the /aI/ sound in *divine* changes to an /I/ in *divinity*. Other examples are as follows:

/aI/—/I/	/eI/—/æ/	/i/—/ɛ/
di*vi*ne—di*vi*nity	expl*ai*n—expl*a*nation	ser*e*ne—ser*e*nity
coll*i*de—coll*i*sion	s*a*ne—s*a*nity	obsc*e*ne—obsc*e*nity

Knowledge of vowel shifting is gained only gradually. A 5-year-old child does not understand the rules, and it is not until age 17 that most individuals learn to apply all the rules.

Stress, or emphasis, is also learned during the school years. The stress placed on certain syllables or words reflects the grammatical function of that unit. In English, stress varies with the relationship between two words and with the word's use as a noun or verb. For example, two words may form a phrase, such as *green house,* or a compound word, such as *greenhouse.* If you repeat the two, you will find that you stress *house* in the phrase and *green* in the compound word. Here are some other examples:

Phrase	*Compound Word*
red *head*	*red*head
black *board*	*black*board
high *chair*	*high*chair

Noun–verb pairs also differ. In the noun *record,* emphasis is on the first syllable, whereas the verb *record* is pronounced with stress on the last. Other examples:

Noun	*Verb*
*pres*ent	pres*ent*
*con*duct	con*duct*

Initially acquired on isolated words, pitch contours are gradually integrated into larger units. The period from age 3 to 5 seems to be particularly important in several languages for the acquisition of stress patterns. It is not until age 12, however, that the full adult stress and accent system is acquired (Ingram, 1986).

SPEECH PRODUCTION

Increased sentence length and complexity requires increased speech motor planning. Although there is a protracted course of speech motor development that lasts well into adolescence, around age 9 years, children begin to use adult-like pre-speech processes to plan the timing of sentence phrases (Sadagopan & Smith, 2008). Although younger children vary considerably in their movement, such as lip-rounding, to produce sounds, these movements may affect and extend across an entire utterance. For both young children and adults, broad chunks of speech have been planned by the time they initiate production of a sentence (Goffman, Smith, Heisler, & Lo, 2008).

Say the following sentence as both a statement or a declarative and as a question or interrogative but do not change the word order: *John's going to the party.* Note the different rhythmic or prosodic patterns in each and the different intonation. Although children as young as age 4 are capable of modifying their lip and jaw movement to mark this declarative–interrogative contrast, refinement of these movements will continue throughout childhood (Grigos & Patel, 2007).

SUMMARY

It is not enough for a child to acquire the sounds of the native language. These are only the building blocks. Throughout the school years, a child learns rules for permissible combinations and for the use of stress, which is related to syntactic and semantic growth as well. Thus, the child is again forming rule systems that bring order to the linguistic world. The child is not just mirroring the speech heard around him or her.

*B*y late elementary school, the language use differences of boys and girls are already evident.

Metalinguistic Abilities

Metalinguistic abilities enable a language user to think about language independently of comprehension and production abilities. As such, a child focuses on and reflects on language as a decontextualized object. It is these "linguistic intuitions" that let us make decisions about the grammatical acceptability of an utterance. Thus, a child treats language as an object of analysis and observation, using language to describe language. This metalinguistic ability develops only gradually throughout the school years.

In adults, comprehension and production are almost automatic, and processing occurs at the rate of communication. There is no inordinate burden. Even children's comprehension strategies seem to be unconscious. Controlled, conscious processes tend to be minimal, because comprehension includes the total linguistic and nonlinguistic contexts.

Although metalinguistic abilities appear in the preschool years, full awareness is not found until age 7 to 8 years. Prior to this age, children view language primarily as a means of communication, rather than focusing on the manner in which it is conveyed. After age 7 or 8, the development of decentration enables a child to concentrate on and process simultaneously two aspects of language: message meaning and linguistic correctness. Thus, a child is able to judge grammatical correctness without being influenced by semantics.

Preschool children tend to make judgments of utterance acceptability based on the content rather than on the grammatical structure. Thus, a 4-year-old might judge "Daddy painted the fence" as unacceptable since, in the child's realm of experience, "Daddies don't paint fences, they paint houses." By kindergarten, a child is just beginning to separate what is said from how it is said, to separate referents from words, and to notice structure. Even so, school-age children may still judge correctness more on semantic intent or meaning than on grammatical form (Sutter & Johnson, 1990).

The ability to detect syntactic errors develops first. A school-age child demonstrates an increasing ability to judge grammatical acceptability and to correct unacceptable sentences.

Ability to perform judgment tasks differs with age, but especially with working memory span and phonological ability (McDonald, 2008). Although school-age children can easily make judgments about grammatical structures, such as word order and article omissions, even 11-year-old children differed from adults on others, such as past tense and third person singular (*she walks*) agreement. Results of several studies indicate a rough developmental order of mastery of grammatical structures in judgment tasks may be (1) simple word order changes; (2) the present progressive morpheme; (3) omitted determiners and auxiliaries; (4) agreement errors, especially third person singular subject–verb agreement and plural agreement; and (5) irregular forms.

Working memory span increases throughout the elementary school years (Gaulin & Campbell, 1994) and among third-graders is significantly correlated with both grammaticality judgment and the ability to correct ungrammatical sentences (Gottardo, Stanovich, & Siegel, 1996). Similarly, working memory is correlated with receptive syntax ability and sentence comprehension in young elementary school children (Ellis Weismer, Evans, & Hesketh, 1999; Montgomery, 2000b).

Metalinguistic abilities usually emerge after a child has mastered a linguistic form. Therefore, it is possible that a young school-age child becomes aware at a metalinguistic level of language forms and content unconsciously used in the preschool years. Some metalinguistic abilities are an almost unconscious or implicit aspect of feedback, whereas others are extremely explicit and conscious. An order of development based on this continuum is presented in Table 10.9.

Metalinguistic awareness may be essential to changes in semantic organization discussed earlier and are important for the development of reading. Morphological awareness of root words, such as *like,* and derived forms, such as *likable, unlike, likely,* and *unlikely,* is necessary for the formation of associational networks. These networks are constructed of highly similar words, and activation of one opens access to others.

Like emerging pragmatic skills, metalinguistic abilities depend on development of all aspects of language. With increased structural and semantic skills, a child is freed from the immediate linguistic context and can attend to how a message is communicated. In addition, metalinguistic skill development is related to language use, cognitive development, reading ability, academic achievement, IQ, environmental stimulation, and play (Kemper & Vernooy, 1993).

Language Difference

Bilingual and non-majority dialectal speakers may or may not experience difficulty developing American English. Children who learned two languages simultaneously should experience no difficulty by school age and may be at an actual advantage in school. Children who are learning English successive to having begun learning a first language may experience some difficulty in school depending on when they began to learn English. Some of these issues have been explored before. Let's discuss two specific issues, code switching among bilingual children and the prejudice some speakers of African American English (AAE) may face.

TABLE *10.9* **Development of Metalinguistic Skills and Awareness**

APPROXIMATE AGE	ABILITIES
Toddler	1. Monitor own utterances ▪ Repair spontaneously ▪ Adjust speech to different listeners
Preschool	2. Check the result of own utterance ▪ Check whether the listener has understood; if not, repair or try again ▪ Comment explicitly on own utterances and those of others ▪ Correct others
	3. Test for reality ▪ Decide whether a word or sentence "works" in furthering listener understanding
	4. Attempt to learn language deliberately ▪ Apply appropriate inflections to "new" words ▪ Practice speech styles of different roles
School age	5. Predict the consequences of using particular forms (inflections, words, phrases, sentences) ▪ Judge utterances as appropriate for a specific listener or setting ▪ Correct word order and wording in sentences judged as "wrong"
	6. Reflect on an utterance (structure independent of use) ▪ Identify specific linguistic units (sounds, syllables, words, sentences) ▪ Provide definitions of words ▪ Construct puns, riddles, or other forms of humor ▪ Explain why some sentences are possible and how to interpret them ▪ Judge utterance correctness

Source: Drawn from Clark (1978).

CODE SWITCHING DEVELOPMENT

Bilingual speakers often exhibit code switching, or shifting from one language to another, especially when both languages are used in the environment, as in the southwestern United States, in Quebec, or in sections of many major U.S. cities. The behavior is not random, nor does it reflect an underlying language deficit. Rather, code switching is the result of functional and grammatical principles and is a complex, rule-governed phenomenon that is systematically influenced by the context and the situation. Code switching is confined almost exclusively to free morphemes, most frequently nouns, and tends to occur where the surface structures are similar. Children begin by code switching single words from one language to another (Lanza, 1992). In contrast, adults tend to substitute whole sentences. Certain words and phrases tend to be switched predictably across different conversations by the same speaker. Individuals vary based on their proficiency in both languages.

Rather than representing the integration of both grammars into a third, new grammar, code switching rules demonstrate the continuing separation of the two languages. For example, code switching occurs only when words are positioned according to the rules for the language from which the word is selected. In other words, code switching occurs at natural word and phrase boundaries that correspond to monolinguals' processing units (Azuma, 1996). Although adults do not code switch within words, this practice is frequently violated by children under 10.

For children, systematic code switching appears to be a function of the participants in a conversation. Three characteristics of the participants are important: their perceived language proficiency, their language preference, and their social identity. In general, children under age 5 combine proficiency and preference decisions. A listener either knows a language or does not, they reason. Older children make finer distinctions and may, therefore, consider their speaker more often. Their behavior reflects the developing presuppositional skills seen in school-age children. Children also identify certain people with certain languages. If unsure, they try to use physical characteristics as a guide. For example, in the southwestern United States, Anglo teachers may be addressed in English even though they are proficient in Spanish.

Other functional variables also influence code switching. Although physical setting alone has little influence, the type of discourse is a factor. Interviews and narratives contain few switches, instead remaining in one language or the other. Conversations, in contrast, are characterized by frequent switches. Adults are more likely to code switch in casual conversations than in public settings in which speech is usually more formal (Zentella, 1999). In addition, code switching can be a stylistic device used for direct quotes, emphasis, clarification or repetition, elaboration, focus on a particular portion of a message, attention getting and maintenance, and personal interjections or asides. Although topics alone do not usually influence switching, the language of a specific group may be used when discussing that group, and code switching may signal topic changes. In the southwestern United States, for example, Spanish-speaking families may use English when discussing Anglos.

The function of code switching may be twofold. First, it may be an aid for retention of the first language while a second is learned. Second, once the two languages are learned, code switching may ensure that both are used.

AFRICAN AMERICAN ENGLISH SPEAKERS AND SOCIETY

For an individual child, the main effects of using the dialect called African American English (AAE) are social and educational. To the extent that AAE is stigmatized within our multidialectal society, a child may also be stigmatized. Unfortunately, many people attach relative values to certain dialects and to the speakers of those dialects and tend to respond in terms of their stereotypes. This response may, in turn, affect other judgments. Employment and educational opportunities may be denied because of dialectal differences. In general, AAE speakers are granted shorter employment interviews, offered fewer positions, and offered lower-paying positions than speakers of dialects with more SAE features. Apparently, this discrimination does not significantly affect the self-concept of AAE speakers. African American children who speak AAE seem to have a higher self-concept than those who do not.

Unfortunately, some educators exhibit a bias in favor of SAE or a regional or majority dialect. Teachers may use any of the following reasons for assuming that minority students are less capable:

1. Lack of verbal capacity in formal or threatening situations.
2. Poor school performance is a result of this verbal deficit.
3. Middle-class speech habits result in better school achievement.
4. Dialectal differences reflect differences in the capacity for logical analysis.
5. Logical thinking can be fostered by teaching children to mimic the formal speech patterns of their teachers.
6. Children who adopt these formal patterns think logically and thus do better in reading and arithmetic.

Scores on norm-referenced tests, usually based on majority language usage, can be, and often are, used to bolster this position.

Although preschool African American children from homes using AAE do not develop all forms ofthe dialect, there is a marked increase in use during school age, especially from grades 3 to 5 (Isaacs, 1996). Prepubescent boys are especially likely to use AAE (Washington & Craig, 1998).

Teachers may assume that students who speak AAE do not understand the predominant regional dialect. But this does not appear to be the case. African American children's comprehension seems to be similar for both dialects. In fact, African American students perform better at sentence completion when cued in the majority dialect. Finally, there is no difference between African American lower-class and white middle-class children in imitation of sentences in the majority dialect. The ability of African American children to comprehend both dialects continues into adulthood. African American adults find child speakers of both dialects equally intelligible, whereas adult majority speakers find children speakers significantly more intelligible in the majority dialect.

Speakers of AAE may have difficulty with reading and spelling. In general, children read orally in accordance with their dialects. The resultant differences are not errors, but phonemic differences that may make it difficult for the teacher to interpret a child's oral reading. Surface phonemic differences may also account for a child's spelling errors. Morphological and syntactic features of AAE are found in the writing of African American school-age children but to a lesser degree than found in their speech (Thompson, Craig, & Washington, 2004).

AAE speakers may not recognize the significance of the grammatical markers that they omit. This suggests that the AAE-speaking child may not hear a difference or may not understand its significance. In one study, 4- to 6-year-old AAE speakers did not understand the third person singular -*s* as a number agreement marker (*he-they take-takes*) nor were they sensitive to its use as a clue to the subject number (Johnson, 2005). It is easy to see how this difficulty could be transferred to other academic areas. Among 5- to 8-year-old African American children, higher familiarity with school English encountered in academic materials and settings is associated with better reading achievement (Charity, Scarborough, & Griffin, 2004).

Conclusion

WITHIN TWELVE YEARS, THE CHILD develops from a dependent newborn to an adolescent. The overall rate of development is amazing.

By kindergarten age, a child has acquired much of the structure of the mature oral language user. Development continues, however, as a child adds new forms and gains new skills in transmitting messages. The process continues throughout life, especially in the semantic and pragmatic aspects of language.

With increased age, a child sharpens word definitions and relationships, resulting in more accurate communication. At the same time, he or she learns to use language figuratively to create nonliteral relationships. As a result of both processes, communication is both more precise and more creative. The language user has gained increased flexibility.

Discussion

PRAGMATICS CONTINUES WITH THE DEVELOPMENT of conversational and narrative skills. Narratives focus on internal narrative development called story grammars.

Vocabulary expands rapidly, thus requiring increasingly better organization. The result is a shift from a word-order type of organization to a categorical, semantic-based organization. The result is flexibility and easy access. New items in the vocabulary are multiple definitions and figurative language.

Syntactic development has slowed, and many forms, such as conjunctions and passive voice, take a long time to develop fully. The development of language form has become very complicated as sentence complexity increases and as morphophonemic changes occur in the child's expanding vocabulary.

At about the time the child begins school, he or she gains an increased ability to manipulate language out of the physical context. Thus, the language of narratives can be used to create the context of the narrative. This ability is called metalinguistics; it lets us consider language in the abstract and make judgments of correctness or appropriateness.

These changes—both pragmatic and semantic—can be subtle, and some deficits may go unnoticed, yet it is just these very deficits that may make some otherwise high-functioning individuals seem odd or inappropriate. Not being able to vary one's style of talking for given contexts, being slightly off in the timing of turns, and even poor eye contact will make a teenager the target of derision by other adolescents. Likewise, not knowing the meaning of slang terms can lead to isolation. It is these differences and more that separate the preschool speaker from the adult.

Main Points

- Narratives develop internally with the emergence of story grammar.

- Intentions or uses increase, especially with the demands of school.

- Conversationally, a child continues to develop more speaking styles, to take more turns per topic and to change topics less abruptly, to produce more indirect requests, to detect and repair more conversational breakdowns, and to use more deictic terms correctly.

- Vocabulary growth increases with education and requires better organization, necessitating the reorganization from categories to more thematic.

- Figurative or nonliteral meanings develop with the use of metaphors, similes, metonyms, idioms, and proverbs over an extended period of childhood and adolescence.

- Morphologic development includes prefixes, derivational suffixes, and morphonemic modifications.

- Noun and verb phrases become longer and more complicated, primarily by the addition of embedded clauses and phrases.

- Passive sentences develop slowly throughout childhood.

- Metalinguistic abilities or the ability to consider language in the abstract and to make decisions of acceptability also develop slowly, most likely in response to educational requirements.

- Bilingual children use code switching, a rule-based use of both languages.

Reflections

1. The conversational abilities of the school-age child increase dramatically. Describe these pragmatic abilities.

2. What are the elements of story grammar?

3. What is the reorganization that occurs in a child's vocabulary? Give examples.

4. Figurative language cannot be taken literally; the child must use other cues to interpret. What are the major types of figurative language? Explain the development of this form of language.

5. Explain the different types of passive sentences and briefly sketch their developmental sequence.

6. Embedding and conjoining, begun in preschool, continue to develop during the school years. Explain this development briefly and give possible reasons for the sequence of conjunction development.

7. Morphophonemic development is the major phonological change present in the school years. Describe the morphophonemic changes and provide an example.

8. Explain metalinguistic abilities.

9. Describe code switching.

11

School-Age Literacy Development

With entry into school, a child is required to learn a new mode of communication through the visual channel. Although there is only moderate overlap between the processes of oral and visual communication, among the best indicators of a child's potential for success with reading and writing are oral language and metalinguistic skills.

Metalinguistic skills enable a child to decontextualize and segment linguistic material. A strong relationship exists between early segmentation skills and reading and spelling. About half of kindergartners and 90% of first-graders are able to segment words into syllables. By the end of first grade, with some formal instruction, approximately 70% of children can segment by phoneme. Awareness of the sound system is also very important. The abilities to recognize and create rhymes and to create words that begin with certain sounds in kindergarten correlate highly with reading success later on.

When you have completed this chapter you should understand

- The process of reading.
- Bottom-up and top-down reading processing.
- The development of reading and writing.
- The development of spelling.
- The following terms:

blending	executive function	phonics
critical literacy	literacy	phonological awareness
decoding	metacognition	print awareness
dynamic literacy	phonemic awareness	segmentation

Companion
Website

To listen to language samples related to chapter content and to peruse other enhanced study aids, please see the Companion Website at www.pearsonhighered.com/owens8e

Literacy is the use of visual modes of communication, specifically reading and writing. But literacy is much more than just letters and sounds. Literacy encompasses language—academic and cognitive processes, including thinking, memory, problem solving, planning, and execution—and is related to other forms of communication.

Although spoken and written language have much in common, they are not just the reverse of each other (Kamhi & Catts, 2005). Nor are reading and writing just speech in print. In addition to the obvious physical difference, reading and writing lacks the give-and-take of conversation, is more permanent, lacks the paralinguistic features (stress, intonation, fluency, etc.) of speech, has its own vocabulary and grammar, and is processed in a different manner.

As in other forms of communication, use of literacy presupposes that the user can encode and decode signals and is able to comprehend and compose messages. In other words, literacy rests on a language base. For example, one of the best indicators of the later reading comprehension abilities of African American preschoolers is their use of complex syntax in their speech (Craig et al., 2003). Of all the factors involved in early reading success, early exposure to reading by parents and a literate atmosphere at home seem to be most important. Children with a history of preschool speech and language problems frequently have difficulty with reading. The relationship between non-mainstream American English dialects and literacy achievement is complex and varies with the aspect of literacy examined and socioeconomic status in the school district (Patton Terry, McDonald Connor, Thomas-Tate, & Love, 2010).

Although both genetic and environmental factors contribute to the relationship between early language skills and reading, genetic factors play a dominant role in the relationship between early speech and reading (Hayiou-Thomas, Harlaar, Dale, & Plomin, 2010). There is a moderate and stable relationship between 4½-year speech and language scores and reading in mid-elementary school.

The Process of Reading

Reading is a language-based skill. As such, it requires the processing of language that is decontextualized from any ongoing event. Decontextualized language is characterized by the fact that the speaker and listener do not directly share the experience being communicated. The speaker must create the context through language, as in narration. It is not surprising, therefore, that poor readers also exhibit poor narrative skills. The narratives of poor readers tend to be shorter and less well developed than those of better readers.

Reading is the synthesis of a complex network of perceptual and cognitive acts from word recognition and decoding skills to comprehension and integration. Beyond the printed page, a skilled reader draws conclusions and inferences from what he or she reads.

Several steps are involved in reading and reading comprehension. Both oral language and the written context play a role in word recognition and in the ability to construct meaning from print (Gillam & Gorman, 2004). Comprehension emerges from the interaction of letter, sound, word meaning, grammatical and contextual processes, and a reader's prior knowledge.

The first step is **decoding** the print, which consists of breaking a word into its component sounds and then blending them together to form a recognizable word. Words are then interpreted based on grammar, word meanings, and context. There is an interaction between the print on the page and linguistic and conceptual information brought to the task by a child (Whitehurst & Lonigan, 2001). Figure 11.1 is a model of this dynamic process of text interpretation. Note all the aspects of language involved.

While phonological skills are essential for decoding, other areas of language—syntax, morphology, semantics, and pragmatics—are needed for comprehension (Nation & Norbury, 2005).

FIGURE *11.1* *Dynamic Process of Text Interpretation*

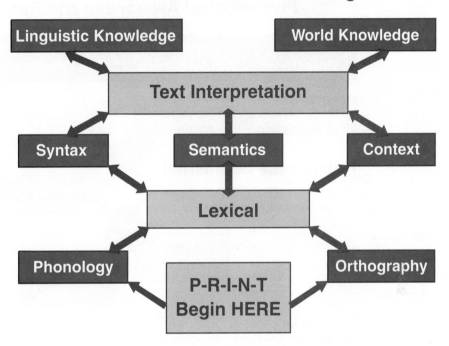

A DYNAMIC Model of Reading

Comprehension requires the active reader to be concerned with self-monitoring, semantic organization, summarization, interpretation, mental imagery, connection with prior knowledge, and metacognition or knowledge about knowledge, to name some of the skills involved. Let's look briefly at two important aspects of reading, phonological awareness and comprehension.

PHONOLOGICAL AWARENESS

Necessary for decoding, **phonological awareness** is knowledge of sounds and syllables and of the sound structure of words. As such, phonological awareness includes **phonemic awareness,** the specific ability to manipulate sounds, such as blending sounds to create new words or segmenting words into sounds. Simply stated, better phonological awareness is related to better reading (Cupples & Iacono, 2000; Hogan & Catts, 2004). Phonological awareness skills also are the best predictor of spelling ability in elementary school (Nation & Hulme, 1997).

Phonological awareness consists of many skill areas including syllabication and phoneme identification, alliteration, rhyming, segmentation, and blending. Not all of these skills are required for reading. Of particular importance for the development of reading are the phonemic skills of **segmentation,** or dividing a word into its parts, and **blending,** or creating a word from individual sounds and syllables.

Phonological representation, or speech sound information in a child's memory, forms the basis for phonological awareness. When children first hear words, they most likely store them holistically in their long-term memory. As a child's vocabulary grows, word memory becomes crowded, and similar-sounding words become confused. In response, a child's brain begins to

FIGURE *11.2* *Dynamic Relationship of Reading and Phonological Awareness*

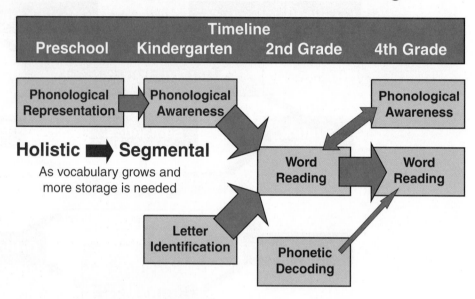

Note: Arrow thickness approximates amount of effect.
Sources: Information from Hogan, Catts, & Little (2005); Sutherland & Gillon (2005).

break words into syllables and phonemes, the basis for phonological awareness. As a result, words become more distinct, and a child is better able to differentiate between them.

The relationship between phonological awareness and reading is dynamic. This relationship is presented in Figure 11.2. Although phonological awareness is the best predictor of reading ability from preschool through kindergarten, after that, the best predictor is reading itself (Hogan, Catts, & Little, 2005). Word reading, in turn, influences phonological awareness.

Socioeconomic status (SES), age, speech sound accuracy, and vocabulary each contribute uniquely to phonological awareness for children between the ages of 2 and 5. In short, the effects of SES and speech sound accuracy on phonological awareness become increasingly important as children get older (McDowell, Lonigan, & Goldstein, 2007).

Among bilingual children, language experience affects phonological awareness in either language (Ibrahim, Eviatar, & Aharon-Peretz, 2007). Reading ability for bilingual children is also affected by the visual complexity of the script. For example, Arabic script seems particularly complex for bilingual children compared to Latin, Cyrillic, and Hebrew script. Examples of several types of script are presented in Table 11.1.

COMPREHENSION

Meaning is actively constructed by the interaction of words and sentences with personal meanings and experiences. Several levels of text comprehension exist. At the basic level, a reader is primarily concerned with decoding. Above this level is **critical literacy** in which a reader actively interprets, analyzes, and synthesizes information and is able to explain the content.

TABLE *11.1* **Examples of Written Scripts**

Arabic:	چَڑِرِ بنُظفَقُكَلُوِي
Greek:	ΠΡΣΦΒγδ
Latin:	ABCDabcd
Kanji:	明清強雄
Hebrew:	בגדהפצקש
Cyrillic:	ДЕЖЗèħѓє
Hangul:	한글 집현전

A reader actively bridges the gaps between what is written and what is meant (Caccamise & Snyder, 2005). At the highest level of **dynamic literacy,** a reader is able to relate content to other knowledge. Dynamic literacy is relating information across multiple texts, comparing and contrasting, integrating and using ideas for problem raising and solving (Westby, 2005).

A reader's meaning is composed of the text and the mental model the reader creates through the comprehension process. Comprehension occurs as a reader builds models based on the text and his or her knowledge and experience (Kintsch, 1998; Sanford & Garrod, 1998).

Reading is a goal-directed activity. Knowing what to do and how to do it is called **metacognition,** knowledge about knowledge and about cognitive processes. Metacogniton has two aspects important for reading, self-appraisal, or knowledge of one's own cognitive processes and how you are using them, and executive function. **Executive function,** mentioned in Chapter 3, is self-regulation and includes the ability to attend, to set reasonable goals, to plan and organize to achieve each goal, to initiate, monitor, and evaluate one's performance in relation to the goal, and to revise plans and strategies based on feedback.

During reading, the efficient reader uses self-regulation. Speed changes with the difficulty of the material. The reader makes hypotheses and predictions and confirms or does not confirm these.

We can describe reading by two processes. Dubbed *bottom-up* and *top-down,* they describe very different processes for print.

Within the bottom-up process, reading is translating written elements into speech. Hence, bottom-up emphasizes lower-level perceptual and phonemic processes and their influence on higher cognitive functioning. Knowledge of both perceptual features in letters and grapheme–phoneme (letter–sound) correspondence, as well as lexical retrieval, aid word recognition and decoding.

In contrast, the top-down, or problem-solving, process emphasizes the cognitive task of deriving meaning. Higher cognitive functions, such as concepts, inferences, and levels of meaning, influence the processing of lower-order information. A reader generates hypotheses about the written material based on his or her knowledge, the content, and the syntactic structures used. Sampling of the reading confirms or does not confirm these hypotheses.

For a skilled reader, printed words are represented only briefly for processing. Automatic and usually below the level of consciousness, each word is represented for less than one-quarter of a second while the brain retrieves all information about that word. At another level of processing, language and world knowledge are used to derive an understanding of the text and monitored automatically to ensure that the synthesized information makes sense (Snow, Scarborough, & Burns, 1999). Both processes are illustrated in Figure 11.3.

In bottom-up processing a child decodes print into speech. In English, the input for a child is *orthography,* or a written alphabetic system containing 26 letters. A child must be able to segment, or divide, each word into phonemic elements and learn the alphabetic code that corresponds. Only when this process is automatic can a child give sufficient attention to the meaning. The progression may be one in which a child gains increasing automaticity at each

FIGURE *11.3* *Theories of Reading Processing*

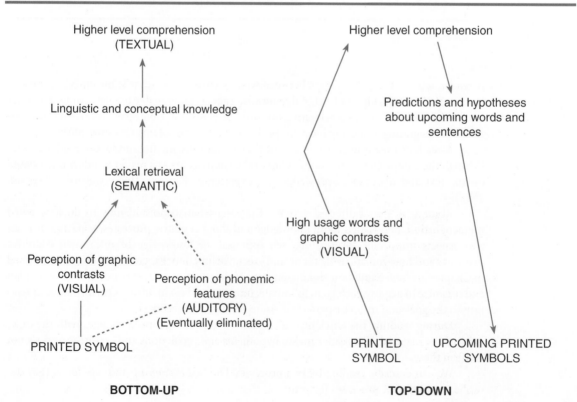

stage as he or she develops and as the process becomes less conscious. Thus, a child first gains automatic processing at the visual and auditory levels; the other stages are still processed consciously (Figure 11.3).

Information processing theory (Chapters 3 and 4) may help to explain how automaticity develops. Each word has a switchboard that activates all the visual, auditory, and semantic features of that word. If a reader has enough information from these features, the information is automatically presented to the other parts of the system for processing. It takes a child approximately 0.5 second to recognize a familiar short word; adults average 0.25 second. If processing facilities are limited, both poor and early readers, who spend relatively more capacity on lower-level decoding, have less available for higher-level, comprehension-type tasks.

The most basic difference between oral and visual language is the input. At the level of word recognition, the two inputs share the same cognitive processes. Auditory and visual features are used to enter a reader's mental dictionary, or lexicon. Initially, a child performs oral reading; therefore, both inputs are available. Eventually, the more indirect auditory route is deleted. A child goes directly from visual analysis to word recognition, just as you're doing right now. The route used depends on the sophistication of the reader. Higher processing involves linguistic and conceptual knowledge. Reading information is stored temporarily in a speech-sound code for processing, regardless of the input mode.

Initial slow learning of reading in English is caused by the lack of correspondence between English speech sounds and letters. The 26 letters of the English alphabet are used to form approximately 24 consonants and 21 vowels or diphthongs. The letters can be combined in over 1,100 ways to form the sounds of English. Most of you have probably seen the example of *ghoti*, which for the uninitiated is pronounced "fish." The analysis is as follows:

$$(\text{enou})\textbf{gh} + (\text{w})\textbf{o}(\text{men}) + (\text{na})\textbf{ti}(\text{on}) = \textbf{ghoti}$$
$$/f/ \qquad\qquad /I/ \qquad\qquad\quad /\int/ \qquad\qquad /fI\int/$$

The letters used in English writing and reading are abstractions that can only be mastered by continual exposure to phonemic patterns.

Bottom-up processing cannot account for the entire reading process, such as sentence comprehension, the effects of context on comprehension, or the use of hypothesis testing with unfamiliar or upcoming words in the text. The top-down, or problem-solving, model of reading addresses these inadequacies by viewing reading as a psycholinguistic process in which a reader uses language and conceptual knowledge to aid in recognizing words sequentially. As he or she reads, a mature reader makes predictions from syntactic and semantic cues about upcoming words and sentences. The text acts as confirmation. At first, a child will learn to recognize high-usage words, such as *the* and *is,* on sight and then use them plus the overall text to form hypotheses regarding unknown words. In other words, a child uses his or her knowledge of language to help figure out the word; much as in speech, when the listener predicts the next word, phrase, or clause.

A mature silent reader doesn't even read whole words. Rather, the reader samples enough of a word to confirm the hypothesis and recognizes others quickly by sight. In this manner, he or she can read rapidly for overall meaning.

Most likely, reading consists of parallel processes, both top-down and bottom-up, that provide information simultaneously at various levels of analysis. This information is then synthesized. The processes are interactive, and relative reliance on each varies with the material being read and the skill of a reader. By third or fourth grade, children employ both a bottom-up strategy when reading isolated words and a top-down strategy when reading text. Thus, faster top-down processes are used with textual material, and slower, bottom-up processes when such support is lacking.

The complex process of reading is closely related to linguistic processing. In addition to the initial use of two input modes, a reader processes material on at least two levels: bit-by-bit and holistically. The relative reliance of the reader on each level varies with reading competence.

Reading Development

Like speech and language, prereading in our culture is acquired through social interaction rather than formal instruction. Reading together is a highly social activity in which both parents and children participate. The adult uses many of the conversational techniques described in Chapter 6 for oral language development, including focusing attention, asking questions, and reinforcing the child's attempts at reading.

EMERGING LITERACY

Reading development begins within social interactions between a child and caregiver(s) at around age 1, as adults begin to share books with toddlers. Book sharing is usually conversational in tone with the book serving as the focus of communication. Here's an example:

ADULT: This book is about a . . .
CHILD: Cow.
ADULT: Well, yes. You found a cow. What do cows say?
CHILD: Moo!
ADULT: Um-hm, cows say, "Moo." Can you find another cow?

Reading the story is secondary to and will be included in the conversation. A parent or caregiver mediates the process by modeling responses for a child, by providing feedback, and by talking about both the text and the pictures (van Kleeck & Beckley-McCall, 2002).

Actual text reading by parents usually begins late in the second year. A relationship exists between the age of onset of home reading routines and a child's oral language skills, especially oral comprehension (Debaryshe, 1993).

Parent–child reading is not the only way of developing a concept of literacy. Television shows, such as *Sesame Street,* and parental activities, such as the use of cookbooks and TV schedules or bill paying, are also important. A child learns that books and writing or print convey information. In short, the child gains a notion of literacy.

There are several phases of reading development. In the prereading phase, which occurs prior to age 6, a child gains an awareness of print and sounds while gradually learning to make associations between the two.

By age 3, most children in our culture are familiar with books and can recognize their favorite books. Through book sharing they have gained the rudiments of **print awareness,** such as knowing the direction in which reading proceeds across a page and through a book, being interested in print, and recognizing some letters (Snow et al., 1999). Later the child will learn that words are discrete units and will be able to identify some letters and use literacy terminology, such as *letter, word,* and *sentence.*

At this age, words may be stored by their visual features, or the way they look, but children lack knowledge of the phoneme–grapheme (sound–letter) correspondence. The connections in the child's memory for printed words are relatively unsystematic at this point.

For most children, emergent story reading in which a child pretends to read a book or uses a book to tell a story begins between ages 2½ and 4 (Kaderavek & Sulzby, 2000). A child uses the vocabulary and syntax associated with specific books and written elements, such as printed words, in this process, even if the words are not interpreted correctly. Gradually, a child moves from language about the text to language that recreates the text (Sulzby & Zecker, 1991). At this age, my granddaughter could recite several of her favorite books, many of the simple ones word for word.

Most 4-year-olds are "consumers" of print and are able to recognize their names and a few memorized words (Dickinson, Wolf, & Stotsky, 1993). Words learned within one context, such as environmental signs and package labels, gradually become decontextualized until they are recognized in print alone. Approximately 60% of 3-year-olds and 80% of 4- and 5-year-olds recognize the word *stop,* and they all probably know McDonald's golden "M." In addition, they gain some general concept that print in books is distinct from the pictures and that books are used in certain ways.

Children who have been exposed to a home literacy environment and to print media have better phoneme awareness, letter knowledge, and vocabulary (Foy & Mann, 2003). Some home literacy practices seem to affect later language and literacy skills more than others. For example, among working-class African American children, these are overall support from the home environment, responsiveness, sensitivity, and acceptance of children's behavior that provides structure, organization, and a positive general emotional climate at home along with stimulating toys and interactions (Roberts, Jurgens, & Burchinal, 2005).

Mothers vary their book-sharing behaviors based on a preschool child's age (van Kleeck & Beckley-McCall, 2002). For example, mothers use more complex books and more sentences with higher levels of abstraction and spend more time sharing books with older preschoolers.

*M*odeling and feedback from a parent aid the child's emerging literacy.

High levels of abstraction include summarizing, making judgments and comparisons, predicting, and explaining. In contrast, mothers use more mediating strategies and spend more time getting and maintaining attention with younger children. In mediating strategies, the parent goes beyond the book to provide a context for the child, as in "*Jonathan lived on a farm. Remember when we went to the farm to pet the animals?*"

As early as age 2 some children show awareness of sounds in their speech, in rhyming, and in sound play (Kamhi & Catts, 1999). Rhyming activities also increase awareness of syllables and smaller units. Most 3-year-olds are unable to segment words into smaller units. Although children are aware of sounds, most will require some formal instruction in order to break words down into individual phonemes.

Phonologic awareness progresses gradually from an awareness of larger segments to smaller ones (Gombert, 1992). By age 4, children are beginning to attend to the internal structure of words such as phonologic similarities and syllable structure.

Syllables are the organizing units for sounds. Each syllable can be divided into its initial phonemes, called the *onset,* and the remaining part of the word or *rime,* which, in turn, consists of a nucleus or vowel and a *coda* (see Figure 11.4). The onset and the coda in English can consist of up to three consonants, so CCCVCCC is possible. For example, in the word *stripes* the onset is /str/ (CCC) and the rime is *ipes,* which can be further divided into the nucleus /aI/ and the coda /ps/ (CC). Many 4-year-olds are able to detect syllables and rimes but are unable to detect phonemes until age 5 or 6.

The child's cognitive and linguistic abilities are also important for early reading development. Especially important are working memory and long-term word storage.

Unfortunately, knowing that a phoneme roughly corresponds to a grapheme is not enough. As discussed previously, the correspondence in English is not one to one. In addition, English orthography sometimes favors morphological stability over phonemic difference, as in using -*ed* for the past-tense marker, even though it may be pronounced as /t/, /d/, or /əd/.

Syllable knowledge is needed in order to decode and pronounce written words. Along with syllable knowledge is a knowledge of syllable stress. The noun "*en*trance" differs from the verb "en*trance*" only in the stress placed on each syllable. A 7-year-old has a rigid stress rule that is the same for all words. This is gradually modified into a more flexible system as the child matures.

FIGURE *11.4* *Syllable Organization*

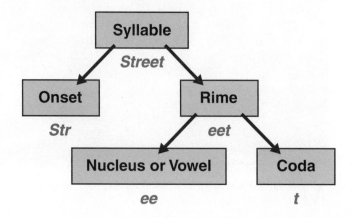

Syllable Organization of *Street*

In the first phase of formal reading acquisition, the alphabetic phase, corresponding to kindergarten through second grade, a child concentrates on decoding single words in simple stories. Undoubtedly, the most difficult part of this learning involves the metalinguistic skills needed in order to integrate the sound and writing systems. In English, the phoneme, as represented by a grapheme or letter, is the basis for the orthographic system. Among such systems, only Korean has phonemic features such as place and manner of sound production included in the written symbols. Other languages, such as Japanese, use an orthography system based on the syllable or word as the basic unit. Alphabetic systems, such as English, German, or Korean, are easier for recovering the phonologic form, although such recovery is unnecessary for mature silent reading (Hardin, O'Connell, & Kowal, 1998).

If the kindergarten curriculum is "literacy rich," children begin to decode the alphabetic system (Snow et al., 1999). Some children learn to recognize words by the word shape, while others begin to "read" based on the first and last letters of a word. Although many kindergartners know letter names, their knowledge is incomplete for vowel sounds and many consonant sounds (Ehri, 2000). In attempting to read, they use a memorized combination of word shapes, letter names, and guessing.

With first grade, children are introduced to reading instruction and to the sound-letter correspondence called **phonics.** Much of a child's cognitive capacity is used in decoding. As the child becomes better able to match sounds to letters, other language skills can be brought to bear on reading, and reading becomes more automatic.

Emerging letter-sound skills vary (Dodd & Carr, 2003). It's relatively easy for children to find a letter that matches a particular sound. Making the sound of a given letter is more difficult, while printing the letter that goes with a sound is even more so.

Although phonology (sound) and orthography (letters) are important for early reading, the contribution of grammar and meaning increases as children begin to read multisyllabic words (Ehri & McCormick, 1998). Knowledge of morphology, for example, may aid students to read all portions of a word and to use their knowledge of word parts in interpretation. Children learn to break words apart, recombine them, and create new words (Berninger, Abbott, Billingsley, & Nagy, 2001).

Although there are strong correlations between phonological and morphological awareness throughout the elementary school years, the relative contribution of each to reading changes in the later elementary grades. Phonological awareness remains correlated with reading through high school, but its importance decreases after second grade (MacDonald & Cornwall, 1995; Scarborough, 1998), while the relative importance of morphological awareness strengthens from third through sixth grades (Deacon & Kirby, 2004). By late elementary school, morphological awareness begins to contribute more to decoding than phonological awareness (Singson, Mahony, & Mann, 2000).

Although phonological and orthographic awareness show greatest growth during the primary grades, additional growth continues thereafter. Morphological awareness is similar, but one type, derivation of words from root words, continues to show substantial growth after fourth grade. While phonological awareness is necessary for development of reading in English, it is not sufficient. All three kinds of linguistic awareness that are growing during the primary grades need to be coordinated and applied to literacy learning (Berninger, Abbott, Nagy, & Carlisle, 2010).

Once a child gains some control over letter discrimination and syllable and word boundaries, he or she becomes a more efficient attender to print, and some higher comprehension skills become evident. Meaningful words in context are read faster than random words. At this stage, a child begins by relying heavily on visual configuration for word recognition by paying particular attention to the first letter and to word length, ignoring letter order and other features. A child is aware of the importance of the letters but is unable to use them in analyzing the word. Next, a child learns sound–spelling correspondence rules and is able, using this phonetic approach, to sound out novel words. Thus, segmental detail, or the arrangement of sound and letter sequences, becomes more important. In addition, a child learns that the text, not the reader, is the bearer of the message and that the text does more than just describe the pictures. Successful first-grade oral readers are able to use the text to analyze unknown words. Along with phonological and orthographics or spelling, semantics is an important factor in word decoding (Swank, 1997). Poor readers tend to guess wildly.

By age 7 or 8, most children have acquired the graphemic (sound-symbol), syllabic, and word knowledge they need to become competent readers. This knowledge is acquired in school in most cultures. Among the Vai, a Liberian population, however, knowledge of written syllabic symbols is learned informally within the family.

In the second or orthographic phase of reading development, roughly third and fourth grades, the child is able to analyze unknown words using orthographic patterns and contextual references. In third grade, the child is expected to use silent independent reading and to use reading texts in different content areas. There is a shift from *learning to read* to *reading to learn* (Snow et al., 1999).

As a child improves, reading becomes more automatic or fluent, especially for familiar words. Fluency is aided by the use of grapheme–phoneme patterns in the child's memory and by analogy, the process of relating unfamiliar words to familiar ones based on similar spelling.

Grades 4 to 8 seem to be a major watershed in which the emphasis in reading shifts to comprehension. Thus, the scanning rate continues to increase steadily.

Children with poor reading comprehension are impaired in their use of supportive context to aid their understanding of opaque idioms (Cain & Towse, 2008). Their difficulty does not seem to result from poor semantic analysis skills.

By secondary school, the adolescent uses higher level skills such as inference and recognition of viewpoint to aid comprehension. Lower level skills are already firmly established. Finally, at the college level and beyond, the adult is able to integrate what reads into his or her current knowledge base and make critical judgments about the material.

The differences between the 7-year-old and the adult reader seem more quantitative, not qualitative, although there are some obvious differences. Adults have a larger, more diverse vocabulary and a more flexible pronunciation system, and they are able to comprehend larger units than elementary school children.

Comprehension is for all readers aided by cohesion within the text. In general, the more cohesive ties in the text, the more understandable it is. More explicit texts are more readable. As in oral development, more mature readers interpret ties more readily and have less difficulty with complex, intersential cohesion.

Not all children follow the same progression. Children have different cognitive styles that influence the manner in which they approach tasks. In addition, which language is being read and whether it is a reader's first or second language will influence the processes emphasized.

MATURE LITERACY

Mature readers use very little cognitive energy determining word pronunciation. At a higher level of processing, language and world knowledge or experiences are used to derive an understanding of the text, which is monitored automatically to ensure that the information makes sense (Snow et al., 1999). A skilled reader then predicts the next word or phrase and glances at it to confirm the prediction. Printed words are processed quickly, automatically, and below the level of consciousness most of the time.

Mature readers don't so much simply read the text as dialog with it. Reading is an active process in which ideas and concepts are formed and modified, details remembered and recalled, and information checked. Although much of this is the unconscious process of the brain partaking of new information, other activities, such as looking up a definition, are very conscious.

As we mature, the types and purposes of reading change, but we can continue to enjoy the process throughout our lives. Reading skill continues to be strong through adulthood if we exercise our ability and do not experience any neuropathologies. Reading is one of the primary ways by which adults increase both their vocabulary and their knowledge.

The Process of Writing

Writing is a social act, and like a speaker, the writer must consider the audience. This demands more cognitive resources for planning and execution than does speaking because no audience is present (Golder & Coirier, 1994; Graham & Harris, 1996, 1997; Scott, 1999).

Nor is written language just transcription of oral language. Children must learn to use constructions other than those they use in speech and to represent phonemes with letters.

In short, writing is using knowledge and new ideas combined with language knowledge to create text (Kintsch, 1998). It's a complex process that includes generating ideas, organizing and planning, acting on that plan, revising, and monitoring based on self-feedback (Scott, 1999).

Writing is more abstract than speech and more decontextualized than conversation, requiring internal knowledge of different writing forms, such as narratives and expository writing. When we write, the entire context is contained in the writing. We create the context from our own language without the help of conversational partners.

The difference between writing and speech fosters two distinct styles of discourse. Spoken communication is usually produced under the pressure of rapid processing. In contrast, writing allows for more planning and monitoring (Chafe, 1994; Strőmqvist, Nordqvist, & Wengelin, 2004). In addition, spoken language is often more personalized and interactive, while written language is more detached and less interactive, with increased time for linguistic encoding (Biber, 1995; Berman, Ragnarsdóttir & Strőmqvist, 2002; Ravid & Zilberbuch, 2003).

Initially, the overall structure of both speech and writing is very close, but children display less maturity in the written form. This is probably because the physical process is so laborious. Once writing becomes more automatic, however, the grammar in writing becomes more advanced than that in speech.

Some structures are common to both speech and writing, while others occur rarely, if at all, in writing. Other structures are more typical of writing than of speech. Structures found almost exclusively in speech include dysfluencies, fillers (*well, you know*), vague expletives (*. . . and all, . . . and everything*), *this* and *these* used for new information (*And there was this man . . .*), and pronoun apposition (*My dog, he got a bath*). Dysfluencies, such as false starts, reformulations, redundant repetitions, and ungrammatical strings of words, are nine times as frequent in the speech of 10-year-olds as in their writing. No doubt this reflects the additional time that writers have to plan, reflect upon, and modify their message. Studies of elementary children who speak majority dialects indicate that dialectal structures also do not occur in written communication.

The ability of elementary school children who speak African American English (AAE) to dialect shift to the majority dialect has significant implications for educational achievement (Craig, Zhang, Hensel, & Quinn, 2009). In short, AAE-speaking students who learn to use a more standard dialect in literacy tasks outperform their peers who do not make this linguistic adaptation. Lower rates of use of AAE in writing accounted for higher achievement in reading.

Writing consists of several processes: text construction, handwriting, spelling, executive function, and memory (Berninger, 2000). Text construction is the process of going from ideas to written texts of words and sentences that support the ideas of the writer. Executive function is the self-regulatory aspect of writing. It's the ability to select and sustain attention, organize perception, and flexibly shift perceptual and cognitive setup, as well as control social and affective behavior (Ylvisaker & DeBonis, 2000).

In general, writing is more formal and more complex, and the structures found more frequently in writing reflect this quality. By ages 12 to 13, the syntax used in writing far exceeds that used in speech (Gillam & Johnston, 1992). This is a gradual process. For example, post-noun modifiers *(the boy at my school)* become more numerous in writing than in speech at about age 8 and embedded clauses at about age 10.

While complex subjects are rare in speech, they are found more frequently in the writing of 9-year-olds than in the speech of adults. This reflects the use of embedded phrases and clauses, some of which, such as those beginning with *whose, whom, on which,* and *in which,* occur almost exclusively in writing. In addition, written sentences include more prepositional and adverbial phrases *(opposite the drug counter . . . , about 5 miles down the beach . . .)*.

In general, by age 9 or 10, writing is free of many of the features of speech. At about this time, writing becomes more mature than speech.

For most of childhood and adolescence, writing ability lags behind reading comprehension. This asymmetry cannot be totally explained by English orthography. Although the sound–letter correspondence is not found in kanji, a Japanese writing system using Chinese characters for words and concepts, the reading–writing asymmetry persists in children even here (Yamada, 1992).

SPELLING

Spelling of most words is self-taught using a trial-and-error approach. It is estimated that only 4,000 words are explicitly taught in elementary school and yet you can spell tens of thousands of words.

Learning to spell is not memorizing words. Good spellers use a variety of strategies (Hughes & Searle, 1997). More specifically, mature spellers, like you, rely on a combination of memory; spelling and reading experience; phonological, semantic, and morphological knowledge; orthographic knowledge and mental grapheme representations; and analogy (Apel & Masterson, 2001). Semantic knowledge is concerned with the interrelationship of spelling and meaning, while morphological knowledge is knowing the internal structure of words, affixes (*un-, dis-, -ly, -ment*) and the derivation of words (*happy, unhappily*). Mental grapheme representations are best exhibited when you ask yourself "Does that word look right?" Your representations are formed through repeated exposure to words in print. Finally, through analogy, a speller tries to spell an unfamiliar word using prior knowledge of words that sound the same.

Writing Development

There is only a moderate amount of overlap between writing and reading. Rather than creating meaning from the text and integrating it with background knowledge as in reading, the writer creates text from concepts.

Writing development is really the development of many interdependent processes. The mechanics of forming letters and learning to spell develops first, with text generation and executive function developing much later.

Although spelling knowledge is working knowledge, not just the applying of memorized rules, it requires a large amount of information to be extracted from memory (Ehri, 2000). Sometimes a speller relies on memory, at others on invention based on spelling and reading experience, and at still others on analogy to familiar words already in memory. Thus, spelling competes for cognitive processing capacity. Excessive energy expended on low-level processing comes at the cost to higher language functions. In other words, poor or inexperienced spellers generally produce poorer, shorter texts.

EMERGING LITERACY

Initially, children treat writing and speaking as two separate systems on the page, writing and drawing are mixed. Three-year-olds, for example, will "write" in their own way but don't yet realize that writing represents sounds. By age 4, some real letters may be included. Figure 11.5 is a drawing by a 4-year-old that shows the beginning stage of graphical communication.

As with reading, in early writing, children expend a great deal of cognitive energy on the mechanics, such as forming letters. Over time, spelling, like reading, becomes more accurate and automatic.

FIGURE *11.5* *A 4-Year-Old's Self-Portrait*

With drawings such as this (entitled Me), children begin to communicate information graphically prior to the development of writing.

Gradually, the spoken and written systems converge, and children write in the same manner as they speak, although speech is more complex. Around age 9 or 10, talking and speaking become differentiated as children become increasingly literate. Written sentences slowly become longer and more complex than speaking. Children display increasing awareness of their use of syntax, vocabulary, textual themes, and attitude. As mentioned, some language forms are used almost exclusively in either speech or writing, such as using *and* to begin many sentences in speech but only rarely in writing.

MATURE LITERACY

In a phase not achieved by all writers, speaking and writing become consciously separate. The syntactic and semantic characteristics of writing are consciously recognized as somewhat different from those of speech, and the writer has great flexibility of style. You may or may not have achieved this phase yet.

SPELLING

Spelling development is a long, slow process. Initial *preliterate* attempts at spelling consist mostly of scribbles and drawing with an occasional letter thrown in (Henderson, 1990). Later, children use some phoneme–grapheme knowledge along with letter names. Gradually, they become aware of conventional spelling and are able to analyze a word into sounds and letters. As mentioned earlier, mature spellers are able to call on multiple learning strategies and different types of knowledge (Rittle-Johnson & Siegler, 1999; Treiman & Cassar, 1997; Varnhagen, McCallum, & Burstow, 1997).

As knowledge of the alphabetic system emerges, a child connects letters and sounds and devises a system called "invented spelling" in which the names of letters may be used in spelling,

*P*ractice in all facets of the writing process helps build proficiency.

as in *SKP* for *escape* of *LFT* for *elephant* (Henderson, 1990). One letter may represent a group of sounds, as in **set** for **street**. Children have difficulty separating words into phonemes (Treiman, 1993). Here are some examples (Pflaum, 1986):

Use vowel names if the vowel is long:

DA = day *LIK = like*

But do not use vowel names if the vowel is short:

FES = fish *LAFFT = left*

Spell the word the way it's pronounced:

BEDR = better *WOODR = water* *PREDE = pretty*

Spell according to placement of the tongue (Temple, Nathan, & Burris, 1982) (Note that different vowels are used for *a* and that medial *n* is often omitted):

PLAT = plant *WOTED = wanted*

Do not use vowels with medial and final nasals (/m/, /n/) or liquids (/r/, /l/):

GRDN = garden *LITL = little*

Write past and plural endings generally as they are heard (*T* is used first, then both *T* and *D*):

STOPT = stopped *DAZ = days* *FESEZ = fishes* *PLATS = plants*

Interestingly, invented spelling demonstrates an analytical approach to spelling and facilitates the integration of phonological and orthographic knowledge, which seems to facilitate the acquisition of reading (Ouellette & Sénéchal, 2008).

In a later phase of inventive spelling, called *phonemic spelling,* a child is aware of the alphabet and the correspondence of sound and symbol. Note the spelling in the following short story (Temple et al., 1982):

HE HAD A BLUE CLTH. IT TRD IN TO A BRD.
(He had a blue cloth. It turned into a bird.)

With school instruction, a child develops a more conventional system.

As spelling becomes more sophisticated, children learn about spacing, sequencing, various ways to represent phonemes, and the morpheme–grapheme relationship (Henderson, 1990). Parallel developments in reading aid this process.

It appears that 6-year-olds initially learn morphological rules for spelling on a word-by-word basis (Chliounaki & Bryant, 2007). This forms a base for later adoption and use of morphological spelling rules.

A child who possesses full knowledge of the alphabetic system can segment words into phonemes and know the conventional phoneme–grapheme (/p/-p) correspondences. As a child begins to recognize more regularities and consolidate the alphabetic system, she or he becomes a more efficient speller (Ehri, 2000). Increased memory capacity for these regularities is at the heart of spelling ability.

Many vowel representations, phonological variations, such as *later-latter,* and morphophonemic variations, such as *sign-signal,* will take several years to acquire (Treiman, 1993). Gradually, children learn about consonant doubling, stressed and unstressed syllables (**report-report**), and root words and derivations (*add-addition*) (Henderson, 1990).

Most spellers shift from a purely phonological strategy to a mixed one between second and fifth grade (Lennox & Siegel, 1996). As words and strategies are stored in long-term memory, the load on cognitive capacity is lessened and access becomes fluent. A child can now focus on other writing tasks.

TEXT GENERATION AND EXECUTIVE FUNCTION

Writing, of course, involves more than spelling. Young writers, like preschool speakers, are often oblivious of the needs of the reader. (See the discussion of presuppositional skills in Chapter 8.) A 6-year-old pays very little attention to format, spacing, spelling, and punctuation.

Often, other aspects of writing will deteriorate when one aspect is stressed. For example, spelling and sentence structure deteriorate when a child changes from printing to script. Writing on a difficult topic may also result in spelling, handwriting, or text deterioration.

Text generation begins with oral narratives. Children become proficient in representing absent entities and events and in describing the internal states, thoughts, and feelings of characters in their narratives at about age 4 (Flavell & Miller, 1991). These skills are important for writing in which a child must create a context through language.

The written stories of young children are often direct and beautiful in their simplicity, as evidenced by the short story that follows. Created especially for this book by my friend Christina, aged 6, the story concerns two frogs (*tow forg*).

Tow forg

Tow forg on a TV. Where anr tow forgs? I will go to The TV. This is My Tow forgs. My forgs are fun. I Love forgs. I Love forgs To.

by Christina

A story by my granddaughter Cassidy is presented in Box 11.1.

Once children begin to produce true spelling, even if it is unconventional, they begin to generate text. In first grade, text may consist of only a single sentence, as in *My sister is yukky* or *Today is Halloween*.

Early text formats are usually of the topic-comment type, as in Christina's story and the following:

I like my birthday parties. I get presents. I eat cake and ice cream.

Early compositions usually lack cohesion and use structures repeatedly, as in the following:

I like going to the zoo. I like monkeys. I like elephants. I like the petting zoo.

Notice both of these patterns in Christina's story.

Older writers use more variety for dramatic effect. The facts and events characteristic of young writers evolve into the older writer's use of judgments and opinions, parenthetical expressions, qualifications, contrasts, and generalizations (Berninger, 2000).

Initially, composition lacks coherence and ideas may be joined with little underlying organization. With the longer writing required in school comes increasing cognitive demands on the child for coherence of ideas.

At first, drawings may be used to highlight important portions and to help organize the text. Later, as in Christina's story, ideas may relate to a central idea, similar to the centering narratives of young children. Very simple narratives, consisting of a list of sequential events, and expository texts emerge next. Early expository writing, seen in essays and reports, includes a unifying sentence to provide coherence. Text forms, such as the letter-writing format, help organize material.

By the middle school years, the length and diversity of children's productions increase. Advanced narratives and expository text develop. Narratives contain temporal events unified

BOX 11.1

Writings of "the Divine Ms. Cassidy Poe," granddaughter par excellence. Age 7.

> I was playing my vidogames. And it was time for Gymnastiks so I stoped and I got my sotes and sowes and cowt. and stared to live from home. It was a loging drive for gram. I thingh? wan we got thar I wated for it to start. So i I was so cold I got undeair grams coat. It was time so we started Gymnastins so we stared. It was so fun that I did a real flip! Bfor I want home I said by to Pallaoa. and stared to leave. ouwer loging dirve. home. we stared in the dor and had a snak and stared up the stars. f or Bed but we did not go to bed but we wacht a movie. and in it was passed ower bedtime and we ware still washing it.

by a topic sentence and the narrative elements of story grammar, character development, plot, and dialog. Expository essays include a unifying topic sentence, comments referenced to the topic, and elaborations on the comments.

With increasing length in both sentences and text comes increases in complexity and variety of sentence types. For example, the types of sentences change. There is a threefold increase in the number of written passive sentences between ages 8 and 13.

At the sentence level, clause length increases in writing, as it does in speech. The mean length of the written clause is 6.5 words for the 8-year-old writer, 7.7 for the 13-year-old, 8.6 for the 17-year-old, and 11.5 for the adult. As in speech, there is also an increase in embedded subordinate clauses and a decrease in coordination or compound sentences. Relative clauses double in frequency between ages 7 and 17 and continue to increase into adulthood. Adverbial clauses, especially those signifying time (*when . . .*), also increase and diversify.

At the phrase level, there is an increase in pre- and post-noun modifiers. By adolescence, writers are modifying nouns with adverbs as well as adjectives and are often using four or more modifiers with a noun. Verb phrases are expanded by increasing use of modality, tense, and aspect.

It is not until early adulthood that most writers develop the cognitive processes and executive functions needed for mature writing (Berninger, 2000; Ylvisaker & DeBonis, 2000). Children begin to proofread and revise as early as third grade. The process is influenced by a writer's syntactic knowledge. Until adolescence, however, young writers need adult guidance in planning and revising their writing. By junior high school, teens are capable of revising all aspects of writing.

Conclusion

ONCE CHILDREN HAVE GAINED a working knowledge of spoken language, most adapt to the new mode of written language with relative ease. Initial difficulties with symbol relationships slow the first stages. The underlying linguistic relationships between spoken and written language, however, make eventual success possible and help explain the process. In addition to a child's linguistic knowledge, emerging metalinguistic skills (mentioned in Chapter 10) enable him or her to use decontextualized language and to understand language in another mode of communication.

Although a child's first introduction to print is informal and conversational, a child learns this new mode of communication by formal instruction, usually in school. Reading and writing open new avenues of exploration and learning for a child and are essential skills in our modern literate society.

Discussion

AS HIGH AS 70% of children with oral language impairments will later exhibit written language impairments. In other words, a child's success in school may be determined to a large extent by toddler and preschool language development. For children at risk, the importance of early intervention can not be overstressed.

SLPs are involved in all aspects of communication—speech, hearing, reading, writing, and augmentative and alternative modes. The importance of literacy for academic and ultimately life success requires that SLPs provide diagnostic and intervention services in those areas of literacy that fall within their purview. These include at least phonological awareness, reading comprehension, spelling, text generation, executive function, and language skills. Each child with oral language impairment should be evaluated for possible literacy problems as he or she approaches school age.

Main Points

- Reading and writing are not mere reverse processes but instead require different skills.

- Reading is decoding and comprehension, a dynamic process that includes all aspects of language plus linguistic and world knowledge.

- Decoding is built upon phonological awareness or awareness of sounds and the ability to manipulate sounds in blending and segmenting of words.

- The relationship of phonological awareness and reading is complex in that phonological awareness initially influences reading, which, in turn, influences phonological awareness.

- Reading is purposeful, requiring metacognition consisting of self-appraisal and executive function or self-regulation.

- Reading can be described by bottom-up and top-down processes.

- Emerging reading literacy moves from print awareness through phonological awareness to phonics or sound–letter knowledge.

- Spelling is not just production of memorized forms, but rather the use of multiple strategies.

- Emerging writing literacy moves from drawing to printing and focus on text.

- Initially, speaking and reading are separate, with speaking the more complex. Gradually, the two merge and a child speaks in the same manner as he or she reads. Later, a child consciously views speaking and writing as different, with writing being the more complex.

- Spelling moves from preliterate attempts through letter-name "invented spelling" to more conventional spelling based on multiple strategies.

- Text generation begins with oral narratives. Written narratives are a step toward expository writing required in school.

- Writing is an active process, and mature writing requires executive function in the use of planning and editing.

Reflections

1. Describe the reading process.

2. Explain the differences between the bottom-up and top-down theories of reading processing.

3. List the major steps in reading development.

4. List the major steps in writing development.

5. Describe the development of spelling.

12

Adolescent and Adult Language

OBJECTIVES

In adolescence and adulthood, the rate of language development slows, and language matures and deepens. Adults are very flexible language users, in part, because of the variety of forms and functions available. Although there are some signs of language and communication decline in some seniors, most adults continue to be effective communicators well into their retirement years. When you have completed this chapter, you should understand

- The conversational abilities of adults.
- The different styles of communication of women and men.
- Adult phonological abilities.
- The following terms:

  coarticulation   genderlect

To listen to language samples related to chapter content and to peruse other enhanced study aids, please see the Companion Website at www.pearsonhighered.com/owens8e

D evelopment slows in adulthood but continues through the lifetime unless hindered by poor health, accident, or injury. As an adult, a person becomes the example for children and sets the standards for mature behavior.

The body usually continues to grow slowly through early adulthood, then steadies, and finally goes into a long slow decline that can be forestalled somewhat with proper diet and moderate exercise. Likewise, cognitive growth also slows but can continue throughout life. As an adult, a person adds new skills, new words, and new problem-solving skills to the formidable ones already possessed.

Measurement of regional cerebral blood flow in the brain suggests that maturation continues. First, myelination or nerve sheathing is not complete until early adulthood. Second, dendritic pruning or trimming, begun in utero and important in increasing neural efficiency, continues into adolescence in higher order cognitive areas, such as the angular gyrus (Devous et al., 2006). In contrast, Heschl's area is neurologically stable by 7 years of age.

In healthy brains engaged in simple language tasks, such as naming, we find that brain activation continues to increase into the senior years in Broca's and Wernicke's areas as well as the correspondingly similar area to Broca's in the right hemisphere (Fridriksson, Morrow, Moser, & Baylis, 2006).

Social and communicative abilities adapt subtly to the many different environments in which an adult functions. With development of a truly impressive set of pragmatic and interactional skills, an adult learns to maneuver in the complex worlds of family, profession, and community, and increasingly in the international multiethnic realm.

As a language user, an adult gains increasing flexibility. The organization of his or her huge vocabulary enables an adult to access concepts both effectively and efficiently. Increased social skills help an adult to choose the most appropriate words and syntactic structures for any given situation. This doesn't mean that language will be error-free or that an adult is an effective communicator in every situation—especially cross-cultural ones—but as you mature you will be even more skilled than you are already.

With aging, there is a slow decline in both oral and written language comprehension, understanding syntactically complex sentences, and inferencing (Nicholas, Connor, Obler, & Albert, 1998). Decline may be related to either overload or processing difficulties in working memory. Although comprehension of figurative language seems unimpaired in healthy older adults, the ability to explain figurative expressions does decline (Gregory & Waggoner, 1996).

The evolution of processing strategies may be reflected in the shifting recall patterns that occur with adult changes. The free recall of complex linguistic material decreases with age. These changes in cognitive operations may be more quantitative than qualitative. The elderly have more difficulty with linguistic processing that requires greater organization in order to recall. In general, the elderly are more sensitive to theme or underlying meaning but are less able than young adults to recall syntax.

The incidence of hearing loss increases with age, being both more common and more severe for the participants in their 80s than for those in their 70s. In addition, men are more affected than women and Caucasian Americans more than African Americans. Other factors, such as education, income, smoking, and cardiovascular disease histories do not seem to be significant (Pratt et al., 2009).

The language difficulties of children with deafness are well documented, but even those with mild-to-moderate hearing loss exhibit language deficits in adolescence (Delage & Tuller, 2007). As adolescents, whatever the cause, children with language impairments tend to be less independent than their typically developing peers, due in part to poor early language and poor later literacy skills (Conti-Ramsden & Durkin, 2008).

In the remainder of the chapter, we'll examine all aspects of language and describe the changes evident in adolescence and adulthood. Special attention will be given to gender differences and phonological skills.

Pragmatics

Adolescents and adults have the linguistic skills to enable them to select, from among several available communication strategies, the one best suited to a specific situation. Mature language is efficient and appropriate. It is efficient because words are more specifically defined and because forms do not need repetition or paraphrasing in order to be understood. It is appropriate because utterances are selected for the psychosocial dynamics of the communication situation. Less mature language users are less able to select the appropriate code because they have a limited repertoire of language forms.

The communication experiences and needs of adults result in a language system characterized by many special *registers,* or styles of speech, not found in childhood. For example, most adults have jobs that require specific language skills—talking on the phone, writing, giving directives—or terminology, called *professional jargon.* Also, special communication rules reflect the power structure of the workplace. Selective styles exist for those with whom an adult is intimate, such as pet names (*poobear, wissycat*) or terms of endearment (*honey, dear*), that are distinct from those reserved for strangers or business associates. Many adults also belong to ethnic, racial, or sexual-orientation minorities or to social groups that require still other styles. These act as a bond for these groups, whether they are African American teenage males, Jewish elders, lesbians, avid CB or shortwave radio enthusiasts, computer geeks, or art patrons. Adults also engage in diverse social functions, such as funerals, public speaking, sports, or even card playing, that require special lexicons and manners of speaking. It is even possible to detect political orientation from the adult's choice of terms. For example, in the present political climate, the contrasts between *women's lib–women's movement, Negroes–African Americans,* and *pro-life–antiabortion* signal conservatism by the first term, liberalism by the second. Most adults use several different registers. Exposure and need are the determining factors in acquisition, and registers disappear from a person's repertoire with infrequent use.

One of the main differences between young children and adults may be in the development of narration and of special styles of communicating found only in adulthood. In general, adult narratives seem to improve steadily in terms of main themes and details into middle age and the early senior years, then decreasing abilities after the late 70s (Marini, Boewe, Caltagirone, & Carlomagno, 2005). Those over 75 have less flexibility and ease with word retrieval and make more morpho-grammatical errors.

SPEAKING STYLES

Styles of speaking are socially conditioned and characterized by differences in syntactic complexity, word choice, phonological from, and the phonetic realization or clarity and speed of speech. Style shifting or changing from one style to another is in part determined by the social distance, context, and listener feedback. For example, we might switch to a slower, clearer speaking style if the other person is very old, speaks English as a second language, or indicates comprehension difficulties. Style shifting in adults is rapid and unconscious. If you have ever talked with a 2-year-old, you have probably noticed that she or he did not change speaking styles in the way that adults do.

Children must acquire relevant social and pragmatic skills before they can develop distinct speaking styles. More specifically, they must be aware that they can adjust their speech to help a listener understand what they are trying to say. Although this awareness may be in place by the end of the second year, being able to style shift depends in part on acquiring adult-like control strategies (Alexander, Wetherby, & Prizant, 1997; Ferrier, Dunham, & Dunham, 2000).

Children acquire distinct speaking styles over several years in early childhood. For example, listeners are unable to differentiate between 3-year-olds' clear speaking style and casual word productions (Redford & Gildersleeve-Neumann, 2009). Listeners are better able to differentiate between those produced by 4-year-olds and are especially able to distinguish between the clear and casual words produced by 5-year-olds. Unlike 4-year-olds, 5-year-olds achieved the consonantal targets associated with different syllable structures better in clear than in casual speech (Redford & Gildersleeve-Neumann, 2009).

Style-dependent differences in 4- and 5-year-olds included shorter vowel durations and lower fundamental frequency in clear compared with casual speech words. Five-year-olds' clear speech words also more fully articulated initial and final phonemes in words. These style differences are unlike those observed in adult clear and casual speech. For example, although preschool children are able to adapt their speech to different social contexts by adjusting articulation timing and pitch, these changes are different from the changes that adults would make under similar social circumstances. Children may not develop adult-like styles until they have acquired expert articulatory control and the ability to highlight the internal structure of words.

Clear speech in adults, for example, is listener oriented and used on formal occasions or when we wish to have no misunderstanding. Adults shift from a casual to a clear speaking style by manipulating some basic control parameters. For example, clearer, more intelligible speech is slower than casual, less intelligible speech. An overall slower rate may lead to secondary changes in articulation, such as decreased overlap in sound production and increased likelihood of attaining the specific sounds desired (Munhall, Kawato, & Vatikiotis-Bateson, 2000).

Communication skills flourish in adulthood and continue into the senior years unless a person experiences a neuropathology, other health-related issue, or accident.

Clear speech also typically has more pauses and greater pitch range than casual speech. These pauses are not uniform and tend to highlight linguistic boundaries (Frazier, Carlson, & Clifton, 2006). Initial and final sounds in words may also be emphasized or more fully produced (Krause & Braida, 2004; Smiljanic & Bradlow, 2008).

CONVERSATIONAL ABILITIES

Through middle and high school, adolescents spend an increasing amount of time with peers. Communication occurs largely in conversations. Management of these interactions becomes increasingly important for acceptance and notions of self-worth. The diversity of communication partners increases as adolescents and young adults enter the workforce or pursue higher education.

In conversations, adolescents frequently gaze at their partner, especially during listening; nodding and showing neutral and positive facial expressions; using feedback and giving contingent responses (Turkstra, Ciccia, & Seaton, 2003). When conversing with their peers, most teens in the United States, regardless of race, are careful to direct their partners' attention, to give positive verbal and nonverbal feedback, and to make responses based on their partner's statements. Verbal feedback occurs on approximately 20% of the utterances and includes words such as *yeah, so yeah,* and *uh-huh* that indicate agreement with or understanding of the previous utterance and encouragement to continue. The overwhelming majority of utterances are contingent on—that's related to—the previous utterance. In other words, the conversation hangs together. In contrast, teens rarely show negative emotions, turning away, requests for clarification, or failure to answer questions in conversations with peers.

The delay markers *uh* and *um* are often used by adult speakers to indicate an upcoming pause, not the end of a conversational turn. Both markers are used in distinct ways. In general, *uh* is used to signal a short delay and to signal a longer one. See if this is true in conversation or when your professor lectures. Both sounds indicate searching for a word, thinking of the next word to say, or holding or ceding the floor in speaking. Three- and 4-year-old children appear to understand the basic use of both markers, but do not yet differentiate between them by the length of the pauses that follow (Hudson Kam & Edwards, 2008).

With more contingent responses, fewer topic changes occur, and, when they do, topics are often related in subtle ways. Adults effectively use *shading,* or modifying the focus of the topic, as a means of gradually moving from one topic to another while maintaining some continuity in the conversation. The topic-shading utterance includes some aspect of the preceding utterance but shifts the central focus of concern.

Although requests for clarification are rare, the ability to detect communication breakdown improves with age and metalinguistic skill. By adulthood, linguistic anomalies are detected almost instantaneously (Fodor, Ni, Crain, & Shankweiler, 1996).

Finally, there is an increase in the variety of intentions expressed in conversations as adolescents mature. Mastery of these intentions comes gradually and varies with the type of intention. Even though 13-year-old adolescents are able to synthesize information rather than parrot what they have heard or read, some 17-year-olds still have difficulty offering and supporting their opinions in a well-formed, logical fashion.

The high-schooler uses language creatively in sarcasm, jokes, and double meanings. These begin to develop in the early school years. It can be a memorable event when a child devises her or his first joke. I remember my daughter's first one very well. We were discussing groupings of animals, such as *herds* of cattle, *flocks* of chickens, *packs* of wolves, and so on when someone asked about bees. One son ventured *hive,* another *school.* At this point Jessica, age 7, chimed in with "If bees went to school, they'd have to ride the school *buzz!*" Even if she heard it elsewhere, she gets some credit for good timing.

High-schoolers also make deliberate use of metaphor and can explain complex behavior and natural phenomena. These changes reflect overall development within all five aspects of language.

GENDER DIFFERENCES

In the early elementary school years, the language of boys and girls begins to reflect the gender differences of older children and adults. These differences can be noted in vocabulary use and conversational style. Although the changing status of women in our society may lessen these differences, they nonetheless exist currently. See how many you note among your peers.

It is important to remind ourselves that males and females have more similarities than differences in their language use (Pillon, Degauquier, & Duquesne, 1992). In addition, other factors such as the context and topic have a greater influence on conversational style than gender (McMullen & Pasloski, 1992).

Other differences may be physiological. For example, gender differences in the production of some phonemes (/f, θ, s, ʃ/) exist as early as age 6 but are more pronounced in post-pubescent adolescents and young adults (Fox & Nissen, 2005). These differences most likely reflect vocal tract variation between men and women, although differences decrease for adults as they age.

Finally, any communicative act must be interpreted in light of context, the conversational style of the participants, the interaction of these styles, and the cultural background of the participants (Tannen, 1994). Interrupting may be interpreted by some speakers as rudeness or pushiness and by others as enthusiastic participation.

Vocabulary Use

The lexical differences between men and women are generally quantitative rather than qualitative. In general, women use less swearing and coarse language in conversation and tend to use more polite words, such as *please, thank you,* and *good-bye.* Other descriptive words, such as *adorable, charming, sweet, lovely,* and *divine,* are also associated with women. In addition, women use a fuller range of color terms.

Considerable differences can be found in emphatic or emotional expressions. Women tend to use expressions, such as *oh dear, goodness,* and *gracious me,* while men tend to use expletives like *damn it.* Even when experimenters equalize a speaker's pitch, first-graders are reasonably accurate at selecting the gender of a speaker who says, "Damn it, you broke the TV" or "My goodness, you broke the TV." In emergency situations in which an active, assertive response is needed, interjections, such as *oh dear,* are rare even for women.

Conversational Style

The caricature of the wife and husband at the breakfast table, she talking while he reads the newspaper, has its basis in adult conversational styles. In short, men talk more in public and less at home. The most frequent reason for divorce given by women in the United States is lack of communication between the two spouses.

Although American English-speaking men and women may possess the same language, they use and understand it in very different ways (Tannen, 1990). While women tend to be more indirect, to seek consensus, and to listen carefully, men tend to lecture and may seem inattentive to women. Women see their role as conversation facilitators, while men see theirs as information providers. Thus, women face their conversational partners, giving vocal or verbal feedback and often finishing the listener's thought. Men, on the other hand, often do not face their partners, looking around the room and making only fleeting eye contact. Body posture differences can be observed in young teens with males more distant and not facing each other. In contrast, girls sit closer and may touch during the conversation (Tannen, 1994).

Much of this difference stems from the different expectations of men and women in conversation. Men see conversations as an opportunity for debate or competition, and thus act combative. When listening, they are silent, giving little vocal feedback, which they may consider to be interruptive.

For men, conversations are events in which talk maintains status and independence. The goal, therefore, becomes "scoring" on one's opponent and protecting oneself. To score, a man may dismiss the topic and, by association, the conversational partner as trivial or unimportant.

Among men in the United States, topics are changed often and rarely involve personal issues or feelings. One unfortunate result may be a lack of intimacy reported by some men throughout adulthood. It is difficult to build intimate relationships based on talk of sports, work, and politics with no personal element.

In contrast, women see conversations as a way to create intimacy. For women, intimacy is built through talking. The topics discussed are not as important as the closeness and sharing of feelings and emotions. Topics are often shared at length and explored thoroughly. In general, girls' and women's topics are more focused, less diffuse than those of boys and men (Tannen, 1994). At all ages, females have less difficulty finding something to talk about, and topics are changed less frequently. As good conversationalists, women see their role as an agreeable and supportive one. When possible, they try to avoid anger and disagreement (Tannen, 1994). Women maintain more eye contact and smile more often than men.

It is not surprising to find that men and women differ in the amount of talking, in non-linguistic devices used, and in turn-taking behaviors. In general, men tend to be more verbose than women. In a conversational context, the longest speaking time occurs when men speak with other men. Contrary to contemporary "wisdom," women's conversations with men or with other women are shorter.

Within a conversation, men and women use different turn-taking styles. In general, adult listeners of either sex are more likely to interrupt a female speaker than a male. Men typically interrupt to suggest alternative views, to argue, to introduce new topics, or to complete the speaker's sentence. In contrast, women interrupt to clarify and support the speaker. In general, however, interrupting is more related to the context than to the gender of the interrupter (Nohara, 1992).

Women relinquish their conversational turns more readily than men. A frequently used device is a question, compliment, or request. Women ask more questions, thus indirectly introducing topics into the conversation. In male–female conversations, only about 36% of these topics become the focus of conversation. In contrast, 96% of male-introduced topics are sustained.

Given these characteristics and the societal roles of men and women, men may feel no need to talk at home because there are no other men to whom they must prove themselves. In contrast, women may feel secure within the home and feel that they are free to talk without offending or being seen as combative.

Development

Maybe these differences reflect how children are raised. Parental speech to children of different sexes varies. As early as 2 years of age, daughters are imitated more by their mothers and talked to longer than are sons. Fathers use more imperatives and more insulting terms, such as butthead, with their sons and address their daughters as *honey* and *sweetie*. These terms may reflect the nature of adult male conversations. Fathers use the diminutive form (adding a suffix to denote smallness or affection) more frequently with daughters and interrupt them more often than sons. The overall effects of these parental behaviors are not known.

Preschool boys seem more aware of the differences between male and female adults than girls do. As early as kindergarten, boys' topics tend to be space, quantity, physical movement, self, and value judgments. In contrast, kindergarten girls talk more about "traditional" female roles. Boys begin to talk about sports and girls about school possibly as early as age 4.

From early childhood, boys' relationships are based less on talking and more on doing. Boys' groups tend to be larger and more hierarchical than those of girls. Actions and talking are used in the struggle to avoid subordination. The listener role is seen as one of passivity and submissiveness, while the talker role is assertive.

In contrast to boys, young girls usually play in pairs, sharing the play, talking, and telling "secrets." Personal problems and concerns are shared, with agreement and understanding by the participants. In this cooperative environment, girls spend considerable time talking, reflecting, and sharing. Their language is more inclusive than that of boys with frequent use of words such as *let's* and *we*.

In the competitive environment of preadolescence and adolescence, however, both girls and boys posture and counterposture, using verbal aggression such as practical jokes, put-downs, and insults. The sense of competition is one in which speech is used by both sexes to assert dominance and to hold attention.

Genderlect, as the collective stylistic characteristics of men and women is called, is well established by mid-adolescence. Communicative competence is valued by adolescents as a way of presenting themselves to peers when great pressure exists to conform.

Conclusion

The communication behaviors of men and women may reflect the traditional status of women within our society. As in other cultures, words associated with masculinity are judged to be better or more positive than those associated with femininity (Konishi, 1993).

Women demonstrate nonlinguistic behaviors, such as increased eye contact, which could also suggest that they hold a less dominant position within conversations. The freedom to interrupt and the sustaining of male-introduced topics reflect a higher relative status for males. In addition, women's use of "feminine" exclamations, such as *oh dear,* suggests a lack of power or a lack of conviction in the importance of the message. Traditionally, the behaviors to which they are expected to conform deny women interactional control and send a devaluing message.

The actual basis for these gender differences has not been determined. It will be interesting to see the effects of more women in the workplace and in college on the communicative behavior of both sexes.

It is impossible to separate conversational behaviors from culture. Men and women around the world interact in very different manners. For example, in Greece, both men and women use indirect styles of address at about the same rate as U.S. women (Tannen, 1994). Nor is the interrupting behavior of U.S. men universal among males. In Africa, the Caribbean, the Mediterranean, South America, Jewish and Arab cultures, and Eastern Europe, women interrupt men far more frequently than in the majority U.S. culture. Finally, many cultures, such as Thai, Japanese, Hawaiian, and Antiguan, exhibit a cultural style of overlapping speech that is cooperative rather than interruptive.

Semantics

Throughout life, the average healthy person will continue to add new words to his or her lexicon. Other than for reasons of poor health, language growth should continue, albeit at a slower rate.

Typical seniors experience some deficits, primarily in the accuracy and speed of word retrieval and naming (Nicholas, Barth, Obler, Au, & Albert, 1997). When compared to younger adults, seniors use more indefinite words, such as *thing* and *one* in place of specific names (Cooper, 1990). These deficits reflect accompanying deficits in working memory and, in turn, affect ability to produce grammatically complex sentences (Kemper, Thompson, & Marquis, 2001). There does not seem to be loss in ability to produce simple sentences when words are provided, possibly because working memory is not taxed in this situation (Davidson, Zacks, & Ferreira, 2003).

Although the ability to access or recall words may rapidly decline for some after age 70, lexical items are not lost. In fact, older adults are as able as younger language users to define words appropriately. In some ways, the language performance of older adults may seem to others to be deteriorating. For example, seniors generally do not hear as well as the young. They may therefore miss critical pieces of information. Senior citizens also tend to use older terminology, which makes them appear to be less adept at using language. Newer terms may be more difficult for them to recall. Thus, the older adult might use the terms *dungarees* and *tennis shoes* in place of *jeans* and *sneakers*. The popular image of the incoherent, rambling older adult with poor word memory is untrue and unfair to most seniors. As Larry, a senior friend of mine, says, "gettin' old ain't for sissies!"

Age, metalinguistic ability, and educational level are all important for the production of well-structured formal definitions (Benelli et al., 2006). In general, adult definitions are more abstract than child definitions. They tend to be descriptive, with concrete terms or references to specific instances used to modify the concept. In addition, adult definitions include synonyms, explanations, and categorizations of the word defined. During adolescence, a number of changes occur in definitions with the inclusion of category membership, the sharpening of core features of a word, and the addition of subtle aspects of meaning (Nippold, Hegel, Sohlberg, & Schwarz, 1999). Frequency of a word's use may be a relatively more important factor in development of definitions by teens and young adults for some types of words, such as adjectives (Marinellie & Johnson, 2003).

Unlike child meanings, adult definitions are exclusionary and also specify what an entity is not. Adult definitions also reflect an individual's personal biases and experiences.

Supplying word definitions is a metalinguistic skill. In general, both quantitative and qualitative improvement in definitions occurs in adolescence. Synonym-type definitions increase. A greater tendency exists to include categorical membership (*an apple is fruit*), function, description, and degree (*almost, nearly*). High-quality definitions develop for root words prior to inflected or derived words.

Figurative language will be a challenge into adulthood. For preteens and adolescents, idioms that are more familiar, supported by context, and more transparent are easier to understand than those that are less familiar, isolated or out of context, and more opaque (Nippold & Taylor, 1995; Nippold, Taylor, & Baker, 1995; Spector, 1996). These factors are also important in the interpretation of proverbs (Nippold & Haq, 1996). Language experience and the development of metalinguistic abilities (see Chapter 10) are important determiners of individual skill with proverbs. For adults in their 20s, concrete proverbs are still easier to interpret than abstract. This difference is not seen in older adults, where the ease of interpreting is related to a person's overall level of education (Nippold, Uhden, & Schwarz, 1997).

Ability to define idioms increases with age as does familiarity with idioms (Chan & Marinellie, 2008). As children move from childhood through adolescence to adulthood, definitions include more critical elements and related or associated concepts.

Syntax and Morphology

The length and syntactic complexity of oral sentences increases into early adulthood and stabilizes in middle age, although there are differences across individual speakers and contexts (Nippold, Hesketh, Duthie, & Mansfield, 2005). Much of the increase in complexity is in the use of dependent clauses. Individual variability exists at all ages with some children using elaborate sentences and some adults simple ones. In general, all speakers produce more complex sentences when explaining how to do something than when in conversational give-and-take. Cohesion in explanations is obtained by relating one sentence to another through the use of various conversation devices, such as articles and use of pronouns and nouns.

Acquisition of increasingly abstract thought enables an adolescent to integrate new information into existing knowledge systems. This is accomplished to support the production of dialogues, such as conversations, and, with increased maturity, the production of social monologues.

Expository monologues are especially challenging because they require production that taps a speaker's knowledge of the topic—however limited or extensive that may be (Nippold et al., 2007). Expository speech places greater demands on a speaker because there is an expectation of an informative monologue in contrast to the more interactive dialogue found in conversation. When children, adolescents, and adults speak in an expository genre, they use greater syntactic complexity than when they are speaking in conversations or relating narratives (Berman & Verhoeven, 2002; Nippold et al., 2005; Nippold, Mansfield, Billow, & Tomblin, 2008; Scott & Windsor, 2000; Verhoeven et al., 2002). Complex thought, supported by a knowledge base, seems to drive the use of complex language.

NOUN PHRASES

The density and variety of nouns and noun phrase types increases dramatically in adolescence and on into adulthood (Ravid, 2006). Because older children do not repeat the same word over and over as do infants and toddlers, the greater density of nouns means more variety and higher linguistic complexity (Berman & Slobin, 1994; Hickmann, 2003; Richards & Malvern, 1997).

As children grow older and mature cognitively, they increase their knowledge, which, in turn, enables them to express increasingly complex concepts in abstract terms (Anglin, 1993; Seroussi, 2004). Even mid-elementary school children, ages 9–10, use fewer concrete nouns, i.e. *ball, backpack, a new car, boy in my class,* than preschool children, and this change continues into adolescence. Through the teen years, there is an increase in categorical and abstract nouns and noun phrases, such as *road to peace, conclusion, authority, his opinion, the teacher's feedback, an annoyance, intervention, prejudices.* Defining abstract nouns, however, is difficult for adolescents, even for 18-year-olds (Nippold, Hegel, et al., 1999). Full mastery of abstract and morphologically complex nouns consolidates only in adulthood (Ravid & Avidor, 1998).

These changes in types of nouns are affected by linguistic, cognitive, and social development, and by modality (spoken versus written) and text genre (narrative versus expository). Beginning in late elementary school, as noted in Chapter 10, narratives become increasingly rich compared to speech in the types of nouns used, especially in adulthood (Ravid & Cahana-Amitay, 2005). There is an increase in the level of abstraction and in the complexity of the syntactic structures in which such nouns occurred. With increased age and education, written texts became richer in complex noun structures (*the small boy from next door who goes to my school*), especially in written expository texts. Cross-linguistic studies report a consistent increase in complex NPs from childhood to adulthood, again more so in written expository texts (Ravid, van Hell, Rosado, & Zamora, 2002).

CONJUNCTS AND DISJUNCTS

In conversation, a child or adolescent slowly learns to link sentences with devices that are peripheral to the clause. By bridging utterances, these devices provide continuity. The devices consist of *adverbial disjuncts,* which comment on or convey the speaker's attitude toward the content of the connected sentence, such as *frankly, to be honest, perhaps, however, yet,* and *to my surprise,* and *adverbial conjuncts,* which signal a logical relation between sentences, such as *still, as a result of,* and *to conclude.* The following are examples of adverbial disjuncts used in conversation:

> *Honestly,* I don't know why you bought that car.
> *In my opinion,* it was a bargain.
> *Well, to be honest,* I think it's a lemon.

Adverbial conjuncts are cohesive and connective devices and may be concordant (*similarly, moreover, consequently*) or discordant (*in contrast, rather, but, nevertheless*). Conjuncts express a logical intersential relationship and are more common in literature than in conversation. In the following example, the conjunct *as a result of* signals the relationship of the two sentences:

> We were up all night. As a result of our effort, our group won the competition.

Development of conjuncts occurs gradually from school age into adulthood. Both production and understanding increase with age, although comprehension exceeds production even in young adults (Nippold, Schwarz, & Undlin, 1992). By age 6, a child uses the adverbial conjuncts *now, then, so,* and *though,* although disjuncts are rare. By age 12, a youth has added *otherwise, anyway, therefore,* and *however,* plus the disjuncts *really* and *probably.* This development continues well into the adult years, with adults using 12 conjuncts per 100 utterances compared to the 12-year-old's four (Scott, 1988).

Phonology

It's important to note that even though the phonetic inventory is mastered by around age 8, finer aspects of speech development extend to the late teens for both males and females (Smith & Goffman, 2004). For example, male–female differences in the laryngeal or formant frequency of speech become evident as early as age 4 but become more apparent later in childhood. Although jumps in the formant frequency accompany growth spurts in the vocal tract, there is an overall decrease in this frequency into adulthood with the most rapid decreases occurring during early childhood and adolescence (Vorperian & Kent, 2007).

Adult phonological knowledge—what they know about American English speech sounds—is multidimensional. It consists of acoustic-perceptual and articulatory knowledge, knowledge of higher level phonological categories, and social-indexical knowledge, which is related to styles of talking (Munson, Edwards, & Beckman, 2005a). Let's discuss each briefly.

The characteristics of a phoneme vary as a function of both (1) the phonetic context or the adjacent speech sounds and (2) the social factors, such as sexual orientation, class, race, regional dialect, gender, and age (Munson, 2004; Munson, Edwards, & Beckman, 2005b). Adults are able to perceive speech sounds with little difficulty; they know the sound characteristics of /s/ and don't confuse it with other speech sounds.

Adults' perceptual knowledge may be based on perception of very fine acoustic characteristics and on knowledge of categories of sounds. For example, adults may base their judgments of a sound on such parameters as frequency, intensity, and duration of the sound. Even children as old as 10 years do not use this variety of perceptual cues (Hazan & Barret, 2000). Children also lack the adult ability to recognize words and sounds from different speakers, suggesting that children have incomplete auditory–perceptual knowledge (Ryalls & Pisoni, 1997).

You will recall that very young children process new words holistically rather than breaking them down into separate sounds. In this situation, high neighborhood density, or the number of words that differ by one sound, can make word learning more difficult. In contrast, among adults high neighborhood density may positively influence the integration of new word representations (Storkel, Armbrüster, & Hogan, 2006). Among both children and adults, phonotactic probability or the likelihood of sound and syllable construction may aid in new word learning.

Articulatory knowledge is knowing the movements needed to produce different speech sounds. These movements vary with the phonetic and prosodic context and such word-specific factors as frequency of use and word similarity. An individual's sound production accuracy is dependent upon recognizing these factors and being sufficiently flexible to adapt to different contexts and task demands.

Acquisition of articulatory knowledge is an extended process. Even adolescent speech differs from adult speech in the length of sounds and words and in characteristics that differentiate one sound from another (Lee, Potamianos, & Naryanan, 1999).

As the development of speech continues into the adult years, there is a steady increase in fluency. This is aided by **coarticulation,** a speech process in which sounds that will be produced later in an utterance are anticipated and the mouth is moved into position on an earlier speech sound. For example, the /k/ in *coat* and *cat* are produced in qualitatively different ways as the speaker anticipates the sound to follow. Produce both words and notice the lip rounding on the /k/ in *coat* that is absent in *cat.*

Adult phonological knowledge also involves the way speech-sound categories are used to convey meaning through morphophonemic changes and the admissible speech-sound combinations in American English. Obviously, such knowledge varies with the language being spoken.

Children do not possess adultlike knowledge that words are composed of strings of phonemes. Such knowledge is acquired throughout childhood and into adolescence. In general, children with larger vocabularies have more higher level phonological skills (Edwards et al., 2004). Most likely, as a child's vocabulary increases, and he or she must store more and more words with similar sound and syllable combinations, a child uses acoustic-perceptual representations and articulatory representations to refine knowledge of word formations. Words become strings of sounds.

Finally, social-indexical knowledge includes knowing how linguistic variability conveys or is perceived to convey a speaker's membership in different social groups (Clopper & Pisoni, 2004; Smyth, Jacobs, & Rogers, 2003). A person's speech may identify group membership and influence a listener's perceptions.

Social-indexical variation, such as gender and dialectal differences, is present even in the speech of very young children. Ability to comprehend speech in an unfamiliar dialect requires greater facility and develops throughout childhood and adolescence (Nathan, Wells, & Donlan, 1998). Dialects will be discussed in detail in the next chapter.

Literacy

The incidence of pleasure reading seems to decrease through adolescence, especially among males (Nippold, Duthie, & Larsen, 2005). Although a moderately popular free-time activity, reading is less desirable than listening to music/going to concerts, watching television or videos, playing sports, or playing computer or video games. The most popular reading materials are magazines, novels, and comics.

Adults read somewhat more than adolescents, often in work-related settings. This generational difference may decrease as more and more adults come from the computer generation. It must not be forgotten, however, that access to the Internet requires considerable literacy skill. Even spell-checkers, grammar-checkers, and word-prediction programs require minimal writing ability to engage their programs.

While adults continue to refine both their writing and reading abilities, these changes are not dramatic. The biggest change in adolescence and adulthood is in executive function, the ability to engage actively with print and to write and read with purpose.

It is not until early adulthood—about where most of you are right now—that writers develop the cognitive processes and executive functions needed for mature writing (Berninger, 2000; Ylvisaker & DeBonis, 2000). It takes this long because of the protracted period of anatomical and physiological development of your brain's frontal lobe where executive function is housed.

Until adolescence, young writers need adult scaffolding or guidance in planning and revising their writing. By junior high school, teens are capable of revising all aspects of writing, which, added to improved long-term memory, results in improved overall compositional quality (Berninger, Cartwright, Yates, Swanson, & Abbott, 1994).

If you find yourself using an enlarged vocabulary when writing or pondering how sentences flow from one to the next, then you are probably a mature writer. As with reading, practice results in improvement, which should continue throughout the lifespan. In general, the writing of adults as compared to adolescents is longer with longer, more complex sentences; uses more abstract nouns, such as *longevity* and *kindness*; and contains more metalinguistic and metacognitive words, such as *reflect* and *disagree* (Nippold, Ward-Lonergan, & Fanning, 2005).

Bilingualism

Immigrant children tend to score lower on English language tests than nonimmigrant children, but their language growth in English continues into adolescence more than nonimmigrant children (Leventhal, Xue, & Brooks-Gunn, 2006). Family SES affects performance also. Poorer children do not have language skills as high as more affluent children.

Although it varies with the brain function in question, there does seem to be a "sensitive" period or a time during development in which the brain is particularly responsive to experiences or patterns of activity (Daw, 1997). In the area of speech and language, native language proficiency cannot be obtained when learning begins after puberty (Bruer, 2001; Werker & Tees, 2005). For example, adults exposed to a second language in early childhood have native-like accents and intonation, while those not exposed until adulthood or late adolescence do not achieve native-like speech (Birdsong & Molis, 2001; Gordon, 2000; Stein et al., 2006). Similarly, early exposure to a second language leads to better judgments of grammatical correctness (Flege, MacKay, & Meador, 1999; Komarova & Nowak, 2001). We should add that these data are complicated somewhat by the differing cognitive processing of adults and children that may enhance the child's ability to learn language (Newport, 1990; Newport et al., 2001).

Non-native child and adult listeners seem to rely less on grammatical analysis for interpretation than native listeners (Felser & Clahsen, 2009). These second language learners may rely more on other cues, such as social. The difference can be explained in part by slower processing speed and cognitive resource allocation by non-native listeners. For example, relatively more cognitive resources may be allocated to lower level phonological analysis, leaving fewer for higher order comprehension processing.

Congratulations!

Well, you made it! You reached the end of this text. Congratulations! And like the folks discussed in this chapter, you have your entire adult life before you. Make it a great one. Take what you've learned and use it with your own children and children in school or in need of special services.

For those of you who will go on to work with children with special needs, you now have a firm foundation to begin to discuss language impairments. Keep an open mind. New ideas come along all the time. Evaluate each in light of research and your knowledge of language development. Good luck. Be well and safe.

Conclusion

BY ADULTHOOD, EACH INDIVIDUAL is a truly versatile speaker who can tailor his or her message to the context and the participants. Adults are able to move flexibly from work to the gym to a cocktail party and home to tuck in the kids and alter their language effortlessly as needed. Within these contexts and many more, the mature communicator can change style and topic rapidly or remain in both almost indefinitely.

The conversational and literacy abilities of adults continue to diversify and to become more elaborate with age if health is maintained. Except for the small percentage of older adults who have suffered some brain injury or disease, most continue to be effective communicators throughout their lives.

Discussion

MOST OF THE QUANTITATIVE DEVELOPMENT of language is behind you, but you can still refine and improve your language as your life progresses. To do so, you must remain actively involved in life and open to new ideas and change. When I began the first edition of this text, I had no more idea how to write a book than many of you. It continues to be a learning experience, and you can judge for yourself how much I have learned and how far I still need to go.

Many of you will be able to participate again in the developmental process through your own children or those of others. Those of you who go into education will help children with the formal aspects of learning language, while those who select special education or speech-language pathology will be involved with children and adults experiencing difficulties. Just because a person has matured into adulthood, it does not follow that speech and language disorders mature into nondisordered communication. In addition, some adults will also experience difficulties because of illness or injury and will also require intervention. You now have some of the knowledge you need to make judgments on the appropriateness of communication among children and adults.

Main Points

- Development continues slowly through adolescence and adulthood, although there are some declines in the senior years.

- Teens and adults are adept and flexible communicators with various styles of talking.

- In the U.S. majority culture, gender differences are obvious in adulthood but may begin as early as late preschool. In general, men and women use different vocabulary and styles of talking that may reflect societal expectations, societal inequalities, and socialization practices.

- Vocabularies continue to grow with some loss in speed and accuracy of word retrieval in the senior years.

- Syntax becomes more complex, and speakers use conjuncts (cohesive devices) and disjuncts (attitudinal markers) to improve the flow and express opinions.

- Adult phonological knowledge enables adults to interpret speech from dialectal speakers and to make rapid speech coarticulatory movements.

- Although adult literacy changes are not dynamic, there are substantial changes in executive function in adolescence. The result is reading and writing with purpose.

Reflections

1. Describe the conversational abilities of adults.

2. Explain the different styles of communication of women and men and their possible origin.

3. Describe the difference between mature adult phonological abilities and those of children.

APPENDIX *A*

American English Speech Sounds

The smallest unit of speech is the phoneme. It consists of a family of sounds that are close enough in perceptual qualities to be distinguished from other phonemes. Thus, although phonemes are meaningless, they make semantic difference in actual use. For example, the final sounds in *kiss* and *kick* are perceptually different enough to alert the listener to differences in meaning. Recognition of this distinction could be crucial, especially on a first date. Phonemes are written between slashes (as in /s/) to distinguish them from the alphabet. The International Phonetic Alphabet (IPA) is used rather than the English alphabet for two reasons. First, a sound may be spelled several ways, as in g*o*, r*ow*, h*oe*, and th*ough*. In contrast, some letters, such as *c*, can be pronounced more than one way (as *s* or *k*). Similarly, the *o* in *comb* differs from the one in *come*. Second, the pronunciation of the English alphabet cannot be applied to other languages. Although French uses an identical alphabet, the pronunciation of the individual letters is quite different.

The actual sound produced by a speaker at a given time is called a **phone**, and no two phones are alike. Phones may be grouped perceptually as **allophones**, but even allophones may differ slightly. For example, the /p/ in *stop* may or may not be accompanied by a puff of air, or aspiration. The /p/ sound in *spot* is not aspirated. These two allophones are similar enough, however, to be classified as the phoneme /p/. A phoneme is thus made up of a group of allophones. As speakers of English, we have no difficulty recognizing the phonemic variations in *pop*, *pot*, *top*, and *tot*. Many English words differ by only one consonant or vowel. Consider *bet*, *get*, *let*, *met*, *net*, *pet*, *set*, *vet*, and *wet* or *bat*, *bet*, *bit*, and *but*. Perception of the different phonemes is extremely important for interpretation.

Each spoken language employs particular phonemes. In English, these sounds are classified as vowels or consonants. The distinction is based mainly on sound production characteristics. Vowels are produced with a relatively unrestricted air flow in the vocal tract. Consonants require a closed or narrowly constricted passage that results in friction and air turbulence. The number of phonemes attributed to American English differs with the classification system used and the dialect of the speaker. In this text we discuss 45 phonemes—21 vowels and 24 consonants.

Phonemes can be described as being voiced or voiceless. **Voiced phonemes** are produced by phonation, or vibration, at the vocal folds of the larynx; **voiceless phonemes** are produced without vibration. All vowels in English are voiced; consonants may be either voiced or voiceless.

Traditional Phonemic Classification

Traditional classification of English phonemes is based on the locus or place of articulation, usually the position of the tongue, and additionally, for consonants, on the manner of articulation, usually the type of release of air. Vowels are classified by the highest arched portion of the tongue and by the presence or absence of lip rounding. Consonants can be described by the site of articulation, by the manner of articulation, and by the presence or absence of voicing.

VOWELS

Vowels can be described in terms of tongue height and front-to-back positioning (Schane, 1973). Heights can be characterized as close, close-mid, open-mid, or open, depending on the position of the highest portion of the tongue and on lip closure. The location of this high point within the mouth can be described as front, central, or back. For example, a vowel can be described as close front, or open back, or any position in between. The English vowels are displayed graphically by position in Figure A.1. Words using each sound are printed next to each phoneme.

FIGURE *A.1* **Classification of English Vowels by Tongue Position**

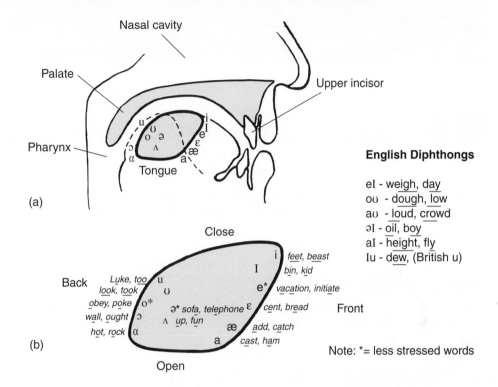

English Diphthongs

eɪ - weigh, day
oʊ - dough, low
aʊ - loud, crowd
ɔɪ - oil, boy
aɪ - height, fly
ɪu - dew, (British u)

Note: *= less stressed words

Lip rounding is an additional descriptive term used in vowel classification. During lip rounding, the lips protrude slightly, forming an O shape. Rounding is characteristic of some, but not all, back vowels, such as the last sound in *construe*. In contrast, there is no lip rounding in *construct*.

One group of vowel-like sounds is more complex than the single-vowel phonemes. These sounds are called diphthongs. A **diphthong** is a blend of two vowels within the same syllable. In other words, the sound begins with one vowel and glides smoothly toward another position. When the word *my* is repeated slowly, the speaker can feel and hear the shift from one vowel to another.

CONSONANTS

Consonant sounds are somewhat more complex than vowel sounds. They are described by their manner of articulation, place of articulation, and voicing (Table A.1). *Manner* refers to the type of production, generally with respect to the release of air. The six generally recognized categories of manner are the following:

- Plosive (/p/, /b/, /t/, /d/, /k/, /g/)—Complete obstruction of the airstream, with quick release accompanied by an audible escape of air; similar to an explosion.
- Fricative (/f/, /v/, /θ/, /ð/, /s/, /z/, /ʃ/, /ʒ /, /h/)—Narrow constriction through which the air must pass, creating a hissing noise.
- Affricative (/tʃ/, /ʒ/)—A combination that begins with a plosive followed by a fricative, as the IPA symbols suggest.

TABLE $A.1$ *Traditional Classification of English Consonants*

PLACE OF CONSTRICTION	MANNER OF PRODUCTION						
	PLOSIVE		FRICATE		APPROXIMANT[†]	LATERAL APPROXIMANT	NASAL[†]
	U	V	U	V	V		V
Bilabial	p (pig)	b (big)			w (watt)		m (sum)
Labiodental			f (face)	v (vase)			
Dental			θ (thigh, thin)	ð (thy, this)			
Alveolar	t (tot)	d (dot)	s (seal)	z (zeal)	ɹ (rot)	l (lot)	n (sun)
Postalveolar			ʃ (shoe, mission)	ʒ (visual, measure)	j (yacht)		
Palatal			tʃ (choke, nature)	dʒ (joke, gentle)			
Velar	k (coat)	g (goat)					ŋ (sung)
Glottal			h (happy)				

U = unvoiced; V = voiced.

[†]All voiced.

- Approximant (/w/, /j/, /ɹ/)—Produced by the proximity of two articulators without turbulence.
- Lateral approximant (/l/)—Produced in similar manner an approximant with the addition of the lateral flow of the airstream.
- Nasal (/m/, /n/, /ŋ/)—Oral cavity closed to exiting air but velum lowered to allow breath to exit via the nasal cavity. Variations result from constriction within the oral cavity.

The *locus* or place of articulation varies across the six manner categories and describes the position where the maximum constriction occurs. Constriction may be partial or complete. The seven locations are the following:

- Bilabial (/p/, /b/, /m/)—Lips together.
- Labiodental (/f/, /v/)—Lower lip touches upper incisors.
- Dental (/θ/, /ð/)—Tongue tip protruding slightly between the lower and upper incisors.
- Alveolar (/t/, /d/, /s/, /z/, /l/, /ɹ/, /n/)—Front of tongue to upper alveolar (gum) ridge.
- Postalveolar (/ʃ/, /ʒ/, /j/)—Tongue blade gently approximates postalveolar ridge area.
- Palatal (/tʃ/, /dʒ/)—Tongue blade raised to hard palate.
- Velar (/k/, /g/, /ŋ/)—Back of tongue raised to soft palate or velum.
- Glottal (/h/)—Restriction at glottis or opening to larynx.

Three sounds are considered combinations because of their location or movement during production. These are /tʃ/, /dʒ/, and /w/.

Many pairs of English consonant sounds differ only in voicing. When two phonemes have the same manner and place of articulation but differ in voicing, they are called **cognates**. For example, the /f/ and /v/ phonemes are cognates. If you repeat the words *face* and *vase*, you can feel the difference at the level of the larynx. The place and manner of articulation do not differ. All English plosives, and fricatives, except /h/, are organized in voiced and voiceless pairs.

You should be aware that the voicing distinction is indefinite. This problem can be explained by **voice onset time** (**VOT**), which is the interval between the burst of a plosive and the commencement of phonation. In other words, no English plosives are truly voiceless; rather, they have a delayed VOT. The VOT is usually less than 30 milliseconds for voiceless plosives. The mean delay is 58 milliseconds for /p/ and 70 milliseconds for /t/ (Lisker & Abramson, 1965).

Theoretically, speech sounds could be produced in almost any tongue position and in all configurations of manner, placing, and voicing. Other languages use some of the phonemes of English, plus additional speech sounds, even some with other production characteristics. Some English distinctions are not present in other languages. In Spanish there is no distinction between /s/ and /z/; they are not separate phonemes. Other languages make finer distinctions. In Zulu, meaning is often differentiated by the degree of aspiration, or breathiness, of a sound. Thus, there are different varieties of /t/, /k/, and /p/ that are not relevant to speakers of English (and are difficult for those speakers to distinguish).

Major Racial and Ethnic Dialects of American English

African American English

Let's discuss some of the more outstanding differences between the majority American English Dialect (MD) and African American English (AAE). The phonemic differences, especially the weakening of final consonants, relate to some of the more evident structural contrasts. Many morphological endings are omitted or not pronounced. Other words tend to sound similar because of omission, weakening, or substitution. The following are a few examples:

MD	↔	AAE	MD	↔	AAE	MD	↔	AAE
guard		god	Carol		Cal	past		pass
sore		saw	fault		fought	boot		boo
court		caught	toll		toe	death		deaf
called		caught	hits		hit	feed		feet

Sociolinguists have yet to determine if the *called–call* contrast reflects consonant cluster simplification or a syntactic rule relating to the fact that the regular past-tense marker is nonobligatory, since past tense can be inferred from the context.

The speech of young African American children does not reflect many of the phonologic contrasts presented in Table B.1. Four- and 5-year-old African American children have not mastered the adult AAE phonological system. Their phonological rules reflect their developmental level. The most consistent syntactic features found in the speech of many African American preschoolers are deletion of the copula and lack of the third-person marker (Washington & Craig, 1994).

Many AAE structural rules reflect a recognition of the redundant nature of many MD constructions. For example, the possessive *'s* is unnecessary when the relationship is expressed by word order. Similar arguments can be made for certain cases of the plural *-s*, the third-person *-s*, and verb-tense markers. If a numerical quantifier such as *five* or *dozen* appears before a noun, the listener knows that the noun is plural and that the plural *-s* is thus redundant. Likewise, the use of *he, she,* or a singular noun subject marks the third person, negating the need for the third-person *-s* on the verb. In addition, context often signals the verb tense. Similar arguments about redundancy have been advanced by linguists to explain the development of some syntactic structures. Other AAE forms introduce redundancy. These include double and triple negatives, pronominal apposition, and certain double modal forms.

The verb *to be* offers a special case. The verb may be nonobligatory in AAE as a contractible copula or as a contractible auxiliary in the present progressive. On the other hand, the verb *to be* is used to mark the future, a habitual state, or the distant past. The verb *to be* is also present in all uncontractible positions. Thus, it appears that the MD rule for contractibility is similar to the AAE rule for nonobligatory use. The rules of the verb *to be* represent not the presence or absence of a structure, but differences in use. Question inversion rules offer a similar example when compared to indirect questions and to the use of the conditional *if* (Table B.2).

In addition to the phonological and structural differences between the MD and AAE, there are also vocabulary differences. In any dialect, words may take on broadened definitions, more restricted meanings, or even new definitions. AAE words and phrases often influence and change the MD. Many expressions used in the MD originated in AAE. These include *rock 'n' roll, cool, rap,* and *jivin'.* Other terms, such as *chitlins* or *crackers,* a derisive term for whites, are

TABLE *B.1* **Phonemic Contrasts Between AAE and the Majority Dialect**

MAJORITY DIALECT PHONEMES	POSITION IN WORD		
	INITIAL	MEDIAL	FINAL*
/p/		Unaspirated /p/	Unaspirated /p/
/n/			Reliance on preceding nasalized vowel
/w/	Omitted in specific words (*I'as, too!*)		
/b/		Unreleased /b/	Unreleased /b/
/g/		Unreleased /g/	Unreleased /g/
/k/		Unaspirated /k/	Unaspirated /k/
/d/	Omitted in specific words (*I'on't know*)	Unreleased /d/	Unreleased /d/
/ŋ/		/n/	/n/
/t/		Unaspirated /t/	Unaspirated /t/
/l/		Omitted before labial consonants (*help–hep*)	"uh" following a vowel (*Bill–Biuh*)
/ɹ/		Omitted or /ə/	Omitted or prolonged vowel or glide
/θ/	Unaspirated /t/ or /f/	Unaspirated /t/ or /f/ between vowels	Unaspirated /t/ or /f/ (*bath–baf*)
/v/	Sometimes /b/	/b/ before /m/ and /n/	Sometimes /b/
/ð/	/d/	/d/ or /v/ between vowels	/d/, /v/, /f/
/z/		Omitted or replaced by /d/ before nasal sound (*wasn't–wud'n*)	

Blends

/stɹ/ becomes /skɹ/
/ʃɹ/ becomes /stɹ/
/θɹ/ becomes /θ/
/pɹ/ becomes /p/
/bɹ/ becomes /b/
/kɹ/ becomes /k/
/gɹ/ becomes /g/

Final Consonant Clusters (second consonant omitted when these clusters occur at the end of a word)

/sk/	/nd/	/sp/
/ft/	/ld/	/dʒ d/
/st/	/ɹd/	/nt/

*Note weakening of final consonants.

TABLE *B.2* *Grammatical Contrasts Between AAE and the Majority Dialect*

AAE GRAMMATICAL STRUCTURE	MAJORITY DIALECT GRAMMATICAL STRUCTURE
Possessive -'s	
Nonobligatory where word position expresses possession	Obligatory regardless of position
Get *mother* coat.	Get *mother's* coat.
It *be* mother's.	It's *mother's.*
Plural -s	
Nonobligatory with numerical quantifier	Obligatory regardless of numerical quantifier
He got ten *dollar.*	He has ten *dollars.*
Look at the *cats.*	Look at the *cats.*
Regular past -ed	
Nonobligatory, reduced as consonant cluster	Obligatory
Yesterday, I *walk* to school.	Yesterday, I *walked* to school.
Double marking	Single marking
I *sawed* 'em both	I *saw* both of them.
Irregular past	
Case by case, some verbs inflected, others not	All irregular verbs inflected
I *see* him last week.	I *saw* him last week.
Regular present-tense third person singular -s	
Nonobligatory	Obligatory
She *eat* too much.	She *eats* too much.
Irregular present-tense third person singular -s	
Nonobligatory	Obligatory
He *do* my job.	He *does* my job.
Indefinite an	
Use of indefinite *a* regardless of first sound in following noun.	Use of *an* before nouns beginning with a vowel.
He ride in *a* airplane.	He rode in *an* airplane.
Pronouns	
Pronominal apposition: Pronoun immediately follows noun for one referent	Pronoun used elsewhere in sentence or in other sentence; not in apposition
Momma *she* mad. She . . .	Momma *is* mad. She . . .
Cases used interchangeably	Case differentiation
Her ate *her* lunch.	*She* ate *her* lunch.
Future tense	
More frequent use of *be going to* (*gonna*)	More frequent use of *will*
I *be going to* dance tonight.	I *will* dance tonight.
I *gonna* dance tonight.	I *am going* to dance tonight.
Omit *will* preceding *be*	Obligatory use of *will*
I *be* home later.	I *will* (I'll) *be* home later.

TABLE *B.2* *Continued*

AAE Grammatical Structure	Majority Dialect Grammatical Structure
Negation	
Triple negative	Absence of triple negative
Nobody don't never like me.	*No one ever* likes me.
Use of *ain't*	*Ain't* is unacceptable form of be + not, have + not, do + not
I *ain't* going.	*I'm not* going.
Modals	
Double modals for such forms as *might, could,* and *should*	Single modal use
I *might could* go.	I *might be able to* go.
Variable use of *do, can, will* and *have.*	Consistent use of *do, can, will* and *have.*
She might been here.	She might have been here.
Questions	
Same form for direct and indirect	Different forms for direct and indirect
What *it is*?	What *is it*?
Do you know what *it is*?	Do you know what *it is*?
Relative pronouns	
Nonobligatory in most cases	Nonobligatory with *that* only
He the one stole it.	He's the one *who* stole it.
It the one you like.	It's the one (*that*) you like.
Use forms such as *hisself* and *theirselves*	*Himself* and *themselves* used
He done saw *hisself*.	He saw *himself*.
Conditional *if*	
Use of *do* for conditional *if*	Use of *if*
I ask *did* she go.	I asked *if* she went.
Past constructions	
Been used for action in the distant past	*Been* not used alone
He *been* gone.	He left a long time ago.
	He has been gone a long time.
Done used for recently completed action	Recently completed action not marked with *done*
I done made the cake.	I just finished making the cake.
Had used with simple past	Simple past used
She had jumped high.	She jumped high.
Copula	
Nonobligatory when contractible	Obligatory in contractible and uncontractible forms
He sick.	He's sick.
Habitual or general state	
Marked with uninflected *be*	Nonuse of *be;* verb inflected
She *be* workin'.	She's *working* now.

Sources: Information from Baratz (1969); Fasold & Wolfram (1970); Washington & Craig (1994, 2002).

TABLE *B.3* *Selected AAE Idioms*

IDIOM	DEFINITION AND EXAMPLE
All that	Excellent, fantastic, superb, all that it seems to be, as in "She bad, she definitely *all that*."
Amen corner	Place where older individuals usually sit in traditional African American church.
Barefoot as a river duck	Not wearing shoes, as in "It too cold for you be runnin' around *barefoot as a river duck*."
Crack on	To insult seriously or in fun, as in "He jus' *crackin on* you."
Eagle-flyin' day	Pay day.
Old head	Older and wiser person.
On it	In control of the situation, as in "Don't worry, I *on it*."
That how you livin'?	Why are you acting like that?
Word	Affirmative response to an action or statement. "Right on, *word up*!"

Source: Information from Smitherman (1994).

used almost exclusively in AAE. A sample of idioms is presented in Table B.3 (Smitherman, 1994). No one AAE speaker uses all of these idioms, and they represent speakers of different ages and geographic locations.

Language use also differs. There is a strong oral tradition in some African American communities, and superior verbal skills are highly regarded. In inner-city groups, youths with good verbal skills are usually in high positions within the group power structure. *Raps,* now popularized in modern music, are used to boast or to humiliate an opponent.

Other nonlinguistic differences may be found between some speakers of AAE and other dialects. For example, touching someone's hair may be considered an offense to some AAE speakers but a sign of affection by users of other American English dialects. Similarly, indirect eye contact, the use of personal questions, and interrupting are acceptable conversational conduct in some African American communities that would be considered rude in others. Conversational silence may signal opposite messages: refutation for AAE speakers and acceptance or agreement for majority speakers. Finally, emotional or demonstrative, even abusive, outbursts may be tolerated in AAE but not in the majority culture.

Latino English

Within the United States, the largest ethnic population is Hispanic. Not all people with Spanish surnames speak Spanish; some do exclusively; and still others are bilingual, speaking both Spanish and English. The form of English spoken depends on the amount and type of Spanish spoken and the location within the United States. The two largest Hispanic or Latino groups in the United States are of Puerto Rican–Caribbean and Mexican–Central American origin. Although both groups speak Spanish, their Spanish dialectal differences influence their comprehension and production of American English. The dialect of American English spoken in the surrounding community also has an effect. As a result, the interference points between the two languages may be very different for individual speakers. We will discuss the general characteristics of these speakers and refer to their dialect as Latino English (LE). Tables B.4 and B.5 summarize the major differences found between LE and the majority dialect of American English (MD).

TABLE *B.4* *Phonemic Contrasts Between LE and the Majority Dialect*

AMERICAN ENGLISH PHONEMES	POSITION IN WORD		
	INITIAL	MEDIAL	FINAL*
/p/	Unaspirated /p/		Omitted or weakened
/m/			Omitted
/w/	/hu/		Omitted
/b/			Omitted, distorted, or /p/
/g/			Omitted, distorted, or /k/
/k/	Unaspirated or /g/		Omitted, distorted, or /g/
/f/			Omitted
/d/		Dentalized	Omitted, distorted, or /t/
/ŋ/	/n/	/d/	/n/ (*sing–sin*)
/j/	/dʒ/		
/t/			Omitted
/ʃ/	/tʃ/	/s/, /tʃ/	/tʃ/ (*wish–which*)
/tʃ/	/ʃ/ (*chair–share*)	/ʃ/	/ʃ/ (*watch–wash*)
/ɹ/	Distorted	Distorted	Distorted
/dʒ/	/d/	/j/	/ʃ/
/θ/	/t/, /s/ (*thin–tin, sin*)	Omitted	/ʃ/, /t/, /s/
/v/	/b/ (*vat–bat*)	/b/	Distorted
/z/	/s/ (*zip–sip*)	/s/ (*razor–racer*)	/s/
/ð/	/d/ (*then–den*)	/d/, /θ/, /v/ (*lather–ladder*)	/d/

Blends
/skw/ and /skr/ become /eskw/ and /eskr/ respectively*
/sl/ becomes /esl/*
/st/ becomes /est/*

Vowels
/I/ becomes /i/ (*bit–beet*)

*Separates cluster into two syllables.

TABLE *B.5* *Grammatical Contrasts Between LE and the Majority Dialect*

LE GRAMMATICAL STRUCTURE	MAJORITY DIALECT GRAMMATICAL STRUCTURE
Possessive -'s	
Use postnoun modifier	Postnoun modifier used rarely
This is the homework of *my brother*.	This is *my brother's* homework.
Article used with body parts	Possessive pronoun used with body parts
I cut *the finger*.	I cut *my finger*.
Plural -*s*	
Nonobligatory	Obligatory, excluding exceptions
The *girl* are playing.	The *girls* are playing.
The *sheep* are playing.	The *sheep* are playing.
Regular past -*ed*	
Nonobligatory, especially when understood	Obligatory
I *talk* to her yesterday.	I *talked* to her yesterday.
Regular third person singular present-tense -*s*	
Nonobligatory	Obligatory
She *eat* too much.	She *eats* too much.
Articles	
Often omitted	Usually obligatory
I am going to store.	I am going to *the* store.
I am going to school.	I am going to school.
Subject pronouns	
Omitted when subject has been identified in the previous sentence	Obligatory
Father is happy. Bought a new car.	Father is happy. *He* bought a new car.
Future tense	
Use *go + to*	Use *be + going to*
I *go to* dance.	I *am going to* the dance.
Negation	
Use *no* before the verb	Use *not* (preceded by auxiliary verb where appropriate)
She *no* eat candy.	She does *not* eat candy.
Question	
Intonation; no noun–verb inversion	Noun–verb inversion usually
Maria is going?	*Is Maria* going?
Copula	
Occasional use of *have*	Use of *be*
I *have* ten years.	I *am* ten years old.
Negative imperatives	
No used for *don't*	*Don't* used
No throw stones.	*Don't* throw stones.
***Do* insertion**	
Nonobligatory in questions	Obligatory when no auxiliary verb
You like ice cream?	*Do* you like ice cream?
Comparatives	
More frequent use of longer form (*more*)	More frequent use of shorter -*er*.
He is *more* tall.	He is tall*er*.

As expected, there are phonological differences between Spanish and English. Some English speech sounds, such as /θ/, /ð/, /z/, /ʃ/, /ʒ/, /I/, /æ/, and /ʌ/, do not exist in Spanish. As a result, these sounds are frequently distorted, or replaced with other sounds, by speakers of LE. In addition, all final plosives are voiceless in Spanish, and initial voiceless plosives are not aspirated. Aspiration is a two-interval release on plosive sounds consisting of an initial burst and a longer, slow release resembling an /h/-like sound. Unaspirated sounds lack the second interval. In LE, sounds may be altered from their English articulation. Finally, Spanish does not distinguish between /b/ and /v/, and the Spanish /ɹ/ and /l/ are produced differently from their English equivalents. As expected, speakers of LE use /b/ and /v/ interchangeably, while they use Spanish /ɹ/ and /l/ in place of their English equivalents.

Spanish vowels are a special consideration. There are five vowels and four diphthongs in Spanish. English has many more. In addition, Spanish vowels have the same quality or length, whether in a stressed or an unstressed syllable. English vowels vary with stressing, as in /o/ and /oʊ/. As a result, English vowels can present a special problem in perception and production for Spanish speakers.

Structural contrasts between LE and the majority dialect (MD) also reflect interference points between Spanish and English. Many redundant MD markers are nonobligatory in LE, as they are in AAE. Other markers, such as the postnoun possessive (house *of Maria*) and placement of adjectives following the noun, reflect Spanish constructions. In addition, the speaker of LE may scatter his or her speech with many vocabulary words of Spanish origin.

Nonlinguistic differences also persist between LE and the MD. In general, a smaller physical distance between speakers is tolerated among many LE speakers, as is a greater incidence of touching. Other differences, such as avoidance of direct eye contact, may signal attentiveness and respect for LE speakers while signaling the opposite for most speakers of American English.

Asian English

Although we shall use the term *Asian English* (AE), it is clearly a misnomer because no such entity exists. It is merely a term that enables us to discuss the various dialects of Asian Americans as a group.

The most widely used languages in Asia are Mandarin Chinese, Cantonese Chinese, Filipino, Japanese, Khmer, Korean, Laotian, Thai, and Vietnamese. Of these, Mandarin has had the most pervasive influence on the evolution of the others. Indian and colonial European cultures, as well as others, have influenced these languages. Each language has various dialects and features that distinguish it from the others. Thus, there is, in reality, no Asian English as a cohesive unit.

Nonetheless, the English of Asian language speakers has certain characteristics in common. These are listed in Tables B.6 and B.7. The omission of final consonants, for example, is prevalent in AE. In contrast to English, most Asian languages, with the exception of Korean, have open or vowel-final syllables.

TABLE *B.6* *Phonemic Contrasts Between AE and the Majority Dialect*

AMERICAN ENGLISH PHONEMES	POSITION IN WORD		
	INITIAL	MEDIAL	FINAL*
/p/	/b/[§]	/b/[§]	Omission
/s/	Distortion*	Distortion*	Omission
/z/	/s/[†]	/s/[†]	Omission
/t/	Distortion*	Distortion*	Omission
/tʃ/	/ʃ/[§]	/ʃ/[§]	Omission
/ʃ/	/s/[†]	/s/[†]	Omission
/ɹ/, /l/	Confusion[‡]	Confusion[‡]	Omission
/θ/	/s/	/s/	Omission
/dz/	/d/ or /z/[§]	/d/ or /z/[§]	Omission
/v/	/f/Ê	/f/[‡]	Omission
	/w/[†]	/w/[†]	Omission
/ð/	/z/*	/z/*	Omission
	/d/[§]	/d/[§]	Omission

Blends

Addition of /ə/ between consonants[‡]

Omission of final consonant clusters[§]

Vowels

Shortening or lengthening of vowels (*seat–sit, it–eat**)

Difficulty with /I/, /ɔ/, and /æ/, and substitution of /ə/ for /æ/[†]

Difficulty with /I/, /æ/, /U/, and /ə/[§]

---

*Mandarin Chinese only.
[†]Cantonese Chinese only.
[‡]Mandarin, Cantonese, and Japanese.
[§]Vietnamese only.
Source: Information from Cheng (1987a, 1987b).

TABLE *B.7* *Grammatical Contrasts Between AE and the Majority Dialect*

AE GRAMMATICAL STRUCTURE	MAJORITY DIALECT GRAMMATICAL STRUCTURE
Plural -s	
Not used with numerical adjective	Used regardless of numerical adjective
three cat	*three cats*
Used with irregular plural	Not used with irregular plural
three sheeps	*three sheep*
Auxiliaries *to be* and *to do*	
Omission: *I going home. She not want eat.*	Obligatory and inflected in the present progressive form:
Uninflected: *I is going. She do not want eat.*	*I am going home. She does not want to eat.*
Verb *have*	
Omission: *You been here.*	Obligatory and inflected: *You have been here. He has one.*
Uninflected: *He have one.*	
Past-tense -ed	
Omission: *He talk yesterday.*	Obligatory, nonovergeneralization, and single marking:
Overgeneralization: *I eated yesterday.*	*He talked yesterday. I ate yesterday. She didn't eat.*
Double marking: *She didn't ate.*	
Interrogative	
Nonreversal: *You are late?*	Reversal and obligatory auxiliary: *Are you late?*
Omitted auxiliary: *You like ice cream?*	*Do you like ice cream?*
Perfect marker	
Omission: *I have write letter.*	Obligatory: *I have written a letter.*
Verb–noun agreement	
Nonagreement: *He go to school.*	Agreement: *He goes to school. You go to school.*
You goes to school.	
Article	
Omission: *Please give gift.*	Obligatory with certain nouns: *Please*
Overgeneralization: *She go the school.*	*give the gift. She went to school.*
Preposition	
Misuse: *I am in home.*	Obligatory specific use: *I am at home.*
Omission: *He go bus.*	*He goes by bus.*
Pronoun	
Subjective/objective confusion: *Him go quickly.*	Subjective/objective distinction: *He gave it to her.*
Possessive confusion: *It him book.*	Possessive distinction: *It's his book.*
Demonstrative	
Confusion: *I like those horse.*	Singular/distinction: *I like that horse.*
Conjunction	
Omission: *You I go together.*	Obligatory use between last two items in a series: *You and I are going together. Mary, John, and Carol went.*

(*continued*)

TABLE *B.7* **Continued**

AE GRAMMATICAL STRUCTURE	MAJORITY DIALECT GRAMMATICAL STRUCTURE
Negation	
Double marking: *I didn't see nobody.* Simplified form: *He no come.*	Single obligatory marking: *I didn't see anybody. He didn't come.*
Word order	
Adjective following noun (Vietnamese): *clothes new.*	Most noun modifiers precede noun: *new clothes.*
Possessive following noun (Vietnamese): *dress her.*	Possessive precedes noun: *her dress.*
Omission of object with transitive verb: *I want.*	Use of direct object with most transitive verbs: *I want it.*

Source: Information from Cheng (1987a, 1987b).

Development Summary

The following tables are presented to help you view the development of communication in perspective with other developments in the areas of motor, cognitive, and socialization. The divisions between tables reflect the organization of this text, and each has been given a name for the major characteristic of a child's behavior.

TABLE *C.1* *The Examiner: 1 to 6 Months*

AGE (MONTHS)	MOTOR	COGNITION	SOCIALIZATION	COMMUNICATION
1	Moves limbs reflexively Lifts head while on stomach but cannot support head while body held upright Has coordinated side-to-side eye movement	Cries from distress Remembers an object that reappears within 2½ seconds	Establishes eye contact with mother Quiets when held; adjusts body to person holding Smiles	Responds to human voice, which usually has quieting effect Cries for assistance Makes pleasure sounds, quasi-resonant nuclei
2	Moves arms in circle smoothly; swipes at objects Holds head up briefly while on stomach; raises head while sitting supported Opens and closes hand; holds for few seconds	Visually prefers face to objects Repeats own actions Excites in anticipation of objects Increased awareness of stimuli	Excites when sees people; has unselective social smile Prefers touch and oral stimulation to social stimulation	Distinguishes different (speech) sounds Makes more gutteral or "throaty" gooing
3	Lifts head and chest while prone; holds head up with minimum bobbing while sitting supported Can swallow voluntarily Reaches and grasps; swipes at dangling objects Kicks more forcefully	Attains full focus; can glance smoothly between objects Visually searches for sounds Exploratory play Stops sucking to attend to voice	Visually discriminates different people and things; recognizes mother Has selective social smile Sleeps most of the night	Coos single syllable (consonant-vowel) Turns head when hears a voice Responds vocally to speech of others Makes predominantly vowel sounds

TABLE *C.1* **Continued**

Age (Months)	Motor	Cognition	Socialization	Communication
4	Can turn head in all directions; complete rollover On stomach: Raises head and chest on arms Occasionally opposes thumb and fingers; grasps small objects put in hand; brings objects to mouth	Localizes to sound Stares at place from which object is dropped Remembers visually for 5–7 seconds Recognizes mother in group; senses strange places and people	Pays attention to faces; discriminates different faces Looks in direction of person leaving room Anticipates being lifted; laughs when played with	Babbles strings of consonants Varies pitch Imitates tones Smiles at person speaking to him
5	Sits supported for up to half an hour Rolls from stomach to back Can be easily pulled to stand Has partial thumb opposition; swaps objects from hand to hand	Recognizes familiar objects; anticipates whole object after seeing a part, is capable of 3-hour visual memory Explores by mouthing and touching Remembers own actions in immediate past	Discriminates parents and siblings from others Imitates some movements of others Frolics when played with Displays anger when objects taken away	Vocalizes to toys Discriminates angry and friendly voices Experiments with sound Imitates some sounds Responds to name Smiles and vocalizes to image in mirror
6	Turns head freely Sits straight when slightly supported or in chair Balances well Reaches with one arm Turns and twists in all directions Creeps	Looks and reaches smoothly and quickly Inspects objects Reaches to grab dropped objects	Differentiates social responses Prefers people games, such as peekaboo Feeds self finger food Explores face of person holding	Varies volume, pitch, and rate Vocalizes pleasure and displeasure: squeals with excitement, intones displeasure

TABLE *C.2* **The Experimenter: 7 to 12 Months**

Age (Months)	Motor	Cognition	Socialization	Communication
7	Transfers object from hand to hand; bangs objects together Cuts first tooth; has better chewing and jaw control; can eat some strained solids Pushes up on hands and knees; rocks	Visually searches briefly for toy that disappears Imitates a physical act if in repertoire Remembers that jack pops up at the end of jack-in-the-box song	Resists Teases (beginning of humor); laughs at funny expressions Raises arms to be picked up	Plays vocally Produces several sounds in one breath Listens to vocalization of others Recognizes different tones and inflections
8	Uses thumb-finger apposition Manipulates objects to explore Pulls up to stand but needs help to get down Crawls Drops and throws objects	Recognizes object dimensions Prefers novel and relatively complex toys Explores shape, weight, texture, function, and properties (example: in/out)	Acts positively toward peers Is clearly attached to mother Shouts for attention Reponds to self in mirror May reject being alone	Recognizes some words Repeats emphasized syllable Imitates gestures and tonal quality of adult speech; echolalia
9	Stands alone briefly; gets down alone; cruises Sits unsupported; gets into and out of sitting position alone Removes and replaces bottle Puts objects in containers	Uncovers object if observes act of hiding first Anticipates outcome of events and return of persons	Explores other babies "Performs" for family ("so big") Imitates play Plays action games	Produces distinct intonational patterns Imitates nonspeech sounds Uses social gestures Uses jargon May repond to name and "no" Attends to conversation
10	Holds and drinks from cup Sits from a standing position Momentary unsupported stand	Points to body parts Attains a goal with trial-and-error approach Searches for hidden object in a familiar place	Helps dress and feed self Becomes aware of social approval and disapproval	Imitates adult speech if sounds in repertoire Obeys some commands

TABLE *C.2* **Continued**

Age (Months)	Motor	Cognition	Socialization	Communication
11	Stands alone; gets up from all-fours position by pushing up Climbs up stairs Feeds self with spoon	Imitates increasingly Associates properties with objects	Seeks approval Anticipates mother's goal and tries to change it by protest or "persuasion"	Imitates inflections, rhythms, facial expressions, etc.
12	Stands alone; pushes to stand from squat Climbs up and down stairs Uses spoon, cup, and crayon; releases objects willfully Takes first steps with support	Can reach while looking away Uses common objects appropriately Searches in location where an object was last seen	Expresses people preferences Expresses many different emotions	Follows simple motor instructions, if accompanied by a visual cue ("bye-bye"); reacts to "no" Speaks one or more words Mixes word and jargon

TABLE *C.3* *The Explorer: 12 to 24 Months*

Age (Months)	Motor	Cognition	Socialization	Communication
15	Walks with rapid runlike gait Walks a few steps backwards and sideways Dumps toys in container Takes off shoes and socks Picks up small objects with index finger and thumb	Imitates small motor acts Uses toy phone like real one	Likes music and dancing Pushes toys Imitates housework Plays in solitary manner; but likes to act for an audience Begins make-believe play Laughs when chased	Points to clothes, persons, toys, and animals named Uses jargon and words in conversation Has four- to six-word vocabulary
18	Walks up stairs with help; walks smoothly, runs stiffly Drinks unassisted Throws ball with whole arm Throws and catches without falling Jumps with both feet off floor Turns pages	Recognizes pictures Recognizes self in mirror Remembers places where objects are usually located Uses a stick as a tool Imitates adult object use	Explores reactions of others; tests others Enjoys solitary play Pretends to feed doll Responds to scolding and praise Little or no sense of sharing	Begins to use two-word utterances Has approximately 20-word vocabulary Identifies some body parts Refers to self by name "Sings" and hums Plays question-answer with adults
21	Walks up and down stairs with help of railing or hand Jumps, runs, throws, climbs; kicks large ball; squats to play; running is stiff Fits puzzle together Responds rhythmically to music with whole body	Knows shapes Sits alone for short periods with book Notices little objects and small sounds Matching objects with owners Recalls absent objects or persons	Hugs spontaneously Plays near but not with other kids Likes toy telephone, doll, and truck for play Enjoys outings Becomes clingy around strangers	Likes rhyming games Pulls person to show something Tries to "tell" experiences Understands some personal pronouns Uses "I" and "mine"

TABLE *C.3* *Continued*

Age (Months)	Motor	Cognition	Socialization	Communication
24	Walks watching feet Runs rhythmically but unable to start or stop smoothly Walks up and down stairs alone without alternating feet Pushes tricycle Eats with fork Transitions smoothly from walk to run	Matches familiar objects Comprehends *one* and *many* Recognizes when picture in book is upside down	Can role-play in limited manner Engages in pretend play constrained by the objects Enjoys parallel play predominately Prefers action toys Cooperates with adults in simple household tasks Communicates feelings, desires, and interests	Has 200–300-word expressive vocabulary Uses short, incomplete sentences

TABLE *C.4* *The Exhibitor*

Age (Years)	Motor	Cognition	Socialization	Communication
3	Walks up and down stairs without assistance; uses nonalternating step Walks without watching feet, marches to music Balances momentarily on one foot Rides tricycle Can spread with knife Explores, dismantles, dismembers	Creates representational art Matches primary colors and shapes Can show two objects: understands concept of two Enjoys make-believe play; is less constrained by objects Knows age but no concept of length of a year	Labels some coins Plays in groups, talks while playing, selects with whom to play Shares toys for short periods Takes turns Insists on being in the limelight	Has 900–1,000-word expressive vocabulary, creates three- to four-word sentences Uses "sentences" with subject and verb, but simple sentence construction Plays with words and sounds Follows two-step commands Talks about the present
4	Walks up and down stair with alternating steps Jumps over objects Hops on one foot Can copy block letters	Categorizes Counts rotely to five; can show three objects; understands concept of three Knows primary colors	Plays and cooperates with others Role-plays	Has 1,500-word expressive vocabulary Asks many, many questions Uses increasingly more complex sentence forms Recounts stories and the recent past Has some difficulty answering how and why Relies on word order for interpretation

TABLE *C.4* **Continued**

Age (Years)	Motor	Cognition	Socialization	Communication
5	Has gross motor control, good body awareness; plays complex games	Carries a rule through a series of activities	Plays simple games	Has expressive vocabulary of 2,100 to 2,200 words
	Cuts own meat with a knife	Knows own right and left, but not those of others	Selects some playmates based on sex	Discusses feelings
	Draws well, colors in lines; creates more recognizable drawings	Counts to 13; can show four or five objects	Enjoys dramatic play	Understands before and after, regardless of word order
	Prints simple words	Accepts magic as an explanation	Shows interest in group activities	Follows three-step commands
	Dresses without assistance	Develops time concepts	Plays purposefully and constructively	Has 90% grammar acquisition
	Has established hand preference	Recognizes relationship of parts to whole		

TABLE *C.5* *The Expert: The School-Age Child*

Age (Years)	Motor	Cognition	Socialization	Communication
6	Has better gross motor coordination; rides bicycle Throws ball well Begins to get permanent teeth	Has longer attention span Is less distracted by additional information when problem solving Remembers and repeats three digits	Enjoys active games Is competitive Identifies with sex peers in groups Transforms egocentric reality to more complex and relative reality view	Has expressive vocabulary of 2,600 words, receptive of 20,000 to 24,000 words Has many well-formed sentences of a complex nature
8	Has longer arms, larger hands Has better manipulative skills Has nearly mature-size brain Has more permanent teeth	Knows left and right of others Understands conservation Knows differences and similarities Reads spontaneously	Enjoys an audience Learns that others have different perspectives Has allegiance to gang, but also strong need for adult support	Talks a lot Verbalizes ideas and problems readily Communicates thought
10	Has eyes of almost mature size Has almost mature lungs and digestive and circulatory systems	Plans future actions Solves problems with only minimal physical input	Enjoys games, sports, hobbies Discovers that he or she may be the object of someone else's perspective	Spends lots of time talking Has good comprehension
12	Experiences "rest" before adolescent growth (girls usually taller and heavier, may have entered puberty) Begins rapid muscle growth with puberty	Engages in abstract thought	Has different interests than those of the opposite sex	Has 50,000-word receptive vocabulary Constructs adultlike definitions

Computing MLU

In general, 50 to 100 utterances are considered a sufficient sample from which to generalize about a speaker's overall production. An utterance may be a sentence or a shorter unit of language that is separated from other utterances by a drop in the voice, a pause, and/or a breath that signals a new thought. Once transcribed, each utterance is analyzed by morphemes; the total sample is then averaged to determine the speaker's MLU.

When analyzing the language of young children, several assumptions about preschool language must be made. Let's use the past tense as an example. The regular past tense includes the verb stem plus -*ed,* as in *walked* or *opened.* Hence, the regular past equals two morphemes, one free and one bound. In contrast, the irregular past is signaled by a different word, as in *eat/ate* and *sit/sat.* As adults, we realize that *eat* plus a past-tense marker equals *ate.* It could thus be argued that *ate* should also be counted as two morphemes. It seems, however, that young children learn separate words for the present and the irregular past and are not necessarily aware of the relationship between the two. Therefore, the irregular past counts as one morpheme for young children. A similar logic exists for words such as *gonna* and *wanna.* As adults, we can subdivide these words into their components: *going to* and *want to.* Young children, however, cannot perform such analyses. Therefore, *gonna* counts as one morpheme for the child, not as the three represented by *going to.*

Although we may not agree with this rationale, for uniformity's sake we must adopt it if we are to discuss language development across children. Guidelines for counting morphemes are presented in Table D.1 (Brown, 1973). Applying these rules, we would reach the following values:

> *Daddy bring me choo-choo-s.* = 5 morphemes
> *Mommy eat-ed a-a-a sandwich.* = 5 morphemes
> *Doggie-'s bed broke baboom.* = 5 morphemes
> *Paddington Bear go-ing night-night.* = 4 morphemes
> *He hafta.* = 2 morphemes

Once the morphemes for each utterance are counted, they are totaled and then divided by the total number of utterances. The formula is very simple:

$$\text{MLU} = \frac{\text{Total number of morphemes}}{\text{Total number of utterances}}$$

Thus, if the total number of morphemes for a 100-utterance sample is 221, the MLU will equal 2.21 morphemes per utterance. Remember that this is an average value and does not identify the length of the child's longest utterance. In other words, an MLU of 2.0 does *not* mean that the child uses only two-word utterances.

TABLE *D.1* *Brown's Rules for Counting Morphemes*

RULE	EXAMPLE
Count as one morpheme:	
Reoccurrences of a word for emphasis	*No! No! No!* (3 morphemes)
Compound words (two or more free morphemes)	*Railroad, birthday*
Proper names	*Billy Sue*
Ritualized reduplications	*Night-night, choo-choo*
Irregular past-tense verbs	*Went, ate, got, came*
Diminutives	*Daddie, doggie*
Auxiliary verbs and catenatives	*Is, have, do, gonna, hafta*
Irregular plurals	*Men, feet*
Count as two morphemes (inflected verbs and nouns):	
Possessive nouns	*Sam's, daddie's*
Plural nouns	*Doggies, kitties*
Third person singular, present-tense verbs	*Walks, eats*
Regular past-tense verbs	*Walked, jumped*
Present progressive verbs	*Walking, eating*
Do not count:	
Dysfluencies, except for most complete form	*C-c-c-candy, bab-baby*
Fillers	*Um-m, ah-h, oh*

Source: Information from Brown (1973).

Background Grammar

Verbs

VERB TYPES

Verb phrases are of three types: *transitive, intransitive,* and *stative.* In mature language, transitive verbs take a direct object and include words such as *love, hate, make, give, build, send, owe,* and *show.* With few exceptions—verbs such as *have, lack,* or *resemble*—transitive verbs can be changed from active to passive voice by exchanging the positions of the two noun phrases.

Active Voice	***Passive Voice***
Mary sent a letter.	A letter was sent by Mary.
Sue loves Fran.	Fran is loved by Sue.

In contrast, intransitive verbs do not have a passive form, nor do they take direct objects. Examples include *swim, fall, look, seem,* and *weigh.* Although we say "She swam the river," it is awkward to say "The river was swum by her." Some verbs may be both transitive and intransitive:

I *opened* the door slowly. (Transitive: *door* is direct object)
The door *opened* slowly. (Intransitive: no direct object)

Overall, transitive verb phrases are more common in English than in other languages.

Intransitive verbs are easier to learn because they don't require a direct object (Valian, 1991). Likewise, verbs that are transitive are first produced by children without a direct object as in *Mommy give* or *I make.* Of interest, this is the way that mothers use these verbs when talking to their young language-learning children (Theakston, Lieven, Pine, & Rowland, 2001).

Stative verbs, such as the copula *to be,* are followed by a *complement,* an element that sets up an equality with the subject. In "She is a doctor," *doctor* complements or describes what *she* is. In other words, she = doctor.

AUXILIARY VERBS

Auxiliary, or helping, verbs in English can be classified as primary, such as *be, have,* and *do,* or as secondary or modal, such as *will, shall, can, may,* and *must.* In general, auxiliary verbs and the copula *be* are the only verbs that can be inverted with the subject to form questions or that can have negative forms attached. Examples of auxiliary forms include the following:

Are you running in the race? (Inverted from the statement "You are running. . . .")
What *have* you done? (Inverted from the statement "You have done. . . .")
I *can't* help you. (Negative form)
I *may* not be able to go. (Negative form)

The copula can also be inverted and made into a negative form, as in *Is she sick?* or *This isn't funny.*

In addition, auxiliary verbs are used to avoid repetition in elliptical responses that omit redundant information and for emphasis. For example, when asked, "Who can go with me?" a respondent avoids repetition by the elliptical reply "I *can.*" To affirm a statement emphatically, a speaker emphasizes the auxiliary verb, as in "I *do* like to dance."

Phrases and Clauses

Sentences are strings of related words or larger units containing a noun subject and a verb or predicate. For example, the sentence "She ate cookies" is a string of words related in a certain way. *She* has acted on *cookies*.

The units within sentences are composed of words, phrases, and clauses. A **phrase** is a group of related words that does not include both a subject and a predicate and is used as a noun substitute or as a noun or verb modifier. For example, the phrase *to fish*, an infinitive, can take the place of a noun. In the sentence "I love candy," *to fish* can be substituted for *candy*, a noun, to form "I love to fish." Other phrases modify nouns, as in "The man *in the blue suit*," or verbs, as in "Loren fought *with a vengeance*." These phrases are said to be embedded within a sentence.

In contrast to a phrase, a **clause** is a group of words that contains both a subject and a predicate. A clause that can stand alone as grammatically complete is a **simple sentence**. Thus, the shortest Biblical verse, "Jesus wept," is a simple sentence. Occasionally, a sentence may contain more than one clause. When a sentence is combined with another sentence, they each become **main clauses**. A **compound sentence** is made up of two or more main clauses joined as equals, as in "*Mary drove to work, and she had an accident.*" Both "Mary drove to work" and "She had an accident" are simple sentences serving as main clauses in the larger compound sentence. Main clauses may be joined by conjunctions, such as *and, but, because, if,* and so on, to form compound sentences. This process is called **conjoining** or coordinating.

Some clauses, such as *whom we met last week*, cannot stand alone even though they contain a subject and a predicate. In this example, *we* is the subject and *met* is the predicate, or main verb. When embedded, such clauses, called **subordinate clauses**, function as nouns, adjectives, or adverbs in support of the main clause. For example, *she is the girl*, a simple sentence, or main clause, can embed the above subordinate clause within it to form "She is the girl whom we met last week."

A sentence such as this, made up of a main clause and at least one subordinate clause, is called a **complex sentence**. The subordinate clause is said to be *embedded* within the main clause even if it's just attached. In general, subordinate clauses are introduced by subordinating conjunctions, such as *after, although, before, until, while,* and *when,* or by relative pronouns, such as *who, which,* and *that*. For example, the sentence "He doesn't know when it began to rain" contains the subordinate clause *when it began to rain*, which serves as the object of the verb *know*. In "the man who lives here hates children," *who lives here* is a subordinate clause modifying *man* and identifying which one.

In the following sections, we shall discuss the development of both embedding and conjoining. As you can imagine, multiple embeddings may result in very complicated sentences.

TYPES OF PHRASES

Phrases other than the noun and verb phrases can be formed in four ways: (1) with a preposition, (2) with a participle, (3) with a gerund, and (4) with an infinitive. A prepositional phrase contains a preposition, such as *in, on, under, at,* or *into,* and its object, along with possible articles and modifiers, as in *on the roof* or *at the school dance*.

Prepositions include the following:

about	among	beneath	except	instead of	onto	through	up
above	around	beside	for	into	out of	to	upon
across	at	between	from	near	outside	toward	with
after	before	by	in	next to	over	under	within
against	behind	down	in front of	of	past	underneath	without
along	below	during	inside	on	since	until	

Many words have other functions. For example, *since* can also be a conjunction, *down* can be an adverb, *past* can be a verb form.

A participial phrase contains a participle (a verb-derived word ending in *-ing, -ed, -t, -en,* or a few irregular forms) and serves as an adjective. Examples of participles include the *setting* sun, a *lost* cause, a *broken* promise, and a *fallen* warrior. In the sentence "The boy riding the bicycle is athletic," *riding the bicycle* is a participial phrase describing or modifying *boy.*

In contrast, a gerund, which also ends in *-ing,* functions as a noun. Gerunds may be used as a subject ("*Skiing* is fun"), as an object ("I enjoy *skiing*"), or in any other sentence function that may be filled by a noun.

Finally, an infinitive phrase may function as a noun but also as an adjective or adverb. An infinitive consists of *to* plus a verb, as in "He wanted *to open* his present." The entire phrase *to open his present* is an infinitive phrase serving as the object of the sentence. The *to* may be omitted after certain verbs, as in "He helped *clean up the mess*" or "He dared not *speak aloud.*"

INTERROGATIVE FORM

There are three general forms of questions: those that assume a yes/no response, those that begin with a *wh-* word and assume a more complex answer, and those that are a statement to which agreement is sought by adding a tag, such as ". . . isn't he?" Yes/no questions seek confirmation or nonconfirmation and are typically formed by adding rising intonation to the end of a statement, as in "You're eating snails?" ↑ ; by moving the auxiliary verb or copula from its position in a declarative sentence (You *are* eating snails) to form "*Are* you eating snails?"; or by adding the auxiliary verb *do* to a position in front of the subject, as in "Do you like eating snails?"

Typical *wh-* or constituent questions begin with words such as *what, where,* and *who.* The verb and subject are inverted, as in yes/no questions, and the *wh-* word appears before the subject (What do you want?) unless it is the subject, as in *who* questions (Who is here?).

In tag questions, a proposition is made, such as "He loves sweets," then negated in the tag: "He loves sweets, doesn't he?" An equally acceptable reverse order might produce "He doesn't love sweets, does he?"

Inverted forms, whether in yes/no or *wh-* questions, require a child to learn the following three rules:

1. The auxiliary verb is inverted to precede the subject.   She can play house. *Can* she play house?
   Tom is eating candy. What *is* Tom eating?
2. The copula is inverted to precede the subject.   They are funny. *Are* they funny?
   Mary is in school. Where *is* Mary?
3. The dummy *do* is inserted before the subject if no copula or auxiliary exists.   Todd loves Joannie. *Does* Todd love Joannie?
   Mike drank a soda. What *did* Mike drink?

SUBORDINATE CLAUSE EMBEDDING

Three primary types of subordinate clauses include the following:

- Nominal ("The dogs knew their master had arrived"), which we'll call *object noun phrase complements* and *embedded wh- complements.*
- Relative ("The dogs that were hungry ran to the door").
- Adverbial ("When they heard their master, the dogs ran to the door").

Object noun-phrase complements consist of a subordinate clause that serves as the object of the main clause. For example, we could say "I know *X* (something)" in which *X* is the object. We could replace *X* with a noun phrase (*a story*) or with a subordinate clause, such as (*that*) *I like it* to form "I know (*that*) *I like it.*"

Indirect or **embedded *wh-* complements** are similar to object noun-phrase complements. In the following sentences, the *wh-* subordinate clause fills the object function, as in "I know *X*":

I know *who did it.*
She saw *where the kitty went.*

Relative clauses are subordinate clauses that follow and modify nouns. Rather than take the place of a noun, these clauses are attached to a noun with relative pronouns, such as *who, which,* and *that.* The earliest relative pronouns are *that, what,* and *where.*

Adverbial subordinate clauses serve as adverbs. For example, in the sentence "Later, they were all sad," *later* is an adverb of time. We could replace it with a clause to form "After we left, they were all sad."

COMPOUND SENTENCES OR CONJOINING

Unlike complex sentences in which one clause is subordinate and cannot stand alone, compound sentences consist of two independent clauses. Each could serve as a sentence. The two clauses are joined by a conjunction, such as one of these:

after	because	in order that	than	when
although	before	now that	that	whenever
as	even if	once	though	where
as if	even though	rather than	till	whereas
as long as	if	since	unless	wherever
as though	if only	so that	until	while

Conjunctions are small overworked words and may have other syntactic functions. Some also serve as prepositions.

Conjoining may include whole clauses or clauses with deleted common elements, called **phrasal coordination**, as in "Mary ran and fell." In full clausal or **sentential coordination**, such as "Mary ran and Mary fell," *Mary* is redundant and may be deleted, as in the first example. Obviously, sentential coordination, such as "Mary ran and John fell," does not lend itself to such shortening. Conjoining by children is relatively independent of the length of the two units to be conjoined, although, obviously, a very young child is not capable of producing adult-length utterances. Initially, sentential coordination seems to be used for events that occur at different times in different locations, while phrasal coordination is used for simultaneous or near-simultaneous events in the same location.

In phrasal coordination, forward reductions are more common and appear earlier than backward reductions. In *forward reductions,* the full clause is stated first, followed by a conjunction, plus the nonredundant information. "Reggie made the cookies by himself and ate them before dinner" is an example of forward reduction. *Reggie* is redundant in the second clause. Conversely, in *backward reductions* the full clause follows the conjunction, as in "Reggie and Noi baked cookies." Ease of processing may be more closely related to the amount of information a child is required to hold than to the direction of reduction. Preschool children have great difficulty with a sentence such as "The sheep patted the kangaroo and the pig the giraffe" because of the amount of information that must be held in short-term memory, especially from the first clause, while deciphering this sentence.

Glossary

Accommodation   Process of reorganizing cognitive structures or schemes or creating new schemes in response to external stimuli that do not fit into any available scheme. Piagetian concept.

Account   A type of narrative in which the speaker relates a past experience in which the listener did not share.

Adaptation   Process by which an organism adapts to the environment; occurs as a result of two complementary processes, assimilation and accommodation. Piagetian concept.

Agent   Semantic case characterized by causing action, as in *Daddy is fixing my bike*.

Allophone   Perceptual grouping of phones of similar speech sounds. Together form a phoneme.

Analogy   A pattern-finding technique that accounts for how children create abstract syntactic constructions from concrete pieces of language by understanding the relationship across schemes. For example, if *X is Y-ing the Z* and the *A is B-ing the C*, then a child sees that X and A play analogous roles, as do C and Z.

Anaphoric reference   Grammatical mechanism that notifies the listener that the speaker is referring to a previous reference. Pronouns are one type of word used in anaphoric reference.

Angular gyrus   Association area of the brain, located in the posterior portion of the temporal lobe, responsible for linguistic processing, especially word recall.

Antonym   A word that differs only in the opposite value of a single important feature.

Archiform   One member of a word class used to the exclusion of all others. For example, *a* may be used for all articles or *he* for all third person pronouns.

Arcuate fasciculus   White, fibrous tract of mostly axons and dendrites underlying the angular gyrus in the brain. Language is organized in Wernicke's area and transmitted through the arcuate fasciculus to Broca's area.

Aspect   The dynamics of an event, noted by the verb, relative to the event's completion, repetition, or continuing duration.

Assimilation   Process by which external stimuli are incorporated into existing cognitive structures or schemes. Piagetian concept.

Associative complex hypothesis   Theory that each example of a meaning category shares something with a core concept. In other words, there are common elements in the meanings of *pants*, *shirt*, *shoes*, and *hat* that classify each as clothing. Vygotskyan concept.

Babbling   Long strings of sounds that children begin to produce at about 4 months of age.

Bilingual   Fluent in two languages; uses two languages on a daily basis.

Blending   Creating a word from individual sounds and syllables and being able to compare initial phonemes in words for likeness and difference.

Bootstrapping   Process of learning language in which the child uses what he or she knows to decode more mature language. For example, the child may use semantic knowledge to aid in decoding and learning syntax.

Bound morpheme   Meaning unit that cannot occur alone but must be joined to a free morpheme; generally includes grammatical tags or markers that are derivational, such as *-ly*, *-er*, or *-ment*, or inflectional, such as *-ed* or *-s*.

Bracketing   Process of breaking a speech stream into analyzable units by detecting end points or divisions through the use of intonational cues.

Broca's area   Cortical area of the left frontal lobe of the brain responsible for detailing and coordinating the programming of speech movements.

Centering   The linking of entities in a narrative to form a story nucleus. Links may be based on similarity or complementarity of features, sequence, or causality.

Central nervous system (CNS)   Portion of the nervous system consisting of the brain and spinal cord.

Cerebrum   Upper brain, consisting of the cortex and the subcortical structures.

Chaining   Narrative form consisting of a sequence of events that share attributes and lead directly from one to another.

Child-directed speech (CDS)   Adult speech adapted for use when talking with young children.

Clause   Group of words containing a subject and the accompanying verb; used as a sentence (independent clause) or attached to an independent clause (dependent clause).

Clustering   Process of breaking speech stream into analyzable units based on predictability of syllables and phoneme structures.

Coarticulation   Co-occurrence of the characteristics of two or more phonemes as one phoneme influences another in perception or in production; may be forward (anticipatory) or backward (carryover).

Code switching   Process of varying between two or more languages.

Cognates   Phoneme pairs that differ only in voicing; manner and place of articulation are similar. For example, /f/ and /v/ are cognates, as are /s/ and /z/.

Communication   Process of encoding, transmitting, and decoding signals in order to exchange information and ideas between the participants.

Communication intention   Purpose of an utterance, i.e., to gain information, request permission, or provide information.

Communicative competence   Degree of success in communicating, measured by the appropriateness and effectiveness of the message.

Complex sentence   Sentence consisting of a main clause and at least one subordinate clause.

Compound sentence   Sentence consisting of two or more main clauses.

Conjoining   Joining two or more main clauses with a conjunction.

Consonant cluster reduction   Phonological process seen in preschool children in which one or more consonants are deleted from a cluster of two or more (/tɹ, stɹ, sl, kɹ/) in order to simplify production.

Constructivist approach   Linguistic theory that argues that children learn language from their environment one construction at a time versus rule learning.

Contingent query   Request for clarification, such as "What?" or "Huh?"

Copula   Form of the verb *to be* as a main verb. Signifies a relationship between the subject and a predicate adjective (*fat*, *tired*, *young*) or another noun (*teacher*, *farmer*, *pianist*).

Corpus callosum   Main transverse tract of neurons running between the two hemispheres of the brain.

Cortex   Outermost gray layer of the brain, made up of neuron cell bodies.

Critical literacy   Above the basic reading level, critical literacy involves active interpretation, analysis, and synthesis of information and the ability to explain the content.

Decentration   Process of moving from one-dimensional descriptions of entities and events to coordinated multiattributional ones.

Decoding   The first step in interpreting print, decoding consists of breaking a word into its component sounds and then blending them together to form a recognizable word.

Deficit approach   Notion that only one dialect of a language is inherently correct or standard and that others are substandard or exhibit some deficit.

Deixis   Process of using the speaker's perspective as a reference. For example, deixis can be seen in words such as *this*, *that*, *here*, *there*, *me*, and *you*.

Diphthong   Vowel-like speech sound produced by blending two vowels within a syllable.

Dynamic literacy   At the highest level of reading, the ability to relate content to other knowledge.

Echolalia   Immediate, whole or partial vocal imitation of another speaker; characterizes the child's speech beginning at about 8 months.

Ellipsis   Conversational device of omitting redundant information. For example, when asked, "Who saw the movie?" we reply, "I did," not "I saw the movie."

Embedded *wh*- complement   Object noun-phrase complement using a *wh*- word as a connector for the dependent clause.

Entrenchment   A pattern-finding technique that accounts for how children confine abstractions about language by doing something in the same way successfully several times, thus making it habitual.

Epenthesis   Process of inserting a vowel sound where none is required.

Equilibrium   State of cognitive balance or harmony between incoming stimuli and cognitive structures. Piagetian concept.

Eventcast   A type of narrative that explains some current or anticipated event. Eventcasts often accompany the play of young children.

Event structure   Set of event sequences including the events, relationships and relative significance.

Evocative utterance   Toddler language-learning strategy in which the child names an entity and awaits adult evaluative feedback as to the correctness of the name or label.

Executive function   The self-regulatory aspect of writing that enables the writer to plan, write according to that plan, and proofread and revise as needed.

Expansion   Adult's more mature version of a child utterance that preserves the word order of the original child utterance. For example, when a child says, "Doggie eat," an adult might reply, "The doggie is eating."

Extension   Adult's semantically related comment on a topic established by a child. For example, when a child says, "Doggie eat," an adult might reply, "Yes, doggie hungry."

Fast or **initial mapping**   Quick, sketchy, and tentative formation of a link between a particular referent and a new name that enables a child to have access to and use the word in an immediate although somewhat limited way. Gradually, the meaning of the referent widens as the word is freed from aspects of the initial context.

Formula   Memorized verbal routine or unanalyzed chunk of language often used in everyday conversation.

Free alternation   Variable use of members of a word class without consideration of different meanings. For example, *the* and *a* may be used randomly.

Free morpheme   Meaning unit that can occur alone, such as *dog, chair, run,* and *fast.*

Fully resonant nuclei (FRN)   Vowel-like sounds that are fully resonated laryngeal tones.

Functional-core hypothesis   Theory that word meanings represent dynamic relationships, such as actions or functional uses, rather than static perceptual traits. Concept usually associated with Nelson.

Functionally based distributional analysis   A pattern-finding technique that accounts for how children form linguistic categories, such as nouns and verbs, based on communicative function. Over time, linguistic items that serve the same communicative function are grouped together into a category based on what these units do.

Genderlect   The style of talking used by men and women.

Generative approach   Also called Nativist, the generative approach assumes that children are able to acquire language because they are born with innate rules or principles related to structures of human languages.

Grammars   Systems of rules or underlying principles that describe the five aspects of language.

Habituation   Over time, with repeated exposure, organisms react less strongly to successive presentation of a stimulus.

Heschl's area (or gyrus)   Area located in the auditory cortex of each hemisphere of the brain that receives incoming auditory signals from the inner ear.

Holophrases   Early one-word utterances that convey a holistic communicative intention.

Hypothesis-testing utterance   Toddler language-learning strategy in which the child seeks confirmation of the name of an entity by naming it with rising intonation, thus posing a yes/no question.

Information processing   Theoretical model of brain function that stresses methods employed in dealing with information.

Integrative rehearsal   Use of repetition or rehearsal to transfer information to long-term memory. Information-processing concept.

Intention-reading   A uniquely human social cognitive skill used in understanding language behavior of others.

Interlanguage   Transitional system in which a person uses rules from two or more languages simultaneously.

Interrogative utterance   Toddler language-learning strategy in which the child attempts to learn the name of an entity by asking *What? That?* or *Wassat?* Not to be confused with adultlike interrogative sentences, which are more varied (*what, where, who, why, how, when*).

Item-based construction   Two-word utterance seemingly based on word-order rules with specific words influenced by how a child has heard a particular word being used.

Jargon   Strings of unintelligible speech sounds with the intonational pattern of adult speech.

Joint action Shared action sequences of mother and child, often routines. Provide basis for many scripts.

Language socialization Process of learning language and culture through interactions with caregivers and others. Language is central to the process of learning culture, and cultural patterns teach children the appropriate way to communicate.

Lexicon Individual dictionary of each person containing words and the underlying concepts of each. The lexicon is dynamic, changing with experience.

Linguistic competence Native speaker's underlying knowledge of the rules for generating and understanding conventional linguistic forms.

Linguistic performance Actual language use, reflecting linguistic competence and the communication constraints.

Literacy Use of visual modes of communication, specifically reading and writing.

Main clause Clause within a multiclause sentence that can occur alone.

Mean length of utterance (MLU) Average number of morphemes per utterance.

Mental maps Complex organizational webs that link concepts within the cognitive systems.

Metacognition Knowing what to do cognitively and how to do it—knowledge about knowledge and about cognitive processes.

Metalinguistic Pertaining to the use of language knowledge to make decisions about and to discuss processes of language.

Metaphoric transparency Amount of literal-figurative relationship. High or strong relationships result in easy interpretation.

Modal auxiliary Auxiliary or helping verb used to express mood or attitude, such as ability (*can*), permission (*may*), intention (*will*), possibility (*might*), and obligation (*must*).

Morpheme Smallest unit of meaning; indivisible (*dog*) without violating the meaning or producing meaningless units (*do, g*). There are two types of morphemes, free and bound.

Morphology Aspect of language concerned with rules governing change in meaning at the intra-word level.

Morphophonemic Term used to refer to changes in sound production related to meaning changes.

Motherese Style of talking used most often by white middle-class American mothers when addressing their 18- to 24-month-old toddlers.

Motor cortex Posterior portion of the frontal lobe responsible for sending nerve impulses to the muscles.

Mutual gaze Eye contact with a communication partner; used to signal intensified attention.

Myelination Process of maturation of the nervous system in which the nerves develop a protective myelin sheath, or sleeve.

Narrative Consists of self-generated story; familiar tale; retelling of a movie, television show, or previously heard or seen story; and personal experience recounting.

Narrative level Overall organization of a narrative.

Nativist approach Linguistic theory associated with Chomsky and his followers, who emphasize innateness of language and contend that there are special mechanisms in the human brain dedicated to the acquisition and use of language.

Neighborhood density The number of possible words that differ by one phoneme and a factor characteristic in shaping a child's emerging lexical system.

Neonate Newborn.

Neurolinguistics Study of the anatomy, physiology, and biochemistry of the brain responsible for language processing and formulation.

Neuron Nerve cell; basic unit of the nervous system.

Neuroscience The study of neuroanatomy or where structures are located and neurophysiology or how the brain functions.

Nonegocentrism Ability to take another person's perspective.

Nonlinguistic cues Coding devices that contribute to communication but are not a part of speech. Examples include gestures, body posture, eye contact, head and body movement, facial expression, and physical distance or proxemics.

Object noun-phrase complement Subordinate clause that serves as the object of the main clause, as in "I remember *what you did to me.*"

Open syllable Syllable, usually CV, ending in a vowel.

Organization Tendency for all living things to systemize or organize behaviors. Piagetian concept.

Otitis media Middle ear infection.

Overextension   Process in which a child applies a word's meaning to more exemplars than an adult would. The child's definition is too broad and is thus beyond acceptable adult usage.

Paralinguistic codes   Vocal and nonvocal codes that are superimposed on a linguistic code to signal the speaker's attitude or emotion or to clarify or provide additional meaning.

Patient   Semantic case characterized as those for whom action is performed, as in *Give the flowers to mommy*.

Pattern-finding   A cognitive skill humans share with other primates that enables us to find common threads in disparate information, such as seeking underlying rules for language.

Peripheral nervous system   All elements of the nervous system outside of the skull and spinal cord.

Phone   Actual produced speech sound.

Phoneme   Smallest linguistic unit of sound, each with distinctive features, that can signal a difference in meaning when modified.

Phonemic awareness   An aspect of phonological awareness, phonemic awareness is the specific ability to manipulate sounds, such as blending sounds to create new words or segmenting words into sounds.

Phonetically consistent forms (PCFs)   Consistent vocal patterns that accompany gestures prior to the appearance of words.

Phonics   Sound–letter or phoneme–grapheme relationship; the primary way in which most children are taught to read.

Phonological awareness   Consideration of phonology at a conscious level, including syllabification; sound identification, manipulation, segmentation, and blending; rhyming; and illiteration. A metalinguistic skill, phonological awareness is necessary for the development of reading.

Phonology   Aspect of language concerned with the rules governing the structure, distribution, and sequencing of speech-sound patterns.

Phonotactic probability   The likelihood of phonemes appearing together and/or in certain locations in words.

Phonotactic regularities   Phonemes, phoneme combinations, and syllable structures typical of the native language and noticed by young children.

Phrasal coordination   Process of conjoining clauses and deleting common elements.

Phrase   Group of words that does not contain a subject or predicate and is used as a noun substitute or as a noun or verb modifier.

Pivot schemas   Two-word utterances in which one word or phrase, such as *want* or *more*, seems to structure the utterance by determining the intent of the utterance as a whole, such as a demand. In many of these early utterances one event-word is used with a wide variety of object labels as in *More cookie, More juice,* and *More apple.*

Pragmatics   Aspect of language concerned with language use within a communication context.

Preemption   A pattern-finding technique that accounts for how children confine abstractions about language based on the notion that if someone communicates to me using one form, rather than another, there was a reason for that choice related to the speaker's specific communicative intention.

Prefrontal cortex   Most anterior or forward portion of the frontal lobe of the brain.

Presupposition   Process of assuming which information a listener possesses or may need.

Print awareness   Knowledge of letters and words, ability to identify some letters by name, and knowledge of the way in which words progress through a book.

Protoconversation   Vocal interactions between mothers and infants that resemble the verbal exchanges of more mature conversations.

Prototypic complex hypothesis   Theory that word meanings represent an underlying concept exemplified by a central referent, or prototype, that is a best exemplar or a composite of the concept.

Quasi-resonant nuclei (QRN)   Partial resonance of speech sounds found in neonates.

Recount   A type of narrative that relates past experiences of which the child and the listener partook, observed, or read.

Reduplicated babbling   Long strings of consonant-vowel syllable repetitions, such as *ba-ba-ba-ba-ba,* that appear in the vocal play of 6- to 7-month-old infants.

Reduplication   Phonological process in which child repeats one syllable in a multisyllabic word, as in producing *wawa* for *water.*

Referencing   Differentiation of one entity from many; noting the presence of a single object, action, or event for one's communication partner.

Reflexes   Automatic, involuntary motor patterns. Although many neonatal behaviors are reflexive, this condition changes quickly with maturity.

Reformulation   Adult recasting of a child utterance that makes it more grammatically correct, adds new information, or changes the form.

Register   Situationally influenced language variations, such as motherese.

Rehearsal   Process of maintaining information within long-term memory; repetition, drill, or practice.

Relative clause   Subordinate clause that follows and modifies a noun, as in "I really like the car *that we test-drove last night*."

Request for clarification   Request from the listener for restatement of or additional information on some unclear utterance of the speaker.

Reticular formation   Unit of neurons within the brain stem responsible for sensory integration and for inhibition or facilitation of sensory information.

Schematization   A pattern-finding technique that accounts for how children create abstract syntactic constructions from concrete pieces of language they have heard by forming schemes or concepts for specific functions and individual words to fill the slots in each.

Scheme   Cognitive conceptual structure used for comparison with incoming sensory information.

Script   Scaffolding or predictable structure of an event that provides "slots" for participation and aids comprehension.

Segmentation   Creating a word when a phoneme or syllable is deleted and breaking a word into its parts.

Selection restrictions   Constraints of specific word meanings that govern possible word combinations.

Selective imitation   Toddler language-learning strategy in which the child imitates those language features that he or she is in the process of learning. Toddlers do not imitate randomly.

Semantic case   Meaning category or class used in constructing and comprehending language.

Semantic-feature hypothesis   Theory that word meanings represent universal semantic features or attributes, such as animate/inanimate and male/female. For young children, meanings represent perceptual attributes. Hypothesis usually associated with Clark.

Semantic features   Perceptual or functional aspects of meaning that characterize a word.

Semantics   Aspect of language concerned with rules governing the meaning or content of words or grammatical units.

Sensitive period   Developmental period that varies for each perceptual and cognitive area during which the brain is more receptive to specific environmental input.

Sentential coordination   Conjoining of full clauses.

Sibilants   Sounds produced by forcing air through a narrow constriction formed by the tongue and palate. The turbulence produced results in a hissing sound. Examples include /s/, /z/, /ʃ/, and /ʒ/.

Simple sentence   Linguistic structure that contains one full clause.

Social smile   Infant's smile in response to an external social stimulus.

Sociolinguistic approach   Considers all dialectal variations to be related to each other and to the idealized standard. Each dialect is a valid rule system and therefore none is better than any other.

Speech   Dynamic neuromuscular process of producing speech sounds for communication; a verbal means of transmission.

Story   Type of narrative, fictionalized.

Story grammar   Narrative framework that specifies the underlying relationship of the story components.

Style shifting   The process of varying the style of talking used, such as shifting between formal and informal styles.

Subordinate clause   Clause that cannot occur alone but functions in support of the main clause.

Supramarginal gyrus   Association area of the brain, located in the posterior portion of the temporal lobe, responsible for linguistic processing, especially of longer syntactic units such as sentences.

Suprasegmental devices   Paralinguistic mechanisms superimposed on the verbal signal to change the form and meaning of the sentence by acting across the elements or segments of that sentence. Examples include intonation, stress, and inflection.

Synapse   Miniscule space between the axon of one neuron and the dendrites of another.

Synaptogenesis   A burst in synaptic growth that occurs at 8 to 10 months of age and is noted in changes in both a child's perception and production of speech.

Synonym   Word that shares the same or a similar meaning with another word.

Syntax   Organizational rules specifying word order, sentence organization, and word relationships.

Tense A marking of the verb, such as past or future, that relates the speech time in the present to the event time or time when the event occurs.

Thalamus Organ located in the higher brainstem that receives incoming sensory information, except smell, and relays this information to the appropriate portion of the brain for analysis.

Theory of Mind (ToM) The ability of individuals to understand the minds of other people and to comprehend and predict their behavior.

Topic Shared focus of a conversation that may contain one or more topics.

Turnabout Conversational device used by a mother with a preschooler to maintain the conversation and aid the child in making on-topic comments. In its usual form, the turnabout consists of a comment on or reply to the child's utterance followed by a cue, such as a question, for the child to reply.

Underextension Process in which a child applies a word meaning to fewer exemplars than an adult would. The child's definition is too restrictive and more limited than in adult usage.

Variegated babbling Long strings of nonidentical syllables that appear in the vocal play of some 8- to 10-month-old infants.

Vernacular Casual, informal, or intimate language register or style.

Voiced phoneme A speech sound produced in part by vibration of the vocal folds.

Voiceless phoneme A speech sound, also called unvoiced phoneme, produced without vibration of the vocal folds.

Voice onset time (VOT) Interval between the burst of a voiced plosive and the commencement of phonation.

Wernicke's area Language-processing area of the brain, located in the left temporal lobe; responsible for organizing the underlying structure of outgoing messages and analyzing incoming linguistic information.

Word combination Two-word utterance consisting of roughly equivalent words that divide an experience into multiple units.

Word knowledge Verbal word and symbol definitions.

Working memory Memory in which information is held while being processed.

World knowledge Autobiographical and experiential understanding and memory of events reflecting personal and cultural interpretations.

References

Abbeduto, L., Nuccio, J. B., Al-Mabuk, R., Rotto, P., & Maas, F. (1992). Interpreting and responding to spoken language: Children's recognition and use of a speaker's goal. *Journal of Child Language, 19,* 677–693.

Abbot-Smith, K., & Tomasello, M. (2006). Exemplar-learning and schematization in a usage-based account of syntactic acquisition. *The Linguistic Review, 23,* 275–290

Abkarian, G., Jones, A., & West, G. (1992). Young children's idiom comprehension: Trying to get the picture. *Journal of Speech and Hearing Research, 35,* 580–587.

Abu-Akel, A., Bailey, A. L., & Thum, Y. (2004). Describing the acquisition of determiners in English: A growth modeling approach. *Journal of Psycholinguistic Research, 33,* 407–424.

Abu-Rabia, S., & Siegel, L. S. (2002). Reading, syntactic, orthographic, and working memory skills of bilingual Arabic-English speaking Canadian children. *Journal of Psycholinguistic Research, 31,* 661–678.

Acredolo, L., & Goodwyn, S. (1988). Symbolic gesturing in normal infants. *Child Development,* 450–466.

Acredolo, L., & Goodwyn, S. (1990). Sign language in babies: The significance of symbolic gesturing for understanding language development. In R. Vasta (Ed.), *Annals of child development* (pp. 1–42). London: Jessica Kingsley Publishers Ltd.

Acredolo, L., & Goodwyn, S. (1996). *Baby signs: How to talk to your baby before your baby can talk.* Chicago: NTB/Contemporary.

Adams, A., & Gathercole, S. E. (1995). Phonological working memory and speech production in preschool children. *Journal of Speech, Language, and Hearing Research, 38,* 403–414.

Adler, S. A., Gerhardstein, P., & Rovee-Collier, C. (1998). Levels-of-processing effects in infant memory? *Child Development, 69,* 280–294.

Akhtar, N., Dunham, F., & Dunham, P. J. (1991). Directive interactions and early vocabulary development: The role of joint attentional focus. *Journal of Child Language, 18,* 41–49.

Akins, M. R., & Biederer, T. (2006). Cell–cell interactions in synaptogenesis. *Current Opinion in Neurobiology, 16,* 83–89.

Akiyama, M. M. (1992). Cross-linguistic contrasts of verification and answering among children. *Journal of Psycholinguistic Research, 21,* 67–85.

Alcamo, E. A., Chiriella, L., Dautzenberg, M., Dobreva, G., Fariñas, I., Grosschedl, R., et al. (2008). Satb2 regulates callosal projection neuron identity in the developing cerebral cortex. *Neuron, 57,* 364–377.

Alexander, D., Wetherby, A., & Prizant, B. (1997). The emergence of repair strategies in infants and toddlers. *Seminars in Speech and Language, 18,* 197–213.

Allen, J., & Seidenberg, M. S. (1999). The emergence of grammaticality in connectionist networks. In B. Macwhinney (Ed.), *The emergence of language.* Mahwah, NJ: Lawrence Erlbaum Associates.

Allen, K., Filippini, E., Johnson, M., Kanuck, A., Kroecker, J., Loccisano, S., Lyle, K., Nieto, J., Feenaughty, L., Sligar, C., Wind, K., Young, S., & Owens, R. E. (2010). Noun phrase elaboration in children's language samples. *Journal of Speech, Language, and Hearing Research.*

Allen, S. (1996). *Aspects of argument structure acquisition in Inuktitut.* Amsterdam: John Benjamins.

Allen, S., Genesee, F., Fish, S., & Crago, M. (2002). Patterns of code-mixing in English-Inuktitut bilinguals. In M. Andronis, C. Ball, H. Elston, & S. Neuvel (Eds.), *Proceedings of the 37th Annual Meeting of the Chicago Linguistics Society* (Vol. 2, pp. 171–188). Chicago: Chicago Linguistics Society.

Allen, S. E. M., & Crago, M. B. (1996). Early passive acquisition in Inuktitut. *Journal of Child Language, 23,* 129–155.

Amayreh, M. M. (2003). Completion of the consonant inventory of Arabic. *Journal of Speech, Language, and Hearing Research, 46,* 517–529.

Amayreh, M. M., & Dyson, A. T. (1998). The acquisition of Arabic consonants. *Journal of Speech, Language, and Hearing Research, 41,* 642–653.

Amedi, A., Stern, W. M., Camprodon, J. A., Bermpohl, F., Merabet, L., Rotman, S., et al. (2007). Shape conveyed by visual-to-auditory sensory substitution activates the lateral occipital complex. *Nature Neuroscience, 10,* 687–689.

Anderson, A. H., Clark, A., & Mullin, J. (1994). Interactive communication between children: Learning how to make language work in dialogue. *Journal of Child Language, 21,* 439–463.

Anderson, E. (1992). *Speaking with style: The sociolinguistic skills of children.* London: Routledge.

Anglin, J. M. (1993). Vocabulary development: a morphological analysis. *Monographs of the Society for Research in Child Development, 58,* 10.

Anglin, J. M. (1995a). Classifying the world through language: Functional relevance, cultural significance, and category name learning. *International Journal of Intercultural Relations, 19,* 161–181.

Anglin, J. M. (1995b, April). *Word knowledge and the growth of potentially knowable vocabulary.* Paper presented at the biennial meeting of the Society for Research in Child Development, Indianapolis, IN.

Apel, K., & Masterson, J. (2001). Theory-guided spelling assessment and intervention: A case study. *Language, Speech, and Hearing Services in Schools, 32,* 182–194.

Arnold, P., & Murray, C. (1998). Memory for faces and objects by deaf and hearing signers and hearing nonsigners. *Journal of Psycholinguistic Research, 27,* 481–491.

Aslin, R. A. (1999, April). *Utterance-final bias in word recognition by eight-month-olds.* Poster session presented at the biennial meeting of the Society for Research in Child Development, Albuquerque, NM.

Aslin, R. N. (1992). Segmentation of fluent speech into words: Learning models and the role of maternal input. In B. deBoysson-Bardies, S. DeSchonen, P. Jusczyk, P. MacNeilage, & J. Morton (Eds.), *Developmental neurocognition: Speech and face processing in the first year of life.* Dordrecht: Kluwer.

Aslin, R. N., Saffran, J. R., & Newport, E. L. (1998). Computation of conditional probability statistics by 8-month-old infants. *Psychological Science, 9,* 321–324.

Astington, J. W. (2003). Sometimes necessary, never sufficient: False belief understanding and social competence. In B. Repacholi & V. Slaughter (Eds.), *Individual differences in Theory of Mind: Implications for typical and atypical development.* New York: Psychology Press.

Astington, J. W., & Jenkins, J. (1995). Theory of mind development and social understanding. *Cognition and Emotion, 9,* 151–165.

Astington, J. W., & Jenkins, J. (1999). A longitudinal study of the relation between language and theory of mind development. *Developmental Psychology, 35,* 1311–1320.

Au, K. (1990). Children's use of information in word learning. *Journal of Child Language, 17,* 393–416.

Axtell, R. E. (1991). *Gestures: The do's and taboos of body language around the world.* Baltimore, MD: Wiley.

Azuma, S. (1996). Speech production units among bilinguals. *Journal of Psycholinguistic Research, 25,* 397–416.

Backus, A. (1999). Mixed native language: A challenge to the monolithic view of language. *Topics in Language Disorders, 19*(4), 11–22.

Baddeley, A. D. (1986). *Working memory.* Oxford: Oxford University Press.

Baddeley, A. D. (1992). Is working memory working? The fifteenth Bartlett lecture. *Quarterly Journal of Experimental Psychology, 44,* 1–31.

Baddeley, A. D. (2000). Short-term and working memory. In E. Tulving & F. I. M. Craik (Eds.), *The Oxford handbook of memory* (pp. 77–92). Oxford, UK: Oxford University Press.

Baddeley, A. D., Gathercole, S., & Papagno, C. (1998). The phonological loop as a language learning device. *Psychological Review 105,* 158–73.

Baker, C. L., & McCarthy, J. J. (1981). *The logical problem of language acquisition.* Cambridge, MA: MIT Press.

Baker, E., Croot, K., McLeod, S., & Paul, R. (2001). Psycholinguistic models of speech development and their application to clinical practice. *Journal of Speech, Language, and Hearing Research, 44,* 685–702.

Baldwin, D. A. (1991). Infants' contribution to the achievement of joint reference. *Child Development, 62,* 875–890.

Baldwin, D. A. (1993). Infants' ability to consult the speaker for clues to word reference. *Journal of Child Language, 20,* 395–418.

Baldwin, D. A., Markman, E. M., Bill, B., Desjardins, N., Irwin, J. M., & Tidball, G. (1996). Infants' reliance on a social criterion for establishing word–object relations. *Child Development, 67,* 3135–3153.

Baldwin, D. A., & Tomasello, M. (1998). Word learning: A window on early pragmatic understanding. In E. V. Clark (Ed.), *Proceedings of the Stanford Child Language Research Forum* (pp. 3–23). Stanford, CA: Center for the Study of Language and Information.

Baratz, J. C. (1969). A bi-dialectal task for determining language proficiency in economically disadvantaged Negro children. *Child Development, 40,* 889–901.

Barker, J., Nicol, J., & Garrett, M. (2001). Semantic factors in the production of number agreement. *Journal of Psycholinguistic Research, 30,* 91–114.

Barrett, M. (1982). The holophrastic hypothesis: Conceptual and empirical issues. *Cognition, 11,* 46–76.

Barrett, M. D., Harris, M., & Chasin, J. (1991). Early lexical development and maternal speech: A comparison of children's initial and subsequent uses of words. *Journal of Child Language, 18,* 21–40.

Barsalou, L. W., Simmons, W. K., Barbey, A. K., & Wilson, C. D. (2003). Grounding conceptual knowledge in modality-specific systems. *Trends in Cognitive Science, 7,* 84–91.

Barton, M. E., & Strosberg, R. (1997). Conversational patterns of two-year-old twins in mother-twin-twin triads. *Journal of Child Language, 24,* 257–269.

Barton, M. E., & Tomasello, M. (1994). The rest of the family: The role of fathers and siblings in early language development. In C. Gallaway, & B. J. Richards (Eds.),

Input and interaction in language acquisition. Cambridge, UK: Cambridge University Press.

Bates, E. (1976). *Language and context: The acquisition of pragmatics.* New York: Academic Press.

Bates, E. (1997). On the nature and nurture of language. In E. Bizzi, P. Catissano, & V. Volterra (Eds.), *Frontiers of biology: The brain of* Homo sapiens. Rome: Giovanni Trecani.

Bates, E. (2003). On the nature and nurture of language. In R. Levi-Montalcini, D. Baltimore, R. Dulbecco, F. Jacob, E. Bizzi, P. Calissano, & V. Volterra (Eds.), *Frontiers of biology: The brain of* Homo sapiens (pp. 241–265). Rome: Istituto della Enciclopedia Italiana fondata da Giovanni Trecanni.

Bates, E., Bretherton, I., & Snyder, L. (1988). *From first words to grammar: Individual differences and dissociable mechanisms.* New York: Cambridge University Press.

Bates, E., Camaioni, L., & Volterra, V. (1975). The acquisition of performatives prior to speech. *Merrill-Palmer Quarterly, 21,* 205–216.

Bates, E., & Carnevale, G. (1993). New directions in research on language development. *Developmental Review, 13,* 436–470.

Bates, E., & Goodman, J. (1999). On the emergence of grammar from the lexicon. In B. MacWhinney (Ed.), *The emergence of language* (pp. 29–79). Mahwah, NJ: Lawrence Erlbaum Associates.

Bates, E., Marchman, V., Thal, D., Fenson, L., Dale, P., Reznick, J., Reilly, J., & Hartung, J. (1994). Developmental and stylistic variation in the composition of early vocabulary. *Journal of Child Language, 21,* 85–123.

Bauer, D. J., Goldfield, B. A., & Reznick, J. S. (2002). Alternative approaches to analyzing individual differences in the rate of early vocabulary development. *Applied Psycholinguistics, 23,* 313–335.

Bauer, P. J. (1996). What do infants recall of their lives? Memory for specific events by one- to two-year-olds. *American Psychologist, 51,* 29–41.

Bavin, E. L., Prior, M., Reilly, S., Bretherton, L., Williams, J., Eadie, P., Barrett, Y., & Ukoumunne, O. C. (2008). The Early Language in Victoria Study: Predicting vocabulary at age one and two years from gesture and object use. *Journal of Child Language, 35,* 687–701.

Beckman, M., & Edwards, J. (2000). The ontogeny of phonological categories and the primacy of lexical learning in linguistic development. *Child Development, 71,* 240–249.

Bedore, L., & Leonard, L. B. (2000). The effects of inflectional variation on fast mapping of verbs in English and Spanish. *Journal of Speech, Language, and Hearing Research, 43,* 21–33.

Beebe, B., Badalamenti, A., Jaffe, J., Feldstein, S., Marquette, L., Helbraun, E., Demetri-Friedman, D., Flaster, C., Goodman, P., Kaminer, T., Kaufman-Balamuth, L., Putterman, J., Stepakoff, S., & Ellman, L. (2008). Distressed mothers and their infants use a less efficient timing mechanism in creating expectancies of each other's looking patterns. *Journal of Psycholinguistic Research, 37,* 293–308.

Behrend, D. A., Harris, L. L., & Cartwright, K. B. (1995). Morphological cues to verb meaning: Verb inflections and the initial mapping of verb meanings. *Journal of Child Language, 22,* 89–106.

Behrens, H. (1998). *Where does the information go?* Paper presented at MPI workshop on argument structure. Nijmegen, The Netherlands.

Benedict, H. (1979). Early lexical development: Comprehension and production. *Journal of Child Language, 6,* 183–200.

Benelli, B., Belacchi, C., Gini, G., & Lucangeli, D. (2006). "To define means to say what you know about things": The development of definitional skills as metalinguistic acquisition. *Journal of Child Language, 33,* 71–97.

Benigno, J. P., Clark, L., & Farrar, M. J. (2007). Three is not always a crowd: Contexts of joint attention and language. *Journal of Child Language, 34,* 175–187.

Bennett-Kaster, T. (1988). *Analyzing children's language.* Oxford: Blackwell.

Berman, R. A. (1982). Verb-pattern alternation: The interface of morphology, syntax, and semantics in Hebrew child language. *Journal of Child Language, 9,* 169–91.

Berman, R. A. (1986). A crosslinguistic perspective: Morphology and syntax. In P. Fletcher & M. Garman (Eds.), *Language acquisition* (2nd ed.). New York: Cambridge University Press.

Berman, R. A., Ragnarsdóttir, H., & Strömqvist, S. (2002). Discourse stance. *Written Language and Literacy, 5,* 255–291.

Berman, R. A., & Slobin, D. I. (1994). *Relating events in narrative.* Mahwah, NJ: Lawrence Erlbaum Associates.

Berman, R. A., & Verhoeven, L. (2002). Cross-linguistic perspectives on the development of text-production abilities: Speech and writing. *Written Language and Literacy, 5*(1), 1–43.

Berninger, V. W. (2000). Development of language by hand and its connections with language by ear, mouth, and eye. *Topics in Language Disorders, 20*(4), 65–84.

Berninger, V. W., Abbott, R. D., Billingsley, F., & Nagy, W. (2001). Processes underlying timing and fluency of reading: Efficiency, automaticity, coordination, and morphological awareness. In M. Worf (Ed.), *Dyslexia, fluency, and the brain* (pp. 383–413). Timonium, MD: York.

Berninger, V. W., Abbott, R. D., Nagy, W., & Carlisle, J. (2010). Growth in phonological, orthographic, and morphological awareness in grades 1 to 6. *Journal of Psycholinguistic Research, 39,* 141–164.

Berninger, V. W., Cartwright, A., Yates, C., Swanson, H. L., & Abbott, R. (1994). Developmental skills related to writing and reading acquisition in the intermediate grades: Shared and unique variance. *Reading and Writing: An Interdisciplinary Journal, 6,* 161–196.

Bertoncini, J., Bijeljac-Babic, R. V., Blumstein, S. E., & Mehler, J. (1987). Discrimination in neonates of very short CVs. *Journal of the Acoustic Society of America, 82,* 31–37.

Best, C. T. (1995). Learning to perceive the sound patterns of English. In C. Rovee-Collier & L. P. Lipsitt (Eds.), *Advances in infancy research* (Vol. 9, pp. 217–304). Norwood, NJ: Ablex.

Beyer, T., & Hudson Kam, C. L. (2009). Some cues are stronger than others: The (non)interpretation of 3rd person present –s as a tense marker by 6- and 7-year-olds. *First Language, 29,* 208–227.

Bialystock, E. (2001). *Bilingualism in development: Language, literacy, and cognition.* New York: Cambridge University Press.

Biber, D. (1995). *Dimensions of register variation: A crosslinguistic comparison.* Cambridge: Cambridge University Press.

Bickerton, D. (2003). Symbol and structure: A comprehensive framework. In M. H. Christiansen & S. Kirby (Eds.), *Language evolution* (pp. 77–93). Oxford, UK: Oxford University Press.

Bijeljac, B. R., Bertoncini, J., & Mehler, J. (1993). How do four-day-old infants categorize multisyllabic utterances? *Developmental Psychology, 29,* 711–721.

Birdsong, D., & Molis, M. (2001). On the evidence for maturational constraints in second-language acquisition. *Journal of Memory and Language, 44,* 235–249.

Blake, J., & deBoysson-Bardies, B. (1992). Patterns of babbling: A cross-linguistic study. *Journal of Child Language, 19,* 51–74.

Blake, J., Quartaro, G., & Onorati, S. (1993). Evaluating quantitative measures of grammatical complexity in spontaneous speech samples. *Journal of Child Language, 20,* 139–152.

Blaye, A., & Bonthoux, F. (2001). Thematic and taxonomic relations in preschoolers: The development of flexibility in categorization choices. *British Journal of Developmental Psychology, 19,* 395–412.

Bliss, L. S. (1992). A comparison of tactful messages by children with and without language impairment. *Language, Speech, and Hearing Services in Schools, 23,* 343–347.

Bloom, K. (1988). Quality of adult vocalizations affects the quality of infant vocalizations. *Journal of Child Language, 15,* 469–480.

Bloom, K., & Lo, E. (1990). Adult perceptions of vocalizing infants. *Infant Behavior and Development, 13,* 209–213.

Bloom, L. (1973). *One word at a time: The use of single-word utterances before syntax.* The Hague: Mouton.

Bloom, L. (1983). Of continuity, nature, and magic. In R. Golinkoff (Ed.), *The transition from preverbal to verbal communication.* Hillsdale, NJ: Lawrence Erlbaum Associates.

Bloom, L. (1993). *The transition from infancy to language: Acquiring the power of expression.* Cambridge, UK: Cambridge University Press.

Bloom, L., Merkin, S., & Wooten, J. (1982). Wh-questions: Linguistic factors that contribute to the sequence of acquisition. *Child Development, 53,* 1084–1092.

Bloom, P. (1990). Subjectless sentences in child language. *Linguistic Inquiry, 21,* 491–504.

Bloom, P. (2000). *How children learn the meanings of words.* Cambridge, MA: MIT Press.

Bookheimer, S. (2002). Functional MRI of language: New approaches for understanding the cortical organization of semantic processing. *Annual Reviews of Neuroscience, 25,* 151–168.

Booth, J. R., MacWhinney, B., Thulborn, K. R., Sacco, K., Voyvodic, J., & Feldman, H. (1999). Functional organization of activation patterns in children: Whole brain fMRI imaging during three different cognitive tasks. *Progress in Neuropsychopharmocology and Biological Psychiatry, 23,* 669–682.

Bornstein, M. H., Cote, L. R., Maital, S., Painter, K., Park, S., Pascual, L., Pêcheux, M., Ruel, J., Venuti, P., & Vyt, A. (2004). Cross-linguistic analysis of vocabulary in young children: Spanish, Dutch, French, Hebrew, Italian, Korean, and American English. *Child Development, 75,* 1115–1139.

Bornstein, M. H., Haynes, O. M., Painter, K. M., & Genevro, J. L. (2000). Child language with mother and with stranger at home and in the laboratory: A methodological study. *Journal of Child Language, 27,* 407–420.

Bortfeld, H., Morgan, J. L., Golinkoff, R. M., & Rathbun, K. (2005). Mommy and me: Familiar names help launch babies into speech-stream segmentation. *Psychological Science, 16,* 298–304.

Bosch, L., & Sebastián-Gallés, N. (1997). Native-language recognition abilities in 4-month-old infants from monolingual and bilingual envirionment. *Cognition, 65,* 33–69.

Boswell, S. (2006, January 17). Signs from the desert. *The ASHA Leader, 11*(1), 12.

Bourgeois, J.-P., Goldman-Rakic, P. S., & Rakic, P. (1999). Formation, elimination, and stabilization of synapses in the primate cerebral cortex. In M. S. Gazzaniga (Ed.), *The new cognitive neurosciences* (pp. 45–53). Cambridge, MA: MIT Press.

Bowerman, M. (1981). *The child's expression of meaning: Expanding relationships among lexicon, syntax and morphology.* Paper presented at the New York Academy of Science Conference on Native Language and Foreign Language Acquisition.

Bowerman, M. (1988). The "no negative evidence" problem. In J. Hawkins (Ed.), *Explaining language universals* (pp. 73–104). London: Blackwell.

Bowerman, M. (1993). Learning a semantic system: What role do cognitive predispositions play? In P. Bloom (Ed.), *Language acquisition: Core readings.* Cambridge, MA: MIT Press.

Boysson-Bardies, B., & Vihman, M. M. (1991). Adaption to language: Evidence from babbling and first words in four languages. *Language, 67,* 297–320.

Bradley, R. H., & Corwyn, R. F. (2002). Socioeconomic status and child development. *Annual Review of Psychology, 53,* 371–399.

Brent, M. R., & Siskind, J. M. (2001). The role of exposure to isolated words in early vocabulary development. *Cognition, 81,* B33–B44.

Bretherton, I. (1984). Representing the social world in symbolic play: Reality and fantasy. In I. Bretherton (Ed.), *Symbolic play: The development of social understanding.* New York: Academic Press.

Brown, C. M., van Berkum, J. J. A., & Hagoort, P. (2000). Discourse before gender: An event-related brain potential study on the interplay of semantic and syntactic information during spoken language understanding. *Journal of Psycholinguistic Research, 29,* 53–68.

Brown, R. (1973). *A first language: The early stages.* Cambridge: Harvard University Press.

Brownell, C. (1988). Combinatorial skills: Converging developments over the second year. *Child Development, 59,* 675–685.

Bruer, J. T. (2001). A critical and sensitive period primer. In D. Ailer Jr., J. T. Bruer, F. J. Symons, & J. W. Lichtman (Eds.), *Critical thinking about critical periods* (pp. 3–26). Baltimore, MD: Paul H. Brookes.

Bruner, J. (1975). The ontogenesis of speech acts. *Journal of Child Language, 2,* 1–19.

Bruner, J. (1977). Early social interaction and language acquisition. In R. Schaffer (Ed.), *Studies in mother–infant interaction.* New York: Academic Press.

Bruner, J. (1983). *Child's talk.* New York: W. W. Norton.

Budwig, N. (1990). The linguistic marking of non-prototypical agency: An exploration into children's use of passives. *Linguistics, 28,* 1221–1252.

Buhl, H. M. (2002). Partner orientation and speaker's knowledge as conflicting parameters in language production. *Journal of Psycholinguistic Research, 30,* 549–567.

Burkhalter, A., Bernardo, K. L., & Charles, V. (1993). Development of local circuits in human visual cortex. *Journal of Neuroscience, 13*(5), 1916–1931.

Butterworth, G. (2003). Pointing is the royal road to language for babies. In S. Kita (Ed.), *Pointing: Where language, culture, and cognition meet* (pp. 9–33). Mahwah, NJ: Lawrence Erlbaum Associates.

Bybee, J. (1995). Regular morphology and the lexicon. *Language and Cognitive Processes, 10,* 425–455.

Bybee, J. (2002). Word frequency and context of use in the lexical diffusion of phonetically conditioned sound change. *Language Variation and Change,* 14, 261–290.

Caccamise, D., & Snyder, L. (2005). Theory and pedagogical practices of text comprehension. *Topics in Language Disorders, 25*(1), 1–20.

Cain, K., Patson, N., & Andrews, L. (2005). Age- and ability-related differences in young readers' use of conjunctions. *Journal of Child Language, 32,* 877–892.

Cain, K., & Towse, A. S. (2008). To get hold of the wrong end of the stick: Reasons for poor idiom understanding in children with reading comprehension difficulties. *Journal of Speech, Language, and Hearing Research, 51,* 1538–1549.

Calkins, S. D., Hungerford, A., & Dedmon, S. E. (2004). Mothers' interactions with temperamentally frustrated infants. *Infant Mental Health Journal, 25,* 219–239.

Cameron-Faulkner, T., Lieven, E., & Tomasello, M. (2003). A construction based analysis of child directed speech. *Cognitive Science, 27,* 843–873.

Campbell, A., & Tomasello, M. (2001). The acquisition of English dative constructions. *Applied Psycholinguistics, 22,* 253–267.

Capirci, O., Iverson, J. M., Pizzuto, E., & Volterra, V. (1996). Gestures and words during the transition to two-word speech. *Journal of Child Language, 23,* 645–673.

Caplan, D. (2001). Functional neuroimaging studies of syntactic processing. *Journal of Psycholinguistic Research, 30,* 297–320.

Capone, N. C. (2007). Tapping toddlers' evolving semantic representation via gesture. *Journal of Speech, Language, and Hearing Research, 50,* 732–745.

Capone, N. C., & McGregor, K. K. (2004). Gesture development: A review for clinical and research practices. *Journal of Speech, Language, and Hearing Research, 47,* 173–186.

Carey, S. (1988). Conceptual differences between children and adults. *Mind and Language, 3,* 167–181.

Carey, S. (1991). Knowledge acquisition: Enrichment or conceptual change? In S. Carey & R. Gelman (Eds.), *The epigenisis of mind: Essays on biology and cognition.* Hillsdale, NJ: Lawrence Erlbaum Associates.

Carpenter, K. (1991). Later rather than sooner: Extralinguistic categories in the acquisition of Thai classifiers. *Journal of Child Language, 18,* 93–113.

Carrell, P. (1981). Children's understanding of indirect requests: Comparing child and adult comprehension. *Journal of Child Language, 8,* 329–345.

Carroll, J. B., & White, M. N. (1973). Age-of-acquisition norms for 220 picturable nouns. *Journal of Verbal Learning and Verbal Behavior, 12,* 563–576.

Case, R. (1992). *The mind's staircase.* Hillsdale, NJ: Lawrence Erlbaum Associates.

Caselli, M. (1990). Communicative gestures and first words. In V. Bolterra & C. Erting (Eds.), *From gesture to sign in hearing and deaf children* (pp. 56–67). New York: Springer-Verlag.

Chafe, W. L. (1994). *Discourse, consciousness, and time: The flow of language in speech and writing.* Chicago: Chicago University Press.

Chaffin, R., Morris, R., & Seeley, R. (2001). Learning new meanings from context: A study of eye movement. *Journal of Experimental Psychology, 27,* 225–235.

Chaigneau, S. E., & Barsalou, L. W. (in press). *The role of function in categorization.* Theoria et Historia Scientiarum.

Chan, A., Lieven, E., & Tomasello, M. (2009). Children's understanding of the agent–patient relations in the transitive construction: Cross-linguistic comparisons between Cantonese, German, and English. *Cognitive Linguistics, 20,* 267–300.

Chan, Y.-L., & Marinellie, S. A. (2008). Definitions of idioms in preadolescents, adolescents, and adults. *Journal of Psycholinguistic Research, 37,* 1–20.

Charity, A. H., Scarborough, H. S., & Griffin, D. M. (2004). Familiarity with school English in African American children and its relation to early reading achievement. *Child Development, 75,* 1340–1356.

Chen, L., & Kent, R. D. (2005). Consonant–vowel co-occurrence patterns in Mandarin-learning infants. *Journal of Child Language, 32,* 507–534.

Cheng, L. (1987, June). Cross-cultural and linguistic considerations in working with Asian populations. *Asha, 29*(6), 33–38.

Childers, J. B., & Paik, J. H. (2009). Korean- and English-speaking children use cross-situational information to learn novel predicate terms. *Journal of Child Language, 36,* 201–224.

Childers, J. B., Vaughan, J., & Burquest, D. A. (2007). Joint attention and word learning in Ngas-speaking toddlers in Nigeria. *Journal of Child Language, 33,* 199–225.

Chliounaki, K., & Bryant, P. (2007). How children learn about morphological spelling rules. *Child Development, 78,* 1360–1373.

Choi, S. (2000). Caregiver input in English and Korean: Use of nouns and verbs in book-reading and toy-play contexts. *Journal of Child Language, 27,* 69–96.

Choi, S., & Gopnik, A. (1995). Early acquisition of verbs in Korean: A cross-linguistic study. *Journal of Child Language, 22,* 497–529.

Chomsky, N. (1957). *Syntactic structures.* The Hague: Mouton.

Chomsky, N. (1965a). *Aspects of the theory of syntax.* Cambridge: MIT Press.

Chomsky, N. (1965b). Three models for the description of language. In R. Luce, R. Bush, & E. Galanter (Eds.), *Readings in mathematical psychology* (Vol. II, pp. 105–124). New York: John Wiley and Sons.

Chomsky, N. (1980). Rules and representations. *Behavioral and Brain Sciences, 3,* 1–61.

Chouinard, M. M., & Clark, E. V. (2003). Adult reformulations of child errors as negative evidence. *Journal of Child Language, 30,* 637–669.

Christiansen, M. H., & Charter, N. (1999). Toward a connectionist model of recursion in human linguistic performance. *Cognitive Science, 23*(2), 157–205.

Clahsen, H., Aveledo, F., & Roca, I. (2002). The development of regular and irregular verb inflection in Spanish child language. *Journal of Child Language, 29,* 591–622.

Clancy, P. M. (2000). *Exceptional casemarking in Korean acquisition: A discourse-functional account.* Paper presented at Conceptual Structure, Discourse, and Language Conference, University of California, Santa Barbara.

Clark, E. V. (1978). Awareness of language: Some evidence from what children say and do. In A. Sinclair, R. Jarvella, & W. Levelt (Eds.), *The child's conception of language.* New York: Springer-Verlag.

Clark, E. V. (1990). On the pragmatics of contrast. *Journal of Child Language, 17,* 417–431.

Clark, E. V. (1996). *Early verbs, event types and inflections* (Vol. 9). Mahwah, NJ: Lawrence Erlbaum Associates.

Clark, E. V., & Bernicot, J. (2008). Repetition as ratification: How parents and children place information in common ground. *Journal of Child Language, 35,* 349–371.

Cleave, P. L., & Kay-Raining Bird, E. (2006). Effects of familiarity on mothers' talk about nouns and verbs. *Journal of Child Language, 33,* 661–676.

Clopper, C., & Pisoni, D. (2004). Some acoustic cues for the perceptual categorization of American English dialects. *Journal of Phonetics, 32,* 111–140.

Coady, J. A., & Aslin, R. N. (2003). Phonological neighborhoods in the developing lexicon. *Journal of Child Language, 30,* 441–469.

Cohen, S., & Beckwith, L. (1975). *Maternal language input in infancy.* Paper presented to the American Psychological Association.

Colombo, J., Shaddy, D. J., Richman, W. A., Maikranz, J. M., & Blaga, O. M. (2004). The developmental course of habituation in infancy and preschool outcome. *Infancy, 5,* 1–38.

Comeau, L., Genesee, F., & Mendelson, M. (2007). Bilingual children's repairs of breakdowns in communication. *Journal of Child Language, 34,* 159–174.

Committee on Language, American Speech-Language-Hearing Association. (1983). Definition of language. *Asha, 25,* 44.

Conti-Ramsden, G., & Durkin, K. (2008). Language and independence in adolescents with and without a history of specific language impairment (SLI). *Journal of Speech, Language, and Hearing Research, 51,* 70–83.

Cooper, P. V. (1990). Discourse production and normal aging: Performance and oral picture description tasks. *Journal of Gerontology: Psychological Sciences, 45,* 210–214.

Cooper, R. P., & Aslin, R. N. (1990). Preference for infant-directed speech in the first month after birth. *Child Development, 61,* 1584–1595.

Coplan, R. J., Barber, A. M., & Lagace-Seguin, D. G. (1999). The role of child temperament as a predictor of early literacy and numeracy skills in preschoolers. *Early Childhood Research Quarterly, 14,* 537–53.

Coulson, A. (1999, August 20). Language is more than words and sentences. Rochester, NY, *Democrat & Chronicle,* 8A.

Crago, M. B., Eriks-Brophy, A., Pesco, D., & McAlpine, L. (1997). Culturally based miscommunication in classroom interaction. *Language, Speech, and Hearing Services in Schools, 28,* 245–254.

Craig, H. K., Connor, C. M., & Washington, J. A. (2003). Early positive predictors of later reading comprehension for African American students: A preliminary investigation. *Language, Speech, and Hearing Services in Schools, 34,* 31–43.

Craig, H. K., & Washington, J. A. (2002). Oral language expectations for African American preschoolers and kindergartners. *American Journal of Speech-Language Pathology, 11,* 59–70.

Craig, H. K., Washington, J. A., & Thompson-Porter, C. (1998). Average c-unit lengths in the discourse of African American children from low-income, urban homes. *Journal of Speech, Language and Hearing Research, 41,* 433–444.

Craig, H. K., Zhang, L., Hensel, S. L., & Quinn, E. J. (2009). African American English–speaking students: An examination of the relationship between dialect shifting and reading outcomes. *Journal of Speech, Language, and Hearing Research, 52,* 839–855.

Crain, S., & Lillo-Martin, D. (1999). *An introduction to linguistic theory and language acquisition.* Malden, MA: Blackwell.

Crnic, K. A., & Low, C. (2002). Everyday stresses and parenting. In M. Bornstein (Ed.), *Handbook of parenting : Volume 5, Practical issues in parenting* (2nd ed., pp. 243–268). Mahwah, NJ: Lawrence Erlbaum Associates.

Cronk, B. C., Lima, S. D., & Schweigert, W. A. (1993). Idioms in sentences: Effects of frequency, literalness, and familiarity. *Journal of Psycholinguistic Research, 22,* 59–82.

Cronk, B. C., & Schweigert, W. A. (1992). The comprehension of idioms: The effects of familiarity, literalness, and usage. *Applied Psycholinguistics, 13,* 131–146.

Crown, C. L., Feldstein, S., Jasnow, M. D., Beebe, B., & Jaffe, J. (2002). The cross-modal coordination of interpersonal timing: Six-week-olds infants' gaze with adults' vocal behavior. *Journal of Psycholinguistic Research, 31,* 1–23.

Cupples, L., & Iacono, T. (2000). Phonological awareness and oral reading skill in children with Down syndrome. *Journal of Speech, Language, and Hearing Research, 43,* 595–608.

Curtin, S. (2009). Twelve-month-olds learn novel word–object pairings differing only in stress pattern. *Journal of Child Language, 36,* 1157–1165.

Cutting, J., & Ferriera, V. (1999). Semantic and phonological information flow in the production lexicon. *Journal of Experimental Psychology: Learning, Memory, and Cognition, 25,* 318–344.

Dąbrowska, E. (2000). From formula to schema: The acquisition of English questions. *Cognitive Linguistics, 11*(1/2), 83–102.

Dąbrowska, E., & Lieven, E. (2005). Towards a lexically specific grammar of children's question constructions. *Cognitive Linguistics, 16*(3), 437–474.

Dale, P. S., & Crain-Thoreson, C. (1993). Pronoun reversals: Who, when, & why? *Journal of Child Language, 20,* 573–589.

Davidson, D. J., Zacks, R. T., & Ferreira, F. (2003). Age preservation of the syntactic processor in production. *Journal of Psycholinguistic Research, 32,* 541–566.

Davis, F. A., & DeCasper, A. J. (1989). *Intrauterine heartbeat sounds are reinforcing for newborns because of active right-lateralized processes.* Paper presented at the Society for Research in Child Development, Kansas City, MO.

Daw, N. W. (1997). Critical periods and strabismus: What questions remain? *Optometry and Vision Science, 74,* 690–694.

Deacon, S. H., & Kirby, J. R. (2004). Morphological awareness: Just "more phonological"? The roles of morphological and phonological awareness in reading development. *Applied Psycholinguistics, 25,* 223–238.

Dean Qualls, C., O'Brien, R. M., Blood, G. W., & Scheffner Hammer, C. (2003). Contextual variation, familiarity, academic literacy, and rural adolescents' idiom knowledge. *Language, Speech, and Hearing Services in Schools, 34,* 69–79.

Debaryshe, B. D. (1993). Joint picture-book reading correlates of early language skill. *Journal of Child Language, 20,* 455–461.

DeCasper, A. J., & Spence, M. (1986). Prenatal maternal speech influences newborns' perceptions of speech sounds. *Infant Behavior and Infant Development, 9,* 133–150.

Delage, H., & Tuller, L. (2007). Language development and mild-to-moderate hearing loss: Does language normalize with age? *Journal of Speech, Language, and Hearing Research, 50,* 1300–1313.

Demuth, K. (1989). Maturation, continuity and the acquisition of Sesotho passive. *Language, 65,* 56–80.

Demuth, K. (1990). Subject, topic and Sesotho passive. *Journal of Child Language, 17,* 67–84.

Demuth, K. (1993). Issues in the acquisition of the Sesotho tonal system. *Journal of Child Language, 20,* 275–301.

Derwing, B., & Baker, W. (1986). Assessing morphological development. In P. Fletcher & M. Garman (Eds.), *Language acquisition* (2nd ed.). New York: Cambridge University Press.

DeThorne, L. S., Petrill, S. A., Hart, S. A., Channell, R. W., Campbell, R. J., Deater-Deckard, K., Thompson, L. A., & Vandenbergh, D. J. (2008). Genetic effects on children's conversational language use. *Journal of Speech, Language, and Hearing Research, 51*, 423–435.

Devescovi, A., Caselli, C. M., Marchione, D., Pasqualetti, P., Reilly, J., & Bates, E. (2005). A crosslinguistic study of the relationship between grammar and lexical development. *Journal of Child Language, 32*, 759–786.

de Villers, J. (2001). Continuity and modularity in language acquisition and research. *Annual Review of Language Acquisition, 1*, 1–64.

de Villiers, J., & Johnson, V. E. (2007). The information in third-person /s/: Acquisition across dialects of American English. *Journal of Child Language, 34*, 133–158.

Devous, M. D., Altuna, D., Furl, N., Cooper, W., Gabbert, G., Ngai, W. T., Chiu, S., Scott, J. M., Harris, T. S., Payne, J. K., & Tobey, E. A. (2006). Maturation of speech and language functional neuroanatomy in pediatric normal controls. *Journal of Speech, Language, and Hearing Research, 49*, 856–866.

Diamond, J. (1993, February). Speaking with a single tongue. *Discover*, 78–85.

Dickinson, D., Wolf, M., & Stotsky, S. (1993). Words move: The interwoven development of oral and written language. In J. B. Gleason (Ed.), *The development of language*. Boston: Allyn & Bacon.

Diessel, H. (2004). *The acquisition of complex sentences*. Cambridge: Cambridge University Press.

Diessel, H., & Tomasello, M. (2001). The acquisition of finite complement clauses in English: A corpus-based analysis. *Cognitive Linguistics, 12*, 1–45

Dionne, G., Dale, P. S., Boivin, M., & Plomin, R. (2003). Genetic evidence for bidirectional effects of early lexical and grammatical development. *Child Development 74*, 394–412.

Dodd, B., & Carr, A. (2003). Young children's letter-sound knowledge. *Language, Speech, and Hearing Services in Schools, 34*, 128–137.

Dodd, B., & McEvoy, S. (1994). Twin language or phonological disorder. *Journal of Child Language, 21*, 273–289.

D'Odorico, L., Carubbi, S., Salerni, N., & Calvo, V. (2001). Vocabulary development in Italian children: A longitudinal evaluation of quantitative and qualitative aspects. *Journal of Child Language, 28*, 351–372.

D'Odorico, L., Cassibba, R., & Salerni, N. (1997). Temporal relationships between gaze and vocal behavior in prelinguistic and linguistic communication. *Journal of Psycholinguistic Research, 26*, 539–556.

Dollaghan, C. (1994). Children's phonological neighborhoods: Half empty or half full. *Journal of Child Language, 21*, 257–271.

Dollaghan, C. A., Campbell, T. F., Paradise, J. L., Feldman, H. M., Janosky, J. E., Pitcairn, D. N., & Kurs-Lasky, M. (1999). Maternal education and measures of early speech and language. *Journal of Speech, Language, and Hearing Research, 42*, 1432–1443.

Donahue, M. L., & Pearl, R. (1995). Conversational interactions of mothers and their preschool children who had been born preterm. *Journal of Speech and Hearing Research, 38*, 1117–1125.

Dore, J. (1974). A pragmatic description of early language development. *Journal of Psycholinguistic Research, 3*, 343–350.

Dore, J. (1975, April). Holophrases, speech acts and language universals. *Journal of Child Language, 2*(1), 33.

Dromi, E., & Berman, R. (1982). A morphemic measure of early language development from Modern Hebrew. *Journal of Child Language, 9*, 403–424.

Duncan, G. J., & Brooks-Dunn, J. (2000). Family poverty, welfare reform, and child development. *Child Development, 71*, 188–196.

Durkin, K., & Conti-Ramsden, G. (2007). Language, social behavior, and the quality of friendships in adolescents with and without a history of specific language impairment. *Child Development, 78*, 1441–1457.

Echols, C. H., Crowhurst, M. J., & Childers, J. B. (1997). Perception of rhythmic units in speech by infants and adults. *Journal of Memory and Language, 36*, 202–225.

Edwards, J., Beckman, M. E., & Munson, B. (2004). The interaction between vocabulary size and phonotactic probability effects on children's production accuracy and fluency in nonword repetition. *Journal of Speech, Language, and Hearing Research, 47*, 421–436.

Ehri, L. C. (2000). Learning to read and learning to spell: Two sides of a coin. *TLD, 20*(3), 19–36.

Ehri, L. C., & McCormick, S. (1998). Phases of word learning: Implications for instruction with delayed and disabled readers. *Reading and Writing Quarterly, Overcoming Learning Difficulties, 14*, 135–163.

Eilers, R., Oller, D. K., Levine, S., Basinger, D., Lynch, M. P., & Urbano, R. (1993). The role of prematurity and socioeconomic status in the onset of canonical babbling in infants. *Infant Behavior and Development, 16*, 297–315.

Eisenberg, S. (1997). Investigating children's language: A comparison of conversational sampling and elicited production. *Journal of Psycholinguistic Research, 26*, 519–538.

Elbers, M. (1990). Language acquisition: Blends, overgeneralization and self-produced input. In P. Coopman, B., Shouten, & W. Lonneveld (Eds.), *OTS Yearbook 1990*. Dordrecht: ICG.

Elias, G., & Broerse, J. (1996). Developmental changes in the incidence and likelihood of simultaneous talk during the first two years: A question of function. *Journal of Child Language, 23*, 201–217.

Ellis Weismer, S., & Hesketh, L. (1996). Lexical learning by children with specific language impairments: Effects on linguistic input presented at varying speaking rates. *Journal of Speech, Language, and Hearing Research, 39,* 177–190.

Ellis Weismer, S., Evans, J., & Hesketh, L. J. (1999). An examination of verbal working memory capacity in children with specific language impairment. *Journal of Speech, Language, and Hearing Research, 42,* 1249–1260.

Elman, J. L. (1993). Learning and development in neural networks: The importance of starting small. *Cognition, 48,* 71–99.

Elman, J. L. (1999). Origins of language: A conspiracy theory. In B. MacWhinney (Ed.), *The emergence of language.* Hillsdale, NJ: Lawrence Erlbaum Associates.

Elman, J. L., Bates, E. A., Johnson, M. H., Karmiloff-Smith, A., Parisi, D., & Plunkett, K. (1996). *Rethinking innateness: A connectionist perspective on development.* Cambridge, MA: MIT Press.

Ely, R., & Berko Gleason, J. (2006). I'm sorry I said that: Apologies in young children's discourse. *Journal of Child Language, 33,* 599–620.

Emmorey, K. (1993). Processing a dynamic visual-spatial language: Psycholinguistic studies of American Sign Language. *Journal of Psycholinguistic Research, 22,* 153–187.

Engel, P. M. J., Santos, F. H., & Gathercole, S. E. (2008). Are working memory measures free of socioeconomic influence? *Journal of Speech, Language, and Hearing Research, 51,* 1580–1587.

Erhard, P., Kato, T., Strick, P. L., & Ugurbil, K. (1996). Functional MRI activation pattern of motor and language tasks in Broca's area (Abstract). *Society for Neuroscience, 22,* 260.2.

Eslea, M. (2002). *Theory of mind,* PS2200 "Virtual Lecture." http://www.uclan.ac.uk/psychology/bully/tom.htm. Last modified August 30, 2002. Accessed June 1, 2006.

Fabiano-Smith, L., & Goldstein, B. A. (2010). Phonological acquisition in bilingual Spanish–English speaking children. *Journal of Speech, Language, and Hearing Research, 53,* 160–178.

Fagan, M. K. (2009). Mean length of utterance before words and grammar: Longitudinal trends and developmental implications of infant vocalizations. *Journal of Child Language, 36,* 495–527.

Farrar, M. J. (1990). Discourse and the acquisition of grammatical morphemes. *Journal of Child Language 17,* 607–624.

Farrar, M. J. (1992). Negative evidence and grammatical morpheme acquisition. *Developmental Psychology 28,* 91–99.

Farrar, M. J., Friend, M. J., & Forbes, J. N. (1993). Event knowledge and early language acquisition. *Journal of Child Language, 20,* 591–606.

Fasold, R. W., & Wolfram, W. A. (1970). Some dialectal features of Negro dialect. In R. W. Fasold & R. W. Shuy (Eds.), *Teaching standard English in the inner city.* Washington, DC: CAL.

Fausett, L. (1994). *Fundamentals of neural networks.* Englewood Cliffs, NJ: Prentice Hall.

Felser, C., & Clahsen, H. (2009). Grammatical processing of spoken language in child and adult language learners. *Journal of Psycholinguistic Research, 38,* 305–320.

Fennell, C. T., Byers-Heinlein, K., & Werker, J. F. (2007). Using speech sounds to guide word learning: The case of bilingual infants. *Child Development, 78,* 1510–1525.

Fenson, L., Dale, P., Reznick, S., Bates, E., Thal, D., & Pethick, S. (1994). Variability in early communicative development. *Monographs of the Society for Research in Child Development, 59* (Serial No. 242)

Fernald, A. (1994). Human maternal vocalizations to infants as biologically relevant signals: An evolutionary perspective. In P. Bloom (Ed.), *Language acquisition: Core readings.* Cambridge, MA: MIT Press.

Fernald, A., & Mazzie, C. (1991). Prosody and focus in speech to infants and adults. *Developmental Psychology, 27,* 209–21.

Fernald, A., & Morikawa, H. (1993). Common themes and cultural differences in Japanese and American mothers' speech to infants. *Child Development, 64,* 637–656.

Ferrier, S., Dunham, P., & Dunham, F. (2000). The confused robot: Two-year-olds' responses to breakdowns in conversation. *Social Development, 9,* 337–347

Ferry, A. L., Hespos, S. J., & Waxman, S. R. (2010). Categorization in 3- and 4-month-old infants: An advantage of words over tones. *Child Development, 81,* 472–479.

Fiebach, C. J., Schlesewsky, M., & Friederici, A. D. (2001). Syntactic working memory and the establishment of filler-gap dependencies: Insights from ERPs and FMRI. *Journal of Psycholinguistic Research, 30,* 321–338.

Flavell, J. H., & Miller, P. H. (1991). Social cognition. In D. Kuhn & R. S. Siegler (Eds.), *Handbook of child psychology, Vol. 2: Cognition, perception, and language development* (5th ed., pp. 851–898). New York: Wiley.

Flege, J. E., MacKay, I. R., & Meador, D. (1999). Native Italian speakers' perception and production of English vowels. *Journal of Acoustical Society of America, 106,* 2973–2987.

Fodor, J. D., Ni, W., Crain, S., & Shankweiler, D. (1996). Tasks and timing in the perception of linguistic anomaly. *Journal of Psycholinguistic Research, 25,* 25–57.

Forbes, J. N., & Poulin-DuBois, D. (1997). Representational change in young children's understanding of familiar verb meaning. *Journal of Child Language, 24,* 389–406.

Fox, R. A., & Nissen, S. L. (2005). Sex-related acoustic changes in voiceless English fricatives. *Journal of Speech, Language, and Hearing Research, 48,* 753–765.

Fox, S. E., Levitt, P., & Nelson, C. A. (2010). How the timing and quality of early experiences influence the development of brain architecture. *Child Development, 81,* 28–40.

Foy, J. G., & Mann, V. (2003). Home literacy environment and phonological awareness in preschool children: Differential effects for rhyme and phoneme awareness. *Applied Psycholinguistics, 24,* 59–88.

Frackowiak, R. S. J., Friston, K. J., Frith, C. D., Dolan, R. J., Price, C. J., Zeki, S. I., et al. (2004). *Human brain function* (2nd ed.). San Diego: Academic Press.

Franco, F., & Butterworth, G. (1996). Pointing and social awareness: Declaring and requesting in the second year. *Journal of Child Language, 23,* 307–336.

Frazier, B. N., Gelman, S. A., & Wellman, H. M. (2009). Preschoolers' search for explanatory information within adult–child conversation. *Child Development, 80,* 1592–1611.

Frazier, L., Carlson, K., & Clifton, C. (2006). Prosodic phrasing is central to language comprehension. *Trends in Cognitive Science, 10,* 244–249.

Frick, J. E., Colombo, J., & Saxon, T. F. (1999). Individual and developmental differences in disengagement of fixation in early infancy. *Child Development, 70,* 537–548.

Fridriksson, J., Morrow, K. L., Moser, D., & Baylis, G. C. (2006). Age-related variability in cortical activity during language processing. *Journal of Speech, Language, and Hearing Research, 49,* 690–697.

Fridriksson, J., Moser, D., Ryalls, J., Bonilha, L., Rorden, C., & Baylis, G. (2009). Modulation of frontal lobe speech areas associated with the production and perception of speech movements. *Journal of Speech, Language, and Hearing Research, 52,* 812–819.

Frieda, E. M., Walley, A. C., Flege, J. E., & Sloane, M. E. (1999). Adults' perception of native and nonnative vowels: Implications for the perceptual magnet effect. *Perception & Psychophysics, 61,* 561–577.

Friederici, A. D. (2001). Syntactic, prosodic, and semantic processes in the brain: Evidence from event-related neuroimaging. *Journal of Psycholinguistic Research, 30,* 237–250.

Friederici, A. D. (2006). The neural basis of language development and its impairment. *Neuron, 52,* 941–952.

Friedlander, M. J., Martin, K. A. C., & Wassenhove-McCarthy, D. (1991). Effects of monocular visual deprivation on geniculocortical innervation of area 18 in cat. *Journal of Neuroscience, 11,* 3268–3288.

Frost, D. O. (1990). Sensory processing by novel, experimentally induced cross-modal circuits. *Annals of the New York Academy of Sciences, 608,* 92–109; discussion 109–112.

Furrow, D., Baillie, C., McLaren, J., & Moore, C. (1993). Differential responding to two- and three-year-olds utterances: The role of grammaticality and ambiguity. *Journal of Child Language, 20,* 363–375.

Furrow, D., Moore, C., Davidge, J., & Chiasson, L. (1992). Mental terms in mothers' and children's speech: Similarities and relationships. *Journal of Child Language, 19,* 617–631.

Galasso, J. (2003). A note on pedagogy, topics and ways of understanding child language acquisition: A working paper. http://www.csun.edu/-galasso/hoff.htm. Posted 2003. Accessed January 27, 2006.

Gardner, H., & Winner, E. (1979, May). The child is father to the metaphor. *Psychology Today,* 81–91.

Gathercole, V. (1989). Contrast: A semantic constraint? *Journal of Child Language, 16,* 685–702.

Gathercole, V., Sebastián, E., & Soto, P. (1999). The early acquisition of Spanish verbal morphology: Across-the-board or piecemeal knowledge? *International Journal of Bilingualism, 3,* 133–182.

Gaulin, C. A., & Campbell, T. F. (1994). Procedure for assessing verbal working memory in normal school-age children: Some preliminary data. *Perceptual and Motor Skills, 79,* 55–64.

Gavin, W. J., & Giles, L. (1996). Sample size effects on temporal reliability of language sample measures of preschool children. *Journal of Speech and Hearing Research, 39,* 1258–1262.

Gawlitzek-Maiwald, I., & Tracy, R. (1996). Bilingual bootstrapping. *Linguistics, 34,* 901–926.

Genesee, F. (1989). Early bilingual development: One language or two? *Journal of Child Language, 16,* 161–179.

Genesee, F., Nicoladis, E., & Paradis, J. (1995). Language differentiation in early bilingual development. *Journal of Child Language, 22,* 611–631.

Genesee, F., Paradis, J., & Crago, M. (2004). *Dual language development and disorders.* Baltimore, MD: Paul H. Brookes.

Genesee, F., & Sauve, D. (2000, March 12). *Grammatical constraints on child bilingual code-mixing.* Paper presented at the Annual Conference of the American Association for Applied Linguistics, Vancouver, Canada.

Gergely, G., Nadasdy, Z., Csibra, G., & Biro, S. (1995). Taking the intentional stance at 12 months of age. *Cognition, 56,* 165–193.

Gerken, L. (1996). Prosody's role in language acquisition and adult parsing. *Journal of Psycholinguistic Research, 25,* 345–356.

Gerken, L., & Asline, R. N. (2005). Thirty years of research on infant speech perception: The legacy of Petter W. Jusczyk. *Language Learning and Development, 1,* 5–21.

Gershkoff-Stowe, L., & Hahn, E. R. (2007). Fast mapping skills in the developing lexicon. *Journal of Speech, Language, and Hearing Research, 50,* 682–697.

Gertner, B. L., Rice, M. L., & Hadley, P. A. (1994). Influence of communicative competence on peer preferences in a preschool classroom. *Journal of Speech and Hearing Research, 37,* 913–923.

Ghera, M., Marshall, P., Fox, N., Zeanah, C., Nelson, C. A., & Smyke, A. (2009). Social deprivation and young institutionalized children's attention and expression of positive affect: Effects of a foster care intervention. *Journal of Child Psychology and Psychiatry, 50*, 253–256.

Gildersleeve-Neumann, C., Kester, E., Davis, B., & Peña, E. (2008). English speech sound development in preschool-aged children from bilingual Spanish-English environments. *Language, Speech, and Hearing Services in Schools, 39*, 314–328.

Gillam, R. B., & Gorman, B. K. (2004). Language and discourse contributions to word recognition and text interpretation. In E. R. Silliman & L. C. Wilkinson (Eds.), *Language and literacy learning in schools* (pp. 63–97). New York: Guilford.

Gillam, R. B., & Johnston, J. R. (1992). Spoken and written language relationships in language/learning-impaired and normal achieving school-age children. *Journal of Speech and Hearing Research, 35*, 1303–1315.

Gindis, B. (1999). Language-related issues for international adoptees and adoptive families. In T. Tepper, L. Hannon, & D. Sandstrom (Eds.), *International adoption: Challenges and opportunities* (pp. 98–107). Meadowlands, PA: First Edition.

Ginsberg, G., & Kilbourne, B. (1988). Emergence of vocal alternation in mother–infant interchanges. *Journal of Child Language, 15*, 221–235.

Girolametto, L., & Weitzman, E. (2002). Responsiveness of child care providers in interactions with toddlers and preschoolers. *Language, Speech, and Hearing Services in Schools, 33*, 268–281.

Girolametto, L., Weitzman, E., van Lieshout, R., & Duff, D. (2000). Directiveness in teachers' language input to toddlers and preschoolers in day care. *Journal of Speech, Language, and Hearing Research, 43*, 1101–1114.

Gleitman, L. R. (1990). The structural sources of verb meaning. *Language Acquisition 1*, 3–55.

Gleitman, L. R. (1993). The structural sources of verb meanings. In P. Bloom (Ed.), *Language acquisition: Core readings.* Cambridge, MA: MIT Press.

Gleitman, L. R., & Wanner, E. (1982). Language acquisition: The state of the state of the art. In E. Wanner & L. Gleitman (Eds.), *Language acquisition: The state of the art.* Cambridge: Cambridge University Press.

Glennen, S. L. (2002). Language development and delay in internationally adopted infants and toddlers: A review. *American Journal of Speech-Language Pathology, 11*, 333–339.

Glennen, S. L. (2007). Predicting language outcomes for internationally adopted children. *Journal of Speech, Language, and Hearing Research, 50*, 529–548.

Glennen, S. L., & Masters, M. G. (2002). Typical and atypical language development in infants and toddlers adopted from Eastern Europe. *American Journal of Speech-Language Pathology, 11*, 417–433.

Glenwright, M., & Pexman, P. M. (2010). Development of children's ability to distinguish sarcasm and verbal irony. *Journal of Child Language, 37*, 429–451.

Glezerman, T. B., & Balkoski, V. (1999). *Language, thought and the brain.* New York: Kluwer Academic.

Goffman, L., Smith, A., Heisler, L., & Ho, M. (2008). The breadth of coarticulatory units in children and adults. *Journal of Speech, Language, and Hearing Research, 51*, 1424–1437.

Gogate, L. J., & Bahrick, L. E. (1998). Intersensory redundancy facilitates learning of arbitrary relations between vowel sounds and objects in 7-month-old infants. *Journal of Experimental Child Psychology, 69*(2), 133–49.

Gogate, L. J., Bolzani, L. E., & Betancourt, E. (2006). Attention to maternal multimodal naming by 6- to 8-month-old infants and learning of word-object relations. *Infancy, 9*(3), 259–88.

Goldberg, A. E. (1995). *Constructions: A construction grammar approach to argument structure.* Chicago: The University of Chicago Press.

Goldberg, A. E. (2006). *Constructions at work: The nature of generalization in language.* Oxford: Oxford University Press.

Golder, C., & Coirier, P. (1994). Argumentative text writing: Developmental trends. *Discourse processes, 18*, 187–210.

Goldfield, B. A. (1993). Noun bias in maternal speech to one-year-olds. *Journal of Child Language, 20*, 85–99.

Goldfield, B. A. (2000). Nouns before verbs in comprehension vs. production: The view from pragmatics. *Journal of Child Language, 27*, 501–520.

Goldfield, B. A., & Reznick, J. (1990). Early lexical acquisitions: Rate, content, and the vocabulary spurt. *Journal of Child Language, 17*, 171–183.

Goldin-Meadow, S. (2003). *Hearing gesture: How our hands help us think.* Cambridge, MA: Harvard University Press.

Goldin-Meadow, S. (2005). *The resilience of language.* New York: Psychology Press.

Goldin-Meadow, S., Nusbaum, H., Kelly, S. D., & Wagner, S. (2001). Explaining math: Gesturing lightens the load. *Psychological Science, 12*, 516–522.

Goldin-Meadow, S., & Wagner, S. M. (2005). How our hands help us learn. *Trends in Cognitive Sciences, 9*, 234–241.

Goldstein, B. A., Fabiano, L., & Swasey Washington, P. (2005). Phonological skills in predominantly English-speaking, predominantly Spanish-speaking, and Spanish-English bilingual children. *Language, Speech, and Hearing Services in Schools, 36*, 201–218.

Goldstein, B. A., & Iglesias, A. (1996). Phonological patterns in normally developing Spanish-speaking 3- and 4-year-olds of Puerto Rican descent. *Language, Speech, and Hearing Services in Schools, 27*, 82–89.

Goldstein, B., & Washington, P. S. (2001). An initial investigation of phonological patterns in typically developing 4-year-old Spanish-English bilingual children. *Language, Speech, and Hearing Services in Schools, 32*, 153–164.

Goldstein, M. H., Schwade, J. A., & Bornstein, M. H. (2009). The value of vocalizing: Five-month-old infants associate their own noncry vocalizations with responses from caregivers. *Child Development, 80*, 636–644.

Golinkoff, R. M. (1993). When is communication a "meeting of the minds"? *Journal of Child Language, 20*, 199–207.

Golinkoff, R. M., Mervis, C. B., & Hirsh-Pasek, K. (1994). Early object labels: The case for a developmental lexical principles framework. *Journal of Child Language, 21*, 135–155.

Gombert, J. E. (1992). *Metalinguistic development.* London: Harvester Wheatsheaf.

Gomez, R. (2002). Variability and detection of invariant structure. *Psychological Science, 13*(5), 431–436.

Goodglass, H., & Lindfield, K. C., & Alexander, M. P. (2000). Semantic capacities of the right hemisphere as seen in two cases of pure word blindness. *Journal of Psycholinguistic Research, 29*, 399–422.

Goodglass, H., & Wingfield, A. (1998). The changing relationship between anatomic and cognitive explanation in the neuropsychology of language. *Journal of Psycholinguistic Research, 27*, 147–165.

Goodman, J. C., Dale, P. S., & Li, P. (2008). Does frequency count? Parental input and the acquisition of vocabulary. *Journal of Child Language, 35*, 515–531.

Goodsitt, J. V., Morgan, J. L., & Kuhl, P. K. (1993). Perceptual strategies in prelingual speech segmentation. *Journal of Child Language, 20*, 229–252.

Gopnik, A., & Choi, S. (1995). Names, relational words, and cognitive development in English and Korean speakers: Nouns are not always learned before verbs. In M. Tomasello & W. E. Merriman (Eds.), *Beyond names for things: Young children's acquisition of verbs* (pp. 63–80). Hillsdale, NJ: Lawrence Erlbaum Associates.

Gordon, N. (2000). The acquisition of a second language [Review]. *European Journal of Pediatric Neurology, 4*, 3–7.

Gottardo, A., Stanovich, K. E., & Siegel, L. S. (1996). The relationships between phonological sensitivity, syntactic processing, and verbal working memory in the reading performance of third-grade children. *Journal of Experimental Child Psychology, 63*, 563–582.

Gottfried, G. M. (1997). Using metaphors as modifiers: Children's production of metaphoric compounds. *Journal of Child Language, 24*, 567–601.

Gow, D. W., & Gordon, P. C. (1993). Coming to terms with stress: Effects of stress location in sentence processing. *Journal of Psycholinguistic Research, 22*, 545–578.

Graham, S., & Harris, K. R. (1996). Addressing problems in attention, memory, and executive functioning: An example from self-regulated strategy development. In G. Reid Lyon & N. A. Krasnegor (Eds.), *Attention, memory, and executive function* (pp. 349–365). Baltimore, MD: Paul H. Brookes.

Graham, S., & Harris, K. R. (1997). Self-regulation and writing: Where do we go from here? *Contemporary Educational Psychology, 22*, 102–114.

Grassmann, S., & Tomasello, M. (2007). Two-year-olds use primary sentence accent to learn new words. *Journal of Child Language, 34*, 677–687.

Graziano-King, J., & Smith Cairns, H. (2005). Acquisition of English comparative adjectives. *Journal of Child Language, 32*, 345–373.

Green, J. R., & Wilson, E. M. (2006). Spontaneous facial motility in infancy: A 3D kinematic analysis. *Developmental Psychobiology, 48*, 16–28.

Gregory, M. E., & Waggoner, J. E. (1996). Factors that influence metaphor comprehension skills in adulthood. *Experimental Aging Research, 22*, 83–98.

Grice, H. (1975). Logic and conversation. In D. Davidson & G. Harmon (Eds.), *The logic of grammar.* Encino, CA: Dickenson Press.

Grigos, M. I., & Patel, R. (2007). Articulator movement associated with the development of prosodic control in children. *Journal of Speech, Language, and Hearing Research, 50*, 119–130.

Groome, D. (1999). *An introduction to cognitive psychology: Processes and disorders.* London, UK: Psychological Press Ltd.

Grossman, A. W., Churchill, J., McKinney, B. C., Kodish, I. M., Otte, S. L., & Greenough, W. T. (2003). Experience effects on brain development: Possible contributions to psychopathology. *Journal of Child Psychology and Psychiatry, 44*, 33–63.

Grunwell, P. (1981). The development of phonology. *First Language, 2*, 161–191.

Guion, S. G., Flege, J. E., Akahane-Yamada, R., & Pruitt, J. C. (2000). An investigation of current models of second language speech perception: The case of Japanese adults' perception of English consonants. *Journal of the Acoustical Society of America, 107*, 2711–2724.

Guo, L.-Y. (2009). *Acquisition of auxiliary and copula be in young English-speaking children.* Unpublished doctoral dissertation, University of Iowa.

Guo, L.-Y., Owen, A. J., & Tomblin, J. B. (2010). Effect of Subject Types on the Production of Auxiliary Is in Young English-Speaking Children. Journal of Speech, Language and Hearing Research, 53, 1720-1743.

Guo, L.-Y. (2011). Personal communication.

Guttierrez-Clellen, V. F. (1998). Syntactic skills of Spanish-speaking children with low school achievement.

Language, Speech, and Hearing Services in Schools, 29, 207–215.

Guttierrez-Clellan, V. F., & Heinrichs-Ramos, L. (1993). Referential cohesion in the narratives of Spanish-speaking children: A developmental study. *Journal of Speech and Hearing Research, 36,* 559–567.

Guttierrez-Clellan, V. F., & McGrath, A. (1991). *Syntactic complexity in Spanish narratives: A developmental study.* Paper presented at the annual convention of the American Speech-Language-Hearing Association, Atlanta, GA.

Haaf, W. L. (1996, March 11). Ohio researchers find better language skills in preschoolers from single parent homes. *Advance for Speech-Language Pathologists and Audiologists,* 5.

Haas, A., & Owens, R. (1985). *Preschoolers' pronoun strategies: You and me make us.* Paper presented at the annual convention of the American Speech-Language-Hearing Association.

Hadley, P. A. (1999). Validating a rate-based measure of early grammatical abilities: Unique syntactic types. *American Journal of Speech-Language Pathology, 8,* 261–272.

Hakuta, K. (1987). The second language learner in the context of the study of language acquisition. In P. Homel, M. Palij, & D. Aronson (Eds.), *Childhood bilingualism: Aspects in linguistic, cognitive, and social development* (pp. 31–55) Hillsdale, NJ: Lawrence Erlbaum Associates.

Hall, D. G., Burns, T. C., & Pawluski, J. L. (2003). Input and word learning: Caregivers' sensitivity to lexical category distinctions. *Journal of Child Language, 30,* 711–729.

Hall, D. G., Corrigall, K., Rhemtulla, M., Donegan, E., & Xu, F. (2008). Infants' use of lexical-category-to-meaning links in object individuation. *Child Development, 79,* 1432–1443.

Hall, D. G., Quartz, D., & Persoage, K. (2000). Preschoolers' use of syntactic cues in word learning. *Developmental Psychology, 36,* 449–462.

Hamayan, E., & Damico, J. (1991). Developing and using a second language. In E. Hamayan & J. Damico (Eds.), *Limiting bias in the assessment of bilingual students* (pp. 40–75). Austin, TX: Pro-Ed.

Hammer, C. S., & Weiss, A. L. (1999). Guiding language development: How African American mothers and their infants structure play interactions. *Journal of Speech, Language, and Hearing Research, 42,* 1219–1233.

Hammock, E. A. D., & Levitt, P. (2006). The discipline of neurobehavioral development: The emerging interface that builds processes and skills. *Human Development, 49,* 294–309.

Hampson, J. (1989). *Elements of style: Maternal and child contributions to the referential and expressive styles of language acquisition.* Unpublished doctoral dissertation, City University of New York.

Hampson, J., & Nelson, K. (1993). The relation of maternal language to variation in rate and style of language acquisition. *Journal of Child Language, 20,* 313–342.

Hane, A. A., Feldstein, S., & Dernetz, V. H. (2003). The relation between coordinated interpersonal timing and maternal sensitivity in four-month-olds. *Journal of Psycholinguistic Research, 32,* 525–539.

Hardin, E. E., O'Connell, D. C., & Kowal, S. (1998). Reading aloud from logographic and alphabetic texts: Comparisons between Chinese and German. *Journal of Psycholinguistic Research, 27,* 413–439.

Harlaar, N., Hayiou-Thomas, M. E., Dale, P. S., & Plomin, R. (2008). Why do preschool language abilities correlate with later reading? A twin study. *Journal of Speech, Language, and Hearing Research, 51,* 688–705.

Harris, M., Barrett, M., Jones, D., & Brookes, S. (1988). Linguistic input and early word meanings. *Journal of Child Language, 15,* 77–94.

Harris, M., Yeeles, C., Chasin, J., & Oakley, Y. (1995). Symmetries and asymmetries in early lexical comprehension and production. *Journal of Child Language, 22,* 1–18.

Harrison, L. J., & McLeod, S. (2010). Risk and protective factors associated with speech and language impairment in a nationally representative sample of 4- to 5-year-old children. *Journal of Speech, Language, and Hearing Research, 53,* 508–529.

Hart, B., & Risley, T. R. (1995). *Meaningful differences in the everyday experience of young American children.* Baltimore, MD: Paul H. Brookes.

Hartsuiker, R., & Kolk, H. (2001). Error monitoring in speech production: A computational test of the perceptual loop theory. *Cognitive Psychology, 42,* 113–157.

Hashimoto, N., McGregor, K. K., & Graham, A. (2007). Conceptual organization at 6 and 8 years of age: Evidence from the semantic priming of object decisions. *Journal of Speech, Language, and Hearing Research, 50,* 161–176.

Hayes, P. A., Norris, J., & Flaitz, J. R. (1998). A comparison of the oral narrative abilities of underachieving and high-achieving gifted adolescents: A preliminary investigation. *Language, Speech, and Hearing Services in Schools, 29,* 158–171.

Hayiou-Thomas, M. E., Harlaar, N., Dale, P. S., & Plomin, R. (2010). Preschool speech, language skills, and reading at 7, 9, and 10 years: Etiology of the relationship. *Journal of Speech, Language, and Hearing Research, 53,* 311–332.

Hayiou-Thomas, M. E., Kovas, Y., Harlaar, N., Plomin, R., Bishop, D. V. M., & Dale, P. S. (2006). Common aetiology for diverse language skills in 4½-year-old twins. *Journal of Child Language, 33,* 339–368.

Hazan, V., & Barret, S. (2000). The development of phonemic categorization in children aged 6–12. *Journal of Phonetics, 28,* 377–396.

Hebb, D. (1949). *The organization of behavior.* New York: Wiley.

Heimann, M., Strid, K., Smith, L., Tjus, T., Ulvund, S. E., & Meltzoff, A. N. (2006). Exploring the relation between memory, gestural communication, and the emergence of language in infancy: A longitudinal study. *Infant and Child Development, 15,* 233–249.

Henderson, E. H. (1990). *Teaching spelling* (2nd ed.). Boston: Houghton Mifflin.

Hensch, T. K. (2005). Critical period mechanisms in developing visual cortex. *Current Topics in Developmental Biology, 69,* 215–237.

Hewlett, N. (1990). Processes of development and production. In P. Grunwell (Ed.), *Developmental speech disorders* (pp. 15–38). Edinburgh, UK: Churchill.

Hickey, T. (1993). Identifying formulas in first language acquisition. *Journal of Child Language, 20,* 27–41.

Hickman, M., Hendriks, H., Roland, F., & Liang, J. (1996). The marking of new information in children's narratives: A comparison of English, French, German, and Mandarin Chinese. *Journal of Child Language, 23,* 591–619.

Hickmann, M. (2003). *Children's discourse: Person, space, and time across languages.* Cambridge, UK: Cambridge University Press.

Hickok, G. (2001). Functional anatomy of speech perception and speech production: Psycholinguistic implications. *Journal of Psycholinguistic Research, 30,* 225–235.

Hirsh-Pasek, K., & Golinkoff, R. M. (1991). Language comprehension: A new look at some old themes. In N. Krasnegor, D. Rumbaugh, M. Studdert-Kennedy, & R. Schiefelbusch (Eds.), *Biological and behavioral aspects of language acquisition.* Hillsdale, NJ: Lawrence Erlbaum Associates.

Hirsh-Pasek, K., & Golinkoff, R. M. (1996). *The origins of grammar: Evidence from early language comprehension.* Cambridge, MA: MIT Press.

Hirsh-Pasek, K., & Golinkoff, R. M. (Eds.). (2006). *Action meets word. How children learn verbs.* Oxford, UK: Oxford University Press.

Hoff, E., & Naigles, L. (2002). How children use input to acquire a lexicon. *Child Development, 73,* 418–33.

Hoff-Ginsberg, E. (1990). Maternal speech and the child's development of syntax: A further look. *Journal of Child Language, 17,* 85–99.

Hoffner, C., Cantor, J., & Badzinski, D. (1990). Children's understanding of adverbs denoting degree of likelihood. *Journal of Child Language, 17,* 217–231.

Hogan, T., & Catts, H. W. (2004). *Phonological awareness test items: Lexical and phonological characteristics affect performance.* Paper presented at the Annual Convention of the American Speech-Language-Hearing Association, Philadelphia.

Hogan, T. P., Catts, H. W., & Little, T. D. (2005). The relationship between phonological awareness and reading: Implications for the assessment of phonological awareness. *Language, Speech, and Hearing Services in Schools, 36,* 285–293.

Hollich, G., Hirsh-Pasek, K., & Michnick Golinkoff, R. M. (2000). Breaking the language barrier: An emergentist coalition model for the origins of word learning. *Monographs of the Society for Research in Child Development, 65* (3, Serial No. 262).

Horn, G. (2004). Pathways of the past: The imprint of memory. *Nature Reviews Neuroscience, 5,* 108–120.

Hornstein, D., & Lightfoot, N. (1981). *Explanation in linguistics.* London: Longman.

Houston-Price, C., Plunkett, K., & Harris, P. (2005). Word-learning wizardry at 1;6. *Journal of Child Language, 32,* 175–189.

Howard, A. A., Mayeux, L., & Naigles, L. R. (2008). Conversational correlates of children's acquisition of mental verbs and a theory of mind. *First Language, 28,* 375–402.

Hudson Kam, C. L., & Edwards, N. A. (2008). The use of *uh* and *um* by 3- and 4-year-old native English-speaking children: Not quite right but not completely wrong. *First Language, 28,* 313–327.

Hughes, C., & Dunn, J. (1998). Understanding mind and emotion: Longitudinal associations with mental state talk between young friends. *Developmental Psychology, 34,* 1026–1037.

Hughes, M., & Searle, D. (1997). *The violet E and other tricky sounds: Learning to spell from kindergarten to grade 6.* York, ME: Stenhouse.

Hurtado, N., Marchman, V. A., & Fernald, A. (2007). Spoken word recognition by Latino children learning Spanish as their first language. *Journal of Child Language, 33,* 227–249.

Huttenlocher, J., Haight, W., Bryk, A., Seltzer, M., & Lyons, T. (1991). Early vocabulary growth: Relation to language input and gender. *Developmental Psychology, 27,* 236–248.

Huttenlocher, P. R., & Dabholkar, A. S. (1997). Regional differences in synaptogenesis in human cerebral cortex. *Journal of Comparative Neurology, 387,* 167–178.

Ibrahim, R., Eviatar, Z., & Aharon-Peretz, J. (2007). Metalinguistic awareness and reading performance: A cross language comparison. *Journal of Psycholinguistic Research, 36,* 297–318.

Imai, M., & Haryu, E. (2001). Learning proper nouns and common nouns without clues from syntax. *Child Development, 72,* 787–802.

Imai, M., Li, L., Haryu, E., Okada, H., Hirsh-Pasek, K., Michnick Golinkoff, R., & Shigematsu, J. (2008). Novel noun and verb learning in Chinese-, English-, and Japanese-speaking children. *Child Development, 79,* 979–1000.

Ingram, D. (1976). *Phonological disability in children.* London: Arnold.

Ingram, D. (1986). Phonological development: Production. In P. Fletcher & M. Garman (Eds.), *Language acquisition* (2nd ed.). New York: Cambridge University Press.

Isaacs, G. J. (1996). Persistence of non-standard dialect in school-age children. *Journal of Speech and Hearing Research, 39*, 434–441.

Iverson, J. M. (2010). Developing language in a developing body: The relationship between motor development and language development. *Journal of Child Language, 37*, 229–261.

Jackson-Maldonado, D., Thal, D., Marchman, V., Bates, E., & Gutierrez-Clellan, V. (1993). Early lexical development in Spanish-speaking infants and toddlers. *Journal of Child Language, 20*, 523–549.

Jaeger, J. J., Lockwood, A. H., Kemmerer, D. L., Van Valin, R. D., & Murphy, B. W. (1996). A positron emission tomographic study of regular and irregular verb morphology in English. *Language, 72*, 451–497.

Jafee, J., Beebe, B., Feldstein, S., Crown, C. L., & Jasnow, M. D. (2001). Rhythms of dialogue in infancy. *Monographs of the Society for Research in Child Development*, Serial No. 265, 66, No. 2.

Jia, G., & Aaronson, D. (2003). A longitudinal study of Chinese children and adolescents learning English in the United States. *Applied Psycholinguistics, 24*, 131–161.

Jia, G., Aaronson, D., & Wu, Y. (2002). Long-term language attainment of bilingual immigrants: Predictive variables and language group differences. *Applied Psycholinguistics, 23*, 599–621.

Joanette, Y., & Brownell, H. H. (Eds.). (1990). *Discourse ability and brain damage:* Theoretical and empirical perspectives. New York: Springer-Verlag.

Johnson, B. W., & Fey, M. E. (2006). Interaction of lexical and grammatical aspect in toddlers' language. *Journal of Child Language, 33*, 419–435.

Johnson, C. J., & Anglin, J. M. (1995). Qualitative developments in the content and form of children's definitions. *Journal of Speech and Hearing Research, 38*, 612–629.

Johnson, J. R., & Wong, M. Y. (2002). Cultural differences in beliefs and practices concerning talk to children. *Journal of Speech, Language, and Hearing Research, 45*, 916–926.

Johnson, M. K. (1998). Brain and cognitive development in infancy. In L. R. Squire & S. M. Kosslyn (Eds.), *Findings and current opinion on cognitive neuroscience* (pp. 345–352). Cambridge, MA: MIT Press.

Johnson, N. S. (1983). What do you do when you can't tell the whole story? The development of summarization skills. In K. E. Nelson (Ed.), *Children's language* (Vol. 4; pp. 315–383). Hillsdale, NJ: Lawrence Erlbaum Associates.

Johnson, V. E. (2005). Comprehension of third person singular /s/ in AAE-speaking children. *Language, Speech, and Hearing Services in Schools, 36*, 116–124.

Joiner, C. (F. Supp. 1979). *Martin Luther King Junior Elementary School vs. Ann Arbor School District*, 1371–1391.

Jones, E. G. (2000). Cortical and subcortical contributions to activity-dependent plasticity in primate somatosensory cortex. *Annual Review of Neuroscience, 23*, 1–37.

Junker, D. A., & Stockman, I. J. (2002). Expressive vocabulary of German-English bilingual toddlers. *American Journal of Speech-Language Pathology, 11*, 381–394.

Jusczyk, P. W. (1999, September 30). *Making sense of sounds: Foundations of language acquisition.* Presentation at State University of New York, Geneseo.

Jusczyk, P. W., & Hohne, E. A. (1997). Infants' memory for spoken words. *Science, 277*, 1984–1986.

Jusczyk, P. W., Houston, D., & Newsome, M. (1999). The beginning of word segmentation in English-learning infants. *Cognitive Psychology, 39*, 159–207.

Jusczyk, P. W., Jusczyk, A. M., Kennedy, L. J., Schomberg, T., & Koenig, N. (1995). Young infants' retention of information about bisyllabic utterances. *Journal of Experimental Psychology: Human Perception and Performance, 21*, 822–836.

Jusczyk, P. W., Luce, P. A., & Charles-Luce, J. (1994). Infant's sensitivity to phonotactic patterns in the native language. *Journal of Memory and Language, 33*, 630–645.

Just, M., & Carpenter, P. (1992). A capacity limitation theory of comprehension: Individual differences in working memory. *Psychological Review, 99*, 122–149.

Kachru, B. B. (2005). *Asian Englishes: Beyond the canon.* Hong Kong: Hong Kong University Press.

Kaderavek, J. N., & Sulzby, E. (2000). Narrative production by children with and without specific language impairment: Oral narratives and emergent readings. *Journal of Speech, Language, and Hearing Research, 43*, 34–49.

Kamhi, A. G., & Catts, H. W. (2005). Language and reading: Convergences and divergences. In H. W. Catts & A. G. Kamhi (Eds.), *Language and reading disabilities* (2nd ed., pp. 1–25). Boston: Allyn & Bacon.

Kan, P. F., & Kohnert, K. (2005). Preschoolers learning Hmong and English: Lexical-semantic skills in L_1 and L_2. *Journal of Speech, Language, and Hearing Research, 48*, 372–383.

Kandel, E. R., & Hawkins, R. D. (1992). The biological basis of learning and individuality. *Scientific American, 266*, 40–53.

Kang, J. Y., Kim, Y.-S., & Alexander Pan, B. (2009). Five-year-olds' book talk and story retelling: Contributions of mother–child joint bookreading. *First Language, 29*, 243–265.

Karmiloff, K., & Karmiloff-Smith, A. (2001). *Pathways to language from fetus to adolescent.* Cambridge, MA: Harvard University Press.

Karmiloff-Smith, A. (1986). Some fundamental aspects of language development after age 5. In P. Fletcher &

M. Garman (Eds.), *Language acquisition* (2nd ed.). New York: Cambridge University Press.

Karrass, J., Braungart-Rieker, J. M., Mullins, J., & Lefever, J. B. (2002). Processes in language acquisition: The roles of gender, attention, and maternal encouragement of attention over time. *Journal of Child Language, 29*, 519–543.

Kärtner, J., Keller, H., & Yovsi, R. D. (2010). Mother–infant interaction during the first 3 months: The emergence of culture-specific contingency patterns. *Child Development, 81*, 540–555.

Kawamoto, A. H. (1994). One system or two to handle regulars and exceptions: How time-course of processing can inform this debate. In S. D. Lima, R. L. Corrigan, & G. K. Iverson (Eds.), *The reality of linguistic rules* (pp. 389–416). Amsterdam: John Benjamins.

Kaye, K., & Charney, R. (1981). Conversational asymmetry between mothers and children. *Journal of Child Language, 8*, 35–49.

Kay-Raining Bird, E., & Chapman, R.S. (1998). Partial representations and phonological selectivity in comprehension. *First Language, 18*, 105–127.

Kehoe, M., Trujillo, C., & Lleó, C. (2001). Bilingual phonological acquisition: An analysis of syllable structure and VOT. In K. F. Cantone & M. O. Hinzelin (Eds.), *Proceedings of the colloquium on structure, acquisition and change of grammars: Phonological and syntactic aspects* (Vol. 27, pp. 38–54). Universität Hamburg, Germany: Arbeiten zur Mehrsprachigkeit.

Kelly, S. D. (2001). Broadening the units of analysis in communication: Speech and nonverbal behaviors in pragmatic comprehension. *Journal of Child Language, 28*, 325–349.

Kemp, N., Lieven, E., & Tomasello, M. (2005). Young children's knowledge of the "determiner" and "adjective" categories. *Journal of Speech, Language, and Hearing Research, 48*, 592–609.

Kemper, R. L., & Vernooy, A. R. (1993). Metalinguistic awareness in first graders: A qualitative perspective. *Journal of Psycholinguistic Research, 22*, 41–57.

Kemper, S., Thompson, M., & Marquis, J. (2001). Longitudinal change in language production: Effects of aging and dementia on grammatical complexity and prepositional content. *Psychology and Aging, 16*, 600–614.

Keren-Portnoy, T. (2006). Facilitation and practice in verb acquisition. *Journal of Child Language, 33*, 487–518.

Killackey, H. P., Chiaia, N. L., Bennett-Clarke, C. A., Eck, M., & Rhoades, R. (1994). Peripheral influences on the size and organization of somatotopic representations in the fetal rat cortex. *Journal of Neuroscience, 14*, 1496–1506.

Kim, M., McGregor, K. K., & Thompson, C. K. (2000). Early lexical development in English- and Korean-speaking children: Language-general and language-specific patterns. *Journal of Child Language, 27*, 225–254.

Kintsch, W. (1998). *Comprehension: A paradigm for cognition.* New York: Cambridge University Press.

Kirjavainen, M., Theakston, A., & Lieven, E. (2009). Can input explain children's me-for-I errors? *Journal of Child Language, 36*, 1091–1114.

Kirkorian, H. L., Pempek, T. A., Murphy, L. A., Schmidt, M. E., & Anderson, D. R. (2009). The impact of background television on parent-child interaction. *Child Development, 80*, 1350–1359.

Kohnert, K., & Goldstein, B. (2005). Speech, language, and hearing in developing bilingual children: From practice to research. *Language, Speech, and Hearing Services in Schools, 36*, 169–171.

Kohnert, K. J., & Bates, E. (2002). Balancing bilinguals ii: Lexical comprehension and cognitive processing in children learning Spanish and English. *Journal of Speech, Language, and Hearing Research, 45*, 347–359.

Komarova, N. L., & Nowak, M. A. (2001). Natural selection of the critical period for language acquisition. *Proceedings of the Royal Society of London. Series B, Biological Sciences, 268*, 1189–1196.

Konishi, T. (1993). The semantics of grammatical gender: A cross cultural study. *Journal of Psycholinguistic Research, 22*, 519–534.

Kovarsky, D., & Maxwell, M. (1997). Rethinking the context of language in schools. *Language, Speech, and Hearing Services in Schools, 28*, 219–230.

Krause, J. C., & Braida, L. D. (2004). Acoustic properties of naturally produced clear speech at normal speaking rates. *The Journal of the Acoustical Society of America, 115*, 362–378.

Kuhl, P., & Miller, J. (1978). Speech perception by the chinchilla: Identification functions for synthetic VOT stimuli. *Journal of the Acoustical Society of America, 63*, 905–917.

Kuhl, P. K. (2004). Early language acquisition: Cracking the speech code. *Nature Reviews Neuroscience, 5*, 831–843.

Kurland, B. F., & Snow, C. E. (1997). Longitudinal measurement of growth in definitional skill. *Journal of Child Language, 24*, 603–625.

Lalonde, C., & Chandler, M. (1995). False belief understanding goes to school: On the social-emotional consequences of coming early or late to a first theory of mind. *Cognition and Emotion, 9*, 167–185.

Landau, B., Smith, L., & Jones, S. (1992). Syntactic context and the shape bias in children's and adults' lexical learning. *Journal of Memory and Language, 31*, 807–825.

Langacker, R. (1991). *Foundations of cognitive grammar, Volume 2.* Stanford, CA: Stanford University Press.

Lanza, E. (1992). Can bilingual two-year-olds code-switch? *Journal of Child Language, 19*, 633–658.

Lanza, E. (1997). *Language mixing in infant bilingualism: A sociolinguistic perspective.* Oxford, UK: Clarendon Press.

Leap, W. L. (1993). *American Indian English.* Salt Lake City: University of Utah Press.

Lee, S. S., Davis, B. L., & MacNeilage, P. F. (2008). Segmental properties of input to infants: A study of Korean. *Journal of Child Language, 35,* 591–617.

Lee, S. S., Davis, B., & MacNeilage, P. (2010). Universal production patterns and ambient language influences in babbling: A cross-linguistic study of Korean- and English-learning infants. *Journal of Child Language, 37,* 293–318.

Lee, S. S., Potamianos, A., & Naryanan, S. (1999). Acoustics of children's speech: Developmental changes of temporal and spectral parameters. *Journal of the Acoustical Society of America, 105,* 1455–1468.

Legerstee, M., Anderson, D., & Schaffer, A. (1998). Five- and eight-month-old infants recognize their faces and voices as familiar and social stimuli. *Child Development, 69,* 37–50.

Lenneberg, E. (1967). *Biological foundations of language.* New York: Wiley.

Lennox, C., & Siegel, L. S. (1996). The development of phonological rules and visual strategies in average and poor spellers. *Journal of Experimental Child Psychology, 62,* 60–83.

Leonard, L. B., Weismer, S. E., Miller, C. A., Francis, D. J., Tomblin, J. B., & Kail, R. V. (2007). Speed of processing, working memory, and language impairment in children. *Journal of Speech, Language, and Hearing Research, 50,* 408–428.

Levelt, W. J. M., & Wheeldon, L. (1994). Do speakers have access to a mental syllabary? *Cognition, 50,* 239–269.

Leventhal, T., Xue, Y., & Brooks-Gunn, J. (2006). Immigrant differences in school-age children's verbal trajectories: A look at four racial/ethnic groups. *Child Development, 77,* 1359–1374.

Levitt, A. G., & Aydelott Utman, J. G. (1992). From babbling towards the sound system of English and French: A longitudinal two-case study. *Journal of Child Language, 19,* 19–49.

Levitt, A. G., Utman, J., & Aydelott, J. (1993). From babbling towards the sound systems of English and French: A longitudinal two-case study. *Journal of Child Language, 19,* 19–49.

Levorato, M. C., & Cacciari, C. (1992). Children's comprehension of production of idioms: The role of context and familiarity. *Journal of Child Language, 19,* 415–433.

Levy, E., & Nelson, K. (1994). Words in discourse: A dialectal approach to the acquisition of meaning and use. *Journal of Child Language, 21,* 367–389.

Lewis, D. J., & Windsor, J. (1996). Children's analysis of derivational suffix meaning. *Journal of Speech and Hearing Research, 39,* 209–216.

Lewis, M., & Freedle, R. (1973). Mother-infant dyad: The cradle of meaning. In P. Pilner, L. Kranes, & T. Alloway (Eds.), *Communication and affect: Language and thought.* New York: Academic Press.

Lewis, R. L. (1996). Interference in short-term memory: The magical number two (or three) in sentence processing. *Journal of Psycholinguistic Research, 25,* 93–121.

Li, P., & Shirai, Y. (2000). *The acquisition of lexical and grammatical aspect.* New York: Mouton de Gruyter.

Lieven, E., Behrens, H., Speares, J., & Tomasello, M. (2003). Early syntactic creativity: A usage-based approach. *Journal of Child Language, 30,* 333–370.

Lieven, E., & Pine, J. M. (1990). Review of E. Bates, I. Bretherton, & L. J. Snyder, From first words to grammar: Individual differences and dissociable mechanisms. *Journal of Child Language, 17,* 495–501.

Lieven, E. V. M., Pine, J. M., & Baldwin, G. (1997). Lexically based learning and early grammatical development. *Journal of Child Language, 24,* 187–219.

Lillo-Martin, D. (1991). *Universal grammar and American Sign Language: Setting the null argument parameters.* Dordrecht, The Netherlands: Kluwer.

Lin, E. L., & Murphy, G. L. (2001). Thematic relations in adults' concepts. *Journal of Experimental Psychology: General, 130,* 3–28.

Lindner, K., & Hohenberger, A. (2009). Introduction: Concepts of development, learning, and acquisition. *Linguistics, 47*(2), 211–239.

Lisker, L., & Abramson, A. (1965). Voice onset time in the production and perception of English stops. *Speech Research, Haskins Laboratories, 1.*

Liszkowski, U. (2005). Human twelve-month-olds point cooperatively to share interest with and provide information for a communicative partner. *Gesture, 5,* 135–154.

Liszkowski, U. (2006). Infant pointing at twelve months: Communicative goals, motives, and social-cognitive abilities. In N. Enfield & S. Levinson (Eds.), *The roots of human sociality: Culture, cognition, and interaction* (pp. 153–178). Oxford, UK: Berg.

Liszkowski, U., Carpenter, M., Henning, A., Striano, T., & Tomasello, M. (2004). Twelve-month-olds point to share attention and interest. *Developmental Science, 7,* 297–307.

Liszkowski, U., Carpenter, M., & Tomasello, M. (2007). Reference and attitude in infant pointing. *Journal of Child Language, 34,* 1–20.

Lively, S. E., Pisoni, D. B., & Goldinger, S. D. (1994). Spoken word recognition: Research and theory. In M. A. Gernsbacher (Ed.), *Handbook of psycholinguistics* (pp. 265–301). New York: Academic Press.

Lleó, C., Kuchenbrandt, I., Kehoe, M., & Trujillo, C. (2003). Syllable final consonants in Spanish and German monolingual and bilingual acquisition. In N. Müller (Ed.), *(In)vulnerable domains in multilingualism* (pp. 191–220). Amsterdam: John Benjamins.

Lleó, C., & Prinz, M. (1996). Consonant clusters in child phonology and the directionality of syllable structure assignment. *Journal of Child Language, 23*, 31–56.

Lloyd, P., & Banham, L. (1997). Does drawing attention to the referent constrain the way in which children construct verbal messages? *Journal of Psycholinguistic Research, 26*, 509–518.

Locke, J. L. (1996). Why do infants begin to talk? Language as an unintended consequence. *Journal of Child Language, 23*, 251–268.

Logan, K. J. (2003). Language and fluency characteristic of preschoolers' multiple-utterance conversational turns. *Journal of Speech, Language, and Hearing Research, 46*, 178–188.

Lohmann, H., & Tomasello, M. (2003). The role of language in the development of false belief understanding: A training study. *Child Development, 74*, 1130–1144.

Love, R., & Webb, W. (1986). *Neurology for the speech-language pathologist.* Boston: Butterworth's.

Lucariello, J. (1990). Freeing talk from the here-and-now: The role of event knowledge and maternal scaffolds. *Topics in Language Disorders, 10*(3), 14–29.

MacDonald, G. W., & Cornwall, A. (1995). The relationship between phonological awareness and reading and spelling achievement eleven years later. *Journal of Learning Disabilities, 28*, 523–527.

MacWhinney, B. (1998). Models of the emergence of language. *Annual Review of Psychology, 49*, 199–227.

MacWhinney, B. (2002). Language emergence. In P. Burmeister, T. Piske, & A. Rohde (Eds.), *An integrated view of language development—Papers in honor of Henning Wode* (pp. 17–42). Trier, Germany: Wissenshaftliche Verlag.

MacWhinney, B. (2004). A multiple process solution to the logical problem of language acquisition. *Journal of Child Language, 31*, 883–914.

Majdan, M., & Shatz, C. J. (2006). Effects of visual experience on activity-dependent gene regulation in cortex. *Nature Neuroscience, 9*, 650–659.

Mandel, D. R., Jusczyk, P. W., & Kemler Nelson, D. G. (1994). Does sentence prosody help infants to organize and remember speech information? *Cognition, 33*, 155–180.

Mandel, D. R., Jusczyk, P. W., & Pisoni, D. B. (1995). Infants' recognition of the sound patterns of their own names. *Psychological Science, 6*, 315–318.

Maneva, B., & Genesee, F. (2002). Bilingual babbling: Evidence for language differentiation in dual language acquisition. In B. Skarabela et al. (Eds.), *The proceedings of the 26th Boston University Conference on Language Development* (pp. 383–392). Somerville, MA: Cascadilla Press.

Marchman, V. A., & Bates, E. (1991). *Vocabulary size and composition as predictors of morphological development.* Technical Report No. 9103, Center for Research in Language, University of California, San Diego.

Marchman, V. A., & Bates, E. (1994). Continuity in lexical and morphological development: A test of the critical mass hypothesis. *Journal of Child Language, 21*, 339–366.

Marcus, G. F. (1995). Children's overgeneralization of English plurals: A quantitative analysis. *Journal of Child Language, 22*, 447–459.

Marcus, G. F. (2001). *The algebraic mind.* Cambridge, MA: MIT Press.

Marcus, G. F., Pinker, S., Ullman, M., Hollander, M., Rosen, T. J., & Xu, F. (1992). Overregularization in language acquisition. *Monographs of the Society for Research in Child Development, 57.*

Marinellie, S. A. (2010). The understanding of word definitions in school-age children. *Journal of Psycholinguistic Research, 39*, 179–198.

Marinellie, S. A., & Johnson, C. J. (2003). Adjective definitions and the influence of word frequency. *Journal of Speech, Language, and Hearing Research, 46*, 1061–1076.

Marini, A., Boewe, A., Caltagirone, C., & Carlomagno, S. (2005). Age-related differences in the production of textual descriptions. *Journal of Psycholinguistic Research, 34*, 439–464.

Markman, E. M. (1992). The whole object, taxonomic, and mutual exclusivity assumptions as initial constraints on word meanings. In J. P. Byrnes & S. A. Gelman (Eds.), *Perspectives on language and cognition: Interrelations in development.* New York: Cambridge University Press.

Masataka, N. (1993). Effects of contingent and noncontingent maternal stimulation on the vocal behavior of three- to four-month-old Japanese infants. *Journal of Child Language, 20*, 303–312.

Masataka, N. (1995). The relation between index-finger extension and the acoustic quality of cooing in three-month-old infants. *Journal of Child Language, 22*, 247–257.

Mashburn, A. J., Justice, L. M., Downer, J. T., & Pianta, R. C. (2009). Peer effects on children's language achievement during pre-kindergarten. *Child Development, 80*, 686–702.

Masur, E. F. (1997). Maternal labelling of novel and familiar objects: Implications for children's development of lexical constraints. *Journal of Child Language, 24*, 427–439.

Masur, E. F., Flynn, V., & Eichorst, D. L. (2005). Maternal responsive and directive behaviours and utterances as predictors of children's lexical development. *Journal of Child Language, 32*, 63–91.

Mattys, S. L., & Jusczyk, P. W. (2001). Phonotactic cues for segmentation of fluent speech by infants. *Cognition, 78*, 91–121.

McCabe, A., & Bliss, L. S. (2003). *Patterns of narrative discourse: A multicultural life span approach.* Boston: Allyn & Bacon.

McCloskey, L. A. (1986). *Prosody and children's understanding of discourse.* Unpublished doctoral dissertation, University of Michigan, Ann Arbor.

McCune, L., & Vihman, M. M. (2001). Early phonetic and lexical development: A productivity approach. *Journal of Speech, Language, and Hearing Research, 44,* 670–684.

McDonald, J. L. (2008). Grammaticality judgments in children: The role of age, working memory and phonological ability. *Journal of Child Language, 35,* 247–268.

McDonald Connor, C., & Craig, H. K. (2006). African American preschoolers' language, emergent literacy skills, and use of African American English: A complex relation. *Journal of Speech, Language, and Hearing Research, 49,* 771–792.

McDowell, K. D., Lonigan, C. J., & Goldstein, H. (2007). Relations among socioeconomic status, age, and predictors of phonological awareness. *Journal of Speech, Language, and Hearing Research, 50,* 1079–1092.

McEachern, D., & Haynes, W. O. (2004). Gesture-speech combinations as a transition to multiword utterances. *American Journal of Speech-Language Pathology, 13,* 227–235.

McGregor, K. K., Friedman, R. M., Reilly, R. M., & Newman, R. M. (2002). Semantic representation and naming in young children. *Journal of Speech, Language, and Hearing Research, 45,* 332–346.

McGregor, K. K., Sheng, L., & Smith, B. (2005). The precocious two-year-old: Status of the lexicon and links to the grammar. *Journal of Child Language, 32,* 563–585.

McKee, C., McDaniel, D., & Snedeker, J. (1998). Relatives children say. *Journal of Psycholinguistic Research, 27,* 573–596.

McLean, J., & Snyder-McLean, L. (1978). *A transactional approach to early language training.* Columbus, OH: Merrill.

McLeod, S., van Doorn, J., & Reed, V. A. (2001a). Consonant cluster development in two-year-olds: General trends and individual difference. *Journal of Speech, Language, and Hearing Research, 44,* 1144–1171.

McLeod, S., van Doorn, J., & Reed, V. A. (2001b). Normal acquisition of consonant clusters. *American Journal of Speech-Language Pathology, 10,* 99–110.

McLoyd, V. C. (1998). Socioeconomic disadvantage and child development. *American Psychologist, 53,* 185–204.

McMullen, L. M., & Pasloski, D. D. (1992). Effects of communication apprehension, familiarity of partner, and topic on selected "women's language" features. *Journal of Psycholinguistic Research, 21,* 17–30.

McNeil, D. (1992). *Hand and mind: What gestures reveal about thought.* Chicago: University of Chicago Press.

Meadows, D., Elias, G., & Bain, J. (2000). Mothers' ability to identify infants' communicative acts consistently. *Journal of Child Language, 27,* 393–406.

Medin, D. L., & Ortony, A. (1989). Psychological essentialism. In S. Vosniadou & A. Ortony (Eds.), *Similarity and analogical reasoning.* Cambridge, UK: Cambridge University Press.

Mehler, J., Jusczyk, P. W., Lambertz, G., Halsted, N., Bertoncini, J., & Amiel-Tison, C. (1998). A precursor of language acquisition in young infants. *Cognition, 29,* 144–178.

Meisel, J. (1994). *Bilingual first language acquisition: French and German grammatical development.* Amsterdam: John Benjamins.

Ménard, L., Davis, B. L., Boë, L-J., & Roy, J.-P. (2009). Producing American-English vowels during vocal tract growth: A perceptual categorization study of synthesized vowels. *Journal of Speech, Language, and Hearing Research, 52,* 1268–1285.

Merriman, W. E., & Bowman, L. L. (1989). The mutual exclusivity bias in children's word learning. *Monographs of the Society for Research in Child Development* (Serial No. 20, Vol. 54).

Merriman, W. E., Marazita, J., & Jarvis, L. (1995). Children's disposition to map new words onto new referents. In M. Tomasello & W. E. Merriman (Eds.), *Beyond names for things: Young children's acquisition of verbs.* Hillsdale, NJ: Lawrence Erlbaum Associates.

Mervis, C. B. (1990). Operating principles, input, and early lexical development. *Communiczioni Scientifiche de Psicologia Generala, 4,* 31–48.

Mervis, C. B., & Bertrand, J. (1993). Acquisition of early object labels: The roles of operating principles and input. In A. P. Kaiser & D. B. Gray (Eds.), *Enhancing children's communication: Research foundations for intervention* (Vol. II). Baltimore, MD: Paul H. Brookes.

Mervis, C. B., & Bertrand, J. (1995). Early lexical acquisition and the vocabulary spurt: A response to Goldfield & Reznick. *Journal of Child Language, 22,* 461–468.

Michaels, S. (1981). "Sharing time": Children's narrative styles and differential access to literacy. *Language and Society, 10,* 423–442.

Michaels, S. (1991). The dismantling of narrative. In A. McCabe & C. Peterson (Eds.), *Developing narrative structure* (pp. 303–352) Norwood, NJ: Ablex.

Miikkulainen, R., & Dyer, M. (1991). Natural language processing with modular neural networks and distributed lexicon. *Cognitive Science, 15,* 343–399.

Miller, C. A. (2006). Developmental relationships between language and theory of mind. *American Journal of Speech-Language Pathology, 15,* 142–154.

Minami, M., & McCabe, A. (1991). Haiku as a discourse regulation device: A stanza analysis of Japanese children's personal narratives. *Language and Society, 20,* 577–599.

Minami, M., & McCabe, A. (1995). Rice balls and bear hunts: Japanese and North American family narrative patterns. *Journal of Child Language, 22,* 423–445.

Mintz, T., & Gleitman, L. (2002). Adjectives really do modify nouns: The incremental and restricted nature of early adjective acquisition. *Cognition, 84,* 267–293.

Mitchell, P., & Kent, R. (1990). Phonetic variation in multisyllabic babbling. *Journal of Child Language, 17,* 247–265.

Miura, I. (1993). Switching pauses in adult–adult and child–child turn takings: An initial study. *Journal of Psycholinguistic Research, 22,* 383–395.

Moerk, E. (1991). Positive evidence for negative evidence. *First Language, 11,* 219–251.

Montgomery, J. W. (2000b). Verbal working memory and sentence comprehension in children with specific language impairment. *Journal of Speech, Language, and Hearing Research, 43,* 293–308.

Montgomery, J. W., Magimairaj, B. M., & O'Malley, M. H. (2008). Role of working memory in typically developing children's complex sentence comprehension. *Journal of Psycholinguistic Research, 37,* 331–356.

Moon, C., Bever, T. G., & Fifer, W. P. (1992). Canonical and non-canonical syllable discrimination by two-day-old infants. *Journal of Child Language, 19,* 1–17.

Moon, C., Cooper, R. P., & Fifer, W. P. (1993). Two-day infants prefer their native language. *Infant Behavior and Development, 16,* 495–500.

Moore, C., Angelopoulos, M., & Bennett, P. (1999). Word learning in the context of referential and salience cues. *Developmental Psychology, 35,* 60–68.

Moore, C., & D'Entremont, B. (2001). Developmental changes in pointing as a function of parent's attentional focus. *Journal of Cognition and Development, 2,* 109–129.

Moore, C., Harris, L., & Patriquin, M. (1993). Lexical and prosodic cues in the comprehension of relative certainty. *Journal of Child Language, 20,* 153–167.

Morales, M., Mundy, P., Delgado, C. E. F., Yale, M., Neal, R., & Schwartz, H. K. (2000). Gaze following, temperament, and language development in 6-month-olds: A replication and extension. *Infant Behavior & Development, 23,* 231–236.

Morford, M., & Goldin-Meadow, S. (1992). Comprehension and production of gesture in combination with speech in one-word speakers. *Journal of Child Language, 19,* 559–580.

Morgan, J., & Demuth, K. (Eds.). (1996). *Signal to syntax: Bootstrapping from speech to grammar in early acquisition.* Mahwah, NJ: Lawrence Erlbaum Associates.

Morgan, J. L. (1994). Converging measures of speech segmentation in prelingual infants. *Infants' Behavior and Development, 17,* 387–400.

Morgan, J. L., & Saffran, J. R. (1995). Emerging integration of sequential and suprasegmental information in preverbal speech segmentation. *Child Development, 66,* 911–936.

Morris, B. J. (2003). Opposites attract: The role of predicate dimensionality in preschool children's processing of negations. *Journal of Child Language, 30,* 419–440.

Mundy, P., Block, J., Delgado, C., Pomares, Y., Vaughan Van Hecke, A., & Venezia Parlade, M. (2007). Individual differences and the development of joint attention in infancy. *Child Development, 78,* 938–954.

Munhall, K. G., Kawato, M., & Vatikiotis-Bateson, E. (2000). Coarticulation and physical models of speech production. In M. B. Broe & J. B. Pierrehumbert (Eds.), *Papers in laboratory phonology V: Acquisition and the lexicon* (pp. 9–28). Cambridge, UK: Cambridge University Press.

Muñoz, M. L., Gillam, R. B., Peña, E. D., & Gulley-Faehnle, A. (2003). Measures of language development in fictional narratives of Latino children. *Language, Speech, and Hearing Services in Schools, 34,* 332–342.

Munson, B. (2004). Variability /s/ production in children and adults: Evidence from dynamic measures of spectral mean. *Journal of Speech, Language, and Hearing Research, 47,* 58–69.

Munson, B., Edwards, J., & Beckman, M. E. (2005a). Phonological knowledge in typical and atypical speech-sound development. *Topics in Language Disorders, 25,* 190–206.

Munson, B., Edwards, J., & Beckman, M. E. (2005b). Relationships between nonword repetition accuracy and other measures of linguistic development in children with phonological disorders. *Journal of Speech, Language, and Hearing Research, 48,* 61–78.

Murphy, V. A., & Nicoladis, E. (2006). When answer-phone makes a difference in children's acquisition of English compounds. *Journal of Child Language, 33,* 677–691.

Murray, A., Johnson, J., & Peters, J. (1990). Fine-tuning of utterance length to preverbal infants: Effects on later language development. *Journal of Child Language, 17,* 511–525.

Myers, J., Jusczyk, P. W., Nelson, D. G. K., Charles-Luce, J., Wordward, A. L., & Hirsh-Pasek, K. (1996). Infants' sensitivity to word boundaries in fluent speech. *Journal of Child Language, 23,* 1–30.

Nagel, H. N., Shapiro, L. P., Tuller, B., & Nawy, R. (1996). Prosodic influences on the resolution of temporary ambiguity during on-line sentence processing. *Journal of Psycholinguistic Research, 25,* 319–344.

Nagy, W. E., Anderson, R. C., Schommer, M., Scott, J. A., & Stallman, A.C. (1989). Morphological families and word recognition. *Reading Research Quarterly, 24,* 262–283.

Nagy, W. E., Diakidoy, I. N., & Anderson, R. C. (1991). *The development of knowledge of derivational suffixes.* Technical Report N. 536, Center for the Study of Reading. Champaign: Univeristy of Illinois at Urbana-Champaign.

Naigles, L. (1990). Children use syntax to learn verb meanings. *Journal of Child Language, 17,* 357–374.

Naigles, L. G., & Gelman, S. A. (1995). Overextensions in comprehension and production revisited: Preferential looking in a study of dog, cat, and cow. *Journal of Child Language, 22,* 19–46.

Naigles, L. R., & Hoff-Ginsberg, E. (1998). Why are some verbs learned before other verbs? Effects of input frequency and structure on children's early verb use. *Journal of Child Language, 25,* 95–120.

Namy, L. L., & Waxman, S. R. (1998). Words and gestures: Infants' interpretations of different forms of symbolic reference. *Child Development, 69,* 295–308.

Nathan, L., Wells, B., & Donlan, C. (1998). Can children with speech difficulties process an unfamiliar accent? *Applied Psycholinguistics, 22,* 343–361.

Nation, K., & Hulme, C. (1997). Phonemic segmentation, not onset-rime segmentation, predicts early reading and spelling skills. *Reading Research Quarterly, 32*(2), 154–167.

Nation, K., & Norbury, C. F. (2005). Why reading comprehension fails: Insights into developmental disorders. *Topics in Language Disorders, 25*(1), 21–32.

National Center for Health Statistics. (2004). *Births of Hispanic parentage, 1980. Monthly Vital Statistics Report.* Washington, DC.

National Coalition for the Homeless. (1999). *Homeless families with children: National Coalition for the Homeless fact sheet #7.* Washington, DC: Author.

Nazzi, T., Bertoncini, J., & Mehler, J. (1998). Language discrimination by newborns: Towards an understanding of the role of rhythm. *Journal of Experimental Psychology: Human Perception and Performance, 24,* 756–766.

Needham, W. P. (1992). Limits on literal processing during idiom interpretation. *Journal of Psycholinguistic Research, 21,* 1–16.

Nelson, C. A., Zeanah, C. H., Fox, N. A., Marshall, P. J., Smyke, A., & Guthrie, D. (2007). Cognitive recovery in socially deprived young children: The Bucharest Early Intervention Project. *Science, 318,* 1937–1940.

Nelson, K. E. (1991). The matter of time: Interdependencies between language and concepts. In S. A. Gelman & J. P. Byrnes (Eds.), *Perspectives on language and thought: Interrelations in development.* New York: Cambridge University Press.

Nelson, K. E. (1995). The dual category problem in the acquisition of action words. In M. Tomasello & W. Merriman (Eds.), *Beyond names for things: young children's acquisition of verbs.* Hillsdale, NJ: Lawrence Erlbaum Associates.

Nelson, K. E., Hampson, J., & Shaw, L. K. (1993). Nouns in early lexicons: Evidence, explanations, & implications. *Journal of Child Language, 20,* 61–84.

Nelson, L. K., & Bauer, H. R. (1991). Speech and language production at age 2: Evidence for tradeoffs between linguistic and phonetic processing. *Journal of Speech and Hearing Research, 34,* 879–892.

Newman, A. J., Pancheva, R., Ozawa, K., Neville, H. J., & Ullman, M. T. (2001). An event-related FMRI study of syntactic and semantic violations. *Journal of Psycholinguistic Research, 30,* 339–364.

Newport, E. L. (1988). Constraints on learning and their role in language acquisition: Studies of the acquisition of American Sign Language. *Language Sciences, 10,* 147–172.

Newport, E. L. (1990). Maturational constraints on language learning. *Cognitive Science, 14,* 11–28.

Newport, E. L., Bavelier, D., & Neville, H. J. (2001). Critical thinking about critical periods: Perspectives on a critical period for language acquisition. In E. Doupoux (Ed.), *Language, brain and cognitive development: Essays in honor of Jacques Mehler* (pp. 481–502). Cambridge, MA: MIT Press.

Nguyen, S. P., & Murphy, G. L. (2003). An apple is more than just a fruit: Cross classification in children's concepts. *Child Development, 74,* 1783–1806.

NICHD Early Child Care Research Network. (2005). Duration and developmental timing of poverty and children's cognitive and social development from birth through third grade. *Child Development, 76,* 795–810.

Nicholas, M., Barth, C., Obler, L. K., Au, R., & Albert, M. J. (1997). Naming in normal aging and dementia of the Alzheimer's type. In H. Goodglass & A. Wingfield (Eds.), *Anomia: Neuroanatomical and cognitive correlates* (pp. 166–188). San Diego, CA: Academic Press.

Nicholas, M., Connor, L. T., Obler, L. K., & Albert, M. L. (1998). Aging, language, and language disorders. In M. T. Sarno (Ed.), *Acquired aphasia* (3rd ed., pp. 413–449). San Diego, CA: Academic Press.

Nicoladis, E., & Genesee, F. (1996). Word awareness in second language learners and bilingual children. *Language Awareness, 5*(2), 80–89.

Nicoladis, E., & Secco, G. (2000). Productive vocabulary and language choice. *First Language, 20*(58), 3–28.

Nicolopoulou, A., & Richner, E. S. (2007). From actors to agents to persons: The development of character representation in young children's narratives. *Child Development, 78,* 412–429.

Ninio, A. (1992). The relation of children's single word utterances to single word utterances in the input. *Journal of Child Language, 19,* 87–110.

Nip, I. S. B., Green, J. R., & Marx, D. B. (2009). Early speech motor development: Cognitive and linguistic considerations. *Journal of Communication Disorders, 42,* 286–98.

Nippold, M. A. (1991). Evaluating and enhancing idiom comprehension in language-disordered children. *Language, Speech, and Hearing Services in Schools, 22,* 100–106.

Nippold, M. A. (2007). *Later language development: School-age children, adolescents, and young adults* (3rd ed.). Austin, TX: Pro-Ed.

Nippold, M. A. (2009). School-age children talk about chess: Does knowledge drive syntactic complexity? *Journal of Speech, Language, and Hearing Research, 52,* 856–871.

Nippold, M. A., & Duthie, J. K. (2003). Mental imagery and idiom comprehension: A comparison of school-age children and adults. *Journal of Speech, Language, and Hearing Research, 46,* 788–799.

Nippold, M. A., Duthie, J. K., & Larsen, J. (2005). Literacy as a leisure activity: Free-time preferences of older children and young adolescents. *Language, Speech, and Hearing Service in Schools, 36*, 93–102.

Nippold, M. A., & Haq, F. S. (1996). Proverb comprehension in youth: The role of concreteness and familiarity. *Journal of Speech, Language, and Hearing Research, 39*, 166–176.

Nippold, M. A., Hegel, S. L., Sohlberg, M. M., & Schwarz, I. E. (1999). Defining abstract entities: development in preadolescents, adolescents, and young adults. *Journal of Speech, Language, and Hearing Research, 42*, 473–481.

Nippold, M. A., Hesketh, L. J., Duthie, J. K., & Mansfield, T. C. (2005). Conversational vs. expository discourse: A study of syntactic development in children, adolescents, and adults. *Journal of Speech, Language, and Hearing Research, 48*, 1048–1064.

Nippold, M. A., Mansfield, T. C., & Billow, J. L. (2007). Peer conflict explanations in children, adolescents, and adults: Examining the development of complex syntax. *American Journal of Speech-Language Pathology, 16*, 179–188.

Nippold, M. A., Mansfield, T. C., Billow, J. L., & Tomblin, J. B. (2008). Expository discourse in adolescents with language impairments: Examining syntactic development. *American Journal of Speech-Language Pathology, 17*, 356–366.

Nippold, M. A., Moran, C., & Schwartz, I. E. (2001). Idiom understanding in preadolescents: Synergy in action. *American Journal of Speech-Language Pathology, 10*, 169–179.

Nippold, M. A., Schwarz, I. E., & Undlin, R. (1992). Use and understanding of adverbial conjuncts: A developmental study of adolescents and young adults. *Journal of Speech and Hearing Research, 35*, 108–118.

Nippold, M. A., & Taylor, C. L. (1995). Idiom understanding in youth: Further examination of familiarity and transparency. *Journal of Speech, Language, and Hearing Research, 38*, 426–433.

Nippold, M. A., Taylor, C. L., & Baker, J. M. (1995). Idiom understanding in Australian youth: A cross-cultural comparison. *Journal of Speech, Language, and Hearing Research, 39*, 442–447.

Nippold, M. A., Uhden, L. D., & Schwarz, I. E. (1997). Proverb explanation through the lifespan: A developmental study of adolescents and adults. *Journal of Speech, Language, and Hearing Research, 40*, 245–253.

Nippold, M. A., Ward-Lonergan, J. M., & Fanning, J. L. (2005). Persuasive writing in children, adolescents, and adults: A study of syntactic, semantic, and pragmatic development. *Language, Speech, and Hearing Service in Schools, 36*, 125–138.

Nittrouer, S. (2002). From ear to cortex: A perspective on what clinicians need to understand about speech perception and language processing. *Language, Speech, and Hearing Services in Schools, 33*, 237–252.

Noel, M., Peterson, C., & Jesso, B. (2008). The relationship of parenting stress and child temperament to language development among economically disadvantaged preschoolers. *Journal of Child Language, 35*, 823–843.

Nohara, M. (1992). Sex differences in interruption: An experimental reevaluation. *Journal of Psycholinguistic Research, 21*, 127–146.

Nohara, M. (1996). Preschool boys and girls use *no* differently. *Journal of Child Language, 23*, 417–429.

Ochs, E. (1982). Talking to children in Western Samoa. *Language and Society, 11*, 77–104.

Oetting, J., & Pruitt, S. (2009). Past tense marking by African American English–speaking children reared in poverty. *Journal of Speech, Language, and Hearing Research, 52*, 2–15.

Oetting, J. B., & Wimberly Garrity, A. (2006). Variation within dialects: A case of Cajun/Creole influence within child SAAE and SWE. *Journal of Speech, Language, & Hearing Research, 49*, 16–26.

Ogura, T. (1991). A longitudinal study of the relationship between early language development and play development. *Journal of Child Language, 18*, 273–294.

Ogura, T., Dale, P. S., Yamashita, Y., Murase, T., & Mahieu, A. (2006). The use of nouns and verbs by Japanese children and their caregivers in book-reading and toy-playing contexts. *Journal of Child Language, 33*, 1–29.

O'Leary, D. D. (1993). Do cortical areas emerge from a protocortex? In M. Johnson (Ed.), *Brain Development and Cognition: A Reader* (pp. 323–337). Oxford: Blackwell.

Oller, D. (1978). Infant vocalization and the development of speech. *Allied Health and Behavior Sciences, 1*, 523–549.

Oller, D., Eilers, R. E., Urbano, R., & Cobo-Lewis, A. B. (1997). Development of precursors to speech in infants exposed to two languages. *Journal of Child Language, 24*, 407–425.

Olmstead, D. (1971). *Out of the mouths of babes*. The Hague: Mouton.

O'Neill, D. K., Main, R. M., & Ziemski, R. A. (2009). "I like Barney": Preschoolers' spontaneous conversational initiations with peers. *First Language, 29*, 401–425.

O'Neill, D. K., & Topolovec, J. C. (2000). Two-year-old children's sensitivity to the referential (in) efficacy of their own pointing gestures. *Journal of Child Language, 28*, 1–28.

O'Neill-Pirozzi, T. M. (2003). Language functioning of residents in family homeless shelters. *American Journal of Speech-Language Pathology, 12*, 220–242.

Oomen, C., & Postma, A. (2001). Effects of increased speech rate on monitoring and self-repair. *Journal of Psycholinguistic Research, 30*, 163–184.

Orsolini, M., Rossi, F., & Pontecorvo, C. (1996). Re-introduction of referents in Italian children's narratives. *Journal of Child Language, 23*, 465–486.

Osborne, J. G., & Calhoun, D. O. (1998). Themes, taxons, and trial types in children's matching to sample: Methodological considerations. *Journal of Experimental Child Psychology, 68*, 35–50.

Otomo, K. (2001). Maternal response to word approximation in Japanese children's transition to language. *Journal of Child Language, 28*, 29–57.

Ouellette, G., & Sénéchal, M. (2008). Pathways to literacy: A study of invented spelling and its role in learning to read. *Child Development, 79*, 899–913.

Owens, R. (1978). *Speech acts in the early language of non-delayed and retarded children: A taxonomy and distributional study.* Unpublished doctoral dissertation, The Ohio State University.

Özçaliskan, S., & Goldin-Meadow, S. (2005). Do parents lead their children by the hand? *Journal of Child Language, 32*, 481–505.

Ozyurek, A. (1996). How children talk about a conversation. *Journal of Child Language, 23*, 693–714.

Pallas, S. L., & Sur, M. (1993). Visual projections induced into the auditory pathway of ferrets: II. Corticocortical connections of primary auditory cortex. *Journal of Comparative Neurology, 337*(2), 317–333.

Pan, B. A., Rowe, M. L., Singer, J. D., & Snow, C. E. (2005). Maternal correlates of growth in toddler vocabulary production in low-income families. *Child Development, 76*, 763–782.

Papaeliou, C., Minadakis, G., & Cavouras, D. (2002). Acoustic patterns of infant vocalizations expressing emotions and communicative functions. *Journal of Speech, Language, and Hearing Research, 45*, 311–317.

Papaeliou, C.F., & Trevarthen, C. (2006). Prelinguistic pitch patterns expressing "communication" and "apprehension." *Journal of Child Language, 33*, 163–178.

Paradis, J. (2001). Do bilingual two-year-olds have separate phonological systems? *International Journal of Bilingualism, 5*, 19–38.

Paradis, J., & Genesee, F. (1996). Syntactic acquisition in bilingual children: Autonomous or interdependent? *Studies in Second Language Acquisition, 18*, 1–25.

Paradis, J., Nicoladis, E., & Genesee, F. (2000). Early emergence of structural constraints on code-mixing: Evidence from French-English bilingual children. *Bilingualism: Language and Cognition, 3*, 245–261.

Pascalis, O., de Haan, M., & Nelson, C. A. (2002). Is face processing species specific during the first year of life? *Science, 296*, 1321–1323.

Pascalis, O., de Schonen, S., Morton, J., Deruelle, C., & Fabre-Grener, M. (1995). Mother's face recognition by neonates: A replication and an extension. *Infant Behavior and Development, 18*, 79–85.

Pascalis, O., Scott, L. S., Kelly, D. J., Dufour, R. W., Shannon, R. W., Nicholson, E., et al. (2005). Plasticity of face processing in infancy. *Proceedings of the National Academy of Sciences of the United States of America, 102*, 5297–5300.

Pashler, H. (1997). *The psychology of attention.* Cambridge, MA: MIT Press.

Patterson, J. L. (2002). Relationships of expressive vocabulary to frequency of reading and television experience among bilingual toddlers. *Applied Psycholinguistics, 23*, 493–508.

Patton Terry, N., McDonald Connor, C., Thomas-Tate, S., & Love, M. (2010). Examining relationships among dialect variation, literacy skills, and school context in first grade. *Journal of Speech, Language, and Hearing Research, 53*, 126–145.

Paul, R. (1990). Comprehension strategies: Interactions between world knowledge and the development of sentence comprehension. *Topics in Language Disorders, 10*(3), 63–75.

Paulesu, E., Perani, D., Blasi, V., Silani, G., Borghese, N. A., De Giovanni, V., et al. (2003). A functional-anatomical model for lipreading. *Journal of Neurophysiology, 90*, 2005–2013.

Paulson, D. M. (1991). *Phonological systems of Spanish-speaking Texas preschoolers.* Thesis, Texas Christian University.

Pearson, B. Z., Fernandez, S., & Oller, D. K. (1995). Cross-language synonyms in the lexicons of bilingual infants: One language or two? *Journal of Child Language, 22*, 345–368.

Pelucchi, B., Hay, J. F., & Saffran, J. R. (2009). Statistical learning in a natural language by 8-month-old infants. *Child Development, 80*, 674–685.

Peña, E., Bedore, L. M., & Rappazzo, D. (2003). Comparison of Spanish, English, and bilingual children's performance across semantic tasks. *Language, Speech, and Hearing Services in Schools, 34*, 5–16.

Perera, K. (1994). Child language research: Building on the past, looking to the future. *Journal of Child Language, 21*, 1–8.

Perez-Pereira, M. (1994). Imitations, repetitions, routines, and the child's analysis of language: Insights from the blind. *Journal of Child Language, 21*, 317–337.

Peterson, C. (1990). The who, when and where of early narratives. *Journal of Child Language, 17*, 433–455.

Petitto, L. A., Katerelos, M., Levy, B. G., Gauna, K., Tétreault, K., & Ferraro, V. (2001). Bilingual signed and spoken language acquisition from birth: Implications for the mechanisms underlying early bilingual language acquisition. *Journal of Child Language, 28*, 453–496.

Petitto, L. A., & Marentette, P. F. (1990, October). *The timing of linguistic milestones in sign language acquisition: Are first signs acquired earlier than first words?* Paper presented at the 15th Annual Boston University Conference on Language Development, Boston, MA.

Petitto, L. A., & Marentette, P. F. (1991, April). The timing of linguistic milestones in sign and spoken language acquisition. In L. Petitto (Chair), *Are the linguistic milestones in signed and spoken language acquisition similar or different?* Symposium conducted at the Biennial Meeting of the Society for Research in Child Development, Seattle, WA.

Pflaum, S. (1986). *The development of language and literacy in young children* (3rd ed.). Columbus, OH: Merrill.

Piaget, J. P. (1952). *The origins of intelligence in children.* New York: International Universities Press.

Piaget, J. (1954). *The construction of reality in the child.* New York: Basic Books.

Pillon, A., Degauquier, C., & Duquesne, F. (1992). Males' and females' conversational behavior in cross-sex dyads: From gender differences to gender similarities. *Journal of Psycholinguistic Research, 21*, 147–172.

Pine, J. M. (1990). *Non-referential children: Slow or different?* Paper presented at the Fifth International Congress for the Study of Child Language, Budapest.

Pine, J. M., Conti-Ramsden, G., Joseph, K. L., Liebergott, J., & Serratrice, L. (2008). Tense over time: Test the Agreement/Tense Omission Model as an account of the pattern of tense-marking provision in early child English. *Journal of Child Language, 35*, 55–75.

Pine, J. M., & Lieven, E. V. M. (1990). Referential style at thirteen months: Why age-defined cross sectional measures are inappropriate for the study of strategy differences in early language development. *Journal of Child Language, 17*, 625–631.

Pine, J. M., & Lieven, E. V. M. (1993). Reanalysing rote-learned phrases: Individual differences in the transition to multiword speech. *Journal of Child Language, 20*, 551–571.

Pine, J. M., Lieven, E. V. M., & Rowland, C. F. (1998). Comparing different models of the development of the English verb category. *Linguistics, 36*, 807–830.

Pinker, S. (1984). *Language learnability and language development.* Cambridge, MA: Harvard University Press.

Pinker, S. (1994). *Language and instinct.* New York: W. Morrow.

Pizzuto, E., & Caselli, M. C. (1992). The acquisition of Italian morphology: Implications for models of language development. *Journal of Child Language, 19*, 491–557.

Plaut, D. C., & Kello, C. T. (1999). The emergence of phonology from the interplay of speech comprehension and production: A distributed connectionist approach. In B. MacWhinney (Ed.), *The emergence of language.* Mahwah, NJ: Lawrence Erlbaum Associates.

Plunkett, K. (1993). Lexical segmentation and vocabulary growth in early language acquisition. *Journal of Child Language, 20*, 43–60.

Plunkett, K., & Marchman, V. (1993). From rote learning to system building: The acquisition of morphology in children and connectionist nets. *Cognition, 48*, 21–69.

Poeppel, D. (1996). A critical review of PET studies of phonological processing. *Brain and Language, 55*(3), 352–379.

Polka, L., & Sundara, M. (2003). Word segmentation in monolingual and bilingual infant learners of English and French. In M.J. Solé, D. Recasens, & J. Romero (Eds.), *Proceedings of the International Congress of Phonetic Sciences, 15*, 1021–1024.

Polka, L., & Werker, J. F. (1994). Developmental changes in perception of non-native vowel contrasts. *Journal of Experimental Psychology: Human Perception and Performance, 20*, 421–435.

Port, R. F., & van Gelder, T. (Eds.). (1995). *Mind as motion.* Cambridge, MA: MIT Press.

Poulin-Dubois, D., Graham, S., & Sippola, L. (1995). Early lexical development: The contribution of parental labelling and infants' categorization abilities. *Journal of Child Language, 22*, 325–343.

Prasada, S., & Ferenz, K. S. (2002). Singular or plural? Children's knowledge of the factors that determine the appropriate form of count nouns. *Journal of Child Language, 29*, 49–70.

Pratt, S. R., Kuller, L., Talbott, E. O., McHugh-Pemu, K., Buhari, A. M., & Xu, X. (2009). Prevalence of hearing loss in black and white elders: Results of the cardiovascular health study. *Journal of Speech, Language, and Hearing Research, 52*, 973–989.

Preisser, D., Hodson, B., & Paden, E. (1988). Developmental phonology: 18–29 months. *Journal of Speech and Hearing Disorders, 53*, 125–130.

Pruden, S. M., Hirsh-Pasek, K., Michnick Golinkoff, R., & Hennon, E. A. (2006). The birth of words: Ten-month-olds learn words through perceptual salience. *Child Development, 77*, 266–280.

Pye, C., Wilcox, K., & Siren, K. (1988). Refining transcription: The significance of transcription "errors." *Journal of Child Language, 15*, 17–37.

Qualls, C. D., & Harris, J. L. (1999). Effects of familiarity on idiom comprehension in African American and European American fifth graders. *Language, Speech, and Hearing Services in Schools, 30*, 141–151.

Quay, S. (1995). The bilingual lexicon: Implications for studies of language choice. *Journal of Child Language, 22*, 369–387.

Rabin, J., & Deacon, H. (2008). The representation of morphologically complex words in the developing lexicon. *Journal of Child Language, 35*, 453–465.

Raichle, M. E. (1994). Images of the mind: Studies with modern imaging techniques. *Annual Review of Psychology, 45*, 333–356.

Raikes, H., Alexander Pan, B., Luze, G., Tamis-LeMonda, C. S., Brooks-Gunn, J., Constantine, J., Banks Tarullo, L.,

Raikes, H. A., & Rodriguez, E. T. (2006). Mother-child bookreading in low-income families: Correlates and outcomes during the first three years of life. *Child Development, 77,* 924–953.

Ravid, D. (2006). Semantic development in textual contexts during the school years: Noun Scale analyses. *Journal of Child Language, 33,* 791–821.

Ravid, D., & Avidor, A. (1998). Acquisition of derived nominals in Hebrew: Developmental and linguistic principles. *Journal of Child Language, 25,* 229–266.

Ravid, D., & Cahana-Amitay, D. (2005). Verbal and nominal expression in narrating conflict situations in Hebrew. *Journal of Pragmatics, 37,* 157–183.

Ravid, D., van Hell, J., Rosado, E., & Zamora, A. (2002). Subject NP patterning in the development of text production: Speech and writing. *Written Language and Literacy, 5,* 69–94.

Ravid, D., & Zilberbuch, S. (2003). Morphosyntactic constructs in the development of spoken and written Hebrew text production. *Journal of Child Language, 30,* 395–418.

Reali, F., & Christiansen, M. H. (2005). Uncovering the richness of the stimulus: Structure dependence and indirect statistical evidence. *Cognitive Science, 29,* 1007–1028.

Redford, M. A., & Gildersleeve-Neumann, C. E. (2009). The development of distinct speaking styles in preschool children. *Journal of Speech, Language, and Hearing Research, 52,* 1434–1448.

Redlinger, W., & Park, T. (1980). Language mixing in young bilinguals. *Journal of Child Language, 7,* 337–352.

Redmond, S. M. (2003). Children's productions of the affix -ed in past tense and past participle contexts. *Journal of Speech, Language, and Hearing Research, 46,* 1095–1109.

Reilly, J., & Bellugi, U. (1996). Competition on the face: Affect and language in ASL motherese. *Journal of Child Language, 23,* 219–239.

Resches, M., & Pérez Pereira, M. (2007). Referential communication abilities and Theory of Mind development in preschool children. *Journal of Child Language, 34,* 21–52.

Rescorla, L. (2002). Language and reading outcomes to age 9 in late-talking toddlers. *Journal of Speech, Language, and Hearing Research, 45,* 360–371.

Rescorla, L. (2009). Age 17 language and reading outcomes in late-talking toddlers: Support for a dimensional perspective on language delay. *Journal of Speech, Language, and Hearing Research, 52,* 16–30.

Rescorla, L., & Alley, A. (2001). Validation of the Language Development Survey (LDS): A parent report tool for identifying language delay in toddlers. *Journal of Speech, Language, and Hearing Research, 44,* 434–45.

Rescorla, L., & Fechnay, T. (1996). Mother-child synchrony and communicative reciprocity in late-talking toddlers. *Journal of Speech, Language, and Hearing Research, 39,* 200–208.

Rescorla, L., Ross, G. S., & McClure, S. (2007). Language delay and behavioral/emotional problems in toddlers: Findings from two developmental clinics. *Journal of Speech, Language, and Hearing Research, 50,* 1063–1078.

Reznick, J. S., & Goldfield, B. A. (1994). Diary vs. representative checklist assessment of productive vocabulary. *Journal of Child Language, 21,* 465–472.

Reznick, S. (1990). Visual preference as a test of infant word comprehension. *Applied Psycholinguistics, 11,* 145–166.

Rice, M. L., Smolik, F., Perpich, D., Thompson, T., Rytting, N., & Blossom, M. (2010). Mean Length of Utterance levels in 6-month intervals for children 3 to 9 years with and without language impairments. *Journal of Speech, Language, and Hearing Research, 53,* 333–349.

Rice, M. L., Taylor, C. L., & Zubrick, S. R. (2008). Language outcomes of 7-year-old children with or without a history of late language emergence at 24 months. *Journal of Speech, Language, and Hearing Research, 51,* 394–407.

Richards, B. J. (1990). *Language development and individual differences: A study of auxiliary verb learning.* New York: Cambridge University Press.

Richards, B. J., & Malvern, D. D. (1997). *The new Bulmershe papers. Quantifying lexical diversity in the study of language development.* Reading, UK: The University of Reading.

Richards, B. J., & Robinson, P. (1993). Environmental correlates of child copula verb growth. *Journal of Child Language, 20,* 343–362.

Rispoli, M. (1994). Structural dependency and the acquisition of grammatical relations. In Y. Levy (Ed.), *Other children, other languages: Issues in the theory of language acquisition.* Hillsdale, NJ: Lawrence Erlbaum Associates.

Rispoli, M. (1998). Patterns of pronoun case error. *Journal of Child Language, 25,* 533–544.

Rispoli, M. (2003). Changes in the nature of sentence production during the period of grammatical development. *Journal of Speech, Language, and Hearing Research, 46,* 818–830.

Rispoli, M. (2005). When children reach beyond their grasp: Why some children make pronoun case errors and others don't. *Journal of Child Language, 32,* 93–116.

Rispoli, M., & Hadley, P. (2001). The leading edge: The significance of sentence disruptions in the development of grammar. *Journal of Speech, Language, and Hearing Research, 44,* 1131–1143.

Rispoli, M., Hadley, P., & Holt, J. (2008). Stalls and revisions: A developmental perspective on sentence production. *Journal of Speech, Language, and Hearing Research, 51,* 953–966.

Rittle-Johnson, B., & Siegler, R. S. (1999). Learning to spell: Variability, choice, and change in children's strategy use. *Child Development, 70,* 332–348.

Robb, M. P., Bauer, H. R., & Tyler, A. A. (1994). A quantitative analysis of the single-word stage. *First Language, 14,* 37–48.

Roberts, J., Jurgens, J., & Burchinal, M. (2005). The role of home literacy practices in preschool children's language and emergent literacy skills. *Journal of Speech, Language, and Hearing Research, 48,* 345–359.

Roberts, J. A., Pollock, K. E., Krakow, R., Price, J., Fulmer, K. C., & Wang, P. P. (2005). Language development in preschool-age children adopted from China. *Journal of Speech, Language, and Hearing Research, 48,* 93–107.

Roberts, R., & Gibson, E. (2002). Individual differences in sentence memory. *Journal of Psycholinguistic Research, 31,* 573–598.

Robinson-Zanatu, C. (1996). Serving Native American children and families: Considering cultural variables. *Language, Speech, and Hearing Services in Schools, 27,* 373–384.

Rollins, P. R. (2003). Caregivers' contingent comments to 9-month-old infants: Relationships with later language. *Applied Psycholinguistics, 24,* 221–234.

Rome-Flanders, T., & Cronk, C. (1995). A longitudinal study of infant vocalizations during mother-infant games. *Journal of Child Language, 22,* 259–274.

Rondal, J., & Cession, A. (1990). Input evidence regarding the semantic bootstrapping hypothesis. *Journal of Child Language, 17,* 711–717.

Rose, S. A., Feldman, J. F., & Jankowski, J. J. (2001). Attention and recognition memory in the first year of life: A longitudinal study of preterms and full-terms. *Developmental Psychology, 37,* 135–151.

Rose, S. A., Feldman, J. F., & Jankowski, J. J. (2004). Dimensions of cognition in infancy. *Intelligence, 32,* 245–262.

Rose, S. A., Feldman, J. F., & Jankowski, J. J. (2005). The structure of infant cognition at 1 year. *Intelligence, 33,* 231–250.

Rose, S. A., Feldman, J. F., & Jankowski, J. J. (2009). A cognitive approach to the development of early language. *Child Development, 80,* 134–150.

Rose, S. A., Feldman, J. F., Wallace, I. F., & Cohen, P. (1991). Language: A partial link between infant attention and later intelligence. *Developmental Psychology, 27,* 798–805.

Rovee-Collier, C. K. (1999). The development of infant memory. *Current Direction in Psychological Science, 8,* 80–85.

Rowe, M. L., Özçaliskan, S., & Goldin-Meadow, S. (2008). Learning words by hand: Gesture's role in predicting vocabulary development. *First Language, 28,* 182–199.

Rowland, C. F., Pine, J. M., Lieven, E. V. M., & Theakston, A. L. (2003). Determinants of acquisition order in *wh-* questions: re-evaluating the role of caregiver speech. *Journal of Child Language, 30,* 609–635.

Rowland, C. F., Pine, J. M., Lieven, E. V. M., & Theakston, A. L. (2005). The incidence of error in young children's *wh-*questions. *Journal of Speech, Language and Hearing Research, 48,* 384–404.

Rowland, C. F., & Theakston, A. L. (2009). The acquisition of auxiliary syntax: A longitudinal elicitation study. Part 2: The modals and auxiliary DO. *Journal of Speech, Language, and Hearing Research, 52,* 1471–1492.

Rozendaal, M. I., & Baker, A. E. (2008). A cross-linguistic investigation of the acquisition of the pragmatics of indefinite and definite reference in two-year-olds. *Journal of Child Language, 35,* 773–807.

Rubino, R., & Pine, J. (1998). Subject-verb agrement in Brazilian Portugese: What low error rates hide. *Journal of Child Language, 25,* 35–60.

Ryalls, B., & Pisoni, D. (1997). The effect of talker variability on word recognition in preschool children. *Developmental Psychology, 33,* 441–452.

Ryan, J. (1974). Early language development: Towards a communicational analysis. In P. Richards (Ed.), *The integration of a child into a social world.* London: Cambridge University Press.

Ryder, N., & Leinonen, E. (2003). Use of context in question answering by 3-, 4-, and 5-year-old children. *Journal of Psycholinguistic Research, 32,* 397–416.

Sabbagh, M., & Gelman, S. (2000). Buzzsaws and blueprints: What children need (or don't need) to learn language. *Journal of Child Language, 27,* 715–726.

Sabbagh, M. A., Bowman, L. C., Evraire, L. E., & Ito, J. M. B. (2009). Neurodevelopmental correlates of Theory of Mind in preschool children. *Child Development, 80,* 1147–1162.

Sachs, J. (1985). Prelinguistic development. In J. Berko Gleason (Ed.), *The development of language.* Columbus, OH: Merrill.

Sadagopan, N., & Smith, A. (2008). Developmental changes in the effects of utterance length and complexity on speech movement variability. *Journal of Speech, Language, and Hearing Research, 51,* 1138–1151.

Saffran, J. R., Aslin, R. N., & Newport, E. L. (1996). Statistical learning by 8-month-old infants. *Science, 274,* 1926–1928.

Salthouse, T. A. (1990). Working memory as a processing resource in cognitive aging. *Developmental Review, 10,* 102–124.

Samuelson, L. K., & Smith, L. B. (1998). Memory and attention make smart word learning: An alternative account of Akhtar, Carpenter, Tomasello. *Child Development, 69,* 94–104.

Sander, E. (1972). When are speech sounds learned? *Journal of Speech and Hearing Disorders, 37,* 55–63.

Sanders, L. D., & Neville, H. J. (2000). Lexical, syntactic, and stress-pattern cues for speech segmentation. *Journal of Speech, Language, and Hearing Research, 43,* 1301–1321.

Sanders, L. D., Neville, H. J., & Woldorff, M. G. (2002). Speech segmentation by native and non-native speakers: The use of lexical, syntactic, and stress-pattern cues. *Journal of Speech, Language, and Hearing Research, 45,* 519–530.

Sanford, A. J., & Garrod, S. M. (1998). The role of scenario mapping in text comprehension. *Discourse Processes, 26,* 159–190.

Santelmann, L., Berk, S., Austin, J., Somashekar, S., & Lust, B. (2002). Continuity and development in the acquisition of inversion in yes/no questions : dissociating movement and inflection. *Journal of Child Language, 29,* 813–842.

Savage, C., Lieven, E., Theakston, A., & Tomasello, M. (2003). Testing the abstractness of children's linguistic representations: Lexical and structural priming of syntactic constructions in young children. *Developmental Science, 6,* 557–567.

Saville-Troike, M. (1988). Private speech: Evidence for second language learning strategies during the "silent" period. *Journal of Child Language, 15,* 567–590.

Saxe, R. R., Whitfield-Gabrieli, S., Scholz, J., & Pelphrey, K. A. (2009). Brain regions for perceiving and reasoning about other people in school-aged children. *Child Development, 80,* 1197–1209.

Scaife, M., & Bruner, J. (1975). The capacity of joint visual attention in the infant. *Nature, 253,* 265–266.

Scarborough, H., Wyckoff, J., & Davidson, R. (1986). A reconsideration of the relationship between age and mean utterance length. *Journal of Speech and Hearing Research, 29,* 394–399.

Scarborough, H. S. (1998). Predicting the future achievement of second graders with reading disabilities: Contributions of phonemic awareness, verbal memory, rapid naming, and IQ. *Annals of Dyslexia, 48,* 115–136.

Schafer, G. (2005). Infants can learn decontextualized words before their first birthday. *Child Development, 76,* 87–96.

Schafer, G., & Plunkett, K. (1998). Rapid word learning by fifteen-month-olds under tightly controlled conditions. *Child Development, 69,* 309–320.

Schaffer, R. (1977). *Mothering.* Cambridge: Harvard University Press.

Schane, S. (1973). *Generative phonology.* Englewood Cliffs, NJ: Prentice Hall.

Scheffner Hammer, C., & Weiss, A. L. (1999). Guiding language development: How African American mothers and their infants structure play interactions. *Journal of Speech, Language, and Hearing Research, 42,* 1219–1233.

Scheffner Hammer, C., & Weiss, A. L. (2000). African American mothers' views on their infants' language-development and language-learning environment. *American Journal of Speech-Language Pathology, 9,* 126–140.

Scherf, K. S., Behrmann, M., Humphreys, K., & Luna, B. (2007). Visual category-selectivity for faces, places and objects emerges along different developmental trajectories. *Developmental Science, 10,* F15–F30.

Schiff-Myers, N. (1992). Considering arrested language development and language loss in the assessment of second language learners. *Language, Speech, and Hearing Services in Schools, 23,* 28–33.

Schlesinger, I. (1971). Production of utterances and language acquisition. In D. Slobin (Ed.), *The ontogenesis of grammar.* New York: Academic Press.

Schmidt, C. L. (1996). Scrutinizing reference: How gesture and speech are coordinated in mother–child interaction. *Journal of Child Language, 23,* 279–305.

Schmidt, C. L., & Lawson, K. R. (2002). Caregiver attention-focusing and children's attention-sharing behaviours as predictors of later verbal IQ in very low birthweight children. *Journal of Child Language, 29,* 3–22.

Schmidt, M. E., Pempek, T. A., Kirkorian, H. L., Frankenfield Lund, A., & Anderson, D. R. (2008). The effects of background television on the toy play behavior of very young children. *Child Development, 79,* 1137–1151.

Schober-Peterson, D., & Johnson, C. J. (1991). Non-dialogue speech during preschool interactions. *Journal of Child Language, 18,* 153–170.

Scopesi, A., & Pellegrino, M. (1990). Structure and function of baby talk in a day-care center. *Journal of Child Language, 17,* 101–114.

Scott, C. M. (1987). *Summarizing text: Context effects in language disordered children.* Paper presented at the First International Symposium, Specific Language Disorders in Children, University of Reading, England.

Scott, C. M. (1988). Producing complex sentences. *Topics in Language Disorders, 8*(2), 44–62.

Scott, C. M. (1999). Learning to write. In H. W. Catts & A. G. Kamhi (Eds.), *Language and reading disabilities* (pp. 224–258). Boston: Allyn & Bacon.

Scott, C. M., Nippold, M. A., Norris, J. A., & Johnson, C. J. (1992, November). *School-age children and adolescents: Establishing language norms.* Paper presented at the annual convention of the American Speech-Language-Hearing Association, San Antonio.

Scott, C. M., & Windsor, J. (2000). General language performance measures in spoken and written narrative and expository discourse of school-age children with language learning disabilities. *Journal of Speech, Language, and Hearing Research, 43,* 324–339.

Sell, M. A. (1992). The development of children's knowledge structures: Events, slots, and taxonomies. *Journal of Child Language, 19,* 659–676.

Senechal, M. (1997). The differential effect of storybook reading on preschoolers' acquisition of expressive and receptive vocabulary. *Journal of Child Language, 24,* 123–138.

Seroussi, B. (2004). Hebrew derived nouns in context: A developmental perspective. *Folia Phoniatrica et Logopaedica, 56,* 273–290.

Serrat, E. (1997). *Acquisition of verb category in Catalan.* Unpublished dissertation.

Shady, M., & Gerken, L. (1999). Grammatical and caregiver cues in early sentence comprehension. *Journal of Child Language, 26,* 163–175.

Shafer, V. L., Shucard, D. W., Shucard, J. L., & Gerken, L. (1998). An electrophysiological study of infants' sensitivity to the sound patterns of English speech. *Journal of Speech, Language, and Hearing Research, 41*, 874–886.

Shapiro, L., Swinney, D., & Borsky, S. (1998). Online examination of language performance in normal and neurologically impaired adults. *American Journal of Speech-Language Pathology, 7*, 49–60.

Shatz, M., & O'Reilly, A. (1990). Conversational or communicative skill? A reassessment of two year-olds' behavior in miscommunication episodes. *Journal of Child Language, 17*, 131–146.

Sheng, M., & Hoogenraad, C. C. (2007). The postsynaptic architecture of excitatory synapses: A more quantitative view. *Annual Review of Biochemistry, 76*, 823–847.

Shipley, K., Maddox, M., & Driver, J. (1991). Children's development of irregular past tense verb forms. *Language, Speech, and Hearing Services in Schools, 22*, 115–122.

Shirai, Y., & Anderson, R. W. (1995). The acquisition of tense-aspect morphology: A prototype account. *Language, 71*, 743–762.

Short-Meyerson, K. J., & Abbeduto, L. J. (1997). Preschoolers' communication during scripted interactions. *Journal of Child Language, 24*, 469–493.

Shrager, J. F., & Johnson, M. H. (1995). Waves of growth in the development of cortical function: A computational model. In B. Julesz & I. Kovacs (Eds.), *Maturational windows and adult cortical plasticity* (pp. 31–44). New York: Addison-Wesley.

Shriberg, L. D. (1993). Four new speech and prosody voice measures for genetics research and other studies of developmental phonological disorders. *Journal of Speech and Hearing Research, 36*, 105–140.

Siedlecki, T., & Bonvillian, J. D. (1998). Homonymy in the lexicons of young children acquiring American Sign Language. *Journal of Psycholinguistic Research, 27*, 47–65.

Singer, B. D., & Bashir, A. S. (1999). What are executive functions and self-regulation and what do they have to do with language-learning disorders? *Language, Speech, and Hearing Services in Schools, 30*, 265–273.

Singson, M., Mahony, D., & Mann, V. (2000). The relation between reading ability and morphological skills: Evidence from derivational suffixes. *Reading and Writing: An Interdisciplinary Journal, 12*, 219–252.

Skipper, J. I., Nusbaum, H. C., & Small, S. L. (2005). Listening to talking faces: Motor cortical activation during speech perception. *NeuroImage, 25*, 76–89.

Slaughter, V., Peterson, C. C., & Carpenter, M. (2009). Maternal mental state talk and infants' early gestural communication. *Journal of Child Language, 36*, 1053–1074.

Slobin, D. (1970). Universals of grammatical development in children. In G. Flores D'Arcais & W. Levelt (Eds.), *Advances in psycholinguistics*. Amsterdam: North Holland.

Slobin, D. (1978). Cognitive prerequisites for the development of grammar. In L. Bloom & M. Lahey (Eds.), *Readings in language development*. New York: Wiley.

Slobin, D. I. (1973). Cognitive prerequisites for the development of grammar. In C. Ferguson & D. Slobin (Eds.), *Studies of child language development*. New York: Holt, Rinehart, Winston.

Slomkowski, C., & Dunn, J. (1996). Young children's understanding of other people's beliefs and their connected communication with friends. *Developmental Psychology, 32*, 442–447.

Smiley, P., & Huttenlocher, J. (1995). Conceptual development and the child's early words for events, objects and persons. In M. Tomasello & W. E. Merriman (Eds.), *Beyond names for things: Young children's acquisition of verbs*. Hillsdale, NJ: Lawrence Erlbaum Associates.

Smiljanic, R., & Bradlow, A. R. (2008). Stability of temporal contrasts across speaking styles in English and Croation. *Journal of Phonetics, 36*, 91–113.

Smit, A. B., Hand, L., Freilinger, J. J., Bernthal, J. E., & Bird, A. (1990). The Iowa articulation norms project and its Nebraska replication. *Journal of Speech and Hearing Disorders, 55*, 779–798.

Smith, A., & Goffman, L. (2004). Interaction of motor and language factors in the development of speech. In B. Maassen, R. Kent, H. Peters, P. van Lieshout, & W. Hulstijn (Eds.), *Speech motor control in normal and disordered speech* (pp. 227–252). Oxford, UK: Oxford University Press.

Smith, C. S. (1997). *The parameter of aspect* (2nd ed.). Norwell, MA: Kluwer.

Smith, J. R., Brooks-Gunn, J., & Klebanov, P. K. (1997). Consequences of living in poverty for young children's cognitive and verbal ability and early school achievement. In G. J. Duncan & J. Brooks-Gunn (Eds.), *Consequences of growing up poor* (pp. 132–189). New York: Russell Sage Foundation.

Smitherman, G. (1994). *Black talk: Words and phrases from the hood to the amen corner*. New York: Houghton-Mifflin.

Smyth, R., Jacobs, G., & Rogers, H. (2003). Male voices and perceived sexual orientation: An experimental and theoretical approach. *Language in Society, 32*, 329–350.

Snow, C. (1986). Conversations with children. In P. Fletcher & M. Garman (Eds.), *Language acquisition* (2nd ed.). New York: Cambridge University Press.

Snow, C. E., Scarborough, H. S., & Burns, M. S. (1999). What speech-language pathologists need to know about early reading. *Topics in Language Disorders, 20*(1), 48–58.

Snow, D. (1998). A prominence account of syllable reduction in early speech development: The child's prosodic phonology of *tiger* and *giraffe*. *Journal of Speech, Language, and Hearing Research, 41*, 1171–1184.

Snow, D. (2006). Regression and reorganization of intonation between 6 and 23 months. *Child Development, 77,* 281–296.

Snyder, L. E., Dabasinskas, C., & O'Connor, E. (2002). An information processing perspective on language impairment in children: Looking at both sides of the coin. *Topics in Language Disorders, 22*(3), 1–14.

So, L. K., & Dodd, B. J. (1995). The acquisition of phonology by Cantonese-speaking children. *Journal of Child Language, 22,* 473–495.

Song, J. Y., Sundara, M., & Demuth, K. (2009). Phonological constraints on children's production of English third person singular –s. *Journal of Speech, Language, and Hearing Research, 52,* 623–642.

Spector, C. C. (1996). Children's comprehension of idioms in the context of humor. *Language, Speech, and Hearing Services in Schools, 27,* 307–315.

Speer, S. R., Kjelgaard, M. M., & Dobroth, K. M. (1996). The influence of prosodic structure on the resolution of temporary syntactic closure ambiguities. *Journal of Psycholinguistic Research, 25,* 249–272.

Speidel, G. E., & Herreshoff, M. J. (1989). Imitation and the construction of long utterances. In G. E. Speidel & K. E. Nelson (Eds.), *The many faces of imitation in children.* New York: Springer-Verlag.

Springer, K., & Keil, F. C. (1991). Early differentiation of causal mechanisms appropriate to biological and nonbiological kinds. *Child Development, 62,* 767–781.

Stanwood, G. D., & Levitt, P. (2007). Prenatal exposure to cocaine produces unique developmental and long-term adaptive changes in dopamine D1 receptor activity and subcellular distribution. *Journal of Neuroscience, 27,* 152–157.

Stark, R. (1986). Prespeech segmental feature development. In P. Fletcher & M. Garman (Eds.), *Language acquisition* (2nd ed.). New York: Cambridge University Press.

Stark, R. E., Bernstein, L. E., & Demorest, M. E. (1993). Vocal communication in the first 18 months of life. *Journal of Speech and Hearing Research, 36,* 548–558.

Steen, F. F. (1997). Theory of mind, a model of mental-state attribution. http://cogweb.ucla.edu/CogSci/ToMM.html. Last modified 1997. Accessed June 1, 2006

Steeve, R. W., & Moore, C. A. (2009). Mandibular motor control during the early development of speech and nonspeech behaviors. *Journal of Speech, Language, and Hearing Research, 52,* 1530–1554.

Steeve, R. W., Moore, C. A., Green, J. R., Reilly, K. J., & Ruark McMurtrey, J. (2008). Babbling, chewing, and sucking: Oromandibular coordination at 9 months. *Journal of Speech, Language, and Hearing Research, 51,* 1390–1404.

Stein, M., Dierks, T., Brandeis, D., Wirth, M., Srtik, W., & Koenig, T. (2006). Plasticity in the adult language system: A longitudinal electrophysiological study on second language learning. *Neuroimage, 33*(2), 774–783.

Stern, D. N. (1977). *The first relationship.* Cambridge: Harvard University Press.

Stokes, S. F., & Surendran, D. (2005). Articulatory complexity, ambient frequency, and functional load as predictors of consonant development in children. *Journal of Speech, Language, and Hearing Research, 48,* 577–591.

Stoll, S. (1998). The acquisition of Russian aspect. *First Language, 18,* 351–378.

Storkel, H. L. (2001). Learning new words: Phonetactic probability in language development. *Journal of Speech, Language, and Hearing Research, 44,* 1321–1337.

Storkel, H. L. (2002). Restructuring of similarity neighbourhoods in the developing mental lexicon. *Journal of Child Language, 29,* 251–274.

Storkel, H. L. (2003). Learning new words II: Phonotactic probability in verb learning. *Journal of Speech, Language, and Hearing Research, 46,* 1312–1323.

Storkel, H. L. (2009). Developmental differences in the effects of phonological, lexical and semantic variables on word learning by infants. *Journal of Child Language, 36,* 291–321.

Storkel, H. L., Armbrüster, J., & Hogan, T. P. (2006). Differentiating phonotactic probability and neighborhood density in adult word learning. *Journal of Speech, Language, and Hearing Research, 49,* 1175–1192.

Storkel, H. L., & Morrisette, M. L. (2002). The lexicon and phonology: Interactions in language acquisition. *Language, Speech, and Hearing Services in Schools, 33,* 24–37.

Streb, J., Hemighausen, E., & Rösler, F. (2004). Different anaphoric expressions are investigated by event-related brain potentials. *Journal of Psycholinguistic Research, 33,* 175–201.

Striano, T., Rochat, P., & Legerstee, M. (2003). The role of modeling request type on symbolic comprehension of objects and gestures in young children. *Journal of Child Language, 30,* 27–45.

Strömqvist, S., Nordqvist, A., & Wengelin, A. (2004). Writing the frog story: Developmental and cross-modal perspectives. In S. Strömqvist & L. Verhoeven (Eds.), *Relating events in narrative: Typological and contextual perspectives.* Mahwah, NJ: Lawrence Erlbaum Associates.

Sudhof, T. C. (2008). Neurotransmitter release. *Handbook of Experimental Pharmacology, 184,* 1–21.

Sulzby, E., & Zecker, L. B. (1991). The oral monologue as a form of emergent reading. In A. McCabe & C. Peterson (Eds.), *Developing narrative structure* (pp. 175–214). Hillsdale, NJ: Lawrence Erlbaum Associates.

Sur, M., Pallas, S. L., & Roe, A. W. (1990). Cross-modal plasticity in cortical development: Differentiation and specification of sensory neocortex. *Trends in Neuroscience, 13,* 227–233.

Sutherland, D., & Gillon, G. T. (2005). Assessment of phonological representations in children with speech impairment. *Language, Speech, and Hearing Services in Schools, 36*, 294–307.

Sutter, J., & Johnson, C. (1990). School-age children's metalinguistic awareness of grammaticality in verb form. *Journal of Speech and Hearing Research, 33*, 84–95.

Swank, L. K. (1997). Linguistic influences on the emergence of written word decoding in first grade. *American Journal of Speech-Language Pathology, 6*, 62–66.

Tamis-Lemonda, C. S., Shannon, J. D., Cabrera, N. J., & Lamb, M. E. (2004). Fathers and mothers play with their 2- and 3-year olds: Contributions to language and cognitive development. *Child Development, 75*, 1806–1820.

Tannen, D. (1990). *You just don't understand: Talk between the sexes.* New York: Ballantine.

Tannen, D. (1994). *Gender and discourse.* New York: Oxford University Press.

Tao, L., & Healy, A. F. (1996). Cognitive strategies in discourse processing: A comparison of Chinese and English speakers. *Journal of Psycholinguistic Research, 25*, 597–616.

Tardif, T. (1996). Nouns are not always learned before verbs: Evidence from Mandarin speakers' early vocabularies. *Developmental Psychology, 32*, 492–504.

Tardif, T., Shatz, M., & Naigles, L. (1997). Caregiver speech and children's use of nouns versus verbs: A comparison of English, Italian, and Mandarin. *Journal of Child Language, 24*, 535–565.

Tare, M., Shatz, M., & Gilbertson, L. (2008). Maternal uses of non-object terms in child-directed speech: Color, number and time. *First Language, 28*, 87–100.

Taylor, N., Donovan, W., Miles, S., & Leavitt, L. (2009). Maternal control strategies, maternal language usage and children's language usage at two years. *Journal of Child Language, 36*, 381–404.

Temple, C., Nathan, R., & Burris, N. (1982). *The beginnings of writing.* Boston: Allyn & Bacon.

Terrell, S. L., & Terrell, F. (1993). African-American cultures. In D. E. Battles (Ed.), *Communication disorders in multicultural populations.* Stoneham, MA: Butterworth-Heinemann.

Thal, D., Tobias, S., & Morrison, D. (1991). Language and gesture in late talkers: A one year follow-up. *Journal of Speech and Hearing Disorders, 34*, 604–612.

Thal, D. J., Bates, E., Goodman, J., & Jahn-Samilo, J. (1997). Continuity of language abilities: An exploratory study of late- and early-talking toddlers. *Developmental Neuropsychology 13*, 239–73.

Theakston, A., Lieven, E. V., Pine, J. M., & Rowland, C. F. (2001). The role of performance limitations in the acquisition of verb-argument structure: An alternative account. *Journal of Child Language, 28*, 127–152.

Theakston, A. L., Lieven, E. V., Pine, J. M., & Rowland, C. F. (2005). The acquisition of auxiliary syntax: BE and HAVE. *Cognitive Linguistics, 16*(1), 247–277.

Theakston, A. L., Lieven, E. V. M., & Tomasello, M. (2003). The role of the input in the acquisition of third person singular verbs in English. *Journal of Speech, Language, and Hearing Research, 46*, 863–877.

Thelen, E. (1991). Motor aspects of emergent speech: A dynamic approach. In N. Krasnegor (Ed.), *Biobehavioral foundations of language* (pp. 339–362). Hillsdale, NJ: Lawrence Erlbaum Associates.

Thompson, C. A., Craig, H. K., & Washington, J. A. (2004). Variable production of African American English across oracy and literacy contexts. *Language, Speech, and Hearing Services in Schools, 35*, 269–282.

Thompson, L. A., Fagan, J. F., & Fulker, D. W. (1991). Longitudinal prediction of specific cognitive abilities from infant novelty preference. *Child Development, 67*, 530–538.

Thomson, J., & Chapman, R. (1977). Who is "Daddy" revisited: The status of two year olds' over-extensioned words in use and comprehension. *Journal of Child Language, 4*, 359–375.

Tincoff, R., & Jusczyk, P. W. (1999). Some beginning of word comprehension in 6-month-olds. *Psychological Science, 10*, 172–175.

Toda, S., Fogel, A., & Kawai, M. (1990). Maternal speech to three-month-old infants in the United States and Japan. *Journal of Child Language, 17*, 279–294.

Toga, A. W., Frackowiak, R. S. J., & Mazziotta, J. C. (Eds.). (1996). *Neuroimage, a journal of brain function. Second International Conference on Functional Mapping of the Human Brain, 3(3) Part 2.* San Diego: Academic Press.

Tomasello, M. (1992a). *First verbs: A case study of early grammatical development.* Cambridge, UK: Cambridge University Press.

Tomasello, M. (1992b). The social bases of language acquisition. *Social Development, 1*, 67–87.

Tomasello, M. (2000). Do young children have adult syntactic competence? *Cognition, 4*, 209–253.

Tomasello, M. (2003). *Constructing a language: A usage-based theory of language acquisition.* Cambridge, MA: Harvard University Press.

Tomasello, M. (2005). Beyond formalities: The case of language acquisition. *The Linguistic Review, 22*, 183–197.

Tomasello, M. (2006). Acquiring linguistic constructions. In W. Damon, R. M. Lerner, D. Kuhn, & R. Siegler (Eds.), *Handbook of child psychology, Vol. 2: Cognitive perception and language* (pp. 255–298). Hoboken, NJ: Wiley.

Tomasello, M. (2008). *Origins of human communication.* Cambridge, MA: The MIT Press.

Tomasello, M., Akhtar, N., Dodson, K., & Rekau, L. (1997). Differential productivity in young children's use of nouns and verbs. *Journal of Child Language, 24*, 373–87.

Tomasello, M., & Cale Kruger, A. (1992). Joint attention on actions: Acquiring verbs in ostensive and non-ostensive context. *Journal of Child Language, 19*, 311–333.

Tomasello, M., & Call, J. (1997). *Primate cognition.* New York: Oxford University Press.

Tomasello, M., Carpenter, M., Call, J., Behne, T., & Moll, H. (2005). Understanding and sharing intentions: The origins of cultural cognition. *Behavioral and Brain Sciences, 28,* 675–735.

Tomasello, M., Carpenter, M., & Liszkowski, U. (2007). A new look at infant pointing. *Child Development, 78,* 705–722.

Tomasello, M., Conti-Ramsden, G., & Ewert, B. (1990). Young children's conversations with their mothers and fathers: Differences in breakdown and repair. *Journal of Child Language, 17,* 115–130.

Tomasello, M., Strosberg, R., & Akhtar, N. (1996). Eighteen-month-old children learn words in non-ostensive contexts. *Journal of Child Language, 23,* 157–176.

Tomblin, J. B., Barker, B. A., Spencer, L., Zhang, X., & Gantz, B. J. (2005). The effect of age at cochlear implant initial stimulation on expressive language growth in infants and toddlers. *Journal of Speech, Language and Hearing Research, 48,* 853–867.

Tompkins, C. A., Lehman-Blake, M. T., Baumgaertner, A., & Fassbinder, W. (2001). Mechanisms of discourse comprehension impairment after right hemisphere brain damange: Suppression in interential ambiguity resolution. *Journal of Speech, Language, and Hearing Research, 44,* 400–415.

Trachtenberg, J. T., & Stryker, M. P. (2001). Rapid anatomical plasticity of horizontal connections in the developing visual cortex. *Journal of Neuroscience, 15,* 3476–3482.

Treiman, R. (1993). *Beginning to spell.* New York: Oxford University Press.

Treiman, R., & Cassar, M. (1997). Spelling acquisition in English. In C. A. Perfetti, L. Rieben, & M. Fayol (Eds.), *Learning to spell: Research, theory, and practice across languages* (pp. 61–80). Mahwah, NJ: Lawrence Erlbaum Associates.

Tritsch, N. X., Yi, E., Gale, J. E., Glowatski, E., & Bergles, D. E. (2007). The origin of spontaneous activity in the developing auditory system. *Nature, 450,* 50–55.

Tronick, E., Als, H., & Adamson, L. (1979). Structure of early face-to-face communicative interactions. In M. Bullowa (Ed.), *Before speech.* New York: Cambridge University Press.

Trotter, R. (1983, August). Baby face. *Psychology Today, 17*(8), 14–20.

Trudeau, M., & Chadwick, A. (1997, February 7). *Language development.* National Public Radio.

Tsao, F., Liu, H., & Kuhl, P. K. (2004). Speech perception in infancy predicts language development in the second year of life: A longitudinal study. *Child Development, 75,* 1067–1084.

Tsushima, T., Takizawa, O., Sasaki, M., Siraki, S., Nishi, K., Kohno, M., Menyuk, P., & Best, C. (1994). *Discrimination of English /r-l/ and /w-y/ by Japanese infants at 6–12 months: Language specific developmental changes in speech perception abilities.* Paper presented at the International Conference on Spoken Language Processing, Yokohama, Japan.

Tucker, G. R. (1998). A global perspective on multilingualism and multilingual education. In J. Cenoz & F. Genesee (Eds.), *Beyond bilingualism: Multilingualism and multilingual education* (pp. 3–15). Clevedon, UK: Multilingual Matters.

Turkstra, L., Ciccia, A., & Seaton, C. (2003). Interactive behaviors in adolescent conversation dyads. *Language, Speech, and Hearing Services in Schools, 34,* 117–127.

Ukrainetz, T. A., Justice, L. M., Kaderavek, J. N., Eisenberg, S. L., Gillam, R. B., & Harm, H. M. (2005). The development of expressive elaboration in fictional narratives. *Journal of Speech, Language, and Hearing Research, 48,* 1363–1377.

U.S. Department of Housing and Urban Development. (2008, July). The third annual homeless assessment report to Congress. Washington, DC: HUD.

U.S. Department of State. (2002). *Number of immigrant visas issued to orphans coming to the U.S.* Retrieved October 10, 2002, at http://travel.state.gov/orphan_numbers.html.

U.S. Department of State. (2009). *U.S. Department of State 2009 Annual Adoption Report.* Retrieved September 11, 2010, from www.adoption.state.gov/pdf/fy2009_annual_report.pdf

Uttal, D. H. (1996). Angles and distances: Children's and adults' reconstruction and scaling of spatial configurations. *Child Development, 67,* 2763–2769.

Valian, V. (1991). Syntactic subjects in the early speech of American and Italian children. *Cognition: International Journal of Cognitive Science, 40,* 21–81.

Valian, V., & Aubry, S. (2005). When opportunity knocks twice: Two-year-olds' repetition of sentence subjects. *Journal of Child Language, 32,* 617–641.

Valian, V., & Casey, L. (2003). Young children's acquisition of *wh-* questions: the role of structured input. *Journal of Child Language, 30,* 117–143.

van den Boom, D. C. (1997). Sensitivity and attachment: Next step for developmentalists. *Child Development, 64,* 259–294.

van Kleeck, A., & Beckley-McCall, A. (2002). A comparison of mothers' individual and simultaneous book sharing with preschool siblings: An exploratory study of five families. *American Journal of Speech-Language Pathology, 11,* 175–189.

van Kleeck, A., Gillam, R. B., Hamilton, L., & McGrath, C. (1997). The relationship between middle-class parents' book sharing discussion and their preschoolers' abstract language development. *Journal of Speech, Language, and Hearing Research, 40,* 1261–1271.

Varnhagen, C. K., McCallum, M., & Burstow, M. (1997). Is children's spelling naturally stage-like? *Reading and Writing: An Interdisciplinary Journal, 9,* 451–481.

Velleman, S. L., & Vihman, M. M. (2002). Whole-word phonology and templates: Trap, bootstrap, or some of each? *Language, Speech, and Hearing Services in Schools, 33,* 9–23.

Veneziano, E., Sinclair, H., & Berthoud, I. (1990). From one word to two words: Repetition patterns on the way to structured speech. *Journal of Child Language, 17*, 633–650.

Verhoeven, L., Aparici, M., Cahana-Amitay, D., van Hell, J., Kriz, S., & Viguie-Simon, A. (2002). Clause packaging in writing and speech: A cross-linguistic developmental analysis. *Written Language and Literacy, 5*, 135–162.

Vihman, M., & Greenlee, M. (1987). Individual differences in phonological development: Ages one and three years. *Journal of Speech and Hearing Research, 30*, 503–521.

Vihman, M. M., & Velleman, S. L. (2000). Phonetics and the origins or phonology. In N. Burton-Roberts, P. Carr, & G. Docherty (Eds.), *Phonological knowledge: Conceptual and empirical issues* (pp. 305–399). Oxford, UK: Oxford University Press.

Visscher, K. M., Kaplan, E., Kahana, M. J., & Sekuler, R. (2007). Auditory short-term memory behaves like visual short-term memory. *Plos Biology, 5*, 0001–0011.

Vitevitch, M. S. (2002). The influence of phonological similarity neighborhoods on speech production. *Learning, Memory, and Cognition, 28*, 735–747.

Vitevitch, M. S., & Luce, P. A. (1999). Probabilistic phonotactics and neighborhood activisim in spoken word recognition. *Journal of Memory and Language, 40*, 374–408.

Vitevitch, M. S., Luce, P. A., & Pisoni, D. B. (1999). Phonotactics, neighborhood activation and lexical access for spoken words. *Brain and Language, 68*, 306–311.

Vogel Sosa, A., & Stoel-Gammon, C. (2006). Patterns of intra-word phonological variability during the second year of life. *Journal of Child Language, 33*, 31–50.

Vorperian, H. K., & Kent, R. D. (2007). Vowel acoustic space development in children: A synthesis of acoustic and anatomic data. *Journal of Speech, Language, and Hearing Research, 50*, 1510–1545.

Vouloumanos, A., Hauser, M. D., Werker, J. F., & Martin, A. (2010). The tuning of human neonates' preference for speech. *Child Development, 81*, 517–527.

Vouloumanos, A., & Werker, J. F. (2007). Listening to language at birth: Evidence for a bias for speech in neonates. *Developmental Science, 10*, 159–164.

Walker, S. J. (2001). Cognitive, linguistic, and social aspects of adults' noun definitions. *Journal of Psycholinguistic Research, 30*, 147–161.

Wallace, I. F., Roberts, J. E., & Lodder, D. E. (1998). Interactions of African American infants and their mothers: Relations with development at 1 year of age. *Journal of Speech, Language, and Hearing Research, 42*, 900–912.

Walley, A. (1993). The role of vocabulary development in children's spoken word recognition and segmentation ability. *Developmental Review, 13*, 286–350.

Walsh, M., Richardson, K., & Faulkner, D. (1993). Perceptual, thematic, and taxonomic relations in children's mental representations: Responses to triads. *European Journal of Psychology of Education, 8*, 85–102.

Walton, G. E., Bower, N. J. A., & Bower, T. G. R. (1992). Recognition of familiar faces by newborns. *Infant Behavior and Development, 15*, 265–269.

Washington, J. A., & Craig, H. K. (1994). Dialectal forms during discourse of poor, urban, African American preschoolers. *Journal of Speech, Language, and Hearing Research, 41*, 618–626.

Washington, J. A., & Craig, H. K. (1998). Socioeconomic status and gender influences on children's dialectal variations. *Journal of Speech, Language, and Hearing Research, 41*, 618–626.

Washington, J. A., & Craig, H. K. (2002). Morphosyntactic forms of African American English used by young children and their caregivers. *Applied Psycholinguistics, 23*, 209–231.

Waters, G., & Caplan, D. (2004). Verbal working memory and online syntactic processing: Evidence from self-paced listening. *The Quarterly Journal of Experimental Psychology, 57*, 129–163.

Watson, M. M., & Scukanec, G. P. (1997). Profiling the phonological ability of two-year-olds: A longitudinal investigation. *Child Language Teaching and Therapy, 13*, 3–14.

Watt, N., Wetherby, A., & Shumway, S. (2006). Prelinguistic predictors of language outcome at 3 years of age. *Journal of Speech, Language, and Hearing Research, 49*, 1224–1237.

Waxman, S., & Booth, A. (2003). The origins and evolution of links between word learning and conceptual organization: New evidence from 11-month-olds. *Developmental Science, 6*, 128–135.

Waxman, S. R., & Kosowski, T. D. (1990). Nouns mark category relations: Toddlers and preschoolers' word-learning biases. *Child Development, 61*, 1461–1473.

Waxman, S. R., & Markow, D. B. (1999). Object properties and object kind: 21-month-old infants' extension of novel adjectives. *Child Development, 69*, 1313–1329.

Waxman, S. R., & Namy, L. L. (1997). Challenging the notion of a thematic preference in young children. *Developmental Psychology, 33*, 555–567.

Weber-Fox, C., & Neville, H. J. (2001). Sensitive periods differentiate processing of open- and closed-class words: An ERP study of bilinguals. *Journal of Speech, Language, and Hearing Research, 44*, 1338–1353.

Weeks, L. A. (1992). Preschoolers' production of tag questions and adherence to the polarity-contrast principle. *Journal of Psycholinguistic Research, 21*, 31–40.

Weist, R. M. (1986). Tense and aspect. In P. Fletcher & M. Garman (Eds.), *Language acquisition* (2nd ed.). New York: Cambridge University Press.

Welch-Ross, M. (1997). Mother–child participation in conversations about the past: Relationship with preschoolers' Theory of Mind. *Developmental Psychology, 33*, 618–29.

Wellman, H., & Liu, D. (2004). Scaling of Theory of Mind tasks. *Child Development, 75,* 523–41.

Wellman, H. M. (2002). Understanding the psychological world: Developing a Theory of Mind. In U. Goswami (Ed.), *Handbook of childhood cognitive development.* Oxford, UK: Blackwell.

Wells, G. (1979). Learning and using the auxiliary verb in English. In V. Lee (Ed.), *Language development.* New York: Wiley.

Wells, G. (1985). *Language development in the pre-school years.* New York: Cambridge University Press.

Werker, J. F., & Curtin, S. (2005). PRIMIR: A developmental framework of infant speech processing. *Language Learning and Development, 1,* 197–234.

Werker, J. F., & Tees, R. C. (1994). Cross-language speech perception: Evidence for perceptual reorganization during the first year of life. *Infant Behavior and Development, 7,* 49–63.

Werker, J. F., & Tees, R. C. (2005). Speech perception as a window for understanding plasticity and commitment in language systems of the brain. *Developmental Psychobiology, 46,* 233–251.

Westby, C. E. (2005). Assessing and remediating text comprehension problems. In H. W. Catts & A. G. Kamhi (Eds.), *Language and reading disabilities* (2nd ed., pp. 157–232). Boston: Allyn & Bacon.

Wetherby, A. M., & Prizant, B. M. (1989). The expression of communicative intent: Assessment guidelines. *Seminars in Speech and Language, 10,* 77–91.

Wexler, K. (1998). Very early parameter setting and the unique checking constraint: A new explanation of the optional infinitive stage. *Lingua, 103,* 23–79.

Wexler, K. (2003). Lenneberg's dream: Learning, normal language development, and specific language impairment. In Y. Levy & J. Schaeffer (Eds.), *Language competence across populations: Toward a definition of specific language impairment.* Mahwah, NJ: Lawrence Erlbaum Associates.

Weyerts, H., Penke, M., Dohrn, U., Clahsen, H., & Münte, T. (1996). Brain potentials indicate differences between regular and irregular German noun plurals. *Essex Research Reports in Linguistics, 13,* 54–67.

Whitehurst, G. J., & Lonigan, C. J. (2001). Emergent readers: Development from prereaders to readers. In S. B. Neuman & D. K. Dickinson (Eds.), *Handbook of early literacy research* (pp. 11–29). New York: Guilford.

Whitmore, J. M., Shore, W. J., & Hull Smith, P. (2004). Partial knowledge of word meanings: Thematic and taxonomic representations. *Journal of Psycholinguistic Research, 33,* 137–164.

Wiley, A. R., Rose, A. J., Burger, L. K., & Miller, P. J. (1998). Constructing autonomous selves through narrative practices: A comparative study of working-class and middle-class families. *Child Development, 69,* 833–847.

Wilson, E. (2003). Lexically specific constructions in the acquisition of inflections in English. *Journal of Child Language, 30,* 75–115.

Windsor, J., Glaze, L. E., Koga, S. F., & the BEIP Core Group. (2007). Language acquisition with limited input: Romanian institution and foster care. *Journal of Speech, Language, and Hearing Research, 50,* 1365–1381.

Wing, C., & Scholnick, E. (1981). Children's comprehension of pragmatic concepts expressed in "because," "although," "if" and "unless." *Journal of Child Language, 8,* 347–365.

Winsler, A., Carlton, M. P., & Barry, M. J. (2000). Age-related changes in preschool children's systematic use of private speech in a natural setting. *Journal of Child Language, 27,* 665–687.

Xu, F., & Pinker, S. (1995). Weird past tense forms. *Journal of Child Language, 22,* 531–556.

Yamada, J. (1992). Asymmetries of reading and writing kanji by Japanese children. *Journal of Psycholinguistic Research, 21,* 563–580.

Yang, C. (2002). *Knowledge and learning in natural language.* New York: Oxford University Press.

Yang, C. L., Gordon, P. C., Hendrick, R., Wu, J. T., & Chou, T. L. (2001). The processing of coreference for reduced expression in discourse integration. *Journal of Psycholinguistic Research, 30,* 21–35.

Ylvisaker, M., & DeBonis, D. (2000). Executive function impairment in adolescence: TBI and ADHD. *Topics in Language Disorders, 20*(2), 29–57.

Zamuner, T. S. (2009). Phonotactic probabilities at the onset of language development: Speech production and word position. *Journal of Speech, Language, and Hearing Research 52,* 49–60.

Zentella, A. C. (1999). *Growing up bilingual.* Malden, MA: Blackwell.

Zubrick, S. R., Taylor, C. L., Rice, M. L., & Slegers, D. W. (2007). Late language emergence at 24 months: An epidemiological study of prevalence, predictors, and covariates. *Journal of Speech, Language, and Hearing Research, 50,* 1562–1592.

Zumach, A., Gerrits, E., Chenault, M., & Anteunis, L. (2010). Long-term effects of early otitis media on language development. *Journal of Speech, Language, and Hearing Research, 53,* 34–43.

Author Index

Subject Index

A

Abbreviated episodes, 325
Accommodation, 104
Accounts, 320
Acquisition
  of consonants, 305, 306
  determinants of order, 278–80
  order, of kinship terms, 259
  of sentence forms, 290–91
  simultaneous, 221–23
  speech sound, 304–6
  successive, 261–64
Action relational words, 255
Action sequences, 323
Adaptation, 104
Adjectives, suffixes, 277–78
Adolescents
  bilingualism, 393–94
  conversational abilities, 385–86
  literacy, 393
  morphology, 390–91
  phonology, 391–92
  pragmatics, 383–88
  semantics, 389–90
  speaking styles of, 383–85
  syntax, 390–91
Adoptions, cross-language, 222
Adults
  bilingualism, 393–94
  conversational abilities, 385–86
  literacy, 393
  morphology, 390–91
  phonology, 391–92
  pragmatics, 383–88
  semantics, 389–90
  speaking styles of, 383–85
  syntax, 390–91
Adult speech, 165–75
  motherese, 165–69
  with preschoolers, 172–75
  to toddlers, 165–72
Adverbial subordinate clauses, 433
Afferent nerves, 58

African American English

African American English (AAE), 28, 30, 31–32, 261, 404–8
  code switching, 352
  development of, 264
  grammatical contrasts between majority dialect and, 406–7
  grammatical contrasts between SAE and, 32
  idioms, 408
  past tense, 339
  phonemic contrasts between majority dialect and, 405
  third person and, 277
  in wider society, 354–55
Agents, 259
Allophones, 398
American English, 7, 31–33, 178, 261, 300, 305, 391
  idioms, 336
  speech sounds, 398–401
American Sign Language (ASL), 7–8, 179, 207
Analogy, 163
Analysis procedures, in research, 52
Anaphoric reference, 261
Angular gyrus, 67
Antonyms, 24
Archiform, 264
Arcuate fasciculus, 68
Articles, 281–82
Articulatory maps, 215–16
Asian English (AE), 28, 33, 411–14
  grammatical contrasts between majority dialect and, 413–14
  phonemic contrasts between majority dialect and, 412
Aspect, 285
Assimilation, 104
  processes, 309
Associative complex hypothesis, 206

B

Attention, 71–72, 101–2
Attentional interactions, 122
Attribution relational words, 257
Auditory maps, 213–14
Auditory patterns, formation of, 86–89
Auxiliary verbs, 283, 430
  use by children, 284

Babbling, 92–93
  reduplicated, 93
  variegated, 94
Baby talk, 113, 128, 130
Bilingual, 32
Bilingualism, 219–20
  adults and adolescents, 393–94
  code switching and development, 352–54
  cross-language adoptions and, 223
  cultural diversity and, 220
  language learning, 220–23
  prevalence of, 219–20
  simultaneous acquisition, 221–23
Blending, 361
Bootstrapping, 157, 167
  lexical, 219
  phonological, 219
  semantic, 157
  syntactic, 157, 219
Bound morphemes, 21, 273–80
Bracketing, 126
Brain, 59
  functions, 61
  hemispheric asymmetry, 62–63
  language processing and, 64–75
  lateral surface of cerebral hemisphere, 60
  maturation, 63–64
  neurological development, 82–84

C

structure, 97–98
  weight of child's, 63
British English, 29
Broca's area, 65, 68, 69
Brown's rules for counting morphemes, 427

Caregivers
  face-to-face communication and, 120, 129
  infant exchange with, 86, 95
  joint action, 139–42
  joint reference, 136–38
  literacy and, 368
  role in cognitive development, 104, 106–7
  speech modifications, 168–69
  turn-taking with, 118, 121, 142–43
Case, semantic, 259
Categorical assumption, 154
Centering, 246
Central nervous system (CNS), 58–64
  brain maturation, 63–64
  hemispheric asymmetry, 62–63
Cerebrum, 59
Chaining, 246
Child development
  age 7 to 12 months, 418–19
  age 12 to 24 months, 420–21
  birth to 6 months, 416–17
  of preschoolers, 422–23
  of school-age children, 424
Child directed speech (CDS), 42
CHILDES, 48
Child language
  analysis procedures, 52
  data collection methods, 45–48, 51–52
  representativeness of data, 50–51
  sample size and variability, 48–49
  study of, 45–52